THE COLLECTED WORKS OF
SAMUEL TAYLOR COLERIDGE 12

MARGINALIA

General Editor: KATHLEEN COBURN
Associate Editor: BART WINER

THE COLLECTED WORKS

1. An inscribed flyleaf of Richard Field *Of the Church* (Oxford 1635) with
Coleridge's verse inscription and annotations. See FIELD headnote
and **61**, **52**, **9**, and **10**
Victoria College Library; reproduced by kind permission

THE COLLECTED WORKS OF

Samuel Taylor Coleridge

Marginalia

II

Camden to Hutton

EDITED BY

George Whalley

ROUTLEDGE & KEGAN PAUL

BOLLINGEN SERIES LXXV
PRINCETON UNIVERSITY PRESS

lw

This edition of the text by Samuel Taylor Coleridge is
copyright © 1984 by Princeton University Press

The Collected Works, sponsored by Bollingen Foundation,
is published in Great Britain
by Routledge & Kegan Paul Ltd
39 Store St, London WC1E 7DD
ISBN 0-7100-02505
and in the United States of America
by Princeton University Press, Princeton, New Jersey
ISBN 0-691-09889-1
LCC 68-10201
The Collected Works constitutes
the seventy-fifth publication in Bollingen Series

The present work, number 12 of the Collected Works,
is in 5 volumes, this being 12: II

Designed by Richard Garnett

Printed in Great Britain
by the University Press, Cambridge

THIS EDITION
OF THE WORKS OF
SAMUEL TAYLOR COLERIDGE
IS DEDICATED
IN GRATITUDE TO
THE FAMILY EDITORS
IN EACH GENERATION

IN THE PREPARATION OF
THIS SECOND VOLUME OF MARGINALIA
THE EDITOR IS INDEBTED FOR SPECIAL KNOWLEDGE
AND CO-OPERATION
TO
Lorna Arnold
James D. Boulger
Merton A. Christensen
Hans Eichner
Lore Metzger
Raimonda Modiano
Willem Schrickx

CONTENTS

──────■ II ■──────

Marginalia

[† designates a "Lost Book"—a book reported to contain marginal notes in C's hand but which the editor has not been able to find and for which no transcript of marginalia is known to exist.]

Contents

Contents

LIST OF ILLUSTRATIONS

A NOTE

George Whalley died on the twenty-seventh of May, 1983. At a desk in his hospital room in Kingston, overlooking the great sweep of Lake Ontario, he made detailed corrections on the page-proofs of this volume; almost invariably each was preceded by a question mark, as if with characteristic modesty he meant to check again, or knew he was raising questions for another to answer. They were the meticulous corrections of a man facing death and yet overcoming the long exhaustion of weakness and pain to demand elegance. On the sixteenth of May he wrote on page 844 of the proofs some suggestions to himself for a "Foreword", the last of which read: "Fuller on bees in winter". On a used envelope later found among his papers he had copied in pencil from the Fuller entry in this volume the following excerpt:

Fuller in *Life Out of Death*:
Sicknesse is a time to suffer, not to do in; Patients are like Bees in winter, no flying abroad to finde fresh flowers, either they must starve, or live on that stock of honey which they have provided in the summer time.

On which Coleridge commented in the margin, probably a few months before *his* death:

A beautiful improvement might be made of this—viz. that God's mercy through Christ *does* supply to his wisest Bees a power of making fresh honey by patience and acknowledgment.

K.C.

FOREWORD

S INCE the first volume of this edition of *Marginalia* began to be printed, the Coleridge family has suffered the loss of the two surviving grandsons of Ernest Hartley Coleridge, sons of Gerard Coleridge, Westcountrymen—early in 1976 the Reverend Nicholas Coleridge, and then in March 1980 his elder brother Alwyne, who for many years held the Coleridge copyright and had been custodian of the "Leatherhead Collection" that descended from Coleridge himself. At the beginning of the thirty-five years of my own work on Coleridge's manuscripts and books the three brothers—Antony, Nicholas, Alwyne—became my friends and joined in the enterprise. I therefore offer this second volume as a tribute to them, particularly because Alwyne's editorial contribution is to be seen here in the difficult and intensely personal copy of Hartley Coleridge's *Worthies of Yorkshire and Lancashire* and in Coleridge's own copy of Henry Nelson Coleridge's *Six Months in the West Indies*.

We have suffered other losses that cannot be passed in silence: Ivor A. Richards, Coleridgian, mountaineer, poet; Chester Shaver, whose work on Wordsworth's Rydal Mount library catalogue was published only a few months before he died; and Reynolds Stone, my friend for many years, calligrapher, engraver in boxwood, whose triumphant version of the *Epitaph* cut in Cumberland slate now watches over Coleridge's grave in the pavement of St Michael's Church, Highgate.

In addition to the work of coeditors described in some detail in the Foreword to Volume I, I wish to acknowledge the work done by Kathleen Wheeler at an intermediate stage of the editing of this second volume in verifying readings as far in the alphabetical sequence for the German entries as Kant and Kluge and in drafting footnotes. In the final preparation of the German copy in this volume Raimonda Modiano—with assistance from the American Council of Learned Societies and from the Graduate School of the University of Washington—checked again the text of philosophical entries and provided additional editorial detail, and has verified copy and prepared fresh material for German entries for the rest of the edition.

To editors of volumes of *The Collected Works* beyond those named in the first volume I am grateful for the answers to particular questions, for suggestions responsive or spontaneous, and for the privilege of consulting their work-in-progress while still in manuscript: W. Jackson Bate and James Engell (*Biographia Literaria*), Owen Barfield (*Lectures 1818–1819: On the History of Philosophy*), and James Mays (*Poetical Works*).

It is a pleasure to record that since Volume I was printed some discoveries of annotated books have been made and some marginalia variously preserved have been identified. The original annotated copy of Thomas Amory *The Life of John Buncle*—Charles Lamb's copy, of which no transcript had been recorded—has come to light in the collection of the Rosenbach Foundation of Philadelphia. (See *CM—CC*—I clxiii and 30.) A clue in Notebook 30 led to the discovery of three annotated books in the Sion College Library: Gilbert Burnet *The Memoires of the Lives and Actions of James and William Dukes of Hamilton and Castleherald* (1677) (the entry for which was ingeniously taken into Volume I at the last minute), *The History of the Troubles and Tryal of...William Laud* (1695), and *The Second Volume of the Remains of...William Laud* (1700), both edited by Henry Wharton. A copy of E. T. A. Hoffmann's *Fantasiestücke in Callot's Manier* (2 vols Bamberg 1819) was recognised by Heather Jackson in the British Library as containing a note in Coleridge's hand. Among the Wedgwood papers deposited in the library of Keele University James Mays found an unpublished manuscript by John Leslie entitled "Some Account of the Life of Josiah Wedgwood" with a few annotations by Coleridge and a few by Thomas Carlyle. The annotated copy of Bernard de Mandeville *Fable of the Bees* (2 vols 1724) that originally belonged to Joseph Henry Green, and had for some years belonged to Christopher Stone and was for a time lost, is now in the library of Nagoya University, Japan, with the second annotated copy of Kant's *Anthropologie*. The annotated copy of William Parnell *An Historical Apology for the Irish Catholics* (Dublin 1807), once Tom Poole's and last reported (1935) in the possession of Alfred Hart in Melbourne, Australia, has now been identified in the State Library of Victoria, Australia. Annotated proofs of part of Thomas Pringle's *African Sketches* (1834), together with three letters from Coleridge to Pringle that had escaped E. L. Griggs's search, were noticed in the South African Library, Cape Town, by a student of history formerly of Queen's University. Two annotated copies of Jeremy Taylor's *Rule and Exercises of Holy*

Living and Holy Dying have turned up—one (1676) in the collection of Nicholas Coleridge (with only one annotation), the other (1710) in the library of Brandeis University. Brandeis University has also acquired the copy of Vindex *The Conduct of the British Government Towards the Church of England in the West India Colonies* (1813), the notes in which had been inaccurately printed in *Notes Theological, Political and Miscellaneous* (1853). The British Library acquired a copy of Esaias Tegnér *Die Frithiofs-Sage* translated by Amalie von Helvig (Stuttgart & Tübingen 1826) in which Coleridge had written a long note on prosody. Of these various books only four had previously been known to have Coleridge's marginalia in them: Amory, Mandeville, Parnell, and "Vindex".

A different kind of evidence came to light in the Humanities Research Center of the University of Texas when Reginald Foakes recognised the importance of a group of transcripts of marginalia that had come from the Leatherhead Collection. Of the seventeen titles from which marginalia had been transcribed all were already known to have been annotated; furthermore, eight of the sets of notes also existed in transcript in the Victoria College collection, and ten of the titles were represented in *Notes Theological*. On closer examination these transcripts were found to include eleven annotations hitherto unrecorded, all written in books from which marginalia had previously been incompletely printed: on John James Park *The Dogmas of the Constitution* (1832), on two numbers of the *Quarterly Review* for 1813–14, and on the lost copy of Richard Baxter's *Reliquiae Baxterianae* (COPY A in Volume I). The Baxter transcript, though incomplete—it runs only from p 314 to the end of the volume, the earlier part of it having been lost—is of particular value: standing closer to Coleridge's original than the selective version in *Literary Remains* does, it corrects the text of some thirty annotations; and while, with its three unrecorded notes, it supersedes the two conjectural notes derived from John Mitford's summary, it also confirms that the conjecture about those two notes was correct, even though the text was not. (See I 277–8.) Also among the Texas transcripts Reginald Foakes noticed two sheets of paper that had been used as file-covers for transcripts of marginalia sent by Tom Poole to Joseph Henry Green after Coleridge's death in response to a request for materials for *Literary Remains*. The use that can be made of these papers in identifying two annotated books as having originally belonged to Poole is discussed in this volume in the headnote to William Hayley *The Life of Milton*.

Despite the long and minute search for Coleridge's books, it is certain that more books annotated by Coleridge remain to be identified—books about which as yet we know nothing or to which we have clues so vague that they will be recognised as evidence only in hindsight; originals for which we have only transcripts and those of questionable quality; and all those books described as annotated but for which there are no transcripts of any kind and descriptions of which are at best brief or ambiguous. (See I clxxiii–clxiv.) The editor will welcome news of any book annotated—or even signed—by Coleridge, or of any manuscript copy of any of his marginalia. He will also welcome, as a mark of that demure courtesy that one scholar pays to another in the restless pursuit of the "dragoun erroure", notice of any detectable oversights, slips, or ignorances that he may have been guilty of.

I wish to thank Mrs Roberta F. C. Cox for the gift of a large group of microfilms of marginalia that her aunt Roberta Florence Brinkley used in preparing her edition of *Coleridge on the Seventeenth Century*, and for sending me after Miss Brinkley's death some papers that she had addressed to me. These have been a great help during necessary absences from the British Library and other great collections.

For various and ingenious contributions to the detail of this and later volumes I wish to thank several persons beyond those noticed in the Foreword to Volume I: Lionel Adey, J. F. Fuggles, and the Reverend Wilfrid J. Little for help with the contents of the lost copy of *A Select Collection of Hymns to be Universally Sung in All the Countess of Huntingdon's Chapels*; H. M. Colvin for a detail in Thomas Fuller; Gerald Finley for information about the Angerstein Collection of paintings; Geoffrey Little for laying to rest a Shakespeare ghost, for identifying the Parnell in Melbourne, and for valuable information about Barron Field; John Lyward for information about his father's copy of John Donne's *Poems*; Anne Mellor for checking the text of the rare copy of Loewe's *Treatise on the Phenomena of Animal Magnetism* in the Beinecke Library; Margaret and Wallace Mills for telling me about the Pringle papers in Cape Town; Barbara Rosenbaum for reporting two Coleridge association books in the Brandeis University Library; Max F. Schulz for verifying readings in William Hayley's *Life of Milton* (1796) in the H. E. Huntington Library; Professor F. S. Scott and the University of Auckland Press for a copy of M. K. Joseph's monograph on Carl Aders (1953); the National Gallery, London, and Mrs Angelina M.

Bacon for archival records of Carl Aders's collection of paintings and the bequest of Ann Eliza Green; T. H. McK. Clough, Keeper of the Rutland County Museum, for information about the distribution of church steeples in Rutland and their liability to lightning-strikes; and Dr Hayim Y. Sheynin, Director of the Library, The Dropsie University, Philadelphia, for locating a copy of Eichhorn's *Allgemeine Bibliothek der biblischen Litteratur* (10 vols Leipzig 1787–1800).

For continued help with queries and special books, and for permission to publish from books in their possession, I am grateful to the staff of the British Library, of Victoria College in the University of Toronto, of the Berg Collection in the New York Public Library, and the Humanities Research Center in the University of Texas; and also to the Philadelphia Athenaeum and Roger N. Ross; Brandeis University Library and Dr Victor A. Berch; the Bristol Central Library and Geoffrey Langley; the Department of Rare Books, Cornell University Library, and Dr Donald D. Eddy; Duke University Library and Janet L. Thomason; the Houghton Library in Harvard University and William H. Bond, and the Widener Library and Rodney G. Dennis; the Henry E. Huntington Library and Art Gallery and Carey S. Bliss; the Milton S. Eisenhower Library of Johns Hopkins University and Carolyn Smith; the library of Keble College, Oxford, and M. B. Parker; the Mosely Collection of Keele University and Ian H. C. Fraser; the Caven Library of Knox College, University of Toronto, and Anna Burgess; the Philip H. and A. S. W. Rosenbach Foundation and Walter C. Johnson; Nagoya Imperial University Library; the library of the Royal College of Surgeons and Mr E. H. Cornelius; Sotheby Parke Bernet, New York, and Susan C. Morace; the South African Library in Cape Town and Miss M. E. Cartwright; the State Library of Victoria and R. G. Anderson; the Humanities Research Center of the University of Texas and Ellen S. Dunlap and Eric Poole; the library of University College, London, and Jane Belson; the Special Collections of Waterloo University and Mrs S. Bellingham (especially for information about the papers of Bertram Davis of Bristol); the Leonard Library of Wycliffe College, University of Toronto.

For various learned courtesies I wish to thank G. Bonner, A. T. Grafton, John Gutteridge, Jane Millgate, and Christopher Tiffin; and in Queen's University, John Baxter, Mary Fraser, Dietmar Hagel, Ross Kirkpatrick, George Logan, Lisa Ann Miller and Tony Riley. Edward Bishop and Mary Silcox made a notable contribution by preparing a working index.

In the transcript of Coleridge's annotations in this and subsequent volumes of *Marginalia* the editor has silently introduced a second parenthesis or quotation mark if C has omitted either.

During the early months of 1979 I found myself treading upon very shadowy ground, and for some months thereafter could not do any work. Those who, throughout that long ordeal, secured for me a stay against dissolution would probably not wish to be named here. Yet I am keenly aware of the contribution they have made to this edition in the past and for the future. I must, however, acknowledge particularly the generous considerateness of the officers of Queen's University, especially Dr Ronald L. Watts, Dr Duncan G. Sinclair, and Dr C. Lougheed. I am also grateful for the unselfish energy with which my colleague A. C. Hamilton agreed without warning to take over my duties and conducted the affairs of the English Department with skill and forbearance at a time when his own scholarly work cried out for attention; and to Douglas Spettigue for his encouragement and for the hospitality that he and the English Department have extended to me since my retirement.

Again I express my gratitude for the grants from the Killam Programme of the Canada Council and for the sustaining grants from Bollingen Foundation through Princeton University Press that have made it possible to bring this volume to completion and to look forward confidently to finishing the rest of the work.

Hartington, Ontario, 1 July 1980   GEORGE WHALLEY

EDITORIAL PRACTICE,
CONVENTIONS,
AND ABBREVIATIONS

For the definition of "marginalia", "textus", and "submargina-lia" see *CM* I xxiii–xxvi. For special terms such as "fly-pages", "annex", "ms transcript", "quasi-marginalia", "lost book", and "marked book" see I xxx–xxxii.

All marginalia are transcribed literatim from the original mss, whenever these were available to the editor: cancelled words and phrases are restored; idiosyncratic spellings and obvious misspellings are reproduced without comment; slips of the pen and accidental repetitions are also reproduced normally with explanation in a textual note. See I xxiii. A second parenthesis or quotation mark omitted by oversight is supplied by the editor without comment unless the placing of the mark is in doubt.

The annotated books are entered in alphabetical order of the authors, and within an author-entry in alphabetical order of title. Reference to annotated books within this edition is made by short title (identifiable from the running headlines) to which the serial number of a particular annotation can be attached: e.g. DONNE *Sermons* COPY B **57**. (Bold figures are used only for serial numbers of marginalia.) Editorial footnotes are identified by attaching the number of the footnote indicator to the abbreviated title of the book: e.g. DONNE *Sermons* COPY B **57** n 2. See also I xxix–xxx.

CONVENTIONS USED IN TRANSCRIPTION

[wild]	A reading supplied by the editor when the word has been lost from the ms by cropping or physical damage
[not]*ᵃ*	A word inserted by the editor to supply an unintentional omission on Coleridge's part, or to clarify the sense of an elliptical or ambiguous phrase. The accompanying textual note *ᵃ* accounts for the insertion
[? wild]	An uncertain reading
[? wild/world]	Possible alternative readings
⌜wild⌝	A reading restored from erasure or obliteration, or from damage to the ms other than cropping—normally accompanied by a textual note

xxi

[. . .]	An illegible word or phrase
[. . . . .]	A passage of undetermined extent illegible through rubbing or offsetting, or lost by cropping or other physical damage
⟨ ⟩	A word or passage inserted between the lines, or marked for insertion from another part of the page (in which case a textual note is provided). An inserted word or passage is not so marked when it follows immediately upon a cancellation in the ms

ABBREVIATIONS

Place of publication is London, unless otherwise noted. Special abbreviations that apply only to certain author-entries or book-entries are given in the appropriate general note or headnote.

AA	*The Annual Anthology* ed Robert Southey (Bristol 1799–1800)
Allsop	[Thomas Allsop] *Letters, Conversations and Recollections of S. T. Coleridge* (2 vols 1836)
AM	S. T. Coleridge *The Rime of the Ancient Mariner*
AP	*Anima Poetae: from the Unpublished Notebooks of S. T. Coleridge* ed E. H. Coleridge (1895)
A Reg	*The Annual Register* (1758–)
AR (1825)	S. T. Coleridge *Aids to Reflection* (1825)
Ashley LC	Thomas J. Wise *The Ashley Library: A Catalogue of Printed Books, Manuscripts and Autograph Letters Collected by Thomas James Wise* (11 vols 1922–36). Coleridge items are principally in Vols I, VIII, X. Items from Wise's collection now in the BM bear the prefix "Ashley" in the press-mark
AV	The "Authorised Version"—or "King James Version"—of the Bible, in modern orthography
BCP	*The Book of Common Prayer and Administration of the Sacraments and other rites and ceremonies of the Church according to the use of the Church of England*
BL (1817)	S. T. Coleridge *Biographia Literaria; or Biographical Sketches of My Literary Life and Opinions* (2 vols 1817)
BL (1847)	S. T. Coleridge *Biographia Literaria* ed. H. N. and Sara Coleridge (2 vols 1847)
BL (1907)	S. T. Coleridge *Biographia Literaria...with His Aesthetical Essays* ed. J. Shawcross (2 vols Oxford 1907)

BL (CC)	S. T. Coleridge *Biographia Literaria* ed James Engell and W. Jackson Bate (2 vols London & Princeton 1983) = *CC* VII
BM	British Library, Reference Division, formerly "British Museum Library"
BMC	*The British Museum Catalogue of Printed Books*
BNYPL	*New York Public Library Bulletin* (New York 1897–)
B Poets	*The Works of the British Poets* ed Robert Anderson (13 vols Edinburgh & London 1792–5; vol 14 1807). The annotated copies are referred to as "ANDERSON"
Bristol LB	George Whalley "The Bristol Library Borrowings of Southey and Coleridge" *Library* IV (Sept 1949) 114–31
C	Samuel Taylor Coleridge
C&S	S. T. Coleridge *On the Constitution of the Church and State, According to the Idea of Each* (2nd ed 1830)
C&S (CC)	S. T. Coleridge *On the Constitution of the Church and State* ed John Colmer (London & Princeton 1976) = *CC* X
C & SH	George Whalley *Coleridge and Sara Hutchinson and the Asra Poems* (1955)
Carlisle LB	Carlisle Cathedral Library Borrowings 1801–2
Carlyon	Clement Carlyon *Early Years and Late Reflections* (4 vols 1836–58)
C at H	L. E. Watson *Coleridge at Highgate* (London & New York 1925)
CC	*The Collected Works of Samuel Taylor Coleridge* general ed Kathleen Coburn (London & Princeton 1969–)
CH	*Coleridge: The Critical Heritage* ed J. R. de J. Jackson (1970)
CIS	S. T. Coleridge *Confessions of an Inquiring Spirit and Some Miscellaneous Pieces* ed H. N. Coleridge (1849)
CL	*Collected Letters of Samuel Taylor Coleridge* ed Earl Leslie Griggs (6 vols Oxford & New York 1956–71)
C Life (C)	E. K. Chambers *Samuel Taylor Coleridge* (Oxford 1938)
C Life (G)	James Gillman *The Life of Samuel Taylor Coleridge* (1838)

C Life (H)	Lawrence Hanson *The Life of Samuel Taylor Coleridge: the Early Years* (1938)
C Life (JDC)	James Dykes Campbell *Samuel Taylor Coleridge* (1894)
CM (*CC*)	S. T. Coleridge *Marginalia* ed George Whalley (London & Princeton 1980–) = *CC* XII
CN	*The Notebooks of Samuel Taylor Coleridge* ed Kathleen Coburn (New York, Princeton & London 1957–)
C Pantheist	Thomas McFarland *Coleridge and the Pantheist Tradition* (Oxford 1969)
CRB	*Henry Crabb Robinson on Books and Their Writers* ed Edith J. Morley (3 vols 1938)
CR (*BCW*)	*Blake, Coleridge, Wordsworth, Lamb, etc. being Selections from the Remains of Henry Crabb Robinson* ed Edith J. Morley (Manchester 1922)
CRC	*The Correspondence of Henry Crabb Robinson with the Wordsworth Circle* ed Edith J. Morley (2 vols Oxford 1927)
CRD	*Diary, Reminiscences, and Correspondence of Henry Crabb Robinson* ed Thomas Sadler (2 vols 1872)
CR Life	Edith J. Morley *The Life and Times of Henry Crabb Robinson* (1935)
C 17th C	*Coleridge on the Seventeenth Century* ed R. F. Brinkley (Durham NC 1955)
C Talker	R. W. Armour and R. F. Howes *Coleridge the Talker* (1949)
CW	*The Complete Works of S. T. Coleridge* ed W. G. T. Shedd (7 vols New York 1853)
DC	Derwent Coleridge
DCL	Dove Cottage Library, Grasmere
DC SC (1888)	*The Philological Library of…Derwent Coleridge* (Sotheby Jul 1888). Marked copy: BM S–C S 956(1)
DC SC (1891)	*A Portion of the Library of…Derwent Coleridge* (Sotheby Jul 1891). Marked copy: BM S–C S 1015(1)
De Q	Thomas De Quincey
De Q to W	John E. Jordan *De Quincey to Wordsworth. A Biography of a Relationship* (Berkeley & Los Angeles 1962)

De Q Works	*The Collected Writings of Thomas De Quincey* ed David Masson (14 vols Edinburgh 1889–90)
Diels	Hermann Diels *Die Fragmente der Vorsokratiker* ed Walther Kranz (3 vols Zürich 1971)
DNB	*Dictionary of National Biography* (1885–)
Durham LB	Durham Cathedral Library Borrowings 1801
DW	Dorothy Wordsworth
DW (S)	Ernest de Selincourt *Dorothy Wordsworth* (Oxford 1933)
DWJ	*Journals of Dorothy Wordsworth* ed Ernest de Selincourt (2 vols 1941)
DWJ (M)	*Journals of Dorothy Wordsworth. The Alfoxden Journal 1798* [and] *The Grasmere Journals 1800–1803* ed Mary Moorman (Oxford 1971)
EC	*The English Catalogue of Books (including the original "London" Catalogue* [of 1786 for 1700–86])...*issued in the United Kingdom...1801–1836* ed R. A. Peddie and Q. Waddington (London 1914)
Ed Rev	*The Edinburgh Review* (Edinburgh & London (1802–1929)
EHC	Ernest Hartley Coleridge
EOT (*CC*)	S. T. Coleridge *Essays on His Times in "The Morning Post" and "The Courier"* ed David V. Erdman (3 vols London & Princeton 1978) = *CC* III
Farington Diary	Joseph Farington *The Farington Diary* ed James Greig (8 vols 1922–8)
Friend (*CC*)	S. T. Coleridge *The Friend* ed Barbara E. Rooke (2 vols London & Princeton 1969) = *CC* IV
Gillman SC (1843)	*Catalogue of a valuable collection of books, including the Library of James Gillman, Esq* (Henry Southgate 1843). Marked copies: BM SC Sg 64 (2) and Sg a 53
G Mag	*The Gentleman's Magazine* (1731–1907)
Göttingen LB	A. D. Snyder "Books Borrowed by Coleridge from the Library of the University of Göttingen, 1799" *Modern Philology* xxv (1928) 377–80
Green List	VCL MS 18. A handlist of Coleridge's books prepared by Mrs J. H. Green c 1863
Green SC (1880)	*Catalogue of the Library of Joseph Henry Green... sold by auction* (Sotheby Jul 1880). Marked copy: BM SC S 805(1)

Green SC (1884)	*Catalogue of scarce and valuable books, including a remarkable collection of Coleridgeiana* (Scribner & Welford, New York 1884)
HC	Hartley Coleridge
HCL	*Letters of Hartley Coleridge* ed Grace Evelyn and Earl Leslie Griggs (Oxford 1936)
HC Essays	*Essays and Marginalia by Hartley Coleridge* ed Derwent Coleridge (2 vols 1851)
HC Poems	*Poems by Hartley Coleridge, with a memoir of his life by his brother* [Derwent Coleridge] (2 vols 1851)
HCR	Henry Crabb Robinson
HEHL	The Henry E. Huntington Library and Art Gallery, San Marino, California
Herbert C SC (1862)	*Catalogue of the Valuable Library of . . . Herbert Coleridge* (Sotheby Apr 1862). Marked copy: BM S–C S 511(3)
Highgate List	Wordsworth LC entries 1186–1299: a handlist in WW's hand of books "Sent to Coleridge" in c 1829
HNC	Henry Nelson Coleridge
H Works	*The Complete Works of William Hazlitt* ed P. P. Howe (12 vols 1930–4)
IS	*Inquiring Spirit: a New Presentation of Coleridge from His Published and Unpublished Prose Writings* ed Kathleen Coburn (revised ed Toronto 1979)
JDC	James Dykes Campbell
JW	John Wordsworth
JWL	*Letters of John Wordsworth* ed C. H. Ketcham (Ithaca NY 1969)
L	*Letters of Samuel Taylor Coleridge* ed E. H. Coleridge (2 vols 1895)
L & L	*Coleridge on Logic and Learning* ed Alice D. Snyder (New Haven & London 1929)
LB	William Wordsworth [and S. T. Coleridge] *Lyrical Ballads with Other Poems* (Bristol 1798 &c); the edition referred to indicated by a bracketed date. "*LB*" following a place-name (e.g. *Durham LB*) means "Library Borrowing"
LCL	Loeb Classical Library

Lects 1795 (CC)	S. T. Coleridge *Lectures 1795: On Politics and Religion* ed Lewis Patton and Peter Mann (London & Princeton 1971) = *CC* I
Lects 1808–1819 (CC)	S. T. Coleridge *Lectures 1808–1819: On Literature* ed Reginald A. Foakes (2 vols London & Princeton 1984) = *CC* VI
LL	*The Letters of Charles Lamb to Which Are Added Those of His Sister Mary Lamb* ed E. V. Lucas (3 vols 1935)
LL (M)	*The Letters of Charles and Mary Anne Lamb* ed Edwin W. Marrs, Jr (3 vols Ithaca NY 1975–8)
L Life	E. V. Lucas *The Life of Charles Lamb* (1921)
LLP	*Letters from the Lake Poets to Daniel Stuart* [ed Mary Stuart and E. H. Coleridge] (1889)
L Works	*The Works of Charles and Mary Lamb* ed E. V. Lucas (6 vols 1912)
Logic (CC)	S. T. Coleridge *Logic* ed J. R. de J. Jackson (London & Princeton 1980) = *CC* XIII
Lost List	A handlist prepared by George Whalley of books known to have been annotated by Coleridge but not located at the time this edition went to press. An incomplete version was published in *Book Collector* XVII (1968) 428–42 and XVIII (1969) 223. A complete list is given in an Appendix in *CM (CC)* V
LR	*The Literary Remains of Samuel Taylor Coleridge* ed H. N. Coleridge (4 vols 1836–9)
LS	S. T. Coleridge *A Lay Sermon, Addressed to the Higher and Middle Classes, on the Existing Distresses and Discontents* (1817)
LS (1852)	S. T. Coleridge *Lay Sermons. I. The Statesman's Manual. II. Blessed are ye that sow beside all Waters* [i.e. *A Lay Sermon*] ed Derwent Coleridge (1852)
LS (CC)	S. T. Coleridge *Lay Sermons* [being *The Statesman's Manual* and *A Lay Sermon*] ed R. J. White (London & Princeton 1972) = *CC* V
M Chron	*The Morning Chronicle* (1769–1862)
Method	*S. T. Coleridge's Treatise on Method as Published in the Encyclopaedia Metropolitana* ed Alice D. Snyder (1934)
Migne *PG*	*Patriologiae cursus completus...series Graeca* ed J. P. Migne (162 vols Paris 1857–1912)

Migne *PL*	*Patriologiae cursus completus...series Latina* ed J. P. Migne (221 vols Paris 1844–64)
Minnow	*Minnow among Tritons: Mrs S. T. Coleridge's Letters to Thomas Poole, 1799–1834* ed Stephen Potter (1934)
Misc C	*Coleridge's Miscellaneous Criticism* ed T. M. Raysor (1936)
M Mag	*The Monthly Magazine* (1796–1843)
M Post	*The Morning Post* (1772–1937)
Mrs C	Sara Coleridge née Fricker (wife of C)
MS Leatherhead	A manuscript formerly in the collection of the Rev Gerard H. B. Coleridge when Vicar of Leatherhead
MW	Mary Wordsworth née Hutchinson (wife of WW)
N	Notebook of Samuel Taylor Coleridge (numbered or lettered) in ms. References are given by folio
NEB	*The New English Bible* (Oxford & Cambridge 1964)
NEB Gk	*The Greek New Testament being the text translated in the New English Bible 1961* ed R. V. G. Tasker (Oxford & Cambridge 1964)
NED	S. T. Coleridge *Notes on English Divines* ed Derwent Coleridge (2 vols 1853)
NLS	S. T. Coleridge *Notes and lectures upon Shakespeare and Some Other Old Poets and Dramatists with Other Literary Remains* ed Sara Coleridge (2 vols 1849)
NT Gk Lex	W. Bauer *A Greek-English Lexicon of the New Testament and Other Early Christian Literature* ed & tr W. F. Arndt and F. W. Gingrich (Chicago & Cambridge 1968)
NTP	S. T. Coleridge *Notes, Theological, Political and Miscellaneous* ed Derwent Coleridge (1853)
NYPL	New York Public Library
OCD	*The Oxford Classical Dictionary* ed N. G. L. Hammond and H. H. Scullard (2nd ed Oxford 1970)
ODCC	*The Oxford Dictionary of the Christian Church* ed F. L. Cross (London 1971)
OED	*The Oxford English Dictionary being a corrected re-issue...of "A New English Dictionary on Historical Principles"* (12 vols Oxford 1970)
OLD	*Oxford Latin Dictionary* (8 vols Oxford 1968–82)

Omniana	*Omniana, or Horae otiosiores* ed Robert Southey [with articles by C] (2 vols 1812)
Orsini	Gian N. G. Orsini *Coleridge and German Idealism* (Carbondale & Edwardsville 1969)
p–d	paste-down. See "Editorial Practice" *CM* I xxx
Peake	*Peake's Commentary on the Bible* ed Matthew Black and H. H. Rowley (1967)
Phil Trans RS	*The Philosophical Transactions of the Royal Society* (1665–1821)
P Lects (1949)	*The Philosophical Lectures of Samuel Taylor Coleridge* ed Kathleen Coburn (London & New York 1949)
PML	The Pierpont Morgan Library, New York
Poole	M. E. Sandford *Thomas Poole and His Friends* (2 vols 1888)
Prelude	William Wordsworth *The Prelude or Growth of a Poet's Mind* ed Ernest de Selincourt, rev Helen Darbishire (Oxford 1959)
"*Prometheus*"	S. T. Coleridge "On the *Prometheus* of Aeschylus: An Essay...read at the Royal Society of Literature, May 18, 1825" as printed in *LR* II 323–59
Proto-*Prometheus*	The ms draft of "*Prometheus*" written c 1821: Duke University
PW (EHC)	*The Complete Poetical Works of Samuel Taylor Coleridge* ed E. H. Coleridge (2 vols Oxford 1912)
PW (JDC)	*The Poetical Works of Samuel Taylor Coleridge* ed J. D. Campbell (1893)
QR	*The Quarterly Review* (1809–1952)
RES	*Review of English Studies* (1925–)
RS	Robert Southey
RS *CPB*	*Southey's Common-Place Book* ed J. W. Warter (4 vols 1849–51)
RSV	The [American] Revised Standard Version of the Bible: NT 1946, OT 1952
RV	The Revised Version of the Bible: NT 1881, OT 1885, Apocr 1895
RX	John Livingston Lowes *The Road to Xanadu* (rev ed Boston 1930)
SC	Sara Coleridge (daughter of C, and wife of HNC)

SC Life	Earl Leslie Griggs *Coleridge Fille. A Biography of Sara Coleridge* (Oxford 1940)
SC Memoir	*Memoir and Letters of Sara Coleridge* [ed Edith Coleridge] (2 vols 1873)
SH	Sara Hutchinson
Sh C	*Coleridge's Shakespearean Criticism* ed T. M. Raysor (2nd ed 2 vols 1960)
SHL	*The Letters of Sara Hutchinson* ed Kathleen Coburn (London & Toronto 1954)
SL	S. T. Coleridge *Sibylline Leaves* (1817)
S Letters (Curry)	*New Letters of Robert Southey* ed Kenneth Curry (2 vols New York & London 1965)
S Letters (Warter)	*A Selection from the Letters of Robert Southey* ed J. W. Warter (4 vols 1856)
S Life (CS)	*Life and Correspondence of Robert Southey* ed C. C. Southey (6 vols 1849–50)
S Life (Simmons)	Jack Simmons *Southey* (1945)
SM	S. T. Coleridge *The Statesman's Manual: or, The Bible, the Best Guide to Political Skill and Foresight. A Lay-Sermon Addressed to the Higher Classes of Society* (1816)
SM (1852)	S. T. Coleridge *The Statesman's Manual* in *Lay Sermons* ed Derwent Coleridge (1852)
SM (*CC*)	S. T. Coleridge *The Statesman's Manual* in *Lay Sermons* ed R. J. White (London & Princeton 1972)
Southey SC (1844)	*Catalogue of the Valuable Library of the Late Robert Southey* (Sotheby, May 1844). Marked copy: BM S–C S 252(1)
Studies	*Coleridge: Studies by Several Hands on the Hundredth Anniversary of his Death* ed E. Blunden and E. L. Griggs (1934)
SW & F (*CC*)	S. T. Coleridge *Shorter Works and Fragments* ed H. J. Jackson and J. R. de J. Jackson (2 vols London & Princeton in preparation) = *CC* XI
TL	S. T. Coleridge *Hints Towards the Formation of a More Comprehensive Theory of Life* ed Seth B. Watson (1848)
TT	*Table Talk of Samuel Taylor Coleridge* ed H. N. Coleridge (rev ed 1836). Cited by date

UL	*Unpublished Letters of Samuel Taylor Coleridge* ed Earl Leslie Griggs (2 vols 1932)
V & A	Victoria and Albert Museum
VCL	Victoria College Library, University of Toronto
Watchman (CC)	S. T. Coleridge *The Watchman* ed Lewis Patton (London & Princeton 1970) = *CC* II
Watson List	Ms list of 21 Coleridge association books that belonged to Mrs Lucy E. Watson (c 1838–1929), granddaughter of James Gillman. Drawn up for EHC after 1889, the list was in the Leatherhead Collection
WL (E 2)	*Letters of William and Dorothy Wordsworth; the Early Years* ed Ernest de Selincourt, rev Chester L. Shaver (Oxford 1967)
WL (L)	*Letters of William and Dorothy Wordsworth; the Later Years* ed Ernest de Selincourt (3 vols Oxford 1939)
WL (L 2)	*Letters of William and Dorothy Wordsworth; the Later Years* ed Alan G. Hill (3 vols Oxford 1980–)
WL (M 2)	*Letters of William and Dorothy Wordsworth; the Middle Years* ed Ernest de Selincourt, rev Mary Moorman (2 vols Oxford 1969–70)
W Library	Chester L. Shaver and Alice C. Shaver *Wordsworth's Library. A Catalogue Including a List of Books Housed by Wordsworth for Coleridge from c. 1810 to c. 1830* (New York & London 1979)
W Life	Mary Moorman *William Wordsworth, A Biography* (2 vols Oxford 1957–65)
Wordsworth LC	Wordsworth Library Catalogue. Harvard MS Eng 880. A handlist of books in WW's library at Rydal Mount from c 1823. Serial numbers supplied by George Whalley. See also *W Library*
Wordsworth SC (1859)	*Catalogue of the ... Library of ... William Wordsworth* (Preston 1859)
W Mem	Christopher Wordsworth *Memoirs of William Wordsworth* (2 vols 1851)
W Prose	*The Prose Works of William Wordsworth* ed. W. J. B. Owen and J. W. Smyser (3 vols Oxford 1974)
WPW	*The Poetical Works of William Wordsworth* ed Ernest de Selincourt and Helen Darbishire (5 vols Oxford 1940–9)
WW	William Wordsworth

MARGINALIA

WILLIAM CAMDEN
1551–1623

Institutio graecae grammatices compendaria, in usum Regiae Scholae Westmonasteriensis. Edited by I. W. [i.e. John Ward (c 1679–1758)]. London 1784 (or 1795?). 12º.

An incomplete copy lacking title-page, being pp 1–42, 49–50 (of viii. 196), distributed through two separate ms documents: Fragment A—pp 1–8 pasted between 6 pp of larger paper sewn together (a single leaf making pp ⁻4/⁻3, and a double leaf making pp ⁻2/⁻1 + ⁺1/⁺2 conjugate) to form a rough booklet; Fragment B—pp 9–42, 49–50 interspersed through a made-up notebook. Both documents are Greek grammars put together by C for his sons, the printed pages of CAMDEN, marked and modified in ms, providing part of the text. The matching of torn leaves in one fragment with cognate leaves in the other shows that only one copy of the printed grammar was dismembered for the two booklets.

Victoria College Library (Coleridge Collection): Fragment A
University of Texas (Humanities Research Center): Fragment B

Fragment A, incorporated into DC's Greek grammar (VCL S MS F 2.6), is annotated and marked on pp 1, 5, 6, 7, 8; C's ms otherwise is on pp ⁻4–⁻1 and ⁺1–⁺2. The whole booklet forms only the beginning of a grammar—the alphabet, accents, etc, and (in ms) the conjugation of the verb εἰμί (of special significance to C: see e.g. *CN* IV 4644, 4697), declensions of the relative pronoun and definite article and of nouns of three of the ten declensions then recognised.

Fragment B, incorporated into HC's Greek grammar, which constitutes an almost complete elementary Greek accidence, is annotated and marked on pp 10, 11, 14, 15, 19, 20, 21, 22, 23, 30, 32, 33, 39(?), 42, 49, the printed pages representing only a small proportion of a considerable ms. The notebook is inscribed: "Hartley Coleridge from his Father, S. T. Coleridge Tuesday, 4 November, 1806. For his Greek Exercises."

DC said that C began to teach HC Greek "before he had learnt any Latin, when he was ten years old, and commenced the compilation of a Greek grammar for his use. This fragment, consisting partly of original matter, partly of leaves cut out of a Westminster grammar, with the English written over the Latin, is now [1851] in my possession.... Beginning Greek nearly at the same time, and being somewhat more regularly instructed, I was soon sufficiently on a level with my brother to share his lessons, and thus became his class-fellow." HC's grammar "contains some curious attempts at simplification, some interesting philological remarks, and some very eloquent writing on the advantages of classical studies, combining in a manner

3

very characteristic of my father's mind, milk for the merest babes, with strong meat for men of ripest years and understanding." *HC Poems* I xxix–xxx. DC printed an incomplete transcript of this grammar in *HC Poems* I clxxxviii–cxcvii; a more complete transcript made by EHC and his clerk, but omitting the printed matter from Camden, is now in VCL (LT 8).

This copy of Camden may have belonged to RS as a Westminster boy. But Camden's grammar had wide circulation beyond Westminster School: first published in 1597 and issued in numerous editions up to at least 1825, it was for more than 200 years the grammar most generally used in schools where Greek was taught. Christ's Hospital had its own Latin grammar (see BAXTER *Reliquiae* COPY B **80** n 1), but—unlike Eton, which had a Greek grammar closely related to Camden's and deriving from it—it did not have a Greek grammar of its own. Lamb repeats a tradition that Camden had been a Bluecoat boy; it is quite possible that C himself learned his Greek from Camden's grammar, and so may WW at Hawkshead grammar school. (There was a "Westminster Greek Gram:" in the Rydal Mount library, edition not identified: Wordsworth LC 122, *W Library* 271.)

C inscribed HC's grammar on 4 Nov 1806, five days after arriving back in Greta Hall from the Mediterranean. The waste paper that served as wrapper for Fragment A originated in Greta Hall, and the local references in the verses to DC all point to Greta Hall; and C stayed on there from 30 Oct until he left to join the Wordsworths at Coleorton, where he arrived on 21 Dec, bringing HC with him but not, as originally intended, DC. DC said that when HC was ten years old C "*commenced* the compilation of a Greek grammar for his use"; it does not appear that he completed it in one concentrated effort. DC's grammar (containing Fragment A), a much smaller affair, could have been put together quite quickly. If C had not made it up before he left Greta Hall for Coleorton, he must have sent it to DC without delay: by 7 Feb 1807 DC had learned the Greek alphabet at least, and on that date C wrote to say that he was "greatly delighted, that you are so desirous to go on with your Greek", finished his letter with "a short Lesson of Greek" (which refers to much that was in DC's grammar), and promised to send "a whole Sheet of Greek Lessons in a few days". *CL* III 1–3; cf 5–6.

DATE. Nov–Dec 1806. There is no reason to doubt EHC's conjecture written on his transcript: "Probable date. November, 1806."

MARGINALIA. The annotations—in Fragment A a few translations inserted and a number of marks to show what is to be studied, in Fragment B mostly translations of Camden's Latin text—cannot be intelligibly separated from the important original ms materials in which they are embedded, of primary interest for C's thoughts on the Greek language. The marginalia will be dealt with in *SW&F* (*CC*) in the examination of these and other grammars that came from C's hand.

BENJAMIN PITTS CAPPER

b 1761

A Topographical Dictionary of the United Kingdom; compiled from parliamentary and other authentic documents and authorities; containing geographical, topographical, & statistical accounts of every district, object, and place in England, Wales, Scotland, Ireland, and the various small islands dependant on the British Empire. [Edition not certainly identified.] Accompanied by forty-seven maps, drawn purposely for this work, on an original plan, with additions and corrections, and the population tables published in 1812. London 1813. 8°.

The 1st ed was published Jun 1808 (*EC*); reissued in revised and expanded form at irregular intervals thereafter.

Not located. *Lost List*.

The annotated copy was in the possession of Fulke Tovey Barnard (b 1797) of 30 Broad Street, Bristol, in 1834. A letter addressed by Joseph Henry Green to Launcelot Wade after C's death went to Barnard, Wade's "Sole Executor", Wade having died in c 1830. (For the few known biographical details of L. Wade and F. T. Barnard, see *CN* III 4179.) In a letter of 15 Oct 1834 Barnard told Green that he had been "in possession of a considerable number of Letters, Books with Marginal Notes, and other papers written by Mr Coleridge, but all went at that time in my House which was destroyed by the Conflagration [in the Bristol riots of 1831]—The annexed is the only Note of Mr Coleridge which I can find...". MS Leatherhead.

MS TRANSCRIPT. MS Leatherhead: transcript by F. T. Barnard in the letter described above, with the heading "Copy of a Manuscript Memorandum of S. T. Coleridge, made in the title page of Capper's Topographical Dictionary", but Barnard describes it as "in Pencil on the first and last leaves".

DATE. Possibly late Oct 1813–early Sept 1814, when C was staying with Josiah Wade at 2 Queen's Square, Bristol.

1   front and back flyleaves, evidently referring to sig 3Y, pencil | Population Returns of 1811. The Cities of London and Westminster

The disproportion of Females to Males, in the population of Towns & Cities, often as 15 Females to 12 Males,[1] is a subject for much

1[1] Capper's table gives figures for Inhabited Houses, Males, and Females, for London City within (and without) the Walls, Westminster City and Liberties,

5

meditation and enquiry.—On the assertions of Travellers (NB *French* in general, and with irreligious prejudices) that in Asia & Africa there are from 2 to 5 women born for a male, Polygamy has been defended. Now Polygamy is demonstrably incompatible with the MORAL Being of Man; therefore the assertion is false, or, the Disproportion is the cause of Polygamy, or some vice tantamount.—

Quere—Whether the equality in numbers of males and females may not be as important an exponent of the Morality of a nation, as the equality in Treatment undoubtedly is.[2] Take 19 Females to 18 Males as the ideal; and let the excess of Females over Males, (not by accident of congregation, but by actual birth) represent the degree of immorality;—This would form a good *Etho*meter = μέτρον ἔθεος.[3]

The perils of Childbirth, and the greater longevity of the prolific power in the Male, sufficiently account for the 19 Females for 18 Males.—

and the Out-Parishes of Middlesex and Surrey within (and not within) the Bills of Mortality. For a total population of 1,009,546, the proportion of Females to Males is 1.207:1; the lowest proportion is for London City within the Walls (1.013:1), the highest is for the Out-Parishes not within the Bills of Mortality (1.360:1). The proportion for the Out-Parishes within the Bills of Mortality (1.225:1) is close to C's figure of 15:12 (1.25:1). His "ideal" of 19:18 (1.056) is similar to the figure for London City without the Walls (1.065:1).

In possible confirmation of this Barnard copy being the 1813 ed, there are no population figures in the 1808 ed; the 1825 ed—too late for this note of C's—has a number of tables, but none showing the general distribution of males and females for the whole, or any part of, the population.

For C's wish "to procure an account of the population of each separate Parish of Bristol" in c May 1807, see *CN* II 3010.

1[2] For a brief series of observations on the equality of the sexes, see *IS* 303–7 (§§227–33).

1[3] "Measurer of morality". "Ethometer" is not in *OED*.

CARMINA

Carmina illustrium poetarum italorum. [Collected and edited by Giovanni Gaetano Bottari.] 11 vols. Florence 1719–1726. 8°.

Victoria & Albert Museum (Dyce Collection)

Inscribed on I ⁻2: "C. P." and "A. Dyce". The catalogue entry from *Herbert C SC* (1862) 75 is pasted in, and below it Dyce has written: "The present copy,—which cost me £5–18–0 at Sotheby's, April 10ᵗʰ 1862. A. D."

Inscribed on the title-pages of Vols I and X, by SC or Mrs C: "S. T. Coleridge Gretahall Keswick". The initials "STC" are also written on the title-page of Vol II and on the half-title of Vol III. On XI ⁺3 (p–d) Herbert Coleridge has written in pencil: "Greater light to rule night—neat speech made by me H. C. Feb 25, 1855, talking to Nell about my bath".

C referred to XI 177 of this set in c May–Jun 1805: *CN* II 2590. For other materials from this collection, see *CN* III 3319 (VIII 167: c May 1808) and perhaps *CN* III 3305 (I 351); *CN* III 4160 (I 42: c May 1812), and *CN* III 4110 (of uncertain date), which is virtually identical with 4160.

DATE. Possibly May–Jun 1805, or later. The marginalia suggest a preliminary early exploration of the volumes rather than a later deliberate reading.

1 I ¹1

Inter meliora

Page.

45. 46. 48.¹

2 VIII ⁻5 (p–d), referring to VIII 7–9 | lines 1–6

*In obitum Philippi Beroaldi, ad Geraldum Cadamustum*¹
Sunt quos bella movent crudi Mavortis, et arma
    Pallados, et Triviae tela pharetrigerae.
Sunt quos plectra decent aurata, sonantia flammas,
    Quae positae hamatis sunt sub harundinibus.
Non me bella movent, non plectra sonantia flammas
    Sed carmen cunctis triste voluminibus....

[*On the Death of Philip Beroaldo, Addressed to Gerald Cadamust*. Some are moved by the wars of cruel Mars, the arms of Pallas, and the weapons of

1¹ Referring "Among the better things" to Latin epigrams by Ignazio Albani of Merate (fl early seventeenth century), five of which are marked in the text: see ANNEX (*a*).

2¹ By Gianfrancesco Quinziano Stoa, formerly Conti (1484–1557), tutor to Francis I of France, and poet laureate.

7

quiver-bearing Diana. Some are pleased by the golden lute singing of the flames that tip the barbed arrows [of Love]. Wars do not move me, nor the lute telling of flames, but the song that's sad in all its windings....]

7 to 9 a most singular Form of the Hex. & Pentameter![2]—Had the Poem ~~but~~ een much shorter, it would have no unpleasing effect

3 viii [+1]

p. 4. 26 to 31.[1] 83[2]

<u>166</u>[a3]

Annex

C refers to the following poems in **1** and **3**. Passages marked with a line in the margin are quoted below.

(*a*) Five poems on i 45–8 by Ignazio Albani of Merate:

Ad Carolum Emanuelem Sabaudiae Ducem
Lis oritur Bellonam inter doctamque Minervam:
Haec sibi prima cupit, quaerit et illa sibi....

[*To Charles Emanuel, Duke of Savoy.* Strife arises between Bellona and learned Minerva: both desire the precedence....]

Eidem
Jam veterum sanxit merito sententia quondam,
Cederet ut doctae Martia turba togae
Ast nunc haud facile est in te discernere, Princeps,
Palladis ars palmam, Martis an arma ferant....

[*To the Same.* A judgement of men of old rightly ordained long since that the warlike throng of Mars should give way to the learned toga. Yet now it is hard to tell, Prince, whether in you the art of Pallas or the weapons of Mars bear the palm....]

In Buccium male ludentem
Cum bene directum certo meditatus in orbem
Jactu indis globulum, Buccie, nemo probat.
Ast male cum jacias; quam belle dirigis! ajunt.
Buccie, si bene vis ludere, lude male.

---

[a] At first glance this figure looks like "100", but closer inspection shows that "166" is the more likely reading

2[2] The main peculiarity is the multi-syllabic endings of the pentameters; this is less frequent later in the poem.

3[1] Referring to two poems by Quinziano: see ANNEX (*b*).

3[2] Referring to a poem by Giulio Ronconi (fl sixteenth century): see ANNEX (*c*).

3[3] No mark in Vol viii certainly identifies the poem referred to. The doubtful reading "166" is perhaps strengthened by the fact that C used a poem on the facing page (167), in c May 1808, as the basis for a sorrowful "Asra poem": see *CN* iii 3319 and ANNEX (*d*). On the difficulty of reading C's 0's and 6's see *CN* iii 4005n.

[*To Bocchio, Playing Badly*. When you calculate, and aim aright, and throw the ball into the circle, Bocchio, no one praises you. But when you throw badly; "How well you aim", they say. Bocchio, if you want to play well, play badly.]

De verâ Justitiâ

Quae Dea? Justitia; et cur torvo lumine? flecti
Nescia sum lacrimis, nec prece, nec pretio.
Quod genus? a superis; genitor quis? Jupiter; ex quâ
Matre? fide; nutrix quae tua? Pauperies.
Quis gremio infantem fovit? Prudentia...

[*True Justice*. Which goddess are you? Justice. And why the stern face? I cannot be bent by tears, nor prayers, nor money. What your descent? From heaven. Who is your father? God. Your mother? Faith. Your nurse? Poverty. Who cherished you as an infant at her bosom? Prudence...]

De falsâ Justitiâ

Quae tu? Justitia; et cur blando lumine? flector
Protinus ante omnes non prece, sed pretio.
Quod genus? a terris; quo patre? Dolo; unde creata?
Ex Spe; quae nutrix? aurea materies.
Quis gremio infantem te fovit? Opinio famae.
Quomodo cognoscis crimina? muneribus.
Cur dextrâ gladium gestas, lancemque sinistra?...

[*False Justice*. Who are you? Justice; and why is your face benign? I am always bent most of all by money, not by prayers. What your descent? From earth. Who is your father? Deceit. Your mother? Hope. Your nurse? Gold. Who cherished you as an infant in her bosom? Reputation. How do you deal with offences? By reward. Why do you hold a sword in your right hand, a balance in your left?...]

(*b*) Two poems beginning on VIII 4, 26, both (like **2** textus) by Gianfrancesco Quinziano Stoa:

Ad Deum

Te Deum coeli colimus parentem,
Te Deum summum dominum fatemur,
Te patrem terrae veneratur omnis
Lingua coruscum....

[*To God*. Thee, O God, parent of heaven, we worship; we confess thee highest Lord; every tongue venerates thee, light-flashing father of the earth....]

Margaretae Scotorum Reginae Monodiae

O coelum, ô superi Lares,
Fatorum ô rabies trium!
An me conjuge proprio
Fraudasse, egregium decus?...

[*Monody of Margaret, Queen of Scots*. O heaven, O gods above, O rage of the three Fates; is it to your honour and glory that you have cheated me of my husband?...]

(*c*) A poem on VIII 83 by Giulio Ronconi:

Ad Torquatum Tassum
Seu canat ardores pastoris Tassus Amyntae,
Sive Cupidineas, quas tulit ipse, faces...

[*To Torquato Tasso*. Whether Tasso sings the loves of the shepherd Amyntas, or the torches of Cupid that he has carried himself...]

(*d*) No poem is marked on VIII 166. On that page a group of five poems by Bernardino Rota on the death of his wife begins, the first two and six of the eight lines of the third being printed on VIII 166. (C transcribed the last poem of the group variatim in *CN* III 3319.)

In Portiae Capiciae conjugis funere. "Dum viridi vernos carpebat gramine flores". [*On the Death of his Wife, Portia Capicia.* "Dino was gathering spring flowers in the green grass".]

Ejusdem tumulus. "Pierides tumulo violas, Venus alma hyacinthos". [*Her Tomb.* "The Muses scatter violets on her tomb, bountiful Venus brings hyacinths".]

Ad eandem. "Dum parere heu sobolem credis dulcissima conjux". [*To the Same.* "Thinking to bring me forth a child, dearest wife, alas".]

WILLIAM CAVE

1637–1713

Scriptorum ecclesiasticorum historia literaria, a Christo nato usque ad saeculum XIV. facili methodo digesta. Qua, de vita illorum ac rebus gestis, de secta, dogmatibus, elogio, stylo; de scriptis genuinis, dubiis, supposititiis, ineditis, deperditis, fragmentis; deque variis operum editionibus perspicue agitur.... Editio novissima, ab autore ipsomet ante obitum recognita et auctior facta. 2 vols. Oxford 1740, 1743. F°.

Not located. *Lost List.*

Wordsworth LC 744 (twice marked as C's) and 1203 (Highgate List) seems to be this copy. Wordsworth LC 288, marked as C's, seems to be another copy: in the catalogue the title "Ecclesiast: Scriptor:" has been crossed out and a note added—"sent to D", i.e. DC. Wordsworth LC 336, a copy of Cave's *Antiquitates Christianae*, is marked as C's but has a note against the entry: "not marked & omitted to be sent to Highgate".

C's notes in BM MS Egerton 2801 ff 237–8 may be quasi-marginalia on this work.

The one annotation printed below is known only from *British Magazine* XI (Mar 1837) 241, reported by "B.".

DATE. Possibly Nov–Dec 1801. For material extracted from this work in late 1801—a list of Duns Scotus' writings, the now-famous Greek epithet (ὁ μυριόνους) that C applied to Shakespeare, and details of the dates and writings of the Fathers—see *CN I* 1000D, 1006, 1070, 1071, 1080.

1   i i | Prolegomena §1 "De instauratione meliorum literarum in Occidente"

In scholis unice regnavit Aristoteles, perperam versus, male intellectus: hunc subsecuti sunt longo satis agmine Theologi scholastici cum suis *accidentibus, instantibus, relationibus, distinctionibus, qualitatibus, quantitatibus, quidditatibus, haecceitatibus, formalitatibus, substantiis individuis, praedicamentis, propositionibus, terminis logicalibus* et *metaphysicalibus*, et *syllogismis* mira arte perplexis et contortis: *Lombardus, Commestor, Albertus, Bonaventura, Thomas, Scotus...Biel...* et sexcenta etiam nominum portenta: hinc nata insana disputandi prurigo, vanae, ineptae, rixosae, et inutiles quaes-

11

tiunculae; usque adeo, ut omnes pene veritates evangelicae in subtilem et spinosam theologiam abierunt.

[*On the Establishment of improved literature in the West.* In the schools Aristotle reigned alone, badly translated and misunderstood: the scholastic theologians followed him in a great long procession with their *accidents, instances, relations, distinctions, qualities, quantities, quiddities, haecceities, formalities, individual substances, predicaments, propositions, terms in logic* and *terms in metaphysics,* and *syllogisms* knotted and tangled with astonishing dexterity: *Peter Lombard, Peter Comestor, Albertus Magnus, Bonaventura, Thomas Aquinas, Duns Scotus...Gabriel Biel...*and a host more of formidable names: hence arose the crazy itch for disputation, the empty, silly, captious, unprofitable subjects for debate; so much so that almost all the gospel truths disappeared into subtle and crabbed theology.]

I have often seen it *asserted*, never *proved*, that the schoolmen used an essentially false translation of Aristotle, and essentially misunderstood and perverted his philosophy. I am, indeed, convinced of the contrary.[1] This whole attack on the schoolmen is mere vulgar common-place, and it is unjust and calumnious. The schoolmen were the true dawn of the restoration of literature: they were the first restorers of it. It is true, they lived before the discovery of the best classics, and wrote in the Latin of their ages, a barbarous Latin; and this attack of Cave's does in reality[a] affect their *style* only, and that fondness for words of classification which is common to systematic thinkers in all ages. Who would not infer, from this whole passage, that the state of learning and religion and good morals had been vastly superior in the ages immediately preceding the scholastic, than

---

a British Magazine reads "really"—probably a printer's error

[1] During the hundred years ending in 1268–72 with Roger Bacon's critique of the Schoolmen and of the translators of Aristotle, the influence of Aristotle was finally established through the gradual transmission of Greek mss from Constantinople, the slow spread of an understanding of the Greek language, the interpretations of Albertus Magnus (c 1200–80) and of St Thomas Aquinas (c 1225–74), and especially the Latin translations of William of Moerbeke (c 1215–56). Aristotle's work had previously been known from Boethius' Latin version of some of the logical works and from Latin translations of some of the philosophical works made from Syriac and Arabic versions of the Greek. C may have made his statement on the basis of his reading of Aquinas' commentary on Aristotle: see e.g. *CN* I 973A (c 25 Jul–24 Aug 1801) and n. At a date so early as this annotation, C may not have been aware that the Schoolmen had indeed succeeded in adapting Aristotle's philosophy to suit and support Church doctrine, and that in the early thirteenth century as reliable texts of Aristotle began to circulate in Latin the direct teaching of Aristotle's philosophy was expressly forbidden by the Schoolmen.

during it? And who so ignorant of history as not to know the falsehood of this? I pray God that I may hereafter be enabled to do justice to these despised schoolmen!²

S. T. COLERIDGE.

1² For C's attempts at acquaintance with the writings of the Schoolmen, in Jul 1801, see n 1, above, and BAXTER *Reliquiae* COPY A **34** n 1 and cf *CL* II 903, 1020. C's instinct was to defend the *heterodoxi* whom others hastily dismissed for the obscurity or strangeness of their terms—e.g. Bruno, Böhme, Swedenborg. In defending the Schoolmen in Lecture 9 of the Philosophical Lectures (22 Feb 1819) he confessed to an unfashionable admiration for them and declared their superiority in intelligence and civility. See *P Lects* (1949) esp 266–7, 275–82, 290–3, 436–40. In Lecture 11 he said that he was "persuaded that to the scholastic philosophy the Reformation is attributable, far more than to the revival of classical literature". *P Lects* (1949) 316–17. Cf *CN* III 3618 (1809), suggested perhaps by Paracelsus; also *SM* (*CC*) 103 and *TT* 20 Apr 1811.

ALEXANDER CHALMERS
1759–1834

The Works of the English Poets, from Chaucer to Cowper; including the series edited, with prefaces, biographical and critical, by Dr. Samuel Johnson...The additional Lives by Alexander Chalmers. Vols III and v (of 21). London 1810. 8°.

Not located. *Lost List.*

The marginalia on Donne printed in *LR* I 148–50 are described as from a copy of Chalmers "belonging to Mr. Gillman". It is not clear whether the single note on Daniel (1), printed in isolation in *LR* II 360 as "Note on Chalmers's *Life of Daniel*", is from the same set. There was no copy of Chalmers in *Gillman SC* (1843); a set in *Green SC* (1880) 184 is not shown as annotated by C. Annotations here reprinted from *LR* II 360–1, I 148–50.

CONTENTS. III. Spenser, Daniel (1), v. Carew, Corbet (2), Davies, Donne (3–7), Drummond, Hall, Shakespeare, Stirling.

DATE. 1820 (Daniel); Sept 1823 (Corbet); and 1829 (Donne)—according to *LR*, whether in ms or supplied by HNC is not clear.

C's scheme for "filtering" Donne's poems, proposed in N 43, apparently belongs to 1830: see DONNE *Poems* headnote. EHC gives 1818 as a conjectural date for the composition of **2**—*PW* (EHC) I 433—but see **2** n 1, below.

SAMUEL DANIEL

1 III 451 | Chalmers's Life of Daniel

[After a quotation of almost a page from "Mr Headly, who appears to have studied Daniel's works with much attention", Chalmers writes:] The justice of these remarks cannot be disproved, although some of them are rather too figurative for sober criticism. Daniel's fatal error was in choosing history instead of fiction; yet in his lesser pieces, and particularly in his sonnets, are many striking poetical beauties; and his language is every where so much more harmonious than that of his contemporaries, that he deserves his place in every collection of English poetry, as one who had the taste or genius to anticipate the improvements of a more refined age.

Most genuine! A figurative remark! If this strange writer had any meaning, it must be:—Headly's criticism is just throughout, but

14

conveyed in a style too figurative for prose composition.[1] Chalmers's own remarks are wholly mistaken;—too silly for any criticism, drunk or sober, and in language too flat for any thing. In Daniel's Sonnets there is scarcely one good line; while his Hymen's Triumph, of which Chalmers says not one word, exhibits a continued series of first-rate beauties in thought, passion, and imagery, and in language and metre is so faultless, that the style of that poem may without extravagance be declared to be imperishable English.[2] 1820.

RICHARD CORBET

2   v 556 | Chalmers "The Life of Richard Corbet, D.D."

As a poet, it will not be found that Corbet stands eminently distinguished. His thoughts, however, are often striking and original, although delivered in the uncouth language of his times, and seldom indebted to correctness of versification. His faults are in general those of the age in which he wrote, and if he fills no conspicuous place in poetical history, it ought not to be forgot that he wrote for the amusement of the moment, and made no pretensions to the veneration of posterity.

I almost wonder that the inimitable humour, and the rich sound and propulsive movement of the verse, have not rendered Corbet a popular poet. I am convinced that a reprint of his poems, with illustrative and chit-chat biographical notes, and cuts by Cruikshank, would take with the public uncommonly well.[1]

September, 1823.

[1] Henry Headley (1765–88), a friend of Bowles at Oxford, published *Poems* in 1786 and *Select Beauties of Ancient English Poetry. With Remarks* (2 vols) in 1787. WW said of him in 1829 that "Headley was a most extraordinary young man—more remarkable for precocity of judgement than any one I ever read or heard of". *WL (L)* I 383.

[2] In spite of what C says here about Daniel's sonnets, he intended in Jan 1804 to "quote the introd. Sonnet to Musophilus" in his projected "Consolations and Comforts" (*CN* I 1796) and in Aug 1805 copied out the opening four lines of the first *Delia* sonnet (*CN* II 2654). Some of his reading of Daniel in 1804, and probably all of it in the Mediterranean, was in *B Poets* IV; but in early 1804 he was also using a 2-vol ed of Daniel that on 8

Mar he sent to Sir George Beaumont "with the eminent Passages of the Hymen's Triumph (for which alone I have sent them) *marked*". *CL* II 1079. Cf *CN* II 1901 and *TT* 15 Mar 1831. For further marginalia on Daniel, see ANDERSON COPY A 3–6, COPY B 10, 11, and DANIEL.

[2] Richard Corbet (1582–1635), bp of Oxford and Norwich, famed for his conviviality and for the rollicking satirical flair of his poems, the best known of which is *The Fairies' Farewell*. His poems were first collected after his death under the title *Certain Elegant Poems* (1647, 2nd ed 1672). Octavius Gilchrist edited all Corbet's printed poems and added others from ms (1807): the volume was reprinted in CHALMERS.

JOHN DONNE

3 v [126], pencil

[added to commendatory verses by Marston, by an unknown writer, and by Jonson:]

> With Donne, whose muse on dromedary trots,
> Wreathe iron pokers into true-love knots;
> Rhyme's sturdy cripple, fancy's maze and clue,
> Wit's forge and fire-blast, meaning's press and screw.[1]

3[1] The figures of contorting and crushing energy that command lines 2 and 4 of the epigram can be seen separately in DONNE *Poems* **28**, **30** (of 1811)—notes that refer, not to the *Songs and Sonets*, but to the *Satyres*. The recent accurate publication of marginalia in a copy of *SL* in the possession of Arthur A. Houghton, Jr suggests that the epigram may have been composed as early as Aug 1798: "This [comment of Lamb's on some lines in *Human Life*] reminds me of some lines I wrote affter leaving Stowey, in a poetic Epistle to my Friend, T. Poole: describing ~~my~~ our pursuits and conversations.

> . . . .
> ~~With~~ Like Donne whose Verse on dromedary trots,
> Wreathe iron pokers into true-love knots,
> Rhyme's sturdy Cripple, Wit's Maze and Clue,
> Thought's Forge and Furnace,
> Mangle-press and Screw...."

Mary Lynn Johnson "How Rare is a 'Unique Annotated Copy' of Coleridge's *Sibylline Leaves*?" *BNYPL* LXXVI (1975) 476, ms reproduced on [459]. The opening three lines of C's fragmentary recollection of the "poetic Epistle" have a parallel in *CN* I 295 (1796–8), a note written some time after C had recorded a project to write "Satires in the manner of Donne". *CN* I 171 (c Oct 1796). In the version of the epigram written in CHALMERS, the figure of Hephaestus—the "sturdy Cripple" who provides the

"Forge and Furnace"—is not altered, but the image of "Brahma's Hydraulic Packing-Engine" in DONNE *Poems* **28** has displaced the domestic "Mangle", and the intensification of "Furnace" to "Fire-blast" conveys some of the force of the unassimilated "Scrouge of Sense" and "Cramp of Strength" that appear in the DONNE *Poems* marginalia. C recalled the "dromedary" epigram when he was correcting and annotating a copy of *SL*, and may have written it down in Gillman's copy of CHALMERS in 1829, when he was again thinking about Donne's poems.

In *LR* I 149 HNC added to C's epigram a second—not by C—with the note: "the publication of No. II. I trust the all-accomplished author will, under the circumstances [i.e. that 'Nothing remains of what was said on Donne in this Lecture'], pardon."

> See lewdness and theology combin'd,—
> A cynic and a sycophantic mind;
> A fancy shar'd party per pale between
> Death's heads and skeletons and Aretine!—
> Not his peculiar defect or crime,
> But the true current mintage of the time.
> Such were the establish'd signs and tokens given
> To mark a loyal churchman, sound and even,
> Free from papistic and fanatic leaven.

The author is not identified. "*Sycophancy* and Cynic Assentation" are ascribed to Dr Johnson in H. COLERIDGE *Worthies* **48**.

4 v (page not recorded)

The wit of Donne, the wit of Butler, the wit of Pope, the wit of Congreve, the wit of Sheridan—how many disparate things are here expressed by one and the same word, Wit!—Wonder-exciting vigour, intenseness and peculiarity of thought, using at will the almost boundless stores of a capacious memory, and exercised on subjects, where we have no right to expect it—this is the wit of Donne! The four others I am just in the mood to describe and inter-distinguish;—what a pity that the marginal space will not let me![1]

5   v 127 | *The Good Morrow* lines 15–18

My face in thine eye, thine in mine appears,
And true plain hearts do in the faces rest;
Where can we find two fitter hemispheres
Without sharp north, without declining west?

The sense is;—Our mutual loves may in many respects be fitly compared to corresponding hemispheres; but as no simile squares (*nihil simile est idem*),[1] so here the simile fails, for there is nothing in our loves that corresponds to the cold north, or the declining west, which in two hemispheres must necessarily be supposed. But an ellipse of such length will scarcely rescue the line from the charge of nonsense or a bull.[2]

January 1829.

---

[4][1] For C on wit, see ATHENAEUM **14** n 1 and *Misc C* 111–30. In drawing a distinction between wit and humour he associated wit with "Cleverness" and with the French race, humour with "Genius and Sense". *Friend (CC)* I 131, 420–1. In a literary lecture of 25 Mar 1819, stimulated to some extent by Richter's *Vorschule der Aesthetik*, he spoke of wit in Shakespeare's Falstaff, and in Young and Butler, and compared Congreve with Shakespeare, Sterne, and Steele, to Congreve's disadvantage. *CN* III 4503. In ANDERSON COPY B **22** he noticed a difference in wit between Cowley and Crashaw, but seems to have given no systematic treatment of the kinds of wit into which the series Donne–Butler–Pope–Congreve–Sheridan might be arranged. He quoted from Butler's *Hudibras* several times and noted with amusement Pepys's accusation of "the want of *wit* in the Hudibras". PEPYS *Memoirs* (2 vols 1825) II i 151; see also ANDERSON COPY A **10** n 1. On C's general view of Pope, see *BL* ch 1 (*CC*) I 18–19. He seldom mentioned Congreve, but see H. COLERIDGE **47–70**.

[5][1] "Nothing similar is identical"—a scholastic maxim. See *C&S* (*CC*) 86 and n 3. See also ESCHENMAYER **35**.

[5][2] R. L. Sharp, in *MLN* LXIX (1954) 493–5, says that Donne was probably thinking of cordiform maps, in which each hemisphere was pictured as a heart. For other marginalia on *The Good Morrow*, see DONNE *Poems* **5, 6**.

6 v 128 | *Woman's Constancy*

A misnomer. The title ought to be—Mutual Inconstancy.[1]

7 v 128 | *The Sun Rising* line 17; *The Progress of the Soul* Song ɪ st 2

> Whether both th' Indias of space and <u>mine</u>[a]
> And see at night thy western land of <u>mine</u>.[a]

This use of the word *mine* specifically for mines of gold, silver, or precious stones, is, I believe, peculiar to Donne.[1]

---

[a] *LR* italicises, presumably to represent C's underlining

6[1] For another marginal note on *Woman's Constancy*, see DONNE *Poems* **8**.

7[1] H. J. C. Grierson repeats this note of C's in his 1912 ed of Donne's *Poems*, adding: "The O.E.D. does not contradict this, for the word had a wider connotation", and quotes the same parallel from *The Progress of the Soul*. (For another reference to *The Progress of the Soul* see BROWNE *Works* **22** n 1.) Grierson provides an extract from Donne's letter of 1624 to Sir Robert Carr: "Your way into *Spain* was Eastward, and that is the way to the land of Perfumes and Spices; their way hither is Westward, and that is the way to the land of Gold, and of Mynes." For another annotation on *The Sun Rising* see DONNE *Poems* **10**.

ROBERT CHAMBRE

fl 1659

Some Animadversions upon the Declaration of, and the Plea for the Army: together with 16 queries thence extracted. Or, an essay by way of answer to the plea for, and declaration of the army, in reference to their interruption of the Parliaments sitting, October the 12. Written November 4. 1659, &c. [Anonymous.] Dublin 1659. 4°.

The title-page of the BM copy is inscribed in ink in a seventeenth-century hand "By Robert Chambre", but *BMC* queries the ascription. Probably originally bound in "CROMWELLIAN TRACTS".

British Museum C 134 b 15

Corrections and marks in an unidentified hand similar to that on the title-page, in ink, on pp 14, 18, 19, 26. A correction on p 15 of "without any vote" to "without any veto" may be C's, as may also be the marking of a passage on p 16 and a question mark on p 21.

MS TRANSCRIPT. VCL BT 37: SC transcript, included in a series "From a Volume of Tracts relating to the times of Cromwell". The volume was evidently broken up before this particular tract reached the BM on 7 Dec 1871.

DATE. Possibly 1818. See "CROMWELLIAN TRACTS" headnote.

1 pp 22–3, pencil

The Tares that have been sown by your means, will not easily be pluckt up; especially whilst they have the Armie for a pale to defend *] them. O that God would convince you that sins against the first Table are greater, and more grievous in the sight of God, then against the second Table; as being immediately against his Majesty!

* On the contrary the Vices against the second Table ~~are~~ would therefore ⟨be⟩ greater (if that were possible/—Epist of St James)[1] because they preclude obedience[a] to the first Table—nay, heap the crime of Hypocrisy on the pretence to obedience.[2]

> [a] "obedience" is written to accommodate the printed signature "D"—"obeDience"

1[1] James 2.8–10: "If ye fulfil the royal law, according to the scripture, Thou shalt love thy neighbour as thyself, ye do well....For whosoever shall keep the whole law and yet offend in one point, he is guilty of all."

1[2] The first table of the Mosaic law was the law of God, with respect to religious duties; the second table dealt with moral duties.

WILLIAM ELLERY CHANNING
1780-1842

A Discourse Delivered at the Installation of the Rev. Mellish Irving Motte, as Pastor of the South Congregational Society in Boston, May 21, 1828. Boston, reprinted in London, 1828. 12°.

Bound as third in "PAMPHLETS—DIVINITY".

British Museum C 126 h 2 (3)

Pencil marks in the margins, and underlining of words, on pp 5, 6, 8, 9, 10, 11, 14, 17, 30, 31, 32 do not appear to be C's.

Channing, lifelong friend and brother-in-law of the American painter Washington Allston (1779–1843), and pastor of a Congregational church in Boston, announced in 1819 his break with orthodox Calvinism and was from that time considered the apostle of Unitarianism in the United States and the leading American opponent of Calvinism. With a letter of introduction from Allston he visited C in Jun 1823. Channing's memorandum book preserves a record of the meeting. C expressed his admiration for Allston, and they spoke of the current state of literature. Channing had particularly admired *BL* and *The Friend* and the "spirituality of the philosophy" in them, and was "struck by the fact that Coleridge never used a word that was empty or even careless". They talked of religion, particularly the doctrine of the Trinity, which C believed to be "the perfection of Reason, which can only be developed in us by our grasping the idea of the relation of the infinite Love and infinite Wisdom in one Spirit, communicated to those who are filial by a free obedience". Channing found nothing to object to in C's formula, except in the phraseology. C also poured out a flood of thoughts: on the transcendental philosophy, on trinitarianism and Unitarianism, "and especially on his idea of the Church of England, which was wholly new to me, and not at all acceptable in England to any party, for he included in the National Church not merely the pulpits and curacies in the Establishment, but all the spiritual forces at work in the land—the great schools and universities, and even the sectarian pulpits!" C did not condemn Unitarians personally, and—Channing said—"he had not become nearly so much a reactionary as Southey, or even Wordsworth". See Arthur W. Brown *Always Young for Liberty: a Biography of William Ellery Channing* (Syracuse NY 1956) 149–50; the quotations are from Channing's memorandum book, now in the Harvard School of Divinity. C wrote to Allston about the meeting, on 13 Jun 1823: "Mr. Channing I could not be said not to have known in part before. It is enough to add, that the reality differed from my previous conception of it only by being more amiable, more discriminating, and more free from prejudices, than my experience had permitted me to

20

anticipate. His affection for the good as the good, and his earnestness for the true as the true,—with that harmonious subordination of the latter to the former, without encroachment on the absolute worth of either,—present in him a character which in my heart's heart I believe to be the very rarest in earth...." *Memoir of the Life of William Ellery Channing* (3 vols 1848) II 218–19; the letter is not in *CL*.

John Wheeler, who was to become president of the University of Vermont in 1833 in succession to James Marsh and who, by making that university "a nursery of American Transcendentalism", forged a link in the chain of circumstances that led to Shedd's edition of C's works in 1853, visited C in Highgate in Jul 1829. C questioned him about Channing—as he was to question Ralph Waldo Emerson on his one visit in 1833—saying that it was "an unspeakable misfortune" that Channing "should have turned out a Unitarian after all". *C Talker* 208–9, 360; but see also **1** n 4, below.

DATE. 1828.

1 pp 5–7

What other men believe is to me of little moment. Their arguments I gratefully hear. Their conclusions I am free to receive or reject. I have no anxiety to wear the livery of any party. I indeed take
*] cheerfully the name of a Unitarian, because unwearied efforts are used to raise against it à popular cry; and I have not so learned Christ, as to shrink from reproaches cast on what I deem is truth. Were the name more honoured, I should be glad to throw it off; for I fear the shackles which a party connection imposes.

* In my humble opinion an insufficing and *illegitimate* "because"; but yet of noble Blood, πατρος ἡμιθεου νοθος Υιος[a][1]—and by no other could D[r] Channing be actuated. I regret it, however: first, because it is a blundering use of the term, which implies the contrary opinion, i.e. a *plurality* united, and differs from the Trini- that is, Tri-unitarian only by leaving the number of the hypostatic proprieties (by the Latin Church most unhappily rendered "*Persons*")[2] in-definites, and 2[ndly] it is *calumnious* in its intent, most uncharitably attributing to the great Body of the Church of Christ that a horrid heresy, of even a denial of the di[vi]nity[b] of the Godhead—or an

[a] C has written Roman "U" for Greek "Υ" (capital *upsilon*)—as he often does
[b] Letters supplied by the editor

1[1] "Bastard Son of a half-divine father".

1[2] C found the term "person" unsatisfactory for formulations of the doctrine of the trinity: it led to "error or ambiguity" (BÖHME **161**), it was an "equivocal word" (DONNE *Sermons* COPY B **7**), a "most unhappy and improper term" (Jeremy TAYLOR *Polemicall Discourses* i 960–3). C discussed this issue in close detail, and with specific reference to Channing, in *CN* IV 5292; see also e.g. *CL* V 88. For C's etymology of *persona* see DONNE *Sermons* COPY A **4** n 3.

acknowlegement that there is more than one God—which we openly denounce & abhor. Adiaphorites, or Uni-personalists, or better still Psilanthropists, are the proper names of the modern Socinians.[3]

But I am vain enough to believe, that an hour's tete a tete with D^r Ch. would leave little difference between him and me, on this point.[4]

S. T. Coleridge.

[3] "Adiaphorites", a variant of "Adiaphorists" (from ἀδιάφορα, "things indifferent")—referring to those who were willing to concede matters of personal judgement and conscience that were considered unprejudicial to Protestant doctrine. (There were two major Adiaphorist controversies, one in the sixteenth century, and one in the seventeenth.) C uses the term here in a general sense to refer to those who are prepared to concede even major points of doctrine in order to secure rational plausibility. For another use of ἀδιάφορα in relation to Kant's *Critik der practischen Vernunft*, see *CL* IV 791–2. "Uni-personalists" (not in *OED*)—from "personality", as distinct from "Uniperson(al)ist" from "person(al)"—refers to those who consider the three "persons" as a single "personality". "Psilanthropists"—a favourite word of C's, ascribed to him by *OED*—refers to those who hold that Christ was a "mere man": see e.g. *LS* (*CC*) 176 and n 4.

[4] In his letter to Allston of 13 Jun 1823 (not in *CL*: see headnote, above) C said: "I feel convinced that the few differences in opinion between Mr. Channing and myself not only are, but would by him be found, to be apparent, not real,—the same truth seen in different relations. Perhaps I have been more absorbed in the depth of the mystery of the spiritual life, he more engrossed by the loveliness of its manifestations."

GABRIELLO CHIABRERA
1552-1637

LOST BOOK

Delle opere di Gabriello Chiabrera tomo primo (secondo, tertio). Vols I–III (of 5) in 2. Venice 1782. 12°.

Not located: marginalia not recorded. *Green SC* (1880) 89: "S. T. Coleridge's copy, with autograph on title, and notes in his handwriting."

In c May 1808 C transcribed three odes of Chiabrera into a notebook; part of one of these appears in a letter of Mar 1811 (*CL* III 313), and another was printed in Italian in *The Friend* (1818). *CN* III 3318; *Friend* (*CC*) I 480. In c Jul–Sept 1809 he also copied out the Italian original of which he was to give a skilful prose version in *The Friend* (1818). *CN* III 3578; *Friend* (*CC*) I 65. In *The Friend* No 14 of 23 Nov 1809 he printed for the first time his sustained "imitation" of Chiabrera, *A Tombless Epitaph*. *Friend* (*CC*) II 184; *PW* (EHC) I 413–14.

WW's translations of Chiabrera's *Epitaphs* numbered ten in all; six of these were first published anonymously in *The Friend* from 28 Dec 1809 to 22 Feb 1810 but were omitted from the 1818 edition. See *Friend* (*CC*) II 248–9, 269–70, 334–5; the series of nine epitaphs is printed in *WPW* IV 248–53, an uncollected tenth in IV 377. For the *Essays upon Epitaphs*—of which the first was published in *The Friend* of 22 Feb 1810, and the second and third requested for *The Friend* (1812) but not sent by WW—see *W Prose* II 49–96. WW owned a copy of this Venice 1782 ed (see *W Prose* II 111n): it is now in the Amherst Wordsworth Collection.

RS *CPB* IV 497 quotes seven passages from Vol II of the Venice 1782 ed of Chiabrera, the editor noting: "It is the Venetian Edition of 1782 that is here referred to. It is before me, and marked throughout.—J. W. W." It seems unlikely that this could have been C's copy or the markings his.

WILLIAM CHILLINGWORTH
1602–1643

Scholar and later fellow of Trinity College, Oxford, and godson of William Laud, Chillingworth engaged in controversy with the Jesuit "John Fisher" (i.e. John Percy) in 1628, at a time when he was one of Laud's Oxford informers. Within a year Chillingworth had been converted to Roman Catholicism by his opponent, went to study at Douai, and returned to Oxford in 1631. Three years later he renounced Catholicism and again engaged in controversy with Jesuits, particularly with "Edward Knott" (i.e. Matthew Wilson). His best-known work, *The Religion of Protestants, a Safe Way to Salvation* (1638), argued that "The Bible, the Bible only, is the religion of Protestants."

C wrote marginalia in a copy of Chillingworth's *Works* (1742) in c Apr 1809: see COPY A. He annotated a second copy of the same edition (COPY B) later, the date not exactly determined, but not much later if HNC's date of 25 Jul 1831 is correct for the remark printed in *TT*: "It is now twenty years since I read Chillingworth's book".

C was strongly of the opinion—and often repeated it—that the Roman Catholics and Protestants had done equal damage to the Church, the one by suppressing the Scriptures, the other by bibliolatrous text-sparring. See e.g. COPY B 2 and n 1, DONNE *Sermons* COPY B 49 PS, and ms note on a copy of *The Friend* (1818) in *Friend* (*CC*) I 135 n 2. See also *CN* III 3743 f 21 and cf 3812. The annotations on Chillingworth mark the earlier phase of C's evolution of his trinitarian position. Here he tends to distinguish the Father as Creator from the Son as eternally generated: later he tends to distinguish the Father as the Good from the Son as the Word, the Jehovah-Word, the I AM (or ῶΝ), Creator, Truth.

Copy A

The Works of William Chillingworth...containing his book, intituled, The Religion of Protestants, a Safe Way to Salvation. Together with his Nine Sermons preached before the King, or upon eminent occasions. His letter to Mr. Lewgar, concerning the Church of Rome's being the guide of faith and judge of controversies. His nine additional discourses. And an answer to some passages in Rushworth's Dialogues, concerning Traditions. The tenth edition, &c. 2 pts in 1 vol. London 1742. F°.

Not located. *Lost List.*

MS TRANSCRIPT. VCL LT 50 (l). The text is here taken from the transcript.

DATE. Apr 1809: see **9**.

1   i 41 | Answer to the Preface (addressed to Chillingworth) of *Mercy and Truth, or Charity Maintained* § 20[1]

To the third, *Whether, seeing there cannot be assigned any visible true Church distinct from the* Roman, *it follows not that she erred not fundamentally?* I say, in our Sense of the Word *Fundamental*, it does follow. For if it be true, that there was then no Church distinct from the *Roman*, then it must be, either because there was no Church at all, which we deny: Or, because the *Roman* Church was the whole Church; which we also deny: Or, because she was a Part of the Whole, which we grant. And if she were a true Part of the Church, then she retained those Truths which were simply necessary to Salvation, and held no Errors which were inevitably and unpardonably destructive of it. For this is precisely necessary to constitute any Man or any Church a Member of the Church Catholick. In our Sense therefore of the Word *Fundamental*, I hope she erred not fundamentally: But in your Sense of the Word, I fear she did: that is, she held something to be Divine Revelation, which was not; something not to be, which was.

If Idolatry in both its kinds, (i.e. worshipping the Supreme God under an Image, and worshipping subordinate Gods) if asserting the merits of creatures so as—tho' not avowedly to deny, yet—effectively to

---

1[1] The full title of Chillingworth's work is *The Religion of Protestants, a Safe Way to Salvation; Or, An Answer to a Book Entitled Mercy and Truth or Charitie Maintained by Catholiques,* *Which Pretends to Prove the Contrary* (1638). In his "Answer", Chillingworth quotes extensively from "Edward Knott's" *Mercy and Truth,* consistently referring to it as *Charity Maintained.*

make vain the sole redemption by and meditation of Christ, if the undermining of the one great purpose of the Gospel by holding out substitutes for *regeneration* (i.e. the practical Hatred of Sin for its exceeding Sinfulness)[2] by doctrines of attrition, priestly absolution as operant in se, & not merely declaratory; finally, if a general corruption of the moral sense produced and favored by the whole compages[3] of its *distinguishing* doctrines and ceremonies added to a bold alteration and repeal of divine Commands, and additions equally bold—as in the Eucharist in one kind only, the dogmas concerning marriage—purgatory &c &c; if these be not *fundamental* Errors what can be? If they be the Romish Church is *fundamentally* erroneous, therefore *heretical*—& Chillingworth seems to play at Fast & Loose. Indeed I cannot but regard it as a proof of the Low-Church[a] Lockian Faction, that this Author is extolled as the Αρχασπιστης Ecclesiæ Anglic:[4] and Stillingfleet's most masterly work ("a rational account &c.") forgotten or neglected.[5] S. T. C.

2   i 43 | §26

To the eighth, *How of disagreeing Protestants, both Parts may hope for Salvation, seeing some of them must needs err against some Truth testified by God?* I answer, the most disagreeing Protestants that are, yet thus far agree; 1. That those Books of Scripture, which were never doubted of in the Church, are the undoubted Word of God, and a perfect Rule of Faith. 2. That the Sense of them, which God intended, whatsoever it is, is certainly true; so that they believe implicitly even those very Truths against which they err; and, why an implicit Faith in Christ and his Word, should not suffice as well as an implicit Faith in your Church; I have desired to be resolved by many of your side, but never could. 3. That they are to use their best Endeavours to believe the Scripture in the true Sense, and to live according to it.

<hr>

a NTP reads "prevalency of Low-Church"

1[2] Cf Rom 7.13.

1[3] *OED* notes that Waterland used "compages"—a complex structure or system of conjoined parts—to refer to "the whole fabrick of the Christian faith".

1[4] "Chief shield-bearer (defender, champion) of the Anglican Church". Cf *EOT (CC)* II 475. Locke, chiefly in his, *Letters Concerning Toleration* (1689–92) and *The Reasonableness of Christianity as Delivered in the Scriptures* (1695), sought to recall Christianity to its original simplicity by arguing for a single all-embracing creed that allowed for variety of individual opinion, maintaining that the only secure basis of Christianity was the Bible as interpreted according to "reason". Chillingworth, like Stillingfleet, was directly attacking Locke's position. See also 9, below.

1[5] See STILLINGFLEET *Origines Sacrae, or a Rational Account of the Grounds of Christian Faith* (1675).

The modern Unitarians who follow Dr Priestly are an exception for they believe the Scripture erroneous in many things de facto, & consequently fallible in any & every thing, except as proved ab extra—i.e. by reason & other histories.[1] S. T. Coleridge.

3 i 55 | Answer to ch 1 § 4

Considering, thirdly and lastly, that if they die not with *Contrition*, yet it is very probable they may die with *Attrition*; and that this Pretence of yours, that *Contrition will serve without actual Confession, but Attrition will not*, is but a Nicety or Fancy, or rather to give it the true name, a Device of your own, to serve Ends and Purposes: God having no where declared himself, but that wheresoever he will accept of that Repentance, which you are pleased to call *Contrition*, he will accept of that which you call *Attrition*: For, though He like best the bright flaming Holocaust of Love, yet he rejects not, * he quencheth not, the smoking Flax of that Repentance (if it be true and effectual) which proceeds from Hope and Fear: These Things, I say, considered (unless you will have the Charity of your Doctrine rise up in judgment against your uncharitable Practice) you must not only be peremptory, in damning Protestants, but you must hope well of their Salvation...

* In the repentance of the Living, I grant it; because such attrition may be a *mean* & a natural step^a from bad to less bad in the process to goodness. Enlightened Selfishness may be the Transit from blind Selfishness to Love of God, & Hatred of Sin even for its exceeding Sinfulness.[1] But that a dying Penitent can be *saved* without Love, without Contrition, first, seems to involve a contradiction, for is it not the same as to be regenerate without regeneration? & secondly, not founded on any and repugnant to very many *express* passages of the N. Testament. This therefore I consider as one of Chillingworth's relicts^b of Popery, more will soon appear. S. T. C.—

P.S. This Error is far less irrational in the Papists who hold a state of Purgatory between Death & the final Judgement.—^c2

^a *NTP* reads "stage"   ^b *NTP* reads "relics"
^c Before **3**, MS TRANSCRIPT notes: "In the following extract some of the words have been cut shorn by a binder. It is all legible and certain."

2[1] Joseph Priestley's Unitarian position (see BAHRDT **1** n 1) represents the narrow "rationalism" and self-styled common-sense that, according to C, threatened to turn Christianity from religion to prudential moralism. See *CN* II 2598, in which C refused to "let the names of Darwin, Johnson, Hume, furr...over" his ideal view of England. See also *CN* II 2448. For C on the inadequacy of the proof *ab extra*, see BAXTER *Reliquiae* COPY A **5** n 1.

3[1] See **1** and n 2, above.
3[2] See FIELD **60** n 3.

4   i 56 | §5

Thus much Charity therefore, if you stand to what you have said, is interchangeably granted by each side to the other, that neither Religion is so fatally *destructive, but that by Ignorance or Repentance Salvation may be had on both sides*: Though with a Difference that keeps Papists still on the more uncharitable side. For whereas we conceive a lower Degree of Repentance (that which they call *] *Attrition*) if it be true, and effectual, <u>and convert the Heart</u>^{*a*} of the Penitent, will serve in them: They pretend (even *this Author* which is most charitable towards us) that *without Contrition* there is no Hope for us.

* i.e. if it end in Contrition. If this be true, the notion is self-destructive—attrition suffices *without* contrition if it end *in* contrition—i.e. if finally it be *with*, or become contrition.

5   i 58 | § 7

But for my part, whatsoever Clamour you have raised against me, I think no otherwise of the Nature of Faith, I mean *Historical Faith*, than generally both Protestants and Papists do; for, I conceive it *An Assent to Divine Revelations upon the Authority of the Revealer*; which though in many Things it differ from Opinion (as commonly the Word *Opinion* is understood) yet in some Things, I doubt not but you will confess, that it agrees with it. As first, that as Opinion is an Assent, so is Faith also. Secondly, that as Opinion, so Faith, is always built upon less Evidence than that of Sense or Science; which Assertion you not only grant, but mainly contend for in your *Sixth Chapter*. Thirdly and lastly, that as Opinion, so Faith admits Degrees; and that, as there may be a strong and weak Opinion, so there may be a strong and weak Faith. These Things if you will grant (as sure if you be in your right Mind you will not deny any of them) I am well contented that this ill-sounding Word *Opinion*, should be discarded, and that among the intellectual Habits you should seek out some other *Genus* for *Faith*. For I will never contend with any Man about Words, who grants my Meaning.

That Faith is but another word for *Opinion*, having its very essence in the perception of the preponderance of probabilities, I hold a *second* Popish Error—indeed the Queen-Bee in the Hive.[1] The

---

^{*a*} The italics, not in the printed text, presumably represent C's underlining

5[1] For this recurrent figure of the queen bee see BAINES 1 n 2.

Romanists have decided, Quod Fides sit essentialiter in Intellectu,[2] & Ch. is right in making their hostility to Faith = Opinion a mere Logomachy. Let Faith be considered, 1. as a *moral act*; 2. as a moral act ripened by Habit into a moral *state*—& *Opinion*, even as elsewhere *Works*, as the natural *consequent* of that state and one of its diagnostics; & Chillingworth's Objections & Fears in this & the following Page will lose all their force.

6   i 59 | § 9

Yet all this I say not, as if I doubted that the Spirit of God, being implored by devout and humble Prayer and sincere Obedience, may, and will, by Degrees advance his Servants higher, and give them a Certainty of Adherence, beyond their Certainty of Evidence. But, what God gives as * a Reward to Believers, is one thing; and what he requires of all Men as their Duty, is another; and what he will accept of, out of Grace and Favour, is yet another.

* St Augustine asserts the *contrary*—viz. that clearness of comprehension is *the* reward of certain adherence—wisely I think & evangelically.[1]

7   i 61 | § 12

For though your Church were indeed as *infallible a Propounder of Divine Truths* as it pretends to be, yet, if it appeared not to me to be so, I might very well believe God most true, and your Church most false. As, though the Gospel of *St. Matthew* be the Word of God; yet, if I neither knew it to be so, nor believed it, I might believe in God, and yet think that Gospel a Fable. Hereafter therefore I must intreat you to remember, that our being guilty of this Impiety, depends not only upon your being, but upon our * knowing that you are so.

* Such knowlege not having been precluded by any wrong moral dispositions, of which God only is the Judge.

5[2] "That Faith is essentially in the Intellect". A patristic commonplace; see e.g. Aquinas *Summa theologiae* 2.2 qu 4 art 2.

6[1] Augustine often quoted, discussed, and made variations upon the Septuagint version of Isa 7.9: "Unless you believe you will not understand." For this version, which makes understanding the *reward* for belief, see *CN* II 3133 and n, *BL* ch 24 (*CC*) II 244. See also *SM* (*CC*) 97n, and cf *CN* III 3888n.

8 i 77 | § 27

"Since then, the visible Church of Christ our Lord, is that infallible *Means whereby the revealed Truths of Almighty God, are conveyed to our Understanding*; it followeth, that to oppose her Definitions is to resist God himself...I conclude therefore with this Argument; Whosoever resisteth that Means which infallibly opposeth us to God's Word or Revelation, commits a Sin, which, unrepented, excludes Salvation: But whosoever resisteth Christ's visible Church ...commits a Sin, which unrepented, excludes Salvation. Now, what visible Church was extant, when *Luther* began his pretended Reformation, whether it were the *Roman*, or *Protestant* Church; and whether he, and other Protestants, do not oppose that visible Church, which was spread over the World, before, and in *Luther's* Time, is easy to be determined, and importeth every one most seriously to ponder, as a thing whereon eternal Salvation dependeth."

If it had been possible 1. to define the visible Catholic Church—2 or (that granted) to conceive either how one man can be the Catholic Church, or how millions of men can be *a Judge*—nay, at once Oracle & Questionists—3. how the opinions of this Judge which must be given in *words*, can be less liable to objections than other express *verbal* sentences—4. or to conceive the infallibility of fallible men, unattested by miracles or by Scripture from men so attested to be infallible—or 5. to clear from a ludicrous *circle* in argument the founding the infallibility of the Church on Scripture, and yet the infallibility of Scripture on the Church[1]—& 6th if the whole were not demonstrated false in fact by the various[a] & gross discrepancies of the supposed Catholic Church in different ages—and 7th idle as well as false by the actual many & gross divisions of opinion in various branches of the existing Catholic Church——then it would be difficult to deny the validity of the Arguments in this Chapter, as it would be unfair, even as it is, not to admit the skill & ability of the arguer, as a sturdy and ingenious Advocate of an indefensible cause. The Protestant may easily answer the Papist, but it will require more to satisfy the Infidel who adopts the Papist's difficulties without the *killing* (*ad hominem*) absurdities of the Papist's creed.[2] Neither can

a NTP reads "obvious"

8[1] The claim to infallibility of the RC Church is Chillingworth's main target. See also COPY B **5** and BLANCO WHITE *Practical Evidence* **12** n 3.

8[2] "Killing"—of a proof or argument that settles the opponent. For "*ad hominem*" see ETERNAL PUNISHMENT **6** n 3.

this be done logically, I think, unless Faith be defined as a *Moral State*, & not a *mere* Intellectual Belief—i.e. but by admitting that the Heart being the same, the saving FAITH is the same, in A. and B., tho' A. should believe and B. disbelieve the Possessions in the Gospel to be *demoniacal* or the like.—

9 p 383*ᵃ*

April 23, 1809. I have been disappointed in this work, which however has confirmed my convictions concerning Mʳ Locke's Taste & Judgement. Similis simili gaudet:[1] I have stated my opinion of Chillingworth's great inferiority to Stillingfleet's Volume on the same plan—it is great indeed.[2] First—this work appears to me prolix, heavy, full of repetitions, & alike deficient in arrangement and that mode of logical acumen which regards the conveyance of Arguments. 2. I do not deny but that a man of sound unprejudiced mind could scarcely read this book & remain a Catholic, or rather Romanist—but the same must be said of 20 other works before Chillingworth. But I do affirm that it is even more probable that from Popery he would be led by it to Infidelity, Socinianism at least, than to regular Protestantism, Arminian or Calvinistic—that the concessions made to the Romanist and the Doctrines laid down concerning Funda-mentals, breathe a principle of Latitudinarianism destructive to all Principle—while with a tiresome repetition of Argument ad hominem & retortions there is a deficiency of direct & affirmative Evidences, and of Learning both Scriptural & from the Fathers. Let a candid Reader turn to Chapt II part the first—and then compare with Chillingworth's Answer to the same[3] (which yet is the master [. . . . .]*ᵇ*

ᵃ MS TRANSCRIPT describes this note as "p. 383. appended to the end of the c."
ᵇ MS TRANSCRIPT ends: "*** desunt caetera by the Bookbinder's carelessness. I seem to detect the tops of the long letters in the name Stillingfleet."

9[1] "Like is pleased with like"—a proverb.
9[2] See **1**, above.
9[3] Ch 2 pt i is entitled: "What is that Means, whereby the revealed Truths of God are conveyed to our Understanding, and which must determine Controversies in Faith and Religion"; Pt ii is "Chil-lingworth's Answer to the same. An Answer to the Second Chapter...".

Copy B

The Works of William Chillingworth, &c. London 1742. F°.

Another copy of the same edition as COPY A.

British Museum C 126 l 1

Inscribed on p ⁻4: "F Sheppard June yᵉ 8ᵗʰ 1745". Inscribed on p ⁻2 by John Duke Coleridge: "C Coleridge Heaths Court 1892 This was STC's". "S. T. C." label on the title-page.

DATE. Probably after 1812. These annotations are certainly later than those in COPY A. A reference to Chillingworth in Jeremy TAYLOR *Polemicall Discourses* i 409 of 1811–12 might mark C's return to this book, but there is no certain evidence for the date of these marginalia.

1   pp iv–vi | The Life of Mr William Chillingworth

[Extract from a letter to a friend on the subject "what Judgment might be made of Arianism from the Sense of Antiquity."] In a Word, whosoever shall freely and impartially consider of this Thing, and how on the other Side the ancient Fathers Weapons against the *Arrians* are in a Manner onely Places of Scripture, (and those now for the most part discarded as impertinent and unconcluding,) and how in the Argument drawne from the Authority of the ancient Fathers, they are almost alwayes Defendants, and scarse ever Opponents; he shall not choose but confesse, or at least be very inclinable to beleeve, that the Doctrine of *Arrius* is eyther a Truth, or at least no damnable Haeresy.

The ⟨best⟩ answer to this Letter seems to be this.—Before Arius the Fathers of the Church lived and expressed themselves under one or other of the two ~~feeling~~ollowing Apprehensions with respect to the right faith[1]—viz. of its corruption, ⟨first,⟩ by the various Sects of the Gnostics, the Marcionites, &c—who blasphemed the God of the Old Testament as an evil Being, or degraded him as imperfect and inferior to the Æon Christ;[2] 2ⁿᵈ, by the Sabellians and Unitarians

[1] Arius (c 250–c 336) taught that the Son was subordinate to the Father, citing Mark 13.32 (for which see n 6, below) as one of his biblical authorities for that view. He was condemned for heresy by the first Council of Nicaea (325). For C's distinction of Arianism, Socinianism, and Unitarianism see DONNE *Sermons* COPY B 8.

[2] The name "gnostic" (from γνῶσις, knowledge) applied to a wide variety of sects, many of them anti-Christian, who believed that true knowledge came by various forms of revelation. Marcion (d 160) is called a gnostic by Tertullian, although his teaching was less fanciful and speculative

who confounded the Deity of the Son with that of the Father, thence called tri[a] Patropassians, teaching that the Father, the unipersonal and only God, having united himself with the man Jesus, or (as some thought) with the Human Nature in the person of Jesus, the latter was on this account the Son of God.[3] What wonder then, that having no forethought of a doctrine, like that of Arius, they were exclusively anxious to affirm & support, first, the primacy of the Father, as the one self-existent self-originated fontal God, *whose* Son and *whose* Wisdom the Word and the Spirit were, and the subordination of the Son to the Father, as self-subsistent indeed but not self-originate—this against the Gnostics; and 2[ndly] (against the Sabellian or Unipersonal Hypothesis) the *alterity* of the Son to the Father, the *Hic* et *Alter* which Tertullian with his accustomed and characteristic Harshness and barbaro-African Latinity expresses by his "aliud et aliud".[4] But that they would have rejected the Arian Conception, had it been fully and avowedly proposed and exposed to them, seems to me clear from these two reasons—first, from the general outcry of the Catholic Bishops as soon as it was proposed in Anti-thesi to the Tri-unitarian & afterwards Nicene Doctrine, & that Arius was conscious of the Anti-thesis—second, that these very Anti-nicene Fathers dwell on the essential ground of the Tri-unity, namely, the opposition of the πρωτογενης to the κτιστης,[5] *begotten* transcendently before all

---

[a] C may have intended to cancel "tri" (as the beginning of some such word as "tripersonist"), or to alter it to "the"

---

than that of the extreme gnostic sects. He believed the Creator to be—from his view of the Old Testament—a cruel, despotic, and treacherous God; Christ was an Aeon, an emanation from the God of love, and would overthrow the Creator. From Tertullian *Adversus Marcionem* (written in several revisions from c 207 onwards)—a work that C refers to several times—we have our chief knowledge of Marcion's teaching. Irenaeus, Clement of Alexandria, Origen, and many other Fathers also wrote against him. In *Adversus Marcionem* Tertullian established, against gnostic dualism, the unity of God and the identity of Christ with the Jewish Messiah. See also FLEURY 32–37 and nn.

1[3] For Sabellians, otherwise Patripassians, see BAXTER *Reliquiae* COPY A 17 n 1 and *CN* III 3968 and n. In *Adversus Praxean* (c 213)—in which the word *trinitas* was first used—Tertullian

attacked their leader and laid down the orthodox doctrine of the trinity.

1[4] "This [person] and the Other". *Alter* means especially the other, or second, of two; *alius* means any other. C is perhaps thinking of the description of Christ in *Adversus Praxean* 9 as "aliud ab alio", Tertullian using the neuter pronoun rather than the masculine (which C prefers). The repetition of *alius*, an idiomatic way of expressing difference, may seem to C overemphatic. See also C's use of the phrase "Alter et Idem" in e.g. BÖHME 172.

1[5] The "first-born" (see FLEURY 49 n 1 and BIBLE COPY B 131 at n 4) and the "creator" (used in NT only of God: see 1 Pet 4.19). For this issue, as posed by esp John 1.14, 18 and Rom 9.5, see BIBLE COPY B 119 and nn. For the Arian and Nicene controversy, see FLEURY 66 and nn.

that was *created*—therefore, Time & Creation commencing together, before all time. Add too even Tertullian's struggles to explain the text of, ουδ' ὁ υιος, & other Arian texts.[a6]—P.S. Chillingworth ought to have shewn that the Anti-nicene Fathers had had the Nicene Faith presented to them & yet rejected it; or the Arian in distinction from the Nicene, and yet affirmed and acknowleged it as their own.—But neither of these could Chillingworth have done. Consequently, his references prove only that men do not express themselves with the same precision, because not with the same caution, on a point not in question, as others after them when the said point has been brought in to frequent controversy, and with a consciousness that their words will be scanned and sifted by sharp-sighted Antagonists.—

2 i 47–9, pencil | Answer to the Preface (addressed to Chillingworth) of *Mercy and Truth* § 27

...though all which is necessary, be plain in Scripture; yet all which is plain, is not therefore written because it was necessary. For what greater necessity was there, that I should know St. *Paul left his Cloak at Troas*, than those *worlds of Miracles* which our Saviour did, which were never written? And when they had done it, it had been to no purpose; there being as matters now stand,* as great necessity of believing those Truths of Scripture which are not fundamental, † as those that are.

* Chillingworth fulfilled *individually* the taunting Prediction of his pontificial Antagonists, that a Protestant beginning from such premises must, if he be consequent and perseverant, end in a Socinian. Chill: himself evidently felt that his own party had *strained* the point of Faith in the Scriptures, as now collected in one Book & made of equal authority.

† A does not believe the whole of the two first Chapters of Matthew, because he believes the 2 first of Luke, and has found no satisfaction in the various attempts of Divines, Roman or Protestant, to harmonize them. Or he feels convinced that both of them were

[a] There is no paragraph break before "P.S."; the postscript continues in the same line as the last phrase

1[6] The Greek phrase, "neither the Son", occurs in the crucial last verse of Mark 13.26–32: "But of that day and that hour knoweth no man, no, not the angels which are in heaven, neither the Son, but the Father." (*NEB* reads "not even the Son".) It does not appear that Tertullian did "struggle" to explain this text, but throughout *Adversus Praxean* he comes to terms with many other passages of Scripture, stressing (because he was arguing against the Patripassians) the distinctness of the persons of the trinity while insisting upon their unity.

prefixed to these enlarged Copies or Editions of the Original common to the three first Evangelists, after the Apostolic Age—say, after A.D. 90.—But A firmly and fully embraces the Nicene Creed and all the *doctrines* contained in the Articles of our Church, respecting Faith. —If A incurs hereby the loss of Salvation—~~in~~ and this be so determined by Protestants—then I dare not arraign the Romanists of Uncharitableness. The Bibliolatry of the Protestants has played and still plays into the hand of Socinianism on one side and of Roman Hagiolatry on the other.[1]—A for instance grounds his christianity on the Divinity of our Lord, and his co-eternal ~~Sun~~onship as declared by Sᵗ John and Sᵗ Paul—and one reason for his rejection of the first Chapters of Matthew & Luke is that he believes them to have been taken from some of those numerous & gossiping Evangelia Infantiæ against which Sᵗ Paul protests.[2] The Unitarian rejects them because he has been accustomed to regard them as favoring the divinity of Christ—tho' Socinus more wisely retained them, as favoring the contrary.[3]

3   i 58–61, pencil | Answer to ch 1 § 7

Christians therefore have, and shall have *Means sufficient* (though not always effectual) *to determine,* not all *Controversies,* but all *necessary to be determined.* I proceed on farther with you, and grant that this Means to decide Controversies in Faith and Religion, *] must be endued with an universal Infallibility in whatsoever it propoundeth for a divine Truth.

2[1] Both C and RS were fond of the word "bibliolatry"; C explains it at the end of 5, below; see also BUNYAN COPY A 4 n 1. C coined other words on the Greek word λατρεία (worship): see BAXTER *Reliquiae* COPY A 38 n 1. But *OED* cites a couplet by Byrom (1763): "If to adore an image be idolatry, | To deify a book is bibliolatry". The word is also found in Lessing's *Theologischer Nachlass* (LESSING *Sämmtliche Schriften* XVII 61—cited by Green in *CIS* xxxiii, referring to C's use on p 50). "Hagiolatry" (saint-worship) was used by William Taylor in 1808: *OED*. See DONNE *Sermons* COPY B 49 PS. See also C's attack on "the Chillingworthian Touch" in *CN* III 3743 f 21 (c Mar 1810) and cf 3812 and 4140.

2[2] C here recognises a difference in

status between a "Christopaedia" (as he elsewhere calls the account of the childhood of Jesus given in the opening chapters of Matt and Luke, inferior in authority to the body of those gospels) and an "evangelium infantiæ", a gospel of the infant Christ (one of those "gossiping" accounts of the divine child that were rejected from the NT canon but nevertheless continued to have wide currency in the Church: see BIBLE *Apocryphal NT* 4 n 4). C's usage, however, is not consistent: see e.g. EICHHORN *Neue Testament* COPY A 19 and *CN* III 3779, 4402. See also DONNE *Sermons* COPY B 9 and n 1. St Paul's protest is presumably Titus 1.10–14.

2[3] For Socinus and Socinianism see BAHRDT 1 n 1.

* Surely, this Concession involves an inconsistency with Chill—'s other declarations—: if at least he make the *belief* in the necessity and actual existence of an infallible Arbitrator itself necessary.

Am I to be damned for having a stronger and more lively faith than others have? damned because I find in the mere *fact* of Christianity, and ⟨in⟩ the philosophy common to the immense majority of Christians, viz. the Roman, the Greek and (with the single exception of the handful of Men, called Unitarians) the Protestant Churches, sufficient both external and internal Evidence to found and support an undoubting Faith in its Verity and a fervent Love so that I would witness the same with my Blood? Am I to be damned, because the mere *contents* of the Gospel of John, ~~and of~~ and the passages in each of the 3 ~~other~~ Gospels *common* to the two others, satisfy me—without any full conviction that the 3 Gospels in their present state were all and each in every part written or attested by Matthew, Mark and Luke?—Among the works of Cicero there are some pasages, found in all the MSS still extant—and yet from their unlikeness to the Style and the Age of Cicero, and their very striking brotherly resemblance to the style and mode of thinking of a later Age, and of the Sophistæ, Rhetores, Grammatici &c the warmest & most learned of Cicero's Admirers have not hesitated to mark them with the asterisk of Doubt or the crotchet of Rejection.[1] While other works rely wholly on one manuscript, and yet bear witness in their own excellence and *Ciceronianism* to their own authenticity.[2]—What if I judge in this way of the six first Chapters of Daniel, and doubt or reject them[3]—while the Chapters *peculiar* to Luke from the 14th

[3][1] For a use of the asterisk as a mark of textual corruption see *C&S (CC)* 69 and n 3. Rudolph Pfeiffer *History of Classical Scholarship* [Vol I] *from the Beginning to the End of the Hellenistic Age* (Oxford 1968) 115, 178, 186, gives a detailed account of the variable use of the asterisk and other sigla in early classical scholarship. Cf BIBLE COPY B **101**, *Apocryphal NT* **4**. C regularly referred to a square bracket as a "crotchet"—a printer's term noted by *OED* from the late seventeenth to the mid-nineteenth century.

[3][2] Among theologians, Cicero was a stock example of an author whose works were—like the Bible—accepted on the grounds of tradition, even though parts might be spurious. E.g. Berkeley in *Alciphron* 6.5 says that the existence of the spurious work *De consolatione* (1583), written in fact by Carlo Sigonio, does not cause us to reject the genuine works of Cicero. As late as 1813 a spurious fourth book of *De natura deorum* was published in Oxford from what the anonymous author claimed was a ms of great antiquity. Cf *Lects 1795* (*CC*) 181 and n.

[3][3] See also BIBLE COPY B **70** and n 1. The first six chapters of Daniel comprise stories about Daniel and his companions under the Babylonian and Median kings, as prelude to the prophecies. They originate in a Persian or Greek setting of the diaspora, unlike the prophecies, which belong to the period of the persecution of Judaism after the destruction of the Temple by Antiochus Epiphanes in 168.

to the 23rd have for me an internal evidence that fully equals the external evidence of the remaining Chapters,[4] the *substance* of which is found both in Matthew, and Mark, and confirmed implicitè by John and Paul—Must I be damned? Damned because believing the same facts and doctrines as Thomas, I like Nathaniel believed in consequence of what Thomas thought insufficient proof?[5] Thank God, Christ, my merciful Redeemer, has left a very different Judgement on record. See John's Gospel, Chapt. IInd.[6] Our Lord seems to smile at the disproportion and the Saltus[7] in Nathaniel's conclusion relatively to the Premiss—but it was a smile of divine Love and parental Complacency in that Affectionateness and habitual unsuspecting Guilelessness of Heart which had integrated the evidence.

4   i 81 | Answer to ch 2 § 7

Thus therefore I conclude; a Writing may be so perfect a Rule, as to need neither Addition nor Interpretation: But the *Scripture you acknowledge a perfect Rule, forasmuch as a Writing can be a Rule*, therefore it needs neither Addition nor Interpretation.

What? A Book in two dead languages not need a translation to those that understand neither? And must not such a Translation either *be* or *require* an interpretation, according as it is equivalent or literal?[1] Oh! this strange *Biblio*latry of the Protestants is a superstition scarcely less depressive of Gospel Liberty, scarcely less suffocative of Gospel Light and the Life of Faith, than the Hagiolatry and

---

3[4] Much material in the third gospel is peculiar to Luke and is now thought by some to represent traditions gathered by him at Caesarea from Palestinian sources. In placing high value on the evidence of the passages peculiar to Luke C is at variance with Eichhorn: see EICHHORN *Neue Testament* COPY A **19**.

3[5] Thomas would not believe that Jesus had risen from the dead until he could "thrust his hand into his side" (John 20.24–31); Nathaniel, who responded to the first news of Jesus with the contemptuous question "Can any good thing come out of Nazareth?" was so impressed by the fact that Jesus (miraculously) knew that he had been sitting under a fig-tree when Philip called him

that he immediately declared his belief that Jesus was the Son of God. John 1.45–51.

3[6] John 2 begins with the miracle of the marriage at Cana, but ends: "Now when he was in Jerusalem...many believed in his name, when they saw the miracles which he did. But Jesus did not commit himself unto them, because he knew all men, And needed not that they should testify of man...".

3[7] "Leap"—sudden transition, breach of continuity (*OED*).

4[1] I.e. an "equivalent" translation is in itself an interpretation; a "literal" (word-for-word) translation needs further interpretation.

Papoduly of the Romanists![2] That the Fathers of the two first Centuries speak of a Rule of Faith which they contra-distinguish from Scripture, has been proved by Lessing[3]—that they were acquainted with the 3 first Gospels in their present *form*, has been made questionable (to say the least) by Eichhorn.[4]

5 i 80–3, referring to **4**, above

On this question as I find little more than windy Attributes with no certain or fixed Subject wherein they inhere (Chimæras bombinantes in Vacuo)[1] in the Books of the pontificial Divines, so I meet with too much Logodædaly or Sleight of Words[2] in too many of our Protestant Controversialists. Surely, the Romanist is in the right when he says, that a Rule doth not by its *excellence* supersede the necessity of an Expounded, tho' possibly it might by its *facility*— which latter not to apply to the Scriptures collectively and in all parts, Scripture itself instructs us. Much mor less will a Rule in a language unknown to the larger portion of those who are bound to follow it supersede the appointment of an Authorized Interpreter—or excellent Laws the office of a Judge. So again, by unwritten Tradition the Romanist means only a sense attached to certain Scriptures by the first teachers of the Church, or ordinances in consequence of such an interpretation, of course not forming a part of the Scriptures—ex. gr. that the words, "till I come", meant the end of the World and not the destruction of the Jewish State: and therefore that the Lord's Supper is of perpetual Obligation.[3]—The Scripture commands us to

4[2] For "hagiolatry" see **2** and n 2, above. "Papoduly" (not in *OED*)— veneration of the Pope—belongs to the family of coinages and compounds discussed in BAXTER *Reliquiae* COPY A **38** n 1.

4[3] E.g. in *Sogenannte Briefe an verschiedene Gottesgelehrte*, with which, however, C found fault when he annotated it: see LESSING XVII 97–171.

4[4] See e.g. EICHHORN *Neue Testament* COPY A **3–10**.

5[1] "Chimæras buzzing in a vacuum"—adapted from Rabelais II vii: "Questio subtilissima, utrum chimera in vacuo bombinans possit comedere secundas intentiones" ("A most subtle question—whether a chimaera buzzing

in a vacuum can consume 'second intentions'").

5[2] *OED* cites the definition of Bailey (1727), "a goodly shew and flourish of words, without much matter", and also records C's use of it as "verbal Legerdemain" in *AR* (1825) 119.

5[3] The phrase "till I come" is in John 21.22–3 (and in Rev 2.25). After Christ had told Peter "by what death he should glorify God", Peter asked what would happen to John and was rebuffed with the reply "If I will that he tarry till I come, what is that to thee?" Word went around that Christ had said that John would never die; but, John adds, "Jesus said *not* unto him, He shall not die; but, If I will that he tarry till I come, what is

honor the Son even as the Father.[4] Is this to be understood absolutely? or only relatively to the Obeying the commands delivered by the Son, even as Kings are accustomed so to credentialize[5] their Plenipotentiaries, relatively (it is not doubted) tho' not by expression, to the Objects of their Mission? And is it nothing that we know by undoubted tradition that the primitive Christians chaunted prayers to Christ, as God? ⟨and consequently, that *they* had been taught to interpret this text absolutely?⟩ The true and effectual way to confute the Romanists is to expose, ⟨either⟩ the utter unmeaningness ~~or~~ and indeterminacy of their *Church-Infallibility*, &c ~~or~~ in whatever they differ from Protestants, or its falsification by *fact* where ever they *have* determined it; with their own ridiculous disagreements as to what or to whom the term, Church, and the attribute Infallibility, are to be determined—(Either A or B or C are infallible, but which neither they nor we know!)—to expose the demonstrable non-tradition of their pretended Traditions—and lastly, not to play into their hands by needless & impossible deifications of a *Book*.[6]

6　i 82 | §10

The Fidelity of a Keeper may very well consist with the Authority of the Thing committed to his Custody. But we know no one Society of Christians that is such a faithful Keeper as you pretend.

Aye, now, *this* is good sound sense, worthy of a Protestant Divine!

7　i 83 | §13

But the Holy Ghost, that speaks in Scripture, can do so, if he please; and when he is pleased, will do so. In the mean time, it will be fit for you to wait his Leisure, and to be content, that those Things of Scripture which are plain should be so, and those which are obscure should remain obscure, until he please to declare them.

I freely confess, that I do not see how without *shuffling*[1] this § can be acquitted of a tendency to Socinianism. Plain to whom? In order to learn what are the *binding* Articles of Faith, we are to find out the *Minimum* of Capacity![2]

---

that to thee?" This would be taken at the time to refer to the Second Coming—hence the dismay when John died. This incident occurred at the supper after the Resurrection. See also C. BUTLER *Vindication* **1** n 7.
　5[4] John 5.23.

5[5] Not in *OED*.
5[6] See also **10**, below.
7[1] Cf C's use of "shuffles" in H. COLERIDGE **1**.
7[2] Cf BLANCO WHITE *Practical Evidence* **2** n 2.

8 i 84 | §14

...there must be a Judge to supply, out of the Principles of Reason, the Interpretation of the Law, where it is defective. But the Scripture (we say) is a perfect Rule of Faith, and therefore needs no Supply of the Defects of it.

What? not reason to assist in the interpretation of Scripture? Chillingworth never outgrew the Sophist.

9 i 84 | §16

And then we suppose that all the necessary Points of Religion are plain and easy, and consequently every Man in this Cause to be a competent Judge for himself; because it concerns himself to judge right as much as eternal Happiness is worth.

The Divinity, incarnation, redemption, regeneration—all plain & easy, as $2 + 2 = 4$! I could pardon this perhaps, if Ch: had said, *I* suppose, *I* conceive, but *we* (i.e. the Protestants in general, and the Church of England in particular)—this is too bad!

10 i 89, pencil | § 35

You proceed: And whereas the Protestants of *England* in the Sixth *Article* have these Words; *In the Name of the Holy Scripture we do understand those Books, of whose Authority was never any Doubt in the Church....* And whereas you infer from hence, *This is to make the Church Judge.* I have told you already, that *of this Controversy we make the Church the Judge*; but not the present Church, much less the present *Roman* Church, but the Consent and Testimony of the *Ancient and Primitive Church...*

It seems to me that the same set of perplexities accompany both parties. The Pr. sees them in the Romanist, and with them attacks the Church, the Pope, &c: the Romanist sees them in the Protestant and with them attacks the Scriptures. In truth, neither Person ⟨n⟩or Book can be a fit subject of Infallibility; but the Book is far less degrading—leaves the Believer in greater independence on the will of other men.

11 i 97 | § 64

[Chillingworth argues that in matters of baptism the Romanist can appeal to no more reliable authority than the Protestant can:] He that will pretend to be certain of it, must undertake to know for a certain all these things.... First, that he was baptized with due Matter. Secondly, with the due Form of Words.... Thirdly, he must know that he was baptized with due Intention...

This doctrine of the Romanists, manifestly traditional and breathing the same spirit as the Language of the early, even of the Ante-nicene, Fathers concerning the mystery of Baptism and the transmission of the Holy Spirit by the Baptist into the Baptized—the early *permission* of Infant Baptism, and consequent admission of the non-necessity of Actual Will and Faith in the Patient,[1] and e contrá this asserted *essentiality* of the concentered Will and right Intention of the Agent—conjoined with the nature and the kind of the Miraculous Cures and Exorcisms of the primitive Church—might furnish the Devil with suggestions of a strange resemblance quibusdam valde recentibus Θαυμασι του Ζωομαγνητισμου. Mem. Πνευμα το τῆς δευτεροψεως, και το μεταλλο-εὐριστικον, παραδοτικα ειναι, πεπιστευται.—[2]

11[1] See BAXTER *Reliquiae* COPY A **8, 11, 12,** and cf ANDERSON COPY A **1** n 4.

11[2] A strange resemblance "to certain very recent Marvels of Zoomagnetism [i.e. Animal Magnetism]. Mem. The spirit of second sight, and the metal-divining [spirit] [i.e. magnetism] have been believed to be transmittable." Cf *Friend* (*CC*) I 59 n 1 (annotation on Copy L). See also BÖHME **26** and n 3.

"CIVIL WAR TRACTS"

[A made-up volume of 39 tracts "relating to the Civil Wars".]
1641–51. 4°.

Not located. *Gillman SC* (1843) 498: "with MS. Notes by S. T. Coleridge".

For a general account of this volume of tracts see "CROMWELLIAN TRACTS".

CONTENTS
Thomas DYMOCK *England's Dust and Ashes Raked Up* (1648).
The Copie of Three Petitions (1647).
VIII Problems Propounded to the Cavaliers (1646).
And 36 other tracts, probably including Charles DALLISON *The Royalist's Defence* (1648).

MS TRANSCRIPTS. (*a*) VCL BT 37: SC transcript of eight annotations in a "Volume of Tracts relating to the Civil War". In this transcript DYMOCK is followed by DALLISON, then by two notes written on a "Blank leaf at the end of the Volume of Tracts during the Civil Wars" (printed below). (*b*) University of Texas (Humanities Research Center): untitled transcript in an unidentified hand, the annotations in a single sequence—WHITFIELD and W. SEDGWICK (from "CROMWELLIAN TRACTS II"), DYMOCK. This transcript may have been made for—or from—*NTP*, in which these three titles appear in this order with only the interposition of HAYLEY 3 (on the trial of Charles I) before DYMOCK. The annotations are here printed from MS TRANSCRIPT (*a*).

DATE. Possibly in the summer or autumn of 1818, if indeed C acquired this volume at that time: see "CROMWELLIAN TRACTS". C cited the title of DALLISON, and quoted from that tract, in *C&S* (*CC*) 97 and 102.

1   "Blank leaf at the end of the Volume..."

In all questions of wide and deep interest it is scarcely less than a fatal Necessity, that the best cause should be the worst defended: the consequence of which is, the temporary Victory of the false and the superficial, and its establishment in the chair of learned as well as popular opinion. The cause is in the instinct of the mind to aim at the highest in the first instance—and hence with imperfect means, and in the absence of all the main conditions of its attainment: The Cherub's aim—the Child's or Savage's wishes, passions, prejudices—Alchemy, Astrology. But the remark was intended chiefly in reference

42

to the Nominalist's controversy with, and temporary (tho' still *continuing*) Victory over the Realists in the 15th Century.[1]—S. T. C.

2 "Blank leaf at the end of the Volume..."

The dispensing power, as completory of the Law and supplying the inherent deficiency of all human provisions expressed in determinate words, is so natural and necessary a prerogative of the supreme Executive's trust, that Charles the First richly deserved death for this alone, that he had treacherously and treasonably perverted a power entrusted to him for the completion of Law into a means of destroying Law, and of evacuating its essential purpose—viz. the ensurance of the subject against individual will.[1]

It was an abuse of terms to say, that the King has the right of dispensing with the Laws. It can only be asserted, the King *had* a dispensing power in such or such a case—or the King has a dispensing power in *this* case. The particular case must be known and specified in order to the determination of the Right—for what is true of all ordinances is eminently true of this—the Reason and ultimate purpose of the ordinance must determine its interpretation.[2]

Since the Revolution we have deemed it necessary to secure this principle by throwing the *onus probandi*,[3] in each instance, on the Dispenser, by *presuming* that he had *not* the power, and this is, perhaps, the wisest plan. But the *substance* is the same: as is evident by the fact, that, in certain emergencies, the Parliament might, and would be bound to, impeach a Minister for not dispensing (advising the King to dispense) with an existing Statute.

1[1] See BAXTER *Reliquiae* **8** n 1 and esp JOANNES **2** n 3.

2[1] For C's view that Charles I deserved to die for "treacherously and treasonably pervert[ing] a power entrusted to him" see e.g. BAXTER *Reliquiae* COPY B **17**, **18** and BEAUMONT & FLETCHER COPY B **54**. BAXTER *Reliquiae* COPY A ANNEX [*b*] reads in a more accurate version (see Foreword, above, II

xvii): "...I confess, that had I been sworn in a judge, I should have given my verdict, as Martin & Colonel Hutchinson did. It is *wicked* injury to the character of our ancestors to similarize the punishment of Charles and the murder of Louis XVIth". See also HAYLEY **3**.

2[2] Cf CROMWELL **1**.

2[3] "Burden of proof".

CLAUDIUS CLAUDIANUS
c 365–c 408

Cl. Claudiani quae exstant: ex emendatione Nicolai Heinsij, &c. Amsterdam (Elzevir) 1650. 16°.

Green SC (1880) 97 and Thomas Arnold (in 1884) give conflicting evidence about the edition; both evidently refer to the same book. *Green SC* cites the 1677 ed (which would be imprinted "Amstelodami, Apud Danielem Elzevirium"), Arnold cites the 1650 ed (which would be imprinted "Amstelodami, Typis Ludovici Elzevirii"). *Green SC* made a small error in citing the title as "Cl. Claudiani Opera quae exstant..."; and since an informed private owner is perhaps less likely to make a mistake about the imprint than is an auction cataloguer describing a large library, the 1650 ed is here preferred. In any case, the 1677 ed is a word-for-word reprint of the 1650 ed and has the same engraved title-page with only the imprint changed.

Not located. *Lost List.*

Thomas Arnold wrote to EHC on 12 Dec 1884: "I have in my possession a very interesting memorial of the intimacy between Coleridge & Southey. It is an Elzevir edition 1650 of Claudianus having on the front fly leaf in schoolboy hand 'E. Libris R. Southey | Regiae Scholae Westminest. | AD 1788' and below this 'S. T. Coleridge | from Robert Southey | June 10. 1810.' in Southey's handwriting." ("Westmonast." in *Green SC*, "Westminest." in Arnold transcript.) Arnold goes on: "The book was purchased some years ago at a booksellers in London. I have verified the handwriting at the M.S. room British Museum. If you would care to see the book I would call with it but as I set great store by it I should not wish to let it out of my hands by leaving it at the Publishers." MS Leatherhead, now University of Texas, Humanities Research Center.

C quoted six lines from Claudian *In Eutropium* in 1794 (*CL* I 68)—like RS, he had probably read Claudian at school. RS's present of this copy left immediate traces in *CN* III 3781, 3876 (both 1810), and later in 4202 (Jun 1814), and in newspaper articles in 1811 and 1814: see *EOT* (*CC*) II 184, 187, 389, 393, 403, 410. See also *CN* II 2728 and *TT* 18 Aug 1833.

MS TRANSCRIPT. University of Texas: Thomas Arnold to EHC, 12 Dec 1884 (quoted in part above), including a transcript of C's annotation and adding that "The writing of the original is somewhat difficult to decipher."

DATE. Unknown: possibly 1810 between 10 Jun and C's departure for London on 18 Oct.

1 "at the end"—i.e. perhaps a back flyleaf or the back paste-down

She sate as square and solemn as an empty chair when you look at it in a half dreamy Mood—. On the reproach of shedding Tears, for a Lady in Pain? Loss of Fortune? Any other cause respecting myself principally? Immediate peril of death? No! never—but treachery unkindness unmerited & implying want of believed goodness, in an instantaneous impression of [?others/those/their] sufferings which my imagination could not limit [?to] a noble act...a Sunset &c &c &c[1]

1[1] Unresponsiveness, "treachery unkindness unmerited"—these are accusations that C was to bring against both SH and WW before and after the serious misunderstanding between C and WW beginning in Oct 1810. See e.g. *CN* III 3303, 3304, 3379, 3555, 3912, 4006, 4148, and nn. "She" may recall the letter ש (*shin*), the initial letter of C's anagram of "Hutchinson", which he sometimes used alone as her name. See *C & SH* 20 and n 3, *CN* II 3222, III 3428, 4164, and nn. "She" could be a disguise for C himself. Yet it is also possible that this agitated note does not record any actual or personal incident, but may rather be a sketch for a poem or for a dramatic episode.

JOHANNES COCCEIUS
(JOHANN KOCH)
1603–1669

LOST BOOK

Opera omnia theologica, exegetica, didactica, polemica, philologica, divisa in decem volumina. Editio tertia, auctior et emendatior. 10 vols. Amsterdam 1701. F°.

Not located; marginalia not recorded. *Lost List.*

A set belonging to a Mr Tudor, with C's notes written before the end of 1827 in Vol v and possibly in other volumes not specified.

The "Mr Tudor" must have been John Tudor (d 1862), one of "The Forty-four" who—including Edward Irving and Henry Drummond, founder of the Irvingite church—met annually at Albury in Surrey 1826–30 to discuss the fulfilment of prophecy. Tudor edited the seven volumes of *Morning Watch, or Quarterly Journal of Prophecy and Theological Review* from Mar 1829 to Jun 1833 ; Irving in a letter of 30 Nov 1829 describes him as "very learned, modest, and devout". In May 1833 Tudor was made an Elder of the Catholic Apostolic Church (the Irvingite church) and in 1835 was appointed Apostle with the charge of Poland and India.

C borrowed this set perhaps in Jul 1825 (see *CL* v 480), was using it in Jan-Feb 1826 (*CN* iv 5319, 5323; *CL* vi 550, 557, 562) and in Jul 1827 (N 33 f 11: *CN* v), and was obliged to return it apparently late in 1827. Between the lines of two successive notebook entries in N 35 C has written: "See the Marginal Notes in Cocceius, Vol. 5—Mem.—To transcribe them into this Book—". These words, written in pencil, C overtraced in ink and continued: "but which, tho' they were long & numerous, I neglected to do till the ten Folios were reclaimed by the Owner, ⟨Mr Tudor, whom the notes scared & scandalized—⟩. So has it been with Volumes of my Marginalia, written indiscriminately in other men's Books. S. T. C." N 35 f 6^v (*CN* v). (Vol v contains *Commentarius in Epistolas Pauli ad Romanos, Corinthios, Ephesios et Philippenses.*) In another notebook entry, dated 16 Jul 1830—which might also be the approximate date of the interlinear note—C bemoaned the gift he had made to Edward Irving of his copy of Pole's *Synopsis*: "The Cocceius I returned, with all my marginal Notes—& these too to a worthy Man, but one who from his Cabbalism will be scandalized rather than *set a thinking* by them.—So that I have not a single commentary, on the Pentateuch—or indeed on the Bible, save only Jerom's Works.—" N 44 f 33^v (*CN* v). See also *TT* 5 May 1830.

C's most enthusiastic response to Cocceius' work (in the absence of the annotations he wrote in the volumes) was recorded in early Feb 1826. C noted (8 Feb) that "It was by an effort of Self-denial that during my late severe indisposition I withdrew my especial study and meditation from the 4ᵗʰ Gospel [etc]...to a careful continuous perusal of the Apocalypse in the original Greek and the Commentary of Coccëius...impelled solely by the rumours, that had reached me, of my friend, Edward Irving's, Aberrations (for such, I fear, they are) into the Cloud-land of Prophecies [of] the approaching fulfilment of certain Prophecies, his Orations on the Millennium, the expulsion of the Gentiles from the Church analogous to that of the Jews, the collection of Gentile False-Believers in Armageddon—& what not of the Faber Insomnia." *CN* IV 5323. He said then that he found Cocceius "the best & most spiritual of all our learned Commentators" (*CL* VI 550); although he said that he "derived little or no assistance...[from] this learned & generally judicious Commentator", and although "unhappily during the whole work the ignis fatuus of the Pope keeps whisking and dancing before the good man's eyes—nothing but this can he see, and this sees every where ", yet "The result...has been such as beyond, nay contrary to my anticipations, I am most thankful for." *CL* VI 557–8 (closely associated with *CN* IV 5323); and cf 562. See EICHHORN *Apocalypse* COPY A passim.

There is some evidence of C consulting particular volumes of COCCEIUS: Vol I—SOUTHEY *The Life of Wesley* (1820) I 297; *CN* IV 5319; Vol IV—N 33 f 11 (a parallel between Micah 7.1 and the parable of the fig-tree in Matt 21.18–22); Vol V—N 35 f 6ᵛ (quoted above); Vol VI—EICHHORN *Apocalypse* COPY A 1, *CN* IV 5323.

SIR GEORGE COLEBROOKE

1729-1808

Six Letters on Intolerance: including ancient and modern nations, and different religions and sects. [Anonymous.] London 1791. 8°.
Privately printed. Preface unsigned.

Not located. *Lost List.*

MS TRANSCRIPT. VCL LT 52: "Remarks written by Mr S. T. Coleridge in the first Page of a Volume containing 'Six Letters on Intolerance' by Sir George Colebrook." This transcript being on a sheet cognate with a transcript of marginalia in Poole's copy of William PARNELL *An Historical Apology for the Irish Catholics* (Dublin 1807) suggests that the COLEBROOKE also belonged to Poole.

DATE. After 1800; if Poole's copy, summer 1807.

1   possibly front flyleaf

The Author of the six letters is inclined to think, that had the Test Act been repealed, the Dissenters from the Established Church would not have become so generally *Republicans*, as it is alledged, they have—This circumstance, if true, proves the policy of the measure when it was proposed to rescind the disqualifying Statutes, in order to unite all Englishmen in a common Interest.[1]

At the same time the Author freely owns, that however much a Friend to general Toleration, he would have suppressed many things, especially what he advanced in the outset, that a neighbouring Nation[2] would be found the truest Asylum for Religious Liberty, if he could have foreseen the mischiefs, to which civilized Society has been exposed by professed Atheists and by ignorant flagitious Reformers.[3]

1[1] The Test Acts of 1673 and 1678—to exclude Roman Catholics and Dissenters from office—required all holders of office under the crown to receive the sacrament according to the use of the Church of England, to take the oaths of supremacy and allegiance to the King, and to make the declaration against transubstantiation; they were finally repealed in May 1828. In 1800, at the time of Union, Pitt had promised Emancipation to the Irish: this seems to be C's allusion in this paragraph.

1[2] France.

1[3] It does not appear that Colebrooke "freely owns" what C here ascribes to him.

HARTLEY COLERIDGE
1796–1849

The Worthies of Yorkshire and Lancashire; being lives of the most distinguished persons that have been born in, or connected with, those provinces &c. 3 pts [all published] in 1 vol. London 1832–3. 8°.

Issued in parts, in paper wrappers, at 5s each; the series planned for 12 pts, each set of 3 pts to be bound in a volume; pts i–iii paginated in one series, 240 pp to a pt. Each pt includes a dated engraving: of Andrew Marvell (1 Jun 1832), of Lady Anne Clifford (1 Oct 1832), and of William Roscoe (Mar 1833). Imprint: "Published by Simpkin and Marshall; and F. E. Bingley, 87, Briggate, Leeds...F. E. Bingley, Printer."

University of Texas (Humanities Research Center)

Inscribed in ink on the dedication page: "H. N. Coleridge Hampstead. 1832." and on the title-page in HNC's hand: "These outer covers to be *bound up*." Inscribed on p ⁻5 (p–d) "H. N. Coleridge—" and at the top of that page "S. Coleridge". On p ⁻4 the signature "Edith Coleridge".

For the circumstances of HC's undertaking this work for the printer and publisher F. E. Bingley in Leeds in Jul 1832 see *Minnow* 166–7, *HC Poems* I ciii–cvi, and *Lives of the Northern Worthies* ed DC (3 vols 1852) I v–vii. See also *HCL* 140. No 1 appeared shortly before 16 Oct 1832 (*HCL* 144); No 2, due on 1 Nov 1832, was "just finished" on 19 Nov and was published shortly thereafter (*HCL* 147); by Dec 1832 Bingley was in financial difficulties (*HCL* 151); No 3 was issued c Mar–Apr 1833.

This book is a moving testament to the silence that had fallen for some years between C and his elder son. It does not appear that HC sent his father a copy of the *Worthies*. His *Poems* was published in Jan 1833 with a dedicatory sonnet addressed to his father, echoing *Frost at Midnight*; Mrs C said that C was "pleased, and much affected *at the dedication* to himself in his poor son's book: he has not seen him for ten years!—" *Minnow* 177. Whether HC sent a copy of the *Poems* to C we do not know; but in Sept 1833 he told HNC: "I will write to Father, perhaps to night—but wholly on literary subjects. I cannot bear, at this first breaking the ice of years, to enter abruptly on any secular affairs." *HCL* 153.

This copy raises special difficulties in presentation. It belonged originally to HNC, was annotated by C—mostly in pencil—and HNC overtraced many of the annotations; it was evidently used later by DC at some stage in preparing his edition of the *Worthies*, coming to him as editor of HC's writings presumably from SC after C, HNC, and HC had all died, but DC clearly did not use this copy as copy-text for his edition. Beyond the marginalia recognisable as C's, it contains a few marginal notes by HNC (e.g. pp 88, 89, 173, 284, 465, 492 ["HNC" written in pencil above this note in an unknown hand], 501, 719; notes in what seems to be DC's hand appear on e.g. pp 355, 396, 403, 453, 715, but the brevity of the notes makes identification questionable in many cases. The volume also shows a large number of markings in pencil and in ink—corrections of printer's errors (about 130, sometimes accompanied by a neat + or × different from C's larger and ragged * as e.g. on p 694), underlinings of words and phrases without comment (about 20), queries of doubtful details, editorial corrections of dates, alterations to preferred spelling or usage (about 30). The concentration of markings in ink in the first 300 pp suggests that DC may have thought at first of using this copy for the printer, but later changed his mind and continued his marking in pencil. But both C and HNC were in the habit of correcting printer's errors and author's slips as they read, and no doubt both did so at times in this copy; and Edith Coleridge's hand may also appear here and there. That DC in his printed text did not follow all the corrections made in this copy increases the difficulty of identification. Even the underlinings of "whose" (as an indiscriminate alternative to "of which") on pp 601, 674, 703, 717, a usage that C deplored, cannot be assumed *prima facie* to be his because HNC is known to have deplored the usage too: see BROOKE 2 and n 1, *CL* VI 787. Again, C sometimes elsewhere jotted exclamation marks in the margin of a text; but the exclamation marks on pp 131, 284, and 301 seem to be HNC's rather than C's. The most difficult question is raised by some thirty instances of "Qu" or "Qy" pencilled in the margin or at a break in the text, for this is also one of C's practices. In this book the notation has two distinct forms: one of these (e.g. p 184) is certainly not C's. The other form, typically rounded in shape (but with a sharper sub-species on pp 131, 301), seemed at first to be C's; but the fact that such a "Qu" on p 337 was evidently written after C's note was on the page holds the identity of these marks in question, even where the "Qu" is associated with an annotation of C's (see 3, 4, and cf 42). Therefore even the apparently most deserving candidates, on pp 156, 172, 251, 337, 344, 402, 422, 443, 576, 617, are excluded.

An interleaved copy of pt i in the Houghton Library, Harvard, bears a note by H. B. Forman: "With fifteen pages of notes written by Samuel Taylor Coleridge"; but the notes are neither in C's hand nor of his composition.

DATE. 1832 (after c 15 Oct)–1833 (after c Apr 1833), if annotated as the parts were issued. C uses the phrase "our Time (1832–3)" in **32** (pt ii).

COEDITOR. A. H. B. Coleridge.

1 title-page verso, pencil, overtraced

The Shuffler.

The Man who *shuffles* in his walk, ~~will~~ runs the risk of being tripped up by the smallest inequalities ~~o~~ in the path of life. The Edge of a Mat may fling him forward on his Nose. S. T. C.

2   pp 240–[240 + 1] (inside back part-cover), evidently referring to pp iv–v, pencil, overtraced | Introductory Essay[1]

We only wish to distinguish the peculiar end, object, and function of History from that of Biography.

In history all that belongs to the individual is exhibited in subordinate relation to the commonwealth; in biography, the acts, and accidents of the commonwealth are considered in their relation to the individual, as influences by which his character is formed or modified,—as *circumstances* amid which he is placed,—as the sphere in which he moves, or the material he works with. The man, with his works, his words, his affections, his fortunes, is the end and aim of all....

There is one species of history which may with great propriety be called biographical, to which we do not remember to have heard the term applied;—we mean that wherein an order, institution, or people, are invested with personality, and described as possessing an unity of will, conscience, and responsibility;—as sinning, repenting, believing, apostatizing, &c. Of this, the first and finest sample is in the Old Testament, where Israel is constantly addressed, and frequently spoken of, as an individual....The scripture *personality* of Israel is something far other, and infinitely more real, than the *personification* of Britannia; and points at a profounder mystery than human sense can ever interpret.

Prothesis
Anthropology.

Thesis	*Mesothesis*	*Antithesis*
State	Statesman	A Man
~~History~~		Biography
History		

Synthesis
Israel or the Church.

2[1] That this annotation refers to HC's Introductory Essay is suggested by DC's note (I 387–8): "On the blank of this life, *S. T. C.* has shown in what way he conceives biography to be related to history, and both to the science of man."

or rather thus—

Man
State   Church   Individual
Statesman.

and correspondingly

Anthropology
History   Church History   Biography
Memoirs of Public Characters.

———

Under Church, or Israel, I place or rather in it I include the History of *Philosophy*: of which I dare avow that I believe—*a2*

---

3   pp 146–7, pencil, overtraced | Richard Bentley[1]

[For his praelection on being elected as Regius Professor of Divinity, Bentley chose to examine critically the textual authority of 1 John 5.7: "For there are three which bear record in Heaven, the Father, the Word, and the Holy Ghost, and these three are One."] The preponderance of outward testimony seems to be against it [the authenticity of the verse], but the logic, the connection of thought, *Qu?] the very *architecture* of the passage, speaks strongly for it. If the seventh verse be rejected, the eighth should be rejected also.

* Hartley here dogmatizes unthinkingly. The words are not only a palpable intertrusion,[2] ~~but~~ not only utterly impertinent to the Apostle's Reasoning, but inconsistent with it, yea, contradictory.[3] They are, doubtless, a marginal Gloss, cited from St Augustine, as

---

a The word "hiatus" is added in another hand, apparently DC's, to suggest that the sentence was left incomplete

2^2 In his Lectures on the History of Philosophy of 1818–19 C had considered the history of philosophy as "an essential part of the history of man", dealing with "questions of deepest concern to all ...What, and *for* what am I made? What *can* I, and what *ought* I to, make of myself? and in what relations do I stand to the world and to my fellow men?" Prospectus in *P Lects* (1949) 67, 66.

3^1 On Bentley see BEAUMONT & FLETCHER COPY B **10** n 1.

3^2 For "intertrude" *OED* quotes two passages from C; there is no entry for "intertrusion".

3^3 The "Johannine Comma" embraces part of 1 John 5.7 and 5.8 (as italicised): "For there are three that bear record *in heaven, the Father, the Word, and the Holy Ghost, and these Three are One*. (8) *And there are three that bear witness in earth*, the Spirit, and the water, and the blood: and these three agree in one." The controversial passage occurs only in late mss, almost exclusively Latin; it was omitted from the first version of Jerome's Vulgate and from the first version of Erasmus' edition of the Greek NT, but later found its way into both the Vulgate and the *Textus Receptus*. It cannot seriously be considered part of the original epistle.

a comment on the passage by some one who had not comprehended the gist and import of Sᵗ John's argument, & afterwards slipped into the Text.[4]

S. T. C.

3A   p 156, pencil

The bursting of the South sea bubble, which awakened thousands from dreams of countless wealth to the sober certainty of ruin, and exhibited a degree of baseness, falsehood, peculation, and depravity, *Qu.*] in high places, which English history has never since rivalled, brought about a change of administration.

3B   p 172, pencil, marked with a brace

Of ancient poetic genius he perhaps knew as little as of English,—as little as any body else; but of the Greek and Latin language he knew *Qu*] more than all men of his time,—of the English language not much more than any tolerably educated woman.

4   p 173, pencil, overtraced

[HC expresses disapproval of Bentley's intention to reject all lines of the *Iliad* "that would not admit of the digamma in every word in which that 'something greater yet than letter' is ever to be found". Footnote on the "Aeolic Digamma":] Of the Digamma nothing is settled, after all the learning that has been employed about it, except that its form is that of a Roman F, though sometimes it rather resembled G, and that it was either a W or a V, or something between both. It is only found on some old marbles, and on coins of the Greek town of Velia, in Italy. However pronounced it must have been an Qu!!!!ᵃ] offence to the ear. The Greeks were right in dropping it, and we are wrong in puzzling about it.

I can scarcely doubt, that the Digamma was nearly the same with the unpronounceable Hebrew gnainᵇ = ng, the sound of a*ng*er heard in an Infant's nang, nang.[1]

ᵃ Not overtraced

ᵇ Overtraced as "Nain"

3⁴ In mentioning Augustine C may have a confused recollection of J. D. Michaelis *Introduction to the New Testament* tr Herbert Marsh (4 vols 1793–1801), which suggests (IV 435–6) that the verse originated in a marginal gloss in the Latin versions and crept into the texts used in Africa, not as early as Augustine but early enough to be used in the Confession of Faith presented by the African bishops at the end of the fifth century. Both Cyprian and Augustine interpret the Spirit, the water, and the blood in a trinitarian sense.

4¹ The existence of the *digamma* (ϝ) is vouched for by Dionysius of Halicar-

5   pp 176–7, pencil, overtraced | Thomas Lord Fairfax

[Footnote:]...Fairfax was, it must be confessed, an unfaithful translator, who, if he sometimes expanded the germ of his author to a bright, consummate flower, just as often spoiled what he was trying *] to improve.

* It is this petulant ipse dixi smartness & dogmatism in which as in a certain Mannerism, a sudden *jerkiness* in the *mood*, and *unexpectedness* of Phrase, something between Wit and Oddity, but with the latter predominant, the Peculiarity certain, the felicity doubtful, ⟨that⟩*a* he has *caught* [from]*b* Southey (the only things in which he might not have profitably taken from his ⟨Maternal⟩ Aunt's Husband[)]—that annoy*c* & mortify me in Hartley's writing[1]

6   p 176, pencil, overtraced

[Footnote continued:]...Probably the Eclogues are "allegorical pastorals". Now, as pastoral, *per se*, is the silliest of all compositions,

a Possibly inserted by HNC
c Overtraced as "annoys", the *s* then cancelled

b Word supplied by the editor

nassus (first century B.C.) and by later grammarians. Bentley was the first to point out that many of the metrical anomalies in Homer would be removed if it were assumed that the *digamma* had dropped out of words the probable etymology of which suggested that it could have been present. There was some controversy whether *digamma* was to be pronounced like English *v* or *w*—as Varro and Dionysius of Halicarnassus implied—or as a weak aspirate—as Priscian and Matthiae preferred. C's suggestion of *ng* arises from both the form and the name of the letter—double *gamma*, ΓΓ, pronounced *-ng* in classical Greek. C had made this same suggestion in A. H. MATTHIAE *Copious Greek Grammar* (2 vols 1824) I xxxiv–xxxvii, but admitted (pp 20–1) that the sound "had already been softened when the Iliad was composed". See also FORBES **9** and n 1, *CN* IV 4765 and n, and *Logic* (*CC*) 25, 92. Hyman Hurwitz in his *Elements of the Hebrew Language* (1807) 1n said of the Hebrew letter *ayin* (which C variously calls *nain, gnain, ngang, gnang*, etc): "The German and Polish Jews pronounce this letter (ע) [*ayin*], like (א) [*aleph*] at the beginning of words, and like (*ng*) at the middle and at the end of them; but the Portuguese and Spanish Jews sound it like (*ngn*) at the beginning, and like (*ng*) at the end of them." In a book C may have used at school, *Hebraicae grammatices rudimenta. In usum Scholae Westmonasteriensis* (1778), ע is called "Gnain" and pronounced *gn*. C's idea that the more primitive language would use infantile sounds may have been inspired by Bentley in a passage cited not by HC but by William VINCENT *The Greek Verb Analysed* (1795) 32 (not annotated): "The legitimate pronunciation of digamma was doubtless our English, w, as Bentley has clearly proved from the Latin *vagitus*, a sound of nature from the wau, wau, of infants, like rugitus, hinnitus, mugitus, the natural sound of the lion, the horse, and the cow."

5[1] See also **9, 17, 24, 37**, below. C was irritated by a tone of smartness in RS's writing and resented the fact that HC had picked it up from him: see e.g. BUNYAN COPY A **12**. HC admired RS's prose style and thought that "my sort of talent had more of Southey than of S. T. Coleridge". See *HCL* 144–5, 275.

so, with due deference to Mantuan and Spenser, the allegorical is the absurdest of all pastorals.
O sad! sad! What? Theocritus?[a] *Bion*! *Moschus*![1]

7 p [240 + 1] (inside back part-cover), referring to p 176; pencil, overtraced
P. 176. I utterly dissent from dear Hartley in his estimation of Pastoral, both as ⟨to⟩[b] what has been done, ex. gr. Solomon's Song, & Theocritus;[1] & as to what it *may* be. Is not Wordsworth's *Brothers* a Pastoral? and Old Michael?[2] Our best Sonnets are Snatches of the Pastoral.

8 p 177, pencil, overtraced

[Footnote continued:]...He was so much affected with the superstitions of his age, as to fancy his children bewitched, and that on so very weak grounds, that the poor wretches whom he prosecuted for this impossible crime were actually acquitted. Yet even the verdict of a jury, little disposed as juries then were, (or dared be), to favour witches, does not seem to have disabused his senses, for he left behind, in manuscript, "Daemonologia: a discourse of Witchcraft, as it was acted in the family of Mr. Edward Fairfax...in the year 1621."

[a] Both ?s overtraced as !

[b] Word inserted by HNC or DC

6[1] Theocritus, Bion, and Moschus were favourites of C's in the time of his earliest association with RS. In *Poems ...by Bion and Moschus* [i.e. RS and Robert Lovell] (Bath 1795), one poem—*The Faded Flower*—bears the pseudonym "Bion" and so, according to the Preface, should be RS's but was in fact C's. See *CN* I 15n.

7[1] Cf "Solomon's Song. There was a time when I thought scorn of this charming Idyll, this prototype of whatever is most beautiful & affecting in Theocritus & (as far as the few precious fragments allow the conjecture) in Sappho, having a *spiritual* sense—in being more than an epithalamium on Solomon's Marriage with a Princess of Egypt. But the more extensive my acquaintance with the Persian Poets, and the more attentively I have studied verse by verse the Song itself, and sought ⟨either⟩ to discover a plan & purpose in the *whole*, or to reduce it to a series of distinct Eclogues or Idylls—the more disposed I find myself to adopt the contrary judgment...." N 47 f 18ᵛ (*CN* v) (c 17 Oct 1830). Milton, remarking upon the tragedy-like quality of Rev, and noticing that Job is a "brief model" of an epic, said that "the Scripture also affords us a divine personal Drama in the Song of *Salomon* consisting of two persons and a double *Chorus*, as *Origen* rightly judges". *The Reason of Church Government* in *A Complete Collection of the Historical, Political and Miscellaneous Works of Milton* ed J. Birch (2 vols 1738) I 60. See also EICHHORN *Alte Testament* **51** and n 1, GREW **26** and n 1, and HAYLEY **1**. Cf also EICHHORN *Apocalypse* **1** n 3.

7[2] C refers to both these Wordsworth poems in *BL* ch 17.

This is an affecting instance of the Evil that a mistranslation of a *word* may effect—viz. *Ob* = Bladder, Ventriloquism by ⟨a⟩*ᵃ Witch*—[1]

9   p 177, pencil, overtraced

Heralds, who amid the darkness of unrecorded antiquity, seldom miss of finding what they seek, have stretched the Fairfax pedigree beyond the Ultima Thule of the Norman Conquest.

and why not? and why the necessity of being always witty, or rather *hitty*—i.e. giving a sly hit?

10   p 178, pencil, overtraced

We have no information concerning his childhood, nor the place of his school education; but, as his father was a zealous Puritan and disciplinarian, and his own character was stern and unbending, we may conclude that the rod was not spared. He studied sometime at St. John's College, Cambridge, to which he was afterwards a benefactor, and acquired a love of learning which never forsook him, and made him, in some of the darkest passages of the civil war, an intercessor for learned books and learned men. He is said to have been deeply versed in the history and antiquities of England, a line of study which for the most part disposes the mind to an almost superstitious reverence for royalty. On Fairfax it does not seem immediately to have taken this effect, though perhaps it had its weight before the close of his career.

The Biogra*pher*'s ⟨Character⟩ should be as the dead-colored Ground of the Biograph**èe**: not a Face peeping over the Shoulder of the Portraited—and more notice-attracting.

11   p 178, pencil, overtraced

But it is a great neglect in the policy of any state to suffer its subjects, at their own discretion, to adopt a foreign service; and a great error in a monarch, to keep his dominions so long in peace, that the art military is forgotten, and the military habits of unconditional obedience, and undeliberative execution become obsolete. "No Bishop, no King," was the favourite maxim of the *Rex Pacificus*. "No Soldier no King," is the doctrine of historic experience. Monarchy,

---

ᵃ Word inserted in pencil by HNC

8[1]   See BIBLE COPY B **10** n 1 and HILLHOUSE **1** and n 9.

at least the feudal monarchy, established on the downfall of the Roman Empire, is an institution essentially military. A crown is a bauble without a helmet; the true sceptre is the sword. Under the feudal system, the whole constitution of society was military; all rank was military; to bear arms was the distinction of free-birth, to be a *lay*man of peace, was to be a churl, a knave, a villain, a slave.

Good—but somewhat too *rash*: but still it is good & a credit ⟨to⟩[a] dear Hartley's Intellect

12 p 179, pencil, overtraced

...the learned King fondly imagined that by maintaining the monarchical principle in the church, he was raising around the throne a host of bloodless champions, who would secure the allegiance of the nation by all the fears of eternal punishment; not considering that, while he bound the Hierarchy to himself, he was setting them at an incommunicable distance from the people, and leaving a gap, for the disaffected, who were sure to make a dangerous use of the favour and attention which the multitude always bestow on those who persuade them that they are not taught or governed as they should be.

very good. *S. T. C.*[b]

13 p 179, pencil, overtraced

He found the church divided into two parties, and thought by his regal authority, to give the victory to the anti-popular side. Thus he hastened the schism which might yet have been prevented; arrayed all the discontent of the country against the doctrines which he patronized, gave to the demagogue preachers the *speciem libertatis*, the shew of freedom and the glory of daring, and brought upon the court ecclesiastics the odium of flatterers and self-seekers. The best arguments of the Arminians and Prelatists were disregarded, because they had too visible an interest in their tenets, while the wildest declamation of the Puritans passed for Gospel, because they declaimed at the risk of their ears.

The error was less in the King than in the Dignitaries of the Church, who ought to have known that the Clerisy is powerful & permanent,

---

a Word inserted by HNC
b The initials are in pencil, not overtraced—possibly inserted by HNC

only while it remains Mediative, the Mesothesis between the Unity and the Multëity, the King and the People, the *State* and the Person.[1]

14　p 179, pencil, overtraced

Even the few expeditions undertaken by command, or with the countenance of the state, were all in behalf of revolted nations; and the assistance afforded to the United Provinces, to the French Hugonots, and to the German Protestants, was a practical acknowledgment of the right of resistance. The alliance of France with the insurgent Americans contributed not more to the French revolution, than the alliance of England with the continental Protestants to the temporary suspension of English monarchy. The Dutch, adopting a republican government, consistently adopted a presbyterian church; and though the German Lutherans retained the name of Episcopacy, the Lutheran Bishop fell so far short of the wealth, pomp, aristocratic rank, and apostolical pretensions of the English prelate, as to bear a much nearer resemblance to the plain, if not humble Presbyter.

Surely H. has left my Essay on the Constitution unread![1] Suppose a *State* consisting wholly of Christians—& that Paul & John lived among them—Would H. grieve to see them acknowleged as Counsellors?

15　p 180, pencil, overtraced

There were no doubt very good and sufficient reasons for the difference, but they are not reasons likely to occur to a young man, whose slender stock of theology was derived from Scripture and his own unlearned judgment, not perhaps wholly unbiassed by that love of novelty, which is as endemic a disease of youth as poetry or love.

excellent.

16　p 180, pencil, overtraced

We have hazarded these observations . . . because these circumstances δ*] belong as it were[a] to the education of young Fairfax's mind . . .

* The *Ease* of Colloquy is a beauty in style, but not the unsteadi-

---

[a] Crossed out in pencil and underlined in ink; both the delete mark and footnote indicator are in pencil, not overtraced

13[1] On "clerisy" see BLOMFIELD 3 n 1.
14[1] I.e. *On the Constitution of the*

Church and State, imprinted 1830 but issued in Dec 1829. There is no record of a presentation copy to HC.

nesses, tutites,[1] hums and has, orange-suckings—or parenthetic expletives, to gain time for recovering the thread of the argument.

17 p 181, pencil, overtraced

For strange as it may now appear, there can be little doubt, that thousands believed that the King was absolutely a captive in the hands of the malignants, deluded and overruled, and that the Parliament army was raised as much for his rescue and protection, as for the defence of the country against the traiterous attempts of courtiers and Irish Papists.

What are the proofs of this? I find no trace of such a *persuasion*, tho' it often occurs as a legal FICTION, a formal pretext. Charles's Character, and that of his wife's,[a] with his uxoriouslyness,[1] were too well known by all parties. There is a *sneeringness* in this § unworthy of H. & discordant with his function as a biographer of Lord Fairfax.

18 p 182, pencil, overtraced

[Footnote on the Queen:] Charles and Henrietta exhibited the singular spectacle of a young couple quarrelling in the honey-moon, making it up, and conceiving in wedlock a passion romantic and violent as first love. Partly owing to the machinations of her French attendants (the priests especially), and partly to the ill offices of Buckingham, she was provoked on her first arrival to a degree of sullenness which obliged the King to use her with something like peremptory harshness; but after her French followers were sent back, and Buckingham removed by assassination, he thought he could not make her sufficient amends, and allowed her a dominion over himself and his affairs which she too often exerted more like an artful mistress than a dutiful wife.

Charles *for* the Queen; but the Queen for Charles? ἐπέχω.[1]

19 pp 184–5, pencil, overtraced

Accordingly, after rejecting a proposal of the Commons, which *] amounted to little less than the abolition of of monarchy, and

a Overtraced as "wife"

16[1] Clumsy and excessive alliteration —from a fragment of Ennius cited by Priscian: "O Tite, tute, Tati, tibi tanta, tyranne, tulisti". Not in *OED*.

17[1] I.e. Charles I and Henrietta Maria. See also **23**, below. C had spoken of Charles as "the poor uxorious Slave of a lewd Virago": N 38 ff 7ᵛ–8 (c Dec 1828).

18[1] "I hesitate"—as in BATEMAN **1** and G. BURNET *History* **8**.

receiving a cargo of arms and ammunition, purchased by the Queen in Holland, he advanced to Nottingham, and there set up his standard, August 22.

* I should rather say the *Suspension*: for it was the too well grounded fear of Charles's own personal character and their absence of all faith in *his* promises, rather than a desire permanently to strip *the Crown* of its essential prerogatives.

20   pp 186–7, pencil, overtraced[a]

At the opening of the year 1643, the King's affairs wore an aspect by no means unpromising. In the preceding summer, when he withdrew from the Metropolis, and found the gates of his own *good* town of Hull shut against him, he had neither ships nor men, nor money.... And here we may be permitted to remark how completely the unprovided condition in which Charles was found in this extremity confutes the assertions and the fears of those who justified their proceedings, upon rumours of armies, and martial preparations in England and Ireland, while in truth the King's adherents had scarce a weapon but the sword worn for fashion by their sides, or the antiquated furniture of their ancestral armories. That Charles *wished* to be free of Parliamentary controul there can be no doubt, any profession of his own notwithstanding; for he was a man, a King, and a High-church-man; but that he was plotting to make himself absolute by force of arms, there is no better proof than the reports of spies, the wild talk of a few hot-brained drunken Cavaliers, and the apprehensions of some who had indeed occasion to dread the exercise of his lawful prerogative. To these weak grounds of suspicion, we perhaps may add the secret insinuations of foreign states, particularly France and Sweden, then respectively governed by Rich⟨e⟩lieu[b] and Oxenstierna, two of the *profoundest politicians* that ever lived.

Is not all this asserted too positively? Charles's Letters to the Duke of Hamilton, and Ld Strafford tend to impress a contrary belief.[1] It was a confusion of the *Idea* or *ultimate* Aim with the historic genesis,

[a] The whole textus is marked with a pencil line in the margin
[b] The correction is in ink, by HNC or DC

20[1] The correspondence of Charles with William Hamilton, 2nd Duke of Hamilton (1616–51) and Thomas Wentworth, 1st Earl of Strafford (1593–1641) can be seen in *The Earl of Strafford's* *Letters and Despatches* ed William Knowler (1739) and in G. BURNET *Memoires of the Lives and Actions of James and William, Dukes of Hamilton and Castleherald* (1677).

in which the Idea gradually, and imperfectly revealed & realized itself, which misled both Charles and his Father.[2] And what James I *thought*, Charles *acted*. Because the Crown had been the seed, out of which grew the Stem, i.e. the Parliamentary Power, James re⟨a⟩soned as if the Stem were still *in*cluded in the Seed—whereas the ~~St~~ Seed had necessarily rotted away, in order to re-appear as the Flower—the Corona[a] & Seed-vessel of the Plant.

21   pp 188–9, pencil, overtraced

[Footnote:]...It was during this abortive negociation, that the Puritan Parliament first demanded, in express terms, the abolition of Episcopacy. This was clearly what neither they, had they been, which they were not, a legitimate representative Parliament, had any right to demand, nor Charles, had he been as absolute a monarch as he was accused of seeking to be, could have had any right to grant, as long as there was one congregation in the empire, who deemed Episcopacy essential to a Christian church, and therefore, in their view, essential to covenanted salvation.... The state may determine the political rank and functions of religious ministers, and over church property it has the same prerogative, be it more or less, as over other property; for property, under whatever denomination, is of the things that be Caesar's. But over the religious character of ministers, the state has no lawful sway. It may deprive a Bishop of his barony, but not of his orders.

But Baxter would have told Hartley: It is not Episcopacy which may be from God, but Prelacy, which certainly is of Cæsar, that we would have removed. But this confusion of Anti-prelatists, who from the *beginning* of the Contest were a numerous body, with anti-episcopalians, who at first were but few & of small influence, is a common error.[1]

22   p 189, pencil, overtraced

...the father and son formed a junction, and resolved to engage the Earl of Newcastle, who was advancing to the siege of Bradford, though their united forces did not exceed 3000, while those of the Earl were 10,000.... The result of this temerity was the defeat of

[a] A slip for "Corolla"

20[2] See e.g. *C&S* (*CC*) 82.

21[1] The distinction, as elucidated in BAXTER *Catholick Theologie* 3, is between "a National Church and its Prelacy" and "the Christian Church and its Episcopacy". See also BAXTER *Reliquiae* COPY B **115**.

Atherton Moor, June 30, 1643. Two thousand were slain or taken in the field, and two thousand more surrendered the next day.[a]
!! *4000* slain or surrendered out of *3000*!!

23   pp 212–15, pencil, overtraced

[Footnote:] It was a most ungentlemanlike act for the weekly-fast-ordaining Parliament or their agents to open Charles's letters to his wife, and all historians who make use of them to blacken his character ought to forfeit the character of gentlemen.

a Υσσειαn[b] Spirit.[1] How could a faithful Historian avoid it? The Parliament ⟨had⟩ acted ⟨ab initio⟩[2] on their convictions of the King's bad faith, and of the utter insincerity of his promises and professions; and surely the justification or condemnation of their acts must depend on or be greatly affected by, the question of[c]—Were these convictions well-grounded, and afterwards proved to be so by evidence, which could without danger to the State be advanced? What stronger presumption can we have of the certainty of the evidences which they[c] had previously obtained, and by the year after year accumulation of which their suspicions had been converted into convictions, and justifying grounds of Action? And was Henrietta an ordinary *wife*?[3] Was Charles to her as Charles of Sweden to his Spouse?[4] The Swede's Queen was only the man's *wife*; but Henrietta

---

a DC (1852) prints: "Four or five hundred were slain or taken in the field, and many more surrendered the next day."

b The first two words not overtraced

c The deletion not overtraced

23[1] "*Huss*eian" refers to RS and to a specific defect that C found in his historical sense. The name seems first to appear in C's comment on a review of RS's in *QR* late 1823, C playing upon the Latin and Greek conventional sounds of grief and pain. "'The Progress of Infidelity', in the last Quarterly—Hugh! Hugh! E. Hugh ⸢Usse Hussee! ['heu! heu! eheu Southey!']—But why an oto-tatoi [ὀτοτατοῖ] or an ! When the Stilts are worn out or lost, the Borrower must stand on his own legs.—" *CN* iv 4985. C's objection, for which he seems to have reserved the adjective "Husseian", was to the anachronistic interpretation of past moral events in terms of present moral taste—precisely the objection here. Cf N 54 f 20ᵛ (of date similar to the

date of these marginalia): "The Doctor —&c—Vol. II. p. 16.—but where indeed is ΥΣΣΕ not?—the dictatorially petulant transmutation of Generals into Universals—and then the exquisite *common-placeness* of the Generals, as far as they are true...". Cf HACKET *Scrinia* 12 n 1.

23[2] "From the beginning".

23[3] See **17**, above.

23[4] Presumably Charles x (1622–60) of Sweden, who made a political marriage with Hedwig Leonora, daughter of Frederick iii, Duke of Holstein-Gottorp, in order to secure an ally against Denmark. In the series of daring military exploits and political manoeuvres in which Charles humiliated and partitioned Denmark, his queen played no part.

was notoriously Charles's QUEEN, or rather the He-queen's She-King—a *Commander* in the War, meddling with & influencing all his Councils. I hold the *Parliament* fully justified ⟨in the publication of the Letters,⟩ much more the *Historian*.[5]

24   pp [241]–3 | Anne Clifford, Countess of Dorset, Pembroke, and Montgomery

The priests of some religions undertake, for a *consideration*, to bear the sins of such of the laity as put trust in them. They may perhaps find, at last, that they have spoken more truth than they meant to do. It is no small portion of the sins of the earth, of which priests shall bear the blame, and the *whole* blame; for the reluctant obedience of those who accepted them for the sake of the Lord, whose commission they had forged, shall not lose its reward. He that said that a cup of cold water, given for *his* sake, should not be given in vain, would take no exception, if for his sake, it were ignorantly given to Judas Iscariot.

These petulant crudities of indigested thoughts from the primæ viæ of Reflection, these temerities of interpocular Talk,[1] vex my Spirit in dear Hartley's Writings: So here! in abusing the Priest he at once justifies the principle, or Assumption, by which he deludes, and removes all the mischief Consequent on the delusion—that is, makes it practically no delusion at all, but a saving truth. So too, Southey has taken pains to quiet the universal Conscience, by the assurance that Prayers offered to the Virgin Mary or S⟨t⟩ Boniface will be equally acceptable to God & bring down the same blessing as those offered to the ~~e~~ ~~the~~ Omniscient thro' the one only Mediator.[2] But in this

23[5] On the publication of this correspondence see also HACKET *Scrinia* **45** and n 1 and HUTCHINSON **15**. DC has added a footnote in his edition (ɪ 361–2): "From the observations of *S. T. C.* on this interesting life, which is written with characteristic moderation and good sense, it appears that while the father takes higher grounds than the son in the Church questions, then as now under discussion, he is nevertheless a much stronger, or at least sterner, parliamentarian. This is significant. It shows first that the Church principles, to which the former attached so much importance, were not those of Laud, or Montague, or of the Caroline divines in general; and secondly, that in his political tenets he was more persistent, and consistent, than has sometimes been taken for granted."

24[1] From the "main streets" and (literally) "among the/his cups", i.e. bibulous table-talk. "Interpocular" is not in *OED*.

24[2] C seems to have misunderstood or misremembered what RS had said in *The Book of the Church* (2 vols 1824) ɪ 299 in his attack on the worship of the Virgin Mary. Through exaggerated and superstitious "representations and fables" of Mary generated by monastics, he said, "the belief of the people became so entirely corrupted, that Christ, instead of being regarded as our Mediator and Redeemer, appeared to them in the character of a jealous God, whom it behoved

charity for the poor benighted Papist what a cruel Bill of Indightment against Wickliff, & Luther; yea, against John & Paul![3]
I would put H. on a year's *Fast* from all Review and Magazine Reading—as one means of getting rid of the constant itch to be witty—which always implies a want of faith in the interest of the Matter itself, of which he is treating.[a][4]

25　pp 248–9

[John, the seventh Lord Clifford, while on service in France, is said to have paid his soldiers at the rate of] "four shillings for every knight; for every Esquire, one shilling; for every archer, six-pence *] per diem." According to the general computation of the value of money in those days, this rate of payment seems enormously high.

* I am strongly inclined to suspect something false, & deceptive in the received comparative values of nominal payments in different Ages. In the times of the Plantagenets Money was so little in actual use, and the necessaries of Life so variable in point of scarcity or abundance from the rude state of Agriculture & the unsettled state of the Times, that the very grounds of a Ratio were wanting. When I read, that Sir Walter's Raleigh's Court-dress was worth 80,000£, & then find, that 80,000£ in Elizabeth's time was equal to almost half a million in 1812—I *feel* sceptical.[1] S. T. C.

26　p 302 | Roger Ascham

[In a footnote, HC quotes Robert Pember in a letter to Ascham.] The words of the original are—"Da operam, aut sis perfectus, non

---

a The word is difficult to read. DC (1852) reads "creating", probably a printer's slip

---

them to propitiate through the mediation of his Virgin Mother, for through her alone could mercy and salvation be obtained." In *Vindiciae Ecclesiae Anglicanae* (1826), the sequel to *The Book of the Church*, RS reiterated this view (p 432).

24[3] Both Wycliffe and Luther had attacked manifest abuses of ecclesiastical authority, particularly the traffic in indulgences, and both refused to remain subject to papal jurisdiction.

24[4] The damage that HC might continue to suffer from reading reviews may be inferred from C's view of the deleterious effects of writing reviews. In a bitter letter to Godwin in Mar 1811, C spoke of anomalies in RS's character and laid the blame, in part at least, on reviewing—a practice that "never fails to produce at certain times on the best minds [as its effects]—presumption, petulance, and callousness to personal feelings, and a disposition to treat the reputations of their Contemporaries as play-things placed at their own disposal". *CL* III 316.

25[1] For C's understanding of the economics of changing wages and prices, see e.g. *CN* III 3987 and n.

Stoicus, ἀλλὰ Λυρικὸς, ut belle pulses lyram."[1] No doubt in the same sense that Socrates was commanded by the Oracle to make music; or, to appeal to a far higher authority, as David "shewed a dark speech on the harp," i.e. opened and exalted the understanding by the aid of the imagination.

Neither has Hartley caught the true meaning of the words, αλλα λυρικος, as opposed to Stoicus. The Stoic = the sovereignty of the Highest by the sacrifice of the inferior—Lyricus, the whole as a beautiful one, by harmonious subordination.

27 p 303

[Quoting from Ascham's *Toxophilus*:] "...Much music marreth men's manners, saith Galen."

Thro' my whole life since the period of reflection I have found the truth of this observation. Music is the Twilight between Sense and Sensuality./[1] For its demoralizing effect, when it is a mastering passion, see "A Ramble among the Musicians of Germany, by a Musical Professor."[2]

28 p 303

That the practice of music no way impairs the faculty of severe thought, is sufficiently evinced by the fact that Milton was a skilful musician, and that most of the German philosophers of the present day, who in mental industry excel the whole world, play on some instrument.

26[1] "Take care that you may be perfect, not as a Stoic, but as a Lyric, so that you may strike the lyre beautifully".

27[1] In view of *TT* 5 Oct 1830 and 6 Jul 1833 one would expect C to say with Beethoven: "Music is the mediator between the spiritual and the sensual life." Cf a notebook entry of late Sept 1833: *IS* 214–15 = N 52 ff 5–6 (*CN* v).

27[2] *A Ramble Among the Musicians of Germany* (anon, 1828) was written by Edward Holmes (1797–1859), a friend of Charles Cowden Clarke, Keats, and Lamb. Pupil and protégé of Vincent Novello, he raised a subscription for Mozart's widow and made his journey to Germany in 1828 to deliver the money to her. The *Ramble* ran through three editions, and in 1845 Holmes published a *Life of Mozart*. C seems to be thinking of pp 5–6 ("Antwerp"): "The genius of our cathedral service and that of the Catholics is essentially different: in the one, all is holy, abstracted, sublime, where the idea of sex and worldly affections cannot interfere with that chilling flesh-creeping solemnity, which 'brings all heaven before the eyes;' in the other, human passions, love and tenderness, are ever awakened, and the eye and ear doth administer to voluptuous sensations. In this religion the imagination and the senses go hand in hand, and music and perfumes, the luxury of an eastern sultan, induce yearnings not always of the most godly kind...".

"*Much* Music" is Galen's Phrase[1]—and see the two last lines of Milton's XXth Sonnet/[2]

29 p 304

About this time he [Ascham] was involved in a most singular controversy, which although the subject be of no very general interest, is yet so characteristic of the times, that we shall briefly describe it. Sir John Cheek and Sir Thomas Smith had introduced some alterations into the pronunciation of the Greek language, which had previously been even more barbarous than at present. Ascham at first opposed the innovation...but his mind was ever open to conviction on all subjects, great and small, and he had adopted the new and improved method, when a more formidable person than any yet engaged in the business thought fit to interfere in a truly despotic manner.... This was the notorious Stephen Gardiner, then Chancellor of the University of Cambridge, who issued his peremptory prohibition of the new pronunciation, and after defining, with great strictness, the sound to be given to each letter, denounced the penalties for disobedience, suspension of degrees for graduates, and private whipping for undergraduates. Sir John Cheek, however... had the courage to defend his system; and the Bishop's attention was soon after diverted to other objects.

It would have been well, if H. had given the *whole* Scheme on each side/ & shewn, in what points *our* present mode of reading Greek at Eton, Westminster &c agrees with one or the other. To my ear it is most cacophonous.[1] Βιργιλιος, Ουιργιλιος—? proof, that the Greek had no V?[2] In the Greek Historians of Roman affairs do we

28[1] Quoting Ascham in **27** textus.

28[2] The last two lines of "Lawrence, of virtuous father..." read: "He who of those delights can judge, and spare | To interpose them oft, is not unwise." Sonnet xx in Lamb's copy of *Paradise Regained and Other Poems* (1751), but not so numbered in all eds of Milton.

29[1] C's rendering of "*our* present mode" of pronouncing Greek is shown by N Q ff 70–69 reporting a conversation of 1795–6. From his phonetic rendering of lines of Homer, C's pronunciation of Greek vowels can be seen to be: ου = *ow* (now), η = *ee* (sheep), ῐ = *i* (thin), ῑ = *ī* (buy). (There is a more sophisticated discussion of the Greek vowels in the

Greek grammar written for HC: see *SW & F.*) When Greek was reintroduced to western Europe the pronunciation was that of the scholars driven from Byzantium by the Turks, which was rather close to that of the Greeks today (see nn 2 and 3 and **30** and **31** textus, below). Ascham's system was roughly as described by C in **31**, below. See also HERMANN 3.

29[2] These alternative spellings of the name of Virgil show that while the Greek pronunciation of β was changing from that of English *b* to *v*, the pronunciation of Latin *v* was changing from English *w* to *v*. C refers to this phenomenon (together with the examples given in nn 3 and 4, below) in *CN* III 3792.

not find one Writer give Titus by Τειτος, and another by Τητος?[3] I can never think o μεγα merely the long o, nor η the long e.[4]

30 p 305

Ascham...declares his adherence to the new pronunciation, and defends the change with considerable humour. Among other absurdities of the exploded system, was that of giving the sound of the English V to the Greek B. Now Eustathius, asserts that the Greek word BH exactly resembled the bleating of a sheep, and therefore it is easy to determine how it is to be pronounced; unless, says Roger, the Greek sheep bleated differently from those of England, Italy, and *] Germany; "Jam utrum ulla ovis effert *ve* ut vos an *be* ut nos, judicetis. Anglae scio omnes et Germanae et Italae pro nobis faciunt; sed fortasse Graece oves olim non *balabant* sed *vilabant*."

[..."Now you will judge whether any sheep utters *ve* as you say, or *be* as we say. I know that all the English, German, and Italian sheep are on our side, but perhaps long ago sheep did not say *baa* but *vee*."]

* a very doubtful ground! Once in Germany, it was in 1799, I observed to a young German Friend the marvellous articulation of the Cuckoo's Note, how complete a dissyllable word it was—to which he warmly assenting, I sang out—Cūck, or rather Cook-koo! Cook-Coo—, No! No! says the German—the Bird clearly says— Gook! Gook![1]—In 5 minutes I could make the Lamb's Bleat *Ba* instead of Bah!—[2]

31 p 305

From the manner in which Ascham speaks of the new pronunciation, it is manifest that the reform was at the date of his letter, (6th of March, 1553) firmly established in England, while the continental

---

29[3] C makes this same point about "Titus" in MATTHIAE *Copious Greek Grammar* I 15; see also *CN* III 3792. Several Greek vowel sounds merged into English *ee*, the sound of the Latin *i* in "Titus".

29[4] *Omega* (ω), ὦ μέγα, "big *o*" as distinct from *omikron* (o), ὁ μικρόν, "little *o*". Cf *CN* III 3792, in which C suspects that η and ω "were not invented merely to express quantity", otherwise we should expect to find *umega, amega,* and *imega* to represent the long values of υ, α, and ι.

30[1] In *CN* IV 4726 C decided to collect from Oken "all the words which he gives as the sounds of the different Birds" in order to compare the perception of consonants by Germans and English. He also recalled his "vain attempt" to persuade a German friend that the cuckoo says "coo! coo!" and not "Gück, gück".

30[2] C also considers the phonetic rendering of the lamb's bleat in MATTHIAE I 15.

nations still adhered to the old method, which was probably derived from the Constantinopolitans by whom the Greek language was revived in the West, as it nearly resembles that of the modern Greeks. Correctness of course is out of the question in either case; but that system is to be preferred which gives to each letter a distinct sound.

The Italian with the English Theta & Diphthongs ⟨& ⟨the⟩ German *ch* = χ⟩ would be the most perfect scheme of pronouncing Greek.[1]

32 pp 335–7, pencil, overtraced

There is another passage, in Aelmer's "Harborough," which defines the three estates of the English constitution so plainly, that we cannot resist extracting it:—"The Regiment of England is not a mere
*] monarchy, as some for lack of consideration think; nor a mere oligarchy, nor democracy; but a rule mixt of all these; wherein each of these have, or should have, like authority. The image thereof, and not the image, but the thing indeed, is to be seen in the Parliament house; where in you shall find these three estates, the King or Queen, which representeth the monarchy, the noblemen, which be the aristocracy, and the burgesses and knights, which be the democracy...."

* I almost wonder, that Hartley should have eulogized such an erroneous Common-place, from Aristotle, Cicero, and Tacitus, as this De Lolmian, or Blackstonian ~~Dictum~~ ⟨Ante⟩dictum of Ælmer's.[1] Alas! it is the aweful Calamity of our Time (1832–3) that it is *beginning* to be true; but as must of necessity be the case, by the (not counterfor[e]sight)[a] the destruction of the two weaker Powers— Our *pledged* House of Commons is *truly* & efficiently a *Democracy*—& therefore a Contradiction, and annulment of Aristocracy & Monarchy—both which change their natures, &

[a] Letter supplied by the editor. DC (1852) reads "counterpoising"

[31][1] This was approximately the system of Ascham, Cheke, and Smith, but they would not have approved of some of the English diphthongs, especially -*ow* for ου.

[32][1] "Aelmer"—i.e. John Aylmer (1521–94), bp of London. Jean Louis de Lolme (c 1740–1807), Swiss advocate, came to England in 1769 and published his *Constitution of England* first in French (Amsterdam 1771), then in English (by another hand, 1775). Perhaps because of its excessive flattery of England, the English version was widely circulated (10th ed 1853). William Blackstone (1723–80) first published his *Commentaries on the Laws of England* in 4 vols 1765–9; it was issued in numerous editions and translations. For an early use of Blackstone's *Commentaries* by C, see e.g. *Lects 1795* (*CC*) 308, 314–15n.

become the Vassals, the κρατούμενοι.[2] The Diamond is mastered by the Oxygen, & becomes ~~carbon~~ charcoal, to supply it with Fuel, till by the repeated action of the mastering Gas, it is volatilized —to exist only as the stifle-damp of a Grotto del Cane.[3] *S. T. C.*

33   p 337, pencil, overtraced

[Footnote:]...[Bishop Aelmer] was a great Hebraist, and a patron of Hebrew scholars, particularly of the celebrated Broughton, who *] first maintained the now approved exposition, that *Hell*, in the Apostle's Creed, means *Paradise*, a very comfortable doctrine for sinners. The word ought to be altered, Hades, the original term, like the Hebrew Schoel, means simply the place, or rather state, of separate spirits; but Hell, in modern English, has no such latitude of signification, therefore, though Hades may signify Paradise, Hell cannot; and though the creed is scriptural in Greek, it is unscriptural in the English translation.

[*] Mem. The Clause was added in the 6[tha] Century; probably to meet some rising Heresy; making Christ's death as state of suspended Animation/ Non verè mortuus est.[1]

34   p 338, pencil, overtraced

Alexander Nowell...Was returned for a Cornish borough in the first parliament of Mary, but declared "not duly elected", as being a Prebendary of Westminster, and therefore a member of the Lower *] House of Convocation. Whence it appears, that holy orders did not of themselves disqualify him for sitting in the House of Commons.

* Worth noticing, as a comment on the distinction between the National Church, Enclesia, and the Church of Christ, Ecclesia.[1]

a DC (1852) reads "sixteenth", mistakenly

32[2] "The ruled".

32[3] The Grotta del Cane near Naples, famous for its carbonic acid gas (carbon dioxide). Cf Berkeley *Siris* § 144. For the basis of C's figure, see Humphry Davy "Some Experiments on the Combustion of the Diamond and Other Carbonaceous Substances" in *Phil Trans RS* CIV (1814) 557–70. Davy pointed out that "the opinion that common carbonaceous substances differ from the diamond by containing oxygene" was not supported by his experiments, and that "the diamond affords no other substance by its combustion than pure carbonic acid gas". "Stifle-damp" (not in *OED*) is the same as "choke-damp" (as distinct from "fire-damp")—i.e. carbonic acid gas.

33[1] "He did not really die"—one of the tenets of the Albigensian heretics. The phrase "He descended into Hell" occurs in the Apostles' Creed but not in the Nicene Creed. For a history of the Apostles' Creed, see BAXTER *Catholick Theologie* 9 n 1.

34[1] For C's use of Ecclesia/Enclesia see HACKET *Scrinia* 33 and n 2.

35 p 339, pencil | John Fisher, Bishop of Rochester

...his death [has been] described as the <u>reward</u> of treason, by others as the testimony of martyrdom.

penalty?

35A p 341, pencil, overtraced

[Margaret of Lancaster, mother of Henry VII] almost merged the ?]*ᵃ* parent in the subject, with a humility rather heroic than christian; for it was too conscious and deliberate to be the spontaneous issue of a soul renewed.

36 p 342, pencil, overtraced

[Lady Margaret signed a letter to her son: "your *humble servant, beadswoman* and mother".] Surely this preposterous reversal of the order of nature, wherein a mother abases herself before her own offspring, before the creature whom she herself had held "muling and puking" in her arms, is a satire upon monarchy.

Lady Margaret's Note is cumbrous; but I can imagine the same spirit in a very winning form. Consider what the *Idea*, the KING, was at that time to a highborn Religionist/ & that the Mother would gratify her Mother's pride in her Humiliation.*

* See my Christmas Day Hymn—
"I am a Woman poor & mean—
"The Mother of the Prince of Peace!"[1]

37 p 354, pencil, overtraced; last sentence marked in the margin in pencil

[James Stanley, son of the Earl of Derby, and son-in-law to the Lady Margaret, was made Bishop of Ely by her interest.] As long as ever the Church is in any degree connected with the property of the country, the superior offices in it must, and will be bestowed on

ᵃ The ? in the margin embraces the whole sentence

36[1] See *PW* (EHC) I 338–49: first published in the *M Post* on Christmas Day 1799 shortly after composition. In st 6 the Virgin speaks:

Tell this in some more courtly scene,
    To maids and youths in robes of state!
I am a woman poor and mean,
    And therefore is my soul elate.

The words "Thou Mother of the Prince of Peace, | Poor, simple, and of low estate!" occur in st 4 and are virtually repeated in the Virgin's words at the close of the poem.

political considerations; and what proof is there that young Stanley was less fit for a Bishop than any other person, whose name might have been drawn in the lottery? As an Earl's son, he had at least a good chance of being a gentleman, which for a man who exercises a somewhat invidious superiority over gentlemen and scholars often his seniors, and it may be, in some respects, his betters, is no small recommendation. As long as patronage is permitted, it is natural and right that the patrons should patronize those whom they know best, and love best.... Even in a land of slaves it will always be found that the higher the rank of the slave-master, the better the condition of the slave.

The worst and yet an *entertaining* fault of H's biographies is his running off on every light occasion into episodes of his ⟨own⟩ wit and reasoning; in which the Wit is sometimes an over-match for the Reason.

37A p 354, pencil

Cardinal Pole was the descendant of kings...yet he was an enemy to persecution. Gardiner and Bonner were both natural children Qu] of men not high enough to dignify their bastardy; they derived their *respectability* solely from their rank in the church, and they were the cruellest of persecutors. !!!

38 p 355, pencil

[St John's College, Cambridge] has always been a resort of students from the northern provinces, who, if less brilliant and mercurial than the children of the south, are not less eminent in *honours*, their slow and sound minds being peculiarly adapted for the patient toil of mathematics, in which branch of knowledge St. John's competes honourably with Trinity.

a *villainous Pittism*[1]

39 p 368, pencil, overtraced

The Commons, who always looked upon the wealth of the clergy with invidious eyes...zealously entered into the King's design of humbling the church of Rome.

envious?

38[1] C had savoured Pitt's style in actual performance thirty-two years earlier: see *EOT* (*CC*) I 152–62, 184–95, and *CN* I 651, 653. At that time he found that "the elegance, & high-finish of Pitt's Periods even in the most sudden replies, is *curious*; but that is all. He *argues* but so so; & does not *reason* at all." *CL* I 568; cf *EOT* (*CC*) I 221–2. The "Pittism" of HC's word "competes" consists in undercutting the rival with an apparent compliment.

40   p 376, pencil, overtraced

So says that stout Church and King man, <u>Tom</u> Fuller...

an unreasonable *Tom* Brownism.[1]

41   p 377, pencil, overtraced

Even the royal right to the appointment of Bishops, &c., to the summoning convocations and synods, and the passing of regulative ordinances for the Church, was not altogether a new claim, though it had been stoutly resisted by the more zealous Church-men. And indeed, however expedient it may be in a secular point of view, that such power be vested in the crown, it is utterly without example in the primitive church, or even analogy in the Jewish theocracy. It is a moot point whether the bishops who purchased of Constantine an establishment for Christianity, and a secular rank for themselves, were not traitors to the Church. The question should be argued on grounds of christian expediency.

Why should Christianity be a greater objection to a Man's being a member & functionary of the Nationalty[1] as a Vicar, Rector, Dean or Bishop, than to his being a Judge, or Chancellor?—to the national *Moralists*, than to the national Legalists? The national *Church* or Clerisy included[a] both.

42   p 378, pencil, overtraced

...and Bishop Fisher in his old age betrayed a degree of ∧ credulity δ] ~~or rather gullibility~~, which the darkness of the times can hardly excuse.

Q[y]?   ∧ *wilful*[b]

43   p 454, pencil, overtraced | The Reverend William Mason

[When Mason took orders, Bishop Warburton advised him to give up the study of poetry.] Mason sensibly took this admonition as words of course, like the common dehortation from fiddling, fox-

---

[a] Overtraced as "includes"
[b] DC (1852) reads: "a degree of credulity, or rather gullibility" and in a footnote ascribes "Query—*wilful* credulity?" to C

40[1] Thomas Brown—one of C's favourite examples of pertness, vulgar slang, and "Thames-Waterman Language". See AURELIUS **62** n 1.

41[1] See e.g. *C&S* (*CC*) 24–9, 39, 57, 108, 194 and BROUGHAM **2** n 2.

hunting, and Pitt-dinner-frequenting, which is one of the common-places of a Bishop's charge.

what can H. mean by this fling?

44 p 634 | Captain James Cook

The Adventure had arrived in Queen Charlotte's Bay on the 7th, and the interval between her arrival and that of the Resolution had afforded such strong instances of the anthropophagous* habits of the New Zealanders, that Furneaux called a particular inlet Cannibal Bay.

[*] For "anthropophagous" substitute "*philanthropic*" in the same ~~spirit, in~~ authority, by which the French Naturalists, and Sentimen-talists, and their Imitators in England, entitle the gratification of a congenerous Appetite ~~at the consequent on~~ obtained by the murder of more than the mere life, *Love*!—The *modern* fashion of this Cannibalism in England & France is commonly philogynic,[1] but in Turkey & China so indifferent, as to ὁ or ἠ, as to be truly *philanthropic*.[2]

45 p 655, pencil, overtraced

And thus ended Cook's second voyage. Its geographical results, though important, were chiefly negative, and therefore not of that kind on which imagination dwells delighted. He had destroyed a vision of fancy, and instead of augmenting the map with new Indies,

44[1] *OED* records "philogyny" but not the form "philogynic".

44[2] This sally—for there is no question about the cannibalism that Cook and his companions witnessed—turns upon the contrast between ἄνθρωπος (a human being) and ἀνήρ/ἀνδρός (a man, as opposed to γυνή, a woman), called to mind by HC's using "anthropophagous" (man-eating) to avoid anticipating the word "cannibal"; C's usual contrast between love and lust is also implied. In the first sentence he points to what he takes to be the French idea of "*Love*"—the murder of the person (presumably the woman) under the licence of gratifying "congenerous Appetite", the lust for a creature of one's own biological genus. This, and the second sentence, is elucidated by a note of 1810 (based on Stavorinus) in *CN* iii 4015: "Chinese Taste in *Love* (as the Gallican, and Philo-gallican English Scribes call their infra-abdominal Inquietudes)—*Porcinellas* in domibus servant! 'I praise the Lord, your Worship, I have a very good *Constitution*—I can —— anything, your Worship!—'" The second sentence then may be glossed: "this Cannibalism ('the murder of more than the mere life' under the name of '*Love*') is nowadays in England and France usually philogynic (woman-loving), but in Turkey and China they are so indifferent as to ὁ and ἠ (he and she) that they are, properly speaking, *philanthropic* (humankind-loving)".

had reduced islands to fog banks and ice shoals, and continents to inconsiderable islets and reefs of coral. He had discovered, in short, *] that a fifth continent was as little to be hoped for as a fifth*a* sense.
* May not New Holland be fairly called so?[1] It contains almost as great a variety of Climate as Europe. If the Coral Insects should ever have stitched*b* together the Polynesia, would it be named a Continent?

46 p 657, pencil, overtraced

On the 12th of December land was seen, which proved to be a group of islands, two of which, in honour of their French discoverers, were *] named Marion and Crozet's Isles. Two, of larger size, were called Prince Edward's Isles. After exploring the coast of Kerguelen's Land...the navigators made for Van Diemen's Land, and anchored in Adventure Bay on the 16th of January, 1777.

* At all events, H. should have transcribed the Longitudes & Latitudes. Without these it is perfect confusion[1]—a play map with the ⌷ and △ slips in a jumble.[2]

47 p 665, pencil, overtraced | William Congreve

[Footnote:] The terms old, middle, and new, applied to the dynasties of Greek Comedy, may with little violence be transferred to the English stage. It must, however, be remarked, that of the two latter races, each originated in the life-time of its predecessor. The old or poetical comedy, composed of a mixture of blank verse and prose, often with a strong infusion of pathetic interest, and very frequently interspersed with songs, dances, &c., flourished under Elizabeth and

---

a Possibly a slip for "sixth", but DC (1852) did not alter the word
b The word was first overtraced as "stretched", then altered to "stitched"—as DC (1852) prints it

45[1] In the seventeenth century the Dutch gave the name "New Holland" to part of western Australia. The name co-existed with "Australia" and "Terre Australe", especially in official circles in Britain, for some time after "Australia" had been established in the 1820s as the official name of the continent. C's favourite name for RS in the early years was "Australis"—a reminder that the pronunciation of RS's name by his contemporaries was "Sou*th*-y".

46[1] C's objection is just. HC, after giving a detailed account of Cook's second voyage, deals perfunctorily with the third (and fatal) voyage and winds up the life abruptly. C wanted to be able to trace out exactly what was happening in the narrative, his eagerness perhaps heightened by his boyhood association with William Wales, Cook's astronomer: see Böhme **66** n 1.
46[2] Representing perhaps the "puzzle-peg" of WW's ms note at ANDERSON COPY A 1.

James.... The second, or middle style, was first perfected by Ben Jonson, though chronology would rather class him with the writers of the old comedy.... The middle comedy became predominant after the Restoration, and numbers many writers of unequal merit; the last were Cumberland and Sheridan.... The new comedy, of which the principal masters are Colman, Morton, Reynolds, Dibdin, Diamond, &c., has been denominated sentimental, or by a French expression, *comedie larmoyant*, crying comedy, an apparent contradiction. It is, in truth, the comic correlative to Lillo's tragedy. Much as it is reviled by the critics, something very like it is occasionally to be found in old Heywood, the prose Shakspeare.... However inferior it may be to the middle or legitimate comedy as a work of art, and still more to the poetic comedy as a birth of imagination, we cannot think it deserves all the vituperation that has been heaped upon it.

This note has less of Hartley's Tact and Discrimination than ⟨from such a subject⟩ I should have expected. Surely a *prose Shakspeare* is not only an overload for Old Heywood[1] but something not very unlike a square Circle.

S. T. C.

48   p 666, pencil, overtraced

It is a pity that the Doctor [Johnson], who, like Boileau, aimed at the character of "a steady and rigorous moralist," did not reflect that sophistry is first cousin, only once removed, to lying, and that an uncharitable piece of special pleading, intended to injure the reputation of the illustrious dead, is not a *very white* lie. Congreve, whatever his faults might be, was not a fool; nor was his convenience or vanity at all concerned in proving himself a Yorkshireman rather than an Irishman.

very sensible[a]
    I could wish to have preserved a long[b] and spirited conclusion of one of my Courses of Lectures on the *Sycophancy* and cynic

a These two words written in the margin beside the textus, the rest in the head- and foot-margins
b DC (1852) reads "lively", but "long" is clear in the overtrace

47[1] HC is—consciously or unconsciously—echoing Lamb, who in his *Specimens of English Dramatic Poets* (1808) called Thomas Heywood (c 1574–1650) "a sort of *prose* Shakespeare". C himself had read the ms of the *Specimens* before publication (see DANIEL headnote DATE); the critical notes to the *Specimens* were reprinted in Lamb's 2-vol *Works* (1818), Vol I of which was affectionately dedicated to C. Cf FLÖGEL **38**.

Assentation of Dr Johnson, both as a Critic, ~~and~~ a Moralist ~~and~~ (&
most strongly as a critico-moral Biographer) to the plebeian envy of
the patrician Mediocres, and the Reading Public.¹

S. T. Coleridge.

48A p 667, pencil, overtraced

[Footnote:] In a school lately established not a hundred miles from
Leeds, the masters are bound by their engagement never to inflict
Bowyer] corporal punishment.¹ What would Orbilius, Busby,
Boye~~y~~er, Parr, and Holofernes say to this?²

49 p 669, pencil, overtraced

The thought of confining a novel to the *unities* was something
original. But French criticism was then the rage...and Congreve, a
precocious mind, might hope to gain a laurel by applying the French
rules to a species of composition never before made amenable to
*] them; as if one should make tea or brew small beer in chemical
nomenclature.

as if? Pray, where is the likeness?^a

* A most infelicitous illustration! and why *might* not a novel &
a very good one in its kind, be written on such a plan? I am sure
that the Pilgrim, Beggar's Bush, and several others of B. and F.'s
Dramas might be turned into very interesting Novels.¹ Had Congreve
said that a good novel *must* be so constructed, then indeed H. might
have slapt him.

^a The queries are written in the margin beside the textus, the rest is written in the head- and foot-margins

48¹ C ascribes "plebeian envy" to
Johnson in *Friend* (*CC*) I 213. This note
is one of his harshest and most compre-
hensive dismissals of Dr Johnson; but see
also BARCLAY *Argenis* COPY A 3 and n
6. C is thinking perhaps of his lecture of
9 Jan 1812 (see *CRB* I 57), or of Lecture
14 of 13 Mar 1818 "On the corruptions
of the English language since the reign of
Queen Ann, in our style of writing
prose", the "spirited conclusion" to
which is not preserved. Cf *CN* III 4188,
and see also **67**, below. On "the Reading
Public", see *SM* (*CC*) 36–8.
48A¹ I.e. Ackworth School, run by the
Society of Friends. It is twelve miles SE
of Leeds. C visited it in c Jul–Aug 1808:
see *CN* III 3348–3351 nn.

48A² HC gives a list of school-
masters notorious for their severity.
For James Boyer—whose name C habi-
tually spelled "Bowyer", perhaps match-
ing the pronunciation still current at
Christ's Hospital—see BAXTER *Reliquiae*
COPY B **112** n 3. When Boyer died, Lamb
wrote to C: "Lay thy animosity against
Jimmy in the grave. Do not *entail* it on
thy posterity." *LL* II 135. For C on
corporal punishment see e.g. *CN* III 3291,
4181 and n.
49¹ C himself had earlier intended
to adapt some Beaumont and Fletcher
plays, not as novels but as plays for the
modern stage: *The Pilgrim*, to be called
"Love's Metamorphoses", and *The
Beggar's Bush* were in mind in Oct
1815. *CL* IV 590; cf *CN* II 2931, III 3736.

But why? supposing the verses worth reading for themselves, would not it be sorry to miss Barrow's & Marvel's poetic Prefaces to the Par. Lost? I fear that the jealousy & still more the unbrother-hood of modern authors have more to do with it than either pride or modesty.
S.T.C.

them to be. Congreve, a templar, and almost a boy, had already heard and partaken the conversation of Dryden, Wycherly, Southerne, and other poets and critics, and frequenters of the theatre, so that he had the benefit of experience, by anticipation, in a line of writing which has been supposed to require more experience than any other. When the "Old Bachelor" was shewn to Dryden, he pronounced that "Such a first play he had never seen." Something, however, was yet wanting to ensure its success, for he added, "It was a pity, seeing the author was ignorant of stage and town, that he should miscarry for want of a little assistance. The stuff was rich indeed, only the fashionable cut was wanting." According to Southerne, it was near miscarrying from another cause:—"When he brought it to the players, he read it so wretchedly ill that they were on the point of rejecting it, till one of them good-naturedly took it out of his hands, and read it." The players must, however, have expected great things from him; for Thomas Davenant, then manager of Drury Lane, gave him what is called the privilege of the house half a year before his play came on the stage, a favour at that time unparalleled. Having undergone a revision from Dryden, Southerne, and Manwairing, the "Old Bachelor" was produced in 1693, before a crowded and splendid audience, and met with triumphant success. The prologue intended to have been spoken was written by Lord Falkland. The play, when printed, was prefaced with three copies of commendatory verses, by Southerne, Marsh, and Higgins. The pride or modesty of a modern writer would revolt at the ancient custom of publishing these flattering testimonials in the vestibule of his own book, where, after all, they could not answer the place of an advertisement. Flattery, wherever she may now abide, no longer rules despotic in first pages.*

The exhibition of the "Old Bachelor" was hailed as a new æra in theatric history. The praise which it fairly earned by its intrinsic merit was aggravated by respect to the author's youth. The critics were glad to display their generosity by applauding, and their candour by forgiving: the play-going public gave their usual hearty welcome to

* Congreve dedicated the Old Bachelor to the Lord Clifford of Lanesborough, son to the Lord Burlington. The allusion to the connection between the families is neat. "My Lord, it is with great pleasure I lay hold on this first occasion which the accidents of my life have given me of writing to your Lordship; for since, at the same time, I write to all the world, it will be the means of publishing what I would have every body know,—the respect and duty which I owe and pay to you. I have so much inclination to be your's, that I need no other engagement, but the particular ties by which I am bound both to your Lordship and family, have put it out of my power to make you any compliment, since all offers of myself will amount to no more than an honest acknowledgment, and only shew a willingness in me to be grateful."

altogether a most unhartleian sentence, too bad to be mended by cutting out one rotten bit and putting a bit of good cloth in the place.

Neat, my dearest Hartley! more clumsy, involved common place I have seldom seen. the thought

2. An annotated page of Hartley Coleridge *The Worthies of Yorkshire and Lancashire* (1832–3). See H. COLERIDGE **51–54**
The Humanities Research Center, The University of Texas at Austin; reproduced by kind permission

50 p 669, pencil

It may be laid down with as much certainty in literature as in politics, that all restriction is evil, *per se*, and can only be recommended or justified by a clear necessity, or a manifest benefit.

Aut erit aut non![1] Oraculous.

51 p 670, pencil overtraced

The play [*The Old Bachelor*], when printed, was prefaced with three copies of commendatory verses, by Southerne, Marsh, and Higgins. The pride or modesty of a modern writer would revolt at the ancient *]custom of publishing these flattering testimonials in the vestibule of his own book, where, after all, they could not answer the place of an advertisement.

* But why? supposing the Verses worth reading for themselves? would not H. be sorry to miss Barrow's & Marvel's poetic Prefaces to the Par. Lost?[1] I fear that the jealousy & still more the *unbrother-hood* of modern authors have more to do with it than either Pride or Modesty. *S. T. C.*

52 p 670, pencil

The praise which it fairly earned by its intrinsic merit was <u>aggravated</u> by respect to the author's youth.

enhanced*a*

53 p 670, pencil, overtraced

The critics were glad to display their generosity by applauding, and their candour by forgiving: the play-going public gave their usual hearty welcome to a new comer: reader and auditor alike were amazed at the stripling whose maiden essay achieved what so many laborious brains had been toiling for the last half century to produce—perpetual excitement and incessant splendour.

altogether a most unhartlëian sentence, too bad to be mended by cutting off out one rotten bit and putting a bit of good cloth in the place.

a Possibly in DC's hand; he also prints (1852) "enhanced"

50[1] "Either it will be or it will not"—ambiguity being the first principle of oracular utterance.

51[1] *In Paradisum Amissum summi poetae Johannis Miltoni* by "S. B., M.D.", i.e. Samuel Barrow (b c 1625), and *On Paradise Lost* by Andrew Marvell, were both prefixed to the 2nd ed, 1674.

54 pp 670–1, pencil, overtraced

[Footnote:] Congreve dedicated the Old Bachelor to the Lord
Clifford of Lanesborough, son to the Lord Burlington. The allusion
*] to the connection between the families is neat. "My Lord, it is with
great pleasure I lay hold on this first occasion which the accidents
of my life have given me of writing to your Lordship; for since, at
the same time, I write to all the world, it will be the means of
publishing what I would have every body know,—the respect and
duty which I owe and pay to you. I have so much inclination to be
your's, that I need no other engagement, but the particular ties by
which I am bound both to your Lordship and family, have put it out
of my power to make you any compliment, since all offers of myself
will amount to no more than an honest acknowledgment, and only
shew a willingness in me to be grateful."

* *Neat*, my dearest Hartley! more *clumsy*, involved common place
I have seldom seen. The thought occurs over and over again in the
Dedications of Massinger & his Contemporaries.[1]

S. T. C.

55 p 671, pencil, overtraced

[Footnote:]...The manifest absurdity and incongruity of Dryden's
allegory [in *The Hind and the Panther*] must have been obvious to
Dryden himself; but perhaps he thought absurdity as necessary for
a superstitious King, as obscenity for a polluted stage.

I confess, that I have ever felt the spotted ~~Hind~~ Panther &c—pleasing
marks of the tranquil feeling in which this ingenious poem was
written, & possibly intended as such by Dryden.[1]

54[1] In his dedication to *The Bondman*
and to *A New Way to Pay Old Debts*
Massinger sought patronage as the son of
a loyal servant of the Herbert family. He
dedicated *The Bondman* to Philip Her-
bert, Earl of Montgomery and 4th Earl
of Pembroke (1584–1650), to whom with
his brother, William, 3rd Earl of Pem-
broke (d 1630) the first folio of Shakes-
peare had been dedicated, offering "to
the noble family of the Herberts" "all
duties and service...descended to me as
an inheritance from my dead father,
Arthur Massinger". In his dedication of
A New Way to Robert Dormer, 1st Earl
of Carnarvon (d 1643) he described him-
self as "born a devoted servant to the
thrice noble family of your incompar-
able lady"—i.e. Anna Sophia Herbert,
daughter of the 4th Earl of Pembroke.
See *The Plays of Massinger* ed William
Gifford (4 vols 1805) ii [3], iii [479].

55[1] *The Hind and the Panther* i
327–30:

The *Panther* sure the noblest, next the
 Hind,
And fairest creature of the spotted
 kind;
Oh, could her in-born stains be wash'd
 away,
She were too good to be a beast of
 Prey!

56   p 671, pencil, overtraced

[Footnote:] Montague seems to have delighted in kicking at the Ex-Laureate. In one of the few copies of indifferent couplets which give him a place among the Poets (!!!) of Great Britain, occur the following lines, in which there is but too much truth,—but it is not truth which a generous mind would have cast in the teeth of a great man, oppressed with years and misfortunes:—

> "Dryden has numbers, but he wants a heart.
>
> *   *   *   *   *
>
> Now sentenced, by a penance too severe,
> For playing once the fool, to persevere."

That Dryden, as a Poet, wants <u>heart</u> (whatever he may have done as a man), his warmest admirers (and we are among them) can hardly deny; but this was not Montague's meaning. In the couplet, he hints that Dryden would gladly have returned to the Church of England if his double apostacy would have been acceptable.

How does H. define *"heart"*?

God save poor Dryden from his Friends! & ⟨from⟩ my Hartley (i.e. as to this note) among them!   S. T. C.

57   p 672, pencil, overtraced

But Montague having the fingering of the public money...<u>hit on</u> a more economical method of securing the adulation of prosemen and versemen than paying them for dedications. Louis XIV. had pensioned poets, and was supposed to have laid out the money at good interest; but Louis was an absolute sovereign, and had no Parliament <u>to overhaul his accounts.</u>

O, dearest H! but this is sadly vulgar!

58   pp 672–3, pencil, overtraced

[Referring to Whig patronage:]...There were Boards, which were furnished with a double set of members,—one for use, which, like the vocal pipes in the body of an organ, were kept out of sight, *i.e.* *] the clerks, deputies, &c., and another, like the pipes in the front of an organ, displayed to public view with all advantages of gilding. Thus, without expense to himself, additional expense to the country, or risk of exposure by appointing an incompetent person to an office of trust, Montague was enabled to make Congreve a Commissioner for licensing hackney coaches, to give him a place in the pipe office, and shortly after another in the customs, worth six hundred a year, and all for writing a single comedy.

* Qu? Take the sum "tottle" of these "front Pipes", or Curæ sine Curis[1]—& how small the amount compared with the plunder from the Nationalty,[2] out of a fraction of which the main Tax-payers furnished them/—and had they been commonly appropriated to even such minds as Congreve's, how little reason would the Public have to complain!

59 p 673, pencil, overtraced

Meanwhile, there is nothing moves the indignation of certain persons more than the evil eye which the poor, and not only the poor, are taught to cast on the gratuities of the Treasury. . . . Hireling and slave are the civilest phrases which any writer may expect who accepts a boon from the rulers of his country. These feelings, however, are but natural to a period of financial embarrassment and general distress.

general *cupidity*, and the malcontentment of almost every man with his lot!

60 p 674, pencil, overtraced

We purposely waive all discussion of these questions on grounds of public economy. We shall not enter into argument with the Utilitarians, as to what abstract science, or fine literature, or fine art, *are worth*, or what use they are of, or whether we might not do very well without them. We will, for the present, take it for granted, that the faculties of pure reason, imagination, and taste, ought to be perfected as much as possible; that philosophy and poetry, truth and beauty, are noble ends of human nature. We will assume—nay, assert—that every man, rich or poor, is, or may be, the better for whatever exalts the imagination, or humanizes the heart: in a short sentence of plain prose, that public money would be well and wisely expended in the promotion of literature, and of fine literature, if the disbursement were really for the benefit of literature or its professors. But "there's the rub."

58[1] "Offices without Duties"—sinecures.
58[2] For "Nationalty" see **41** n 1, above. DC adds a note (III 304): "By 'plunder of the Nationalty' *S. T. C.*

means Church property, not merely secularized, but rendered *private* and *heritable*, at the Reformation. See 'Church and State' [i.e. *C&S* (*CC*) 35–6]."

What the deuce has become of the Old Bachelor?[1] H. has left him on the road, & galloped off on the back of a Dromedary Digression.

61 p 677, pencil, overtraced

Even now there are many, who think that so-called *sinecures* might be rendered most beneficial, in giving leisure to intellect; so that the genius and the scholar, free from worldly toil and anxiety, may labour for glory and posterity, and repay their country's bounty with deathless honour. The advantages of "learned leisure" to the church establishment have been asserted with Paley's plausibility and Southey's upright zeal; and might not "learned leisure," wit in easy circumstances, imagination with a moderate independence, be serviceable to the state also? Shall there be no cushions, where unconsecrated heads may slumber *pro bono publico?*

This, it must be confessed, sounds well; but if the actual history of modern authorship were honestly written, we should discover that the expectation of patronage has ruined more geniuses, both in purse and character, than the liberality of patrons has ever benefitted.... But patronage should never be accorded to the presumptive evidences of genius, or even to the *promise* of excellence. The bounty, whether of kings, or of commonwealths, or of nobles, honours itself and its object, when it is bestowed on the veteran scholar, or grey-headed poet,—when it provides peace, comfort, and competence to venerable age. But it should be given unsought. No encouragement should be afforded to vain youth, who, by a servile display of flashy fantasies, and a presumptuous rivalry of well-bred vices, endeavour to insinuate themselves, canker like, into the opening blossoms of nobility; nor should the more prudent advances of the middle-aged be suffered to outstep the bounds of modesty.

All I can say on these pages is, that the reasoning is *crude*, compared with what H. would have produced, had I been blest with his society, & what of himself he will yet produce.[1]

62 p 678, pencil, overtraced

> And *crazy* Congreve scarce could spare
> A shilling to discharge his chair,
> Till prudence taught him to appeal
> From Paean's fire to party zeal:

60[1] HC had begun discussing *The Old Bachelor* on p 670: see **54** textus.

61[1] C had not seen HC since Oct/Nov 1822. See BÖHME **149** n 2.

Not owing to his happy vein
The fortunes of his latter scene;
Took proper principles to thrive,
And so might any dunce alive.

In this last line the Dean [Swift] is deplorably in the wrong. Dunces never thrive but in the way of honesty. Had not Congreve been a splendid wit, he would not have been worth purchase. We cannot conjecture why he calls Congreve crazy. There is no madness isn his writings,—neither the *fine madness* of poetry, nor the rant and fury of a disordered brain: and in his private conduct, whatever virtue he might want, he possessed an ample store of prudence. With so little of truth or reason could the man write, who, of all his contemporaries, *might* have been the greatest philosopher. ∧

∧ i.e. if with equal genius he had *not* been Dean Swift, but almost the very contrary.[1]

63   p 680, pencil, overtraced

But it is much easier to shine in depicting a moral than an immoral character; and of all characters, the truly virtuous female is the most difficult to draw satisfactorily in a dramatic poem. It is easy enough to describe, for it is not unfrequently seen; it is very easy for a poet to praise.... But when the woman is to speak and act, when she is to shed the perfume of her goodness spontaneously, and shine by her own light, and yet not overstep the reserved duties of her sex—there is a task beneath which human genius is in danger of breaking down. We really cannot recal to memory a single dramatic female whom we should recommend for a wife, or for an example.

Genuine Comedy is, I fear, almost incompatible with Christianity, as it exists among the *Many*, who neither can nor will *abstract*. Now Comedy *is* an Abstraction/[1]

62[1] DC (1852) adds a footnote: "*Secundae curae.* I believe the word crazy, in Swift's time, was generally applied to bodily, not mental infirmity. Congreve was gouty, and the Dean in alluding to the chair probably hinted that Congreve, too lame to walk, was too poor to be carried."

63[1] I.e. comedy presents persons and events that do not directly represent actual persons and events. See *Sh C* I 151–2, in which C observed that Shakespeare's comedies and old comedy are "ideal" in the same way that Greek comedy and tragedy were "ideal". Yet (*Sh C* II 7) "Christianity in its worst state was not separated from humanity".

64   p 681, pencil, overtraced

But though the heroine of a comedy can hardly be a good example to her sex, there is no necessity that she should be an offensive insult to it. Her faults should be such as a good woman might feel it possible for herself to have committed,—such as a moderate degree of self-delusion might pass off for virtues. The ladies were quite right in resenting the exhibition of Lady Touchwood. An innocent heart would require much and sad experience to convince it of the possibility of such a being. There are degrees of wickedness too bad to laugh at, however they may be mingled with folly, affectation, or absurdity.

Wickedness is no Subject for Comedy. This was Congreve's great error, & almost peculiar to him. The Dram. Personæ of Dryden, Wycherly &c are often *vicious*, obscene, &c but not like Congreve's, *wicked.*[1]   S. T. C.

65   p 683, pencil, overtraced

Yet the Mourning Bride is assuredly the effort of no common ability. It contains a passage which Johnson pronounced superior to any single speech in Shakspeare, and which appears to us more *poetical* than any thing in Rowe or Otway.

!!! Oh! Oh! oh D[r] J! D[r] J. oh![1]

66   p 683, pencil, overtraced

It is a rare thing for a serious drama to be hissed off the stage.

No! only *silenced* and *thin-audienced* off.

67   p 686, pencil

[Footnote:] Mr. Dibdin tells us that it [Collier's *Ecclesiastical History*] might once be had for the price of waste paper, but that the days of *book-vandalism* are passed—so much the worse for poor book-worms. There are few branches of learning on which even well-educated Englishmen are so ill-informed as upon ecclesiastical history, surely the most interesting that a christian or a philosopher can study. Southey's "Book of the Church" will go far to remove this reproach as far as England and the Church of England are concerned.

64[1] See also **69**, below.   65[1] See **48** and n 1, above.

Whoo! any compliment to S. is amiable in you, dear H.! but this is *too* gross. With exception of the beautiful first §ph,[a] it is the weakest of Southey's works.[1]

68 p 688, pencil, overtraced

Whatever refinement may have taken place in the public taste for diversion...is to be ascribed to other causes than the severity of satirists, or even the fulminations of the pulpit. The chief of these are, the general good education of females, the purifying influences of female society, the higher value set upon the domestic affections, the greater freedom of choice in marriage, and the more frequent intercourse between the religious and the fashionable world. ∧

∧ And more than all, the attendance of all classes on the theatres, except the gloomier sects/—at least, till of late.[1]

69 p 689, pencil, overtraced

[The *Way of the World*] has no moral interest. There is no one person in the *dramatis personae* for whom it is possible to care. Vice may be, and too often has been, made interesting; but cold-hearted, unprincipled villainy never can.

Virtue and Wickedness are sub eodem genere.[1] The absence of *Virtue* is no defecticiency in a genuine Comedy; but the presence of Wickedness a great Defect.[2]   *S. T. C.*

70 p 693, pencil, overtraced

The conduct of Congreve in leaving £10,000, the amassings of a close economy, to this Duchess [of Marlborough], has been severely reprehended. If his relations were poor, he had certainly much better have bestowed his fortune on the poor than on the wealthy. Still, it was not by inheritance from parents, nor by aid of kinsfolk, that he became rich. To the great he owed his property, and to the great ?] he returned it. He offended no rule of justice by so doing.

Lax Morality,[b] Master H. But this & the like comes from the cacoethes dogmatizandi.[1]—From whom H. caught this Itch, I shall

---

[a] Over "first §ph" DC has written in pencil "prose stile"   [b] DC (1852) gives no more of this note

[67][1] For the controversy aroused by RS's *Book of the Church* see C. BUTLER and BLANCO WHITE.
[68][1] Cf, however, THE AGE 2.
[69][1] "Under the same genus".

[69][2] See **64**, above.
[70][1] "The itch to dogmatise"—on the analogy of Juvenal 7.52, "scribendi cacoethes". Cf **24** (at n 4), above.

not say;[2] but the Pustules are the only Disornaments of his fair Skin.   S. T. C.

71 p 694, pencil, overtraced | Dr John Fothergill

In a very entertaining little essay, prefixed, we believe, by the late Dr. Beddoes, of Bristol, to an edition of the works of John Brown, is a classification of physicians, according to the Linnaean method,—as the *canting doctor*, the *wheedling doctor*, the *Adonis doctor*, and the *bully quack doctor*....But we do not recollect any mention of the *] Quaker philanthropist doctor. Yet such a one was John Fothergill...

* Had Beddoes added the *"fond pawing* Doctor", the Quaker Doctor would have been *inclusive*.[1]

72 p 713, pencil

The object of the first [anecdote] was a poor clergyman, a class who, considering the rank they are expected to support, the expense of their education, and the wealth of their more opulent brethren, which operates as <u>a direct tax</u> upon the laborious and slenderly-provided, may be called the poorest of the poor.

how?

73 p 713, pencil

[Footnote:] "Vines," said he [Peter Collinson], "will thrive well in your country [Virginia]; but...don't keep them close to the ground ...your summer heats exceed, as much as ours fall short; allow them, therefore, longer stems...as in the warmer countries of Europe."

Hence bad a low vine!!!

70[2] C's annotations have already identified the source of infection.

71[1] John Fothergill (1712–80) had a distinguished medical and scientific career. "Pawing", which usually means handling clumsily or fondling obscenely, seems here to mean taking money in hand—a sense not recorded in *OED*. C commonly accused modern Quakers of being zealous money-makers: see e.g. AURELIUS **47** n 1 and *LS* (*CC*) 185.

HENRY NELSON COLERIDGE
1798–1843

"Life and Writings of Hesiod." [Review article in] *Quarterly Review* no 93. London 1832. 8º.

pp 1–39 of Vol XLVII pt i, published nominally Mar 1832. In grey-brown paper wrapper.

Victoria College Library (Coleridge Collection)

Inscribed by HNC on the outside of the front cover: "H. N. Coleridge Hampstead. from Mr Murray." In another hand: "Hesiod by HNC. Notes by *STC*."—this inscription repeated on the outside of the back cover. HNC made a correction in ink on p 38.

The cardboard case in which this copy of *Quarterly Review* No 93 is stored contains the cover of *Quarterly Review* No 103 (Aug 1834) inscribed: "~~Crabbe~~ Coleridge's Poet Works by H. N. C.", but the copy of HNC's essay—his review of *PW* (1834), for which see *CH* 620–51—is not now with the cover.

The books noticed in this essay are: A. Twesten *Commentatio critica de Hesiodi carmine...Opera et Dies* (Kiel 1825); G. Hermann *Epistola ad C. D. Ilgenum Hymnorum Homericorum editioni Lips. praemissa* (Leipzig 1822); F. Creuzer *Symbolik und Mythologie der alten Völker, besonders der Griechen* (Darmstadt 1828); G. Hermann and F. Creuzer *Briefe über Homer und Hesiodus* (Heidelberg 1829). Of these only Hermann *Epistola* is given more than passing notice.

DATE. 1832, after 7 Aug: see *CL* VI 919.

1   pp 8–9

We are next presented with the original of that often-copied picture of the successive ages of gold, silver, brass, and iron—with reference to which favourite allegory it is observable that, although the notion of a gradual degeneracy of mankind from their primitive state was almost universal among those nations of the old world, with whom
*] we are at all acquainted, a fact of a Fall—a disobedience and forfeiture of *one*, with which the obedience and redemption of *one* should be commensurate—is nowhere, unless we are to except the story of Pandora and Epimetheus, and a single shadowy glimpse or guess of Plato, to be met with in the profound and glowing records of pagan philosophy.

But sure, dear Henry! if you are on the *Literal* Tack, there were *two*—or was *M^rs* Adam nobody? And most assuredly there was no such duality of the God-man, the second Adam.—S. T. C.*a*
P.S. The truth is, there was Adam and the Adam, and ⟨both⟩ the former l̶i̶k̶e̶ and his "Better Half" were included in the Latter— Individuum pro genere primario, sensu representativo.[1]

2 p 8

[continuing immediately on **1** textus:] That most beautiful, most wonderful tale of Cupid and Psyche we do *not* except; because, though its origin has never been precisely discovered, and its external dress is pagan, we can never believe but that the *motive*, the
⎰επεχω—[1]⎱ germ of the romance, must have been found by
⎱   ⎰ Apuleius in the scriptures of the New Testament.

a note from the §ph in the "Aids to Ref." would not have been amiss.[2]

3 p 9

Between the brazen period and that of iron, or his own times, the poet places the heroes of Greece—the warriors against Thebes and Troy—the morning of history clearing up from the bewildering Twilight of tradition, yet still streaked with the flying clouds of ignorance, and rendered magically <u>lustrous</u> by the setting moon of fiction.

a very sweet passage, save & except "lustrous"—a strange effect of a moon, much more of a "setting Moon."

4 p 9

...Hesiod enters into a palpable imitation of that very remarkable passage in the Odyssey, in which the curious mention is made of fish being plentiful under a good government—<u>an oddity</u> which it is quite intelligible that an imitator should omit...

a The initials may not be in C's hand

1[1] "The individual [standing] for the primary genus, in a representative sense".
2[1] "I hesitate". See H. COLERIDGE **18** and n 1.
2[2] In *AR* (1825) 277–8 C noticed how, after the spread of the gospel had awakened the need to provide some solution of the great problem of "Original Sin, or the corrupt and sinful Nature of the Human Will", "the beautiful Parable of Cupid and Psyche was brought forward as a *rival* FALL OF MAN: and the fact of a moral corruption connatural with the human race was again recognized. In the assertion of ORIGINAL SIN the Greek mythology rose and set."

With $\frac{1}{20}$th of Lord Bacon's ingenuity it would be easy to alchemize this "oddity" into a very shrewd & pregnant specimen of political economy. The safety of unarmed fishing smacks in those times of piratical Coasters, the excellent Roads implied, &c &c— —S. T. C.

5 p 13

Hesiod and Virgil were both poets in the truest sense of the word...

Mentiris, Carissime![1] V. in *no* sense but that of having a good ear.[2] But I forgot—you are an *Etonian*, & swear per Maronem/[3] S. T. C.

6 p 13

[Hesiod's description of a land-storm in *Works and Days* 506ff] whence Milton seems to have taken a pregnant hint for a part of his grand description of a storm in the wilderness in Paradise Regained [IV 413]...

Now on my Conscience, Henry! this is the only *flat* remark, I ha ever heard from YOU or knew of your making.

7 p 18

A strong instance of such an inconsistency [i.e. suggesting an interpolation] may be found in a comparison of [*Theogony*] vv. 217–18 with vv. 904–6; in the former of which passage, the Fates, Clotho, Lachesis and Atropos, are said to be the offspring of Night, while in the latter they are declared to be the daughters of Jupiter and Themis.

But are not such seeming inconsistencies incidental to all allegoric personages? Both *Gĕnĕsēs* were true.[1] S. T. C.

8 p 18

Hermann has, with great ingenuity and show of probability, pointed out no less than seven distinct beginnings to the Theogony; and he thinks it reasonable to conclude that an equal number of rhapsodists have had a hand in the compilation of the poem, as we now see it.

[5][1] "Not true, my dearest boy!"
[5][2] For a similar judgement of Virgil's poetic quality see ARGENS 10 and n 3.
[5][3] Swear "by Maro"—i.e. Virgil.
[7][1] Here, as in 8, below, HNC is reviewing Hermann's letter to C. D. Ilgen, with which he had introduced his edition of HOMERIC HYMNS. C here defends the unity of the *Theogony*, although he had long rejected the unity of the Homeric poems (for early and late expressions of which see HOMER 9 and GREW 19).

O absurdissime Hermann![1]—They were evidently the different
Tunes, to which the Rhaps. might sing the Psalm ad libitum/
Salisbury or York &c[2]

8A p 38

That several and various literary dialects should contemporaneously
exist at all, is, beyond a doubt, mainly to be explained by that
permanent absence of metropolitan centralization ~~peculiar~~ to so
characteristic of ancient Greece.

8[1] "O most absurd Hermann!" In
view of what follows, a pun may lurk:
absurdus, "out of tune", and *surdus*,
"deaf".

8[2] The Homeridae or rhapsodes—
"singers of stitched lays" (cf ῥαπτῶν
ἐπέων in Pindar *Nemean* 2.1–3) or
"stitchers together of lays"— developed
skill in improvisation as professional re-
citers or singers of epics. See also FLÖGEL
45 and HOMERIC HYMNS 1. Various
traditions ascribe the establishment of a
standard text of Homer to Solon, Peisi-
stratus, or Lycurgus (see also GREW 19),
but since these texts were themselves
superseded and the witness of the ancient
scholia is confused it is impossible to
reconstruct the exact manner of the
rhapsodes' performance. For C on the
impossibility of reconstructing the sound
of Greek lyric see EICHHORN *Alte
Testament* 50. C evidently accepts the
proposal that the multiple opening of
Hesiod's *Theogony* represents not a
single complex opening but a sequence of
alternative openings; the rhapsode's
choice "ad libitum" would then presum-
ably be his decision about which opening
best suited his "tune", or individual style
of performance.

C's strongly musical analogy, with the
reference to psalms and psalm-singing,
suggests that he is not thinking so much
of the rhapsode's practice of interpolating
improvised material as of the need to
match music to words (as e.g. in

plainsong or speech-rhythm chanting) or
to match words to a tune (as e.g. in
metrical psalms and hymns). (That such
matters are not utterly esoteric is implied
by Mistress Ford's account of Falstaff:
"his words...no more adhere and keep
place together than the Hundredth Psalm
to the tune of 'Green Sleeves'". *Merry
Wives of Windsor* II i 63.) C must have
heard a good deal of church music in his
youth, but there is no evidence for the
quality of what he heard or that he took
any critical or informed interest in the
vocal performance of church music. In
this annotation he may refer to the
practice (that still prevails) of assigning
different tunes to various parts of a psalm
or canticle to suit changes in the
psalmist's mood, subject, or tone. By
"Salisbury or York &c" he may be using
the names of tunes or chants, but the
phrase seems rather to point towards
differences in liturgical usage than of
musical performance—the differences
that the Act of Uniformity (1549) sought
to discipline through the "First Prayer
Book of Edward VI" (1549) which
declares in its Preface: "And where
heretofore, there hath been great diuersitie
in saying and syngyng in churches within
this realme: some followyng Salisbury
use, some Hertford use, some the use of
Bangor, some of Yorke, and some of
Lincolne: Now from henceforth, all the
whole realme shall haue but one use."

Notes on the Reform Bill. By a Barrister [i.e. Henry Nelson Coleridge]. [First edition.] London 1831. 8°.

Published by Roake and Varty, 31 Strand; cf DIALOGUE. Bound as third in "PAMPHLETS ON THE REFORM BILL".

British Museum C 126 h 15(3)

On p 62 "vetet" is corrected in ink to "vetat", not in C's hand; the correct form of the word is printed in the 2nd ed (1831).

BMC ascribes this tract to John Taylor Coleridge (1791–1876), but Edith Coleridge, in a copy of the 3rd ed, ascribed it to her father, HNC. *CL* VI 858n. C wrote to HNC on 23 May 1831: "I have carefully read over your second Edition—and on reading the excellent paragraph against the scoffers of virtual representation...I could not help feeling that tho' representation is far more appropriate than delegation, yet that both terms are fallacious—". *CL* VI 858–9. The passage C refers to is a paragraph of 34 lines on p 11 of the 2nd ed, inserted at p 10 of the text of the 1st ed. The "Advertisement to the Second Edition" is signed "Lincoln's Inn, April, 1831"; the 2nd ed had probably already been published by 23 May 1831.

An interleaved preliminary proof copy of the 1st ed, comprising 58 pp and a provisional title-page, is preserved in the BM (8138 c 8). This is not HNC's working proof, but has at the end in an unidentified hand—perhaps the printer's—"A few sentences to be added". The "few sentences" came to 56 lines of type, bringing the text to an end near the foot of p 63 in the published version.

DATE. Apr–23 May 1831.

1	pp 39–41, pencil

...generally in all the places which are to return members to Parliament, *two-thirds* of the voters will be persons holding houses from 10*l.* to 20*l.* value....Hence "the majority of voters in every town will belong to the very lowest class of houses, and, consequently, the effective Representation of the WHOLE EMPIRE will be thrown into the hands of one single class, and that, too, a very *narrow* class of the NATION!" ["Mr Croker's Speech"]—the small Shopkeepers—precisely the most dependent race of men in the whole empire!

An additional evil is that it will not only assuredly excite but morally justify, yea, necessitate the demand for Elect. by Ballot. Without the Ballot the Elective Franchise would be a Deianira's Shirt to the Shopkeeper[1]—exposing him to the alternative of affronting his wealthy Customers or being mobbed by the poorer—which those *on his books* would probably take the first pretext to carry into effect.—[2]

[1] Deianeira, hoping to regain the love of her unfaithful husband Hercules, unwittingly sent him a poisoned shirt: it killed him. Cf *CL* VI 889 (to HNC, 1 Mar 1832) and *C&S* (*CC*) 158.

[2] In the 2nd ed, HNC made an addition to his text at this point, whether in response to C's marginal note, or his conversation, does not appear.

Six Months in the West Indies in 1825. [Anonymous.] London 1826. 8°.

First edition, published Feb 1826 (*CL* vi 560n). The edition was withdrawn at the command of HNC's father, Colonel James Coleridge. Second edition (London 1826) omitted part of pp 3–7 and made some additions.

Gerard P. D. Coleridge

Inscribed in ink by HNC on front flyleaf: "Samuel Taylor Coleridge with the Author's best respects". A note by EHC pasted in: "Presentation Copy from H. N. Coleridge to his uncle S. T. C. vid. MS note p. 37 and the omitted portion, 5, 6 & 7 from later editions. E. H. C." The cancelled section (actually parts of pp 3–7) gave offence because the two "cousins" Margaret and Lucy there described—"sisters well stricken in years" who "for more than half their lives have lived within hail of each other" ministering with food and medicines to the poor of the parish—were too easily recognisable as the widowed sister-aunts "George" and "Luke", née Jane and Sarah Hunt. See [Bernard] Lord Coleridge *The Story of a Devonshire House* (1905) 288–9.

Late in 1824 HNC accompanied his cousin William Hart Coleridge (1789–1849), first Anglican bishop of Barbados (1824–41), to the West Indies. For HNC the purpose of the visit was to seek relief from a rheumatic complaint that had forced him earlier that year to cancel plans of visiting Scotland and the Lakes. The purpose of the northern visit was to see C's daughter Sara, whom he had first met in Highgate on 29 Dec 1822; by 21 Mar 1823 they had become "solemnly engaged to each other", but secretly. Colonel James, having married an heiress and established himself as a country gentleman, refused to give permission for the engagement: he disapproved of the marriage of first cousins, and did not want to see his brilliant son marry the penniless daughter of the black sheep of the Coleridge family. Sara, who (as HNC noted in his diary) had "promised never to marry any one but me", refused to accept Colonel James's demand that the engagement be broken off; but HNC and Sara had to wait until the autumn of 1829 before they could marry.

In Jun 1824 HNC had raised with C—very obliquely—the question of first cousins marrying. C was inclined to disapprove but was reluctantly prepared to accept the authority of Augustine in the matter. *TT* 10 Jun 1824; see also his ms note in *CL* vi 590n. C might have wondered a little when he read on p 117: "I love a cousin; she is such an exquisite relation, just standing between me and the stranger to my name, drawing upon so many sources of love and tieing them all up with every cord of human affection—almost my sister ere my wife!"; he might also have noticed the yearnings for "Eugenia" uttered later in the book. But he did not mark any of these passages; his earliest written comment on the engagement was to Edward Coleridge in Jul 1826: see *CL* vi 589–91. For C's critical reaction to the book see **1** n 1, below.

A copy of the 1st ed in the BM (C 126 c 9), with the "S. T. C." label on the title-page verso, came from Green's library but has no annotation or mark in C's hand.

DATE. 1826, by 8 Feb. See *CL* VI 560.

COEDITOR. A. H. B. Coleridge.

1   p 37, pencil | Madeira

[HNC, seeing a pretty young nun in a convent, asks her whether she is happy. While his companion engages the abbess in conversation, Maria answers] with an air of gaiety, "O sim, muito feliz" ["O yes, very happy"]. I shook my head as in doubt. A minute elapsed, and the abbess was occupied again. Maria put her hands through the grating, took one of mine, and made me feel a thin gold ring on her little finger, and then, pressing my hand closely, said, in an accent which I still hear; "Naō, naō, naō; tenho dor do coraçaō" ["No, no, no; I have the heart-ache"].

The service began; the old nuns croaked like frogs, and the young ones paced up and down, round and about, in strange and fanciful figures, chaunting as sweetly as caged Canary birds. I gazed at them for a long time with feelings that cannot be told, and when it was time to go, I caught Maria's eye, and made her a slight but earnest bow. She dropped a curtesy which seemed a genuflection to her neighbour, raised a violet behind her service-book to her mouth, held it, looked at it, and kissed it in token of an eternal farewell.

I wish to know whether there would have been any harm in my accepting the captain's offer of his coxswain and gig's crew, and running away with Maria Clementina. The thing was perfectly easy, as we all agreed at the time; at the principal door there was no grating, and in the court none but maimed or decrepit persons; three men should stand at the outer gate and prevent any egress till we had brought our prize down to the Loo Rock; in a quarter of an hour we should be on board a man of war, and even if they had taken the alarm and fired from the battery, it is perfectly well known that the Portugueze government never allows more than one half of the due charge of powder to its artillery, and so we might have laughed at their impotent attempts. But what could I have done with my nun? Her lover was, heaven knows where, and as to conjugating myself, although Maria was a very lovely girl, I happen to have my hands quite full for the present.

O Henry Coleridge! Henry Coleridge. If this be all a romance, it is very *Derwentish*—i.e. gallocristan, if true, most ruthlessly indiscreet.[1]

1[1] "Gallocristan" (not in *OED*): coxcombical—from *gallus* (cock) + *crista* (crest); perhaps also "Frenchified" as from "*Cristogalli*...French Christians,

I myself know the misery & persecution which Blabs of this sort have brought on individuals & whole families in Sicily & Minorca. S. T. C.

2   p 210, cropped | St Christopher's

The height is more than 3,700 feet, and is the most tremendous precipice I ever beheld. But the ruggedness of this central cluster only renders the contrast of the cultivated lands below more striking, and the entire prospect is so charming, that I could not help agreeing with the captain's clerk who said he wondered that Colon, who was so delighted with this island as to give to it his own name, should not have made a full stop upon its shores. I do not uphold the pun, but upon the whole it was well enough for a hot climate and a captain's clerk.

[In your cor]rections [? read] come to.[1]

3   p 287, pencil, cropped | Barbados

I dislike the man, swordsman or not, who deliberately trifles with the affections of a woman. I would rather shake hands with a highwayman than with a gentleman who has sacrificed to his own vanity the lifelong happiness of an inexperienced girl.

young nuns excepted? Vid[e] p. 36[1]

---

or Coxcombs" in LUTHER 230–1. Cf C's comment on DC to Edward Coleridge: "the *Genus* is (as you say) Self-conceit; but the *species* is Coxcombry". *CL* VI 563. Earlier in the same letter C had said that he had "read almost half" of "Henry's Book" and then discussed it more at length and in a more genial tone than in this annotation. He had received "both amusement & instruction from it"; but it had one fault that he would like to have seen removed—"an imitation of Southey, especially in his Letters from Portugal & Spain in the frequent obtrusion of offensive images, Sweating &c"; and he could "almost be angry with Henry for that very indiscreet & ex omni parte objectionable Episode on *Maria*".

CL VI 560. C's letter to HNC is not preserved. SH thought the book a "conceited work". *SHL* 323. HC, writing to DC, shared his father's view: "The *Six Months* is very clever, and tolerably sensible, but there is a flippancy, a vulgarity about it, which I cannot esteem. It might have past in a magazine article, written in a feign'd character, but surely it suits not the accredited confidante and relative of a Bishop. Neither do I think he feels sufficiently the moral enormity of the slave system—". *HCL* 93–4. In conformity with the last sentence see *CN* IV 5402n.

2[1] HNC did not alter the text in the 2nd ed.

3[1] See **1**, above.

WILLIAM COLLINS
1721–1759

The Poetical Works of Mr. William Collins. With memoirs of the author; and observations on his genius and writings. By J. Langhorne...A new edition. London 1781. 8°.

British Museum Add MS 47552

Inscribed on p ⁻4 in ink above the signature of J. T. Coleridge: "J. T. Coleridge Montague Place   August, 1838   From Heath's Court—". Typographical errors corrected on pp 117, 151, in ink, in an unidentified hand.

Lamb told Henry Francis Cary that in his youth C "*fed* himself on Collins". R. W. King "*Parson Primrose*": *The Life...of Henry Francis Cary* (New York 1925) 193. This may be seen in his helping a friend during his first vacation from Cambridge (summer 1792) to prepare a paper on the superiority of Collins's Odes to Gray's. *BL* ch 1 (*CC*) I 20; cf *TT* (1917) 318–19. In 1796 he included among his projected works "Edition of Collins & Gray with a preliminary Dissertation", but he seems not to have begun it. *CN* I 161[*i*], 174 (15). In Dec of that year he told Thelwall that part of the *Ode on the Poetical Character* "has inspired & whirled *me* along with greater agitations of enthusiasm than any the most *impassioned* Scene in Schiller or Shakspere" but admitted a greater loyalty to Bowles and Burns. *CL* I 279; cf *CN* I 383. The pristine enthusiasm was never to return.

DATE. Possibly summer or autumn 1793. The occasion of the two poems written in this book is briefly recounted—with the text of both poems—in two letters to George Coleridge written in late Jul and early Aug 1793. *CL* I 57–8, 60. According to the letters, *The Rose* was written first, but EHC printed them in reverse order. The variants between the versions in COLLINS and those in the letters suggest that the COLLINS versions are the earlier.

1   pp ⁻2–⁻1, footnote on p ⁻3, pencil

Cupid turn'd Chymist.

Cupid (if ancient legends tell aright)
Once fram'd a rich Elixir of Delight:
A cauldron o'er love-kindled flames he fix'd,[1]
And in it Nectar and Ambrosia mix'd.

[1] In all printed versions the "cauldron" became a "Chalice", in defiance of normal alchemical usage.

With these the magic dews, which evening brings,
Brush'd from th' * Idalian Star by fairy wings,
Each tender pledge of sacred Faith he join'd
Each gentler pleasure of th' unspotted mind;—
Fond Hopes, the blameless parasites of woe,
Fond Dreams, whose tints with beamy brightness glow.
With Joy he view'd the chymic Process rise,
The steaming cauldron bubbled up in sighs
Sweet sound's transpir'd as when th' enamour'd Dove
Pours the soft murmurs of responsive Love.
The finish'd work not Envy's self could blame,
And "Kisses" was the precious compound's name.
With part the God his Cyprian Mother blest,
And breath'd on Nesbitt's lovely lips the rest—[3]

S T Coleridge
Friday Evening—July
1793

* Idalian Star—Venus, the Evening Star: a planet, which from its superior Beauty, and the time of its appearance has been (time out of mind) appropriated to Love.[2]

2 pp [+1]–[+2], pencil

On presenting a Moss Rose to Miss F. Nesbitt

As late each flow'r that sweetest blows
    I pluck'd, the garden's pride;
Within the petals of a Rose
    A sleeping Love I 'spy'd.

[1][2] Venus was called *Idalaea* after Idalus, a mountain in Cyprus (hence she is "Cyprian Mother" in the penultimate line), and after Idalium, the town at the foot of the mountain that had a grove sacred to her. Venus, although commonly called "the Evening *Star*", is in fact a planet, as C observed in this note.
[1][3] Fanny Nesbitt, the "Miss F. Nesbitt" of the title of *The Rose*, of whom no biographical record seems to exist; C told his brother George on c 5 Aug 1793 that she was his "fellow-traveller in the Tiverton diligence from Exeter.—I think a very pretty Girl.—" *CL* I 60. In *PW* (1852) a note was added to these two poems: "This *Effusion* and *The Rose* were originally addressed to a Miss F. Nesbitt, at Plymouth, whither the author accompanied his eldest brother, to whom he was paying a visit, when he was twenty-one years of age." According to an itinerary evolved from the letters (*CL* I 60n), *The Rose* was written at Exeter, *Cupid Turn'd Chymist* at Tiverton, and the date of "Friday evening" was 26 Jul.

In a footnote to *Poems* (1796), (1797), and (1803) C provided from *Carmina Quadragesimalia* (Oxford 1723, 1748) II the Latin text of the poem of which *Cupid Turn'd Chymist* is an "imitation".

Around his brows a lucid wreath
    Of many a mingled hue;
All purple glow'd his cheek beneath
    Inebriate with dew.

I softly seiz'd th' unguarded power,
    Nor scar'd his balmy rest,
And plac'd him cag'd within the flower
    On lovely Nesbitt's[1] breast.

But when all reckless of the guile
    Awoke the slumberer sweet,
He struggled to escape awhile
    And stamp'd his angry feet.

Ah! soon the soul-entrancing Sight
    Subdued th' impatient Boy!
He gaz'd—he thrill'd with deep delight,
    Then clapp'd his wings for Joy.

And oh! he cry'd, what charms refin'd
    This magic Throne endear!
Some other Love let Venus find—
    I'll fix my Empire here.—

                                S T Coleridge

2[1] Variously "Angelina's" (letter), "Anna's" (MS Estlin), "Sara's' (*Poems*—1796—and all later eds).

PATRICK COLQUHOUN
1745–1820

A Treatise on Indigence; exhibiting a general view of the national resources for productive labour; with propositions for ameliorating the condition of the poor, and improving the moral habits and increasing the comforts of the labouring people, particularly the rising generation, &c. London 1806. 8°.

Published Jan 1807 (*EC*).

Not located. *Lost List.* Annotations reprinted from Richard Herne Shepherd in *Philobiblion* I (1862) 65–6.

Thomas Poole's copy with his name on the cover.

Patrick Colquhoun, manufacturer, metropolitan police-magistrate, and collector of statistics, also published a *Treatise on the Police of the Metropolis* (1796) that went through many editions. For C's later reading of other works of his see *SM* (*CC*) 38 and n 2 and *LS* (*CC*) 158 n 3, 204 n 5.

DATE. Probably summer 1807, while C was staying with Poole in Nether Stowey.

1 front flyleaf

There appear to me many and important exceptions to several of the doctrines and proposals advanced in this Treatise; yet it is an excellent Book spite of these exceptions. S. T. C.

2 pp 8–9 | Introduction

Poverty is... the state of every one who must labour for subsistence. *Poverty* is therefore a most necessary and indispensable ingredient in society, without which nations and communities could not exist in a state of civilization. It is the lot of man—it is the source of *wealth*, since without poverty there would be *no labour*, and without labour there could be no *riches*, no *refinement*, no *comfort*, and no *benefit* to those who may be possessed of wealth—inasmuch as without a large proportion of poverty surplus labour could never be rendered productive in procuring either the conveniences or luxuries of life.

Certainly! if the present state of general Intellect and morals be supposed a fair average of the capabilities of society. Otherwise I can not see why without this *Poverty* (even as here contra-distinguished from Indigence) A. might not agree to make Shoes, B. Cloth, C. Breeches, &c: and the whole Alphabet of Labor carry on a similar Barter to the present, even tho' one third of Society were *not* devoted to the production of useless & *debasing* Luxuries for those who are privileged to live in Idleness.—For mark, the definition of Poverty is invidious—he is not a poor [man]*ᵃ* whose subsistence depends on constant Industry, but he whose bare wants can not be supplied without such unceasing bodily Labor from the hour of waking to that of sleeping, as precludes all improvement of mind—& makes the intellectual Faculties to the majority of mankind as useless a boon as pictures to the Blind.[1] Such a man is poor indeed: for he has been robbed by his unnatural Guardians of the very house-loom of his *human nature*, stripped of the furniture of his Soul. S. T. C.

See Milton's Comus. line 765 to 779.[2]

ᵃ Word supplied by the editor

2[1] In 1795 C had expressed himself strongly on the distribution of labour: see *Lects 1795 (CC)* 11–12, 223, and cf 235. In those days he believed that no one needed to work more than two hours a day. With "pictures to the Blind" cf WW *Tintern Abbey* line 24: *WPW* ii 260.

2[2] *Comus* lines 765–79:

Means her provision onely to the good
That live according to her sober Laws,
And holy dictate of spare Temperance:
If every just man that now pines with
    want
Had but a moderate and beseeming
    share
Of that which lewdly-pamper'd
    Luxury
Now heaps upon som few with vast
    excess,

Natures full blessings would be well
    dispenc't
In unsuperfluous eeven proportion,
And she no whit encomber'd with her
    store,
And then the giver would be better
    thank't,
His praise due paid, for swinish
    gluttony
Ne're looks to Heav'n amidst his
    gorgeous feast,
But with besotted base ingratitude
Cramms, and blasphemes his feeder.

C wrote six marginal notes on *Comus* in MILTON *Poems upon Several Occasions* (1791).

PHILIPPE DE LA CLYTE
SIRE DE COMMINES
c 1447–1511

The History of Philip de Commines, Knight, Lord of Argenton. The fourth edition corrected. London 1674. F°.

Princeton University Library

This book—a history of France from 1464 to c 1498, conceived as memoirs—belonged to Charles Lamb, who has written a note of some length on p ⁻3 (p–d). J. S. Finch, in "Charles Lamb's Copy of *The History of Philip de Commines*" *Princeton University Library Chronicle* ix (1947–8) 30–7 (which gives a detailed account of the dispersal and destruction of Lamb's library, the two sales of Lamb's books in New York in 1848, and the provenance of this book), suggests that the note may have been addressed to C. "Read Chapters 7.8.9.10.11. & 12ᵗʰ of the 6ᵗʰ Book of this History, of the pleasant end of King Lewis the 11ᵗʰ of France; particularly of his shifting his servants (page 206) alledging that Nature delighteth in variety; together with his ingenious contrivances (page 208) not to be thought dead; with the ⟨singular⟩ opinions of honest Comines concerning the virtues of the said Lewis, & how he was the best of all the sovereign princes he had known in his time.—A touch of his ⟨Royal⟩ character, by way of commendation I take it, occurs in page 39 near the bottom, and many such like panegyrical observations are scattered *passim*.—" A short note by Lamb on p 214 and textual corrections on pp 47, 56. Many passages are marked throughout; some of the vertical pen slashes, distinguishable by weight and colour, may well be C's. The volume, still in the original livery of Lamb's "ragged regiment", is now preserved in a solander case of full red morocco.

Gillman's library included another copy of the *History* (1665) described as "with MS. Notes by S. T. Coleridge", but it has disappeared. *Gillman SC* (1843) 525.

DATE. Possibly 1811–12.

1 p +3, referring to pp 44–5ᵃ | Bk ii ch 2 "How the Liegeois Brake the Peace with Duke of Burgundy..."

Notwithstanding great Conquerors have just cause to desire the Battel to abridge their labour, as have also the *English* and *Switzers*, both because they are better Foot-men than their Neighbors, as appeareth by the great Victories they have obtained, (which notwith-

---

ᵃ The textus for this note—as for the other two notes—is marked with an ink line in the margin

standing I write not to the dispraise of other Nations) and also because their men cannot keep the Fields long without doing some exploit, as *French-men* and *Italians* can, who also are more full of practice and easier to be governed than they. Now on the other side, he that abtaineth the Victory, increaseth his honor and estimation, his Subjects are the more obedient, they deny him nothing that he demandeth, his Souldiers also was thereby the hardier, and the more couragious. Notwithstanding oftentimes the Princes themselves after a Victory obtained, are so puffed up with pride and vainglory, that commonly their good success turneth to their harm, all the which hapneth by Gods disposition, who sendeth alterations according to mens deserts.

Memorabilia.[a]

44–45. (the character of the English, as Soldiers, the same in all ages—and hid only for a small time by D. of Ys, & Generals of German-King-mongrel Choice.)[1]

2   p [+]3, referring tó pp 47–8 | II 3 "How...the L. of Hymbercourt Found Means to Enter into [Liege] for the D. of Burgundy"

...for he [the Duke of Burgundy] durst hardly have craved at Gods hands the good success he gave him, which great honor and goodly Victory in the judgment of all Vertuous and wise men hapned to him, for the favour and mercy shewed to the Hostages above mentioned. This I write because both Princes and others oftentimes find fault as

---

[a] "Memorabilia" is evidently intended to be the heading for the three page-references and notes written one after the other on the back flyleaf

[1] Frederick Augustus, Duke of York (1763–1827), second son of George III, had already, in Flanders in 1793, shown his military incapacity before being appointed Commander-in-Chief in 1795. A further spectacular display of soldierly incompetence in 1799 did not lead to his dismissal, and the disgraceful Convention of Cintra (see 3 n 1, below) was negotiated in 1808 during his command. He continued as Commander-in-Chief until, in early 1809, he was forced to resign because of the disclosure of the traffic of his mistress Mrs Clarke in military commissions. In 1811 he was reinstated, and—as C observed in a suppressed article for the *Courier* of 12 Jul 1811—"The moment of public agitation and joy at our successes in Portugal was cunningly chosen for announcing the re-appointment of the Duke of York as commander in chief, with the design obviously, of evading popular notice and animadversion." C asked whether "that bold indecent measure" were not "a national insult without pretence or palliation"; for "What has occurred to render the Duke of York's presence necessary at the head of the army, or to weaken the force of the charges that were proved against him?—Nothing." *EOT* (*CC*) III 221. Wellington's alarm at the quality of generals sent him for the Peninsular campaign found expression in a quizzical epigram; and the Duke of York's military prowess found its monument in a nursery rhyme.

it were with themselves, when they have a pleasure or good turn to own, saying, that they were accursed when they did it, and will beware hereafter how they pardon so lightly, how they bestow any such benefit, or shew any such favour to any man, all the which notwithstanding, are things appertaining to their Duty and Office.

47—& seq. It is to be regretted that Commines gives no Light as to the causes of the War on the part of Liege—what they complained of &c. In Germany, in this & the preceding Ages, the Free Towns were always in the Right, & the Princes always the oppressors, & finally the successful oppressors—a sad proof, that small Republics cannot wage war in the long run against arbitrary Princes, tho' of domains equally small, with success, unless they admit a large portion of Kingship & ~~perhaps~~ of Aristocracy into their ~~Composi~~institution.—

2A   p 82 | III 5 "How by King Lewis His Aide, the Earl of Warwick Chased King Edward out of England"

Besides this, he i.e. the E. of W. made a Marriage between the Prince of *Wales* and his (the Earl of Warwick) second Daughter.

3   p +3, referring to p 91 | III 8 "How the Wars Revived Between King Lewis and Charles Duke of Burgundy"

In all treaties of peace concluded between the *English* and *French* nations, the *French* have alwayes shewed more fineness, subtilty, and cunning than the *English*, so far forth that the said *English* men have a common proverb, as once they told me, when I treated with them: that in all battels fought with the *French*, ever or for the most part they have obtained honour and victory, but in all treaties that have been concluded between them they have ever received loss and damage.

91. The old adage that the English lose in the Cabinet what they win in the Field.[1]

3[1] I.e. what they have won in battle, they lose in the negotiations for a treaty—as e.g. the Convention of Cintra.

ABRAHAM COWLEY
1618–1667

The Works of Mr Abraham Cowley. Consisting of those which were formerly printed: and those which he design'd for the press, now published out of the authors original copies. [Fly-title to Pt vii:] The Second Part of the Works of Mr. Abraham Cowley. Being what was written and published by himself in his younger years. And now reprinted together. The fourth edition. [Together] The seventh edition. London 1681. 7 pts in 1 vol. London 1681. F°.

The first six parts of the one-volume "7th edition" are paginated separately, with individual fly-titles, but are signed continuously. The "Second Part" is here treated as Pt vii; many copies of the 7th ed (1681) include this "Second Part" (pp vi 162) bound in the same volume.

University of Indiana (Lilly Library)

WW's copy with the signature "Wm Wordsworth" in pencil, overtraced in ink, on the title-page. Signatures of "Anthony Whitwell 1769" and "H & R Whitwell" in ink on p ⁻1 (recto of portrait facing the title-page). WW mentions this copy in the "Essay, Supplementary to the Preface" to *Poems* (1815): see *WPW* II 417, *W Prose* III 71. A note by Edward Dowden attached to p ⁻2 (and attested at the end in another hand: "*Note by Edward Dowden.*"): "WORDSWORTH & COLERIDGE This is N°. 508 of the Catalogue of Wordsworth's Library sold at Rydal Mount in 1859. His name is on the title—On the last end-paper is a faintly pencilled head (such as a child might draw) with the words pencilled in S. T. Coleridge's handwriting:—[transcript (var) of 3] In Cowley's The Preface to Miscellanies (p C. 2) is a long note in pencil by S. T. Coleridge & in his handwriting. Wordsworth had two copies of Cowley—this, and an earlier edition." See also *W Library* 68.

In c Sept 1800 C copied into a notebook 4 lines of Cleve's translation of *De plantis* from *B Poets* (*CN* I 816), but traces in his notes of his reading of Cowley are connected with WW's copy in 1807–8, later than with the writing of these marginalia. *CN* II 3196–3199, 3203.

In *BL* C spoke of "The seductive faults, the dulcia vitia of Cowley, Marini, or Darwin", which had proved capable of "corrupting the public judgement for half a century". *BL* ch 4 (*CC*) I 74; cf II 235–6n. Again, "for competitors in barbarism with Cowley's Latin Poem de Plantis, or even his *not quite so bad* Davideid Hexameters, we must go I fear to the Deliciae Poetarum Germanorum/or other ~~similar~~ Warehouses of Seal-fat, Whale Blubber and the like Boreal Confectionaries selected by the delicate Gruter." BM MS Egerton 2800 f 54, in *IS* 157; see also *BL* ch 4 (*CC*) I 84, and cf FIELD 5 and n 4. But Cowley, he also said, although he had "a discursive intellect, *naturally* less vigorous and daring", was yet a legitimate child of Donne; and "with the omission of quaintness here and there, is probably the best model of style for modern imitation in general". DONNE *Poems* 11; *Misc* C 219. See also PEPYS *Memoirs* (2 vols 1825) II i 110.

CONTENTS. i An Account of the Life and Writings of Mr. Abraham Cowley; *Elegia Dedicatoria*; The Preface of the Author (1); *Miscellanies*. ii *The Mistress* (1A–1C). iii *Pindarique Odes*. iv *Davideis*. v *Davideis* (Latin). vi *Verses Written on Several Occasions*; *A Proposition for the Advancement of Experimental Philosophy*; *A Discourse by Way of Vision*; Several Discourses by Way of Essays, in Verse and Prose. vii [prefatory matter;] *Constantia and Philetus*; *Piramus and Thisbe* (1D, 1E); *Sylva*; *Loves Riddle* (1F); *Naufragium joculare*.

DATE. 10 Oct 1801: dated in 3.

1   sig C2, pencil, corrections in ink, cropped | "The Preface of the Author"

...I have cast away all such pieces as I wrote during the time of the late troubles, with any relation to the differences that caused them; *] as among others, *three Books of the Civil War it self*, reaching as far as the first *Battel* at *Newbury*, where the succeeding *misfortunes* of the *party* stopt the *work*.

As for the ensuing Book, it consists of four parts: The first is a *Miscellanie* of several Subjects, and some of them made when I was very young, which it is perhaps *superfluous* to tell the *Reader*; I know not by what chance I have kept *Copies* of them; for they are but a very few in comparison of those which I have lost, and I think they have no extraordinary virtue in them, to deserve more care in preservation, than was bestowed upon their *Brethren*; for which I am so little concerned that I am ashamed of the *arrogancy* of the *Word*, when I said *I had lost them*.

* Strange that a respect for the Subject of two of these Poems viz that on his Friend Hervey & the othe[r] on the Poet Crash[aw], and both funera[l] Poems, should not have preve[n]ted him from speaking in thi[s] light Manner.—But there is here a deal of affectation.

^aI have fallen into a mistake in the above—The contemptuo[us] tone in which he speaks is not the one to apply to the whole *miscellany* but only to ~~those~~ the juvenile part of it.—It gives me pleasure to have observe[d] this & to correct the mistake in this manner rather than ~~to erase~~ erase the Note.—~~It is~~ The whole may serve as a warning against careless reading which leads to rank censure.

^a C has drawn a line below the first paragraph (in the outer margin) and written the PS immediately below the line, in the outer margin and at the foot

1A ii 29, pencil, braces and line in the margin | *The Mistress.* "Counsel"

1.

Gently, Ah gently, Madam, touch
  The wound which you your self have made;
That pain must needs be very much,
  Which makes me of *your hand* afraid.
Cordials of *Pity* give me now,
For I too weak for *Purgings* grow.

.   .   .   .

5.

Thy *Tongue* comes in, as if it meant
  Against thine *Eyes* t' assist my *Heart*;
But different far was his intent;
  For straight the *Traytor* took their part.
And by this new Foe I' am bereft
Of all that *Little* which was left.

6.

The Act I must confess was wise,
  As a dishonest Act could be:

1B ii 30, pencil line in the margin | "Resolved to be Beloved"

1.

'Tis true, I' have lov'd already three or four,
  And shall three or four hundred more;
I'll love each fair one that I see,
Till I find one at last that shall *love me*.

2.

That shall my *Canaan* be, the fatal Soil,
  That ends my wandrings and my toil.
I'll settle there and happy grow;
The *Country* does with *Milk* and *Honey* flow.

1C ii 56, pencil line in the margin | "Resolved to Love"

4.

If *learn'd* in other things you be,
  And have in *Love* no skill,

For Gods sake keep your Arts from me,
    For I'll be *ignorant* still.
Study or *Action* others may embrace;
My *Love*'s my *Business*, and my *Book*'s her *Face*.

5.

These are but *Trifles*, I confess,
    Which me, weak Mortal move;
Nor is your *busie Seriousness*
    Less trifling than my Love.
The wisest *King* who from his sacred brest
Pronounc'd *all Van'ity*, chose it for the *best*.

1D   vii 26, pencil | *Piramus and Thisbe* st 6

For age had crack'd the Wall which did them part,
This the unanimate couple soon did spy,   animate
And here their inward sorrows did impart,
Unlading the sad burthen of their heart.
    Though Love be blind, this shews he can descry
    A way to lessen his own misery.

1E   vii 30, pencil | st 30

She blames all-powerful *Jove*, and strives to take
His bleeding body from the moistned ground.
She kisses his pale face, till she doth make
*   It red with kissing, and then seeks to wake
    His parting Soul with mournful words, his wound
    Washes with tears, that her sweet speech confound.

1F   vii 78 | *Loves Riddle* ii i

Hylace. She came last to you.
Bellula. She hath another love;
    And kills *Palaemon* with her cruelty,
    How can she expect mercy from another;
Cal.   In what a labyrinth doth love draw mortals,
And then blind-folds them! what a mist it throws
Upon their senses! if he be a God,
As sure he is (his power could not be so great else)
He knows the impossibility which nature
Hath set betwixt us, yet entangles us,

And laughs to see us struggle. ∧ D' ye both love me?[1]
Bell. I do I'm sure.
Hyl. And I as much as she.
Callidora. I pity both of you, for you have sow'd
Upon unthankful sand, whose dry'd up womb
Nature denies to bless with fruitfulness,
You are both fair, and more than common graces
Inhabit in you both...

2　p $^{+3}$ (p–d), pencil

30
56
28 2nd part
22[1]

3　p $^{+3}$ (p–d), pencil, written above and beside C's drawing of a head

Drawn by S. T. Coleridge, entirely out of his own fancy, Oct. 10,
1801—he being then only 29 years of age—yea, not 29, by 10 days.[1]

1F[1] C suggests that Bellula's speech,
as printed, should be interrupted—as
marked—by Callidora, to be resumed at
the point marked with a caret.
　2[1] For the first two page-references,
see **1B** and **1C**. "2nd part" refers to Pt vii
(see citation of title), but there is no mark
on either page.
　3[1] For once, C has his age right. See
BAXTER *Reliquiae* COPY B **91** n 4.

OLIVER CROMWELL

1599–1658

His Highnesse the Lord Protector's Speeches to the Parliament in the Painted Chamber, the one on Munday the 4th of September; the other on Tuesday the 12. of September. 1654. Taken by one who stood very near him, and published to prevent mistakes. 2 pts in 1 vol. London 1654. 4º.

"Printed by T. R. and E. M. for G. Sawbridge at the Bible on Ludgate-hill." Pt ii has a separate title-page, differing only in the date of the speech. Bound in "CROMWELLIAN TRACTS".

Not located. *Lost List.*

MS TRANSCRIPT. VCL BT 37. Here used as text in preference to *NTP.*

DATE. Unknown. See "CROMWELLIAN TRACTS" headnote.

---

1   ? front flyleaf

Query—how long it has been since and how long it is likely to be before a Mʳ Recorder has made or will make such another speech, of equal solidity in the substance, and dignity in language? S. T. C.

2   i 15ff

...if I say they were but Notions, they were to be let alone. Notions will hurt none but them that have them. But when they come to such practises, as to tell us, that Liberty and Property, are not the Badges of the Kingdome of Christ; and tell us, that instead of regulating Lawes, Lawes are to be abrogated, indeed subverted; and perhaps would bring in the Judaical Law, instead of our known Lawes setled amongst us. This is worthy of every Magistrates Consideration: especially, where every stone is turned to bring Confusion.

Notions not punishable however erroneous; but the drawing and publishing of *consequences* from the same, that is, of practical consequences, inconsistent with the social rights and obligations; or with the fundamental laws of the State; and tending to their subversion, is an *overt act*, as rightfully within the sphere of the civil Magistrate's office, as theft, forgery, or any other *crime*: tho' the degree of guilt, of which God alone is the competent Judge, may be very different.

To this dictum of the Lord Protector I know of no sound objection, *in genere*. There is, however, a practical difference, the annexment of which would render the principle at once more safe and more complete: namely, that in cases of the first kind (the publication of speculative opinions with unsafe consequences) the Magistrate is or should be entrusted with a larger discretional power, and in deciding the question, not only respecting the nature and quantum of the punishment, but likewise whether he shall interfere at all, he will in each case be determined by the greater or lesser probability of the consequences being acted on, or the public peace being disturbed by the attempt; still more, perhaps by the question, whether his interference may not do more harm than good, and aggravate the evil, he wishes to remedy—both by spreading the contagion and increasing the susceptibility of the persons exposed to it.[1] This last caution would apply particularly to the offence of questioning or denying the truth or divine authority of the Scriptures or any main article of the Established Faith. In such cases it is ordinarily wiser to proceed (where the occasion is given) against the *manner*, as indecency, wanton outrage of the Feelings of the Community, for *incivism*,[2] in short, and nuisance, than against the *matter*, had it been calmly and modestly worded, addressed to the Reason and Understanding, not to the passions or appetites of the Readers—and (as probable by the style, price and circumstances of publication) intended for competent Judges.—

3   ii 7

And that there was high cause for their Dissolving, is most evident, not onely in regard there was a just fear of the Parliaments *] perpetuating themselves; but because it was their designe. And had not their heeles been trod upon by importunities from abroad, even to threats, *I* believe there would never have been thoughts of Rising, or of going out of that Roome to the worlds end.

After reading this cloudy *Tiberian* Speech,[1] and comparing these

2[1] Cf "CIVIL WAR TRACTS" 2.

2[2] *OED*, noting that "incivism" was originally (1794) used to mean want of loyalty to the principles of the French Revolution, ascribes to C (in Allsop I 92)

the first use of the word as applying—as here—to other states and times.

3[1] In the debate in the Senate that took place after the death of Augustus to decide who should be emperor, Tiberius

impudent assertions with the measures and declared intentions of the Republican Parliament, it should be impossible to doubt the baseness of Cromwell. Even supposing some truth in *, yet what more can be wished from a Parliament than that they should yield to the desires from abroad? S. T. C.

made a speech (Tacitus *Annals* 1.11) expressing his reluctance to assume the burden of empire, while he had every intention that the Senate should eventually persuade him to accept it. This not uncommon manoeuvre is proverbially, in public life, called "Tiberian".

"CROMWELLIAN TRACTS"

Gillman SC (1843) enters as lots 498, 499, and 500 three volumes of seventeenth-century tracts, for each volume giving the number of tracts, the inclusive dates of publication, and the titles of three or four tracts. For lot 498, described in *Gillman SC* as containing a variety of tracts "relating to the Civil Wars", see "CIVIL WAR TRACTS". Of the other two volumes, the catalogue describes the first (lot 499) as containing tracts "relating to Cromwell" but gives no such general description of the contents of the second volume (lot 500). Although MS TRANSCRIPT (*a*) distinguishes between the tracts "relating to the civil wars" and the tracts "relating to the times of Cromwell" it does not recognise the Cromwell tracts as divided into two volumes. The inclusive dates of lot 500—1630–79—carry the contents of this second volume twenty years beyond the date of Cromwell's death; but because SC (who was able to examine the volumes) considered that at least the annotated tracts in both volumes were adequately described as "relating to the times of Cromwell" the first volume (lot 499) is here entered as "CROMWELLIAN TRACTS I" and the second (lot 500) as "CROMWELLIAN TRACTS II". *NTP*, which evidently drew upon MS TRANSCRIPT (*a*) for its text and sequence of these tracts, does not offer independent evidence of contents or order of Volume II; the slight variations from the transcript are readily explainable in terms of the topical arrangement and editorial principles of *NTP*.

In reconstructing the relative order of the named and annotated tracts in the two Cromwellian volumes two assumptions have been made: (1) that *Gillman SC* gives the correct number of tracts for each volume and the correct inclusive dates of publication, and that the three or four titles given as a sample of the contents of each volume are the first—or at least among the first—tracts bound in each volume; (2) that when SC made her MS TRANSCRIPT (*a*), having the actual volumes in hand, she worked through the two volumes by transcribing the annotations as they occurred, and that the order of the annotated items in her transcript represents the relative order in which the annotated tracts occurred in the bound volumes.

While C was preparing Vol III of *The Friend* in the summer or early autumn of 1818 he "met with a volume of old tracts, published during the interval from the captivity of Charles the First [c May 1646] to the restoration of his son [1660]." *Friend* (*CC*) I 410. As motto to the first essay of Section II "On the Grounds of Morals and Religion" he chose a passage from John HALL *An Humble Motion* (in II, below), and in the same essay "filtered" an extensive section of William SEDGWICK *Justice upon the Armie Remonstrance* (also in II, below). *Friend* (*CC*) I 409, 411–14.

C seems to have acquired the "CROMWELLIAN TRACTS" in about the middle of 1818; and his footnote in *Friend* (*CC*) I 411 is a version, only slightly revised, of the third sentence of his one annotation on SEDGWICK. Whether C's expression there of Aubrey-ish regret (for which see BYFIELD headnote) at the dispersal of such precious and ephemeral writings through the caprice of Sir Gilfrid Lawson at Broughton near Keswick records the circumstances in which C acquired these tracts is to be doubted. Whether he acquired the "CIVIL WAR TRACTS" and the "ENGLISH TRACTS" (from which no annotations are preserved) at the same time as the "CROMWELLIAN TRACTS" is not known; the apparently later statement in *TT* 4 Jan 1823 seems to refer rather to the "CROMWELLIAN" or "CIVIL WAR TRACTS", yet nothing appears in C's writing from the "CIVIL WAR TRACTS" until he quoted from one of the tracts in that volume in *C&S* (Dec 1829): see DALLISON headnote.

I

[A made-up volume of 26 tracts "relating to Cromwell".] 1654–60. 4°.

Not located. *Gillman SC* (1843) 499: "with MS. Notes by S. T. Coleridge".

CONTENTS

William STEELE *Mr Recorder's Speech to the Lord Protector* (1653).
Oliver CROMWELL *His Highnesse the Lord Protector's Speech to the Parliament...on...the 4th of September, 1654.* [and]...*on...the 12th of September, 1654* (1654). (Entered as two titles in MS TRANSCRIPT (*a*).)
Sir Harry VANE *A Healing Question Propounded* (1660).
And 23 other tracts unidentified.

I I

[A made-up volume of 24 tracts.] 1630–79. 4°.

Not located. *Gillman SC* (1843) 500: "with MS. Notes by S. T. Coleridge".

CONTENTS

John Geree *The Character of an Old English Puritane* (1646).
John HALL *An Humble Motion to the Parliament...Concerning the Advancement of Learning* (1650) [1649 in MS TRANSCRIPT (*a*)]. (HALL 1 begins: "This third Tract...".)
The Lyer Laid Open (1648).
Newes from Turkie (1648).
And 20 other tracts, probably including:
[Robert CHAMBRE] *Some Animadversions upon the Declaration...of the Army* (1659).
Thomas WHITFIELD *A Discourse of Liberty of Conscience* (1649).
William SEDGWICK *Justice upon the Armie Remonstrance* (1648). (C's one annotation, written on "Blank page at the end of the Volume of Tracts", begins: "8.th Tract 1649 | Justice upon the remonstrance of the Army...".)

MS TRANSCRIPTS. (*a*) VCL BT 37: SC transcript "From a Volume of Tracts relating to the times of Cromwell": I—STEELE, CROMWELL, VANE; II—HALL, CHAMBRE, WHITFIELD, SEDGWICK. This transcript is associated with a transcript of annotations on "CIVIL WAR TRACTS", which see. (*b*) University of Texas (Humanities Research Center): untitled continuous transcript in an unidentified hand: WHITFIELD, SEDGWICK; DYMOCK (from "CIVIL WAR TRACTS").

CHARLES DALLISON

fl 1648

The Royalist's Defence: vindicating the King's proceedings in the late warre made against him. Clearly discovering, how and by what impostures the incendiaries of these distractions have subverted the knowne law of the Land, the Protestant religion, and reduced the people to an unparallel'd slavery. [Anonymous.] [? London] 1648. 4°.

Possibly bound in "CIVIL WAR TRACTS". The title-page of the BM copy, E 1948(37), is inscribed "~~Matthew~~ Charles Dallison". See also *C&S* (*CC*) 97 n 1.

Not located.

C quotes (var) from this tract in *C&S* (*CC*) 97 (see **4** n 1, below), describes it on p 98, and quotes again from it (var) on p 102. On p 103 he says that the author was "evidently a Tory Lawyer of the genuine breed, too enlightened to obfuscate and incense-blacken the shrine, through which the kingly Idea should be translucent...".

MS TRANSCRIPT. VCL BT 37: SC transcript; here used as text.

DATE. Possibly 1829, at the time of writing *C&S*.

1   p [vi] | The Epistle to the Readers

Now amongst those, he who hath once got the *reputation* of an *Antiquary*, and hath accustomed himself to discourse of things out of the common *roade, ipso facto*, is Master of this Art. It is then but making use of some dull *expressions* found in an old *worm-eaten Record*, selecting the mistaken opinions of some *Iudges obiter*, ·delivered in Arguments, or some *dark Sentences* taken out of a *rotten Manuscript*. And if any *printed Book* be daigned the mentioning, it must not be the *known authentique Authours*...but some *antiquated* thing whose *Authour* is unknowne, and his meaning as *obscure*. These *rules* being observed, his work is done; the people observing this *Cynicks* discourse to be different from other men, presently conclude him to be *far* more learned in his profession, then his *fellow Lawyers*, and gaze upon him as an *infallible* guide.

113

Palpably a sneer at Selden.[a1]

2 p [vii]

And the *King* on the other side, with *wonderfull* expressions of *loyalty*...was told *He should be made more Glorious, then any of His Ancestors or Predecessours*: But the *Members* having thus *encreased* the flame, between the *King* and the *Subject*, and having by these false *surmises* and cunning *dissemblings*, gulled the people into a belief, *That whatever the Members declared*...*the one was good Law, and the other true Gospel*; which the Members perceiving, they instantly made use thereof, and upon that score voted it a *high Breach of the Priviledge of Parliament for any*...*either to oppose their Commands, or to deny that to be Law, which they declared so to be*: By which sleight, their whole work was finished...and both *King* and *people*...*inslaved*, to their *will* and *doome*.

How strange, if, under the influence of party-spirit, anything can be thought strange, that this Royalist, evidently a man of sense and learning, should have suffered himself to forget, who and what portion of the nation these *members* were, in the two or three first Parliaments of Charles I.—Vide Clarendon's own Confession.[1]

3 p [ix]

And for those of the latter *ranke*, how far their following the *dictamen* of their owne conscience, in point of *Divinity* may excuse them, I will

---

a In MS TRANSCRIPT each annotation ends with the initials "S. T. C.". Since this is SC's usual way of identifying C's note in her transcript, it is omitted as probably not present in C's original

1[1] John Selden (1584–1654), jurist and son of a wandering minstrel, a man of prodigious learning in the law and in oriental studies, was well known also for his provocative *History of Tythes* (1617), of which C owned a copy. His "Address to the Reader" attached to Drayton's *Polyolbion* made an early impression on C: see ANDERSON COPY B **3** n 1 and *CN* II 3086. For Selden's "masculine intellect", a "genuine *English* Mind whose erudition, broad, deep, and manifold as it was, is yet less remarkable than his robust healthful common sense", see *SM* (*CC*) 107, 111; cf *AR* (1825) 360n. C annotated a copy of some version of Selden's *Table Talk*: see SELDEN.

2[1] In the first three Parliaments in

Charles I's reign (Jun–Aug 1625, Mar–Jun 1626, Jun 1628–Mar 1629) the Commons with increasing confidence defied the King and challenged his prerogative to govern. After dissolving the third Parliament, Charles ruled for eleven years without calling Parliament. Clarendon's recognition of Charles's inept judgement and overbearing behaviour in dealing with Parliament can be seen in the *History of the Rebellion* (6 vols Oxford 1888) I 5–8 (Bk I §§6–10). For Clarendon as "Hypocrite, Liar in all his characters", see BUNYAN COPY A **11** n 1. For C's reading of Clarendon in c Mar 1810, and the edition he was using at that time, see *CN* III 3740–3742 and nn.

not *dispute*, but, certaine I am by the *constitutions* of this Realme, in *Temporall* things, it neither *extenuates* the crime, nor *mitigates* the punishment.

One sophism pervades the whole of this reasoning—*pars pro toto*[1]—or the confusion of the individual and what he *represents* but does not possess. Our King represents the whole power of the nation and its Laws, but does not possess it.[2]

4   p 48 | Ch 4 "That the King... have not an unlimited power to make Laws..."

By this it appears, that when the *two* Houses have passed a Bill for an *Act* of Parliament, and to it the Kings *Royale Assent* is had, the Parliaments power *ends*, and then *begins* the *authority* of the Judges of the Realme, whose office is... first to judge, whether the Act it selfe be *good*, and if *binding*, then to declare the *meaning* of the words thereof. And so the *necessity* of having a power upon *emergent* occasions to make new Laws is supplied, and yet the *fundamentall* grounds of the Law, by this limitation of the power of the *Law-maker*, with reference to the Judges to determine which Acts of Parliament are binding, and which void, is *preserved*.[1]

In a state of society, in which the active and influencive portion of the inhabitants was small, scarcely perhaps trebling the number of the members of the two Houses—the right and power here contended for might have been wisely vested in the Judges of the Realm. It is curious to observe, that the thinner the Realm was (the less both the wealth & influence and the less they were *diffused*) the greater was the division of power. It is now almost merged in the House of Commons.—Formerly, the Convocation, the Judges &c. shared in it.—[2]

3[1] "The part for the whole"—the logical fallacy of assuming that what is true of the part is necessarily and without qualification true of the whole.

3[2] For C's use of this tract in *C&S* see headnote, above. For the king as representing the unity of the nation see e.g. *C&S* (*CC*) 20, 77, 108.

4[1] C quotes this page (var) in *C&S* (*CC*) 97, his comment being an expanded version of **4**.

4[2] *NTP* continues this note with two more paragraphs. MS TRANSCRIPT shows that they were written on a back flyleaf of this volume of tracts; they are printed as "CIVIL WAR TRACTS" **2** and **3**.

SAMUEL DANIEL
1562–1619

The Poetical Works of Mr. Samuel Daniel, author of the English
History. To which is prefix'd, memoirs of his life and writings. 2 vols.
London 1718. 8°.

Harvard University (Houghton Library)

Charles Lamb's copy, presented by Mary Lamb after his death to William
Hazlitt the younger. Autograph signature "W C Hazlitt" on I ⁻6, and a note
by him on I ⁻7: "This copy is particularly interesting as having belonged
to Charles Lamb and having been enriched by him and by S T Coleridge
with MSS notes & Corrections. It also contains two or three letters by
S T H C which are not published. Critically speaking, it is a very poor
edition. The errors of the press are both numerous & gross, so gross, however
that in many cases they almost correct themselves. W C H." Autograph
signature of "S! Clair Baddeley. 1893." on I ⁻4, and pasted to I ⁻5 the
descriptive entry for a copy of Daniel's *Delia and Rosamond Augmented*
(1598), lot 300 of the Sotheby catalogue of 22 Mar 1905.

Lamb has written a long biographical note on Daniel "from Fuller's
Worthies" on I ⁻1, and on the Contents page (I [1]) has entered "Song at
a Court Masque 246" referring to I 246, and after the title "A Defence of
Rhime..." has noted "(by Tho! Campion)". He has also written a short
note on II 419, and on II 425 at the end of *To the Angel Spirit of the Most
Excellent Sir Philip Sidney*: "This seems written *by*, or *for*, the Countess of
~~Pemfr~~ Pembroke, Sister to Sir P. Sidney, who joined with him in the Psalms;
elegant, and Anglo-courtly not not true Hebrew, like Milton's." Textual
corrections by Lamb are made on I 8, 28, 31, 33, 38, 40, 51, 57, 75, [89], 95,
108, 122, 131, 194, 201, 207, 220, 222, 223, 242, 271, 293, 318, 332, 362, 364,
368, 377; II 27, 84, 133, 139, 170, 186, 209, 286, 314, 323, 336, 359, 377, 421,
422, 423, 424, 425. The correction on II 422 could be C's, being the same
correction of "weaves" to "veins" that appears in ANDERSON COPY B 11A.
Several passages in *The History of the Civil War* are marked with a line in
the margin, but it is difficult to say who made these: II 6–7 (bk I st 5), 34–6
(sts 93–9), 143 (bk V st 5, and lines 3–4 underlined), 178 (bk VI st 1 lines 7–8),
302 (bk VIII st 103 lines 7–8), 303 (st 107 lines 2–5), 383; the last three of
these are probably by Lamb.

C noted in N 16 that he "Read Daniel" at midnight 31 Dec 1803/1 Jan
1804; shortly thereafter he jotted down two quotations from *Hymen's
Triumph*—the second evidently of personal import—and made memorandum
to quote "the introd. Sonnet to Musophilus" in his projected *Consolations
and Comforts*. *CN* I 1793–1796. He was staying at Dove Cottage at the time,
and was using, not Anderson's text (*B Poets* IV), but WW's copy of the 2-vol

116

1718 cd (Wordsworth LC 638, now in DCL). On 8 Mar 1804 he sent Lady Beaumont "Daniel's Poems, 2 Volumes", "with the eminent passages of the Hymen's Triumph (for which alone I have sent them) marked". *CN* II 2055, *CL* II 1079. In a notebook entry of c Apr 1804 he assigned to SH the name "Isulia" (*CN* II 1079)—the name of the girl in *Hymen's Triumph* who returns from pirate captivity to her lover "a pure, | A chaste, and spotless maid". See also 3 n 6, below. Although there are no marginalia on *Hymen's Triumph*, it was of this and of the *Civil War* that C later said the style and language were "such as any very pure and manly writer of the present day— Wordsworth, for example—would use". *TT* 15 Mar 1834; cf 11 Sept 1831, *BL* chs 18, 22 (*CC*) II 78, 146–7, and *CN* II 2224 f 85ᵛ.

For further marginalia on Daniel, see ANDERSON COPY A 3–6, COPY B 10, 11, and CHALMERS 1.

C owned a copy of Daniel's *History of England* (ed not identified) with Trussell's *Continuation*; he left it at Allan Bank in Oct 1810, and it is included in WW's list of books to be sent to Highgate in c 1829–30. Wordsworth LC 729–30, 1205–6; *W Library* 324, 358, and (for WW's copy) 73.

CONTENTS. I Some Account of the Life and Writings of Mr. Samuel Daniel; *A Defence of Rhime*; *The Complaint of Rosamond*; *A Letter from Octavia to Marcus Antonius*; *Hymen's Triumph*; *The Queen's Arcadia*; *The Vision of the Twelve Goddesses*; *The Tragedy of Cleopatra*; *The Tragedy of Philotas*; *The Apology* [for *Philotas*]. II *The History of the Civil War* (5–23); *A Funeral Poem upon the Death of the...Earl of Devonshire*; *A Panegyric Congratulatory, Deliver'd to the King's Most Excellent Majesty*; *Certain Epistles* (to Sir Thomas Egerton; Lord Henry Howard; Lady Margaret, Countess of Cumberland; Lady Lucy, Countess of Bedford; Lady Anne Clifford; Henry Wriothesly, Earl of Southampton); *The Passion of a Distressed Man*; *Musophilus*; *Sonnets to Delia*; *An Ode*; *A Pastoral*; *A Description of Beauty* (translated out of Marino); *To the Angel Spirit of...Sir Philip Sidney*; *To the Right Reverend James Montague, Lord Bishop of Winchester*.

MS TRANSCRIPT. Lord Abinger's library (microfilm at Duke University): William Godwin's incomplete transcript of the marginalia.

DATE. c 9–10 Feb 1808 (1, 3), or a little earlier, and possibly later. C arrived in London 23 Nov 1807 and began his first literary lectures at the Royal Institution 15 Jan 1808, by which time he was lodging at the *Courier* office in the Strand. He had visited Lamb some days before 2 Feb, having "walked to and from Lambe's to procure his Mss selections from the Dramatists of the Age of Shakspeare"—i.e. *Specimens of English Dramatic Poets*, which was to be published in Jul 1808. Lamb may not have been at home when C called on that occasion, but 1 points to a notable meeting on 9 Feb. In May or Jun 1809 Lamb recovered from the *Courier* office several of the books he had lent to C, including this annotated DANIEL, Sidney's *Arcadia*, and all but Vol III of Dodsley's *Old Plays*. *LL* II 75.

1 ii ⁻4

Tuesday, Feb. 10. 1808. (*10ᵗʰ or 9ᵗʰ?*)
Dear Charles,
   I think more highly, far more, of the "Civil Wars", than you
seemed to do (on Monday night, Feb. 9ᵗʰ 1808)—the Verse does not
teize *me*; and all the while I am reading it, I cannot but fancy a plain
England-loving English Country Gentleman, with only some dozen
Books in his whole Library, and at a time when a "Mercury" or
"Intelligencer" was seen by him once in a month or two, making
this his Newspaper & political Bible at the same time/ & reading
it so often as to store his Memory with its aphorisms. Conceive a
good man of that kind, diffident and passive, yet *rather* inclined to
Jacobitism; seeing the reasons of the Revolutionary Party, yet by
disposition and old principles leaning, in quiet nods and signs at his
own parlour fire, to the hereditary Right—(and of these characters
there must have been many)—& then read this poem assuming in
your heart his Character—conceive how grave he would look, and
what pleasure & ⟨there would be, what⟩ unconscious, harmless,
humble self-conceit, self-compliment in his gravity; how *wise* he
would feel himself—& yet after all, how forbearing, how much
calmed by that most calming reflection (when it is really the mind's
own reflection)—aye! it was just so in Henry the 6ᵗʰ'ˢ Time/ always
the same Passions at work—&c—. Have I injured thy Book—? or
wilt thou "like it the better there*fore*?"¹ But I have done as I would
gladly be done by—thee, at least.—²

                                    S. T. Coleri[dge]ᵃ

2 ii ⁻4, at the head, written through the beginning of 1

— means either a long syllable, or, symbolically, less than, as
2−1 = 2 1. = the same as, or equal to— + more by: thus
3+5−2 = 6. × means multiplied by. 5+5 = 10; but 5 × 5 = 25.—

ᵃ Signature cropped

1¹ The italics mark some idiomatic
jest shared by C and Lamb; it appears
again e.g. in a doggerel verse that C wrote
in Lamb's copy of LUTHER *Colloquia
Mensalia* (1652) 370. See also BROOKE 1
(at n 2). There may be some connexion
with *Merry Wives of Windsor* ii i 186: "I
like it never the better for that."
1² Cf Luke 6.31. For similar mock
apologies for writing marginalia in other
people's books see e.g. BLOMFIELD 1,

DONNE *Poems* 61, HOWIE 4. Lamb
responded graciously on 7 Jun 1809,
when he recovered his book "enriched
with manuscript notes": "I wish every
book I have were so noted. They have
thoroughly converted me to relish
Daniel, or to say I relish him, for, after
all, I believe I did relish him. You well call
him sober-minded. Your notes are
excellent. Perhaps you've forgot them."
LL ii 75.

3 ii ⁻3 ⁻2

Second Letter/ 5 hours after the first.

Dear Charles

You must read over these Civil Wars again. We both know what a *mood* is. And the genial mood will, it shall come, for my sober-minded Daniel. He was a Tutor, and a sort of Steward in a noble Family in which Form was religiously observed, and Religion formally; & yet there was such warm blood & mighty muscle of substance within, that the ~~iron~~ moulding Iron⟨s⟩ did not distort tho' ~~it~~ they stiffened the vital man within. Daniel caught & recommunicated the Spirit of the great Countess of Pembroke, the glory of the North/ he *formed* her mind, & her mind inspirited him.[1] Gravely sober in all ordinary affairs, & not easily excited by any—yet there is one, in which his Blood boils—whenever he speaks of English Valour exerted against a foreign Enemy. Do read over—but some evening when ~~we are~~ I am quite comfortable, at your fire-side—and O! where shall I ever be, if I am not so there—that is the last Altar, on the horns of which my old Feelings hang, but alas! listen & tremble/—Nonsense!—well! I will read it to you & Mary—the 205, 206 and 207th page (above all, that 93rd* Stanza)[2] What is there in

3[1] Mary Herbert, Countess of Pembroke (1561–1621), younger sister of Philip Sidney, married Henry Herbert, 2nd Earl of Pembroke, in 1577, and made her country house at Wilton a gathering place for distinguished writers. Daniel, having entered her household for a time as tutor to William Herbert, won her admiration and patronage. Sidney's first *Arcadia* was written for her amusement; she inspired Daniel's *Cleopatra* and Kyd's *Cornelia*; she is the Urania of Spenser's *Colin Clout*, and was patron of Ben Jonson, Nicholas Breton, and other poets. Her own literary accomplishment and neoclassical taste are to be seen in her revision of *Arcadia*, in the collaboration with her brother in a metrical version of the Psalms, and in her elegy for her brother appended to Spenser's *Astrophel*. In the opening of his *Defence of Rhime*, addressed to William Herbert, Daniel acknowledged his gratitude to the Countess for having "first encourag'd and fram'd" his talents (i 6, not annotated). But C is merging two generations. The

"glory of the North" was Daniel's later pupil, Anne Clifford (1590–1672), daughter of the Earl of Cumberland. Born in Yorkshire, she was married first to the Earl of Dorset, then (1630) to Philip Herbert, 4th Earl of Pembroke. Widowed again in 1650, she returned to the north and was noted for her learning and hospitality and for the building and restoration of castles and churches. HC later gave an account of her life in his *Worthies of Yorkshire and Lancashire*, in which he noticed that some had incorrectly spoken of Daniel as tutor to the earlier Countess.

Lamb had lent C his copy of Sidney's *Arcadia* at the same time as this DANIEL: see headnote (DATE).

3[2] *Poetical Works* ii 205–7 contains *Civil War* vi 87–96; vi 93 reads:

> Whilst *Talbot* (whose fresh Ardor
>   having got
> A marvelous Advantage of his Years)
> Carries his unfelt Age as if forgot,
> Whirling about where any Need
>   appears.

description superior even in Shakspere? only that Shakespere would have given one of his *glows* to the first Line, and flatter'd the mountain Top with his sovran Eye[7]—instead of that poor "a marvellous advantage of his Years"—/[8] but this however is Daniel—and he must not be read piecemeal. Even by leaving off, & looking at a Stanza by itself, I find the loss.   S. T. Coleridge—
O Charles! I am *very*, very ill. Vixi.[9]

* and in a different style, the 98th Stanza, p. 208:[3] ⟨& what an Image in 107, p. 211.—⟩[4] Thousands even of educated men would become more sensible, fitter to be members of Parliament, or Ministers, by reading Daniel—and even those few, who quoad intellectum[5] only gain refreshment of notions already their own, must become better Englishmen. O if it be not too late, write a kind note about him/[6]
S. T. Coleridge

His Hand, his Eye, his Wits all present, wrought
The Function of the Glorious Part he bears:
Now urging here, now cheering there, he flies;
Unlocks the thickest Troops, where most Force lies.

In the text and running headlines of this edition the poem is entitled *Civil War*, not *Civil Wars*, as the Contents lists it and as C calls it, following normal usage (as in the first separate editions of 1595 and 1609 and the first collective edition of 1623).

3[3] *Civil War* VI 98:

Which Blood not lost, but fast laid up with heed
In everlasting Fame, is there held dear,
To seal the Memory of this Day's Deed;
Th' Eternal Evidence of what we were:
To which our Fathers, We, and who succeed,
Do owe a Sigh, for that it touch'd us near.
Nor must we sin so much, as to neglect
The Holy Thought of such a Dear Respect.

3[4] *Civil War* VI 107:

Like as proud *Severn* from a private Head,

With humble Streams at first both gently glide,
Till other Rivers have contributed
The springing Riches of their Store beside;
Wherewith at length (high-swelling) she doth spread
Her broad-distended Waters laid so wide,
That coming to the Sea, she seems from far,
Not to have Tribute brought, but rather War:

3[5] "So far as they have understood".

3[6] C is evidently thinking of Lamb's *Specimens of English Dramatic Poets*, the ms of which he had borrowed in early Feb 1808: see headnote, above. Lamb included three extracts from *Hymen's Triumph* under the titles "Love in Infancy", "Love after Death", And "The Story of Isulia", but he did not write a "kind note" about Daniel; when he got back his copy of Daniel, with C's injunction, on 7 Jun 1809, the *Specimens* had been in print for almost a year. That C remembered Lamb's treatment of Daniel in the *Specimens* is seen in *BL* ch 18 (*CC*) II 78–9.

3[7] Cf Shakespeare Sonnet 33: "Full many a glorious morning have I seen | Flatter the mountain tops with Sovereign eye".

4 II ⁻1

Is it from any hobby-horsical Love of our old Writers¹ (& ⟨of⟩ such a passion respecting Chaucer, Spenser, & Ben Jonson's Poems I have ~~at~~ occasionally seen glaring proofs in one, the string of whose Shoe I am ~~un~~ not worthy to unloose)² or is it a real Beauty./ the interspersion, I mean, (in stanza poems), of rhymes from polysyllables—such as Eminence, Obedience, Reverence?³ To my ear they convey not only a relief from variety, but a *sweetness* as of repose—and ~~to~~ the Understanding they gratify by reconciling Verse with the whole wide extent of good Sense. Without being distinctly conscious of such a Notion, having it rather than reflecting it (for one may think in the same way as one may see & hear) I seem to be made to know, that I need have no fear; that there's nothing excellent in itself which the Poet cannot express accurately & naturally, nay, no good word.—

THE HISTORY OF THE CIVIL WAR

5 II 171, referring to v 101

But as he to his judged *Exile went,
Hard on the Shore he came encountered
By some, that so far off his Honour sent,
As put his Back-Return quite out of Dread:
For there he had his rightful Punishment,
Tho' wrongly done; and there he lost his Head.
Part of his Blood hath Neptune, Part the Sand;
As who had Mischief wrought by Sea and Land.

[Daniel's note:] * As the Duke [of Suffolk, accused of responsibility for the "shameful Loss of France", banished for five years] was

---

3⁸ *Civil War* VI 93 line 2. See **3** n 3, above.

3⁹ "I have lived"—that is, I have come to the end of life, I am dying. C wrote the same sort of thing to Lamb in two other sets of marginalia three years later: see DONNE *Poems* **61** (May 1811) and BEAUMONT & FLETCHER COPY A **13** (Oct 1811).

4¹ The hobby-horse had been established for a couple of centuries as figure for ridiculous preoccupation, and so C uses it in *BL* ch 4 (*CC*) I 85 (cited by *OED*). But "hobbyhorsical" (which C

also used in Feb 1808 in *CL* III 56) is Laurence Sterne's word, first used in *Tristram Shandy*.

4² C is evidently thinking of WW. The last phrase echoes Mark 1.7; Lamb, who was inclined to make irreverent play upon his own name and Mary's, drew upon this same text when he sent his folio edition of Aquinas to C in Oct 1829: see *LL* III 230.

4³ These rhyme-words occur in *Civil War* VII 5, which C regarded as "a fine Stanza": see **21**, below.

sailing into France, he was encounter'd with a Ship of War apper-
taining to the D. of Exeter; who took him, and brought him back to
Dover; where his Head was stricken off, and his Body left on the
Sands, Anno Regni 27.

Considering the style of this poem & how it is pitched, it is
unpardonable in the Author to have put the particulars of Suffolk's
Death in a *Note*; & yet havinge inserted a Stanza unintelligible
without it. Concerning the abuse of *Notes* in modern works an Essay
might be written usefully.[1]

6 ii 172–5, referring to v 102–5, Queen Margaret's speech

> "And art thou *Suffolk*, thus (said she) betray'd?
> And have my Favours thy Destruction brought?
> Is this their Gain, whom Highness favoureth;
> Who Chief preferr'd, stand as preferr'd to Death?

> "O fatal Grace! without which Men complain,
> And with it perish—What prevails, that We
> Must wear the Crown, and other Men must reign;
> And cannot stand to be, that which We be?
> Must our own Subjects limit and constrain
> Our Favours, whereas they themselves decree?
> Must We our love at their Appointment place?
> Do We Command, and They Direct Our Grace?

> . . . .

> "But well;—We see, altho' the King be Head,
> The State will be the Heart. This Sov'reignty
> Is but in Place, not Pow'r; and governed
> By th' equal Sceptre of *Necessity*.
> And we have seen more Princes ruined
> By their immod'rate Fav'ring privately,
> Than by Severity in general:
> For best He's lik'd, that is alike to all."

5[1] Neither C nor RS had shown
much restraint in adorning their early
poems with illustrative and explanatory
gear: see e.g. *Religious Musings* and *Joan
of Arc*. Another "abuse of *Notes*" to
which C objected a few months later was
the introduction of "*personal* themes in
this AGE OF PERSONALITY" in "the patch-
work Notes (which possess, however, the
comparative merit of being more poetical
than the Text)". *Friend* (*CC*) ii 138 (19
Oct 1809), i 210 and n 3.

This is the most inappropriate Speech in the whole Work: it is indeed so very much ~~off~~ out of character, that I should not be surprised if some thing of nearly the same import were to be in our Old English or Latin Chronicles/ for Daniel is a man of excellent good sense, and had he had to *invent* a speech for the Queen, would, I would fain think, have entered decently, at least, *Racinishly* if not Shakspearianly, into her character[1]—and yet meeting the speech in the shape of history would have [been]*a* seduced by its coincidence with his own modes of reflection to have inserted & versified it. The recommencement of the narration, "Thus *storms* the Lady",[2] is truly *humorous*. Like a Phlegmatist, who conversing with his Lip-brother, the Pipe, in his Mouth, observed—"I know, I'm too—apt—to speak—pre-cip-cipi-cipitately."[3]

7   ii 175 | v 113

> Then as for those who were his Followers
> *   (Being all Choice Men for Virtues, or Deserts)
> He so with Grace and Benefits prefers,
> That he becomes the Monarch of their Hearts.

It is perhaps worth noticing as an excellence suited to the style of the Poetry (whatever may be thought of that) that the accents and scansion of Daniel's Lines more assist the reading & the sense, than in any work, I know. If the Line runs ill to you, you may be sure, you have not read it in its exact sense. The whole represents a grave easy man talking seriously to his friends. Sometimes too he breaks up, for a moment, the feeling of versification; but never by a *contradiction to* it, but by heightening the feeling of conversation—ex. gr. by putting 3 important words in the most important Line of an aphorism: as if at each of the 3 words the Speaker gave a wise nod aided by the motion of the forefinger—[1]

a Word supplied by the editor

6[1] That is, with the polished, even artificial, elegance of Racine, if not with the vigorous natural force of Shakespeare. In the 1809 version of "Satyrane's Letters", C was to deplore "the *kind* of Drama, which is now substituted every where for Shakespeare and Racine", admitting that "I offer violence to my own feelings in joining these names", yet declaring that "the French Tragedies are consistent works of art, and the Offspring of great intellectual power". *Friend* (*CC*) ii 216 (7 Dec 1809). Later comments suggest that for C, Shakespeare and Racine represent the polarity of imagination and fancy: see *SM* (*CC*) 79, *BL* chs 1, 23 (*CC*) i 23, ii 210.

6[2] The opening words (var) of the next stanza, v 106.

6[3] Lamb's stammer could on occasion—as C delighted to recall—produce "Tungstic Acid": see e.g. *CN* i 977.

7[1] C makes the same point about Donne's verse and Beaumont and Fletcher's, in DONNE *Poems* 1, 2 and n.

8 ɪɪ 173, 175 | v 114

> "He only treads the sure and perfect Path
> * To Greatness, who Love and Opinion hath.[''']
>   1   2   3

"To *Greatness*, who *Love* and *Opinion* hath—"
p. 192. 1. 14—where there are 3 emphatic and 3 subemphatic words.[1]

9 ɪɪ 178 | vɪ 2

> When as the King thereof ascertained,

I do not recollect to have seen this word elsewhere, accented as a Pæon Secundus ◡ – ◡ ◡ / but it gives the meaning & brings out the *sensorium*-syllable far better than the present anapestic or Pæon-tertius emphasis.[1] That is "*tain'd*" or "*tained*"?

10 ɪɪ 182 | vɪ 14, referring to Warwick

> He intimates his Mind; and openly
> The present bad Proceedings discommends;
> Laments the State, the People's Misery,
> * And (that which such a Pitier seldom mends)
> Oppression, that sharp two-edged Sword,
> That others wounds, and wounds likewise his Lord.

We can not too highly praise the strain of political morality thro' this Work. No success, no Heroism ever makes the Author forget the immutable Right & Wrong. And if it be objected, that the Right to the Throne is confounded with the right to common property, to an estate or house, yet still this was the Creed of those Ages/ as much the Creed of Henry the IVth & V^th & as Richard the *Second*—yet Daniel was ⟨not⟩[1] *blinded* by it so as to overlook the guilt of

8[1] See **15**, below. "Subemphatic" is not in *OED*.
9[1] I.e. ◡ ◡ – ◡. A paeon—a foot consisting of one long and three shorts—is named *primus, secundus*, etc according to the position of the long syllable. Cf **19**, below.
10[1] Probably Lamb's inserted word (in a different ink and hand). Instances of C's omitting "not" can be seen e.g. in DONNE *Sermons* COPY A **4**, COPY B **11**, and EICHHORN *Alte Testament* **50**. Aware of the psychological interest of habitually omitted words, C made a note in c 1807–8 of "the Law of Mind, by which in writing earnestly while we are thinking, we omit words necessary to the sense...". *CN* ɪɪ 3217 f 70. Several years later he noted: "Mem. The words, you omit in writing... will be generally found to express subjective *Acts*, determining the relation of the Object to your own Being, not objects (i.e. Noun Substantives) themselves. Thus 'not' you will very often have occasion to overline with an ∧ ", and formulated a rule that "the

involving a nation in civil war on an old tho' rightful Claim—see p. 155, Stanza 46.—[2]

11 II 183 | VI 16

"*Anjou* and *Main*, (the Mai[n] that foul appears;
Th' eternal Scar of our dismember'd Land)
Guien, all lost; that did Three Hundred Years
Remain subjected under our Command...."

In the first Line of Stanza 16. of this Book is a Pun in its right place & passion. Had Puns never been used less judiciously than in this Instance & that of the fallen Angels in the 6th Book of Paradise Lost,[1] they would still have been considered as Beauties.—

12 II 186–92 | VI 26–7

. . . .

Artillery, th' Infernal Instrument
New brought from Hell, to scourge Mortality
With hideous Roaring and Astonishment.

[a]Poor Daniel! [? he curses the practical]! Aye! a [...][b] artillery [...] flings out, or will annoy [...]! The very malice prepense of imputing

a Three lines of ms at the foot of II 186, three lines on II 187, and one line and about three words at the foot of II 188 have been heavily obliterated in ink, making reconstruction difficult
b One word illegible

Subjective is the [most] liable to omission ...⟨The *very* frequent omission of the 'not' gives strong confirmation of the Rule...⟩". N 36 ff 5, 22ᵛ–23ᵛ.

10[2] *Civil War* v 46 reads:

His Father's End, in him no Fear
could move
T' attempt the like, against the like of
Might;
Where long Possession now of Fear
and Love,
Seem'd to prescribe ev'n an innated
Right.
So that to prove his State, was to
disprove
Time, Law, Consent, Oath and
Allegiance quite:
And no Way but the Way of Blood
there was,
Thro' which (with all Confusion) he
must pass.

11[1] The speech of Belial uttered in "gamesom mood" after the surprise discharge of "devilish Engins" which "in the second dayes Fight put *Michael* and his Angels to some disorder": the "terms" of Belial's speech being cannon-balls:

Leader, the terms we sent were terms of
weight,
Of hard contents, and full of force
urg'd home,
Such as we might perceive amus'd them
all,
And stumbl'd many: who receives them
right,
Had need from head to foot well
understand;
Not understood, this gift they have
besides,
They shew us when our foes walk not
upright.

Paradise Lost VI 621–7. C refers to this passage again in DONNE *Poems* **51**, remarking upon "Malice the Mother of bad Puns".

to Pandora artillery argues but a [...] case—charges so [...] as [...]ᵃ
[? ʿΡαχιζαλαλαγος]!¹—[.....]ᵇ a [? paltry notion] [...] that
[? agreeable with] [.....]ᶜ
But the passage vexes me: it has spoilt, and discharactered, the
poem, the best of its kind in any language: for spite of a few dazzling
Passages in the Pharsalia it is as much superior to Lucan's (meâ
quidem sententiâ)² as the steady staid gait of manhood to the
all-sort-of-motions of a Hobbitihoy, or as plain and often deep sense
to Stoical declamations. The Pharsalia is really a Hobbitihoy poem
—neither man nor boy. It is to me just what I should have expected
from a youth well educated & of strong natural Talents at 19: and
great works might have followed if he had lived/³ but more probably,
if this work had been composed in his head, & forgotten by
himself—For no man is proof against the popularity of his own
writings.—But in this long [passage]ᵈ what vexes one is, that the whole
might so well have been said in the Author's own person, the
philosophy being shallow indeed & short-sighted (a cowardice of
present evil is the character of the Writers of that age) but it is of
a piece, it harmonizes/ and in the morally, tho' not *intellectually* (for
that is scarcely possible) nobler æra that succeeded even Milton fell
into the nonsense of abusing Fire-arms.—⁴

ᵃ Two words illegible
ᵇ Six words illegible

ᶜ Four words illegible
ᵈ Word supplied by the editor

12¹ "Spine-chilling shouting"—a compound adjective from ῥαχίζω (cleave down the spine) and ἀλαλαγή (shout, war-cry).

12² "In my opinion, at least".

12³ "Hobbitihoy" (hobbledehoy, etc) —an awkward youth between boyhood and manhood. Cf Lamb in "A Dissertation upon Roast Pig": "things between pig and pork—those hobbydehoys".

Marcus Annaeus Lucanus (39–65), as precocious in public life as in writing, was made augur and quaestor by Nero before the required age, and was less than twenty-six when he chose suicide rather than execution for his part in the Pisonian conspiracy against Nero. Of his many writings only *De bello civili* (commonly called the *Pharsalia*) survives in ten books, unfinished, the first three books having been written in his teens. His verse, technically monotonous, is often bombastic and obscure despite his

deep feeling for his subject; Scaliger accused him of barking rather than singing. RS's early admiration for Lucan was probably aroused more by Lucan's expression of republican sentiment than by his poetic accomplishment, and C's use of an epigraph from Lucan in *The Plot Discovered* was evidently so informed. C said later that, although Lucan's "taste was wretched", "the Pharsalia is...a very wonderful work for such a youth as Lucan was". *TT* 2 Sept 1833. To C's contemporaries Lucan was seen as a member of the company of precocious poets killed by the world's insensitivity—e.g. Otway, Chatterton, and (for RS) Kirke White.

12⁴
...yet haply of thy Race
In future dayes, if Malice should abound,
Some one intent on mischief, or inspir'd
With dev'lish machination might devise

13 II 189 | VI 34

> And that abused *Pow'r which thus hath wrought,
> Shall give her self the Sword to cut her Throat.

[Daniel's note:] * *The Church.*

The Poets of Elizabeth & still more of James's time had a half in half hankering for Popery—We see it in Spenser, in Drayton, in Massinger. In dignity of moral character they were wofully inferior to the succeeding age—a fact honorable to Liberty, & therefore to human nature.

14 II 191 | VI 42

> ...and all her People toss'd
> With <u>unkind</u> Tumults, and almost all lost.

the etymon of KINDE is here preserve[d]*a* & unkind = unnatural.

15 II 192 | VI 46

> All round about her Blood and Misery;
> *   Powers betray'd, Princes slain, Kings massacred;

See 175, l. 20ᵗʰ, & the note.[1]

16 II 208 | VI 99

> Yet happy-hapless Day, blest ill-lost Breath,
> Both for our better Fortune, and your own!
> For what foul Wounds, what Spoil, what shameful Death,
> Had by this forward Resolution grown;
> If at St. *Albans, Wakefield, Barnet-Heath,*
> It should*b* unto your Infamy been shown?
> Blest you, that did not teach how great a Fault
> Ev'n Virtue is in Actions that are naught.

an stanza obscure from mismanagement of syntax—a defect, of which there is scarce a second example in our "well-languaged

---

a Letter supplied by the editor
b Lamb underlined "should" and substituted "had", then cancelled "had"

Like instrument to plague the Sons of men
For sin, on Warr and mutual slaughter bent.

Paradise Lost VI 501–6. In ANDERSON COPY B **10–11** C also comments adversely on Daniel's condemnation of gunpowder.

15[1] See **8**, above. Here the "subemphatic" words are so strong as to produce an entirely different effect from that noted in **8** or in **19**.

Daniel", as Spenser most appropriately, as to this fact, calls him, tho'
the phrase stands in contrast to the sense—[1]
Southey! rarely will the English Tongue admit ~~of~~ participles of
substantives.—[2]

17   ıı 209 | vı 101

The wŏrkĭng Spírĭt cĕás'd not, tho' Work dĭd cease,

A whole Book might be written, neither diffuse or uninstructive, on
the metrical excellence of the 5ᵗʰ line of the CIst Stanza.

The pause after Spirit compels a stress on ceas'd, & so makes ceas'd
not, by addition of the pause after not, = to a spondee—a fine effect
after the Tribrach, or ᴗ ᴗ ᴗ.—

Spirit, Body, money, honey, & two or 3 more perhaps which I do
not recollect, are remnants of genuine *metre* in our language—they
are, at least always may be, Pyrrhics, i.e. ᴗ ᴗ = -: as a a delicate
Ear may instantly perceive & prove that Accent, contrary to the
almost universal opinion, shortens the syllable on which it rests; for
~~on~~ in these words there is an equal accent on both syllables—hence
they are both short—The wŏrkĭng Spírĭt (a pause equal to ᴗ) ceás'd
nŏt, tho' Work dĭd ceàse. N.B. This is a valuable Remark.

18   ıı 210 | vı 105

A stirring Humour gen'rally possess'd
Those Peace-spilt Times, weary of being well:

either (or = to) spoilt

19   ıı 211 | vı 106

Th' abused World so hastily is led,
(Some for Revenge, some for Wealth, some for Delight)

16[1] "Well-languaged"—which C in
BL ch 18 (*CC*) ıı 78 considered a
"well-merited epithet" as applied to
Daniel—comes not from Spenser but
from William Browne *Britannia's Pas-
torals* ıı ii 303; but Spenser does praise
Daniel in *Colin Clout* lines 416ff. C
notices in passing that Spenser (i.e.
Browne), in the act of praising Daniel's
conduct of language, has himself com-
mitted the solecism of forming a par-
ticiple on a noun: see n 2, below.
16[2] In Jun 1814, in SOUTHEY *Joan
of Arc*, C remarked of "The mother's
anguish'd shriek": "Not English. A
Participle presupposes a verb— now there
is no such verb as 'to anguish.' ergo, there
can be no such participle as
'anguished'."

p. 192 & 175.[1]

◡◡◡ – / ◡◡◡ – / ◡◡◡ – /: two Pæon quarts with an anapest interposed,[2] 14 instead of 15, the pauses more than making up the deficient time/ so very much more indeed, that I cannot but admire the metrical judgement of the Poet—[3]

20   II 216–17 | VII 2

> The Queen abroad, with a revenging Hand
> (Arm'd with her own Disgrace, and others Spite,
> Gath'ring th'Oppressed Party of the Land)
> Held over him the threatning Sword of Might;
> That forc'd him in the Terms of Awe to stand,
> (Who else had burst-up Right, to come t'his Right)
> And kept him so confus'd, that he knew not
> To make use of the Means which he had got.

In the mind of a man like Daniel, neither Priest or Lawyer, too honest to falsify a notion of Duty, and too good by nature to stifle a sense of general misery, this mistake (common to all his Contemporaries except Buchanan, Knox, & Raleigh)[1] (I speak of Authors) of the Jus Individui de re individuâ for the Munus Individui *propter* rem publicam[2] occasioned a civil war, bloodless indeed, yet as perplexed as that which the same mistake called into action by ambition produced in the *real* World. See Judge Foster's excellent animadversions on Hales ~~obs~~ concerning Kings de jure & de facto.—[3]

19[1] See **15** and **8**, above.

19[2] A *pæon quart[us]*—a paeon with the accent on the fourth syllable; see **9**, above.

19[3] I.e. 8 short syllables + 3 long syllables (the equivalent of 6 short syllables) make 14 metrical units; on the same calculation, the iambic pentameter makes 5 × 3 = 15 metrical units. For C's conviction that the prosodic measurement of a line of verse depends upon a sense of duration and upon the pauses in meaningful utterance see DONNE *Poems* **1** n 1.

20[1] George Buchanan (1506–82), John Knox (1505–72), and Sir Walter Ralegh (c 1552–1618).

20[2] The common error was to mistake "the Right of the Individual in a personal matter" for "the Duty of the Individual *for the sake of* the state"—a distinction that C often drew. See e.g. *Friend* (*CC*) I 192, and 191–2.

20[3] Sir Matthew Hale's views on the status of kings de jure and de facto, as expressed in his *Pleas of the Crown* (1678), were refuted by Sir Michael Foster (1689–1763) in *A Report of Some Proceedings on the Commission...for the Trial of the Rebels in the Year 1746...to which are added Discourses upon a Few Branches of the Crown Law* (1762).

21   ii ⁻3 referring to ii 217ᵃ | vii 5

> Whether it be, that Form and Eminence,
> Adorn'd with Pomp and State, begets this Awe;
> Or whether an in-bred Obedience
> To Right and Pow'r, doth our Affections draw:
> Or whether Sacred Kings work Reverence,
> And make that Nature now, which was first Law;
> We know not—But the Head will draw the Parts;
> And Good Kings, with our Bodies, have our Hearts.

p. 217. V. a fine Stanza.—[1]

22   ii 218 | vii 8

> As usually it fares with those that plot
> These Machines of Ambition, and high Pride;

The word was pronounced, sometimes, *Matchins*, sometimes
Mackins, from máchĭnă.[1]

23   ii 220 | vii 14

> Wrapt in a strong and curious Ordinance
> Of many Articles, bound solemnly:

curious = careful in the extreme, solicitously guarded.[1]

ᵃ Written above 3, but later

21[1] See **4**, above.
22[1] "In 17–18th c.... often stressed on
the first syll." *OED* "machine".

23[1] *OED* "curious" i 1 *a* and *b*. C
copied *Civil War* vii 14–15 into N 18 in
c Nov–Dec 1809: *CN* iii 3655.

DANTE ALIGHIERI
1265–1321

C's earliest known exploration into Dante was his borrowing of Henry Boyd's translation of the *Inferno* from the Bristol Library in late Jun 1796. *Bristol LB* 80; cf 31, 32. Soon after, he noted a project for a "Poem in one Book in the manner of Dantè on the excursion of Thor—". *CN* I 170; cf II 2919. His desire to read Dante in the original blossomed as his departure for the Mediterranean approached: in Feb 1804 he asked the Wordsworths to send him in London "Dante & a Dictionary". *CL* II 1059. The Beaumonts also gave him a copy of the *Divina Commedia* (Venice 1774) as a going-away present. By c May 1805 he could say: "Dante, Ariosto, Giordano Bruno [shall] be my Italy" (*CN* II 2598), and from that year transcripts of favourite passages in Dante begin to appear in the notebooks, usually from the *Canzone*. See *CN* II 3012–3014, 3017, 3108; but cf 3014 for C's difficulty in reading *Canzone* XIV. Page-references to Dante in *CN* II and III match the *Opere* (5 vols Venice 1793)—a book C seems to have acquired in the Mediterranean and that survived to be catalogued as *Green SC* (1880) 152.

C's only surviving extended discussion of Dante is in *CN* III 4498—a literary lecture prepared for 11 Mar 1819. In Feb 1818 he told Cary that he intended to publish his earlier "Critique...devoted to the names of Dante, Donne, and Milton" (of 27 Feb 1818), but did not do so. For his advocacy of Cary's translation of Dante, in the same lecture, see COPY B, below.

Copy A

Dante [Divina Commedia] con una breve e sufficiente dichiarazione del senso letterale [by P. Venturi] diversa in più luoghi da quella degli commentatori. Alla santita' di N. S. Clemente XII. [Ed G. B. Placidi.] 3 pts. Lucca 1732. 8°.

Collection of N. F. D. Coleridge

Inscribed on the title-page of Vol I, by Mrs C or by SC in her youth: "S. T. Coleridge Gretahall Keswick". Signature of "Edith Coleridge 1852", who has written at the end of *Purgatorio* (II 273) "Nov. 5th 1887" and at the end of *Paradiso* (III 294) "Dec. 22nd 1887 Eldon Lodge Torquay".

This seems to be the copy sent to London by WW in response to C's request of Feb 1804, the Beaumont gift being the Venice 1774 edition. C left the book behind at Allan Bank in Oct 1810; it is twice marked as C's in Wordsworth LC and was included in WW's list of books to be sent to Highgate in 1829–30.

DATE. Possibly 1804–5.

1   II 5

Pacchiaretti[1]

1[1] C seems first to have encountered in Germany this "sweet dessert wine from the south of Spain... 'well known on the tables of the rich'", called *Pajarete*, for which see *CN* I 371n. In a letter of 8 Nov 1798 he referred to it obliquely as "A Spanish Wine—I have forgot the name" (*CL* I 439), but by the time he had revised that letter as part of "Satyrane's Letters" (Dec 1809) he had identified the wine as "Pacchiaretti". *Friend* (*CC*) II 216. The first occurrence of the name—always so spelled by C—is in *CN* I 371 (c 1798–9); it occurs twice in isolation in notebooks—*CN* II 3040 (May 1807) and 4107 (1811)—is written on a front flyleaf of RS's copy of PASCAL *Les Provinciales* (Sept 1803), and was once legible in pencil on a sheet of azure laid paper used as a wrapper for several "packets" of paper on which WW's poems were transcribed (Dove Cottage MS 44 [MS M]). Possibly the word had some secret personal meaning for him.

Copy B

The Vision; or Hell, Purgatory, and Paradise, of Dante Alighieri. Translated by the Rev. Henry Francis Cary, A.M.... The second edition corrected. With the life of Dante, additional notes, and an index. 3 vols. London 1819. 8°.

British Museum C 45 d 4–6

Perhaps a presentation copy from Cary, but there is no record of the transaction. James Gillman's bookplate on p ⁻5 (p–d) of each volume. A passage in ɪ xliii is marked in pencil.

Henry Francis Cary (1772–1844) published his translation of the *Inferno*, with Italian text, in 2 vols 1805–6; the first edition of the complete translation was in 3 vols in 1814. C had read Cary's juvenile *Sonnets and Odes* (1787) when he wrote the introduction to his "Sheet of Sonnets" in 1796: *PW* (EHC) ɪɪ 1140 and n 2. When C met Cary by chance at Littlehampton in Sept 1817, Cary immediately recognised the man whose work he had quoted in his 1814 Preface, and lent C a copy of the 1814 edition. After reading only "two books and passages here and there of the other" C told Cary on 29 Oct 1817 that "In itself the Metre is, compared with any English Poem of one quarter the length, the most varied and harmonious to my ear of any since Milton...". *CL* ɪv 779; see also 780–2. Determined to see the translation more widely recognised, C praised it in his lecture of 27 Feb 1818 and in the 1818 *Friend*. See *Friend* (*CC*) ɪ 429. The effect was prompt and impressive: "The work, which had been published four years, but had remained in utter obscurity, was at once eagerly sought after. About a thousand copies of the first edition, that remained on hand, were immediately disposed of; in less than three months a new edition was called for." Henry Cary *Memoir of the Rev. Henry Francis Cary* (2 vols 1847) ɪɪ 28. Samuel Rogers later dismissed the younger Cary's account of the Littlehampton meeting as "a mistake", saying that "Moore mentioned the work [i.e. Cary's Dante] to me with great admiration; I mentioned it to Wordsworth; and he to Coleridge, who had never heard of it till then, and who forthwith read it". *Recollections of the Table-Talk of Samuel Rogers* (New York 1856) 282–3. Rogers's evident desire to establish that Cary's translation "owes some of its celebrity to me" does not negate either account of how C first came to read the translation—see e.g. *WL* (*M* 2) ɪɪ 382, *CL* ɪv 592—but it did lead him to report as an eye-witness that at the lecture in which C praised Cary there were "about a hundred and twenty persons in the room". C took prompt and vigorous action to interest a publisher in a new edition of Cary's translation; with the support of WW and Rogers it was published in Jul 1819 by Taylor and Hessey, who were later to become C's publisher. See *CL* ɪv 823–4, 827–8, 832–3, 834–5, 953. In his Preface Cary wrote: "Amongst the few into whose hands [this translation] fell, about two years ago, Mr. Coleridge became one; and I have both a pride and a pleasure in acknowledging that it has been chiefly owing to the prompt and strenuous exertions of that gentleman in recommending the book to public notice, that the opportunity has been afforded me of sending it forth in its present form." Cary became Assistant Keeper of Printed Books in the BM in 1826. For C's request for help and advice in preparing an annotated edition of Asgill's *Collection of Tracts* in 1832, see ASGILL headnote.

DATE. Possibly autumn 1819, soon after publication in Jul.

1   II 193, pencil, cropped | *Purgatory* XXI 92–4

> Statius they name me still. Of Thebes I sang,
> And next of great Achilles: but i' the' way
> Fell* with the second burthen.

[footnote:] * Statius lived to write only a small part of the Achilleid. This is the general belief; but I think, erroneous. It se[ems] to me an entire poem—Achilles Puer.[1]

2   III 4–5 | *Paradise* I 12–17

>   Benign Apollo! this last labour aid;
> * And make me such a vessel of thy worth,
> As thy own laurel claims, of me belov'd.
> Thus far hath one of steep Parnassus' brows
> Suffic'd me; henceforth, there is need of both
> For my remaining enterprize.

* A very difficult passage. I speak with much diffidence. But I am inclined to think that the sense of

> "si fatto vaso
> Come dimanda dar l'amato lauro"

is = "a Vessel such As doth demand the loved laurel's gift."[1]

1[1] The *Achilleid* of Publius Papinius Statius (c 45–96), which describes the education and boyhood exploits of Achilles up to his departure for Troy— "Achilles as a Boy", in C's phrase—is now generally held to have been "brought to a conclusion in the second book by the poet's death". *OCD*. Nevertheless, C's view has the substance of intuition, as does the judgement of those who regard *Kubla Khan* as a complete poem in the face of C's apparent acknowledgement of its incompleteness. WW's library included ten unspecified volumes of "Statius, Apollodorus, Homer, &c &c Gr. & Latin" "with the autographs of Coleridge and Wordsworth": *Wordsworth SC* (1859) 436.

2[1] COPY A (Lucca 1732), Venice 1774, and Venice 1793 (see DANTE general note) have the same readings. C quotes exactly, except "si" for "sì" and "amato lauro" for "amat' alloro", the latter no doubt a slip, influenced by the Latin and English words. His translation too is exact, leaving by inversion the same possible ambiguity as the Italian.

The line following[2] refers, I conjecture, to the division of all objects of Thought into Form, and Essence, το γινομενον και το οντως ον[3]—the former sufficed for Hell & Purgatory. In Heaven alone true Reality subsists. In other words, the Poet says—Hitherto, the Poet & Moralist has sufficed; but henceforward the *Philosopher* must be added: my "Paradiso" *must* be metaphysical. Yet how to make this compatible & co-present with the equally necessary Element of Poetry—hic labor est![4] Both the Powers of Intellect, the Discursive & Sensuous, and the Rational Super-sensuous, must unite at their summits.[5]

Thus too: Dante did not mean to speak of Apollo's *own* Song in his strife with Marsyas; but asks for an evacuation and exinanition of all *Self* in *him* (Dante) like the unsheathing of Marsyas[6]—that so he (Dante) might become a mere Vessel, or Wine-skin, of the Deity.

3   iii 5 |*Paradise* i 24–7

> Thou shalt behold me of thy favour'd tree
> Come to the foot, and crown myself with leaves:
> For that to honour thou and my high theme ·
> Will fit me.

1. 24. I am tempted and yet ashamed to suggest the possibility of "al" having taken place of the original "il" by mistake or carelessness of the earliest Copyists. Venir vedràmi il tuo diletto legno = This beloved Tree shall behold me come and crown me with those leaves, of which the Theme and Thou shalt make me

2[2] Lucca 1732 and Venice 1793 both suggest that the two peaks represent philosophy and theology. Cary's note reads: "He appears to mean nothing more than that this part of his poem will require greater exertion on his part."

2[3] "That which is becoming [coming into being] and that which actually *is*"—Greek philosophical terms to which the mediaeval abstractions "Form and Essence" are approximate equivalents. The term το γινομενον corresponds to "Form" in the Aristotelian sense that everything being-what-it-is assumes form in the process of becoming-what-it-must.

2[4] The phrase "hoc opus, hic labor est" (*Aeneid* 6.128)—"this is the work, this is the task"—refers to the difficulty of retracing one's steps back from Avernus. It occurs many times in C's writing; for an early context see e.g. *CL* ii 810.

2[5] Cf *CN* iii 4498 f 139ᵛ.

2[6] The invocation to Apollo continues, in Cary's version: "Do thou | Enter into my bosom, and there breathe, | So as when Marsyas by thy hand was dragg'd | Forth from his limbs, unsheathed." The satyr Marsyas, having taken over the flute (or oboe) from its dissatisfied inventor Athena, challenged Apollo to a contest in music. Apollo won, and, acting on their agreement that the winner could do what he liked with the loser, flayed Marsyas alive.

worthy.[1]—But those only who see the difficulty of the Original can do justice to M[r] Carey's Translation—which may now & then not be Dante's *Words*, but always, always, *Dante*.

4 III 6, pencil and ink[a] | *Paradise* I 36–41

> Through divers passages, the world's bright lamp
> Rises to mortals; but, through that which joins
> Four circles with the threefold cross, in best
> Course, and in happiest constellation set,
> He comes; and, to the worldly wax, best gives
> It's temper and impression..

Admirably translated. O how few will appreciate its value! Genius is not alone sufficient—it must be present, indeed, in the Translator, in order to supply a *negative* Test by its Sympathy; to *feel* that it *has been* well done. But it is *Taste, Scholarship, Discipline,* TACT, that must do it.[1]

5 III 6 | *Paradise* I 41–2

> Morning there,
> Here eve was well nigh by such passage made;

l. 42. ? Is not the "*quasi*" here enclitic on "foce"? This *Gorge*, as it were?[1]—mem. To recommend Mr Carey to run his eye thro' Swedenberg's Arcana Cœlestia.[2]

---

[a] The first two words are in pencil. The second sentence is in pencil, overtraced in ink evidently by C; the rest in ink in a smaller hand than the opening

3[1] All C's editions read:

Venir vedràmi al tuo diletto legno,
  E coronarmi allor di quelle foglie,
  Che la matera e tu mi farai degno.

By emending "al" to "il" C accounts for the apparent third person "vedrà": "Thy beloved tree shall see me come...". Modern editors read "vedra'" (for "vedrai")—"Thou shalt see me come...". C's "and crown me" is at best ambiguous: the text means "thou shalt see me crown myself".

4[1] In C's view the sense of touch serves an especially important cognitive function, in the moral and intellectual fields as in the physical. As early as 1802 he had used the word "tact" to indicate

an exquisite critical discrimination: see *CL* II 810, and cf 856 (cited in *OED*). See also BÖHME **24** n 9.

5[1] C's suggestion is made less plausible by the use of "foci" in line 36, without any such qualification. The word can indeed mean gorge, throat, mouth, narrow valley, pass, etc. Cf φάραγξ in AESCHYLUS *Prometheus* 1 and n 1. C takes *quasi* in the Latin sense of "as it were", not in Italian, "almost".

5[2] Emanuel Swedenborg (1688–1772) *Arcana coelestia* (8 vols 1749–56), a massive exposition of the internal and spiritual sense of Genesis and Exodus. C annotated several works of Swedenborg, but no marked or annotated copy of *Arcana coelestia* is recorded.

6 III 9, pencil | *Paradise* I 74–6

> Whenas the wheel which thou dost ever guide,
> Desired Spirit! with it's harmony
> * Temper'd of thee and measur'd, charm'd mine ear;

* Not in my dear & honored Friend's *own* style—né Car- nè Dant-esca.[1] Better as well as more literal—"made me attent."? I doubt, whether "desiderato" is here a Vocative. I rather think—tho' the o final is against me—that it is an objective governed by the active-transitive verb, "sempiterni"—dost sempiternalize A thing desired.[2]

7 III 10, pencil | *Paradise* I 97–9

> Whence, after utt'rance of a piteous sigh,
> She tow'rds me bent her eyes, with such a look,
> As on her frenzied child a mother casts;

l. 99. "frenzied" too strong for "deliro"—dreaming? feverous? brain-wilder'd?[1]

8 III 58–9, pencil | *Paradise* VII 33–4

> The nature with it's maker thus conjoin'd,
> * Created first was blameless, pure and good;

* I interpret the Mosaic "GOOD" by equal and fitted to the wise and gracious purposes of the Λογου του Δημιουργου.[1] How otherwise could it be applied to the bestial and even to the Inanimate? Jacob Boehm, who took the word in ~~its~~ the common sense and yet saw that the Fall of Man *could* not on this supposition be cleared

6[1] "Neither Cary- nor Dante-esque".
6[2] All C's editions read:

Quando la ruota, che tu sempiterni
Desiderato, a se mi fece atteso
Con l'armonia, che temperi, e
discerni…

John D. Sinclair (3 vols Oxford 1971) translates: "When the wheel which Thou, being desired, makest eternal held me intent on itself by the harmony Thou dost attune and distribute…"—which makes "desiderato" nominative rather than vocative, and implies, as also does

C's suggestion, that the Love that rules the universe does so by being desired. C's "objective" is more forced and less probable. "Sempiternalize" is not in *OED* (but "sempiternize" is).
7[1] All C's eds read: "Che madre fa sopra figliuol deliro".
8[1] "Of the Word of the Creator"—i.e. the Jehovah-Word, for which see BIBLE COPY B 11 and n 1, **119** n 1. The "Mosaic 'GOOD'" is in the formula that, in Gen 1, closes each phase of creation: "and God saw that it was good".

from inherent contradictions, too boldly cut the Knot: affirming that in the 1st C. of Gen. the Veil was on Moses's face, relatively to his own Vision as well as for others.[2]

8[2] Moses put a veil over his face, not in the presence of God, but when he gave the commandments to the children of Israel, who were afraid of the shining of his face after he came down from Mt Sinai: see Exod 34.30–5. For Böhme on Moses's veil see *Aurora* ch 18 and *The Three Principles* ch 17 §§4, 20–1, 36: *Works* ɪ i 171, ɪ ii 146ff.

ALEXANDER CHARLES LOUIS D'ARBLAY
1794–1837

The Vanity of All Earthly Greatness. A funeral sermon on His Majesty, George the Fourth, preached in Camden Chapel, St. Pancras, on Sunday, July XVIII, MDCCCXXX.... Second edition, corrected, &c. London 1830. 8°.

Bound as fourth in "Pamphlets—Divinity".

British Museum C 126 h 2 (4)

Inscribed on the half-title verso: "S. T. Coleridge Esq^e. From one of the humblest admirers of his genius   The Author".

Alexander d'Arblay, son of Fanny Burney, was tenth wrangler at Cambridge in 1818, took orders, and was Perpetual Curate, Camden Town 1824–37.

DATE. Perhaps 1830, soon after publication.

1   p 27

But with that Ancient of Days "who is of purer eyes than to behold *] iniquity," there is but one source of pardon and of life, even the precious blood of Christ shed upon the cross: of Christ, who, like that unvarying nature which He rules, hath no respect of persons or of times: of Christ, the sole fulfiller of the law, the Sun of Righteousness shining on all alike, "the same yesterday, to-day, and for ever:" of Christ, the beams of whose mercy gild with equal rays of hope the sceptre of the sovereign, and the fetters of the slave!

[*] Deeply convinced that in Christ alone God loveth the World, and resting wholly on *Him* as our alone Life, Righteousness and Resurrection, I nevertheless never hear from the lips or read from the pen of a Clergyman of the Ch. of Engl. the words, "precious Blood of Christ shed on the Cross" without yearning for a definite *comment*, a precise interpretation.[1]

[1] See 1 Pet 1.18–19: "ye know that ye were not redeemed with corruptible things...But with the precious blood of Christ, as of a lamb without blemish and without spot". The phrase was carried into the Prayer of Humble Access in the Communion service: "Grant us ...that...our souls [may be] washed through his most precious blood". For C on redemption see FIELD 12 and ETERNAL PUNISHMENT 4 (last clause).

GEORGE DARLEY

1795-1846

Sylvia; or, the May Queen. A lyrical drama. London 1827. 8°.

Victoria College Library (Coleridge Collection)

Inscribed on the half-title: "S. T. Coleridge Esqr With the Author's Respects".

George Darley, Irish poet and mathematician, educated at Trinity College, Dublin (BA 1820), travelled in Italy, and settled in London in 1822. As a contributor to the *London Magazine* he made the acquaintance of Lamb, who, in Feb 1825, recognised a paper of Darley's on the dramatists as representing "the only clever hand they have". *LL* ii 460. Darley soon became acquainted with the circle of Lamb's younger friends, Allan Cunningham and Bryan Procter particularly, and with C's friend and contemporary, H. F. Cary. *LL* iii 158, 167, 383. Whether Darley knew of C from Lamb and his friends, or directly through Cary, or perhaps through the younger Irishman John Anster, does not appear; there seems to be no record of Darley and C meeting.

DATE. Perhaps 1827. But cf Lamb's sending a copy of *Sylvia*—"Darley's very poetical poem"—to Bernard Barton in Mar 1829: *LL* iii 213.

1 pp +2-+3, pencil

Yes!—There is much & of no ordinary *promise* in this Man's Volume! and sad it is that the very points and passages that attest his merits will be the last, that the popular Judgement would notice—or perhaps *notice*, but as the demerits. And yet accuse not the Popular Judgement—That which is *best*, it declares such, but that which is all but *worst*, it places in the next place to the Best.—Of the *comparative* highest it misjudges, only because it is not positively *the High*—Meantime, the Low it judges by another standard/ its fitness to its *existing* Self—Wordsworth appeals to the Ideal in every man's Mind—i.e. what he knows, he ought to be—Sir W. Scott to the actual, at the poor Beast that dances to his Chains.[1]—O what an awful Thing is a *Poet*!—Logician, *Linguist* in the purest sense, for

---

[1] Cf Thomas Gray *The Progress of Poesy* line 80: "And coward Vice that revels in her chains", and *Ode for Music* line 6: "Servitude that hugs her chains". Cf *Friend* (*CC*) i 90 and n.

it must be at once the particular & yet in its essence a *universal* language, the identity of *Idiom* & *Catholism*[2]—And—but I have said all in saying this—for Words are the whole communicable utterable Man!

S. T. Coleridge

1[2] C has refracted the relation between "particular" and "universal" into two terms proper to a discussion of language, one of them eroded by special use, the other not in *OED*: "idiom" (ἰδίωμα—peculiarity, specific property, unique feature) and "Catholism" (from τὰ καθόλου—"universals" in Aristotle's memorable distinction between poetry and history in *Poetics* 1451^{b}7, for C's awareness of which see e.g. BEAUMONT & FLETCHER COPY A 5 and n 2).

JOHN DAVISON

1777–1834

Discourses on Prophecy, in which are considered its structure, use, and inspiration; being the substance of twelve sermons preached in the Chapel of Lincoln's Inn in the Lecture founded by the Right Reverend William Warburton, &c. Second edition. London 1825. 8º.

Not located. *Lost List.* Annotations here reprinted from *LR* IV 385–99.

Probably Edward Coleridge's copy. In a letter of c 11 Nov 1825 from Ramsgate, C told Edward Coleridge that he had read this book and "the two Volumes of Skelton"—which he also annotated. He had found Davison's book "a most valuable Accession to our Theological Literature" but confessed that "the first 120 pages excited an expectation, which the remainder of the Volume did not *quite* answer": the marginalia begin on p 140; of two quasi-marginalia in *CN* IV 5269, 5271, the first refers to pp 145–55. He considered the subject of prophecy "a Mine, the richest Veins of which still remain to be opened", and hoped that Edward would distinguish himself by continuing the inquiry. *CL* V 510; see also **13**, below. On 31 Jan 1826 he told Edward that he had returned the Davison book, the two volumes of Skelton, and his copy of Matthiae's *Copious Greek Grammar*. *CL* VI 549. MATTHIAE and SKELTON are known to have been Edward's; the DAVISON probably was too.

Edward Coleridge (1800–83), youngest son of Col James Coleridge and brother of HNC, was a master at Eton 1824–50, and took Henry Gillman into his house in 1825. *CN* IV 5214. In 1823 he began to show an interest in C's published works (*CL* V 285–7); presentation copies of C's books and C's annotations in some of Edward's books amplify the special trust that C placed in Edward in allowing him, in Sept 1825, the privilege of reading "some of the Memorandum Books of old date". See *CL* V 492–3, 501, VI 585. Edward first brought Gioacchino de' Prati to see C in Highgate (*CL* V 452), and C arranged for Edward to meet Lamb, Irving, and Blanco White (*CL* V 521).

DATE. Nov 1825, at Ramsgate; the book was returned by 31 Jan 1826 (see above).

---

1 p 140 | Discourse IV pt i "State of Prophecy Contemporary with the Promulgation of the Mosaic Law"

As to systems of religion alien from Christianity, if any of them have taught the doctrine of eternal life, the reward of obedience, as a dogma of belief, that doctrine is not their boast, but their burden and difficulty, inasmuch as they could never defend it. They could neither justify it on independent grounds of deduction, nor produce their warrant and authority to teach it. In such precarious and unauthenticated principles, it may pass for a conjecture, a pious fraud, or a splendid phantom: it cannot wear the dignity of Truth.

Ah, why did not Mr. Davison adhere to the manly, the glorious, strain of thinking from p. 134. (*Since Prophecy*, &c.) to p. 139. (*that mercy*) of this discourse?[1] A fact is no subject of scientific demonstration speculatively: we can only bring analogies, and these Heraclitus, Socrates, Plato, and others did bring; but their main argument remains to this day the main argument—namely, that none but a wicked man dares doubt it. When it is not in the light of promise, it is in the law of fear, at all times a part of the conscience, and presupposed in all spiritual conviction.

2 p 160

Some, indeed, have sought the <u>Star</u> and the <u>Sceptre</u>[a] of Balaam's prophecy, where they cannot well be found, in the reign of David; for though a Sceptre might be there, the Star properly is not: and perhaps that vision of the prophet's mind carried far into futurity, "I shall see him, but not now; I shall behold him, but not nigh," is expressive of something more than an ideal vision, the mirrour of

---

[a] These two words, in italic in *LR* but in roman in the printed text, are taken to have been underlined by C

1[1] For C's dissatisfaction with the later part of the book see headnote, above. In pp 134–9 Davison invites "the religionist" to consider "that the obligation of man to obedience under the divine law, does not rest upon any specific pledge, or institution, of reward or punishment, at all", affirming that "The relation of man to God, as his Creator and Sovereign Lord, is the immediate reason and principle of duty; and the perception of this relation is the evidence of the duty" (p 134). "...It is the piety and virtue of mind directed to Him as the object of homage and obedience, that gives to our action whatever degree of rectitude it can have....A virtuous man, conforming to his conscience as to the will of God, has his virtue in that conformity, whether he know of any distinct reward or not" (p 136). "...The essence of the obligation, and the virtue of compliance with it, are independent of the kind, or the degree, of the retribution annexed" (p 137). In the end he submits it "to the Christian religionist, whether he can take just offence at the omission of the doctrine of an eternal reward in the Mosaic Code, when he adverts to the important principle of his own faith, that such a reward is not attainable by that Law" (p 138). "In his own time, when God, by the work of Redemption, restored man to the confessed capacity of eternal life...then it was his gracious purposes were fully disclosed..." (p 139). In *CN* IV 5269 C noted of pp 145–55: "Not so satisfactory as the rest of this excellent Volume—."

prophecy; perhaps it is nothing less than the mysterious foreboding of that real sight, which all shall have in beholding Him who is the chief object of prophecy, when "he cometh with the clouds, and *every eye shall see him*; and they also which pierced him, and all kindreds of the earth shall wail because of him." [Rev 1.7]

Surely this is a very weak reason. A far better is, I think, suggested by the words, *I shall see him—I shall behold him*;—which in no intelligible sense could be true of Balaam relatively to David.[1]

3 p 162

The Israelites could not endure the Voice and Fire of Mount Sinai. They asked an intermediate messenger between God and them, who should temper the awfulness of his voice, and impart to them his will in a milder way.

Deut. xviii. 15.[1] Is the following argument worthy our consideration? If, as the learned Eichhorn, Paulus of Jena, and others of their school,[2] have asserted, Moses waited forty days for a tempest, and then, by the assistance of the natural magic he had learned in the temple of Isis, *initiated* the law,[3] all our experience and knowledge of the way in which large bodies of men are affected would lead us

2[1] Balaam's vision of "a Star out of Jacob, and a Sceptre [that] shall rise out of Israel" is in Num 24.17, the whole story of Balaam being in Num 22–4. The Star of David is traditionally associated with the Messiah; the "Sceptre" of AV is more properly rendered "comet" (as in *NEB*). Both Davison and C wish to establish the prophecy as messianic, not historical. C's "far better" argument, based on Num 24.17, is that Balaam (contemporary with Moses) could not see David in this life, but he will see Christ at the Second Coming.

3[1] "The Lord thy God will raise up unto thee a Prophet from the midst of thee, of thy brethren, like unto me; unto him ye shall hearken"—from Moses' second address to the people of Israel. Davison had quoted this on the previous page.

3[2] C sometimes referred to Eichhorn and Paulus, and other founders of the Higher Criticism, as "Neologists":

see BAXTER *Reliquiae* COPY B **45** n 1 and *CN* III 4401. On Paulus see also DE WETTE **18** n 3.

3[3] The assertion that Moses borrowed the magic and institutions of Egypt was common among rationalistic German biblical critics: see e.g. Carl F. Dornedden "Erläuterung der aegyptischen Götterlehre in besonderer Rücksicht auf den Ursprung des Mosaischen Kosmogonie und des Mosaischen Gottes" in EICHHORN *Allgemeine Bibliothek* x (1800) 548–9, on which C commented in *CN* IV 4794 f 34ᵛ (c 1820–23), agreeing that Moses probably took the "purest" elements of the Egyptian doctrine. See also *CN* IV 5219 (7 May 1825), on Acts 7.22. The detail of Moses waiting for a tempest, however, has not been traced in the published works of Eichhorn or Paulus. C may have heard of it in one of Eichhorn's lectures: see also EICHHORN *Alte Testament* **29** and n.

to suppose that the Hebrew people would have been keenly excited, interested, and elevated by a spectacle so grand and so flattering to their national pride. But if the voices and appearances were indeed divine and supernatural, well must we assume that there was a distinctive, though verbally inexpressible, terror and disproportion to the mind, the senses, the whole *organismus* of the human beholders and hearers, which might both account for, and even in the sight of God justify, the trembling prayer which deprecated a repetition.[4]

4   p 164

To justify its application to Christ, the resemblance between him and Moses has often been deduced at large, and drawn into a variety of particulars, among which several points have been taken, minute and precarious, or having so little of dignity or clearness of representation in them, that it would be wise to discard them from the prophetic evidence. The great and essential characters of similitude between Christ and Moses are in the fulness and luminous intuition of their communications with God.... In these points, none of the other prophets were like to Moses; and in these, Moses is like to Christ, as the less to his greater.

With our present knowledge we are both enabled and disposed thus to evolve the full contents of the word *like*;[1] but I cannot help thinking that the contemporaries of Moses (if not otherwise orally instructed), must have understood it in the first and historical sense, at least, of Joshua.[2]

5   p 168 | note to p 133

A distinguished Commentator on the Laws of Moses, Michaelis, vindicates their *temporal* sanctions, on the ground of the Mosaic code being of the nature of a *Civil* System, to "the statutes" of which the rewards of a future eternal state would be incongruous and unsuitable. But this solution of the matter is inadmissible, inasmuch as the Law comprehends both a *moral* and a *civil* code, and prescribes to the

---

3[4] See Deut 18.16.
4[1] Deut 34.10: "And there arose not a prophet since in Israel like unto Moses...".

4[2] Deut 34.9: "And Joshua the son of Nun was full of the spirit of wisdom; for Moses had laid his hands upon him: and the children of Israel hearkened unto him...".

private as well as the *public* duty. It was a Law of Religion, as well of Government. The perfect love of God, which is one commandment of Moses; the Tenth commandment of the Decalogue, and many others, never can be reduced to "statutes of the land," to be administered and enforced on the rules of a civil government. [Citing J. D. Michaelis *Mosaic Law* Art xiv.]

I never read either of Michaelis's Works,[1] but the same view came before me whenever I reflected on the Mosaic Code. Who expects in realities of any kind the sharp outline and exclusive character of scientific classification? It is the predominance of the characterizing constituent that gives the name and class. Do not even our own statute laws, though co-existing with a separate religious Code, contain many *formulæ* of words which have no sense but for the conscience? Davison's stress on the word *covet*, in the tenth commandment, is, I think, beyond what so ancient a Code warrants;[2] —and for the other instances, Michaelis would remind him that the Mosaic constitution was a strict theocracy, and that Jehovah, the God of all, was their *king*. I do not know the particular mode in which Michaelis propounds and supports this position; but the position itself, as I have presented it to my own mind, seems to me among the strongest proofs of the divine origin of the Law, and an essential in the harmony of the total scheme of Revelation.

6   p 180 | Discourse IV pt ii "On the Temporal Prophecy Concurrent with the Promulgation of the Law"

Thirdly, Hereby the atheist may learn to suspect that bold objection of his upon which he most relies. He would impute to Revealed Religion the choice of the sanction of a future unseen reward and

5[1] Johann David Michaelis (1717–1791), professor of Hebrew, Syriac, and Chaldee in Göttingen University from 1750 (as C knew: *CL* I 477), wrote numerous books, including a commentary on OT (1769–83). The passages referred to by Davison are *Mosaisches Recht* (1771–5) Art 14, and *Syntagm[a] Commentat[ionum]* (1759–67) II 210. C borrowed both volumes of Michaelis's *Introduction to the New Testament* tr H. Marsh (Cambridge 1793) in Jun 1795, and intended to bring back from Germany the works of Semler and

Michaelis. *Bristol LB* 59, 60; *CL* I 209; cf *CN* I 404 and *Lects 1795* (*CC*) 175–6 n 2, 177 and nn, 179–88, 190. See also HACKET *Century* 5 n 1.

5[2] The tenth commandment reads: "Thou shalt not covet thy neighbour's house, thou shalt not covet thy neighbour's wife, nor his manservant, nor his maidservant, nor his ox, nor his ass, nor any thing that is thy neighbour's." Exod 20.17. Davison had stated that "the Tenth commandment of the Decalogue, and many others, never can be reduced to 'statutes of the land'".

punishment, for the convenience of the uncertainty and disguise which seem to cover that distant scene. But the first Law meets him on his own terms: it stood upon a present retribution; the execution of its sentence is matter of history, and the argument resulting from it is to be answered, before the question is carried to another world.

This is rendered a very powerful argument by the consideration, that though so vast a mind as that of Moses, though perhaps even a Lycurgus,[1] might have distinctly foreseen the ruin and captivity of the Hebrew people as a necessary result of the loss of nationality, and the abandonment of the law and religion which were their only point of union, their centre of gravity,—yet no human intellect could have foreseen the perpetuity of such a people as a distinct race under all the aggravated curses of the law weighing on them; or that the obstinacy of their adherence to their dividuating institutes in persecution, dispersion, and shame, should be in direct proportion to the wantonness of their apostasy from the same in union and prosperity.

7   p 234 | Discourse v pt ii "State of Prophecy in the Reigns of David and Solomon"

Except under the dictate of a constraining Inspiration, it is not easy to conceive how the master of such a work, at the time when he had brought it to perfection, and beheld it in its lustre, the labour of so much opulent magnificence and curious art, and designed to be "exceeding magnifical, of *fame* and of *glory* throughout all countries" [1 Chron 22.5], should be occupied with the prospect of its utter ruin and dilapidation, and that too under the *opprobrium* of God's vindictive judgment upon it; nor to imagine how that strain of sinister prophecy, that foreboding of malediction, should be ascribed to him, if he had no such vision revealed.[1]

Here I think Mr. Davison should have crushed the objection of the Infidel grounded on Solomon's subsequent idolatrous impieties. The Infidel argues, that these are not conceivable of a man distinctly conscious of a prior and supernatural inspiration, accompanied with supernatural manifestations of the divine presence.

6[1] The Spartan lawgiver. See e.g. *LS* (*CC*) 223n.

7[1] Solomon had prophesied that the Temple would be destroyed after it had been completed: 1 Kings 9.7–8.

8 p 283 | Discourse VI pt i "Temporal Prophecy...from the time of Solomon to the Restoration from Babylon"

There is a depth and a combination of prescience in the prolonged succession of his [Isaiah's] predictions, which oblige us to ask, whence it came, when it could come, if not from the revelation of Him "who calleth the things that are not as though they were?" In order to evade this conclusion, nothing is left but to deny that Isaiah, or any person of his age, wrote the book ascribed to him; which is to affirm that the Jewish people knew nothing of the Book which they placed at the head of their Prophetic Canon...

This too is my conclusion, but (if I do not delude myself) from more evident, though not perhaps more certain, premisses. The age of the Cyrus prophecies is the great object of attack by Eichhorn and his compilers;[1] and I dare not say, that in a controversy with these men Davison's arguments would appear sufficient. But this was not the intended subject of these Discourses.

9 p 289 | Pt ii "On the Christian Prophecy Within That Period"

For what does the Prophet profess to promise? A restoration to "national happiness:" so it is said, and perhaps truly. But how does he express that promise? In the images of the resurrection and an immortal state. Consequently, there is *implied* in the delineation of the lower subject the truth of the greater.

This reminds me of a remark, I have elsewhere made respecting the expediency of separating the arguments addressed to, and valid for, a believer, from the proofs and vindications of Scripture intended to form the belief, or to convict the Infidel.[1]

10 p 325 | Pt iv "Last Age of Ancient Prophecy..."

When Cyrus became master of Babylon, the prophecies of Isaiah were shewn or communicated to him, wherein were described his victory, and the use he was appointed to make of it in the restoration of the Hebrew people. (Ezra i. 1, 2.)[1]

8[1] Cyrus' name appears in Isa 44.28 and 45.1, both of which belong to Deutero-Isaiah (chs 40–55)—a collection of prophecies, oracular rather than literary in character, composed in the time of Cyrus immediately before the release of the children of Israel in 538 B.C.

The reference is to EICHHORN *Alte Testament* III 70–180, on which section C wrote six marginalia.
9[1] Cf CHILLINGWORTH COPY A (at n 2).
10[1] Ezra 1.1–2: "Now in the first year of Cyrus king of Persia, that the

This I had been taught to regard as one of Josephus's legends; but upon this passage who would not infer that it had Ezra for its authority,[2]—who yet does not expressly say that even the prophecy of the far later Jeremiah was known or made known to Cyrus, who (Ezra tells us) fulfilled it? If Ezra had meant the prediction of Isaiah by the words, *he hath charged me*, &c., why should he not have referred to it together with, or even instead of, Jeremiah? Is it not more probable that a living prophet had delivered the charge to Cyrus? See *Ezra* vi. 14.[3]—Again, Davison makes Cyrus speak like a Christian, by omitting the affix *of Heaven* to the *Lord God* in the original. Cyrus speaks as a Cyrus might be supposed to do,—namely, of a most powerful but yet national deity, of a God, not of God. I have seen in so many instances the injurious effect of weak or overstrained arguments in defence of religion, that I am perhaps more jealous than I need be in the choice of evidences. I can never think myself the worse Christian for any opinion I may have formed, respecting the price of this or that argument, of this or that divine, in support of the truth. For every one that I reject, I could supply two, and these ἀνέκδοτα.[4]

11 p 366

Meanwhile this long repose and obscurity of Zerubbabel's family, and of the whole house of David, during so many generations prior to the Gospel, was one of the preparations made whereby to manifest more distinctly the proper glory of it, in the birth of the Messiah.

In whichever way I take this, whether addressed to a believer for the purpose of enlightening, or to an inquirer for the purpose of

word of the Lord by the mouth of Jeremiah might be fulfilled, the Lord stirred up the spirit of Cyrus king of Persia, that he made a proclamation throughout all his kingdom, and put it also in writing, Thus saith Cyrus king of Persia, The Lord God of heaven hath given me all the kingdoms of the earth; and he hath charged me to build him an house at Jerusalem, which is in Judah." Davison quotes this directly after the summary given as textus, above, omitting—as C notes below—"of heaven".

[2] Josephus *Antiquitates Judaicae* XI–XIII, written in A.D. 93, dealt with the period from Ezra to Maccabeus, using much legendary material, some of which Eichhorn was able to trace to its sources.

[3] "And the elders of the Jews builded, and they prospered through the prophesying of Haggai the prophet and Zechariah the son of Iddo. And they builded, and finished it, according to the commandment of the God of Israel, and according to the commandment of Cyrus, and Darius, and Artaxerxes king of Persia."

[4] C provides an accurate gloss in *CN* III 3740: "ἀνέκδοτα = inedita". In Greek, and in earlier English usage, an "anecdote" is an unpublished or secret account.

establishing, his faith in prophecy, this argument appears to me equally perplexing and obscure. It seems, *prima facie*, almost tantamount to a right of inferring the fulfilment of a prophecy in B., which it does not mention, from its entire failure and falsification in A., which, and which alone, it does mention.

12 p 370

And now, when Prophecy was about to be withdrawn from the ancient Church of God, its last light was mingled with the rising beams of "the Sun of Righteousness." In one view it combined a retrospect to the Law with the clearest specific signs of the Gospel advent. "*Remember* ye the *law of Moses* my servant, which I commanded him in Horeb, for all Israel, with the statutes and judgments. *Behold,* I *will send* you *Elijah* the *prophet,* before the *great and dreadful day of the Lord.*" (Malachi iv. 2.) Prophecy had been the oracle of Judaism, and of Christianity, to uphold the authority of the one, and reveal the promise of the other. And now its latest admonitions, were like those of a faithful departing minister, embracing and summing up his duties. Resigning its charge to the *personal Precursor* of Christ, it expired, with the Gospel upon its tongue.

Almost every page of this volume makes me feel my own ignorance respecting the interpretation of the language of the Hebrew Prophets, and the want of the one idea which would supply the key. Suppose an Infidel to ask me, how the Jews were to ascertain that John the Baptist was Elijah the Prophet;—am I to assert the pre-existence of John's personal identity as Elijah? If not, why Elijah rather than any other Prophet? One answer is obvious enough, that the contemporaries of John held Elijah as the common representative of the Prophets; but did Malachi do so?[1]

13 p 373 | Recapitulation ["Of the Structure, and Use, of Ancient Prophecy"]

I. It has been shewn that the character of Prophecy is not simple and uniform, nor its light equable. It was dispensed in various degrees

12[1] Mal 4.5, the penultimate verse of OT (as we have it), is the first reference to Elijah as forerunner of the Messiah (the "Sun of righteousness" of 4.2), and may well be an editorial note. Elijah was of all the prophets a natural type of the Messiah (see e.g. Matt 11.14, 16.14, 17.12, 27.47–9; Mark 6.15, 9.4–13; John 1.20) because he had not died on earth but had been taken up into heaven. He was held in such special honour among the Jews that in later times a place was laid for him at the Passover meal; it was confidently expected that he would return to prepare the people for the crisis that would usher in the messianic age.

of revelation; and that revelation adapted, by the wisdom of God, to purposes which we must explore, by studying its records, and considering its capacity of application....

III. The *subjects* of Prophecy varied. Whilst it was all directed to one general design, in the evidence and support of religion, there was a diversity in the administration of the Spirit, in respect of that design. In Paradise, it gave the first hope of a Redeemer. After the Deluge, it established the peace of the Natural world. In Abraham, it founded the double covenant of Canaan and the Gospel. In the age of the Law, it spoke of the Second Prophet, and foreshadowed, in Types, the *Christian* doctrine, but foretold most largely the future fate of the selected People, who were placed under that preparatory dispensation. In the time of David, it revealed the *Gospel Kingdom*, with the promise of the Temporal. In the days of the later Prophets, it presignified the changes of the Mosaic Covenant, embraced the history of the chief Pagan kingdoms, and completed the annunciation of the Messiah and his work of Redemption. After the Captivity, it gave a last and more urgent information of the approaching Advent of the Gospel.

Thus ancient Prophecy ended as it had begun.... But its *earliest*, and its *latest* use, was in the preparatory revelation of Christianity....

I cannot conceive a more beautiful synopsis of a work on the Prophecies of the Old Testament, than is given in this Recapitulation. Would that its truth had been equally well substantiated! That it can be, that it will be, I have the liveliest faith;—and that Mr. Davison has contributed as much as we ought to expect, and more than any contemporary divine, I acknowledge, and honor him accordingly. But much, very much, remains to be done, before these three pages merit the name of a Recapitulation.[1]

14   p [374] | Discourse vii "Of the Divine Foreknowledge, and Its Union with the Liberty of Human Action"

If I needed proof of the immense importance of the doctrine of Ideas, and how little it is understood, the following discourse would supply it.[1]

13[1] Cf *CL* v 510 (quoted in part in headnote, above).

14[1] A complaint that C often uttered against theologians: see e.g. BAXTER *Catholick Theologie* 10.

The whole discussion on Prescience and Freewill, with exception of the page or two borrowed from Skelton,[2] displays an unacquaintance with the deeper philosophy, and a helplessness in the management of the particular question, which I know not how to reconcile with the steadiness and clearness of insight evinced in the earlier Discourses. I neither do nor ever could see any other difficulty on the subject, than what is contained and anticipated in the idea of eternity.

By Ideas I mean intuitions not sensuous, which can be expressed only by contradictory conceptions, or, to speak more accurately, are in themselves necessarily both inexpressible and inconceivable, but are suggested by two contradictory positions.[3] This is the essential character of all ideas, consequently of eternity, in which the attributes of omniscience and omnipotence are included. Now prescience and freewill are in fact nothing more than the two contradictory positions by which the human understanding struggles to express successively the idea of eternity. Not eternity in the negative sense as the mere absence of succession, much less eternity in the senseless sense of an infinite time; but eternity,—the Eternal; as Deity, as God. Our theologians forget that the objection applies equally to the possibility of the divine will; but if they reply that prescience applied to an eternal, *Entis absoluti tota et simultanea fruitio,*[4] is but an anthropomorphism, or term of accommodation, the same answer serves in respect of the human will; for the epithet human does not enter into the syllogism. As to contingency, when did Mr. Davison learn that it is a necessary accompaniment of freedom, or of free action? My philosophy teaches me the very contrary.[5]

14[2] C was reading *The Complete Works of Philip Skelton* (6 vols 1824) at the same time that he was reading DAVISON, and wrote marginalia in Vols I, III, IV. If Davison did borrow from Skelton, he did not acknowledge the debt.

14[3] For a central account of C's doctrine of ideas see *L & L* 135–7. For a series of observations on ideas as "Truth-powers of the pure Reason", see DONNE *Sermons* COPY B esp **60, 62, 64**. See also *SM* (*CC*) 23, 24, 113–14, and *BL* ch 9 (*CC*) I 156.

14[4] "The complete and simultaneous fulfilment of an absolute Being".

14[5] C develops this thought more fully in *CN* IV 5271: "Dr Davison has threshed over again the bruised, and chopped Straw of the ? respecting the compossibility of Prescience with Free Will; but setting aside the passage borrowed from (at least, pre-existing in) Phil. Skelton, without beating out a single additional grain—a mournful proof of the incommunion with IDEAS in the ablest men of the present Age...".

15 p 392

He [Pearson][1] contends, without reserve, that the free actions of men are not within the Divine Prescience; resting his doctrine partly on the *assumption*, that there are no strict and absolute predictions, in Scripture, of those actions in which men are represented as free and responsible; and partly on *the abstract reason*, that such actions are in their nature impossible to be certainly foreknown.

I utterly deny contingency except in relation to the limited and imperfect knowledge of man. But the misery is, that men write about freewill without a single meditation on will absolutely; on the idea κατ᾽ ἐξοχὴν without any idea;[2] and so bewilder themselves in the jungle of alien conceptions; and to understand the truth they overlay their reason.

16 p 416 | Discourse viii "On the Inspiration of Prophecy" § 2

In some measure to open this proof, take the following characteristic predictions of Isaiah; "It shall come to pass in the last days that the *mountain* of the *Lord's house* shall be *established* in the top of the mountains, and shall be *exalted above* the hills; and all *nations shall flow* into it. And *many people* shall go and say, Come ye, and let us go up to the mountain of the Lord, to the house of the God of Jacob; and he will teach us of his ways, and we will walk in his paths: for out of *Zion* shall go forth *the law*, and the *word of the Lord* from Jerusalem. And he shall *judge among the nations*, and *rebuke many people* (Isaiah ii. 2–4):" i.e. *instruct* them by reclaiming from error.

It would not be easy to calculate the good which a man like Mr. Davison might effect, under God, by a work on the Messianic Prophecies, specially intended for and addressed to the present race of Jews,—if only he would make himself acquainted with their objections and ways of understanding Scripture.[1] For instance, a learned Jew would perhaps contend that this prophecy of Isaiah (c. ii. 2–4,) cannot fairly be interpreted of a mere local origination of a religion historically; as the drama might be described as going forth

---

15[1] Edward Pearson (1756–1811) in *Twelve Lectures on the Subject of the Prophecies Relating to the Christian Church* (1811).

15[2] "In the higher sense, *eminenter*"; here, "*as* an idea".

16[1] Ever since he had made friends with Hyman Hurwitz in 1816, C had had the advantage of appreciating the Jewish "ways of understanding Scripture". See BOOK OF COMMON PRAYER COPY B 25 n 2 and HURWITZ headnote.

from Athens, and philosophy from Academus and the Painted Porch,[2] but must refer to an established and continuing seat of worship, *a house of the God of Jacob*. The answer to this is provided in the preceding verse, *in the top of the mountains*; which irrefragably proves the figurative character of the whole prediction.

17 p 431

One point, however, is certain and equally important, *viz.* that the Christian Church, when it comes to recognise more truly the obligation imposed upon it by the original command of its Founder, "Go teach all nations," a command, which, having never been recalled or abrogated, can never be obsolete, will awaken another energy of its apostolic office and character, than has been witnessed in many later ages, in this most noble work of Piety and Charity combined...

That the duty here recommended is deducible from this text[1] is quite clear to my mind; but whether it is the direct sense and primary intention of the words; whether the first meaning is not negative,— (*Have no respect to what nation a man is of, but teach it to all indifferently whom you have an opportunity of addressing*)—this is not so clear. The larger sense is not without its difficulties, nor is this narrower sense without its practical advantages.

18 pp 453–4 | Discourse ix "On the Inspiration of Prophecy..."

The striking inferiority of several of these latter Discourses in point of style, as compared with the first 150 pages of this volume, perplexes me. It seems more than mere carelessness, or the occasional *infausta tempora scribendi*,[1] can account for. I question whether from any modern work of a tenth part of the merit of these Discourses, either in matter or in force and felicity of diction and composition, as many uncouth and awkward sentences could be extracted. The paragraph in page 453 and 454, is not a specimen of the worst.[2] In

---

16[2] I.e. from the schools of Plato and of Zeno (the Stoic).
17[1] Matt 28.19.
18[1] "Unfortunate occasions of writing".
18[2] The paragraph reads: "5. Lastly; the prophecies which relate to the subversion of the Jewish state, and the introduction of Christianity, are raised in the evidence resulting from them, by their joint and coincident completion. Upon one aera and crisis of things there falls an aggregate of prophetic fulfilment. Either event, so modified as each was, would have been a memorable fact. Together, they are a congeries of a rare and wonderful fabric of providence. Nor is prophecy without its indications that this coincidence should take place. For the two events are not

Discourses on Prophecy

155

a volume which ought to be, and which probably will be, in every young Clergyman's library, these *maculæ*[3] are subjects of just regret. The utility of the work, no less than its great comparative excellence, render its revision a duty on the part of the author;[4] specks are no trifles in diamonds.

19 p 519 | Discourse xi "On the Inspiration of Prophecy..."

Four such ruling kingdoms did arise. The first, the Babylonian, was in being when the prophecy is represented to have been given. It was followed by the Persian; the Persian gave way to the Grecian; the Roman closed the series.[1]

This is stoutly denied by Eichhorn, who contends that the Mede or Medo-Persian is the second—if I recollect aright.[2] But it always struck me that Eichhorn, like other learned Infidels, is caught in his own snares. For if the prophecies are of the age of the first Empire, and actually delivered by Daniel,[3] there is no reason why the Roman Empire should not have been predicted;—for superhuman predictions, the last two at least must have been. But if the book was a forgery, or a political poem like Gray's Bard or Lycophron's Cassandra,[4] and later than Antiochus Epiphanes,[5] it is strange and

only each foretold, but they are sometimes so brought together in the prediction, that their concurrence appears to be manifestly intended to be expressed; and if this interpretation which unites them is not imperative from the text, it is at least the most fair and direct. Such is the impression of the prophecies of Moses and Isaiah, as well as some others. But whether this concurrent accomplishment can be strictly deduced from the text of prophecy, or no; still it is, in the fact, such a mark of a special providence in the consummation of things so produced, and such a key to the exposition of the Divine Economy, as well as to the solution of the mixt oracles of prophecy, that we shall be warranted in laying some stress upon it, on each of those accounts."

18[3] "Spots, blemishes".

18[4] Davison's book reached a 4th ed in 1839.

19[1] Davison is interpreting the "four kingdoms" in Dan 2.36–40.

19[2] Eichhorn *Alte Testament* III 350, not annotated by C. See also **22** n 2, below.

19[3] For the authorship and date of Daniel see BIBLE COPY B **70** n 1 and CHILLINGWORTH COPY B **3** n 3.

19[4] Thomas Gray's *The Bard* was "founded on a Tradition current in Wales, that EDWARD THE FIRST, when he compleated the Conquest of that country, ordered all the Bards, that fell into his hands, to be put to death" (Advertisement 1757), because they "encouraged the Nation to rebellion" (Gray's Commonplace Book). For C's general appreciation of Gray's poetry see GRAY headnote. *Cassandra* (or *Alexandra*) is the only surviving composition of Lycophron (b c 320 B.C.)—a dramatic monologue of notorious obscurity in which a slave reports to Priam the prophecies of Cassandra regarding the destruction of Troy, the return of the Greeks, and the struggle between Europe and Asia.

19[5] Antiochus IV, surnamed Epiphanes, King of Syria and fourth of the Seleucid dynasty (reigned 175–163 B.C.), attempted to hellenise the Jews, then by trying to suppress Judaism provoked the

most improbable that the Roman should have escaped notice. In both cases the omission of the last and most important Empire is inexplicable.

20 p 521

Yet we have it on authority of Josephus, that Daniel's prophecies were read publicly among the Jews in their worship, as well as their other received Scriptures, and he knows nothing of any doubts of their genuineness, or their authority, having disturbed their reception.

It is but fair, however, to remember that the Jewish Church ranked the book of Daniel in the third class only, among the Hagiographic[1]—passionately almost as the Jews before and at the time of our Saviour were attached to it.

21 pp 522–3

But to a Jewish eye, or to any eye placed in the same position of view, in the age of Antiochus Epiphanes, it is utterly impossible to admit that this superior strength of the Roman power, to reduce and destroy, this heavier arm of subjugation, could have revealed itself so plainly, as to warrant the express, deliberate, description of it.

Quære. See Polybius.[1]

22 p 523

We shall yet have to inquire how it could be foreseen that this Fourth, this yet unestablished, Empire, should be the *last* in the line. The prophecy delineates *four*. So many there were: and no more; for not a fifth empire of general dominion, but a multitude of separate kingdoms were erected on the ruins of the Fourth.

---

revolt of the Maccabees. In 169/8 he clashed unsuccessfully with the expanding Roman empire over control of Egypt. The records of his reign provide "outside" evidence of Roman power and policy during the time of these Hebrew prophecies.

20[1] See EICHHORN *Alte Testament* **46** n 1.

21[1] Polybius (c 203–c 120 B.C.), in his *Universal History* (40 bks, of which only I–V survive intact, the rest in excerpts in other writers), shows an acute critical

perception of the growth of Roman power and of its implications. He began his history well before the Roman conquest of Greece. For the period 220–168 B.C. he traces with admiration the strength and stability of Roman institutions as they reached imperial fulfilment in the protectorate over Greece. But in the history from 168 to 144 he sees the onset of a process of degeneracy and considers the possibility of cyclic process in history.

This is a sound and weighty argument, which the preceding does not, I confess, strike me as being. On the contrary, the admission that by a writer of the Maccabaic æra the Roman power could scarcely have been overlooked,[1] greatly strengthens this second argument, as naturally suggesting expectations of change, and wave-like succession of empires,[2] rather than the idea of a last. In the age of Augustus this might possibly have occurred to a profound thinker; but the age of Antiochus was too late to permit the Roman power to escape notice; and not late enough to suggest its exclusive establishment so as to leave no source of succession.

22[1] The family or dynasty of Maccabees, beginning in 168 B.C., led a revolt against the persecution of Antiochus Epiphanes, which resulted in the reconquest of Jerusalem in 165, the purification of the Temple, and the restoration of the Jewish rites. On the death of Antiochus, the Maccabees through an alliance with the Romans recovered most of the Davidic monarchy and prospered until Hyrcanus died in 78 B.C. Thereafter their power declined rapidly; the last of the Maccabees, Antigonus, was killed by Antony in 37 B.C. Their history is recorded by Josephus and in the apocryphal 1 and 2 Maccabees.

22[2] See also BIBLE COPY B 70 and n 1, and 19, above. The succession of empires was: Assyrian, Median, Medo-Persian, Greek, Roman.

DANIEL DEFOE

1660–1731

The Life and Adventures of Robinson Crusoe, &c. [Anonymous.] 2 vols. London 1812. 12º.

Princeton University Library (Robert H. Taylor Collection)

Inscribed in ink on I ⁻4: "To Henry Gillman from his Affectionate Friend.—J. Watson.—" On II ⁻4 a similar inscription, erased and almost illegible, in another hand, possibly a bookseller's. On the half-title of Vol I: "Grandmama Gillman to Arthur Riley"; and on II ⁻2: "Grandmama Gillman to Arthur Riley 1855—", and below this, "Henry Gillman". On the half-title of Vol II: "Arthur Riley".

A note in an unidentified hand is written on I 312; the apparent underlining of the words "there, which" on I 313 is an offset from the note on I 312. At the top of II 352 an illegible word or combination of letters, not in C's hand.

J. L. Lowes incorrectly stated that this copy was in the Norton Perkins Collection of the Harvard Library (*RX* 318, 574 n 44), but he had seen the book somewhere; F. D. Klingender found it "on a second-hand book-stall" some time before his announcement in *TLS* 1 Feb 1936. It was later, for a time, in the collection of Mr Dudley Massey in London.

Robinson Crusoe was one of the books that made a profound impression upon C's imagination in his early childhood (see *CL* I 347, VI 979), and he was pleased to record that Sir Alexander Ball had entered the Navy at an early age "in consequence of the deep impression and vivid images which were left on his mind by the perusal of Robinson Crusoe". *Friend (CC)* II 288. For Defoe as ranking with Shakespeare, Milton, Fuller, and Hogarth see FULLER *History* 2; and see 1 and n 1, below. See also *BL* ch 22 (*CC*) II 133. C wrote at least one note in a copy of Walter WILSON *Memoirs of the Life of Defoe* (3 vols 1830).

MS TRANSCRIPT. VCL E 6 (12): a complete transcript, from which the *LR* I version was printed.

DATE. Jul–Aug 1830, and perhaps later. Two notes are dated in ms: 1830 (2), 30 Jul 1830 (5). See also 17 n 1.

1   I ⁻2, pencil, overtraced

Compare the contemptuous Swift with the contemned De Foe: and how superior will the latter be found.[1] But by what test?—Even by

1[1] C said of Asgill: "I think his and Defoe's irony often finer than Swift's." *TT* 30 Apr 1832; cf 15 May 1833.

this. The Writer who makes me sympathize with his presentations with the *whole* of my Being is more estimable than the Writer, who calls forth & appeals to but a *part* of my Being—my sense of the Ludicrous, for instance—

and again he, who makes me forget my *specific* class, character, & circumstances ~~of~~ raises me into the Universal *Man*—Now this is De Foe's Excellence, you become a Man while you read.[2]

2   ı 4–5, pencil, overtraced

He bid me observe it, and I should always find, that the calamities of life were shared among the upper and lower part of mankind; but that the middle station had the fewest disasters, and was not exposed to so many vicissitudes as the higher or lower part of mankind; nay, they were not subjected to so many distempers ʌ and uneasinesses, either of body or mind, as those were, who, by vicious living, luxury, and extravagances, on one hand, or by hard labour, want of necessaries, and mean and insufficient diet, on the other hand, bring distempers upon themselves by the natural consequences of their way of living...

ʌ rather malapropos from a gentleman laid up with the *Gout*. Alas, the evil is, that such is the pressure of the Ranks on each other, and with exception of the ever increasing Class of Paupers so universal is the ambition of Appearances, that morally & practically we scarcely have a Middle Class at present![1]—S. T. C. 1830.

3   ı ⁻4, referring to ı 5–6, pencil, overtraced

...I resolved not to think of going abroad any more, but to settle at home according to my father's desire. But alas! a few days wore it all off...

P. 5. A[a] most impressive instance & illustration of my Aphorism, that the wise only possess ~~an~~ ideas, but that the greater part of man-kind are possessed by them.[1] Robinson Crusoe was not

[a] Mistraced as "As"

[1][2] See also **15**, below. In the 1818 literary lectures, C said that "The charm of De Foe's works, especially of Robinson Crusoe, is founded on the same principle" as many tales in the *Arabian Nights*: they "cause no deep feeling of a moral kind...but an impulse of motion is communicated to the mind without excitement". *LR* ı 188–9.

[2][1] One of C's chief objections to Napoleon was that he had destroyed, as far as was within his power, the one source of civilisation—the middle class. See e.g. *Friend* (*CC*) ı 231, *EOT* (*CC*) ıı 76, 348.

[3][1] This aphorism also appears (var) in *C&S* (*CC*) 13.

conscious of the master-impulse—because it *was* his Master, and had taken full possession of him.

4 I ⁻4⁻⁻2, referring to I 16, pencil, overtraced

But my ill fate pushed me on now with an obstinacy that nothing could resist; and though I had several times loud calls from my reason, and my more composed judgment, to go home, yet I had no power to do it. I know not what to call this, nor will I urge that it is a secret overruling decree that hurries us on to be the instruments of our own destruction, even though it be before us, and that we rush upon it with our eyes open.

P. 16. Notice this §ph. "But my ill fate"—

When once the Mind in despite of the remonstrating Conscience has once abandoned its free power to a haunting Impulse or Idea—then whatever tends to give depth and vividness to this Idea, or indefinite Imagination, increases *its* despotism and in the same proportion renders the Reason and Free Will ineffectual. Now fearful Calamities, Sufferings, Horrors, & Hair breadth Escapes will have this effect, far more than even sensual pleasure & prosperous incidents/ Hence the evil consequences of Sin in such cases instead of retracting and deterring the sinner, goad him on to his Destruction. This is the moral of Shakespear's *Macbeth*:[1] and this is the true solution of this §ph—not any over-ruling decree of Divine Wrath, but the tyranny of the Sinner's own evil Imagination which he has voluntarily chosen as his Master.

5 I 73–4, pencil, overtraced

I smiled to myself at the sight of this money: "O drug!" said I aloud, "what art thou good for?...e'en remain where thou art, and go to the bottom, as a creature whose life is not worth saving." However, *] upon second thoughts, I took it away; and wrapping all this in a piece of canvass, I began to think of making another raft...

* worthy of Shakespear; and yet the simple semi-colon after it, the instant passing on without the least pause of reflex consciousness is more exquisite & masterlike than the Touch itself. A meaner writer,

4[1] C noticed, in SHAKESPEARE *The Dramatic Works* (6 vols Oxford 1786–99) [COPY C] VI 186, 190, that in the case of Macbeth one crime leads to another "even by the very virtues of the agent", through the increase of terror.

a Marmontel would have put an !—after "away", and have commenced a fresh Paragraph.[1] S. T. C. 30 July 1830.

6 I 100–1, pencil, overtraced

...I must confess, my religious thankfulness to God's providence began to abate too, upon the discovering that all this was nothing but what was common; though I ought to have been as thankful for *] so strange and unforeseen a providence, as if it had been miraculous: for it was really the work of Providence...

[*] To make men feel the truth of this, is one characteristic object of the miracles worked by Moses—the providence miraculous, the miracles providential.[1]

7 I 114–15, pencil, overtraced

The growing up of the corn, as is hinted in my Journal, had, at first, some little influence upon me, and began to affect me with seriousness, *] as long as I thought it had something miraculous in it...

* By far the ablest vindication of Miracles, that I have met with. It is indeed the true ground, the proper purpose & intention of a Miracle[1]

8 I 127, the corner of the leaf torn

I descended a little on the side of that delicious vale, surveying it with a secret kind of pleasure... to think that this was all my own; *] that I was king and lord of all this country indefeasibly, and had a right of possession...

* By the bye, what *is* the law of England re[specting]*a* this? Suppose, I ~~or~~ had discovered or been wrecked [on an]*a* uninhabited island— would it be mine or t[he] Ki[ng's]?*a*[1]

a Words from the missing corner of the leaf are supplied from *LR* I 192

5[1] C seems to be thinking of the *Moral Tales* of Jean François Marmontel (1723–99), first published 1761, extensively translated and reprinted.

6[1] Cf *CN* III 3581: "...Miracles are not the *proofs* but the necessary results of Revelation". See also e.g. *CN* III 3897 ff 48ᵛ, 49.

7[1] See **6** n 1, above.

8[1] The law was that new-found land became a possession of the country the discoverer represented, provided the act of possession was publicly declared and recorded; in no circumstances did the fact of discovery entitle the discoverer to claim the land as his personal property.

9 I 201–2

I considered that... as I could not foresee what the ends of divine wisdom might be in all this, so I was not to dispute his sovereignty, *] who, as I was his creature, had an undoubted right, by creation, to govern and dispose of me absolutely as he thought fit.

* I could never understand this reasoning, grounded on a compleat misapprehension of St Paul's Potsherd. Rom. IX.[1] Or rather I do fully understand the absurdity of it. The susceptibility of pain and pleasure, of Good and evil, constitutes a *Right* on every creature endowed therewith, in relation to *every* rational & moral Being—a fortiori, therefore, to the Supreme Reason, to the absolutely *Good* Being.[2]

10 I 209, concluded in pencil

...I rather prayed to God as under great affliction and pressure of mind, surrounded with danger, and in expectation every night of *] being murdered and devoured before morning; and I must testify from my experience, that a temper of peace, thankfulness, love, and affection, is much the more proper frame for prayer than that of terror and discomposure; and that under the dread of mischief impending, a man is no more fit for a comforting performance of the duty of praying to God, than he is for a repentance on a sick bed; for these discomposures affect the mind, as the others do the body; and the discomposure of the mind must necessarily be as great a disability as that of the body, and much greater; praying to God being properly an act of the mind, not of the body.

* As justly conceived as it is beautifully expressed,^{a} and a mighty motive for habitual prayer:[1] for this cannot but greatly facilitate the performance of rational prayer even in moments of urgent distress.

^{a} Words following are in pencil

9[1] Rom 9.20–1: "Nay but, O man, who art thou that repliest against God? Shall the thing formed say to him that formed it, Why hast thou made me thus? Hath not the potter power over the clay, of the same lump to make one vessel unto honour, and another unto dishonour?" C may also have in mind the parallel in Isa 45.9–10, in which the word "potsherd" occurs.

9[2] *LR* I 192–3 adds: "Remember Davenant's verses" and quotes *The Death of Astragon* sts 88–90. But C had transcribed these stanzas in BIBLE COPY A 5 under the heading of Rom 9.19–21.

10[1] For C on the habit of praying, see BOOK OF COMMON PRAYER COPY B 1.

11 I 220–1, pencil

...that this would justify the conduct of the Spaniards in all their barbarities practised in America, where they destroyed millions of these people who, however they were idolaters and barbarians, and had several bloody and barbarous rites in their customs, such as sacrificing human bodies to their idols, were yet, as to the Spaniards, very innocent people; and that the rooting them out of the country is spoken of with the utmost abhorrence and detestation by even the Spaniards themselves at this time, and by all other Christian nations in Europe, as a mere butchery, a bloody and unnatural piece of cruelty, unjustifiable either to God or man; and for which the very name of a Spaniard is reckoned to be frightful and terrible to all people of humanity, or of Christian compassion; as if the Kingdom of Spain were particularly eminent for the produce of a race of men who were without principles of tenderness, or the common bowels of pity to the miserable...

De Foe was a true philanthropist, who had risen above the antipathies of nationality—but he was evidently partial to the Spanish Character, which, however, it is not, I fear, possible to acquit of cruelty— America, the Netherlands, the Inquisition, the late Guerilla warfare,[1] &c. &c.—

12 I ⁻5, referring to I 225

That I shall not discuss, and perhaps cannot account for; but certainly they are a proof of the converse of spirits...

P. 225. "I cannot account for; *but* certainly &c—"
This reminds me of a conversation, I once overheard—"*How* a statement so injurious to Mʳ S.*ᵃ* and so contrary to the truth, should have been made to you by Mʳ Mahony,*ᵇ* I *do not pretend to account for*; only I know of my own knowlege, that Mahony is an inveterate Liar, and has long borne malice against Mʳ S: and I can prove, that

---

ᵃ Changed to "A." in *LR*   *ᵇ* "Mr. B." in *LR*

11¹ By "America" C would be thinking particularly of Cortes's conquest of Mexico and Pizzarro's conquest of Peru. The "Netherlands" recalls the brutality inflicted upon the Flemish by the Duke of Alba, as described with horrifying illustrations in Michael Eytzinger *De Leone Belgico* (Cologne 1583): see *CN* III 3601 and *EOT* (*CC*) II 54–64, 68–71. For "the Inquisition", see BAXTER *Reliquiae* COPY B 1 n 6 and **105** n 1. The "late Guerilla warfare"—the Peninsular War 1808–14, fought by Britain, Portugal, and the Spanish guerillas against the occupying French.

he has repeatedly declared ~~from~~ that, in some way or other he would do M[r] S. a mischief."[1]

13   I 229

The place I was in was a most delightful cavity or grotto of its kind, *] as could be expected, though perfectly dark; the floor was dry and level, and had a sort of small loose gravel upon it...

* How accurate an observer of Nature De Foe was! The Reader will at once recognize Prof. Buckland's Caves & the deluvial gravel.[1] S. T. C.

14   I 278–81

...I entered into a long discourse with him about the devil, the original of him, his rebellion against God, his enmity to man, the reason of it, his setting himself up in the dark parts of the world to be worshipped instead of God...

I presume, that Milton's Par. Lost must have been bound up with one of Crusoe's Bibles; or I should be puzzled to know, where he found all this history of the Old Gentleman. Not a word of it in the Bible itself, I am quite sure.—But to be serious. De Foe did not reflect, that all these difficulties are attached to a mere fiction, or at the best an allegory, supported by a few popular phrases & figures of Speech used incidentally or dramatically by the Evangelists; and that the existence of ~~an~~ Personal intelligent Evil Being, the Counterpart and Antagonist of God, is in direct contradiction to the most express declarations of Holy Writ! Is there evil in the city, and I have not done it? saith the Lord. I do the evil, and I do the good.[1]

12[1] If "M[r] S." is RS, the Mahony episode has not been traced. A PS has been added in pencil in another hand: "Do not see how the above is applicable to ⟨the reference⟩ page 225, but would fain ask a competent person." C, however, is merely difflating the illogical sequence implied in the sentence given as textus.

13[1] William Buckland (1784–1856), geologist and reader in geology at Oxford 1819–25, whose *Reliquiae Diluvianae; or Observations on the Organic*

Remains, Contained in Caves, Fissures and Diluvial Gravel (1823) provided geological evidence in general support of the Mosaic account of the flood. In Oct 1823 C noted that "our *biblical* philosophers, as Grenville Penn, Dr. Copleston, and the other Oxford Parsons are on tiptoe with Prof. Buckland's antediluvian Hyenas". *CN* IV 5061.

14[1] A conflation of Amos 3.6 and Isa 45.7. *LR* I 194 adds, on unknown authority: "This is the deep mystery of the abyss of God."

15 ɪ ' 1 – ⁺3, pencil, overtraced

One excellence of De Foe among many is his sacrifice of lesser interest to the greater because more universal. Had he (as without any improbability he might have done) given his Robinson Crusoe any of the turn for natural history which forms so striking and delightful a feature in the equally uneducated Dampier[1]—had he made him find out qualities and uses in the before (to him) unknown plants of the Island, discover a substitute for Hops for instance or describe Birds &c—many delightful pages & incidents might have enriched the Book—But then Crusoe would cease to be the Universal Representative—the person, for whom every reader could substitute *himself*—But now nothing is done, thought, or suffered, ⟨or desired⟩ but what every man can imagine himself doing, thinking, ⟨feeling⟩ or wishing for,. ~~what every ma~~

Even so very easy a problem as that of finding a substitute for ink, is with exquisite judgement made to baffle Crusoe's inventive faculties. Even in what he does, he arrives at no excellence/ he does not make Basket-work like Will Atkins,[2] the Carpentering, Tailoring, Pottery, are all just what will answer his purposes—and those are confined to needs that all men have, and comforts that all men desire. Crusoe rises only where all men may be made to feel that they might, and that they ought to, rise—in religion—in resignation, in dependence on & thankful acknowlegement of the divine Mercy and goodness.

S. T. Coleridge

15[1] William Dampier (1652–1715), successively pirate and adventurer, Captain RN, and hydrographer. At the turn of the year 1807–8 C drew four passages from the 1729 edition of Dampier's *Collection of Voyages* (*CN* ɪɪ 3224, 3226, ɪɪɪ 3239, 3240); the second he used in *The Friend*, and the fourth provided the basis for his recommendation that WW alter the "Household Tub, like one of those | Which women use to wash their clothes" in *The Blind Highland Boy* to a giant tortoise shell. See *Friend* (*CC*) ɪɪ 289, ɪ 541; *WPW* ɪɪɪ 91, 447–8. A series of variatim extracts from *The Voyages and Adventures of Capt. William Dampier* (2 vols 1776) is preserved in BM MS Egerton 2800 ff 105ʳ⁻ᵛ (watermarked 1795). See also *TT* 17 Mar 1832, 4 Sept

1833. For Dampier's possible contribution to the sea-snakes of *AM*, see *RX* 49–51. This annotation on DEFOE is a reminder of the delight C took in the detailed accounts of trees, plants, flowers, animals, birds, and fishes which are a notable feature of BARTRAM and of many of the records of discovery collected by Hakluyt and Purchas.

15[2] Will Atkins was indeed a remarkable craftsman: he had "made himself such a tent of basket-work, as, I believe, was never seen; it was one hundred and twenty paces round on the outside...the walls were as close worked as a basket, in pannels or squares of thirty-two in number, and very strong, standing about seven feet high". *Robinson Crusoe* ɪɪ 120.

16 II 2–3

I have often heard persons of good judgment say, that all the stir people make in the world about ghosts and apparitions, is owing to the strength of imagination, and the powerful operation of fancy in *] their mind; that there is no such thing as a spirit appearing, or a ghost walking, and the like...

* I cannot conceive a better definition of *Body* than "Spirit appearing": or of a *flesh & blood* Man than a rational Spirit apparent. But a Spirit per se appearing is tantamount to a Spirit appearing without its appearances. And as for Ghosts, it is enough ~~to~~ for a man of common sense to observe that a Ghost and a Shadow are concluded in the same definition, viz. Visibility without Tangibility.[1]

17 II ⁻5 (p–d), referring to II 8

But, in the middle of all this felicity, one blow from unseen Providence unhinged me at once.... This blow was the loss of my wife.... She was...the stay of all my affairs, the centre of all my enterprises, the engine that, by her prudence, reduced me to that happy compass I was in, from the most extravagant and ruinous project that fluttered in my head, as above, and did more to guide my rambling genius than a mother's tears, a father's instructions, a friend's counsel, or all my own reasoning powers, could do.

P. 8. The Story, of ~~my~~ his Affairs, the Center of ~~my~~ his Interests, the Regulator of ~~my~~ his schemes and movements, whom it *soothed* his pride to submit to, and in complying with whose wishes the conscious sensation of his own *activeing* will increase ~~while it disg~~ the impulse, while it disguised the coercion, of Duty! the clinging Dependent, yet the strong Supporter, the Comforter, the Comforter, and the Soul's living Home!—

~~Such~~ This is De Foe's comprehensive Character of the Wife, as She Should be—and to the honor of Womanhood be it spoken, there are few neighborhoods in which one name at least might not be found for the Portrait.[1] S. T. C.—

16[1] An extension of this note, with close verbal parallels, is given in *TT* 3 Jan 1823.

17[1] C's altering "my" to "his" betrays the personal force of the observation: he had decided more than twenty-five years earlier that Mrs C could not fulfil this "Character of the Wife, as She Should be". See BROWNE *Religio* 23 n 1 and e.g. *CN* III 4006.

A revised version of this annotation, in C's hand, signed and dated "Grove, Highgate, December 1831" is in PML: "A Husband's Eulogy on a departed Wife, partly taken from, partly suggested by, a passage in Robinson Crusoe, Vol. II.

18   ii ⁻3, referring to ii 8–9

*a*I was happy in listening to her tears, and in being moved by her entreaties; and to the last degree desolate and dislocated in the world by the loss of her. When she was gone, the world looked awkwardly round me. I was as much a stranger in it, in my thoughts, as I was in the Brazils, when I first went on shore there; and as much alone, except as to the assistance of servants, as I was in my island. I knew neither what to think nor what to do. I saw the world busy around me; one part labouring for bread, another part squandering in vile excesses or empty pleasures, equally miserable, because the end they proposed still fled from them; for the men of pleasure every day surfeited of their vice, and heaped up work for sorrow and repentance; and the men of labour spent their strength in daily struggling for bread to maintain the vital strength they laboured with: so living in a daily circulation of sorrow, living but to work, and working but to live, as if daily bread were the only end of wearisome life, and a wearisome life the only occasion of daily bread.

P. 8. 9. These exquisite paragraphs in addition to others scattered tho' with a sparing hand, thro' the Novels, afford sufficient proof that De Foe was a first-rate Master in periodic style; but with sound judgement and the fine tact of Genius had avoided it, as adverse to, nay incompatible with, the every-day matter-of-fact *Realness* which forms the charm and the character of all his Romances. The Rob. Crusoe is like the Vision of a happy Night-mair, such as a Denizen of Elysium might be supposed to have from a little excess in his Nectar and Ambrosia Supper. Our imagination is kept in full play, excited to the highest; yet all the while we are touching or touched by, common Flesh and Blood. S. T. C.

---

a This textus follows immediately upon 17 textus

p. 8., but which pleases me, as being a sort of Miniature of Mʳˢ Gillman.

"The Stay of his affairs, the Center of his interests, the Regulator of his feelings and movements! his gentler Second Thought! in complying with whose wishes the genial Sensation of a prevenient and conspiring Free Will in himself hid the coercion, while it enlivened the impulse, of Duty; and Submission to whom, like the Bending-down of the Head to a Kiss, fed and flattered the pride, it overcame!

—the meek Dependent yet strong Supporter! her Husband's Comfort, Comforter, and living Home!

"Here behold the true Portrait of THE WIFE: and to the honor of Womanhood be it spoken, there are few Neighborhoods, in Gr. Britain at least, in which the Likeness ought not be justly claimed for more than one Original. Would to Heaven, that the correspondent Husband were no rarer Character."

19 II 61

It was not above a week after they had these arms, and went abroad,
*] but the ungrateful creatures began to be as insolent and
troublesome as before.

* How should it be otherwise? They were *idle*. And when *we* will not
sow *Corn*, the *Devil* will be sure to sow *weeds*—Nightshade, Hensbane
& Devil'sbit!—[1]

20 II 74

"How, Seignior Atkins, would you murder us all? What have you
to say to that?" The hardened villain was so far from denying it, that
*] he said it was true: and G—d d—mn him, they would do it still,
before they had done with them.

* Observe—when a Man has once abandoned himself to wickedness,
he cannot stop, and does not join the Devils til he has become a Devil
himself. Rebelling against his Conscience, he becomes the Slave of
his own furious Will

19[1] Nightshade and hensbane are
both poisonous, hensbane also being
narcotic; devil's-bit has no such proper-
ties, but is so named because its root
looks as though bitten or gnawed by
"some Divel". All three appear in the
long list of vernacular flower-names that
SH transcribed into N 21 from Wither-
ing's *British Plants*: *CN* I 863.

RENÉ DESCARTES
1596–1650

Opera philosophica. Editio ultima, nunc demum hac editione diligenter recognita, et mendis expurgata. 3 pts in 1 vol. [Amsterdam 1685, 1677, 1685.] 4°.

Each pt has a full title-page, the first and third imprinted "Amstelodami, ex typographia Blaviana, MDCLXXXV", the second "Amstelodami, apud Danielem Elzevirium, MDCLXXVII." The general title is a half-title without imprint, with "Contenta" on the verso; the sheet is completed with "Typographus ad lectorem" on the recto of the second leaf, portrait of Descartes on verso.

University of Vermont Library

Inscribed on the first fly-title: "Thomas Knight. 1798". It seems likely that this was Thomas Knight (d 1820), actor and dramatist, and that he gave the book to C, but there is no clue to how or when. Knight played a variety of parts in Bath and Bristol 1787–95 and seems to have lived in Bath until his wife—Margaret Farren, sister of the Countess of Derby—died there in 1804. In 1795 he made his first appearance at Covent Garden, and was lessee and manager of the Liverpool Theatre 1803–20. See also *WL* (*E* 2) 197–8.

Inscribed in pencil below C's note 4 on p $^-3$ (p–d): "by Coleridge"; and in ink: "W G T. Shedd's Formerly belonged to S. T. Coleridge. Has notes of his on this page, and on De Passionibus pp. 2, 8, 82–84." Bookplate of the Library of the University of Vermont and State Agricultural College. A letter from W. G. T. Shedd to Professor H. A. P. Torrey, dated from 148 East 38th Street, New York, 20 May 1891, is tipped in at pp $^-3/^-2$: "I send to your address Express, a copy of the Works of Descartes, formerly owned by S. T. Coleridge, to be placed in the Library of the University. It contains a few marginal notes by him. There is no place so well suited for it in this country, as the shelves of the Library of that institution which was the earliest to direct attention to the principles and method of that extraordinary man, and to give them explanation & impulse in the Western World." On p $^+3$ (p–d) a large signature has been overwritten with an elaborate design of interlaced loops, below which Shedd has written three page-references. Shedd, originally a member of the University of Vermont, was the first to attempt a collective edition of C's work: *CW* (7 vols New York 1853). Torrey included the Descartes marginalia in footnotes to his *The Philosophy of Descartes* (New York 1892). The marginalia were published more carefully and with a commentary by J. I. Lindsay, also of the University of Vermont, in *PMLA* xlix (1934) 184–95.

There are pencilled X's, with pencil strokes in the margin ("possibly by

Coleridge", according to Lindsay) on *Principia* pt i arts 51, 52–3 (i 14), 63–4 (i 18), and "Ego cogito, ergo sum" in art 7 (i 2) is underlined. A section of the Index is marked with two small x's in ink (see **3** n 1, below); these seem not to be C's. Notes in another hand on i 4, 7, 29, ii 6, 10, 79, and a printer's error corrected on iii 80.

Although C spoke of reading Descartes at Stowey, he seems not to have made any systematic study of his work until he had established in Keswick, particularly in the winter of 1800–1 (see *CN* I 886 and n, 937G, 975), the immediate fruits being the philosophical letters "of prodigious length" addressed to the Wedgwoods in Feb 1801. See *BL* ch 10 (*CC*) I 200, and cf 145; *CL* II 678–703. In the Jun 1803 plan for the *Logosophia* a chapter or section was to be devoted to Descartes: *CL* II 947. For a detailed discussion of Descartes in Aug–Sept 1809, see *CN* III 3605. See also **1** n 4, below.

CONTENTS. *Principia philosophiae*; *De passionibus animae*; *Specimina philosophiae: seu dissertatio de methodo*.

DATE. 1800–15, and perhaps later (see **2** n 1, below). Lindsay assigns **2** and **3** to c 1815, **1** to "fairly late date", and the others to "chance encounters during desultory reading" of earlier date.

Textus translation: Descartes *Philosophical Works* tr E. S. Haldane and G. R. T. Ross (Cambridge 1931).

DE PASSIONIBUS ANIMAE

1   ii 2–3 | Pt I Art 3 "Qualis regula eum in finem sit sequenda"

Qua in re non magna reperietur difficultas, si animadvertatur id omne quod experimur esse in nobis, et quod videmus etiam posse inesse corporibus plane inanimatis, soli nostro corpori tribuendum esse; Et è contrario id omne quod nobis inest et quod nullo modo concipimus posse alicui corpori convenire, nostrae animae tribui debere.

["What rule we must follow to bring about this result". As to this we shall not find much difficulty if we realise that all that we experience as being in us, and that to observation may exist in wholly inanimate bodies, must be attributed to our body alone; and, on the other hand, that all that which is in us and which we cannot in any way conceive as possibly pertaining to a body, must be attributed to our soul.]

This utter disanimation of Body, and, its, *not* opposition, but contrariety, sicuti omninó heterogeneum,[1] to Soul, as the assumed Basis of Thought and Will; this substitution, ef I say, of a merely logical *negatio* alterius in omni et singulo[2] for a philosophic Antithesis

---

[1] "Just as [it is] absolutely different in kind". *OED* cites Browne *Pseudodoxia Epidemica* for "disanimation" as "deprivation of life"; here C may mean by it "privation of *soul*", unsoulment. Cf

"disensoul" in BLANCO WHITE *Practical Evidence* **7** and n 2.

[2] "*Negation* of the other in the general and in particular".

necessary to the manifestation of the Identity ⟨of both⟩ 2 = 1, as the only form in which the human Understanding can represent to itself the 1 = 2;³—is the peccatum originale⁴ of the Cartesian System.

2 ii 8ª | I 16 "Quomodo omnia membra possint moveri per objecta sensuum, et per spiritus, absque opera animae"

Denique notandum est machinam nostri corporis ita constructam esse, ut omnes mutationes quae accidunt motibus spirituum, efficere possint ut aperiant quosdam poros cerebri magis quàm alios; et reciproce, ut cum aliquis ex his poris paulo magis vel minus solito est apertus per actionem nervorum qui sensibus inserviunt, hoc mutet aliquid in motu spirituum, et efficiat ut deducantur in musculos qui inserviunt movendo corpori, eodem modo quo ordinario movetur occasione talis actionis. Ita ut omnes motus qui nobis eveniunt, voluntate nostra nihil ad eos comferente (ut saepe evenit nos respirare, ambulare, et denique omnes actiones facere quae nobis cum bestiis communes sunt) non aliunde pendeant quam à conformatione nostrorum membrorum, et cursu quem spiritus excitati per calorem cordis naturaliter sequuntur in cerebro, in nervis, et in musculis: Eodem modo quo ᵇmotus automatiᶜ producitur sola virtute manuclae et figura suarum rotularum.

["How all the members may be moved by the objects of the senses and by the animal spirits without the aid of the soul". We must finally remark that the machine of our body is so formed that all the changes undergone by the movement of the spirits may cause them to open certain pores in the brain more than others, and reciprocally that when some one of the pores is opened more or less than usual (to however small a degree it may be) by the action of the nerves which are employed by the senses, that changes something in the movement of the spirits and causes them to be conducted into the muscles which serve to move the body in the way in which it is usually moved when such an action takes place. In this way all the movements which we make without our will contributing thereto (as frequently happens when we breathe, walk, eat, and in fact perform all those actions which are common to us and to the brutes), only depend on the conformation of our members, and on the course which the spirits, excited by the heat of the heart, follow

ᵃ Written beside Arts 13–15 on the page facing Art 16
ᵇ⁻ᶜ Underlined in pencil, not by C

1³ For C's formulation of the dynamic interaction of thesis and antithesis (in this case soul and body) as "2 = 1" see BÖHME 6 and n 10. See also *BL* ch 8 (*CC*) I 129–30, which seems to be a reworking of this involute note. For soul and body in terms of action and passion

see *IS* 63–4 (BM MS Egerton 2801 ff 43–46ᵛ). See also *Friend* (*CC*) I 94n.

1⁴ Lit "original sin", but in this context more probably the Latin equivalent of πρῶτον ψεῦδος (fundamental error), for which see BAXTER *Reliquiae* COPY B 92 n 1.

⊥

naturally in the brain, nerves, and muscles, just as the movements of a watch are produced simply by the strength of the springs and the form of the wheels.]

Can the Bruckers and German Manualists have read this work of Des Cartes—which yet was his most popular Treatise—that they should (one, I guess, copying from the other) talk of Spinoza's having given Leibnitz the *Hint* of his pre-established Harmony?— What is this XVIth Article if not a clear & distinct statement of thise Theory?/[1]

3   ii 82–4 | iii 187 "Quomodo Generosiores hoc Affectu tangantur"

At tamen Generosiores et qui sunt animo fortiori, ita ut nihil mali sibi metuant, et se supra fortunae imperium statuant, non carent Commiseratione: cum vident infirmitatem aliorum hominum, et eorum querelas audiunt. Pars enim est Generositatis, bene velle unicuique. Verum hujus Commiserationis Tristitia amara non est, sed instar ejus quam producunt casus tragici qui in Theatro re-praesentari videntur, magis est in exteriori et in sensu, quàm in ipsa anima, quae interim fruitur satisfactione cogitandi se defungi suo officio dum compatitur afflictis. Atque in hoc differt, quod cum vulgus misereatur eorum qui queruntur, quia putat mala quae patiuntur valde gravia esse, praecipuum contra objectum Commis-erationis maximorum virorum sit imbecillitas eorum quos queri vident, quia censent, nullum accidens posse dari quod tam grave sit

2[1] C made a similar statement in his ms essay "On the Passions" (BM MS Egerton 2801 f 44[v], written in 1828: in *IS* 64), pointing to "The Histori-ographers of Philosophy from Brucker to Tennemann". C had borrowed Vols I and II of Johann Jakob Brucker (1696–1770) *Historia critica philos-ophiae* (2nd ed 6 vols Leipzig 1766–7) from the Bristol Library Society in the spring of 1797, after first trying William Enfield's abridgment (2 vols 1791). *Bristol LB* 93, 94; cf *CL* I 323. It is not clear whether C used Brucker at a later date, but in 1815 he spoke of Enfield's abridg-ment with contempt, and of Brucker's work as "a Wilderness in six huge Quar-tos". *CL* IV 589, 591–2. In the Prospectus to the Philosophical Lectures he spoke of Enfield and Brucker—and of Stanley's *History of Philosophy*, which he did con-sult and annotate—as "little more ...than collections of sentences and extracts...with no *principle* of arrange-ment, with no *method*" and turned to TENNEMANN *Geschichte der Philosophie* (10 vols Leipzig 1798–1819), which pro-vided him with much primary material for his lectures and became the repository for a mass of marginalia. *P Lects* (1949) 67 and marginalia introduced by the editor *passim*. The ascription of pre-established harmony appears in e.g. JACOBI *Lehre des Spinoza*; see also *BL* (*CC*) I 130. Brucker (IV ii 384–5) and Tennemann (x 474) mention that some persons (not named) had detected such a connexion between Spinoza's deter-minism and Leibniz's pre-established harmony, but dismiss the connexion; C became convinced of it—see e.g. *BL* ch 8 (*CC*) I 130–1.

malum ac Pusillanimitas eorum est qui id ferre non possunt
constanter; et quamvis odio habeant vitia, non ideo tamen oderunt
eos quos illis vident obnoxios, sed solum eorum miserentur.

["How the most noble-minded are touched by this passion".
Nevertheless those who are most generous and strongest in mind, inasmuch as they fear
no ill for themselves and hold themselves to be beyond the powers of fortune,
are not exempt from compassion when they see the infirmity of other men
and hear their plaints; for it is a part of generosity to wish well to one and
all. But the sadness of this pity is no longer bitter, and, like that *caused by
the tragic actions* which we see represented in a theatre, it is more external
and in the senses than in the interior of the soul, which has yet the satisfaction
of thinking that it does its duty in compassionating the afflicted. And there
is this difference here that while the ordinary man has compassion on those
who lament their lot because he thinks that the evils from which they suffer
are very vexatious, the principal object of the pity of the greatest men is the
weakness of those whom they see bemoaning their fate, because they do not
consider that any accident which might possibly happen would be so great
an ill as is the cowardice of those who cannot endure it with constancy; and
although they hate vices, they do not for all that hate those whom they see
subject to them, but only pity them.]

Not always. A man of great fortitude & nobleness of character may
at the same time possess great constitutional sensibility with a lively
imagination. a Now the latter will represent to him, & the distresses
of another, whether known by verbal description or by the usual signs
and visual language of Pain or Grief, with great vividness and
distinctness of impression/ and thus produce in his own passive Life
perhaps even more acute feelings & stronger sentiments of Grief than
the actual Sufferer's Nature is susceptible of—while he cannot take
for granted an equal share of fortitude with himself. He fancies
himself suffering the distress without the power of enduring it—and
apart from the alleviations & compensations with which it would be
accompanied in his own instance and this may be a very painful
sympathy.[1] S. T. C.

DE METHODO

4 p ⁻3, referring to iii 8–9 (marked with an ink line in the margin)

Sed quod ad eas opiniones attinet, quas ego ipse in eum usque diem
fueram amplexus, nihil melius facere me posse arbitrabar, quàm si

---

[3][1] On grief see *IS* 68 (also from "On
the Passions"). Lindsay noticed that a
long passage on fountains had been
marked in the index with two small x's in
ink—*Principia philosophiae* pt iv art
64—and wondered whether these were
C's marks in connexion with the projected
Hymn to the Elements. The marks,
however, seem not to be C's: see
headnote.

omnes simul et semel è mente mea delerem, ut deinde vel alias meliores vel certè easdem, sed postquam maturae rationis examen subiissent, admitterem: credebamque hoc pacto longè meliùs me ad vitam regendam posse informari, quàm si veteris aedificii fundamenta retinerem, iisque tantùm principiis inniterer, quibus olim juvenilis aetas mea, nullo unquam adhibito examine an veritati congruerent, credulitatem suam addixerat. Quamvis enim in hoc varias difficultates agnoscerem, remedia tamen illae sua habebant, et nullo modo erant comparandae cum iis quae in reformatione publicae alicujus rei occurrunt. Magna corpora si semel prostrata sunt, vix magno molimine rursus eriguntur, et concussa vix retinentur, atque omnis illorum lapsus est gravis. Deinde inter publicas res si quae fortè imperfecta sunt, ut vel sola varietas quae in iis apud varias gentes reperitur, non omnia perfecta esse satis ostendit, longo illa usu tolerabilia sensim redduntur, et multa saepe vel emendantur vel vitantur, quibus non tam facile esset humanâ prudentiâ subvenire; ac denique illa fere semper ab assuetis populis commodiùs ferri possunt quàm illorum mutatio. Eodem modo quo videmus regias vias quae inter amfractus montium deflexae et contortae sunt, diuturno transeuntium attritu tam planas et commodas reddi solere, ut longè melius sit eas sequi, quàm juga montium transcendendo et per praecipitia ruendo rectius iter tentare. Et idcirco leves istos atque inquietos homines maximè odi, qui cùm nec à genere nec à fortuna vocati sint ad publicarum rerum administrationem, semper tamen in iis novi aliquid reformare meditantur. Et si vel minimum quid in hoc scripto esse putarem, unde quis me tali genere stultitiae laborare posset suspicari, nullo modo pati vellem ut vulgaretur. Nunquam ulteriùs mea cogitatio provecta est, quàm ut proprias opiniones emendare conarer, atque in fundo qui totus meus est aedificarem.

[But as regards all the opinions which up to this time I had embraced, I thought I could not do better than endeavour once for all to sweep them completely away, so that they might later on be replaced, either by others which were better, or by the same, when I had made them conform to the uniformity of a rational scheme. And I firmly believed that by this means I should succeed in directing my life much better than if I had only built on old foundations, and relied on principles of which I allowed myself to be in youth persuaded without having inquired into their truth. For although in so doing I recognised various difficulties, these were at the same time not unsurmountable, nor comparable to those which are found in reformation of the most insignificant kind in matters which concern the public. In the case of great bodies it is too difficult a task to raise them again when they are once thrown down, or even to keep them in their places when once thoroughly shaken; and their fall cannot be otherwise than very violent. Then as to any imperfections that they may possess (and the very diversity that is found between them is sufficient to tell us that these in many cases exist) custom has doubtless greatly mitigated them, while it has also helped us to avoid, or insensibly corrected a number against which mere foresight would have found it difficult to guard. And finally the imperfections are almost always more supportable than would be the process of removing them, just as the great roads which wind about amongst the mountains become, because of being frequented, little by little so well-beaten and easy that it is much better to follow them than to try to go more directly by climbing over rocks and descending to the foot of precipices. This is the reason why I cannot in any way approve of those turbulent and unrestful spirits who, being called neither by birth nor fortune to the management of public affairs, never fail to have always in their minds some new reforms. And if I thought that in this treatise there was contained the smallest justification for this folly, I should be very sorry to allow it to be published. My design has never extended beyond trying to reform my own opinions and to build on a foundation which is entirely my own.]

De Methodo, ⟨P⟩ 8, 9.—The part to be transcribed is that between the [   ]*ᵃ¹*

ᵃ C has not inserted [ ]; the textus is marked with an ink line in the margin

4¹ The Descartes motto in *Friend* (*CC*) ɪ 204 is from iii 8, preceding this marked passage.

ANTOINE DESMOULINS

1796–1828

Histoire naturelle des races humaines du Nord-est de l'Europe, de l'Asie boréale et orientale, et de l'Afrique australe, d'après des recherches spéciales d'antiquités, de physiologie, d'anatomie et de zoologie, appliquée à la recherche des origines des anciens peuples, à la science étymologique, à la critique de l'histoire, &c. Paris 1826. 8°.

British Museum C 43 b 21

DATE. Possibly c 1827.

1 half-title, pencil

This work is the quintessential French—and Desmoulin's the pure & *intense* Frenchman. No other nation could have produced the Author of this work./[1]

2 half-title, pencil

To M. Desmoulin I must not speak of God or Providence—Well! it shall be Nature then.—Now only abstract the palpable glaring effects of Savagery & Misery, and I call on Mr Desmoulins to shew any instance of five or six aboriginal Species in the whole Catalogue of the Mammalia so slightly distinguished from each other or passing so imperceptibly into each other, as in this 5 or 6 ~~Species~~ Races of Man.—The last fact, the approximation I mean, is a direct contradiction to the conception, SPECIES.[1]

3 title-page verso, pencil

The immense tracts in New Holland and in America without inhabitants—the proof that the Islanders in the South Sea came

[1] C's prejudiced revulsion from French writing and the French way of mind is even more forcefully expressed in DUBOIS. On the unconnectedness of French writing see e.g. *P Lects* Lect 5 (1949) 190, and cf *Friend* (*CC*) II 150 (I 20–1), I 143 and n 1, *SM* (*CC*) 76–7. For C as self-confessed "anti-Gallican" in 1808 see *CL* III 81, 88; and for "the present illogical age" that in the French manner has rejected "all the *cements* of language" see *CL* III 234, 237.

[2] Desmoulins posits sixteen kinds of humans, with races assigned to each: e.g. under "Scythians" appear Indo-German, Finnish, and Turkish. The scheme is displayed in a table at the end of the volume.

thither the miserable unfitness of the poor Savage for his Circumstances—the amazing differences between the inhabitants of neighboring Islands—but why waste reasons on so irrational a Tirade?

Yet as few absurdities, that have not some dim likeness to a truth, so here—the diversity of character implied in the μύθῳ of Cain and Abel, and afterwards of Shem, Ham & Japhet is a necessary *Idea*,[1] but difficult to account for.[2]

4   p vii, cropped | Introduction (a letter addressed to Baron Cuvier)[1]

O Gallia ter felix, ranarum rararumq[ue] avium rariorumque piscium ferax! ut crocitas, ut glocitas, ut gallicinaris! qualem Quac-quac et Splash-spleish fecisti semper et u[bique] facis!—[2]

5   p xxix, pencil

G. CUVIER

Cuvier

Cuvier

Cavier

Cu

3[1] For the "myth" of Adam's judgement against Cain (the elder son, "tiller of the ground", then murderer and outcast) in favour of Abel (the younger son, shepherd and victim), and the story of the division of "the earth after the flood" among Shem (eldest and chosen one), Ham (accursed for seeing Noah's nakedness, and condemned to subservience to his younger brother), and Japheth (the youngest, favoured above Ham), see Gen 4.4–16, 9.18–27, and 10. C implies that each of these is not a mere legendary story but a true myth, a commanding figure—"a necessary *Idea*", a shaping principle—the action of which we can perceive and recognise, even though we do not understand the cause of it. **3**[2] In his historical first book, Desmoulins ignores the evidence of the Bible and cites only those secular authors who had written about the races known to the ancients. For C on the theory of races, see BLUMENBACH **4**.

4[1] At the head of Desmoulins' introductory letter Cuvier's name is adorned with nine lines of titles and distinctions. **4**[2] C's Latin. "O thrice-fruitful France, abounding with frogs and rare birds and rarer fishes! how you croak and cluck and crow! [*a*] what a quack-quack and splish-splosh [*b*] you have always made and make everywhere! [*c*]" "Gallicinate" (see *a*) provides a modulating pun on *Gallicanus* (French) and *gallinaceus* (hen-like) to produce "quack-quack"; (*b*) recalls the excremental couplet in e.g. *CL* II 924 and *CN* III 4103; (*c*) may be a play on the Vincentian canon—"quod semper, quod ubique, quod ab omnibus". Cf DE WETTE **15**. What probably offended C most of all was the way Desmoulins had used the apparently honorific letter addressed to Cuvier as an occasion to direct a highly personal and emotional attack on a man of science whom C greatly admired.

6   p 2, pencil, lightly cropped | "Exposition et division du sujet"

D'autres hommes à peau également jaune habitent aussi, de temps immémorial, l'Asie à l'est du Gange et des monts de Belur. Ils s'étendent sur toute la côte nord-est de l'Asie, sur le rivage opposé de l'Amérique jusqu'au 50ᵉ parallèle, et sur les îles Aléoutes jetées en avant du détroit de Bering. Mais ces peuples ont [*Q]ʸ? suieux?] des cheveux soyeux, rectilignes, roides, très-fournis et plus longs que chez les autres hommes...

[Other men with just as yellow skin have also lived, from time immemorial, in Asia east of the Ganges and the Belur mountains. They spread over the whole north-east side of Asia, on the coast facing America up to the 50th parallel, and on the Aleutian Islands lying in the approach to the Bering Strait. But these people have hair that is glossy, straight, stiff, very thick, and longer than that of other men...]

* It must be *sooty*. Silky (*soyeux*) and *roides* are contradictions.¹

6¹ C is puzzled because *soyeux* usually means "silky" and *roide* (*raide*) means "stiff, straight". However, *che-* *veux soyeux* is a special term for hair that is glossy and thick. The adjectival form of *suie* is not used in French.

WILHELM MARTIN LEBERECHT
DE WETTE
1780–1849

Theodor oder des Zweiflers Weihe. [Title-page of Vol II adds the subtitle:] Bildungsgeschichte eines evangelischen Geistlichen. [Anonymous.] 2 vols. Berlin 1822. 8°.

Originally in grey paper wrappers, now in a late Victorian marbled paper and calf binding. In rebinding, the back wrapper of Vol II was transposed to the front of Vol I, becoming I $^-2/^-1$ (instead of II $^+1/^+2$), the front wrapper of Vol I consequently becoming I $^-4/^-3$. The note written on what is now I $^-2$ refers to a passage in Vol II: see **36** and n *a*.

The Athenaeum of Philadelphia

Autograph signature "Carl Aders" on I $^-4$, II $^-2$; and "H. C. Robinson" on I $^-1$, I $^-3$ (original wrapper of Vol II). Bookplate of Edwin Wilkins Field, executor of HCR, on the front p-d of each volume. (Field, solicitor and amateur artist, died in 1871 only four years after HCR's death; Mrs Koblenzer-Hill bought this copy in Eastbourne at a sale that consisted mostly of Field's books.) Inserted in Vol I, there was previously a letter of 28 Aug 1943 from F. G. Rendall of the BM identifying the author; on the verso of the letter, a biographical note on De Wette evidently written by Mrs Koblenzer-Hill (who first drew these volumes to the editor's attention); this letter is no longer in the book. An incomplete list of the marginalia is written on I $^-1$, $^-3$, II $^-2$, drawn up after the volumes had been rebound. There are many pencilled lines and several notes (usually single words) in pencil in an unidentified hand; these are not recorded here.

Carl (or Charles) Aders, a wealthy young German merchant living in London, attended C's 1811 lectures and had "enthusiasm enough to relish [them] greatly". *CRB* I 56. HCR, already a friend of Aders, saw to it that Aders and C met at dinner on 17 Jan 1812. *CRB* I 59. A year later HCR and Aders were visiting C to talk about Goethe, and C discovered not only that Aders had a fine collection of German and Italian paintings and was a lover of music, but also that he had a good collection of German books, which (as Lamb put it) "pant for that free circulation which thy custody is sure to give them". *LL* II 134. Through HCR first, then directly, Aders became an important source from which C could borrow or acquire German books not otherwise available to him, and by Feb 1830 at latest Aders belonged to a "German Book-Club" that extended C's range of borrowing. See CR (*BCW*) 63 and *CL* III 407, 422, 461, 698, VI 553, 828. By 1818, if not before, Aders had acquired a house in Euston Square and arranged his pictures there as though in a picture-gallery for the enjoyment of his friends.

For C the music at Aders's house was a strong attraction (*CRB* I 122, 288, 293, *CL* v 261–2); but it was the paintings that drew Lamb into close friendship with Aders and made him a frequent member of the big dinner parties that Aders gave as a bachelor and then on an even more splendid scale after his marriage on 6 Jul 1820 to Eliza Smith, daughter of the painter and engraver John Raphael Smith, who had herself exhibited paintings at the Royal Academy 1799–1808. Their acquaintance included William Hazlitt, Thomas Campbell, Flaxman, Irving, Landor, Sir Thomas Lawrence, John Linnell, Basil Montagu, Samuel Rogers; and it was at their house that C's only meeting with HCR's friend William Blake occurred. C, who seems to have visited the Aderses seldom after taking up residence in Highgate (*CL* v 129), was enchanted with Eliza Aders and formed a deep friendship with her that lasted to the end of his life; his poem *The Two Founts* (1826) was addressed to her. *PW* (EHC) I 454–5. See esp *CL* VI 581, 651, 662–5. By Aug 1823 Aders had acquired an estate in Godesberg on the Rhine while continuing to live in Euston Square. The Rhine tour that C and WW took in 1828 was largely planned and arranged by Aders and included at least two visits to Godesberg, where Mrs Aders was spending the summer. *CL* VI 747n. For C's discussion of the design of his gravestone with Eliza Aders in Nov 1833 see *CL* VI 968–70 and GREW **44** and nn.

Only one other of Carl Aders's books with C's marginalia has been identified—RICHTER *Museum* (Stuttgart & Tübingen 1814), bound with HCR's copy of SCHELLING *Einleitung zu seinem Entwurf eines Systems der Naturphilosophie* (Jena & Leipzig 1799); the STEFFENS *Caricaturen des Heiligsten* (2 vols Leipzig 1819–21) that came to the BM from the Green Sale (1880) was probably the copy C asked Aders to lend him on 16 Jan 1825 (*CL* v 407). HCR noted on 3 Feb 1837 that "Mrs. Aders insisted on my accepting some books (German philosophy) in which Coleridge had written notes", but we don't know what these were. *CRB* II 511 (Edith Morley's note that "Some of these are in Dr. Williams's Library" seems now to apply only to RICHTER *Museum*). The wholesale loss of the books marks the decline in the Aders's affairs beginning in 1832/3 with the dissolution of the household at 11 Euston Square and ending three years later in "a terrible reverse in trade" that destroyed Aders's personal fortune. The process can be traced indistinctly through records of the dispersal of Aders's collection of paintings from a public exhibition of them in the Gallery of British Artists in Pall Mall in Feb 1832 through a private sale in 1833 and two public auctions in 1835 and 1839. After the sale of 26 Apr 1839 no more is heard of Carl Aders, and except for a few diary entries by HCR up to 1848 little is recorded about Eliza Aders except that she painted an unsuccessful portrait of WW in 1842. But fourteen Netherlandish paintings from Aders's collection are now in the National Gallery: one came by bequest in 1876, and one by purchase in 1904; the other twelve were bequeathed by Mrs Joseph Henry Green in 1880.

HCR took the annotated DE WETTE to Rydal Mount at the turn of the years 1847/8, when WW was still stricken with grief for the death of his daughter Dora; HCR "looked over Browne's Vulgar Errors with Coleridge's notes", and began reading *Theodor* "expect[ing] amusement independent of some manuscript notes by Coleridge". A fortnight later, apparently not sharing the enthusiasm of many Protestant theologians of his day, he was still reading it doggedly—"a book I go on with, having begun it, though neither itself nor Coleridge's notes are worth much". *CRB* II 671–2. A translation of *Theodor* (2 vols Boston 1841) by James F. Clarke, Unitarian minister and friend of Emerson and Channing, has provided useful information in its introduction and notes: see e.g. **8** n 1 and **10** n 1. Green's library included a copy of De Wette *Vorlesungen über die Sittenlehre* (2 vols Berlin 1823): *Green SC* (1880) 477. On 16 Jan 1825 C asked Aders to get him a copy of De Wette *Lehrbuch der historisch kritischen Einleitung in die kanonischen und apokryphischen Bücher des Alten Testaments* and of Johann Leonhard Hug *Einleitung in die Schriften des neuen Testaments* but there is no further record of such a transaction. *CL* v 407.

DATE. After 1822; possibly 1825–6. C was reading DE WETTE c 7 May 1826: *CN* IV 5371, 5375, 5381.

COEDITOR. Hans Eichner.

1 I 26–7, pencil, overtraced | Pt I bk i ch 1

Die Kantische Lehre von der Gottheit, welche von der Vernunft gefodert werde, damit sie die Herrschaft der Tugend in der Welt herstelle und sie durch Glückseligkeit belohne, fiel wie ein Wetterstrahl in seine Seele, der das heilige Feuer der Andacht in ihr auslöschte, und eine grauenvolle Finsterniss in ihr zurückliess. Die Tugend an sich bedarf Gottes nicht, sie hat ihr Gesetz und ihre Kraft in der Vernunft; nur damit sie im Kampfe mit der Sinnlichkeit desto leichter siege, muss ein allmächtiger Gott seyn als Richter und Belohner: welch ein stolzer, aber auch trostloser Gedanke! Gott *ist* nicht, und wir sind nicht durch ihn und von ihm und für ihn, sondern die Vernunft ist und er um ihretwillen und durch sie.

[The Kantian doctrine of the godhead, which [Kant teaches] is required by reason in order to establish the rule of virtue in the world and to reward virtue with happiness, pierced his soul like a flash of lightning, which extinguished the sacred fire of devotion in it and left behind a horrible darkness. Virtue in itself does not need God; it has its laws and its strength in reason; only in order that virtue might all the more easily triumph in its struggle with sensuality must there be an almighty God as a judge and rewarder. What a proud, but also dismal thought! God does not *exist*, and we do not exist through Him and by Him and for Him, but reason exists and He for its sake and through it.]

How grievously is this doctrine of Kant's misunderstood![1] Kant is[a] speaking of the *Science* of pure Ethics: and if Ethics are to be

a Mistraced as "as"

[1] For the "Kantian doctrine of the godhead" see KANT *Die Religion innerhalb der Grenzen der blossen Vernunft* III v (1794) esp 147–9 and cf III vii *Allgemeine Anmerkung* esp 211–15, 219–22.

scientifically constructed, there remains for the Deity only the completion of the Law by a harmony of Consequences![2] How should it be otherwise? The Logos, the Intelligence & Holiness of God had been already given in the Practical Reason—and what remained but his Almighty Power of Providence? But does he say, that Religion is to be identical with *Science*? No more, than Westminster Bridge with the mathematical Theory of Arches![3]

S. T. Coleridge—

2 ɪ +1, referring to ɪ 27

Er fühlte sich so allein und trostlos mit seiner selbstständigen sich selbst genugsamen Vernunft, gleich einem Kinde, das seinen Vater verloren hat.... Er machte bald mit Schrecken die Entdeckung, dass er nicht mehr beten könne.... Kraft und Trost von oben konnte er sich nicht mehr erflehen; von einem solchen Gott etwas bitten, hiess ja von sich selbst bitten. Ein solcher Gott, der nichts ist als die ewige Ordnung der Welt, die Gewähr der sittlichen Gesetzgebung, kann nichts thun, als was in sich selbst nothwendig und von Ewigkeit her so bestimmt ist: wie sollte das Gebet seinen Willen umlenken und eine Wirkung hervorbringen, die nicht von selbst schon auch ohne dasselbe erfolgen würde?

[He felt himself so alone and comfortless with his independent, self-sufficing reason, like a child who has lost its father.... Suddenly with terror he came to realise that he could no longer pray.... He could no longer pray for strength and comfort from above; for to request something from such a God meant merely to request it from oneself. Such a God, who is nothing more than the eternal order of the world, the protector of the moral law, can do nothing more than what is in itself necessary and has been so determined from eternity: how could prayer bend his will and bring forth any effect, which would not have come of itself, regardless of that prayer?]

P. 27.—But where did Theodore find in Kant that the Practical Reason was his individual Self? That Theodore was Reason?—Kant, as a form of Science, uses the Moral Law in which God revealeth himself to man, as the Equation, ⟨or Representative,⟩ of the

---

1[2] See Kant *Critik der praktischen Vernunft* (of which there is no annotated copy) ɪɪ ii 5, in which the phrase "harmony of consequence" is also suggested.

1[3] C refers to the mathematical analysis made by George Atwood (1746–1807) in 1801–4 of Thomas Tel-

ford's proposal for a single iron arch of 699-foot span to replace London Bridge. C had already used this illustration in greater detail to make the same point in the 1818 *Friend*: see *Friend* (*CC*) ɪ 496–7, *CL* vɪ 789. For more general reference to the theory of arches see *CL* ɪv 875, *C&S* (*CC*) 159.

Supreme Reason, contemplated abstractly from the Divine Power.[1]
But what difference can this make in the Argument? Are not the same
Objections to prayer deducible from the Perfection of the Deity &
his the consequent immutability of his Decrees? And must not the
answers that apply to Calvin, apply *here*?—Nay, Kant himself (the
first who has done so since Duns Scotus and Occam)[2] supplies the
answer: viz. The Idea of God is *altogether* transcendent:[3] what
therefore we are to believe concerning him must be determined by
the Conscience & the Moral Interest, under the *negative* condition
⟨only⟩ of not contradicting Reason.

3 1 41 | 1 i 2

Christus hat selbst gesagt, dass auch Andere vor ihm Götter genannt
worden, und dass er, den der Vater geheiliget und in die Welt gesandt
habe, um so eher Gottes Sohn genannt zu werden verdiene.

[Christ himself has said that others before him were called gods, and that
he, whom the Father had hallowed and sent into the world, deserved so
much the more to be called the Son of God.]

I am greatly mistaken if this, tho' the usual, be the true import of
our Lord's Reference to that singular Verse in the Psalms.[1] I seek
for the interpretation in the words of the Evangelist—He came to
his own: and his own received him not[2]—i.e. included in himself, as
the Universal *Idea*, in whom God contemplated the World,[a]

4 1 45–6, lightly cropped at the foot of 45

Unwillkührlich sprach er das kurze Gebet...welches die Hoffnung
der Auferstehung enthielt. Er besann sich, dass ihm durch die neuere

[a] The note remains incomplete

2[1] Theodore may have found this
notion in Kant *Grundlegung zur Meta-
physik der Sitten* II 36, for C's early
objection to which see *CN* I 1717. For
Kant on the moral law as equatable with
Supreme Reason see *Religion* II §1 B (not
annotated).

2[2] C's admiration for Joannes Duns
Scotus (with Thomas Aquinas) and
Occam is to be seen in e.g. *P Lects* Lect
9 (1949) 280, and for Occam particularly
as "the true transitional mind" in *P Lects*
(1949) 51, Lect 9 266n, 280–1, JOANNES
2 (i 1285), and TENNEMANN VIII ii +6
(referring to 956). In *CN* IV 5087 C says

that, in contrast to Duns Scotus' "strict
proof" of the existence of God, which
amounts to the assertion that "what *is*,
is", "His great scholar & *seeming*
Antagonist, W. Occam speaks out. The
Existence of God is an article of Faith,
inaccessible to Reason, underivable from
Experience. I agree in toto with
Occam...". See also HOOKER 6 and n 1
and TENNEMANN VIII ii 872.

2[3] For Kant on God as transcendent
see e.g. *Critik der reinen Vernunft* (2nd
ed) 611–70.

3[1] John 10.34, citing Ps 82.6.

3[2] John 1.11.

Theologie auch dieser Glaube genommen, und dafür die Idee einer
*] bloss geistigen Unsterblichkeit gegeben war.

[Involuntarily he said the short prayer...that contained the hope of the
resurrection. He called to mind that this belief had also been taken from
him by modern theology and had been replaced by the idea of a merely
spiritual immortality.]

* In what part of the N. T. is the Resurrection of *the* Body taught!
Not by the two highest authorities, John & Paul, I am certain. The
Resurrection of the Dead in the Body (i.e. no mere Ghosts but living
Persons & real Men)—this I do find asserted & this I belie[ve.[1] To
the] other Judæo-egyptian Dogma, I answer with the great Apostle—
Thou Fool! *not* that, which goeth into the Grave, riseth again! Flesh
and Blood cannot inherit the kingdom of Heaven!—[2]

5 I 49

*] Das Gesetz, sagte er, ist nichts weiter, als das Mosaische Gesetz,
und da wir diesem nicht mehr anhangen, so ist auch für uns jene
Lehre von keiner Bedeutung mehr.

[The law, he said, is nothing but Mosaic law, and as we no longer adhere
to the latter, the former doctrine also no longer has any meaning for
us.]

* So say the generality of our Clergy; & if St Paul had been as
shallow a Thinker & Moralist as themselves—it might have been a
plausible interpretation.[1]

6 I 53

Man solle nur um geistliche Güter, um Tugend und Weisheit, bitten,
und alles, was unsere leibliche Wohlfahrt betreffe, in Gottes Hände
legen, indem man sich ganz in seinen Willen ergebe, und, was er uns
sende, Glück oder Unglück, mit Selbstverleugnung annehme; wenn
man so bete und es ernstlich thue, so könne man der Erhörung gewiss
seyn, indem das ernstliche Gebet auch den ernstlichen Willen, sich
*] der geistlichen Güter theilhaftig zu machen, mit sich führe, und so
der menschliche Wille mit dem göttlichen eins werde.

4[1] The phrase "the resurrection of
the body" occurs in both the Apostles'
and the Nicene Creed but not in NT; but
"the resurrection of the dead" occurs in
Acts 24.15 and 21 (ascribed to St Paul)
and in 1 Cor 15.12; cf John 5.21, "the
Father raiseth up the dead" (cf 28–9). C's
interpretation would rest particularly
upon Luke 20.35–8, John 11.25, and 1
Cor 12–44.
4[2] 1 Cor 15.36–8, 50.
5[1] St Paul discussed the relation
between the law and grace particularly in
Romans. For C on St Paul's attitude to
the law see BUNYAN COPY B **16**. Cf also
AR (1825) 189–95.

[One should only ask for spiritual blessings, for virtue and for wisdom, and place everything that concerns our bodily welfare in God's hands by surrendering wholly to His will, and by accepting with self-abnegation whatever He may send us, happiness or misfortune; if one prays thus and does it earnestly, one may be sure that one's prayer will be granted; for the fervent prayer also implies the serious intent to possess spiritual blessings, and so the human will becomes one with the divine will.]

* Doubtless, this ought to form the larger and predominant portion of our Prayers—& should be the only unconditional petitions & the *ultimate* end of all the rest. But I can ~~no~~ see no good reason for forbidding or excluding the latter: and no argument that would not apply equally against my lifting my hand to my mouth to feed myself.[1]

7 86–7, cropped | I i 4

Ein Gott, der um sich selbst zu erkennen, sich in die Welt schaffend ergiesst, und sich in ewigen Umwandlungen immer wieder selbst vernichtet und von neuem gebiert, schien ihm zwar lebendiger und wesenhafter zu seyn, als der Gedanken-Gott, den ihm die Kantische Philosophie gelehrt hatte, aber auch unheiliger und irdischer...

[A God who, in order to know Himself, enters creatively into the world, and who time and again destroys Himself and gives birth to Himself anew in eternal transformations, seemed to him more vital and more substantial than the purely abstract God that Kantian philosophy had taught him, but also less holy and more worldly...]

I can never without indignation read these most groundless attacks on Kant's System: which I distinguish from Kant's own personal opinions respecting Prayer & Miracles.[1] But his System is most

6[1] For C on prayer see 7 n 1.

7[1] The central epistemological thesis of the *Critik der reinen Vernunft*. See also *Critik der praktischen Vernunft* I i §1.

On prayer Kant wrote in *Die Religion innerhalb der Grenzen der blossen Vernunft* IV §2 and Allgemeine Anmerkung (Königsberg 1795) 264–5, 298–9, 302–8, as follows. Whether a man prays aloud or writes his prayers on banners or whirls them heavenward on a wheel is immaterial and worthless. Nothing depends on outward ceremonial, but all on becoming acceptable to God by moral actions. True worship of God is an inward service of the heart. Prayer is "a superstitious

delusion", a wish spoken to a Being who does not need the information. Therefore, by prayer nothing is accomplished and no duties to God are discharged. To pray for something is to wish to be able to work miracles. On miracles Kant wrote in *Religion* III Allgemeine Anmerkung pp 116–24: when man has "attained a true religion that can subsist... by itself and on its own evidence in reason", it is pointless to question miracles or even interpret them. Sensible people admit that miracles are possible, but discount them. Since there are no practical benefits from miracles, man should act as if there were none and, obeying the dictates of reason, should act as though the inner

friendly to the Christian Faith—were it only, that it proves the utter worthlessness of all the Grounds against its doctrines. There is nothing (says Kant) in right Reason *against* it—tho' Reason has no means of demonstrating its truth/ for this plain reason, that Religion is not *Science* but Faith![2] And all the other Constituents of our proper Humanity plead for it and demand it—Our Conscience, our Love of the Good, our Love of the Beautiful, Hope and Affection and Reverence of the Enduring, and yearnings after a satisfying Object and an ultimate end, tho' Experience had shewn us neither the one nor the other.—But these Assailants of this genuine Philosopher overlook the fact, that Kant's Ethics & Vernunft-Religion are to the practical Divine what Mathematics a[re to the] [?Architect...]

8 ı 111 | ı i 6

Theodor besuchte zuerst einige Vorlesungen, welche in sein jetziges Fach einschlugen. Bald aber konnte er der Lust nicht widerstehen, die philosophischen Vorträge eines berühmten Lehrers zu hören, welche sehr häufig besucht wurden.

Das System dieses Philosophen schien ihm zwischen dem Kantischen und Schellingischen mitten inne zu stehen, und beide zu vereinigen.

[Theodore at first attended some lectures that were connected with his present subject. Soon, however, he could no longer withstand the desire to listen to the philosophical lectures of a famous teacher that were very well attended.

The system of this philosopher seemed to him to stand exactly between the Kantian and the Schellingian and to unify them both.]

Solger? or Eschenmeyer? or Jacobi?[1]

man depended solely on his own exertions.
For C on prayer see e.g. BOOK OF COMMON PRAYER COPY B **1** and **29** and n 9, *CN* III 3355, 4183; and on miracles *CN* III 3278, 3897, 4381, 4452.

7[2] In **1**, above, C had denied that Kant held that "Religion is to be identical with *Science*". See KANT *Religion* pp xivff, 63, 77–8, 183–4, 205, 247–8.

8[1] De Wette stated, in correspondence with J. F. Clarke, the American translator of *Theodor* (2 vols Boston 1841), that "this philosopher" was J. F. Fries (1773–1843), professor of philosophy at Heidelberg from 1805 and at Jena from 1816, who tried to reconcile Kant's doctrines with Jacobi's psychology. "The philosophy of Fries," De Wette told Clarke, "taught me how to reconcile understanding and faith in the principle of religious feeling". *Theodore* tr J. F. Clarke I xxxi. Charlotte Broicher observed, in "Fries und Coleridge" *Preussische Jahrbücher* CXLVII (1912) 250, that "the fact remains surprising and noteworthy, that Fries and Coleridge, without knowing of each other, developed Kant's *Critik der Urtheilskraft* in the same direction...".

9 i 112–13

Er ging von einem Urbewusstseyn des menschlichen Gemüths aus,
das er Glauben nannte… Erkenntniss aber sey nur das unvollkom-
mene Abbild des Wesens der Dinge, von welchem das Urbild in jenem
Urbewusstseyn beschlossen liege, und man könne die höchste
Wahrheit und die Befriedigung des Geistes nur im Glauben
finden… Er unterschied zwischen Verstand und Vernunft: jenen
nannte er das niedere mittelbare Bewusstseyn, wodurch die Welt in
Zeit und Raum und in ihren Naturgesetzen begriffen werde; unter
dieser verstand er die unmittelbare Erkenntniss und das ganze Leben
des Geistes in allen seinen Thätigkeiten, und als deren Urquell und
*] Mittelpunkt bezeichnete er den Glauben. Er zeigte, dass die
Erkenntniss nur die eine Seite des menschlichen Gemüths sey, dass
ihr zur Seite das Gefühl und das Thatvermögen stehe, und dass nur
durch alle drei Vermögen das Leben des Geistes vollendet werde,
welche sowohl durch die Erkenntniss als durch das Gefühl und die
That mit der Welt in Berührung trete.

[He proceeded from a primal consciousness of the human mind, which he
called faith.…Knowledge, however, was only the imperfect copy of the
essence of things, the archetype of which lay hidden deep in the primal
consciousness; the highest truth and fulfilment of the spirit can only be
found in faith.…He distinguished between understanding and reason; the
former he called the lower mediate consciousness, by which the world is
understood in terms of space and time and the laws of nature; by the latter
he meant the immediate knowledge and the entire life of the mind in all its
activity; as the primal source and the midpoint, he designated faith. He
showed that knowledge was only one aspect of the human mind, that feeling
and the capacity for action stood side by side with it, and that only all three
faculties together completed the life of the spirit, which came into contact
with the world through knowledge as well as through feeling and action.]

* Is not this the very essence of the *System* of Kant?[1] Those who
cannot distinguish between the System & with its *legitimate* Conse-
quences, and this or that opinion which Kant himself inwove with
his Evolution of the System, are not competent to read Kant, at all.
But if this mean something other and more than what is asserted or
involved in Kant's Critique der Urtheilskraft, & yet ⟨is⟩ not the same
with the *Ideas* of Schelling[2]—what *does* it mean? Much as I dislike

9[1] For Kant's discussion of the
faculties as completing the life of the
spirit see *Critik der Urtheilskraft* Intro-
duction §3 and n.

9[2] C saw the distinction between
Kantian and Schellingian as correspond-
ing to the "two genera generalissima of
Philosophizing"—Platonist and Aris-
totelian. TENNEMANN i 107–8.

Schelling's Jesuitical character, and wholly as I reject his system as far as it is *his*; yet I find his reply to Eschenmeyer respecting this pretended Glaubenskraft, this bewusstlose ideenlose Urbewüsstseyn,[a3] the decisions of which are nevertheless expressible in dogmas, quite unanswerable!—[4]

10 I 114–15

Die Vernunft hat ihren Namen vom *Vernehmen*...

[The etymological root of *Vernunft* (reason) is *Vernehmen* (to perceive)...]

Herder will have it from Verneinen; but more probable than either, from the Theotiscan Nunft for Zunft, a Guild or Company, a consociation—and Wahr = Verum.[1] In short, the original sense of Vernunft was a translation of *Veritas*/ das ist vernunftig—i.e. that belongs to the class of Truths, or that is according to the *faculty* of Truth.—But my wonder is to find this distinction between Reason & Understanding, spoken of as *new*—as a doctrine which a Reader of Kant, Schelling, &c hears for the first time from a Harmonist of their Systems!—

11 I 117

"Sie sind zu rasch, lieber Freund! Ich unterscheide noch zwischen der Vernunft und der ihr einwohnenden Offenbarung. Diese ist der letzte, unbedingte Grund oder der Urquell von jener, gleichsam die

a A slip for "Urbewusstseyn"

9³ "This pretended power of faith, this non-conscious, idealess primal consciousness"—from De Wette I 111.

9⁴ C refers to an exchange between Eschenmayer and Schelling in *Allgemeine Zeitschrift von Deutschen für Deutsche* (1813). Schelling specifically rejects Eschenmayer's "pretended Glaubenskraft" etc on the grounds that true faith is inseparable from thought and knowledge (VIII 185 tr): "The word faith... really expresses only the confidence in the conviction and agreement of the heart with certain knowledge. True faith is itself no other than a believing, confident knowing, in which, as in all true knowing, heart and mind agree; but in no sense of the word is it, as you and some others claim, a complete negation of all knowing."

10¹ The Herder reference has not been traced; it may be a slip of memory. The ms clearly reads "Verneinen" (deny, contradict); this may be a slip for *vermeinen* (think, consider). In SCHELLING *Denkmal* pp 192–3, in which Schelling cites Hamann as deriving *Vernunft* from *vernehmen* (perceive, understand), C gives the same account of *Vernunft* as related to *verus* (true). The received etymology is that given by Schelling. C referred to "THEOTISCAN" as "the transitional state of the Teutonic language from the Gothic to the old German of the Swabian period". *BL* ch 10 (*CC*) I 209. He received instruction in it from Thomas Christian Tyschen (1758–1834) at Göttingen and said in May 1799 that "I can now read it pretty well". *CL* I 494; cf V 491.

Sonne, aus welcher alle Strahlen der Erkenntniss und des geistigen Lebens fliessen...."

"Herrlich, herrlich! das macht mir Alles klar."

["You are in too much of a hurry, my dear friend! I also distinguish between reason and the revelation that is inherent in it. The latter is the last unconditioned ground or the primal source of reason, exactly like the sun, from which all rays of knowledge and the life of the mind emanate...."

"Marvellous, marvellous! that makes everything clear."]

Marvellous! What then is the Reason? a *passive* Consciousness of the Revelation? If not, but a power of affirming by its own light the *truth* of the Revelation, which ~~can~~ must of course consist wholly in its accordance with the reason itself, what is gained by this more than by Kant's Doctrine, that certain truths of Reason ~~have~~ derive their objective reality from the Conscience![1]

12 i 145–7 | i i 8

"...halten Sie es für schlechthin unmöglich, dass Jesus diese körperliche Eigenschaft, auf dem Wasser, wie auf dem Lande, zu gehen, gehabt habe?"

"Allerdings; denn es streitet diese Annahme mit dem Gesetz der Schwere, welches wir ganz genau kennen."

"Aber ich habe Menschen gekannt, welche, ohne schwimmen zu können, niemals im Wasser untersanken, und wenn sie sich untertauchten, immer wieder von selbst in die Höhe kamen."

["...do you take it to be absolutely impossible that Jesus had the physical quality of being able to walk on water just as on dry land?"

"Of course; for this assumption conflicts with the law of gravity, which we know for certain."

"But I have known men who could not swim and yet never sank down in water, and if they dived under, they always rose up again effortlessly."]

It is well known, that the human Body in a passive or unagitated state of the feelings is nearly of the same specific gravity as water: else how could men swim or float? It is not improbable that some men may be exactly of the same sp. gr. or even a fraction less—and such men would of course rise like cork.[1] But what has this to do with walking

---

11[1] *Critik der praktischen Vernunft* i i §1.

12[1] The specific gravity of a human body is slightly greater than that of water. If a body weighs less than the water it displaces it will float, if more, it will sink; for a body sinks if its average density is greater than the density of water. Fresh water weighs about 62.4 lbs per cubic foot, salt water about 64 lbs; a person floats higher in salt than in fresh water because of the greater density of salt water. In recent years it has been shown that the flotation of air in the lungs can

on water? In order to this, the Water and not the man must be altered and cease to act equally in all directions—i.e. must lose the lubricity of its parts as happens in the case of Frost. Consequently, our Lord's Act must have been super-natural: and doubtless a Will that could expand the repressive Power which with us is confined within the outline of the Soles of the Feet a yard or more in all directions, like a pair of invisible Snow-shoes, would enable a man to walk on the Sea with as much ease as a Duck swims.[2] A vast rapidity of motion would have the same effect, but then this would not be walking, but skimming.

13 ɪ 175 | ɪ i 11

Ist nicht, dachte er, jeder dieser Tänze, sey es Walzer, Menuet, Quadrille oder Ecossaise eine Allegorie der Geschlechtsliebe?...Es kann nicht gut seyn, dass die Jugend, beiderlei Geschlechts, in dieser erhöheten sinnlichen Stimmung sich einander nahe kommt...

[Is not every one of these dances, he thought, be it a waltz, a minuet, a quadrille, or an ecossaise, an allegory of sexual love?...It cannot be a good thing if the youth of both sexes approach each other in this heightened sensual mood...]

Against this reasoning I protest. In England at least, our young Ladies think as little of the Dances representing the moods and manœuvres of Sexual Passion as of the Man-in-the-Moon's whiskers: & woe be to the Girl, who should so dance as to provoke such an interpretation. Es mag anders getanzt seyn in Teutchland.[1] I My recollections of Germany in 1799 incline me to fear, that it is so.[2] But still this is beginning at the wrong end. Bring about a revolution in the Books that the Girls read, and the conversation they hear: and the Dancing will be ~~more~~ as harmless as the Dancers. But while Wieland, and Goethe are idolized;[3] and even religious & philos-

---

offset the small negative specific gravity and establish a slow rhythmic movement in which the head sinks below the surface and then rises above it for long enough to recharge the lungs. This rhythm can be sustained for very long periods, but only if the swimmer remains "passive or unagitated" i.e. does not swim.

12[2] On 25 Aug 1978 an American army sergeant, Walter Robinson, walked across the English Channel from Dover in eleven and a half hours, using home-made "water shoes" that he had

developed (in appearance a cross between oversized snowshoes and pontoons). Reported in *The Times* 26 Aug 1978.

13[1] "Perhaps they dance differently in Germany."

13[2] For C on German dancing see *CL* ɪ 458, 506–7, *CN* ɪ 414, 448. Cf also THE AGE 2.

13[3] I.e. by popular romantic reputation in Germany. For Wieland's immorality see *Sh C* ɪɪ 64, 158, *BL* ch 15 (*CC*) ɪɪ 22. In 1815 C considered that parts of Goethe's *Faust* would be

ophical popular works abound in discussions and ~~phy~~ psychologico-moral disquisitions on the sexual relations; the Reformation of Walzing & Ballets would but effect a quaker-like suppression of the ~~display~~ Symptoms, while the Distemper would prey inwardly on the vital parts of their moral Being.

14   I 212–13 | I ii 1

"Die dichterische Bedeutung des Lachens liegt noch tiefer. Es entsteht aus einem Widerspruch, einer Verkehrtheit. Um einen Widerspruch zu fassen, muss man eine Regel haben, nach der man ihn messe. Diese Regel ist keine andere als das Urbild des menschlichen Lebens, mit welchem die Erscheinung des Lächerlichen kontrastirt; und indem wir darüber lachen, kommt uns jenes Urbild dunkel zum Bewusstseyn, wir erheben uns über den Widerspruch in die freie Region des Urbildlichen...."

["The poetic significance of laughter lies still deeper. It arises from a contradiction, an absurdity. In order to grasp an incongruity, there must be a rule to compare it with. Such a rule is none other than the ideal of human life, with which the appearance of the laughable is contrasted; and insofar as we laugh at that, this ideal comes darkly into the consciousness; we raise ourselves above the incongruity into the free realm of the ideal..."]

Laughter is a physical phænomenon: and must be physically explained. The contrast of an act or image with our Ideal of Humanity may be the accompaniment of Laughter in particular instances; but when we laugh at a sweet Infant's droll looks? Where is the contradiction here? It is the Law of Pleasure to pass into Pain, and this is especially the case where from the unimportant nature of the incident the nerves are unprepared & withdrawn from the control of the Will: and Laughter is the nascent Convulsion by which Nature breaks off the train of sensations before they reach a painful state. Hence it is, that the suppression of Laughter is always painful, and sometimes even dangerous.—[1]

15   I 226–7 | I ii 3

Der Grundfehler der Kantischen Forschung über die Sittlichkeit lag darin, dass er das Gefühl verkannte, und fälschlich annahm, dass der

---

"highly obnoxious to the Taste & Principles of the present righteous English Public". *CL* VI 1036.

14[1] C made a note in Oct–Nov 1799 to "Analyse the causes why the ludicrous weakens the Memory" and how by laughter "associations [are] suddenly

shattered". *CN* I 501, 502; see also *CN* I 1586, *CL* III 506, and *TT* 25 Aug 1833. For the suggestion that C drew from Richter's *Vorschule der Aesthetik* much of what he said about the laughable in Lect 9 of 24 Feb 1818 see *Misc C* 117–18, 440–6.

*] Wille durch die Erkenntniss bestimmt werde. So ward seine Sittenlehre die Beute des Verstandes, und das Gefühl und mit ihm die Wärme und das Leben hatte daran keinen Theil.

Theodors Lehrer sah hingegen richtig, dass das Gefühl, welches im Herzen wohnt, ein ursprüngliches Vermögen ist, worin die Wurzel der sittlichen Gesetzgebung und dasjenige liegt, wodurch der Wille angeregt und bestimmt wird, nämlich, die *Liebe*. Liebe im Herzen tragen, und den Willen ihrem reinen Dienste unterwerfen, das war ihm der Hauptgedanke der Sittenlehre; und dadurch erhielt die Kantische Idee des kategorischen Imperativs Leben und Fülle.... Die Fülle der Liebe ist unergründlich und verliert sich in die Tiefe der Gottheit, welche die Liebe ist; aber eine Regel ist uns klar gegeben, das ist die Liebe des Nächsten und unser selbst, als des Ebenbildes der Gottheit.

[The basic error of Kant's investigation of morality was that he failed to appreciate feeling and assumed incorrectly that the will is determined by cognition. Hence his moral philosophy fell prey to reason; and feeling, and along with it warmth and life, had no part in it.

On the other hand, Theodore's teacher saw correctly, that the feeling which resides in the heart is an original capability, in which the root of the moral law lies, as well as that through which the will is stimulated and determined, namely, *love*. To carry love in the heart, and to submit the will to her pure service, *that* was the primary thought of the moral doctrine and through this the Kantian idea of the categorical imperative gained its life and fullness.... The fullness of love is unfathomable and loses itself in the profundity of the Godhead, which is love; but one rule is clearly given to us, and that is the love of our neighbour and ourselves, which is also the love of the image of God.]

* I am really ashamed of the ingratitude of the modern German Writers towards Kant.[1] Kant does no such thing; but enforces the important truth, that the finite Will should be subordinated to the Practical Reason, not as Will to Cognition (Erkenntniss) generally, but as a finite Will to the Absolute or Divine Will, of which the Practical Reason is *our* only immediate representative.[2]—All this ~~gabble~~ verbiage about Gefühl, Love &c lies between Goose & Duck—Gabble and Quackery.[3] Love is as its object—the Object of

---

15[1] For C on the ingratitude of the modern German writers to Kant see e.g. *CRB* i 70 (3 May 1812).

15[2] See *CN* i 1710 and 1717, and KANT *Grundlegung zur Metaphysik der Sitten* ii 15–16, 36 (not annotated). Cf also FICHTE *Bestimmung* 16.

15[3] For similar onomatopoeic foolery see e.g. DESMOULINS 4. Here, however, C combines the sense of silliness and charlatanism. *OED* notes "quackery" as behaving like a quack in 1707, of "quackery" as the sound of ducks in 1828.

Religious Love is God; but God is a pure *Act*—in Action therefore must the Love of God subsist.⁴ To love ~~Christ~~ God, says Christ himself, is to obey ~~my~~ his commandments/⁵ ~~and to~~ love your neighbor *as* you love yourself.⁶ Now Schl. and the other Syncretists and Compounders of Kant's, Fichte's, and Schelling's Philosophies, would have us pretend to love God, in the same way that we love each other—instead of what Christ commanded—Love your neighbor *as* yourself; but God *above* all.—⁷

16   ɪ 230

[De Wette quotes from Schleiermacher's *Reden über die Religion*:]
"Die Wissenschaft ist das Seyn der Dinge in uns, in unsrer Vernunft; Kunst und Bildung ist unser Seyn in den Dingen, in ihrem Maass und ihrer Gestalt; und beides kann in uns nicht zum Leben gedeihen, als nur sofern die ewige Einheit der Vernunft und Natur, sofern das *ᵃ*allgemeine Seyn alles Endlichen im Unendlichen unmittelbar in uns lebt."

["Science is the being of things in ourselves, in our reason; art and culture are our being in things, in their order and form; and neither can come alive in us except in so far as the eternal unity of reason and nature, the general being of everything finite in the infinite, is immediately alive in us."]

I have no other objection to this but that it *means* nothing: if it does not mean what is neither Truth nor Christianity. Remove the *allgemeine*: and it is in every Catechism/.¹

17   ɪ 266–7 | ɪ ii 6

Ich habe kürzlich über das Wunder der Speisung gesprochen; aber *]ich konnte mich nicht dabei aufhalten, dass Jesus auf wunderbare Art den geringen Vorrath an Speise vermehrt hat (was nicht einmal ausdrücklich gesagt wird), weil darin nichts für das Gemüth erweckliches liegt...

ᵃ An ink line in the margin runs from here to the end of the textus; C begins his annotation with a similar line

15⁴ See Donne *Sermons* copy b **44** and cf *Friend* (*CC*) ɪ 117n.

15⁵ John 14.15.

15⁶ Matt 22.37–9, Mark 12.30–1, Luke 10.27.

15⁷ In e.g. Schleiermacher *A Critical Essay on the Gospel of St. Luke* and *Über den sogenannten ersten Brief des Paulos an den Timotheos*. On syncretism

see Baxter *Reliquiae* copy b **47** n 1 and e.g. *CN* ɪɪɪ 4251 (May 1815).

16¹ By removing *allgemeine* (here tr "general") the term *Seyn* would lose its pantheistic implications. The relation between *Vernunft* and *Natur* could then correspond to the description of a sacrament as given in the Catechism: "an outward and visible sign of an inward and spiritual grace". Cf **31** n 1, below.

[I preached recently about the miracle of the feeding of the five thousand; but I could not dwell on the fact that Jesus miraculously increased the meagre supply of food (which is not even expressly stated), because there is nothing inspiring for the mind in it...]

* Nicht ausdrücklich gesagt??—As well might it be said, that in relating that I had gone in the Stage to Euston Square,[1] I might possibly have gone without Horses—for I had not expressly mentioned them!—And the question of no importance!! What is it of no importance whether the only Authorities for *all*, we know of Jesus, were honest sensible Men, or Dupes, and Fablers?—Away! away! with such dishonest Toleration! Plain Atheism is Religion compared with it.—

18 I 288–9, pencil, overtraced | I ii 8

O wie verfehlen doch, rief Theodor aus, als er allein war, diejenigen Gottesgelehrten, welche ihren Scharfsinn auf die natürliche Erklärung der Wunder und die kritische Beleuchtung der biblischen Geschichte wenden, und dabei der hohen Bedeutung, welche darin *] für das fromme Gefühl liegt, vergessen, wie verfehlen sie ihres Zieles!

[O, Theodore cried out when he was alone, how they miss their goal, those theologians who apply their acumen to the natural explanation of miracles and to the critical exegesis of biblical history, and in doing so forget *the great significance* these things have *for pious feeling!*]

* Fromme Gefühl? fromme Teufel! Was frommes can there be in impostures,[1] or in exaggerations and misconceptions of plain incidents so gross & blind as to be first Cousins to imposture? And *how* can an honest man arrive at the hohen Bedeutung[2] without looking at the road, thro' which he must travel thither? Either—as is *my* faith—there exists no ground or fair pretext for questioning the miraculous in the New Testament Narratives—or there does. And if there does, Paulus of Jena acts as an honest man ought to act.[3] Truth! The whole Truth! Nothing but the Truth! This is the only foundation on which *my* Religion can stand.

17[1] Carl and Eliza Aders lived in Euston Square.
18[1] "Pious feeling? Pious, the devil! What piety can there be...". Cf **39**, below.
18[2] "Great   significance"—underlined in the textus.

18[3] For H. E. G. Paulus (1761– 1851) as a "Neologic Divine" see DAVISON **3** n 2. In the introduction to PAULUS *Das Leben Jesu* (2 vols Heidelberg 1828) he stated his position on the question of miracles: (tr) "*My greatest wish is that my observations on the*

19 ɪɪ 28 | ɪɪ i 3

[Theodore and a Catholic clergyman discuss the validity of the ecclesiastic tradition as a complement of Scripture.]

I do not know, which has managed this most interesting Argument of Tradition as co-ordinate with Scripture weakest, the Protestant Plaintiff or the Catholic Defendant.

20 ɪɪ 29

*] [THEODOR:] "Ich gebe Ihnen auch zu, dass die Kirche höher steht als die Schrift, weil die Stiftung derselben durch das lebendige Bekenntniss, dass Jesus Gottes Sohn sey, nicht aber durch die Anerkennung der Schrift geschah."

["I also grant you that the Church ranks above the Scriptures, because it was founded by the living acknowledgement that Christ is the Son of God, and not by the recognition of the Scriptures."]

* This is *my* Conviction; but in the mouth of Theodore, after his definition of the Church on p. 15 it seems to me either a contradiction or a bubble.[1] The Church is here spoken of as an *authority*, a governing and directing Power, in like manner as the Scriptures. But how is this predicable of the whole multitude to be governed & guided? It is like the Jacobin nonsense of the Sovereignty of the People.[2]

---

accounts of the miraculous be by no means taken as the main point. Oh, how empty would be a devotion to God or a religion the genuineness of which depended on a belief or a disbelief in miracles. . . . The main point is certain in advance, that the most inexplicable alterations in the course of *nature* can neither invalidate nor establish any *spiritual* truth, for it cannot be observed in any natural event what spiritual design has made it happen in this manner and no other. . . . In itself the proof from miracles demands . . . that the assertions should be worthy of the divine and not contrary to reason. If they be so, miracle is no longer necessary as proof of them." ɪ x, xi, xiv. C commented on all three of these passages with some qualification. De Wette studied under Paulus in 1800 in Jena, where Paulus was professor until in 1811 he became

professor at Heidelberg. C also annotated HCR's copy of Paulus's edition of Spinoza *Opera* (1802–3).

20[1] On ɪɪ 15 a passage is marked with a pencil line, possibly by C: (tr) "The Church is a spiritual association based on a common conviction and mood, and to this extent it ought to be quite free; but for the same reason it is not a private matter, but the most general association that is to be found among men. It extends over the whole earth and throughout all ages." Theodore argues against the hierarchical authority of the Church, and insists that authority comes from *die Völker.*

20[2] For C's rejection of "the sovereignty of the people" see e.g. *SM* (*CC*) 16; but see also *EOT* (*CC*) ɪ 70, 109, 116, 123, 135–8 (all 1800), etc.

21 II 39 | II i 4

*] Wenn einst die reine Geistigkeit des Protestantismus sich mit einer anschaulichen glänzenden Hülle umgibt: dann wird etwas viel Höheres zu Stande kommen, als die katholische Kirche jetzt aufweisen kann.

[If in days to come the pure spirituality of Protestantism will clothe itself in a visible, lustrous cloak, then something much higher will come into being than anything the Catholic Church can now boast of.]

* This is sad Lack of Thought! Had the Author only bethought him of our familiarity with Opera-Houses, Splendid Scenery, Vauxhall,[1] &c!! What can a lustrous Hülle be but a splendid Coat?

22 II 56–7 | II i 6

Ich war längst so glücklich, einen mir von Jugend an eng verbundenen Freund zu besitzen; aber an dem Gute der Freundschaft kann man nicht reich genug seyn. Und je mehr man liebt, desto fähiger wird man der Liebe, und desto mehr kann man davon den Freunden zuwenden.

[I had long been so fortunate as to have one friend who was closely bound to me by youth; but one can never be rich enough in the goodness of friendship. And the more one loves, the more capable one becomes of love, and the more of it one can bestow on one's friends.]

21[1] A garden on the south bank of the Thames in the borough of Lambeth, named Falkes Hall (or Fox-hall) after the thirteenth-century manor on that site, had been a pleasaunce for the people of London long before the new garden called Spring Gardens was laid out in 1661. Pepys used to resort there often, finding it "a great refreshment" and "mighty diverting" to listen to "the nightingale and the birds, and here fiddles and there a harp, and here a Jew's trump, and here laughing and there fine people walking". The gardens had become highly fashionable before the middle of the eighteenth century and so continued in C's day. In his *Walks Through London* (1817) 302–3 David Hughson gave a description of Vauxhall Gardens as he saw them. "These extensive gardens contain a variety of walks, illuminated with coloured lamps, and terminated by beautiful transparent paintings. Opposite the west door is a magnificent Gothic orchestra, and on the left, an elegant rotunda, in which the band perform, in rainy or cold weather. At ten o'clock, a bell announces the opening of a cascade, with the representation of a water-mill, a mail coach, etc. Fireworks of a most brilliant description are also among the attractions of this charming place....The respective boxes and apartments are adorned with a vast number of paintings, many of which are executed in the best style of their respective theatres. The labours of Hogarth and Hayman are the most conspicuous....Upwards of 15,000 lamps have been used to illuminate the gardens at one time....Those who have never visited the 'fairy land of fancy', can form an idea of its fascinating appearance only by conceiving themselves to be in some of those enchanted palaces and gardens, so admirably described in the Arabian Nights' Entertainments."

Among many other proofs, which I have noted elsewhere, this may be added, of the difference in kind between Friendship and Love: and in confutation of the debasing but alas! the common opinion, that the purest Love is no more than Friendship + Lust.[1] Were this the truth, a woman might be in love with half a dozen Persons. But all, who are capable of Love, know that it must be exclusive—and the reason is evident, when it is seen that Friendship is Sympathy, but Love Correspondence—not a juxta-position of homonimous poles (gleichnämigen[a] Polen) but the Union of opposite Poles.—Hence too the more intense the Individuality in a man, the more necessarily is his Love exclusive.

23   II 96–7 | II i 10

*] Also auch von dieser Seite kam Theodor im Streite nicht vorwärts, und er überzeugte sich, dass es überall im Denken und Handeln auf etwas Erstes ankomme, auf welches sich alles Andere gründe. Dieses Erste lässt sich nicht beweisen und rechtfertigen, ja nicht einmal in einen bestimmten Begriff fassen; es ist ein Gefühl, ein Trieb, eine Richtung.

[So also from this point of view Theodore could make no headway in the dispute, and convinced himself that what mattered everywhere in thought and action was some first principle, on which everything else was based. This first principle cannot be proved or justified, and indeed cannot even be expressed in a definite concept: it is a feeling, an instinct, a tendency.]

* This is very true, and the whole dialogue highly instructive. The only way is to detect the πρῶτον ψευδες[1] the first principle or Postulate, from which all that follows derives its semblance of sense and pertinence—and then to return to this point, and shew its arbitrariness—that the individual can only say—It is so: because I choose to think, that so it is.

24   II 100, pencil, roughly overtraced

[WALTHER:] "Mein sündhaftes Ich sehe ich tief unter mir... hoch dagegen in himmlischer Glorie strahlend steht Christus über mir, von dem meine Seele alles Licht empfängt."

a A slip for "gleichnamigen"

22[1] C objected to the view he attributed to WW that love is simply friendship combined with lust: see *CN* III 3284. See also KANT *Metaphysik der Sitten* 3. For C on love and friendship see e.g. BROWNE *Religio* 22 and nn and BÖHME 132 and n 1; also the *Improvisatore* and *Love and Friendship Opposite*: *PW* (EHC) I 462–8, 484.

23[1] An admissible variant of πρῶτον ψεῦδος—"fundamental error". See BAXTER *Reliquiae* COPY B 92 n 1.

[THEODOR:] "Auch ich, wenn ich meinen Gemüthszustand prüfe und im innern Kampfe mit mir selbst begriffen bin, richte meine *] Seele nach Christo hin, dem Urbild aller Wahrheit und Vollkommenheit, und frage mich 'was er über mich urtheilen würde, ob ich vor seinem prüfenden Richterblick bestehen möge'; aber meine höchsten Gemüthserhebungen verdanke ich dem Aufschwung des Geistes zu Gott, dem unsichtbaren Vater."

[[WALTHER:] "I see my sinful self far below me... but Christ, from whom my soul receives all light, stands high above me, radiant in heavenly glory."

[THEODORE:] "I too, when I examine my state of mind and am caught up in an inward struggle with myself, turn my soul towards Christ, the prototype of all truth and perfection; and I ask myself, 'how would He judge me? Would I be able to justify myself before his examining, judging gaze?'; but I owe my most sublime spiritual exaltation to the flight of my mind towards God, the invisible Father."]

* If Walther's be enthusiasm, surely this borders on Superstition.[1]

An "Urbild *aller* Wahrheit und Volkommenheit"/[a][2] but he is yet not God—

25 ii 101–2

*] Was ist der Sinn der Lehre von der Dreieinigkeit...

[What is the meaning of the doctrine of the Trinity...]

* Note to last line but 8.

The sense & import of the Trinity is to me abundantly clear—viz. that God is—not an abstract barren Unity, such as we conceive in Space; nor yet an exclusive Unity, = A because not = B, not = C, not = D &c, as when I say, this is *one* billiard ball; but he is a positive all-including Unity, containing all distinctions of Being, that verily *are* and that are verily distinct. Now all real distinctions ⟨are⟩ resolved into three genera generalissima, or absolute Ideas—1. Absolute Will. 2. Realized Will, or real, i.e. Spiritual Being, Idea, pure Intelligence—these being but different terms for the same Conception. 3. Communicate Unitive Life: Feeling and Act, Spirit, Love.—And the Deity exists entire and absolute at once in each of these.[1]

a A slip for "Vollkommenheit"

24[1] C often drew a distinction between enthusiasm and fanaticism, and in BAXTER *Reliquiae* COPY A 51 said that "Fanaticism is the *fever* of *superstition*."

See also BIRCH 1 and n 1 and BUNYAN COPY B 4.

24[2] A "prototype of *all* truth and perfection"—from textus.

25[1] See also 37 and n 1, below.

26 II 113 | II i 11

[Theodore says of the New Jerusalem:]...des Mondes Schein wird
seyn wie der Sonnen Schein, und der Sonnen Schein sieben Mal
heller, denn jetzt...

[...the light of the moon will be as the light of the sun, and the light of the
sun will be seven times brighter than it is now...]
I hope, we shall have *Goggles* provided!

27 II 117 | II i 12

*] [Theodor:]...dass es nur in der Ansicht der Menschen, nicht aber
an sich und wirklich Böses gibt.

[...that evil does not really exist in itself but only in the opinion of man.]

* This is a Sophism below a School-boy! Wherein but the Will, and
the Intention can *Evil* exist?[1] Pain may; but where actual Evil exists,
Pain may be a Blessing.[2]

28 II 121–2

Theodor antwortete: dass das Böse an sich nicht sey, haben die
rechtgläubigsten Kirchenlehrer behauptet; sie erklären es für einen
Mangel.

[Theodore answered: that there is no evil in itself has been asserted by the
most orthodox doctors of the Church; they interpret it as a lack.]

Even Schelling would have taught this omne et nihil christian[1] the
shallowness of this pseudo-platonic Opinion of some of the Fathers
respecting the negativity of Evil.[2] It suits very well, however, with
a pantheistic christianity, a religio hybrida or compound of Spinoza
& St Paul!

29 II 130

Das Christenthum vereinigt in seiner Dreieinigkeitslehre alle Ele-
mente der Religion in vollkommenem Einklang, und die Idee des
heiligen Geistes, als der dritten Person in der Gottheit, scheint mir
eben pantheistisch zu seyn. Denn das ist der wahre Pantheismus,

27[1] For C on the relation between
will and evil see e.g. *AR* (1825) 278–80.

27[2] See LEIBNIZ **4** (ii 134), in which
C asserts that "physical Evil" (pain) is
"subordinate" to moral evil.

28[1] This "all and nothing"

Christian—i.e. pantheist. For if God is
all, he is nothing: see HILLHOUSE **1**.

28[2] See e.g. St Augustine *City of
God* 11.8, 12.1, 22.1. See HACKET *Scrinia*
24 and n 1. For a summary of C's varying
view of the nature of evil see *Lects 1795*
(*CC*) 107–8n.

überall, in allem Lebendigen, eine göttliche Urkraft zu ahnen, welche alle endlichen Kräfte trägt und bewegt. Der falsche hingegen besteht darin, dass man, das Endliche in das Unendliche auflösend, alle *] besondere Wesenheit aufhebt, und die besondern Erscheinungen der Dinge für Ausflüsse des Urwesens ansieht.

[Christianity unifies in the doctrine of the Trinity all the elements of religion in complete harmony. The idea of the Holy Ghost as the third person in the Godhead just seems to me to be pantheistic. For true pantheism senses everywhere, in all that lives, a divine primeval power that supports and moves all finite forces. False pantheism, on the other hand, consists in rarefying all particular being by dissolving the finite in the infinite, and in regarding the individual phenomena of things as emanations of the primal being.]

* And how does the Author avoid this Aufhebung der Wesenheit?[1] By a visual image, a crude metaphor—der Allgemeine Heilige Geist *trägt* die endliche*ª* Kräfte—![2]—so much for this newest Urgefühl-religion!—[3]

30 ii 140–1 | ii i 13

*] ...derjenige Gedanke ist der richtigste, welcher dem Gefühl am angemessensten ist.

[...that thought is the most correct which is most commensurate with feeling.]

* The necessary consequence of which would be, that every man, woman and child must have a several & different Creed. The Brahmin finds the Thought of Deva incarnate in a horned Beast, perfect God and perfect Cow, morest admensate[1] to his Feeling—the African finds the Fetisch that which he feels most &c—But what can be more demoralizing than to adjust the Reason to the Feeling, instead of framing our feelings to our Reason! The Author will reply—This is not what I mean by *dem* Gefühle.[2] But if you do ⟨not⟩

ª A slip for "endlichen"

29[1] "Suspension of all particular being"—variant of a phrase in textus.
29[2] "The universal Holy Ghost *carries* the finite forces"—quoted from the sentence immediately preceding the textus. C frequently asserted that the spiritual can be represented "in the idea alone, and never as an image or imagination": see e.g. *Friend (CC)* i 501.
29[3] Religion based on "primal (*or* pure) feeling". For C's rejection of

Fichte's derivation of knowledge and belief from something akin to *Urgefühl* see FICHTE *Bestimmung* **4, 5, 10**.
30[1] Commensurate—from *admetior*, *admensus* (measure out)—a direct rendering of *angemessensten* (in textus) through Latin into English. Not in *OED*.
30[2] For the importance to C of the interaction of reason and feeling see e.g. *CN* i 1623 and cf *Friend (CC)* i 398.

mean Gefühl by Gefühle, why do you use the word? And what *do* you mean?

31 ɪɪ 141

Die Ahnung einer allmächtigen Geisteskraft, erwiederte Theodor, welcher unser Geist am ersten verwandt ist, die er im Glauben erfassen kann—einer Kraft, die unsichtbar und einfach, Alles, das Grösste wie das Kleinste, bildet und erhält, ist mir der wahre Bedanke in dieser [biblischen] Lehre....Von dieser Kraft lebt ein Keim auch in mir, der durch Glauben und Liebe ins Unendliche wachsen kann...

[The true thought in this [biblical] doctrine, Theodore replied, is in my opinion the intimation of an omnipotent spiritual power, to which our spirit is most closely related and which our spirit can comprehend in faith—a power that, invisible and simple, forms and maintains everything, the greatest as well as the smallest....A germ of this power lives in me, too, a germ that can grow through faith and charity into infinity...]

Ein Keim, a Seed, Bud, or Germ, of a simple omnipresent Power—how shall I makinge ⟨a⟩ meaning out of this? What should we think of a *Germ* of the Power of Gravitation?[1]

32 ɪɪ 143

Ach! es ist das Gefühl des irdischen Wechsels, dem wir unterworfen sind, die Sorge des Verlustes, was die Begierde weckt. Wir wollen das, was uns entgehen kann, eng' an uns schliessen; und was wir gierig an uns reissen, ist eben nur das Vergängliche und Irdische, die äussere Erscheinung; und nur zu leicht verliert sich der Blick in den irdischen Reiz der nahe gerückten Gestalt, und erblindet für den Himmelsschein, der sie umgibt.

[Alas! it is our awareness of the temporal change that we are subject to, the fear of loss, that arouses desire. We want to hold tight to what can be lost to us; and what we greedily seize is only the ephemeral and the worldly, the outward appearance; our gaze loses itself all too easily in the worldly fascination of the shapes that are close to us, and becomes blind to the light of heaven that surrounds them.]

Equally just in the thought, & beautiful in the expression. A thousand times have I said or sighed the same.—[1]

31[1] C's objection is to the "crude metaphor": see **29** and n 2, above. Cf, however, C's view that each of the elements of the Bible is "at the same time a living Gᴇʀᴍ, in which the Present involves the Future, and in the Finite the Infinite exists potentially". *SM (CC)* 49, and cf **30** and 99.

32[1] Between **32** and **33** occurs the discussion of William Tell "leaping out of the boat" to which C refers in *CN* ɪv 5371, 5375 (c 7 May 1826).

33 ɪɪ 191–3 | ɪɪ i 17

[Defending his belief in the legend reporting that Niklaus von Flüe had totally abstained from food towards the end of his life, Theodore argues:] Der eine kann zwei, der andere vier, ein dritter vielleicht sechs Tage fasten; und möglich, dass es ein vierter vielleicht noch weiter treibt: warum soll es nicht auch einen Menschen geben können, der Jahre lang so viel als nichts geniesst? Alles was nicht einen reinen Widerspruch in sich schliesst, was nur auf einem Mehr oder Weniger beruht, ist für möglich zu halten.

[One person can fast for two days, another for four, and a third for six days perhaps; and it is possible that a fourth can hold out perhaps even longer. Why should there not be a man who for years eats almost nothing at all? Everything that does not contain a pure contradiction in itself but depends only upon a question of degrees should be considered possible.]

Here is a triple confusion or at least confusing indistinction in the word, möglich. X may ⟨be⟩ logically possible—and in this sense Swift's Lilliput and Brobdignag are possible; i.e. there is no contradiction in the terms. Yet the same X may be really impossible—i.e. involve a contradiction to a Law of Nature/ Again it may even in this sense be *negatively* possible—i.e. it may not contradict any Law of Nature, as far as we know; and yet not according with any known result of the Laws of Nature, it is more probable, that it does. Lastly, the question respecting any given Miracle is not, whether it be possible in either of the three senses of the word, logically, negatively, or positively, but whether it be *credible*. And Theodor's vindication of old Nic von der Flue is very weak reasoning.[1] Of the pretended instances on record the two most recent, after having stood a much closer & more vigilant ex Investigation than was or could be given in the case of Nicolaus, with credit and triumph, wasere at last detected to be impostures—and in one instance by a mere and extraordinary accident.[2]

34 ɪɪ 218–20 | ɪɪ i 19

Sind die Menschen selbst sehr geistig ausgebildet, so ist es natürlich, dass sie sich Gott auch geistig denken; und doch kann dabei dasjenige fehlen, was das Wesentliche in Gottesglauben ist, ich meine *]* die Ahnung eines unerreichbar, unbegreiflich Höheren, dem wir

33[1] Niklaus von Flühe (1417–87), a hermit who played an important part in holding the Swiss Confederation together, was canonised in 1947. His hermitage is still visited by pilgrims.

33[2] The "two most recent...impostures" have not been identified.

uns demüthig unterwerfen. Ist der Mensch zu einem hohen Grad von Bewusstseyn gelangt, dann reicht es nicht mehr hin, Gott als ein menschlich bewusstes Wesen zu denken.

[If men are very highly trained intellectually, then it is natural that they also think of God as intellectual. And yet in this view the essential element of faith in God, that is, the intimation of some unattainably, incomprehensibly higher being, to whom we humbly subject ourselves, may be missing. If man has achieved a high level of consciousness, then it is no longer enough to think of God as a being with some sort of human consciousness.]

* With all Schelling's faults, he is too clear a Thinker to sanction such Ahnung-drivel as this[1]—the trite Verbiage of the Alexandrine Philosophy. What cannot be comprehended may yet be contemplated; and what can neither be comprehended nor contemplated, cannot possibly be expressed. And it does seem strange to me, that a man of so fine a mind as the Author of this work, should have imposed on him⟨self⟩ a faith in the limitedness of his own intellect for an Attribute of the Supreme Being. God may have attributes which he has not revealed to us, nor given us faculties capable of knowing—but this we know, that they cannot contradict the Attributes, he has revealed to us—ex. gr. that his name is, I AM I Am.[2]

35 ɪɪ 256 | ɪɪ i 21

Kann man an das Evangelium des Johannes, dem das Leben seines göttlichen Meisters in einer höhern Verklärung erschien, in welcher das Himmlische das Irdische überstrahlte, den Massstab legen, nach welchem man die Glaubwürdigkeit eines gewöhnlichen Denkwürdigkeiten-Schreibers misst? Da wo ein neues geistiges Leben entsteht...lässt sich da eine Geschichtschreibung erwarten, welche Alles in pragmatischem Zusammenhange und in gemeiner Deutlichkeit darstellt?

[Can the Gospel written by John, who saw the life of his master in a sublime transfiguration, in which the heavenly element eclipsed the earthly, be judged by the standards that are normally applied to the author of memorabilia? At a time when a new spiritual life begins...can we expect a historical account that presents everything in a plausible context and with everyday clarity?]

34[1] Drivel about "intimations". On the fault of trying to express the inexpressible see **45**, below, and cf **29** and n 2, above.

34[2] See *BL* ch 12 (*CC*) ɪ 272–5 and cf Bɪʙʟᴇ ᴄᴏᴘʏ ʙ **57** and n 1, **119** and n 1.

In the name of German Uprightness & English Common Sense what can this mean? *Because* John's mind was enlightened and expanded—*therefore* we must expect that his relations of what he had seen & heard must be ex riddle my ree—& such that what he actually saw & heard, no living Soul can decypher!

36 I ⁻2 (in rebinding misplaced from II ⁺1/⁺2), referring to II 256

Setzen Die den Fall, die Geschichte des Christenthums enthielte keine Undeutlichkeiten, Räthsel und Wunder, und läge vor uns so klar, wie das Tageslicht: könnte es dann seinen Charakter als eine höhere Erscheinung behaupten? Alles was gross und ausserordentlich ist, bringt auch sein Wunderbares und Räthselhaftes mit sich.

[Suppose that the history of Christianity were to contain no obscurities, mysteries, and miracles, but were as clear to us as day: could it then preserve its character as a higher manifestation? Everything that is great and extraordinary brings with it elements of wonder and mystery.]

P. 256. 1. 9.*ᵃ*

What gross sophistry! Doubtless, if Christianity be a fact, i.e. an immediate outward Revelation (God manifest *in the Flesh*)[1] it would be strange indeed if a faithful Narrative of the same contained nothing but events of common History—. But what is this to do with the question—which is, whether the facts therein recorded are truly or falsely stated? This Bread that I am eating is converted into flesh/—the Water at Cana was converted into Wine—The first is an ordinary event: the latter what without troubling themselves about a definition all men would call a miracle (supposing, no trick were suspected). But how can this affect the relation of the facts? Why might not the one be recorded as distinctly and intelligibly as the other? The ⟨intelligibility of the⟩ *relation* of the facts, not the intelligibility of the facts themselves, is the point in dispute.—Properly speaking, we comprehend the one conversion as little as the other.—

37 II 270 | II i 22

Sie [fast alle christlichen Lehren] tragen mehr oder weniger das Gepräge der Zeit, in welcher sie zuerst zum Bewusstseyn gekommen sind; andern hat eine spätere Zeit ihre Farbe geliehen, wie der Lehre *] von der Dreieinigkeit und der Gottheit Christi.

ᵃ That this flyleaf was misplaced in rebinding is confirmed by a pencilled note on II 256 in an unidentified hand: "See End of Vol"

36[1] 1 Tim 3.16.

[To a greater or lesser extent, they [i.e. almost all the Christian doctrines] bear the stamp of the age in which they were first conceived; others, such as the doctrine of the Trinity and of the divinity of Christ, were given their colour by a later age.]

* Will, Mind, Life—The Good, the True, the Wise—το αγαθον, η αληθεια, η σοφια[1]—what other *colour* or meaning could this sublime doctrine ever have had?

Of the holy Spirit the Scripture is not so explicit, as a Protestant might wish. But of the first and second Person what can be more express than both John & Paul?

38   II 272–5

*]...In Christo, dem reinen vollkommenen Menschen...

[...in Christ, the pure and perfect man...]

* This a favorite phrase, a fashionable point of view, with the sentimental Theologians of Herder's and Schleiermacher's School.[1] But I want to know, when they assert that in Jesus the Human Character was realized in ideal perfection, by what standard they measure & appreciate? Before *I* can form any judgement of a person's Character, I must ascertain who and what he is, his rank, circumstances, aims, objects. If I thought of Christ, as the English Unitarians think, my opinions would not be the same respecting his moral excellence, as they would be if I denied or questioned his possession of miraculous powers & privileges with sundry German Divines. Still more, nay, altogether different will my appreciation be, if I regard him as Luther & the Catholic Church generally believe—viz. as the incarnate Word, the co-eternal Son of God who became Man. What I could not help deeming presumption, and fanatical arrogance on the former supposition strikes me with grateful awe as the most astonishing humility on the latter. And similarly in other points of character—sincerity, fortitude & so forth—In short, theseis finde sentimental Complimentsing of our Lord seems to me a part of that scheme, which I utterly dislike—that of making Christ & the Christian Religion a lump of soft Wax, to play with & try fancies on.—

37[1] Two formulations of the Trinity, the Greek terms—"the good, truth, wisdom"—virtually equivalent to the second triad. See **25**, above, and **42** and n 1, below.

38[1] On "the Schleiermacher School" cf **HEINROTH 2** n 5.

39 ii 279

In Allem, was lebt, ist ein Strahl des göttlichen Lichts; aber erst in der Allheit der Welt, in welche alle einzelne Strahlen zusammenlaufen, erscheint uns die ewige Sonne. So trägt auch jeder Mensch das Ebenbild Gottes an sich, aber nur in demjenigen, welcher alle menschliche Vollkommenheit in sich vereinigt und gleichsam der All-Mensch ist, erscheint der Abglanz der Gottheit.

[In everything that lives, there is a ray of the divine light; but the eternal sun only appears to us in the totality of the world in which all individual rays converge. Thus, every man is made in the image of God, but the reflection of the Godhead appears only in him who unites all human perfection in himself and who is, as it were, the universal man.]

In the last § ph. but one I find, first a metaphor (Ray of divine Light), 2. an eternal Soun,[1] not a source of Radiance, but a product or unit of Aggregation, by the concurrence of Rays, which Sun & which concurrence are neither a Sun nor a concursion but the *Allness* of the World—which, I suppose, means all the World/[2] 3. a bold Assertion—& 4th another Metaphor, the Abglanz der Gottheit,[3] from a metallic Mirror.—Verily, my uninitiated cold Common Sense is too sick to smile—& does not care, how soon das fromme Gefühl[4] takes hold of it!—

40 ii 282–3 | ii i 23

...das Vertrauen zur menschlichen Kraft wächst durch die Erfahrung *] die wir von einer ausserordentlichen Kraft in andern Menschen machen; ja, auch die Lust und der Eifer wächst, wenn wir Andere das Vollkommene leisten sehen.

[Confidence in human power grows with our experience of an extraordinary power in other men; and indeed, our eagerness and zeal increase when we see others achieve perfection.]

* When the disproportion is great, the very contrary takes place. So in the present case, the sinless perfection of our Lord renders his *life* & *actions* the only safe *Model*, for mankind, but ~~disqualifies him from being~~ but not in ~~ex~~ himself an *example* that ~~excites~~ excites by hope to imitation. In the Drama this is universally acknowleged. All that

39[1] On "Sun/Son" see AURELIUS 35 n 2.

39[2] For C's use of the term "ray" (αὐγή) in a scheme of the relation between God, Christ, and man see BÖHME 169 and n 1.

39[3] "Reflection of the Godhead"— from textus.

39[4] "Pious feeling"—as in **18**, above.

follows on p. 283[1] I can only answer by denying—except as these relations of Christ to us are proofs of his Love & Goodness and thus inspire the hope of being aided by his spirit, and pardoned thro' his intercession. These indeed *are* most powerful influences. Besides, what unprejudiced man will deny that the New Testament represents Christ as reconciling God to us, and not merely us to ourselves.

41 ii 285

Dieser Art von Menschen [den Kantischen Moralisten] fehlt einmal die Demuth, welche die Rechtfertigungslehre voraussetzt und emp-
*] fiehlt; die Anerkenntniss, dass das Sittengesetz nicht vollkommen erfüllt werden kann; sodann der Hinblick auf eine alles übertreffende, nie ganz erreichbare Vollkommenheit; endlich die wahre beseligende Gewissensruhe, deren Stelle ihnen die anmassliche Zuversicht auf sich selbst ersetzen muss.

[This kind of man [the Kantian moralist] lacks first of all the humility that is presupposed and recommended by the doctrine of justification; he lacks the knowledge that the moral law cannot be entirely implemented; the awareness of a perfection that surpasses everything and can never be entirely attained; and finally the true blissful peace of conscience, which he must put in the place of a presumptuous reliance on himself alone.]

* Here again an unjust attack. If there be one writer who has expressed this more forcibly than another, it is Immanuel Kant. But I am convinced that Kant is more talked of than read—one proof of which is, that this very theory of Justification was first started by Kant himself—& is one of the weakest parts of his Writings.[1]

42 ii 287

Christus ist das Urbild der Wahrheit und der Güte...Seine Weisheit...hat alle andere Weisheit zu Schanden gemacht, und die höchsten Grundsätze der Wahrheit hergegeben.
[Christ is the archetype of truth and goodness...His wisdom...has triumphed over all other wisdom and has provided the highest principles of truth.]

Christ was indeed, in my belief, the Wisdom of God from the beginning. But if this Writer means his moral precepts & parables,

---

40[1] De Wette argues (p 283) that Christ lived and suffered in order to communicate his perfection to us, that we thereby participate in his perfection, his perfection becoming our own.

41[1] For Kant on justification see *Religion* ii §1c.

the substance of all which pre-existed in the Old Testament, I must remind him—that it was [not]*a* Christ's *wisdom* in *this* sense that Paul preached,[1] but Christ only and him crucified.[2] Even so was the world christianized—by faith in Christ crucified for the forgiveness of Sins.

43   II [307] (fly-title to Bk II)

This Second Book and indeed all the Dialogues on Catholicism[1] are so well written and for the far greater part so just and in so truly Christian a Spirit, that I should scarcely have attributed them to the same Author.

44   II 422, pencil | II ii 12

Alles, was den Glauben betrifft, selbst die Auslegung der heil. Schrift, soll im Katholicismus dem Urtheil der Kirche unterworfen werden; die Kirche aber ist nichts weiter, als die Gesammtheit der Bischöfe, nach dem System des römischen Stuhls sogar der Pabst selbst, in welchem die Fülle aller bischöflichen Gewalt ruhen soll; wenn nun der katholische Christ nichts glauben darf, als was die Bischöfe gut geheissen, so ist ja klar, dass er an diese, und nicht an Christum glauben darf.

[In Catholicism, everything that concerns faith, even the interpretation of Holy Writ, is to be subjected to the judgement of the Church; but the Church is nothing but the aggregate of the bishops, including—according to the system of the Roman See—even the Pope himself, in whom the sum total of all episcopal power is said to reside. Now if the Catholic Christian is to believe nothing but what the bishops have approved, then it is obvious that he must believe in them and not in Christ.]

Might not a R. Catholic retort—that on the same ground the Prot[nt] might be said to believe the Scripture not Christ?

45   II 483 | II ii 17

[Having been accused of sharing the error of the Patripassians, who held that God the Father had shared Christ's sufferings, Theodore

a Word supplied by the editor

42[1] Cf **37** and n 1, above. C maintains, in N 36 f 72 (*CN* v), that in the OT (Septuagint) the terms Λόγος, Σοφία, and Πνεῦμα Θεοῦ (Spirit of God) are used without distinction as synonyms for the spirit of God: in this sense, Λόγος (of Ps 33.6) and Πνεῦμα Θεοῦ (of Gen 1.2) are the same as the Σοφία of Prov 8.16.

The Christ-Logos of John 1.1–4 is thus the *Wisdom* of God, and all three terms represent the second person of the Godhead. Cf BIBLE *NT Gospels* **3** n 1, DONNE *Sermons* COPY B **75** n 1, and EICHHORN *Apocrypha* **11** n 3.
42[2] 1 Cor 2.2.
43[1] I.e. in *Theodor.*

replies:] Ich vermeide diesen Fehler...indem ich Gott nur, insofern er in der Welt erscheint, am Leiden Theil nehmen lasse.

[I avoid this error...by assuming that God participates in suffering only in as far as He appears in the world.]

An insufficient answer, but in fact no answer can be given *in words*. We must refer to *the Idea* itself. So it is. Not indeed the Father, but yet the eternal Word, θεος κοσμητωρ,[1] did suffer.

45[1] "God as creator"—literally "God giving order to the world".

DIALOGUE

A Dialogue on Parliamentary Reform. London 1831. 8°.

Published by Roake & Varty, 31 Strand, publisher of H. N. COLERIDGE
Notes on the Reform Bill, bound in this same volume. Bound as fifth in
"PAMPHLETS ON THE REFORM BILL".

British Museum C 126 h 15 (5)

Since the "Barrister" of the anonymous *Notes on the Reform Bill* (1831) has
now been identified as HNC, and that tract was issued by the same publisher
as the *Dialogue*, HNC might seem a likely author of the *Dialogue*. Roake
& Varty, however, published a large number of controversial tracts at that
time—it seems to have been their main business. Furthermore, the setting
of the *Dialogue*, the use of Lincolnshire dialect, and the tone of this rough
piece of invective make HNC's authorship unlikely. It is also unlikely that
if C had thought this was written by HNC he would have written notes so
dismissive in tone, or that he would have spoken of it as one of "all these
Anti-reform tracts".

DATE. 1831. Month of publication is not recorded.

1   p † 1, referring to p 6, pencil

[A Radical and a Tory are arguing with a Grazier about "bribery,
corruption, and boroughmongering":]
>   *Rad.* Because it is against the constitution!
>   *Tory.* Where *is* the constitution, sir?
>   *Rad.* Where!—the Lord knows where; any where, but where it
> ought to be.
>   *Graz.* The Lord deliver me from such a rigmarole; the constitution
> any where!—odds, mun, thee dostn't mean to sai ould England ha'nt
> a constitution?—What's all to do, at Westminster there?

P. 6—In all these Anti-reform tracts I see one error or defect—the
absence of *all* concessions. I would, because I must, admit, that the
language of sundry Statutes and Resolves of Parliament being what
it is, a notorious contravention to this express Law-language in actual
practice, is an evil.[1] The Evil may be in the language of these

---

1[1] See *SM* (*CC*) 64: "RIGHT in its
most proper sense is the creature of law
and statute, and only in the technical
language of the courts has it any
substantial and independent sense. In
morals, Right is a word without meaning
except as the correlative of Duty." The
"evil" arises from confusing "right" as
defined by law with moral right.

Statutes—or in the Acts incompatible with it—but as long as they co-exist, *an Evil* is./

2   pp 18–19, pencil

Tory.... What reasonable ground have you to suppose, that six hundred men, of honourable life and character, at least, *generally*— *]* (for exceptions must ever present themselves in large bodies of men however chosen,—of birth, rank, and education,—men, who in their private conduct are unimpeachable), should, when assembled together in a body, become at once, rogues, plunderers, and tyrants?

* *Mem*—And who *are* in fact the notorious *Exceptions?*—Even the notorious Bawlers, Menacers, and Slanderers *for* the *Reform*!!:— Whittle—neither Wit nor Wit-tol—Harvey—Long *Wellesley*— Hunt/[1]

2[1] On the "sophists and incendiaries of the revolutionary school" and "mob-sycophants" see *LS* (*CC*) 125, 144, and cf 152–5. C names three radical politicians who, in their various ways, made themselves obnoxious to the Tory party. Daniel Whittle Harvey (1786–1863)— "neither Wit nor Half-wit (or Cuckold)" —eloquent orator and radical agitator, MP for Colchester (1818–20, 1826–34), giving strong support to the dissenters of that riding, voted for the Catholic Relief Bill (1829) and for the Reform Bill (1831). It was said of him as an orator that "He could thrill you in his best days by reading the alphabet". *G Mag* NS XIV (1863) 662. William Pole Tylney Long-Wellesley (1788–1857)—his name was parodied in [James and Horace Smith] *Rejected Addresses* (Edinburgh 1812), and C's italics may be a silent comment on his being nephew to the Duke of Wellington—MP for Wiltshire (1818–20) and for St Ives (1830–1), was one of the recalcitrant Tories who defeated the Wellington ministry in 1830. Committed to the Fleet for contempt of court in 1831, he nevertheless became MP for Essex 1831–2. A notorious spendthrift and adulterer, he lived off his uncle's bounty for the last years of his life and was described in his obituary as "redeemed by no single virtue, adorned by no single grace". Henry Hunt (1773–1835), radical mob-orator—referred to in *TT* 28 Apr 1823, and perhaps in *LS* (*CC*) 125, 144—active in Bristol politics 1806–17 and a friend of Cobbett, had agitated for parliamentary reform particularly since his imprisonment for presiding at the meeting that turned into the Peterloo Massacre (1819). Regarded by his opponents as "an unprincipled demagogue", he eventually gained the seat for Preston (by default) 1831–3, but behaved in debate in a way that endeared him to no individual or party. On losing his seat he retired from politics and became a blacking manufacturer.

HENRY AUGUSTUS DILLON-LEE
VISCOUNT DILLON
1777–1832

The Life and Opinions of Sir Richard Maltravers, an English gentleman of the seventeenth century, &c. [Anonymous.] 2 vols. London 1822. 8°.

Not located; marginalia not recorded. *Green SC* (1880) 163: "Presentation copy from the author, with autograph inscription to S. T. Coleridge and MS. notes in the handwriting of the latter."

JOHN DONNE

1573–1631

Poems, &c. By John Donne, late Dean of St. Pauls. With elegies on the authors death. To which is added divers copies under his own hand, never before printed. London 1669. 8°.

Yale University (Beinecke Library)

Charles Lamb's copy. Bought by George T. Strong in New York in 1848: the initials "G. T. S." are written on the title-page, and the number "388" is written in pencil in the top corner of p ⁻3. This volume was in the possession of W. Harris Arnold in 1903.

Notes in a seventeenth-century hand are written on pp 3, 47, 155, 162, 169, 184, 200, 231, 304, 322, 321 (misprinted for 323), 333, 396. Passages are marked, and textual corrections made, apparently by Lamb, on pp 5, 6, 22, 31, 48, 66, 75, 80, 84, 97, 119, 121 (misprinted 221), 125, 130, 134 (possibly C's), 147, 164, 168, 206, 227, 234, 237, 255, 263, 281, 288, 308, 311, 363, 364, 370, 373, 376, 380. Short notes are written on pp 222, 365, 366, 376, also apparently by Lamb; some of C's notes are in direct response to Lamb's markings, corrections, and notes. A brief comment on p 2 in a neat small hand has been traditionally assigned to C but seems not to be in his hand. The comment "How excellent!" on p 365, also traditionally ascribed to C, is in Lamb's hand. On pp 414 and ⁺1 the word "Mass" is written in ink, sideways, in an unidentified hand.

C seems to have read Donne's poems in 1796 in the corrupt text and small type of Anderson's *British Poets*. (*B Poets* reprints the 1719 ed and follows the eccentric grouping used in Bell's *Poets of Great Britain* 1779: see Grierson II lxxv n.) Like Ben Jonson, C admired the *Satyres* first, and made note in c Oct 1796 to write "Satires in the manner of Donne—", and did so in a verse letter to Poole. See CHALMERS 3 n 1, *CN* I 171; cf *IS* 152–3. It is possible that Donne's accounts of the Azores expedition, *The Storme* and *The Calme*—a verse letter "To Mr. Christopher Brooke"—left their mark on *AM*. Late in 1803 C made some notes on the *Elegies* and verse *Letters* (*CN* I 1786–1789; cf 698) and at this time wrote a note on the supposititious poem *On the Blessed Virgin Mary* thinking it Donne's (ANDERSON COPY A 2). When he began to annotate Lamb's copy of the *Poems* in 1811, he brought to it some years of enthusiastic critical reflection, the experience of attempted imitation, and an exceptionally fine ear.

On 27 Feb 1818 C lectured on Donne, Dante, and Milton. "I am vain enough," he told H. F. Cary before the lecture, "to set more than usual value on the Critique, I have devoted to the names of Dante, Donne and Milton (the middle name will, perhaps, puzzle you) and I mean to publish it singly, in the week following it's delivery." *CL* IV 827. He did not publish the lecture; although part of what he said about Dante and Milton on that occasion is recorded, nothing on Donne survives even in the notes for the lecture as repeated in the following March. See *CN* III 4494; cf *BL* ch 1 (*CC*) I 23 and *C Talker* 239.

At the back of N 43 ff 80ᵛ–79 (*CN* v) C has written: "The FILTER | By successive Chipping the rude Block becomes an Apollo or a Venus. By leaving behind I transmute a turbid Drench into a chrystalline Draught, the Nectar of the Muses!: the Whole is mine. To eject is as much a living Power, as to assimilate: to excrete as to absorb...." He then devoted three pages to poems of Donne (referred to by ordinal numerals); the five poems to which the "Filter" is applied in part are *Breake of Day*, *A Valediction: of the Booke*, *Loves Growth*, *Loves Exchange*, and *A Valediction: Forbidding Mourning*. Cf *TT* 23 Oct 1833; and for two "Adaptations" from Donne included in *The Friend* (1818) see *PW* (EHC) II 1117.

Although some of C's annotations on Donne's *Poems* were among the earliest of his marginalia to be published, by chance they did not have the wide currency, even in incomplete form, that their intrinsic interest warranted. William Hone, through his friendship with Lamb, included some of them in *The Every Day Book* (1826). G. T. Strong's purchase of the annotated copy after Mary Lamb's death led to the publication of many of the marginalia in the *Literary World* (30 Apr, and 2, 14, 28 May 1853); he also communicated the notes to DC for inclusion in *NTP*, published later in that year, but too late for inclusion in Shedd's *CW* in the same year. By the time T. M. Raysor began to collect C's critical writing the volume had disappeared, with the help of MS TRANSCRIPT (*a*) he constructed a more complete version than had hitherto been published and, by including this in *Misc C* (1936), placed the Donne marginalia in the mainstream of C's critical observation. It remained for K. Davis, after the original had come into the possession of Mr Weld Arnold, to publish the first reasonably complete and accurate transcript of the marginalia on Donne's *Poems* in *N&Q* May 1963. The unusual number of MS Transcripts is a mark of the interest these marginalia have aroused in those who, from c 1825 onwards, were able to catch a glimpse of the original.

MS TRANSCRIPTS. (*a*) Harvard MS Eng 966: a section of the notes transcribed by Barron Field (1786–1846) in preparing for the Percy Society his unpublished ms "The Songs and Sonnets of Dr. John Donne, with Critical Notes by the Late Samuel Taylor Coleridge". The prefatory note reads in part: "The following Notes were written by the Poet Coleridge in his and my friend Charles Lamb's copy of Donne; and Mr. Lamb permitted me to transcribe them into mine, thirty years ago. I expected that they would be published...in the 'Literary Remains'...but the learned Editor of that work has lamentably died without collecting them....[F]ew as they are they are too precious to be lost to the world; and the Poems of Donne are so little read, that there will be no harm in affording the Members of the Percy Society with opportunity of refreshing their acquaintance with this learned and fanciful poet...." See *C 17th C* 519–20n. Despite omissions, this transcript includes four notes not found in previously published versions.

(*b*) Not located: notes transcribed by Barron Field into his copy of the 1669 ed of *Poems*: see (*a*), above.

(*c*) Not located. Formerly in the collection of George A. Lyward, Tenterden, Kent: ms facsimile, notes transcribed in an unidentified hand into a copy of the 1669 ed. Comparison with the printed version by Strong and with the Field ms suggests that this transcript is based on the Strong version.

(*d*) Harvard EC.D7187.633 pg(B): ms facsimile, notes transcribed by Charles Eliot Norton into a copy of the 1669 ed, with other notes of Norton's not deriving from C. Only about a dozen of C's notes are included, but three of these are not found in any other transcript.

DATE. Early 1811: **61** is dated 2 May 1811. Although there are parallels between some of these marginalia and the 1808 marginalia on Lamb's copy of DANIEL, and with AURELIUS marginalia that may belong to 1808, there is no evidence that any of the annotations in DONNE *Poems* were written much before the date given in **61**. (C was seeing a good deal of Lamb in Mar–May 1811.) The notebook entries most closely related to these marginalia are *CN* III 4073 (c Apr–May 1811) and 4152 (May 1812).

SPECIAL ABBREVIATIONS. "Gardner"—*John Donne: The Elegies and The Songs and Sonnets* ed Helen Gardner (Oxford 1965); "Grierson"—*The Poems of John Donne* ed Herbert J. C. Grierson (2 vols Oxford 1912); "Milgate"—*John Donne: The Satires, Epigrams and Verse Letters* ed W. Milgate (Oxford 1967).

INDEX TO THE MARGINALIA

	CHALMERS	DONNE *Poems*
Commendatory Verses	3	
Air and Angels		**18**
Canonization		**12**
The Dissolution		**23A**
The Extasie		**20A, 21**
A Feaver		**17**
The Flea		**4, 4A**
The Good-morrow	5	**5, 6**
The Indifferent		**11**
Loves Deity		**22**
A Nocturnal upon S. Lucies Day		**19**
The Primrose		**23**
Song: "Goe, and catch a falling starre"		**7, 7A**
Song: "Sweetest Love, I doe not goe"		**14, 16**
The Sun Rising	7	**10**
The Triple Fool		**(12), 13**
Twicknam Garden		**18A**
The Undertaking		**9**
A Valediction Forbidding Mourning		**20**
Womans Constancy	6	**8**

(ANDERSON COPY A **2** is an annotation on the supposititious poem *On the Blessed Virgin Mary*.)

1   p ⁻3

To read Dryden, Pope &c, you need only count syllables; but to read Donne you must measure *Time*, & discover the *Time* of Each word by the Sense & Passion.[1]—I would ask no surer Test of a Scotch-man's *Substratum* (for the Turf-cover of Pretension & they all have) than to make him read Donne's Satires aloud. If he made manly Metre of them, & yet strict metre,—*then*—why, then he wasn't a Scotchman, or his Soul was geographically slandered by his Body's ~~being~~ first ~~apparent~~aring there.—[2]

2   pp ⁻2-⁻1

Doubtless, all the Copies, I have ever seen, of Donne's Poems are grievously misprinted. Wonderful that they are not more so, considering that not one in a 1000 of his Readers have any notion how his Lines are to be read—to the many 5 out of 6 appear anti-metrical.—How greatly this aided the Compositor's negligence or ignorance,[1] & prevented the Corrector's remedy, any man may ascertain by examining the earliest Editions of Blank Verse Plays, Massinger, Beaumont & Fletcher, &c[2]—Now Donne's Rhy~~mes~~thm ~~were~~as as inexplicable to the many as Blank Verse, spite of his

---

[1]¹ See also **16**, **24**, below, and DANIEL **7**. C later discussed the relation in Donne of sense, passion, and metre: see BEAUMONT & FLETCHER COPY B **10**, **26**, **41** PS. This note draws attention to one of C's most unusual endowments as a prosodist—the sense of (what may be called) the "absolute duration" of the verse line. For C timing shipboard manoeuvres according to "pulses in

poetry", see *CN* II 2064 §6. Cf *CN* I 1610 f 72.

[1]² For C's use of the Scotchman as type of dullness see e.g. ANDERSON COPY B **8** and n 1.

[2]¹ The closing petition of the Litany includes the formula "to forgive us all our sins, negligences, and ignorances".

[2]² See e.g. BEAUMONT & FLETCHER COPY B **16** and **22**.

Rhymes—Ergo, as Blank Verse, misprinted.—I am convinced that where no mode of rational Declamation, by pause, hurrying of voice, or apt, ~~and~~ some times double, Emphasis can ⟨at once⟩ make the verse ~~at once~~ metrical & *bring out* the sense & passion more prominently, that there we are entitled to alter the Text, when it can be done by simple omission or addition of That, Which, And, & such "small Deer"[3]—or by mere new-placing of the same Words.—I would venture nothing beyond.

S. T. C.

3 p ⁻1

N.B. Tho' I have scribbled in it, this is & was Mʳ Charles Lamb's Book, who is likewise the Possessor & (I believe) lawful Proprietor of all the Volumes of the "Old Plays" excepting one.[1]

SONGS AND SONETS

4 p 1, written vertically in the outer margin | *The Flea*

On Donne's first Poem.[1]

Be proud, as Spaniards. Leap for Pride, ye Fleas!
In Nature's *minim* Realm ye're now Grandees.
Skip-jacks no more, nor civiller Skip-Johns,
Thrice-honor'd Fleas! I greet you all, as *Dons.*
In Phœbus' Archives register'd are ye,
And this your Patent of Nobility![2]

2[3] Cf Shakespeare *Lear* III iv 138: "mice and rats, and such small deer".

3[1] Lamb wrote to C on 7 Jun 1809: "...I fetch'd away my books [from the *Courier* office]...and found all but a third volume of the old plays, containing 'The White-Devil', 'Green's *Tu Quoque*', and the 'Honest Whore',—perhaps the most valuable volume of them all—*that* I could not find. Pray, if you can, remember what you did with it, or where you took it out with you a walking perhaps; send me word; for, to use the old plea, it spoils a set." *LL* II 75. (Dodsley's *Collection of Old Plays*—12 vols 1744; Vol III contains Greene's *Tu Quoque* and Dekker's *The Honest Whore* but not Webster's *The White Divil*.) This oversight on C's part, which Lamb mentioned again six years later (*LL* II 131, 136), led to some vexation between them (see *CL* IV 655–6), but was later celebrated in "The Two Races of Men". C's plea to be forgiven for "bescribbling" Lamb's book is repeated in **61**; see also **15**, below.

4[1] In eds 1635–69 *The Flea* stands as the first poem of *Songs and Sonets*.

4[2] These lines represent a revised and sharpened state of the opening lines of the draft poem *On Donne's First Poem*, which includes what was later printed as *Limbo* and *Moles*, written in N 18 in c Apr–May 1811: see *CN* III 4073. *PW* (EHC) II 980–1 prints the epigram from N 18 but does not notice this version.

4A　p 1 | line 3

　　　　1　　　　2　　　　6　5
　　Me it suck'd first, and now it sucks thee,[1]

5　p 2 | *The Good-morrow* lines 17–18

　　Where can we find two fitter hemisphears
　* Without sharp North, without declining West?

* I do not understand this Line.[1]

6　p 3 | lines 19–21

　　What ever dies is not mixt equally;
　　If our two loves be one, both thou and I
　　Love just alike in all, none of these loves can die.

Too good for mere wit. It contains a deep practical truth—this Triplet.

7　p 3 | *Song* "Goe, and catch a falling starre"[a]

Life from Crown to Sole.

7A　p 4 | lines 25–7
　　　　　　　Yet she
　　　　　　　Will be
　　I?] False, ere she come, to two or three.[1]

8　pp 4–5 | *Womans Constancy*

After all, there is but one Donne! & now tell me yet, wherein *in his own kind* he differs from the *similar* power in Shakespere? Sh. was all men potentially except Milton—& they differ from him by negation, or privation, or both.[1] This power of dissolving orient

---

[a] The title is marked with three oblique strokes in ink

4A[1] Reading: "Me first it suck'd, it now sucks thee". The 1669 ed was the first to read "Mee it suck'd first" for "It suckt mee first" of 1633, but is also the only ed to read "and now it sucks" for "and now sucks". Grierson and Gardner both read: "It suck'd me first, and now sucks thee".

5[1] See CHALMERS **5**.

7A[1] Both Grierson and Gardner read: "False, ere I come, to two, or three." For C's principle of emendation based on "the philosophy of metre", see BEAUMONT & FLETCHER COPY B **10**.

8[1] Cf the recurrence of the words "Negation/Privation" near the end of the draft of *Limbo* in *CN* III 4073. Cf the verse letter *To M. T. W.* "Hast thee harsh verse" (pp 169–70 in this ed, unmarked by C) esp lines 7–8: "And 'tis decreed, our hell is but privation | Of him, at least in this earths habitation".

pearls, worth a kingdom! in a health to a Whore! i̶s̶ this absolute
Right of Dominion over all thoughts, that Dukes are bid to clean
his Shoes, and are yet honored by it!—But, I say, in th̶e̶i̶s̶ Lordliness
of opulence, in which *the* Positive of Donne agrees with *a* Positive
of Shakespere, what is it that makes them *homoi*ousian indeed; yet
not homoousian?²

9 pp 5–6 | *The Undertaking*

A grand Poem; and yet the Tone, the *Riddle* character, is painfully
below the dignity of the main Thought. Addressed to those who
understand & feel it, it lends sympathy & admiration, no wonder-
ment—to the rest, it is a Lie—& it was mean[t]ᵃ therefore to turn
the discourse to them.

10 p 7 | *The Sun Rising*

Fine vigorous Exultation! Both Soul & Bódy in full puissance!¹

11 pp 7–10 | *The Indifferent* lines 1–9

> I can love both fair and brown,
> Her whom aboundance melts, and her whom want betrayes,
> Her who loves lovers best, and her who sports and playes,
> Her whom the country form'd, and whom the Town,
> Her who believes, and her who tries;
> Her who still weeps with spungie eyes,
> And her who is dry Cork, and never cries;
> I can love her, and her, and you and you,
> I can love any, so she be not true.

How legitimate a child was not Cowley of Donne;¹ but C. had a
Soul-*mother* as well as Soul-*Father*—& who was she? what was
that?—Perhaps, sickly Court-Loyalty, conscientious per accidens, a
discursive Intellect *naturaly* less vigorous, & daring—& then *cowed*
by King-Worship. The populousness, the activity, is as great in C.
as in D; but the *vigor*—the insufficiency to the Poet of active Fancy

---

ᵃ Letter supplied by the editor

8² For ὁμοιούσιος ("of like sub-
stance")...ὁμοούσιος ("of the same
substance")—two credal terms sur-
rounded with early controversy—see
FLEURY **56** nn 1, 2. For another later
annotation on this poem see CHALMERS

6. Cf ὁμοίωμα in *Sermons* COPY B **93** and
n 3.

10¹ For another and later annotation
on this poem see CHALMERS **7**.

11¹ See COWLEY headnote.

without a substrate of profound, tho' mislocated, Thinking—The Will-worship in squandering golden Hecatombs on a Fetisch, ⟨on⟩ the first stick or straw met with at rising! this pride of doing what he likes with his own—fearless of an immense surplus to pay all lawful Debts to ⟨self-subsisting⟩ Themes that rule, while they create, the moral will—this is Donne! He was an orthodox Christian, only because he could have been an Infidel *more* easily, & therefore *willed* to be a Christian: & he was a Protestant, because it enabled him to lash about to the Right & the Left—& *without a motive* to say better things for the Papists than they could say for themselves. Oh! it was the Impulse of a purse-proud Opulence, of innate Power! In the sluggish Pond the Waves roll this or that way: for such is the wind's direction/ but in the brisk Spring or Lake boiling with Bottom-winds—this way, that way, all ways—most irregular in the calm, yet inexplicable by the most violent ab extra Tempest.—[2]

12 p 10 | *Canonization* or *The Triple Fool*

One of my favorite Poems.[1] As late as 10 years ago, I used to seek and find out grand lines and fine stanzas; but my delight has been far greater, since it has consisted more in tracing the leading Thought thro'out the whole. The former is too much like coveting your neighbour's Goods: in the latter you merge yourself in the Author— you *become He*.—[2]

13   pp 11 | *The Triple Fool* lines 12–16

>   But when I have done so
>   Some man his art or voice to show,
>   Doth Set and sing my pain,
>   And, by delighting many, frees again
> *   Grief, which Verse did rest[r]ain.

[11][2] Cf *CL* v 447. The one quotation given by *OED* is for 1849: "The Bottom-Wind has its name from being supposed...to arise from the bottom of those lakes which are situated amongst mountains." Lakes enclosed by steep hills (e.g. Windermere) are subject to unpredictable winds (often catabatic), which can be disconcerting to vessels under sail and produce effects difficult to explain in terms even of "the most violent Tempest from outside".

[12][1] This note is written in the space between the end of *Canonization* and the opening of *The Triple Fool*, and continues down the margin beside *The Triple Fool*. Although the placing of the note suggests at first that it refers to *The Triple Fool*, C's comment is more richly applicable to *Canonization*; and it is to this poem that the note is traditionally referred.

[12][2] Cf *CN* i 383, 921, and 1016.

* $- \cup | - \cup \cup | -$. a good instance, how D. read his own verses. We should write, The Grief, Verse did restrain. But D. roughly emphasized the two main words, Grief & Verse, and therefore made each the first Syllable of a Trochee: $- \cup$, or Dactyl.

14   p 13 | *Song* "Sweetest Love, I doe not goe" lines 21–4

> But come bad chance,
> And we joyn to 't our strength,
> And we teach it art and length,
> It self o'r us t'advance.

The anapest judiciously used, in the eagerness of haste to confirm & aggravate.

15   p 13

N.B. Spite of Appearances, this Copy is the better for the Mss. Notes. The Annotator himself says so.   S. T. C.

16   p 13

This beautiful & perfect Poem[1] proves by its Title "*Song*", that *all* Donne's Poems are equally *metrical* (misprints allowed for) tho' *smoothness* (i.e. the metre necessitating the proper reading) he deemed appropriate to *Songs*;[2] but in Poems where the Author *thinks* & expects the Reader to do so, the Sense must be understood in order to ascertain the metre.

17   p 16 | *A Feaver* lines 25–8

> And here as my minde, seising thee,
> Though it in thee cannot persever.
> { Yet I had rather owner be
> {   Of thee one hour, than all else ever.

Just & affecting *as dramatic*, i.e. the out-burst of a transient Feeling,

16[1] C is reported to have said in 1834 that this *Song* "for sweetness and tenderness of expression, chastened by a religious thoughtfulness and faith, is, I think, almost perfect". R. A. Willmott "S. T. Coleridge at Trinity, with Specimens of His Table-Talk" in *Conversations at Cambridge* (1836) 15.

16[2] That Donne expected some at least of his "Songs" to be sung, probably to tunes already current, is suggested by *The Triple Fool* lines 12–14 and is consonant with Jacobean practice. For what little is known about musical settings of Donne's poems in his own time see Grierson II 54–7 and Gardner 238–47. A setting of "Sweetest Love" is discussed in Gardner 239–40; a setting also exists for "Goe, and catch a falling starre"—see **7**, above, and Gardner 240–1.

itself the symbol of a deeper Feeling, that would have made *one* Hour, *known* to be *only* one Hour (or even one year) ~~or~~ a perfect Hell! All the preceding Verses are detestable. Shakespere has nothing of this. He is never *positively* bad, even in his Sonnets. He *may* be sometimes worthless (N.B: I don't say, he *is*) but no where is He *un*worthy.

18   p 17 | *Air and Angels*

> Twice or thrice had I loved thee,
> Before I knew thy face or name;
> So in a voice, so in a shapeless flame,
> *Angels* affect us oft, and worship'd be,
>   Still when, to where thou wert, I came,
> Some lovely glorious nothing did I see,
>   But since, my soul, whose child love is,
> Takes limbs of flesh, and else could nothing do;
>   More subtil then the parent is,
> Love must not be, but take a body too,
>   And therefore what thou wert, and who
>   I bid love ask, and now,
> That it assume thy body, I allow,
> And fix it self in thy lips, eyes, and brow.
>
> Whilst thus to ballast love, I thought,
> And so more steddily to have gone,
> With wares which would sink admiration,
> I saw, I had loves pinnace overfraught;
>   Thy Every hair for love to work upon
> Is much too much, some fitter must be sought;
>   For, nor in nothing, nor in things
> Extream, and scattering bright, can love inhere;
>   Then as an Angel, face, and wings
> Of air, not pure as it, yet pure doth wear,
> So thy love may be my loves sphear;
>   Just such disparitie
> As is 'twixt Airs and Angels puritie,
> 'Twixt womens love, and mens will ever be.

The first Stanza is noble—& reminds me of Wordsworth's *apparition-* poem.[1] The 2ⁿᵈ I do not understand.[2]

18[1] *She Was a Phantom of Delight*, composed in 1804 and first published in *Poems in Two Volumes* (1807), was being prepared for the press when C was with the Wordsworths at Coleorton. *WPW* II 213–14.

18[2] For an unravelling of some hard knots in this poem see Gardner 205–6.

18A   p 22 | *Twicknam Garden* line 8

> And that this place may thoroughly be thought[1]

19   p 35 | *A Nocturnal upon S. Lucies Day Being the Shortest Day* lines 22–7

> ...Oft a flood
> Have we two wept, and so
> Drown'd the whole world, us two; oft did we grow,
> To be two Chaosses, when we did show
> Care to ought else; and often absences
> Withdrew our souls, and made us carcasses.

When I love thee not,
Chaos is come again[1]

20   p 40 | *A Valediction Forbidding Mourning* [sts 7–9]

> If they be two, they are two so
>   As stiff twin Compasses are two,
> Thy soul the fixt foot, makes no show
>   To move, but doth, if th' other do.
>
> And though it in the center sit,
>   Yet when the other far doth rome,
> It leans, and harkens after it,
>   And grows erect, as that comes home.
>
> Such wilt thou be to me, who must
>   Like th' other foot, obliquely run.
> Thy firmness makes my circle just,
>   And makes me end, where I begun.

An admirable Poem which none but D. could have written. Nothing were ever more admirably made out than the figure of the Compass.—

20A   p 42 | *The Extasie* lines 41–2

> When love with one another so
> Interinanimates two souls,[1]

18A[1] Both Grierson and Gardner read "thoroughly".

19[1] Shakespeare *Othello* III iii 91–2.

20A[1] The 1st ed (1633) reads "inter-animates", but the authority of many mss encourages both Grierson and Gardner to read "interinanimates". "Interanimate" is in *OED* (citing Donne 1650 ed); "interinanimate" is not.

21   p 43 | lines 65–end

> So must pure lovers souls descend
> T' affections, and to faculties,
> Which sence may reach and apprehend,
>   Else a great Prince in prison lies,
> To our bodies turn we then, that so
>   Weak men on love reveal'd may look;
> Loves mysteries in Souls do grow,
>   But yet the body is the book,
> And if some lover such as we,
>   Have heard this dialogue of one,
> Let him still mark us, he shall see
>   Small change when we are to bodies grown.

I should never find fault with metaphysicall Poems, were they all like this,—or but half so excellent.—[1]

22   p 44 | *Loves Deity*

> I long to talk with some old lovers ghost,
>   Who dyed before the god of Love was born:
> I cannot think that he, who then lov'd most,
>   Sunk so low, as to love one which did scorn.
> But since this god produc'd a destiny,
> And that vice-nature custom lets it be;
>   I must love her that loves not me.
>
> Sure they, which made him god, meant not so much,
>   Nor he, in his young godhead practis'd it
> But when an even flame two hearts did touch,
>   His office was indulgently to fit

[21]¹ C must have encountered early, either by word of mouth or directly from Johnson's "Life of Cowley", the special term "metaphysical poets" used in a pejorative sense: they were, Johnson said, "men of learning, and to shew their learning was their whole endeavour; but, unluckily resolving to shew it in rhyme, instead of writing poetry they only wrote verses, and very often such verses as stood the trial of the finger better than of the ear....Their attempts were always analytick: they broke every image into fragments: and could no more represent by their slender conceits and laboured particularities the prospects of nature, or the scenes of life, than he who dissects a sun-beam with a prism can exhibit the wide effulgence of a summer noon." C, coming to his conclusion through the poems of Donne rather than Cowley, thought otherwise; as early as 1799, speaking of the weak effect of Gray's *The Bard*, he said that it was for its clarity and precision that "what *I* call metaphysical Poetry gives me such delight". *CN* I 383.

Actives to Passives, Correspondency
Only his *Subject* was; it cannot be
Love, till I love her that loves me.

But every modern god will now extend
His vast prerogative as far as *Jove*,
To rage, to lust, to write to, to commend,
All is the purlue of the God of Love.
Were we not weak'ned by this Tyranny
To ungod this child again, it could not be
I should love her, who loves not me.

But for the last Stanza, I would use this poem as my Love-creed.[1]

23   p 50 | *The Primrose*

I am tired of expressing my admiration: else I could not have passed
by The Will, the Blossom, & this Primrose, with The Relique./[1]

23A   p 53 | *The Dissolution* line 12

(But ne̸ar worn out by loves securitie)[1]

ELEGIES

23B   p 71 | *Elegie* iv. *The Perfume* lines 71–2

All my perfumes, I give most willingly
To embalm thy fathers coorse; <u>What</u>, will he dy?

When (?)[a1]

SATYRES

24   p 125 | *Satyre* iii

If you would teach a Scholar in the highest form, how to *read*, take
Donne, and of Donne this Satire. When he has learnt to read Donne,

---

[a]   C's query was later crossed out with a bold "X", presumably by Lamb

22[1] The fourth and last stanza reads:

Rebel and Atheist too, why murmure I,
  As though I felt the worst that love
    could do?
Love may make me leave loving, or
    might try
A deeper plague, to make her love
    me too,
Which, since she loves before, I'm loth
    to see;

Falshood is worse than hate; and that
    must be,
If she whom I love, should love me.

23[1] *The Will, The Blossom, The Primrose, The Relique* appear in this sequence on pp 45–51.
23A[1] The 1633 ed reads "ne'r"; mss, Grierson, and Gardner read (as 1635–69) "neere". C's emendation is not noted by the editors.
23B[1] A guess on C's part, unsupported by mss or printed versions.

with all the force & meaning which are involved in the Words—then send him to Milton—& he will stalk on, like a Master, *enjoying* his Walk.[1]

25 p 126, cropped | III lines 42–54

> Give this flesh power to tast joy, thou dost loath,/.
> Seek true Religion, O where:/ ?...
> . . . .
> *Grants* to such brave Loves will not be inthrall'd,
> * But loves her only, who at *Geneva* is call'd
> Religion, plain, simple, sullen, young,
>
> Contemptuous yet unhandsome./;As among
> Lecherous humours, there is one that judges
> No wenches wholsome, but coarse country drudges.[1]

* [But loves | her on]ly, who't | Gene | va's call'd |[2]

26 p 126 | III 55–60

> *Grajus* stayes still at home here, and because
> Some Preachers, vile ambitious bawds, and laws
> Still new like fashions, bids* him think that she
> Which dwels with us, is only perfect, he
> Imbraceth her, whom his Godfathers will
> Tender s to him, being tender;

* bid? or bids, sing. verb to a conjunct nom. Plural, as Nouns neuter in Greek?[1]

27 p 127 | III 65–9

> *Gracchus* loves all as one, and thinks that so
> As women do in divers Countries go

24[1] Cf BEAUMONT & FLETCHER COPY B **10**. In *CN* III 4152 C drew attention to *Satyre* III under the title of "Donne's Spleen" (from the opening words "Kind pity chokes my spleen"), but for its argument, not its prosody.

25[1] Milgate punctuates in all three places as C does, but makes a paragraph at "Seek true...".

25[2] Milgate reads "who'at Geneva's call'd".

26[1] Grierson and Milgate read "bid", following mss rather than eds 1633–69. In *CN* IV 5135 f 145—in *SW&F* (*CC*)—C explains that in Greek a neuter plural governs a singular verb because "*Singleness* belongs to Persons only...a 1000 Stones are regarded but as *Stone*". See also **36**, below.

> In divers habits, yet are still one kind;
> So doth, so is Religion; and this blind-*
> ness too much light breeds.

* a fine instance of free, vehement, verse-disguising Verse. Read it as it ought to be read; and no Ear will be offended.—

28 p 127 | III 69–75

> But unmoved thou
> Of force must one, and forc'd but one allow;
>   3   1   2   4
> ~~And~~ ⸜The right⸝ to ask thy Father which is she,[1]
> Let him ask his. Though truth and falshood be
> Near twins, yet truth a little elder is.
> Be busie to seek her; believe me this,
> He's not of none, nor worst, that seeks the best.

Here's Brama's Hydraulic Packing-Engline![2] a *scrouge* of Sense!—[3]

29 p 127 | III 79–88

> On a huge hill,
> Cragged, and steep, Truth stands, and he that will
> Reach her, about must, and about it goe:
> And what the hills suddenness resists, win so,
> Yet strive so, that before age, deaths twilight,
> Thy Soul rest, for none <u>can</u> work in that night.
> To <u>will</u> implyes delay, therefore now <u>do</u>:
> Hard deeds, the bodies pains; hard knowledge to*
> The minds indeavours reach; and mysteries
> Are like the Sun, dazling, yet plain to all eyes.

28[1] C apparently means to read: "The right to ask thy Father which is she". Grierson and Milgate accept the printed version.

28[2] See also **30**, below. By the application of "Pascal's paradox", the Bramah hydraulic press, patented in 1795 by Joseph Bramah (1748–1814), converted a small force applied at one place into a very large force applied at another. It was used originally for flanging boiler plates, forging large ingots of steel, and pressing bales.

28[3] "Scrouge", as a noun, is given by *OED* as meaning a crush, or crowd [of people], a variant of the verb "scruze", to press or squeeze—which is evidently C's meaning here. Cf the "Mangle-press and Screw" of the first version of the "dromedary epigram" on Donne, CHALMERS **3** n 1. See **30** and n 1, below.

* i.e. The body's pains reach hard deeds; & likewise so do the mind's Endeavors reach hard Knowlege.[1]

29A   p 128 | III 101–2

Those past, her nature, and name are chang'd; to be,
Then humble to her, is Idolatry.[1]

30   p 128, referring to *Satyre* III

Knotty, double-jointed Giant! Cramp of Strength![1]

30A   pp 129–30 | IV 38–9, 47–8, 67–9

He speaks one language/. If strange meats displease/,[1]
Art can deceive...

.   .   .   .

Out-flatter favorites, or outlie either/,
Jovius, or Surius, or both together.[2]

.   .   .   .

                    I said, not alone,
My loneness is/; but Spartanes fashion/.[3]
To teach by painting drunkards doth not last,

31   p 136 | V 9–11

                    If all things be in all,
        As I think, since all, which were, are, and shall
        Be, be all made of the same elements:

an impracticable Line: perhaps, insert "all" after the 2nd be.[1]

29[1] Cf Grierson's gloss (II 116): "Hard deeds are achieved by the body's pains (i.e. toil, effort), and hard knowledge is attained by the mind's efforts." On lines 79–82 see also Milgate App C (pp 290–2).

29A[1] Grierson and Milgate agree about the first comma, but continue: "to be | Then humble to her is idolatrie".

30[1] This note, with **28**, above, provides the germ for the second part of C's well-known epigram on Donne, for which see CHALMERS 3 and n 1. It is clear that he intended the epigram to refer to the *Satyres* rather than to the *Songs and Sonets*.

30A[1] Milgate reads: "He speakes one language; If strange meats displease,".

30A[2] Milgate has no punctuation after "either".

30A[3] Milgate reads: "My lonenesse is. But Spartanes fashion,".

31[1] There is no ms or editorial support for this insertion. The line scans without it, but the insertion need not make the line hypermetrical.

31A p 136 | v 23–30, marked in the margin with a broken line

They [i.e. Suiters] are the mills which grind you, yet you are
The wind which drives them; and a wastful war
Is fought against you, and you fight it; they
Adulterate law, and you prepare the way,
Like wittals, th' issue your own ruin is.
Greatest and fairest Empress, know you this?
Alas, no more than Thames calm head doth know
Whose meads her arms drown or whose corn o're-flow.

32 pp 136–8 | v 37–8

    *   The iron Age was, when justice was sold, now
           Injustice is sold dearer far, allow...

    *   In th' Iron Age was Justice sold; (but) now

Donne sometimes makes a dissylable of liquid monos.—sōōld, fi*er*,
cāēr, wi*er*, for sold, fire, care, wire. But rather throw a very strong
emphasis on "Justice", & you will find the Line read.[1]

33 p 137 | v 48–51, marked in the margin with a dotted line

            But if the injury
    Steel thee to dare complain, Alas, thou go'st
    Against the stream upwards, when thou art most
    Heavy and most faint;

one feels oneself yielding to the Stream after vain efforts, in these fine
Lines.

34 p 137 | v 63–8

      Would it not anger/
    A Stoick, a Coward, yea a Martyr,/
    To see a Pursivant come in, and call/
    All his clothes, Copes; Books, Primers; and all/

32[1] A difficult passage because of the punctuation in the 1st ed. Grierson reads: "The iron Age *that* was, when justice was sold; now | Injustice is sold dearer farre. Allow...", preserving the "*that*" of 1633–54 and mss. He glosses the passage: "*That*...was the iron age when justice was sold. Now...injustice is sold dearer." Milgate repeats Grierson's note, and prints "Th'iron Age *that* was". C's emendation makes the line metrically more regular but rhetorically weaker.

His Plate, Chalices, and mistake them away,/
And ask a fee for comming?/

The Text suspicious.[1]

35 p 137 | v 68–73

> Oh; n'er may
> Fair laws white reverend name be strumpeted,
> To warrant thefts: she is established
> Recorder to Destiny, on earth, and she/   δ er?
> Speaks Fates words, and tells who must be/   eth eth
> Rich, who poor, who in chairs, who in jayles;/

R. *and* w. p., in chairs who, who in j.[1]

35A p 138 | v 84–5

> for all hast paper
> Enough to cloath all the great Charricks Pepper.
>   Carack's[1]

36 p 138, referring to *Satyre* v lines 63–91

The last 30 lines ου ραδιως ρυθμιζεται;[1] but no haste in altering.
Satyrs (for in the age of Donne they took the literal meaning) were
supposed to come all rough from the woods, with a rustic accent.[2]

34[1] Except that they print a semi-colon after "Challices", Grierson and Milgate print the text as in 1669, and record the single variant of "lack" (1633–54) for "ask" in line 68; they make no comment, beyond quoting a parallel from the *Sermons*.

35[1] Grierson and Milgate read:

> she is established
> Recorder to Destiny, on earth, and
> shee
> Speakes Fates words, and but tells us
> who must bee
> Rich, who poore, who in chaires,
> who in jayles:

which produces the effect C wanted in line 72. C's inserted "and", however, has the same smoothing effect upon Donne's abrupt texture as his insertion of "all" in **31**.

35A[1] Eds 1633–5 read "Carricks" (which Grierson and Milgate adopt); 1639–69 read "Charricks". A carrack (or carack) was a large armed merchant ship used by the Portuguese in trading with the East Indies, and pepper a desirably profitable homeward cargo. See also Milgate 170n.

36[1] "Is not easily scanned"—a singular verb after a neuter plural, as in **26**, above.

36[2] For the derivation of the word *satire* see FLÖGEL **6** textus. Later critics, with C in FLÖGEL **6**, tended to accept a combination of all three of the derivations there given, but modern scholars prefer that from *satura* (a mixed dish). Donne's

37   p 138 | vi lines 1–4[1]

> Sleep, next,/ Society and true friendship
> Mans best contentment, doth securely slip./
> His passions and the worlds troubles : rock me./,
> O sleep, wean'd from thy dear friends company,

Evidently corrupt.[2]

38   p 142, referring to *Satyre* vi

A most strange Poem! & purposely obscure, I guess. Yet enough is plain to have risked the Author's neck, I should have thought—at least, his Ears.[1]

FUNERAL ELEGIES

39   p 202, written at the end of *To the Praise of the Dead, and the Anatomy*

? BEN JONSON?[a][1]

---

[a] The name is written more carefully than most of C's notes in this volume, but it looks more like C's hand than Lamb's

---

Satyres are in the tradition of Roman satire; the precedent for careless versification is to be found in Lucilius (see Horace *Satires* 1.4.9–10 in FLÖGEL **4** textus) and in Horace himself (*Satires* 1.4.42, for which see DYER **1** and n 1 and FLÖGEL **8** and n 2). See also FLÖGEL **7**, **9**, and **10** and "Donne as Satirist" in Milgate pp xvii–xxv.

37[1] The poem *To Sr Nicholas Smyth*, called "Satyre vi" in this ed, is probably by Sir John Roe (1581–c 1608), to whom Grierson ascribed eight other poems that had been drawn into the Donne canon. See Grierson ii cxxix–cxxxv.

37[2] Grierson reads:

> Sleep, next Society and true friendship,
> Mans best contentment, both securely
>   slip
> His passions and the worlds troubles.
>   Rock me
> O sleep, wean'd from my dear friends.
>   company,

38[1] C did not recognise that this poem was not by Donne, but it is a mark of his sensitive reading that he registered a failure to meet the complex expectations he had formed from the genuine *Satyres*. For Grierson's assessment of the quality of the supposititious poems that he ascribed to John Roe, see ii cxxxii.

39[1] It is not certain that this is in C's hand; if it is, it is in answer to Lamb's query on p 222: "Q^y Who the author of this and the Copy of verses prefix'd to the First Anniversary." Grierson conjecturally ascribes the introductory poem *To the Praise of the Dead, and the Anatomy* to Joseph Hall (1574–1656), on the evidence of Jonson's conversations with Drummond of Hawthornden. See Grierson ii 187. C discusses the *Anniversaries* in **45**, below.

LETTERS [in prose]

40 p 266 | *De libro cum mutuaretur, impresso*...lines 13–22

> *Si veterem faciunt, pueri, qui nuperus, Annon*
> *Ipse Pater, Juvenem, me dabit arte, senem?*
> *Hei miseris senibus! nos vertit dura senectus*
> *Omnes in pueros, neminem at in Juvenem.*
> *Hoc tibi servasti praestandum, Antique Dierum,*
> *Quo viso, et vivit, et juvenescit Adam.*
> *Interea, infirmae fallamus taedia vitae,*
> *Libris, et Coelorum aemula amicitia.*
> *Hos inter, qui a te mihi redditus iste libellus,*
> *Non mihi tam charus, tam meus, ante fuit.*

I. D.[1]

[*On a printed book which, when he borrowed it, was torn to pieces* [reading *frustatim*] *at home by his children, and was later returned written out by hand. To his very learned and dear friend, Dr. Andrews.*

...If boys make [this book] old, which was so fresh and new, will not their father [who was a medical doctor] by his skill make me, an old man, young? Alas for old men! cruel age turns us all into children but not one of us into a young man. You, Ancient of Days, have reserved to yourself this as your function—that when a man sees you Adam lives and takes on youth. Meanwhile we beguile the weariness of infirm old age with books and with friendship matching the heavens. Among these, this book you have returned to me will be more dear, and more mine, than it was before.]

fine Lines—& the whole Poem is pleasing, spite of the Wilfulness & Wrench of the Analogy.

41 p 267 | To Sir H. G.

...For my Letters are either above or under all such offices, yet I write very affectionately, and I chide and accuse my self of diminishing that affection which sends them, when I ask my self why.

A noble Letter in that *next* to the best Style of Correspondence, in which Friends communicate to each other the accidents of their meditations, and baffle absence by writing what, if present, they would have talked. Nothing can be tenderer than the sentence, I have lined.

40[1] I.e. John Donne, the younger.

42 p 268

And when we get any thing by prayer, he gave us before hand the
*] thing and the petition: for, I scarce think any ineffectual prayer
free from both sin and the punishment of sin*.*

> *   Great omnipresent Teacher! He shall mould
>   Thy Spirit, and *by giving make it ask.*
>   ⟨Coleridge's Frost at Midnight.⟩[1]

43 p 271 | To the La. G., 7 Feb 1611

MADAM I am not come out of *England*, if I remain in the noblest part
of it, your minde; Yet I confess, it is too much diminution to call your
mind any part of England, or this world, since every part even of
your body, deserves titles of higher dignity.* No Prince would be
loath to die, that were assured of so fair a tomb to preserve his
memory: But I have a greater advantage then so; for, since there is
a religion in friendship, and a death in absence, to make up an intire
friend, there must be a heaven too: and there can be no heaven so
proportional to that religion, and that death, as your favour, and I
am gladder that it is a heaven, than that it were a Court or any other
high place of this world, because I am likelier to have a room there,
than here, and better cheap: Madam, my best treasure is time, and
my best imployment of that (next my thoughts of thankfulness for
my Redeemer) is to study good wishes for you, in which, I am by
continual meditation, so learned, that any creature (except your own
good Angel) when it would do you most good, might be content to
come and take instructions from

                      Your humble and affectionate
                                servant,
                                  J. D.

Contrast this Letter with that in p. 281.[1] There is perhaps more wit
and more vigor in this; but the thoughts played upon are of so serious
a nature, and the exception in the Parenthesis so aweful, that the Wit
instead of carrying off aggravates the Flattery—and Donne must
either have been literally sincere, or adulatory to extravagance, &
almost to Blasphemy.

42[1] For the context of these lines (63–4) in *Frost at Midnight*, see *PW* (EHC) I 242. The reading "omnipresent", for "universal", is not elsewhere recorded.

43[1] I.e. the letter to the Countess of Bedford, given in **47**, below.

44   p 271 | **43** textus

*] No Prince would be loath to die, that were assured of so fair a
tomb to preserve his memory...

> *   Thou in our wonder & astonishment
>   Hast built thyself a live-long Monument;
> *   And there sepulchred in such state dost lie
>   That Kings for such a Tomb might wish to die.
>   Milton's Lines on Shakespere[1]

45   pp 273–4 | To my honored friend G. G. Esquire (14 Apr 1612)

Of my Anniversaries, the fault that I acknowledg in my self, is to have
descended to print any thing in verse, which though it have excuse
even in our times by men who profess, and practise much gravity:
yet I confess I wonder how I declin'd to it, and do not pardon my
self; But for the other part of the imputation of having said too much,
my defence is, That my purpose was to say as well as I could: for
since I never saw the Gentlewoman, I cannot be understood to have
bound my self to have spoken just truths, but I would not be thought
to have gone about to praise her, or any other in ryme; except I took
such a person, as might be capable of all that I could say: If any of
those Ladies think that Mistris *Drewry* was not so, let that Lady make
her self fit for all those praises in the book, and they shall be hers.

This excuse reminds me of Sallust's (the Greek Platonic Philosopher's)
apology for the Pagan Mythology, viz. that the Fables are so
excessively silly & absurd, that they were incapable of imposing on
any man in his Senses, and therefore to be acquitted of
falsehood.[1]—To be sure, these Anniversaries were the strangest
Caprice of Genius upon Record. I conjecture, that Donne had been
requested to write something on this Girl, whom he had never seen—&
having no other Subject in contemplation, & Miss Drewry herself
supplying Materials, he threaded upon her name all his thoughts, as
they crowded into his mind—not careless how extravagant they
became, when applied to the best Woman on Earth.[2] The idea of

---

44[1] Milton *On Shakespear. 1630*
lines 7–8, 15–16 (var). The last two lines
read: "And so Sepulchr'd in such pomp
dost lie, | That Kings for such a Tomb
would wish to die." C also quoted these
lines in *The Friend* No 25: (*CC*) ii 346.

45[1] C had noted this argument of

Sallust's (*Concerning the Gods and the
Universe* §3) in c Jun 1810: see *CN* iii 3902
and n.

45[2] Donne wrote *The Anatomie of
the World* and *Of the Progresse of the
Soul* in memory of Elizabeth Drury, who
died in 1610 at the age of fifteen,

degradation & frivolity which Donne himself attached to the character of a professed Poet, & which was only not universal in the reigns of Elizabeth & James, which yet ~~pr~~ exhibited the brightest Constellation of Poets ever known, gives a *settling* answer to the fashionable outcry about Patronage—nothing but Patronage wanting to Midas-ize Mein Herr Füssly into Michael Angelo Buonaroti, Mister Shee to a Rafael, & Rat Northcote into a Titian![3]

46   p 275 | To my honored friend G. G. Esquire (7 Jan 1630)

It hath been my desire (and God may be pleased to grant it) that I might die in the Pulpit, if not that, yet that I might take my death in the Pulpit, that is, die the sooner by occasion of those labours.

This passage seems to prove that Donne retained thro' life the main opinions defended in his Biothanatos[1]—at least, this *joined* with his

daughter of the wealthy and influential Sir Robert Drury of Hawsted. Drury rewarded Donne handsomely for the poems. Although the two *Anniversaries*, the first of Donne's poems to be published in his lifetime (1611, 1612), were conceived as "an impassioned and exalted *meditatio mortis*", they gave offence to Donne's earlier patrons and friends who suspected that he had been willing, for the sake of large patronage from a stranger, to extend his poetic powers in extravagant eulogy of a girl whom he had never met. See Grierson II 187–8.

45[3] Johann Heinrich Fuessli (1741–1825), born in Zurich, changed his name to Henry Fuseli when he came to England in 1764. With Reynolds's encouragement, he abandoned orders for an artist's career, studied the work of Michelangelo and the Italian masters in Rome for eight years, and began exhibiting regularly at the Royal Academy in 1780. He hoped to revive the grand style of Michelangelo and Raphael in defiance of the current taste for landscape painting, but his inflated reputation was won by the *Nightmare* and his illustrations of Shakespeare rather than by the Michelangelesque drawings that were his best work. For C on Fuseli, see e.g. *CRB* I 34, *CL* I 135. Sir William Archer Shee, portrait painter, RA (1800) and founder

of the British Institution (1807), was to become—as president of the Royal Academy from 1830—a vigorous defender of the Academy against well-deserved criticism. James Northcote (1746–1831), portrait painter (of whom one of his contemporaries said that "he looks like a rat who has seen a cat"), was for a time assistant to Reynolds, and after studying in Italy became a regular exhibitor in the Royal Academy. (For his portrait of C painted from one sitting in Mar 1804, see *CN* II 1976, 1984, and nn.) B. R. Haydon and his friends, hoping to restore to England the scope of Michelangelo's art, tried to persuade Parliament to commission paintings by such men as Haydon himself, Fuseli, Archer Shee, and Northcote (none of whom were of the first class) for public buildings in the way that sculptures had been publicly commissioned, but they were not successful.

46[1] *Biathanatos* (1646). For another comment on this book see AURELIUS **28**. Here, as in AURELIUS **28** and in *CN* III 4050, C silently alters Donne's acceptable, though little documented, Greek word. In earlier Greek it was βιαιοθάνατος, in patristic Greek βιοθάνατος—as C has it here and in *CL* III 52 (2 Feb 1808). This latter form carries an interesting ambiguity: though always used of a person who dies a violent death (βία, "violence") it

dying command that the Treatise should not be destroyed tho' he did not think the Age ripe for its Publication, furnishes a strong presumption of his perseverance in the defensibility of Suicide in certain cases.[2]

47   p 281, two textual corrections by Lamb | To the Countess of Bedford

Happiest and worthyest Lady,

I do not remember that ever I have seen a petition in verse, I would not therefore be singular, nor adde these to your other papers. I have yet adventured so near as to make a petition for verse, it is for those your Ladiship did me the honour to see in Twicknam garden, except you repent your making and *ª*having mended your judgment by thinking worse, that is, better, because juster,*b* of their subject. They must needs be an excellent exercise of your wit, which speak so well of so ill. I humbly beg your Ladiship, with two such promises, as to any other of your compositions were threatnings: That I will not shew them, and that I will not believe them; And nothing should be so used which comes from your brain or heart. If I should confess a fault in the boldness of asking them, or make a fault by doing it in a longer letter, your Ladiship might use your stile and old fashion of the Court towards me, and pay me with a pardon. Here therefore I humbly kiss your Ladiships fair learned hands, and wish you good wishes and speedy grants.

Your Ladiships servant,
JOHN DONNE.

a truly elegant Letter, and a happy specimen of that dignified Courtesy to Sex and Rank, of that white Flattery, in which the Wit unrealizes the Falsehood, and the sportive exaggeration of the Thoughts blending with a delicate tenderness faithfully conveys the Truth as to the Feelings[1]

---

a–b Corrections in another hand, presumably Lamb's, to read: "have mended... because more justly,"

---

also suggests death-in-life or life-in-death (βίος, "life"). During the last part of his sojourn in the Mediterranean and for some time after his return to England, C had been entertaining thoughts of suicide: see e.g. *CN* ii 2100, 2510, 2527, 3148 f 44ᵛ, iii 3309. Whether he found in Donne's unimpassioned treatise any solace or resolution in his own distress does not appear.

46[2] For the history of the publication of *Biathanatos*, and for the argument of the book, see AURELIUS **28** nn 2, 3.

47[1] See **43**, above.

ELEGIES UPON THE AUTHOR

48 p 364 | H[enry] K[ing] *To the Memory of My Ever Desired Friend Doctor Donne*

There are occasions, on which Regret expresses itself not only in the most manly, but likewise in the most natural way, by intellectual effort & activity in proof of intellectual admiration. This is one: & with this feeling should these poems be read.[1]—*S. T. C.*

49 p 364 | lines 1–28

> [a]To have liv'd eminent, in a degree
> Beyond our lofty'st flights, that is, like Thee,
> Or t'have had too much merit, is not safe;
> For, such excesses find no Epitaph.
> At common graves we have poetique eyes,
> Can melt themselves in easie Elegies,
> Each quill can drop his tributary verse,
> And pin it, like the Hatchments to the Hearse:
> But at Thine, Poem, or Inscription,
> (Rich soul of wit, and language) we have none.
> Indeed a silence does that tomb befit,
> Where is no Herald left to blazon it.
> Widow'd invention justly doth forbear
> To come abroad, knowing thou art not here,
> Late her great Patron; Whose Prerogative
> Maintain'd and cloath'd her so, as none alive
> Must now presume to keep her at thy rate,
> Though he the Indies for her dowr estate.
> Or else that awful fire, which once did burn
> In thy clear brain, now faln into thy Urn
> Lives there, to fright rude Empericks from thence,
> Which might prophane thee by their Ignorance.
> Who ever writes of thee, and in a stile
> Unworthy such a Theme, does but revile
> Thy precious Dust, and wake a learned Spirit
> Which may revenge his Rapes upon thy Merit.
> For, all a low pitcht fancie can devise,
> Will prove, at best, but Hallow'd Injuries.

[a] The whole poem is marked into two sections, lines 1–28 and 29–end, with ragged vertical lines; in the margin opposite the first section (p 165) "How excellent!" is written, and below this on the same page, and again on p 366, "Ditto". These words, previously assigned to C, are in Lamb's hand

48[1] For C's general view of elegiac writing see ATHENAEUM **17** and n 1.

This fine poem has suggested to me many Thoughts for "An apology for Conceits", as a sequel to an Essay, I have written, called an "Apology for Puns".[1]

50 p ⁺1, referring to p 365

Page 365. We cannot better illustrate the weight and condensation of metal in the old English Parnassian Guinea, or the immense Volume of French Writing which it would cover & ornament if beat into Gold Leaf, than by recurrence to the funereal Poems of our elder Writers from Henry the 8th to Charles the 2nd—These on Donne are more than usually excellent—their chief, and indeed almost only fault, being want of smoothness, flow, & perspicuity from too great compression of thought—too ~~much~~ many Thought⟨s⟩, & often too much Thought in each.—*S. T. C.*

51 p 367 | Daniel Darnelly *In obitum venerabilis viri Johannis Donne* lines 15–27

> *Verum hac nolente coactos*
> *Scribimus audaces numeros, et flebile carmen*
> *Scribimus (O soli, qui te dilexit)̀, habendum⌡!)ᴵ*
> *ᵃSiccine perpetuus liventia lumina somnus*
> *Clausit? et immerito merguntur funere virtus,*
> *Et pietas? et quae poterant fecisse beatum,*
> *Caetera: sed nec te poterant servare beatum.*
> *Quo mihi doctrinam? quorsum impallescere chartis*
> *Nocturnis juvat? et totidem olfecisse lucernas?*
> *Decolor et longos studiis deperdere Soles*
> *Ut prius aggredior, longamque accessere famam.*
> *Omnia sed frustra: mihi dum, cunctisque minatur*
> *Exitium, crudele et inexorabile fatum.*

[But I defy her [i.e. the Muse, who departed with you and bids other poets despair] and boldly write the numbers forced from me; I write the tearful song that is to be sung only by one who loved you. Has eternal sleep thus

ᵃ The last ten lines marked by Lamb in the outer margin, with the comment: "quite *classical*! and be damned to it!—'*Sic* cine'." This note was previously ascribed to C

49¹ The more-than-once-projected "Essay on/ Apology for Puns" has not been discovered. For C on punning generally see BAXTER *Reliquiae* COPY B 112 and BÖHME 60 and n 1. See also *CN* III 3542 and n, 3762 and n, 4444; and **51**, below, and *Sermons* COPY A 7.

51¹ Grierson reads: "Scribimus (ô soli qui te dilexit) habendum", following the printed text; but C appears to be correct, and the translation here follows his emendation.

Cœpta, nec officii contemnens pignora nostri
Aversare tua non dignum laude Poetam.

  O si Pythagoræ non vanum dogma fuisset :
Inque meum à vestro migraret pectore pectus
Musa, repentinos tua nosceret urna furores.
Sed frustra, heu frustra hæc votis puerilibus opto :
Tecum abiit, summoque sedens jam monte Thalia
Ridet anhelantes, Parnassi & culmina vates
Desperare jubet. Verum hac nolente coactos
Scribimus audaces numeros, & flebile carmen
Scribimus (O soli qui te dilexit habendum!)
Siccine perpetuus liventia lumina somnus
Clausit ? & immerito merguntur funere virtus,
Et pietas ? & quæ poterant fecisse beatum,
Cætera : sed nec te poterant servare beatum.
  Quo mihi doctrinam ? quorsum impallescere chartis
Nocturnis juvat ? & totidem olfecisse lucernas ?
Decolor & longos studiis deperdere Soles
Ut prius aggredior, longamque accessere famam.
Omnia sed frustra : mihi dum, cunctisque minatur
Exitium, crudele & inexorabile fatum.
  Nam post te sperare nihil decet : hoc mihi restat
Ut moriar, tenues fugiatque obscurus in auras
Spiritus : O doctis saltem si cognitus umbris,
Illic te (venerande) iterum (venerande) videbo,
Et dulces audire sonos, & verba diserti
Oris, & æternas dabitur mihi carpere voces.
Queis ferus infernæ tacuisset Janitor aulæ
Auditis : Nilusque minus strepuisset : Arion
Cederet, & sylvas qui post se traxerat Orpheus.
Eloquio sic ille viros, sic ille movere
Vociferos potuit ; quis enim tam barbarus ? aut tam
Facundis nimis infestus non motus, ut illo
Hortante, & blando victus sermone sileret ?

[handwritten marginal notes:] quite classical: and he damned it! "Siccine"—yes, one might continue to be sick, since all this Non-sense.! N. B. Malice the Mother of bad Puns; & Shoot the Father. vide Par. Lost Book VI.

Sic

[handwritten at foot:] —? rus potuit ??

3. A page of John Donne *Poems* (1669) annotated by Charles Lamb and Coleridge.
See DONNE *Poems* headnote and **51–52**
The Beinecke Rare Book and Manuscript Library, Yale University; reproduced
by kind permission

closed your leaden eyes? and are goodness and piety thus sunk in undeserved death with all the other merits that were able to make you fortunate yet could not keep you so? To what purpose is my learning? Why do I choose to grow wan over midnight papers? to snuff up the nightly lamps? even as in my pallor I first begin to lose long sunny days in study and summon [reading *arcessere*] long-delaying fame. But all is in vain, when over me, as over everyone, death looms, a cruel and inexorable fate.]

"*Sic* cine"[a]—O yes! one might contrive to be *sick*, sine all this Nonsense!—[2]

N.B. Malice the Mother of bad Puns; & Sport the Father: vide Par. Lost, Book VI.[3]

52   p 367 | lines 31–8

> *Illic te (venerande) iterum (venerande) videbo,*
> *Et dulces audire sonos, et verba diserti*
> !! *Oris, et aeternas dabitur mihi <u>carpere</u> voces.*
> *Queis ferus infernae tacuisset Janitor aulae*
> *Auditis: Nilusque minus strepuisset: Arion*
> *Cederet, et sylvas qui post se traxerat Orpheus.[b]*
> *Eloquio sic ille viros, sic ille movere*
> *Vociferos potuit;*

[There I shall see you again, venerable friend, and I shall be granted to hear the sweet sounds and the words of your eloquent mouth and to *enjoy* [lit. pluck, gather] your immortal voice, at which the fierce doorkeeper of the halls of Hades would have been silent, the Nile have stilled its tumult, Arion have given place, and Orpheus too who drew woods to follow him. So too could he move men by his voice; so could he [reading *voce feros*] move savages by his eloquence.]

—? *rus* potuit??—[1]

---

[a] The last ten lines marked by Lamb in the outer margin, with the comment: "quite *classical*! and be damned to it!—'*Sic* cine'." This note was previously ascribed to C

[b] This line and the two preceding are marked, apparently by Lamb, with a line in the margin and a bold "!"

51² C is responding to Lamb's note: see textual note *a*. The pun on *siccine*, a malformation of *sicine* (so, thus), depends upon C's now-outmoded English pronunciation of Latin.
51³ For the pun in *Paradise Lost* VI 621–7 see DANIEL 11 and n 1. On punning generally see **49** n 1, above.
52¹ Grierson's text is differently punctuated; otherwise the only variant is that he prints "Voce feros potuit". The printer's omission of a space between

Voce and *feros* distracted C from the correct reading: treating the two words as a single compound, he first emended *Voceferos* to *Vociferos* in the text, then at the foot of the page revised it again to *Vociferus* by writing with a query: "[*Vocife*]rus potuit". His reading *Vociferos* would translate: "So too could he move vociferous men"; the final reading *Vociferus* would translate: "So too could he, vociferous, move men".

53   p 368 | lines 47–9

> *Nunc habet attonitos, pandit mysteria plebi*
> *Non concessa prius, nondum intellecta: revolvunt*
> *Mirantes, tacitique arrectis auribus astant|.,* [a]

[Now he holds them amazed, expounds mysteries not formerly vouchsafed
to the people nor understood by them; marvelling, they ponder them and
stand silent with ears pricked up.]
i.e. *bray*less Asses.[1]

53A   p 369 | line 88

> *Quin nusus (Venerande) Vale, vale* ...[1]

[Again [reading *rursus*], venerable friend, farewell, farewell...]

54   p 369 | at the end

The careful Perusal of modern Latin Verses is not without its use.
They furnish instances of every species of vice characteristic of
modern English Poetry: & in some measure are ~~in~~ perhaps a cause.
But even Virgil & Horace (in his serious *odes*) will do the same, tho'
in a less glaring way—Yet compare them or the best of their
Successors with Lucretius, Catullus, Plautus, & even Terence—the
difference is—as between Row, D[r] Johnson &c, & the writers of Eliz.
& James[1]

55   p 373 | [Izaak Walton] *An Elegie upon Dr. Donne*

> Our *Donne* is dead; England should mourn...

an admirable Poem.

55A   p 373 | lines 15–16

> God hath rais'd Prophets to awaken them   ~~then~~
> From stupefaction...   ~~Their~~[b1]

---

[a] At the end of the line C has written a comma over the printed full point so that his gloss follows directly
upon the closing Latin phrase
[b] The corrections and underlining are Lamb's, but C has cancelled the corrections

53[1] C is probably punning on
"*astant*".
53A[1] C's emendation is correct:
nusus is meaningless.
54[1] The verse of Nicholas Rowe
(1674–1718) is in *B Poets* vii and his tr of

Lucan in *B Poets* xii. C's low opinion of
Rowe was of long standing—see *CL* ii
743, and cf *TT* 20 Mar 1834. C seldom
discusses Johnson's verse.
55A[1] Grierson gives no variant
from the 1669 text.

56   p 375 | lines 59–64

> Or, knowing, grief conceiv'd, conceal'd, consumes
> Man irreparably, (as poyson'd fumes)
> Do waste the brain) make silence a safe way
> To inlarge the Soul from these wals, mud, and clay, [1]
> (Materials of this body) to remain
> With *Donne* in heaven.

—instance of unhappy Alliteration. In a climax of similar thoughts, it aids; in a disjunction of separate thoughts, it confuses. Read as below*

* Or knowing that ~~deep~~ a hidden grief, ~~suffers~~, consumes

56A   p 375 | lines 67–76

> Dwell on this joy, my thoughts; oh, do not call
> Grief back, by thinking of his Funerall;
> Forget he lov'd me; Waste not my sad years, !
> (Which haste to *Davids* seventy,) fill'd with fears
> And sorrow for his death,)! Forget his parts,
> Which find a living grave in good mens hearts,!
> And, (for my first is daily paid for sin)
> Forget to pay my second sigh for him,!
> Forget his powerful preaching,! and forget
> I am his *Convert.*

56B   p 375 | lines 76–81

> Oh my frailty! let
> My flesh be no more heard, it will obtrude
> This Lethargy: so should my gratitude,   and so my Gratitude;
> My flows of gratitude should so be broke:[1]   My Flows &c
> Which can no more be, than *Donne's* virtues∧ spoke
>   ⟨i.e.⟩ can be spoken)
> By any but himself,!

56[1] Grierson reads: "(as poyson'd fumes | Do waste the braine) make silence a safe way | To'enlarge the Soule from these walls, mud and clay,".

56B[1] In line 79 Grierson reads "vowes" for "flows".

57 p 375, at the end of the *Elegie*

Is not this sweet Poem Isaac Walton's?—[1]

58 p 376 | Sidney Godolphin *Elegie on D. D.* lines 13–14[a]

> Thou mad'st our sorrows, which before had bin
> Onely for the * Success, sorrows for sin,

noticeable use of success for *result* or *consequences.*

58A p 376 | lines 23–4

> Pious dissector: theyou one hour didst treat
> The thousand mazes of the hearts deceit:

59 p 377 | lines 36–8

> That fancy findes some check, from an excess
> Of merit: most, of nothing, it hath spun,
> And truth, as reasons task and theam, doth shun.

Of Merit. Most of nothing it, i.e. My Muse, hath spun[1]

60 p +1[b]

> C̣ Ḥ Ḷ R T Ṭ
> Ạ E O

LATCH[1]

---

[a] Lamb has drawn a line down the margin against lines 11–32 and written against line 23: "Noble Lines"
[b] This note is written above **50**

57[1] In the 1st ed (1633) this elegy bears the signature "Iz. Wᴀ."; the signature was omitted in this ed probably through the printer's oversight. Izaak Walton submitted the poem to considerable revision; after it had appeared in all eds of the *Poems* (1633–69), it was transferred to the enlarged *Life of Donne* (1670).

59[1] Although "it" evidently refers to "fancy", C refers it back to the subject of the previous sentence, "My Muse".

60[1] C has arranged the letters of the name "CHARLOTTE" in order to derive an anagram, at which "LATCH" is an abortive attempt. For ten years or more he had made anagrams of SH's name, the most usual being "Asra", thereby distinguishing her from Sara his wife and later from Sara his daughter. In a note of 5 Nov 1807 he achieved an almost completely successful anagram of the name of Charlotte Brent, sister of John Morgan's wife, Mary: see *CN* ɪɪ 3186. The words "Yram" and "ettolrach" in *CN* ɪɪɪ 4166 (c Oct 1812) are "Mary" and "Charlotte" spelled backwards. For C's relations with the Morgan family, see ᴀɴᴅᴇʀsᴏɴ ᴄᴏᴘʏ ʙ headnote; in Apr–May 1811 he saw a good deal of them in Hammersmith before he began to live with them there.

61 p ⁺1*ᵃ*

I shall die soon, my dear Charles Lamb! and then you—will not be vexed that I had bescribbled your Books. 2 May, 1811.[1]

ᵃ This note is written below **50**

61[1] For a notebook entry of Apr 1811 ending "But I shall soon die", see *CN* III 4071. For two similar expectations of death—one allegedly in Apr 1807, the other in Oct 1811—see BEAUMONT & FLETCHER COPY A (Lamb's copy) **13** and n 1. Cf *CN* III 3276.

On 3 May 1811 C gave up his lodgings in Southampton Buildings and moved into the Morgan household in Hammer-smith. On the day he wrote this note on the back flyleaf of Donne's *Poems* he also wrote a long letter to Longman agreeing to an edition of his poems (*CL* III 324–5); the agreement was not fulfilled, but his request for an immediate advance of £20 is a mark of his straitened circumstances. It looks as though he wrote this last note in order to return the book to Lamb before leaving for Hammersmith.

Sermons

Whether or not C had read any of Donne's sermons before, his annotations in *LXXX Sermons* COPY A were probably written in 1809–10. The notes in COPY A are all on sermons late in the volume (Nos XXXI–LXXII); the notes in COPY B are, with one exception, on early sermons (Nos I–XIX, XLVI). That *LR* and *NED* printed the two sets of marginalia in a single sequence has concealed the distinctive tone of the notes written in COPY A at a time when C was carefully evolving his own trinitarian position and when the first impact of Donne's sermons was fresh. C noted in SHAKESPEARE *Works* (8 vols 1773) [COPY A] VIII 145: "I have (and that most carefully) read Dr Donne's Sermons"; but that particular annotation is not dated (c 1810–14).

When C paid his last visit to Cambridge in 1833 he is reported as saying: "The prose works of this admirable Divine, are Armouries for the Christian Soldier. Such a depth of intellect, such a nervousness of style, such a variety of illustration, such a power of argument, are to be looked for only in the writings of that race of Giants. Donne's poetry must be sought in his prose...". Willmott in *Conversations at Cambridge* 15. See also *Poems* 16 n 1.

Henry Alford (1810–71), prompted by C's remark "Why is not Donne's volume of sermons reprinted at Oxford?" (*TT* 4 Jun 1830, as in 1838 ed; later altered to "volumes"), was the first to attempt a collective edition of Donne's sermons. First conceived as a selection in modernised spelling and punctuation, the edition was published in 6 vols in 1839 and stood alone for more than a hundred years.

SPECIAL ABBREVIATION. "Potter & Simpson"—*The Sermons of John Donne* ed George R. Potter and Evelyn M. Simpson (10 vols Berkeley & Los Angeles 1953–62). All known sermons arranged chronologically, the *LXXX Sermons* following the text of 1640 that C used. Individual sermons can be identified through Appendix B (x 414–17) "List of Sermons in the Folios, the Present Edition, and Alford's Edition". Appendix C (x 418–21) provides a means of identifying each sermon through its biblical text.

From *NED*, Potter & Simpson quoted, usually in part, only ten of the more than 100 marginalia taken variatim from Donne's *Sermons*.

Copy A

LXXX Sermons preached by that learned and reverend divine, Iohn Donne, D[r] in Divinity, late Deane of the Cathedrall of S. Pauls London. London 1640. F°.

Includes Izaak Walton's *Life and Death of Dr. Donne* in its earliest published form. For full bibliographical description of this edition see Potter & Simpson I 1–5. In this copy, between correctly numbered pp 550 and 551 the text continues on four pages misnumbered 545, 546, 549, 550.

Harvard University (Houghton Library)

WW's copy; it later belonged to John Livingston Lowes, who bequeathed it to the Harvard Library.

Signed on the title-page: "Ant: Johnson", and on p 21: "Anthony Johnson 168[ ]". On the title-page below Johnson's signature: "John Beadsmoore his book March y[e] 20th 1799. God gave me it." Beadsmoore signed his name again on p [xxx], and on p 45 "John Beadesmoore his book 1738", and has written notes on pp [iii] and [v].

Below Johnson's signature on the title-page, written over an earlier erasure: "W[m] Wordsworth, ⟨bought at Ashby de la Zouch 1807⟩ Ashby de la Zouche". Inscribed on p ⁻7: "Bought at Wordsworth's Sale, for a Beloved Pastor, the Rev[d] Thomas Vores. by an Affectionate Member of his Flock. July 19th 1859." The donor is identified on p ⁻4 as Mrs Vernon. A list of "Ms. observations" with page references is pasted into the front, together with newspaper clippings of 1876 and 1882 and a Pickering catalogue entry of Jan 1880 to supply the provenance. Bookplate of the Rev Edward Marshall, M.A., F.S.A., Sandford St Martin. Inscribed on p ⁻3: "John Livingston Lowes. The gift of Corliss Lamont. October 20, 1925".

There are a number of pencil and ink markings in the margins, probably by Beadsmoore and Johnson, and notes—not by C—on pp 117, 120, 121. Passages in Sermons XLVI and LXXI marked probably by C in the margin with a pencil line are assembled in the ANNEX to this entry.

MS TRANSCRIPTS. (*a*) EHC transcripts on sheets of paper tipped in at pp 304/5 (**1–3, 4** pt), pp 724/5 (**6, 7**), 726/7 (**8** pt), and a blank leaf at pp 728/9. These transcripts were made after the margins had been cropped in rebinding. EHC has also written a column of topical references on p ⁻1. (*b*) VCL 41: EHC's transcript of **6**.

DATE. Probably c Jan 1809–May 1810, at Allan Bank.

The Wordsworths spent the winter of 1806–7 in Sir George Beaumont's Hall Farm at Coleorton, two miles from Ashby de la Zouca, arriving at the end of Oct 1806 and leaving on 10 Jun 1807. C was with them from 21 Dec 1806 until they all went up to London together on 4 Apr 1807; C went on to the West Country and was not to see the Wordsworths again until the following spring. Although C could have written these marginalia at Coleorton, the notes are remarkably assured for a date earlier than the series of marginalia written at Poole's in the summer of 1807, which represent his first fluency in this kind of writing (see Introduction, I p lxxxiv).

SERMONS PREACHED UPON WHITSUNDAY

1 p 305, cropped | Sermon XXXI, on Gen 1.2

The Jews...take the word [Spirit] here...to signifie onely a *winde*, and then that that addition of the name of *God*...which is in their Language a denotation of a vehemency...induces no more but that a very strong winde blew upon the face of the waters, and so in a great part dryed them up.

If the Earth were waste & wild—and a fluid confused mass—how can this confusi[on] of Elements be imagined withou[t] *winds*?—Let Lime meet with an acid—& then with a strong Hea[t,] will there not b[e] a violent rush of fixed air?[1]—Doubtless, the Gloss of the Jews is accurate/ tho' still it would be a wretched Taste to translate it, as Dr Geddes has done—a violent wind—:[2] for this may be the cold truth of the *Thing* but by no means a fear^a transfusion of the Prophet's meaning—or in the spirit of the theocratic Theology, which attribute all things to God *immediately*, that were powerful enough to [. . . . .][3]

^a A slip for "fair"

1[1] "Fixed air"—the name given by Joseph Black (1728–99) in 1756 to the carbon dioxide released in the reaction between lime and acid. For a note on the production of fixed air, taken by C at Humphry Davy's lectures of 1802, see *CN* I 1098 f 2^v. For Davy's lectures of 1808, known to C, see AURELIUS **51** n 1.

1[2] Alexander Geddes (1737–1802) gave up his parochial duties as a Roman Catholic priest in order to make a revised catholic version of the Bible, and published his version of Genesis–Joshua in 1792 and of Judges–(apocryphal) Prayer of Manasseh in 1797. His work was placed on the Index as heretical in interpretation. His tr of Gen 1.2 reads: "The earth was yet a desolate place, with darkness upon the face of the deep, and a vehement wind oversweeping the surface of the waters...", with a footnote—"Literally, *a wind of God*...". C may have met Geddes, for he referred to him in 1805 as "that bubbling ice-spring of cold-hearted mad-headed Fanaticism". *CN* II 2396.

1[3] C is trying to correct Donne's argument. The sermon, preached on Whitsunday 1629, seeks to establish that "In this Text [Gen 1.2] is the first mention of this Third Person of the Trinity". "The Jews who are afraid of the Truth, lest they should meete evidences of the doctrine of the Trinity, and so of the Messias", translate AV "The Spirit of God" as "a very strong wind". If only the Jews had said this, Donne continued, he would let it "flye away with the winde"; but Theodoret had said it too, so it must be answered. Donne's answer is "That it is a strange anticipation, that Winde, which is a mixt Meteor, to the making whereof, divers occasions concurre with exhalations, should be thus imagined, before any of these causes of Winds were created, or produced, and that there should be an effect before a cause, is somewhat irregular." C is arguing on scientific evidence that the causes were indeed present as the chaos moved towards definition. See **3**, below.

2   pp 313–14, cropped | Sermon XXXII, on 1 Cor 12.3

Now as this death hath invaded every part and faculty of man, understanding, and will, and all, (for though originall sin seem to be contracted without our will, yet *Sicut omnium natura, ita omnium voluntates fuere originaliter in Adam,* sayes S. *Augustine,* As the whole nature of mankinde, and so of every particular man, was in *Adam,* so also were the faculties, and so the will of every particular man in him) so this death hath invaded every particular man; Death went over all men, for as much as all men had sinned.

As the one and yet all, the synthesis inclusive and yet annihilative of all & each Antithesis, is & must ever remain the great mystery of Deity, so is the original Sin—(i.e. *Guilt*: for taken as mere imperfection is it is a contradiction or a nullity: for what sin is it in the Mole to have a deficient Vision—& if that be all the meaning, Sin means only that Man is now born less capacitated morally & intellectually than Adam was) so, I say, is the connate Guilt of man (a fact) and its compatibility with the free will, the [. . . . .] [*a*]*rbitrement* of man (arbitrium as distinguished from their unreal Volition) which is likewise a *Fact*/ the great mystery of Human Nature.[1] And they are grievously mistaken, who suppose that this difficulty rises or [fa]lls with, ~~or~~ or [an]y way [de]pends on, [the] Truth [o]r [F]alsehood [of] *Historical* Christianity/ and one proof of this is, that [th]ose Sects, who [l]east attend to, [o]r care for, [th]e external Evidences of [R]evealed Religion, are most affected by, & most [mo]uld their feelings upon, this very Tenet—Their Will is [t]he sole possible Fountain of all *Virtue* (as [d]istinguished from *Luck*) ~~is [i]n the~~ & that Fountain is itself polluted—& therefore the Redemption must come from without:[2] S. T. C.—

3   p 318, cropped

That Giant in all kinde of Learning, *Plato,* never stopped at any knowledge, till he came to consider the holy Ghost: *Unum inveni quod cuncta operatur,* I have (saies *Plato*) found One, who made all things; *Et unum per quo cuncta efficiuntur,* And I have found another, by whom all things were made; *Tertium autem non potui invenire,* A third, besides those two, I could never finde.

2[1] For C on original sin see e.g. *AR* (1825) 276–86, 301ff.

2[2] Generally, the Pelagians, and in particular the Unitarians. Cf **5**, below, and *Lects 1795* (*CC*) 107 n 1, 108 n 1. C wrote an essay on luck in *The Friend* of 28 Dec 1809: see *Friend* (*CC*) II 251ff (I 529ff).

a False [T]ranslation of Plato/[1] [I] have found one who [e]ffects all things; & [a]nother, which [i]s the *condition*, [as] it were, the [*m*]*atter* of all [a]gency—i.e. *mind* and *Being*; a third I could [n]ever find.—We find a [t]hird in [c]onceiving the mutual re-action of mind participant of Being on Being, and of Being participant (by effluence from itself) of Mind on its own offspring—and this is the Spirit = Air + Motion = Wind.[2]—& these three ~~dis~~ or three by distinction are ~~as~~ by the same necessity of conception indivisibly *One*.—[3]

4   pp 335, 338–40, cropped | Sermon xxxiv, on Rom 8.16

But by what manner comes he from them? By proceeding. That is a very generall word; for, Creation is proceeding, and so is Generation too: Creatures proceed from God, and so doth God the Son proceed from God the Father; what is this proceeding of the holy Ghost, that is not Creation, nor Generation?...

There is *processio corporalis*, such a bodily proceeding, as that that which proceeds is utterly another thing then that from which it proceeds: frogs proceed (perchance) of ayre, and mise of dust, and worms of carkasses; and they resemble not that ayre, that dust, those carkasses that produced them. There is also *processio Metaphysica*, when thoughts proceed out of the minde; but those thoughts remaine still in the mind within, and have no separate subsistence in themselves: And then there is *processio Hyperphysica*, which is this which we seek and finde in our soules, but not in our tongues, a proceeding of the holy Ghost so from Father and Son, as that he remaines a subsistence alone, a distinct person of himselfe. This is as far as the Schoole can reach....Consider him in his proceeding, so he must necessarily have a relation to another, Consider him actually in his person, so he subsists of himselfe. And *De modo*, for the manner of his proceeding, we need, we can say but this, As the Son proceeds *per modum intellectus*, (so as the mind of man conceives a thought) so the holy Ghost proceeds *per modum voluntatis*; when the mind hath produced a thought, that mind, and that discourse and ratiocination produce a will; first our understanding is setled, and that understanding leads our will. And nearer then this (though God

[3][1] A literal translation of the Latin might read: "I have found one that operates all things, [and] one through which all things are effected...". Both Donne and C take *operor* and *efficio* to be synonymous. Donne's version seems to identify the two gods, whereas C distinguishes creator and ground, or cause and ground. See e.g. FIELD 13.

[3][2] Cf BIBLE *NT Gospels* 3 n 2. See also **4**, below.

[3][3] For a similar view of the Trinity see e.g. BIBLE *NT Gospels* **2** and n 2. Cf BÖHME **169** and n 2, **172** and n 1.

knows this be far off) we cannot goe, to the proceeding of the holy Ghost.

If this mystery be considered, as words or rather *sounds* vibrating on some certain ears, to which their Belief assigned a supernatural cause—well and good! Wh[at] else can be said! Such were the sounds—Wha[t] their meaning is, we know not/ but such sounds not being in the ordinary cour[se] of nature, we of course attribute them to some thing extra-natural. Bu[t] if God made man in hi[s] own Image therein, as in a mirr[or] misty, no doubt[,] at best, & now *cracked* by peculiar & inherited defects, yet still our only mirror, & therein to re contemplate all we can of God,—this word " proceeding " may admit of an easy sense. For if man first used it to express as well as he could a notion found in himself, as Man in genere, we have to look into ourselves—& there we may find, that two events of vital Intelligence may be conceived—the first, a necessary and eternal outgoing of *Intelligence* (Νοῦς) from *Being* (Το ὄν)*ᵃ* *with the will as an accompaniment*, but not *from* it, as a cause, in *order* tho' not necessarily in *time*, precedent—/ this is true *Filiation*; the second, [an] act of [*th*]*e Will & Reason*, [in] their purity strict [Id]entities/ & therefore [n]ot *begotten* or [fi]liated, but [P]ROCEEDING from [in]telligent essence [a]nd essential [i]ntelligence [c]ombining in [a]ct/ necessarily [i]n deed, & [c]o-eternally/ [f]or the co-existence [o]f absolute Spontaneity with [a]bsolute necessity is involved in the very Idea of *God*, one of whose intellectual Definitions is, the Synthesis generative a[d] extra, and annihilative tho' inconclusive quod se,[1] of all conceivable Antitheses: even as the best moral Definition—(and O how much more godlike to *us*, in this state of antithetic Intellect is the moral beyond the intellectual!)—the best moral Definition is—God *is* LOVE![2]—and this is (to *us*) the high prerogative of *the moral*, that all its dictates immediately reveal [truths]*ᵇ* of intelligence, whereas the strictly Intellectual only by more ⟨distant & cold⟩ deductions carries us towards the Moral.—For what is Love? Union with the desire of union—/ God therefore is the Cohesion & the

---

ᵃ A slip for ὄν
ᵇ The only legible detail is the top of the ascender of *h* or *l*. *LR* reads "the truths", but that is too long for the space

4[1] God synthesises all antitheses in two ways: "generatively", proceeding "outwards" (cf "outgoing", above), to form a *tertium aliquid*; and "annihilatively", so that they cancel each other out, though "not conclusively [i.e. not completely] with respect to themselves". C's meaning is perhaps best understood as a gloss on his preceding account of "Filiation" and "Proceeding".

4[2] 1 John 4.8, 16.

Oneness of all Things—& dark & dim is that system of Ethics, which does [not]*a* take *"Oneness"* as the *root* of all Virtue!

*b*Being, Mind, Love in action = holy Spirit, are ideas—distinguishable, tho' not divisible, but *Will* is ~~both~~ equally incapable of distinction & or division—It is equally implied in 1. vital Being, [2]. in [e]ssential [I]ntelligence/ [an]d 3. in [re/co]-effluent Love or [h]oly Action/ Now Will [i]s the true [p]rinciple & meaning of *Identity*, of *Selfness*: even in our common Language.—The Will therefore being indistinguishably [o]ne, but the possessive Powers [t]riply distinguishable do perforce involve the notion expressed by three *Persons* and one *God*. There are three "Personæ *Per quas sonat"*[3] three forms of manifestation co-eternally co-existing, in which the one will is totally, all in each/ the truth of which we may *know* in our own minds, & can understand by no analogy—for the wind*c* ministrant to diverse at the same moment, in order then either to aid the fancy, borrows ⟨or rather steals,⟩ from the mind the idea of [the] total in omni parte,[4] which alone furnishes the Analogy—but that both it & a myriad of other material Images do inwrap themselves in these veste non sua,[5] & would be even no objects of conception, if they did not—yea, that even the very words, "conception, comprehension," & all in all languages that answer to them—suppose this transinfusion[6] from the Mind (even as if the Sun be imagined visual, it must first irradiate from itself in order for itself to perceive) is an argument better than all analogy

a Word supplied by the editor
b At the top of p 338 C has written "note continued from p. 335—"
c A slip for "mind"

4[3] "Persons through whom he [i.e. God] speaks". C tries to find a radical meaning for "person" by stressing the derivation (given by Aulus Gellius 5.7, but no longer accepted), from *per* (through) and *sono* (I sound); a *persona* (mask) was originally used in drama to magnify the voice of an actor. C uses this figure also in Henry MORE *Philosophical Poems* (Cambridge 1647) back flyleaf and later in *CN* IV 5244 f 34, 5297 PS.

4[4] The whole "in each and every part". "Totus in omni parte" is expected, but cf "totally, all in each" earlier in the sentence.

4[5] "A garment not its own"—the phrase being in the correct case and idiomatically singular in spite of the preceding "these".

4[6] Not in *OED*, which, however, quotes from this annotation the incorrect *LR* III reading "trans-impression". Cf "transelemented" and "transnatured" in COPY B 6, "translocation" in FIELD 33 and n 3, "transsensual" in Andrew FULLER 4 n 7, "trans-*conceive*" and "transimagine in GREW 3, and "transnihilation" in *Friend* (*CC*) I 522–3n, quoted in BAXTER *Catholick Theologie* 13 n 1.

5   pp 342–3, cropped at the end | Sermon xxxv, on Matt 12.31

§] First then, for the first terme, *Sin*, we use to ask in the Schoole, whether any action of man can have *rationes demeriti*, whether it can be said to offend God, or to deserve ill of God; for whatsoever does so, must have some proportion with God....

If then we can sin so against God, as we can against the King, and against the Law, and against Propriety, and against Parents; wee have wayes enow of sinning against God. Sin is not therefore so absolutely nothing, as that it is (in no consideration) other than a privation, onely *Absentia recti*, and nothing at all in it selfe: but...we rest in this, that sin is *Actus inordinatus*, It is not only an obliquity, a privation, but it is an action deprived of that rectitude, which it should have; It does not onely want that rectitude, but it should have that rectitude, and therefore hath a sinfull want.

This § appears to me to furnish an interesting Instance of the bad effects, in reasoning as well as morals, of the "*cui bono? cui malo?*" system of Ethics:[1] that system which places the *good* and *evil* of actions in their painful or pleasurable effects on the sensuous or passive nature of sentient Beings; not in the Will, the "pure act" itself.[2] For according to this system God must either be a passible dependant Being, i.e. not God, or else he must have no Interest, and therefore no motive, or impulse to reward Virtue or punish Vice. (Corollary, the Epicurean Veil of their Atheism is itself an implicit Atheism—) Nay, the World itself could not have existed: & as it does exist, the origin of Evil, (for if Evil means no more than Pain in genere,/[3] Evil has a true Being in the order of Things) is not only a difficulty of impossible solution, but it is a fact immediately & necessarily implying the non-existence of an omnipotent & infinite Goodness, i.e. of God. For to say, I believe in a God, but not that he is omniscie[nt,] omnipotent, and all-goo[d,] is as mere a

[1] A calculation according to the question "to whose advantage? to whose disadvantage?" would in C's view not be an ethical judgement at all, any more than the utilitarian criterion of "the greatest good (i.e. happiness) for the greatest number" seemed to him, in his mature years, to have any moral reality. For his earlier view, akin to utilitarianism, see e.g. *Lects 1795 (CC)* 228 and n 2, *Watchman (CC)* 99. For the phrase *cui bono* see *SM (CC)* 21 n 4.

[2] For will as act cf COPY B **44** and n 1. See also **4** par 2, above.

[3] On the relation between pain and evil see COPY B **114**. In LEIBNIZ *Theodicee* ii 134 C objects to "the subordination of moral to physical Evill: in consequence of which the latter in reality constitutes the true evil of the former—now as the latter is evidently avoidable by omnipotence...the former becomes unintelligible", and so "the first Principle of morality" is removed.

contradiction in Terms, as to say—I believe in a circle; but not that all the ray[s] from its cent[er] to its circumfer[ence] are equal.[4]

I cannot read the profound truth so clearly expressed in the last Line but four of p. 342[5]—I[n] the very next Paragrap[h—] without an uneasy wond[er] at its incongruity with the former Dogmata.

SERMONS PREACHED UPON THE CONVERSION OF S. PAUL

5A   p 460 | Sermon XLVI, on Acts 9.4

So ill a Historian as to say, God hath called *Saul*, a Persecutor... And *that mind toward*] therefore if he have a minde to me, he will deale so with me too, and, if he have no such minde, no man can imprint, or infuse a new minde in God? God forbid.[1]

SERMONS PREACHED AT COURT, AND ELSE-WHERE

6   pp 724–5, pencil, lightly cropped[1] | Sermon LXXI, on Matt 4.18–20

Which present obedience of theirs is exalted in this, that this was freshly upon the imprisonment of *Iohn Baptist*, whose Disciple *Andrew* had been; And it might easily have deterred, and averted a man in his case, to consider, that it was well for him that he was got out of *Iohn Baptists* schoole, and company, before that storme, the displeasure of the state fell upon him; and that it behoved him to be wary to apply himselfe to any such new Master, as might draw

5[4] C's illustration is not at random: see BÖHME **6** and n 9.

5[5] I.e. the last sentence in the textus.

5A[1] Sermon XLVI is the only sermon that C marked in COPY A and also annotated in COPY B. T. A. Methuen recalled that in 1814–15 when he knew C in Calne, C had repeated "the following description by *Donne* of the conversion of St Paul 'CHRIST was the lightning flash that melted him, CHRIST was the mould that formed him'—". VCL SMS 11.6 and *C Talker* 310 (var). If this is exactly what C said, it is an epigrammatic transformation of a passage in the paragraph immediately preceding **5A** in Sermon XLVI, the first of the four "Sermons Preached upon the Conversion of S. Paul" and the only sermon that C marked in both COPY A and COPY B, pp 460–1 being especially memorable. The "light of heaven" (Acts 9.3) that blinded Saul C has turned into "lightning", thereby at a stroke rendering the abruptness of the conversion (as e.g. of "Men that opened a window to take ayre, and saw an Execution in the street") and Donne's image of metal melted to be poured into a mould. "...Whereas Christs other Disciples and Apostles, had a breeding under him, and came... first to be Disciples, and after to be Apostles; S. *Paul* was borne a man, an Apostle, not carved out, as the rest in time; but a fusil Apostle, an Apostle powred out, and cast in a Mold; As *Adam* was a perfect man in an instant, so was S. *Paul* an Apostle, as soone as Christ tooke him in hand." See also COPY B **130** and n 1.

6[1] For marked passages in this sermon, beginning at p 717, see ANNEX.

him into as much trouble; which Christs service was very like to doe. But the contemplation of future persecutions, that may fall, the example of persecutions past, that have falne, the apprehension of imminent persecutions, that are now falling, the sense of present persecutions, that are now upon us, retard not those, upon whom the love of Christ Jesus works effectually; They followed for all that. And they followed, when there was no more perswasion used to them, no more words said to them, but *Sequere me, Follow me.*[a]

... The way of Rhetorique in working upon weake men, is first to trouble the understanding, to displace, and discompose, and disorder the judgement, to smother and bury in it, or to empty it of former apprehensions and opinions, and to shake that beliefe, with which it had possessed it self before, and then when it is thus melted, to powre it into new molds, when it is thus mollified, to stamp and imprint new formes, new images, new opinions in it. But here in our case, there was none of this fire, none of this practise, none of this battery of eloquence, none of this verball violence, onely a bare *Sequere me, Follow me*, and *they followed.**

* It is a sort of sophism peculiar, as far as I know, to the reasoning in behalf of Christianity, first, actually tho' perhaps indirectly to assume the Truth of the Gospels, & then from that assumption to prove the assumption/ Every $A = A$ But A is A Ergo, $A = A$. If I believe literally all that is written in the Gospels, what more have you, or any uninspired Being, a right to demand of me? If I do not believe them, how silly must those arguments be, quoad *me*,[2] which take its Truth for granted? The argumentum in circulo,[3] d I own, is common enough in all parties; but by inadvertence—or at least in particular reasonings—but to make it the Queen-Axiom of a whole System,[4] and that not by one man, or by men of one Age, but by a whole sect of 200 millions for a succession of ages is, as I said, as far as my Knowlege extends, peculiar to the Christians. S. T. C.

---

7   p 725, pencil, lightly cropped

But still consider, that they did but leave their nets, they did not burne them. And consider too, that they left but nets; those things, which

---

[a] This paragraph is marked with a pencil line in the margin, probably by C. See also ANNEX for other passages probably marked by C but not annotated

[2] "As far as *I* am concerned".
[3] "Circular argument"—arguing in a circle.

[4] A telescoped version of the recurrent figure of "the queen-bee in the hive of error": see BAINES 1 n 2. Cf CHILLINGWORTH COPY A 5.

might entangle them, and retard them in their following of Christ. And such nets, (some such things as might hinder them in the service of God) even these men, so well disposed to follow Christ, had about them. And therefore let no man say, *Imitari vellem, sed quod relinquam, non habeo*, I would gladly doe as the Apostles did, leave all to follow Christ, but I have nothing to leave; alas, all things have left me, and I have nothing to leave. Even that murmuring at poverty, is a net; leave that. Leave thy superfluous desire of having the riches of this world; though thou mayest flatter thy selfe, that thou desirest to have onely that thou mightest leave it, that thou mightest employ it charitably, yet it might prove a net, and stick too close about these to part with it.

an excellent Paragraph grounded on a mere *Pun*!—Suc[h] was the taste of the Age/ & it is an awful joy to observe that not great Learni[ng,] great Wit, great Talen[t,] or even (as far without great virtue that *can* be) no, not even great Genius, were effectual to preserve the man from the contagion, but only the deep & wise enthusiasm of moral Feeling.[1] Compare in this light Donne's theological prose with that even of the honest Knox;[2] and above all, compare Cowley with Milton[3]

8   pp 727–8, pencil, cropped | Sermon LXXII, on Matt 4.18–20

And yet, though for the better applying of God to the understanding of man, the Holy Ghost impute to God these excesses, and defects of man (lazinesse and drowsiness, deterioration, corruptiblenesse by ill conversation, prodigality and wastfulnesse, sudden choler, long irreconci[l]ablenesse, scorne, inebriation, and many others) in the Scriptures, yet in no place of the Scripture is God, for any respect said to be proud; God in the Scriptures is never made so like man, as to be made capable of Pride; for this had not beene to have God like man, but like the devill.

It is amusing to see the use, w̄ch the Xtian Divines make of the very facts in favor of their own religion, with which they triumpha[ntly]

[1] An unusually negative view of the possible functions of punning. See, in contrast, *Poems* 49 and n 1.

[2] Presumably John Knox (c 1513–72), whose *First Book of Discipline* (1560) was the only coherent book of systematic theology widely current in Britain after the dissolution of the monasteries.

[3] On Cowley's wit see CHALMERS 4 n 1 and COWLEY headnote. For Milton's punning see DANIEL 11 and DONNE *Poems* 51 and n 3. Cf "Milton had a highly *imaginative*, Cowley a very *fanciful* mind": *BL* ch 4 (*CC*) I 84.

batter that of the Heathen[;] viz. th[e] gross & sinful anthropomorphitism of thei[r] representatio[ns] of Divin[ity;] & yet the Heathen Philosophers and Priest[s] (Plutarch for instance) tell us as plainly as Donne or Acquinas can do, these are only accomodations to human modes of conception/[1] the divine nature in itself is impassible/ how otherwise could it be the prime Agent, but that we name it, abusivè,[2] by the effects, it produces on our passions. Pain is commonly inflicted in anger—therefore & for no *reason* but from this *cause*, we say God [. . . . .]*[a]* Plutarch = Donne. Paganism needs a true philosophical Judge—condemned it will be[3]—more heavily perhaps then by the [p]resent Judges but not from the same Statutes or [o]n the same Evidence.[4]

Annex

Several passages in Sermons LXXI and LXXII are marked with pencil lines in the margin, which are distinguishable from the many other markings in this volume. Their association with **6** and **7** (on Sermon LXXI) and **8** (on Sermon LXXII) suggest that these markings are probably C's. The passage marked on p 723 D–E is included in **6** textus, above; all other marked passages in Sermon LXXI precede **6**, and all the marked passages in Sermon LXXII follow **8**.

(*a*) SERMON LXXI

p 717 C. . . . the mercy of Christ is not lesse active, not lesse industrious then the malice of his adversaries, He preaches in populous cities, he preaches in the desart wildernesse, he preaches in the tempestuous Sea: and as his Power shall collect the severall dusts, and atomes, and Elements of our scattered bodies at the Resurrection, as materialls, members of his Triumphant Church; so he collects the materialls, the living stone, and timber, for his Militant Church, from all places, from Cities, from Desarts, and here in this Text, from the Sea, (*Iesus walking by the Sea, &c.*)

p 718 A. . . . And then we note their readinesse, they obeyed the call, they did all they were bid, They were bid *follow*, and they *followed*, and *followed presently;* And they did somewhat more then seemes expresly to have been required, for, *They left their Nets, and followed him.*

p 719 A. Which Lake [the Sea of Galilee] being famous for fish, though of ordinary kinds, yet of an extraordinary taste and relish, and then of extraordinary kinds too, not found in other waters, and famous, because

---

[a] The cropped words could begin: "[is angry...]" The note continues from p 727 to p 728 without change of textus

8[1] Plutarch of Chaeronea, Platonic philosopher and priest at Delphi for thirty years, frequently points out that the stories about the gods are not to be taken literally, and looks for the meaning behind them. See e.g. *Moralia* 358F, 378A, 379E (*Isis and Osiris*).

8[2] "Abusively", i.e. by a misuse of language.
8[3] The "philosophical Judge" would, no doubt, condemn paganism on grounds of pantheism. Cf DUBOIS **8**.
8[4] For marked passages in Sermon LXXII, beginning at p 731, see ANNEX.

divers famous Cities did engirt it, and become as a garland to it, *Capernaum*, and *Chorazim*, and *Bethsaida*, and *Tiberias*, and *Magdalo*, (all celebrated in the Scriptures) was yet much more famous for the often recourse, which our Saviour (who was of that Countrey) made to it; For this was the Sea, where he amazed *Peter*, with that great draught of fishes, that brought him to say, *Exi à me Domine, Depart from me, O Lord, for I am a sinfull man*...

p 719 B–D. ... Hee [Christ] is come... from his *Iuda* and *Levi*, the foundations of State and Church, to an *Andrew* and a *Peter* fisher-men, sea-men; and these men accustomed to that various, and tempestuous Element, to the Sea, lesse capable of Offices of civility, and sociablenesse, then other men, yet must be employed in religious offices, to gather all Nations to one houshold of the faithfull, and to constitute a Communion of Saints; They were Sea-men, fisher-men, unlearned, and indocil; Why did Christ take them? Not that thereby there was any scandall given, or just occasion of that calumny of *Iulian* the Apostat, That Christ found it easie to seduce, and draw to his Sect, such poore ignorant men as they were; for Christ did receive persons eminent in learning, *(Saul* was so) and of authority in the State, *(Nicodemus* was so) and of wealth, and ability, *(Zacheus* was so, and so was *Ioseph* of Arimathea) But first he chose such men, that when the world had considered their beginning, their insufficiency then, and how unproper they were for such an employment, and yet seene that great work so farre, and so fast advanced, by so weake instruments, they might ascribe all power to him, and ever after, come to him cheerfully upon any invitation, how weake men soever he should send to them, because hee had done so much by so weak instruments before: To make his work in all ages after prosper the better, he proceeded thus at first. And then, hee chose such men for another reason too; To shew that how insufficient soever he received them, yet he received them into such a Schoole, such an University, as should deliver them back into his Church, made fit by him, for the service thereof. Christ needed not mans sufficiency, he took insufficient men; Christ excuses no mans insufficiency, he made them sufficient.

p 720 A–B. When *Peter* and *Iohn* preached in the streets, *The people marvelled*, (sayes the Text) why? *for they had understood that they were unlearned.* But *beholding also the man that was healed standing by, they had nothing to say*, sayes that story. The insufficiency of the Instrument makes a man wonder naturally; but the accomplishing of some great worke brings them to a necessary acknowledgement of a greater power, working in that weake Instrument. For, if those Apostles that preached, had beene as learned men, as *Simon Magus*, as they did in him, *(This man is the great power of God*, not that he had, but that he was the power of God) the people would have rested in the admiration of those persons, and proceeded no farther. It was their working of supernaturall things, that convinced the world. For all *Pauls* learning, (though hee were very learned) never brought any of the Conjurers to burne his bookes, or to renounce his Art; But when God wrought extraordinary works by him, That sicknesses were cured by his napkins, and his handkerchiefs, (in which cures, *Pauls* learning had no more concurrence, no more cooperation, then the ignorance of any of the fisher-men Apostles) And when the world saw that those Exorcists, which went about to doe

Miraclcs in the Name of Jesus, because *Paul* did so, could not doe it, because that Jesus had not promised to worke in them, as in *Paul*, Then the Conjurers came, and burnt their bookes, in the sight of all the world, to the value of fifty thousand pieces of silver. It was not learning, (that may have been got, though they that heare them, know it not; and it were not hard to assigne many examples of men that have stolne a great measure of learning, and yet lived open and conversable lives, and never beene observed, (except by them, that knew their Lucubrations, and night-watchings)...)...

p 721 B–C. Such men then Christ takes for the service of his Church; such as being no confidence in their ownc fitnesse, such as embrace the meanes to make them fit in his Schoole, and learne before they teach. And to that purpose he tooke *Andrew* and *Peter*; and he tooke them, when he found them *casting their net into the Sea.* This was a Symbolicall, a Propheticall action of their future life; This fishing was a type, a figure, a prophesie of their other fishing. But here (in this first part) we are bound to the consideration of their reall and direct action, and exercise of their present calling...

p 723 A. ...And that God loves; that a naturall, a secular, a civill fraternity, and a spirituall fraternity should be joyned together; when those that professe the same Religion, should desire to contract their alliances, in marrying their Children, and to have their other dealings in the world (as much as they can) with men that professe the same true Religion that they do. That so (not medling nor disputing the proceedings of States, who, in some cases, go by other rules then private men do) we doe not make it an equall, an indifferent thing, whether we marry our selves, or our children, or make our bargaines, or our conversation, with persons of a different Religion, when as our Adversaries amongst us will not goe to a Lawyer, nor call a Physician, no, nor scarce a Taylor, or other Tradesman of another Religion then their owne, if they can possibly avoid it.

(*b*) SERMON LXXII

pp 731 E–732 A. ...Take heed therefore of going on with thine owne inventions, thine owne imaginations, for this is no following; Take heed of accompanying the beginners of Heresies and Schismes...And therfore to follow Christ doctrinally, is to embrace those Doctrins, in which his Church hath walked from the beginning, and not to vexe thy selfe with new points, not necessary to salvation. That is the right way, and then thou art well entred; but that is not all; thou must walke in the right way to the end, that is, to the end of thy life. So that to professe the whole Gospel, and nothing but Gospel for Gospel, and professe this to thy death, for no respect, no dependance upon any great person, to slacken in any fundamentall point of thy Religion, nor to bee shaken with hopes or feares in thine age, when thou wouldst faine live at ease, and therefore thinkest it necessary to do, as thy supporters doe; To persevere to the end in the whole Gospel, this is to follow Christ in Doctrinall things.

pp 734 E–735 A. Because it was *Nomen primitivum*, their owne, their former name. The Holy Ghost pursues his owne way, and does here in Christ, as hee does often in other places, he speaks in such formes, and such phrases, as may most worke upon them to whom he speaks. Of *David*, that was a shepheard before, God sayes, he tooke him to feed his people. To those *Magi* of the East, who were given to the study of the Stars, God gave a Star to be their guide to Christ at Bethlem. To those which followed him to Capernaum for meat, Christ tooke occasion by that, to preach to them of the spirituall food of their souls. To the Samaritan woman, whom he found at the Well, he preached of the water of Life. To these men in our Text accustomed to a joy and gladnesse, when they tooke great, or great store of fish, he presents his comforts agreeably to their tast, They should be fishers still. Beloved, Christ puts no man out of his way, (for sinfull courses are no wayes, but continuall deviations) to goe to heaven. Christ makes heaven all things to all men, that he might gaine all: To the mirthfull man he presents heaven, as all joy, and to the ambitious man, as all glory; To the Merchant it is a Pearle, and to the husbandman it is a rich field. Christ hath made heaven all things to all men, that he might gaine all, and he put no man out of his way to come hither. These men he calls Fishers.

p 736 c–d. The Scriptures will be out of thy reach, and out of thy use, if thou cast and scatter them upon Reason, upon Philosophy, upon Morality, to try how the Scriptures will fit all them, and beleeve them but so far as they agree with thy reason; But draw the Scripture to thine owne heart, and to thine owne actions, and thou shalt finde it made for that; all the promises of the old Testament made, and all accomplished in the new Testament, for the salvation of thy soule hereafter, and for thy consolation in the present application of them.

pp 736 d–737 a. Now this that Christ promises here, is not here promised in the nature of wages due to our labour, and our fishing. There is no merit in all that we can doe. *The wages of sin is Death*; Death is due to sin, the proper reward of sin; but the Apostle does not say there, That eternall life is the wages of any good worke of ours. (*The wages of sinne is death, but eternall life is the gift of God, through Iesus Christ our Lord*) Through Jesus Christ, that is, as we are considered in him; and in him, who is a Saviour, a Redeemer, we are not considered but as sinners.... God shuts no man out of heaven, by a lock on the inside, except that man have clapped the doore after him, and never knocked to have it opened againe, that is, except he have sinned, and never repented. Christ does not say in our text, Follow me, for I will prefer you; he will not have that the reason, the cause. If I would not serve God, except I might be saved for serving him, I shall not be saved though I serve him; My first end in serving God, must not be my selfe, but he and his glory. It is but an addition from his own goodnesse, *Et faciam*, Follow me, and I will doe this... The Moone is at such time just betweene the Earth and the Sunne, therefore the Sunne must be Eclipsed; for upon the Sunne, and those other bodies, God can, and hath sometimes wrought miraculously, and changed the naturall courses of them; (The Sunne stood still in *Ioshua*, And there was an unnaturall Eclipse at the death of Christ) But God cannot by any Miracle so worke upon himselfe, as to make himselfe not himselfe, unmercifull, or unjust; And out of his mercy he makes this promise, (Doe this, and thus it shall be with you) and then, of his justice he performes that promise, which was made meerely, and onely out of mercy, If we doe it, (though not because we doe it) we shall have eternall life.

Copy B

LXXX Sermons. [Another copy.] London 1640. F°.

Bodleian Library

C's copy, which remained in possession of the Gillman family after his death, and is evidently referred to in a letter from HNC and SC to Gillman dated "Thursday 10" (i.e. Sept or Dec 1835): "Baxter and Donne must still wait." Ms at Blackwell's 1948, now unlocated. HNC and SC were then completing *LR* I and II; the marginalia on Donne's *Sermons* did not appear in print until *LR* III (1838). A note to Watson List 21 shows that this copy was "given to the Rev. H. A. Harvey Oxford by my father"—i.e. by the Rev James Gillman. Henry Auber Harvey (b 1824), vicar of St Mary Magdalen, Oxford, 1876–84, has marked Sermons IV, V, VI, and IX in the Table of Contents and noted "Read" twice there; and against Sermons XVIII (p 178) "Read 1904"; and against Sermon LXXVI (p 766): "Read, esp. last part, August 3, 1905."

The title-page shows damage to the outer edge, and a triangle (about 4 × 5 inches) is cut from the top corner; both had been repaired before C annotated that leaf.

Passages are marked in pencil with a rough "X" or with a ragged vertical line on pp 32, 33, 34, 36, but these cannot be certainly identified as C's. In addition to the usual editorial check-marks made by HNC and SC, passages are marked with crosses and lines on a number of pages, and with a distinctive mark like a large flourished German 7: these are presumably Harvey's, as are a few short notes, on sig C2 (Contents), and on pp 25, 29, 32, 37, 55, 60, 67, 175, 178 ("Read 1904"), 557; the note on p 37 is printed as C's in *C 17th C*. In view of the number of non-Coleridgian markings, marked passages have been sparingly identified as C's. For the "insert" bearing some of C's notes, see **4** n *a*, below; and for C's distinctive mark "R", see **4**.

When Professor S. G. Dunn was teaching in India between the wars and beginning to form his collection of editions of all the works of his blood-relation John Donne, he received this copy from Blackwell's (there is a Blackwell's label at the foot of the front board) in place of a finer copy that had been sold by the time Dunn's order reached Oxford; the marginalia had not then been identified as C's and the copy was described as heavily marked up and in poor condition. Dunn bequeathed this copy to the Bodleian.

DATE. Oct 1831 to the end of 1832; and possibly earlier (see **5A** and n 1). Notes dated in ms: Oct 1831 (**3**, **16**), 6 Dec 1831 (**75**). In **16** and **132** C speaks of himself as sixty years old, which—with his customary mistake of one year in his age—places those notes between Oct 1831 and Oct 1832. There are close affinities between these annotations and those on HACKET, HEYLYN, and HOOKER.

1 p ⁻3

There have ⟨been⟩ many and those illustrious Divines in our Church, from Elizabeth to the present day, who over-valuing the accident of antiquity, and arbitrarily determining the appropriation of the words, ancient, primitive, &c to a certain date—ex. gr. to all before the 4ᵗʰ, or 5ᵗʰ, or 6ᵗʰ Century, were resolute Protesters against the corruptions and tyranny of the Romish Hierarch; and yet lagged behind Luther and the Reformers of the first generation.—Hence I have long seen the necessity or expedience of a three-fold Division of Divines. There are many whom, God forbid! I should call *papistic*, or like Laud, Montague, Heylin, longing for a Pope at Lambeth, whom yet I dare not ~~call~~ name Apostolic.[1]—Therefore I divide our Theologians into

      1. Apostolic, or *Pauline.*
      2. Patristic.—
      3. Papal.

Even in Donne, ⟨(see p. 80)⟩[2] still more in Bishops Andrews and Hackett, there is a strong *patristic* leaven—.[3] In Jeremy Taylor, this Taste for the Fathers, and all the Saints and Schoolmen before the Reformation amounted to a dislike of the Divines of the Continental protestant Churches, Lutheran or Calvinist—But this must in part at least be attributed to Taylor's keen feelings, as a Carlist and a Sufferer by the Puritan, anti-prelatic Party.[4]

S. T. C.

[1] For William Laud (1573–1645) see LAUD, also BAXTER *Reliquiae* COPY B 76 n 1. Laud, impeached in 1640 on several charges including "Popery", was condemned and executed. Richard Montagu (1577–1641), bp of Chichester and Norwich, and Peter Heylyn (1600–62), prebendary of Westminster, were both followers of Laud and violent controversialists in defending and promoting Laud's policies. Heylyn—whom C refers to in **15**, below, as "Laud's Creature"—wrote a life and defence of Laud entitled *Cyprianus Anglicus* (1668), a copy of which (1671) C annotated.

[2] See **68**, below.

[3] Cf **70** and **74**, below; and see HERBERT **16** and n 1. The "*patristic* leaven" arose, C thought, from too uncritical admiration of the early Church Fathers: see **22**, below (which, however, includes the twelfth-century St Bernard), and FIELD **59** nn 1, 2. See also HACKET *Century* **12** and **24** and e.g. *TT* 12 Jan 1834. For Lancelot Andrewes (1555–1626) cf **132**, below, and see HEYLYN **12** and n 1 and ANDERSON COPY B **32** n 1.

[4] Through Laud's influence, Jeremy Taylor (1613–67) was appointed chaplain to Charles I at an early age and in 1642 became chaplain to the Royalist army. Forced to withdraw from public life after the death of Charles I, he was appointed bp of Down and Connor after the Restoration; his episcopate was much troubled by the resistance of both Presbyterians and Roman Catholics. C annotated at least four of Taylor's works, Lamb's copy of the *Polemicall Discourses* (1678) containing more marginalia than any other book that C annotated.

2 p ⁻3

Is it not a lamentable inconsistency that the For. & Br. Bible Society should exclude all notes & comments, not offend ~~the~~ a handful of infidels under the name of *Unitarians*—and withhold the Scriptures from the R. Catholics, rather than suffer the Apocrypha to be bound up in the same Volume![1]

3 p ⁻2

An assured faith in a future State, and with a distinct appropriation of it to our own person, cannot but be a heightening and enlivening of all other moral and rational Supports. It is a grace to be earnestly prayed for by all, a blessing most devoutly to be acknowleged with thanksgiving by as many as feel it. Nevertheless, I can well understand how the religious Hebrews before Christ, ~~mig~~ with very dim & indistinct views of ⟨personal⟩ immortality—tho' certainly not under a positive negation or disbelief of the same—might derive great consolation and effectual Support from the simple trust in the divine Love & Wisdom/ O there is a marvellously tranquillizing power ⟨~~even~~⟩ in the ⟨mere⟩ Sense of *Necessity*—that it *must* be. How much more when this is united with the assurance, that whatever must be, therefore only *must* be because it *ought* to be—that ~~it is nec~~ the Necessity is the Offspring of the freeest Love and the most perfect Wisdom. ~~Every~~ The collective impulses and energies of our proper humanity converge and concenter in that inward act uniting Will and Reason, by which say—Almighty God! Heavenly Father! thy Will be done![1]   Octʳ 1831.

4 p ⁻1, title-page verso, and insert pp 1–4ᵃ

Paragraphs that peculiarly pleased or struck me—and opposite to which, in the margin, I have written R. i.e. recollige.[1] I began this

---

ᵃ "Insert"—a double leaf of writing paper, 4 pp, watermarked 1831, tipped in after the title-page, containing the conclusion of **4** and the text of **100** (pt), **102**, **103**, **105**, **107–109**, **111**, **118**, **120–122**

2[1] See BIBLE COPY B **68** n 1; and for a brief history of the British and Foreign Bible Society see *LS* (*CC*) xxxvi–xxxvii n 6. The first rule of the Society was that its Bibles were to have "*No Notes! No Comment! Distribute the Bible and the Bible only among the Poor!*"—*LS* (*CC*) 201—and another rule was that the Apocrypha should not be included. Both policies were no doubt informed by the desire for doctrinal neutrality reinforced by the conviction (which C could not share) that the Bible could speak perfectly clearly for itself. In a ms fragment (collection of Kathleen Coburn) C made a memorandum to write a series of letters, the second of which was to be "on the Babel Society, alias, boy-bull, or *Calf*, of Idolatry".

3[1] See **122**, below.

4[1] "Collect". Passages so marked, when not included in textus, are given as sub-marginalia.

at the 35ᵗʰ page; but will look over the preceding pages, & therefore leave a space for prefixing the numbers.[2]

P. 35.—	p 115. A.
p. 35. B.C.[3]	129. A.B.C.
p. 38 C.E.	134, 135. . . .
p. 39. D. . . .[4]	P. 163. . . .
39. E.—. . .	P. 164. . . .
40 B.	P. 165. B. . . .
42. C. . . .	165. C.D. . . .
58, 59.—. . .	E. . . .
60. . . .	166. D.—. . .
69 D.E.—70. A.—. . .	P. 167. A.—. . .[b]
70 D.E. . . .	— B.C.D.—. . .
P. 71. . . .	167. 168.—. . .
P. 77. . . .	176.—. . .
P. 78. . . .	177. C.—. . .
P. 84. D.E.—	178 A. . . .
P. 90 B./[a]	
94. A.B.	

5　title-page verso[c]

It might be noticed, as seeming to attest the privilege of Sᵗ John, as the *beloved* Apostle,[1] that to him alone the Church owes the record of the first and the last Miracle of Christ—that at the Marriage-Feast at Cana, and the raising of Lazarus—one in honor of ⟨conjugal⟩ Love, the other of Friendship[2]

---

[a]　In the ms, the references to pp 90–135 are written in one line
[b]　Insert p 1 begins
[c]　This note was written after **49** and runs through the beginning of it

---

4[2]　No passage is marked "R" in the text before p 35.

4[3]　Each page of the text is printed in a fifty-eight-line format, with marginal letters A–E to divide the page into four twelve-line sections and a final section of ten lines.

4[4]　A page reference followed by an elision means that the note written by C on p ⁻1 or insert has been transferred to the appropriate position in the sequence of pages of text.

5[1]　Cf John 13.23, 19.26, etc.

5[2]　For these two miracles see John 2.1–11 and 11.17–44; and on the Lazarus miracle cf **92**, below. On the relation between love and friendship see e.g. BROWNE *Religio* **22** and n 1, DE WETTE **22** and n 1.

SERMONS PREACHED UPON CHRISTMAS-DAY

5A   p 1 | Sermon I, title

$$1816^1$$
PREACHED...*upon* Christmas *day*. <u>1622</u>.
$$194$$

6   fly-title verso, continued on p 1, pencil, completed in ink | Sermon I, on Col 1.19–20

Hath God reconciled me to God; And reconciled me by way of satisfaction? (for, that I know his justice requires) What could God pay for me? What could God suffer? God himselfe could not; and therefore God hath taken a body that could.

God forgive me! or those who first set abroad this strange μεταβασιν εις αλλο γενος,[1] this Debtor and Creditor Scheme of expounding the mystery of Redemption! or both![2] But I never can read the words, "God himself could not, and therefore took *a body* that could" without being reminded of the Monkey that took the Cat's paw to take the chesnuts out of the Fire, and claimed the merit of Puss's sufferings. I am sure however that the ludicrous Images under which this Gloss of the Calvinists embodies itself to my fancy, never disturb my recollections of the adorable Mystery itself. It is clear, that a Body, remaining a Body, can only suffer *as*[a] a Body; for no faith can enable us to believe, that the same thing can be at once A and −A. Now, that the Body of our Lord was not transelemented or tra[b]nsnatured[3] by the pleroma indwelling, we are positively assured by Scripture. Therefore, it would follow from this most unscriptural doctrine, that the divine justice had satisfaction made to it by the suffering of a Body which had been brought into existence for this special purpose, in lieu of the debt of eternal misery due from and leviable on, the Bodies and Souls of all Mankind. It is to this gross perversion of the sublime Idea of the Redemption by the Cross, that we must attribute the rejection of Redemption by the Unitarian, and of the Gospel in toto by the more consequent Deist.—

---

[a] Word inked over by C   [b] Continued from here in ink

5A[1] This folio volume may have been given to C as a gift on his first Christmas at Highgate.

6[1] "A shift [in argument, from one kind, or basis of reference] to another kind". See BAXTER *Reliquiae* COPY A **29** n 1.

6[2] See also FIELD **12** and cf BAHRDT **2** n 3.

6[3] For other Coleridgian words with prefix *trans*- see COPY A **4** and n 6. *OED* cites a use of "transelemented and transnatured" in 1567, and also quotes this use by C (from *LR*).

7 p 2

In the qualification of the person, we finde *plenitudinem*, fulnesse, and *omnem plenitudinem*, all fulnesse; and *omnem plenitudinem inhabitantem*, all fulnesse dwelling, permanent. And yet, even this dwelling fulnesse, even in this person Christ Jesus, by no title of merit in himselfe, but onely *quia complacuit*, because it pleased the Father it should be so.

This in the intention of the Preacher may have been *sound*—but was it *safe*—Divinity? In order to the latter, methinks, a less equivocal word than *Person* ought to have been adopted[1]—as the Body and Soul of the Man, Jesus, considered abstractedly from the Divine Logos, who in it took up humanity into deity, & was *Christ* Jesus.[2] Dare we say, that there was no self-subsistent, tho' we admit no self-originated, merit in the CHRIST? It seems plain to me, that in this & sundry other passages of S[t] Paul, the Father means the total tri-une Godhead.

8 pp 3–4

...there was a fulnesse to be added to God, for this work, to make it *omnem plenitudinem*, for Christ was God before; there was that fulnesse; but God was not Christ before, there lackcd that fulnesse. Not disputing therefore, what other wayes God might have taken for our redemption, but giving him all possible thanks for that way which his goodnesse hath chosen, by the way of satisfying his justice, (for, howsoever I would be glad to be discharged of my debts any way, yet certainly, I should think my selfe more beholden to that man, who would be content to pay my debt for me, then to him that should entreat my creditor to forgive me my debt) for this work, to make Christ able to pay this debt, there was something to be added to him.

It appears to me, that dividing the Ch. of E. into two Æras, the first from Ridley to Field, or Ed. VI. to the commencement of the latter Third of James the First's Reign—and the second ending with BULL and Stillingfleet[1]—we might characterize their comparative

---

7[1] For C's view of the inappropriateness of the term "person" in credal and trinitarian use see e.g. CHANNING 1 and n 2.

7[2] *Christ*—"anointed", the Greek tr of Hebrew "messiah", "anointed [of Yahweh]".

8[1] The first period would be c 1547–1615. Nicholas Ridley (c 1500–55), one of the compilers of the Book of Common Prayer (1549), discovered the distinctive force and colour of his Protestantism when he was appointed bp of Rochester in 1547; Edward VI reigned

excellencies thus: that the Divines of the first Æra had a deeper, more genial, and more practical ⟨Insight⟩ into the mystery of Redemption, in the relation of Man toward both the Act and the Author, viz. in all the inchoative states, the regeneration, & the operations of saving Grace generally: while those of the second Æra possessed clearer & distincter Vision concerning the nature & *necessity* of Redemption, in the relation of God toward Man, in and concerning the connection of Redemption with the article of the Tri-unity, and above all, that they surpassed their Predecessors in a more safe and determinate scheme of the divine es Esconomy of the three Persons in the one undivided Godhead.—This indeed was mainly owing to Bishop Bull's masterly Work de Fide Nicenâ,[2] which in the next generation Waterland so admirably maintained against the Psilosophy of the Arians,[3] the combat ending in the Death & Burial of Arianism, & its descent & metempsychosis into Socinianism, and thence into modern Unitarianism/[4] and on the other extreme against the *oscillatory* creed of Sherlock, now swinging to Tritheism in the recoil from Sabellianism, and again to Sab. in the recoil from Tritheism.[5]

1547–53. Richard Field (1561–1616) published in 1606–10 his noncontroversial apology for the Church of England under the title *Of the Church*—a favourite book of C's, which he annotated heavily. James I reigned 1603–25. The second period would end in 1685 with the publication of George Bull's *Defensio fidei Nicaenae*. C's annotated copy of BULL is lost, but annotations in copies of works of Edward Stillingfleet (1635–99) are preserved. For other remarks on the chronology of the early English divines, see **22** and **56**, below.

8[2] See also BIBLE *Gospels* **2** n 2, and BULL.

8[3] The writing of Daniel Waterland (1683–1740), two of whose books C annotated, was—with Bull and Leighton—central in C's consideration of the doctrine of the Trinity. For "psilosophy"—*OED* recognises it as a C word, citing *BL* (*CC*) I 67n, 185—which C glosses as pseudo-philosophy or "slender wit", see *CN* II 3121 (c May–Sept 1807), *LS* (*CC*) 244, *Friend* (*CC*) I 94, and *CL*

IV 922n, 972n. Cf "psilanthropism" in CHANNING **1** and n 3, and for other words compounded with "psilo-" see HOOKER **22** and n 1.

8[4] A condensed version of C's understanding of the origins of "modern Socinianism" is given in CHILLINGWORTH COPY B **1**; see also *LS(CC)* 181–4n and cf 176–7, 254–8. See also BAHRDT **1** n 1.

8[5] William Sherlock (c 1641–1707) by his *Vindication of the Doctrine of the Trinity* (1690)—of which C annotated a copy—aroused a controversy in which he was accused of tritheism, and in 1695 his trinitarian views were condemned by the Hebdomadal Council of Oxford. He responded with *The Present State of the Socinian Controversy* (1698), in which he abandoned most of his earlier theological position. The Sabellians held that the three persons of the Trinity are merely different aspects or modes of the one divine person. Tritheism is a doctrine of three gods not unified in one god.

9 pp 4–5

First, we are to consider this fulnesse to have been in Christ, and then, from this fulnesse arose his merits; we can consider no merit in Christ himselfe before, whereby he should merit this fulnesse; for, this fulnesse was in him, before he merited any thing; and but for this fulnesse, he had not so merited. *Ille homo, ut in unitatem filii Dei assumeretur, unde meruit?* How did that man, (sayes St. *Augustine* speaking of Christ, as of the son of man) how did that man merit to be united in one person, with the eternall Son of God? *Quid egit ante? Quid credidit?* What had he done? nay, what had he beleeved? Had he eyther faith, or works, before that union of both natures?

Dr Donne and St Augustin said this without offence; but I much question whether the same would be endured now by our Bishops & their Chaplains. That it is, however, in the spirit of Paul and of the Gospel, I doubt not to affirm; and that this great truth is obscured by the (in my judgement) *post-apostolic* Christopædia, concorporated with the first, & prefixed to Luke's Gospel, I am inclined to think.[1]

10 p 5

What canst thou imagine, he could fore-see in thee? A propensnesse, a disposition to goodnesse, when his grace should come? Eyther there is no such propensnesse, no such disposition in thee, or, if there be, even that propensnesse and disposition to the good use of grace, is grace, it is an effect of former grace, and his grace wrought, before he saw any such propensnesse, any such disposition; Grace was first, and his grace is his, it is none of thine.

One of many instances in dogmatic theology, in which the half of a divine Truth has passed into a fearful Error by being mistaken for the whole Truth.[1]

11 pp 6–9[a]

Gods justice required bloud, but the bloud is not spilt, but poured from that head to our hearts, into the veines, and wounds of our owne soules: There was bloud shed, but no bloud lost.

[a] Written in the foot-margins of the four pages, the last paragraph in the head and outer margins of p 7

9[1] Luke 1.5–2.52, which is indeed post-apostolic, is the only "Christopaedia" ("Childhood of Christ", which C in *CN* III 4402 also calls *evangelium infantiae*) in a canonical gospel; a few details are included ("concorporated") in Matt 1.18–2.23 ("the first" gospel in order of presentation). See also BLANCO WHITE *Letters* 7 and CHILLINGWORTH COPY B 2 n 2. In this note, however, C is concerned not with the chronology of the synoptic gospels but—as 16 at n 3 also shows—with the question of the origins of the doctrine of the Trinity. See also *CL* VI 611 (8 Sept 1826).

10[1] See also 119, below.

It is affecting to observe, how this great man's mind sways & oscillates between his Reason, which demands in the word "blood" a symbolic meaning, a spiritual interpretation, and the habitual awe for the *letter*—so that he himself seems uncertain whether he means the physical lymph, serum and globules that trickled from the wounds of the nails & thorns down the face & sides of Jesus—or the blood of the Son of Man, which he who drinketh not, cannot live.[1] But it is a deep subject—the true solution of which may best, God's Grace assisting, be sought for in the collation of Paul with John—specially in Paul's assertion, that we are baptized into the Death of Christ, that we may be partakers of his Resurrection & Life.[2] It was not on the visible Cross, it was [not][a] directing attention to the blood-drops on his Temples and Sides, that our Blessed Redeemer said—*This* is my body—and *this* is my Blood[3]

Yea, it is most affecting to see the Struggles of so great a mind to preserve its inborn fëalty to the Reason under the servitude to an accepted article of *Belief* which was, alas! confounded with the high obligations of *Faith*—Faith, the co-adunation of the finite individual Will with the universal Reason by the submission of the former to the latter.[4] To reconcile redemption by the material blood of Jesus with the mind of the Spirit, he seeks to spiritualize the material blood itself in all men! And a deep truth lies hid even in this!

12   p 9

But if we consider those who are in heaven, and have been so from the first minute of their creation, Angels, why have they, or how have they any reconciliation? How needed they any, and then, how is this of Christ applyed unto them?

The history and successive meanings of the term, Angels, in the O. and N. Testament, and the Idea, that shall reconcile all, as so many several forms, & as it were *perspectives*, of one and the same truth—this is still a desideratum in Christian Theology[1]

---

a Word supplied by the editor

11[1] Cf John 6.54, 56.
11[2] Rom 6.3–10.
11[3] Matt 26.26, Mark 14.22, Luke 22.19; also incorporated from 1 Cor 11.23–6 into the order of administration of the Sacrament.

11[4] On the distinction between faith and belief see **30** and n 2, and cf **62**, below. For faith as the coadunation of will and reason see also **122** (at n 3), below.
12[1] Cf HACKET *Century* **16** and nn.

13 p 9

For, at the generall resurrection, (which is rooted in the resurrection of Christ, and so hath relation to him) the creature shall be delivered from the bondage of corruption, into the glorious liberty of the children of God; for which, the whole creation groanes, and travailes in paine yet. The deliverance then from this bondage, the whole creature hath by Christ, and that is their reconciliation. And then are we reconciled by the blood of his Crosse, when having crucified our selves by a true repentance, we receive the seale of reconciliation, in his blood in the Sacrament. But the most proper, and most literall sense of these words, is, that all things in heaven and earth, be reconciled to God, (that is, to his glory, to a fitter disposition to glorifie him) by being reconciled to another, in Christ; that in him, as head of the Church, they in heaven, and we upon earth, be united together as one body in the Communion of Saints.

A very meagre and inadequate interpretation of this sublime text! The Philosophy of Life, which will be the corona et finis coronans[1] of the Sciences of Comparative Anatomy and Zoology, will hereafter supply a fuller and *nobler* Comment.[2]

14 p 10

The blood of the sacrifices was brought by the high priest, *in sanctum sanctorum*, into the place of greatest holinesse; but it was brought but once, *in festo expiationis*, in the feast of expiation; but, in the other parts of the Temple, it was sprinkled every day. The blood of the Crosse of Christ Jesus hath had his effect *in sancto sanctorum*, even in the highest heavens, in supplying their places that fell, in confirming them that stood, and in uniting us and them, in himselfe, as Head of all. In the other parts of the Temple it is to be sprinkled daily. Here, in the militant Church upon earth, there is still a reconciliation to be made; not only toward one another, in the band of charity, but in our selves.... In a word, till the flesh and the spirit be reconciled, this reconciliation is not accomplished. For, neither spirit, nor flesh must be destroyed in us; a spirituall man is not all spirit, he is a man still. But then is flesh and spirit reconciled in Christ, when in all the faculties of the soule, and all the organs of the body we glorifie him in this world; for then, in the next world wee shall be glorified by him, and with him, in soule, and in body too, where

13[1] The "crown and crowning end"—proverbial.   13[2] Possibly a hope for the *Theory of Life* to fulfil.

we shall bee thoroughly reconciled to one another, no suits, no controversies; and thoroughly to the Angels; when we shall not only be *sicut Angeli*, as the Angels in some one property, but *aequales Angelis*, equall to the Angels in all . . . [but] this shall be the blessednesse of them both, to be united in one head, Christ Jesus.

a truly excellent & beautiful paragraph.

15 p 10

If you will mingle a true religion, and a false religion, there is no reconciling of God and Belial in this Text. For the adhering of persons born within the Church of Rome, to the Church of Rome, our law sayes nothing to them if they come; But for reconciling to the Church of Rome, by persons born within the Allegeance of the King, or for perswading of men to be so reconciled, our law hath *] called by an infamous and Capitall name of Treason, and yet every Tavern, and Ordinary is full of such Traitors. Every place from jest to earnest is filled with them; from the very stage to the death-bed; At a Comedy they will perswade you, as you sit, as you laugh, And in your sicknesse they will perswade you, as you lye, as you dye.

* A strange transition from the Gospel to the English Statute-Book! But I may observe, that if this statement could be truly made under James the first, there was abundantly ampler ground for it in the following Reign. And yet with what bitter Spleen does not Heylin, Laud's Creature, arraign the Parliamentarians for making the same complaint.[1]

16 pp 11–14 | Sermon II, on Isa 7.14

The fear of giving offence, especially to good men, of whose faith in all essential points we are partakers, may reasonably ~~make sure~~ induce us to be slow, and cautious in making up our minds finally on a religious question—may, & ought to, influence us to submit our conviction to repeated revisals and re-hearings. But there may arrive a time of such perfect clearness of view respecting the particular point, as to supersede all fear of Man by the higher duty of declaring the whole truth in Jesus. Therefore, now having overpassed six-sevenths of the ordinary period allotted to Human Life,[1] resting my whole & sole hope of Salvation and Immortality on the Divinity of

15[1] Cf HEYLYN 6, 7, and esp 14.
16[1] C was born 21 Oct 1772 but often regarded himself as a year older than he was and usually antedated his birthday by one day: see BAXTER *Reliquiae* COPY B 91 n 4. Cf 132, below.

Christ, and the Redemption by his Cross & Passion, and holding the doctrine of the Tri-une God as the very ground and pediment of the Gospel Faith, I feel myself enforced by Conscience to declare & avow, that, in my deliberate Judgement the Christopædia prefixed to the third Gospel and concorporated with the first,[2] but according to my belief, in its *present* form, the latest of the four, was no part of the Original Gospel,[3] was unknown or not recognized by the Apostles Paul and John, and that instead of supporting the doctrine of the Trinity, and the filial Godhead of the Incarnate Word, as set forth by John (Ch. 1.) and by Paul, if it ⟨be⟩ i̶s̶ not altogether irreconcilable with this faith, doth yet greatly weaken and bedim its evidence—& by the too palpable Contradictions between the Narrative in the first Gospel and that attributed to Luke, has been a fruitful magazine of doubts respecting the historic character of the Gospels themselves. No learned Jew can be expected to receive this as the true primary sense of the text in Greek—in which the Hebrew word does not correspond to Virgin, Virgo, or παρθενος, but to Lass)(L̶a̶d̶, to Puella)(Puer, to νεᾱνις)(νεανιας. Accordingly, νεᾱνις is the Greek Term, by which the severely literal Aquila renders.[4]— What *sign* indeed could Mary's pregnancy have been for King Ahaz? Or rather how could that which in its very nature could only have been known to herself, h̶a̶v̶e̶ be called a *Sign* for any one?

S. T. Coleridge Octob^r 1831.[a]

[a] Here, at the head of p 13, C has drawn a line to mark the end of the note; below the rule, " ∧ ", and at the foot of the page the PS is introduced by " ∧ "

16[2] See also **9** and n 1, above.

16[3] C refers to Matt as the "first" gospel from its traditional placing in the Bible. C argues that, although there may be grounds for a version of Matt earlier than Luke, Matt "in its *present* form" is later than Luke because it "concorporates" material from Luke. If "four" is not a slip for "three"—i.e. synoptic gospels— C would place Matt "in its *present* form" later than John; cf e.g. *CL* VI 784. By "the Original Gospel" C means the *Urevangelium* postulated by Eichhorn and others (see e.g. EICHHORN *Neue Testament* COPY A **17** and n 1) as the primitive source from which all four gospels, along different lines, derive. On the date of Matt see also BAXTER *Catholick Theologie* **7** and n 1.

16[4] Matt 1.23 alone of the gospels takes the phrase " Behold a virgin shall be with child" from the "sign" given to the reluctant King Ahaz by Isaiah in Isa 7.14: hence C's appeal to the Hebrew word for "virgin". Matt 1.23 takes the word παρθένος (virgin) from the Septuagint version of Isa 7.14. The Hebrew word in Isa 7.14, however, is *almah* (which Donne evidently meant to include in his text)—a young woman of marriageable age whether or not virgin. C refers to the Greek tr of Aquila Ponticus (fl c 120), the third text in Origen's *Hexapla*, notable for its rigid literal adherence to the Hebrew: it reads νεᾱνις (girl, young woman). C may have had this detail from RHENFERD *Opera philologica* (Utrecht 1772) p 159 (a passage annotated by C), in which Aquila Ponticus is cited from Irenaeus. *NEB* reads "A young woman is with child".

P.S.—But were it asked of me—Do you then believe our Lord to have been the Son of Mary by Joseph? I reply—It is a point of religion with me to have no belief one way or the other—I am in this way like St Paul more than content not to know Christ himself ως κατα σαρκα.[5] It is enough for me to know, that the Son of God "became flesh", εγενετο σαρξ, γενομενος εκ γυναικος[6]—and more than this, it appears to me, was unknown to the Apostles or if known not taught by them as appertaining to our saving faith in Him.

S. T. C.

17 p 14

One of the most convenient Hieroglyphicks of God, is a Circle. . . . His Sun, and Moone, and Starres, (Emblemes and Instruments of his Blessings) move circularly, and communicate themselves to all. His Church is his chariot; in that, he moves more gloriously, then in the Sun; as much more, as his begotten Son exceeds his created Sun, and his Son of glory, and of his right hand, the Sun of the firmament. . . . As the Sun does not set to any Nation, but withdraw it selfe, and returne againe; God, in the exercise of his mercy, does not set to thy soule, though he benight it with an affliction.

The affinity in sound of Son and Sun, Sohn and Sonne, is not confined to the Saxon & German—or the Gothic Dialects generally. I find the same in Helios and Filius—[1]

Item—Conciliare, versöhnen, = Confiliare, i.e. facere esse cum filio—one with the Son./[2]

16[5] "As after the flesh"—i.e. from a human point of view. See 2 Cor 5.16. C elsewhere refers to the synoptic gospels as gospels κατὰ σαρκά: see e.g. BLANCO WHITE *Practical Evidence* 1 and n 2, *CL* VI 894.

16[6] John 1.14 (AV), "was made flesh" (cf FLEURY 98 and n 4); Gal 4.4 (AV), "made of a woman". This PS, with which cf FIELD 26, explains C's persistent objection to "parthenolatry": see HACKET *Century* 11, BLANCO WHITE *Practical Evidence* 11, and cf H. COLERIDGE 24 and n 2.

17[1] C's pun on "Son" and "Sun" had become, ever since the early years, almost a habit of writing: see AURELIUS 35 n 2. C had made this same fanciful etymological connexion between Greek ἥλιος (sun) and Latin *filius* (son) in an annotated copy of *SM*: see *SM* (*CC*) 56n. Donne's frequent play on Son/Sun in the sermons, and his use of the Sun as the sign of God, of the Logos, of Messiah, and of the Son, is discussed in Potter & Simpson x 302–6.

17[2] A second punning nexus: *conciliare* and *versöhnen*, to reconcile— *confiliare*, to make to be "one with the Son". Also in the *SM* annotation cited above.

18 p 17

That which *Gellius*, and *Plinie* say, that a Virgin had a child, almost
200. yeares before Christ, that which *Genebrard* saies, that the like
fell out in France, in his time, are not within our faith, and they are
without our reason . . . of this Virgin in our text, If that be true, which
Aquinas cites out of the Roman story, that in the times of *Constantine*
and *Irene*, upon a dead body found in a sepulchre, there was found
this inscription, in a plate of gold . . . Christ shall be borne of a Virgin,
and I beleeve in that Christ . . . If this be true, yet our ground is not
upon such testimonie; If God had not said it, I would never have
beleeved it.

One of the sad relics of patristic super-moralization aggravated by
papal Ambition, which clung to too many of Divines, especially those
of the second or third generation after Luther.[1]

   Luther himself was too Spiritual, an of too heroic a faith, to be
thus blinded by the declamations of the Fathers—of whom with the
exception of Augustine, he held in very low esteem—[2]

19 p 17

There are three Heresies; all noted by S. *Augustine* that impeach the
virginity of this most blessed Woman: The Cerinthians said she
conceived by ordinary generation; *Iovinian* said, she was delivered
*] by ordinary meanes; And *Helvidius* said, she had children after:
All against all the world besides themselves, and against one another.

* *Helvidius*? If there be any meaning in words, the New Testament
asserts the same, over and over again.[1]

18[1] Donne continues: "And there-
fore I must have leave to doubt of that
which some of the Roman Casuists have
delivered, That a Virgin may continue a
virgin upon earth, and receive the
particular dignity of a Virgin in Heaven,
and yet have a child, by the insinuation
and practise of the Devill; so that there
shall be a father, and a mother, and yet
both they Virgins." He then quotes St
Cyprian: "It is not enough for a virgin to
bee a virgin in her owne knowledge, but
she must governe her selfe so, as that
others may see, that she is one" and
adds some amplifying commentary by
Tertullian on this statement.

18[2] See also **74**, below.
   19[1] The fourth-century Latin theo-
logian Helvidius, seeking to defend
marriage against the prevailing exaltation
of virginity, argued that Jesus' brothers
were the natural sons of Joseph and
Mary; Jerome, in *De perpetua virginitate
B. Mariae adversus Helvidium*, identified
them as the sons of another Mary.
C's "over and over again" would in-
clude Matt 12.46 ("his mother and his
brethren"), 13.55 (four brothers are
named), 27.56; Mark 3.31–4, 15.40,
16.1; Luke 8.19–21; Acts 1.14.

20   p 19, at the end of Sermon II

I think, I might safely put the question to any serious, spiritual-minded Christian—what one inference tending to edification, in the discipline of Will, Mind, or affections he can draw from these speculations of the last two or three pages of this Sermon respecting Mary's pregnancy & parturition. *Can* ~~the~~ such points appertain to our faith as Christians which ~~no~~ every Parent would decline speaking of before a family & and which, if the questions were propounded by another in the presence of my Daughter, aye, or even of my (no less in mind & imagination) innocent Wife I should resent as an indecency?

21   p 20 | Sermon III, on Gal 4.4–5

"*But when the fulnesse of time was come, God sent forth his Son,* *] *made of a woman, made under the law, to redeem them that were under the Law, that we might receive the adoption of Sonnes.*"

* I never can admit that γενομενον, εγενετο, &c in John and Paul are adequately or rightly rendered by the English, *made.*[1]

22   p 21

What miserable revolutions and changes, what downfals, what break-necks, and precipitations may we justly think our selves ordained to, if we consider, that in our comming into this world out of our mothers womb, we doe not make account that a childe comes right, except it come with the head forward, and thereby prefigure that headlong falling into calamities which it must suffer after?

The taste for these forced and fantastic Analogies Donne with the greater number of the learned ⟨prelatic⟩ Divines from James I to the Restoration acquired from ~~a~~ that too great partiality for the *Fathers*, from Irenæus to St Bernard, by which they sought to distinguish themselves from the Puritans.[1]

21[1] The words γενόμενον (as in Rom 1.3, Gal 4.4, Phil 2.7) and ἐγένετο (as in John 1.14, 1 Cor 15.45) are translated in AV as "made" (past participle) and "was made". (Cf **16**, above, in which C has "became flesh".) The many shades of meaning of this verb—come into being, come to be, become; variously, be born or begotten, arise or come about, be made or created, happen or take place, and appear or exist—make this term crucial in any attempt based on the text of NT Greek to establish verbally the precise divine/human status of Jesus. C had discussed the difficulty, and the limitations of the word "proceeding", in COPY A **4**.

22[1] This stylistic mannerism is part of what C meant by "patristic leaven", which he deplored in Field, Jeremy Taylor, and Hooker, as well as in Donne (see **1** n 3, above), and was as-

23 p 21

So fully was the time of the Messias comming, come, that though some of the Jews say now, that there is no certain time revealed in the Scriptures when the Messias shall come, and others of them say, that there was a time determined...but by reason of their great sins he did not come at his time, yet when they examine their own supputations, they are so convinced...that this was that *fulnesse of time*, that now they expresse a kinde of conditionall acknowledgement of it, by this barbarous and inhumane custome of theirs, that they always keep in readinesse the blood of some Christian, with which they anoint the body of any that dyes amongst them, with these words, if Jesus Christ were the Messias, then may the blood of this Christian availe thee to salvation...

!!—Is it *possible*, that DONNE could have given credit to this absurd legend![a]

It was, I am aware, not an age of critical acumen—Grit, Bran & Flour were swallowed in the unsifted mass of their Erudition—Still that a man like Donne should have imposed on himself such a set of idle tales for facts of History is scarcely credible—that he should have attempted to impose them on others, most melancholy.

24 p 22, pencil

...but <u>thou</u> shalt feele the joy of his third birth in thy soul, most inexpressible this day, where he is born this day (if thou wilt) without

---

[a] C has drawn a line here as though to mark the end of the note, but the following paragraph continues in the same hand and ink

---

sociated with a distinctive doctrinal allegiance with the early Fathers. In the period indicated—c 1603–60—the efforts of the "learned Divines" were directed to establishing the distinctness of the Church of England from the Church of Rome, in opposition not only to the Church of Rome but also to the Calvinistic Puritans who demanded express scriptural warrant for all details of public worship and rejected the prelatic hierarchy that Laud and his followers sought to perpetuate. From their study of the early Fathers they hoped to recover the purity of Christian belief and ritual; but, since the early Fathers were often engaged in bitter anti-heretical controversy, purity of doctrine was not easy to discover in what survived of their writing. In naming Irenaeus and Bernard, C indicates a period from the second to the twelfth century. St Irenaeus, bp of Lyons (c 130–c 200), "the first great Catholic theologian", placed great value upon episcopal tradition and "the co-ordinate authority of all four Gospels". *ODCC*. Cf *CN* III 4215 and n. St Bernard of Clairvaux (1091–1153), a model of austere orthodoxy, saintliness, and mysticism—the "good and holy Bernard" that Donne often quoted in his sermons— argued that the work of salvation could not be accomplished without the co-operation of free will and grace.

father or mother; that is, without any former, or any other reason then his own meere goodnesse that should beget that love in him towards thee, and without any matter or merit in thee which should enable thee to conceive him.

Qu? does the Will in man precede or follow or is it co-existent

25 p 22, pencil

In the first alone, are two degrees too [in the manner of his comming], that he takes the name of the Son of a woman, and wanes the glorious name of the Son of God; And then, that he takes the name of the son of a woman, and wanes the miraculous name of the son of a Virgin.

Very ingenious, but likewise very presumptuous, this arbitrary attribution of St Paul's *silence* repecting, & presumable ignorance of, the virginity of Mary to Christ's own determination, to have the fact passed over.[1]

26 p 22

Christ waned the glorious Name of Son of God, and the miraculous Name of Son of a Virgin to; which is not omitted to draw into doubt, the perpetuall Virginity of the Blessed Virgin, the Mother of Christ; she is not called a woman, as though she were not a Maid...

Is "wane" a misprint for "wave" or "waive"?—It occurs so often as to render its being an erratum improbable. Yet I do not remember to have met elsewhere *wane* used for *decline*, and as a verb active.[1]

27 pp 22, pencil^a

...when it is said, Joseph *knew her not, donec peperit, till she brought forth her Son*, this does not imply his knowledge of her after, no more, then when God sayes to Christ, *donec ponam*, sit at my right hand, till I make thine enemies thy footstoole, that imports, that Christ should remove from his right hand after: For, here is a perpetuall *donec* in both places...

Fabling admits of no stop/ the Negative here is mere impudence. Would not the Evangelist have said—Joseph had never known her/

---

^{a} The note is written higher on the page than **26**, but later, **26** having already been written in the space that would be natural for **27**

25[1] Referring to Gal 4.4—the text of this sermon.

26[1] "Wane", printed three times on this page, is corrected to "waive" in the errata at the end of the volume.

28 p 23, pencil

But behold here is a greater then *Solomon*, and he sayes now in action, by being borne of a Virgin, as he had said, long before, in Prophesie....If this had been spoken of such a woman, as were no Maid, this had been no new thing: As it was, it was without example, and without naturall reason...If there were reason for it, it were no miracle, if there were precedents for it, it were not singular; and God intended both, that it should be a miracle and that it should be done but once...

~~No~~ The relation of the first Comet that had ever been observed might excite doubt in the mind of an Astronomer, ⟨to⟩ who⟨m⟩ from the place, where he lived, it had not been visible. But his *reason* could have been no objection to it.—Had God pleased all Women might have conceived without a Male/ as many of the Polypi & Planariæ do.[1]—Not on any such ground do I decline this as an Article of faith—but because I doubt the *evidence*/

29 p 25

Though therefore we may think, judging by the law of reason, that since Christ came to gather a Church, and to draw the world to him, it would more have advanced that purpose of his, to have been borne at *Rome*...then in *Iury*, and...better to have been borne at *Ierusalem*...then at obscure *Bethlem*...Though we may thinke in the law of Reason,[a] that his work of propagating the Gospel, would have gone better forward, if he had taken for his Apostles, some *Tullies*, or *Hortensii*, or *Senecaes*, great, and perswading Orators, in stead of his *Peter*, and *Iohn*, and *Matthew*, and those Fishermen, and tent-makers, and toll-gatherers...yet...sayes the Lord, *your way is not my way, your law is not my law*; for...*it became him* [Christ] *to fulfill all righteousnesse*, that is, all that Decree of God, which he had accepted, and acknowledged as Righteous.

It is and has been a misfortune, a grievous and manifold loss & hindrance, for the interests of moral & spiritual truth, that even our best & most vigorous theologians & philosophers of the age from

[a] "Reason" underlined in indelible pencil, and in the margin—not in C's hand—"See Flyleaf & Margin"

28[1] Polypi (e.g. sea anemone, jelly-fish, coral) and planariae (flatworms with unsegmented bodies)—types, respectively, of *Coelenterata* and *Turbellaria*— reproduce without differentiation into male and female. When C discussed polyps in *TL*, he was concerned to trace the rising scale of individuation, without particular reference to sexual differentiation: *TL* (1848) 71–3, 75–6.

Edward VI. to James II., so generally confound the *terms*, and so *too* often confound the subjects themselves—Reason and Understanding.[1] Yet the diversity, the difference *in kind*, was known ⟨to,⟩ and clearly admitted, by, many of them: by Hooker, for instance,[2] and ⟨it is⟩ *implied* in the whole of Bacon's Novum Organum.[3] Instead of "the law of Reason," Donne *meant* and ought to have said—"judging according to the ordinary presumptions of the *Understanding*"—i.e. the faculty which generalizing particular experiences judges of the future by analogy of the past—See "Aids to Reflection".[4]

30 p ⁻2, referring to p 25

Sermon III. p. 25.

All the §ph. from B. to F. I most deliberately protest against[1]—& should cite its dicta with a host of others, as sad effects of the Confusion of Reason and Understanding and the consequent abdication of the former—instead of the bounden submission ~~to~~ of the Latter, ⟨to a higher Light.⟩

FAITH itself is but an Act of the Will assenting to the Reason on its own evidence, ⟨without, and⟩ even against, the Understanding. This indeed is, I fully agree, to be brought into captivity to the Faith.[2]

29[1] For the confusion between reason and understanding see BAXTER *Reliquiae* COPY B **42** and n 2.

29[2] See e.g. HOOKER **28** (at n 5).

29[3] See *AR* (1825) 207–8.

29[4] *AR* (1825) 209–10, 217–18, 245–6 and n. See also BAXTER *Catholick Theologie* **14** n 3. The theme is developed further in **30** and **122**, below. In *CN* IV 5293 C noted: "Let me by all the labors of my life have answered but one end, if I shall have only succeeded in establishing the diversity of Reason and Understanding, and the distinction between the *Light* of Reason in the Understanding, viz. the absolute Principles presumed in all Logic and the Conditions under which alone we draw universal and necessary Conclusions from contingent and particular facts, and the Reason itself, as the Source and birth-place of IDEAS...". C said that he had first seen the distinction

"Thirty Years" before writing *C&S*—i.e. c 1799: *C&S* (*CC*) 58.

30[1] A slip for "from B. to E". C refers to the long paragraph beginning at p 25 A—the substance of which is **29** textus—and ending in p 25 D: "And so we have done with our second part, The manner of his comming."

30[2] See also **11**, above, and **62**, **67**, **68**, **122**, below; and cf BAXTER *Reliquiae* COPY B **42**, BLANCO WHITE *Letters* **1**, CHILLINGWORTH COPY A **5**. Aphorism VIII of the "Aphorisms on Spiritual Religion", which opens the discussion of reason and understanding in *AR* cited in **29** n 4, above, is taken from Leighton: "Faith elevates the soul not only above Sense and sensible things, but above Reason itself. As Reason corrects the errors which Sense might occasion, so supernatural Faith corrects the errors of natural Reason judging according to Sense." *AR* (1825) 200.

31   p 26

...All these, and all others, whom the searching Spirit of God, seales to his service, in all the corners of the earth, because they are *] strangers in the land of Israel, should not be under the Law, and so should have no profit by Christs being made under the Law, if the Law should be understood, onely of the Law of *Moses*. And therefore to be *under the Law*, signifies here, thus much, To be a debter to the law of nature, to have a testimony in our hearts and consciences, that there lyes a law upon us, which we have no power in our selves to performe; that to those lawes, *To love God with all our powers*, and *to love our neighbour as our selves*, and *to doe, as we would be done to*, we find our selves naturally bound, and yet wee finde our selves naturally unable to performe them, and so to need the assistance of another, which must be Christ Jesus, to performe them for us...

* This exposition of the term, *Law*, in the epistles of S[t] Paul is most just, and important. The whole should be adopted among the Notes to the Ep. to the Romans, in every Bible printed with Notes.[1]

32   pp 27–9

And this was his first worke, *to Redeeme*, to vindicate them from the usurper, to deliver them from the intruder, to emancipate them from the tyran, to cancell the covenant betweene hell, and them, and restore them so far to their liberty, as that they might come to their first Master, if they would; this was *Redeeming*.

There is an absurdity in the notion of a finite divided from and superaddible to, the Infinite; of a particular Quantum of Power separated from, not included in, Omnipotence, i.e. the All-power./ But alas! ~~men~~ we too generally use the terms that are meant to express the *Absolute*, as mere *Comparatives* taken superlatively. In one thing only are we permitted & bound to assert a diversity—viz. God and Hades, the Good and the Evil Will. This aweful Mystery, this Truth—at once certain and incomprehensible, is at the bottom of *all* Religion; and to exhibit this truth free from the evil phantom of the Manichæans,[1] or the two co-eternal & co-ordinate Principles of Good and Evil, is the Glory of the Christian Religion.[a]

[a] Here C has written " ∧ ", and resumed the note with " ∧ " in the blank space at the end of Sermon III

31[1] The central discussion is in Rom 6–8. See also DE WETTE **5** and n 1.

32[1] For manichaeism see BÖHME **73** n 2.

But this mysterious dividuity[2] of the Good and Evil Will, the Will of the Spirit and the Will of the Flesh,[3] must not be carried beyond the terms, Good & Evil. There can be but one *good* Will.—the Spirit in all—and even so all evil Wills are one evil Will, the Devil, or evil Spirit.—But then the *one* exists for *us*, as finite intelligences, necessarily in a two-fold relation—Universal and Particular. The same Spirit *within us* pleads *to* the Spirit as without us, and in like manner is every evil mind in communion with the evil spirit—But—o Comfort!—the Good alone is the *Actual!*—the Evil essentially *potential*. Hence the Devil is most appropriately named, the *Tempter*, and the Evil hath its essence in the WILL.[4] It cannot pass out of it. *Deeds* are called evil in reference to the individual Will, expressed in them; but in the great scheme of Providence they are, only as far as they are good—coerced under the conditions of all true Being—and the Devil is the *Drudge* of the All-good./[5]

---

33   pp 30–2 | Sermon IV, on Luke 2.29–30

...we shall consider, that that preparation, and disposition, and acquiescence, which *Simeon* had in his Epiphany, in his visible seeing of Christ then, is offered to us in this Epiphany, in this manifestation *] and application of Christ in the Sacrament; And that therefore every penitent, and devout, and reverent, and worthy receiver, hath had in that holy action his *Now*, there are all things accomplished to him, and his *For, for his eyes have seen his salvation*; and so may be content, nay glad *to depart in peace*.

* O! would that Donne, or rather that Luther before him, had carried this just conception to its legitimate consequents! that as the Sacrament is the Epiphany for as many as receive it in faith, so the Crucifixion, resurrection and ascension of Christ himself in the Flesh were the Epiphanies, the sacramental Acts and Phænomena, of the *Deus Patiens*,[1] the visible Words of the ⟨invisible⟩ Word that was in the Beginning, Symbols in time & historic fact of the redemptive functions, passions, and procedures of the Lamb crucified from the foundation of the World[2]—the reincarnation, cross, and passion,

---

32[2] Apart from an appearance in Blount's *Glossographia* (1656), this is the only use of "dividuity" noticed in *OED*.
32[3] Cf John 1.13.
32[4] Cf GREW **25** n 3.
32[5] See also **122**, below, and COPY A **3** and **5**.

33[1] "Suffering God"—Christ on the cross, of whom the figure of the suffering servant in Isa 53, vicariously suffering for the sins of the many, is one of the prefigurations in OT.
33[2] Rev 13.8.

~~and~~ in short, the whole life of Christ in the flesh, dwelling a man, among men, being essential & substantive parts of the process, the whole of which they represented—& on this acount proper SYMBOLS of the acts & passions of the Christ dwelling *in* man, as the Spirit of Truth, & *for* as many as in faith have received him—in Seth and Abraham no less effectually than in John [and]*a* Paul. (For this is the true definition of a Symbol as distinguished from the Thing on one hand, and from a mere metaphor or conventional exponent of a Thing, on the other.)[3] Had Luther mastered this great Idea, this Master-truth, he would never have entangled himself in that most mischievous Sacramentary Controversy or had to seek a murky Hiding-hole in the figment of Consubstantiation.[4]

                                                                S. T. C.

34   p 30

§] In the first part then, in which we collect some marks, and qualities in *Simeon* which prepared him to a quiet death, qualities appliable to us in that capacity, as we are fitted for the Sacrament, (for in that way only, we shall walk throughout this exercise) wee consider first, the action it self, what was done at this time. At this time our Saviour Christ, according to the Law, by which all the first born were to be presented to God in the Temple, at a certain time after their birth, was presented to God in the Temple, and there acknowledged to be his; And then, bought of him again by his parents, at a certain price prescribed in the Law. A Lord could not exhibite his Son to his Tenants, and say, this is your Land-lord; nor a King his Son to his Subjects, and say, this is your Prince; but first he was to be tendred to God; his they were all; He that is not Gods first, is not truly his Kings, nor his own. And then God does not sell him back againe to his parents, at a racked, at an improved price; He sels a Lord, or a King back againe to the world, as cheap as a Yeoman, he takes one and the same price for all; God made all Mankinde of one blood, and with one blood, the blood of his Son, he bought all Mankinde again: At one price, and upon the same conditions, he hath delivered over all into this world; *Tantummodo crede*, and then *fac hoc, et vives*, is the price of all; Beleeve, and live well: More he asks not, lesse he

                    a Word supplied by the editor

33[3] Cf e.g. *SM* (*CC*) 30.

33[4] On symbol and sacrament see BOOK OF COMMON PRAYER COPY B **6**

and n 2 and C. BUTLER *Vindication* 1 (with n 2 on Luther and the sacramentary controversy).

takes not for any man, upon any pretence of any unconditioned decree.

§. a *beautiful* §ph—well worth extracting, aye, and re-preaching.

35 pp 35–7

When thou commest to this seale of thy peace, the Sacrament, pray that God will give thee that light, that may direct and establish thee, in necessary and fundamentall things; that is, the light of faith to see that the Body and Bloud of Christ, is applied to thee, in that action; But for the manner, how the Body and Bloud of Christ is there, wait his leisure, if he have not yet manifested that to thee: Grieve not at that, wonder not at that, presse not for that; for hee hath not manifested that, not the way, not the manner of the presence in the Sacrament, to the Church. A peremptory prejudice upon other mens opinions, that no opinion but thine can be true, in the doctrine of the Sacrament, and an uncharitable condemning of other men, or other Churches that may be of another perswasion then thou art, in the matter of the Sacrament, may frustrate and disappoint thee of all that benefit, which thou mightst have, by an humble receiving thereof, if thou wouldest exercise thy faith onely, here, and leave thy passion at home, and referre thy reason, and disputation to the Schoole.

O! I have ever felt & for many years thought, that this rem credimus, modum nescimus,[1] is but a poor evasion. It is a seems to me an attempt so to *admit* an irrational proposition as to have the credit of denying it—or to separate an irrational proposition from its irrationality. Ex. gr. I admit that $2+2 = 5$; *how* I do not pretend to know; but in SOME way not in contradiction to the multiplication ⟨table⟩. To spiritual operations, in the very term, *mode*, is perhaps inapplicable—for these are *immediate*. To the linking of *this* with that, of A with Z by intermedia; the term, mode, the question how? is properly applied. The assimilation of the Spirit to of a man to the Son of God, to God as the Divine Humanity, this spiritual transsubstantiation, like every other process of Gr operative grace, is necessarily modeless.—The whole question is concerning the transmutation of the sensible Elements. Deny this—and to what does the *modum* nescimus refer. We cannot ask, *How* is that done which

35[1] "We believe *what is done*, but we do not know *how* it is done". The source of the Latin phrase is not traced; C also used it in Jeremy TAYLOR *Polemicall Discourses* i 227.

we declare not done at all. Admit this transmutation and you necessarily admit by implication the whole absurdity of the Romish Dogma, viz. the separation of a sensible thing, from the sensible accidents which constitute all we ever meant by the thing.

35A p 35

R]As thou wouldest be well interpreted by others, interpret others well; and, as when thou comest to heaven, the joy, and the glory of every soule, shall bee thy glory, and thy joy; so when thou commest to the porch of the Triumphant Church, the doore of heaven, the Communion table, desire that that joy, which thou feelest in thy soule then, may then be communicated to every communicant there.

36 p 35

R]When I pray in my chamber, I build a Temple there, that houre; And, that minute, when I cast out a prayer, in the street, I build a Temple there; And when my soule prayes without any voyce, my very body is then a Temple: And God, who knowes what I am doing in these actions, erecting these Temples, he comes to them, and prospers, and blesses my devotions; and shall not I come to his Temple, where he is alwaies resident? My chamber were no Temple, my body were no Temple, except God came to it; but whether I come hither, or no, this will be Gods Temple: I may lose by my absence; He gaines nothing by my comming. He that hath a cause to be heard; wil not goe to Smithfield, nor he that hath cattaile to buy or sell, to Westminster; He that hath bargaines to make, or newes to tell, should not come to doe that at Church; nor he that hath prayers to make, walke in the fields for his devotions.... In cases of necessity, Christ in the Sacrament, vouchsafes to come home to me; And the Court is where the King is; his blessings are with his Ordinances, wheresoever: But the place to which he hath invited me, is his house. Hee that made the great Supper in the Gospel, called in new guests; but he sent out no meat to them, who had been invited, and might have come, and came not. Chamber-prayers, single, or with your family, Chamber-Sermons, Sermons read over there; and Chamber-Sacraments, administred in necessity there, are blessed assistants, and supplements; they are as the almes at the gate, but the feast is within... he that hath a handfull of devotion at home, shall have his devotion multiplyed to a Gomer here; for when he is become a part of the Congregation, he is joynt-tenant with them, and the devotion of all the Congregation, and the blessings upon all the Congregation, are his blessings, and his devotions.

Good; but it would be better to ~~place~~ regard solitary, family, and templar devotion as distinctions in *sort*, rather than differences in *degree*. All three are necessary.   S. T. C.

37   p 35

...without holinesse, no man shall see God; not so well, without holinesse of the place; but not there neither, if he trust onely to the holinesse of the place, and bring no holinesse with him. Betweene that fearefull occasion of comming to Church, which S. *Augustine* confesses and laments, That they came to make wanton bargaines with their eyes, and met there, because they could meet no where else; and that more fearfull occasion of comming, when they came onely to elude the Law, and proceeding in their treacherous and traiterous religion in their heart, and yet communicating with us, draw God himselfe into their conspiracies, and to mocke us, make a mocke of God, and his religion too...

What then was their guilt who by terror & legal penalties tempted their fellow Christians to this treacherous mockery? Donne should have asked himself that question.[1]

38   p 37

We say the Sacramentall bread is the body of Christ, because God hath shed his Ordinance upon it, and made it of another nature in the use, though not in the substance; Almost 600. years agoe, the Romane Church made *Berengarius* sweare, *sensualiter tangitur, frangitur, teritur corpus Christi*, That the body of Christ was sensibly handled, and broken, and chewed. They are ashamed of that now, and have mollified it with many modifications; and God knowes whether 100. yeares hence they will not bee as much ashamed of their Transubstantiation, and see as much unnaturall absurdity in their Trent Canon, or Lateran Canon, as they doe in *Berengarius* oath.

Mem. To rationalize this frightful figment of his Church, Bossuet has recourse to Spinozism, & dares make God the Substance & sole ens reale[1] of all body—& by this very hypothesis baffles his own end and does away ~~all~~ miracle in the particular instance.[2]

37[1] See **15**, above.
38[1] "Real existence". Cf **76** and n 1, below.

38[2] Jacques   Bénigne   Bossuet (1627–1704), bp of Meaux, exceptional preacher, and controversialist, sought to

38A   p 38

R] At least, make this an argument of your having been worthy receivers thereof, that you are in *Aequilibrio*, in an evennesse, in an indifferency, in an equanimity, whether ye die this night or no. For, howsoever S. *Ambrose* seem to make it a direct prayer, that he might die, he intends but such an equanimity, such an indifferency....If thou desire not death...if thou beest not equally disposed towards death...yet if thou now feare death inordinately, I should feare that thine eyes have not seen thy salvation to day; who can feare the darknesse of death, that hath had the night of this world, and of the next too? who can feare death this night, that hath had the Lord of life in his hand to day?...When wilt thou dare to goe out of this world, if thou darest not goe now, when Christ Jesus hath taken thee by the hand to leade thee out?

   ...and yet, as a man that should love the ground, where his prison stood, we love this clay, that was a body in the dayes of our youth, R] and but our prison then, when it was at best; <u>wee abhorre the graves of our bodies; and the body, which, in the best vigour thereof, was but the grave of the soule. we over-love.</u>

39   p ⁻1, referring to p 39 | Sermon v, on Exod 4.13

It hath been doubted, and disputed, and denied too, that this Text, *O my Lord, send I pray thee, by the hand of him, whom thou wilt send*, hath any relation to the sending of the Messiah, to the coming of Christ, to Christmas-day; yet we forbeare not to wait upon the ancient Fathers, and as they said, to say, that *Moses* having received a commandement from God...and having excused himselfe by some other modest and pious pretences, at last, when God pressed the imployment still upon him, he determines all in this, *O my Lord, send I pray thee, by the hand of him, whom thou wilt send....* It is a work, next to the great work of the redemption of the whole world, to redeem Israel out of Aegypt; And therefore doe both workes at once, put both into one hand, and *mitte quem missurus es, send him, whom* I know, *thou wilt send*, him, whom pursuing thine own decree, *thou shouldest send*, send Christ, send him now, to redeem Israel from Aegypt.

---

reconcile the Protestants with the Roman Church. His works include *Exposition de la doctrine de l'Église catholique sur les matières de controverse* (1671), *Discours sur l'histoire universelle* (1681), *Histoire des variations des Églises protestantes* (1688), and devotional works published posthumously. Cf *CN* III 3917 and n. The source of C's statement is not identified.

P. 39 D. as one of the happier accomodations of the Gnosis, i.e. the science of detecting the mysteries of faith in the simplest texts of Old Testament History, to the contempt or neglect of the literal & contextual sense—a sort of Katterfelto Solar Microscope, that discovered in any drop of transparent Water ~~as~~ scores of animals, each as large as the Conjuror's own black Cat.[1]—It was *Gnosis*, and not Knowlege, as our English Testaments absurdly render the words, that Paul warns against, & most wisely, as *puffing* up—inflating the heart with self-conceit, and the head with idle fancies.[2]

40 p ⁻1, referring to p 39

...But, as a thoughtfull man, a pensive, a considerative man, that stands for a while, with his eyes fixed upon the ground, before his feete, when he casts up his head, hath presently, instantly the Sun, or the heavens for his object, he sees not a tree, nor a house, nor a steeple by the way, but as soon as his eye is departed from the earth where it was long fixed, the next thing he sees is the Sun or the heavens; so when *Moses* had fixed himselfe long upon the consideration of his own insufficiency for this service, when he tooke his eye from that low peece of ground, Himselfe, considered as he was then, he fell upon no tree, no house, no steeple, no such consideration as this, God may endow me, improve me, exalt me, enable me, qualifie me with faculties fit for this service, but his first object was that which presented an infallibility with it, Christ Jesus himselfe, the Messias himselfe, and the first petition that he offers to God is this, *O my Lord send I pray thee, by the hand of him whom thou wilt send.*

P. 39. E.—beautifully imagined & happily applied.

41 pp 40–1

That *Germen Iehovae*, as a Prophet *Esay* calls Christ, that Off-spring of Jehova, that Bud, that Blossome, that fruit of God himselfe, the Son of God, the Messiah, the Redeemer, Christ Jesus, growes upon every tree in this Paradise, the Scripture; for Christ was the occasion before, and is the consummation after, of all Scripture.

39[1] For Katterfelto, his black cats, and solar microscope see BLANCO WHITE *Practical Evidence* **10** n 1 and *CN* IV 5207 and n.

39[2] C refers to 1 Cor 8.1: "Knowledge [γνῶσις] puffeth up". See also EICHHORN *Neue Testament* COPY B **5**.

The definition of *gnosis* that C takes here to be St Paul's meaning—the science of detecting the mysteries of faith in the simplest OT texts—is not the heretical gnosticism noticed in e.g. CHILLINGWORTH COPY B **1** n 2.

If this were meant to the neglect or exclusion of the primary sense, if we are required to believe, that the sacred Writers themselves, had such thoughts present to their minds—it would doubtless throw the doors wide open to every variety of folly and fanaticism—But it may admit of a safe, sound and profitable use, if we consider the Bible, as *one* Work, intended by the Holy Spirit for the edification of the Church in all ages, & having, *as such*, all its parts synoptically interpreted, the eldest by the latest &c./ Moses or David, or Jeremiah, (we might in this view affirm) meant so and so, according to the context, and the light under which and the immediate or proximate purposes, for which he wrote—but we, who command the whole scheme of the great dispensation, may see a higher & deeper sense, of which the literal meaning was a symbol or type.—& this we may justifiably call the Sense of the Spirit.

S. T. C.

42 p 41

Therefore as S. *Stephen* saw Christ, standing at the right hand of his Father... so in our Liturgie, in our Service, in the Congregation, we stand up at the profession of the Creed, at the rehearsing the Articles of our Faith, thereby to declare to God, and his Church, our readinesse to stand to, and our readinesse to proceed in that Profession.

Another Church might sit down, denoting a resolve to abide in this profession.—These things are indifferent: but charity, love of peace, & on indifferent points to prefer another's liking to our own—⟨& to observe an order once established, for order's sake,—⟩ these are *not indifferent*.

43 p ⁻1, referring to p 42

As long as the devill doth but say, Doe this, or thou wilt live a foole, and dye a begger; Doe this, or thou canst not live in this world, the devill is but a devill, he playes but a devils part, a lyer, a seducer; But when the devill comes to say, Doe this, or thou canst not live in the next world, thou canst not be saved, here the devill pretends to be God, here he acts Gods part, and so prevails the more powerfully upon us. And then, when men are so mis-transported, either in opinions, or in actions, with this private spirit, and inordinate zeale... sayes the same Father, Though the devill hath not quenched faith in that man himselfe, yet he hath quenched that mans charity towards other men; Though that man might be saved, in that opinion which he holds, because (perchance) that opinion destroyes no fundamentall point, yet his salvation is shrewdly shaked, and endangered, in his uncharitable thinking, that no body can be saved that thinks otherwise. And as it works thus to an uncharitablenesse in private, so doth it to turbulency, and sedition in the publique.

42. C. ΙΡΦΙΝΓ.[1] D.—all excellent.[2]

44   p 46

...God declares to *Moses*, his bosome name, his viscerall name, his radicall, his fundamentall name, the name of his Essence, *Qui sum, I am; Goe, and tell them, that he whose name is I am, hath sent thee.* It is true, that literally in the Originall, his name is conceived in the future; it is there, *Qui ero, I that shall be....* Howsoever, all intend, *] that this is a name that denotes Essence, Beeing: Beeing is the name of God, and of God onely.... The name of the Creator is, *I am*, but of every creature rather, I am not, I am nothing.

* Rather, I should say—the eternal Antecedent of Being—I that shall be in that I will to be—the absolute Will, the ground of Being—the Self-affirming Actus purissimus.[1]

45   p ⁻1, referring to pp 58–9 | Sermon vi, on John 12.38

O, beloved, that wee would not be afraid of giving God too much glory...or of making God too imperious over us, by acknowledging...that all our changes are acts of the right hand of God, and come from him. But we are not onely subject to the Prophets increpation, *Quis credit*, that we doe not beleeve Gods warnings of future judgements, but to the Euangelists increpation, in the person of

---

43[1] "IRVING" Edward Irving (1792–1834). C first met him c Jul 1823 (*CL* v 280, 284); thereafter Irving became a virtual disciple of C's, but by 1827 C had begun to have misgivings about Irving's theology and then of his sanity: see *TT* 17 Aug 1833. See also BAXTER *Reliquiae* COPY B **47** n 5. For annotated copies of Irving's books see IRVING and LACUNZA.

43[2] Donne gives a "pregnant, and ...aplyable example" from Eusebius' life of the Emperor Constantine. "In his time, there arose some new questions, and new opinions in some points of Religion; the Emperor writ alike to both parties, thus...Doe you move no questions, in such things, your selves; and if any other doe, yet be not too forward, so much as against them.... Disturbe not the peace of the Church, upon Inferences, and Consequences, but deale onely upon those things, which are evidently declared in the Articles, and necessarily enjoyned by the Church."

44[1] "Absolutely pure Act". See BAXTER *Catholick Theologie* 1 n 2; cf BÖHME 177 n 2 and DE WETTE 15. See also **54**, below.

Christ, *Quis credidit?* we do not beleeve present judgements to be judgements. An invincible navy hath beene sent against us, and defeated, and we sacrifice to a casuall storme for that; wee say the winds delivered us. A powder treason hath been plotted, and discovered, and we sacrifice to a casuall letter for that; we say, the letter delivered us. A devouring plague hath raigned, and gone out againe, and we sacrifice to an early frost for that; we say, the cold weather delivered us. Domestique encumbrances, personall infirmities, sadnesse of heart, dejection of spirit oppresses us, and then weares out, and passes over, and we sacrifice for that, to wine, and strong drinke, to musique, to Comedies, to conversation, and to all *Iobs* miserable comforters; wee say, it was but a melancholique fit, and good company hath delivered us of it. But when God himselfe saies, *There is no evill done in the City, but I doe it*, we may be bold to say, there is no good done in the world but hee does it. The very calamities are from him; the deliverance from those calamities much more. All comes from Gods hand; and from his hand, by way of hand-writing, by way of letter, and instruction to us.

58, 59.—on general and particular Providence—only to the unbelieving heart diverse—a noble passage.

The whole (VIth) a noble Sermon—in thought and in diction.

46 p 59

Therefore we have a clearer light then this; *Firmiorem propheticum sermonem*, says S. Peter, *We have a more sure word of the Prophets*; that is, as S. *Augustine* reads that place, *clariorem*, a more manifest, a more evident declaration in the Prophets, then in nature, of the will of God towards man, and his rewarding the obedient, and rejecting the disobedient to that will.

The sense of this text, as explained by the context, is—that in consequence of the fulfilment of so large a proportion of the Oracles the Christian ⟨Church⟩ has not only the additional light given by the Teaching & Miracles of Christ, but even the Light vouchsafed to the old Church (the Prophetic) stronger & clearer[1]

46[1] The text under discussion is 2 Pet 1.19: (AV) "We have also a more sure word of prophecy"—lit. "And we have the prophetic word [made] more certain". Cf *CN* IV 4644 (31 Mar 1820): "Can it be that so celebrated a passage as Peter's more sure word of Prophecy should have been universally mistranslated?—Yet so it appears to me—The words seem plainly to be—Therefore *we* have an additional confirmation of the prophetic word."

47 p 60

...He spake personally, and he spake aloud, in the declaration of Miracles; But, *Quis credidit auditui filii?* who beleeved even his report? did they not call his preaching sedition, and call his Miracles *] conjuring? Therefore we have a clearer, that is, a nearer light then the written Gospell, that is, the Church.

* True; yet he who should now venture to assert this truth, or even, as I in my letters on the religious & superstitious veneration of the Scriptures have done,[1] contended for a co-ordinateness of the Church and the Written Word, must bear to be thought a Semi-papist, an Ultra-HighChurchman. Still the Truth is the Truth.

48 p ⁻1, referring to p 60*ᵃ*

For, the principall intention in Christs Miracles, even in the purpose of God, was but thereby to create and constitute, and establish an assurance, that he that did those Miracles, was the right man, the true Messias, that Son of God, who was made man for the redemption and ransome of the whole world. But then, that which was to give them their best assistance, that that was to supply all, by that way, to apply this generall redemption to every particular soule, that was the establishing of a Church, of a visible and constant, and permanent meanes of salvation, by his Ordinances there, *usque ad consummationem*, till the end of the world....So that here is the case, if the naturall man say, alas they are but dark notions of God which I have in nature; if the Jew say, alas they are but remote and ambiguous things which I have of Christ in the Prophets; If the slack and historicall Christian say, alas they are but generall things, done for the whole world indifferently, and not applyed to me, which I

ᵃ Two passages, here given as textus, are marked with a pencil line in the margin, apparently not by C

47[1] These "letters" were published by HNC in 1840 as the leading item in *Confessions of an Inquiring Spirit*, under the title "Letters on the Inspiration of the ·Scriptures" with the prefatory description "Seven Letters to a Friend concerning the bounds between the right, and the superstitious, use and estimation of the Sacred Canon...". Written perhaps as early as 1823, the letters were in the hands of Taylor and Hessey by the early summer of 1824, C's intention being that they be printed as an appendix to *AR*. *CL* v 486. They were considered too long for inclusion; C announced in *AR* that they would "appear in a small volume by themselves". *AR* (1825) 381. The ms remained in the publisher's hands until 30 Jun 1826: *CL* v 435, 486 n 2. An outline for the *Opus maximum* dated 27 May 1828 includes as its fifth part "the inquiry (already instituted by me in my Eight Letters on the right and the superstitious Estimation of the Scriptures)". *L&L* 7. See also **48**, below.

reade in the Gospell, to this naturall man, to this Jew, to this slack Christian, we present an established Church, a Church endowed with a power, to open the wounds of Christ Jesus to receive every wounded soule, to spread the balme of his blood upon every bleeding heart; A Church that makes this generall Christ particular to every Christian, that makes the Saviour of the world, thy Saviour, and my Saviour; that offers the originall sinner Baptisme for that; and the actuall sinner, the body and blood of Christ Jesus for that...a Church, in contemplation whereof, God may say, *Quid potui Vineae*, what could I doe more for my people then I have done? first to send mine only Son to die for the whole world, and then to spread a Church over the whole world, by which that death of his might be life to every soule.

60. Admirable. Mem to quote this if ever I publish my letters on the right ⚹ to the superstitious veneration of the Scriptures.—[1]

49   title-page verso referring to p 60

P. 60—

    * Thus I class the Pentad of Operative Christianity[1]

Prothesis
Christ, the
WORD

Thesis	Mesothesis	Antithesis
The Written Word	The H. Spirit.	The Church

Synthesis
The Preacher.

    * The Papacy elevated the Church to the virtual exclusion or suppression of the Scriptures; the modern Church of ~~Languages~~ England, since Chillingworth, have so raised up the Scriptures as to annul the Church[2]—both alike have quenched the Holy Spirit, as the mesothesis of the two, and substituted an alien Compound for the genuine Preacher, who should be the Synthesis of the Scripture and the Church, and the sensible Voice of the H. Spirit.

48[1] *CIS* (1840) opens with two epigraphs, one from Hooker, the other presumably C's. The "Letters" do not have any epigraph, nor is Donne mentioned in the text of them.

49[1] "The Pentad of Operative Christianity" printed as prefix to the "Letters" in *CIS* (1840) differs from this only in adding "or the Indifference" to the term *Mesothesis*. Cf "my *Logical Pentad*, or Heptad, of *forms*" in *CL* VI 816 and the Pentad in BUNYAN COPY A 7 (c 1830).

49[2] See CHILLINGWORTH COPY B 2 and n 2.

50   pp 62–3 | Sermon VII, on John 10.10

Since the Revolution in 1688 our Church has been chilled and starved too generally by Preachers & Reasoners, Stoic or Epicurean—first, a sort of pagan Morality, = Virtue, substituted for the Righteousness by faith, & lastly, Prudence, Paleyianism, substituted for Morality.[1] A Christian Preacher ought to preach *Christ* alone—and all things in him & by him. If he finds a dearth in this, if it seem to him a circumscription, he does not know Christ, as the Pleroma, the Fullness—It is not possible, that there should be aught *true*, or seemly, or beautiful, in thought, will or deed, in speculative or practical,[2] which may not & which ought not, to be evolved out of Christ, and the Faith in Christ—no folly, no error, no evil to be exposed or warred against, which may not and should not be convicted & denounced from its contrariancy or enmity to Christ.

   Christ in all, all things in Christ[3]—the Christian Preacher should abjure every argument, that is not a link in the chain of which Christ is the Staple & Staple Ring.[4]

S. T. Coleridge.

51   p 64

He to us, God to man; all to nothing: for upon that we insist first, as the first disproportion betweene us, and so the first exaltation of his mercy towards us. *Man is*, sayes the Prophet *Esay, Quasi stilla situlae, As a drop upon the bucket.* Man is not all that, not so much as that, as a drop upon the bucket, but *quasi*, something, some little thing towards it; and what is a drop upon the bucket, to a river, to a sea, to the waters above the firmament? Man to God? *Man is*, sayes the same Prophet in the same place, *Quasi momentum staterae*; we translate it, *As small dust upon the balance*: Man is not all that, not that small graine of dust, but *quasi*, some little thing towards it: And what can a graine of dust work in governing the balance? What is man that God should be mindfull of him? Vanity seemes to be the lightest thing, that the Holy Ghost could name; and when he had named that, he sayes, and sayes, and sayes, often, very, very often, *All is vanity*. But when he comes to waigh man with vanity it selfe, he findes man lighter then vanity...

50[1] For Paley's prudential scheme see AURELIUS **38** n 1 and BLANCO WHITE *Practical Evidence* **1** n 1. With "Stoic or Epicurean" cf "the Epicurean Veil of their Atheism" in COPY A **5**.

   50[2] Cf Phil 4.8.

50[3] Cf Col 3.11.

50[4] For C's use of the figure of the staple and the link see e.g. *Friend (CC)* I 455, *BL* ch 12 (*CC*) I 266, and *Misc C* 19, 21. See also EICHHORN *Neue Testament* COPY A **44**.

In this page Donne passes into rhetorical extravaganza, after the manner of too many of the Fathers, from Tertullian to St Bernard.[1]

52 p 66

Some of the later Authors in the Roman Church...have noted in [several of the Fathers]...some inclinations towards that opinion, that the devill retaining still his faculty of free will, is therefore capable of repentance, and so of benefit by this comming of Christ...

If this be assumed, viz. the free-will of the Devil, the consequence would follow—his capability of repenting, & the possibility that he may repent. But then, he is no longer what we mean by the Devil, i.e. he is not *the* evil Spirit, but an wicked Soul./—[1]

53 p ⁻2, referring to p 67[a]

God is so omnipresent, as that the Ubiquitary will needs have the body of God every where: so omnipresent, as that the Stancarist will needs have God not only to be in every thing, but to be every thing, that God is an Angel in an Angel, and a stone in a stone, and a straw in a straw.

P. 67. "The Stancarist"—i.e. as appears by the context, the Pantheist or what we now call Spinosist. Q^y Is this a misprint?—The name is utterly new to me.[1]

S. T. C.

54 pp 68–9

So God fed that old world with expectation of future things, as that that very name by which God notified himself most to that people, in his commission by *Moses*, to *Pharaoh*, was a future name; howsoever our Translations and Expositions run upon the present, as though God had said *Qui sum*, my name is *I am*, yet in truth it is *Qui ero, my name is I shall be.*

[a] See **130** n *a*, below

51[1] Cf **22**, in which the span is indicated by Irenaeus and St Bernard. Tertullian (c 160–c 220) was about thirty years younger than Irenaeus.

52[1] Cf **32**, above.

53[1] Followers of Francesco Stancaro (1501–74) of Mantua, one of the Italian reformers in Poland. Stancaro taught that Christ mediated only through his human (corporal) nature, "since only thus can we avoid implying that he is not equal to God, being inferior to Him with whom he intercedes". See Frederic C. Church *The Italian Reformers 1534–1564* (New York 1932) 338.

Nay—I *will* be or I shall be in that I will to be.[1] I am that only one who is self-originant, causa sua,[2] whose Will must be contemplated as antecedent in idea to his own co-eternal Being, or deeper than.—But antecedent, deeper, &c are mere vocabula IMPROPRIA, words of accomodation, that may suggest the idea to a mind purified from the intrusive phantoms of Space and Time, but falsify and extinguish the truth, if taken as adequate exponents.

55 p 69

Wee know that Christ is come, and we avow it, and we preach it, and we affirm, that it is not onely as impious, and irreligious a thing, but as senslesse, and as absurd a thing to deny that the Son of God hath redeemed the world, as to deny that God hath created the world...

A bold but true Saying. The man who cannot see the redemptive agency in the Creation, has but dim apprehension of the creative power.

56 p ⁻1, referring to pp 69–70

First then in this last part, we consider the gift it self, the treasure, Life, *That they might have life.* Now life is the character by which Christ specificates and denominates himselfe; Life is his very name, and that name by which he consummates all his other names, *I am the Way, the Truth, and the Life*; And therefore does *Peter* justly and bitterly upbraid the Jews with that, *Ye desired a murderer,* (an enemy to life) *to be granted unto you, and killed the Prince of Life.* Acts 3.14. It is an honour to any thing that it may be sworn by; by vulgar and triviall things men might not sweare, *How shall I pardon them this?* sayes God, *They have sworn by things that are not gods.* And therefore God, who in so many places professes to sweare by himself, and of whom the Apostle sayes, *That because he could sweare by no greater, he swore by himselfe,* because he could propose no greater thing in himself, no clearer notion of himself then life, (for his life is his eternity, and his eternity is himselfe) does therefore through all the Law and the Prophets still sweare in that form, *Vivo ego, vivit Dominus, As I live, saith the Lord, and as the Lord liveth*; still he

---

54[1] The Hebrew word for "I am" can be (in tense) past, present, or future. On "I Am" see BIBLE COPY B **119** n 1. See also **44**, above.

54[2] "His own cause". Cf **110**, below.

sweares by his own life; As that solemne Oath which is mentioned in *Daniel*, is conceived in that form too…that is, by God, and God in that notion as he is life.…God is life, and would not the death of any. We are not sure that stones have not life; stones may have life; neither (to speak humanely) is it unreasonably thought by them, that thought the whole world to be inanimated by one soule, and to be one intire living creature; and in that respect does S. *Augustine* prefer a fly before the Sun, because a fly hath life, and the Sun hath not.… This is the reward proposed to our faith, *Iustus fide sua vivit*, To live by our faith: And this is the reward proposed to our works, *Fac hoc et vives*, to live by our works; All is life. And this fulnesse, this consummation of happinesse, Life, and the life of life, spirituall life, and the exaltation of spirituall life, is the end of Christs comming, *I came that they might have life*.

69 D.E.—70. A.—A noble instance of giving importance to the single words of a text—each word by itself a pregnant text. Here, too, lies the excellence, the imitable but alas! unimitated excellence, of the Divines from Elizabeth to William IIIrd.[1]

---

57   pp 70–1

And therefore as there is *copiosa redemptio*, a plentifull redemption brought into the world by the death of Christ, so…there is *copiosa lux*, a great & a powerfull light exhibited to us, that we might see, and lay hold of this life, in the Ordinances of the Church, in the Confessions, and Absolutions, and Services, and Sermons, and Sacraments of the Church: Christ came *ut daret*, that he might bring life into the world, by his death, and then he instituted his Church, *ut haberent*, that by the meanes thereof this life might be infused into us…

O that our Clergy did but know & see that their Tythes &c belong to them,[1] as Officers & Functionaries of the Nationalty, as *Clerks* & not exclusively as Theologians, ⟨and not at all as Ministers of the Gospel;⟩ but that they *are* likewise Ministers of the Church of *Christ*, and that their claims & the powers of that Church, are ~~not alien~~ no more alienated or affected by their being at the same time, the

---

56[1] A period (1560–1700) that embraces the great divines in whom C was most interested: Hooker, Field, Donne, Fuller, Leighton, Jeremy Taylor, Henry More, Launcelot Andrewes, Richard Baxter, Barrow, Burnet, Stillingfleet, Waterland, Pearson, Bull. Cf **8** and n 1 and **29**, above.

57[1] For C on tithes see GREW **35** n 1.

established Clergy, than they are by the casual co-incidence of being Justices of the Peace, or Heirs to an Estate or Fund-owners.—The Romish Divines placed the Church *above* the Scriptures, our present Divines give it no place at all.[2]

58   p ⁻1, referring to p 70

70 D.E. Donne and his great Contemporaries had not yet learnt to be *afraid* in announcing and enforcing the claims of the Church, distinct from, and co-ordinate with, the Scriptures.—This is ~~the~~ one evil consequence, tho' most unnecessarily so, of the Union of the Ch. of Christ with the National Church, and of the claims of the Christian Pastor and the Preacher with the legal and constitutional Rights & Revenues of the Officers of the National Clerisy.[1]—Our Clergymen are thinking of the Tythes, and feeling the weakness of their claim as grounded on the Gospel, forget the rights which depend on no human Law.

59   title-page verso, referring to p 71

This is the difference betweene Gods Mercy, and his Judgements, that sometimes his Judgements may be plurall, complicated, enwrapped in one another, but his Mercies are always so, and cannot be otherwise; he gives them *abundantiùs, more abundantly.*

P. 71. A a just sentiment beautifully expressed.

60   pp 71–2

Whereas the Christian Religion is, as *Greg. Nazianz.* sayes, *Simplex et nuda, nisi pravè in artem difficilimam converteretur*: It is a plaine, an easie, a perspicuous truth, but that the perverse and uncharitable wranglings of passionate and froward men, have made Religion a hard, an intricate, and a perplexed art...

A Religion of *Ideas*, = Spiritual Truths or Truth-powers—not of notions, and conceptions, the factory of the Understanding—therefore simplex, et nuda—i.e. immediate./[1] Like the clear blue

---

57[2] Cf **49**, above. For a fuller discussion of the clergy as functionaries of nationalty, see *C&S* ch 6 (*CC*) 56–7, esp 53–5.

58[1] See *C&S* (*CC*) 56–7 and nn. For the authority of the church in collecting tithes, see also **57**, above.

60[1] For ideas as "Truth-powers" see also **62**, below, and HOOKER **28** and n 2. In N 47 f 28 (*CN* v) C distinguishes "the Saving *Ideas*, the regenerating *Truth-powers*" from "the Conceptions generalized from the notice of the Senses".

Heaven of Italy, deep and transparent, an ocean unfathomable in its depth, yet groun[d]ed[a] all the way. Still as meditation soars upwards, still it meets the arched *Firmament*, with all its suspended Lamps of Light.

O let ǂ not the simplex et nuda of Greg. Nazian[z]en[a2] be perverted to the Socinian " plain and easy for the meanest Understandings! "[3]— The Truth of Christ, like the *Peace* of Christ, passeth *all Understanding*.[4] If ever there was a mischievous misuse of words, the confusion of the terms, Reason and Understanding, Ideas and Notions or Conceptions, is most mischievous, a Surinam Toad with a swarm of Toadlings sprouting out of its Back and Sides![5]

SERMONS PREACHED UPON CANDLEMAS-DAY

61　title-page verso, referring to p 77 | Sermon VIII, on Matt 5.16

Now, when God received lights into his Tabernacle, hee received none of Tallow, (the Oxe hath hornes) he received none of Waxe, (the Bee hath his sting) but he received only lampes of oyle. And, though from many fruits and berries they pressed oyle, yet God admitted no oyle into the service of the Church, but only of the Olive; the Olive, the embleme of peace. Our purification is with an oblation, our oblation is light, our light is good works; our peace is rather to exhort you to them, then to institute any solemne, or other than occasionall comparison between faith and them.

P. 77. D.E. The illustration of the day would be censured as *quaint* by our modern Critics!—Would to heaven! we had but even a few Preachers capable of such *quaintnesses*.

---

[a] Letter supplied by the editor

60[2] Gregory of Nazianzus (329–89), with the two other Cappadocian Fathers Basil the Great and Gregory of Nyssa, was influential in establishing the Nicene faith and in securing the defeat of Arianism at the Council of Constantinople in 381. His description of the Christian faith as "simplex et nuda"— "clear and naked"—characterises his own combination of simplicity and strength, zeal and self-effacement. C regarded him as one of the three great masters of rhetoric among the Fathers: *TT* 12 Jul 1827.

60[3] Cf *SM* (*CC*) 45, *LS* (*CC*)

176–81, 250–1, and EICHHORN *Neue Testament* COPY B **27**.

60[4] Phil 4.7.

60[5] C found the image of the Surinam toad in J. G. Stedman *Narrative of a Five Years' Expedition Against the Revolted Negroes of Surinam* (2 vols 1776). *CN* I 124n suggests that C may have known the book as early as 1796. See e.g. *CL* I 535, *Friend* (*CC*) II 212, *CN* II 2794; and cf *CL* III 95, *TT* 14 Jun 1834, *CRB* II 632. See also T. FULLER *Holy State* **11** n 1. On the confusion of reason and understanding see **29** and **30**, above, and **122** (at n 6), below.

62   p [76], referring to p 77 | **61** textus continued

And it is observable, that in all this great Sermon of our Saviours in the Mount...there is no mention of faith, by way of perswasion or exhortation thereunto, but the whole Sermon is spent upon good works. Every good work hath faith for the roote; but every faith hath no good works for the fruit thereof....For, good works presuppose faith; and therefore he concludes that they have but little faith; and therefore he concludes that thcy had but liltle faith, because they were so solicitous about the things of this world....And as Christ concludes an unstedfastnesse in their faith, out of their solicitude for this world, so may the world justly conclude an establishment in their faith, if they see them exercise themselves in the works of mercy, and so *Let their light shine before men...*

Faith i.e. fidelity, the fealty of the finite Will and Understanding to the Reason! = the Light that lighteth every man that cometh into the World,[1] as one with and the representative of the Absolute Will, and to the Ideas—i.e. Truths or rather Truth-powers of the pure Reason, the super-sensuous Truths which in relation to the finite Will and as meant to determine the Will, are moral LAWS, the voice and dictates of the Conscience——

this Faith is properly a state and disposition of the Will, or rather of the whole Man, the "*I*", i.e. the finite Will self-affirmed—It is therefore the Ground, the Root, of which the Actions, the Works, the Believings, as acts of the Will in the Understanding, are the Trunk and Branches.—But these must be in the *Light*. The disposition to see must have Organs, Objects, Direction and an *outward* Light. These three latter of these our Lord gives to his Disciples in this Sermon, preparatorily—and as Donne rightly observes, presupposing Faith as the ground & root./[2]

63   title-page verso, referring to p 78

...to every one of us...(from him, that rides with his hundreds of Torches, to him that crawles with his rush-candle) our Saviour sayes, *Let your light so shine before men, that they may see your good works, &c.*

P. 78. line the first.—But the whole page affords a noble Specimen, how a Minister of the Church of England should preach the doctrine

62[1]   John 1.9 (var).
62[2]   Cf **30**, above, **68**, below, and BAXTER *Reliquiae* COPY B **42**. An "Essay on Faith", extending this position in greater detail, was printed by HNC in *LR* IV 425–38 and again in *CIS* 103–21 (see esp 119).

of *Good* Works, purified from the poison of the Romish doctrine of
Works, as the Manioc[1] is evenomated[2] by fire & rendered safe,
nutritious, a bread of life. To Donne's exposition the heroic Solifidian,
Martin Luther, himself would have Subscribed, hand and heart.—[3]

64 p 78

And therefore our latter men of the Reformation, are not to be
blamed, who for the most part, pursuing, S. *Cyrils* interpretation,
interpret this universall light, *that lightneth every man*, to be the light
of nature.

The error here—and it is a grievous error—consists in the word
"Nature". There is, there can be no Light *of* Nature. There may be
a Light *in* or *upon* it; but this is the Light, that shineth down into
the Darkness—i.e. in Nature; and the Darkness comprehendeth it
not.[1] All Ideas, i.e. spiritual truths, are supernatural.[2]

S. T. Coleridge.

65 p 79

...*faith is dead*, without breath, without spirit, if it be *without
workes.*... We are created, we are baptized, we are adopted for good
works; and it is beyond them all, even that of faith; for, though faith
have a preheminence, because works grow out of it, and so faith (as
the root) is first, yet works have the preheminence thus, both that
they include faith in them, and that they dilate, and diffuse, and
spread themselves more declaratorily, then faith doth. Therefore, as
our Saviour said to some that asked him, *What shall we do that we*

63[1] Manioc, a name for cassava
(*Manihot utilissima*), a plant with a fleshy
tuberous root used for food in tropical
America, from which tapioca is prepared.
The sweet cassava is prepared as a
vegetable; the bitter cassava contains a
virulent volatile juice that can be expelled
by heat. *OED*.

63[2] *OED* cites this passage (from
LR) as the only use of "evenomate".

63[3] Solifidianism, the doctrine of
justification by faith alone (*sola fides*),
was originally based on Luther's trans-
lation of πίστει in Rom 3.28 as *allein
durch den Glauben*—"only by faith". The
Protestant reformers used this doctrine in
assailing the mediaeval doctrine of the

merit of good works. Luther's teaching
on justification by faith only, in opposi-
tion to the RC doctrine of works, is
generally approved in the Thirty-nine
Articles (XI–XIII) with the recognition that
"Good Works, which are the fruits of
Faith, and follow after Justification", are
"pleasing and acceptable to God in
Christ". See also FLEURY **8** and n 1,
HOOKER **43**.

64[1] See John 1.5. For "Light of
Nature" see FORBES **6** and n 1.

64[2] Cf "Whatever is spiritual, is *eo
nomine* supernatural; but must it be
always and of necessity miraculous?"
CIS 78.

might work the work of God?...This is the work of God, that ye beleeve in whom he hath sent, and so refers them to faith, so to another that asks him, *What shall I do, that I may have eternall life?...*Christ sayes, *Keepe the Commandements,* and so refers him to works.... This then is the light that lighteth every man that goes out of the world, *good works*; for, *their works follow them.* Their works; they shall be theirs, even after their death; which is our second branch in this first part, the propriety, *lux vestra,* let *your light* shine.

I cannot alwaies call the works that I do, my works; for sometimes God works them, and sometimes the devill... Yet, for all this diverse, this contrary working, as S. *Augustine* sayes of the faculty of the will, *Nihil tam nostrum, quam voluntas,* there is nothing so much our owne, as our will before we worke, so there is nothing so much our owne, as our workes, after they are done. They stick to us, they cleave to us; whether as fomentations to nourish us, or as corrasives, to gnaw upon us, that lyes in the nature of the worke; but ours they are; and upon us our works work. Our good works are more ours, then our faith is ours. Our faith is ours as we have received it, our worke is ours, as we have done it. Faith is ours, as we are possessors of it, the work ours, as we are doers, actors in it. Faith is ours, as our goods are ours, works, as our children are ours.

In this page Donne rather too much plays the rhetorician. If the Faith worketh the Works, what is true of the former, must be equally affirmed of the Latter. Causa causæ causa causati.[1] Besides, he falls into something like a confusion of Faith with Belief, taken as a Conviction or Assent of the Judgement. The Faith and the Righteousness of a Christian are both alike his and *not* his—the f. of Christ in him, the r. of Christ in and for him. See Ep. to the Galatians, Ch. 1. 20.[a][2]

Donne was a truly great man; but he did not possess that full, steady, deep ~~and~~ yet comprehensive Insight into the nature of Faith and Works, which was vouchsafed to Martin Luther. ~~And~~ But

---

[a] Here the note, in the outer margin, breaks off with a rule and " ∧ ∧ "; it is resumed at the foot of the page with " ∧ ∧ "

65[1] "The cause of a cause is the cause of the effect." This logical maxim occurs in this form in e.g. Thomas Aquinas *Quaestiones disputatae de malo* 3.1.4, but it occurs not uncommonly elsewhere in the Schoolmen. C also used the phrase (var) in GREY 2 and in Jeremy TAYLOR *Polemicall Discourses* i 388–9. Cf *C&S* (*CC*) 154 for a variant.

65[2] The correct reference is Gal 2.20—to which add 2.21. On faith and belief see **30** and n 2, above, and **68**, below.

Donne had not attained to the reconciling of distinctity with unity—ours yet God—God, yet ours.[3]

66　p 79

Velle et nolle nostrum est, to assent or to dis-assent is our own; we may choose which we will doe...

?—too nakedly expressed.

67　p 79

...and certainly our works are more ours then our faith is, and man concurres otherwise in the acting and perpetration of a good work, then he doth in the reception and admission of faith.

Why? because Donne confounds the *act* of Faith with the Assent of the fancy and understanding to certain words and conceptions.

68　p 80

With all my reverence for D[r] Donne, I warn against the contents of the preceding page, as scarcely tenable in Logic, unsound in Metaphysics, and unsafe, slippery Divinity.—principally, that he confounds Faith, essentially an *act,* the fundamental *Work* of the Spirit, with Belief, which is then only good, when it is the effect and accompaniment of Faith.[1]

69　pp 80–1

Because things good in their institution, may be depraved in their practise, *Ergonè nihil ceremoniarum rudioribus dabitur, ad juvandam eorum imperitiam?* Shall therefore the people be denied all cere-monies, for the assistance of their weaknesse? *Id ego non dico*; I say not so, sayes he [Calvin].

Some Ceremonies may be for the Conservation of Order, & Civility, or to prevent Confusion & Unseemliness; others are the natural or conventional language of our feelings,—as shaking hands, bowing the head &c—and to neither of these two sorts do I object. But as to "poor Men's books", the "ad juvandam imperitiam, &c &c" I

65[3] For distinctity and unity see *C&S* (*CC*) 118–19 and 118 n 2. *OED* ascribes "distinctity" to C, citing this note (from *LR*) and also the "Formula fidei de Sanctissima Trinitate" (from *LR* III 2).

68[1] See **30** and n 2, above.

protest against them & the pretexts for them, in toto.[1] What? Can any ceremony be more instructive than the words required to explain the ceremony? I make but one exception—& that where the truth signified is so vital, so momentous, that the very occasion & necessity of explaining the sign are of the highest spiritual value.—Mem. Bread and Wine. Yet alas! to what gross & calamitous superstitions has not even this visible Sign given occasion?[2]

70 p 81

We have a story delivered by a very pious man, and of the truth whereof he seemes to be very well assured, that one *Conradus* a devout Priest, had such an illustration, such an irradiation, such a coruscation, such a light at the tops of those fingers, which he used in the consecration of the Sacrament, as that by that light of his fingers ends, he could have reade in the night, as well as by so many Candles; But this was but a private light...It did not shine out, so that men might see it. Blessed S. *Augustine* reports, (if that Epistle be S. *Augustines*) that when himselfe was writing to S. Hieromc, to know his opinion of the measure and quality of the Joy, and Glory of Heaven, suddenly in his Chamber there appeared *ineffabile lumen*, sayes he, an unspeakable, an unexpressible light...such a light as our times never saw, and out of that light issued this voyce, *Hieronymi anima sum*, I am the soule of that *Hierome* to whom thou art writing, who this houre dyed at *Bethlem*, and am come from thence to thee, &c. But this was but a private light...this light did not shine so, as that men might see it.

This ridiculous Legend is one instance of what I have called the *patristic* leaven in Donne[1]—who assuredly had no belief in the authenticity of this letter, but himself considered spurious. But yet it served a purpose. As to Master Conradus, he must have recently shaken hands with Lucifer.

71 p 83

As it is *Davids* recognition...*The Lord is the portion of mine inheritance*, so the *Possedi virum à Domino*, was *Eves* recognition upon the birth of her first son, *Cain, I have gotten, I possesse a man from the Lord.*

69[1] The Latin phrase, from the textus, is translated there; "poor Men's books" is a truncated version of "Pic-tures are the books of the poor", for which see e.g. *CN* II 2420.

69[2] Cf **33** and n 4, above.

70[1] See **1**, above.

"I have got the Jehova-man"—is, I believe, the true rendering and sense of the Hebrew Words. Eve full of the promise, supposed her first-born, *the* first-born, to be the promised Deliverer/.[1]

72 p 84 and title-page verso, referring to p 84

Mem.] For, it were better God disinherited us so, as to give us nothing, then that he gave us not the grace to use that that he gave us, well: without this, all his bread were stone, and all his fishes serpents, all his temporall liberality malediction. How much happier had that man beene, that hath wasted thousands in play, in riot, in wantonnesse, in sinfull excesses, if his parents had left him no more at first, then he hath left himselfe at last? How much nearer to a kingdome in Heaven had hee beene, if he had beene borne a begger here?... There cannot be a more fearfull commination upon man, nor a more dangerous dereliction from God, then when God saies, *I will not reprove thee for thy sacrifices*; Though thou offer none, I care not, Ile never tell thee of it, nor reprove thee for it, I will not reprove thee for thy sacrifices.... When God shall say to me, I care not whether you come to Church or no, whether you pray or no, repent or no, confesse, receive or no, this is a fearfull dereliction; so is it, when he saies to a rich man, I care not whether your light shine out, or no, whether men see your good works or no; I can provide for my glory other waies. For, certainly God hath not determined his purpose, and his glory so much in that, to make some men rich that the poore might be relieved... as in this, that he hath made some men poore, whereby the rich might have occasion to exercise their charity; for, that reaches to spirituall happinesse; for which use, the poore doe not so much need the rich, as the rich need the poore; the poore may better be saved without the rich, then the rich without the poore.

P. 84. D.E.—

73 p 90 | Sermon IX, on Rom 13.7

Mem.[1]] That soule, that is accustomed to direct her selfe to God, upon every occasion, that, as a flowre at Sun-rising, conceives a sense of

---

71[1] Gen 4.1 reads (AV): "and she conceived, and bare Cain, and said, I have gotten a man from the Lord"; (*NEB*): "and she conceived and gave birth to Cain. She said, 'With the help of the Lord I have brought a man into being.'" Donne suggests that the name Cain may be a pun on *qanah*, "to acquire" and also "to beget". C's version suggests that the "Jehova-man" prefigures Christ (the "last Adam", 1 Cor 15.45) the "Jehovah-word": see BIBLE COPY B 55 and n 3 and BROWNE *Works* 39 and n 1.

73[1] For a possible echo of this passage in c 1815–16 see *CN* III 4291 and n.

God, in every beame of his, and spreads and dilates it selfe towards him, in a thankfulnesse, in every small blessing that he sheds upon her; that soule, that as a flowre at the Suns declining, contracts and gathers in, and shuts up her selfe, as though she had received a blow, when soever she heares her Saviour wounded by a oath, or blasphemy, or execration; that soule, who, whatsoever string be strucken in her, base or treble, her high or her low estate, is ever tun'd toward God, that soule prayes sometimes when it does not know that it prayes.

73A   p 94 (referred to in 4)

Sileat licèt fama, non silet fames, says good and holy *Bernard*, fame may be silent, but famine will not: perchance the world knowes not this, or is weary of speaking of it, but those poore wretches that starve by thy oppression, know it, and cry out in his hearing, where thine own conscience accompanies them, and cryes out with them against thee. Pay this debt, this debt of restitution, and pay it quickly; for nothing perishes, nothing decayes an estate more, nothing consumes, nothing enfeebles a soule more, then to let a great debt run on long.

But if they be poore of Gods making, and not of thine... (for though God have inflicted poverty upon them for their sins, that is a secret between God and them, that which God hath revealed to thee, is their poverty, and not their sins) then thou owest them a debt of almes, though not restitution: though thou have nothing in thy hands which was theirs, yet thou hast something which should be theirs; nothing perchance which thou hast taken from them, but something certainly which thou hast received from God for them; and in that sense S. *Bernard* says truly, in the behalfe, and in the person of the poore, to wastfull men, *Nostrum est quod effunditis*, you are prodigall, there is one fault; but then you are prodigall of that which is not your own, but ours, and that is a greater; and then we whose goods you wast, are poore and miserable, and that is the greatest fault of all.

74   pp 112–13 | Sermon xii, on Matt 5.2

We dealt in the reformation of Religion, as Christ did in the institution thereof; He found ceremonies amongst the Gentiles, and he took them in, not because he found them there, but because the Gentiles had received them from the Jews, as they had their washings, and their religious meetings to eat and drink in the Temple, from the Jews Passeover. Christ borrowed nothing of the Gentiles, but he

took his own where he found it: Those ceremonies, which himself
had instituted in the first Church of the Jews, and the Gentiles had
purloined, and prophaned, and corrupted after, he returned to a good
use againe. And so did we in the Reformation, in some ceremonies
which had been of use in the Primitive Church, and depraved and
corrupted in the Romane.

The disposition of the Church Divines, under James I. to bring back
the stream of the Reformation ~~within~~ to the channel & within the
banks, formed in the first six centuries of the Church; and their
alienation from the great patriarchs of ~~the~~ Protestantism, Luther,
Calvin, Zuinglius, &c,[1] who held the Saints & Fathers of the
Ante-papal Church, with exception of Augustine, in light esteem—
this disposition betrays itself in this & many other parts of Donne.[2]
Here Donne plays the Jesuit, disguising the true fact, viz. that even
as early as the third Century the Church had begun to *paganize*
Christianity under the pretext & no doubt in the hope, of chris-
tianizing Paganism.[3] The mountain would not go to Mahomet:
& therefore Mahomet went to the Mountain.[4]

74A   p 115 (referred to in **4**)

*...Christ came downe, and stood in the plaine, and a great multitude
of people about him.* Both must be done; we must preach in the
Mountaine, and preach in the plaine too; preach to the learned, and
preach to the simple too; preach to the Court, and preach to the
Country too. Onely when we preach in the mountaine, they in the
plaine must not calumniate us, and say, This man goes up to
Jerusalem, he will be heard by none but Princes, and great persons,
as though it were out of affectation, and not in discharge of our duty,
that we doe preach there: And when we preach on the plaine, they
of the mountaine must not say, This man may serve for a meane

74[1] Huldreich Zwingli (1484–1531),
admirer of Erasmus and trained in
humanist learning, was elected minister
at Zürich in 1518 and laid the foundations
of the Swiss Reformation with his
lectures on the NT in 1519, owing little
debt to Luther, of whose influence he
became jealous. He took the Gospel as
the sole basis of truth and rejected the
authority of the Pope, the doctrine of
sacrifice in the Mass, invocation of
saints, and clerical celibacy. In bitter
controversy with Luther on the divine

presence in the Mass (see BLANCO
WHITE *Poor Man's Preservative* **2** n 1), he
upheld a purely symbolic interpretation
of the sacrament, rejecting the doctrines
of transubstantiation and consubstan-
tiation.

74[2] See also **1** (at n 4) and **18**, above,
and HACKET *Century* **24** (at n 2).

74[3] Cf *Friend* (*CC*) I 38.

74[4] C had used this figure in his
"Essay on Fasts" 9 Mar 1796: *Watchman*
(*CC*) 52.

Auditory, for a simple Congregation, for a Country Church, as though the fitting of our selves to the capacity, and the edification of such persons, were out of ignorance, or lazinesse, and not a performance of our duties, as well as the other. Christ preached on the mountaine, and he preached in the plaine; he hath his Church in both; and they that preach in both, or either, for his glory, and not their owne vain-glory, have his Example for their Action.

75   pp 117–18

...And therefore when the Prophet saies, *Quis sapiens, et intelliget haec, Who is so wise as to finde out this way*, he places this cleannesse, which we inquire after, in Wisdome. What is Wisdome?...The Wisdome that accomplishes this cleannesse, is the knowledge, the right valuation of this world, and of the next...

E. The primitive Church appropriated it to the third Hypostasis of the Trinity—hence Sancta Sophia became the distinctive name of the Holy Ghost, and the Temple at Constantinople dedicated by Justinian to the Holy Ghost is called the Church, alas! now the Mosk, of Sta Sophia.[1] Now this suggests, or rather implies, a far better & preciser definition of Wisdom than this of Dr Donne's. The distinctive title of the Father, as the Supreme *Will*, is The Good; that of the only-begotten Word, as the Supreme Reason (= Ens realissimum, Ὁ ὤν, The BEING)[2] is The True; and the Spirit proceeding from the Good thro' the True is the Wisdom. Goodness in the form of Truth is Wisdom: or Wisdom is the ~~Holy~~ pure Will realizing itself intelligently. or again, the Good manifested as the Truth and realized in the Act.—Wisdom, Life, Love, Beauty, the Beauty of Holiness,[3] are all Synonyma of the Holy Spirit.

S. T. C.   6^a December, 1831.

76   p 121

He [S. *Augustine*] professes ingenuously...That he could be more easily brought to attribute so much too much to the body of man,

---

^{a} The "6" is written over "5" by way of correction

75[1] For the variable identification of *Sophia* (Wisdom) with the Logos (second hypostasis) and with the Holy Ghost (third hypostasis) see BIBLE *Gospels* **3** n 1. The Church of Santa Sophia, built under Justinian 532–7, one of the most perfect examples of Byzantine architecture and celebrated for its great dome and splendid mosaics, was converted into a mosque by the Turks in 1453. The mosaics, covered up and partly destroyed at that time, were not restored until after C's death.

75[2] For C's special meaning of ὁ ὤν see BIBLE COPY B **119** n 1.

75[3] "The beauty of holiness" is found in 1 Chron 16.29, 2 Chron 20.21, Ps 29.2, 96.9 (cf 110.3).

as to say that with these bodily eyes he should see God, then to derogate so much from God, as to say that he had a body that might be seen; but because he saw that one might follow on the other, he denyed both, and did no more beleeve that mans eyes should see God, then that God had a body to be seen.

And this negative opinion of his, S. *Augustine* builds upon S. *Ambrose*, and upon S. *Hierome* too, who seem to deny that the Angels themselves see the Essence of God; and upon *Athanasius*, who, against the Arrians opinion, That God the Father only was invisible, but the Son, (who was not equall to the Father) and the Holy Ghost, (who was not equall to the Son) might be seen, argues and maintains, that the whole Trinity is equall in it self, and equally invisible to us.

A   Here we have an instance—one of many—of the inconveniences & contradictions that rise out of the assumed contrary essences of Body and Soul—both Substances, each independent of the other, yet so absolutely diverse as that the one is to be defined by the negation of the other.[1]

SERMONS PREACHED IN LENT

76A p 129 (referred to in **4**) | Sermon XIII, on Job 16.17–19

Therefore does *Origen* say of *Iob*...I doe verily beleeve, and therefore may be bold to say, that for constancy and fidelity towards God, *Iob* did exceed...Not onely men, but Angels themselves; for, saies *Origen*, *Iob* did not only suffer *Absque culpa*, without being guilty of those things to which his afflictions were imputed, but he suffered *Cum gratiarum actionibus*, he said grace when he had no meat, when God gave him Stones for Bread, and Scorpions for Fish; he praised God as much for the affliction it self, as for his former, or his subsequent benefits and blessings. Not that *Iob* was meerly innocent, but that he was guilty of no such things, as might confer those conclusions, which, from his afflictions, his enemies raised. *If I justifie my self*, sayes *Iob*, *Mine own mouth shall condemn me*; Every self-justification is a self-condemnation; when I give judgement for my self, I am therein a witnesse against my self.... *Iob* felt the hand of destruction upon him, and he felt the hand of preservation too; and it was all one hand; This is Gods Method, and his alone, to preserve by destroying.... Gods first intention even when he destroyes is to preserve, as a Physitians first intention, in the most distastfull

76[1] See also **79, 83, 95, 125,** below; and cf e.g. BÖHME 155 and n 2 and esp HUGHES 1 (at n 7).

physick, is health; even Gods demolitions are super-edifications, his Anatomies, his dissections are so many re-compactings, so many resurrections; God windes us off the Skein, that he may weave us up into the whole peece, and he cuts us out of the whole peece into peeces, that he may make us up into a whole garment.

But for all these humiliations, and confessions, *Iob* doth not wave his protestation....Every nights sleep is a *Nunc dimittis*; then the Lord lets his servant depart in peace. Thy lying down is a valediction, a parting, a taking leave, (shall I say so?) a shaking hands with God; and, when thou shakest hands with God, let those hands be clean. Enter into thy grave, thy metaphoricall, thy quotidian grave, thy bed, as thou entredst into the Church at first, by Water, by Baptisme; Re-baptise thy self every night, in *Iobs Snow water*, in holy tears that may cool the inordinate lusts of thy heart, and with-hold uncleane abuses of those hands even in that thy grave, thy Bed...

77   title page verso, referring to pp 134–5

This then is *Iobs*, and our first comfort, *Quia in coelis*, because he is in heaven, and sits in heaven, and dwels in heaven, in the highest heaven, and so, sees all things....And therefore, as God, from that heighth, sees all...as God is to this purpose, all eye, and sees all, so for our farther comfort, he descends to the office of being a Witnesse, There is a Witnesse in heaven.

But then, God may be a Witnesse, and yet not my Witnesse, and in that, there is small comfort, if God be a Witnesse on my adversaries side, a Witnesse against me....And that is that which *Iob*, with so much tendernesse apprehended, *Thou renewest thy witnesses against me*....All this while God was a Witnesse, but not his witnesse, but a witnesse on his adversaries side. Now, if our own heart, our owne conscience condemne us, this is shrewd evidence, saies S. *Iohn*; for mine owne conscience, single, is a thousand witnesses against me. But then, (saies the Apostle there) God is greater then the heart; for, (saies he) he knowes all things; He knowes circumstances of sinne, as well as substance; and, that, we seldome know, seldome take knowledge of. If then mine owne heart be a thousand, God, that is greater, is ten thousand witnesses, if he witnesse against me. But if he be my Witnesse, a Witnesse for me, as he alwaies multiplies in his waies of mercy, he is thousands of thousands, millions of millions of witnesses in my behalfe, for *there is no condem[n]ation*, no possible condemnation, *to them that are in him*; not, if every graine of dust upon the earth were an *Achitophel*, and gave counsell against me, not if every sand upon the shoare were a *Rabshakeh*, and railed against me, not if every atome in the ayre were a Satan, an Adversary, an Accuser, not if every drop in the Sea, were an Abaddon, an Apollyon, a Destroyer, there could be no condemnation, if he be my Witnesse.... For, he is in Heaven, and he sits in Heaven, and he dwels in Heaven, in the highest Heaven, and sees all, and is a Witnesse, and my Witnesse; there is the largenesse of our comfort.

But will all this come home to *Iobs* end and purpose...? herein lyes his, and our finall comfort, That he that is my Witnesse, is in the highest Heaven, there is no person above him, and therefore He that is my Witnesse, is my Judge too. I shall not be tried by an arbitrary Court, where it may be wisdome enough, to follow a wise leader, and think as he thinks. I shall not be tried by a Jury, that had rather I suffered, then they fasted, rather I lost my life, then they lost a meale. Nor tryed by Peeres, where Honour shall be the Bible. But I shall be tryed by the King himselfe, then which no man can propose a Nobler tryall, and that King shall be the King of Kings too.... He that is my Witnesse, is my Judge, and the same person is my Jesus, my Saviour, my Redeemer; He that hath taken my nature, He that hath given me his blood. So that he is my Witnesse, in his owne cause, and my Judge, but of his owne Title, and will, in me, preserve himselfe; He will not let that nature, that he hath invested, perish, nor that treasure, which he hath poured out for me, his blood, be ineffectuall. My Witnesse is in Heaven, my Judge is in Heaven, my Redeemer is in Heaven, and in them, who are but One, I have not onely a constant hope, that I shall be there too, but an evident assurance, that I am there already, in his Person.

134, 135. (admirable)

78 pp 144–5 | Sermon xv, on 1 Cor. 15.26

Who then is this enemy? An enemy that may thus far thinke himselfe equall to God, that as no man ever saw God, and lived; so no man ever saw this enemy and lived, for it is Death; And in this may thinke himselfe in number superiour to God, that many men live who shall never see God; But *Quis homo*, is *Davids* question, which was never answered, *Is there any man that lives, and shall not see death?* An enemie that is so well victualled against man, as that he cannot want as long as there are men, for he feeds upon man himselfe. And so well armed against Man, as that he cannot want Munition, while there are men, for he fights with our weapons, our owne faculties, nay our calamities, yea our owne pleasures are our death. And therefore he is *Novissimus hostis*, saith the Text, *The last enemy*.

D. This borders too close on the Irish Franciscan's conclusion to his Sermon of Thanksgiving/—"Above all, Brethren! let us thankfully laud and extol God's transcendent mercy in putting Death at the end of Life and thereby giving us all time for repentance."—Dr Donne was an eminently *witty* man in a very witty age; but to the honor of his judgement let it be said, that tho' his great wit is evinced in numberless passages in a few only is it *shewn off*. This §ph is one of these rare exceptions.

                                                              S. T. C.

79 p 144

...we shall see him [Death] destroyed....But how? or when? At, and by the resurrection of our bodies; for...as soone as my soule enters into Heaven, I shall be able to say to the Angels, I am of the same stuffe as you, spirit, and spirit, and therefore let me stand with you, and looke upon the face of your God, and my God; so at the Resurrection of this body, I shall be able to say to the Angel of the great Councell, the Son of God, Christ Jesus himselfe, I am of the same stuffe as you, Body and body, Flesh and flesh, and therefore let me sit downe with you, at the right hand of the Father in an everlasting security from this last enemie, who is now destroyed, death.

Mem. Nothing in Scripture, nothing in Reason, commands or authorizes us to assume or suppose any bodiless *creature*. It is the incommunicable attribute of God. But all bodies are not *flesh*; nor need we suppose, that all bodies are corruptible. There are celestial bodies![1]

                                                              S. T. C.

80 p 145

We begin with this; That the Kingdome of Heaven hath not all that it must have to a consummate perfection, till it have bodies too. In

---

79[1] Cf references in **76** n 1, above. C is thinking of the same chapter from which Donne drew his text—1 Cor 15.35–54, esp 39–40: "All flesh is not the same flesh....There are also celestial bodies, and bodies terrestrial: but the glory of the celestial is one, and the glory of the terrestrial is another." See, however, HACKET *Century* **22** and n 2.

those infinite millions of millions of generations, in which the holy, blessed, and glorious Trinity enjoyed themselves one another, and no more, they thought not their glory so perfect, but that it might receive an addition from creatures; and therefore they made a world, a materiall world, a corporeall world, they would have bodies.

Alas! in E.A.B.[a] we trace the wild fantastic position grounded on the arbitrary notion of Man as a *mixture* of two heterogeneous Components—which Des Cartes shortly afterwards carried into its extreme/—[1]

On this doctrine the Man is a mere phænomenal *result*, a sort of Brandy-Sop, or Toddy-punch![2] It is a doctrine unsanctioned by, & inconsistent with, the Scriptures.

81 pp 144–5, pencil

There must be bodies, Men, and able bodies, able men; Men that eate the good things of the land, their owne figges and olives; Men not macerated with extortions: They are glorified bodies that make up the kingdome of Heaven; bodies that partake of the good of the State, that make up the State. Bodies, able bodies, and lastly, bodies inanimated with one soule...the Immortall soule, one supreame soule, one Religion. For as God hath made us under good Princes, a great example of all that, Abundance of Men, Men that live like men, men united in one Religion, so wee need not goe farre for an example of a slippery, and uncertaine being, where they must stand upon others Mens men, and must over-load all men with exactions...

N.b.—Answer to Bentham's Vindication of Usury[1]—or Vindication of the Wisdom of States in the Discouragement of Usury.—This

[a] I.e. pp 144 E and 145 A.B.—part of **79** textus, and **80** textus as given

80[1] Descartes asserted that mind or spirit is pure consciousness, and that matter is mere extension; these attributes are mutually exclusive; hence these two "created substances" can be united—as in man—only through the intervention of God. Body and mind do not affect each other; processes in the nerves and brain are merely the *occasion* of God's producing in us a corresponding mental result. See DESCARTES 1.
80[2] Cf **126**, below.

81[1] Jeremy Bentham (1748–1832) *Defence of Usury* (1787). HCR noted on 29 Jan 1811 that C "differed from Bentham, who censures the laws of usury, contending that those laws by exciting a general contempt against usurers prevented many from degrading themselves by being addicted to it. Genoa fell by becoming a people of money-lenders instead of merchants. In money-loans one party is in sorrow; in the traffic of merchandise both parties gain and rejoice." *CRB* I 22.

done, *then* to consider the National Debt, i.e. the Funds, as an enormous Encouragement of Usury, first, preventing the dispersion of Capital & removing the natural Check which trade-gained Wealth would otherwise receive from the increasing Price of Land—and thus preventing Emigration and Colonization, the natural Relief of old Communities.[a2]

Capital may be defined in one word & the same number of syllables, viz. Briareus,[3] i.e. 100 arms under one Head, a plurality of Powers directed by one intellect and activated by one will.

82   title-page, referring to p 145

P. 145. Capital improvement on our modern political Economists' in Donne's definition of a prosperous State—"Man animated with a common soul, abundance of men, but of men that live like Men."

83   p 146

It is not that Body + Soul = Man—i.e. Man is not the Syntheton[1] or *Compositum* of Body and Soul,—as the two component Units: No! Man is the unit, the Prothesis; and Body and Soul are the two Poles, the − & +, the Thesis & Antithesis of the Man; even as Attraction & Repulsion are the two Poles, in which one & the same Magnet manifests itself.

84   p 146, pencil

...for it is not so great a depopulation to translate a City from Merchants to husbandmen, from shops to ploughes, as it is from many Husbandmen to one Shephcard, and yet that hath beene often done.

Ex. gr. in the Highlands of Scotland.[1]

---

a The last paragraph is written at the foot of p 145 above the closing sentence of the first paragraph

81[2] Cf *C&S* (*CC*) 90 and n 4. This note may be a memorandum for an article in a newspaper or journal. C had discussed the national debt and the funds in 1811 in articles in the *Courier* but had not come to grips with defending paper money against gold as not causing inflation and depressing the economy. See also *LS* (*CC*) 212 and n and *Friend* (*CC*) I 233–4; and cf *CL* VI 978 (18 Mar 1834).

81[3] Briareus (in Greek, trisyllabic) —one of three monsters called Hecatoncheires (of a hundred hands): Hesiod *Theogony* 147ff. Cf *LS* (*CC*) 122 and n 3.

83[1] "A thing put together", the Greek equivalent of "*Compositum*" following.

84[1] On agricultural conditions in the Highlands of Scotland see *LS* (*CC*) 209–11.

85 p 147

Doth not man die even in his birth? The breaking of prison is death,
  Mem.]and what is our birth, but a breaking of prison? Assoon as
we were clothed by God, our very apparell was an Embleme of death.
In the skins of dead beasts, he covered the skins of dying men. Assoon
as God set us on work, our very occupation was an Embleme of
death; It was to digge the earth...

86 p 148

The ashes of an Oak in the Chimney, are no Epitaph of that Oak,
to tell me how high or how large that was; It tels me not what flocks
it sheltered while it stood, nor what men it hurt when it fell. The
dust of great persons graves is speechlesse too, it sayes nothing, it
distinguishes nothing: As soon the dust of a wretch whom thou
wouldest not, as of a Prince whom thou couldest not look upon, will
trouble thine eyes, if the winde blow it thither; and when a
whirle-winde hath blowne the dust of the Church-yard into the
Church, and the man sweeps out the dust of the Church into the
Church-yard, who will undertake to sift those dusts again, and to
pronounce, This is the Patrician, this is the noble flowre, and this the
yeomanly, this the Plebeian bran.

very beautiful

87 p 149

But when I lye under the hands of that enemie, that hath reserved
himselfe to the last, to my last bed, then when I shall be able to stir
no limbe in any other measure then a Feaver or a Palsie shall
shake them, when everlasting darkesse shall have an inchoation in
the present dimnesse of mine eyes, and the everlasting gnashing
in the present chattering of my teeth, and the everlasting worme in
the present gnawing of the Agonies of my body, and anguishes of
my minde, when the last enemie shall watch my remedilesse body,
and my disconsolate soule there, there, where not the Physitian, in
his way, perchance not the Priest in his, shall be able to give any
assistance, And when he hath sported himselfe with my misery upon
that stage, my death-bed, shall shift the Scene, and throw me from
that bed, into the grave and there triumph over me, God knowes,
how many generations, till the Redeemer, my Redeemer, the Re-
deemer of all me, body as well as soule, come againe...

All this is too much in the style of the Monkish Preachers—papam redolet.[1] Contrast with this Job's description of Sheol, and S[t] Paul's Sleep in the Lord.[2]

88   p 150

Neither doth *Calvin* carry those emphaticall words, which are so often cited for a proofe of the last Resurrection: *That he knows his Redeemer lives, that he knows he shall stand the last man upon earth, that though his body be destroyed, yet in his flesh and with his eyes shall he see God*, to any higher sense then so, that how low soever he bee brought, to what desperate state soever he be reduced in the eyes of the world, yet he assures himself of a Resurrection, a reparation, a restitution to his former bodily health, and worldly fortune which he had before. And such a Resurrection we all know *Iob* had.

I incline to Calvin's opinion;[1] but am not decided.—"After my Skin" must be rendered, according to, or as far as my Skin is concerned./ tho' the flies & maggots in my ulcers have destroyed my skin, yet still, and in my flesh, I shall see God as my redeemer./[2] Now St Paul says—Flesh *cannot* inherit the Kingdom of Heaven[3]—i.e. the spiritual world.—Besides, how is the passage, as commonly interpreted, consistent with the numerous expressions of doubt & even of despondency?

89   p 150

...Thus far [in Ezekiel's vision of the dry bones] God argues with them *à re nota*; from that which they knew before, the finall Resurrection, he assures them that which they knew not till then, a present Resurrection from those pressures: Remember by this vision that which you all know already, that at last I shall re-unite the dead, and dry bones of all men in a generall Resurrection: And then if you remember, if you consider, if you look upon that, can you doubt, but that I who can do that, can also recollect you, from your present desperation, and give you a Resurrection to your former

---

87[1] "It stinks of the Pope".
87[2] Job 7.7–10, 15.20–30, and 1 Thess 4.13–18, esp 4.14, "which sleep in Jesus".
88[1] As given by Donne in textus.
88[2] Job 19.25–6: "For I know that my redeemer liveth, and that he shall stand at the latter day upon the earth: And though after my skin worms destroy this body, yet in my flesh shall I see God". See also *TT* 29 May 1830. For C's rendering of this passage in a different sense see BIBLE COPY B 27 and cf HACKET *Century* 22 (at n 1).
88[3] 1 Cor 15.50 (var).

temporall happinesse? And this truly arises pregnantly, necessarily out of the Prophets answer; God asks him there, *Son of man, can these bones live?* And he answers, *Domine tu nôsti, O Lord God thou knowest.* The Prophet answers according to Gods intention in the question. If that had been for their living in the last Resurrection, *Ezekiel* would have answered God as *Martha* answered Christ, when he said, *Thy brother Lazarus shall rise again, I know that he shall rise again at the Resurrection at the last day*; but when the question was, whether men so macerated, so scattered in this world, could have a Resurrection to their former temporall happinesse here, that puts the Prophet to his *Domine tu nôsti,* It is in thy breast to propose it, it is in thy hand to execute it, whether thou do it, or do it not, thy name by glorified...

B.C.—I cannot but think, that Dᵣ Donne by thus antedating the distinct belief of the Resurrection destroys in great measure the force & sublimity of this Vision. Besides, it was but a mongrel egyptian catacomb sort of faith, or rather superstition, that was the later Jews entertained.

90 p 152, at the end of Sermon xv

This is one of Donne's least estimable Discourses—/ The worst Sermon on the best text.

91 p 153 | Sermon xvi, on John 11.35

The Masorites (the Masorites are the Critiques upon the Hebrew Bible, the Old Testament) cannot tell us, who divided the Chapters of the Old Testament into verses; Neither can any other tell us, who did it in the New Testament.

How should they, when *their* Hebrew Scriptures were not divided into Verses?—The Jews adopted the invention from the Christians—who were led in to it by in the construction of Concordances.[1]

92 pp 154–5, pencil

If they killed *Lazarus,* had not Christ done enough to let them see that he could raise him againe? for *Caeca saevitia, si aliud videtur*

[1] The division of books of the OT into chapters may have been the work of Stephen Langton (d 1228). Hugo of St Cher (d 1263) first subdivided the chapters into smaller units, using marginal letters A–G, to simplify the making of a concordance. Isaac Nathan ben Kalymos, in c 1437, similarly subdivided the Hebrew Bible, also for a concordance.

mortuus, aliud occisus; It was a blinde malice, if they thought, that Christ could raise a man naturally dead, and could not if he were violently killed.

Malice, above all, Party-Malice, is indeed a blind passion; but one man can scarcely conceive the Chief Priests such dolts, as to think "that Christ could raise &c." Their malice blinded them as to the nature of the Incident, made them suppose a conspiracy between Jesus and the Family of Lazarus—a mock-burial, in short—

and this may be one, tho' it is not, I think, the principal reason for this greatest miracle being omitted in the 3 other Gospels.[1]

93   p 155, pencil

Christ might ungirt himselfe, and give more scope and liberty to his passions, then any other man: both because he had no Originall sin within, to drive him, no inordinate love without to draw him, when his affections were moved; which all other men have.

How then is he said to have conquered sin in the flesh?[1] Without *guilt*, without *actual* Sin, assuredly he was—but εγενετο σαρξ[a][2]—and what can we mean by Original Sin relatively to the *flesh*, but that Man is born with an animal life, and a material organism that renders him *temptible* to evil, that tends to dispose the life of the *Will* to contradict the Light of the Reason. Did Paul by ομοιωμα mean a deceptive resemblance?[3]

94   p 155, pencil

Christ was alwayes safe; *He was led of the Spirit*: of what spirit? his own Spirit: *Led* willingly *into the wildernesse, to be tempted of the devill*. No other man might do that; but he who was able to say to the Sun, *Siste sol*, was able to say to Satan, *Siste Lucifer*. Christ in another place gave such scope to his affections, and to others interpretations of his actions, that his friends and kinsfolks thought

[a] Here C has written " ∧ " and continued in the foot-margin with " ∧ "

92[1] See **5**, above.

93[1] Cf Rom 8.3: "...God sending his own Son in the likeness of sinful flesh, and for sin, condemned sin in the flesh". See also n 3, below.

93[2] Cf **16** and n 5, above. The phrase, which C often repeats, is from John 1.14: (AV) "was made flesh".

93[3] AV renders ὁμοίωμα "likeness"

where it occurs in Rom 6.5, 8.3 and Phil 2.7. Cf *NT Gk Lex* p 570: "In the light of what Paul says about Jesus in general it is safe to assert that his use of [ὁμοίωμα] is to bring out both that Jesus in his earthly career was similar to sinful men and yet not absolutely like them." C, whose question is directed rhetorically to Donne, implies such an interpretation.

him mad, besides himself: But all this while, Christ had his own actions, and passions, and their interpretations in his own power: he could do what he would.

I can see no possible edification that can arise from ⟨these⟩ ultra-scriptural Speculations respecting our Lord.

S. T. C.

95 p 157, pencil

!!] Though the Godhead never departed from the Carcasse, (there was no divorce of that Hypostaticall union) yet because the Humane soule was departed from it, he was no man.

Donne was a poor Metaphysician, i.e. never closely questioned himself as to the absolute meaning of his words. What do you mean by the *Soul*? What by the Body?[1]

96 p 157, pencil, completed in ink[a]

...And I know that there are Authors of a middle nature, above the Philosophers, and below the Scriptures, the Apocryphall books...

—a whimsical instance of the disposition in the mind ~~for~~ to every two Opposites to find an intermediate, a mesothethis[b] for every Thesis and Antithesis. So here. Scripture ⨉ Philosophy—and the Apocrypha is Philosophy[c] ~~in~~ relatively to Scripture, and Scripture relatively to philosophy &c.[1]

97 p 159

And therefore the same Author [*Epiphanius*] sayes, That because they thought it an uncomely thing for Christ to weep for any temporall thing, some men have expunged and removed that verse out of S. *Lukes* Gospell, That Jesus when he saw that City, wept: But he is

[a] C has overtraced the first three words of the note in ink
[b] A slip for "mesothesis"
[c] From here the note is concluded in ink

95[1] See **126** n 1, below.

96[1] The name "Apocrypha" (hidden things)—on which see BIBLE *NT Apocrypha* **4** n 4—referred originally to those books which were added in the Greek version of the OT but were not included in the Hebrew Bible. As far as the Church of England was concerned, the status of the Apocrypha was estab-lished by Article VI of the Thirty-nine Articles, which prescribes those books which may be taken "for example of life and instruction of godly manners" but not "to establish any doctrine": the Apocrypha was printed as a separate section between OT and NT in AV of 1611.

willing to be proposed, and to stand for ever for an example of weeping in contemplation of publique calamities...

This by the bye rather *indiscreetly* lets out the liberties, which the early Christians took with their sacred writings. Origen who in answer to Celsus's reproach on this ground Confines the practice to to the Heretics furnishes proofs of the contrary himself, in his own Comments.[1]

98   p 161

And yet...sayes S. *Gregory*, as wittily as S. *Augustine*...that world which findes it selfe truly in an Autumne, in it selfe, findes it selfe in a spring, in our imaginations.

Worthy almost of Shakespear.

99   title-page verso, referring to p 163 | Sermon XVII, on Matt 19.17

R] The Scriptures are Gods Voyce, The Church is his Eccho; a redoubling, a repeating of some particular syllables, and accents of the same voice. And as we harken with some earnestnesse, and some admiration at an Eccho, when perchance we doe not understand the voice that occasioned that Eccho; so doe the obedient children of God apply themselves to the Eccho of his Church, when perchance otherwise, they would lesse understand the voice of God, in his Scriptures, if that voice were not so redoubled unto them. This fasting then, thus enjoyned by God, for the generall, in his Word, and thus limited to this Time, for the particular, in his Church, is indeed but a continuation of a great Feast: Where, the first course (that which we begin to serve in now) is Manna, food of Angels, plentifull, frequent preaching; but the second course, is the very body and blood of Christ Jesus, shed for us, and given to us, in that blessed Sacrament, of which himselfe makes us worthy receivers at that time....

The words [of the text] are part of a Dialogue, of a Conference, betweene Christ, and a man who proposed a question to him; to whom Christ makes an answer by way of another question, *Why*

97[1] C refers to *Contra Celsum* (2.27), Origen's reply to Celsus' Ἀληθὴς Λόγος (*The True Word*) (c 178), which is the earliest written attack on Christianity of which there is record. C considered Origen superior to Jerome and "almost the only very great scholar and genius combined among the early Fathers". *TT* 12 Jan 1834. He also considered "Origen, Jerome, and Augustine to be the three great fathers in respect of theology". *TT* 12 Jul 1827.

callest thou me good, &c. In the words, and by occasion of them,
R] we consider the Text, the Context, and the Pretext: Not as three
equall parts of the Building; but the Context, as the situation and
Prospect of the house, The Pretext, as the Accesse and entrance to
the house, And then the Text it selfe, as the House it selfe, as the
body of the building: In a word, In the Text, the Words; In the
Context, the Occasion of the words; In the Pretext, the Pretence, the
purpose, the disposition of him who gave the occasions.

P. 163. The compendium of Christianity, and in E an example of
elegant and happy Division of a Subject. Our great Divines were not
ashamed of the learned Discipline, to which they had submitted their
minds under Aristotle and Tully—but brought the purified products,
as sacrificial Gifts to Christ. They BAPTISED the logic & p and manly
Rhetoric of ancient Greece.

100   title-page verso and insert p 1, referring to p 164

We begin with the Context; the situation, the prospect; how it stands,
how it is butted, how it is bounded; to what it relates, with what it
is connected... a man comes to Christ, inquires the way to Heaven,
beleeves himselfe to be in that way already, and (when he heares of
nothing, but keeping the Commandements) beleeves himself to be far
R] gone in that way; But when he is told also, that there belongs to
it a departing with his Riches, his beloved Riches, he breakes off the
conference, he separates himselfe from Christ; for, (saies the Story)
This Man had great possessions. And to this purpose, (to separate us
from Christ) the poorest among us, hath great possessions. He that
starves, as well as he that surfets, he that lies in the spitting places,
and excrementall corners of the streets, as well as he that sits upon
carpets, in the Region of perfumes, he that is ground and trod to durt,
with obloquie, and contempt, as well as he that is built up every day,
a story and story higher with additions of Honour. Every man hath
some such possessions as possesseth him, some such affections as
weigh downe Christ Jesus, and separate him from Him, rather then
from those affections, those possessions....

There are some sins so rooted, so riveted in men, so incorporated,
so consubstantiated in the soule, by habituall custome, as that those
sins have contracted the nature of Ancient possessions....But then
there are lesse sins, light sins, vanities; and yet even these come to
possesse us, and separate us from Christ....Men perish with
whispering sins, nay with silent sins, sins that never tell the conscience

R] they are sins, as often as with crying sins: And in hell there shall meet as many men, that never thought what was sin, as that spent all their thoughts in the compassing of sin; as many, who in a slack inconsideration, never cast a thought upon that place, as that by searing their conscience, overcame the sense and feare of the place.

P. 164. Excellent illustration of fragmentary Morality: in which each man takes his choice of his virtues & vices.—& mark, *D*. I almost doubt,[a] whether the truth here so boldly asserted is not of more general necessity for [co]ngregations[b] in general, than the denunciation of the large Sins, that cannot remain [IN]COGNITO.[b]

101   p 165

...And then, sayes S. *Mark*, handling the same story, *Venit procurrens. He came running. Nicodemus* came not so, *Nicodemus* durst not avow his comming; and therefore he came creeping, and he came softly, and he came seldome, and he came by night.

But we trust in God, that they *came*. The adhesion, the thankfulness, the love, that arise & *live after* the having come, whether from spontaneous liking, or from a beckoning Hope, or from a compelling Goad—are the truest Criteria of the man's christianity.

102   insert p 1, referring to p 165

R.] Of all proofes, Demonstration is the powerfullest: when I have just reason to think my superiours would have it thus, this is Musique to my soul; When I heare them say they would have it thus, this is Rhetorique to my soule; When I see their Laws enjoyne it to be thus, this is Logick to my soul; but when I see them actually, really, clearly, constantly do thus, this is a Demonstration to my soule, and Demonstration is the powerfullest proofe: The eloquence of inferiours is in words, the eloquence of superiours is in action.

P. 165, B. A just representation, I doubt not, of the general feeling & principle at the time Donne wrote. Men regarded the gradations of Society as God's Ordinances, & had the elevation of a self-approving Conscience in every feeling and exhibition of respect to those of rank superior to themselves. What a contrast with the present times!

Mem. a beautiful sentence—The Eloquence of Inferiors is in words, the Eloquence of Superiors is in action!!—

---

[a] Insert p 1 begins   [b] Letters effaced by tipping-in of the insert

103   insert p 1, referring to p 165

He came to Christ; hee ran to him; and when he was come, as S. *Mark* relates it, *He fell upon his knees to Christ....*He was no ignorant man, and yet he acknowledged that he had somewhat more R] to learn of Christ, then he knew yet. Blessed are they that inanimate all their knowledge, consummate all in Christ Jesus. The University is a Paradise, Rivers of knowledge are there, Arts and Sciences flow from thence. Counsell Tables are *Horti conclusi...* *Gardens that are walled in*, and they are *Fontes signati, Wells that are sealed up*; bottomlesse depths of unsearchable Counsels there. But those *Aquae quietudinum*, which the Prophet speaks of, *The waters of rest*, they flow *à magistro bono*, from this good master, and flow into him again; All knowledge that begins not, and ends not with his glory, is but a giddy, but a vertiginous circle, but an elaborate and exquisite ignorance. He would learn of him, and what? *Quid boni faciam*, What good thing shall I do? Still he refers to the future; to do as well as to have done: and still to be doing so. Blessed are they that bring their knowledge into practise; and blessed again, that crown their former practise with future perseverance.

165. C.D. But I doubt whether in his desire to make every particle *exemplary*, to draw some Christian moral from it, Donne has not injudiciously attributed, quasi per *prolepsîn*,[1] merits inconsistent with the *finale* of ~~its~~ a wealthy would-be proselytes.—At all events, a more natural and perhaps not less instructive, interpretation might be made of ⟨the sundry movements of⟩ this religiously earnest & zealous Admirer of Christ & Worshipper of Mammon. O I have myself known such./ However, the passage is beautiful, as an independent truth.—But from D to E all is *pure gold.*[2] Without being aware of this passage in Donne I had expressed the same conviction, or rather declared the same experience, in the Appendix to my first "Lay Sermon"—or the Statesman's Manual./[3] O if only one day in a week, Christians would consent to have the Bible as the only Book—& their Ministers labor to make them find all substantial good of all other books in their Bible.—

103[1] "As though by *prolepsis*"— i.e. by anticipation, or by assuming that an event that has not yet occurred is operative at present. Cf e.g. BIBLE COPY B **8** n 1.

103[2] I.e. textus, beginning at "The University is a Paradise".
103[3] *SM* (*CC*) 70 (and n 2).

104   p 165

I remember one of the Panegyriques celebrates and magnifies one of the Romane Emperours for this, That he would marry when he was yong; that he would so soon confine and limit his pleasures, so soon determine his affections in one person.

It is surely some proof of the moral effect, Christianity has produced, that in all protestant countries at least, a writer would be ashamed to assign this, as a ground of *panegyric*: as if promiscuous intercourse with those of the other sex had been a natural Good, a privilege, which there was a great merit in foregoing! O! what do not *Women* owe to Christianity! As Christians only, do they or ordinarily *can* they, cease to be *Things* for men—instead of Co-persons in one spiritual I AM.[1]

105   insert p 1, referring to p 165

R.] When a yong man comes to Christ, Christ receives him with an extraordinary welcome; well intimated in that, that that disciple whom Christ loved most, came to him yongest.

E. Mem. Apply this to the Deacons of the Church—in a discourse on the moral advantages of THE CHURCH *as a* PROFESSION.

106   p 166

But such is often the corrupt inordinatenesse of greatnesse, that it only carries them so much beyond other men, but not so much nearer to God; It only sets men at a farther, not God at a nearer distance to them...

Like a Balloon—away from earth, but not a whit nearer the Arch of Heaven.[1]

107   insert p 1, referring to p 166

When he [Nicodemus] enquired of Christ after salvation, Christ doth not say, There is no salvation for thee, thou Viper, thou Hypocrite,

---

104[1] For C's disgust at the view of women as instruments of male lust see e.g. BEAUMONT & FLETCHER COPY B **49** n 1; and cf ANALYSIS **7** and n 2. "Co-person" is not in *OED*. On "I AM" see e.g. **54** n 1, above, and **110** n 2, below.

106[1] Cf *CL* v 98 (*IS* 144). When C wrote this note, the art of manned flight by balloon was almost fifty years old, beginning from the pioneer work of the brothers Montgolfier in France in 1783 and of James Tytler and James Sadler in England in 1784–5. In Oct 1813 C met a man who had accompanied Sadler on one of his ascents. *CL* III 444.

thou Pharisee, I have locked an iron doore of predestination between salvation and thee...But Christ teaches him the true method of this art: for, when he sayes to him, *Why callest thou me good? There is none good but God,* he only directs him in the way to that end, which he did indeed, or pretended to seek. And this direction of his, this method is our third part...you may now be pleased to look farther into the house it self, and to see how that is built; that is, by what method Christ builds up, and edifies this new disciple of his; which is the principall scope and intention of the Text, and that, to which all the rest did somewhat necessarily prepare the way.

166. D.—There is a praise-worthy *relativeness* & *life* in the morality of our best old Divines. It is not a cold Law in Brass or Stone—But *this* I may & should think of my neighbor—& yet not quite *this* dare I soothe myself with—*this* I will say *of* a great man, a prince—yet not *to* him—& this he must not say to himself.—

108   insert p 2, referring to p 167

Christ was pleased to redeem this man from this error, and bring him to know truly what he was, that he was God. Christ therefore doth not rebuke this man, by any denying that he himself was good; for Christ doth assume that addition to himself, *I am the good Shepheard.* R] Neither doth God forbid, that these good parts which are in men, should be celebrated with condigne praise. We see that God, as soon as he saw that any thing was good, he said so, he uttered it, he declared it, first of the Light, and then of other creatures: God would be no author, no example of smothering the due praise of good actions. For, surely that man hath no zeale to goodnesse in himself, that affords no praise to goodnesse in other men.

P. 167. A.—Very fine. But I think, an other, not however a different, view might be taken, respecting our Lord's intention in these words. The young noble, who came to him, had many praise-worthy traits of character; but he failed in the *ultimate* end and aim.[1] What ought only to have been valued by him, as a *means*, was *loved* and had a *worth* given to it, as an *end* in itself. Our Lord, who knew the hearts of men, instantly, in the first words, applies himself to this—/ takes occasion by an ordinary phrase of courtesy to make him aware of the difference between a mere *relatively* good & that which is absolutely good—that which *may* be called good, when regarded as

108[1]   Matt 19.16–24—the subject of this sermon.

a *Means* to Good, but which must not be mistaken for or confounded with that which *is* good, and itself the *End.*

109   insert p 2, referring to p 167

...For as there is Treason, and petty-treason, so there is Sacriledge, and petty-sacriledge; and petty-sacriledge is to rob Princes and great persons of their just praise. But then, as we must confer this upon them, so must they, and we, and all transfer all upon God: for so R]*Iudith* proceeds there, with her Priests and Elders, Begin unto my God, with Timbrels, sing unto the Lord with Cymbals, exalt him, and call upon his name. So likewise *Elizabeth* magnifies the blessed Virgin *Mary, Blessed art thou amongst women*: And this was true of her, and due to her; and she takes it to her self, then she sayes there, *From henceforth all Generations shall call me blessed*; but first, she had carried it higher, to the highest, *My soule doth magnifie the Lord, and my spirit doth rejoyce in God my Saviour.* In a word, Christ forbids not this man to call him good, but he directs him to know in what capacity that attribute of goodnesse belonged to him, as he was God...

Now this leads us into two rich and fragrant fields; this sets us upon the two Hemispheares of the world; the Western Hemispheare, the RR] land of Gold, and Treasure, and the Eastern Hemispheare, the land of Spices and Perfumes; for this puts us upon both these considerations, first, That nothing is Essentially good, but God, (and there is the land of Gold, centricall Gold, viscerall Gold, gremiall Gold, Gold in the Matrice and womb of God, that is, Essentiall goodnesse in God himself) and then upon this consideration too, That this Essentiall goodnesse of God is so diffusive, so spreading, as that there is nothing in the world, that doth not participate of that goodnesse; and there is the land of Spices and Perfumes, the dilatation of Gods goodnesse.

—B.C.D.—all excellent; and D. most so. Thus, thus, ~~old~~ our old Divines shewed the depth of their love & appreciation of the Scriptures—& thus led their congregations to feel and see the same—

110   p 167

So that now both these propositions are true, First, That there is nothing in this world good, and then this also, That there is nothing *] ill: As, amongst the Fathers, it is in a good sense, as truly said, *Deus non est Ens, Deus non est substantia*, God is no Essence, God is no substance, (for feare of imprisoning God in a predicament) as it is said by others of the Fathers, that there is no other Essence, no other Substance but God.

* This, *this*, is what I have so earnestly endeavored to shew—that God is Ens super Ens,[1] the *Ground* of all Being, but therein likewise absolute Being, in that he is the Eternal Self-Affirmant, the I AM in that I AM:[a] And that the key of this mystery is given to us in the pure idea of the WILL, as the alone *causa sui*/—[2]

111   insert p 2, referring to pp 167–8

First then, there is nothing good but God: neither can I conceive any thing in God, that concerns me so much as his goodnesse; for, by that I know him, and for that I love him. I know him by that, for, as *Damascen* sayes, *primarium Dei nomen, Bonitas*; Gods first name, that is, the first way by which God notified himself to man, was Goodnesse; for out of his goodnesse he made him.... By that I know him, and for that I love him: For, the object of my understanding is truth; but the object of my love, my affection, my desire, is goodnesse. If my understanding be defective, in many cases, faith will supply it; if I beleeve it, I am as well satisfied, as if I knew it; but nothing supplies, nor fills, nor satisfies the desire of man, on this side of God; Every man hath something to love, and desire, till he determine it in God...

167. 168.—O compare this manhood of our Church Divinity with the feeble dotage of the Paleyean School, the *Natural Theology*, the Watch-making Scheme, that knows nothing of the Maker but what it can be proved out of the Watch[1]—the unknown Nominative Case of the Verb Impersonal, Fit, et Natura est./[2] The "It" of *it* rains, *it* snows, *it* is cold, &c.!—

112   p 167

R.—] His name of Jehova we admire with a reverence; but we cannot expresse that name: not only not in the signification of it, but not

---

[a] "I AM", in both cases, is written in larger letters than the rest of the writing

110[1] "Being above Being".

110[2] On "I AM" see e.g. FLEURY 56 n 6. For the will as the "self-cause", see also **54**, **62**, and **75**, above.

111[1] William Paley in his *Natural Theology* (1802) gave widest currency to the analogy of the universe to a watch

and of God to the watchmaker: see *Lects 1795 (CC)* 98 and n 3. For what C commonly called "the Grotio-Paleyan scheme" see e.g. BAHRDT 2 n 2.

111[2] "It is made, and Nature is"—a laconic play on the divine fiat of Gen 1.

confidently, not assuredly in the sound thereof; we are not sure that we should call it Jehova; not sure that any man did call it Jehova a hundred yeares agoe.

O rather say, *Jehova, his name.* It is not so properly *a* name of God, as God, the Name, God's Name and God.[1]

112A   p 168

R] How abusively then doe men call the things of this world, Goods? They may as well call them (so they do in their hearts) Gods, as Goods: *for there is none good but God.* But how much more abusively do they force the world, that call them *Bona quia beant*, Goods because they make us good, blessed, happy? In which sense, *Seneca* uses the word shrewdly, *Insolens malum beata uxor*, a good wife, a blessed wife, says he, that is, a wife that brings a great estate, is an insolent mischiefe.... Except thou see the face of God upon all thy money, as well as the face of the King, the hand of God to all thy Patents, as well as the hand of the King, Gods *Amen*, as well as the Kings *fiat*, to all thy creations, all these reach not to the title of Goods, for *there is none good but God.*

113   p 169

Land, and Money, & honor must be called Goods, though but of fortune; Fortune her self, is but such an Idol, as that S. *Aug.* was ashamed ever to have named her in his works...

We should distinguish between the *conditions* of our possessing good, and the goods themselves. Health, for instance, is ordinarily a condition of that working & rejoicing in and for God, which are *goods* in the end of, *themselves.*

Health, Competent Fortune, & the like, are good, as negations of the preventives of Good, as *clear Glass* is good in relation to the Light, which it does not exclude. Health & Ease without the love of God are crown Glass in the Darkness.[1]

114   pp 170–1

And... *Philo Iudaeus,* sayes well... God hath made nothing, in which he hath not imprinted, and from which he hath not produced some

---

112[1] Cf BIBLE COPY B 33 and n 1.
113[1] The futility of the translucence of clear window-glass in the absence of light is akin to the futility of "a sun-dial by moonlight": see *SM (CC)* 57 and n 2.

good: He follows it so far, (and justly) as to say, that God does good, where that good does no good: He takes his examples from Gods raining in the Sea; that rain does no good in the Sea: And from Gods producing fresh springs in the desart Land, where, not only no beasts come to drink, but where the very salt tide overflows the fresh spring. He might have added an example from Paradise, that God would plant such a garden, for so few houres; that God would provide man such a dwelling, when he knew he would not dwell a day in it. And he might have added an example from the Light too; That God would create light, and say it was good, then when it could be good for nothing, for there was nothing made to see it, nor to be seen by it: so forward, so early was God, in diffusing his goodnesse. Of every particular thing, God said *it was good*, and of all together, that *it was very good*; there was, there is nothing ill.

Much of this page consists of Play on Words, ex. gr. that which is useful, as Rain & that which is *of use*, as Rain on a Garden after drouth—& much of Sophistry/[1] ~~as if~~ Pain is not necessarily an *ultimate* Evil/ as the means of ultimate good, it may be a relative Good—but surely that which makes Pain, Anguish, Heaviness, necessary in order to Good must be Evil. And so the Scripture determines. They are the Wages of *Sin*;[2] but God's infinite mercy raises them into sacraments, means of Grace—Sin is the only absolute evil, God the only absolute Good—but as myriads of things are good relatively thro' participation of God, so are many things evil, as the fruits of evil.[3]

115   p [172] (blank page), possibly referring to **114** and pp 170–1[a]

What is the Apostasis, or Fall of Spirits?[1]

Answer.—That that which from the essential perfection of the absolute good could not but be *possible*, i.e. have a potential Being, but never ought to have become ~~p~~ *actual*, did strive to be actual—but this involved an impossibility—& it actualized only its own *potentiality*.

What the consequence of the Apostasis? That no philosophy is possible of Man & Nature but by assuming at once a *Zenith* and a

---

[a] Possibly a continuation of **114**. The foot-margins of pp 170, 171 are filled with **114**, the next available space being p [172], at the head of which this note is written

114[1] Cf COPY A **7**.
114[2] See Rom 6.20, 23. On the relation between pain and evil see LEIBNIZ **4**.

114[3] Cf **32**, above.
115[1] For C's use of *apostasis* to mean "the Fall" see BÖHME **158** n 5.

Nadir—God and Hades./ An ascension from the one thro' and with a condescension from the other—or redemption by *prevenient*, and then auxiliary, Grace.[2]

116 p 171

And therefore, as *Origen* said...Though it be strangely said, yet I say it, That Gods anger is good; so saies S. *Augustine, Audeo dicere*, Though it be boldly said, yet I must say it, *Utile esse cadere in aliquod manifestum peccatum*, Many sinners would never have beene saved, if they had not committed some greater sin at last, then before; for, the punishment of that sin, hath brought them to a remorse of all their other sins formerly neglected. If neither of these will serve my turne, neither that sin is nothing it selfe, and therefore not put upon me by God, nor that my sin, having occasioned my repentance, hath done me good, and established me in a better state with God, then I was in before that sin, yet this shall fully rectifie me, and assure my consolation, that in a pious sense I may say, Christ Jesus is the sinner, and not I.

no doubt, a sound sense *may* be forced into these words; but why use words, into which a sound sense must be *forced*?—Besides, the subject is too deep & too subtle for a Sermon./

117 p 171

Since sin is nothing, no such thing as is forced upon thee by God, by which thy damnation should be inevitable, or thy reconciliation impossible, since of what nature soever sin be in it selfe, thy sins being truly repented, have advanced, and emproved thy state in the favour of God, since thy sin, being by that repentance discharged upon Christ, Christ is now the sinner, and not thou, *O my Soule, why art thou so sad? why art thou disquieted within me?* And this consideration of Gods goodnesse, thus derived upon me, and made mine in Christ, ratifies and establishes such a holy confidence in me, as that all the morall constancy in the world, is but a bulrush, to this bulwark...

Donne is here too deep, & not deep enough. He *treads waters*, & dangerous waters—Mem. The familists.[1]

115[2] Cf **32**, above.

117[1] An Anabaptist sect founded in Holland by Hendrik Niclaes (c 1502–c 1580), called "Familia Caritatis" (*Huis der Liefde*, Family of Love), was later active in England. Although Elizabeth ordered them to be imprisoned and their books burned, branches of the Family lingered in East Anglia until, at the end of the seventeenth century, they merged

118   insert pp 2–3

When, after reading the biographies of Isaac Walton, and his Contemporaries I reflect on the crowded Congregations, on the thousands, who with intense interest came to these hour and two hour-long Sermons, I cannot but doubt the fact of any true progression, moral or intellectual, in the mind of the Many.—The tone, the matter, the anticipated sympathies, in the sermons of an Age form the best moral criterion of the character of the Age.—[1]

SERMONS PREACHED UPON EASTER-DAY

119   p [173] (fly-title, blank) | Sermon xviii, on Acts 2.36

The first word of the Text, must be the last part of the Sermon, *Therefore*; Therefore let all know it. Here is something necessary to be knowne, And the Meanes by which we are to know it...

Therefore—id.e. there is a sufficing reason, or motive, why I should communicate a certain ~~truth or fact~~ matter to you, or why you should give attention of it. But Truth is a common Interest—it is every man's duty to convey it to his Brother, if only it be, first, a truth that concerns or may profit him, & secondly, if he [be][a] competent to receive it—for we are not bound to *say* the Truth, where we know, we can not *convey* it, but very probably may emplant a falsehood instead.[1] & no falsehoods more dangerous than Truths misunder stood! Nay, the most mischievous Errors on record have been Half-Truths, taken as the whole.—[2]

But let it be supposed, that the matter to be communicated be a Fact of general Concernment, a truth of deep and universal Interest, a momentous Truth involved in a most awe-striking Fact, which all responsible Creatures are competent to understand, and of which no man can safely remain in Ignorance. ~~In this case we may confidently say on the~~ Now this is the case with the matter, on which I am now to speak; and it being such, I can with good reason say—*Therefore* let *all* of the H. of I. know assuredly &c[3]

[a] Word supplied by the editor

with the Quakers and other bodies. The society preached a form of mystical pantheism with antinomian features. Cf HOOKER 7. For C's view that the Familists "and similar enthusiasts of later date" overlooked the essential point of the "law of liberty" see *AR* (1825) 16–17 and nn.

118[1] C made a similar remark in *LS* (*CC*) 197–8. The *LXXX Sermons* (1640) included the earliest version of Izaak Walton's Life of Donne.

119[1] On saying truth and conveying falsehood see e.g. *Friend* (*CC*) i 43, 48–9.

119[2] Cf **10**, above, and *LS* (*CC*) 228.

119[3] "House of Israel"—cf Acts 2.36.

119A   p 176

First then, the Apostle applies himself to his Auditory, in a faire, in a gentle manner; he gives them their Titles, *Domus Israel, The house*
R] *of Israel.* We have a word now denizened, and brought into familiar use amongst us, Complement; and for the most part, in an ill sense; so it is, when the heart of the speaker doth not answer his tongue; but God forbid but a true heart, and a faire tongue might very well consist together: As vertue it self receives an addition, by being in a faire body, so do good intentions of the heart, by being expressed in faire language.

120   insert p 3, referring to p 176

I remember a vulgar Spanish Author, who writes, the *Iosephina,* the life of *Ioseph,* the husband of the blessed Virgin *Mary,* who moving that question, why that Virgin is never called by any style of Majesty, or Honour in the Scriptures, he sayes, That if after the declaring of her to be the Mother of God, he had added any other Title, the Holy Ghost had not been a good Courtier, (as his very word is) nor exercised in good language, and he thinks that had been a defect in the Holy Ghost in himself....

That Spanish Author need not be suspitious of the Holy Ghost in that kinde, that he is no good Courtier so; for in all the books of the world, you shall never reade so civill language, nor so faire expressions of themselves to one another, as in the Bible: When *Abraham* shall call himself *dust, and ashes*...If God shall call this *Abraham,* this Dust, this Worme of the dust, *The friend of God*...when *David* shall call himself *a flea, and a dead dog,* even in respect of *Saul,* and God shall call *David, A man according to his own heart,* when R] God shall call us, *The Apple of his own eye, The Seale upon his own right hand,* who would go farther for an Example, or farther then that example for a Rule, of faire accesses, of civill approaches, of sweet and honourable entrances into the affections of them with whom they were to deale?

176.—True Christian Love not only permits, but inspires *Curtesy*— God himself, says Donne, gave us the example./

120A   pp 176–7

R] It is one thing to sow pillows under the elbows of Kings, (flatterers do so) another thing to pull the chaire from under the King, and popular and seditious men do so. Where Inferiours insult over their Superiours, we tell them, *Christi Domini, they are the Lords anointed, R.R.*] and the Lord hath said, *Touch not mine anointed*; And when such Superiours insult over the Lord himselfe, and think themselves Gods without limitation, as the God of heaven is, when they doe so, we must tell them they doe so...though you be the Lords anointed, yet you crucifie the anointed Lord...

121   insert p 3, referring to p 177

The Holy Ghost is a Dove, and the Dove couples, paires, is not alone; Take heed of singular, of schismatical opinions; & what is more singular, more schismaticall, then when all Religion is confined in one R.] mans breast? The Dove is *animal sociale*, a sociable creature, and not singular; and the Holy Ghost is that; And Christ is a Sheep, *animal gregale*, they flock together: Embrace thou those truths, which the whole flock of Christ Jesus, the whole Christian Church, hath from the beginning acknowledged to be truths, and truths necessary to salvation; for, for other Traditionall, and Conditionall, and Occasionall, and Collaterall, and Circumstantiall points, for Almanack Divinity, that changes with the season, with the time, and Meridionall Divinity, calculated to the heighth of such a place, and R.] Lunary Divinity, that ebbes and flowes, and State Divinity, that obeyes affections of persons, *Domus Israel*, the true Church of God, had need of a continuall succession of light, a continuall assistance of the Spirit of God, and of her own industry, to know those things that belong to her peace.

And therefore let no Church, no man, think that he hath done R.] enough, or knowes enough....No man knowes enough; what measure of tentations soever he have now, he may have tentations, through which, this knowledge, and this grace, will not carry him; and therefore he must proceed from grace to grace. So no man hath sinned so deeply, but that God offers himself to him yet; *Sciant omnes*, the wisest man hath ever something to learn, he must not presume; the sinfullest man hath God ever ready to teach him, he must not despaire.

177. C.—*excellent.*—and E[1] of a deeper worth./ "No man knows enough"—All that is wanting here, is to determine the true sense of "knowing"—i.e. that sense, in which it is revealed that to know God is Life Everlasting—

121[1] I.e. the last paragraph of textus.

122 insert pp 3–4, referring to p 178

Now the universality of this mercy, hath God enlarged, and extended very farre, in that he proposes it, even to our knowledge, *Sciant*, let all know it. It is not only *credant*, let all beleeve it; for the infusing of faith, is not in our power: but God hath put it in our power to satisfie their reason, and to chafe that waxe, to which he himself vouchsafes to set to the great seale of faith.... And truly it is very well worthy of a serious consideration, that whereas all the Articles of our Creed, are objects of faith... yet God hath left that, out of which, all these Articles are to be deduced, and proved (that is, the R.] Scripture) to humane arguments; It is not an Article of the Creed to beleeve these, and these Books, to be, or not to be Canonicall Scripture; but our arguments for the Scripture are humane arguments, proportioned to the reason of a naturall man. God does not seale in water, in the fluid and transitory imaginations, and opinions of men; we never set the seale of faith to them; But in Waxe, in the rectified reason of man, that reason that is ductile, and flexible, and pliant, to the impressions that are naturally proportioned unto it, God sets to his seale of faith....

As therefore it is not enough for us, in our profession to tell you, *Qui non crediderit, damnabitur*, Except you beleeve all this, you shall be damned, without we execute that Commission before, *Ite praedicate*, go and preach, work upon their affections, satisfie their reason; so it is not enough for you, to rest in an imaginary faith, and R] easinesse in beleeving, except you know also what, and why, and how you come to that beliefe. Implicite beleevers, ignorant beleevers, the adversary may swallow; but the understanding beleever, he must chaw and pick bones, before he come to assimilate him, and make him like himself. The implicite beleever stands in an open field, and R] the enemy will ride over him easily; the understanding beleever, is in a fenced town, and he hath out-works to lose, before the town be pressed; that is, reasons to be answered, before his faith be shaked, and he will sell himself deare, and lose himself by inches, if he be sold or lost at last; and therefore *sciant omnes*, let all men know, that is, endeavour to informe themselves, to understand.

178 A. A problem here affirmatively stated, of highest importance, of deepest interest—viz. Faith a *so* distinguished from Reason, cred*et* from sciat,[1] that the former is an infused grace, "*not in* our power";

122[1] "'He *will* believe' [distinguished] from 'let him know'."

the latter, an inherent quality or faculty, on which we [are]^a able to calculate, as man with man.^{2}—I know not what to say to this.—Faith seems to me the co-adunation of the individual Will with the Reason, enforcing adherence alike of Thought, Act, and Affection to the Universal Will, revealed i whether in the Conscience or by the light of Reason, however the same may contravene or apparently contradict the will and mind of the flesh/—the presumed experience of the senses & of the Understanding, as the faculty of intelligential yet animal Instinct, by which we generalize the notices of the senses, and *substantiate* (*understand*, facio apparentiæ *aliquid sub*-stare)^3 the spectra or phænomena/ In this sense, therefore, & in this only I agree with Donne—Not a man (says Christ) cometh to me unless the Father leadeth him—.^{4} The corrupt will cannot without prevenient as well as auxiliary Grace be unitively subordinated to the Reason;^{5} & again without this union of the Moral Will the Reason itself is latent.— Nevertheless, I see no *advantage* in not saying, *the Will*; and but putting first the term Faith. But the sad Non-distinction of Reason from the Understanding, throughout Donne/ and the confusion of ideas and conceptions under the same term, "*rationibus*", painfully inturbidates his theology./^{6} Till this distinction (of Reason & Understanding, νους & φρονημα σαρκος)^7 be seen, nothing *can* be seen aright. Till this great truth be mastered, and with the Sight that is *In*sight, other truths may casually take possession of the mind, but the mind cannot possess them.^{8}—And yet Mr Hare writes of it, as a sort of inessential arbitrary refinementing in *Words*.—much like *sweat* and *perspire*, p—— and make water!!^{b}—So little had *he* comprehended me.^{9}—If you do not know *this*, you *know*, you *can*

---

^{a} Word supplied by the editor
^{b} Here C made a stroke to mark the end of the note, but continued

---

122^2 See **30** and n 2, above.

122^3 "I make *something* to stand *under* the appearance". For the relation between "*sub*stance" and "*under*standing" see BIBLE COPY B **136** n 2. On faith as the coadunation of will and reason cf **11**, above.

122^4 John 6.44 (var); cf 6.65.

122^5 Cf **129**, below, last line.

122^6 Cf **29** and n 1, above. This use of "inturbidates" is one of only two cited in *OED*.

122^7 "Reason" and the "mind of the flesh"; cf "the will and mind of the flesh" a few sentences earlier. For the recurrent term φρόνημα σαρκός see BAXTER *Reliquiae* COPY B **115** n 10.

122^8 On mankind possessed by ideas see **60, 62, 64**, above; and e.g. DAVISON **14** and n 3.

122^9 Julius Charles Hare (1795–1855)—"of all Coleridge's disciples, one of the most loyal....No other disciple knew Coleridge better or was better equipped to understand him." C. R. Sanders *Coleridge and the Broad Church Movement* (Durham NC 1942) 123; for an account of the relations between C and Hare, see ch 5. C is probably thinking of Hare's *The Children*

know *nothing*: for if you do not know the diversity of Reason from the Understanding, you do not know *Reason*—and Reason alone is Knowlege.—

What follows, p. 178. B. is admirable—/[10] worthy of a~~n~~ Divine of the Church of England, the National and the Christian, and indeed proves, that Donne felt, *was possessed by*, the truths, I have here labored to enforce—viz. that Faith is the *Apotheosis* of the Reason in Man;—the *Complement* of Reason, the Will in the form of the Reason. As the Basin-water to the fountain-shaft, ~~of~~ such is Will to Reason in *Faith*—The whole Will shapes itself in the image of God, in which it had been created, and shoots toward Heaven.

S. T. C.

123 p 178

Suppose an impossibility...If we could have been in Paradise, and seen God take a clod of red earth, and make that wretched clod of contemptible earth, such a body as should be fit to receive his breath, an immortall soule, fit to be the house of the second person in the Trinity, for God the Son to dwel in bodily; fit to be the Temple for the third person, for the Holy Ghost, should we not have wondred more, then at the production of all other creatures?

---

of Light, a Sermon Preached Before the University of Cambridge (Cambridge 1828), in which Hare had spoken of "Reason" with adverse qualification: see pp 5–6, 18–19. In the Preface he enlarged on the subject, responding to representations that "the sentences on the aberrations and extravagances of the reasoning faculty may easily be misinterpreted into a dissuasive from all severe exercise of thought". He distinguishes (pp iv–v) between two uses of the term "Reason": as signifying "the whole complex of the reflective faculties" and as "restricted with greater propriety to the logical faculty or the power of drawing inferences". "In the former sense Reason is much less likely to err; although even then it needs to be evermore refreshed and replenished by influxes from the imagination and the heart....It is in the latter sense however that Reason has been...so fruitful a parent of errour and mischief: and in such a sense have I used the word, when speaking against it. This sort of Reason is fallible in the extreme....And yet the first and essential axiom of the Reason is its own infallibility." In discussing Bacon's view of reason (p vii) Hare concludes that "the Reason...is so far from being self-sufficient in itself, that, without the ministerial offices of the other faculties, it has no hold and is utterly unable to act upon anything external...". See also James H. Rigg *Modern Anglican Theology* (1857) 57–8: "Nowhere does he [Hare] seem to make reason a supreme, intuitive power, whose sphere is above and aloof from that of the understanding. Nor does his nomenclature uniformly agree with that of the Coleridgeans. Sometimes, indeed, especially in his 'Victory of Faith' [a collection of Hare's sermons, 1840], he appears to use the words 'reason' and 'understanding' in senses altogether different from Coleridge's...". Rigg then quotes at length the passage in pp iv–v summarised above.

122[10] I.e. the last paragraph of the textus.

A sort of pun on the Hebrew word, Adam, or red earth;[1] common in Donne's Age, but unworthy of Donne—who was worthy to have seen deeper into the scriptural sense of "*the Ground*"—i.e. Hades, the Multëity, the Many absque ⟨numero⟩ et infra numerum/[2]—that which is *below*, as God is that which transcends intellect.

124 p 179

We place in the Schoole, (for the most part) the infinite Merit of Christ Jesus...rather *in pacto*, then *in persona*, rather that this contract was thus made between the Father, and the Son, then that, whatsoever that person, thus consisting of God and Man, should doe, should, onely in respect of the person, bee of an infinite value, and extention, to that purpose; for then, any act of his, his Incarnation, his Circumcision, any had been sufficient for our Redemption, without his death.

O this is sad misty divinity! far too scholastic for the pulpit, far too vague & unphilosophic for the Study!/

125 p 180

Quis nisi Infidelis negaverit, apud inferos fuisse Christum? saies S. *Augustine*; Who but an Infidell, will deny Christs descending into hell?

Q.ʸ In what part of Augustine?[1]—Pearson asserts the clause, Descended into Hell, not to have been introduced into the (so called) Apostle's Creed, till the sixth Century[2]—And even now the sense of these words is in no reformed Church determined, as an article of faith—or those pronounced heretical, who render them = *verè*

123[1] As with the name "Cain" (**71** and n 1, above), the meaning of the name "Adam" was sought in common words that seemed to come from the same root. The connexion between Adam and red earth is in Gen 2.7, in which there is play on *adamah*, meaning both "earth, ground" and "red clay". Donne noticed this connexion in three sermons, none of which C annotated. C could have satisfied himself about Donne's "clod of red earth" by referring to his Hebrew lexicon. But in *CN* IV 4702 (c Jul 1820) there is a list of Hebrew words with transliterations and English translations, in Hurwitz's hand, including "...adom = red...adam [=]Adam...adamah[=]ground".

123[2] "Without number and below number". On "the Ground" see e.g. FIELD **13** n 1.

125[1] The reference is to St Augustine Letter 164 ch 2 §3, referring to Acts 2.24, 27 (Migne *PL* XXXIII 710).

125[2] John Pearson *Exposition of the Creed* (Oxford 1710) 225. The first creed to include the descent into hell was formulated at Sirmium in 359; Athanasius gives the text in *De symbolis* (Migne *PG* XXVI 692–3). C is known to have annotated two copies of Pearson.

mortuus est[3]—i.e. ~~to~~ in contra-distinction from a trance, or suspended animation.

126   p 181

Never therefore dispute against thine own happinesse; never say, God asks the heart, that is, the soule, and therefore rewards the soule, or punishes the soule, and hath no respect to the body...Never go about to separate the thoughts of the heart, from the colledge, from the fellowship to the body...All that the soule does, it does in, and with, and by the body.

Had Donne but once asked himself, what he meant by the Body, as distinct from the carcase, he must have detected the fallacy, the mischievous fallacy, of this reasoning.[1]—It is not Soul + Body = Man, as Brandy + Water = Toddy;[2] but the Unity, Man, that is Soul and Body as the + and − Poles of the same Magnet.

127   p 182

Audacter dicam, saies S. *Hierome*, I say confidently, *Cum omnia posset Deus, suscitare Virginem post ruinam, non potest*: Howsoever God can do all things, he cannot restore a Virgin, that is fallen from it, to virginity againe.

One instance among hundreds of the wantonness of phrase & fancy in the Fathers. What did Augustin mean? Quod Deus τὸ Hymenis membranum luniforme ~~non potes~~ reproducere nequit?[1]—No!—That were too absurd—What then? That God cannot make what has been not to have been!—Well then—Why not say *that*: since that is all you can mean—

128   pp 184–5, pencil | Sermon XIX, on Rev 20.6

The literall sense is always to be preserved; but the literall sense is not always to be discerned: for the literall sense is not always that,

125[3] "He- *really* died". See H. COLERIDGE **33** n 1. C considered that the formula "he descended into hell" was introduced into the Apostles' Creed in order to affirm that Christ really died, but that it had opened the way to various Arian and Socinian interpretations. Cf WATERLAND *Importance* 238–43.

126[1] Cf **95**, above, and see HUGHES **1** n 7.
126[2] Cf **80**, above.
127[1] "That God ~~cannot~~ is unable to reproduce the luniform membrane of the hymen?" The statement that C questions is in fact Jerome's; his eye must have caught Augustine's name in the preceding sentence.

which the very Letter and Grammer of the place presents... But the literall sense of every place, is the principall intention of the Holy Ghost, in that place: And his principall intention in many places, is to expresse things by allegories, by figures; so that in many places of Scripture, a figurative sense is the literall sense, and more in this Book [Revelation] then in any other.... [Donne then offers various interpretations.] And these foure considerations of the words; A Resurrection from persecution, by deliverance; a Resurrection from sin, by grace; a Resurrection from tentation to sin, by the way of death, to the glory of heaven; and all these, in the first Resurrection, in him that is the roote of all, in Christ Jesus, These foure steps, these foure passages, these foure transitions will be our quarter Clock, for this houres exercise.

A lively instance of how much excellent good sense a wise man, like Donne, can bring forth on a passage, he does not understand/ For to say, it may either mean X. or Y. or Z., is to confess I do not know what it means.—*But* if it be X, *then*—& if it be Y, then—and lastly if it be it be Z, then.—i.e. he understands X, Y, Z, but not the text.

S. T. C.—

129   p 185

We wonder, and justly, at the effusion, at the pouring out of blood, in the sacrifices of the old Law.... Seas of blood, and yet but brooks, tuns of blood, and yet but basons, compared with the sacrifices, the sacrifices of the blood of men, in the persecutions of the Primitive Church. For every Oxe of the Jew, the Christian spent a man, and for every Sheep and Lamb, a Mother and her childe; and for every heard of cattle, sometimes a towne of Inhabitants, sometimes a Legion of Souldiers, all martyred at once...

Whoo!!!—Had the other nine so called Persecutions been equal to the *tenth*, that of Diocletian,[1] the only one of any great efficiency, Donne's assertion would still be extravagant.

SERMONS PREACHED UPON THE CONVERSION OF S. PAUL

130   p ⁻2, referring to p 461 | Sermon XLVI, on Acts 9.4

But to that presumptuous sinner, who sins on, because God shewed mercy to One at last, we must say, a miserable Comforter is that Rule,

129[1] C follows the traditional account given by Paulus Orosius (fl 417): "This persecution [of Diocletian (284–305)], the tenth in succession from Nero's, was longer and more cruel than any that had preceded it." *Seven Books of History Against the Pagans* 7.25: tr I. W. Raymond (New York 1936).

that affords but one example. Nay, is there one example? The Conversion of *Saul* a Persecutor, and of the Theife upon the Crosse, is become *Proverbium peccatorum*, The sinners proverb, and serves him, and satisfies him in all cases. But is there any such thing? Such a story there is, and it is as true as Gospel, it is the truth of Gospel it selfe; But was this a late Repentance? Answer S. *Cyril*... Tell me, Beloved, Thou that deferrest thy Repentance, doest thou do it upon Confidence of these examples?... Thou deludest thine own soule; The Theife was not converted at last, but at first; As soone as God afforded him any Call, he came; And at how many lights hast thou winked? And to how many Cals hast thou stopped thine ears, that deferrest thy repentance? Christ said to him, *Hodie mecum eris, This day thou shalt be with me in paradise*; when thou canst finde such another day, looke for such another mercy; A day that cleft the grave-stones of dead men; A day that cleft the Temple it selfe; A day that the Sunne durst not see; A day that saw the soule of God... depart from Man; There shall be no more such dayes; and therefore presume not of that voyce, *Hodie*, This day thou shalt be with me, if thou make thy last minute that day, though Christ, to magnifie his mercy, and his glory, and to take away all occasion of absolute desperation, did here, under so many disadvantages call, and draw S. *Paul* to him.

A noble passage on death bed Repentance, p. 461.[a1]

SERMONS PREACHED UPON THE PENITENTIALL
PSALMES

131   p 557 | Sermon LV, on Ps 6.8–10

...there are not in all the world so eloquent Books as the Scriptures; and that nothing is more demonstrable, then that if we would take all those Figures, and Tropes, which are collected out of secular Poets, and Orators, we may give higher, and livelier examples, of every one of those Figures, out of the Scriptures, then out of all the Greek and Latine Poets, and Orators...

See Paradise Regained.[1]

---

[a]   C first wrote "491" and corrected it by deleting "9" and writing "6" above it in pencil; he then wrote "p. 461" in pencil in the space between **130** and **3**. **53** was written after **130**, at the head of the page, in the space left above **130**

130[1]   This textus comes from the same paragraph as COPY A **5A**, following it at an interval of three sentences. The passage echoed in BAXTER *Reliquiae* COPY A **10** (1811) and in more detail in *EOT* (CC)

II 475 (2 Apr 1817) is in the paragraph following this textus on p 461. See also COPY A **5A** n 1.

131[1]   *Paradise Regained* IV 321–50, esp 336–8: "Our Hebrew Songs and

132   p ⁺5

If our old Divines in their homiletic expositions of Scripture *wire-drew* their Texts, in the anxiety to evolve out of the words the fulness of their meaning, expressed, involved or suggested, our modern Preachers have erred more dangerously in the opposite extreme, making their Text a mere *theme*, or *motto*, for their discourse. Both err in *degree*, the old Divines, especially the Puritan, by excess—the modern, by defect. But there is this difference to the disfavor of the latter—that the *defect* in *degree* alters the *kind*. It was ever God's holy Word, that our Donnes, Andrewses, Hookers preached, th it was *Scripture* Bread, that they divided according to the needs & seasons—the Preacher of our Days expounds or appears to expound his own sentiments & conclusions—& thinks himself evangelic enough, if he can st make the Scripture seem in conformity with them.—

Above all, there is something to my mind ⟨at once⟩ elevating & soothing in the idea of an order of learned Men making reading the many works of the Wise & great in all many languages for the purpose of making one book contain the life and virtue of all for their Brethren who have but that one to read—What then, if that one book be such, that the greatest increase of Learning is shewn by more & more enabling the mind to *find* them all in it. But such, according to my experience, turned as I am of 3 score,[1] the Bible is—as far as all moral, spiritual and prudential, private, domestic, or political, truths & interests are concerned. The Astronomer, Chemist, Mineralogist must go elsewhere; but the Bible is THE BOOK for the MAN—[2]

Harps in *Babylon*, | That pleas'd so well our Victors ear, declare | That rather *Greece* from us these Arts deriv'd...". Cf AESCHYLUS *Agamemnon* **1** (at n 4).

132[1] The date, then, is at earliest

Oct 1832—if C remembered his birth-date correctly. See **16** and n 1, above.

132[2] Cf **103**, above. This closing affirmation repeats the dominant theme of both *SM* and *CIS*.

JEAN ANTOINE DUBOIS

1765–1848

Description of the Character, Manners, and Customs of the People of India; and of their institutions, religious and civil. By the Abbé J. A. Dubois, missionary in the Mysore. Translated from the French manuscript. London 1817. 8°.

Large-paper copy.

British Museum C 44 g 3

A set of notes in pencil in an unidentified hand on pp 9, 10, 21, 23, 33, 34, 36, 39, 51, 82, 83, 112, 194, 214, 266, 277, 307, 312, 316, 345, 362, 460, 474, 475, 486, 545; and on 558 a note in another hand—EHC thought it might be Mrs Gillman's, but it may be John Morgan's. Many pencil markings throughout, some of which—and perhaps some or all of the notes—were made before C annotated the book: see 6, below.

On p 316 (pt II ch 31) Dubois writes: "...the fire of the Yajna bears the appellation of *Yajneswara*, or the god fire; and the word Yajna is derived from *Agni*, fire; as if it were to this god that the sacrifice were really offered. I need not point out the resemblance between the word *Agni* and the Latin *Ignis*." Beside this, in pencil, in an unidentified hand: "hence αγνος as purus from πυρ & castus from καιω". Cf *CN* III 4418 f 15ᵛ (c Aug 1818), and see the reference to IRVING *Sermons*, below.

In c 1796–7 C had drawn upon the oriental work of Sir William Jones (1746–94), especially his *Institutes of Hindu Law* (1794) and the *Asiatic Researches* (see e.g. *CN* I 302 and n, II 3130 and n), and upon Thomas Maurice *The History of Hindostan* (2 vols 1795) (see *CN* I 240–5 and "*Prometheus*" in *LR* II 327). In 1809 he read the accounts written by William Carey (1761–1834), a Baptist missionary in India, published in *Periodical Accounts Relative to the Baptist Missionary Society* (Clipstone 1800). See *CN* III 3505, 3507, 3511; cf *AR* (1825) 10–11. There are connexions between the marginalia on DUBOIS and the undated marginalia on Lodewijk VALCKENAER *Diatribe de Aristobulo Judaeo* (Leyden 1806). Also the long annotation on IRVING *Sermons* (3 vols 1828) II 33–49 is connected with DUBOIS p 367 ("The Origin of the Trimurti") and with the unidentified pencil note on p 316 (see above).

DATE. Perhaps between 1818 and 1828.

1 p 323, pencil | Pt II ch 33 "Opinions of the Hindu Philosophers on the Nature of God..."

The professors of the last doctrine designate the foundation of their system by the two technical expressions *Abhavana Bhava-nasti*: *From nothing nothing comes*. They maintain that *Creation* is an impossibility, and that, on the other hand, a pre-existing and eternal substance is absolutely chimerical. From these premises they infer, that, whatever we imagine to be the universe, and the various objects which appear to compose it, is nothing but a pure illusion, or *Maya*.

The Eleatic School of Greece. See Zeno's Paradox.[1]

2 p 324, pencil

There is still another scheme of philosophy, which is utterly rejected by the Brahmans, and is said to be followed and taught by the Jainas and the votaries of Buddha. This system is nothing else than the pure *Materialism*, which Spinosa and his disciples have endeavoured to pass for a new discovery of their own. The materialists of India appear to have long preceded them in this doctrine...

Nonsense! Spinosa was no Materialist, but the sternest & most consistent of *Adwitam*ists.[1]—Again: these Buddhists are not Materialists, but Hylozoists,[2] by Dubois' own account. I question

[1] The Eleatic philosophy, founded c 540 B.C. by Xenophanes (though some deny that he was the founder: see *OCD* "Xenophanes"), flourished until c 440 B.C., its principal members in the fifth century being Parmenides, Zeno, and Melissus. The central doctrine of the school was monism, either theological or physical, and the assertion of "the impossibility of any change, any true transition from any one thing or state to another". *P Lects* Lect 3 (1949) 122. C wrote extensive marginalia on the Eleatics in TENNEMANN I; see also GRAY **6** and n 3. Zeno of Elea (b c 490 B.C.) was a brilliant critic of the paradoxes involved in a belief in plurality and change. For C's account of "Zeno's Paradox"—a logical demonstration that a tortoise given a small head-start can never be overtaken by a hare—see *P Lects* Lect 3 (1949) 122–4; and for C's analysis of the sophism involved in the paradox see

KANT *Vermischte Schriften* COPY C **29** and TENNEMANN I ⁻3, referring to I 337ff.

[1] For C on the importance of distinguishing between Spinoza and Spinozism see e.g. SPINOZA *Opera* II 59–61. C has devised his term "Adwitamist" (not in *OED*) from Dubois' account of two Hindu sects of philosophers: *Dwitam*, "which admits of two essences, *God* and *Matter*", and *Adwitam*, "those who acknowledge one being, one substance, one God".

[2] Hylozoism—the theory that matter (ὕλη) is endowed with life (ζωή) or that life is merely a property of matter: *OED*. The term is Cudworth's; for his condemnation of "The Numen, which the hylozoic Corporalist pays all his devotions to" as "a certain blind she-god or goddess, called Nature" see *Lects 1795* (*CC*) 93 n 1. See also *BL* ch 8 (*CC*) I 131–2 and JACOBI **10**.

whether there was ever exact knowlege enough of Geometry in India to render a pure Materialism possible.[3]

3   p 328, pencil

At any rate, it must be admitted, that, if the Bauddhists actually hold the odious and detestable tenets which are ascribed to them...these have no visible influence on their behaviour, or the slightest effect in relaxing the social ties which bind them, equally with other casts, to the great stock of society.

These Bauddhists seem to have referred all knowlege to Sensation, in the first place, as Locke (as far as he was consistent with his premises) Hartley, Condillac &c—then to have explained the palpable difference between knowlege & sensation, a pin-prick and a pro-position, by the *partiality* of the Sensation. In short, the result would be *as usual*, that the Philosopher had called Jack Tom, and Tom Jack; but *bating that*, was no greater Fool (& no greater Solomon) than his Neighbors.

S. T. C.

4   pp 409–10, pencil | iii ch 3 "Of the Temples of the Hindus and the Ceremonies There Practised"

In fact, there is no country on earth where population is so much encouraged as amongst the Hindus. Their domestic institutions are in this respect pre-eminent over those of other nations, who are vaunted as at the very summit of civilization, although they have, in reality, sunk to the lowest degree of vice, by the love of luxury, the thirst after distinction and wealth, or other propensities not less despicable in the eyes of the philosopher; which have driven a vast number of their most distinguished members to the horrid necessity *] of resisting nature in the most general, most invariable, and also the sweetest of her inspirations: by opposing meditated obstacles to her principle of propagation, and sometimes even by means which cannot be alluded to without disgust.

* This is the honestest book of its kind as written by a *Frenchman*, that I have ever read—but still *the Frenchman* is conspicuous. So the line marked *—and the utter unconnectedness of Thought./[1] There

2[3] Cf *P Lects* Lect 11 (1949) 333–4. But here C means that the Buddhists did not know enough geometry to become Cartesian.

4[1] For C's condemnation of the French mentality see DESMOULINS 1 n 1. See also 8, 16, and 18, below, and *P Lects* Lect 5 (1949) 190.

is throughout not so much a confusion, as a contradiction between the opinions of the writer (ex. gr. in his eulogy on Casts)[2] and the facts which prove the *effects* to be equally horrible and degrading/ Compare this §, and the abuse of Christian Europe compared with the praise of the Hindus with the Facts on p. 411, 412!![3]

5   p 422, pencil, marked with a pencil line in the margin

The miracles of the Christian religion, however extraordinary they must appear to a common understanding, are by no means so to the Hindus. Upon them they have no effect. The exploits of Joshua and of his army, and the prodigies they effected by the interposition of God, in the conquest of the land of Canaan, seem to them unworthy of notice, when compared with the achievement of their own Rama, and the miracles which attended his progress when he subjected Ceylon to his yoke. The mighty strength of Samson dwindles into nothing, when opposed to the overwhelming energy of Bali, of Ravana and the giants. The resurrection of Lazarus itself is, in their eyes, an ordinary event; of which they see frequent examples in the Vishnu ceremonies of the Pahvahdam.

Well worthy the attention of those modern Divines, who represent miracles as the fundamental proof of Religion instead of one of the means of introducing it. O when will Divines read the Gospel according to John with the head and heart of the inspired Writer!

6   pp 422–3, pencil, marked wath a line in the margin (not by C)

And had not God Himself condescended to impart to us the knowledge of his attributes, and of the worship that is pleasing to Him, never could our limited understanding, warped as it is by passion and prejudice, have arisen to just notions on the subject; and we must have been still groping in the thick darkness of idolatry...

  The modern Deists of Europe, I know, will not agree with these *] sentiments. They presumptuously maintain that human reason, when purged from the prejudices of education, is of itself sufficient to form just notions of the Divinity; and, arrogantly, attribute those which thcy themselves entertain to the vigour of their own genius;

4[2] In Pt ɪ chs 1–5 (pp 1–34) Dubois describes the caste system. For C on castes see *P Lects* Lect 2 (1949) 99–101.

4[3] In pp 411–12 Dubois gives an account of various "abominable prac-

tices" used in India by barren women in search of "the gift of fruitfulness"—collecting ordure, drinking sewer water, and the like.

while it is easy to see that they are only the fruit of the Christian education which they have received, and for which they are indebted solely to the high privilege of having been born in a country where the revealed religion alone is professed.

* Well and wisely, *me saltem judice*,[1] has the reader, whoever it was marked this sentence by the marginal pencil-line.—But then more & other than Dubois had in mind, must have been meant by him. For it would be dangerous to young Christians to assert what could not be proved.—viz. that Pythagoras &c had read the Old Testament,[2] or the Philosophers had not in the most emphatic words taught that the practice of the Godlike could alone be acceptable to God. How could the Heathens otherwise have been "without excuse" as S[t] Paul asserts?[3] How could Paul himself have received Christ crucified as a *new creation*?[4] It will not be pretended, that Paul was ⟨previously⟩ ignorant of the divine Oracle—What more doth God require of thee, O man! than to do justice, and love mercy, and walk humbly before the Lord thy God.[5]—As a descriptive Anatomist to the vital Principle in the body described, such is the Best of ancient and modern Philosophy (aye, alas! and the fashionable Theology too) to the vital truths of Christianity.

7   p 423, pencil

Socrates, the wisest and most renowned of all [the philosophers] . . . was not able completely to shake off the fetters of superstition. For after he had taken the hemlock, surrounded by friends, who were cheering ?] him with the prospects of a better life, he felt inward remorse, and whispered to his disciple Crito that he had vowed the sacrifice of a cock to Esculapius; which he entreated his friend, most earnestly, to offer in his name.... The history of all mankind shews us that God has never been truly known or worshipped but by nations who have had Him for their only Lord.

Assuredly, there was some meaning, some Hint or Doctrine which Socrates wished to convey by this Enigma—*possibly*, that the Sacrifice of the first annunciators of a revolutionary Truth was a necessary to heal the feverous state of the public mind, and by the

6[1] "In my opinion, at least".
6[2] "Pythagoras &c" would presumably include Heraclitus and Plato. See *Friend* (*CC*) I 503–4, quoted in "*Prometheus*" (*LR* II 332–3); and for an imaginary account of a meeting between Pythagoras and Daniel see *CN* IV 5439.
6[3] Rom 1.20.
6[4] Gal 6.14–15 (var); cf 2 Cor 5.17.
6[5] Micah 6.8 (var).

natural re-action of human feelings the most certain means of spreading the Truth. The Cock = the morning Herald.[1]

By the bye, how coolly this Roman Catholic speaks of "their only Lord". Have not his own Religionists Lords many and Gods (Divi) many?[2] The idolatry of the Romanists is not so foul, but it is equally gross.

8 p 425, pencil

...however gross and evidently absurd the worship and doctrines of the Hindus are, their religion appears to me, under its worst aspect, to be preferable to Atheism.

What does Dubois mean by *Atheism*? Brahmanism is and the Hesiodic Greek Mythology are themselves species of polytheistic Atheism.[1] It is Pantheism carried by Fancy into the *possible* results/ viz. as the τὸ πᾶν[2] has produced man, why not gods?—The proper Question therefore is this: whether Atheism in the form of Polytheism is better or worse than Atheism in the form of A Sebanthropism, i.e. the reverence of *man*[3] as the highest known impersonation of the One and All—which is Spinozism.[4] I should reply: the Question is useless—for the number of those who are wise enough and yet not too wise to be of the latter Faith must for ever be small & composed of speculative tranquil minds—Were it otherwise, I should not hesitate to include the latter.

9 p 425, pencil

I would far rather believe in the doctrine of the Maru Jelma, the metempsychosis of the Hindus, than in that which teaches that death *] is an eternal sleep, or, in other words, that the crimes of the wicked are buried with them for ever in the grave.

7[1] The usual explanation is that the sacrifice to Aesculapius, the god of healing, was a thank-offering for death as the release of the immortal soul from all ills and from the trammels of the body.

7[2] 1 Cor 8.5–6. *Divi*—the title of Roman emperors deified after death, later used by the Renaissance humanists (cf BOCCACCIO 1 on their use of pagan instead of Christian terms) to describe the saints, as opposed to *Deus* (God). C may

also be playing on the Zoroastrian use in which *divi* are evil spirits.

8[1] Cf *P Lects* Chronological Assistant (1949) 72.

8[2] "The All", as in the pantheist phrase C uses below—"the One and All": see n 4, below.

8[3] From σέβας (reverential awe) + ἄνθρωπος (man)—not in *OED*.

8[4] On Spinozism, pantheism, and τὸ πᾶν see BAXTER *Reliquiae* COPY A 2 n 2.

* This does not merit the name of an opinion or doctrine: it was the mere frenzy of Wickedness—a rank Steam from the putrid Dunghill of the Gallo-jacobinical *Heart*.[1] "The FOOL sayeth in his HEART, &c"[2]

10 p 427, pencil

[Montesquieu *De l'Esprit des lois* xxiv 2:] "In order to diminish the abhorrence of atheism, idolatry is overloaded. It is not true that when the ancients erected altars to any vice, they shewed that they loved that vice; but on the contrary that they hated it...."

No!—that they *feared* it. I repeat, that speculative negative Atheism, which rejects as inconclusive all the proofs hitherto adduced of the existence of any impersonation of the unconscious Wisdom (= cogitatio infinita, sine centro)[1] of Nature higher than the human Intellects, ⟨as it⟩ existings in States as well as Individuals, is of necessity confined to a *very* Few—: and that the Hypothesis is only logically, but and not really, possible: and therefore no comparison can be grounded on it. Far better to impress and prove this most certain truth—that philosophic Atheism will necessarily pass into immoral Polytheism in its transfer to a People.[2]

11 p 430, pencil | III 4 "Of the Principal Divinities of India"

They say that Brahma, in his first essay to create a human being, made him with only one foot; which not answering, he destroyed the work, and formed the next with three; but the third foot being more an incumbrance than a help, he destroyed this model also, and finally resolved upon the two legs.

Who can doubt that the ground-work of Brahmanism is physiological—and that the Powers and Laws of the Material Universe are taken as antecedents of Intellect and Moral Will—just as the Titanic Deities are elder than Jove &c?—[1]

9[1] On the *monstrum hybridum* of Jacobinism see *SM* (*CC*) 63–4.

9[2] Ps 14.1 (and 53.1): "The fool hath said in his heart, There is no God...".

10[1] "Infinite (unbounded) thought, without a centre." For C's view of Spinoza's *cogitatio infinita* see BÖHME **10** n 2.

10[2] This is one of the themes of the essay "On the *Prometheus* of Aeschylus", drafted largely 1820–1, delivered to the Royal Society of Literature 18 May 1825. See *LR* II 330 and FIELD **23** and n 1. On negative atheism see *P Lects* Lect 6 (1949) 209.

11[1] How the Greeks, by studying "the Powers and Laws of the Material Universe" established philosophy, "not...as the product [of philosophising], but as = the producing power—the productivity", is the principal theme of "*Prometheus*": see *LR* II 333–8.

12 p 433, pencil

[Dubois is outlining the ten Avataras or metamorphoses of Vishnu, giving for each its name and mythological story, and has reached the fourth Avatara (called *Narasingha*), where C has written this note.]

Spite of the fantastic admixtures (which are perhaps only *literal translations*/ into *words*) of the inessential minutiæ of the original rude *Picture*-language, it is easy to see a caricature of the Mosaic Cosmogony/ from Shell-fish to Fish, thence to Amphibii, thence to Beasts, thence by an other intermediate to the Centaur, or Pindar's θηρ διος, to the ~~divine~~warf Man—the Hanuman or rational Ape = πυγμαιων γενος[1]—thence to the Hero Man, *the Son* of &c—

13 p 435, pencil

[An account of the seventh Avatara, the metamorphosis of Vishnu into the hero Rama, which is described "in a very prolix and tedious way, in the Ramayana". A central exploit is Rama-Vishnu's recovery of his beloved Sita (abducted by the Giant Ravana) with the help of an army of Apes led by "the great Ape *Hanuman*".]

Every where the Atheism, which is ground-work of *all* Polytheism, peeps out.—i.e. Intellect is falsely taken as the result of limitation/ and hence derived *to* the infinite Mind in and from the *limitations*, that is, the finite Minds. Vishnu, ignorant of Tactics, is taught by the Apes.[1]

14 p 436, pencil

The Tenth Avatara is the transformation into a *Horse*. This last *] Avatara has not yet taken effect; but the Hindus trust that it will be realized. They expect it with the same ardour as the Jews look forward to their Messiah.

12[1] C's sequence passes from the "divine beast"—actually φὴρ θεῖον, the centaur Chiron, of Pindar *Pythian* 4.119—to the "race of pygmies". The sequence of avatars of Vishnu as summarised by Dubois is: 1 fish, 2 tortoise, 3 boar, 4 half man, half lion (C's "Centaur"), 5 dwarf Brahman (C's "dwarf Man"), 6 god Paraswama, 7 hero Rama, 8 god Krishna, 9 tree, 10 horse. Hanuman—the great Ape in command of the army of apes which Rama (avatar 7) called to his service in his search for his wife Sita (p 435). Chiron, of divine origin, conspicuous in legend as the teacher of Aesculapius, Jason, Achilles, and other heroes, has affinities with the Hanuman as instructor of Rama.

13[1] "Rama...being ignorant of war, received instruction from the Apes, who taught him to build bridges, to draw up an army in array, and to surprize the enemy...". Dubois p 435.

* Q︮y︮—The powers of Nature will be finally domesticated by man, the symbol being that of the most generous and beautiful of the herbivorous Quadrupeds in the service of the human Race.[1]

15   p 451, pencil | iii ch 5 "Of the Worship of Animals, and That of the Butam or Malevolent Beings"

All nations of the earth, civilized or barbarous, have acknowledged the existence of certain evil spirits, whose nature and constant employment it is to injure men in various ways. Revealed religion *] alone gives just and rational views of the subject.

* That is to say: none at all.

16   p 457, pencil | iii ch 6 "Of the Pariahs and Other Inferior Casts of Hindus"

It cannot be questioned that the want of delicacy on the part of the Europeans, in admitting Pariahs into their menial service, gives more offence and occasions more disgust to the Hindus, than any thing besides, and is the principal cause of preventing persons of a decent cast from serving them in that capacity. They are exposed, therefore to faithless domestics, in whom they cannot confide.

What truly *French* Contradictions! Has he not told us a score of times, that neither Honesty or Fidelity or disinterested affection in any form can be expected from a Hindu? What is the whole Book, but a catalogue of their Vices, positive or negative? And at what point was the accommodation to their endless superstitions to begin or end?

17   p 461, pencil

[An account of the various outcasts, some held to be below the Pariahs.]

How evidently both here and in the instance of the Pariahs has the Frenchman confounded the effects with the causes! Even from his own account I should conclude that the Pariahs were, on the whole, less morally hateful than the Brahmans.

18   p 462, pencil

The cast of *Potiers* and that of *Utarans*, whose principal employment consists in building walls of earth, digging tanks, and keeping their

14[1] With this "most generous and beautiful" creature, C never established   a satisfactory rapport. He may also have in mind Swift's Houyhnhnms.

banks in repair, are likewise considered as low tribes, by the Sudras. The education of these people corresponds to the meanness of their origin. Their mind is as uncultivated as their manners; and every thing seems to justify the small esteem in which they are held.

Truly *French*—and so far justifiable. For a Frenchman feels that he is *born* a Frenchman—he is the Peccatum originale of the animal vis vitæ plastica[1] of the Planet, which m there⟨-fore⟩ re-appears in the Link which connected ⟨the Frenchman, as⟩ *its* highest result, with the spiritual Life; namely, in Man. So much of Vice, in the primary impulse, so much Frenchman.[2]

19 p 469, pencil

[Indian snake-charmers practise "rank imposture":] When they enter into an agreement with any simpleton, who fancies that his house is infested with serpents...they artfully introduce...one of their tame snakes, which comes up to its master, as soon as it hears his flute.

This is utterly improbable/ they doubtless have at least as much power, as our Rat-catchers in England.

20 p 477, pencil | III ch 7 "Of the Metempsychosis"

Several writers, both ancient and modern, have been of opinion that Pythagoras was the author of the system of the Metempsychosis...and that it was communicated by that philosopher to the sages of India, when he visited their country. But all who are acquainted with the spirit and education of the Brahmans, both ancient and modern, will be easily satisfied of the contrary...

It might have been as well, if it had been first prove[d][a] that Pythagoras really taught the doctrine of Transmigration, relative to the Soul or reason of Man.[1] In any other sense we might as well call

---

[a] Letter supplied by the editor

18[1] "The first Error (or original Sin) of the shaping life-force". For the *vis vitæ* see e.g. *TL* (1848) 44. The notion of a "plastic force" operative in nature, which commended itself to Cudworth, Sir Thomas Browne, Stillingfleet, and the early C, was giving way to the advance of science by the 1830s.

18[2] Cf **4** and n 1, above. See also H. COLERIDGE **44** and n 2.

20[1] Cf *P Lects* Lect 2 (1949) 99–100, in which C supposes the doctrine of metempsychosis "a common feeling spread thro' many nations" but not necessarily originating in Pythagoras.

~~manure~~ a chemical treatise on the nature of *Manure* a doctrine of Metempsychosis—

21   p 478, pencil

It appears wonderful that Empedocles, Socrates, and Plato, philosophers otherwise so enlightened, should have adopted it [the doctrine of metempsychosis], without examination.

O for the proofs!

WILLIAM DUNBAR

c 1460–c 1520

LOST BOOK

The Poems of William Dunbar, now first collected. With notes, and a memoir of his life. By David Laing. 2 vols. Edinburgh & London 1834. 8°.

Not located; marginalia not recorded. *DC SC* (1891) 894: "a few autograph notes of S. T. Coleridge, and bookplate of Rev. D. Coleridge".

GEORGE DYER

1755–1841

George Dyer left Christ's Hospital in 1774, took his degree at Emmanuel College in 1778, and by 1792 was established in Clifford's Inn, where he lived in rooms over an attorney's chambers, "like a dove over an asp's nest". Leigh Hunt remembered him as a man "whose life was one unbroken dream of learning and goodness, and who used to make us wonder with passing through the school-room (where no other person in 'town clothes' ever appeared) to consult books in the library". Whether or not C had met him at Christ's Hospital, he was taken by a fellow Grecian to breakfast with Dyer in Sept 1794 and the meeting was a great success: see *CL* I 97–8. It is from Lamb, however, that we know most about Dyer's amiable unworldliness, his agonised poetic conscience, and the industry and learning that drove from his pen much that is now forgotten. See e.g. *LL* I 262–3, II 28–30. Drawn into the periphery of the C–Lamb–RS–WW circle, Dyer contributed to both volumes of the *AA* (1799, 1800). For his activities in preserving Chatterton's work see the ms collection in BM C 39 h 20 (1). In Mar 1804 C protested against an anecdote that Dyer had published in the *M Mag* that C was afraid would offend Samuel Butler or J. H. Frere (*CL* II 1091 and headnote); Dyer referred to the episode in his *Privileges of the University of Cambridge* (1824), a copy of which he presented to C. In a letter of 6 Jun 1828 C addressed Dyer as "Brother Blue, Brother Grecian, Brother Cantab., Brother Poet, and last best Form of Fraternity, a Man who has never in his long life by tongue or pen uttered what he did *not* believe to be the truth from *any* Motive". *CL* VI 746.

The other Dyer books that C read, owned, or knew are described in the Appendix of Marked Books.

Academic Unity; being the substance of a general dissertation contained in The Privileges of the University of Cambridge, as translated from the original Latin: with various additions.... With a preface, giving some account of the Dissenting Colleges in the United Kingdom, and of the London University. London 1827. 8°.

Victoria College Library (Coleridge Collection)

Inscribed on p ⁻2: "S. T. Coleridge Esq: From the Author." Corrections by the author in ink on pp xxx, xxxiii, ii (second pagination), 49, 78, 96, 130.

DATE. 1827, after Apr.

1   pp 63–4 | Ch 32 "A Comparison Made Between the Modern and Ancient Subscriptions and Oaths"

Why, Are not all *in statu pupillari*—as they are wont to put the question—required to use according to custom the form, and creeds, and prayers of the Church of England? Are they not bound to receive the Lord's Supper according to the rites of administering it in the *] Church of England? And he who subscribes, that he is *bonâ fide* a member of the Church of England, what else does he subscribe— only more fully—but that on what as a mere youth he professed, he is now of an age competent to give his judgement; that he now in *foro conscientiae* believes, and in sincere faith professes it?

* I do not agree with my friend, G. D. in this point. A man may rightly call himself a bonâ fide *Member* of the Church of England, who attends its assemblies, uses its ordinances, and prefers its communion on the whole to any other Religious Society, which it is in his power to connect himself with—who believes, that tho' it may have both errors and defects, yet they are not such as to present any serious obstacles to his Salvation, or sto counter-balance the aids and comforts which its many excellencies afford him.—More than this is required of a *Minister* of the Church but no more of a Member.

S. T. Coleridge.

Poems, by George Dyer. London 1800, 1801. 8°.

This copy includes the unique copy of the cancelled Preface of 1800 (title-leaf + 68 pp). Bound as first with GODWIN and FITZGIBBON.

British Museum C 45 f 18 (1, 2)

Charles Lamb's copy, inscribed by him in ink on p ⁻3: "This Book contains Poems by G. Dyer Godwin's Reply to Parr, Mackintosh &c. Speech of Lord Baron Fitzgibbon on Catholic Question." On p 161 Lamb has cancelled two stanzas that the printer had repeated in error; on p 208 he has altered "Darwin" to "Rogers", and "doctor" to "banker", writing "1ˢᵗ edit." in the margin (for Dyer's anxiety about these words, see *LL* III 300); on p 234, in *The Balance*, he has corrected "would" to "'twould".

On the Advertisement to the *Poems* (1801) (leaf following the title-leaf), Lamb has written beside Dyer's notice of the cancellation of the 1800 Preface: "one copy of this cancelled preface, snatch'd out of the fire, is prefixed to this volume". (The Preface shows no sign of having suffered ordeal by fire.) For Lamb's account of Dyer's dramatic decision to cancel the Preface and later giving Lamb the "burnt" Preface see *LL* (M) I 262–3, II 29. The whole volume was evidently set up late in 1800, with the Preface: the "Introductory Poems"—the beginning of the prefatory matter as issued in 1801—begin at p lxix. On p lxv of the Preface, Lamb has altered Mrs. "Donne" to Mrs. "Drury"; and on p lxxxiv, "laurels" has been altered to "laurel", by Lamb or C.

DATE. Probably Nov 1801–Feb 1802, in London, when C was seeing much of Lamb.

1   pp xxvi–xxvii | cancelled Preface

Panegyric, in the hands of a mere rhymster, is almost sure to sink into insipidity; in the hands of a poet, it may swell into flattery. Here, probably, Pindar and Horace grew extravagant.

PINDAR—and—who?——*Horace*!!! and pray, good George Dyer! in what ode or fragment of the Theban Republican do you find Flattery? I can remember no one word, that justifies the charge. As to Horace, ~~thanks~~ praise be to him as an amiable gentleman, & man of fine courtly sense—thanks & thanks for his Satires & Epistles, & whatever is "sermoni proprius"¹—& his little translations or

1¹ By correcting *sermoni proprius* to *sermoni propius* ("nearer to [common] speech" or "to prose") C draws attention to its source in the phrase *sermoni propiora* in Horace *Satires* 1.4.42 (cited by Dyer on p liv), to his own earlier use of it, and to an Elian jest that stuck in C's memory. He had chosen *sermoni propiora* as epigraph to his *Reflections on Having Left a Place of Retirement* in *Poems* (1797), but the second word was misprinted *propriora*. PW (EHC) I 106. Lamb, a good Latinist and fond of Horace, not only noticed the slip but

originals of light & social growth, thanks for them too!—But as a Poet, a Lyric Poet, a Companion of *Pindar*, or the Author of the Atys—(be he Catullus or some unknown Greek—)²—it won't do! No!—

2 p 214 | *The Poet's Fate*

[Footnote to "But should I poems eucharistic pen":] JOSHUA BARNES was Greek professor in the university of Cambridge, at the close of the last century; eminent and learned, though inclined to trifling and pomposity....He was...no unsuccessful versifier of Greek, and turned the book of Esther into Greek heroics, with as much ease as he made the following lines kick * with k, and rattle with r.

> "Three blue beans in a blue bladder,
> "Rattle, rattle, rattle."

* Alludes, I suppose, to the Greek Translation of the Lines, which was not by Barnes—

Τρεις κυαμοι κυανοι κυανῳ ἐνι κῦστι κεχεῦντο.¹

S. T. C.

3 p 299 | *Poetic Sympathies*

[Footnote to "Thus gay Anacreon felt the Lesbian's strain":] Sappho, loved by Anacreon. Her celebrated ode beginning,

Φαινεται μοι κηνος ισος θεοισιν,

made capital of it, translating it as "properer for a sermon". *TT* 26 Jul 1832. C, however, claimed that version in a letter to Sotheby on 10 Sept 1802 (*CL* II 864), and again in *BL* ch 1 (*CC*) I 26, writing *propriora* to point the joke—a detail lost by silent editorial correction in both eds of 1847 and 1907.

1² Several of Catullus' poems are translated or imitated from Greek originals; internal evidence strongly suggests that the *Attis* (or *Atys*) is one of them, though the brilliant management of subject matter and metre is surely Catullus' own. The poem describes the self-castration of the Greek youth Attis as an act of devotion to Cybele, and his journey in an ecstatic frenzy to the forests of Mt Ida, the dwelling-place of the goddess. Cf ACTA SEMINARII 1.

2¹ A tongue-twister in the form of a hexameter: "Three blue beans have been bundled up in a blue bladder." The author of the Greek is not identified. Joshua Barnes (1654–1712) was a Bluecoat; perhaps the Greek jingle was still current at Christ's Hospital in Dyer's time, and in C's.

is produced by Longinus as one of the noblest and completest examples of the <u>sublime;</u> and it has been transferred into all languages that have attempted poetry.

—no such thing. Longinus was no very profound critic; but he was no Blunderer.[1] Of the energetic, of the language of high excitement, elevated from passion, in short, ὑψοτητος παθητικης,[2] of this indeed it was, is, & probably ever will be, the most perfect specimen. But as to Sublime you might as well call it Blue, or Snub-noscd.

4   pp 325–6 | *The Redress*

[Footnote to "But genuine wit is sure to find a sale":]...That the principal and immediate aim of poetry is, to please, has been opposed by Julius Scaliger, and some other critics. But though I must admit that,

      Omne tulit punctum, qui miscuit utile dulci,[1]

yet will I still abide by Aristotle's and Plutarch's opinion, that the immediate object of poetry is, to please, and that even in solemn subjects poetry is used to render them more engaging and agreeable.

Damned Nonsense! But *why* does it please? Because it pleases! O mystery!—If not, some cause out of itself must be found. Mere utility it certainly is not—nor mere goodness—therefore there must be some third power—& that is Beauty, i.e. that which *ought* to please./

    My benevolent Friend seems not to have made an obvious

3[1] C is correct. What Longinus says (9.15–10.4), in answer to his own question "What else can make style elevated?", is that Sappho shows her excellence "in the skill with which she selects and combines the most striking and intense of those symptoms"—i.e. of "erotic mania". He quotes four strophes of Sappho beginning φαίνεταί μοι κῆνος ἴσος θεοῖσιν but only to illustrate "the skill with which she chooses the most striking [symptoms] and combines them into a single whole". Tr W. Hamilton Fyfe (LCL 1927). See also HERDER *Kalligone* **4**.

3[2] "Of elevation through passion". C objected to the translation of τὸ ὕψος as "the Sublime" on the grounds that the theme of Περὶ ὕψους is in fact "the elevated style of writing", and as a reminder that the eighteenth-century meaning of "the Sublime" as a term distinguished from "the Beautiful" should not be anachronistically ascribed to "Longinus". Cf HERDER *Kalligone* **6**. In *The Friend* C cites a passage from Jeremy Taylor as "at least in Longinus's sense of the word...*sublime*": *Friend* (*CC*) II 176, I 347n. See also ACTA SEMINARII **2** n 1. C, apparently thinking of ὕψος as an adjective, has coined the noun ὑψότης (not in Liddell & Scott), the correct (though rare) form being ὑψηλότης.

4[1] "He has won *every* vote who has combined utility with pleasure." Horace *Ars poetica* 343.

distinction, between end and means—The Poet *must* always aim at Pleasure as *his* specific *means*; but surely Milton did & all ought to aim at something nobler as their end—viz—~~the~~ to cultivate and predispose the heart of the Reader &c.—[2]

4[2] C was forcibly confronted with this issue when he co-operated with WW in the Preface to *LB* 1800 and 1802, as his letters to Sotheby show: see *CL* II 808–19, 855–9, 862–7. For C's doctrine that the immediate end of poetry is pleasure, the ultimate end truth see *BL* ch 14, esp (*CC*) II 12; see also II 8, 134, 214, 217–18 (on poetic faith). Shawcross printed this annotation from the BM ms in *BL* (1907) II 307 as a contrast to the definition of poetry that C gave in "On the Principles of Genial Criticism"—"the excitement of emotion for the purpose of *immediate* pleasure, through the medium of beauty".

THOMAS W. DYMOCK

fl 1648

Englands Dust and Ashes Raked Up, or, The King and People Beguiled. Being an historical narration, or a generall treatise upon the present warre, whose unlawfulnesse and authors are so plainly set out, as present his Majesties sufferings, and the malice of his adversaries, to a more neer and convincing discovery...penned at the last siege and surrendry of Newark upon Trent, &c. [? London] 1648. 4°.

Bound in "CIVIL WAR TRACTS".

Not located. *Lost List.*

MS TRANSCRIPTS. (*a*) VCL BT 37: SC transcript. (*b*) University of Texas (Humanities Research Center): ooo "CIVIL WAR TRACTS" headnote. The annotations are here printed from MS TRANSCRIPT (*b*)

DATE. Possibly autumn 1818, if the marginalia were written at about the same time that C acquired "CROMWELLIAN TRACTS".

1   p [vii] | To the Reader

[Commenting on a sermon of Latimer: "If the King should require of thee an unjust request, yet art thou bound to pay it, and not resist nor rebell against the King":]...yet now for humane ends, thou seest we are forc'd to forsake the Almighty, to deny the blessed conduct of his most holy Word, and turn our beliefe to a new piece of Parliament Divinity, which compels to pay no tribute to *Caesar*, but rather take violently from him his own inheritance, & royall patrimony, while he refuses to be under command.

The King (which in the New Testament ought to have been translated Emperor) means the Supreme Power, in whomever placed. In England it was placed in the King and two Houses of Parliament. The King separately from these was no more than a Constable without a warrant. S. T. C.

2   p [xii] | Preface

That if the King being seated at the top, and placed highest, as superior of the body, cannot be legally subject to the inferior

357

members at all, nor by conspiracie, without their owne finall detriment: For when the rest of the parts will combine to offer violence against their head, they are said in a desperate phrase to doe it, either by dashing out their braines, or cutting their owne throats, from both which they derive to themselves the just recompence of inevitable death: the King therefore cannot be capable of constraint from his vassals; for whom if they miscarry for want of temper ate his corrections, he is said in a qualified sense, to be generally accountable, which could by no meanes be, if his power were not above all men, and his dominion absolute.

Here we have an open avowal of arbitrary Monarchy, which Charles I encouraged in his followers, while he disavowed it in the public papers, written for him and in his name, but with his full consent and authority by Clarendon, Falkland and Culpepper.—[1]

2[1] Edward Hyde (1609–74), 1st Earl of Clarendon, Lucius Cary (c 1610–43), 2nd Viscount Falkland, and John Colepeper (d 1660), 1st Baron, rallied to Charles's support when he moved to York in Jan 1641/2. These three, at the King's direction, managed the King's parliamentary affairs, Falkland as secretary of state, Colepeper as chancellor of the exchequer, and Clarendon as chancellor in succession to Colepeper. For three years Clarendon drew up all the King's declarations; Falkland and Colepeper spoke for the King, presented the King's position to Parliament, and negotiated with Parliament on his behalf. See e.g. Clarendon *History of the Rebellion* Bk IV §§121–6 (1707) I 339–44. Cf HACKET *Scrinia* **38**.

ECLECTIC REVIEW

The Eclectic Review. Part of Vol IX, for June 1813. London 1813. 8°.

An incomplete copy of the June 1813 issue, comprising pp 637–46 of 565–678.

British Museum Add MS 34225 ff 170–4

The *Eclectic Review*, published monthly from Jan 1805, produced from C and RS an indignant reaction to an attack on Shakespeare in Apr 1807: see *CN* III 3246n, *Sh C* I 177n, *S Life* (CS) III 255. It reviewed WW's *Convention of Cintra* (1809) favourably, and in Oct 1811 devoted a long and perceptive review to *The Friend*. See *Friend* (*CC*) II 502, I lxxiv–lxxv; and cf *WL* (*M* 2) II 14. In Apr 1814, when RS was trying to persuade C to return to Keswick and earn a competence by reviewing, the two periodicals he had in mind were *QR* and the *Eclectic*, but C did not take up the suggestion. *S Letters* (Curry) II 94–5. In *AR* (1825) 331 C referred to the *Eclectic* as "our ablest and most respectable Review".

CONTENTS. The incomplete issue comprises (pp 637–43) a review of James Wardrop *History of James Mitchell, a Boy Born Blind and Deaf, with an Account of the Operation Performed for the Recovery of His Sight* (Edinburgh 1813) [not annotated]; (pp 643–6) a review of Thomas Morton *An Essay on the Trinity; Containing a Brief Enquiry into the Principles on Which Mysterious and Contradictory Propositions May Be Believed* (1813).

DATE. c 1813, after Jun. For parallels to the trinitarian material in the one annotation, of date before and after Jun 1813, see *CN* III 3934, 3968, *CL* III 480–6.

1   pp 645–6 | Review of Thomas Morton *An Essay on the Trinity* (1813)

[Quotation from Morton pp 10–11:] "It is certain, that our senses can never bear evidence on the subject of the Deity's non-relation to number, any more than they can on His non-relation to time and place: but, that the senses do not help us, is no proof that reason is our sole guide in this enquiry. Mortals are undoubtedly capable of receiving testimony on this subject; and this is certainly a subject on which testimony, compared with reason, is a superior and more valid species of evidence."

But if the words of the Testimony convey neither forms to the Imagination, nor relations to the Understanding, nor notions (ideas, at least) to the Reason—what *do* they convey? ~~but~~ s *Sound!* Let an

Angel descend or a prophet work wonders in proof of his veracity, and then ~~act out~~ utter certain sentences in the language of the third Heaven[1]—what can I believe but his *veracity*? or that *a something* had been spoken, which was *true*?[2]—O this weak way of arguing has done incalculable injury ⟨not only⟩ to the sublime Doctrine of the Trinity, in which are hidden all the treasures of knowlege; ~~&~~ but likewise to all the ~~other~~ aweful Truths *peculiar* [to]*a* Christianity, which the Doctrine of the Trinity is not: tho' it is the Rock on which they all rest as far as their ideal *possibility* is in question. For their *reality* we rely wholly on Revelations.—This most important ~~distinction between~~ interdependence of the distinct tho' inseparable, and equally necessary functions of Reason and Testimony, is the point, which our dissenting Divines are for ever overlooking—and pray, where did Mr Morton find the definition of Reason, contained in his *i.e.*?[3] I doubt, whether his words would not have been more apropós, had he been attempting to define a Turnip!

a Word supplied by the editor

1[1]. I.e. incomprehensible words. See 2 Cor 12.2–4 for a man "caught up to the third heaven...into paradise" who heard "unspeakable words, which it is not lawful for a man to utter".

1[2] For C's use of the word "veracity" see BAXTER *Reliquiae* COPY B **46** n 1.

1[3] C refers to the reviewer's quotation (p 646) from Morton pp 26–7: "reason, *i.e.* the conformity of a doctrine to the knowledge we possess".

EDINBURGH MEDICAL JOURNAL

The Edinburgh Medical and Surgical Journal: exhibiting a concise view of the latest and most important discoveries in medicine, surgery, and pharmacy. With plates. Vols XIV, XXIV, XXXIII. Edinburgh 1818, 1825, 1830. 8°.

Not located. *Lost List*. Annotations printed from MS TRANSCRIPT.

From James Gillman's set, which is shown in *Gillman SC* (1843) 376 as Vols I–XXXVIII (1805–32). George Grove, in his transcript of the notes (see MS TRANSCRIPT, below), stated that "These volumes having been in Mr Gillman's Library and bearing his Book-plate They were lent to me by E. J. Waring—in October 1843—who bought them from a man ["Smith" in the marked catalogue] who had purchased them at Mr Gillmans Sale at Southgate."

The notes in Vol XIV have been slightly cropped; those in Vols XXIV and XXXIII have suffered severe loss from cropping. Note 11 implies that there may have been other notes, either not transcribed from these three volumes or written in volumes Grove did not see.

In a letter to Green on 10 Apr 1824, C referred to a comment by the editor of "the Eding. Medical Review, last number"—i.e. *Edinburgh Medical and Surgical Journal* Vol XVII (no 34) of 1824. *CL* v 349. For Thomas Bateman as founder-editor of this journal, see BATEMAN headnote.

MS TRANSCRIPT. VCL BT 21 (12): George Grove's transcript—"Notes written by Mr Coleridge in different Volumes of the Edinburgh Medical & Surgical Journal"—dated "Thurlow Terrace Wandsworth Rd Decr 20th 1843", guarded in with a series of EHC transcripts of marginalia in a made-up volume. His transcript of C's annotation on Thomas MORE *Utopia* follows the notes on EDINBURGH MEDICAL JOURNAL.

DATE. Apr–Oct 1818; Jul 1825; Jan 1830—on the assumption that C read and annotated the numbers shortly after they were issued.

---

1   XIV 131, pencil[a] | John H. Fuge "Case of Gunshot Wound of the Heart"

On the day subsequent to that of his death, the body was opened.... On raising the sternum, the left side of the thorax was found to contain about two quarts of a serous fluid, slightly tinged with blood...on cutting into it [i.e. the pericardium], about half a pint of the same coloured fluid, as that found in the cavity of the pleura, was collected....

[a] Grove: "[At bottom of p 131 in pencil without any reference to particular passage.]"

361

In this very extraordinary [other] case, life was prolonged for nearly 14 days.... It is by no means difficult to account for the prolongation of life, where a sword or any other sharp instrument have been the weapons used; but how to explain the circumstance of the non-effusion of blood into the pericardium, at the moment of the accident, as well as subsequently, is a difficulty which hitherto I have been unable to solve.

n.b. what will the Unitarians, who rest the proof of Christ's actual Death on the water from the side[1] say to this and similar cases? They would gladly get rid of the ascension [i].e. the physical ascension recorded by Luke and yet this is the only *proof* of the Death, in *that* sense of the word proof.[2]

2   xiv 486–9[a] | Robert Hamilton "On the Early History and Symptoms of Lues"

The most common mode of inoculation, however, is by the lips and mouth, from sucking, kissing, using the same spoon, glass, pipe, &c. It is therefore to be regarded as contagious in the most accurate sense of the word...

Dr John Wynell [who wrote in London in 1659]... observed that the disease was not communicated by the air, and therefore contends, *a fortiori*, that it was not contagious!

If proof were needed of the general, only not *universal*, neglect of Logic among the medical professors in G. Britain and of the most important part of logical discipline, the appropriation of Terms, the words contagious and infectious would suffice—99 times in a 100 the etymological sense is inverted—the Itch called infectious, and the scarlet fever contagious. Now surely nothing but ignorance of the Latin Originals could have prevented us from appropriating the word "*contagious*" to those diseases which ordinarily require immediate *contact* for their communication and "*infectious*" to those which are supposed to stain, corrupt, or *infect* the air for a lesser or larger sphere round the body of the Patient, whether by the Miasmata floating in the air or by a specific change produced in the air itself.[1] Betwixt these

[a] Grove: "[written in Ink on bottom of pages 486, 7, 8, & 9]"

[1] See John 19.34.

[2] For C's reaction to the claim that Christ did not really die on the cross see DONNE *Sermons* COPY B **125** and n 3.

[1] C characteristically wishes to desynonymise the terms "infectious" and "contagious". Although some bacteria had been identified in his day (see BROWNE *Works* **50** n 1), infection had not yet been correctly defined and the various ways in which infection can be transmitted—especially through intermediate hosts—were not fully understood. If diseases were in fact transmitted in only two distinct ways—(*a*) by direct physical contact (contagious), or (*b*) by the

two lies the epidemic i.e. disease produced on many in different places at the same time, having its common cause in local circumstances, not orginating in animal disease, whether from the atmosphere or gasses from the soil, as in Marshes.[2]

3 XIV 487

Fifty years ago, it [i.e. sibbens] committed great ravages in the south of Scotland.... After what I have said, it will not appear strange that it should spread rapidly and be easily overcome. What is more contagious than the itch? What is more disreputable than its existence? Dr. Adams, when in this part of the world, could with considerable difficulty see only six cases. Dr Collingwood of Wigton informs us that it is now altogether unknown in the south of Scotland.

Credat Judæus Apella: non ego.[1]

4 XIV 487,[a] cropped

The disease still exists in some[b] force in the north of Scotland. They do not deny that it is an old acquaintance. They are, however, very unanimous in ascribing its introduction to the English soldiers who came among them under Oliver Cromwell, about the year 1650.

Some. When [. . . . .][c] a fine and matronly woman with an itchy child at her itch-scabrous Bosom used the following words "O Sir! for full sixty miles around us the Itch is the plague of Egypt! We bring it from the Womb into the Cradle and we carry it with us from the Coffin into the Grave. And why? the smallest number can afford to

---

[a] Grove: "[in ink on p 487.]"
[b] Underlined twice by Grove, presumably following C
[c] Grove has written above the elision: "(cut off in binding)"

---

medium of (say) air or water (infectious)— C's proposal would hold; this rule of thumb, applicable to treatment of infected patients at home or in a community suffering from epidemic disease, is still useful even if not philosophically precise or complete. For C's division into two kinds of "contagious diseases" see *TT* 7 Apr 1832. In his "Essay on Scrofula" (Sept–Nov 1816) C had also attacked the medical profession for lack of logical consistency and the use of imprecise terms.

2[2] For a discussion of contagion and epidemic diseases see *Friend (CC)* I 101–2 and n 1.

3[1] "Let Apella the Jew believe it; not me." Horace *Satires* 1.5.100–1. See also e.g. *Lects 1795 (CC)* 309, *AR* (1825) 309n. For C's direct observation of sibbens (sivvens) in Scotland see **4**, below.

burn their Clothes—so we are cured only to catch it again from our own garments."[1] S. T. Coleridge

5 xxiv 120, cropped | Review of C. F. H. Marx *On the Origin of the Doctrine of Contagion* (Carlsruhe & Baden 1824)

[Gregory of Nyssa is quoted, attempting to prove that those who minister to the sick poor run no risk of contagion:] "Some diseases," says he, "as pestilential attacks, and such as depend on an external cause, when they proceed from corruption of air or water, are suspected by many, of passing from those previously affected, to those who approach them. The disease, however, does not, as I think communicate the sickness by contagion; but while the common attack produces similarity of sickness, the disease arises from those who had first taken it, and proceeds to the others. Hence, therefore, the disposition to this complaint being established, and the blood undergoing a certain degree of corruption from the confusion of destructive fluids, the disease is confined to the individual patient...."

I doubt or rather I do *not* doubt, that this is a mistranslation—Probably the Greek runs thus—"but while the common infective cause (malaria, Airblight, Blasts from stagnant waters, or the like) produced [.....] similar[a] [.....] the Disease begins in those who were first exposed to the noxious influence, or were from peculiarity of depressive causes least able to resist it—and so proceeds in its attacks—i.e. and the [.....]"][b1]

[a] Grove: "[?]"   [b] Grove: "[a line cut off in binding]"

4[1] This observation recollected from the Scotch Tour of Aug 1803 is not recorded either in the journal C kept at the time (in *CN* i) or in the letters he wrote from Scotland. The medical terms are indistinct. "Lues"—the subject of the article C is annotating—a general term for contagious diseases of the skin, ill-specified but including leprosy and syphilis (*Lues venerea*). "Sibbens" (Gaelic for raspberry), the subject of 3 and 4—a non-venereal contagious disease of the skin epidemic at times in Scotland. "Itch"—generally scabies or eczema, but here perhaps a local term for sibbens.

5[1] The passage is in Gregory of Nyssa *De pauperibus amandis* ii (Migne *PG* xlvi 485–8), not cited by the reviewer. The Greek, as well as the translation, is confused. C gives Gregory's reasoning correctly. A modern editor, Arie von Heck (Leyden 1964), tries to save the situation by revising the punctuation, and would make the second sentence read: "...(The disease, however, does not, as I think, communicate the sickness by contagion; but the common attack produces similarity of sickness.) [They suggest that] the disease arises...". Gregory's opinion is resumed with "Hence, therefore".

6 xxiv 148–9, cropped | Review of J. H. Dierbach *Die Arzneimittel des Hippocrates* (Heidelberg 1824)

[The reviewer is discussing ch 2, a number of specifics used in antiquity:] The mixture of wine with honey, *mulsum*, Μελιχρος οἶνος, Οἰνομελι, vinegar Ὄξος, and oxymel Ὄξυμελι are well known; not, however, the mixture of milk with wine, Ὀινόγαλα,* which indeed was the least used of all the preparations of wine.

* An eminent Poet, had been married eight years, and his Lady still childless—I prescribed the οινογαλα in the form of Devonshire clouted cream and port wine [. . . .]*a* 3 wine glasses after dinner to each Patient, and nine months afterwards a large healthy Child was born—As far as could be conjectured three repetitions of the medicine in the dose above mentioned sufficed for the cure.[1] S. T. C.

N.B. The wine must be genuine Port, Old, strong bodied, and if it can be procured of a fruity flavour. The Cream must be [. . . . .]*b*

7 xxxiii 25, cropped*c* | James Syme "Quarterly Report of the Edinburgh Surgical Hospital from August to November 1829"

How then are the wounds healed by granulation?

Lymph being effused over the surface and organised into a granular pellicle, lymph and serum are effused into the subjacent cellular tissue so as to distend it more or less. In what is called a healthy granulating ulcer, the quantity is very small, so as hardly to affect the elevation of the surface, or induration of subjacent parts, but when the process proceeds in a morbid manner, then many remarkable phenomena are thus induced.

This appears to me far more than plausible—In the complexly organised Animals, in which the total organismus is a unity of many and perfectly distinct Integers—Brain, Vessel, Gland, and Nerve—I understand the reproduction is to be [. . . . .]*d1*

---

a Grove has written "over" above the elision, presumably marking the turn of the leaf
b Grove: "[cut off in binding]"; "clouted" is his conjecture for the first word
c Grove, at the beginning: "[apparently refering to no particular sentence in the Text]"
d Grove: "[cut off]"

6[1] The "eminent poet" who benefited from this miraculous cure is not identified. It could be RS: he was married Nov 1795, and almost seven years later, in Aug 1802, his first child Margaret was born.

7[1] On the superiority of "that individual which, as a whole, has the greatest number of integral parts" see *TL* 44; and on "granulation" see ibid 75–6.

8 xxxiii 27, cropped

And here I dare say it will be asked, if morbid structures be reproduced, why cannot the healthy tissues be regenerated? To which I answer by asking, Since the legs of salamanders and lobsters are reproduced after removal; why are not the limbs of man also *] reproduced? In studying the operations of nature we ought always to prefer facts to reasoning.

* A wretched answer to a question, to which it would not be difficult to return a rational and perhaps a satisfactory one—ex. gr. would any Physiologist hesitate if he were asked which of the two least resembled the substance of Polype[a]—a hand or a morbid[. . . .] tumour[b1]

9 xxxiii 28 | "At end of the paper"[c]

With deficiencies rather than defects a superior and very instructive paper. S. T. C.

10 xxxiii 39, cropped | R. Arrowsmith "Abstract of the Prize Essay of Dr William Horn...on the Poison Contained in German Sausages"

Dr Horn terminates his essay by saying, that he cannot concur in any of the opinions put forth as to the nature of this poison; and that it appears to him to be some matter developed by spontaneous putrefaction, and that this spontaneous putrefaction arises perhaps in improperly made farcimina.

It may be safely said, however, that putrefaction is not the proper term to apply here, for it is distinctly stated in the essay, that farcimina, known to be poisonous, were not to be distinguished either by their odour or taste. Some kind of degeneration may be correctly assumed; and it is highly probable that a principle of a peculiar nature, and poisonous, is thereby developed.

Thereby—*Whereby*—A peculiar poison it is highly probable is produced by a peculiar action—*Producing* very *probably* Inære[1]—is

[a] A slip for "Polypi"
[b] Grove queries his reading of the last two words, and above the elision has written "[cut off]"
[c] Grove's description

8[1] For the polypi as "individuality in its first dawn" see *TL* 72.

10[1] The meaning of this word—if correctly transcribed by Grove—is uncertain. "Without air", indicating e.g. an organism (anaerobe) that can live without free oxygen, seems unlikely, since such organisms were first identified and named by Pasteur in 1863. A more likely meaning occurs if the word is extended to "anaeretic" (ἀναιρετικός, destructive, poisonous), which in medical usage indicates an agent that destroys tissue, especially in the digestive tract.

it not possible that the poison may in these Sausages have originated in the skin or gut enveloping them? The mucus from the stomach after death is reported to form the base of a most deadly yet slow poison—in Turkey—At all events, the attempts to hunt down a poison of this kind by destructive destil[. . . . .]ᵃ

11 xxxiii 42, cropped | James Rankine "Case in Which Hydatids Were Contained in the Synovial Sheaths of the Flexor Tendons of the Hand"

Whether these hydatids are animalculae, as some have pretended, and that they belong to a genus of which they assure us there are different species, I cannot presume to decide; but in this instance they certainly appear to me to have been the production of disease; and it must be confessed it is rather a stretching of the known laws of
*] animal life, to suppose that a series of the same animals can be inclosed in one another like pill-boxes, as in some instances have been asserted.

* Why not? [. . . .] not every [. . . .] [. . . .]aved law [. . . .] Rabbit [. . . .]n? And why *must* we or need we assume that a [. . . .]tusᵇ a[. . . .]ant chasm every where subsists between partial life and integral? between *growth*, and self [se]parativeᶜ projective production?¹ In a former number of this Journal I have written a *Marginale*² on the so boldly asserted absurdity of admitting an exception to the "omnia ex ovo"³ i.e. that every [. . . . .]ᵈ

12 xxxiii 159, pencilᵉ | Review of William Stoker *Pathological Observations* Pt ii

He conceives that one of the great purposes of the liver is to contribute to the decarbonization of the blood.

I very easily draw the inference that the spleen probably assisted in carbonizing the Blood, the Liver in distributing the Carbon, and (so

ᵃ Grove: "[cut off]"
ᵇ Grove: "[*hiatus*?]"
ᶜ Grove supplies "[se]" and adds "[operative?]"
ᵈ Grove, after a long line of dots: "[cut off]"
ᵉ Grove's description

11¹ Cf the "*projective* reproduction" ascribed to the generation of fishes in *TL* 80–1. According to C, "growth" below the order of fishes does not have enough nisus towards individuation to be regarded as "projective"—i.e. shaping its development towards an end that is not implicit in its environment (*ab extra*).

11² For C a rare—if not unique—use of the singular form of *marginalia*. Either the volume that he refers to was not preserved or Grove failed to transcribe the note.

11³ For the principle of *omnia ab ovo* (everything comes from an egg), established in biology by Harvey, see Browne *Works* 50 n 1. Cf **13** n 2, below.

to speak) dis carbonizing, and so far indeed de-carbonizing, but that this function more especially belonged to the Liver.[1] S. T. C.

13 xxxiii 358, pencil, rubbed and cropped[a] | Review of Thomas Bell *The Anatomy, Physiology, and Diseases of the Teeth*

Now, without denying the well-established fact, that the teeth are often the seat of acute pain, and that this pain implies sensation, we think it more than doubtful that pain indicates the presence of nerves. It is quite certain that there are in the animal body textures in which nerves have never been traced by the most careful anatomists, and which, nevertheless, become the seat of most acute pain when inflamed.

Perfectly just—it is really refreshing in this paralogical age[1] to meet with such a chain of [. . . .] nervous substance [. . . .] molluscæ to the Mammalia—if the powers that in *it* become *manifest* had not subsisted as latent power in the inferior and antecedent textures.[2]

[a] Grove, at the end: "[In Pencil—very indistinct and cut off in binding]"

12[1] In *CN* iv 5425 (c 2–6 Aug 1826) C wrote: "Cyanic Gas/Carbon + Nitro-gene—explosive, forming rather ⟨than⟩ formed—this alternating with the pre-dominance of Carbon by aid of Hyd-rogen, and thus constituting a vital dynamic carbonization of the Blood, I suspect to be the Function and character of the Liver."

13[1] Cf "This is not a logical age" in *TT* 4 Jan 1823. See also **2**, above.

13[2] Cf "The Power which comes forth and stirs abroad in the bird, must be latent in the egg." *TL* 49. On individuation generally see *TL* 42, 75–6, 86; and cf 70: "the progress of Nature is more truly represented by the ladder, than by the suspended chain, and . . . she expands as by concentric circles".

JOHANN GOTTFRIED EICHHORN
1752–1827

Eichhorn, one of the chief founders of the Higher Criticism and of the rational school of Biblical criticism, Professor of Oriental Languages at Jena from 1775, was appointed Professor in 1788 at Göttingen, where C first met him in the spring of 1799. Eichhorn, like Blumenbach, paid C "the most flattering attentions" (*CL* I 494, cf 477); Carlyon in his account of the Göttingen episode reported that C was "well acquainted with Eichhorn" but that Eichhorn "is a coward, who dreads his arguments and his presence". Carlyon I 100n. At that time C studied Eichhorn's work with some care, saying some years later that Eichhorn's "lectures on the New Testament were repeated to me from notes by a student from Ratzeburg, a young man of sound learning and indefatigable industry". *BL* ch 10 (*CC*) I 207; cf *CL* II 861. There is no evidence that C brought any of Eichhorn's works home with him in 1799; but in Sept 1802 he cited Eichhorn's theory of the authorship of the *Wisdom of Solomon* in opposition to William Taylor's view (*CL* II 860–2), and in 1826 he said that he had had Vol I of the *Commentarius in Apocalypsin Joannis* "for years" (*Apocalypse* COPY B 1).

In the spring of 1810 C was testing HC's precocity with arguments about Esther from the *Einleitung in das Alte Testament* (*CL* III 286); the earliest marginalia in that work were written between that time and about 1812. Intensive reading and annotation of Eichhorn came later, in 1818–19—some of it, at least, in connexion with a projected series of literal and metrical translations from the prophetic and poetic books of the Old Testament: see *CL* IV 811. By Mar 1819 he had written extensive notes in four of the five Eichhorn works that he is known to have annotated, for he told DC that he must read "Eichhorn's introductions to the O. & N. Testament, and to the Apocrypha, and his Comment on the Apoc[al]ypse (to all which my Notes and your own previous studies will supply whatever antidote is wanting)". FIELD 1.

When C undertook a systematic study of the Bible in 1827 and began to prepare in his notebooks a detailed commentary intended for publication, he regularly consulted Eichhorn's works. These provided him with some fruitful suggestions and the resistance of argument; but, as his note to DC testifies, he was not uncritical of Eichhorn's way of mind and was determined that his own exegesis should rectify any errors of fact or judgement that he found in Eichhorn. In c Jul 1827 he noted: "The great defect in Eichhorn's work is, in my opinion, not so much the several arbitrary and improbable Points in his Theory, as the deficiency of determinate Dates and Circumstances, when and under which he supposes it possible that such momentous additions [to] the Facts narrated orally by the Apostles might have been made...". N 34 ff 14–14ᵛ (*CN* v). He noticed at times instances of "shocking impudence, almost blindness of heart, in Eichhorn". N 41 f 38ᵛ (*CN* v) (c Jun/Jul 1829).

C's sympathetic but wary feeling for the Higher Criticism, however, brought him under suspicion in some clerical circles. See e.g. BM MS Egerton 2801 f 232 (also *IS* 387): "The poltroonery of our clergy in their anxiety to suppress the arguments of Infidels or Heretics. Ex. gr. I was speaking of Eichhorn's Theory of the three first Gospels, and his View of the Apocalypse to an Oxford & lettered Clergyman—and the answer was—I don't wish to hear anything about [that]. Let them keep it to themselves. And recommended silence to me, lest some busybody may translate it.—As if Truth were to be prized because and as far as it happened to be Christianity, and not Chr. because it is the Truth."

ARRANGEMENT OF ENTRIES. After *Allgemeine Bibliothek*, the Eichhorn titles are here arranged according to the order of the parts of the Bible to which they refer. Within the EICHHORN author-entry abbreviated short-titles are used in referring to the annotated works:

AT—Einleitung ins Alte Testament
Apocrypha—Einleitung in die apokryphischen Schriften des Alten Testaments
NT—Einleitung in das Neue Testament
Apocalypse—Commentarius in Apocalypsin Joannis

Allgemeine Bibliothek der biblischen Litteratur, von J. G. Eichhorn. 10 vols. Leipzig 1787–1800. 8°.

Articles by various authors, compiled and edited by Eichhorn.

Not located

In an unfinished letter of 4 Jan 1820 intended for Hyman Hurwitz C supports his discussion of the incapability of the Jews "alike to submit to or successfully to resist the yoke of the Romans" with the remark: "see my Mss Note on the blank leaves of Eichhorn, Vol. X.". *CL* v 3. No volume of the known annotated works of Eichhorn can be plausibly identified as "Eichhorn, Vol. X.", and no recorded marginal note on Eichhorn corresponds to the description in C's letter. The work is identified as *Allgemeine Bibliothek der biblischen Litteratur* by a reference to "C. F. Dornedden, Eich. Bibl. X. p. 360" in *CN* IV 4625 (c Oct–Dec 1819) and, in the same notebook entry, by detailed reference to articles in x 177–88. Other notebook entries—*CN* IV 4626, 4794, and 4796—also make detailed use of articles in IX and X.

It is not known who owned these volumes, nor is it certain that C had access to a full set.

MS TRANSCRIPT. BIBLE COPY B pp 904/5: a loose sheet of paper inserted, with two copies in an unidentified hand of a note by C that opens with a reference to "Vol. 9. p. 216"—i.e. *Allgemeine Bibliothek* IX 216. (This sheet is loosely inserted in the volume, not tipped in as described in BIBLE COPY B **75** n 1.)

DATE. c 1819 (*CL* v 3 and *CN* IV 4625) and perhaps later.

1 IX 216 | Review of *Die Orakel des Propheten Mica* ed Arnold Heinrich Grosschopf (Jena 1798)

[To this edition of Micah there is attached a little essay "On the Oracles of the Hebrews" in which "the writer says absolutely nothing new to those familar with biblical literature"; then:] Hierauf folgt eine prosaische Uebersetzung des Micha, die wir zwar grösstentheils treu und fliessend gefunden haben, wodurch aber doch der hohe Genius des Dichters gar sehr verloren hat. Den schönen 4ten Vers des 1sten Kap. übersetzt z.B. Hr. Gr.: "Es zerrinnen die Berge unter seinen Tritten, und die Thäler zerfliessen; wie Wachs vor dem Feuer, wie Ströme, die von Abhängen herabstürzen!" Vielleicht lässt folgende metrische Uebersetzung eher den Geist des Dichters ahnen:

> Gebirge schmelzen unter ihm, wie Wachs am Feuer,
> Und Thäler spalten sich,
> Wie Wasser, das vom Abhang stürzt!

Im Original finden wir eigentlich ein Hetrostichon, da das Bild von Wachs nur auf das Schmelzen der Gebirge, und das Stürzen des

Wassers vom Abhang, nur auf das Spalten der Thäler bezogen werden kann.

[There follows a prose translation of Micah that, to be sure, we find for the most part accurate and fluent, but in which the high genius of the poet is very much lost. The beautiful 4th verse of the 1st chapter, for example, Herr Grosschopf translates: "The mountains dissolve under his steps, and the valleys melt away, like wax before fire, like streams plunging from cliffs!" Perhaps the following metrical translation gives a better impression of the spirit of the poet:

> Mountains melt under him, like wax in fire,
> And valleys split open,
> Like water plunging from a cliff!

Indeed, in the original we find a heterostich, since the image of wax can be referred only to the melting of the mountains, the plunging of waters from the cliff only to the splitting of the valleys.]

Vol. 9. p. 216

Micah I.iv.[1]—If the Hebrew word translated wax could bear the sense of Cedar or Pine Wood, incomparably more just and sublime would the image be thus: As the Cedar-wood (or the varnished Cedarwood) in the fierceness of the dry Heat, the Valleys split—and the mountains melt under them as Waters that plunge from the Precipice.—[2]

The thunder or cannon-like explosions of the splitting Deal & Cedar-wood, yea even of the stoutest Oak & Mahogany, in the heat of Summer, must have struck & astonished every traveller in Sicily, Malta, and West Asia![3]—S. T. C.

2   x "blank leaves"

[A note commenting upon the incapability of the Jews "alike to submit to or successfully to resist the yoke of the Romans—(N.B. not from defect of power, but of union, not from any thing impracticable in the thing itself, but from the unfitness in the temper of the People—see my Mss Note on the blank leaves of Eichhorn, Vol. X.)..." *CL* v 3.]

[1] AV: "And the mountains shall be molten under him, and the valleys shall be cleft, as wax before the fire, *and* as the waters *that are* poured down a steep place."

[2] *NEB* reads:

Beneath him mountains dissolve
  like wax before the fire,
valleys are torn open,
as when torrents pour down the
  hill-side...

[3] See *CN* II 2628 (2–3 Aug 1805) and *CL* VI 937 (25 Apr 1833).

Einleitung ins Alte Testament.... Zweyte verbesserte und vermehrte Ausgabe. 3 vols. Leipzig 1787. 8°.

In uniform binding with *Apocrypha* and *NT* COPY A to form a set of 7 vols.

British Museum C 126 h 5

"S. T. C." label on the title-page of each volume. John Duke Coleridge's monogram on I ⁻5 (only).

Eichhorn's *Einleitung ins Alte Testament*, made up largely from his public lectures and from lectures given at Göttingen University and first published Leipzig 1780–3, provides background materials from the history of Israel, a history of the text and canon of the Old Testament, with linguistic aids and introductions to the several books. The book-by-book commentary begins at II 211 (§ 405). He develops the theory that the sacred literature of Israel was a human production developing slowly through various stages of semi-civilisation; at the same time he takes account of the divinely inspired ideas of which the Old Testament is an expression. He first used the term *die höhere Kritik*—the Higher Criticism—to distinguish the study of origin, content, significance, and development from the purely textual studies that had proceeded on the assumption of divine origin, declaring that this mode of inquiry was as applicable to sacred writings as to secular literature.

A copy of the Leipzig 1803 edition of *AT*—BM C 126 d 6—has "S. T. C." labels but no marginalia. It evidently belonged to Green, and includes in Vol III an undated letter addressed to Green by William Otter, first Principal of King's College, London, 1830–6.

DATE. Possibly 1810 (see *CL* III 286 on Esther) to c 1812 (if the "15 years" of **41** is taken literally); and as late as 1827 (**41** is dated 5 Jan 1827). On the questionable evidence of handwriting alone, the following notes appear to be early: **2, 11, 25, 32, 36, 40, 41** (first sentence), **45**; and perhaps **44, 48–51**.

COEDITOR. Merton A. Christensen.

1   I 44 | Ch 1 "Von der Hebräischen Litteratur überhaupt..." § 9

Wollte man nun diese alten Volksideen auch auf einen Hebräischen *Nabi* übertragen (welches aber meines Wissens bisher noch kein Schriftsteller gethan hat); so könnte man auch alle die Schriftsteller, von denen wir etwas im A. T. übrig haben, *Nebiim* oder Propheten nennen.

[If one were to assign these old folk ideas as well to a Hebrew *Nabi* (which so far as I know, however, no writer has yet done), he could also call all the writers from whom we have anything at all in the Old Testament *Nebiim* or Prophets.]

Spinoza in Tractatu Theol.–Polit.—[1]

2 1 +1 (original wrapper), referring to 1 62 | §15

[Footnote]...Allein 1. es ist falsch, dass die Juden keinen Unterschied zwischen den alten heiligen Büchern ihrer Nation und den so genannten *Apocryphis* gemacht haben sollen. Josephus, der doch auch mit den Griechischen Juden, deren Uebersetzung er in seinen Werken überall zu Grund legt, bekannt war, sagt ganz allgemein, von allen Juden überhaupt: "wir haben nur 22 Bücher, die bis auf Artaxerxes Longimanus Zeit abgefasst worden. Seit Artaxerxes bis auf unsre Zeiten ist zwar auch viel geschrieben worden; aber alle diese neuen Schriften haben gar das Ansehen jener ältern bey uns nicht."

[But 1. it is untrue to say that the Jews made no distinction between the old holy books of their nation and the so-called *Apocrypha*. Josephus, who was familiar with the Greek Jews and who used their translation everywhere as the foundation of his works, says quite generally of the Jews as a whole: "We have only 22 books, which were composed up to the time of Artaxerxes Longimanus. From Artaxerxes to our own time many more indeed have been written; but certainly none of these new writings have the esteem with us of those older ones."]

62. It seems to me, that Josephus's "δια το μη γενεσθαι την των προφητων ακριβῆ διαδοχην"[1] contains a full and most satisfactory solution of the Problem respecting the Jewish Canon, and its difference in kind from the Apocryphal Writings[2]—especially, when we conjoin with it the circumstance of the great majority of the latter existing only in the Greek Language—nay, a majority originally Greek—and the others in all probability in the spoken Language of Palestine, the difference of which from their Ancestral Hebrew, even

1[1] C may be thinking of *Tractatus theologico-politicus* ch 1: "...we must not suppose that everything is prophecy or revelation which is described in Scripture...". Cf ch 2: "...prophecy never rendered the prophets more learned... and...we are, therefore, not at all bound to trust them in matters of intellect." Tr R. H. M. Elwes. Cf **49** at n 1, below. C borrowed HCR's copy of the Paulus edition of SPINOZA *Opera* (2 vols Jena 1802–3) on 3 Nov 1812 and returned it with annotations on 26 Nov 1813. *CRB* 1 112, *CL* III 461. There are no annotations on the *Tractatus*.

2[1] Eichhorn quoted this phrase in 1 60 n *u* from Josephus *Contra Apionem* 1 8: "because of the failure of the exact succession of the prophets". Tr H. St J. Thackeray (LCL 1961).

2[2] Eichhorn 1 99–109 discusses Josephus' view of the formation of the Jewish canon in *Contra Apionem*: that the canon was closed in the reign of Artaxerxes Longimanus (465–425 B.C.), and that it contained 22 books divided into three classes—5 books of Moses, 13 of the Prophets, and 4 of "Morality".

as it is found in Malachi, must have [been]*a* felt as strongly by the Jews at & just before the Christian Æra, as we feel the difference of Pope from Chaucer, or as the Arabs their present Arabic compared with that of the Koran.—But the Διαδοχη³ alone would suffice. Suppose a high Court to have existed for a number of Centuries, & then to have ceased—but that a number of Volumes, containing the Dicta of ~~the~~ successive Lord Chancellors or Chief Justices—. How could any Publications of private Jurists be placed by their side?

3 I 109 | § 44

3... Daniel war ihm [Josephus] ein sehr wichtiger Prophet, dessen Weissagungen er öfters, in einer sehr starken Sprache, die genaue Erfüllung nachrühmt (§. 46). Und doch rechnet er sein Buch nur unter *] die βιβλους ʿΕβραιων, und αρχαια βιβλια, aus denen er seine Geschichte schöpft.

[To Josephus, Daniel was a most important prophet, the exact fulfilments of whose prophecies he often lauds in very emphatic terms (§ 46). And yet he considers the book only among the "books of the Hebrews", and "ancient books", from which he builds his history.]

* I have rarely found Eichhorn reason so weakly as on this Subject. From this expression contrasted with Josephus's infatuation in favor of Daniel I should draw the very contrary Conclusion/

4 I 109

It weighs with me somewhat against the belief of the universal admission of Josephus's Notion, that the Canonical or inspired Writers ceased under or immediately after Artaxerxes—that the early Church gave equal honor to several books of our Apocrypha.¹

---

a Word supplied by the editor

2³ "Succession"—from the Josephus quotation at n 1, above.

4¹ The books now included in the Apocrypha came to the Church from Hellenistic Judaism and were written c 300 B.C.–A.D. 100, mostly 200 B.C.–A.D. 70 before the separation of the Church from Judaism. The Septuagint accepted all of them except 2 Esdras and did not distinguish them from the books of OT (see *AT* I 73–95); the Vulgate included them for the most part (but see *Apocrypha* 1 n 1). In AV and other non-Roman versions they are either included in a separate section between OT and NT or omitted altogether. Eichhorn notices that Melito included Esdras (I 122), and that Origen included Baruch and 1 and 2 Macc (I 125–6).

5 I 132 | § 57

Kurz, die Geschichte spricht dafür, dass nach dem Babylonischen
*] Exil, und zwar bald nach der neuen Gründung des Hebräischen
Staats in Palästina, der Kanon fest gesetzt, und damahls alle die
Bücher darein aufgenommen worden, welche wir jetzt darin finden.

[In brief, history attests the fact that after the Babylonian Exile, and indeed
shortly after the re-establishment of the Hebrew state in Palestine, the canon
was definitively drawn up, and all the books that we find in it now were placed
in it then.]

* How does this agree with Eichhorn's own theory respecting the
VI first Chapters of Daniel[1]—As to Josephus's praises of Daniel, they
are = 0—does he not copy the fables of Maccabees II. &c &c—[2]

6 I 133–5 | Ch 2 "Geschichte des Textes der Schriften des A. T." § 58

Eine vollständige Geschichte des Hebräischen Textes würde alle
wesentliche und zufällige Veränderungen, welche er durch Jahrtau-
sende und Menschenhände, zu seinem Vortheil und Nachtheil, seit
seiner Abfassung bis und auf die neuesten Zeiten herab erlitten hat,
nach Ursachen und Folgen melden; und Integrität und Kritik auf
unbewegliche Felsen gründen, und unumstösslich beweisen, dass wir
selbst bey den Unvollkommenheiten unsres jetzigen Hebräischen
Textes dennoch die weisesten Anstalten Gottes zu verehren haben.

[A complete history of the Hebrew text would report all the fundamental
and inconsequential alterations which it suffered, to its advantage and
disadvantage, through thousands of years and human hands, with causes and
effects, from its original composition down to the most recent times; and
it would establish integrity and criticism on unshakable grounds, and
incontestably prove that, even with the imperfection of our present Hebrew
text, we nevertheless have the most profound precepts of God for our
reverence.]

5[1] Eichhorn is not consistent on this
point. In III 361–4 he states that Dan is
made up of three documents: chs 1–2, an
historical memoir written by Daniel
himself; chs 3–6, an exaggerated account
of Daniel written by somebody else; chs
7–12, an oracle written by Daniel.
Contrary to the present statement, he
says in III 183 that the book in its present
form was admitted into the canon only
within the Hagiographa (for which see **46**
n 1, below) because it reached the
compilers of OT after the books of the
Prophets had already been closed. See
also **48** and n 1, below.

5[2] C here seems to accuse Josephus of
copying "the fables of Maccabees" Book
II. But C is in error. Josephus takes his
historical authority from 1 Macc and
ignores the fabulous retelling in 2 Macc.

My best judgement on this most important point is: that at or shortly after the completion of the Temple and the City Walls all the Books composed in Hebrew, and of a moral and religious character, which were in possession of the Priests and of the Heads of Families, were collected and placed in the Temple—that the collection was probably begun by Ezra, and carried on by Nehemiah, at the same time that I doubt not measures were taken, if not a body of men (the Scribes) instituted to prepare authentic Copies of the Law for the Magistrates, and of the Law, the Prophets & the Psalms, for such as were able & desirous to pay the cost of their transcription, as well as for the Temple Service, and the Synagogues.[1] The Psalms were, I doubt not, like the Greek Anthologies, appeared in two or three successive Collections—first, those extant before the Captivity & then, those that were composed during the Captivity, and on the Return, or during the Building & on the opening of the Temple—third, the two were united, and others of all the 3 Periods that had escaped the former Compilers, added.[2]—Of the other Hagiographa, I doubt not that such as had existed before the Captivity, (the abridged Annals continued under the supervision of Ez[r]a,[a] Nehemiah, or other Priests or Prophets,) formed part of this collection or Temple-Library, at that was extant as a *Bible* or Bibliotheca Sacra, at the close of the Reign of Artaxerxes.—But that after the plunder & defilement of the Temple, & furious war of extirpation waged against the sacred Books of the Jews, by Antiochus Epiphanes, and on the recommencement of the Temple Worship under the Maccabees, none were added/—this the style, idiom, above all the Contents, of two or three—(Daniel, Esther, Ecclesiastes) prevent me from believing: tho' I can readily understand, that such Books only were added that pretended to revered names.[3] The Assertion of the Talmud respecting the confacciamento[4] of Daniel by the Great Synagogue; the arguments afforded by the Septuagint; Origen's Annumeration of Baruch:[5] are of no decisive force indeed but yet

---

6[1] C is largely summarising *AT* I 59–132.

6[2] See *AT* III 83–140, 390–448, esp 418–26, which makes the same general point as C makes here. For the history of the Psalms see BIBLE COPY B **34** n 1.

6[3] C is drawing on *AT* I 59–61, 100–1 for most of this.

6[4] "Conflation"—i.e. of the three elements in Dan: see **5** n 1, above. C

seems to have constructed the word *confacciamento* on the analogy of the word he often applied to the 1818 revision of *The Friend—rifacciamento* (more usually *rifacimento*), reworking.

6[5] For the view that the Talmud put Dan in the canon see *AT* I 129–30, III 369n. On the formation of the Jewish canon, and Origen's inclusion of Baruch, see **4** n 1, above.

not to be slighted, as confirmations of a supposition so probable in itself.—We have abundant reason to bless the divine providence that the books of equivocal character are so few & [of]^a so little importance. S. T. C.

7 ɪ 138 | § 65

Lernte nun auch der grosse Theil der Hebräischen Nation (welches mir nicht einmahl wahrscheinlich ist) vor ihrem Auszug aus Aegypten schreiben: so musste es unter Anleitung Aegyptischer Lehrer geschehen, und die Hebräer mussten sich, wie nothwendig folgt, an Aegyptische Buchstabenschrift gewöhnen.

Aber, hatte auch kein einziger Hebräer vor dem Auszug aus Aegypten schreiben lernen: so war doch Mose, ihr Heerführer, darin geübt; und er schrieb gewiss mit keiner andern, als mit Aegyptischer Buchstabenschrift...

[Even if most of the Hebrew nation learned to write (which to me seems not at all probable) before their Exodus from Egypt, they would have had to do so under the direction of Egyptian teachers, and the Hebrews, as follows by necessity, would have had to become familiar with Egyptian writing.

But even if not a single Hebrew before the Exodus from Egypt had learned to write, still Moses, their army commander, was practised in it; and certainly he wrote in nothing other than Egyptian writing...]

But surely the Documents, from which Moses compiled the History from Adam to the Call of Abraham, were not Egyptian?

8 ɪ 142 | § 67

[In commenting that the Hebrew nation was much altered by admixture with the Babylonians during the Captivity, c 596–526 B.C.:] 70 Jahre darauf kehrte zwar ein grosser Theil in das Land ihrer Vorfahren wieder zurück; aber an eine Rückkehr zu den alten Sitten, der alten Sprache und der alten Schrift war gar nicht zu denken...

[After 70 years a large part did indeed return to the land of their former sojourn; but a return to the old customs, the old speech, and the old writing was not to be imagined...]

On what authority can Eichhorn have grounded this assertion? A comparative Handful of men (not 80,000) in all) appeared to have returned from Captivity, either under Cyrus, or Artaxerxes.—[1]

^{a} Word supplied by the editor

8[1] Ezra 2.64–5 and Neh 7.66–7 both give the same figure: 49,697.

9   ɪ 321 | Ch 3 "Hülfsmittel zur kritischen Bearbeitung des A. T." pt ɪv §164

[In regard to the Septuagint translation of the Old Testament:] Auch die Rechtschreibung der *nominum propriorum* ist in den Chroniken ganz anders, als in den Büchern Mosis. Richter, Ruth, Samuel und Könige zeichnen sich durch einen Sprachfehler, den sonderbaren Gebrauch εγω ειμι für εγω aus. So steht Richter V, 3 Ασομαι εγω ειμι τω Κυριω, εγω ειμι für ασομαι εγω τω Κυριω, εγω.

[Even the orthography of *proper names* is entirely different in the Chronicles from that in the books of Moses. Judges, Ruth, Samuel, and Kings distinguish themselves with a solecism, the unusual use of εγω ειμι [I am] for εγω [I]. Thus Judges 5.3 reads "I-am will sing unto the Lord, even I-am" instead of "I will sing unto the Lord, even I".]

Mallem, idioma insolens, et a Linguâ Græcanicâ alienum, quam peccatum grammaticum dicere. Werde Singen, ich setze mich, dem Herrn—mich setze ich.—Sic Anglicè: I myself quó "myself" in casu objectivo stat, verbo "mean", vel "put" subintellecto.[1] S. T. C.

10   ɪ 322 | §165

Alle schrieben in einer Griechischen Sprache, die ein starkes Hebräisches Colorit hat, oder, wie andre sprechen, in der Sprache der Hellenisten; alle haben den Fehler, den keine zum gemeinen Gebrauch bestimmte Uebersetzung haben sollte—den Fehler der Wörtlichkeit. Nur einer übersetzt immer noch sclavischer als der andre; und der Uebersetzer des Prediger scheut sich so wenig, wie Aquila, die *nota accusativi* את durch συν auszudrücken...

[All write in a Greek that has a strong Hebrew tinge, or as others have it, in the Hellenistic dialect; all have the fault that no translation intended for general use should have, the fault of literalness. One translates even more slavishly than the other, and the translator of Ecclesiastes has as little aversion as Aquila to expressing the mark of the accusative *eth* by συν...]

This is not however, without interest, to the general Philologist, as marking the primary force of the Greek συν—as equivalent to the

---

9[1] "I should prefer to call it strange usage, one foreign to a Graecising language, rather than a grammatical error. [I] Will sing, I set myself, to the Lord—myself set I.—So in English [we have] 'I myself', where 'myself' is in the objective case with the word 'mean' or 'put' understood."

To C, εἰμί (I am)—the verb substantive, as the old grammars call it, the name of God in Exod 3.14 (see BIBLE COPY B 119 n 1)—means *me pono*, I set myself, I posit or affirm myself; it is etymologically connected, he thought, with ἕζω, "I set", or (in the middle voice) "I sit". These ideas occur often in the later notebooks, especially in the Greek grammar of c May 1825 (*CN* ɪv 5227, in *SW&F*).

Hebrew *eth*, our *with*, the German *mit*, the Gothic *ga* or *go*, the Latin *cum*—all having the same import, namely, what *meets*, follows close upon, (σευω) objicit se verbo antecedenti—.[1]

---

11   ɪ 355 | §182

[On the Septuagint:] Die erste Frage gründet sich auf einige zwey-deutige Ausdrücke der Epistel des falschen Aristeas. Sie braucht von der Arbeit jener der Sage nach aus Palästina verschriebenen Gelehrten die Ausdrücke μεταγραφη, αναγραφη, γραμμασι ἑλληνικοις μεταγραφεσθαι, welche eine blosse Abschrift des Hebräischen Textes mit Griechischen Buchstaben anzeigen könnten. Allein dieselbe Epistel nennt ihre Arbeit auch ἑρμηνεια, διασαφεια u.s.w., und sollte man die erstern zweydeutigen Ausdrücke nicht aus den letzten bestimmteren erklären müssen?. . . Endlich *wem* konnte *damahls* eine Abschrift des Hebräischen Texts mit Griechischen Buchstaben nützen? Den Ptolemäern nicht: denn die verstanden wohl Griechisch, aber kein Hebräisch;—den Aegyptiern nicht, denn die alte Aegyp-tische, d.i. Koptische Sprache, hatte gar keine Verwandtschaft mit der Hebräischen;—den Juden in Aegypten nicht, denn durch eine Hebräisch-Griechische Abschrift wurde ihnen das Verstehen des Hebräischen Textes nicht erleichtert, sondern vielmehr erschweret. Und konnten sie die Hebräischen Originalschriften, ohne die Nothhülfe einer Abschrift mit Griechischen Buchstaben nich lesen; so war bey ihnen die Kenntniss der Hebräischen Sprache wohl schon ziemlich erloschen, und eine Griechische *Uebersetzung* war ihnen unentbehrlich.

[The former consideration is based on several ambiguous expressions in the *Letter* of pseudo-Aristeas. Of the work of those scholars who, according to the story, were recruited from Palestine, it uses the terms "transcript, copy, transcribed in Greek letters", which could indicate a mere transliteration of the Hebrew text in Greek characters. But the same Epistle also calls their work "interpretation, elucidation", etc; should we not therefore allow the former ambiguous expressions to be interpreted by the latter, more precise ones?. . . Finally, *to whom at that time* could such a transcript of the Hebrew text in Greek letters have been useful? Not to the Ptolemies, for they would

---

10[1] "Throws itself in the way of the preceding word". C's suggestion that σεύω is cognate with σύν is supported, though unemphatically, by Johan Daniel van Lennep (1724–71) *Etymologicum linguae graecae* ed E. Scheidius (2 vols Utrecht 1790). Cf *CN* ɪɪɪ 3276n for a copy C may have owned. C approved of Lennep's derivation of prepositions and conjunctions from verbs. Cf *TT* 7 May 1830: "All that is true in Horne Tooke's book ['Επεα πτερόεντα] is taken from Lennep." See also FLEURY **35** and n 1.

understand Greek but not Hebrew; not to the Egyptians, for the old Egyptian—that is, Coptic—bore no kinship whatsoever to Hebrew; not to the Jews in Egypt, for a Hebrew–Greek transcript would make an understanding of the Hebrew text not easier but much more difficult for them. And if they could not read the original Hebrew text without the help of a transcript in Greek characters, their knowledge of Hebrew was probably close to extinction, and a Greek *translation* essential.]

That the Alexandrine Copy delivered to the Græco-ægyptian Government was a Translation of Characters merely, I fully agree with Eichhorn in rejecting as absurd.[1] But yet that such a Work might have been undertaken for Masoretic uses,[2] does not seem to me improbable—⟨What if the Masora was executed after the Jews had rejected the Septuagint from hatred to the Christ[ians]*a*?⟩

12 II 5 | Ch 3 pt v § 339a

Inzwischen müssen wir doch bey Josephus, seiner Geburt, seines Vaterlands und ehemahligen Standes wegen, Kenntniss der Hebräischen Sprache voraus setzen; er war auch in dem Besitz eines vorzüglichen Exemplars der Hebräischen Nationalbücher... also die *Möglichkeit*, dass Josephus den Hebräischen Text bey seiner Arbeit zu Rath gezogen habe, wird niemand läugnen.

[With Josephus, however, because of his birth, his fatherland and former station, we must suppose a knowledge of the Hebrew language; he was also in possession of a superior copy of the Hebrew national books...thus no one will deny the *possibility* that Josephus consulted the Hebrew text in the course of his work.]

must? So far from its being a necessary, I do not think it even a probable, inference. Whatever he made himself in after life, yet neither by birth, breeding or Station was Josephus a Man of Letters—& the Hebrew was at that time a *learned* Language.[1] I

---

a This word is written scramblingly at the extreme foot of the page but is not cropped

11[1] The "Masora"—the Massoretic text of OT, now standard, prepared by Jewish grammarians between the sixth and tenth century A.D. with vowel points and accents to preserve exactly the oral tradition of pronouncing the (unpointed) Hebrew text. The word *Masoreth* probably means "tradition". The Septuagint—so called because it was said to have been prepared by seventy-two translators for the Museum at Alexandria at the order of Ptolemy Philadelphus, according to Aristeas reported by Josephus (see T.

FULLER *Pisgah-Sight* **3** and n 1)—was a translation of the Hebrew OT into Greek, finished c 132 B.C. Until the later fourth century A.D. it was regarded as the standard form of OT among Greek-speaking Christians.

11[2] I.e. to provide the correct pronunciation.

12[1] In *Jewish Antiquities* 10.10.6 Josephus himself speaks of translating "the books of the Hebrews" into Greek. See also *AT* I 109.

should almost as soon expect to find a deep Sanscript Scholar in a Sepoy Serjeant.[2] That he might have frequently consulted ~~the~~ some Syro-chaldaic Commentary is much more likely.

EINLEITUNG IN JEDES EINZELNE BUCH
DES ALTEN TESTAMENTS

13   II 224–6, pencil[a] | Moses § 409

[On the theory that the Pentateuch could not have been written after the time of Moses:] Hingegen waren nur diese fünf Bücher bey der Trennung der beyden Reiche schon vorhanden; so mussten sie bey den Priestern, die sich in den zehn Stämmen aufhielten, in mehreren Exemplaren zu finden seyn. Diese sprachen nach der Trennung, wie vor dem, daraus das Recht, und so erhielt sich der Samaritanische Pentateuch in dem Ansehen eines heiligen Nationalbuchs auch in diesem Reiche. Nun hat dieser schon alle die Glossen und Einschiebsel, die auch in der Abschrift der Juden vorkommen; und da sich wieder bey dem Hass der beyden Reiche nicht begreifen lässt, wie eines dem andern diese Glossen hätte abborgen mögen: so folgt, dass sie schon bey der Trennung der beyden Reiche eingetragen waren, oder, welches einerley ist, dass diese Bücher damahls schon ein Alter hatten, welches manche Erläuterungen nothwendig machte.

[On the other hand, if only these five books already existed at the time of the separation of the two kingdoms, they must have existed in several copies among the priests who remained with the ten tribes. After the division, as well as before it, they gave the Law out of them, and so in this kingdom too the Samaritan Pentateuch had the status of a sacred national book. It even has all the glosses and interpolations that also occur in the version of the Jews, and since it is not conceivable how, in view of the hatred between the two kingdoms, one could borrow these glosses from the other, it follows that these already existed at the time of the division or—which is the same thing—that these books were at that time so old that they needed much elucidation.]

Far, very far, am I from refusing a weight and worth to this celebrated Argument, first stated in its full force by Sir Isaac Newton.[1] But I

---

[a] The parts of the note written in the head- and foot-margins of pp 224 and 225 are confusingly offset upon each other and very difficult to read

12[2] Troops recruited by the British from among the natives of India and used as second-class troops were called Sepoys. C may have had in mind Josephus' record as a minor military organiser and leader before his removal to Rome.

13[1] Isaac Newton *Observations on the Prophecies of Holy Writ*...pt 1 ch 1 § 4: *Works* ed Samuel Horsley (5 vols 1779–85) v 299. C had known the work since 1796: see *CN* I 82, 83, and nn.

Juda: aber ehe es ein ächtes Exemplar davon aus
Reiche Juda kommen ließ, sezte es lieber ein ne
Buch Josua aus allerley verdorbenen Sagen und
genden zusammen, das die Samaritaner noch jezt
sizen. Hingegen waren nur diese fünf Bücher bey
Trennung der beyden Reiche schon vorhanden; so m
ten sie bey den Priestern, die sich in den zehn St
men aufhielten, in mehreren Exemplaren zu finden s
Diese sprachen nach der Trennung, wie vor dem,
aus das Recht, und so erhielt sich der Samaritani
Pentatevch in dem Ansehen eines heiligen Natio
buchs auch in diesem Reiche. Nun hat dieser s
alle die Glossen und Einschiebsel, die auch in der
schrift der Juden vorkommen; und da sich wieder
dem Haß der beyden Reiche nicht begreifen läßt,
eines dem andern diese Glossen hätte abborgen mö
so folgt, daß sie schon bey der Trennung der bey
Reiche eingetragen waren, oder, welches einerley
daß diese Bücher damahls schon ein Alter hatten,
ches manche Erläuterungen nothwendig machte.

Von dieser Zeit an bis auf seine Zerstörung d
Nebukadnezar wird im Reiche Juda fast alle fun
Jahre eine Erneuerung der Geseze und eine Refo
des Gottesdienstes nach ihnen vorgenommen. J
phat befiehlt den Leviten, in allen Städten seines Re
herum zu reisen und das Volk zu unterrichten: und
nehmen in dieser Absicht das Gesezbuch (תורה
1 Chronik XVII, 9) mit. Beyde, Jojada (2 Chro
XXIII, 18) und später hin Hiskias (2 Chronik XX
3), stellen den Gottesdienst so her, wie er „im Ge
Mosis vorgeschrieben war" (כתיב כתורת משה
Aber gleich darauf verfiel er auch unter Manasse's i
ligiöser Regierung wieder; und Josias schreitet zu
ner neuen Reforme nach der Vorschrift dieser Büc
(2 Chronik XXXIV, XXXV). Von dieser lezten Re
gu

ng des Gottesdienſtes bis auf den Untergang des
taats und ſeine Wiederherſtellung unter Cyrus ver-
ſſen nur einige Menſchenalter. Kurz vor dem Exi-
fordert Jeremias ſeine Zeitgenoſſen ununterbrochen
r Beobachtung dieſer Geſetze auf; in demſelben ge-
nkt Daniel (IX, 11. 13) der häufigen Uebertretungen
ſſen, „was in dem Geſetz geſchrieben war," und
r wirklich eingetroffenen Strafen, die den Uebertre-
en im Geſetz gedrohet waren; und nach demſelben
d dieſe Bücher die einzige Norm der neuen Einrich-
ngen. Die erſte Colonie ordnete nach ihrer Vor-
rift den öffentlichen Gottesdienſt, die Brandopfer,
s Lauberhüttenfeſt und die Neumonden an (Eſr. III, 2
ככתוב בתורת םש), und nach ihnen richteten ſich
ras und Nehemias ungefähr achtzig Jahre nachher
y der neuen Reforme der ſchon wieder halb verwilder-
n Colonie (Nehem. VIII, 1. 3. 8. 14. 18; IX, 3).

§. 410.
Eſras kann ſie nicht abgefaßt haben.

So folgt alſo von Jahrhundert zu Jahrhundert,
en von Joſua an, bis auf Eſras und Nehemias her-
, von der Exiſtenz dieſer Bücher eine Nachricht auf
e andere. Wie können ſie nun aus ſpäteren Zeiten
erſtammen? Und wer hätte ſie erdichten können?
Eſras, rufen ihre Feinde — Eſras nach dem Baby-
niſchen Exil! So müßte er denn auch alle andre
Schriften des A. T., die ſich an jene wie Glied an
Glied anſchließen, erdichtet haben? Dieß überſteigt
chtbar alle menſchlichen Kräfte! Wie hätte er im
Stande ſeyn ſollen, ſich in ſo verſchiedene Charaktere
u werfen, ſo oft ſeine Schreibart zu verändern, und
der Schrift und jeder Erzählung die natürliche Farbe
es Inhalts und der Stelle, in der ſie ſteht, zu geben?

II. Theil.   P   wie

do seem to see that too much has been attributed to it—that it has been unduly raised from a presumptive fact to an apo[dictic ?] "x y z"—not a probable [. . .] so impossible [. . .] [. . . .] and the impossibility [. . . .] tho' I allow the comparative [. . .] probability, I cannot even see any *positive* improbability in the supposition that the Kingdom of Israel, so confessedly inferior to that of Judea in Arts and Learning, should in some one of the brief alliances of the two Governments, have received or sent for a Copy of the Law Code, bearing the name of a Hero (Moses) of whom all 12 tribes were equally proud. The Baal Party were not always in the ascendant in the Kingdom of Israel. I say, I can see nothing *very* unlikely in this even tho' the present arrangement of the Pentateuch had been later than the reign of Rehoboam—which, however, on other grounds I hold to be grossly improbable.[2] On the other hand, I strove in vain hitherto to reconcile my feelings with the assumption that the first 12 or 14 Chapters of Exodus were written by Moses or any Contemporary Historian. They have a *traditional* character so sharply contrasting with all the following portions of the Pentateuch—that I am tempted to the conjecture, that they form a sort of biographical Introduction, connecting the Acts & Laws of Moses with the history of Joseph—i.e. with the conclusion of Genesis.[3] *S. T. C.*

14   II 239, pencil | § 414

Also, in der Voraussetzung, dass eine Cuschitinn aus Aethiopen in Afrika her seyn müsse, liessen die spätern Leser Mosis aus einer Araberinn eine Mohrinn aus Afrika werden, und verlegten den Anfang der Ehe mit ihr in die Zeit des ersten Aufenthalts Mosis in Aegypten (ob gleich der Umstand, dass Moses wegen dieser Ehe in *] der Wüste Vorwürfe hören muss, eine neue, erst in der Wüste geschlossene, Ehe, und keine, die schon über vierzig Jahre gedauert hätte, voraussetzt).

13[2] Cf N 26 ff 110v–116v (*CN* v) of 7 Jun 1827 (cf date of **41**, below)—a long note that begins: "First, endeavor to form a distinct notion of the Habits of thinking and feeling with regard to Literature, in the *most* (or rather in an *ultra*-) extensive Sense of the Word as comprizing all set forms of Words, oral and written, from a proverb...to a Book —the Pentateuch for instance,—of a People such as we know the Jews to have been from B.C. 975 to 445—i.e. from Jeroboam to Nehemiah..." and ends by referring to **40** or **41**, below. It is not known when the Pentateuch was arranged in the form now known to us.

13[3] Modern scholars do not hold such a view, but consider that these chapters of Exod were constructed throughout from a number of documents. See *Interpreter's Bible* I 833–5. See also **18** and **29**, below.

[Thus, on the assumption that a Cushite woman must be from Ethiopia in Africa, later readers of Moses made an Arabian woman into a blackamoor from Africa, and erroneously placed the marriage with her in the time of Moses' first sojourn in Egypt (although the circumstance that Moses had to hear reproaches out in the wilderness because of this marriage suggests a new marriage, concluded in the wilderness, and not one that had lasted for over forty years already).]

Where is the *proof* that the Cushites were Blackamoors in the time of Moses? It may have been so; but where is the Proof?[1]

15   ii 240–1, pencil | **14** textus

* This cuts both ways. Far more probable (might it be said) and more in character of a mutinous Malcontents to warm up an old reproach than of a Legislator and Chieftain, like Moses, to have set an example of transgressing his own regulations.[1] With his whole head and heart not merely filled but oppressed by the various and incessant Duties and Objects of his high Station, it was surely not the most likely time for him to have fallen in Love!—

16   ii 246–7, pencil | Moses bk i (Genesis) § 416a

Wäre sie aus blosser *mündlicher* Ueberlieferung geschöpft: dennoch würde mir das Buch wichtig und seine Quelle heilig seyn. Vorausgesetzt die grössere Lebenslänge der Menschen, so konnte in der ältesten Welt nicht so leicht und stark wildes Wasser in historische Quellen strömen. Denn da Lamech noch Adam, und Sem noch *?]Lamech, und jener noch Abraham, und Jacob noch diesen, und viele von Mosis Zeitgenossen noch Jacob könnten gesehen haben: so durfte eine mündliche Nachricht aus der ältesten Welt sich weder durch den Mund viele Glieder drängen und sich dabey formen, vergrössern und verunstalten lassen, noch durften andre etwas jüngere Nachrichten bis auf Mosen lange unaufgezeichnet im Umlauf seyn, ohne dass man noch ihretwegen, wo nicht beym ersten,

14[1] Num 12.1 AV: "And Miriam and Aaron spake against Moses because of the Ethiopian [*margin*: Cushite] woman whom he had married; for he had married an Ethiopian [*margin*: Cushite] woman." *NEB* reads only "Cushite". Gesenius glossed *kush* as the people and land of Southern Nile (Upper Egypt); some modern writers think that the reference is to the *kushi* of northern Arabia. See *Interpreter's Bible* i at Num 12.1. There is still no proof that the Cushites were black.

15[1] For the law against foreign marriage—Moses' "own regulations"—see Exod 34.14–16, Deut 7.2–3. Eichhorn (*AT* ii 241) notes another story, not in OT, about Tharbis, who, seeing the commander-in-chief Moses from the walls of beleaguered Saba, fell in love with him and offered herself to him after the city fell.

doch bey einem zuverlässigen Gewährsmanne hätte Rücksprache halten können.

[Even if it were made up simply from *oral* reports, still to me the book would be significant and its sources holy. If we grant the greater life span of mankind, it was not so easy in these earliest times for wild waters to flow into the historical sources. For since Lamech could have seen Adam, and Shem could have seen Lamech, and Abraham could have seen Shem, and Jacob could have seen Abraham, and *many of the contemporaries of Moses could still have seen Jacob*, an oral account from earliest times could not have been allowed to become exaggerated and disfigured by the creation of many additions from word of mouth, nor could somewhat newer accounts be long unnoticed in circulation until the time of Moses without there being someone who could have made reference back, if not to the first source, at least to a reliable guarantor in regard to them.]

* Has not Eichhorn forgotten the deluge and the shortening of human life? ~~How could Lamech who died before the Flood have seen Abraham?~~[1]—~~and~~ t Taking 500 years for the time from the migration of Jacob into Egypt to the Exodus of the Hebrews, and the then life of man at 120 years, how could a Contemporary of Moses have seen Jacob?

17   II 250, pencil | § 416b

Höchstens bleibt eine Reihe bedeutender Nahmen übrig, deren Erklärung mit dem Fortrücken der Zeit immer dunkler und ungewisser wird. Nun werden sie mit verschieden gewendeten Erzählungen begleitet; die Nachwelt erlaubt sich nach einer möglichen Bedeutung eines Nahmens eine neue Geschichte für ihn zu erfinden, die Witz und Vorliebe zu eigenen Einfällen dem Nahmen selbst bald angemessener finden wird, als die, welche noch in dunkeln Spuren übrig ist. So kommen wohl von Einem Manne Erzählungen verschiedener Art in Umlauf, die sich auf mögliche Ableitungen gründen *y*), und Etymologie wird eine Hauptquelle der ältesten Geschichte. [Footnote:] *y*) Der Fall ist bey Isaak 1 B. Mose XVIII, 15 vergl. XXI, 5. Andre Beyspiele s. 1 B. Mose XXX, 1–24 unten in der Denkschrift mit dem Nahmen Elohim. Aus dem Griechischen Mythus liessen sich unzählige Beyspiele der Art beybringen. Z.B. Argus hiess πανοπτης; daher geben ihm einige vier Augen, andre einen ganzen Leib voll Augen, u.s.w....

16[1] Eichhorn says that Shem could have seen Lamech and Abraham could have seen Shem. C acknowledges his own mistake by cancelling his question.

[At best there remains a list of significant names, the explanation of which grows ever more obscure and uncertain with the passage of time. Now they are accompanied by variously contrived tales; later generations permit themselves from a possible meaning of a name to invent a new history for it, which ingenuity and a predilection for one's own notions will soon find fit the name itself better than the old history, which has survived in obscure traces. Thus probably there come into circulation various tales about one man based on possible derivations *y*), and etymology becomes a major source of the most ancient history.

[Footnote:] *y*) The case with Isaac, Gen 18.15; cf 21.5. For other examples see Gen 30.1–24, below, in the document with the name Elohim. Countless examples of this kind may be adduced from Greek mythology. For example, Argus was called *panoptes*; from this, some gave him four eyes, others a whole body filled with eyes, etc....]

The Life of Homer by the ψευδο-Herodotus is a yet more striking Instance—blind, from α and οραω, a Hostage from Ὅμηρος, a cyclical Bard, from ομηρευεσθαι, concinere, &c.[1]

18 II 253–5

Die alten Lieder verlieren sich zwar allmählig; die Härte der alten Sprache, die Dunkelheit und Zweydeutigkeit des Ausdrucks bringt sie in den Zeiten der fortgeschrittenen Bildung aus dem Mund des Volks: aber die poetischen Ideen aus der Vorzeit bleiben doch; die spätern Dichter kleiden sie nur um, und die Stämme singen sie wie ehedem, nur aber in wohlklingendern und leichtern Poesien. Und da es überhaupt der menschlichen Natur so gemäss ist, alles *] Vergangene sich besser und edler, als die Gegenwärtige zu denken: ist es nicht sehr verzeihlich, wenn die späte Nachwelt blosse Bilder und poetische Ideen im historischen Sinn genommen hat?

[The old songs fade slowly enough; the crudity of the old language, the obscurity and ambiguity of the expression serve to hinder their use among the people in times of more advanced learning: but the poetic ideas from earlier times still remain; the later poets merely recast them, and families sing them as before, but in easier and more musical poetry. And since it

17[1] No one source has been traced for this. The pseudo-Herodotean *Life of Homer* (§13) says only that he was called Homeros after he was blinded, because ὅμηρος means blind in the Cumaean dialect. C must have meant to write μὴ ὁράω but made a natural slip: ά (but not μή, "not") is regularly and freely used as a negative prefix. (Cf ἀόρατος in *Apocrypha* 6 and n 5.) The etymology of ὅμηρος from μὴ ὁρᾶν by metathesis (from Theopompus in Harpocration) appears in Stephanus *Thesaurus graecae linguae* (1572), immediately followed by a general reference to Eustathius and the writers of the Lives of Homer. Ὅμηρος is the normal word for "hostage", and Plutarch's *Life* tells a tale of Homer's being a hostage. For "ομηρευεσθαι, concinere, &c" see HOMERIC HYMNS 1 n 1.

is generally characteristic of human nature to look on everything past as better and nobler than the present, is it not most forgivable that the later world has taken mere images and poetic ideas in an historical sense?]

* These universal Solvents too rarely prove satisfactory when applied to any *one* problem. Would that Eichhorn had made the attempt in the particular instance of Moses' and Aaron's negociation with Pharaoh, from the first Defection of the mirific Rod to the Passover![1]—If the wonders done & plagues induced were but physiosophic Predictions,[2] many of which were in the Almanachs, or figured Lamina, of the Court-Astronomers[3]—can this hypothesis be reconciled with the chronology given by the Books themselves?[4] Had the Negociation, like ours on the Abolition of the Slave-trade, lasted from 20 to 2 40 or 50 years, then indeed—[5]

Vide Shaksp's Dramatic Histories & our oldest *Ballad* Chronicles— for the crowding of Events.—*

* But Eichhorn's universal Solvents from p. 249[6] are not only Panaceas that make a poor figure as Specifics, but they force on his Readers the question—If E. was not laughing in his sleeve in §416, first half of p. 246,[7] what need of all these *might-be's*? Was it Lamech who told th a Lie to Noah, or Adam w that hum-bugged Lamech? Adam at least could not have been deceived. At least, it would suppose a strange colluvion[8] of belief-throttling Semi-possibles.

18[1] See Exod 3–14, esp 4.20. No internal chronology appears; the negotiations may have extended over a number of years and the accounts have been telescoped. Cf **29**, below.

18[2] I.e. predictions drawn from an "assumed knowledge of nature" (*OED*). C could, however, apply the word 'Physiosophs" less neutrally to the *Naturphilosophen*: see e.g. BÖHME ANNEX n 5. In C's mind there may be some connexion between "the mirific Rod" (cf Exod 4.20) in the previous sentence and the magnetic baguet (wand) of animal magnetism: see *CN* IV 4624 f 20. See also **38** and n 1, below.

18[3] See BIBLE COPY B 7 nn 1, 3.

18[4] The "chronology given by the Books" of the Pentateuch has so far defied the efforts of scholars to synchronise it with external history, with different versions of the Pentateuch, and within

the books themselves. See *Interpreter's Bible* I 142–52.

18[5] The slave-trade was abolished in the British sphere of authority in 1807 after almost half a century of agitation. Universal abolition was not achieved until Aug 1833. See ANALYSIS 7 and n 1.

18[6] Eichhorn assists his arguments with various general assumptions that C calls "universal solvents": here, that "it is generally characteristic of human nature to look on everything past as better and nobler than the present"; at II 251, that primitive people were proud of their ancestry, as shown by the genealogies in the Pentateuch; at II 252, that the language of primitive peoples was rude and "ganz poetisch".

18[7] See **16** textus, above.

18[8] *Colluvion*, from the Latin *colluvio* (a jumble), particularly appropriate in its literal sense (washing together) to the

ex. gr. All Adam's Fellow-men destroyed by Earth-quakes & Inundations—himself drowned & his body half-imbedded in the sediment of umber o̶r̶ Sludge—humane-societied by the heat of the S̶o̶n̶ Sun[9] after the waters had dried away—but from fright &c with the entire loss of his memory—&c &c.—

19 ii 256–7, pencil

It would be amusing, aye and instructive, to place two collateral tables before the eye—the first column or side being a catalogue of the Positions asserted and presumed by Moses, & all who receive the Book of Genesis as a history of actual facts/ the second, a catalogue of all the *sup*positions necessary to or implied in, Eichhorn's ⟨*bar-miracle*⟩ *theory* of Nature & the Natur-mensch.[1]

20 ii 261, pencil | § 417

Einige Kapitel des ersten Buchs Mosis tragen das deutliche Gepräge einzelner für sich bestehender Urkunden, deren Verfasser sonst weiter keinen jetzt noch sichtbaren Antheil an den übrigen Theilen desselben haben. Gleich das zweyte Kapitel vom vierten Vers an und das ganze dritte machen so ein eigenes, abgesondertes Document aus. Mit dem ersten hängt das zweyte vom vierten Vers an nicht zusammen.

[Several chapters of Genesis carry the clear imprint of single independent documents, the authors of which have no detectable hand in the other parts. Thus the second chapter from the fourth verse onward and the entire third constitute such an individual separate document. The second from the fourth verse onward has no connexion with the first.]

---

drowning of Adam. Not in *OED* but see "colluvies", citing *Rees's Cyclopaedia* (1819): "a term which...writers on the universal deluge have applied to the fluid mass into which...the strata of the antediluvian world were dissolved". See also FABER **11** and nn 1, 2.

18[9] For C's frequent merging of "Son" and "Sun" see AURELIUS **35** n 2. The Humane Society was on its formation (1774) named the Society for the Recovery of Persons Apparently Drowned, its motto being "Lateat scintillula forsan [peradventure a little spark may yet lie hid]". Cf HERDER *Von der*

Auferstehung **17** n 1. See also in FABER **11** n 2 "the fat ooze & mud of the Retiring Flood", quoted from N 36.

19[1] Eichhorn supposed that in the earliest stages of the cultural evolution of the human race man was simple, childlike, and artless—hence his term *Natur-mensch* (nature-man, man in a state of nature). C's underlining "*sup*positions" and "*theory*" is a reminder of his distinction between hypothesis (supposition) and hypopoiēsis (subfiction), and between theory and hypothesis. See *NT* COPY A **12** n 3.

It seems plain enough to me, that the 1st Ch.—II.4 contains the physical theory of the Earth, the IInd from v. 4. and the IIIrd the moral or spiritual theory or philosopheme of Man/[1] Both make one Double-nut.

21 ii 262–3, pencil

Im ersten Kapitel bis zum vierten Vers des zweyten wird von Gott ohne Ausnahme *Elohim*; und von da wiederum bis zum Ende des *]$ dritten ohne Ausnahme *Jehova Elohim* gebraucht. Sollte wohl dieser Unterschied im Ausdruck das Werk eines blossen Zufalls seyn? oder sollte nicht vielmehr diese Verschiedenheit von der Verschiedenheit der Verfasser herrühren?

[In the first chapter up to the fourth verse of the second *Elohim* is used for God without exception; and from there to the end of the end of the third *Jehovah Elohim* without exception. Is it probable that this difference of expression would be the result of a mere accident? Or does not this difference originate rather from a difference of authors?]

* This is one possible Solution/ but not the only one possible—& it is exposed to some striking objections—that Moses, the Zealous Monotheist should have adopted and retained the language of Polytheism, = Dii immortales[1]—or that Moses was ignorant of its origin and import and left it for Professor Eichhorn to discover! Likewise, his hypothesis would be much more plausible, if the one set of Chapters had Elohim only, and the other Jehova singly—and not, as it is, Jehova Elohim./[2] What if Elohim expressed the Absolute

20[1] In *"Prometheus"* C favoured the word "philosopheme"—a philosophical statement, theory, system, or axiom—a word current in English in C's day, and used in German (*Philosophem*) by e.g. Schelling and Creuzer. Eichhorn seems simply to be pointing to the documentary independence of the two passages; C, acknowledging the distinction, also recognises that in Gen as we have it the two sources are not in conflict. Documentary analysis now classifies Gen 1–2.4a as P (Priestly—i.e. mythical and/or liturgical material) and Gen 2.4b–3.24 as J–E (Jahwist–Elohist—i.e. each distinguished by the use of the name Jahweh or Elohim). In C's day the distinction, recognising only the J and E sources, was less refined; identification of the P source

was made by Wellhausen in the late nineteenth century.
21[1] "Immortal Gods".
21[2] *Elohim* is a plural form. In *CN* iv 5321 C describes *Elohim* as a collective noun, identifying it with "Robora, the Strengths, connected with the image & notion of the *Trunk* of an Oak". See also *Apocrypha* **6** (at n 2) and a close parallel in *CL* v 134 and 135. Eichhorn seems to have hoped to find in the different uses of the name of God evidence for the evolution of the religion of Israel, the Elohistic document coming from an early polytheistic stage, the Jahwist from a more advanced monotheistic stage. But the solution—as C noticed—is more complex: not only is J earlier than E, but subtle problems are posed by the use of the name *Jehovah Elohim*.

Will, as the all-causative *Omnipotence*—/ and Jehova, or Jehova
Elohim, the Godhead in its moral and spiritual relations to Man, as
his Judge &c?

22   II 280–3, pencil | § 420

[Eichhorn's summary on II 281 of his whole argument in II 264–81:]
So wäre also das erste Buch Mosis aus zwey Werken Stückweis
zusammen getragen: aber auch aus Werken zweyer verschiedener
Verfasser?

[The book of Genesis is, then, patched together from two works, but is it
also from works of two different authors?]

I am not so well satisfied with this very plausible Hypothesis, as I
was for the 4 or 5 first years of my Acquaintance with it. Had it been
limited to the first ten Chapters of Genesis, I should probably have
been less disposed to quarrel with it. But two documents, with
Authors of a diverse faith, the one a Worshipper of the Gods, the
other of Jehovah, for the biography of one Family—!—

   I regard the Chapters respecting the Flood as by far the strongest
nail in the fastening of Eichhorn's Hypothesis.[1] And yet the present
form of the whole Pentateuch I cannot help thinking later than
Moses.[2]

23   II 288–9 | § 422

[Eichhorn traces a parallel wording between Genesis 1 and a
Chaldean cosmogony in order to show that the Israelite, Ishmaelite,
Edomite, and other creation stories from contiguous peoples come
from one source, while the Chaldean and Egyptian are corruptions
of the Mosaic account:] Wer fühlt nicht in dieser Vorstellung einen
verdorbenen Ausfluss der Mosaischen Worte? "Alles war (vor der
Bewohnbarmachung) auf der Erde öd' und leer, und Finsterniss
ruhte auf dem allgemeinen Ocean....Gott theilte das Wasser über
*]und unter der Atmosphäre...und so ward Himmel und trockenes
Land".

22[1] Eichhorn pointed out that the
story of the flood (Gen 6.9–8.22) does not
disturb the geographical consistency of
passages preceding and following it (Gen
2.1–17; 10.7; 15.18), and argued that the
story of the flood had come from an
independent document later edited into a
document that did not include that story:
see II 278–97. Later documentary analysis
designates the story of the flood as J–P
and not a separate document.

22[2] This view is now generally held.

[Who does not sense in this presentation a corrupt derivative of the Mosaic words? "All on the earth (before its being made habitable) was waste and void, and the darkness rested upon the universal ocean....God divided the water above and below the atmosphere...and thus were made the heavens and the dry land".]

* If E. meant these five last lines to pass for the Mosaic Account, it is a trick—There is no such word as Atmosphere in 1 Gen—and the Dry Land stands in no connection with this Halving of the Waters.[1] Perhaps, Moses represented the process thus—Water passed into Air—the ~~remainder~~ other Part by a sort of precipitate formed Earth, a Bed—so that the final Remainder was what we now see as Water. Consequently, the Process would stand thus

> Water
> Air
> Water
> Earth.

The division of the latter Pair is the subject of a following distinct process.—

---

24   ɪɪ 296, pencil | § 424

Und der Ausleger—hat ihm nur erst die höhere Kritik Document von Document geschieden, so darf er nicht mehr mit Schwierigkeiten streiten, die vor dem für unauflöslich gehalten wurden. Er wird nun nicht mehr Mosis zweytes Kapitel aus dem ersten, und das erste aus *] dem zweyten erklären; er wird nicht mehr behaupten, dass aus den Worten der Mosaischen Nachrichten von der Noachischen Fluth ihre Allgemeinheit nothwendig folge...

[*And the commentator*—the Higher Criticism has now distinguished document from document for him, so that he need no longer wrestle with difficulties hitherto held as insoluble. He will no longer explain the first chapter of Genesis from the second, and the second from the first; he will no longer assert that from the words of the Mosaic account of the Noachian flood its universality follows of necessity.]

* a Flood, that destroyed *all* ~~life~~ atmospheric Life on the Earth and left the Arc on the Summit of a Mountain—*could* it be other than universal?

23[1] Gen 1.2, 7, 9–10 confirm C's statement. Cf *CN* ɪɪɪ 4418.

25 II 327–9 | § 427

[Eichhorn is answering the objection that if Genesis is composed word for word from two previously written documents, there is an inconsistency in the fact that one of the writers uses the name *Jehovah* for God in even the very earliest times whereas in Exod 6.3 God tells Moses that He was not known to the patriarchs by this name. Eichhorn's reply is that in Exod 6.3–8 God is assuring Moses and the Hebrew people that he will fulfil the promises made to their forebears in regard to Canaan, that the third verse is a prologue to this statement, that the significance in this prologue regarding the names by which God is known to men lies not in the *forms* of the names, the words used, but in the *meanings* of these names, that *El Shadai* means God Almighty and was the concept by which God was known to the patriarchs and *Jehovah* means The Unchangeable and was the concept by which God meant to be known to Moses and Israel as one who fulfils his word.] Leicht und natürlich ist also der Sinn des Verses: "eure Vorfahren kannten mich nur als den allmächtigen Gott; nicht aber als den, der bey seinen Gesinnungen unveränderlich bleibt." So (diess ist der Inhalt der folgenden Verse) sollt ihr mich nun kennen lernen.

[Thus the sense of the verse is easy and natural: "Your forebears knew me only as Almighty God; but not as the one who remains unchanged in his intent." It is thus (this is the point of the following verses) that you shall now know me.]

No better answer could be given: and it is both ingenious and plausible; but I confess, it does not quite satisfy me. Nay, I doubt the interpretation of JEHOVAH, as = the immutable; & believe it rather to refer to Ex. C. III. 14.[1] To Abraham I was known as a power pre-eminent to all others; but to you first have I revealed mey Self-existence, and necessary Being = I AM (in) that I AM. The[y][a] knew me as the King of all Gods—a God above all other Gods; but you shall know me as the one, only God!—And why may we not suppose, that Moses for the edification of his People altered in his transcription the various names of God or perhaps periphrastic allusions to him, to the one true name ~~used~~ appointed by God himself?—Had the word, Jehovah, been only annexed marginally on

---

a Letter supplied by the editor

25[1] Exod 3.14: "And God said unto Moses, I AM THAT I AM: and he said,   Thus shalt thou say unto the children of Israel, I AM hath sent me unto you."

all such occasions, the marginal note would soon be received into the Text.—[2]

26   ii 339–40 | § 428

6. Endlich, stellt man die Nachrichten in Mose mit den ältesten andrer Völker in Vergleichung: so lässt sich's fühlen, dass dort reine Quellen strömen. Unter allen alten Nationen ist nicht eine einzige, die etwas Aehnliches aufzuweisen hätte, oder das in der ältesten Geschichte nur den Schatten von Simplicität, Genauigkeit und philosophischer Wahrheit dieses Buchs erreichte.... Zum Beyspeil, ihre älteste Philosophie über den Ursprung der Dinge, welche in den Theogonien und Kosmogonien andrer Völker durch spätere Missdeutungen oft ein lächerliches und sinnloses Ansehen bekommen hat, ist bey den Hebräern so voll Einfalt, Würde und Wahrheit, und so frey von den Chimären andrer Völkerstämme, dass sie um dieses einzigen Stücks willen allein schon einer Krone werth wären.

[Finally, if the accounts from Moses are compared with those of other peoples of earliest times, it will be seen that the former come from unadulterated sources. Among all other ancient nations there is not a single one which has anything similar to offer, or which in its earliest histories has even the shadow of the simplicity, precision, and philosophic truth which this book achieves.... For example, their earliest philosophy of the origin of things, which in the theogonies and cosmogonies of other peoples has taken on so often a ridiculous and senseless character because of later misinterpretations, is with the Hebrews so full of simplicity, dignity, and truth, and so free of the chimerical notions of other peoples, that for the sake of this one section they would deserve a crown.]

So *I* think, who take Gen. I literally and geologically: and so *did* I think, when I interpreted the Chapter as a Morning Hymn, in which the Creation is represented under the analogy of the daily emergence of visible Nature out of Night thro' all the successive appearances till full Sun rise/ a se and hence ⟨explained⟩ the posteriority of the Sun = the visible Orb, to the Light, its far earlier Harbinger.[1] But would not *Eichhorn* deem *this* too refined, and the former visionary?— If so, in what *third* can he find the Dignity, Truth, & freedom from all chimerical notions? *I* haved deduced the same process from grounds wholly independent of the Mosaic Cosmogony; in fact, without thinking of the latter and unconscienous of the coincidence.

25[2] Scribes in making fair copies often carried marginal and interlinear corrections and glosses into the text without differentiation.

26[1] Cf *CN* iii 4418; but C's interpretation of Gen 1 "as a Morning Hymn" has not been identified.

394 *Johann Gottfried Eichhorn*

But surely Eichhorn would denounce the separation of the Vegetable from the Animal Creation by an intermediate Creation of the present Solar System, Forests elder than the Sun, as mo a Chimæra κατ' εμφασιν.[2] S. T. C.—

27 II 340–2, pencil | § 429

Aus I B. Mose XII, 6 "damahls waren die Kananiter im Lande" wollte man ehedem folgern, dass die Genesis erst nach der Eroberung von Palästina und der Vertreibung der Kananiter daraus müsse abgefasst seyn. Denn die Anmerkung setze voraus, dass sie nun *nicht mehr* im Lande seyen.—Aber bessere Ausleger Mosis haben diese Stelle schon längst aus der Nachricht Herodots, dass die Phönicier keine in Palästina einheimische, sondern eine dahin eingewanderte Nation seyen, erläutert, und ihr den Sinn beygelegt: damahls waren die Kananiter *schon* im Lande, also *schon* vom rothen Meere nach Palästina gezogen.

[From Genesis 12.6—"And the Canaanite was then in the land"—it had heretofore been deduced that Genesis must have been composed only after the conquest of Palestine and the expulsion of the Canaanites. For the statement supposed that they were *no longer* in the land.—But better commentators on Moses have long since clarified this passage from the report given by Herodotus that the Phoenicians were not a nation indigenous to Palestine but one which had migrated there, and they have given this text the meaning: at that time the Canaanites were *already* in the land, thus had *already* migrated from the Red Sea to Palestine.]

This is very erudite and really ingenious and plausible, nay, I am ready to admit that it is sufficient to break the force of the Blow, to d extract the mortal fang from the proof, if it does not leave it toothless. But still it does not seem to be the natural sense of the Words. I cannot see in it what is so obvious in the ordinary interpretation any reason for the remark. Had it been *Moses* instead of Herodotus who had recorded the emigration of the Canaanites from the Red Sea—*then* indeed it would be satisfactory./[1] Surely it is much easier to consider this, as we *must* do several other annotation-like sentences in the Pentateuch as ⟨a⟩ Glosses.

28 II 341

"In Edom regierten Könige, ehe ein König über Israel herrschte" I B. Mose XXXVI, 31—dieses soll niemand vor Davids Zeit haben

26[2] "Par excellence".

27[1] Because Herodotus was writing about eight centuries after the Exodus.

schreiben können. Allein, stand denn in den Unterredungen Gottes mit Abraham und Jacob I B. Mose XVII, 6.16; XXXV, 11 nicht die Verheissung, dass Könige von ihnen abstammen sollten? Konnte nun nicht der Anordner des Buchs bey der Liste der Edomitischen Könige mit Rücksicht auf jene Unterredungen die Anmerkung machen, dass die Edomiter früher ein freyes, einer eigenen Constitution fähiges Volk gewesen, und von Königen beherrscht worden wären, als ihr Halbbrüder, die Hebräer?

["In Edom kings ruled before there was a king over Israel" (Genesis 36.31)—it is asserted that no one could have written this before the time of David. But was there not included in the conversation of God with Abraham and Jacob (Genesis 17.6, 16; 35.11) the promise that kings would stem from them? Could not the compiler of this book, considering the roll of Edomite kings in reference back to these conversations, have made the observation that the Edomites were a free people, capable of their own constitution and ruled by kings earlier than their half brothers the Hebrews?]

Not satisfactory. May it not more probably allude to the settling of the Hebrews in Egypt, and allude to the Pharaohs?[a] But why *not* consider this as a gloss introduced by the Editors of the Pentateuch, or Preparers of the Copy that was to be layed up in the Temple of Solomon? The authenticity of the Books would be no more compromised by ~~this~~ such glosses, that[b] that of the Book before me by this marginal Note of mine.

---

29 II 358–9, pencil | Moses bks II–V (Exodus–Deuteronomy) § 435

[On II 356 Eichhorn has briefly stated, without analysis, that Exod 3–14 comprises a group of narratives of the Exodus; some of the narratives (e.g. Exod 4.14–27) are incomplete, others (e.g. Exod 12.1–28, 43–50; 13.3 ff) were edited later. For the most part, however, he has taken his examples from Lev, Num, and Deut.] Diese Gestalt der Bücher kann niemand anders, als aus der Zusammensetzung einzelner Aufsätze erklären, welche der Ordner so zusammen stellte, wie sie von Zeit zu Zeit abgefasst waren.

2. Sodann ist in den einzelnen Büchern eine Art von systematischer Anordnung nicht zu verkennen. Das zweyte Buch enthält die Fundamentalgesetze, die das ganze Volk angingen, sammt der Geschichte ihrer Promulgation. Voraus also eine Nachricht, wie die Nachkommen Jacobs in Aegypten zu einem Volk heran wuchsen, wie sie darauf von Aegypten los kamen, und ein freyes, einer eigenen

---

[a] The note continues in a different pen and hand, without paragraph break, and seems to have been written later   [b] A slip for "than"

Constitution fähiges, Volk wurden, zuletzt die allgemeine Constitution am Sinai selbst....[a] Das dritte Buch sammelt die Bestandtheile eines Priestercodex, dessen Inhalt nicht allen Gliedern der Nation so geläufig seyn durfte, wie dem Stamm Levi.

[No one can explain this form of the books other than on the basis of a collection of individual pieces that the arranger put together as they were composed from time to time.

2. In that case, it is impossible not to recognise a kind of systematic arrangement in the individual books. The second book contains the fundamental laws that applied to all the people, together with the history of their promulgation. Thus there is an account in advance of how the descendants of Jacob grew into a nation in Egypt, how they came up out of Egypt, and how they became a free people ready for their own constitution. Finally there is the general constitution itself at Sinai....The third book collects the constituent parts of a priestly code, the contents of which were not necessarily so well known to all parts of the nation as to the tribe of Levi.]

Beyond doubt Eichhorn has purposely *slurred over* the first 14 Chapters of Exodus—omitted, perhaps, this part of his esoteric & very much softened the corresponding part of his public Lectures—prudentiæ causa.[1] See the...or hiatus, overleaf, p. 361, l. 6.[2]—My own opinion—*astra* singula *memorabantur* ⟨*memorandum'd*⟩, vel Mose vel Aharono seriatim forsan, nullo tamen intervallo definite designato—Hæc omnia vidit Samuel, seu vir Samueliticus *in planum* posita, et *Cassiopëiam* finxit.[b] ita ut sub ⟨singulis⟩ diebus annos, imo biennia intelligas, oportet[3]—*Poiηtik Hist.*[4]—*Psalms* ♓ *Chronicles,*

[a] The ellipsis is so printed in the text

[b] Here, at the foot of p 359, C has written "+" and has resumed the note at the head of the page with "+ *from below*." The full point is a slip for a comma

29[1] "For prudence' sake". See **18** and **19**, above. C, having heard some of Eichhorn's lectures in Göttingen in 1799 (see *CL* I 480–1, 494), was familiar with his theory that the accounts of miracles as we have them in OT were later poetic renderings of natural phenomena reshaped for teleological purposes.

29[2] At n *a* in textus.

29[3] "Individual *stars* were *memorandum'd*, either by Moses or Aaron, perhaps one by one, yet at no definitely specified interval—All these Samuel, or someone like Samuel, saw arranged *in a plane figure*, and imagined *Cassiopeia*, so that by single days you have to understand years, or even two-year periods."

29[4] "*Poietic* (?poetic) *History*—Psalms as opposed to Chronicles, Diplomatic [history] [as opposed to] *theocratic*, Esemplastic (imaginative) [history]... [e.g.] Shakespeare's Richard II." The Greek phrase, "to shape into one", is the basis for C's new word "Esemplastic": see BÖHME **46** n 4. C is presumably thinking of the relation between *Richard II* and Holinshed's *Chronicles*, from which Shakespeare derived much of his historical detail. Cf **43**, below. For Shakespeare's telescoping of historic time for purposes of imaginative clarity, see **18**, above.

Diplomatic [)(]*[a]* θεοκρατικ/ Esemplastic εις εν πλασσειν—Shak: Rich. 2ⁿᵈ.

30   ɪɪ 368, pencil | § 437

[In making the point that the last three chapters of Deuteronomy are a later addition, Eichhorn gives detailed examples (in his footnote *r*) of late Hebrew expressions in Deut 32.]

The allusion in v. 7.8. to X Genesis seems almost Cabalistico-Rabbinical.[1]

31   ɪɪ 372, pencil | § 439

*] 1. Inzwischen—glaubt es die ganze vernünftige Welt, dass Homer Verfasser der Iliade und Odyssee sey, weil kein Grieche jemahls an der Wahrheit dieser Ueberlieferung gezweifelt hat:—warum sollten wir nicht auch einer ähnlichen, unter den Juden herab geerbten und von ihnen nie bezweifelten Tradition glauben, dass diese Bücher von Moses verfasst seyn?

[However—if the whole reasoning world believes that Homer was the author of the *Iliad* and the *Odyssey* because no Greek has ever doubted the truth of this tradition, why should we not believe a similar one, handed down among the Jews and never doubted by them, that Moses was the author of these books?]

* An unlucky Argument. Within how few years from the publication of this Work, glaubte nicht die ganze vernünftige Welt der Teutchsen*[b]* Gelehrten, das der, oder vielmehr die, Verfasser der Iliade nicht der Verfasser Odyssee seyn könnte/[1]

---

[a] Symbol supplied by the editor

[b] A slip for "Teutschen"

30[1] Gen 10–11 sets forth in genealogical sequence the establishment of peoples and kingdoms by descent from the sons of Noah. Deut 32.7–8 reads: "Remember the days of old, consider the years of many generations: ask thy father, and he will shew thee; thy elders, and they will tell thee. When The Most High divided to the nations their inheritance, when he separated the sons of Adam, he set the bounds of the people according to the number of the children of Israel." C suggests that Deut 32.7–8 may be a cabalistic reminder of Gen 10 made by the rabbis.

31[1] "...did the whole reasoning world of the learned Germans not believe that the author, or rather the authors, of the *Iliad* could not be the author of the *Odyssey*". Prolonged and continuing controversy had been aroused by Friedrich August Wolf (1759–1824), who, in his *Prolegomena ad Homerum* (1795), argued that it would have been impossible to compose such long poems as the *Iliad* and *Odyssey* without the help of writing, which was not introduced into Greece until long after the supposed time of Homer; that we know nothing of the two poems before they were fitted together by

32 II 377 | § 440

[Arguments that Moses could not have been the author of the four last books, including:] Vielleicht, weil von Mose meistens in der dritten Person und nicht in der ersten gesprochen wird?—Aber das ist gerade die den morgenländischen Schriftstellern eigenthümliche Beschiedenheit!

[Perhaps because Moses for the most part speaks in the third person and not in the first? But that is precisely the form characteristic of Oriental writers!]

I can think only of one weighty Objection, that an Infidel reasoning with Infidels could make to the position, that Moses himself was the Writer of the 5 Books—viz—that they afford the only instance, in which a really & undeniably great man relates miracles as performed by himself.

33 II 408–11, pencil | Joshua § 450

2. Auch vor der Trennung des Staats der Hebräer in zwey Reiche kann es nicht geschrieben worden seyn. Denn es spricht schon vom Gebirge *Juda* und *Israel*...und diese Eintheilung ist nicht älter, als der Ursprung der beyden Reiche selbst, von dennen die Nahmen *] geborgt sind. Sodann, wäre das Buch früher in seiner jetzigen Gestalt vorhanden gewesen: so würden wir es wohl auch bey den Samaritanern finden.

[Also it cannot have been written before the division of the Hebrew state into two kingdoms. For already it speaks of the mountains of *Judah* and *Israel*...and this distinction is not older than the origin of the two states themselves, from which the names are taken. And also, if the book had been extant earlier in its present form, we would have found it in the Samaritan Version.]

* This is a Point on which I especially want and wish information. Where and what are the proofs, that the two Kingdoms Judea and

sixth-century editors; and that the text as we have it goes back only to Alexandrian times. He concluded that if we may believe in the existence of a poet called Homer, the name was probably best applied to the original author of a comparatively small part of the present text. Wolf had developed his views from the "higher criticism" (Wolf uses the term) and from contemporary interest in folk literature, known to C from Herder and Schlegel. See Friedrich Schlegel *Geschichte der alten und neuen Litteratur* (2 vols Vienna 1815) I 27, 218, 257, on which C was making notes in *CN* IV 4637. See also GREW **19** n 2 and cf HOMERIC HYMNS esp **1** n 1.

Israel were at all times & without any intervals of kinder feelings, mortal enemies?—Is it probable, that even during the different Dynasties of the Priests of Baal in the Israelitish Courts the Priests & Prophets of Jehova should have had no communication with their established Church in Judea? The great Revolution under J Rehoboam must have deprived the Documents collected in the Book, Joshua, of most of their *legal* value, for the Kingdom of Israel at least.—On what ground then can we expect that the Israelites should have taken and continued to preserve & multiply Copies of the Work, supposing it to have existed as early as David or Solomon? Sufficient reference is not made to the comparative Illiterateness of the Israelites. The *Contents* of the Book were, I doubt not, written and placed in the Archives shortly after the death of Joshua—and at what period they were *edited* with explanatory Notes, in the present form, is of little Consequence: as neither the Credibility nor the interpretation of the Narratives is at all affected thereby. Not so the Life & Diplomacy of Moses.

34 ii 408, pencil

Ist es aber erst nach ihrem [Israels] Abfall von den Juden abgefasst worden: so ist es sehr begreiflich, dass sie es, als ein Werk, bey ihren Erbfeinden, den Juden, entstanden, nicht annahmen; dagegen aber, weil sie doch von Urkunden über die Vertheilung des Landes, aus Josua's Zeiten her, wussten, dass sie eine Chronik von der Eroberung und Vertheilung des Landes aus allerley Sagen und Ueberlieferungen zusammen stoppelten, um sie unsrem Buch Josua entgegen zu stellen.

[If it was not composed until after Israel's break from Judah, it is quite understandable that they did not accept it, it being a work originating with their hereditary enemy, Judah; on the other hand, however, it was because they were aware of documents from Joshua's time concerning the division of the land, that they composed a chronicle of the conquest and division of the land, put together from all sorts of myths and traditions, to set against our present book of Joshua.]

But at what time?—

35 ii 470, pencil | Samuel § 469

Bey den Juden war es auch nicht ungewöhnlich, ein schon vorhandenes Geschichtbuch zur Basis zu machen, und in dasselbe alles das einzuschalten, was man noch anderwärts als dahin gehörig auftreiben konnte. Bey dem Evangelio nach den Hebräern lag unser Matthäus zu Grunde, war aber mit allerley Erzählungen und Anekdoten bereichert, die in Palästina von Christo mündlich im Umlauf waren.

[Among the Jews it was not unusual to use an already existing history as a basis, and to insert in this everything that could be hunted up elsewhere as relevant to it. The Gospel according to the Hebrews had our Matthew as its foundation, but was enriched with all sorts of tales and anecdotes concerning Christ that were in oral circulation in Palestine.]

I am strongly inclined to believe, that our *Greek* Matthew is itself a translation from such an enriched Gospel of the Hebrew Churches— to which the name of Matthew was given as that of Paul to the Epistle to the Hebrews: & from similar motives.[1]

36   II 483 | § 476

[Footnote *r*:] Gegen allen Sprachgebrauch und mit sichtbarer Härte übersetzen manche die Worte לישפט שמלאל את־ישראל כל ימי חייל "Samuel ward zum Richter auf sein Lebtag gewählt." Leichter ist die obige Vorstellung, die auch von der innern Einrichtung der Bücher Samuels begünstiget wird.

[Against all usage and with obvious forcing, many translate *ispat Samuel eth Israel kal imi hi'io* "Samuel was elected judge for his lifetime". The suggestion given above is more natural, and it is supported by the interior structure of the book.[1]]

I doubt this. How naturally might an Historian of the French Revolution, writing in the present time or hereafter, say: "and Buonaparte became Consul for Life."

35[1] Although Matt is recognised as the gospel with the strongest Jewish colour, its special authority for the Church rests upon the emphasis given by its location in a Christian community. The view that Matt was a Greek translation of a Hebrew gospel had a long tradition behind it but does not consort with the conclusions of later study. Even those who, following Eusebius' quotation from Papias, argue that Matt came from an Aramaic original acknowledge that it was worked out in Greek, that it relied upon a Greek gospel of Mark, and that any Aramaic source is at best at second remove. The ascription of this gospel to "Matthew" is "late" and the reason not clear. On the traditional ascription of Hebrews to Paul see e.g. BIBLE COPY B 134 and n 1. Cf EICHHORN *NT* COPY A 1 and 13.

36[1] In the text to which this is a footnote (II 483) Eichhorn says: "Also here and there accounts occur that can have been cast in the wording used only if they had been set down at once in writing in this form. Instead of reporting that Samuel was chosen as Judge over Israel for his entire life, the writer states merely that Samuel, as the choice and early will of the people had indicated, remained Judge until the end of his life…(1 Sam 7.15). Now, he must have known, since—according to later indications—he lived in the latter part of the Hebrew monarchy, that the will of the people changed later." For 1 Sam 7.15 AV reads: "And Samuel judged Israel all the days of his life"; Luther reads: "Samuel aber richtete Israel sein Leben lang"; *NEB* reads: "Samuel acted as judge in Israel as long as he lived".

37   II 606–7 | Esther §510

15. ...Inzwischen, sollten nicht alle diese Lösungen eine genaue Prüfung unpartheyischer Forscher aushalten, so rechne man solche Stücke der Geschichte unsres Buchs zu denen, deren Unwahrscheinlichkeit sich nicht heben lässt. Es ist wenigstens schwer zu begreifen, wie Haman schon im ersten Monath die Erlaubniss *öffentlich* bekannt machen konnte, am zwölften das Blut aller Juden im Persischen Reich fliessen zu lassen und noch weniger, wie die Juden sich so *] dabey betragen *mochten* und betragen *durften*, wie das Buch ihr Betragen schildert.

[However, if not all of these explanations hold up under the precise scrutiny of an impartial investigator, these bits of history in our book may be relegated to those the improbability of which cannot be explained away. At least it is difficult to comprehend how Haman could make public in the first month the permission to shed the blood of all the Jews in Persia in the twelfth, and even less easy to understand how in those circumstances the Jews *might* have conducted themselves, and *dared* to, in the manner that the book depicts that conduct.[1]]

* This objection may be in great measure removed, ~~by~~ if we interpret this (as we well may) as an edict for compulsory emigration of the Jews from the Persian Provinces—such as that for the expulsion of the Moors from Spain. If you are found this time 12 month, you are outlawed. This edict therefore of Outlawry after a given time was evidently to *prevent* the Massacre—& it is not improbable that the reversal of the same is made to *cover* some tumultuary proceedings of the Jews on this change of Ministry in which a numbers of the Ex-minister's party had been maltreated or lost their lives.

38   III 31–4 | Propheten § 517

Hauptsächlich aber hatten die Propheten ihre scharfen Blicke in die Zukunft und die Weisheit ihrer Vorschläge dem hohen Geist zu danken, der sie beseelte, und sie so hoch über ihre Zeitgenossen erhob. Wie der beschaffen war, sagen sie uns nirgends; sie beschreiben nur hie und da, *wie Dichter*, die Anwandlung ihrer Begeisterung, in einer Sprache, in der alle Begeisterte aller frühen Zeiten sie geschildert haben...

[Mainly, however, the prophets owed their penetrating insights into the future and the wisdom of their recommendations to the elevated spirit that

37[1]   See Esther 3.9, 13; 8.9–11; 9.1–19.

animated them and that raised them so high above their contemporaries. Of this condition they say nothing to us; only here and there, *like poets*, they describe the agitations of their inspired state, in a language in which all those who were inspired in all ancient times have described it...]

I have no other objection to these Views than that they leave the main point, the prophetic state itself, the focal moment, out of sight. They Prophets do *not* describe their inspiration as Poets; but relate sudden changes produced without any conscious act of their own will, both on their bodies and their minds—and the sum of all is, that with more or less excitement, equ greater or less disturbance of their nervous system they passed into a state of *inner vision*, a *state* (tho' not the occurrences and presentations during the same) in all points identical with that of Extasy or Clair-voyance, from whatever cause and by whatever means induced or super-vening.[1] In every age, tho' more numerously since the discovery of Mesmer's and Puysegur's Discoveries of the mode of exciting it in predisposed Persons under certain conditions of bodily health,[2] this State has been described by thos Patients or Eye-witnesses, and in all instances concurrently in all essential points. Now it is asserted, and according to my inmost convictions truly asserted, that in the Hebrew Prophets this state was used instrumentally by the Divine Spirit, as the congruous Base or Suscipient of his immediate spiritual Agency—even as the eye, optic nerve, and the correspondent in the Brain are the congruous and Correlative Recipients of the material Light.

Supposing as is generally supposed that Moses beheld the flaming Bush with his bodily eyes, does it alter the nature of the Object seen or detract from its *miraculous* character, that the instrument of vision was the same as men ordinary men possess and use on objects not miraculous? Perhaps, all deep Affections unmixed with appetite, all that we refer to the pectoral region and call *Heart*, ex. gr. Love, the

---

38[1] Cf reference to the "6th or ecstatic state of zoomagnetism" in *NT* COPY A 33, and to "the different magnetic Grades" and to "clairvoyants of the Fifth Grade" in KLUGE 6 and 7. See also n 2, below.

38[2] Franz Anton Mesmer (1734–1815), convinced that there was healing power in his own hands, conceived of this power as permeating the whole universe and in 1775 named it "animal magnetism". See BÖHME 26 n 3. Armand Marie Jacques de Chastenet, Marquis

de Puységur (1751–1825), a disciple of Mesmer, was particularly interested in hypnotism and somnambulistic phenomena. For evidence of C's prolonged and well-informed interest in animal magnetism, see ESCHENMAYER, JAHRBÜCHER, JUNG, KLUGE, and MESMER; cf KANT *Vermischte Schriften* COPY C 31. For signs that C kept animal magnetism in mind as a possible solution for some puzzling questions in biblical interpretation, see e.g. 18 and n 2, above, and *NT* COPY A 24, 33, COPY B 19.

Sense of the Beautiful, &c, may be the *nascent* quantities of this inward Vision—even as outward Sight seems to commence in a *sensation* of Light and Color, or rather a *Having* of them, as the next step to the *being* they.[3]

39   III 38 | § 519

Hingegen zuweilen wussten sie schon zum voraus, wovon sie zu sprechen hatten; zuweilen hatten sie so gar durch symbolische Handlungen auf ihre Reden vorbereitet: und in diesen Fällen lässt sich's denken, dass sie ihre Vorträge vorher entworfen, und dass wir sie in diesem Concept noch übrig haben können. Dürfte man voraus setzen, dass wir noch viele Stücke in den Propheten bis auf jedes Wort so lesen, wie sie vom umstehenden Volk gehört worden sind: so würde aus der innern Beschaffenheit der Stücke selbst eine schriftliche Ausführung vor der Declamation nothwendig folgen. So mahlt z. B. Ezechiel seine Gotteserscheinung so prächtig, vielseitig und gross, *] dass schwerlich ihre Darstellung ein Impromtü seyn kann, sondern von ihm mit Kunst angelegt und ausgearbeitet seyn muss.

[Occasionally they already knew in advance, however, what they were to discuss; occasionally thus they had prepared themselves, with completely symbolic devices for their statements; and in these cases it may be presumed that they sketched out their discourses in advance and that possibly we still have them in this form. If it might be supposed that we are reading every word in many passages from the prophets just as they were heard by the people around them, it would necessarily follow from the inner character of the passage itself that there was a written preparation prior to the declamation. Thus, for example, Ezekiel describes his vision of God with such majesty, complexity, and grandeur that it can scarcely have been extemporaneous, but must have been prepared and worked out with artistry.]

* From the analogy of Dreams during an excited state of the Nerves, which I have myself experienced, and the wonderful intricacy, complexity, and yet clarity of the visual Objects, I should infer the contrary. Likewise, the noticeable fact of the words descriptive of these Objects rising at the same time, and with the same Spontaneity and absence of all conscious Effort, weighs greatly with me, against the hypothesis of Pre-meditation,[1] in this and similar Passages of the Prophetic Books.[2]

S. T. C.

38[3] Cf *NT* COPY B **18** n 2 and **19** n 2.

39[1] C gave a detailed account of precisely this experience in his prefatory ' note to *Kubla Khan*: *PW* (EHC) I 295–6. See also GOLDFUSS **7** and n 1.

39[2] The visions of God referred to are in Ezek 1.4–28 and 10.1–22.

40 III 70–3, pencil | Isaiah § 525

Freylich könnte man klagen: so verlieren wir die Weissagungen mit den speciellsten Darstellungen Jahrhunderte vor ihrer Erfüllung! Die verlieren wir allerdings; aber es bleiben doch die allgemeinern, die in so späte Zeiten gehen; und jene verlieren wir mit grossem Gewinnst. Viele Zweifel sind dadurch gelöst, viele Schwierigkeiten gehoben, viele Fragen beantwortet, die man sonst nicht lösen, heben und beantworten kann. Für wen sollten doch die speciellsten Darstellungen der Ereignisse in der spätesten Zukunft seyn? Doch wohl für uns aus der spätern Nachwelt nicht, die wir durch andere stärkere Gründe überzeugender belehrt sind, als diese Orakel uns belehren können, dass Jehova der einzige allmächtige Regierer der Welt sey...

[Certainly it may be lamented that thus we lose the prophecies with the most exact predictions centuries before their fulfilment! These we lose, of course; but there still remain the more general ones, which extend just as far in time; and the former we lose with great gain. Many uncertainties are thus resolved, many difficulties removed, many questions answered that otherwise cannot be resolved, removed, and answered. For whom anyhow are these exact predictions of events in the most distant future? Certainly not for us of the modern world, who may be more convincingly instructed by other and stronger means than these oracles can provide, that Jehovah is the single, almighty ruler of the world. .]

Oh, Eichhorn! this is Sophistry with a vengeance! Not that there is an intelligent Governor of the World chiefly do we seek to learn from the Prophecies; but that God has specially, even as Father to Child, as Man to man, REVEALED his intentions and conveyed his *promises*, respecting the destiny of the Human Race. What plain and simple man (= ἰδεωτης)[1] ever witnessed the life of an aged Parent languish & *go out*, without needin[g to bear in mind the]ᵃ Revelation, that the Departed "is not *dead*, but sleepeth"?[2] Whether there are, or can be, ~~satis~~ Proofs of Revelation satisfactory to a full and active Understanding, is not here the Question: but *supposing* the existence of such

---

ᵃ Words suplied by the editor. The foot of the page has been lightly trimmed, apparently with scissors

40[1] Properly ἰδιώτης (C's spelling deflected by his habitual use of the English form "ideot")—in this context, a layman, an unlearned person (a standard meaning in Greek, as distinct from the primary meaning of a private person, a person with a world of his own, which informs WW's *The Idiot Boy*). For

C's refusal to take sides in the quarrel between Priestley and Horsley about Tertullian's meaning in referring to non-trinitarians as *idiotae* (as "idiots" or "unlearned persons") see *CN* III 3675n.

40[2] Cf Matt 9.24; Mark 5.39; Luke 8.52.

proofs, would not the ⟨Human⟩ Heart derive a more feeling assurance from *them*, than from all the arguments, which mere Reason or Metaphysics have afforded? Let it be, that the latter gives all, that it is fit for us to receive, yet still Eichhorn plays the Sophist—for the *Wish* for more remains, & *this* Wish it is, which we seek to gratify in the Prophecies of special Events, not that Faith in a God, which is pre-supposed in the very conception of the possibility of a Prophecy.[3]—*S. T. C.*

41   III 71, pencil, concluded in ink

Und was konnten sie [die Hebräer] aus diesen speciellesten Darstellungen für Nutzen ziehen, den ihnen nicht auch die allgemeineren gewähren konnten? "Vielleicht grössere Beruhigung? dass sie den Ausgang ihrer Schicksale gelassener erwarteten?" Aber diese Folge hatten sie sichtbar nicht; die Hebräer im Exilium waren voll Verzweifelung bey der Zögerung ihrer Rückkehr in ihr Vaterland. Und konnten sie die specielle Darstellung in den meisten Stücken auch durchschauen?

[And what could they [the Hebrews] draw to their advantage from these special representations, which the more general ones could not also assure them? "Perhaps a greater comfort? so that they could await more calmly the release from their fate?" But this clearly was not the consequence of them; the Hebrews in exile were filled with despair at the delay in the return to their homeland. And could they even see through the special representations in most of the passages?]

Not for the Exiles principally, but for *us*, for the whole Human Race. The *ª*greater their Doubts,*ᵇ* the *ª*higher our Satisfaction.*ᵇ* ⟨S. T. C.⟩*ᶜ*

Softly, softly, Master Coleridge of 15 years ago![1] This might tell for something, *if* only the inspiring Deity had provided some satisfying evidence for *us* of the actual Date of the Oracle, some *proof* of its having been delivered by Isaiah—whereas we are ignorant even of the name & age of the compilers of the Canon; but are certain that they were fallible Men, by undeniable instances of their fallibility—in

ᵃ⁻ᵇ Words overtraced in ink by C
ᶜ Here C has written " ∧ + " and resumed the note at the head of the page with " ∧ + ", writing in ink, the continuation of the note being written both above and below the first pencilled paragraph

40³ See **41** n 1, below.
41¹ At the end of a long note, dated 7 Jun 1827, in which he reflects upon the possible history of the composition and compilation of the prophetic books (see also **13** n 2, above), C added: "See my MSS marginal note on Eichhorn's Introduction, Isaiah." N 26 ff 110ᵛ–116ᵛ (*CN* v).

sundry of the Titles of the Oracles—and even *they* no otherwise assign this Oracle to Isaiah than by prefixing his name as the introductory Title of the whole collection.[2]—But so are the Psalms entitled collectively Psalms of David.[3] S. T. C. 5 June 1827.

42   III 87 | § 529

Die Natur der Orakel verträgt es schlechterdings nicht, dass man sie wie ein Geschichtbuch behandle, und die Bilder in einzelne Facta auflöse. Aus der Reihe der Dichtungen und Bilder muss immer bloss eine Hauptidee ausgehoben, und das Uebrige alles dem Dichter als Darstellung, als Schmuck, als Verzierung seines Werks zurück gegeben werden—ich appellire an Dichterkenner und kundige Leser. Und würde man nicht diese Behandlungsart gänzlich verlassen müssen, wenn man alles, was hinter Jesaias Nahmen steht, auch für seinen Ausspruch, seine Rede, seine Ahnung ausgeben wollte?

[The nature of the oracles definitely does not allow of their treatment as a historical book and of the resolution of their figures into independent events. From the series of poems and figures one leading idea must always be abstracted, and all the remainder surrendered to the poet as representation, ornament, embellishment—I appeal to those who understand poets and to informed readers. And would not this mode of treatment have to be abandoned entirely if all that stands under Isaiah's name were taken as his own utterance, his own speech, his own sentiments?]

Not only the genuine Poet, but every genial Critic who has formed his taste and judgement on the works of genuine Poets, will reply to this over-confident Appeal in the Negative. Eminently must the Poet have a distinct meaning and reason for every word, he uses: for herein chiefly does Poetry differ from Prose. But a religious, an inspired Poet, and a Commissioned Prophet—that *he* should scatter about flighty fancies, and sentences senseless, is too absurd.[1] The Half and Half of Eichhorn will never do! S. T. C.

41[2] For the authorship of various sections of Isaiah see **45** n 1, below. Cf also BIBLE COPY B **61** n 1 and DAVISON **8** n 1.

41[3] See BIBLE COPY B **34** n 1.

42[1] C said of his schoolmaster James Boyer: "I learnt from him, that Poetry, even that of the loftiest and, seemingly, that of the wildest odes, had a logic of its own, as severe as that of science; and more difficult, because more subtle, more complex, and dependent on more, and more fugitive causes. In the truly great poets, he would say, there is a reason assignable, not only for every word, but for the position of every word...". *BL* ch 1 (*CC*) I 9; cf ch 18 II 60–1. On the difference between poetry and prose, see e.g. *CN* III 3611, *TT* 12 Jul 1827, 3 Jul 1833.

43   III 88 | § 530

...alle, ohne Ausnahme, trügen überall das Gepräge eines weit höhern Alters in der Sprache an sich.—Prüfe, wer dieses behaupten mag, doch nur einmahl die Spuren von spätern Ausdrücken, die ich oben...zur Probe gesammelt habe; halten diese die strengste *] kritische Untersuchung nicht aus, so habe ich noch eine beträchtliche Anzahl anderer in Bereitschaft.

[...all, without exception, bear everywhere in the language itself the stamp of a much greater age.—Only examine, whoever asserts this, the traces of later expressions that I have collected above...for specimens; if these will not stand the strictest critical investigation, I have yet a considerable number of others ready.]

* How weak this argument must be respecting a Language, all the remains of which are contained in a single thick Octavo Volume, may be easily shown in a hundred instances from ⟨English⟩ MSS of the age of Richard II, and downward to Henry 8th, of words that had been supposed quite modern.—

44   III 90

Sollten aber...die Ordner und Sammler unsres A. T. nicht gewusst haben, dass sie auf diese Weise frühere Orakel mit späteren mischten?...Ihre Absicht war ja nicht, nach dem Alter zu sammeln, sondern bloss alle Orakel ohne Nahmen ihrer Urheber auf Eine Haut zu bringen, und zwar auf die, welche mit Jesaianischen anfing, weil ihnen diese Methode am bequemsten schien.

[But would not the arrangers and collectors of our Old Testament have known that they were mixing earlier and later oracles in this manner?...Their purpose indeed was not to collect by age, but merely to put all the oracles not bearing the names of their originators on one parchment, and indeed on the one which began with Isaiah's, because this seemed to them the most convenient method.]

a poor evasion grounded on a mere assertion.

45   III 101 | § 534

Nach der Zeit wurde diese Sammlung von Orakeln als ein Werk angesehen, dessen Urheber Jesaias allein sey, weil man bald vergass, ∧ und wahrscheinlich auch nur wenige wussten, dass er aus der Zusammenstellung ganz verschiedener von den verschiedensten Propheten zu den verschiedensten Zeiten ausgesprochenen Orakeln erwachsen war.

[After a time this collection of oracles was viewed as one work, the author of which was Isaiah alone, because it was soon forgotten, and probably only a few ever knew, that it was made up of a collection of entirely different oracles spoken by the most various prophets at the most various times.]

∧ and no one recollected, till P.C. 1785 the fact revived in the inventiv[e][a] Brain of Professor Eichhorn &c! I abominate Sneering; but really the cool complacency with which in the course of a few pages E. elevates a mere Guess of his own into a portion of History, and *narrates* the same, is *too* provokingly cavalier.—[1]

46　ɪɪɪ 183–7 | Ezekiel § 549

[Eichhorn is arguing against the theory that Ezek 40–48 comprise a second book, distinct from the first thirty-nine chapters and *] composed by the Samaritans:] Und hätten auch die Samaritaner durch die feinsten Kunstgriffe ihren Betrug zu verbergen gewusst; hätte wohl das von ihnen untergeschobene Stück seinen jetzigen Platz in ihren Nationalbüchern erhalten können? Es wäre doch erst nach vollendetem Tempelbau in die Hände der Juden gelangt: war damahls nicht schon die Bibliothek der Propheten geschlossen? Musste nicht Daniel seinen Platz unter den Hagiographis höchst wahrscheinlich deshalb nehmen, weil er in die Hände der Sammler des A. T. erst zu der Zeit kam, als die Propheten schon ein geschlossenes Ganzes ausmachten...?

[And even if the Samaritans had known how to disguise their fraud by the finest strokes of art, is it likely that this piece interpolated by them could have been received into its present place in their national books? It would have reached the hands of the Jews only after the completion of the Temple: was not the canon of the prophets already closed at that time? Did not Daniel have to take its place in the Hagiographa in all probability simply because it did not reach the hands of the collectors of the Old Testament until the time that the prophets had been made up into a closed entity?]

[a] A letter missed, or cut off, at the outer edge of the page

45[1] The view of the book of Isaiah now established conflicts with the positions of both Eichhorn and C, but is closer to C's. Three sections are distinguished in the book as we now have it: (ɪ) by Isaiah—chs 1–12, 16–22, 28–32; (ɪɪ) chs 40–55, by "Deutero-Isaiah", written in the post-exilic period; (ɪɪɪ) chs 56–66, by "Trito–Isaiah". (Chs 36–9 are taken over from 2 Ki 18–19 with the "Song of Hezekiah".) Against Eichhorn, the unity of the Isaianic corpus is recognised, but the unity is seen to be editorial, the work of a school working from the eighth century to the time of the building of the Temple (520–516 B.C.), in which Deutero-Isaiah was a commanding figure. Chs 40–66—and modern scholars discern subdivisions in chs 56–66—are seen as a collection of oracles originally oral rather than written; although these are of independent origin, they represent not a haphazard collection but a studious and considered arrangement.

* And how came it, that the Selecters and Compilers of the Hebrew Canon omitted to annex an explanation of their degrading Daniel to the Hagiographi,[1] to the Authors of which they conceded only the lowest grade or sort of inspiration—scarcely more than we attribute to favorite devotional Books, the Whole Duty of Man for instance,[2] when we say, the Writer was eminently favored by God's grace, and the like or still stronger expressions—how happened this, if they were in possession of satisfactory proofs of its Authenticity?— Besides, what an absurd notion, that the ⟨prophetic⟩ Canon was *closed*! What? degrade a Prophet, a great prophet, whose prophecies both in definiteness, in importance, and in deep national interest transcend all the other Oracles of the O. T. & strip the Book of the very name of Prophet, rather than insert or annex it in the next public Copy made by ~~the~~ authority—!—*if*, I say, they had documents decisive of the Age of the Book and that Daniel, Premier and Archimage, of the Babylonian Empire, was the Writer, or the Deliverer at least of the Contents! I cannot believe it: even tho' I attached greater worth and solidity to Eichhorn's Hypothesis of the 4 Skins, than I am inclined to do![3] What was more easy than to make room for the six Chapters of Daniel (VII–XII) on the Isaiah Skin by omitting the historical Chapters inserted from the Chronicles merely (according to Eichhorn) to fill up the Skin of Parchment.—Is it not strange that neither Ezekiel (who yet mentions Daniel's name) nor Zachariah should not once allude to such prophecies—nor any later Prophet—nor Ezra?—[4]

46[1] *Hagiographa* (Holy Writings): i.e. *Kethubim* (Writings), the third of the three Jewish divisions of OT, the group of books not included in the Law or the Prophets and the last to achieve canonicity: Ps, Prov, Job; Ruth, Lam, Song of Songs, Eccles, Esther; Dan, 1 and 2 Chron, Ezra, Neh. Cf *NT* COPY A **45**.

46[2] *The Practice of Christian Graces: or, The Whole Duty of Man Laid Down in a Plain and Familiar Way* (c 1658)—a devotional work popular in England until the beginning of the nineteenth century, frequently reprinted and incorporated into many collections of devotional writings. Probably written by Richard Allestree (1619–81), it has been variously ascribed to Henry Hammond (1605–60), John Fell (1625–86), Dorothy Lady Pakington (d 1679), and Richard Sterne (c 1596–1683).

46[3] Eichhorn's theory (III 81) was that at the time the OT canon was being drawn up the works of the prophets were placed on four skins or scrolls. The first two contained the oracles of Jeremiah and Ezekiel, the two prophets from whom the redactors had complete works; the third contained oracles from prophets known by name but whose work had survived only in part—hence the scroll of the twelve minor prophets; the fourth contained fragments from Isaiah and parts of oracles from various unidentified prophets. Eichhorn supposed that all the miscellaneous fragments of the fourth scroll were put down under the name of the only prophet in this group who was identified by name—Isaiah. See also **45** n 1, above.

46[4] Daniel is mentioned by name in Ezek 14.14, 20, and 28.3. C is correct in

47 III 188–9 | § 551

Alle Entzückungen und Visionen sind, meinem Urtheil nach, blosse
Einkleidung, blosse poetische Dichtungen; und ein Dichter aus
einem andern Zeitalter und von einer andern Stimmung, von
geringerer Phantasie und Dichtungsgabe würde denselben Ideen
ein ganz andres Kleid angelegt haben.

[All the raptures and visions are, according to my judgement, mere drapery,
mere poetic fiction; and a poet from another age and of another cast of mind,
of more limited imagination and poetic genius, would have set the same ideas
forth in entirely different garb.]

It perplexes me to understand, how a Man of Eichhorn's Sense,
Learning, and Acquaintance with Psychology could form, or attach
belief to, so cold-blooded an hypothesis. That in Ezechiel's Visions
Ideas or Spiritual Entities are presented in visual Symbols, I never
doubted; but as little can I doubt, that such Symbols did present
themselves to Ezechiel in Visions—and by a Law closely connected
with, if not contained in, that by which sensations are organized into
Images and mental sounds in our ordinary sleep.

48 III 388 | Daniel § 618

Aber auf alle Fälle kann unser Hebräisch-Chaldäischer Daniel keine
Uebersetzung aus dem Griechischen seyn.

[But at all events, our Hebrew-Chaldaic Daniel cannot be a translation from
the Greek.]

My own Conjecture is—that there were many floating Traditions of
Daniel among the Jews, and old fragments of his Oracles attributed
to him—just as our Ancestors had of Merlin, Nostradamus &c, and
the Greeks & Romans of the Sibyls[1]—and that during the tyranny

noticing a gap in Eichhorn's reasoning
about Dan and the canon. Eichhorn
argues that shortly after the Exile the
canon was closed with all the books we
now have, but he later said that Dan was
taken in after the canon had been closed.
See **5** and n 1, above. If, as Eichhorn also
recognises, Ezekiel and Daniel were
almost exact contemporaries and knew
each other (III 165, 340), and if the
compilers of the canon had devoted a
whole scroll to Ezek, it is difficult to see
how Daniel's work could have escaped
their notice. For a possible reason for

Eichhorn's ambiguous treatment of Dan,
see **49** n 2, below.

48[1] Merlin, magician and prophet,
perhaps in part historically identi-
fiable with a fifth-century Welshman,
and/ or a sixth-century Caledonian, of
the same name, is not supposed to
have left any collection of written
oracles, but the Arthurian Legend
includes many accounts of his prophetic
powers and oblique style. Nostra-
damus—Michel de Nostredame (1502–
66)—Provençal-Jewish medical doctor
and astrologer, favourite of Catherine de'

of Antiochus Epiphanes some Man of Genius of the Maccabæan Party framed the Oracles from C. VIII, as a political Pamph[l]et,[a] circulated secretly among the[b] ~~among~~ the Jewish Nobles. Of course, the purity of the Style would be included in the ~~writer him~~ Writer's Object—but no such object would exist for the later Compiler of the biographic Traditions (C. VI–VII) prefixed to the Copy of the oracles, when they were placed together with Esther among the Sacred Books.[2]

49 III 389

Sollte (um bey dem System zu bleiben, das selbst Porphyrius von den Propheten gehabt zu haben scheint)—sollte der Gott, welcher Propheten wecken und einzelne Begebenheiten Jahrhunderte vor ihrer Ereigniss bekannt machen kann, nicht auch ganze Reihen von Begebenheiten offenbaren können? und sollte der Gott, welcher seine Propheten dunkel in die Zukunft blicken lassen kann, nicht auch seinen Dienern die Zukunft hell vor Augen stellen können? Aber lagen auch dem Daniel wirklich die Aussichten, die er beschreibt, so hell vor Augen, wie dem Porphyrius, und uns, die wir nach ihrer Erfüllung leben? Und wer zu unsern Zeiten ohne Bekanntschaft mit der Geschichte Daniels Geschichte liest: kann der irgend ihr heiliges Dunkel durchschauen? und konnte es daher wohl Daniel?

[Should (to follow what appears to have been Porphyry's method of dealing with Prophets) not God, who could raise prophets and make individual events known centuries before their occurrences, have also been able to reveal entire series of events? and should not God, who can let his prophets see darkly into the future, also be able to set the future clearly before the eyes

---

[a] Letter supplied by the editor
[b] Having filled the foot-margin, C continued in the outer margin with "*(from the bottom)*"

Medici and physician-in-ordinary to Charles IX of France, declared himself a prophet in 1547 and thereafter published two collections of *Centuries* of predictions (1555, 1558) written in rhymed quatrains in an enigmatic manner. The ecstatic prophecies of the Sibyl or Sibyls (of whom the Cumaean was the most revered), written in Greek hexameters of an impenetrable obscurity, were preserved for later study with such cumulative authority that as they were destroyed from time to time they were replaced with others, usually forged, which became progressively contaminated with Hebrew and Christian accretions. Virgil in *Aeneid* 6.77–102 described Sibylline ecstatic utterance, and because of the Cumaean Sibyl's prophecy in his *Eclogue* IV Sibylline prophecies were accorded a position of regard almost equal to that of the Old Testament.

48[2] The book of Daniel divides into two sections: chs 1–6, stories about Daniel; chs 7–12, his visions (four in number), with ch 7 as a pivot. It is now generally held that the book was put together in its present form during the reign of Antiochus Epiphanes (175–163 B.C.). See also **5** n 1, above.

of his servants? But did the prospects that Daniel describes really stand as
clearly before his view as they do for Porphyry and us, who live after their
fulfilment? And who in our day, reading Daniel's history without benefit of
historical knowledge, can penetrate its sacred obscurity? and is it then likely
that Daniel could?]

I cannot comprehend this Reply of Eichhorn to Porphyry either on
the ground of Truth or of Policy. Not on the former; for how can
such professions be reconciled with Eichhorn's adoption of Spinoza's
Scheme of interpretation ⟨in his introductory Chapter,⟩:[1] or with his
objection to the Authenticity of the latter prophecies of ~~Danie~~ Isaiah/
And having published these—not on the latter.[2] For who can be
deceived?

50   III 441 | Psalms § 628

Sie [die Psalmen] wurden nicht zum Lesen gemacht sondern zum
Singen; die Musik, mit der sie der Dichter begleitete, können wir
nicht wieder herstellen; und das Instrument, dem er sie bestimmte,
ist uns nach seinem Affect ganz unbekannt. Wir entbehren als aus
Zeitferne und Unbekanntschaft mit vielen Gegenständen des
Hebräischen Alterthums, der wirksamsten Mittel, unser Herz zu
öffnen, und der Empfindungen fähig zu machen, mit denen der
Dichter auf seine Lieder vorbereitete, die er im Fortgang desselben
*] unterhielt, und mit denen er es verhallen liess. Und das ist gewiss
ein grosser Verlust für einen geschmackvollen Leser und Ausleger.

[They were written not for reading but for singing; we cannot restore the
music with which the poet accompanied them, and the effect of the
instrument for which he intended them is totally unknown to us. From the
passage of time, then, and ignorance of many circumstances of Hebrew
antiquity, we are deprived of the most effective means of opening our hearts
and of making ourselves receptive to the feelings with which the poet
introduced his songs, which he maintained as they continued, and with which
he let them die away. And this is certainly a great loss for the reader and
interpreter of taste.]

49[1] See **1** and n 1, above.

49[2] Eichhorn reckoned Daniel to be as
genuine a Hebrew prophet as Jeremiah or
Ezekiel: see III 343. In his introductory
chapter on the prophets (III 13) he said
that the prophets' ability to "see the
future" rested not on pictorial or eidetic
revelation from God but on a heightened
ability to sense the nature and trend of
present events and so to infer future
events accurately. In this passage, how-
ever, Eichhorn seems to suggest that
Daniel *saw*, but did not always under-
stand, the precise events that would occur
in the future. C seems to have overlooked
the possibility that here Eichhorn is
arguing forensically, seeking to demolish
Porphyry's view (which was close to the
orthodox eighteenth-century position) in
order to establish the view that he had
expressed in the earlier chapter.

* Is not this equally true of the Greek Lyrics?[1] The loss of the metre is indeed a serious loss:[2] if any other metre existed than a mere arrangement of the Words to the Music, as in Handel's Messiah.[3] But the mere loss of the *Music* can [not][a] effect the *merit* of the *Poetry*.

51   III 491 | Job §640

Man hat das Buch Hiob oft ein Drama genannt: und wenn man das Wort in seiner ersten einfachsten Bedeutung nimmt, nach der es ein Dialog war, so will ich mit niemand darüber streiten.

[The book of Job has often been called a drama: and if the word is taken in its first, simplest sense, to mean a dialogue, I have no quarrel with anyone on the matter.]

Milton far more judiciously considers [it][b] as a didactic Epic Poem.—[1]

52   III 513 | § 642

2. Aber die grosse Cultur (kann vielleicht ein anderer ausrufen), die in dem Buch durchleuchtet, erlaubt wohl schwerlich, ihm ein so hohes Alter beyzulegen. Freylich, so wenig die Funken des Genius des

---

[a] A characteristic slip

[b] Word supplied by the editor

50[1] C implies, correctly, that since we have lost the music and the whole ambience of Greek lyric we cannot feel the full original effect of it, even though the metre, so far as it consists of a regular arrangement of long and short syllables, is not lost. In Hebrew, with its less effective alphabet, the metre was entirely lost. Cf Charles Burney *A General History of Music* (4 vols 1776–89) I 83, on dramatic lyrics: "We can be certain of nothing, concerning the music applied to the ancient chorus, except the *relative lengths* of the notes as they are determined by the *prosody*; in what manner the ancients divided them by *beats*, I do not even presume to guess."

50[2] Robert Lowth *De sacra poesi Hebraeorum praelectiones* (Oxford 1753), "epoch-making in its insistence on the parallelism of Hebrew poetry" (Saintsbury *History of Criticism* III 617), was the principal work on the subject. C borrowed a copy of the first edition from the Bristol Library Society 16–22 Sept 1796

(*Bristol LB* 84). Eichhorn refers to the book in III 24–5. Lowth argues (Lecture 3) for an original metrical scansion, and (Lectures 18 and 19) for the still detectable division into lines and the parallel arrangement of lines and verses.

50[3] The libretto of Handel's *Messiah* is a cento of unversified passages from AV—from which any reconstruction of the music would be highly problematical. *Messiah*, composed in twenty-four days in 1742, was first performed in Dublin on 13 Apr 1742, at Covent Garden on 23 Mar 1743, and thereafter frequently.

51[1] In the Introduction to *The Reason of Church Government* (1641) Milton discussed his meditations on a composition "of highest hope, and hardest attempting", whether epic or tragedy, and spoke of the book of Job as "a brief model" of the "Epic Form". *A Complete Collection of the Historical, Political, and Miscellaneous Works* ed Thomas Birch (2 vols 1738) I 60. See also H. COLERIDGE **7** n 1, GREW **25** (at n 3), and HAYLEY **1**.

Verfassers in allen Arabern seines Zeitalters brannten, eben so wenige möchten die Strahlen der Cultur, die aus seinem Werke leuchten, alle Winkel von Arabien erleuchtet haben. Aber Idumäa war von je her der Sitz morgenländischer Weisen, und Edomitische Weisheit war bey den Alten zum Sprüchwort worden...

[But (another can perhaps cry out) the high culture that shines out from the book scarcely allows the attribution of such a great age to it. Indeed, as little as the sparks of genius of this author burned in all the Arabs of his times, just so little could the rays of culture that shone from his work have illuminated every corner of Arabia. But Idumaea was from the beginning the abode of Oriental wise men, and Edomite wisdom had became a proverb among the ancients...]

Not to mention, that this Objection grounds itself on an arbitrary and in many respects improbable Hypothesis, that the human Race commenced in Savagery. Most unscriptural at all events is the Supposition: and in my humble opinion not less unphilosophical. If we credit the Book of Genesis (& what other historic document have we that comes near to it in age & authenticity?) we must admit, that the most important of the Arts were discovered or invented before the Flood—and that a Monarchy had risen before the dispersion of the Human Race. I can find nothing in Job, that might not have been written by a Contemporary of Abraham: tho, if I were to fix on any period, it would be between the times of Joseph and Moses.[1] *S. T. C.*

52[1] C is here taking Eichhorn's side: cf GREW **25** n 2. Present scholarship, finding no accurate chronological evidence, dates Job conjecturally c the fourth century B.C.—i.e. at least 1000 years later than C's guess. In *BL* ch 10 (*CC*) I 202 C referred to Job as "the sublimest, and probably the oldest, book on earth".

Einleitung in die apokryphischen Schriften des Alten Testaments. Leipzig 1795. 8°.

Bound uniformly with *AT* and *NT* COPY A.

British Museum C 126 i 5

"S. T. C." label on the title-page. John Duke Coleridge's monogram on p ⁻6. On p 121 C has corrected, in ink, μεταλλένει to μεταλλευει ("perverteth" —Wisd 4.12): cf **13**, below.

In this work, prepared and published between his *AT* (1780–3) and *NT* (1810–14), Eichhorn continued his systematic historical study of the religion of the writings of Israel. His principal conclusion was that the apocryphal writings reflect the mingling of Hellenistic with Hebrew thought in the period between the closing of the Old Testament canon and the beginning of the Christian era.

DATE. c 1812–13, with additions to before 28 Mar 1819—see FIELD **1** (quoted in general note, above)—and later.

COEDITOR. Merton A. Christensen.

1   p [ii] (title-page verso), pencil

I cannot help regretting that Eichhorn had not deviated so far from his plan as to have given us, if only in a note, his opinions of third and fourth Books of Esdras.[1] They seem to me to have been the work of different centuries, from the 2ⁿᵈ to as low [as]*ᵃ* the 7ᵗʰ P.C.[2]

ᵃ Word supplied by the editor

1[1] I.e. 1 and 2 Esdras in Apocrypha. In the Septuagint there were two books entitled Esdras (the Greek and Latin form of the name Ezra): Esdras A—a Greek book based on parts of 2 Chron, Ezra, and Neh, with an interpolated story not extant in Hebrew; and Esdras B—a straightforward form of the Hebrew Ezra and Neh as one book. In the current Vulgate four books of Esdras are given: I and II Esdras (Jerome's rendering of Esdras B into two separate books); III Esdras (the Old Latin version of Esdras A, derived independently from Hebrew canonical sources and not—as was once supposed—from Septuagint Esdras B); IV Esdras (a composite, the central "Ezra Apocalypse" originally written in Hebrew but extant only in Syriac and other non-Hebrew versions). Jerome rejected III and IV Esdras as uncanonical; the Council of Trent (1546) also rejected them from the canon but placed them, with the Prayer of Menasses, in an appendix to the NT. The Geneva Bible (1560) established the AV arrangement, placing I and II Esdras in OT as Ezra and Neh, III and IV Esdras in the Apocrypha as 1 and 2 Esdras. For more detail see *ODCC* "Esdras".

1[2] Present scholarship dates III Esdras (Apocryphal 1 Esdras) c 200–c 50 B.C.; IV Esdras (Apocryphal 2 Esdras) not later than A.D. 117–138.

2 p [ii]

Arbitrary signs used in my Marginal notes, in this & other Books—
  = equal to.
  + in addition to: likewise, the mark of the Positive Pole.
  − less by: likewise, the mark of the Negative Pole
  ✗ disparate from. Ex. gr. Attraction ✗ Contraction, or Repulsion ✗ continuous Dilation.
  ✷ opposed to. Ex. gr. Attraction ✷ Repulsion, or Contraction ✷ Continuous Dilation.
  ✷ Contrary to. Ex. gr. Sweet ✷ Sour; but ✷ Bitter[1]

3 p [ii]

B.C.[1]
430. Hist. of O. T. finishes
401. Cyrus killed in his Expedition against his Brother, Artaxerxes. Retreat of the 10,000./ 401. Socrates' Death/
338. Battle of Cheronæa. 335. Alexander enters Greece.—Temple built on Mount Gerizim.[2]
3223. Death of Alexander—.[3] Praxiteles obiit.—The year after, Demosth. Hyperides, Demades put to death by Antipater.
320. Ptolemy carries 100,000 Jews Captive into Egypt.
312. Seleucus takes Babylon, and the æra of the Seleucidæ begins
306. Successors of Alexander the G. assume the name of King/
284. Supposed Date of the Septuagint—probab. of the Pent. only—[4] 280. Pyrrhus—278. Brennus.
267. Ptolemy m. canal from Nile to Red Sea. 175. An. Epiph. suc[c]eeded Antiochus the Gr.
*172. Antiochus Epiph. Egyptian Exp. in returning from which he plundered Jerusalem. 165. Judas M. purified the Temple—

[*] ?169[5]

2[1] See FICHTE *Bestimmung* 1 n 1.

3[1] A chronological table intended to provide a framework of historical reference for the period of Israelite history during which the apocryphal books were written and compiled.

3[2] Built by the Samaritans (elements of the ten northern tribes of Israel from before the Babylonian captivity) to rival the Temple at Jerusalem.

3[3] Alexander died in 323, the others—as C first wrote—in 322.

3[4] The Septuagint—a Greek translation of the Hebrew scriptures made by Jews living in Alexandria, so called from the tradition that it was the work of seventy-two translators: see *AT* 11 n 1. Whether only the Pentateuch (the first five books of OT) was completed in 284 B.C. is still matter of conjecture. Cf *AR* (1825) 193–4.

3[5] Antiochus Epiphanes attacked Jerusalem and defiled the Temple in 170 B.C.—the same year in which, in his

4   p [vii] | Inhalt

I apprehend, that the second book of the Apocryphal Esdras was not translated by Luther and forms no part of the Apocrypha in the German Bibles.[1] It is to be regretted, however, that Eichhorn had not thought it worthy of his researches—the more so, if he believed it the fiction of some Christian, heretical or orthodox.[2]

5   p 3, lightly cropped | Ueber die Apokryphen

So waren, als sie [die Juden] nach Palästina zurückkehrten, ihre Begriffe von Gott und Vorsehung nicht mehr die alten Mosaischen mit den Erweiterungen und Verfeinerungen, die ihnen ihre früheren Dichterphilosophen und Propheten gegeben hatten, sondern sie waren nach der Religionsphilosophie der Nationen, unter denen sie in Babylonien, Assyrien, und Medien sechzig bis siebenzig Jahre gelebt hatten, verändert, umgebildet und erweitert. Dort war Licht der Gegenstand der Anbetung, weil nach dem Klima von der Läuterung und Mischung des Lichts drückende und verdorrende Hitze, wie belebende und erquickende Kühle so sichtbar abhängt...

[Thus when they [the Jews] returned to Palestine, their concepts of God and Providence were no longer the old Mosaic ones, with the amplifications and refinements given them by their earlier poet-philosophers and prophets, but they were altered, transformed, and expanded by the religious philosophies of the nations under which they had lived in Babylon, Assyria, and Media for sixty to seventy years. There light was the object of worship, for, according to the climate, both oppressive and withering heat and invigorating and quickening coolness so obviously depend on the purity or impurity of the light...]

I have lived myself in the very hottest Climates of Europe, viz Naples, Sicily and Malta: and have been in habits of Intercourse with natives

invasion of Egypt, he captured Ptolemy VI. C may be thinking of Antiochus' second attack on Jerusalem in 168 after Roman intervention in the siege of Alexandria prevented Antiochus from taking command of the whole of Egypt. The harsh regulations instituted after the second defilement of the Temple with the purpose of destroying the Jewish religion led at once to the Maccabbean revolt.

4[1] Luther did translate the whole Apocrypha; his first complete Bible with Apocrypha was published in 1534. For C's copy (or copies) of Luther's Bible, which did not include the Apocrypha, see *NT* COPY A **57** n 2.

4[2] In a notebook entry of c Jan 1828 C regretted that Eichhorn had not "included" in his inquiry the "2nd & 3rd Books" of Esdras—a slip for "3rd & 4th Books", i.e. apocryphal 1 and 2 Esdras —and that, not having "Grabe's Septuagint—nor Fabricius—nor any other source of information", he had no way of testing or enlarging the "Strong interest he felt in them". N 36 f 44ᵛ.

of Barbary, Egypt, and Persia. But I never could trace any other influence of Climate on their minds but that of Languor from Heat, and great feebleness of the imagination not less than of the Understanding/ Even this I suspect attributable still more to despotism and superstition.[1] I will venture to assert that there is more imagination & fancy in Shakespear, than all South Asia has produced from the creation.

6　pp 3–5 | **5** textus continued

...dort [im Babylonien, Assyrien, und Medien] stellte man sich die Gottheit als ein reines Lichtwesen vor, und dachte sich die Entstehung der Dinge als Läuterung des Lichts nach unendlich verschiedenen Graden, weil in jenen Ländern die Einbildungskraft so leicht bis zu Ekstasen und Entzückungen aufglüht.... Je näher nun schon vor dem die althebräischen Feuervorstellungen an diese Lichttheorie angränzten, desto empfänglicher mussten die Exulanten und ihre mit Persien eng verbundene Nachkommen für die Aufnahme der in vielen Stücken anders und eigen modificirten Lichtvorstellungen der höheren Asiaten seyn....

　Diese in ihrem Exilium angefangene Umkehrung ihrer Denkart und Begriffe vermehrte nach der Zeit der Umgang mit den Griechen.... Seit diesem neuen Verkehr bemerkten sie bald, dass ihre alten Nationalbegriffe und ihre aus Moses, ihren Dichterphilosophen und Propheten abgeflossene religiöse Vorstellungen mit griechischer Weisheit und Aufklärung in einem nachtheiligen Contrast stunden, und dass sie sich den Griechen nähern müssten, woferne sie nicht dem Spott dieser ihrer Nachbaren Preis stehen, und mit ihren Kinder-Ideen von Gott und der menschlichen Beziehung zu ihm nicht sich selbst verächtlich scheinen wollten....

　So stellte schon Plato die Gottheit als ein reines Licht vor, und die Juden hatten seit ihrem Aufenthalt in Chaldäa und seit ihrem Umgang mit den Persern ihren alten Feuerbegriff in einen Lichtbegriff verfeinert.

[...there [in Babylonia, Syria, and Media] the Divinity was thought of as a pure essence of light, and the origination of things was conceived of as a refinement of light in infinitely various degrees, for in those lands the imagination flared up so easily to ecstasy and rapture.... Therefore, the nearer the ancient Hebrew concept of fire approached to this theory of light,

5[1] For another argument from C's experience of the Mediterranean climate see e.g. JAHRBÜCHER 25.

the more the exiles and their descendants, so closely tied to the Persians, must have been receptive to absorb the modified ideas of light....

This subversion of their mode of thought and ideas, begun during their exile, increased after the time of their association with the Greeks.... Soon after this new association they noticed that their old national ideas and their religious ideas, flowing from Moses and from their poet-philosophers and prophets, stood at a disadvantage in contrast to Greek wisdom and enlightenment, so that they would have to move closer to the Greeks so as not to win the ridicule of these their neighbours, and not to have their childish ideas of God and his relations to man appear ridiculous....

Thus even Plato depicted the Divinity as pure light, and after their sojourn in Chaldea and after their intercourse with the Persians, the Jews refined their old fire-concept into a light-concept.]

The Creation so simply asserted in six Words:[1] and this name of the Creator, the Self-existent, the Strengths;[2] the distinction plainly made between the timeless creative Act, and the subsequent formative; that not any thing visible but a *Word* gave existence to Light, by polarizing the Indifference; and then by Light and its Antagonist successively evolving the several forms of the Universe—;[3] the silence concerning Elements; the terms of the ⟨first⟩ Revelation to Moses;—&c &c—conjoin to disprove Eichhorn's Assertion concerning a Fire-god, and the progressive refinement of the Jewish Faith during the Captivities. How absurd to suppose that a Jew taught from Childhood to consider Light as a creature, and God as a *Person*, should accept Light for a God! Greek Wisdom!! and the Nursery faith of Moses & the Prophets! To what extravagances will not Infidelity seduce even men of Sense and Learning? What other Nation or School ever combined the Unity, the Personëity[4] and the Omnipresence in their conception of God, as the Jewish did? I scarcely know, which of the two E. most libels, Plato or Moses: as if by pure Light Plato meant Light physically and not pure Intelligence—φως αшορᾶτον[5]

6[1] In the Hebrew text, Gen 1.1—"In the beginning God created the heaven and the earth"—consists of only six words.

6[2] The Hebrew name for God in Gen 1 is *Elohim*, a plural form—hence C's "Strength*s*". See *AT* **21** n 2.

6[3] For C's view of the cosmogony arising out of the polarity of light and darkness see Böhme passim, esp **31, 100, 139, 140, 169**. Cf *AT* **26**, and see *CN* iii 4418.

6[4] Cf *NT* COPY A **30, 31** and nn. On

"personëity" (person-ness) generally see BAXTER *Reliquiae* COPY B **42** n 1.

6[5] "Light invisible". Cf θεὸς ἀόρατος (invisible God) in e.g. Col 1.15, 1 Tim 1.17. C repeats from Eichhorn the phrase "pure light": see textus. By his reference to Plato, Eichhorn perhaps reminded C of *Republic* 6.507E–508D, in which Socrates likens the idea of good, the presence of which produces knowledge of truth and reality in the soul, to the light of the sun, which (in full splendour) induces the "pure vision" that brings us

7 p 7

Die palästinischen Juden...konnten sich lange nicht von der Geist
und Herzen lähmenden Vorstellung los machen, dass ihr Jehova den
Hauptkreis seiner Wirkungen innerhalb der Gränzen ihres Landes
habe...

[The Palestinian Jews...for long were unable to free themselves from the
spiritually and emotionally paralysing idea that their Jehovah had the chief
centre of his workings within the boundaries of their land...]

This is downright Falsehood. In what part of the Law or the Prophets
had they not the most direct assertions of the Contrary?

8 p 8, pencil, completed in ink

Doch kann sie [die heilige Bibliothek] nicht zu seiner [Esras] Zeit
zugleich auch geschlossen worden seyn, da der Augenschein lehrt,
dass wenigstens ein weit später geschriebenes Buch, die Weissagungen
*] Daniels, die in die Zeiten kurz nach Antiochus Epiphanes zu setzen
sind, einen Platz darinn erhalten hat...

[Yet it [the collection of sacred books] cannot have been closed exactly at
his [Ezra's] time, for evidence indicates that a book written far later at least,
the prophecies of Daniel, which are to be placed in the time shortly after
Antiochus Epiphanes, received a place in it...]

* I should like to know the secret History of the odd discrepance
between this, ⟨&⟩ Eichhorn's[a] marvellously orthodox Opinion in his
introduction to the Old Test. in the Chapter on Daniel.[1]

9 pp 22–5

Während dass im Palästina noch lange das schwache Licht eines
neuen Tags der Aufklärung mit den Finsternissen der frühen Nacht
rang, war es schon in Aegypten unter den Juden durch die wohl-
thätigen Einflüsse der griechischen Philosophie helle und in manchen
edlen Köpfen völlig lichter Tag geworden, und sie dachten und
philosophirten über Gott, Vorsehung und Unsterblichkeit so rein
und moralisch, als wenige Philosophen von erhabenem und gött-
lichem Geist aus den Zeiten vor Christus, wovon wir ein schönes

a The note continues from here in ink; the preceding inserted "&" is also in ink

knowledge of the world. (In the same
passage occurs the statement that the eye
is "the most sunlike—ἡλιοειδής—of all
the instruments of sense".) But cf **12** and
n 5, below.

8[1] On the history of the introduction
of Dan to OT see *AT* **48** and **49** and nn.

Beyspiel an dem vortrefflichen Verfasser des Buchs der Weisheit haben.

[While in Palestine the weak light of a new day of enlightenment struggled for long with the darkness of the earlier night, among the Jews in Egypt, under the beneficial influences of Greek philosophy, it was broad daylight, and in many noble minds it had become complete daylight, and they thought and philosophised about God, prophecy, and immortality as purely and morally as did few philosophers of elevated and godly spirit in the times before Christ, of which we have an excellent example in the admirable writer of the Book of Wisdom.]

Eichhorn in the *vornehm* style of the philosophists of the time[1] begins by taking for granted the falsehood of all pretences to Revelation, Inspiration, &c. in the Jewish Religion, and treats the Hebrew Nation as a barbarous tribe slowly improving according to their opportunities of becoming acquainted with more refined Races, the Persians, and Greeks. And into what gross inconsistencies with his own facts does not this Theory lead him? According to his Theory the later works of the Jews ought to have been the best; according to his facts they are the worst—nay, such paltry patch-work as [not][a] to deserve Comparison. Meanwhile his instances of refinement in their conceptions of the Deity are mere fancies—or attempts of one or two individuals to adapt—not their scriptural faith to Platonism; but—Platonism to the more religious philosophy of their inspired Scriptures. All History and the concurrent suffrages of all Historians, present the fact that the Jews on from the Captivity to the Birth of Christ were a degenerating not an improving People.

10   p 65, pencil | Ueber das Sittenbuch Jesus des Sohns Sirach

Dieses Verhältniss des Verfassers zu den reiner denkenden und besser aufgeklärten Juden vor dem christlichen Zeitalter, war sehr natürlich, da bis zu ihm die griechische Weisheit noch nicht gelangt war, mit deren Bekanntschaft sich die Periode der moralischen Aufklärung unter den Juden anfängt. Noch weiss er von allen den Kenntnissen nichts, welche seit der Vereinigung der griechischen Philosophie mit der NationalLiteratur der Hebräer keinem Gelehrten fehlen durften... Noch sind ihm die religiosen Begriffe seiner Nation nicht veraltet; noch kennt er keine allegorische Auslegung um den

a Word supplied by the editor

9[1] *Vornehm*—superior. C often implies disapproval when he uses this word: see e.g. HERDER *Von der Auferstehung* **15** ("*quality*-like") and **17** and KANT *Vermischte Schriften* COPY C **24** ("affected quality tone").

Mangelhaften derselben nachzuhelfen, ihre Lücke auszufüllen, und ihre Unvollkommenheit zu vervollkommnen. Noch weiss er nichts von einer Bearbeitung der alten hebräischen Geschichte nach moralischen Geschichtspunkten, sondern er bleibt bey dem Buchstaben ihrer Aufzeichnung...

[This relationship of the author to the Jews of purer thought and greater enlightenment before the time of Christ was most natural, for Greek wisdom had not extended to him yet, with the knowledge of which began the period of moral enlightenment among the Jews. He knew as yet nothing of that learning, which after the union of Greek philosophy with the national literature of the Hebrews no scholar could be without...The religious concepts of his nation are not yet old-fashioned to him; he is not yet capable of an allegorical interpretation, to help out their deficiences, fill in their gaps, and make good their imperfections. He still has no idea of a rewriting of early Hebrew history from a moral point of view but follows its records literally...]

the poor Man[1] did not know how to tell Lies with Theological Decorum

11   pp 87–91 | Ueber das Buch der Weisheit

Weisheit (חָכְמָה, σοφία) diente in der philosophisch-armen Sprache der Hebräer zur Bezeichnung einer Menge von Begriffen, welche die philosophisch–ausgearbeiteten Sprachen anderer Nationen genau zu unterscheiden pflegten....Schon die alten Hebräer sprachen gern von ihrer Vielseitigkeit, und waren unerschöpflich in ihrem Lob. Sie war ihnen die Erstgebohrene des Himmels, Rathgeberin, Gehülfin und Vertraute Gottes bey seinem grossen Werk der Schöpfung....Das ganze Buch der Sprüche Salomo's ist an solchen Aeusserungen reich...

[Wisdom (*ḥakmah, sophia*) served in the philosophically impoverished language of the Hebrews to designate a whole mass of concepts that the more philosophically developed languages of other nations were accustomed to distinguish more precisely....The more ancient Hebrews already loved to speak of its many-sidedness, and were untiring in its praise. To them it was the firstborn of Heaven, counsellor, companion and confidante of God in his great work of creation....The entire book of the Proverbs of Solomon is rich in such expressions...]

Count Zinzendorf, a man of Genius tho' somewhat extra-zodiacal, promulgated the bold Idea, that the Father, Θεος αορατος,[1] God, as the Absolute, the Source & Ground of Being, was unknown to the Jews under the Law & was first revealed by Christ, from whom

---

10[1] I.e. Jesus, son of Sirach.   **11**[1] "God invisible": see **6** n 5, above.

as by a reflected Light Θεος without the article is named ο πατηρ.[2]—
Whether the Count was led to this Assertion by the *Idea*, which I
take as the Ground of my Philosophy, I do not know. At all events,
it is a splendid Conception—and for as many as receive the doctrine
of a miraculous origin of the Scriptures, it would remove many
difficulties & clear up many Obscurities. Ex. gr.—Many Divines have
found or tried to find the Second Person of the Trinity in *the Wisdom*
of the Proverbs; but this, the Santa Sophia, of the Greek Church,
is every where in the Christian Fathers the name of the Holy
Ghost[3]—and assuredly to the Holy Ghost the functions described in
the Proverbs, in Ecclesiasticus, and in the Wisdom of Solomon, are
appropriate rather than to the Logos.—But so according to
Zinzendorf it ought to be. The Son is the Jehovah, the Supreme *Being*
or Reason; and the Abysmal WILL, the Eternal Antecedent of Being,
not having been declared to the Elder Church, the subordinate
Godhead could only be the Holy *Spirit*. In short, the Fathers under
the Law knew only Jehova God, the Lord, and the Spirit of the Lord.
The Absolute WILL, essentially immanifestable in itself but eternally
begetting the Supreme Reason, or Absolute Being as its manifesta-
tion, or person, or essential Form, Deus Alter et Idem,[4] was indeed
from the beginning manifest *in* the co-eternal I Word, but first
declared or made known *by* the Word Incarnate.—Do I believe that
the Writers of the old Testament were conscious of any such
Ideas?—What if they were not?—The Bible *is* that which it is capable
of reflecting—It is the Mirror of Faith.—[5]

12   pp + 1 and [544], referring to p 106 | Ueber den ersten Theil des Buchs der Weisheit

Plato äussert sich über die WeltSeele in vielen Stücken eben so wie
der anonyme Verfasser der Weisheit über seinen Geist Gottes. Plato
dachte sich Gott nicht mehr wie die frühern Philosophen als Feuer
oder Aether, sondern als ein Licht, sey es nun, dass er die gröbere
Feuer- und AetherTheorie in die feinere LichtTheorie veredelt, oder
dass er sie (wovon man aber keine sichere Spuren kennt) aus dem

11[2] "God...the father". Nikolaus
Ludwig, Count Zinzendorf (1700–60)
propounded his view in *Theologischer
und dahin einschlagender Bedencken*
(1741). See also BROOKE **25** n 2.
11[3] On Sophia and Santa Sophia see
BIBLE *NT Gospels* **3** n 1, DONNE *Sermons*
COPY B **75** n 1, and the annotation quoted

in *SM* (*CC*) 67 n 2. See also DE WETTE
37 and **42** and *CN* IV 4870.
11[4] For "Deus Alter et Idem" (God
the Other and the Same) see esp BÖHME
172 and n 1, **178** and n 1. See also **23** n 3,
below.
11[5] Cf Gregory the Great *Moralia* 2.1.

Morgenland erborgt hat. Nach ihm ist der Verstand (νοῦς) zuerst von der Gottheit erzeugt worden; in ihm haben die Ideen, welches lauter Substanzen sind, ihren Sitz; folglich ist in ihm die Ideen- oder IntellectualWelt. Das Erste, was Gott ausbildete, war die WeltSeele, ein Compositum aus Licht und Materie; er vereinigte mit ihr einen Theil seiner Substanz, indem er seine Ideen, die göttlicher Natur und Theile von der göttlichen Substanz sind, mit Materie verband. Nun setzte er die WeltSeele in die Mitte der Welt, dehnte sie durch die ganze Welt aus, und hüllte alles Körperliche in sie ein, so dass auch von aussen die Seele das grosse Ganze um schliesst und zusammenhält.

Setzt man zu diesen orientalisch-platonischen Ideen noch die NationalBegriffe der Hebräer von Gott, so ist der Ursprung der obigen Schilderung des Geistes der Weisheit nach ihrem ganzen Umfang erklärt.

Schon der *frühern Hebräern* war der Geist Gottes, ein Hauch Gottes, ein heiliges, wohlthätiges, menschenfreundliches, alles Gute liebendes Wesen...

[In many passages Plato expresses himself in regard to the World-Soul exactly as the anonymous author of the Wisdom does in regard to his Spirit of God. Plato no longer thought of God in the manner of the earlier philosophers, as fire or ether, but as a light; whether it was that he refined the cruder fire- and ether-theory into the light-theory or that he borrowed it from the East (although no certain traces of this borrowing are recognised). According to him Reason (νοῦς) was created by God at the beginning; in it the ideas, which are pure substances, have their seat; therefore in it is the world of ideas, or of the intellect. The first thing that God gave outward form was the world-soul, a compound of light and matter; he united with it a portion of his own substance, by combining his ideas, which are of divine nature and part of the divine substance, with matter. Now he set the world-soul in the middle of the world, extended it throughout the whole world, and enveloped in it all that has body, so that from the outside too the soul encloses and holds together the whole universe.

If the national concepts of God among the Hebrews are put with these oriental-platonic ideas, the source of the foregoing description of Wisdom in its whole extent is clear.

To even the *earlier Hebrews* the Spirit of God was a breath of God, a holy, beneficent essence, favourably disposed to man and loving all that is good...]

106. Has not Plato declared that by intellectual Light he does not mean the Light which is an Object of the senses?[1] If they are the same, or different only by purification, how can the Light-Theory be

12[1] See *Republic* 6.508ff and cf **6** and n 5, above.

deemed a finer or more spiritual Theory than that of Fire? Is it not as easy to conceive a pure, elementary Fire as a pure, elementary Light? Has not Heraclitus written as loftyily and spiritually of his monad that can be conceived by the mind only as two, each opposed to the other, ερως και νικη, and πυροειδης?[2]—So again with regard to the ὕλὴ of Plato & his followers, the το μη ον, whose essence is negation,[3] did it mean any thing but that finiteness, which must be permitted if there were to be any thing but God as God—and therefore so far necessary & co-eternal, as God's communicatin[g][a] Goodness is necessary. το εν = το αγαθον—whereas Νους, το καλον,[4] &c are not in that absolute sense identical, but posterior in order of Thought. I would as soon believe that Plato taught the equality of an equilateral Triangle to a Pound Sterling, or the identity of a pure Circle with a plum-pudding, or a Pound Weight, as that he held God to be Light, or that Light, i.e. the material Image which and by which we see bodily, could be νοερον, φιλαγαθὸν, φιλάνθ-ρωπον, &c.[5] That the visual Light may have its ground or causative principle in the immaterial Light, what is that but to say—that the sensuous is but a shadow & unsubstantial Creation of the super-

---

[a] Letter supplied by the editor

12² "Love and strife"—but C has written νικη (victory) in error for νεῖκος (strife)—and "fire-like". Love (φιλία rather than ἔρως) and strife were, in Empedocles' system, the forces of attraction and repulsion that caused the coming together and separating out of the four elements. To Empedocles also is attributed the view that τὸ τῆς μονάδος νοερὸν πῦρ (the intellectual fire of the monad) is God. Diels I 289.1. Heraclitus is said to have described the soul as πυρῶδες (fire-like): Diels I 109.15. The term *monad*, however, does not appear in the surviving fragments of Heraclitus; it is found principally in the Pythagoreans or as the "One" in Parmenides, and is appropriate to the universe under the predominance of love in Empedocles' scheme. For C's fondness for compounds with -ειδής cf BIBLE COPY B **116** and n 1.

12³ "Matter...not-being".

12⁴ "The one is the same as the good—whereas Mind, the beautiful".

12⁵ Some of the epithets of wisdom as given in Wisd 7.22–3, quoted by Eichhorn pp 108, 117, and here ascribed by C

to the φῶς ἀόρατον (cf **6** at n 5): (AV) "for in her is an understanding (νοερόν) spirit, holy, one only, manifold, subtil, lively, clear, undefiled, plain, not subject to hurt, loving the thing that is good (φιλαγαθόν), quick, which cannot be letted (ἀκώλυτον), ready to do good, kind to man (φιλάνθρωπον), stedfast, sure, free from care, having all power, overseeing all things, and going through all understanding, pure, and most subtil spirits". See also **23** and n 3, below.

Eichhorn, in giving as Plato's the view that God is a light, cites (p 105) *Phaedrus* (perhaps 250B–C, but there is some error in his reference to the Bipontine ed) and *Republic* 7.517C–D, 616B–617D (in the first of which the idea of good is "the author of light"). All these references are to "myths"; Eichhorn seems to take them literally in spite of Plato's warnings. On pp 109–10, however, Eichhorn says that Plato does not say *ausdrücklich* (explicitly) that God is a *Lichtwesen* (of the essence of light) but that such a view is implied.

sensual/ and that as *we* can name the cause only from or in relation
to the effects, so we may call God Light—even as we call Calorique
Heat, i.e. a Heat-causing.—[6]

13   p ⁻1, evidently referring to pp 117–21, or a continuation of 12

When Eichhorn had before him such a case in point as the free and
comparatively elegant Version from an Hebrew Original in the
apocryphal Esdras, see p 336[1]—one wonders, he had not stated the
possibility if not probability of the Book of Wisdom being likewise
eine wirkliche ⟨übersetzung,⟩ ob es gleich ~~nich~~ keine sklavische
über~~setzung~~tragung der hebräischen Worte in griechische ist, weil der
U. sich die vernünftige freiheit nahm die gar zu harten Hebraismen
zu vermeiden.[2]—To my feeling at least it is not a *Greek* Original; and
yet the work of one who wished to make it as much Greek, as fidelity
would allow. Even the many far-fetched, unusual, and newly-
compounded * Words[3] seem to me confirmations that this Work is
a translation, and that the Author had to ask himself or inquire—what
is the Greek for such a word, or such a phrase!—for odd words are
not apt to crowd on a man who thinks in the Language in which he
is composing:—Some however of the words marked by Eichhorn are
far from peculiar to the Wisd. of. Sol.—as νοερον, a favorite word
with the Alexandrine Abstraction-mongers, & distinguished by them
from νοητον, as νοερον και νοητον, i.e. intellectual & intelligible[4]—
thus the first hypostasis of the Eclectic Trinity would be νοερον

12[6] *Calorique*—Lavoisier's term (c
1790) for "a supposed elastic fluid to
which the phenomena of heat were
formerly attributed" (*OED*). In a long
note on the difficulty of reaching an exact
functional definition of terms, C examines
"Caloric", and continues: "By Caloric
are we [to] understand a Quality, Prop-
erty, Function or particular modifica-
tion of some higher Power (Repulsion,
for instance)—Or a distinct kind of
Matter, a peculiar Fluid for in-
stance....Is Caloric a thing, in the
sense in which Water is a thing, or a mode
in which a thing exists, as a Wave?...The
answer will, I imagine, greatly depend on
the answers given to the same question
put concerning Light?..." *CN* IV 5144.

13[1] "However, an exact comparison
of this with the Hebrew Ezra has
convinced me that this latter obviously

lies at the foundation of the former, and
that the apocryphal book, in the places
where it is parallel to the canonical, is
nothing more than a free translation of
the Hebrew Ezra as we have it." See also
1 n 1, above.

13[2] "An actual translation, although
it is not a slavish rendering of the Hebrew
words into Greek, since the translator
took the reasonable liberty of avoiding
the over-harsh Hebraisms" (p 338 var).

13[3] Eichhorn writes about these words
on pp 117, and 121 n *h*.

13[4] On νοερόν (intellectual) and
νοητόν (intelligible) see BROWNE
Works 53 n 4 and BIBLE *NT Gospels* 3 n
2. C is apparently thinking of Philo's
system, in which God is the intellect
creating the universe that he intellects, as
in *De opificio mundi* 4.16.

perhaps, but not νοητον, the second, or Λογος, both νοερον και νοητον. Ακωλυτος, I think, occurs either in Epictetus, or Marc Antonine.[5]—The Play on Words would supply some proof of its being originally Greek, but the two only instances which E. gives in the Note, may be accidental, and are not striking[6]—and the Balancing of Sentences is pure Parallelismus. In short, the Book was either ~~written in Greek~~ composed, as it now is: the Author trying to hebraize ~~the style~~ his Greek; or translated from the Hebrew, the Translators endeavoring to ~~soften~~ Greecize & accommodate the Hebraisms.—[7]

* I retract the above Remark. A man could not *think* so in Hebrew.—

14 p 146 | Ueber den zweyten Theil des Buchs der Weisheit

Im ersten Theil ist Freygeisterey und Atheismus Quelle aller Laster (Cap. II.), im zweyten ist es Abgötterey (Cap. XIV, 12.); im ersten Theil ist Tugend Grund der Unsterblichkeit (I, 15. II, 23–III, 4.), im zweyten ist es Bekanntschaft mit der Grösse des Jehova, d. i. intuitive Kenntniss von ihr (XV, 3.); im ersten Theil trifft man nicht leicht Aeusserungen im engherzigen JudenGeist an; der zweyte Theil ist davon voll.

[In the first part scepticism and atheism are the sources of all depravity (Ch 2), while in the second it is idolatry (Ch 14.12); in the first part virtue is the basis of immortality (1.15; 2.23–3.4), while in the second it is acquaintance with the greatness of Jehovah—that is, intuitive knowledge of it (15.3); in the first part there are few pronouncements done in the restricted spirit of Judaism, while the second part is filled with them.]

Had E. forgotten his New Testament? forgotten, that "to know God & him whom God hath sent" is Life everlasting[1]—i.e. the Ground and efficient Cause of all those moral & spiritual perfections of that sanctity of the whole Man without which no man can have "intuitive Kenntniss" of God?

13[5] "Unhindered"—in Eichhorn pp 117, 121, from Wisd 7.22 (see **12** n 5, above). The word ἀκώλυτος occurs often in Epictetus but not, apparently, in Marcus Aurelius. Eichhorn had pointed out (p 108) the Cabbalistic nature of the passage (see **18** and n 3, below) and

(p 117) that the words are current among Alexandrian Platonists.
13[6] Eichhorn p 122 n *i*: Wisd 1.8: ἄδικα—δίκη; 5.10: ἄτραπον—τρόπιος.
13[7] Scholars now consider that Wisd was not a translation, but that it was written in Greek by Alexandrian Jews.
14[1] John 17.3 (var).

15 p 148

Endlich das Buch der Weisheit ist schon von mehreren Gelehrten für ein defectes Werk gehalten worden, weil es viel zu abgebrochen endiget. Gehört der letzte Theil desselben gar nicht zu dem Hauptwerk, so lässt sich der Ursprung dieser Erscheinung leicht und *]natürlich erklären. Entweder fügte man den letzten Theil hinzu, um einen leeren Raum der Haut, welche das Buch der Weisheit nicht ganz füllte, nicht ungenützt zu lassen; oder um auf einen Raum etwas vollständige philosophische Betrachtungen über die älteste Geschichte der Hebräer oder kunstreiche Combinationen aus derselben beysammen zu besitzen.

[Finally, the Book of Wisdom has before now been taken by many of the learned for an incomplete work because it ends much too abruptly. If this last part of it does not belong at all to the main work, the reason for this phenomenon is easy and natural to explain. Either the last part was added in order to fill up an empty space on a parchment that the Book of Wisdom did not entirely fill, so as not to leave it unused; or to have in one place some completed philosophic considerations concerning the earliest history of the Hebrews, or some artistic combinations from it.]

* This hypothesis has had "hot service"[1]—it has been a very *Mungo*[2] to Eichhorn—but verily, frames of Iron will wear out at last. S. T. C.

16 p 148

[Eichhorn suggests that the original writer of the Book of Wisdom has accompanied his recommendations of wisdom with such moralisings over the earlier history, up to Moses, as would serve as an example and spur to his readers, and that then some ancient Jew or other added further examples from another work covering the Egyptian–Arabian period of Jewish history.] Durch diese Hypothese würde der Ursprung von der veränderten Einkleidung des Buchs der Weisheit und der auffallenden Inconsistenz seiner Grundsätze, und dem Fragmentarischen desselben am Ende von selbst in die Augen fallen.

[Through this hypothesis the reason for the change of style of the Book of Wisdom and the striking inconsistencies of its basic principles, and its fragmentation at the end, would be perfectly clear.]

15[1] See EICHHORN *AT* **46** and n 3.
15[2] Don Diego's black servant in Isaac Bickerstaffe's comic opera *The Padlock* (1768). Cf Act I sc vi: "Poor black man must run; | Mungo here, Mungo dere, | Mungo every where; | Above and below, | Sirrah come, Sirrah go, | Do so, and do so. | Oh! Oh!"

The shallow Morality of Paley, Garve, Faber &c,[1] which Kant crushed with elephantine feet,[2] and the constitutional Lack of all religious Sensibility, fitted E. admirably for the Scavenger office of removing Rubbish; but—in short, Scavengers are not Architects!—

17   pp 156–7

Als *ägyptischen Juden* bezeichnet sich der Verfasser der zweyten Hälfte der Weisheit, durch seine genaue Kenntniss von Aegypten, und manches andere, das ägyptischen Juden eigenthümlich war.... Den WürgEngel, welcher die ägyptische ErstGeburt erschlug, nennt er λόγος πανδύναμος, ein Name, den gerade die ägyptischen Juden gern von Engeln gebrauchten *p*) [Footnote *p*:]...Und Philo nennt die Engel sehr häufig λογους...

[It is as an *Egyptian Jew* that the author of the second half of the Wisdom identifies himself—by his exact knowledge of Egypt, and by much else that was peculiar to the Egyptian Jews. The Angel of Death which struck the firstborn of Egypt he calls "omnipotent word", a name the Egyptian Jews were fond of using for angels *p*)...[Footnote *p*:]...And Philo very frequently calls angels "words"....]

It is strange that Eichhorn should not have noticed the distinction between the plural Λογοι and the singular with the epithet π̄ omnipotent![1]—Where ⟨else⟩ has Philo called a single Angel τον λογον.[2]—The Logos was the divine Pleroma, Idea Ideas omniformes continens, perpetuè parturiens[3]—With Pythagoras the Messengers or Secondary Agents of the Absolute Will were Numbers; with Plato Ideas; with the Platonizing Jews Words.[4]

16[1] For Paley see BLANCO WHITE *Practical Evidence* 1 n 1 and *LS (CC)* 186 n 2. Christian Garve (1742–98) translated Paley's *Principles of Moral Political Philosophy* (1785) into German, and—with J. J. Engels—adversely reviewed Kant's *Critique of Pure Reason*. Johann Melchior Faber (1743–1809) published a series of "Programmata" (1776–87) on Wisdom.

16[2] Cf KANT *Vermischte Schriften* COPY C 32, review of Herder's *Ideen zur Philosophie der Geschichte der Menschheit*, which C considered "a perfect *model* of a Review" and declared that it left Herder "defunct as a Philosopher". Cf *NT* COPY A 22 and 54.

17[1] Referring to πανδύναμος in the textus—Eichhorn's slip for παντοδύναμος.

17[2] Hans Leisegang's *Index verborum* in Philo's *Opera* (Berlin 1896–1926) under λόγος IV confirms that Philo did indeed call the angels Logoi, but it gives no example of λόγος used of an angel (singular). Philo explains a single angel as an allegory of the divine Logos in e.g. *Quod Deus immutabilis sit* 37.182. For Philo on Logos see e.g. 23, below, and *NT* COPY A 32. C's inserted "else" suggests that here he is thinking of Philo as the author of Wisd: cf 18 and n 1, below. See also FLEURY 87 and n 1.

17[3] "The Idea containing the omniform Ideas, perpetually bringing to birth".

17[4] For numbers as ideas see HOOKER 6 n 4.

18 p 158, probably a continuation of 17[a]

N.B. In this Book (assuming that it is elder than Philo's Works)[1] I find the first Gleam, the *Dawn* of the Idea of the Trinity.—as Νους, Λογος & Σοφια,[2] in a Jewish Writer.—I conjecture, that the Cabalistic School commenced between the Maccabæian æra and the date of this Book, supposing it about a Century before the Birth of our Lord[3]—The failure of the Nation's Messianic Hopes in so many successive Instances would naturally lead the nobler Minds, especially after their acquaintance with the philosophy of Pythagoras, Heraclitus & Plato, to *spiritualize* their Messiah.—But it is requisite to have entered into the heart & soul of the *Realist* Scheme ⚹ Nominalist, before we can do common justice to the Masters of the Cabala.[4]

19 p 157

...er [der Verfasser] verbindet platonische Philosophie mit seinem väterlichen Glauben, wie von ägyptischen Juden seit ihrer Niederlassung in Alexandrien gewöhnlich geschah. Platonisch ist es, dass er die Welt aus einem ungestalten Klumpen (ὕλη ἄμορφος) durch Gottes Kraft gebildet lässt...

[...[the author] combines Platonic philosophy with the beliefs of his fathers, as occurred customarily among the Egyptian Jews after their domicile in Alexandria. Platonic it is that he has the world formed out of a figureless *clump* (matter without form) [Wisd 11.17] through the power of God.]

---

[a] Note 17 is written in the foot-margins of pp 156, 157. The outer margin of p 157 being filled with **19** and **20**, the continuation of **17** was written in the margin of p 158

18[1] Philo lived c 20 B.C.–A.D. 50. Eichhorn's various discussions appear to date Wisdom between 200 B.C. and the early Christian era. He dismisses the possibility of Philo's authorship after a detailed comparison of style and teaching.

18[2] "Mind, Word, & Wisdom". In Wisd God is called Θεός, never Νοῦς (Mind); his ministers are his Word (Λόγος) and Wisdom (Σοφία). Philo (according to the *Index verborum*) often described God as Νοῦς, and described λόγος and σοφία as his agents. It is not certain from the passages referring to λόγος or to σοφία that Philo identified Word and Wisdom as C implies at the end of **23**, below.

18[3] In N 33 f 9[v] (*CN* v) C considered that the Cabbalistic school could not have been later than the beginning of the Maccabaean era, c 167–100 B.C. See also *P Lects* Lect 10 (1949) 299, 444 n 21. For Eichhorn's argument that Wisd was not earlier than the beginning of the Cabbalistic school, on the evidence of the Cabbalistic nature of Wisd 7.22, see **13** n 5, above.

18[4] For C's account of the difference between Realists and Nominalists see *P Lects* Lect 9 (1949) 290–1; see also BAXTER *Reliquiae* COPY B **8** n 1, *TT* 30 Apr 1830 and JOANNES Scotus Erigena **2** n 3. The point that C is making here is made less elliptically in *P Lects* Lect 10 (1949) 300.

a wanton mistranslation—ὕλη, of which Sylva is the Italian Dialect-form, means materia indistinctè confusa[1]—Hence *Sylva* for a Miscellany.[2] How can a *Clump* be figureless? Who talks of a Clump of *Water*?

20 p 157[a]

Platonisch ist es...dass er die intuitive Kenntniss für den höchsten Gipfel der Weisheit hält; vielleicht auch das παραληφθῆναι [Wisd 15.3], welches er von der Trennung der Seele von ihrer groben körperlichen Behaussung gebraucht...

[It is Platonic...that he holds intuitive knowledge to be the highest peak of wisdom; perhaps also the word "being received", which he uses for the division of the soul from its rude physical housing.]

In order to the ψυχη[1] having any definite meaning, there must be Insight into the antagonist Factors of organic Life—Geneic[b] Nature ⚹ Prin. Indiv.[c2] The Soul is opposed to the Corpus *phænomenon* only. Of the Corpus *reale* seu *noumenon*,[3] it is one of the Poles, viz + ⚹ −, or Actual ⚹ Potential.

21 pp 172 and +1, referring to p 172 | Ueber das Buch der Weisheit überhaupt

Nach dem Buch der Weisheit braucht ein Kind zehn Monathe zu seiner Bildung in Mutterleib (Weish. VII, 2.); nach Philo hingegen nur sieben Monathe, und wenn es später gebohren wird, so geschieht es mit Gefahr seines Lebens.

[According to the Book of Wisdom, a child requires ten months for formation within its mother's body (Wisd 7.2); according to Philo, on the other hand, only seven months, and if it is born later, its life is endangered.]

---

[a] Both **19** and **20** are written in the outer margin. C has drawn a line below **19**
[b] Possibly a slip for "Generic", but see **20** n 2, below
[c] Here C has written * and continued the note with * in the head-margin

19[1] "Matter indistinctly jumbled together".

19[2] *Sylva*—more correctly *silva*—primarily a wood or forest, could also, like ὕλη, mean raw material, undifferentiated matter. Perhaps through the sense of a forest-like abundance, the word was extended to apply to a literary work of varied content, and was so used by Statius and by Renaissance writers. Cf *CN* IV 5136: "...ὕλη, hyle. Materia, matter taken *collectively*, or miscellaneously (hence a *miscellany* of any sort, of Poems,

or Annotations, or &c is called a *Silva*—. So Statius's Sylvæ, or Miscellanies.)..." Cf *SM* (*CC*) 55–6 n 4 (ms note) on etymologies, including this one.

20[1] Psyche, "Soul".

20[2] "Generic Nature as opposed to the Principle of Individuation". Cf FLEURY **85** n 1 (from N 35). "Geneic" (not in *OED*) could be C's formation of an adjective from γένος, γένεος rather than from Latin *genus, generis*. Cf γενικός in LACUNZA II 182–3.

20[3] "The *real* or *noumenal* Body".

Vide p. 545, M.S.S.*a*

172. Eichhorn has strangely misunderstood the Passage in Philo, and attributed to him an ignorance ~~beyond~~low that of old Women and Girls of 14. The meaning is—"Who does not know, that of Infants *some* are born in the 7th month, but others who are born later, as in the 8th month, run great risk"—which is a well known fact—and Philo is speaking of both the one and the other as exceptions to the natural order of 9 or 10 months.[1]

22 pp 180–1

Das Buch der Weisheit lehrt einen Zustand der Belohnung und Bestrafung nach diesem Leben, und der glückliche Zustand nach diesem Leben heisst ihm Unsterblichkeit, und dagegen der unglückliche Zustand nach demselben Tod (I, 12–16. II, 21–III, 3.)...

Das Buch der Weisheit lehrt Präexistenz der Seelen von doppelter, guter und böser Art. Auch Philo nimmt zweyerley Gattungen von Seelen, gute und böse, an, mit denen die Luft angefüllt sey...

[The Book of Wisdom teaches a condition of reward and punishment after this life, and the felicitous condition after this life it calls immortality, and against this the unfortunate condition afterwards it calls death (1.12–16; 2.21 to 3.3)...The Book of Wisdom teaches the pre-existence of souls of two kinds, good and evil. Philo too assumes two kinds of souls, good and evil, with which the air is filled...]

Nothing can shew more ~~completely~~ clearly the true Source of Man's faith in a conscious existence after death, and how completely it is a moral source, than ~~th~~ our consummate indifference ~~about~~ with regard to the Question of our Pre-existence, and the fact that it has been mooted only by two or three speculative Virtuosi, seemingly as a divertisement of their superabundant Leisure![1] And yet intellectually it is a Question of great Interest.

a I.e. p +1, the inside of the original grey wrapper

21[1] Eichhorn gives the Greek of Philo *De legum allegoria* 1.4.13: "Who does not know that seven months' infants come to the birth, while those that have taken a longer time, remaining in the womb eight months, are as a rule still-born." Tr F. H. Colson and G. H. Whittaker (LCL 1929). C is evidently unaware of the context: Philo is accumulating illustrations of the proposition that "nature delights in the number seven".

22[1] C is perhaps overreacting—as he did in the case of Jacobinism—against a belief he had once held. The image of the pre-existence of the soul that set WW's *Immortality Ode* in motion two years after it had stranded at the end of strophe IV is supposed to have come from Proclus and to have come to WW through C. See, however, *BL* ch 22 (*CC*) II 147, in which, after giving a memorable description of the qualifications needed in a good reader of the *Ode*, C peremptorily

23 p +1, evidently referring to p 189*a*

[Eichhorn is considering the Book of Wisdom as a Judaic work incorporating its basic ideas from Alexandrian Platonism.] Indessen der λόγος ist überhaupt den spätern Juden die personificirte Weisheit: mag es seyn, dass dieser Begriff aus der Vereinigung der Chaldäer- und PerserWeisheit mit alt-hebräischen Begriffen von der Weisheit, die schon im Hiob und den Sprichwörtern Rathgeberinn Gottes bey der WeltSchöpfung ist, sich gebildet habe: muss ein jüdischer Schriftsteller, der ihn hat, gerade in den Zeiten gelebt haben, als Zoroaster aufstund, dessen Schule auch alles durchs Wort werden lässt?... Es wäre wenigstens wahrscheinlich, wenn auch alles Uebrige zoroastrisch im Buch der Weisheit wäre; wenn es chaldäisch-mystisch, wenn es von Amuleten, Beschwörungen und magischen Künsten redete. Allein von allem dem ist es ganz frey, und hält sich vielmehr an Worte und Sprüche der platonischen Schule.

[At the same time, among the later Jews the *logos* is generally wisdom personified: may it be that this concept grew up out of the union of Chaldean and Persian wisdom with ancient Hebrew ideas of wisdom, which in Job and Proverbs is already a counsellor to God at the creation? Must a Judaic writer who held it have lived exactly at the time Zoroaster arose, whose school also had everything made by the Word?...It might at least be plausible if everything else in the Book of Wisdom were Zoroastrian, if it were Chaldaic-mystic, if it spoke of amulets, conjurations, and magic arts. But it is entirely free of all that, and holds itself much more to words and expressions of the Platonic school.]

It betrays an unacquaintance with the writings of the Alexandrine Philosophers, from Philo to Proclus, at least with the spirit of their writings, to call the Λογος a *personification* of wisdom—as if Philo meant no more than a modern Poet, or Allegorist—or as Prudentius in his Psychomachia.[1] The very essence of this Philosophy is the Abstractorum—i.e. Universalium Realismus[2]—The Wisdom of God in Philo, or Word, is a distinct Being from God, as distinct as any of the Angels, altho' not divided or divisible.[3]

a This note is written in the middle of p +1 below **21** (with its reference to p 172); note **12**, written below **22** and overrunning backwards to the preceding p [544], was written last

dismisses the possibility that WW believed the doctrine (cf WW's comment in *WPW* iv 464) and dismisses the possibility that Plato "ever meant or taught it". Cf FLEURY 36 n 2.

23[1] In the *Psychomachia* Aurelius Clemens Prudentius (c 348–c 410) depicts the struggle of Christianity with paganism under the allegory of a conflict between Christian virtues and pagan vices.

23[2] "The Realism of Abstracts, i.e. Universals".

23[3] See *TT* 23 Jun 1834, paragraph 2, in which C lists some epithets that show Philo thinking of the personality—as

24 p 240 | Ueber das Erste Buch der Makkabäer

[Eichhorn points out that the author of 1 Maccabees makes mistakes when he writes about lands far from his own: he had Darius rule Greece, Alexander divide his kingdom among his generals rather than vaguely nominate "the worthiest man" as his successor, etc.]

This is surely hyper-critical.

25 p [544]

O that none were called Christians, who were not Christians!— Then all would be Christians, who were not Beasts or Devils. I see no medium between sceptical Deism, & Xtnty, considered as Redemption.

---

distinguished from personification—of the Logos and the distinctness of its being from God. Cf **11** (at n 4), above, on God as "Alter et Idem": Philo describes the Logos as "second God" (an alternative meaning for *alter* being "second") in *Quaestiones in Genesin* 2.62. See also *NT* COPY A **32** and n 1.

It may not be a coincidence that C's attitude to Philo is very like that of Jacob Bryant (1715–1804) in *The Sentiments of Philo Judeus Concerning the* ΛΟΓΟΣ, *or*

Word of God; together with large extracts from his writings compared with the Scriptures on many other particular and essential doctrines of the Christian religion (Cambridge 1797). Bryant finds much evidence of Christian influence in Philo, and lists (pp 108–54) sentences from Philo about the Logos, with parallels from NT. These include all the phrases in the list given in *TT*, including "second divinity".

Copy A

Einleitung in das Neue Testament. 3 vols. Leipzig 1804, 1810–11, 1812–14. 8°.

Vols II and III were issued in two parts each, each vol paged in a single series. Series title (facing title-page) in each volume: "J. G. Eichhorn's Kritsche Schriften" v, vi, vii. This set bound uniformly with *AT* and *Apocrypha* to form a set of 7 vols.

British Museum C 126 f 5

"S.T.C." label on the title-page verso of each volume. John Duke Coleridge's monogram on I ⁻5.

Coleridge's copy. On 7 Feb 1829 he wrote to Green: "The second Volume of my Eichhorn's Einleitung to the New Testament has been long ago alibi in terra incognita ["adrift in an unknown land"]—and now the first part of Volume 3rd is missing—just at the very time, that I am beginning my notes, chapter by Chapter, on the Epistles of Paul.... I should be much obliged to you therefore... to bring with you the two intermediate Volumes." *CL* vi 784. (In fact, the discussion of the Pauline epistles begins with III i.) Green's set is COPY B.

In this work Eichhorn's purpose was to complement the work of the "lower critics"—i.e. the textual critics—by demonstrating what factual conclusions about the date, authorship, meaning, and historical context of the books of the New Testament could be reached by the process that he called "the Higher Criticism" (see Vorrede, I v–viii). His main conclusions were that behind the four canonical gospels lay an *Urevangelium* that all four evangelists had used; that the accounts of the miracles were amplifications of natural events informed by oriental modes of thought and by a desire to magnify the life and work of Jesus; and that many of the so-called Pauline epistles were actually the work of other hands. In all this he distinguishes between the Christianity set forth by Jesus and the later Apostles at Jerusalem and the Christianity preached by St Paul.

DATE. c 1816–19 and 1827–8, **57** being after Jul 1828.

COEDITOR. Merton A. Christensen.

DISTRIBUTION OF MARGINALIA IN THE TWO COPIES

	Text	COPY A	COPY B	Subject
I	9–406	**1–14**		Earliest gospels
	430–512	**15–22**		Matthew
	576	**23**		Mark
	598	**24**		Luke
	634–49	**25–27**		Gospels generally
II	40–1	**28, 29**		Acts
	109–57	**30–38**	1	John
	158–210		2–6	

DISTRIBUTION OF MARGINALIA IN THE TWO COPIES

Text	COPY A	COPY B	Subject
213–65	39–42	7–10	
303		11	1 John
346–77		12–15	Revelation
387	43	16	
469	44		
III 1–14	45–46	17–21	Pauline Epistles
61		22, 23	1 Thessalonians
71–81		24–25	Galatians
102–59	47–49		1 Corinthians
202–15	50–51	26	Romans
289–90		27	Colossians
340	52		1 Timothy
413–63		28–30	Hebrews
497	53		
580	54	31	James
603–16	55	32	Peter
618–21	56–58		1 Peter
631–2	59, 60		2 Peter
646–8	61, 62		Jude

1 1–2, referring to I 10 (actually I 9) | Evangelien 1 Evangelium der Hebräer § 2

[Eichhorn, pp 6–10, discusses three titles of this no-longer-extant Gospel: (*a*) εὐαγγέλιον καθ᾽ Ἑβραίους, (*b*) Evangelium secundum Apostolos, (*c*) Evangelium secundum Matthaeum.]

P. 10. How strikingly does not this confirm my old & constant hypothesis, that the κατα in the titles of ~~our~~ the 3 first Gospels must be interpreted by the καθως of Luke![1] Κατα τους Ἑβραιους, would be a Collection of the Κηρηυγματα (testimonies given publicly by the Apostles) as they were *reported* by converted Hebrews—the Notes or *Reports* ~~of~~ taken of the words of the *Heralds*, evangeligzing—ο των κηρυκων τῶν εὐαγγελιζομένων, in use and circulation among the Churches of Palestine;[2] and to which as being written in the same

1[1] AV renders κατά in the titles of the Gospels as "according to". The "καθως of Luke" occurs in Luke 1.2: "Forasmuch as many have taken in hand to set forth a declaration of those things which are most surely believed among us, even as (καθώς) they delivered them unto us, which from the beginning were eyewitnesses, and ministers of the word". C's hypothesis is that κατά in the

titles of the synoptic Gospels stands for—as it does not in that of John—"the καθως of Luke", the whole statement in Luke 1.2 (above). If so, these Gospels would not represent the actual words of the Apostle but merely edited (as in the Gospel According to the Hebrews) reports of their words.

1[2] The Greek phrase is C's translation of "of the *Heralds*, evangelizing".

language, in which they were first announced, and (as far as these *Reports* contained τοῦ Κυριου Λογους as well as πραξεῖς και παθήματα)³ in which they were first spoken—viz. in the *then* Hebrew or Syro-chaldaic Dialect—a great & superior value would naturally be attributed. And more than this need not, in my opinion, be supposed in order to explain the assertion of the Gentile Fathers, the inveterate Slanderers of the Palestine Churches, that the Nazarenes & Ebionites rejected all other Gospels,⁴ but that κατα τους Ἑβραιους, which they afterwards (possibly from some tradition, that it had been revised or sanctioned by Sᵗ Matthew; or that the things were recorded καθως ἐκήρυξεν ὁ Ματθαιος, = i.e. taken down from Matthew's Mouth) entitled κατα τον Ματθαιον.⁵

2 ɪ 14–15, pencil | § 4

In jedem Falle gehörten sie zu den Christen aus Petrus Schule, und *] hiessen Nazaräer und Ebioniter zur Unterscheidung von der Paulinischen Schule, die für sich den Namen Christen (Apostelgesch. 11, 26) erfunden hatte...

[In any event, they belonged to the school of Peter, and were called Nazarenes and Ebionites as a distinction from the Pauline school, which had coined the name Christian (Acts 11.26) for itself...]

* Eichhorn seems not to have been acquainted with Rhenferd's excellent Disquisition on the Ebionites & Epiphanius's slanderous Blunders respecting them,¹ at the same time exposing this father of the Petrine Anti-pauline School;² most unworthy of Eichhorn's adoption. S. T. C.

1³ "The Words of the Lord as well as his acts and sufferings". Cf BIBLE COPY ʙ **82**. For Hone's confusing the *Gospel According to the Hebrews* with the *Gospel of the Birth of Mary* see BIBLE *Apocryphal NT* **2** and n 1.

1⁴ The Nazarene sect of early Jewish Christians held to the Law of Moses for themselves but did not demand such observances of Gentile Christians. The Ebionite sect, which lasted from the first to the fourth century, declared that they were Christians but rejected much of the NT, including the doctrine of the miraculous divinity of Christ, and held to much of the traditional Jewish belief. This information is in Eichhorn—e.g. ɪ 13–17.

1⁵ "Recorded 'according as (even as) Matthew preached'...entitled 'according to Matthew'". Cf *CL* vɪ 611 (8 Sept 1826) and DONNE *Sermons* COPY ʙ **9** n 1.

2¹ Jacob RHENFERD *Operaphilologica* (Utrecht 1722) 109ff, esp 159. C wrote twelve marginalia on this section in Jul 1827, including a comment (p 114) on "the malignant credulity of the Fathers respecting those whom they considered as Heretics".

2² Epiphanius (d 403), bp of Constantia, attacked eighty heresies in his *Panarion*. For his attack on the Ebionites see *Adversus haereses (Panarion)* 2.2.66 (Migne *PL* xLII 125–47); but the substance of it is in RHENFERD.

3　ɪ ⁻1, pencil, referring to ɪ 76 | 2 Marcion's Evangelium §17

Es scheint nemlich dasselbe Evangelium, das in einer unvollendeteren Gestalt in Marcion's Hände kam, eine der Quellen des Evangelisten Lukas gewesen zu seyn, und ihm zur Grundlage seines Evangelienbuchs gedient zu haben.

[It appears that precisely the same gospel that came into Marcion's hands in a less finished form was one of the sources of the Evangelist Luke, and served him as the basis of his gospel.]

Eichhorn's Reasoning respecting the Marcionite Gospel all unsatisfactory, saving the one point—its relation to our Luke.[1] E. seems to have proved pretty fairly, that it was not an intentional correlation—but gives no proof, that it might not have been a transcript, perhaps a careless tr^pt, of Luke's in its first form. Many requests and applications would be made to Luke by the new Churches for a Copy of his Work—or permission to send a trusty Scribe with all the materials, Parchment &c—& in every Copy (I judge by myself) Luke maybe found occasion to make some improvement availing himself as a sensible Author would do, of his friends' judgements and his own experience—Such a passage had been misunderstood—another not understood—& so forth—a far more probable hypothesis than Eichhorn's of its arriving at its present state thro' *many* hands—.

4　ɪ 76–8, pencil

[Eichhorn had said (ɪ 72) that Marcion's gospel cannot be a garbled version of the canonical Luke because before the end of the second century the Church did not have the four canonical gospels. He summarises the patristic theory and the defence by the Marcionites, stating (ɪ 75) that the Church Fathers attacked Marcion's gospel as a garbled version in order to preserve the authenticity of Luke.] Die Kritik aber kennt bey ihren Untersuchungen keine Partheyen und kein Partheyeninteresse, und kann nach den bisher vorgetragenen

---

3[1] Coming to Rome in 140, Marcion established a community and worked vigorously to propagate his view that the Christian Gospel was entirely a gospel of love involving rejection of the Law, the Old Testament, and the God of the Old Testament. He accepted only the recension of Luke henceforth known as the Marcionite Gospel, and ten of the Pauline epistles (excluding the pastoral epistles). The Marcionite Gospel— Eichhorn discuses it in ɪ 40–78, arguing that it was not a recension of Luke but that it had a common source with Luke—can be substantially reconstructed from Tertullian's attack on Marcion.

Gründen nichts anders, als beyde Evangelien, das des Marcion so gut als das des Lukas, für zwey von einander verschiedene, aus gleichen Quellen abgeflossene, unverfälschte Urkunden des Christenthums erklären, wovon die eine, die Marcion besass, und die nun bis auf einzelne Fragmente verlohren ist, als die kürzere und unausgebreitetere noch durch wenigere Hände; die andere aber, die wir von Lukas noch besitzen, als die reichere, vollkommenere und ausgearbeitetere durch mehrere Hände gegangen war.

[But criticism in its investigations recognises no parties and no party interests, and on the grounds previously advanced can explain the two gospels, Marcion's as well as Luke's, as no other than two gospels distinct from one another deriving from the same source and as genuine Christian documents, the one that Marcion possessed, now lost except for a few scattered fragments, being the shorter and less elaborated because coming down through fewer hands, and the one by Luke, which we still have, being the richer, more complete, and more elaborated because it came through more hands.]

A more natural supposition can scarcely be wished for, that in that about the commencement of the 3rd Century, A.D. 200, the ⟨the growth of Heresies & the⟩^{a} number of Gospels, all containing the substance at least of the original κηρυγματα,[1] but with more or fewer & various traditional anecdotes, rendered it expedient that the Bishops of the most celebrated Churches should endeavor to ascertain which of all these could be traced to any definite Authority—of which of the Gospels it could be proved or made highly probable, that they were compiled, or ⟨had⟩ at least been sanctioned, by Apostles or Apostolic Men?[2]—and that the result of this investigation was the establishment of the 4 we now have.[3] And surely we have every reason to be satisfied with their decision.—The only difficulty (and it *is* a great difficulty) is the silence of ecclesiastic History respecting any such Committee of Tryers.

---

^{a} This phrase, prefixed with " ∧ ", is written above the first line of the note. The corresponding " ∧ " can be indistinctly seen

4[1] "Testimonies".

4[2] The phrase "Apostles or Apostolic Men" is from Tertullian *Adversus Marcionem* 4.5, not in Eichhorn but in Michaelis III i 206.

4[3] C follows Eichhorn in ascribing a date of c 200 for the official recognition of the primacy of the four Gospels. Most scholars accept (disagreeing with Eichhorn) that the unique authority of Matt, Mark, Luke, and John, however, was fully established earlier, as witness Tatian's *Diatessaron* (c 150) and Irenaeus (c 130–200). Marcion's canon, with his prefaces to the epistles that found their way into some good mss of the Vulgate, certainly accelerated the process by which the Church distinguished between true and spurious works and set about to construct its own canon.

5 I 79–81, pencil | 3 Justin's Denkwürdigkeiten der Apostel § 18

Was er in seinen ächten Werken, nemlich der Ermahnung und der Rede an die Griechen, den beyden Apologien, dem Gespräch mit dem Juden Tryphon, und seinem Buch von der Monarchie Gottes, von dem Leben und den Reden Jesus beybringt, das ist alles aus einem eigenen Werke genommen, das er ἀπομνημονεύματα τῶν Ἀποστόλων (Commentarien, Memoiren, Denkwürdigkeiten der Apostel) betitelt *i*).

[Footnote *i*:] Apol. I. 66 οἱ γὰρ ἀπόστολοι ἐν τοῖς γενομένοις ὑπ᾽ αὐτῶν ἀπομνημονεύμασι, ἃ καλεῖται εὐαγγέλια, οὕτως παρέδωκαν...

[Whatever of the life and sayings of Jesus he [Justin] cites in his genuine works, namely the Hortatory Address and the Discourse to the Greeks, the two Apologies, the Dialogue with the Jew Tryphon, and his book of the Monarchy of God, all is taken out of one particular work, which he entitles "...(Commentaries, Memoirs, Memorabilia of the Apostles" *i*).

[Footnote *i*:] *Apologies* 1.66: "For the Apostles, in the memoirs composed by them, which are called Gospels, have thus delivered..."]

i) betitelt?—and this with the blank contradiction at the bottom of the same page, ἃ καλεῖται εὐαγγέλια.[1] Indeed, all Eichhorn's arguments are Moonshine!—or rather the fire-fly scintillations of minute Criticism: Justin Martyr was arguing with a Jew, to whom the names of Matthew, Mark, Luke, and John would have been worse than indifferent & have appeared almost ludicrous compared with Isaiah, Moses, &c.—[2]

6 I 110 | 5 Tatian's Harmonie § 28

Tatian, der am Ende des zweyten Jahrhunderts (A. 170) blühte, verfertigte ein aus den Evangelien zusammengesetztes Evangelien-buch unter dem Namen διὰ τεσσάρων, von dem man bisher für ausgemacht angenommen hat, dass es eine harmonische oder synoptische Darstellung unsrer vier Evangelien gewesen sey... aber ist es eben so gewiss, dass es aus *unsern* vier Evangelien zusammengeschrieben war?

[Tatian, who flourished (anno 170) at the end of the second century, prepared a gospel book put together from the Gospels, under the name "Through the Four", from which it has hitherto been taken as certain that this was a

5[1] "Which *are called* gospels". The Greek phrase is in the textus.

5[2] Eichhorn's footnote continues with two quotations from the *Dialogue with*

[the Jew] *Trypho*, also referring to the "memoirs of the Apostles" and the "'euangelion' as it is called".

harmonic or synoptic presentation of our four Gospels...but is it equally certain that it was put together from *our* four gospels?]

How is this to be reconciled with the introduction of Tatian's name in the Note, p. 577?[1]

7   I 113, pencil | 6 Von den Evangelium der apostolischen Väter § 29

[Footnote *o*:] *Epiphanius* in haeresi 46. n. 1. vom Tatian: λέγεται δὲ τὸ διὰ τεσσάρων Εὐαγγελίων ὑπ' αὐτοῦ γεγεννῆσθαι, ὅπερ κατὰ Ἑβραίους τινὲς καλοῦσι.

[Epiphanius *Against Heresies* (*Panarion*) 46.1 says of Tatian: "It is said that *Dia Tessarōn Evangeliōn* [the *Through Four Gospels*], which some call *According to Hebrews*, was produced by him."]

If not ov, it may still be rendered the Book of four evangelies,[1] i.e. matter of good tidings—viz. th̶ Κυριου 1. πραξεις: 2. λογος η διδαχη: 3. παραβολαι: 4. παθηματα:[2]—Bold, [a]nd new, at all events, Master Coleridge!—

8   i 130, pencil | § 32

Hat aber der zweyte Clementinische Brief ein solches, von unsern Evangelien verschiedenes Evangelium gebraucht, so ist dieser Umstand ein Beweis von seinem hohen Alter.

[If, however, the Second Epistle of Clement made use of such a gospel, different from our gospels, this circumstance is proof of its great antiquity.]

In the 2nd and spurious Epistle of Clement the References to and citations from the Canonical Scriptures of the Catholic Church come in shoals sic mihi visum est, dum istum legebam.[1]

6[1] There Eichhorn cites Tatian as evidence in support of the genuineness of Mark 16.9–20, yet here he claims that that gospel did not then exist. Cf "By the bye, Eichhorn's defence of the Authenticity of the last 11 verses of Mark (believing, as he does, in authenticity of the Gospel generally) surprizes me! But Eichhorn wants to be always original...." N 26 f 55 *CN* v: c May 1826).

7[1] C considers emending the title to mean the "Gospel (or Evangely) through four", i.e. through the four types of material he enumerates. Even without his emendation it could, he says, have substantially this same meaning.

7[2] The four "evangelies" in C's scheme are "the Lord's 1. Acts: 2. his word or teaching: 3. his parables: 4. his sufferings". See also **1** n 3, above.

8[1] "So it seemed to me while I was reading him"—i.e. c Apr 1826: see BIBLE *Apocryphal NT* headnote. In an extended series of notes on the Apocryphal NT in *CN* IV 5351 C comments on the Epistles of Clement to the Corinthians.

9 I 130–1, pencil

[If the Second Epistle of St Clement is not by Clement of Rome]...so muss er doch nicht blos in die Periode vor dem Concilium von Nicea (vor 325) gehören, sondern gewiss vor dem Ausgang des zweyten Jahrhunderts geschrieben seyn, weil er von unsern Evangelien noch keinen Gebrauch macht, da diese im Anfang des dritten Jahrhunderts bey allen christlichen Schriftstellern zum Grunde gelegt sind, und ihr Gebrauch allgemein eingeführt ist.

[...nevertheless, it must belong not merely in the period before the Council of Nicaea (before 325), but must have been written before the close of the second century, inasmuch as it makes no use of our Gospels, for these were introduced as a basis in all Christian authors and came into general use at the beginning of the third century.]

And how is this possible, if there had existed constant tradition? And who not blinded by neology could avoid the obvious interpretation of the Words, υπο των αποστολων, και των εκεινοις παρα-κολουθησαντων[1] as distinguishing between Matthew & John, & Mark with Luke?[2]

The 2nd Epist. of Clement seems to me to have been forged for the very purpose of removing the difficulty occasioned by the entire absence of any distinct reference to the Catholic Gospels and Epistles in the first and undoubtedly genuine Letter, and by th its psilanthropic tone.[3] The 2nd is nothing else almost so far am I from thinking as Eichhorn does.

10 I 144–5, pencil | § 35

Um die wahren Nachrichten von dem Leben Jesus...der Nachwelt in der möglichen Unverfälschtheit zu übergeben, hob die Kirche endlich am Ende des zweyten und im Anfang des dritten Jahrhunderts der christlichen Zeitrechnung aus den vielen Evangelien vier aus, welche die meisten Kennzeichen der Wahrheit und zum allgemeinen Gebrauche die nöthige Ausarbeitung hatten. Denn da vor dem Ende des zweyten und dem Anfang des dritten Jahrhunderts alle Spuren von unserm gegenwärtigen Matthäus, Markus und Lukas fehlen; da *] erst Irenäus (um das Jahr 202) entschieden von vier Evangelien

9[1] "In the memorials that I say were compiled 'by his Apostles and those who followed them'". The phrase is from Justin's *Dialogue with Trypho*, quoted in *NT* I 79n, continuing 5 textus.

9[2] I.e. Matthew and John as apostles, Mark and Luke as their followers.

9[3] Asserting "the *mere* humanity of Christ". See CHANNING 1 n 3. Cf 41 (at n 2), below.

spricht und allerley Ursachen aussinnt, warum es so viele Evangelien geben müsse?...

[In order to deliver the true accounts of the life of Jesus...to posterity without possible distortion, the Church finally selected, at the end of the second century and beginning of the third in the Christian epoch, from the many gospels, four which had the greatest marks of truth and the necessary elaboration for common use. For since before the end of the second century and the beginning of the third, all traces of our present Matthew, Mark, and Luke are absent; since Irenaeus (in the year 202) is the first to speak decisively of four gospels and so laboriously produces all manner of reasons why there should be so many gospels...]

Yet this according to E. was the *very time* when the Church, of which Irenæus was a Leader, was employing itself in making the selection!! —and how pitifully does E. pass over the odd Circumstance of the Diatessaron of Tatian! how criminally falsify the ἃ καλεῖται εὐαγγέλια of Justin Martyr!—[1]

11 ɪ 208–9 | ɪɪ Von den drey ersten katholischen Evangelien überhaupt 1 Urevangelium § 58

Hätte Lukas den Matthäus vor Augen gehabt, so würde er nicht Christus *vierzig Tage lang* versucht werden lassen (Luk. 4, 2), da nach Matthäus erst die Versuchung nach dem *Verlauf von vierzig Tagen* mit dem entstandenen Hunger anfängt (Matth. 4, 2. 3.)....

Es bleibt daher wiederum nichts anderes übrig, als anzunehmen, dass eine *hebräische* Urquelle im Fortgang der Zeit mehrmahls in ihrer hebräischen Ursprache abgeschrieben und dabei mit der ausführlichern Darstellung der Versuchungen bereichert worden ist.

[If Luke had had Matthew['s gospel] before his eyes, he would not have had Christ tempted *for forty days* (Luke 4.2), since according to Matthew the temptation begins merely after *the period of forty days* of growing hunger (Matthew 4.2, 3)....

Consequently there remains nothing other than to assume that an original source in *Hebrew* was copied down again and again in the course of time, in its original Hebrew tongue, and thereby was enriched with more detailed depiction of the temptation.]

This hypothesis not only supposes a boldness of interpolation amounting to forgery, not probable at so early a period, under the

10[1] The *Diatessaron* (see **6**, above), compiled from the four Gospels to provide a continuous narrative, became the standard text of the Gospels in the Syriac-speaking churches until the end of the fifth century; it was intended both as a harmony of the four traditional Gospels and as an apologia for them. For Justin Martyr's phrase "which are called Gospels" see **5** textus, above; see also **15**, below.

very eyes of the Apostles; but it takes away all meaning from the incident, and precludes all resolution of its Origin. In all probability, our Lord related it as a Parable.[1]

12 1 +1, referring to 1 398 | § 95

Die erste Hypothese von mehreren Hülfsschriften, die bey unsern katholischen Evangelien gebraucht worden, ist von ihren Vertheidigern zu wenig bestimmt worden, als dass sie sich mit Bestimmtheit widerlegen liesse. Sie kann wahr und falsch seyn, je nachdem man sie wendet: wahr, wenn man die verschiedenen mit Bereicherungen versehenen Ausgaben des Urevangeliums für verschiedene Schriften, und die grosse Einschaltung des Lukas (von 9, 51–18) für eine eigene Schrift ansieht; falsch, wenn man lauter kleine, von einander völlig verschiedene und für sich bestehende Schriften für die Grundlage unserer katholischen Evangelien erklären wollte.

[The first hypothesis, of several written aids that were used for our catholic gospels, is too undefined by its defenders for it to be decisively controverted. It can be true or false, depending on how it is approached: true if the various versions of the original gospel, with their elaborations, are considered as various documents and the great interpolation of Luke (from 9.51–18) is considered as one document; false if mere small, completely separate and independent writings are interpreted as the basis of our catholic gospels.]

P. 398. "falsch, wenn man lauter kleine————Schriften für die Grundlage unserer katholischen Evangelien erklären wollte."[1]

And yet after year-long thinking on the subject, and repeated revisals of my thoughts by comparison with other Schemes, and by testing them by whatever fresh information my Reading turned up, it is this Hypothesis to which with some modifications I continue to adhere, first as the only one, which does not contradict the declarations of Luke, I.1–4,[2] at least, because the Scheme grounded on this hypothesis duly qualified and distinctly stated seems to me the only one, which fully coincides with Luke's Statement; and 2[ndly] because this alone is more than a mere Supposition—or if I may use this word in its original but obsolete Sense, because this alone has a *Subpositum* (videlicet, the Testimony of a *Contemporary*, himself an Evangelist)—The proto-evangelium, and the Book entitled, Marks

11[1] See **17**, below.
12[1] At the end of the last sentence of textus.
12[2] For Luke 1.1–2 see **1** n 1, above; vv 3–4 continue: "It seemed good to me also, having had perfect understanding of all things from the very first, to write unto thee in order, most excellent Theophilus, That thou mightest know the certainty of those things, wherein thou hast been instructed."

of the Messiah, on which Eichhorn's Edifice is founded,[3] are Suf*ficta*, not Sup*posita*, hypo*poiēsis* not hypo*thesis*.[4]

13   I $^+$1, referring to I 401 | § 96

Und dass von Matthäus, Markus und Lukas die drey ersten katholischen Evangelien herrühren, dafür war die allgemeine Tradition der Kirche, die wir nicht bezweifeln dürfen, wofern wir nicht durch starke Gründe das Gegentheil beweisen können.

[And for the fact that the first three catholic gospels originated from Matthew, Mark, and Luke there was the common tradition of the Church, which we may not doubt insofar as we cannot on strong grounds prove the contrary.]

P. 401.—Luke scarcely needs the support of the Church Tradition—for the *authenticity* of Mark's I readily admit it, as sufficient proof; but I do feel the ~~same~~ like conviction with regard to the first Gospel, as attributable to Matthew in the same sense, as the second to Mark and the third to Luke/ and this too not only from difficulties of internal Evid[ence.]*a*

14   I 406, pencil | § 97

Diese Entdeckung des Urevangeliums ist für die Worterklärung des Evangelisten und die richtige Auffassung ihres Sinnes, für die allgemeine Kritik des Neuen Testaments und für die Specialkritik der Evangelisten, ja für die gesammte Theologie, von grosser Wichtigkeit.

[This discovery of an original gospel document is of great importance for the linguistic interpretation of the gospel writers and correct comprehension of their meaning, to the general criticism of the New Testament and to the special criticism of the gospel writers—indeed, for theology generally.]

Verily, my respected Friend Eichhorn! this is rather too much! A conjecture without a single testimony!—& call this *a Discovery*!

15   I 430/1, on a slip of wove unwatermarked paper tipped in, referring to I 430ff | III Von Matthäus, Markus und Lukas insbesondere 1 Matthäus § 100

[Eichhorn argues that the first two chapters of Matthew were not written by Matthew, that the content of them is neither contemporary

---

a The corner of the back wrapper is rubbed, to the loss of these characters

12[3] This is mentioned, only, in *NT* I 483. Perhaps C remembered, as he may have done in *AT* **29**, something he heard in Eichhorn's lectures. Cf DAVISON **3** n 2.

12[4] See e.g. *CN* III 3587: "Where both the position and the fact are imagined, it is Hypopoeēsis not Hypothesis, subfiction not supposition." See also BÖHME **31** n 4 and ARGENS **6** n 2.

nor historical, and that they were produced very much later than apostolic times. He compares the accounts of the childhood of Christ in Matt and Luke.]

Eichhorn—Vol. I. P. 430 &c.

There are, it must be confessed, great, very great Difficulties: insuperable perhaps; but yet it is scarcely credible, that the additions should have been of so late a date as Eichhorn would suppose.—For how can we account for the whole Christian Church submitting to the authority of the Canon?/ how account for the Selectors themselves not rejecting such open and palpable contradictions, had it been in their power?[1] If with any probability the CHURCH (whatever be meant thereby) *could* have attributed a later Date to these Chapters than to the other parts—How easy would it have been to have omitted St Matthew's and have taken Luke's far more splendid account?—Besides the α καλεῖται ευαγγελια, and of Justin Martyr, and the Διατεσσαρων of Tatian are mighty difficulties on the against Eichhorn—[2]

16 i 450, pencil | §101

Die ganze Erzählung von der Auferweckung der verstorbenen Heiligen im Moment des Todes Jesus gehört zu den Sagen, welche Autorität keines Apostels vor sich haben. Ihrer erwähnt auch weder ein anderer Evangelist noch sonst ein anderer Schriftsteller...

[The entire tale of the resurrection of righteous dead at the moment of the death of Jesus belongs among those myths which have no authority from the Apostles. It is referred to by no other Evangelist, not even by any other writer...]

Much more naturally explained by a blunder in the *Greek*ing of the Syro-chaldaic original—in which the Verb, like our "went" to was capable of a double meaning—either passive or active.[1] The Bodies went into the City—i.e. were carried/ and as the Hebrew Soul, Person, Corse are thus each designated by the same word, the Greek Translator (some Jewish Christian) made a ghost-story out of an unearthing of sundry Corses by the Earthquake—

15[1] C refers to the discrepancies between the *evangelia infantiae* in Matt 2 and Luke 2.
15[2] See 10 and n 1, above.
16[1] In Matt 27.52–3 "many bodies of the saints", coming out of (ἐξελθόντες) the graves "after his resurrection", "went into (εἰσῆλθον) the

holy city". If the bodies came and went actively, they would be walking; if passively, they would be carried. See also Eichhorn at i 448. For C on the possibility of a primitive Syro-Chaldaic original gospel see H. E. G. PAULUS *Das Leben Jesu* (2 vols Heidelberg 1828) ii vi–vii (Sept 1828).

17 I 456/7, on a slip of paper tipped in,[a] referring to I 452 | §102

[Eichhorn argues that the story of the temptation is too full of local superstitions and "drapery" to have been the work of an Apostle. He advances the theory that the *Urevangelium*, the only version from apostolic times, had none of the "magical" qualities added to the story that we find in Matthew and Luke, and that perhaps Matthew found a version of the Evangelium enriched by some of these and simply left them there.]

Vol. I. p. 452.

It is somewhat droll to see Eichhorn, after leaping a series of five-bar Gates of canonical and ecclesiastical Assertions and Declarations, stopping and reining in at this one tradition of S[t] Matthew, nine tenths of which he considers as false, and ridiculous! And equally humorous is the sudden idealising of the Apostles—the Proto-evangelium itself was no work of an *Apostle*—they were men of Quality—but some Journeyman assistant &c!!—[1]

With regard to the Temptation, it seems much more probable to me that it was a Parable related by our Lord on the occasion of the Dispute between the Sons of Zebedee, the request to call down Fire from Heaven &c.[2]

18 I 456/7, on a slip tipped in, referring to I 455 | §103

[Eichhorn proceeds to analyse the order, arrangement, and bases of the canonical gospels on the assumption that only those sections which the gospels obviously have in common from the Urevangelium are of certain apostolic authority.]

p. 455.

This Urevangelium is a downright Will o' the Wisp of Eichhorn/ ~~and~~ It is for ever leading him out of his way, and his[b] undoubtedly rendered his Introduction a work of much less value than with his great Learning and Acuteness it would have been if this Fancy had not fascinated his Judgement.

19 I 456/7, on a slip tipped in, referring to I 457

Indessen ist der zweite Fall wahrscheinlicher, dass eine von Matthäus verschiedene Person der erste Concipient gewesen, und Matthäus

---

[a] The slip of paper also contains **18** and **19** 　　　　[b] A slip for "has"

17[1] Eichhorn had stated (I 435) that the *Urevangelium* produced by eyewitnesses was later copied by scribes who, misunderstanding the events, fell into occasional errors.

17[2] See Luke 9.51–6 and cf **11**, above.

bloss der Revisor zu einer Zeit, wo schon Abschriften von dem ersten Entwurf gemacht waren, von denen die Exemplare abstammten, welche Markus und Lukas gebraucht haben.

[Nevertheless the second case is more probable, that a person other than Matthew was the first author, and Matthew merely a revisor at a time when copies from the first draft had already been made, from which the exemplars used by Mark and Luke originated.]

p. 457. ~~What~~ Is it not absurd to suppose the truth of the Tradition, to take for granted that the Christian Church had evidence of the first Gospel having been written or revised by Matthew; and yet that they permitted his Gospel to be so interpolated as to make it impossible to ascertain what was written or at least sanctioned by Matthew, and what was added by unauthorized persons?—In fact, the supposition evacuates the meaning of the demonstrative Pronoun—*this* Gospel[1]—the Church knew that Matthew had composed or revised *a* Gospel—but where it was, they were so far from knowing that they received instead of it a Gospel according to Eichhorn incomparably more unlike the original, than Mark's—or Luke's. For ~~from~~ of Luke's the Evang. Infantiæ is no organic part, as in the spurious Matthew?[2] Even "the visibly righter Order"[3] of the events in the first Gospel is asserted without proof. ~~The~~ Its appearance might be explained by a contrary ground.—viz. the arrangement in ~~Ma~~ the 1st G. being quite as the convenience of the compiler suggested. Who expects in a History the Sequence of time given in a Novel?—

20　ɪ 484, pencil | §106

Matth. 8, 21. wird von Jesus auf die Bitte eines seiner Schüler, dass ihm sein Meister, ehe er dessen beständiger Nachfolger werde, erlauben möge, erst seinen Vater zu beerdigen, ganz paradox geantwortet: ἄφες τοὺς νεκροὺς θάψαι τοὺς ἑαυτῶν νεκρούς. Stand מֵתֵיהֶם מְתִים, so könnte dieses schon heissen: "überlass andern, die bey ihnen Verstorbenen zu beerdigen" und der griechische

19[1] Matt 24.14: κηρυχθήσεται τοῦτο τὸ εὐαγγέλιον—"And this gospel... shall be preached".

19[2] Cf **15**, above. For the *evangelium infantiae* in Luke and Matt see Chillingworth copy b **2** n 2 and Donne *Sermons* copy b **9** n 1. See also *CL* vɪ 611 (8 Sept 1826). By "spurious Matthew" C means the gospel traditionally but

incorrectly ascribed to Matthew as author: see Herder *Von der Auferstehung* **11** n 1.

19[3] Eichhorn does not use this exact phrase, but it is implied in his statement (ɪ 165–6) that Matthew "corrected" the *Urevangelium*, as Luke did not. See also Eichhorn ɪ 239, 306, 370, 395, 490–2.

Uebersetzcr hätte nur beyde Mahle מֵתִים (Todte, Verstorbene) ausgesprochen. Nimmt man... ܣܥܒ̈ܪ für ܠ̣ܣܥܒ̈ (den Todten-gräbern, Ezech. 39, 15) so entsteht der verständliche Sinn: "überlass die Todten denen, deren Pflicht es ist, die bey ihnen Verstorbenen zu beerdigen."

[In Matt 8.21, when one of his proselytes asks his Master if he may be permitted to bury his father before he becomes a regular disciple, Jesus answers most paradoxically: "let the dead bury their dead". If the wording is [Hebrew] "those who had the duty of burying the dead", this could mean: "Leave the burying of those who have died among you to others", and the Greek translator merely rendered [Hebrew] (the dead, the deceased) both times. If we take...[Syriac] "the buriers of the dead" for "the dead" (the buriers of the dead of Ezek 39.15) there emerges the comprehensible meaning: "Leave the dead to those whose duty it is to bury the dead among you."]

This is the art of *flatt'ning* with a vengeance![1] "My Father is dead." Ans. "Never mind! the Undertaker will see to his burying!" And this from him who said—"If ye love not your earthly Father whom ye have seen, how can ye &c.—"[2]

21   I 509, pencil | § 114

*] Im apostolischen Zeitalter taufte man blos auf Jesus, wie es durchweg in der Apostelgeschichte und den Briefen des Apostels Paulus heisst: im Matthäus wird auf Vater, Sohn und Geist getauft: die neue Taufformel führt uns über das apostolische Zeitalter hinaus, und eine Schrift, die sie vorschreibt, muss erst nach demselben entstanden seyn.

[In apostolic times baptism was only in Jesus, as it is given throughout the Acts of the Apostles and the epistles of the Apostle; in Matthew it is in the Father, Son, and Spirit; this new baptismal form takes us beyond the apostolic age, and a document that prescribes it must have been produced only after this.]

* How is this to be proved? Surely not by an Historian and Letter-writers having used words of the same import as our "He was *christen'd*", or such a Minister baptized him into the faith of Jesus.—[1]

20[1] In an annotation on PAULUS I 173 C suggested that Paulus "ought to take out a Patent for his *Flatting-mill*". See also **42**, below.

20[2] A free variant of 1 John 4.20: "for he that loveth not his brother whom he hath seen, how can he love God whom he hath not seen?" See also BROOKE **14**.

21[1] See also FLEURY **75** and n 3 and **100** and n 4 and cf BAXTER *Catholick Theologie* **7**.

22 I 512, pencil

Jetzt steht im Matthäus alles unschuldig vergossene Blut "von Abel bis auf Zacharias *den Sohn Barachias*". Von der Ermordung eines Zacharias, der Barachial Sohn war, findet sich nichts im Alten Testament... aber während des Jüdischen Kriegs ward ein Zacharias der Sohn Barachias (oder Baruchs) mitten im Tempel von den Zeloten ermordet...

*] Diese einzige Stelle reicht hin, um unwiderleglich zu beweisen, dass der katholische Matthäus in seinem Alter nicht über das Jahr Chr. 70 hinaufreiche, sondern eher spätern Ursprungs seyn könne.

[Now Matthew speaks of all innocent blood shed "from Abel down to Zacharias the son of Barachias". Of the murder of a Zacharias who was the son of Barachias there is nothing to be found in the Old Testament... but during the Jewish War a Zacharias the son of Barachias (or Baruch) was murdered by the Zealots in the centre of the Temple...

This single instance suffices to prove incontestably that the catholic Gospel of Matthew is no older than the year A.D. 70, but rather could be of later origin.]

* This *is* an argument of weight. To *me* it appears, I own, decisive; but on *my* scheme of the Evidences not at all alarming. How the Grotians and Paleyans will digest it and the deducibilia therefrom, I know not.[1]

23 I 576–7, pencil, continued in ink | 2 Markus §122

Und wenn in Antiochien, einer von Christen so stark besuchten Stadt, so frühe, schon bald nach dem Jahr 37... das griechische Evangelium Marci den Christen zum Gebrauch in die Hände *] gegeben war, wie kam es, dass der Gebrauch des katholischen Markus bey den Kirchenvätern nicht früher anfängt? dass bis gegen das Ende des zweyten Jahrhunderts keine Spur von ihm vorkommt? dass niemand von seinem Evangelium etwas weiss? Sollte wohl Markus Evangelium an einem Orte in griechischer Sprache erschienen seyn, der in so starkem Verkehr mit der übrigen christlichen Welt gestanden hat?

[And if in Antioch, a city so heavily visited by Christians, so early, indeed shortly after the year 37... the Greek Gospel of Mark was put into the hands of the Christians for use, how does it come that a use of the catholic Gospel of Mark does not begin earlier with the Church Fathers? that not until the

22[1] For C's contemptuous view of the "Grotio-Paleyans" see *Apocrypha* 16, BAHRDT 2 n 2 and e.g. *CN* II 2640 and n. "*Deducibilia*"—apparently C's Latin back-formation from "deducibles", inferences.

end of the second century does any trace of it appear? that no one knows anything of his gospel? Would Mark's Gospel have appeared in Greek in a place that had such busy communication with the remainder of the Christian world?]

* This is nimis = nihil[1]—If it prove any thing, it would prove that Mark's Gospel was written no where..[a] Of mere Conjectures I prefer my own mere conjecture, that Luke's for *all*, or for the Gentiles, & the Proselytes to Judaism of Gentile origin as well as the Jews, who used the Septuagint; Mark's for Jews out of Palestine, & specially in Alexandria, (yet why not Antioch, Babylon, & wherever Jewish Settlements were?) Matthew's for Palestine Jews.

24 ɪ 598–600, pencil | 3 Lukas § 127

Die Alten suchten die Glaubwürdigkeit des Lukas dadurch zu sichern, dass sie sein Evangelium auf Paulus zurückführten, aus dessen Vorträgen er seine Nachrichten genommen habe. Selbst Paulus habe es nachher durch sein apostolisches Ansehen bestätiget, und es wegen seiner Richtigkeit in der Darstellung gerade zu *sein* Evangelium gennant (Röm. 2, 16). Wer möchte aber diese Folgerung der Kirchenväter, die eine falsche Auslegung eines Ausdrucks der Paulinischen Briefe, bey welcher man Paulus Lehre (εὐαγγέλιον) mit Paulus Lebenbeschreibung von Jesus verwechselte, zur Grundlage hat, der ausdrücklichen Erklärung vorziehen, die Lukas (1, 1–3) über die bey seinem Evangelium gebrauchten Quellen giebt? Unter diese zählt er aber Paulus Lehrvorträge nicht.

Seine Glaubswürdigkeit hängt einzig und allein von der Güte seiner Quellen und seiner vorzüglichen Fähigkeit ab, diese zu beurtheilen.

[The ancients sought to validate the credibility of Luke by deriving his gospel from Paul, from whose discourses he had taken his information. They even have Paul later give it his apostolic seal of approval, and call it *his* gospel because of its correctness of depiction (Rom 2.16). But who would prefer this deduction of the Church Fathers, which has as its basis a false interpretation of an expression in the Pauline epistles that confuses Paul's teaching (*evangelium*) with his biography of Jesus, to the explicit account that Luke gives of the sources he used (1.1–3) for his gospel? Among these he does not list Paul's teachings.

[a] After "no where" two full points are written, one in pencil, the second in ink; the note then continues, without a paragraph break, in ink

23[1] "Too much" amounting to "nothing". Cf Jeremy Taylor *Polemicall Discourses* sig c5[r]—"No more ingenious way of making nothing of a thing than by making it every thing" —and De Wette **28**.

His credibility depends solely upon the worth of his sources and his outstanding competence to assess these.]

Even Eichhorn, the best of the *historical* Critics among Theologians, presumes too much on the truth of the notion, that the biography of Jesus formed the whole or the principal part of the Apostolical Preaching—too little on the share which the divine Philosophy, the revealed *Religion* itself had—the everlasting Gospel that was from the Beginning, the Christ that was even in the Wilderness. St Paul scarce ever refers to historic facts but in confirmation or exemplification of some doctrine, as in his account of the Lord's Supper, and the Resurrection—no where, I think, to any particular miracle. They who had received the doctrines, did not need them—they believed them a fortiori. Those who refused the doctrines, would either deny the facts or account for them according to the general fancies of their age—ex. gr. of magic, or of connate δυναμεῖς,[1] as those of our Greatrakes or Greatorix and others.[2]

---

25   I 634, pencil | IV Bemerkungen über die drey ersten Evangelisten zusammen § 133

Und aus eben der Ursache, weil es ihren Verfassern gar nicht in den Sinn kam, dass ihre Evangelien auf die Nachwelt kommen würden, und sie dieselben nur bestimmten Personen in die Hand gaben... sorgten ihre Verfasser gar nicht... in denselben allerley Kenntzeichen niederzulegen, welche den Werth und die Wichtigkeit ihrer Schrift jedem Leser... hätten bezeichnen können.

[And on the plain grounds that it never entered the minds of the writers that their gospels would reach the modern world and that they put them into the hands of particular persons only... the writers took no care at all... to set down in them any manner of indications that could have shown the worth and importance of their writings to every reader.]

This is surely a groundless assertion/[1]

24[1]   "Powers".

24[2]   Valentine Greatrakes (also known as Greatorix) (1629–83) attracted wide attention as a healer capable of curing scrofula and other diseases by "stroking" and by the laying on of hands. Later it was thought that his cures were effected by animal magnetism. RS's long note on him in *Omniana* II 144–55 consists almost entirely of quotation from Henry More *Enthusiasmus Triumphatus*. Cf **33** and n 3, below, and COPY B **19** and n 2.

In *CN* IV 4603 (c Oct 1819) C referred to this annotation—"I have written (in pencil) a serviceable Note ending p. 600, Vol. I. Eichhorn: Einl. in das Neue Test."— and discussed at length the historicity of the Gospels and the authority based on historicity.

25[1]   In N 26 ff 59–60 (*CN* V: c 27 Jul 1827) he wrote a note on Luke, referring to I 631, and in f 60^v referred to I 633–4 as "a grand specimen of the Indefinite and the Hum and Ha Round-about".

26 I 632/3, a slip of paper tipped in, referring to I 639–40 | §135

Nur seufzt man über das Wunderbare in der von ihnen dargestellten
!] Lebensgeschichte! In den Begebenheiten selbst liegt es nicht,
sondern blos in der Darstellung, in der Ansicht, in welcher sie gefasst
sind, in den Volksdeutungen, welche mit den Erzählungen von ihnen
zusammengeflossen sind....Schwer wird zwar für uns nun in einem
völlig anders gestimmten Zeitalter das Auffassen der Begebenheiten
und ihre Trennung von der Volksdeutung: abcr konnten auch die
Evangelisten auf uns rechnen? bestimmten sie uns ihre Aufsätze?
liessen sie es sich, da sie nichts weniger als Schulgerechte Schriftsteller
waren, nur träumen, dass ihre Schriften, für bestimmte Personen
geschrieben, nach Jahrtausenden in einem grossen Theil der be-
wohnten Welt gelesen werden würden?

[One only sighs over the miraculous in the biographical accounts that they
set forth! It does not exist in the events themselves, but merely in the telling,
in the point of view from which they were written, in the folk beliefs that
have flowed in upon them in the recounting....Indeed it is difficult for us
in an age of completely different orientation to comprehend the events and
to separate them from popular interpretations: but could the Evangelists
have reckoned with us? Did they intend their treatises for us? Did they even
dream, since they were anything but regular and academic writers, that
their works, addressed to particular persons, would be read thousands of
years later in a large part of the inhabited world?]

Eichhorn Vol. I. p. 6439, 640. §135.

This dishonesty absolutely provokes an English Reader.—
Death!— Did the Apostles believe that they were commissioned to
found a Religion? If so, could they be such Oafs, with the example of
the Jewish Sacred Books before them, as not to foresee that written
Documents must exist & would be preserved, if the Gospel was
received?—Matthew, an eye-witness, revised at least, arranged and
augmented the supposed Original Gospel!—And *could* he as a man
of common honesty give his sanction to the assertion, that Jesus fed
4000 men with 7 Loaves & a few small Fishes, & with a surplus of
seven Baskets full of Fragments—when all this was merely what the
Mob thought who did not know that Jesus had previously layed up
Provender for the mat number/ and S[t] Matthew, forsooth, meant only
to record Christ's humane Fore-thought?[1] And Jesus himself—he
cures diseases at once, by word of mouth—or a little sand.—Were

---

26[1] Eichhorn does not specifically
propose such an interpretation but his
treatment of miracles generally suggests
it: see e.g. I 630–9, II 133.

ever Diseases in such numbers epilepsy, mania, &c cured without Medicine—or Leprosy? If given, either Christ concealed it & was an impostor—or his Apostles—& then they were Liars—And what in the name of common sense does Eichhorn believe? What remains after he has taken away the Divinity, Incarnation, mysterious Redemption, and all the miraculous coloring of the Facts?—A Quack doctor, who interspersed his Cures with ~~mor~~ teaching, the moral part of the old Testament separated from the legal—that which belonged to Individuals as men, from that which belonged to the Jews nationally, as Subjects of a particular Statute-Book!—This seems to me the most puerile and at the same time the most sneeking Form of Deism. For the evidence of ~~the~~ Historical Christianity is wholly *moral*/ the men report, nay, the thousand-fold attestation of marvellous Cures, proves nothing but what it proves daily, even at this day—viz. Quackery and Credulity. If a Difference, an essential Difference, is not made by the Doctrine and the Character of the Recorders, there is none at all.

27 ɪ 649, pencil | § 138

Die...hergebrachte Gewohnheit, mit dem Texte des Urevangeliums nach Belieben Veränderungen vorzunehmen, hier etwas zuzusetzen, und dort etwas wegzunehmen...wurde auch auf die drey katholischen Evangelien übergetragen, und zwar nicht bloss, seitdem sie allgemein in der Kirche neben einander gebraucht wurden, sondern auch wahrscheinlich schon viel früher...denn die uralte Itala ist schon von solchen eingeschobenen Lesarten voll.

[The...traditional custom of altering the text of the original gospel document according to whim, adding something here and taking away something there...was also carried over to the three catholic gospels, and not merely after they came into common use in conjunction with one another in the Church but probably also much earlier...for the ancient Itala is already filled with such interpolative readings.]

How unfair! Of the interpolations with which the eldest Itala is FILLED (!!!) how many are there, that really give a new or other sense? Is there even one, that affects seriously any one doctrine of Christianity or act of Christ.[1]

28 ɪɪ 40–1, pencil | v Von der Apostelgeschichte § 149

Seine [Paulus] mündlichen Reden halten sich von der Parenthesen-reichen, nicht selten dunkeln und verworrenen Sprache seiner Briefe

27[1] The *Itala* were Latin translations of the Bible in use in the Church until, in the fourth century, Jerome prepared the Vulgate version.

völlig frey, und folgen der Deutlichkeit und Klarheit des Vortrags, die in den erzählenden Theilen dem Geschichtschreiber eigen ist. Nach seiner Vertheidigungsrede vor dem im Aufruhr begriffenen Volk (22, 17) kehrt Paulus unmittelbar nach seiner Bekehrung wieder nach Jerusalem zurück; nach seinen Briefen hingegen (Gal. 1, 17) begiebt er sich unmittelbar nach seinem Uebertritt zum Christenthum nach Arabien, und besucht erst mehrere Jahre nachher wieder Jerusalem: können wir die eigenen Worte des Apostels in der Apostelgeschichte lesen?

[[Paul's] oral discourses are completely divorced from the style of his Epistles, which is rich in parentheses and not infrequently obscure and confused expressions, and are characterised by the intelligibility and clarity of exposition in the narrative parts, typical of a writer of history. After his speech of self-defence before the crowd that was clamoring against him (22.17) Paul returns to Jerusalem immediately on his conversion; according to his epistles, on the other hand (Gal 1.17), he goes immediately after his conversion to Christianity into Arabia and does not visit Jerusalem until several years later: can we be reading the very words of the Apostle in Acts?]

An assertion alike groundless and tasteless.

The Letters of a man overloaded with important Business, of an eager, full mind, and habitually ratiocinative, and who has a perplexing number of Points to decide and explain in the same Dispatch, might be confidently expected to swarm with Parentheses, abrupt transitions, &c—consequently obscure to others tho' perfectly intelligible to his Correspondents.[1] But to infer from this, that his set premeditated Orations before Kings, Magistrates, Senatorial Courts, &c must have had the same character, is illogical almost to absurdity. The seeming Contrad[n] of Gal. 1.17[2] may be easily removed by supposing Paul to speak only of Apostolic Missions *after* his acknowlegement by the Apostles at Jerusalem/ and of these the Arabian was the first.[3]

28[1] In BIBLE COPY B 116 C noticed that in following the intricacies of St Paul's involute style there would be advantage in separating out some of the parenthetic subordinations by deflecting them into footnotes. That C in that note should cite the example of his own parenthetic style and his own use of footnotes endorses the impression that in this note there is more than a hint of self-portraiture. For C's "Labyrinth of Parentheses" (of which *CN* IV 4603, cited in **24** n 2, is an extreme example) see *CN* II, 2431, 2670; and cf *CL* III 94–5 (Apr 1808), 541–2 (3 Nov 1814), v 98–9 (c Aug 1820).

28[2] "Neither went I up to Jerusalem to them which were apostles before me; but I went into Arabia, and returned again unto Damascus."

28[3] In Acts 22.1–21 Paul says that after his conversion he returned to Jerusalem but was warned in a trance in the Temple to flee the city because the people there would not accept his testimony about Jesus; he had in any case been commissioned to serve the Gentiles. Gal 1.18–19 (continuing from the verse

29 ii 41, pencil

Schwerer lässt sich der Brief des Lysias in einer Abschrift in Lukas
Händen denken; da es eben so unglaublich ist, dass er dem Officier,
der Paulus mit einem Commando Soldaten begleitet hat, offen
mitgegeben worden, als dass dieser ihn, wenn es geschehen wäre, dem
Apostel Paulus zum Abschreiben würde mitgetheilt haben...

[It is even more difficult to think of a copy of the letter of Lysias in the hands
of Luke; for it is just as unbelievable that it was given unsealed to the officer,
who escorted Paul with a troop of soldiers, as that this man, if such were
the case, gave it to the Apostle Paul so that he could copy it.]

Nothing more likely than either or all of these three pretended
Incredibles![1]

30 ii 109–10, pencil | vi Ueber die Schriften des Apostels Johannes 1 §156

Sein Evangelium hat, wie das des Matthäus, Markus und Lukas, die
*] Absicht, zu erweisen, dass Jesus der verheissene Messias sey; es
führt aber den Erweis nicht auf eine reine palästinische, sondern auf
eine palästinisch-hellenistische Weise.

[His gospel, like that of Matthew, Mark, and Luke, has the purpose of
demonstrating that Jesus is the promised Messiah; it rests its proof,
however, not on a purely Palestinian, but rather on a Palestinian-Hellenistic
system.]

* But, I should add, not in the same sense. I would therefore say,
that it was John's purpose to represent the Messias as the Regenerator
and Redeemer of Man. Master this one truth: that it was the object
of John to emancipate the idea of personëity[1] from the phænomenal
notion of Outline, and (generally) from the sensuous Definite in space
and time, and you will meet with few difficulties in the fourth Gospel.

31 ii 110, pencil

Doch scheint dem Verfasser desselben die Idee des λόγος keine ihm
durch Erziehung angebildete und geläufige, sondern eine von ihm

---

quoted in n 2, above) reads: "Then after
three years I went up to Jerusalem to see
Peter, and abode with him fifteen days.
But other of the apostles saw I none, save
James the Lord's brother."

29[1] See Acts 23.12–35. Claudius
Lysias was the centurion who sent Paul
under guard to Felix the governor in
order to remove him from the band of

Jews who had sworn to kill him. Lysias'
letter to Felix is recorded in Acts
23.26–30.

30[1] On "personëity" see **31** and n 2,
below, and see *Apocrypha* **6** n 4. For
John's purpose see *TT* 6 Jan 1823. C
reiterates the point in COPY A **31**, **32**,
and COPY B **1**, **38**. See also **44**,
below.

blos um seiner Leser willen angenommene Idee gewesen zu seyn. Geläufiger war ihm die Idee eines Gesandten Gottes wie man sich in Palästina den Messias gewöhnlich dachte. Er spricht daher nirgends, wie die Hellenisten, von einem Emanirten, von einem *] Ausgeflossenen und Zurückfliessenden; nirgends von einem Ausstrahlen, Durchstrahlen und Zurückstrahlen, sondern von einem Senden: er palästinirt den λόγος der Hellenisten in den Ausdrücken, die er von ihm gebraucht.[1]

[All the same, the idea of the *logos* appears not to have been one that was furnished by and made familiar from this writer's background, but rather one adopted purely for the sake of his readers. To him the idea of one sent from God would have been more familiar, as it was customary in Palestine to think of the Messiah. Hence he speaks nowhere, as the Hellenists do, of one emanated, of one proceeding and flowing back; nowhere of a shining forth, a shining through, and a shining back, but of a sending: he "Palestinises" the Logos of the Hellenists in the expressions about it that he uses.]

* The very first Chapter of John's Gospel gives the reason of this. It was John's Object to assert the personëity (the only true reality) of the Λογος:[2] how then could he adopt phrases conveying images of passive things & mere forms of matter?

32 ıı 111, pencil

Ein Theil der Redensarten, die von Christus gebraucht werden, scheinen sich allerdings an die Idee des λόγος anzuschliessen. Hieher kann schon die Benennung μονογενὴς παρὰ πατρὸς (1, 14), noch mehr μονογενὴς υἱός, ὁ ὢν εἰς τὸν κόλπον τοῦ πατρός (1, 17), ὁ υἱὸς τοῦ θεοῦ μονογενής (3, 16. 18), ὁ υἱὸς τοῦ ἀνθρώπου, ὢν ὁ ἐν τῷ οὐρανῷ gehören, wie auch Philo seinen λόγος den ersten und ältesten Sohn Gottes nennt *: (denn der Gedanke im Menschen, der vor jeder Ausführung hergeht, ist immer das Ersterzeugte; in Gott also der erste und älteste Sohn)...

[Some of the expressions used of Christ seem, to be sure, to connect closely with the idea of the Logos. To these could belong the designation "only begotten of the Father" ([John] 1.14), still more "only begotten Son, which is in the bosom of the father" (1.17 [18]), "the only begotten Son of God" (3.16, 18), "the Son of man, which is in heaven" [3.13], just as Philo calls his Logos the first and eldest son of God *: (for the thought that precedes every execution is always the first-begotten: in God, therefore, it is the first and eldest son)]

31[1] C comments on the same textus in COPY B 1.

31[2] For the family of words that "personëity" belongs to see BAXTER *Reliquiae* COPY B **42** n 1.

[In Footnote *s* Eichhorn quotes two passages from Philo. *De confusione linguarum* (1691) 329 = 14. 63. "For that man is the eldest son, whom the Father of all raised up, and elsewhere calls him His first-born [πρωτόγονον] and indeed the Son thus begotten followed the ways of his Father, and shaped the different kinds, looking to the archetypal patterns which that Father supplied." *Philo* tr F. H. Coleson and G. H. Whitaker LCL (10 vols 1929–) IV 45. *De migratione Abrahami* 389 = 1. 6. "...the Word who is antecedent to all that has come into existence, the Word, which the Helmsman of the universe grasps as a rudder to guide all things on their course. Even as, when He was fashioning the world, He employed it as an instrument, that the fabric of His handiwork might be without reproach." LCL IV 134.]

A most unfair account. Philo names the Logos the only-begotten Son of God to distinguish the Word from a Thought[1]—The very term, the Word, implies this distinction, and was chosen by the Jewish Platonists to express self-subsistence without self-origination.

33   II 119, pencil | §157

Zu einem poetischen Werk, voll Dichtungen der lebendigsten Einbildungskraft, wie sie die Apokalypse enthält, hat ein so hohes Alter die Kraft nicht mehr...

[For a poetic work so filled with materials of the liveliest imaginative power as the Apocalypse is, a person of such an advanced age no longer has the ability...]

Did not Milton write the Paradise Lost in old Age?[1] Who does not know the story of Sophocles?[2] But indeed the whole Hypothesis is gratuitous. If ever there was a Vision (of which the 6th or ecstatic state of zoomagnetism supplies recent proofs)[3] the Apocalypse was

32[1] See the two quotations from Philo in Eichhorn's footnote *s* (textus), and cf, on πρωτόγενής, CHILLINGWORTH COPY B 1 and n 5, FLEURY 49 and n 1. Eichhorn's interpretation would seem better supported by Philo *De opificio mundi* 4.16 (paraphrased in *Apocrypha* 13 n 4). See also *TT* 6 Jan 1823: "Philo expressly cautions against anyone's supposing the Logos to be a mere personification, or symbol. He says, the Logos is a substantial, self-existent Being." "Only begotten" is not found in Philo, and indeed C's statement is contrary to

Philo's "eldest son"; John 1.18, a passage often quoted by C.

33[1] Milton composed *Paradise Lost* 1658–65, aged forty-nine to fifty-six; he died one month before he reached sixty-six. See also COPY B 8.

33[2] Sophocles won his first prize at the age of twenty-eight in competition with Aeschylus, who was thirty years older. His twentieth prize, won at the age of ninety-one, filled him with such delight that he is said to have died of it.

33[3] Animal magnetists recognised a series of grades of access to zoomagnetic power. See *AT* 38 and nn.

a Vision, not a Poem.—Whether divine and bonâ fide prophetic, I do not here determine/[4]

34 II 122–3, pencil

[Eichhorn argues that, contrary to Church tradition, the Apocalypse was not composed on the Isle of Patmos during the persecutions of the Christians under Domitian (c A.D. 94), when John was banished thence, but in Ephesus shortly after the destruction of Jerusalem, between A.D. 71 and 78, as its symbolic references show. The reference in Rev 1.9 to the Isle of Patmos and John's tribulations he explains as poetic, not historical; and Tertullian's story that John was cast into boiling oil, emerged unscathed, and consequently was banished to Patmos he dismisses as a fable akin to the other obviously fabulous tales among which it is found.]

Had this been any other man's hypothesis, with what contempt would E. have asked why John at Ephesus should have hit on *Patmos*, and been so well acquainted with this obscure Roman Law—& this years before any Christians had been banished thither? And where is the proof that the Law, which condemned Proselyters to desert on thinly peopled Islands, had particularized Patmos? Meantime this whole Hypothesis rests on one very doubtful and another certainly false position: the first, that the Apoc. is a Poem, not a Vision actually presented—the second, that a fine Poem cannot be written by an old man.

Had even Printing and Newspapers existed, E.'s argument would not be convincing; but at that time to deny the existence of any secure historical source, when thirty years after the event a Writer records [it][a] as the universal belief—if this be allowed, what faith can we give to $\frac{19\text{ths}}{20}$ of ancient History, in general? Why must the story of the Oil be a fable? Are *all* the recorded facts of *Ordeals* in the middle ages

---

[a] Word supplied by the editor

33[4] In *C&S* (*CC*) 139–40n C rejects Luther's conclusion about Rev that "I cannot hold it to be either apostolic or prophetic" and declares it to be "the most perfect specimen of symbolic poetry". But the question is a very complex one, as the marginalia on **BIBLE** *NT Revelation*, **JAHN** *Appendix*, and **MORE** *Theological Works* show. In **EICHHORN** *Apocalypse* COPY A C agrees with Eichhorn's general proposition that Rev is symbolically historic rather than prophetic but quarrels with the crudity of Eichhorn's symbolic interpretation. For C's projected translation of "the Apocalypse into verse, holding a mid place between the Epic Narrative and the Choral Drama" see *LS* (*CC*) 147n and n 3. On the absurdity of projecting Rev into a prophecy of future historical events see e.g. *C&S* (*CC*) as cited above.

fables? As the priests then, so might not here the humanity of the Officer have made it a *shew* merely? Why may it not have been a previous ignominy (like the American Pitching and Tarring)[1] put on him first, and then sending him off to the transportation-vessel, or Convict-ship?—

35 ıı 123, pencil

Kann die Insel Patmos, wo Johannes die Gesichte zu Theil worden, nicht eben so gut zur Dichtung gehören, als der Tag, an dem sie ihm geworden sind? Muss sie nicht Dichtung seyn, da alle übrigen Scenen Dichtung sind?

[Cannot the Isle of Patmos, where John had a part of the vision, just as easily belong to the fictitious as the day on which it came to him? Must this not be poetic fiction, inasmuch as all the other scenes are poetic fiction?]

Had Eichhorn attributed the work to an unknown Author, and included the I, John, in the fiction, like the "I, Solomon", in the Ecclesiastes, there would be some plausibility.[1] But to make John tell a lie in his own name is too bad.

36   ıı 131, pencil | § 159

So eine Schrift von allgemeinem Gebrauch bey den Christen war dem Johannes gewiss lange vor der Abfassung seines Evangeliums bekannt, das Urevangelium, gesetzt dass er auch seine Bearbeitung in den drey ersten Evangelisten nicht gekannt haben sollte.

[Such a work as the original gospel document, in common use among the Christians, was certainly known to John long before the composition of his gospel, allowing that he might not have been acquainted with the version of it in the three first Evangelists.]

This is so plausible, nay, so probable, that I am always detecting myself in the act of taking it as *proved*. It is necessary, however, still to bear in mind that it is an hypothesis, the result of *combinations* of facts, not itself an attested fact. I know, indeed, no other way of solving the problem of the Gospels, but this, and ergo, so it is—is presumptuous Logic.

34[1] Tarring, or tarring and feathering —unlike the cropping of ears and slitting of noses—was never legalised.

35[1] Cf Eccles 1.12: "I the Preacher was king over Israel in Jerusalem." Solomon is traditionally the author of Eccles, but the words "I, Solomon" do not appear in the text.

37   II 133, pencil

Die Speisung der 5000 Mann (Matth. 14, 14. Mark. 6, 35. Luk.
9, 12) erzählt er vollständig (5, 1–15), nicht blos als Einleitung zu den
Reden, welche darauf folgen, (denn da hätte sie sich kürzer fassen
lassen) sondern auch recht geflissentlich in der Absicht das Ereignis
in seinen wahren Zusammenhang zu stellen. Nach der Urevangelium
hatte sich Jesus, um sich dem Volk, das ihm nachgegangen war,
heimlich zu entziehen, über den See Genezareth übersetzen lassen;
das Volk, das ihn auf dem jenseitigen Ufer vermuthete, war ihm zu
Fuss um den See nachgefolgt, und schon am jenseitigen Ufer
angekommen, als Jesus ans Land stieg.... Nun setzt man doch
schneller über einen See, als man um ihn herumkommen kann,
zumahl wenn er, wie der See Genezareth, eine länglichte Gestalt hat.
Schon einem frühen Leser war es bekannt, das Jesus von einem Berg
kommend das Volk gespeisst habe; er trug daher eine zweyte
Speisung Jesus (wie ihm keine Tradition sagte) von 4000 Mann in
seinem Evangelienbuch nach, die einer der Nachträge des Urevang-
eliums geworden ist, welche unser katholischer Matthäus mit
Markus gemein hat.... Nach Johannes war Jesus früher, als ihm das
Volk um den See nachkam, an das Land gestiegen; er hatte sich
darauf mit seinen Jüngern in die Einsamkeit auf einen Berg zurück-
gezogen, von dem herab er das Volk um den See Genezareth
herumkommen sieht, um ihn aufzusuchen, und weil er vermuthet,
dass ihm bey seinem langen Weg die Speisevorrath ausgegangen seyn
möchte, entschliesst er sich, dasselbe zu speisen.

[He relates in detail (5.1–15) the feeding of the five thousand (Matt 4.14,
Mark 6.35, Luke 9.12), not merely as an introduction to the sermon that
follows (for then he would have made it briefer) but quite intentionally so,
with the purpose of placing the event in its true context. According to the
Protogospel, Jesus had crossed the Sea of Gennesaret in order to escape the
people who followed him; the people, who supposed him to be on the other
shore, followed him around the sea on foot and were already on the other
shore when Jesus stepped out on to the land.... Now it is quicker to cross
a sea than to go around it, especially when it is oval-shaped as the Sea of
Gennesaret is. To an earlier reader it was already known that Jesus had come
down from a mountain when he fed the people; from this he added to his
gospel a second feeding, of four thousand, by Jesus (which he had from no
tradition), and this became one of the supplements to the Protogospel that
our catholic Matthew has in common with Mark.... According to John,
Jesus came to the shore before the people came around the sea, at which
time he had withdrawn with his disciples into the solitude of a mountain,
from which he saw the people coming around the Sea of Gennesaret seeking

him, and because he supposed that they might have run out of provisions on their long journey, he decided to feed them.]

How was it *possible*, that the Writer of this page should yet speak elsewhere of the miracles as mere *modes* of *thinking*, which we cannot at present *exactly explain*?[1]

38   II 156/7, on a slip of paper tipped in[a] | § 161

Indessen hatte Johannes nicht blos aus Jesus Mund göttliche Weisheit gehört, sondern ihn auch mit der Kraft zu ausserordentlichen Heilungen und Belebungen ausgerüstet gesehen, die aber Jesus nie für seine Hauptbestimmung ausgegeben, sondern nur als Mittel gebraucht hatte, die Menge auf sich aufmerksam zu machen.

[At the same time, John not only had heard divine wisdom from the mouth of Jesus, but also had seen him endowed with extraordinary powers of healing and life-giving, which Jesus, however, had never set forth as his main mission but used only as a means for drawing the attention of the multitude.]

One argument in support of the Catholic Faith occurs to me, which I do not remember to have met with—that on the Socinian Scheme the Gospel of John has no conceivable Object.—It does not collate the life and Mission of Jesus with the Messianic Signs collected from the Prophets, like the three earlier Gospels: and the Miracles are ever related as occasions of his Doctrinal Discourses, not advanced as proofs of his Mission. Indeed, there has often seemed to me a feeling directed thro' the whole, as of one who feared that the attention of Christians had been too strongly fastened upon the Miracles, to the injury of the higher and more spiritual faith.—What then was the purpose of this Gospel? Evidently to prove that in Jesus, the Jewish Messiah, was the Christ, the co-eternal Son of the living God, the Redeemer of the *World*, of Man and all other Creatures. Admit this: and the whole Gospel from first to last is clear and luminous.—

Eichhorn's Scheme is not worth confuting, being in flat contradiction to the very introduction of the Gospel, which places John Baptist in the same rank as the Prophets thro' whom the Logos had spoken in times of old, and declares that he was *not* the Logos—but that the Logos was Christ.[1]—What can this mean but to contra-

---

[a] The laid paper includes part of a watermark but without date

37[1] See Eichhorn I 638–9.
38[1] John 1.1–16 and 14.23. Eichhorn states (II 124) that the gospel of John had a twofold purpose: to prove that Jesus

was the expected Jewish Messiah, and to provide a more accurate account of certain events in the life of Jesus than had hitherto been given.

distinguish him from all inspired Teachers, as *possessing* the πνευμα θεου,[2] not merely gifted by it?—"My Father and I will come, and *we* will dwell in you."[3]—These are the Texts that separate the doctrine of John equally from Socinianism and Pantheism.[4]

39   II 216, pencil | §170

[Eichhorn is answering arguments against the Johannine authorship of John 21.] 1. "Habe nicht Johannes schon 20, 31. durch eine Unterschrift sein Evangelium geschlossen? was hinter ihr folge, müsse *fremder* Zusatz seyn."—Zusatz wohl; aber nicht nothwendig ein fremder, wofern nicht besondere Umstände auf eine fremde Hand führen. "So sey es wirklich; denn

2. "der Styl des Capitels sey nicht der des Johannes. Sonst spreche er immer von sich in der dritten Person; hier aber in der ersten: οἶμαι 'ich glaube'"....Konnte der Verfasser dieses Zusatzes, der doch (durch sein ὁ γράψας ταῦτα) für Johannes angesehen seyn will, sich so vergessen, dass er οἴδαμεν geschrieben hätte, wenn der Pluralis in dieser Wortfolge nicht diesen bestimmten Sinn gehabt hätte? Ja kann es nicht der Verfasser (wie andere Schriftsteller in ähnlichen Fällen) gerade zu für οἶδα gesetzt haben, da er mit οἶμαι in der einfachen Zahl zu reden fortfährt?

[1. "Has not John already closed his gospel in 20.31 by means of a signature? Whatever follows it must be a postcript by *another* hand."—Postscript probably, but not necessarily one foreign to the work, inasmuch as no marked circumstances indicate another's hand. "But so it is in fact, for 2. the style of the chapter is not that of John. Elsewhere he speaks of himself in the third person, but here in the first: οἶμαι (I suppose)"....Could the writer of this postscript, who (through his "who wrote these things") wishes to be taken for John, so forget himself that he wrote οἴδαμεν (we know), when the plural in this context would not have carried this precise sense? Indeed, could not the author (like other authors in similar circumstances) simply have written this instead of οἶδα (I know), since with οἶμαι (I suppose) he continues in the singular number?]

Both the 1st and 2nd Objection is most weakly answered by Eichhorn. Where is the *necessity* that ὁ γράψας ταῦτα should mean the P.S. or Appendix? Why not, the Gospel of which the *Postscriber* is speaking—ο γραψας ταυτα = the Writer of this Work.—[1]

38[2] "The spirit of God". The Greek phrase occurs in Matt 3.16 in the account of John baptising Jesus. Cf John 1.31–3.

38[3] See John 14.23: "If a man love me...my Father will love him, and we will come unto him, and make our abode with him."

38[4] See **31**, above. Socinians denied the divinity of Christ; pantheists dissolved God by identifying him with everything.

39[1] The reference is to John 21.24: "This is the disciple which testifieth of these things (ὁ μαρτυρῶν περὶ τούτων),

40   II ⁻2, referring to II 230 | § 172

Wie Herakleon, Valentin's Schüler, so scheinen auch Valentin und die übrigen Valentinianer das Evangelium Johannes für ächt angenommen zu haben...

[Like Heracleon, Valentine's disciple, Valentine also and the other Valentinians appear to have accepted the Gospel of John as genuine...]

p. 230 It appears to me a most forcible argument in proof of the Authenticity of John's Gospel that the Deniers suppose it gnostic— Valentinian—and first mentioned by Heracleon, a friend & probably follower of Valentin in the former half of the 2ⁿᵈ Century/[1] And yet the Catholic Fathers, the bitter enemies of Gnosticism and who made it the reproach of Valentine's Sect that it had another Gospel beside the four Catholic, received it without a scruple!

41   II 253, pencil | § 173

Nach diesen Gründen bedarf es keiner Beleuchtung der Hypothese, dass ein vom Apostel Johannes verschiedener Schriftsteller, der mit den alexandrinischen Vorstellungen vom λόγος vertraut gewesen, wenigstens die Einleitung dem Evangelium möge vorangestellt haben. Was das Evangelium vom λόγος beybringt, ist nicht das alexandrinische Philosophem von ihm...

[On these grounds there is no necessity for an examination of the hypothesis that another writer than the Apostle John, familiar with the Alexandrian representations of the λόγος, might have written at least the introduction to the gospel. That which the gospel sets forth regarding the λόγος is not the Alexandrian philosophy of it...]

Eichhorn's Appetite for Doubting had by excess of feeding satiated itself[1]—besides the Tempering of Age. In this assertion I see the struggle of old Psilanthropism[2] with sound Learning. He could not deny the authentʸ of the Gospel—& *would* not admit its obvious meaning.

---

and wrote these things (ὁ γράψας ταῦτα)". The point at issue is whether περὶ τούτων (about these things) and ταῦτα (these things) refer to "this postscript" or to "this work". See also COPY B 7.

40[1] Valentinus (fl c 136–160), founder of the most famous sect of gnostics; his scheme of the universe included a system of spiritual emanations set above the material world. See also FLEURY 37 n 2. Heracleon, mystic and follower of Valentinus, wrote a commentary on John.

41[1] Cf e.g. Shakespeare *Two Gentlemen of Verona* III i 219–20 and *Twelfth Night* I i 1–3.

41[2] See **9** n 3, above.

42   II 264–5 pencil | §175

Wenn von Jesus nach seiner Austreibung der Käufer und Verkäufer aus den Tempelgebäuden ein Beweis gefodert wird, dass er zu dieser Machthandlung ein Recht habe, und er antwortet (2, 19.): "brechet diesen Tempel ab und in kurzer Zeit soll ein anderer wieder da stehen"; so kann er nur den Tempel als Bild des religiösen Instituts *] der Juden betrachtet und gesagt haben: "gebt euer ganzes bisheriges religiöses Institut auf; ein anderes werde ich in kurzer Zeit an seine Stelle gesetzt haben."

[When Jesus, after he had driven the buyers and sellers from the Temple buildings, was asked to give proof that he had the right to make this forcible expulsion, and he had answered (2.19), "Destroy this Temple and in a short while another will stand here"; he could only have envisioned the Temple as a symbol of the religious institutions of the Jews, and have said, "Destroy your entire previous religious institution; in a short while I shall have set another in its place."]

* This is bold even for Eichhorn: and (let me add) as flat as it is bold. A more appropriate as well as sublime Reply can scarcely be imagined than this allusion to the Character of the Messiah as the Schechinah/ whose presence constituted the proper Holiness, the *Templarity*, of the Temple.[1]

43   II 387, pencil | 5 Ueber Johannes Offenbarung §191

Aber die Verschiedenheit in Manier und Schreibart abgerechnet, welche Alter, Lage und Inhalt jedem Schriftsteller unvermeidlich *] machen, kehren in der Apokalypse alle wesentlichen Eigenthümlichkeiten der Einkleidung und Schreibart wieder, durch welche sich Johannes Evangelium und Episteln auszeichnen...

[Making allowance, however, for differences in manner and style that age, location, and content make inevitable in every writer, there recur in the Apocalypse all the essential characteristics of form and style that are indicative of John's Gospel and epistles...]

* Surely not. The Resemblances consist in words and phrases borrowed from St John, which of course the dullest Personator would take care to do—but the whole *Soul* and *Spirit* are diverse. I think,

---

42[1] *Shekinah* (the word is late Aramaic, not Hebrew)—"the Glory of the Lord" as displayed to man in the form of an angel of fire, a pillar of fire, or the "devouring fire" on Mt Sinai, but especially marking the presence of God in the tabernacle or Temple (Exod 40.34–8, Lev 9.23–4, and esp 2 Chron 7.1–3). See also COPY B **10** and *P Lects* Lect 10 (1949) 299.

I could almost give a psychological Demonstration of its not being John the Evangelist's Work.[1]

44 II 469, pencil | § 197

"[Offenbarung] 3, 14. heisst Christus ἀρχὴ τῆς κτίσεως τοῦ θεοῦ, *das erste Geschöpf Gottes*: wie konnte Johannes den Messias also nennen, von dem er im Evangelium sagte: ἐν ἀρχῇ ἦν ὁ λόγος?"...

Entweder, weil ἀρχὴ τῆς κτίσεως τοῦ θεοῦ *Ersterstandener aus den Todten* ist (wenn bey dieser Stelle auf πρωτότοκος ἐκ τῶν νεκρῶν (Apok. 1, 5) zurückgesehen wird); denn Auferstehung kann sehr schicklich eine neue *Schöpfung Gottes* heissen: oder weil der Ausdruck *Oberhaupt des neuen Volks Gottes* heisst, so dass ἀρχὴ für ἄρχων, und κτίσις θεοῦ für das sonst gewöhnliches κτίσις καινὴ...gesetzt ist. So wurde ja Israel auch nach einem ähnlichen Verhältniss zu Gott κτίσμα θεοῦ genannt.

[[Rev] 3. 14 calls Christ "the beginning of the creation of God"; how could John refer to the Messiah thus, of whom he said in his gospel: "in the beginning was the Word"?...

Either because ἀρχὴ τῆς κτίσεως τοῦ θεοῦ means "first-arisen from the dead" (if the "first begotten of the dead" (Rev 1.5) is referred to in this passage); for resurrection can very appropriately be called a new creation of God; or because the expression means "ruler of the new people of God", with ἀρχὴ (beginning) substituted for ἄρχων (ruler), and κτίσις θεοῦ (creation of God) for the otherwise customary κτίσις καινὴ (a new creation). Indeed, Israel also was called, because of a similar relation to God, κτίσμα θεοῦ (a creature of God).]

ἀρχὴ signifies not only here and elsewhere in the N. T. but even in Aristotle, the antecedent *principle*, the ground, & actuating power in one;[1] & not a first effect:—the staple, not a Link.[2]

45 III 1–2, pencil | VII Ueber die Briefe des Apostels Paulus § 202

Als Jesus von seinen Jüngern schied, war sein Lehrbegriff nur erst in schwachen Umrissen vorhanden. Die Lehre von Gott, Vorsehung und Unsterblichkeit hatte er als allgemeine Wahrheiten vorausgesetzt, ohne sie zu beweisen, oder ihren Zusammenhang mit dem

43[1] For C's conviction that the John of Rev was not John the Evangelist, see COPY B **16**.

44[1] A central statement of the meaning of ἀρχή; see also BLUMENBACH **4** n 2 and BAXTER *Reliquiae* COPY B **92** n 1. Cf **30–32**, above, and COPY B **1**. The opening words of John 1.1—and corres-

pondingly the opening words of Gen 1.1 in Septuagint—are ἐν ἀρχῇ. See also BÖHME **161** n 4.

44[2] For the image of the staple and the link (or ring), familiar from the "Essays on Method" in *The Friend*, see DONNE *Sermons* COPY B **50** and n 3.

allgemeinen Wahrheitssinn zu zeigen. Gott hatte er als Ideal der Heiligkeit und als Muster dargestellt, dem die Menschen unablässig nachzustreben hätten, und das Sittengesetz als göttliches Gebot, an dessen Befolgung die Bedingung des göttlichen Beyfalls und der Glückseligkeit geknüpf sey.

[When Jesus departed from his disciples, his system of doctrines existed only in vague outlines. His doctrines concerning God, providence, and immortality he had set forth as general truths, without proving them and without indicating their connexion with a general apprehension of truth. He set God forth as the ideal of holiness and as a pattern that mankind had faithfully to strive after, and the moral law as a divine order, on observance of which the blessing of God and a state of bliss depended.]

Merciful Heaven! What must a pious and learned Jew think and feel of this §. 202.? What? And did a Reader of Moses, the Prophets, and the Hagiographa[1] need to be *informed* (however much he might need to be reminded) of *these* truths?[2]

46 III 14

Zur Quelle, aus welcher er [Paulus] seine Anfangs etwa noch mangelhaften Kenntnisse der Lehren Jesus ergänzte, scheint ihm das Urevangelium[k)] nach der Bearbeitung gedient zu haben, in welcher es das Evangelium der Hebräer hiess.

*] [Footnote *k*:] Den Gebrauch eines Evangeliums beweisen die Stellen, in welchen Paulus die Befehle des Herrn von seiner Meynung, die er aus dem Geist seiner Lehre (1 Kor. 7, 40) geschöpft haben will, unterscheidet 1 Kor. 7, 6. 12. 25. 40; und einzelne ausdrücklich angeführte Verbote und Gebote des Herrn, wie sein Verbot willkührlicher Ehescheidungen 1 Kor. 7, 10., die Erlaubniss vom Evangelium zu leben 1 Kor. 9, 14.

[As the source from which Paul supplemented his at first rather imperfect knowledge of the doctrines of Jesus, the original gospel document[k)] appears to have served him, in the recension in which it was called the Gospel of the Hebrews.

[Footnote *k*:] The use of a gospel is indicated by the places in which Paul distinguishes (1 Cor 7.40) between the commands of the Lord and his own opinions, which he wants to draw from the spirit of his teaching (1 Cor 7.6, 12, 25, 40); and by his explicit introduction of single prohibitions and

---

45[1] The last of the three Jewish divisions of OT, embracing all that was not included in the "Law" or the "Prophets". See *AT* **46** n 1.

45[2] For other notes on Eichhorn's § 202 see COPY B **17–21**.

commandments of the Lord, such as the prohibition against arbitrary divorce (1 Cor 7.10) and the command to live according to the gospel (1 Cor 9.14).]

* Why not from the Apostles at Jerusalem? Surely, if Paul had had a Gospel before him, some citations, at least some more distinct references, would have appeared.[1]

47   III 102, pencil | Erster Brief an die Korinther § 217

[Eichhorn argues the spuriousness of the Armenian Epistle of Paul to the Corinthians.] [Footnote *p*:]...Wie häufig kämpft Paulus in seinen unstreitig ächten Briefen gegen den Vorwurf, dass er ein Schüler der frühern Apostel sey (z. B. Gal. 1, 12), und könnte er an die Korinthier geschrieben haben: er habe ihnen vorgetragen, was ihm von den frühern Aposteln gelehrt worden?

[How often Paul protests in his indisputably genuine Epistles against the reproach that he was a disciple of the earlier apostles (e.g. Gal 1.12), and could he have written to the Corinthians that he expounded to them what he had been taught by the earlier apostles?]

This does not, I owe,[a] appear to me so strong an objection as it does to Eichhorn. The ~~anee~~ biographical facts Paul would surely have received from the Eye-witnesses, tho' not the great essential doctrines of Christianity.

48   III 110, pencil | § 218

[Eichhorn argues that the salutation in 1 Cor 1.2, "to all who call upon the name of Our Lord Jesus Christ in every place, both theirs and ours", has reference to the dissenting parties among the Corinthians themselves rather than to Corinthians everywhere, whom he would not be saluting in a letter addressed to the Corinthians.] Aber weil sich schon manche getrennt hatten, so musste er, um seinen Brief an alle Christen zu Korinth zu bestimmen, im Grus hinzusetzen, "an welchem Orte sie sich versammeln mögen, an dem von mir gewählten (dem Hause des Justus), oder an dem ihrigen". [Footnote:] Welche andere Erklärung von (χαίρειν λέγω) *]τοῖς ἐπικαλουμένοις τὸ ὄνομα τοῦ Κυρίου ἡμῶν Ἰησοῦ Χριστοῦ ἐν παντὶ τόπῳ, αὐτῶν τε καὶ ἡμῶν (1 Kor. 1, 2) man annehmen mag, so ist sie unnatürlich.

a A slip for "own"

46[1] For other notes on this passage see COPY B **20, 21**.

[But because so many had seceded he had, in order to direct his Epistle to all the Christians at Corinth, to add to the salutation: "in whatever place they may assemble, either that chosen by me (the house of Justus) or that chosen by them". [Footnote:] Any other explanation of [the Greek of 1 Cor 1.2] that one may consider is unnatural.]

* Why, should not του Κυριου be understood as repeated here—? Our Lord J. C. in every place their Lord and ours.[1]—Besides, is ἐν τοπῳ ημων, even Hellenistic Greek for ἐν οικῳ ἡμετερῳ?—[2]

49 III 159, pencil | § 222

6) [Über 1. Korinther 15] Den Verzweiflern der Auferstehung der Todten wiederholt Paulus zuerst die durch so viele Zeugen bestätigte Gewissheit der neuen Belebung Jesus, durch welche die Möglichkeit einer Auferstehung der Todten erwiesen sey (15, 1–13).

[6)[On 1 Cor 15] To those who doubt the resurrection of the dead, Paul reviews first the certainty of the resurrection of Jesus, confirmed through so many witnesses, from which the possibility of a resurrection of the dead may be inferred (15.1–13).]

This §.6. contains, I am aware, the common interpretation of the famous Chapter; but false, I am persuaded.

50 III 202–3, pencil | Brief an die Römer § 228

[Footnote *x*:]...Ein Paulinisches Christenthum war höher gestellt, als das der übrigen Apostel, und konnte nur von dem Apostel oder seinen Schülern gelehrt worden...

[Pauline Christianity was constituted on a higher plane than that of the other apostles, and could be taught only by the apostle or his disciples...]

[x] In order to this we must not only reject the epistles of Peter and James, with Eichhorn, who plainly rejects them for no other cause than their incompatibility with this supposition of a Pauline Chris-

---

48[1] C disposes of Eichhorn's argument ingeniously by making "in every place" qualify "our Lord": "all who call upon the name of Christ, who is in every place their Lord and ours". AV is partly ambiguous. *NEB* reads: "with all men everywhere who invoke the name of our Lord Jesus Christ—their Lord as well as ours"—which is firmly against Eichhorn's version without supporting C's.

48[2] This objection seems not to be well founded. "In our place" could well mean, in the context, "in our house", i.e. the house we have chosen for our meetings. The use of the genitive case of personal pronouns—e.g. ἡμῶν (of us)—instead of possessive adjectives agreeing with the noun they qualify—as ἐν οἴκῳ ἡμετέρῳ (in our house)—can lead to ambiguity, though both are idiomatic in classical as well as NT Greek. Cf **59**, below, and *CN* III 3778 and n (on John 8.44).

tianity, but we must likewise reject the Gospel of John, which Eichhorn receives, and degrade Luke's Acts of the Apostles in[a] the work of a Romancer not an Historian. For give what extent you will to the Licence implied in the τοιαυτα λεγει of the Speeches, yet a Poet only dare invent a vision like Peter's.[1]

51   III 206/7, stuck in with black wax at the top corner, referring to III 206

Die Judenchristen in Palästina hielten so streng auf Beschneidung und Beobachtung der herabgeerbten jüdischen Nationalgebräuche, dass so gar die Apostel zu Jerusalem dem Apostel Paulus bey seiner Ankunft daselbst den Rath gaben, sich einem Mosaischen Ritus zu unterziehen, um die vielen tausend Christen, die grosse Eiferer für das Mosaische Gesetz wären, zu überführen, er sey kein Verächter Mosis (Apg. 21, 20–24).

[The Jewish Christians in Palestine held so firmly to circumcision and observance of the traditional Jewish national customs that even the apostles at Jerusalem counselled Paul upon his arrival there to submit to a Mosaic rite in order to convince the many thousand Christians who were zealous for the Mosaic Law that he was no despiser of Moses (Acts 21.20–4).]

p. 206

It is easy to conceive, that the Apostles, Peter and James, whose apostolic duties were at that time assigned to Judæa and in Judæa especially to Jerusalem and its Vicinity, and who had heard our Lord's express declaration that till the entire subversion of the Jewish State, Church, Government, and People (the meaning of "till Heaven & Earth shall pass away"[1]) no Christian, an inhabitant of Palestine, should presume to disobey the least part of the ceremonial Law, or anticipating the final operation of the Gospel make such fore-sight the pretext for present sedition—it is, I say, easy to conceive, that these Apostles might be apprehen[sive][b] of Paul's being carried too

---

[a] Perhaps a slip for "as"

[b] Letters obliterated by the seal

50[1] For Peter's vision see Acts 10.9–20. C refers—in the formulary phrase τοιαῦτα λέγει (he spoke in this way)— not to any expression in NT, but to the practice of ancient historians of putting speeches into the mouths of their characters of the kind they would have been likely to have made in the circumstances. The *locus classicus* is Thucydides 1.22 (but without this formula); but C several times in discussing NT uses Livy as an example of this procedure. As for Luke's

account of Peter's vision, C feels that it is not such a justifiable piece of imaginative reconstruction; it is either a romance or else a true account of Peter's vision as he himself described it.

For a similar shorthand reference by C cf "the καθως of Luke" in **1**, above.

51[1] Matt 5.18: "For verily I say unto you, Till Heaven and earth pass, one jot or one tittle shall in no wise pass from the law, till all be fulfilled." Cf Luke 16.17. See also *CN* III 4402.

far—and still more probable, that their warnings to the converted Hierosalamites not to apply Paul's principles, meant for Pagan Converts or Jewi[sh][a] Subjects in other States, as condemnations of the principles themselves—& that the prejudiced part of their Auditors might have believed themselves armed with apostolic Authority to oppose Paul's Attempts to present the Religion of Christ as the Substitute for the Law of Moses, or rather as superseding it. On this ground only can the conduct of the Bishops of Jerusalem for so many successions, who combined the Gospel with the Mosaic ordinances, be rationally explained—To assert, that they wittingly acted in defiance of the first Council, and the solemn Decision of the Apostles at Jerusalem, & that the Apostolic Churches connived at this disobedience from motives of Tolerance, is absurd. Doubtless, they stood justified as Bishops of *Jerusalem*. Nay, I hold that even now the Jews are bound by Christ's authority to observe all such Laws as have not been repealed by the removal of the Subject-matter of the Law. Cessante causâ, cessat Lex.—[2]

52   III 340–1, pencil | Erster Brief an Timotheus § 248

Wie konnte an einen Mann, der etwa im October oder November des Jahrs 59 der ausgebildetste und vollendeste Lehrer des Christenthums durch Unterricht und Erfahrung (1 Kor. 4, 17) geheissen hat, etwa im Anfang des nächsten Jahrs geschrieben werden: "damit du weissst, wie du dich in der Gemeine Gottes zu Ephesus zu benehmen hast, so gebe ich dir die Grundlehren des Christenthums an" (1 Tim. 3, 15. 16)?...

Wollte man erwiedern: "alles was im ersten Brief an den Timotheus stehe, das stehe nicht um seinetwillen, sondern um der Gemeine willen da..."

[How could a man, who in about October or November of the year 59 was called (1 Cor 4.17) the best instructed and most complete teacher of Christianity by virtue of training and experience, be addressed about the beginning of the following year: "I give you the basic teachings of Christianity so that you will know how to comport yourself in the community of God at Ephesus" (1 Tim 3.15, 16)?...

If the answer is: "Everything in the first Epistle to Timothy is there, not for his sake, but for the sake of the community..."]

Whatever Eich[n] may object to this argument, it completely answers Eichhorn's former—But the whole Train of Reasoning is Feather

---

[a] Letters obliterated by the seal

51[2] "When the reason [for a law] is gone, the law ceases to hold."

and Snow-flake/ any ordination sermon answers the whole. Besides, an old man writing to a young & filial friend, how naturally he goes over again his old Lessons, familiar indeed to the Receiver but with how many revivings of pleasure connected for the Writer!—

53   III 497, pencil | Brief an die Hebräer § 269

Man könnte zwar auf alexandrinische Judenchristen rathen, weil der Brief [an die Hebräer] ganz in ihrem Geiste geschrieben ist, und schon eine alte Sage im Fragment des Muratorius...ihn für eine *epistola ad Alexandrinos* erklärt....[Aber] der alexandrinische Character des Briefs bezeichnet mehr den Verfasser als Zögling der alexandrinischen Schule, weniger die ersten Leser desselben als Alexandriner...

[One could indeed guess at an Alexandrian Jewish Christian, because the Epistle to the Hebrews is written entirely in their spirit, and an old legend in a fragment of Muratorius...interprets it as an epistle to the Alexandrians ...[But] the Alexandrian character of the Epistle indicates the writer as a student of the Alexandrian school rather than the first readers of it as Alexandrians.]

Surely, the argumenta ex concessu,[1] as the Delivery of the Law by Angels, are proofs of the *ad*-Alexandri*nos* scarcely less strong than of the *ab*-Alexandri*no*.[2]

54   III 580, pencil | VIII Ueber die katholischen Briefe 1 Jacobus § 279

Beyde [Jacobus und Paulus] stimmen zwar in ihrem Lehrbegriff mit *] einander überein, bey Paulus sind die ἔργα die ἔργα νόμου, die Beobachtung der mosaischen Gesetze, und die πίστις ist das Vertrauen auf Christus...

[Both [James and Paul] certainly agree with one another in their doctrines; in Paul the "works" are the "works of the law", the observation of the Mosaic laws; and the πίστις (faith) is the belief in Christ...]

* As shallow in the philosophy of Morals as false in fact and interpretation.[1]

53[1] I.e. arguments based on what is generally accepted.

53[2] C refers to Heb 2.2—"the word spoken by angels". C argues that the statement here of the tradition that the Law was delivered by angels (also in Acts 7.53 and Gal 3.19) is as strong evidence that the epistle was delivered *to* people who believed in that tradition, and so was delivered *ad* Alexandri*nos* ("to Alexandrians"), as it is evidence that it was delivered *by* a man who believed the tradition, and so was delivered *ab* Alexandri*no* ("by an Alexandrian").

54[1] For a longer note on this textus see COPY B 31. For Eichhorn's "shallow Morality" see *Apocrypha* 16.

55   III 603, pencil | 2 Erster Brief Petrus § 282

Da der Briefsteller [1 Pet 5, 13] von seiner Frau sagt, dass sie zu Babylon sich aufhalte, so mag es seyn, dass auch er selbst sie einst dahin gebracht, folglich auch sich einst daselbst befunden hat; aber jetzt, da er den Brief schreibt, kann dieses wenigstens der Fall nicht gewesen seyn. "Meine Frau zu Babylon" setzt voraus, dass der Briefsteller, zu der Zeit da er von ihr grüsst, bey ihr nicht gegenwärtig, sondern an einem andern Orte befindlich ist: sonst würde er bloss geschrieben haben: "euch grüsst meine Frau."

[Inasmuch as the writer of the Epistle [1 Pet 5.13] says that his wife is in Babylon, it may have been that he took her there, consequently that he also was once there; but now, as he writes the letter, this at least cannot be the case. "My wife at Babylon" presumes that the writer of the Epistle at the time that he sends greetings to her is not at that time with her, but in another place; otherwise he would merely have written: "My wife greets you."]

1 Does the word γυνη εμη found^a in any MSS. In my Gr. Test. it is simply η εν Βαβυλῶνι—which our Translators interpret by *Church*.[1]

56   III 618, pencil | § 285

Und könnte der Gruss, welcher von Markus an die Leser des Briefes Petri (1 Petr. 5, 13.) bestellt wird, nicht dahin gedeutet werden, dass *] er Theilhaber an der Ausfertigung des Briefes gewesen sey?

[And could not the greeting that Mark sends to the readers of Peter's epistle (1 Pet 5.13) indicate that he had been a participant in the preparation of the Epistle?]

* Is not this inconsistent with the Author's remarks on Peter's Wife—if Wife it must be./[1]

57   III ii $^{-}1^b$, referring to III 618

P. 618.

It is strange that Eichhorn does not even *notice* the fact, that in all the common Editions of the New Testament no such words, ⟨as⟩ η εμου γυνὴ, or γυνὴ εμη εμου, are to be found, but simply η εν Βαβυλωνι συνεκλεκτη, και Μαρκος ο υιος μου[1]—and that the

---

^{a} Confusion of "Is the word...found" and "Does the word...[occur/ appear/ exist?]"
^{b} I.e. verso of the original front flyleaf of III ii, bound in

55[1] AV reads (with italics): "The *church that is* at Babylon", but *NEB* reads: "her who dwells in Babylon". No ms listed by Griesbach supplies γυνὴ ἐμή (my wife), but some mss supply ἐκκλησία (church). See **56–58**, below.

56[1] See **55** textus, above, and **58** textus, below.

57[1] "...no such words, as 'my wife' [repeated in two forms]": see **55** n 1, above. C then quotes the *Textus Receptus* of 1 Pet 5.13, which AV renders: "The

Lutheran, the English, and the Dutch Versions supply the noun by Church, or Congregation.[2] And is not συνεκλεκτη[3] a strange epithet for a single female, in connection with all the Christians of the Circumcision scattered through out Pontus, Galatia, Cappadocia, Asia and Bythinia—whereas nothing could be more appropriate from the fellow-elect in Babylon—and would do away ~~in~~ Eichhorn's inference that the Epistle could not have been written from Babylon—. If any thing, the words would prove the contrary.—If I should address a circular Letter to the Brunswicke̶r̶-Clubs all over G. Britain & Ireland, what more natural than that I should say Our Club at Highgate ~~are~~ is staunch to the cause, and sends greetings to all true Brunswickers, and so does Mr Gillman, my House-mate.—[4]

58 III 620–1, pencil | § 286

Als Ort der Ausfertigung des Briefs nimmt man Babylon an, weil der Verfasser "von seiner Frau zu Babylon" grüsse (1 Petr. 5, 13.). Schon einen trägen Leser hätte der Zusatz *in Babylon* auf den Gedanken bringen können, dass der Verfasser sich dadurch als einen von seiner Frau Abwesenden darstelle.

[The place of writing of the Epistle is assumed to be Babylon, because the writer sends greetings from his wife in Babylon (1 Pet 5.13). But the postscript *in Babylon* could have brought to the mind of an inattentive reader that the writer was thereby indicating an absence from his wife.]

And yet it seems strange that Peter at a distance from Babylon writing to the Christians scattered throughout Pontus, Galatia, &c

---

church that is at Babylon, elected together with *you*, saluteth you; and *so doth* Marcus my son."

57[2] C bought a copy of "Luther's Bible" in Hamburg 28 Sept 1798 (*CN* I 346); this may have been the copy left at Allan Bank— Wordsworth LC 1062 (twice marked as C's), 1095 (marked as C's). *Green SC* (1880) 37 was a copy of *Die Bibel nach der deutschen Uebersetzung D. M. Luthers* (Dresden 1818), not shown as C's. *Green SC* (1880) 772 was a copy of *Nieuwe Testament door H. M. Heeren* (Maastricht 1691); cf Wordsworth LC 1106 "Dutch Bible" (twice marked as C's).

57[3] AV "elected together": see n 1, above. Cf C's "fellow-elect", below, equally correct.

57[4] Brunswick Clubs were first formed in Jul 1828 by ultra-Protestant peers and MPs in reaction to the growing political pressure for Catholic emancipation. The name originally proposed for the club was "Protestant Club" but the camouflage name "Brunswick Constitutional Club" was quickly substituted to avoid charges that political "clubbing" was an intrusion on parliamentary authority. (The Brunswick Club may indeed have been unconstitutional, and some influential sympathisers declined to join for that reason.) The name of the club was "taken from the dynasty which was, according to the ultras, peculiarly committed to Protestant Ascendancy through the circumstances of its accession to the throne". G. I. T. Machin *The Catholic Question in English Politics, 1820 to 1830* (Oxford 1964).

&c should send a greeting from his absent Wife! What! had he informed his Wife by a Letter that he was going to write a letter to the Strangers scattered &c: and had received her answer in time to include it? In my Test. no *wife* is found.[1]

59 III 631–2, pencil | Zweyter Brief Petrus § 290

Im lauf des Briefs entschlüpft dem Verfasser eine Stelle, in welcher er sich von den Aposteln ausschliesst. "Ich schreibe euch (sagt er 3, 2.) einen zweyten Brief, um euch zu ermahnen, eingedenk zu seyn der Vorausverkündigungen der heiligen Propheten und der Vorschrift, unsrer Apostel, (καὶ τῆς τῶν ἀποστόλων ἡμῶν ἐντολῆς)." Durch diesen Ausdruck "*unsrer Apostel*" verräth der Verfasser, dass er sich nicht zu den Aposteln rechne. Die Ausleger räumen zwar dieses dadurch hinweg, dass sie übersetzen: "ich ermahne euch eingedenk zu seyn *der Vorschriften von uns, den Aposteln.*" Dies ist aber der Sprache entgegen; in diesem Sinn hätte der Verfasser schreiben müssen καὶ τῆς ἡμῶν τῶν ἀποστόλων ἐντολῆς und nicht καὶ τῆς τῶν ἀποστόλων ἡμῶν ἐντολῆς.

[In the course of the Epistle there slips out from the author a passage in which he excludes himself from the Apostles. "I write you (he says in 3.2) a second epistle in order to admonish you to be mindful of the words spoken before by the holy prophets and of the precepts of our Apostles (καὶ τῆς τῶν ἀποστόλων ἡμῶν ἐντολῆς)." By this expression, "*our Apostles*", the writer reveals that he does not count himself among the Apostles. The commentators certainly dispose of this difficulty by translating it "I admonish you to be mindful *of the precepts of us, the Apostles*". But this is contrary to linguistic usage; in this sense the writer would have had to write καὶ τῆς ἡμῶν τῶν ἀποστόλων ἐντολῆς and not καὶ τῆς τῶν ἀποστόλων ἡμῶν ἐντολῆς.]

—I cannot admit this, in a *Letter*, and that written by a Palestine Jew. I should construe the word, and the Apostles', *our*, Prescript.[1] Besides, why *might* not, how often *have* not, modest and humble Clergymen admonished their correspondents or flock—"be attentive to your Pastors.—."[2] Eichhorn's Habit of Scept. misleads him into hundreds of puerilities.

60 III 632, pencil

In einer zweyten Stelle, 3, 15. 16. spricht der Verfasser des Briefs... gleich als ob Paulus Briefe noch während seines Lebens gesammelt worden wären: und wer kann dieses glaublich finden?

58[1] See **55–57**, above.
59[1] C is right. Cf the similar ambiguity in **48**, above, which demonstrates that word-order in NT Greek cannot be taken as seriously as Eichhorn takes it here. Modern editors read ὑμῶν (your), which removes the difficulty.
59[2] Echoing 2 Pet 3.2, in textus.

[In a second place, 3.15, 16, the writer of the epistle speaks...as if Paul's letters were collected while he was still living, and who can find this credible?] Why not? Cicero's were—Pliny's were—Politian's, &c &c.[1] But in this instance, it would have been strange, had they not been.

61   III 646–7, pencil | Judas § 294

Seinem Brief zufolge war er kein Apostel: denn, indem er (V. 17.) *] sagt: "errinert euch an das, was euch von den Aposteln unsers Herrn Jesus Christus vorausgesagt worden," schliesst er sich deutlich genug von den Aposteln aus.

[According to his epistle, he was not an apostle, for when he says (v 17), "Remember that which was spoken to you by the apostles of our Lord Jesus Christ", he clearly enough excludes himself from the apostles.]

* What should prevent a Judge from saying to a Barrister— Remember what was decided by the Bench/ or a Bishop from referring to the unanimous Votes of the Bench of Bishops on such or such a measure—tho' he himself was one? The passage following is ⟨more⟩ satisfactory—and yet if we might suppose James to have had a Martyr's death or ⟨in⟩ any other way become a famous name, Jude might have been led by this + to brotherly Love/[1]

62   III ii ⁻1–title-page of III ii,[a] referring to III 648

Judas, der leibliche Bruder Christus, war zwar kein Apostel und könnte sich daher bloss δοῦλον Χριστοῦ genannt haben, wie in Gruss dieses Briefs steht; aber dennoch scheint es nicht, dass dieser Judas Verfasser des Briefs unter diesem Namen gewesen seyn könne.... Denn von diesem Jacobus, dem leiblichen Bruder Jesus, hat die Geschichte nichts Merkwürdiges, sie hat nichts als zufällig seinen Namen erhalten (Matth. 13, 55. Mark 6, 3.): man kann nur vermuthen, dass er etwa den ersten Lesern des Briefs eine merk- würdige, hochgeehrte Person gewesen sey, die dem Verfasser des Briefs und seiner Schrift zur Empfehlung habe dienen können; aber beweisen kann man es nicht.

a The note begins on the verso of the original front flyleaf of III ii

60[1] Cicero (106–43 B.C.) was thinking of publishing a collection of his letters four years before he died (*Letters to Atticus* 16.5.5). Pliny the younger (c A.D. 61–112) himself published nine of the ten books of his letters, beginning twelve years before his death. The letters of Angelo Ambrogini (Angelo Poliziano) (1454–94) were collected during his lifetime.

61[1] See **62**, below.

[Jude, Christ's own brother, was indeed not an apostle and could, therefore, have called himself simply "servant of Christ" as in the salutation of this epistle; nevertheless it does not appear that this Jude can have been the writer of the epistle under this name.... For of this James, the actual brother of Jesus, history says nothing remarkable. It has nothing more than a fortuitous retention of his name (Matt 13.55, Mark 6.3): it can only be supposed that to the first readers of the epistles he might have been a remarkable, highly esteemed person who could have served the writer as a recommendation of the epistle and his writing; but this cannot be proved.]

P. 648. A slender argument might perhaps be advanced in favor of the Letter-writer's being the Son of Joseph & Mary—viz. that the ~~Author~~ Writer wished to express the fact of his being Christ's Brother & yet to avoid the presumption of so calling himself—He was only the *Servant* of Christ, tho' the Brother of James[1]—and this Trait of Nature would be an argument for the Authenticity of this Epistle.[2] S. T. C.

62[1] Eichhorn states that Jude, because he was not an apostle, referred to himself as the brother of James (who was the brother of Jesus—see **28** n 3, above—but not an apostle) so that he could secure for his epistle an authority that would otherwise be denied to a man who was not an apostle. The James who was the author of the epistle was an apostle and was not the brother of Jesus.

62[2] C's explanation of Jude's lack of presumption is very similar to that attributed to Clement of Alexandria in Eichhorn's footnote on this page. The application of this to the question of the authorship is C's. Eichhorn's footnote reads: "What Clement Opp T. II p 1007 says on this subject, that the actual brother of Jesus called himself not Jesus' brother but James's brother out of humility, is too schematic"; Eichhorn then quotes in Latin a fragment of Clement's *Adumbrationes in Epistolam Judae* from *Opera* (Venice 1757) II 1007. There is, however, no conclusive evidence against the traditional presumption that the author of Jude's epistle was the brother of Jesus.

Copy B

Einleitung in das Neue Testament. [Another copy.] 3 vols. Leipzig 1804, 1810–11, 1812–14. 8°.

British Museum C 126 d 5

Green's copy with his autograph signature "Joseph Henry Green" on II ⁻5 and III ⁻5. "S. T. C." label in all three volumes. There is an inked line in the margin of II 449.

For C's mislaying II and III i of his own set (COPY A) and his request of 7 Feb 1829 that Green lend him these "two intermediate volumes", see COPY A headnote. C wrote no notes in Green's Vol I. Presumably both the 2-pt Vols II and III of Green's set were already bound as single volumes when Green left them with C, not only because C has written notes on II i as well as on II ii and on III ii as well as on III i, but because a noticeable feature of this set is that all but one of C's notes in Vol II, and all but three of those in Vol III, are written on flyleaves. (The part-division in Vol II occurs at pp 330/331, in Vol III at pp 410/411.)

DATE. 1829, after 7 Feb: see *CL* VI 784 (quoted in COPY A headnote).

COEDITOR. Merton A. Christensen.

1   II ⁻4, referring to II (i) 110 | VI Ueber die Schriften des Apostels Johannes 1 Ueber Johannes Evangelium § 156

[Eichhorn is arguing that John was a Palestinian Jew, and that he was not—as many theologians think—influenced by Alexandrian philosophy in his doctrine of the Logos:] Er spricht daher nirgends, wie die Hellenisten, von einem Emanirten, von einem Ausgestossenen und Zurückfliessenden; nirgends von einem Ausstrahlen, Durchstrahlen und Zurückstrahlen, sondern von einem Senden: er palästinirt den λόγος der Hellenisten in den Ausdrücken, die er von ihm gebraucht.[1]

[Hence he speaks nowhere, as the Hellenists do, of one emanation, of one proceeding and flowing back; nowhere of a shining forth, a shining through, and a shining back, but of a sending: he "Palestinises" the Logos of the Hellenists in the expressions about it that he uses.]

P. 110.

    Eichhorn was no philosopher—a sensible Conceptualist, but who contemplated nothing in the light of the *Idea*.[2] There is, however, in the mid §ph. of this page an obtuseness beyond what I could have expected even from him.—How was it possible that John should have

[1] C comments on the same textus in COPY A 31.

[2] On the distinction between idea and conception see 31 and n 1, below.

uscd the idly sensuous forms of the Emanationists, the Eradiation, Reflection &c[3]—all which represent the Efflux of *a Thing*—when he begins his Gospel by the sublime annunciation of the *Personality* of THE WORD?[4] And of a Person what other terms can be used both[a] those of "coming, sending, being sent, &c"?[5]

2   II ⁻4⁻⁻3, referring to II 158–61, pencil, overtraced in part | §162

Weil aber Jesus nicht blos lehrte, sondern auch that, was kein anderer vermochte, so schien es dem Evangelisten, dass seinen Lesern beydes erklärt werden müsste; und er nimmt zur Erklärung des erstern an, dass mit Jesu die Weisheit Gottes, und des letztern, dass mit ihm die Macht Gottes vereiniget gewesen sey....

Alle Religionen giengen von rohen, sinnlichen Begriffen aus, weil ihre Anfänge in die Zeiten der Rohheit und der ersten Bildung des menschlichen Verstandes fallen, in denen die Vorstellungen von Gott und den Beziehungen der menschen zu ihm nicht anders als kindisch-klein und sinnlich-roh seyn konnten. Sie sind aber nicht lange so geblieben. Mit dem Wachsthum der Erfahrungen, mit der Erweiterung des Verstandes durch wissenschaftliche und Kunstkenntnisse, mit der Erhöhung und Veredelung der Geistesbildung durch Nachdenken, ändern sich Begriffe und Vorstellungen: und den geistigen Veränderungen, die mit dem Menschen vorgehen, müssen auch seine ursprünglichen religiösen Begriffe weichen....

[But because Jesus did not merely teach but also did what nobody else could do, it appeared to the Evangelist that both must be explained to his readers...and as an explanation of the former he supposed that Jesus was united to the wisdom of God, of the latter the fact that he was united to the power of God...

All religions proceeded from crude sensual concepts, for their origins lie in ages of crudity and of the first formation of the human understanding, when ideas of God and of man's relation to him can be no other than childishly narrow and sensually crude. But they did not remain so for long. With the growth of experience, with the widening of the understanding through scientific and artistic learning, with the elevation and ennoblement of the mind through contemplation, concepts, and ideas change: and to the spiritual changes, which go forward as men go forward, their original religious concepts must yield also.]

a A slip for "but"

1[3] See BÖHME 110 n 2; cf ETERNAL PUNISHMENT 4 and FLEURY 96.
1[4] See also COPY A 30, 31 (esp n 1), and 32 and n 1.
1[5] In John 1 only the word "coming" applies strictly to Christ: see John 1.11, 15, 27. The cluster "coming, sending, being sent" applies specifically to John the Baptist (see John 1.6–9), but John later uses these words of Christ as the Word.

P. ᵃ158 and the following pages present to my mind a fine Figure of self-complacent Aufklärungs-stolz declaiming in the chill Moonshine des Verstandeswesen¹ with ~~its~~ nose cocked up into the Air & Head thrown backward, to the utter Overlooking of all the palpable Facts that lay ~~before it~~ at its very feet. Ex gr. the last §ph. of p. 159ᵇ—Popery, eine ᵃSache derᵇ Uberlieferung, ᵃProtestantismᵇ durch Religionsurkunden²—how ADMIRABLY they exemplify Eichhorn's position—But p. 161—"Moses und die Propheten &c" is still more exquisite.—Beneath God's Dignity to concern himself with trifles—he keeps his thought for matters of state!³ This, the very Dregs of Popery in J. G. Eichhorn—is it not almost incredible? and it was kindisch-klein and sinnlich-roh⁴ in Moses to worship the Omnipresent Spirit, before whose infinitude all difference of Great and Small vanishes!—Ohe!!!. s. t. c.

3 II ⁺3–⁺4, referring to II 161

P. 161.

The influence of Voltaire was great even in Protestant Germany, tho' modified by the peculiar attributes of the German Mind & character—.¹ To this influence it was owing, that to think & speak of the Jews and of the Hebrew Writers as a poor, barbarous unenlightened Set, whom it was the absurdity of supersitious prejudice to compare otherwise than by contrast with the Legislators, Philosophers, Poets & Historians of Greece and Rome, had become the indispensable Mark and Criterion of a liberal and enlightened Person. This Prejudice was at its height when Eichhorn began to form

ᵃ⁻ᵇ Overtraced in ink

2¹ Self-complacent "Enlightenment-pride" declaiming in the chill moonshine of "the Understanding-system" (or "the rational man").

2² Adapted from Eichhorn, who remarks ("last §ph. of p. 159") that the NT is a vehicle for delivering religious ideas that are understood differently and in a more refined way by future generations (*die Nachwelt*): for Popery "a matter of tradition", for Protestantism "by way of religious documents".

2³ "Moses and the Prophets attributed all occurrences in the world to God himself; their Jehovah was in constant activity; he effected each trifle without an intermediate agent; he was active equally with the good and with the evil. There were indeed moments when it occurred to the wiser ones among them that it might be beneath the dignity of an almighty Being to concern himself with every little detail...".

2⁴ "Childishly narrow and sensually crude"; in textus.

3¹ Voltaire hated orthodox Christianity and the Roman Catholic Church. Yet he strongly recommended a deistic position, and considered that a belief in the existence of God and in personal immortality was necessary for the government of the masses. *ODCC.*

his mind under Semler:[2] and only by the force of this Prejudice is it to be explained, that a man of so much sound Learning and of so clear a Head should have fallen into the gross mistatements and misrepresentations of the Morals & Theology of the Old Testament, that unfortunately abound in this even more than in his elder Work, the Introd. to the Hebrew Canon.[3]—I shall therefore regard it as a service of no mean value to the English Student if I should do what I propose to do in my own work,[4] i.e. extract the numerous medicinal herbs free from the hemlock & other noxious weeds.—

4   II ⁻3, referring to II 180 | §163

Während er [Johannes] getauft habe (d. i. wie die andern Evangelien ergänzen, als sich auch Jesus seiner Taufe unterworfen habe), sey ihm in einer Vision bemerklich geworden, wie göttliche Gaben und Einsichten (das πνεῦμα ἅγιον) mit ihm vereiniget worden; und Gott habe ihm dabey geoffenbahrt...

[While John was baptising (i.e. as the other Evangelists fill out the account, when Jesus had submitted himself to his baptism), there were made known to him in a vision the divine gifts and insights (the Holy Ghost) being united with him; and through this God revealed to him....]

P. 180. Observe—the Baptist makes this declaration *before* Jesus had entered on his public Functions, as a Teacher.[1]

5   II ⁻3–⁻2, referring to II 190 | §166

Gnosticismus war Verfeinerung der Lehre von Gott nach den Bedürfnissen der Zeiten und Länder und deren Aufklärung: er war Annäherung der Religionslehren an die zeitigen moralischen und philosophischen Ideen, zur Vollendung des Unvollendeten, zur Vervollkommnung des Unvollkommenen in metaphysischen und moralischen Grundsätzen.

3[2] Johann Salomo Semler (1725–91), professor of theology at Halle from 1752, an important pioneer of the historical method in biblical criticism. When C first thought of going to study in Germany, Semler, Michaelis, and Kant were three Germans whose works he intended to bring home. *CL* I 209 (May 1796). In c Mar 1818 he noted down Semler's dates (*CN* III 4399), and later mentioned "the different Patristic & Ecclesiastico-historical tracts of Semler". LUTHER

Colloquia mensalia 349–51. In the light of his own biblical studies, C came to distrust the "rationalism" of the "Neological School", which included Semler, Eichhorn, Paulus, and Schleiermacher. See *CN* III 4401n and e.g. *CN* IV 5322 and N 43 f 65ᵛ (*CN* v).

3[3] I.e. *Einleitung ins Alte Testament*.

3[4] Presumably in some part of the *Opus maximum*.

4[1] See John 1.29–34.

[Gnosticism was a refinement of the doctrines concerning God according to the needs of the time and place, and of their state of enlightenment: it was a bringing closer of religious doctrines to contemporary moral and philosophical ideas, to complete the uncompleted, to perfect the unperfected, in metaphysical and moral principles.]

P. 190. A very deceptive and unhistoric account of the Gnostics—whose common and characteristic error was, the divulsion of Christianity from all *previous* History, and then from *all* history, so as to leave it a pure speculative Edifice, a new Polytheism with arbitrary personifications of General or Abstract Words in the place of *Ideas*. Thus they would have destroyed both the Factors of Revealed Religion, fa Fact and Idea—and confounded a *lunacy* of the Understanding for with the supersensual Light of Reason[1]—Such were the Gentile Gnostics. Among the Jewish Christians the Professors of the Gnosis were distinguished by the abuse of allegorical interpretation—Solvers of Riddles, which they had themselves made. Among these as among their successors, our modern *Improvers* of Scripture Texts, who find in the latter half of the Text—Let those on the House Top not come down—a prophetic Prohibition of Ribbons = Top (k)not! Come down/[2] there were many well-meaning and orthodox Christians. In the Epistle attributed (and I think justly) to S[t] Barnabas you may find a throughout rich Specimens of the Gnosis,[3] and a proof of the truth and wisdom of S[t] Paul's Remark—

5[1] Cf the "chill Moonshine" of 2 at n 1.

5[2] Mark 13.15. C is burlesquing the well-intentioned but uninspired new translations that swam in the wake of the Higher Criticism, of which an example could be (see *CIS* 80) William Newcome (1729–1800), Abp of Armagh, *An Attempt Towards Revising Our English Translation of the Greek Scriptures* (2 vols Dublin 1796, but withheld from general publication until after Newcome's death in 1800). Thomas Belsham (1750–1829) made for the Unitarians an unauthorised and anonymous sectarian version, which was severely attacked in *QR*: *The New Testament in an Improved Version upon the Basis of Archbishop Newcome's New Translation* (1808). C owned a copy of "Newcome on Bibl: Transl:"—*An*

Historical View of the English Biblical Translations: the expediency of revising by authority our present translation: and the means of executing such a revision (Dublin 1792). Wordsworth LC 294 (marked as C's but apparently sold with WW's library).

5[3] For the apocryphal *Epistle of Barnabas* see BIBLE *Apocryphal NT*. A series of notes in N F° shows C reading it in Hone's collection in Apr 1826. He found chs 5 and 6 "somewhat too philo-judaic, alexandrine, edging on the fantastical"; the whole epistle, he considered, "may be *authentic*; it *is* not a *Catholic* Epistle. It may have been written by Barnabas with a holy intention; it was not outbreathed from the Holy Ghost...." *CN* IV 5353, 5354.

that the Gnosis puffeth up—which word, gnosis, our Translation[s][a] have no less mischievously than absurdly rendered *knowlege*!—[4]

6   II ⁻2–⁻1, referring to II 210 | §168

Historisch gewiss ist nur dieses, dass manche Schüler des Täufers Jesum wegen des grössern Zulaufs, den er hatte, beneidet haben, woraus allerdings folgt, dass sie ihn nicht für den Messias angesehen haben. Doch konnte der letzte Glaube zu den Lebzeiten des Täufers unmöglich aufkommen, da er dieser Vermuthung, auf die manche Juden verfallen waren, so öffentlich und feyerlich widersprochen hatte. Und hätte auch die Anfrage, die er von seinem Gefängnis aus bey Jesu durch einige von seinen Schülern thun liess, ob denn er nicht der Messias sey? oder ob man auf einen andern warten solle (Matth. 11, 7)? ihren Ursprung von seiner Wankelmuth genommen, so konnte sie doch nicht auf die Vermuthung führen, er, der Täufer selbst, sey der Messias...

[Historically only this much is certain: that because of the greater following that Jesus had, many of the disciples of John the Baptist were envious, from which it follows, of course, that they did not regard him [Jesus] as the Messiah. Nor could this latter belief [i.e. that John was the Messiah] possibly have prevailed in the lifetime of the Baptist, since he so openly and solemnly had spoken against this supposition, upon which many Jews had fastened. And even if the inquiry, which from his prison he [John] had made of Jesus through some of his own disciples, as to whether Jesus was the Messiah or if they should expect another (Matt 11.7), had its grounds in his indecision, it could not have led to the supposition that he, the Baptist himself, was the Messiah...]

P. 210. What need of suspecting inconstancy (*Wankelmuth*) in the Baptist, when he sent his disciples with these questions to Jesus?—Are we under any obligation to suppose him free from all the Jewish Prejudices respecting the Messiah, from which the Apostles themselves were not exempt, even after their Lord's resurrection? Why might not the Baptist have expected that Christ would have given *the Sign*, which the Scribes and Pharisees required—i.e. the open assumption of the kingly Character, and the Sceptre of David?—But so it is. We are always passing from one extreme to the opposite—.

---

[a] Letter supplied by the editor

5[4] For an explication of γνῶσις (knowledge) in 1 Cor 8.1 see DONNE *Sermons* COPY B **39** and n 2. For gnosticism see CHILLINGWORTH COPY B **1** n 2 and cf FLEURY **37**. For "the extinction of all the Writings of the Gnostics [as] among the heaviest losses of ecclesiastical Literature" see FLEURY **32** n 1.

Because the Baptist possessed only a *measure* of the Spirit, and was not *the* Light, but only *a* Light,[1] therefore he must have been of an inconstant and unsettled mind!—

7 II ‾1, referring to II 213–23 | §170

[Eichhorn here counters various arguments that have been advanced to prove that the last chapter of the Gospel of St John (ch 21) is not John's. He considers the Evangelist the author.]

P. 213–223. Notwithstanding all Eichhorn's ingenuity, it appears to me abundantly the more probable and satisfactory Hypothesis, that the Post-script or Appendix was added by the Successor in the Church after John's Death—and for a good and sufficient cause, viz. to remove an objection grounded on a Saying of our Lord's that had been inaccurately reported.[1]—I cannot doubt, that the last Chapter—or at least the latter Half of it—was written after the death of both Apostles—Peter and John.[2]

8 II 256 | §174

Die Apokalypse muss, nach der darinn durchweg herrschenden lebendigen Dichtungskraft, die früheste und die Briefe...müssen die spätesten Schriften des Johannes seyn...

[The Apocalypse, judging by the vigorous poetic power prevailing throughout, must be the earliest, and the Epistles...the latest...of the writings of John...]

Nonsense!—Milton's Par. Lost: Dryden's Ode.[1]

9 II ‾4–‾5(p–d), referring to II 262 | §175

[Eichhorn is here arguing that the ungrammatical elements in the Greek of the Gospel of St John stem from the fact that the author

[6][1] John 1.8 reads (AV): "He [John] was not that Light, but was sent to bear witness of that Light".

[7][1] John 14.3: "And if I go and prepare a place for you, I will come again, and receive you unto myself; that where I am, there ye may be also." This statement may have led the disciples to believe that Jesus would return in their lifetime. C suggests that the epilogue to the fourth Gospel was written to declare that this might not be the case—see esp John

21.23: "Then went this saying abroad among the brethren, that that disciple [John] should not die: yet Jesus said not unto him, He shall not die".

[7][2] Scholars are not agreed that the epilogue (John 21) was not written by the Evangelist himself. Cf *NT* COPY A 39 and BIBLE *Apocryphal NT* 4 n 4.

[8][1] See COPY A 33 and n 1. Dryden was sixty-six when he wrote *Alexander's Feast*.

was thinking in Aramaic as he was writing in Greek, and not from the fact that the gospel is a poor translation from an Aramaic original.] Joh. 19, 11. ist dem Pilatus die Macht, Jesum zum Tode zu verdammen, δεδόμενον ἄνωθεν, d. i. von Gott (ἄνωθεν Joh. 3, 31.) zugelassen: wo wäre da ein Misverstand eines aramäischen Originals? Wollte man das ἄνωθεν auf das Synedrium ziehen, so würde der ungereimte Sinn in den Johannes getragen, dass Pilatus seine Macht dem Synedrium verdankt habe; und wo wäre selbst bey dieser Deutung Misverständnis eines aramäischen Worts nothwendig?

[In John 19.11 Pilate has the power to condemn Jesus to death "given from above", i.e. from God ("from above" John 3.31); where in this would there be a misunderstanding of an Aramaic original? If the "from above" is applied to the Sanhedrim, there is carried into John the absurd meaning that Pilate derived his power from the Sanhedrim; and even with this interpretation, where is the necessity of a misunderstanding of an Aramaic word?]

262. So far from admitting the interpretation of ανωθεν as relating to the Sanhedrim to be absurd, "ungereimt", I have little doubt that it is the true sense of the passage.[1] Eichhorn was so blinded by his infra-socinian scheme[2] as not to see that the Charge against Jesus for claiming the Messiahship was a mere ruse of the High Priest, as the only way of bringing the affair before the Roman[a] Governor, who alone could pass a capital sentence; but that the real offence, for which according to *their* Law (the law of Moses) he was worthy of Death, was tour Lord's Affirmative to the perfectly distinct question— Art thou (i.e. dost thou assert thyself to be) the Son of the Living God? *Then* first Caiaphas rent his robes and cried—Blasphemy!—It was no crime among the Jews for a man to believe himself the Messiah—tho' in the Jewish meaning of the Messiah it was no less than high treason in the view of the Roman Government.—

10 II +4–+5 (p–d), referring to II 264

Wenn von Jesus nach seiner Austreibung der Käufer und Verkäufer aus den Tempelgebauden ein Beweis gefodert wird, dass er zu dieser

---

[a] Notes **1** and **2** having taken up the rest of II ⁻4, C has written " ∧ ∧ " and resumed the note on p ⁻5 (p–d) with " ∧ ∧ "

9[1] See also BIBLE COPY B 111 and n 1. This is now the accepted understanding of ἄνωθεν (from above) in John 19.11. C gives the same explication in more detail in *TT* 20 May 1830.

9[2] For C on Eichhorn's Socinianism see e.g. COPY A **38** and cf **31, 34**; and for his "psilanthropism" see COPY A **41**.

Machthandlung ein Recht habe, und er antwortet (2, 19.): "brechet diesen Tempel ab und in kurzer Zeit soll ein anderer wieder da stehen"; so kann er nur den Tempel als Bild des religiösen Instituts der Juden betrachtet und gesagt haben: "gebt euer ganzes bisheriges religiöses Institut auf; ein anderes werde ich in kurzer Zeit an seine Stelle gesetzt haben".

[When Jesus, after he had driven the buyers and sellers from the Temple buildings, was asked to give proof that he had the right to make this forcible expulsion, and he had answered (2.19), "Destroy this Temple and in a short while another will stand here"; he could only have envisioned the Temple as a symbol of the religious institutions of the Jews, and have said, "Give up your entire previous religious institution; in a short while I shall have set another in its place."]

P. 264. In this instance, at least, John understood the words of his Friend and Master better than Pr. Eichhorn. When did Christ wish or require his Countrymen to give up, or abolish, their national institutions? The act of scourging the Money-changers out of the Temple was a proof of the contrary—i.e. of his zeal & reverence for them. But when it was demanded of him that he should shew by what right he exercised this power, could any possible reply be more to the point, thatn the implied Assertion that *he* was the Lord of that *Temple*? that theiris ~~Temple~~ Pile of Stone was now only in a secondary and a far meaner sense the ~~true~~ temple of Jehova (i.e. the Jehova-word)[1] which power belonged to his own Body, in which the Jehova εσκηνωτε,[2] did then tabernacle? That I have authority over the meaner & merely nominal temple ~~you~~ there will soon be proof—for in three days I will raise up the *true* Temple, the tabernacle of the Shechinah of the living Jehova,[3] after that you have levelled it to the ground. There are at least three other passages in which our Lord *involved* (συνετοισι φωνουντα[a])[4] the same affirmation of his Jehova hood—and whence did Paul learn *his* doctrine, that Christ was in the Wilderness—that he was the Rock—that he filled all things?[5] ~~From~~

[a] For φωναεντα

10[1] For the "Jehovah-Word" see BIBLE COPY B 11 and n 1, 55 and n 3, 119 n 1 and BROWNE *Works* 39 and n 1. See also 14 (at n 6), below.

10[2] Lit. "lived in a tent" or "tabernacle". Cf John 1.14 and Rev. 21.3, and, for σκήνωμα meaning "body", 2 Pet 1.13, 14.

10[3] For *Shekinah*—the Glory of the Lord, as a presence especially in the Temple—see COPY A 42 n 1 and cf 14 (at n 3), below.

10[4] For this recurrent phrase from Pindar *Olympian Odes* 3.85—"speaking to the enlightened"—see BÖHME 9 n 5. Speaking to the enlightened, Christ *involved* (wrapped up) his meaning.

10[5] See 1 Cor 10.4; cf Rom 9.33, 1 Pet 2.8.

By immediate Revelation from Christ? Then why should not Christ have declared the same in his discourses? If not by Revelation, then whence but from these discourses could he derive it?—

11 II ⁻1 and title-page, referring to II 303 | 2 Ueber Johannes ersten Brief § 180

Nun lehrte Cerinth, der Aeon, Christus, sey auf Jesum erst bey seiner Taufe herabgekommen, und habe ihn bey seinem Tod wieder verlassen: es scheine daher Cerinth in dem ersten Brief Johannis bestritten zu werden. Wer könnte aber ἐν σαρκὶ ἔρχεσθαι sprachrichtig durch "*gebohren werden*" erklären? dem Sprachgebrauch nach kann es nicht anderes bedeuten, als φανερωθῆναι ἐν σαρκὶ "im Aeussern andern Menschen gleich seyn".

[But Cerinthus taught that the Aeon, Christ, descended upon Jesus only at his baptism, and departed again from him at his death: it would appear, therefore, that Cerinthus is being attacked in the First Epistle of John. But who could interpret ἐν σαρκὶ ἔρχεσθαι in proper linguistic terms as "to be born"? According to the customary usage it can mean nothing other than φανερωθῆναι ἐν σαρκὶ "in outward appearance to be like other men".]

P. 303. I am not *quite* satisfied as to the mere equivalence of εν σαρκι ερχεσθαι to σαρκα (= σωμα) εχειν:[1] it seems to me to involve the notion of pre-existence.[2] But I fully agree with Eichhorn, that it could not have ⟨been⟩ the object of John's Gospel to vindicate the union of the Logos with Jesus in the Womb against Cerinthus. Had this been the Evangelist's aim & purpose, he would like the Redactor of our Greek Matthew, and the Prefixer of the Christopædia to Luke's G.[3] have begun with the Birth instead of passing it over, and with it the whole first 30 years of our Lord's Life, in silence.

12 II ⁺1, referring to II 346 | 5 Ueber Johannes Offenbarung § 189

Die ganze Symbolik des Dichters gieng von Kenntniss der zeichnenden und plastischen Kunst aus... Durch die Hülfe dieser Kenntniss vereinfachte er den etwas zu künstlich zusammengesetzten Wagenthron Gottes beym Ezechiel, in einen schlichten Thron, von vier lebendigen (den Cherubim) getragen...

[The writer's whole symbolism derived from a knowledge of the graphic and plastic arts... With the aid of this knowledge he simplified the rather too

---

11[1] "To come in the flesh", in textus; and cf 1 John 4.2, 2 John 7. The second Greek phrase—"to have flesh (i.e. a body)"—is not in NT.

11[2] The gospel phrase involves Christ's existence before his coming in the flesh.

11[3] For the *evangelia infantiae* see COPY A **19** n 2.

artfully done chariot-throne of God in Ezekiel into a plain throne drawn
by four living creatures (the Cherubim)...]

P. 346. I confess that I prefer Ezekiel's, as conveying the omnia in
singulis[1]—and altogether I cannot find the faults in Ezekiel's
Symbolik which Eichhorn does.[2] And I please myself with the
thought, that Milton would have been of my mind. *S. T. C.*

13   II 376 | §191

Woher dieser frühe Glaube geflossen ist, ob aus dem Zeugniss
gleichzeitiger Männer, die aus dem Umgang mit dem Apostel
wussten, dass er die Apokalypse verfasst habe? Oder aus dem Buche
*] selbst, das allerdings für eine Arbeit des Evangelisten und Apostels
Johannes angesehen seyn will (1, 1. 2. 9. 22, 8)? das ist völlig
ungewiss.

[Whence flows this early belief—from the witness of contemporary persons
who knew from their association with the Apostle that he wrote the
Apocalypse? or from the book itself, which, of course, wants to be taken
as a work of the Evangelist and Apostle John (1.1, 2, 9; 22.8)? that is
completely uncertain.

* No such assertion is made in either: and in XXII.8. the contrary
seems inferred.[1]

14   II +1–+2, referring to II 376 | 13 textus

P. 376.

If either I.9: or XXII.8. contained this assertion, it was impossible
that Eusebius should have thought John the Elder the more probable
Author than J. the Evangelist.[1] But it was too common with
Eichhorn to find in a text what he wished to find—Ex.gr. Exodus
XXV.40.[2]—The Hebrew does not say nor must the words necessarily
be believed to imply, that the Cherub-shaped corresponded to a
celestial Prototype, or that they were intended as types or copies of
an Original actually existing in Heaven. In ⳥ the Hebrew, Jehova

---

12[1] "Everything in the particulars"—
a variant of the principle of *totus in omni
parte*, for which see BLANCO WHITE
Practical Evidence 13 n 7. See also FIELD
32 (at n 6) and *CN* III 3962.
12[2] See Ezk 1.4–28 and Rev 4.1–11.
13[1] The John who speaks in the first
person in Rev nowhere explicitly says
that he is the Apostle and Evangelist.

Rev 22.8 reads: "And I John saw these
things, and heard *them*...."
14[1] On Eusebius see 16, below.
14[2] "And look that thou make them
[the furnishings of the tabernacle] after
their pattern, which was shewed thee in
the mount." The cherubim are described
in Exod 25.18–20.

simply refers Moses to the Forms or Patterns, which he *had been
caused* to see on the Mount, i.e. within the inclosure filled by the
~~Cloud~~ Glory and curtain⟨ed⟩ by the Cloud.[3]—The great Question
is—*what* did Aaron, Alihu and the 70 Princes or Elders *see*, & yet
lived?—By analogy of Genesis XXXII.24–31.[4] ~~it is f~~ one would most
naturally suppose that it was the Human Form in which God was
seen by them: and if so, it seems impossible for a Christian, who
believes that v. 18 of Ch. I. of St John's Gospel is inspired Scripture,[5]
to deny that the Jehova on the Mount was Christ, the only begotten
WORD, the Son of God and God.[6]—Those Critics, however, who
hold that ~~that~~e Hebrews worshipped God as ein *Licht* und *Feuer-
wesen,*[7] may evade perhaps this conclusion/ but not, I think, without
shewing in what the *essential* difference could have subsisted between
these Elders and the People at large. For the latter beheld the Light
and the Fire.—I adhere therefore to the first interpretation: and am
at no time other than well-content to understand a passage as I am
certain the Apostles, John and Paul understood it. S. T. Coleridge.

---

15   II +2, referring to II 377

[By citing linguistic parallels in the Gospel of St John and the
Revelation, Eichhorn argues that John the Evangelist is the author
of both.] . . . wie er nach dem Evangelium die Sünden der Welt gebüsst
hat (Joh. 1, 29, 36), so auch in der Apokalypse (1, 5. 5, 9. 7, 14. 12,
11). . .

[. . . just as he, according to the Gospel, atoned for the sins of the world (John
1.29, 36), so also in the Apocalypse (1.5, 5.9, 7.14, 12.11). . .]

p. 377. gebüsst hat.—First of all, the words here alluded to by
Eichhorn are John the Baptist's[1] and secondly, the words ~~ware~~ ὁ
αιρων την αμαρτιαν του κοσμου—i.e. taking away or (which I
prefer) *lifting up* (as we lift up a burthen from the shoulders of an
over-loaded Porter) not as E. renders it, expiating or atoning for—and
την αμαρτιαν, the *sin* of the world—i.e. the burthen of a corrupt

---

14[3] The whole passage refers to Exod
24–31, esp 24.9–18, 25.40.

14[4] The account of Jacob wrestling
with the angel ends (v 30): "I have seen
God face to face, and my life is
preserved".

14[5] John 1.18: "No man hath seen
God at any time".

14[6] See **10** n 1, above, and cf DONNE
Sermons COPY B **71** n 1.

14[7] "A *light-* and *fire-being*". See
Apocrypha **6** and cf **12** n 6.

15[1] In John 1.29, 36 the words
"Behold the Lamb of God, which taketh
away the sin of the world" and "Behold
the Lamb of God" are spoken by John
the Baptist.

nature—not the *sins* or trespasses of Individuals taken collectively. αμαρτια from αμαρτω, *frequentatively* αμαρτανω, a turning aside from its original direction, a missing of its aim.[2] And I am so far from considering this as any proof of the identity of the Author of the ~~Gospel~~ Apocalypse and ~~the Author of~~ the Evangelist, that I am inclined to cite the I. 5, and other similar Sentences of the Apocalypse[3] as forming a Contrast with the scheme of redemption set forth in the 4th Gospel, not easily to be reconciled with the supposition of ~~th~~ one man being the Author of both.

16   II +3,[a] evidently referring to II 387

Und eben darum ist auch Eusebius Einfall, dass Johannes Presbyter die Apokalypse, das Evangelium aber und die Episteln Johannes der Apostel verfasst haben möge, keiner ernsthaften Beachtung werth.

[Thus on that score Eusebius' notion that John the Presbyter might have written the Apocalypse, and John the Apostle the Gospel and Epistles, is not worthy of serious consideration.]

I can find nothing in the Apocalypse є incompatible with the Eusebian Hypothesis of John an Elder of Ephesus under the Evangelist John, being the Author.[1] Doubtless, the majority of the Church at Ephesus were Jews—the same Palestino-hellenistic Style might therefore be expected in the one John as in the other—and that the favorite words and phrases of the Bishop (i.e. the evangelist John) should be adopted by one of his Elders & Converts was so natural that the contrary would have surprised us. Twenty Co-incidences of this sort would not ~~prove as~~ furnish as strong a presumption *in favor* of the Evangelist John's being the Author, as a single discrepance in doctrine would *against* it. Now this discrepance I seem to *find* in two or three texts, and to *feel* in very many—and I have greater trust in the latter, in that Luther felt the same.[2]   S. T. C.

17   III 1, concluded on p iv, pencil | VII Ueber die Briefe des Apostels Paulus § 202

Als Jesus von seinen Jüngern schied, war sein Lehrbegriff nur erst in schwachen Umrissen vorhanden. Die Lehre von Gott, Vorsehung

---

[a] Written in the upper part of the page, above 3

15[2] C's comments on the meanings of the Greek words are sound.

15[3] "Unto him that loved us, and washed us from our sins in his own blood." For "other similar sentences" in Rev see e.g. 7.14 and 12.11.

16[1] Eusebius *Ecclesiastical History* 3.39.5–6—a view still held in the unresolved controversy about the authorship of Rev. Cf BIBLE *NT Revelation* 4 and n 1.

16[2] In Luther's Preface to the Apocalypse.

und Unsterblichkeit hatte er als allgemeine Wahrheiten voraus-gesetzt, ohne sie zu beweisen, oder ihren Zusammenhang mit dem allgemeinen Wahrheitssinn zu zeigen. Gott hatte er als Ideal der Heiligkeit und als Muster dargestellt, dem die Menschen unablässig nachzustreben hätten, und das Sittengesetz als göttliches Gebot, an dessen Befolgung die Bedingung des göttlichen Beyfalls und der Glückseligkeit geknüpft sey.

[When Jesus departed from his disciples, his system of doctrines existed only in vague outlines. His doctrines concerning God, providence, and immortality he had set forth as general truths, without proving them and without indicating their connexion with a general apprehension of truth. He set God forth as the ideal of holiness and as a pattern that mankind had faithfully to strive after, and the moral law as a divine commandment, on observance of which the blessing of God and a state of bliss depended.]

A false Theory both of the Religion and the Character of Christ is at the bottom of all these remarks in § 202.[a]

Eichhorn every where reasons, as if Christ stood in the same relation to Christianity, as Euclid to the Elements of Geometry. But Christ himself is the Stuff, Substance and main Object of the Christian Faith/ & no Scheme of theological or ethical doctrines other than as deduced from, & dependent on, him.[1]

18   III ⁻5 (p–d), referring to III 1 | **17 textus**

P. 1.

Glück-seligkeit?—In vain would Eichhorn seek in the writings of Paul or John such an abuse of language, so self-contradictory a term![1]—But generally, let me leave on record that as far as sound and extensive book-learning, unfettered research, and acute judge-ment, in determining the Age of Writings and the grounds of their attribution to this or that traditionary Name are concerned, I gladly & thankfully take Eichhorn, as my Guide. But as to the philosophy, the *religion* by the performed comprehension of which alone the Contents of these Writings can be interpreted, I would soon[b] trust a blind man in a question of Colors.[2]

S. T. Coleridge.

[a] Here C has written " ∧ ", and resumed the note with " ∧ " on p iv
[b] Perhaps a slip for "sooner" or "as soon"

17[1] With **17, 18, 20,** and **21** cf COPY A **45** and **46**.

18[1] *Glück*—happiness, as good luck, good fortune; *Seligkeit*—blessedness. The word *Glück-seligkeit* is sound German but offends C's sensitivity to original meanings.

18[2] In *CN* IV 5322 (c Jan–Feb 1826) C comments on *NT* III 11 and "this one incident of the Flash" in St Paul's conversion (**19**), saying that in only four years he had collected reports of "similar instances, where the persons had been struck off their horse, heard voices,

19 iii ⁻4, referring to iii 12

Aber unterwegs, als er [Paulus] Damaskus schon nahe war, trift ihn ein Blitz bey heiterem Himmel und blendet ihn; er sieht ihn nach dem Glauben der Alten Welt für ein Omen an, das ihn vor der Fortsetzung seines Verfolgungseifers, mit welchem er seine Reise nach Damaskus angetreten hatte, warnen wolle.

[But on the way, when Paul was already near Damascus, a bolt of lightning from clear skies struck and blinded him; in the manner of belief of the ancient world, he regarded this as an omen that would warn him against the continuation of his zeal for persecution, for which he had undertaken his journey to Damascus.]

P. 12.

Of the force or weakness of E's explanation of St Paul's sudden Conversion, I say nothing.* But the Assertion, that Paul himself did not regard the incident, as miraculous and an actual presence of Jesus, when he grounds his apostleship and equality with the other Apostles, on the fact, that he no less than they had been in personal Communion with the Lord—this is too bad! Fair Play is a Jewel in all games. A psychological exposition of the *Causes* of a Man's Belief is one thing: an historical statement of the Belief is another. And how are we ⟨to⟩ account for the cöincident Vision of Ananias, and the instantaneous Restoration to Sight?[1] From whom could Luke have received the Account but from his Friend and Comrade, St Paul? or if from common report, is it credible that he should never have ascertained its truth and correctness from Paul himself?

N.B. Amaurosis and Blindness from nervous distemperature inter *casus*, in quibus Ζωο-μαγνητισμος multum valere creditur.[2]

---

struck with blindness & recovered their sight after two or three days". Cf **24** and n 3, below, and DONNE *Sermons* COPY A **5A** n 1. C in his mind implicitly connected St Paul's conversion, Milton's amaurosis, and certain visual and tactual phenomena of animal magnetism: see **19** n 2, below, and *AT* **38**.

19[1] Ananias, a disciple in Damascus, received a vision showing that he was to restore sight to Saul of Tarsus: see Acts 9.10–18.

19[2] Amaurosis—partial or total loss of sight from disease of the optic nerve, not outwardly observable (*OED*), for which "Gutta serena" is another name—

the cause of Milton's blindness (see BUNYAN COPY A **14** n 3). "Amaurosis...among the *cases* in which Zoomagnetism [i.e animal magnetism] is believed to have much virtue". In his marginalia on SOUTHEY *Life of Wesley* (see **24** n 4, below) C considered in several places the possible relation between zoomagnetism and the enthusiastic and ecstatic states ascribed to some of the early Methodist preachers and converts. In a comment on apparent miraculous cures by a lay-preacher (ii 338) C distinguishes between "a *surgical* case" (a young woman cured of cancer of the breast) and "that class which have been

* I am bound to confess, that it would in my judgement strengthen and facilitate the evidence of Christianity, if it could be shewn, that *miracles* in the highest & speciallest sense of the word were predicable of Christ alone.

20 III ⁻1, referring to III 14

Zur Quelle, aus welcher er [Paulus] seine Anfangs etwa noch mangelhaften Kenntnisse der Lehren Jesus ergänzte, scheint ihm das Urevangelium*ᵏ* nach der Bearbeitung gedient zu haben, in welcher es das Evangelium der Hebräer hiess.

[As the source from which Paul supplemented his at first rather imperfect knowledge of the doctrines of Jesus, the original gospel document*ᵏ* appears to have served him, in the recension in which it was called the Gospel of the Hebrews.]

P. 14.—In addition to other objections, which might be brought, against this hypothesis of Sᵗ Paul's using a written Gospel during his Lehrjahre in Arabia, the character of the three first Gospels, even of Luke's, compared with the Gosp. according to Sᵗ John, & the perfect harmony, nay, identity of Paul's Ideas in the Ep. to the Ephesians with *this* Gospel, written after Paul's Death, weighs greatly with me.[1]

21 III 14

*] [Footnote *k*:] Den Gebrauch eines Evangeliums beweisen die Stellen, in welchen Paulus die Befehle des Herrn von seiner Meynung, die er aus den Geist seiner Lehre...geschöpft haben will, unterscheidet...

[The use of a gospel is indicated by the places in which Paul distinguishes between the commands of the Lord and his own opinions, which he wants to draw from the spirit of his teaching...]

---

found *most often*, and *most* influenced by stimulants of Imagination, sudden acts of active and passive Volition, and ...by regular friction—*touching*—on-breathing—& the like", and associates with the second class the preacher's possible ability to cure an "amaurotic, or a case of disordered function, not organic disease or defect". There, as here, C apparently uses the absence of outwardly observable disease in amaurosis as a metaphor for neurotic blindness, which not only does not exhibit any "organic" symptom of disease but is also an apparent blindness from which—as for St Paul—full sight can be restored without any adverse effect. On animal magnetism in healing and in prophetic vision see COPY A **24** and n 2 and **33**; for animal magnetism generally see *AT* **38** nn 1 and 2 and BÖHME **26** n 3.

20[1] With **20** and **21** cf COPY A **46**.

* But why necessarily of a *Book*? Why not from the Evangelists, or those who expounded the prophecies as fulfilled in the Life & Works of Jesus?

22 III ⁻3⁻⁻2, referring to III 61 | A 1 Erster Brief an die Thessalonicher § 207

Ein eigener Abschnitt ist der Erwartungen der Rükkehr Christi von Himmel gewidmet (4, 13–18). Jesus hatte in seinen letzten Lebenstagen viel von seiner Rükkehr gesprochen; er hatte vor dem Synedrium die Frage des Hohenpriesters, ob er der Messias sey? bejahet, und beygefügt: er werde nächstens seine Mitregentschaft bey Gott antreten, und als himmlisches Wesen auf Wolken wiederkommen (Matth. 26, 64): die Christen erwarteten daher Christus zum Antritt seines Reichs nächstens zurück, voll des Wunsches, dass jeder diese glückliche Zeit erleben möchte.

[A special section is devoted to expectations of the return of Christ from heaven (4.13–18). In the last days of his life, Jesus had spoken much of his return; before the Sanhedrim he had answered affirmatively to the high priest's question as to whether or not he was the Messiah, and had added that he would shortly enter his co-regency with God and return in the clouds as a heavenly being (Matt 26.64): the Christians expected, therefore, that he would shortly enter on his kingdom, and each was filled with the desire that he might live to experience this blissful occasion.]

P. 61.—Eichhorn is often sadly inconsistent. Because it suited his present purpose, he attributes the impatient millennary expectations of the Thessalonians to our Lord's words as found in Matthew 26. v. 64:[1] and of course, assumes the historical accuracy ⟨of,⟩ & evangelical & apostolical testimony for, the relation. For a contrary purpose, he would have been the first to have denounced the passage, as found *only* in the first Gospel as spoken on *this* occasion, and as irreconcilable with the consistent and masterly narration of an Eye-witness, that of John. This, he would have remarked, is not the first, second or third instance of Speeches held at one time & on one occasion being transferred by the Redactor of our Matthew's Gospel to another time & occasion/. But even so, Eichhorn's

---

22[1] Matt. 26.64: "Jesus saith unto him, Thou hast said: nevertheless I say unto you, Hereafter shall ye see the Son of man sitting on the right hand of power, and coming in the clouds of heaven." 1 Thess 4.16–17 (part of Eichhorn's reference) reads: "For the Lord himself shall descend from heaven with a shout, with the voice of the archangel, and with the trump of God: and the dead in Christ shall rise first: Then we which are alive and remain shall be caught up together with them in the clouds, to meet the Lord in the air: and so shall we ever be with the Lord."

paraphrase is no feuair or necessary interpretation of the words—the proper meaning of which every Believer in Christ must now hold to be—the time will come, when you will experience the truth of my Dispensation, and in the destruction of your own Temple & State, and find my power in the dark and terrible Events & Judgements in which as in clouds it will be veiled. Briefly, whom you reject as a Saviour you will hereafter sink prostrate before as an avenging Providence.—That the Church at Thessalonica understood our Lord's words literally, and that St Paul himself had no prophetic revelation authorizing him to undeceive them, are neither matters to excite surprize except in those who fondly attribute little less than omniscience to the Apostles, in the very face of their own declarations to the contrary and the proofs of their fallibility recorded in the ACTS—nor form any excuse for us who have learnt the true Sense of the Prophecy from its fulfilment.

23 III ⁻3, perhaps referring to **22**

Mem.

The infallibility attributed to the Apostles has been scarcely less injurious to Theology than the Infall.⁷ assumed by the Pope$ has proved to Religion.

24 III ⁺1–⁺2, evidently referring to III 71–91 | A 3 Brief an die Galater §§ 211–15

Galatians. In few words—Judaism as expounded by the Scribes, Pharisees and Rabbis, in short, by the Jewish Church of the Apostolic Age regarded *Reformation* as the appointed and sufficient Means of Salvation. Men were to become Good, and the Natural Will to be rendered holy and meritorious by a continued series of voluntary Acts, in obedience to the Law delivered by Moses: which Law comprized in its several ordinances all the works and all the abstinences requisite to make men well-pleasing and conformable to God.

In opposition to Reformation, which as derived from this source and exacted in this extent was declared impracticable and the Law requiring the same a Law of *Condemnation*, Christianity proposes and offers REGENERATION—not the ruinous Adam *repaired*, but a new man born of the Spirit into Christ, the Medium and Mediator between God and Man. In allusion to the primary and most proper sense of βαπτω, baptō, the etymon or root of baptism (βαπτω, = intingo, to dip into a *die*,) Christ, the Word incarnate, is what

Dyers call the MORDAUNT.[1] As the Corollary to this—the crimes and vices which the Jew was to shrink back from for their illegality, the Christian is exhorted to rise above, & to leave behind him, on account of their now *alien* nature—but to attribute no merit to such negative duties, and no saving efficacy: which ⟨last⟩ must be sought for, not in the doings and *not* doings of the *Living Soul*, but in the powers and presence of the *life-making Spirit* thro' faith; which is itself a gift and product of the Spirit. Such is the doctrine of the Apostles John and Paul: ⟨a doctrine,⟩ which ~~our Divine~~ whoever preaches without caution must *expect*, ~~th~~ and even with caution must be *prepared* for, the charge of Antinomianism.[2]

Thus Wesley having with his Skillet or Shallow Scull-pan skimmed a portion of the Froth from the rocky Basin into which the impetuous Luther precipitates his waters, ~~of~~ eloquentiæ θεοπνευστῆς[a] flumen et fulmen,[3] mistakes it for the rabid foam of ~~sin~~ Licentiousness & screams out, Poison! Madness! Blasphemy!—⟨See Southey's Life of Wesley.⟩[4]   S. T. C.

---

[a] A slip for θεοπνευστης. C often (as here) provides an illicit iota subscript for a first-declension genitive singular

24[1] A substance used in dyeing to fix certain colours by chemical reaction—"a well-known phrase from technical chemistry", as C remarks in *BL*, having probably read Claude-Louis Berthollet (1748–1822) *Élemens de l'art de la teinture* (Paris 1791) tr William Hamilton (1791): see *CN* III 3606n. For uses of "morda(u)nt" by C see e.g. *Friend (CC)* I 463 (noted in *OED*), *BL* ch 18 (*CC*) II 71.

24[2] A belief, chiefly in the Reformation and later, and mainly in smaller sects such as the Anabaptists, that the inner workings of grace were more important than obedience to the moral law. Cf BUNYAN COPY A **24** n 1 and (on Ranters) FLEURY **34** n 2. The reference to SOUTHEY *Life of Wesley* at the end of this annotation suggests that C had in mind particularly the antinomianism towards which early Methodism strongly tended, despite John Wesley's determination in his later years to prevent his work from being destroyed by "the wild boars, the fierce, unclean, brutish, blasphemous Antinomians": II 316–19.

24[3] "A flood and flash [or lightning-river] of god-inspired eloquence". (The pun on *flumen*, river, and *fulmen*, thunderbolt, does not turn exactly into English.) C also referred to Luther as "the German 'Son of Thunder'" (cf Mark 3.17). *Friend (CC)* I 132 (II 113). He also acknowledged that "Phrases equally strong and Assertions no less rash and startling [than in the works of Calvin] are no rarities in the Writings of Luther: for Catachresis was the favourite Figure of Speech in that age." *AR* (1825) 154.

24[4] SOUTHEY *Life of Wesley* (2 vols 1820)—which C called "the favourite of my Library...this darling Book" (I 218)—draws in minute and sympathetic detail a portrait of John Wesley as greatly endowed with physical and emotional energy, moral fervour, and evangelical passion but somewhat lacking in intellectual power, being inconstant in doctrine (II 287) and given to credulity (II 184). Wesley's pugnacity tempted him at times into a violent and extravagant language that often had the air of desperation rather than of policy; and his habit of combativeness led him to reject in turn the Moravians, then the Calvinists, and finally the Church of England, which he had always hoped his work would serve

25 III ⁻2–⁻1, referring to III 81 | § 213

Christus habe sich daher als einen Schuldbaren darstellen lassen,
oder sey zur Bestätigung seiner Lehre gestorben, damit sich niemand
mehr an das nichtsvermögende Mosaische Gesetz halten, sondern
jeder durch die Lehre des Christenthums vom vernünftigen Glauben
oder zweifellosen Vertrauen auf Gott zu Gottes Wohlgefallen
gelangen möchte, wie auch Abraham wegen jenes vernünftigen
Glaubens dazu gelangt sey...

[With this purpose had Christ let himself be represented as a criminal, or
had died in ratification of his doctrines, so that no longer should anyone be
bound to the inoperative Mosaic law, but that each might succeed to the
favour of God through the Christian teaching of a reasoned belief or
confident faith in God, even as Abraham succeeded to this because of his
reasoned belief...]

P. 81. last line but 13. *oder sey zur Bestätigung &c—*
This reminds me of a droll fellow who telling a story about a
Methodist Butler to a Methodist Preacher, said—Well, Sir! as
Scripture says, He ascended into the high places—*or* as *we* ~~may~~ say,
he gets me down into the Wine-vault.

Verily, such effrontery as this of Eichhorn's scarcely permits a
more serious confutation: or it would be a sufficient answer, that this
was not the point for which our Lord was sentenced to the Cross,
it was not the point which our Lord confirmed by his crucifixion—but
that he was the Son of the Living God, therein asserting himself to
be of one Substance with the Father—and that in his death he
fulfilled the annunciation of the Baptist—Behold the Lamb of God
that taketh away the Sins of the World.[1] What Pharisee was there
who did not profess a firm belief in the truth and ultimate fulfilment
of God's Promises? What was this more than a belief in the divine
Veracity—which an Atheist only or a gross Pagan could doubt?—But
the Faith demanded in a Christian is Faith in Christ, as the Promise
and ~~the~~ Consummation of the Promises. And for *what* promised? For
the remission of Sinss thro' faith in his *Blood!* And for the victory
over Sin itself, namely, Corruption, and the Body corruptible, to a
permanent or everlasting Life,[2]—by the Blood of the Son of Man!—

and strengthen. C considered Luther by
contrast a man of Pauline mentality and
stature (see e.g. *CL* VI 561, *TT* 12 Jul
1827, and cf **31** at n 3, below), called him
"the heroic Solifidian" and one of "the
great Patriarchal Protestants", and ad-
mired him particularly for his "full,

steady, deep yet comprehensive Insight
into the Nature of Faith and Works".
DONNE *Sermons* COPY B 63, **74, 65.**
25[1] John 1.29 (var).
25[2] See 1 Cor 15.52–7 and cf Rom
3.25, Eph 1.7, Col 1.14.

26 III 215 | A 6 Brief an die Römer § 230

Er [Paulus] schildert es [das Christenthum] als eine Weltreligion, durch deren Befolgung man, zu welchem Volk man auch gehören möge, zu Gottes Wohlgefallen gelangen könne. Wie schwer fiel es damahls einem Judenchristen, sich zu diesem Gedanken zu erheben! Lukas legt zwar auch dem Apostel Petrus diese Ueberzeugung in den Mund: "wer tugendhaft lebe, der sey Gott angenehm, aus welchem Volk er auch seyn möge (Apg. 10, 34. 35)"....

[[Paul] depicted [Christianity] as a world religion, through the adherence to which one might win the favour of God whatever one's nationality. How difficult it was at that time for a Jewish Christian to raise himself to this thought! To be sure, Luke puts this conviction into the mouth of the Apostle Peter: "Whoever lives righteously is pleasing to God, from whatever nationality he might be (Acts 10.34–5)"....]

At all events Luke would not have put into Peter's mouth a sentiment opposite to his known principles.

27 III +3, referring to III 289–90 | A 8 Briefe an die Kolosser § 240

[Eichhorn here argues, in regard to Col 1.12–23 in general and verses 15–18 in particular, that St Paul's description of Christ as the One by which "all things consist" means only that Jesus was the chief figure of the Church, and not necessarily of the entire universe.]

P. 289, 290. A notable example of the Figure of Speech, called Meiosis, by which Mountains are turned to Mole-hills—or a Mountain Text made to bring forth the blind Mouse (Mus typhlus) of a Socinian.[1] "It *only* means so and so."—Strange that it should not have seem[ed][a] strange to Eichhorn, that these monstrous Hyperboles (for if Coloss. I. v. 12–23 *mean only* what Eichhorn states as the meaning,[2] more outrageous Bombast, more bellowing Bull-froggery

a Letters supplied by the editor

27[1] With splendid effect C combines his inversion of a common example of hyperbole with Horace's proverbial line, "parturiunt montes, nascetur ridiculus mus" (*Ars Poetica* 139), and makes Horace's "ridiculous mouse" into the blind cave-dwelling rat of scientific nomenclature (see *CN* III 4356 f 28). The "blind mouthes" of *Lycidas* 119 may also have been at the fringes of his attention. With "a Mountain Text" cf (also with Horace in mind) "a mountain-birth" in *Dejection* line 129: *PW* (EHC) I 368.

27[2] Cf Col 1.15–18: his dear Son... "Who is the image of the invisible God, the firstborn of every creature: For by him were all things created, that are in heaven, and that are in earth, visible and invisible, whether they be thrones, or dominions, or principalities, or powers: all things were created by him, and for him: And he is before all things, and by him all things consist. And he is the head of the body, the church: who is the beginning, the firstborn from the dead; that in all things he might have the preeminence."

is not be found in Rabelais's wildest Mock-heroic!)[3] are to be met with in no other part of Paul's Writings, and on no other Subject—. When P. speaks of himself, of the Apostles, of the Prophets, or of the Churches, all is calm, and sober, tho' earnest, *prose*—strong sound Sense, with complete Self-possession!—And that such a Man should not have foreseen what the least reflection must have shewn him to be inevitable, that all his Readers for 18500 years would misunderstand him!—& with exception of a handful of men, whom the great Body of Christians will not allow to be Christians,[4]—I might have said, for eighteen hundred years!

                                                        S. T. C.—

28   III +4, possibly referring to III 413 | A 14 Briefe an die Hebräer § 256

Sie [die christliche Lehrer] setzten die Richtigkeit und Wahrheit aller von der mosaischen Religion gangbaren Vorstellungen voraus, und bemüheten sich nur zu zeigen, dass die Vorzüge derselben auch in der christlichen, aber viel vollkommener, vorhanden wären.

[They [the Christian teachers] presumed the rightness and truth of everything in the current concepts of the Mosaic religion, and endeavoured only to show that the excellence of all this was also present in the Christian religion, but much more fully.]

Singular! that a work (the Epistle to the Hebrews) written for the purpose of elevating and spiritualizing the gross conceptions of the Jews should have been (as yet it has been) the chief occasion and mean of f literalizing and debasing those of the Christians!—

29   III +4, referring to III 441 | § [2]58

[Eichhorn argues that much of the style and wording of the epistle is over-elaborate and artificial. He illustrates by paraphrasing Heb 3:2.] So wollte der Verfasser (3, 2.) sagen: "wenn gleich der Stifter der neuen Religion über Mosen erhaben ist, so wird er deswegen noch nicht Gott gleich; denn Gott als Sender der beiden Gesandten bleibt immer der Höchste": wie künstlich ist dieses ausgedrückt...

27[3] For C on Rabelais see BROOKE 10. "Bull-froggery": not in *OED*—a happy coinage from the name of *Rana pipiens*, a large American frog, first reported from Carolina in 1738: "It hath its English Name from its Noise, which seems not unlike the Bellowing of a Bull at a Distance."

27[4] I.e. Unitarians. On the difficulty of St Paul's style see **31** (at n 3), below, and COPY A **28** and n 1.

[The author wished (3.2) to say: "Although the founder of the new religion is elevated over Moses, he is not therefore equal to God; for God, as the sender of both, is still the highest": how artificially is this expressed...]

P. 144. A difficulty and fault of Eichhorn's own making.[1]

30 III +4, referring to III 463 | § 260

Und in welcher Zeit seines Lebens sollte der Brief an die Hebräer von Paulus geschrieben worden seyn? Man setzt ihn in die Zeit nach seiner Entlassung aus seiner Gefangenschaft zu Rom, als er noch durch *Italien* reisete, um nach Griechenland und Palästina zu gehen...

[And in what period of his life would the Epistle to the Hebrews have been written by Paul? It has been placed in the time after his release from his imprisonment at Rome, while he was still travelling through *Italy* on his way to Greece and Palestine...]

P. 462.[a] I think it probable, that the notion of S[t] Paul's dismission from, and second Journey to, Rome was deduced, by help of the assumption of the plenary inspiration of every sentence in the canonical Books, from Paul's confident Anticipation of revisiting his Churches in the Ep. to the Philippians.[1]

31 III +4, referring to III 580 | VIII Ueber die katholischen Briefe 1 Jacobus § 279

Beyde [Jacobus und Paulus] stimmen zwar in ihrem Lehrbegriff mit einander überein, bey Paulus sind die ἔργα die ἔργα νόμου, die Beobachtung der mosaischen Gesetze, und die πίστις ist das Vertrauen auf Christus...

[Both [James and Paul] certainly agree everywhere with one another in their doctrines; in Paul the ἔργα (works) are the ἔργα νόμου (works of the law), the observation of the Mosaic laws; and the πίστις (faith) is the belief in Christ...]

p. 580. To the want of PHILOSOPHY, as the Science of IDEAS in contra-distinction from CONCEPTIONS,[1] must it be attributed, that a Man of so much Learning and Perspicacity, as Eichhorn, and so intimately acquainted with Paul's Writings, has deigned to take

a A slip for "463"

29[1] Heb 3.2 speaks of Christ as "faithful to him that appointed him, as also Moses was faithful in all his house".

30[1] See Phil 2.24: "But I trust in the Lord that I also myself shall come shortly."

31[1] See also **1**, above. On the distinction between ideas and conceptions see DAVISON **14** (at n 3) and FIELD **35** n 3; and for the danger of mistaking conceptions for ideas see e.g. DONNE *Sermons* COPY B **60** (at n 5) and FLEURY **63**.

refuge in the vulgar pretence, that ⟨by⟩ *Works* i̶n̶ St Paul meant εργα νομου, the ceremonial ordinances of the Mosaic Code exclusively.[2] But who indeed *has* understood the Pauline Writings? Who *has* mastered the Spirit of the great Apostle, since MARTIN LUTHER?[3]

32   III + 5, referring to III 616 | 2 Erster Brief Petrus § 284

Soll also der Brief nach der einstimmigen Ueberlieferung der Kirche beym Papias, Polykarp, Irenäus, Origenes und Eusebius dem Apostel Petrus zugehörig bleiben; so muss der Concipient desselben die mit den paulinischen Briefen so mannichfaltig zutreffenden Stellen mehr aus den mündlichen Vorträgen des Apostels Paulus, als aus der Sammlung seiner Briefe genommen haben: und wer könnte dieses unmöglich finden, wenn er nur ein häufiger Anhörer von Paulus Lehrvorträgen gewesen wäre? Wer über dieselben Materien häufig gesprochen hat, der wird sich zuletzt bey ihrer Darstellung, schriftlich wie mündlich, fast immer derselben Worte bedienen; und wenn sein Schüler auf dieselben Materien zu reden kommt, wird er sie, so bald er sich nur nicht der Ausdrücke seines Lehrers recht geflissentlich zu enthalten sucht, in dieselben Worte finden....

...Und dies ist das Verhältniss, in welchem Petrus's erster Brief mit dem ersten Brief an den Timotheus steht, der doch nach allen Umständen von einem unbekannten paulinischen Schüler geschrieben worden. Beide stimmen mit einander, wo sie von gottesfürchtigen christlichen Frauen und dem Anstand reden, mit welchem sie in christlichen Versammlungen zu erscheinen haben, so in Ideen und im Ausdruck zusammen, wie ihnen ohngefähr das Gedächtniss aus einst angehörten Vorträgen des Apostels Paulus liefern konnte.

[So if, following the unanimous tradition of the Church in Papias, Polycarp, Irenaeus, Origen, and Eusebius, the epistle must be attributed to the apostle Peter, the author of it must have taken the many passages parallel with the Pauline epistles more from the oral discourses of the apostle Paul than from the collection of his epistles: and who could find this impossible if he happened to be a frequent listener to Paul's spoken discourses? After all, anyone who has spoken frequently on the same subjects will end up by almost always using the same words in presenting them, in writing as well as in speaking; and if his pupil comes to speak about these same matters, he will put them in the same words unless he consciously seeks to avoid the exact expressions of his teacher....

31[2] Cf COPY A **54.**

31[3] See **24** and n 4, above, and cf *TT*

15 Jun 1833: "The only fit commentator on Paul was Luther."

...And this is the relation in which Peter's first epistle stands to the first Epistle of Timothy, and from all evidence this was written by an unknown disciple of Paul. Where they speak of God-fearing Christian women and the propriety with which they are to appear in Christian congregations, idea and expression so agree in both that they can only have been transmitted as a proximate memory from a once-heard discourse of the apostle Paul.]

616. With all due respect for Papias, Polycarp, Irenæus, Origen, ~~and~~ Eusebius and the Tradition of the Church, I must confess, that my Judgement inclines to the opinion, that even the *first* Epistle of Peter was composed after Peter's Death, by some one of his Scholars: and that it is in all points analogous to the ⟨I⟩ Epistles to Timothy.[1] To give to the Pauline Doctrines and Terminology the additional Sanction of the Chief of the Apostles[2] might, perhaps, have been one of the motives of the Writer: even as to give the sanction of Paul's Name to the Judæo-Christian *Gnosis*, which had its head-quarters in the Church of Alexandria, occasioned the Alexandrian Fathers against all internal evidence to force the Great Apostle's name on the Epistle to the Hebrews.—[3]

32[1] For C's view that 1 Tim, if not by Paul, is "Paul-like" (Παυλοειδής) see BIBLE COPY B **133** and n 1. Eichhorn accepts that Peter was the author of 1 Pet, but not of 2 Pet. For C's view of the authorship of the pastoral epistles see BIBLE COPY B **116** and n 1, and *CN* IV 5312 (12 Jan 1826), 5372 (c 7 May 1826), both referring to *NT* III 315–410.

On 8 Feb 1826 C said that he had been "impelled" by his concern for Irving to turn from his study of the pastoral epistles to a detailed study of Rev: see *Apocalypse* COPY A headnote.

32[2] I.e. Peter.

32[3] On the authorship of Heb see BIBLE COPY B **134** and n 1. Cf *TT* 6 Jan 1823, 31 Mar 1832.

Copy A

Commentarius in Apocalypsin Joannis. 2 vols (in 1). Göttingen 1791.
8°.

British Museum C 126 c 8

"S. T. C." label on the title-page of Vol ɪ. Inscribed on a slip of ruled paper
pasted to p ⁻6: "Transcr. E. H. Coleridge Nov. 20 1889". In the transcript
itself EHC noted: "Presumably the new *second volume* bought in 1826 was
bound with the *old odd first* vol: and the new *second volume* henceforth
became an odd volume." MS TRANSCRIPT. In the last clause, "*second
volume*" is a slip for "*first volume*"—i.e. the inscribed Vol ɪ here called COPY
B. The binding of the old Vol ɪ and the new Vol ɪɪ into one volume was Green's
work, not C's.

There is clear evidence that C worked through Cocceius' commentary with
the Greek text of Rev between c 1 and 8 Feb 1826 (see **1** n 1, below)—that
is, some days before he acquired the new set of *Apocalypse* on 19 Feb to
complete the odd Vol ɪ that he had had "for years...among my Odd Books".
See COPY B 1. For the circumstances that in 1826 precipitated C's study of
Cocceius and Eichhorn on Rev see COCCEIUS. In the records of the Cocceius
reading (N F° and letters) there is no mention of Eichhorn; the marginalia
on COPY A are as much a reaction to Cocceius as to Eichhorn; of the four
annotations in the old Vol ɪ only **2** and **4** could have been written before
C had completed his study of Cocceius' commentary on Rev (c 8 Sept 1826):
cf FIELD 1. The reason for annotating the old Vol ɪ rather than the
elaborately inscribed new Vol ɪ (now COPY B) could simply have been that,
once he had finished his study of Cocceius on Rev, and driven by the urgency
of his task, he annotated the old Vol ɪ without waiting to see whether he could
get a copy of Vol ɪɪ. If he decided to annotate the old Vol ɪ *after* acquiring
the new set on 19 Feb, it could have been because **4** was already written on
a back flyleaf.

These annotations on Eichhorn are associated not only with Cocceius'
commentary but particularly with Edward Irving: C (as he said on 8 Feb
1826) was "impelled" to turn aside from his study of the Gospels and the
pastoral epistles in order to make a detailed study of the Apocalypse "solely
by the rumours, that had reached me, of my friend, Edward Irving's,
Aberrations (for such, I fear, they are) into the Cloud-land of Prophecies
[of] the approaching fulfilment of certain Prophecies..."—"studies that
were against my inclinations & cravings". *CN* ɪᴠ 5323; see also COCCEIUS.
This examination of Irving's "historico-chronological Arrangement"—or
"liberal Chronological Scheme of Interpretation"—had important results
for C. *CL* ᴠɪ 557 (8 Feb 1826), *CN* ɪᴠ 5329 (18 Feb 1826). On 1 Feb 1826
he had said that he was "not ashamed to say, that a single Chapter of St
Paul's Epistles or St John's Gospel is of more value to me, in light & in life,
in love & in Comfort, than the Books of the Apocalypse, Daniel &
Zachariah, all together". *CL* ᴠɪ 550. Yet a week later he wrote that "even
more unexpected [than his recent detailed comparison of the synoptic

Gospels] have been the enlightening & enlarging Insights obtained by the study of the Apocalypse—which now for the first time I perceive to be an important and even necessary Supplement of the Gospels according to the Flesh, the Gospel according to the Spirit, with the Epistles—the Apocalypse uniting both & at the same time crow[n]ing the whole ". *CN* IV 5323; cf *CL* VI 557–8. This illuminating study of Rev, however, did not at once have as wholesome an effect on Irving as C had hoped. A year later, on 13 Apr 1827, when he was trying to come to terms with Irving's translation of LACUNZA *The Coming of Messiah* (2 vols 1827) with his 124-page "Preliminary Discourse", C regretted that Irving had not yet found (as C was still confident that he would "ultimately find") that "the Exposition of the Apocalypse—which (the Child of much Thought and many Prayers!) I was prepared to place before him & in [the] past did place, will not always remain dead in his Bosom". N F° f 60 (*CN* v).

For C's translation of Rev projected in c Feb 1829 see **1** n 3, below; and for annotations that C wrote on Rev in Oct–Nov 1833 see BIBLE *NT Revelation*.

Eichhorn in this work develops a theory that the author of Revelation is giving a poetic and obscurely symbolic representation of the triumph of Christianity over Judaism: Act I, the fall of Jerusalem; Act II, the fall of Rome or the victory of the Christians over the Gentiles; Act III, the heavenly Jerusalem. C agrees on the whole that the book is historical rather than prophetic; his objection to Eichhorn is that, although he is treating Rev symbolically not literally, he is too unimaginative to come at the poetic truth of the vision.

MS TRANSCRIPT. VCL BT 21: in EHC's hand, transcribed 20 Nov 1889.

DATE. c 8–21 Feb 1826, and perhaps later. If **4** was written before c 8 Feb 1826 (see above), it could have been written at any time from c 1817 onwards: see *CN* III 4307 (c 1815–16) and FIELD **1** (28 Mar 1819).

COEDITOR. Merton A. Christensen.

1 I ⁻1

How can it have happened, that Eichhorn should have made no mention of Joannes Coccëius, born Aug. 1603, died 1669[1]—the first rational Commentator on the Apocalypse and to whom the ⟨merit

---

1[1] C had borrowed a set of COCCEIUS *Opera omnia* (10 vols Amsterdam 1701) in Jul 1825 and had it in his possession until in late 1827 he had to return the volumes without having transcribed the notes he had written in them. See COCCEIUS (Lost Book). In the early days of Feb 1826 C had occupied "the larger portion of the time, my Strength allowed me", "as a duty of friendship" to Edward Irving, in studying the Apocalypse "verse by verse in the original with the commentary of Cocceius". *CL* VI 550 (1 Feb), 556–7 (8 Feb), 557–8. Cf **3**, below, and parallel statements quoted from N F° (*CN* IV 5323) in COCCEIUS. Cocceius' commentary on Rev is in VI iii 31–119. C had finished his study of Rev with Cocceius' commentary before he acquired the new set of *Apocalypse* on 19 Feb: see headnote, above.

of the first⟩ exposure of Ireneus's fiction respecting the Nicolaitans is due?[2]—His views respecting this grand prophetic Drama,[3] the Cassandra of the Christian Lycophron,[4] in general, & of the 7 Churches in particular, are so strikingly coincident with those of Eichhorn, as to render the Latter's Silence respecting his great Predecessor subject of regret—[5]

S. T. Coleridge

2 I 22 | on Revelation 1.5

Messiam igitur in tam alto dignitatis fastigio collocatum, et de toto praeterea humano genere praeclare meritum quis non veneretur, quis non adoret?

[Who would not then venerate, who would not adore the Messiah, placed on so lofty a summit of worthiness and so pre-eminent in his services to the whole human race?]

quis *adorare* audeat?—N̶ si non sit verè Deus verus[1]

[1][2] This statement is substantially repeated in *CL* VI 557–8 and in N F°. See 3 n 2, below.

[1][3] In c Feb 1829 he considered "my long ago thought of translating the Apocalypse into a Symbolico-dramatic Poem sui generis" according to the scheme: 1. Dedication (Rev 1.9–3.22), 2. Prologue (Rev 1.1–8), 3. The Drama (Rev 4.1–22.21 [end]). N 39 f 34 (*CN* v). Illness, and the preparation of the two eds of *C&S* and of *AR* (1831), interrupted the project, if indeed he intended to take it in hand in 1829. See also BIBLE *NT Revelation* and *LS* (*CC*) 146–7n. Another of C's schemes was: Act I: The fall of Jerusalem; Act II: The fall of Rome and the victory of the Christians over the Gentiles; Act III: The heavenly Jerusalem. Milton in his preface to *Sumson Agonistes* (lines 13–17) noted that "*Paraeus* divides the whole Book [of Rev] as a Tragedy, into Acts distinguished each by a Chorus of Heavenly Harpings and Song between"—an observation he also made in *The Reason of Church Government*: Milton *Works* ed Birch (2 vols 1738) I 60. See also H. COLERIDGE 7 and n 1 on the Song of Solomon as "a divine pastoral Drama".

[1][4] Cocceius saw Rev, not as drama or history, but as heaven-inspired prophecy relating to the history of the Christian Church. *Cassandra* (or *Alexandra*), the only surviving composition of Lycophron

(b c 320 B.C.), recounts a series of prophetic utterances made by Cassandra during the Trojan war. According to legend, Cassandra was a truthful seer, but Apollo's punishment was that her oracles should never be believed. The obscurity of the poem won for Lycophron the title *tenebrosus*.

[1][5] C observed that Cocceius "interprets [the] Chapter on the Millennium [Rev 19] as of events already past"—i.e. as events now past to us, though not past to the writer of Rev—as against the view of Irving and "the prognosticating Commentators" that the millennium was in the future. See *CL* VI 550 and **17** and n 4, below.

In the treatment of Rev 2 and 3 there is some resemblance between the attitudes of Cocceius and Eichhorn: both take the letters to be intended as actual exhortations to the churches named, with lessons to be deduced in similar circumstances by all Christians at all times. Of the passages directly commented on in these notes, only **13** and **14** represent Cocceius as saying anything that C—but not Eichhorn —would approve on factual (as opposed to spiritual) interpretation: viz. that Rome is alluded to in Rev 9. 13–15, though Cocceius takes it to be papal, not imperial, Rome.

2[1] "Who would dare to *adore* him? if he were not truly the true God".

3 1 77, pencil | on Rev 2.6

[Eichhorn equates the Nicolaitans mentioned here with "them that hold the doctrine of Balaam" in Rev 2.14, and suggests that there was no heretical sect of this name. Both terms—*Nicolaitans* and *Balaamites*—he says, are used (the Greek *Nikolaos* being a translation of the Hebrew *Balaam*) to signify merely all teachers of false *] doctrines who put a stumbling block in the ways of believers.] At omnes tamen praeter Ianum et Heumannum, quotquot adhuc in haeresium historiis condendis operam collocarunt, ad hanc tam claram lucem coecutierunt, quod creditu esset difficile, nisi, qui noctu immanibus spectris terreantur, cum iisdem eos interdiu adeo pugnare saepius, constaret. Irenaeum, inquiunt, seculi secundi scriptorem, Nicolaitarum nomen in haereticorum catalogum retulisse, ex quo salva ecclesiasticae traditionis auctoritate expungi non possit.

[Yet, except for Jan and Heumann, all who have employed themselves in the composition of histories of heresies have been blind to this clear light, which fact would be difficult to believe were it not known to be the case that men who are terrified by monstrous apparitions at night will often also fight with the same in broad daylight. They say that Irenaeus, a writer of the second century, includes the name of the Nicolaitans in his list of heretics, from which it cannot be removed without impugning the authority of ecclesiastical tradition.]

* The merit of this exposure and of all sound comment on the Apocalypse is due to Coccëius,[1] long before Janus and Heumann.[2]

4 1 +2 pencil

The Councils of Basel and Constance & Pisa before them instances of the Melancholy Truth, that no corrupt System ever has been or probably can be, effectually reformed by a legitimate Convention or Assembly consisting of authorized accredited Potentiaries of that

3[1] Cf 1 and nn 1 and 2, above.

3[2] In *CN* IV 5323 C said that to Cocceius "long before Janus and Heumann the credit belongs of expunging the Nicolaitans from the list of Heresies, and evincing the little reliance that can be placed on the assertions of Irenæus and the Fathers generally, taken apart from their authorities...". Cf *CL* VI 558. Cocceius makes this point in *Opera* V iii 41, 43. Irenaeus declared that the Nicolaitans of Rev 2.6, 15 were followers of

Nicolas, a proselyte of Antioch mentioned in Acts 6.5—*Adversus haereses* 2.27. There is no supporting evidence for this view. Eichhorn in a footnote refers to Johann Wilhelm Jan *De Nicolaitis ex haereticorum catalogo expungendis, ad Apoc. ii. 6, 14, 15* (1723) in Theodor Hase and Conrad Iken *Thesaurus novus theologico-philologicus* (2 vols Amsterdam 1732) II 1016, and to Christian August Heumann (1681–1764) in *Acta eruditorum* (1712) 179.

System.[1] Even when they mean well and are earnest in their wishes to reform, the dread of Insecurity, the preservation οτου Νυν,[2] which is the proper function of such Assemblies, will predominate—& *Fear* will dictate Counsels that will baffle & paralyse every scheme of *Hope*/—

They will content themselves with pruning abuses, and in the fear of having even in this gone too far, & anxious to excuse themselves with the Advocates of existing Power will turn savage against those, who would lay the ax to the root of the Upas Tree/[3]

4[1] The Council of Pisa (1409), called to end the Great Schism that had divided the Western Church since 1378, made matters worse; for in deposing two rival popes and appointing a third it succeeded in establishing the existence of three popes. The Council of Constance (1414–18) aimed not only to end the schism, but also to deal with various heresies, and to reform the Church. It resolved the schism by deposing or discrediting the two rival popes and the anti-pope and by unanimously electing Martin v; it dealt severely with the heresy of John Wycliffe, and savagely condemned John Huss; but it failed to attempt any radical reform within the Church. The Council of Basle (1431–49), called by Martin v to continue the work of reform intended at Constance, dissolved by his successor Eugenius iv and then reinstated, returned to the dispute over papal authority, assumed a strongly anti-papal attitude, and declared itself a General Council that (according to a decree of the Council of Constance) had its authority directly from God and must therefore be obeyed even by the pope. By procedural manipulation the directors of the council deprived the papal minority of any effective voice, proceeded to claim control of papal policy and prerogative, and finally after Eugenius had withdrawn his minority to Ferrara in 1437, deposed the pope as a heretic and appointed an anti-pope. These excesses deprived the Council of its prestige; gradually all nations came to accept the authority of the legitimate pope, and in 1448 the Council was moved to Lausanne and the anti-pope abdicated. Eighteen years of bitter conflict had settled the question of papal authority; but the Council of Basle in failing to effect reform within the Church made irresistible the growing momentum of "the Reformation" in reaction against the corruptions and obtuseness of papal monarchy. For C's objection to the pre-and anti-reformation councils see JURIEU 2 and cf *CN* iii 4143. In Jeremy TAYLOR *Polemicall Discourses* i 1014–16 C wrote: "It may be & in fact it is, very questionable whether any Council, however large and fairly chosen, is not an absurdity, except under the universal faith that the Holy Ghost miraculouly dictates all the decrees—& this is irrational, where the same superseding Spirit does not afford evidence of its presence by producing unanimity. I know nothing more ludicrous than the supposition of the Holy Ghost contenting himself with a Majority...."

4[2] "Of the way things are now".

4[3] For C's early and unfulfilled poetic designs upon the poisonous upas tree see *CN* i 37 and n, 174 (25). *Antiaris toxicaria* of the Malayan archipelago is a genuine enough tree; only its legendary properties are open to question, as C had them from Erasmus Darwin *Botanic Garden* (1791) ii 186: "This...is certain, though it may appear incredible, that from fifteen to eighteen miles round this tree, not only no human creature can exist, but that, in that space of ground, no living animals of any kind has ever been discovered. I have also been assured by several persons of veracity, that there are no fish in the waters, nor has any rat, mouse, or any other vermin, been seen there; and when any birds fly so near this tree that the

5   ɪɪ [2] (title-page verso), pencil

A[a] Child accustomed once a week with strongly excited feelings and all sorts of vague dim Notions, to behold a collection of Prints thro' a magnifying Glass—& then let the Prints themselves be shewn him one by one, out of the Puppet-shew Box, and to his unarmed eye—Such is the effect of the real truth of Scripture Language on the minds of men at large. In vain, would you point out beauties in the Prints never seen before—the Glass, the Magnitude, the indefinableness & the Mystery are gone/

6   ɪɪ ⁻2, referring to ɪɪ [9–]10 | on Rev 8.10–11

[On the sounding of the Third Angel, and the star that falls from heaven turning a third part of the waters to bitterness:] *Aqua amara* Israëlitis desertum Arabicum peragrantibus tam molesta fuit, ut de ea tanquam publica calamitate querelas funderent Exod. 15, 23. Hinc a Nostro inter publicae calamitatis signa adoptatur. Repraesentari hoc in theatro non potuit, nisi re aliqua, in oculos et sensus incidente, in aquam iniecta, quae amaritudine illam corrumpere posset. Fingitur igitur stella de coelo delapsa, quae in nomine suo omen habebat, hoc est, nomine, quam produceret amaritiem, prodebat.

[To the Israelites wandering in the Arabian desert the *bitter water* was so vexing that they poured forth complaints about it as of a public calamity (Exod 15.23). Hence it has been used by our author as one of the symbols for a public calamity. This could not be represented dramatically except by something accessible to the sight and senses and which, being cast into the water, could corrupt it with its bitterness. A star is invented, therefore, fallen from heaven, which had a sign in its own name: that is, it expressed in its name the bitterness it would produce.]

P. 10. All this is good as far as it goes. But we may be assured, that in the mind and intent of the Seer[b] each Trumpet represents some one particular Calamity, or class of Calamities.[1] Thus the Star that shot from the Heaven, like a fiery Meteor (Shakespear, Midsummer Night's Dream, in the celebrated allusion to the Duke of Norfolk & Mary Queen of Scots)[2] signified I doubt [not]ᶜ ~~the~~ some Leaders,

---

[a] The first word in ink, the rest in pencil
[b] Written in large letters
ᶜ Word supplied by the editor

---

effluvia reaches them, they fall a sacrifice to the effects of the poison." See *RX* 18 and nn, and for the currency of the legend, *Friend (CC)* ɪ 47n.
6[1] See **7** textus, below.

6[2] "And certain stars shot madly from their spheres"—*Midsummer Night's Dream* ɪɪ i 153. Thomas Howard, 4th Duke of Norfolk of the Howard house (1536–72), one of the commissioners

from ⟨one of⟩ the Princely Houses, that put himself at the head of the Robbers that so frightfully infested Judæa—And in whom did his Calamity ~~rise~~ commence?—Josephus tells us. In *Amarus*[a] and Eleazer![3]—Who does not at once see the *Marah*, Bitterness, the waters of Marah, Ex. XV—&c.—.[4]

7   ii 14–15 | on Rev 8.13

[Eichhorn has asserted (ii 6) that the angels sounding the first four trumpets in Rev 8.6–12, are, in a general way, the heralds of a public calamity. The last three, in Rev 9–10, represent the outbreak of the Zealots, the attack of the Romans, and God's promises to his servants.]

I cannot agree with Eichhorn here/ The 4 first Trumpets denote the Evils that preceded and prepared the way for, the Outbreak of the Zelotæ,[1] Terrorists, and Septembrizers[2] of Jerusalem, with antici-

---

[a] Written in large letters and underlined

---

inquiring into Scottish affairs at York in 1568, devised a scheme to marry Mary, Queen of Scots, which she conditionally accepted. When it was discovered that Norfolk was involved in the Ridolfi plot for a Spanish invasion of England to secure the marriage to Norfolk and to place Mary on the throne, Norfolk was imprisoned and executed for treason. The source for C's allusion is not known; modern Shakespeare scholars do not recognise such a connexion.

6[3] According to Josephus (*Jewish War* 2.17.2 [2.409]), the war with the Romans broke out when Eleazer, son of Ananias and governor of the Temple, refused to accept sacrifices from Nero as a foreigner and so in A.D. 64 touched off the revolt of the Zelotae. See 7 n 1, below. Cf *CN* IV 5329: "18 Feb[y] 1826—. I hold it far more probable than I imagined, I should at the first Suggestion of the hypothesis, that the third Trumpet refers to the dreadful System of Robberies, High-road, Oppidan, and even in the Streets & Synagogues of Jerusalem itself the *commencement* of which was in Amarus (Marah, Bitterness: Exodus XV. 23.) and Eleazar". C goes on to say that Josephus' works make it difficult not to interpret the

first four Trumpets as "the Factions... that preceded the War", "the 5th of the Zelotae or Terrorists during the Siege; and the 6th of the Collection of Roman Forces that executed the final Judgement on the murderous City and the rebellious People". Amarus seems to be a slip for the high priest Ananus, for whom see Josephus *Jewish War* 4.3.9 (160)ff and 4.4.3 (238)ff. Cf **19** textus, below, and FLEURY **21**.

6[4] Exod 15.23: "And when they came to Marah, they could not drink of the waters of Marah, for they were bitter: therefore the name of it was called Marah." Rev 8.11 reads: "And the name of the star is called Wormwood [Ἄψινθος]...and many men died of the waters, because they were made bitter."

7[1] The Zelotae (Zealots), a Jewish party of revolt, not only opposed the Romans with such fanatical ferocity that the Romans in retaliation destroyed Jerusalem in A.D. 70, but also showed great cruelty in treating those of their fellow-countrymen who did not support the revolt with appropriate dedication. See Josephus *Jewish War* 4.3.9ff.

7[2] Terrorist and terrorism, words that seem to belong peculiarly to the second

pation of their horrors during the War & Siege—For remember that in a Chain the higher link has its lower portion below the link that follows./

8 ɪɪ ⁻2, referring to ɪɪ 19–20 | on Rev 9.1

...Attamen hanc stellam persona indutam cogitemus necesse est, quae manu aliquid tenere possit, nisi ineptus in fingendo poëta versetur, adeoque *angelum, stellam* claro lumine et *splendore imitantem*, ut adeo ipse ἀστὴρ diceretur, ex eadem fere ratione, qua angelus ille, aquilae audacia in volando usus, c. 8, 13 ἀετός dicebatur. Denique εἶδον πεπτωκότα quod de stella recte sensu vulgari dicitur, cum autem de angelo stellae instar lucente et splendente h. 1. praedicetur, positum est pro εἶδον καταβαίνειν, hoc tamen consilio, ut ipsa, qua in terram descendit, celeritas declaretur.

[But we have to think that this star is personified, since it can hold something in its hand (unless the poet is ineptly inventing) and therefore an *angel, so like a star* in bright light and *splendour* that he himself was called ἀστήρ (a star), for much the same reason as the angel that flew with the audacity of an eagle (8.13) was called ἀετός (an eagle). Finally "I saw fallen", which is rightly said of a star in the literal sense—since, however, it is here said (v 1) of the angel shining and blazing like a star—is put in the place of "I saw descending" to emphasise the speed with which it descended to earth.]

P. 20.—Here again, I cannot coincide with Eichhorn in interpreting the Star that fell from Heaven to Earth of an Angel. It must assuredly signify some one of the Nobles, or Archiereis[1] (the Princely or Pontifical Houses) who like the Duke of Orleans in the early part of the French Revolution had encouraged the Terrorists.[2]—Or it may be, that the Apostle meant merely to intimate that the Downfall & plebicolar Debasement of the legitimate Authorities had given the occasion and the opportunity to the Anarchists & Agitators. Both may indeed have been meant.

---

half of the twentieth century, became current during the Terror of the French Revolution. See also **8**, below. "Septembrizers"—people who behaved like the Septembrists, members of the Paris revolutionary Commune who on 2 and 3 Sept 1792 ordered the execution of hundreds of supposed royalists without trial.

8[1] ᾽Αρχιερεῖς—high priests.
8[2] Louis Philippe, Duc d'Orléans (1747–93) renounced his titles during the Revolution, took the name Philippe-Égalité, and worked with Danton and Mirabeau. Nevertheless, his estates were eventually confiscated, he was imprisoned, found guilty of conspiracy, and guillotined.

9 II 25, written in a column, in swash capitals[a]

APRIL 13[b1]

10 II −1 (referring to II 25) | on Rev 9.7

[Eichhorn quotes the Greek text, AV of which reads: "...and on their heads were as it were crowns like gold".]

Chapt. IX.

V. 7.—latter half.—και επι τας κεφελας αυτων <u>ως</u> στεφανοι <u>ομοιοι</u> χρυσω[1]—Who but must call to mind Milton's "What *seem'd* his Head, the *Likeness* of a Kingly Crown had on"[2] and Burke's masterly accomodation of the Passage to the first Constitution of the French Demagogues,[3] the Zelotæ of Paris? And their philanthropic preambles, the Rights of *Man*, &c, the *faces* put on their iniquitous measures by these voracious Locusts and ~~on~~ venomous Scorpions--/ ~~Each~~very Rapscallion a sort of *King*—a Vice-roy at least, as the Representative of the Sovereign People![4]

> [a] Written in the outer margin, the book turned upside down
> [b] The numeral has been altered from "11" and/or "12"

9[1] The reason for the ceremonious treatment of this date does not appear; nor is it clear which year the date belongs to. There is a notebook entry for 13 Apr 1826 in N F° (*CN* IV 5355) but it does not record anything momentous. On 13 Apr 1827 C noted: "...Good Friday.—I have begun to study E. Irving's 'Coming of the Messiah'.—When I think of the barbarisms, solecisms, all isms but Anglicism, in my honored Friend's 'Orations' [1825]...the perfection of the Style... [and] the projected Image of Irving's proper Soul, impresses me even with wonder—/ As to the Work, I dare not speak of it in the unmeasured terms of rejection and regret, which the greater number even of his friends and Admirers use...". N F° ff 59ᵛ–60 (*CN* v). When he began to read Irving's LACUNZA C might well have turned back to the marginalia made for him on the same theme a year earlier. On 10 Apr 1827 Canning was chosen by George IV to be prime minister after Liverpool's stroke in Feb: this was reported in the papers on the 11th, and will have marked the end of C's hopes of a pension—hardly an event to be cele-

brated in swash capitals. The Catholic Emancipation Bill received royal assent on 13 Apr 1829.

10[1] C has supplied ὅμοιοι, necessary to the sense but omitted by Eichhorn. His underlinings call attention to the similarity in the Greek words translated by AV "as it were" and "like" and in the Milton passage.

10[2] *Paradise Lost* II 672–3: the figure of Death, with Sin guarding the gates of Hell.

10[3] Edmund Burke (1729–97) on the first National Assembly in Sept 1789: *Reflections on the Revolution in France* in *Works* (1807) III 84–6. For C's early admiration for Burke and his detailed acquaintance with his writings see *Lects 1795* (*CC*) Index. This reading of Eichhorn evidently recalled vividly to C his first response to the Terror: see also **15**, below.

10[4] For the specious arguments of revolutionaries drawing upon the text of Rev see *LS* (*CC*) 143, 146. C expresses his contempt for the "plebs", for the concept of the "sovereignty of the people", and the fiction of the "social contract" in

11 II ⁻1 (referring to II 26) | on Rev 9.8

[Eichhorn quotes the Greek text, AV of which reads: "And they had hair as the hair of women, and their teeth were as the teeth of lions."]

V. 8.—The fashion of our Cavaliers during the Civil Wars mi was perhaps the party-mark of the Jerusalem Round-heads and Levellers.[1] Most assuredly, Charles's Forces under Sir R. H.[2] in the West of England could not have been more aptly described than as Woman-haired & with the teeth of Lions.[3]

12 II ⁻1, referring to II 27–9 | on Rev 9.11

[Eichhorn quotes the Greek text, AV of which reads: "And they had a king over them, which is the angel of the bottomless pit, whose name in the Hebrew tongue is Abaddon, but in the Greek tongue hath his name Apollyon." This, according to Eichhorn, signifies the demonlike leadership of the insurgent groups ravaging Judea shortly before the fall of Jerusalem—no one leader, but a succession of tyrants.]

V. 11.—Very fine!—These ANARCHISTS had a King, whose Slaves and blind Drudges they were even when they were trampling all authority under their feet—the *Devil* himself.

⟨Eichhorn's great error is in carrying his *general meanings*, & his resolution of particular images into mere poetic garnish, to an excess. But semper in extremis is the motto of Germans.⟩[a1]

---

[a] The smaller hand, and the way the two sentences are crowded into the available space, show that this is a later insertion

---

Samuel JOHNSON (rector of Corringham) *Works* esp pp 153, 156, 209–10; see also *LS* (*CC*) 12–13n (quoting this annotation) and 16.

11[1] Cf LAUD *Second Volume of the Remains* i 12 (which C annotated): "...the Brethren of the Separation [i.e. the men of the Parliamentary party]... are commonly called *Round-heads*, from their Fashion of cutting close and rounding of their Hair"; in a note Laud adds that the Grecians and Romans wore long hair, that "Rounding of the Head" was sometimes "a sign of superstitious sorrowing", sometimes "an effeminate and luxurious Fashion", sometimes "a mark of Servitude and Vassalage". Cf BIBLE COPY B 120 and n 1.

11[2] Ralph Hopton, 1st Baron Hopton (1596–1652), a Somerset cavalier, commanded the King's forces in Cornwall and Devon for a time with great success.

11[3] Rev 9.8: "And they [the locusts that came out of the bottomless pit] had hair as the hair of women, and their teeth were as the teeth of lions."

12[1] "Always at extremes". Throughout this section Eichhorn had been considering Rev 8–11 as a poetic account of the Jewish War.

13 II 33 | on Rev 9.13–15

Huius autem carceris locus in *desertis ad Euphratem regionibus* ponitur, quorsum etiam Zacharias (c. 5, 11) daemonem illum, idolatriae praesidem, in vincula coniiciendum, relegavit, quod homines in Palaestina nati atque educati ad nullam forsitan terram magis horrerent.

[But the location of this prison is set in the *desert near the Euphrates*, whither Zechariah also (Zech 5.11) banished that devil, guardian of idolatry, to be bound in chains, because people born and brought up in Palestine perhaps had a horror of no region more than of that.]

As Romane was to be Babylon, the River must of course be Euphrates.

14 II 35 and pp +1–+2, referring to II 35 | on Rev 9.14

Iubet igitur coelestis vox vinculis liberari τοὺς τέσσαρας ἀγγέλους τοὺς δεδεμένους ἐπὶ τῷ ποταμῷ τῷ μεγάλῳ Εὐφράτῃ, in deserto ad Euphratem usque pertingente vinculis constrictos daemones malos: qui carceris locus soli debetur poëtae ingenio, nullamque patitur ex historia excidii Hierosolymitani interpretationem.

[Therefore the voice from heaven commands that "the four angels which are bound in the great river Euphrates", that is, the evil spirits bound in chains in the desert that reaches as far as the Euphrates, be loosed from their bonds; but this place of imprisonment is due solely to the imagination of the poet and allows of no interpretation from the history of the fall of Jerusalem.]

See the blank page ad finem.

P. 35. I wonder at this assertion from so acute and ingenious a Man as Eichhorn. First, as I have noted—if Rome was to be symbolized as *Babylon*, the River must be Euphrates. But that the four mighty Destroyers were bound in up the ~~mighty~~ great River—"up a great River, great as any *Sea*"[1] is in according to the code of popular Beliefs—the bad Spirits are sent bound to the bottom of the Red Sea—.[2] But a *Sea* would not have been appropriate or designative of the Roman Power—while the Tiyber was a perfect Synonime of Rome, and the trite poetic Exponent of the Roman Empire—n Now the Tyber could not but be changed into the Euphrates—Therefore the επι τω ποταμω τω μεγαλω Ευφρατη is no mere poetic Ornature; but a very significant & requisite amplification/

14[1] *Osorio* IV 232: *PW* (EHC) II 574.
14[2] A common rabbinic legend dispersed through the Babylonian Talmud: see *Pesahim* 112a, *Alphabet of Ben-Sira* 23a–b, 33a–b, and *The Testament of Solomon* passim.

Four giant Dæmons could not be imagined bound or chained up in a ~~city~~ vast *City*[3]—[a]this would have been far too indefinite—But neither in any Dungeon or Tower in the Babylon—That would have been as much too narrow, & besides too gross an outrage to probability, & above all, too little ghostliness/—With great Judgement therefore the sublime Seer transfers their prison to the River but amplifies the River into all the magnificence of a Sea for the Imagination of the Readers. Only read the Greek words aloud ore rotundo:[4] and you will feel the effect.—Add to all this the Hebrew Associations with the Euphrates—Captivity after a bloody Wars, and the Siege, Sack, and utter Destruction of their Chief City & Temple!—Is it not, I again say, wonderful that Eichhorn should overlook all these so striking and exquisite proprieties in a "soli debetur poetæ ingenio"!!—[5]

15 II +2, referring to II 36 | on Rev 9.15

[Eichhorn quotes Rev 9.15 in Greek, AV of which reads: "And the four angels were loosed, which were prepared for an hour, and a day, and a month, and a year, to slay the third part of men"] h.e. *daemones mali* (quorum est τὸ ἀποκτείνειν) *ad mala inferenda semper parati a vinculis liberabantur*. Enimvero ἐτοιμασμένοι εἰς τὴν ὥραν, ἡμέραν, μῆνα, ἐνιαυτόν sunt *vel* ad hoc tempus fatale a Deo praedestinati; sed tum nominum accumulatorum commoda ratio reddi nulla posset: *vel* ἐτοιμασμένοι εἰς τὴν ἡμέραν κ.τ.λ. positum est pro ἐν ἡμέρᾳ ἑκάστῃ ut dicantur, *quovis tempore* ad mala inferenda parati; rei enim universitas a poëtis saepe vocabulorum fere synonymorum copia exprimitur.

[that is, the *evil spirits* (whose task is "to slay") *always prepared to inflict evil, were loosed from their bonds*. So indeed they are "prepared for the hour, day, month, year", *either* as being foreordained by God for this fatal moment—but then no proper reason could be given for the cluster of nouns: *or* "prepared for the day etc" is used for "on every day" in order that they may be said to be prepared to inflict evil *at any time*; for often the universal implication of a thing is expressed by poets by a cluster of almost synonymous terms.]

P. 36. Doubtless, the second is the true sense of the words—& most poetic & vivid they are—. See Ode on the Departing Year, and the

a Here the ink and hand change, as though what follows had been added later

14[3] In Hebrew symbolism river and city are equivalent.
14[4] "In round, full voice"—Horace *Ars poetica* 323.

14[5] In textus—"It is due solely to the imagination of the poet."

Personification of Destruction, with lidless dragon eyes Dreaming ⟨on the marge of a Volcano⟩ of the predestined prey—The Fiend-hag on her perilous Couch doth leap Muttering distempered Triumph in her charmed Sleep.[1] So here—the four Spirits of Vengeance

Impatient wai~~ting with unsleeping~~
~~to~~ By hour, by day, by month, by year—[2]

No measure of time so small as to relax their Ward, None long enough to exhaust & weary out/

16   II ⁺3, referring to II 40 | on Rev 9.19

[Eichhorn quotes the Greek of Rev 9.19, AV of which reads: "For their power is in their mouth, and in their tails: for their tails were like unto serpents, and had heads, and with them they do hurt." He has explained the strange form of the horses by saying that they are monsters and portents, to express the idea of a terrible army. On this verse he says merely that they are unlike ordinary horses in having "their power in their mouths" and gives no particular symbolic interpretation of the form of their tails.]

P. 40. It appears, I own, somewhat fanciful; but I cannot frown away the suggestion, that the power being in the Mouths, and even the Tails having Mouths, is meant to express the fact that the great superiority of the Roman Armies over the Zelotæ, and other Fanatics of Judæa & Jerusalem (the Scorpion-Locusts)[1] consisted not in Courage or Warlike Skill; but in the admirable *Officering* even of the lowest portions of the ~~Arm~~ Forces brought by Vespasian & Titus—[2]

It was the Discipline—the Voice—the Word of Command—

17   II ⁺3, referring to II 58 | on Rev 11.1–3

[Eichhorn explains the temple and the altar as representing the worship of the one God, and the court as the ceremonial through which God was approached by ignorant men; the temple is that part of the Mosaic religion which was to survive in Christianity; the

15[1] *Ode on the Departing Year* lines 140–8: *PW* (EHC) I 167–8. In a long footnote to this passage C quoted Nahum 3.8–19 but made no reference there—or elsewhere in the notes on this poem—to Rev.

15[2] A variant of Rev 9.15—perhaps a venture in versification.

16[1] See Rev 9.7, 10.

16[2] Vespasian (9–79) led expeditions to subdue the revolts in Palestine in 68–9 during the rule of Nero, and conquered Galilee and most of Judea. After he returned to Rome in the summer of 69 to be proclaimed emperor, his son Titus (c 40–81) destroyed the Jewish state by besieging and sacking Jerusalem in Oct 70.

surrounding buildings, walling off the approach, were to perish, to be given to the Gentiles, as profane. On II 54 Eichhorn says:]... Primum, cui decempedam admovere iubetur est ὁ ναὸς τοῦ θεοῦ... quod, ubi atrio opponitur (uti h. 1. v. 2 factum videmus), *sanctum* est (quod vulgo dicitur) sive templum proprie sic dictum, exclusis multis illis, quibus obseptum erat,˸ aedificiis et atriis, quae incluso templo uno nomine τὸ ἱερόν, ὁ οἶκος dicebantur. Alteram erat τὸ θυσιαστήριον, sive *altare suffitus*, quo templum (ναός) instructum erat, ad suffitum inter preces adolendum, adeoque adorationis verae cultusque divini mente et animo peragendi optimum emblema.

[The first object he is told to measure is "the temple of God...", which, when it is opposed to the "court" (as we see it is in v 2), is the *sanctum*, as it is commonly called, or the temple properly so called, excluding the many other buildings and courts by which it was walled round; these including the temple were called by the one name τὸ ἱερόν [the holy place] or ὁ οἶκος [the house]. The second was the altar of incense, with which the temple proper (ναός) was provided, for the burning of incense amid prayers; it was therefore an excellent emblem for the true adoration and divine worship to be performed with heart and mind.]

[Eichhorn proceeds to examine the meaning of the 42 months and the 1260 days. He closes on II 58 his search for a literal application in the history of the fall of Jerusalem, goes on to draw the conclusion that they are fictitious and symbolical, and finally pronounces them to be standard expressions for the long duration of a public calamity.]

P. 58. Here Eichhorn's Genius dormitates.[1]—a brief *parenthestisc* of Snore. *Zzs*—If the Sanctum, the ναος του Θεου with its Θυσιαστηριον[2] are to be interpreted spiritually (as E. *has* and in my opinion very soundly and successfully interpreted them)—the ιερον, ο οικος, η αυλη,[3] must have a spiritual or theological, and not an historical, import. E. falls stands here into on the very same ⟨Line of⟩ Error, with only at the other end of the line, as the prognosticating Commentators—/[4]—*Both* 1260 Eichhorn DAYS, the

17[1] Not in *OED*, though "dormitation" is recorded. Cf Horace *Ars poetica* 359: "dormitat Homerus" ([even] Homer nods)—now proverbial.

17[2] "The temple of God" with its "altar" (for sacrifice)—from Rev 11.1.

17[3] The "holy place (temple), the house, the court"—of which only the third appears in the Greek text of Rev 11.2.

17[4] Protestant commentators, particularly some Evangelicals, commonly interpreted the time period of Dan 7 and 9 and these passages in Rev as symbolising periods of years (on the basis of Ezek 4.6 and Num 14.34, in which a day is reckoned as a year), and took them for prognostications of the end of the world. C is here thinking particularly of Henry Irving and Hatley Frere as of "the Revd G. S. Faber School": see *CL* VI 557 (which includes C's awkward question to

Nostradamuses *Years/*—[5]
   The symbolic Ἑβδομάς ἡμερων[6] is measured by the Horologe of
divine Predestination, by E̶v̶e̶n̶t̶spochs & ⟨the⟩ Procession of the
Plan of Providence—not subject to any *external* measure, but like
the Sun & Planets self-measured by their own movements.

18   II 66, pencil | on Rev 11.6

[Eichhorn quotes the Greek of Rev 11.6, AV of which reads: "These
have power to shut heaven, that it rain not in the days of their
prophecy: and have power over waters to turn them to blood, and
to smite the earth with all plagues, as often as they will"—referring
to the "two witnesses" of Rev 11.3.] Qui ad haec declaranda res ex
historia belli Judaici expiscari vellet, nae is misere argutaretur.

[The man who would choose to fish out incidents from the history of the
Jewish War in order to elucidate these statements would get hopelessly
tangled in subtleties.]

= Eichhorn.

19   II 74, referring to II 61–74 | on Rev 11

[Eichhorn writes (II 61) on Rev 11.3–14:] *Cui* autem *urbi* excidium
paretur, nondum a poëta expositum est. Interponitur igitur, (quod
acutum Herderi ingenium iam vidit) Anani et Jesu, pontificum
maximorum laudatio sollennis, quod illi, dum vivebant, Zelotarum
furore precibus, minis, consiliis, eloquentia represso, rei Judaeorum
publicae fere soli optime consuluerunt, donec nocte illa, Idumaeorum
inter saevam tempestatem in urbem irruptione, calamitosa a Zelotis
interimerentur, quod urbi inprimis et reipublicae Judaeorum fatale
fuit.

[The poet has not yet revealed of *what city* the destruction is being prepared.
He therefore interposes (as Herder's acute genius has already perceived) a
solemn panegyric of Ananus and Jesus, the high priests, because during their
lives by suppressing the madness of the Zealots by their prayers, threats,
advice, and eloquence they were almost alone in consulting the best interests
of the Jewish state, until that night, already disastrous from the irruption
of the Idumaeans under cover of a heavy storm, when they were murdered

---

Irving "from what *date* do you com-
mence?") and **19** n 2, below. For similar
numerological calculations see BIBLE *NT
Revelation* esp **5** and **6**. C's marginalia on
BIBLE *NT Revelation* takes up the argu-
ment of Rev where it had been dis-
continued in the marginalia on Eichhorn.

[17][5] On Nostradamus see EICHHORN
Alte Testament **48** n 1.
   [17][6] "A period of seven days". Cf Dan
10.2 and 3, though this is not a prophetic
passage.

by the Zealots, a crime that boded great evil for the city and the Jewish nation.]
[Eichhorn (II 74) reminds the reader to bear in mind throughout Rev 11 that vv 1–14 give an account of the end of the war not as a prophecy of future events, which would be an imposture, but to make it impossible not to see that Jerusalem is represented in the following scene, vv 15–19, the fall of the city.]

I beg Eichhorn's and Herder's pardon/ but of all interpretations this seems to me the most wild and improbable/[1] Faber himself could not surpass it.[2]

20   II 181 | on Rev 16.7

Καὶ ἤκουσα τοῦ θυσιαστηρίου (h.e. τοῦ ἀγγέλου τοῦ θυσιαστηρίου quandoquidem vox ab altari progressa ab eodem altari quasi edita videri poterat) λέγοντος...

["And I heard the altar (i.e. 'the angel of the altar' since a voice proceeding from the altar could seem as though it was uttered by that same altar) saying"...]

The common Editions have αλλου εκ[1]

19[1] Eichhorn gives no reference for Herder's discussion. C could have read it—"Johannes Offenbarung"—in HERDER *Sämmtliche Werke* XVIII (not annotated). Cf FLEURY 21.
19[2] George Stanley Faber traced the 1260 days of Rev 11.3 as prognostications of detailed events that occurred between 1790 and 1800 in *A Dissertation on the*

Prophecies (2 vols 1807), which C evidently read: see *CN* III 3793n. See also 17 n 4, above.
20[1] *Textus Receptus* reads: καὶ ἤκουσα ἄλλου ἐκ τοῦ θυσιαστηρίου, λέγοντος ("And I heard another out of the altar say"). Griesbach and all modern eds omit ἄλλου ἐκ.

Copy B

Commentarius in Apocalypsin Joannis. [Another copy.] Vol I (of 2).
Göttingen 1791. 8°.

British Museum C 126 c 7

Inscribed by C on the title-page: "E libris S. T. Coleridge Grove,
Highgate". Bookseller's mark in pencil on p 2: "2 Vols 12s 6 10/6".
"S. T. C." label on the title-page.

Vol I of a new set bought on 19 Feb 1826. C had had an "*old odd*" copy
of Vol I (see COPY A headnote) "for years" and had wanted to complete it
since c 1815–16. *CN* III 4307. His critical reading of Rev c 1–8 Feb made
the need urgent: see COPY A headnote and COCCEIUS. On 16 Feb HCR called
at the Red Cross Library to try to get a copy of Eichhorn *Apocalypse* for
C, but "To its reproach [it was] not there." *CRB* I 332. C then bought—or
commissioned to be bought—the new set. C annotated the "*old odd*" copy
of Vol I, which Green later had bound with the annotated Vol II of the new
set, making a mixed set here called COPY A and leaving the new Vol I, with
its long acquisition inscription, as an odd volume.

MS TRANSCRIPT. VCL BT 21: in EHC's hand.

DATE. 19 Feb 1826.

COEDITOR. Merton A. Christensen.

1 I ⁻2–⁻1

S. T. Coleridge purchased at Priestley's, High Holborn,[1] for half a
guinea—

With *such* paper (plusquam Germanico–cakcistiᴎη (κακιστη))[2]
and no greater number of pages, five Shillings should have ⟨been⟩
supererogatory—But Booksellers are themselves absolute Papishes
in super-*rogue*-ation this article of Miscreance, and Master Priestley
⟨κατ᾽ ἐξοχὴν⟩[3] a *super-rogue!*—whether a tory likewise, I know not/
but by his name he should be High-Church, at least, ⟨which is⟩ as

1[1] Richard Priestley (1771–1852), for
many years a bookseller at 143 High
Holborn, stocking mainly classical works
and printing many classical editions
prepared by editors of great ability.
In 1815 his stock was worth £30,000.
His catalogue of 1819 (in BM) listed
15,004 titles (456 pp), including Eichhorn
Commentarius in Apocalypsin Joannis
(Göttingen 1791), 12*s* for 2 vols
sewn—perhaps the copy C bought

seven years later. Priestley was declared
bankrupt on 3 Aug 1827.

1[2] "More than Germanic-*shit*tiest
(worst)". The word *caciste*, evolved from
cacata carta of Catullus *Carmina* 36.1,
merges the meanings of Latin *caco* (from
κακκάω) and Greek κάκιστος. For a
similar complaint about the paper in
German books see BIBLE *NT Revelation*
7.

1[3] "Eminently, especially".

close to Tory as Gown to Black-coat. But I *wanted* the Book:[4] and so Good-*by*, Half Guinea!

?Good *Buy*?

Monday, 19 Feb[y] 1826.   S. T. C.

Mem. I have had, for years the first Volume, among my Odd Books—& should have so filled the Margins before this time, that it would have been fairly worth th~~is~~e 10$\frac{1}{2}$ Blood-drops ⟨wrung⟩ from the ~~Aorta~~ pinched Hippocratic Nose of my Poverty, (£0,,10,,6) to any Friend of mine of an Apocalyptic Turn—But the villa[i]nous[a] paper, the spongy Goodwin Sands, that would suck in a Galleon of Ink-wit, baffles every attempt/ tho' you still see sundry black Wrecks hulling shapeless in the Margins.[5]

N.B. The Reward of my Thanks offered to Sir Humphrey Davy, Guy de Lussac, D[r] Woolaston, or any other of the Chemical Magnates of this All-chemical Generation,[6] for the discovery of a new Pounce or other Additament, fluid or solid, that shall render the papyrus cacatoria[7] of German Books as retentive of the *forms*, as it is absorbent of the *Stuff*, of Marginal Msspta—. It will be an act of true Christian Charity to prevent such a waste of ~~a~~ our poor Scholars' Ink-hum[8]

S. T. C.—

---

[a] Letter supplied by the editor.

[1][4] The reason for his need is explained in COPY A 1 n 1 and COCCEIUS. C's indignant complaint ignored the evidence of the front flyleaf: the price of the book had been reduced by 2*s*.

[1][5] C's comment describes aptly enough some of his attempts to write in ink in his German books, but not on the volumes of Eichhorn. The difficulty now in reading some of his notes on Eichhorn —e.g. in *AT*—is not from the blotting of ink but from the rubbing and offsetting of what he wrote in soft pencil. The reference to the Goodwin Sands is well informed: once C began to spend regular holidays at Ramsgate he became witness to shipwrecks and heard firsthand accounts of them. See e.g. *CL* v 396 (Nov 1824) and cf 511. The Goodwin Sands— "The Shippe Swallower"—lying about six miles easterly from the North Foreland presented for centuries one of the gravest menaces to ships approaching Dover and the Thames Estuary. See e.g. G. G. Carter *The Goodwin Sands* (1953). See also Editor's Introduction *CM* I lxxiii. "Hulling"—drifting, without sails set, under the action of wind and current on the hull.

[1][6] Sir Humphry Davy, Joseph Louis Gay-Lussac (1778–1850), and William Hyde Wollaston (1766–1828)—names to be conjured with for inventive ingenuity in chemistry. The pun of "All-chemical" may hold a parable for our own time.

[1][7] "Toilet paper"—another improvised variant of Catullus *cacata carta*: see n 2, above.

[1][8] "Ink-hoax"—also "Income": cf "my Poverty".

ΕΙΚΩΝ ΒΑΣΙΛΙΚΗ

Εικων Βασιλικη. The Portraicture of His Sacred Majestie in his Solitude and Sufferings: together with his private prayers used in the time of his restraint, and delivered to Dr Juxon, Bishop of London, immediately before his death. [London] 1649. 8°.

Lacking the title-leaf. This copy corresponds to the issue represented by BM 599 e 11.

University of Illinois

Bookplate of "John Waugh—Chancell^r of Carlisle" on front p-d. On p ⁻5 in ink: "Tullie Cornthwaite. 1832".

C's letter of 13 Jul 1825 to the Rev Samuel Mence, evidently referring to the reading that produced these marginalia, is tipped into the front of this copy of Εικων Βασιλικη. The letter begins: "It must (I am almost ashamed to confess it) have been more than 20 years since I had read the Εικὼν Βασιλική. I determined therefore, ⟨after having skimmed the first 20 pages of Dr Wordsworth,⟩ to give it a careful re-perusal, before I entered on the controversy as to its true Author. This I have done...". *CL* v 477. There are, however, traces of Εικων Βασιλικη in a notebook of c Jul–Sept 1809, both referring to ch 27 (*CN* III 3528, 3529): C may have acquired this copy at about this date. But it is possible that this was WW's copy, shown in *Wordsworth SC* (1859) 99 as lacking the title-page. The only copy of Εικων Βασιλικη in Wordsworth LC (809)—perhaps this same copy—is not marked as C's. Cf *W Library* 52 (under Charles I).

DATE. Jul 1825, shortly before writing to Samuel Mence on 13 Jul 1825: see *CL* v 477–8.

1   pp ⁻4–⁻3, pencil

It is well worth a Christian's meditation, what important events are apparently linked to ~~an~~ accidents of Nature & bodily Constitution. Such was timidity on any sudden danger, want of presence of mind, in the Stuart Family. They could suffer nobly: i.e. they could *act* in accordance with a previous meditation, *or a making up of their mind* on the proposed subject—but not when ~~it~~ the Call came unexpected.

Charles's misfortunes may be traced with great probability to the undue terror, with which the mobs & tumults of the Apprentices & Rabble had stricken him—and his frequent reverting to this subject in the Εικων Βασιλικη may be placed foremost among the numerous internal evidences of its Authenticity—altogether inexplicable on the hypothesis of the Scoundrel Gauden's being the Antony of this Cæsar's Will./[1]   Εστησε[2]

P.S. Clarendon has noticed that neither James I nor Charles I could stand the force of an eye fixed on their eyes. It was so painful, that they hastily granted even impudent requests, to get rid of the fascination.[3] Hence Charles's total want of a commanding influence on his Followers, even after victory—the more striking, that his deportment was grave & his Countenance majestic. Hence too we may derive the explanation of the proximate cause of his troubles— that which his enemies interpreted as *lying*—in other words, the unsatisfying nature of his first determinations to him, & their frequent inconsistency with his after-thoughts—which almost forced him to seek relief in Casuistry. Saunderson de juramentis was one of his favorite Books.[4] Alas! poor man! had he been more great or less good, Cromwell would have been a New England Elder & he an admired Monarch.—

1[1] Εικων Βασιλικη, published anony-mously on the day of Charles I's burial, purported to have been written by the king in prison, being reflections upon his tribulations up to the time of imprison-ment in Carisbrooke and his meditations and prayers upon the death that he foresaw with the patience and composure of a Christian martyr. The book—issued without licence and without a printer's name, and provided (at Jeremy Taylor's suggestion) with a Greek title that concealed the nature of the book for long enough to capture public imagination and avoid prosecution—immediately became known as "The King's Book", sold at high underground prices, and passed through more than thirty printings in a year. John Gauden (1605–62), at the Restoration, claimed to have written the book from papers given him by Charles at about the time of the Newport Treaty (Sept–Oct 1648). His "elevation to a bishopric by Charles II suggests that the claim was not groundless" (C. V. Wedg-wood *The Trial of Charles the First*— 1964—206); indeed his authorship is now widely accepted as probable. C, however, shared Christopher Wordsworth's view

that Charles I was the author: see **2** n 2, below.

In *Julius Caesar* III ii, Antony used Caesar's will as a clever rhetorical means to turn the people of Rome against Caesar's assassins, whom at first they were disposed to favour.

1[2] "S. T. C." See ANNUAL ANTHO-LOGY **10** n 3.

1[3] No record of this striking detail has been traced.

1[4] Robert Sanderson (1587–1663), regius professor of divinity at Oxford from 1642 until ejected in 1648, issued his *De juramenti promissorii obligatione praelectiones septem* in Latin 1647. There is a tradition that Charles I translated it while a prisoner on the Isle of Wight. The English tr of 1655 is entitled *De jura-mento. Seven Lectures Concerning the Obligation of Promissory Oathes* "Trans-lated into English by His late Majesties speciall Command, and afterwards re-vised and approved under His Majesties own hand." Reinstated in his professor-ship at the Restoration and appointed bp of Lincoln, Sanderson took a leading part in the Savoy Conference (1661) called to review the Book of Common Prayer. Cf *AR* (1825) 157–8.

2   p 86, pencil | Ch 12 "Upon the Rebellion, and Troubles in Ireland"

And certainly, 'tis thought by many wise men, that the preposterous rigour, and unreasonable Severity, which some men carried before them in *England*, was not the least incentive, that kindled and blew up into those horrid flames, the sparks of discontent, which wanted not pre-disposed fewell for Rebellion in *Ireland*; where... it was easie to provoke to an open Rebellion, a people prone enough... both to exempt thcmsclvcs from their present restraints, and to prevent those after rigours, wherewith they saw themselves apparently threatned, by the covetous zeal and uncharitable fury of some men, who think it a great Argument of the truth of their Religion, to endure no other but their own.

Compare this with p 75, last §.ph.[1]

This evident tolerance of Romanism compared with Puritanism appears to me a strong presumption of Charles, & not Gauden, being the Author of the Work.[2]

3   p 102, pencil | Ch 14 "Upon the Covenant"

The *Presbyterian Scots* are not to be hired at the ordinary rate of Auxiliaries; nothing will induce them to engage, till those that call them in, have pawned their souls to them, by a Solemne League and Covenant:

Where many engins of religious and fair pretensions are brought chiefly to batter, or rase Episcopacy...

I should suspect myself of Bigotry, if I did not concede a considerable if not force yet plausibility to Dr Walker's argument drawn from this Chapter on the Covenant.[1] But on the other hand it is to be

2[1] "But as to the main matters propounded by them at any time, in which is either great noveltie, or difficultie, I perceive that what were formerly look'd upon as Factions in the State, and Schismes in the Church, and so punishable by the Laws, have now the confidence, by vulgar clamours, and assistance (chiefly) to demand not onely Tolerations of themselves, in their vanitie, noveltie, and confusion; but also Abolition of the Laws against them, and a totall extirpation of that Government, whose Rights they have a mind to invade."

2[2] C said that his reading of Christopher Wordsworth's "*Who Wrote* ΕΙΚΩΝ ΒΑΣΙΛΙΚΗ" *Considered and Answered* (2 vols 1824–5) "does not sensibly weaken my total and final impression—first, that the work was written by the King—tho' I think it probable that many passages were composed from his recollection of the public papers, published in his name, but (as we learn from Clarendon) written by himself, or Lord Falkland." *CL* v 477: 13 Jul 1825. But cf HACKET *Scrinia* **45** for the statement that Charles lied about the authorship.

3[1] The two chief witnesses that Christopher Wordsworth cites as assigning authorship to Gauden are Gauden's wife

considerableed that the intent & spirit of the whole Book is to *mediate*, soften, reconcile.[2]

4 p 121, pencil | Ch 15 "Upon the Many Iealousies Raised, and Scandals Cast upon the King..."

'Tis strange, that so wise men, as they would be esteemed, should not conceive, That differences of perswasion in matters of Religion may easily fall out, where there is the samenesse of duty, Allegiance, and subjection. The first they own as men, and Christians to God; the second, they ow to Me in Common, as their KING...

Is it not strange, that Charles should not have adverted to the extremes of the contrary policy enforced by him against all other sectarians?[1]

4A p 173, marked in the margin | Ch 20 "Upon the Reformations of the Times"

For I conceive, that where the Scripture is not so clear and punctuall in precepts, there the constant and Universall practice of the Church, in things not contrary to Reason, Faith, good manners, or any positive Command, is the best Rule that Christians can follow.

4B p 236, marked in the margin | "Meditations upon Death..."

Death being an eclipse, which oft happeneth as well in clear, as cloudie dayes.

---

and Anthony Walker (c 1622–92), Gauden's curate at Bocking (from 1648) and author of *A True Account of the Author of a Book Entituled* Εικων Βασιλικη (1692). Walker (according to Wordsworth p 27n) claimed that Gauden was the author on the grounds that "Gauden, though now a most hearty friend of the King, had himself taken the covenant, which we may rationally conclude, had induced him to write more favourably of it, than any of the King's party and friends, or the King himself, would ever have done". C wrote: "tho' I cannot help conceding to Dr Walker's argument drawn from the chapter on the Covenant more force, or at least greater plausibility than Dr Wordsworth is disposed to allow

it, it does not sensibly weaken my total and final impression—first, that the work was written by the King...". *CL* v 477; continued in n 2, below.

3[2] Cf *CL* v 477–8: "Second, that the Book was written with the intent & foresight... of conciliating the judgement and affections of his subjects, in favor of himself... or at all events of his Children....A man, whose object is to mediate, soften, bring together *for a time* contending parties, will naturally, and may innocently, go as far as he can— even beyond his wishes, if not beyond his intentions."

4[1] See also BAXTER *Reliquiae* COPY B 12 and n 1.

EKKEHART I
DEAN OF ST GALL
c 910–973

LOST BOOK

De prima expeditione Attilae regis Hunnorum in Gallias ac de rebus gestis Waltharii Aquitanorum principis carmen epicum saeculi VI. Ex codice manuscripto membranaceo optimae notae summa fide descriptum, nunc primum in lucem productum, &c. [Ed Friedrich Christoph Jonathan Fischer (1750–97).] 2 pts in 1 vol. Leipzig 1780, 1792. 4°.

Not located; marginalia not recorded. *Green SC* (1880) 272 (author entered as F. C. J. Fischer, as in *Lost List*): "With autograph, and several MS. Notes by S. T. Coleridge".The book was included in *Green SC* (1884) 13 and was sold in New York at that time. It was last sold by Parke-Bernet 2–4 Apr 1941 (cat. no 272): "Samuel T. Coleridge's copy, with his autograph signature on the title-page...a few marginal notations in pencil." Sold again by Parke-Bernet 15 Dec 1953 lot 119.

C referred to "the Latin Hexameter Romance on Attila" in *IS* pp 152, 424. BM MS Egerton 2800 f 53 (watermarked 1796): "Memoranda for a History of English Poetry".

The poem has been traditionally ascribed to Ekkehart I on the statement of Meister Ekkehart (c 1260–1327) that Ekkehart I wrote a poem on this subject. This attribution is now questioned: one Geraldus is also suggested as author of the poem, which is usually now called *Waltharius*.

ENCYCLOPAEDIA LONDINENSIS

Encyclopaedia Londinensis; or, Universal Dictionary of Arts, Sciences, and Literature. Comprehending, under one general alphabetical arrangement, all the words and substances of every kind of dictionary extant in the English language....Compiled, digested, and arranged, by John Wilkes...assisted by eminent scholars of the English, Scotch, and Irish, Universities. Vols VI and XII (of 24). London 1810, 1814 (of 1810–29). 4º.

The volumes were issued at irregular intervals: Vols I–VIII in 1810, IX and X in 1811, and thereafter a volume a year except for 1813, in which no volume was issued. Vol VI of this copy lacks its title-page.

Princeton University Library (Rare Books Department)

Heraldic bookplate of Stephen Coleridge (1854–) on the front paste-down of each volume. The bookplate in Vol VI has been pasted over a descriptive note in pencil: all that can be seen is "[...]leridge". Each volume is signed on a front flyleaf recto: "Stephen Coleridge 7 Egerton Mansions ⟨'SW' in Vol VI⟩ 1900."

Apparently John Morgan's copy of a set that may not have advanced beyond Vol XII (1814). On 19 Apr 1819 C wrote to an unknown correspondent, probably Charlotte Brent, asking for "the Loan of the Volume of your Encyclopaedia, containing the Article, Fluxions"—i.e. Vol VII. *CL* IV 936. A notebook entry on the Elzevir family, written c Oct 1810, is definitely assignable to *Encyclopaedia Londinensis* VI: see *CN* III 3978 and BARCLAY COPY A **2** n 1; cf *CN* III 4269 f 26 (c Aug–Sept 1815), which may also be assignable to Vol VI. In the autumn of 1810 C was living with the Morgans in Hammersmith; in the autumn of 1815 he was living with them in Calne. In 1810 John Morgan was still prosperous, although soon to find himself in financial difficulties; by 1814–15, although he had not recovered his fortunes, he had emerged from the shadow of bankruptcy and might have been able to buy Vols IX–XII (issued 1811–14).

MS TRANSCRIPT. (*a*) VCL LT 50(i): **2–10** with textus, in an unidentified hand (endorsed "Copied S. D."). This seems to have been the copy from which *NTP* 218–20 was prepared. (*b*) Kathleen Coburn Collection: EHC transcript of **7** only.

DATE. c Nov 1810–c May 1811 (**1–6**), and early 1815 at Calne. A few details in the annotations seem to be parallel to notebook entries of late 1810–early 1811.

1 vi 461 | "Elephas"

[quoting from John Corse "Observations on the Manners, Habits and Natural History, of the Elephant" *Trans RS* (1799), which begins on p 458:] "...nor have elephants, so far as I have been able to observe, any particular seasons of love, like horses."

This detestable use of the word "love" was introduced by the French;[1] and is a good instance of the filthiness of mock-modesty. In order to avoid the plain and appropriate word "Lust" or "Sexual Heat", we are to blaspheme the noblest Affection of Human Nature —nay, which God himself has chosen as most descriptive of His Essence: "God is Love!"[2]   [S. T.] C.[a]

2 vi 824 | "Entomology"

ENTOMOLOGY...The science which investigates the nature, structure, and economy, of insects; called likewise *insectology*.

By what son of Babel?[1]

3 vi 825

The number of <u>ideas</u> with which a skilful botanist must load his memory, before he can acquire an accurate knowledge of plants, is no doubt great: his task, however, bears no proportion to that of the entomologist...

terms & perhaps Images; but I know of few *Ideas* peculiar to Botany.[1]

3A vi 825

The Chinese, whose progress in many of the arts is deservedly celebrious,[1] avail themselves of the labours of certain insects in

---

[a] Part lost in the gutter

[1][1] In the course of a series of notes on John Splinter Stavorinus *Voyages to the East-Indies* tr S. H. Wilcocke (3 vols 1798), C remarked upon the "Chinese Taste in *Love* (as the Gallican, and Philo-gallican English Scribes call their infra-abdominal Inquietudes)". *CN* III 4015 (c 1810). See also H. COLERIDGE **44** n 2.

[1][2] 1 John 4.8. For C on the difference between love and lust see—among numerous references—KANT *Metaphysik der Sitten* **3** and n 1.

[2][1] C's distaste is presumably for the hybrid form of the word: Bonnet had introduced it (1744) because the "barbarous sound [of *entomology*] terrify'd" him. *OED*. The fact that "insectology" had come into English from French would not mitigate C's revulsion.

[3][1] On the relation of botany to ideas, see *Friend* (*CC*) I 466–70, esp 466–7.

[3A][1] *OED* records uses of the word from the seventeenth to the nineteenth century.

procuring a rich dye, and an elegant varnish, which is provided by a certain species of winged ant.

4   VI 886 | "Equus"

The horse, like the other domestic animals, has, no doubt, been originally tamed by human art. Wild horses are still found in various parts of the world. But this species of animals have been so long known in a domestic state, and their useful qualities have caused them to be diffused so generally over the globe, that it is impossible to discover, with any degree of certainty, of what country they were originally natives. Wild horses are found in the country lying round the lake Aral;...in the southern part of Siberia; in the great Mongolian deserts; and...north-west of China. These horses are smaller than the domestic...

Doubtful.[1] The Germans wisely distinguish wilde Pferden from verwilderten Pferden—wild from those that have run wild. Of the latter are the immense Herds of S. Amer.

5   VI 891 | "Erasmus"

In conformity with the pedantic taste then prevailing among men of letters, of assuming names of Greek or Latin etymology, he translated his family name of *Gerard*, signifying *amiable*, into the equivalent ones of *Desiderius* in Latin, and *Erasmus* in Greek.

And why pedantic?[1] What man of the least Taste would have preferred Mynheer Groot to Grotius, Reuchlin to Capnio, or Schwarzerdt to Melancthon?[2] While the Latin was the Lingua Communis of Europe, such Translations were fit & graceful.

6   VI 891

He first lodged with sir Thomas More, and amused himself with writing his *Moriae Encomium*; or, Praise of Folly: a facetious and satirical composition, which became popular.

4[1] Przewalski's horse, first scientifically described in 1881, a truly wild horse, smaller than the domestic species, is found in Mongolia.

5[1] Cf "pedantry consists in the use of words unsuitable to the time, place, and company. The language of the market would be in the schools as *pedantic*...as the language of the schools in the market." *BL* ch 10 (*CC*) I 170.

5[2] Hugo Grotius (1583–1645), theologian and jurist (see BAHRDT **2** and n 2); Johann Reuchlin (1455–1522), humanist and Hebraist; Philipp Melanchthon (1497–1560). C often referred to Grotius and Melanchthon, rarely to Reuchlin (see *CN* III 4497 and n).

And is that all that can be said of the (perhaps) most exquisite Work of wit & wisdom extant! In its kind certainly the most exquisite.[1]

S. T. Coleridge

7 xii 585–6 | "Liberty"

It were endless to enumerate all the *affirmative* acts of parliament, wherein justice is directed to be done according to the law of the land; and what that law is, every subject knows, or may know if he pleases; for it depends not upon the arbitrary will of any judge; but is permanent, fixed, and unchangeable, unless by authority of parliament.

Mere declamation! In a rich & populous, a commercial and manufacturing people, the practical Law exists in Precedents, far more than in Statutes—and every new Judge furnishes new Precedents. Hence the "glorious uncertainty of the Law".[1]—How can it be truly affirmed, that every *man* may know, when it requires the study and practice of a Life to be qualified even to give an opinion; & when nothing is more common than for two men equally qualified to give opposite opinions. Not to mention the ruinous expences of a Law suit to all but rich men: so that the power of appeal from lower to higher Court instead of protecting the poor man enables a rich Tyrant, such as the late Lord Lonsdale to ruin whom he chooses.[2] I write this not in complaint for the evil is inevitable, & results from the very nature of Property in the present state of human Nature;[3] but because the strongest arguments of Jacobinism are drawn from these rash assertions, & the actual state of things so opposite to them.[4] These

6[1] Cf "I think the praise of Folly is the most pleasant Book of Erasmus." Allsop ii 190. C used a passage from *Moriae encomium* as epigraph in *Friend* (*CC*) i 363. For Erasmus' style see *Friend* (*CC*) i 130–2. For a clue to C's edition of *Moriae encomium* (Oxford 1668) see *CN* iii 4262n (ed cited in *CN* iv 4808).

7[1] A toast ascribed to a Mr Wilbraham in 1756; the phrase appears (var) in Charles Macklin *Love à la Mode* (1759). See *OED* "Glorious" 5.b.

7[2] James Lowther (1736–1802), 1st Earl of Lonsdale, the "bad Lord Lowther", "unrivalled in the art of electioneering", repeatedly MP for Cumberland, and for Westmorland and Cockermouth. His failure to repay a substantial sum borrowed from his agent and attorney, WW's father, resulted in a distressing delay in the devolution of the Wordsworth inheritance until the "good Lord Lowther", William Lowther (1757–1844), succeeded on the death of his third cousin James. See *W Life* (Moorman) i 167–9, 558–61.

7[3] Private property results in the formation of a class of rich and a class of poor, the rich wielding political power. See e.g. *EOT* (*CC*) i 32 and n 2, 372–3 and n 10, iii 225–6.

7[4] C claimed that it was he, in an essay in *M Post* in 1802, who "gave the first fair and philosophical statement and definition of Jacobinism and of Jacobin". *Friend* (*CC*) ii 144n. See *EOT* (*CC*) ii 369, *SM* (*CC*) 63–4, and *CN* iii 3742.

positions should be treated as the declared *Ideal* and ultimate *Object* of Legislation, which every man is bound to hold in view in his administration of Law, not as the actual Result of Law: and men should be taught, that the Evils here stated are great indeed yet cannot be removed without far greater Evils, & that there are advantages on the other hand, resulting from those very evils, & in some measure counterbalancing them/ such as the existence of a large & learned Profession; a Check on Litigiousness; and not least a general sense of the insufficiency of Law, & the consequent praise & value attached to Honor & Morality as contradistinguished from *Legality*.[5]

8 XII 587 | "Liberty of Conscience"

With religion, Christian governments have no farther concern than as it tends to promote the practice of virtue.

No! If this were once admitted, even the Inquisition might be defended. Not the practice of *Virtue*, but the peace of Society and the *Legality* of the Individuals, are the Objects of Law: these secured, it trusts & may safely trust, to Religion, Education, Civilization, for the rest.[1]

9 XII 587

That the civil magistrate has a right to check the propagation of opinions which tend to sap the foundations of virtue, and to disturb the peace of society, cannot, we think, be questioned; but that he has no right to restrict mankind from publicly professing any system of faith, which comprehends the being and providence of God, the great laws of morality, and a future state of rewards and punishments, is as evident as that it is the object of religion to fit mankind for heaven, and the whole duty of the magistrates to maintain peace, liberty, and property, upon earth.

But who is to be the Judge, what opinions do tend to sap &c? —Will any orthodox Xtian allow, that the Denial of the Christian Revelation does not tend to sap the foundations of virtue?

7[5] For C's attack on the confounding of morality with law see *Friend* (*CC*) II 313–14 (I 314–15). See also *ibid* II 66–7 and *SM* (*CC*) 64.

8[1] On the proposition that "the sharp limits and exclusive *proprieties* of Science, Law and Religion should be kept distinct" see *Friend* (*CC*) I 94–5.

10 XII 588

It is indeed a hardship to deprive a man of his living for conscientiously illustrating what he believes to be a truth of the gospel, only because his illustration may be different from that which had formerly been given by men fallible like himself; but, if the establishment of human compilations of faith be necessary, this hardship cannot be removed, but by making such compilations as simple as possible, and drawing them up in scripture language.

This is utterly impracticable: for the question is what is the meaning of the Scripture Language. If you take only a certain set of Texts, the opponent has another set to refer to—and by these he will interpret the former. Thus, the Socinian & Trinitarian would both subscribe to the same words—and the whole purpose of Subscription be baffled.[1] The Church of England has no occasion for Subscription, inasmuch as all her Articles of Faith are interwoven in her Liturgy; but for this very reason there can be ground of Objection to Subscribing. For will you hestitate to subscribe what you do not believe in the presence of a Bishop, & yet not hestitate to offer up a Lie to your Maker ~~twic~~ in the most solemn part of [?Religion][a]?—

---

[a] MS TRANSCRIPT reads "solemn part of Religion", but in ms there is no word between "solemn" and "of"; the reading of the last word is uncertain

10[1] For the legal requirement of subscription to the Thirty-Nine Articles of Religion, which remained on the statute books until 1828, see BOOK OF COMMON PRAYER COPY B **28** n 1.

"ENGLISH TRACTS"

LOST BOOK

[A made-up volume of 6 tracts 1748, 1756, etc.] 8°.

Not located: marginalia not recorded. *Gillman SC* (1843) 435: "with Autograph of W. Hone, and Index in MS. by Mr. Coleridge". Acquired, directly or indirectly, from the sale of Hone's books at Southgate's 22–3 Feb 1827, lot 251, described as "Towgood's Essay towards a true idea of Charles I &c." Whether this was already a made-up volume, or whether the other tracts were added by C, does not appear.

CONTENTS. *Gillman SC* 435 gives the total number of tracts in the volume, but cites only two titles:

Michaijah Towgood (1700–92) *An Essay Towards Attaining a True Idea of the Character and Reign of King Charles the First, and the Causes of the Civil War* (London 1748)

Address to the Commons (London 1756)

ADOLPH CARL AUGUST ESCHENMAYER
1768–1852

Psychologie in drei Theilen als empirische, reine und ungewandte.
Stuttgart & Tübingen 1817. 8⁰.

British Museum C 126 f 6

"S. T. C." label on title-page verso.

Eschenmayer, physician, professor of philosophy at Tübingen 1811–36, was associated with Schelling in the early stages of the *Naturphilosophie* and contributed to at least two of Schelling's periodicals: see JAHRBÜCHER (Tübingen 1805–8) item 8 and ZEITSCHRIFT *für speculative Physik* (Jena & Leipzig 1800–1). He became interested in animal magnetism, spiritualism, and demonology, and edited *Archiv für den thierischen Magnetismus* from 1817: see "Maxilian" in *Miscellanies* (1885) 272 n 1 and JUNG headnote.

MS TRANSCRIPT. VCL BT 22 (omitting half the notes).

DATE. From 1818—or a little later—onwards: see *CN* III 4435 f 56ᵛ and n (c Aug–Sept 1818). As early as 8 Jul 1817 C had retracted the outright dismissal of animal magnetism that—in part at least—arose from his respect for Gillman's professional scepticism: see BM Add MS 36532 ff 5, 7–12 (in *SW&F*) and marginalia on the 1818 *Friend*: (*CC*) I 59 n 1. See also **29–32** and nn. C mentions Eschenmayer by name in SOUTHEY *Life of Wesley* (c 1820–2) and in SWEDENBORG *De cultu et amore Dei* (c Sept 1821).

COEDITORS. Lore Metzger, Raimonda Modiano.

1   p 8, pencil | Einleitung

Das Selbstbewusstseyn ist: 1) das kombinirteste Factum, was der empirische Psycholog aufzufassen vermag.

[Self-consciousness is: (1) the most combined fact that the empirical psychologist is able to conceive.]

1) not a happy phrase. Who would [have]ᵃ called Oxygen the kombinirteste, most combined, to express the number of different things, with which singly it is found in combination? Das am

---

ᵃ Word supplied by the editor

1¹ "That which combines most readily".

2 p 8, pencil

Das Selbstbewusstsein ist...2) das bewährteste Factum, weil die Identität der Ichheit sich durch alle Gedanken, Gefühle und Handlungen hindurchzieht. Es ist keiner Skepsis unterworfen; denn indem ich mein Selbstbewusstseyn läugnen würde, müsste ich sein Daseyn voraussezen. Affirmation und Negation erhalten den Grund ihrer Möglichkeit nur durch die Identität der Selbstbewusstseyns.

*] Mit diesem Factum, mit dem die empirische Psychologie endet, fängt die rationale an.

[Self-consciousness is...(2) the best substantiated fact since the identity of selfhood pervades all thoughts, feelings, and actions. It is not subject to scepticism; for in order to deny my self-consciousness, I should have to postulate its existence. The possibility of affirmation or negation is established only through the identity of self-consciousness.

With this fact, with which empirical psychology ends, rational psychology begins.]

Why so? It being das bewährteste Factum keiner Skepsis unterworfen,[1] why should *empirical* Psychology not begin with it, as well as rational Psychology?[2]

3 p 23, pencil, lightly cropped | I Psychologie § 9

Nehmen wir *die Seele als Urkraft* an, so sind alle Vermögen nur verschiedene Abdrüke, alle Functionen nur verschiedene Richtungen und Aeusserungen, alle Ideen nur verschiedene Bilder ihrer selbst. Sie ist die Eine, ungetheilte Substanz, worinn alle Erscheinungen nur gleichsam Accidenzen darstellen.]

[If we postulate *the soul as the primal power*, then all faculties are but different moulds, all functions but different directions and expressions, all ideas but different images of the soul itself. It is the one undivided substance, wherein all phenomena represent, as it were, mere accidents.]

Wherein then does the term, Soul, differ from the term, God?[1] Is there

[2][1] "The best substantiated fact [or the most [fully] authenticated fact] beyond all doubt"—the phrase compounded from the first two sentences of textus.

[2][2] Eschenmayer elaborates upon this argument (p 2): "...the springs of the mental functions...hide themselves from empirical observation. Only once they emerge into the light of day, like the streams of the earth, can we observe their course and accompany it with our sense.

Hence there is an *empirical self-knowledge*, which follows the course of the functions that emerge into the daylight, and a *speculative self-knowledge*, which goes back to the hidden source." For C's view that self-consciousness is the ultimate source of all knowledge and must therefore inform natural philosophy see *BL* ch 12 and *SM* (*CC*) 78–9.

[3][1] C detects a pantheistic bias in Eschenmayer's failure to distinguish

any sense in the words, My Soul? Or have we all one and the same Soul?[2] and what is the meani[ng] of *we, I*?[3]

4 p 25, pencil | Pt I Empirische Psychologie §13

Das Kind führt im Mutterschoos ein bloses Pflanzenleben. Es beschäftigt sich mur mit seiner eigenen Plastik und ist allen äussern Eindrüken verschlossen.

[The child in the womb leads a mere vegetative existence. It occupies itself only with its own shaping and is closed off from all outside impression.]

The Deuce and all! but how much better is he employed than he is likely to be at any period after his Birth[1]—what incomparably greater Science does he manifest. "The child is Father of the man" with a vengeance in this sense![2]

5 pp 30–1, pencil | I §19

Dieser Annahme kommt eine merkwürdige Thatsache entgegen, nemlich dass das Kind, wenn es schon Sprache, Sach- und Namenkenntniss hat, doch sein Ich noch nicht ausspricht, sondern anfangs von sich als einer dritten Person redet. Der Carl—will das—u. s. w.

[This hypothesis is confirmed by the strange fact that the child, having already learned language, things, and names, nevertheless does not yet express his ego but in the beginning speaks about himself in the third person. Carl wants this—etc.]

§19. This is one of the *very few* silly remarks of Immanuel Kant: all of which very few are to be found in his Anthropology.[1] This therefore suited Eschenmayer. I is but αυτου κηρ,[2] *this here*; and this

between a universal spirit and an individual soul. Cf *AR* (1825) 4–5, which includes the statement that "Life is the one universal soul…'And man became a living soul.' He did not merely *possess* it, he *became* it. It was his proper *being*, his truest *self*, *the* man *in* the man." See also HEINROTH 15, KANT *Metaphysische Anfangsgründe* 3, and *CL* IV 807.

3[2] Cf *The Eolian Harp* lines 44–6 and 26–9, added possibly in the 1820s: *PW* (EHC) I 101–2.

3[3] For C's early speculations on the "I" see e.g. *CN* I 921. On the problem of defining the "I" see FICHTE general note

and especially the marginalia on *Die Bestimmung des Menschen*.

4[1] On the importance and interest of uterine life see BROWNE *Religio* 17.

4[2] WW *My Heart Leaps Up* line 7: *WPW* I 226. C quoted the poem in *The Friend* 10 Aug 1809: *Friend (CC)* II 41 (I 40). See *BL* ch 22 (*CC*) II 138–41.

5[1] C comments on the passage in KANT *Anthropologie* COPY A 1 and COPY B 1.

5[2] "His heart"—a recollection of Homer, the heart being in both *Iliad* and *Odyssey* the centre of thought and emotion. See e.g. *Iliad* 1.44, 491.

"Carl" does as well as "I"—δεικτικῶς.³—The whole amount of this *merkwürdige Thatsache*⁴ is that the Child learns the meaning of the words, *This and That*: and that a universal + an act of shewing = a Noun: *That-there*, with the finger pointed = a stone, &c. The remark reminds one of the Irishman, enquiring which was the other side of the way.

6 p 34, pencil | 1 § 23

Die Erkenntniss Gottes tritt an die Stelle der Selbsterkenntniss und die Selbstgesetzgebung verwandelt sich in einen unbedingten Gehorsam gegen göttliche Gebote.

[*The knowledge of God takes the place of self-knowledge, and self-government is transformed into absolute obedience to divine laws.*]

And so—good bye, Urcraft Seely, Esquire!¹

7 p 35, pencil, line in margin beside 5), lightly cropped | 1 § 26

Ordnen wir diese Reihen in bestimmte dem Stufenalter des Menschen parallelgehende Abschnitte, so können wir dieselbe in eben so viele Grundverhältnisse absondern: Sie sind 1) das *Sinnliche*...2) Das *Intellectuelle*...3) Das *Gemüthliche*...4) Das *Sittliche*...5) Das *Religiöse*, der höchsten Reihe und zugleich dem Greissenalter am meisten angemessen.

[If we classify these series as definite epochs paralleling the stages of man's development, then we can divide these in just as many basic relationships: they are (1) the *sensual*...(2) the *intellectual*...(3) the *sentimental*...(4) the *moral*...(5) the *religious*, most appropriate at once to the highest series and to old age.]

Notoriously false! The selfish Bead- and Prayer-book-ery is indeed "the Toys of Age".¹ But Childhood, and Boy (or Girl) hood is the true *religious* Æra.—²

5³ "By way of demonstration".
5⁴ "Strange fact"—from the textus.
6¹ Facetious play on *Urkraft Seele* (as in 3 textus, above)—"Soul the primal power". See also 8, below.
7¹ Pope *Essay on Man* ii 280: "And beads and pray'r-books are the toys of age". Cf *CL* vi 577 (18 Apr 1826).

7² Cf *Sh C* ii 111–12. In *The Friend* 22 Feb 1810 C remarked upon the "early, obstinate, and unappeasable inquisitiveness of Children upon the subject of origination"; cf his statement that "the minds of very young Children meditate feelingly upon Death and Immortality". *Friend* (*CC*) ii 337.

8 p 36, pencil | I § 27

Und nun kann uns auch die Bedeutung der Seele klarer werden. Sie selbst ist kein Vermögen, sondern vielmehr die Innhaberin dieses ganzen geistigen Schemas von Vermögen.... Im Glauben übt die Seele ihre höchste Kraft... In der Empfindung übt sie ihre niederste Kraft; denn durch sie ist die Seele an den Boden des Zeitlichen und Vergänglichen gefesselt.

[And now we can also clarify the significance of the soul. It is itself no faculty, but rather the proprietor of this whole spiritual system of faculties.... In faith the soul exercises its highest power... In sensation it exercises its lowest power, because through sensation the soul is fastened to the ground of the temporal and the transient.]

§ 27. Here comes Urcraft Seele again: but O! how shorn of its Beams![1]

Who does not see, that Soul is here a mere general term, like *the King* in our Law-books/ the King never dies[2]—the King übt seine niederste Kraft in the Turnkey and Jack Ketch/![3]

9 p 38, pencil | I § 30

Der organischen Beschaffenheit nach ist jede Empfindung eine Affection des Nervensystems und der Sitz derselben im Gehirn. Darauf leiten uns schon empirische Schlüsse. Lähmung, Unterbindung oder Zerschneidung der Nerven hebt alle Empfindung auf.

[In accordance with its organic nature, every sensation is an affection of the nervous system and has its seat in the brain. Empirical deductions already lead us to this point. Injury, blockage, or severance of the nerves destroys all sensation.]

These have ever appeared to me very imperfect proofs. Apply the reasoning to the strings of a Violin.[1]

10 p 43, pencil | I § 37

Wenn irgend ein Theil des Leibes an Brand oder Lähmung leidet, so hört alle Empfindung davon auf. Es findet hier, warum die Seele den Schmerz ausser dem Sitz der Empfindung referire... Jedes Organ

---

8[1] See 6 and n 1, above.

8[2] C cited "The King never dies" as one of "the most venerable maxims of English Law". *Friend* (*CC*) I 177n.

8[3] The King "exercises his lowest power" (in textus) in the gaoler and the executioner—Jack Ketch (d 1686) being a public hangman and executioner, notorious for clumsiness. He is still celebrated in the Punch-and-Judy show.

9[1] C seems to imply a figurative equation: Violin = Brain, Strings = Nerves, Music = Sensation. His objection is to Eschenmayer's failure to notice the "integrative action of the nervous system", of which he was himself acutely aware. Cf BROOKE 24. Or C may have heard of Paganini's trick of breaking one or more strings in performance and completing the music on the remaining strings.

giebt eine specifische Art von Empfindung für den innern Sinn, die aber nie dem Totaleindruck der Einheit gleichkommt. Daher muss die Seele den Eindruck als verschieden von dem Werthe, den der innere Sinn hat, wahrnehmen und ihn ausser dem Sitz der Empfindung referiren.*

[When some part of the body suffers from burns or paralysis, it loses all sensation. This explains why the soul refers the pain to a place outside the seat of sensation... Every organ transmits a specific kind of sensation to the inner sense, which, however, never equals the total impression of the whole. Therefore the soul must evaluate the impression differently from the inner sense and must refer it to a place outside the seat of sensation.]

* This seems to illustrate the fact, that we do not feel in the Brain; but why do we refer the feeling *determinately* elsewhere? By mere guess?—And certainly we are often deceived.[1]

11   p 67, pencil, lightly cropped | I § 71

Provinzen müssen da seyn, in welchen die Zeichen eingegraben werden und diese mögen an Fruchtbarkeit oder Unfruchtbarkeit von sehr verschiedenem Gehalt seyn. Ein grosses und sehr geübtes Gedächtniss scheint dem Judicium Abbruch zu thun, ohne Zweifel, weil das Zuströmen der Bilder, Zeichen, Wörter, Begriffe die Festhaltung der Einzelen verhindert.

[There must be areas in which the signs are engraved, their substance differing in degree of fertility or sterility. A large and well-trained memory seems to be detrimental to judgement, doubtless because the streaming in of images, signs, words, conceptions prevents the fixation of any single one.]

A strange Jumbl[e,] methinks, of Materialism and I know not what! *Engraving Brain-plates*, in a more or less *fertile soil, streamin*[g] *on*, &c &c.—[1]

12   p 68, pencil | I § 73

Die Aufmerksamkeit hat verschiedene Grade.... Die gröste Intensität derselben erfordert der Tiefsinn in der Spekulation. Es ist die Sammlung der Seele in allen ihren Richtungen auf einem Punct.

10[1] C had for years studied by introspection the phenomena of the projected physical locality of sensation and the hallucinatory delusions of "double touch". See e.g. *CN* II 2399, 2405, 3215, and **28** nn 1, 3, below. See also FICHTE *Bestimmung* **6** n 2.

11[1] For C's rejection of the representation of the mind—by Locke and "Empirism"—as "receiving impressions from things" in the way that "the melted Sealing wax has the power or property of receiving an impression from the Seal" see *CN* III 3605 ff 120–119^v (c Aug–Sept 1809) and cf e.g. *CL* II 682 (18 Feb 1801). See also **27** n 3, below.

[Attention has different degrees.... Its greatest intensity is demanded by profound speculation. It focuses all the directions of the soul upon one point.]

Patience! Patience!

13   p 76, pencil | ɪ § 85

Da nun die Summe der Vorstellungen, Begriffe, Zeichen, Wörter und Bilder unermesslich ist, so können die Spuren der Einzelen im organischen Raum des Gehirns nur wie punctirte Abdrücke erscheinen.

[Since the sum total of ideas, conceptions, signs, words, and images is immeasurable, the traces of each single one can appear only like dotted impressions in the organic chamber of the brain.]

Such a crude unimaginable Image is strange in a Natur-philosoph![1] As well might Esch. suppose Traces in the Muscles, of the Arms for instance, of all the ropes, sticks, stones, &c &c that had been raised or moved by them.

14   p 77, pencil | ɪ § 86

Wie beim Vorstellen das Räumliche des Objects verschwindet und nur sein Zeitverhältniss als Zahl, Ziffer, als Moment der Kraft übrig *]bleibt, so wird beim Einbilden zu diesem Zeitverhältniss auch wider das Räumlich des Objects gefunden, und dadurch erhält das Differential des Objects wider einen endlichen Werth.

[Just as in the act of representation the spatial dimension of the object disappears and only its temporal relation as number, cipher, or moment of the power remains, accordingly in the act of imagination the spatial dimension of the object is found again along with its temporal relation, and thus the differential of the object receives its finite value.]

* The absurdity of this is exquisite! If the Soul can by its own intellectual powers supply the dimensions of *Space* for integration,

13[1] *Naturphilosoph* and *Naturphilosophie*—terms denoting an ill-defined group of late-eighteenth- and early-nineteenth-century German philosophers, e.g. Schelling, Fichte, Schubert, Oersted, Oken, Steffens, who emphasised an organic concept of nature, most of them embracing some form of transcendental idealism and using the guiding figures of organicism and vitalism. See also HEINROTH and ZEITSCHRIFT *für speculative Physik* ed Schelling (1800–1). For C's qualified view of the *Naturphilosophie* in general see **38** n 3, below, *CL* ɪv 792, and e.g. GOLDFUSS **2**. For C's coinage "Physiosophy" see e.g. *CL* ɪv 654 and cf EICHHORN *Alte Testament* **18** n 2.

why not the schematic moment of *Time* for the Differential? Why not *rather* indeed, Time being far more = the mind than space.—[1]

15 p 79, pencil | I § 88

[Eschenmayer has been pointing out the analogy between the process of obtaining representations of external objects and the operation of differentials in mathematics (pp 78–80).] Wie nun die Ziffer beschaffen seye, welche das Vorstellungsvermögen von den Objecten im Gedächtniss...aufbewahre, das können wir nicht gerade bestimmen. Es ist genug, die <u>Wahrscheinlichkeit</u>! <u>solcher</u>! Ziffer gezeigt zu haben.

[We cannot determine exactly just how the figures that store up the representations of objects in memory might be obtained. It is sufficient to have shown the probability of such figures.]

!!!!![a]

16 pp 94–5 pencil | I § 109

Um das Wundervolle, was im menschlichen Zeugnungsacte liegt, wegzuräumen, dürfen wir nur annehmen, dass in ihm, mit ihm und
*] durch ihn ein geistiges Prinzip mit den organischen Keimen in Verbindung trete, und somit schon im Schlagpuncte des Lebens Seele
*] und Körper in Eins verschmolzen seye. Der geistige Theil des Menschen gibt im Zeugnungsacte eben so wohl einen Bestandtheil zum neuen Producte als der organische.

[To remove the wonderful inherent in the act of human procreation, we have only to assume that in it, with it, and through it a spiritual principle merges with the organic seeds, and that body and soul are thus fused into one at the inception of life. In the act of procreation the spiritual part of man plays as much of a rôle in the creation of the new product as the organic.]

** We have *only* to—&c—and this removes the *Wonderful*!!!! Um das Wundervolle (i.e. in the production of such d—n'd Nonsense) wegzuräumen, we have *only* to assume, that in, with and thro' the Author a nonsensical Spirit passed into combination with the first Drop of Ink, after its entrance into a *Quill* with a *Slit* in it. N.B. Ein *geistiger Keim sich ablöse*!!![1]

[a] Written in the margin beside the two underlined words

14[1] For C on space and time see *Logic* (*CC*) 155–73 and Maass 2 n 2. Cf *BL* ch 7 (*CC*) I 126: "The act of consciousness is indeed identical with *time* considered in its essence."

16[1] "*A spiritual seed detaches itself!*" —modified from § 111 (tr): "When a spiritual seed is to detach itself in order to fan a new life [into being] it can originate only from the centre point

17   p 95, pencil | I § 110

...müssen wir annehmen, dass der Mittelpunkt des geistigen Organismus, *welches das Gefühlvermögen ist,* gleichsam über-ströme, und...an die organische Keime der beyden Geschlechter ...übergehe. *Dieses Ueberströmen des Gefühlvermögens und sein Durchgang durch den Körper an den organischen Keim zu neuem Leben ist durch ein unverkennbares Phänomen bezeichnet,—es ist die Intensität der Lust, die jeden Zeugungsact begleitet.*

[...we must assume that the central part of the spiritual organism, *which is the faculty of feeling,* overflows, as it were, and...transfers itself...to the organic seeds of both sexes. *This overflowing of the faculty of feeling and its passage through the body to the organic seed of future life is characterised by an unmistakable phenomenon—the intensity of pleasure accompanying every act of procreation.*]

A dirty subject—and the assertion not always nor necessarily true. Not the Secretion, nor the Transportation, but the Ejaculation is marked by this Intensity—nor is it certain, that this *feeling* in the + is necessary to the impregnation of the − ./[1]

18   p 104, pencil | I § 122

Jeder Pflanzenkeim, jeder Saamentropfen, jedes Blumenstäubgen ist wie ein organisches Differential zu betrachten, das implicite schon die Natur seiner künftigen Grösse und Bildung in sich trägt, und nur integrirt zu werden braucht, um als lebendige Einheit sich zu ent-wikeln.... Saamen und Eychen werden als organische Differentiale sich zu einander verhalten, wie diese der Abscisse und Ordinate...Er [der Analytiker] setzt, wenn er z. B. aus der Subtangente der Parabel + 2x die Curve selbst wieder finden will, sie der allgemeinen Formel

$+\dfrac{ydx}{dy}$ gleich, und erhält dann das Verhältniss der Differentiale der

Abscisse und Ordinate in einen doppelten Ausdruck—ydx = 2xdy, welche nach übertragener Analogie wie weibliches und männliches Prinzip einander gleichgesetzt sind.

[Each vegetative germ, each grain of seed, each particle of pollen has to be regarded as an organic differential that potentially contains within itself the

(focus, hearth) of the spiritual organism itself. In the same way the physical seed must detach itself from the focus of the physical organism." Cf **37** and n 1, below.

17[1] The signs + and − here stand for male and female. See **16** and n 1, above, and GOLDFUSS **4**. Cf *CN* III 4435 and n.

nature of its future size and shape; it only needs to be integrated in order to develop as a living entity....Sperms and ovules relate to one another like organic differentials, similar to the differentials of abscissae and ordinates...If, for example, the mathematician wants to recover the curve out of the subtangent of the parabola +2x, he equates it with the general formula $+\dfrac{ydx}{dy}$, and then obtains the ratio of the differentials of abscissae and ordinates in a double expression—ydx = 2xdy, which, according to the analogy conveyed above, are equated with the female and male principle.]

There seems one defect at least in this analogy—that E. supposes that figure ac̶t̶u̶really produced by the differential motion of the point—but it is only imagined, and the figure itself ⟨is⟩ made by the ink, slate, chalk, or sand. Far more intelligible is the idea of Behmen who derives the Body from Death, as the residuum inertiæ of a potential not entirely actualized.[1]

19 p 105, pencil | I §123

Die Seele ist keine *Tabula rasa*, wie Aristoteles meint, die sich erst aus der Erfahrung füllen müsste, sie hat vielmehr schon die ursprünglichste und allgemeinste Proportionen, Gleichungen, Geseze, Ideale und Grundsäze in sich, und kommt mit denselben dem Erfahrungs- und Inductionswissen entgegen, oder vielmehr, sie sucht alle Erfahrung und Induction mit ihren Ideen zu indentificiren.

[The soul is not, as Aristotle maintains, a *tabula rasa*, which must first be filled with experience; on the contrary, it already contains within itself the most fundamental and most universal proportions, equations, laws, ideals, and principles, and brings these to bear upon empirical and inductive knowledge—or rather it seeks to identify all experience and induction with its own ideas.]

Aristotle speaks of Images, Actualities, εξεις, and affirms that these are ingenerated thro' the Senses by impregnation ab extra. Consequently, he impl̶y̶ies an ovarium in the Soul[1]—Thus too what Lock

18[1] See BÖHME I i 261 (*Aurora* ch 26): "The *Flesh* is not the Life, but is a dead inanimate Being, which when the Government or Dominion of the Spirit *ceases* to qualify or operate therein, soon becomes a dead *Carcase*, and putrefies and turns to Dust or Ashes." C wrote six marginalia on ch 26 but none on this passage. "Residuum inertiae"—"inert residue", related to *corpus* (or *caput*) *mortuum*: see BÖHME 71 and n 2 (in which "worthless residue" should read "inert residue"). Cf also BÖHME 74.

19[1] In Aristotle the word for "images" is εἴκονες or φαντάσματα, and for "actuality" is ἐντελεχεία or ἐνεργεία; ἕξεις are states, conditions, habits, traits of character or predispositions. C seems to be giving a not very lucid impression of Aristotle's theory, perhaps from some secondary source (cf his use of Maass on Aristotle in

verbally denies as *in*nate *Ideas*, he admits in reality under the name of Predispositions—unless he means by the form⟨er⟩ only *con*nate *Images*, i.e. a mere truism.²

20   p 110, pencil | I §130

Vernunft sucht alle Erkenntniss auf ursprüngliche Principien zurückzuführen, und sie so viel möglich der Idee der Wahrheit zu nähern....Im Willen hingegen ist von keinem Erkennen die Rede, sondern von einem Handeln...*Der Karakter der Vernunft ist Gesetzmässigkeit, der des Willens Freyheit—und darinn sind sie völlig entgegengesezt.*

[Reason seeks to refer all knowledge back to primary principles and to bring it as close as possible to the idea of truth....With regard to the will, on the other hand, it is not a question of knowledge but of action...*The essence of reason is lawfulness, that of will is freedom—and herein they are diametrically opposed.*]

This is not a bad account of *the secondary* Will, consequent on the establishment of the antithesis of Action and Intellection; but a most erroneous view of ~~the~~ a *Will* in itself, as the universal Antecedent.¹

21   p 112, pencil | I §133

Wenn der Astronom auf Jahrhunderte hinaus Sonn- und Mondfinsternisse vorhergesagt, so ist diss keine Divination, es geschieht zufolge eines steten Naturgesetzes...Das wahre Vorhersehungsvermögen ist das *prophetische*, gleichsam als ob ein höherer Geist uns *] in den Spiegel der Zukunft blicken lasse. Wir finden solche Männer im alten und neuen Testament. Und hier die Frage: Sollten wohl jene tugendhafte und fromme Männer, welche die Schicksale der Menschen und Völker im Spiegel der Religion betrachten, sie nicht vorhersagen können?

BL). Aristotle apparently nowhere uses the analogy of impregnation in this context, but key passages C might have in mind are e.g. *Posterior Analytics* 99b–100b (in which ἕξις is used of the innate capacity of apprehension of immediate first principles) and *De anima* 417b (in which, in a literal sense, the part of the male parent in the formation of an offspring capable of sensation is mentioned), 418a–432a. Cf *CN* IV 5133 ff 99ᵛ–98.

19² Locke *Essay Concerning Human Understanding* esp bk I ch 2. Cf **11** n 1, above. See also *CL* II 678–703 (esp 693) and *AR* (1825) 72–3.

20¹ Cf *SM* (*CC*) 67n: "I know indeed but one other truth of equal worth and pregnancy—and that is the Primacy of the Will, as deeper than and (in order of *thought*) antecedent to, Reason." Cf BÖHME **178** and *C&S* (*CC*) 182.

[When the astronomer has predicted solar and lunar eclipses for centuries to come, he does not, however, exercise [the power of] divination; these occur according to a fixed law of nature... The true power of foresight is that of *prophecy*, as if, so to speak, a higher spirit permitted us a glimpse into the mirror of the future. We find such persons in the Old and New Testament. Hence the question: Should not those virtuous and devout men who viewed the destinies of man and nations through the mirror of religion, be able to predict them?]

* in what one instance? E. should have given one example of the *Fact* instead of referring to *Persons*. The moral world has its laws as well as the physical—and true Religion is the Science of the former/.[1] Hence the Prophecies of the Bible are all *conditional* in proportion as they are particular.—[2]

22 p 113 | ɪ § 134

Es sind die geistige Mittheilungen solcher, die sich mit Liebe und Innigkeit vertrauen, selbst aus weiter Ferne. Es sind die dunkle Ahnungen von dem Tode geliebter Freunde, Verwandten und Eltern. In einem Lichtgewand schweben die Gestalten an der Seele vorüber und füllen uns mit ihrem Andenken.

[These are the spiritual messages of those who entrust each other with their love and devotion even at a great distance. They are the dark presentiments of the deaths of dear friends, relatives, and parents. These figures float past the soul in a robe of light and fill us with their memory.]

Nothing more an antipathy to a truly poetic Mind, than poetic Frippery in philosophy. Light from a Robe I can understand; but what is a Robe of Light?[1]

23 p 150, pencil | ɪ § 182

Der Organismus involvirt ein selbstthätiges inneres Prinzip.... Wenn ein Rad stokt, so steht die ganze Uhr still, da hingegen der Organismus seine innere Missverhältnisse aus innerer Kraft auszugleichen sucht.

[The organism involves an independent inner principle.... When one wheel stops turning, then the whole watch stops, whereas an organism tries to adjust its inner disturbances through its inner power.]

21[1] See *AR* (1825) 15–16.

21[2] On religion as "the Consideration of the Particular and Individual" see *SM* (*CC*) 62, 64.

22[1] But Eschenmayer's phrase has biblical sanction. Cf *AR* (1825) 16–17:

"The scheme of grace and truth that *became* through Jesus Christ, the faith that *looks down into* the perfect law of liberty, has 'light for its *garment*' [Ps 104.2 var]: its very '*robe* is righteousness' [Isa 61.10]."

May not the same be said of a Fly-wheel in Water-machines, by which the Machine accomodates itself to the too much and too little?

24 p 152, pencil | I §184

Der Chymiker kann zwar einwenden, dass gerade nach aufgelöster Form, z. B. bei der Fäulniss des Fleisches, eine neue Formenwelt, nemlich die Infusorien zum Vorschein kommen, und somit der umgekehrte Satz richtiger scheine, dass vielmehr die Mischung höher stehe als die Form. Allein ich finde die ganze Infusorienwelt von weit geringerem Werth, als den Muskel, wenn er gleich nur Theil eines Ganzen ist.

[No doubt the chemist may object that particularly after the dissolution of form, as for instance in the case of putrid meat, there emerges a new world of forms, namely the infusoria, and therefore the opposite thesis might appear more accurate, that composition is superior to form. However, I consider the whole world of infusoria to be of much smaller value than the muscle, even if the latter is only part of a whole.]

a whimsical Objection as whimsically answered. And where are the proofs that the Infusory animals are any more the Product of Putridity, than the Fish are of the Rivers, or Caterpillars of Leaves?[1] All the Attempts at Proof, that I have yet seen, are drawn from ignorance against knowlege and analogy.[2]

25 p ⁻1, pencil, badly rubbed | 24 textus

The Gobe-mouche[a] or fly-catcher/ the least and most beautiful of Lizards, all green and gold[1]—passes its whole life in pursuit of fleas, flies &c; and after death [? finds/has] all its glittering colors, changed to a dusky grey—apply to fashionable Virtues—184[2]

26 p 165, cropped | I §195

Die Elemente, die uns die chymische Analyse liefert, sind im Flüssigen wie im Festen als nähere Bestandtheile, *Fibernstoff*,

[a] The reading is uncertain: "Gobe-mouche/Gat-mouth/Gap-mouth"

24[1] Infusoria—a class of protozoa found in infusions of decaying animal or vegetable matter. C was familiar with Oken's classification and treatment of various types of infusoria in OKEN *Lehrbuch der Naturgeschichte* V; see also *CN* IV 4984 esp f 87ᵛn. Cf *CL* V 422.

24[2] On analogy and the misuse of it see e.g. GOLDFUSS **8** and n 1.

25[1] If, as seems likely, "Gobe-mouche" (flycatcher, bird or plant) is indeed what C wrote, he refers to *Lacerta ocellata*, a lizard of spectacular emerald green with "eyed" spots, which C certainly encountered in the Mediterranean: see e.g. *CN* II 2198 (in Sicily).

25[2] I.e. the "fashionable virtues" (the green and gold) turn to nothing at death.

Eiweissstoff und das wässerige Extract. Beyde zusammen lassen sich auf die chymische Basen reduciren, nemlich Sauer- Stik- Wasser- und Kohlenstoff, die als Urstoffe sowohl der inorganischen als der organischen Natur gemein sind.

[The elements furnished to us by chemical analysis are, as proximate [i.e. pending further analysis] constituents, in liquids as in solids, *fibre, albumen, and the watery extract.* Both alike may be reduced to the chemical bases, namely oxygen, nitrogen, hydrogen, and carbon, which as primal "stuffs" are common to inorganic as well as organic nature.]

Festina lente![1] No[t] yet—neither Sulp[hur] nor Phosphorus n[or] the Base of Lime. It is not even like[ly] that any true Base is reduc[i]ble practically: however plausib[le] it may be, that they subsist in a series of vary[ing] proportions of Carbon + azote, or of − and + Magnetism.[2]

27   p −1, referring to p 170 | I §199

Das dritte System bilden die Kopforgane, grosses, kleines Gehirn, verlängertes Mark sammt ihren Häuten. Die Form ist nun die höchste geworden, und hat sich am weitesten von allen physischen Formen entfernt. Die Intensität und Kraft des organischen Lebens- prinzips erreicht ihr Maximum. Im Kopf liegen die eigentliche Animalitätsorgane. Die Functionen derselben nennt man Sensation und Locomotion. Das Gehirn ist der Wendepunct zwischen dem geistigen und organischen Leben, und zugleich der Träger und das Instrument der geistigen Functionen, und in dieser Beziehung nennen wir es *Seelenorgan.*

[The third system is formed of the organs of the head: the cerebrum, the cerebellum, and the medulla oblongata, together with their membranes. The

26[1] "Hurry slowly"—proverbial.

26[2] Eschenmayer is correct in saying that chemical analysis has shown albu- men, etc to be composed of C, H, N, and O. These four elements are not only the fundamental elements in organic chemis- try; they are also the elements in the compass of nature proposed in STEFFENS *Grundzüge der philosophischen Natur- wissenschaft.* In the compass of nature, however, they were the *dynamic* con- stituents of all chemical substances (see e.g. *CN* III 4420), and are not shown by laboratory analysis to be the "primal matter" of inorganic nature. Hence C is correct: S, P, and calcium (the base of lime) had not then—and have not even now—been reduced chemically, though *dynamic* chemistry made it plausible that they were constituted primarily of powers symbolised by carbon and nitrogen—a proposition unacceptable to most English chemists of the day. (In *Elements of Chemical Philosophy*—1811—Humphry Davy classified sulphur and phosphorus among the undecompounded substances, along with H, O, C, chlorine, and the metals. For his discussion of S and P see *Collected Works* IV 200–20.) For C on sulphur cf BROWNE *Works* 29. Cf GOLDFUSS 2.

form has now become the highest and has reached the point furthest from all physical forms. The intensity and power of the organic life-principle reaches its maximum. It is in the head that the actual organs of animal existence lie. Their functions are called sensation and locomotion. The brain is the turning-point between spiritual and organic life and, at the same time, it is the transmitter and instrument of spiritual functions; in this connexion we call it the *soul-organ*.]

P. 170. All the difficulties in Psychology (i.e. in the attempt to harmonize the facts of common sense with the laws of the *Conceivable*) seem reducible to the one mystery of the KIND-diversity (= heterogeneity) of the Body material and of the Soul or Spirit intellectual. We cannot conceive the union of hardness, figure, and discerpibility[1] with Consciousness, memory, volition, pain &c in the same, as as constituting the same, Subject or individuum.—If not, the same heterogeneity renders all action and reaction of the one and on the other equally inconceivable. I can as easily understand the oneness of the Body and Soul, as the relation of the former to the latter as its *organ*. Both arc alike inconceivable. The scheme of Idealism, or psilo-phænomenonism (esse sensuale = percipi)[2] makes indeed easy work of it. But this is = to deny, not to reconcile, the facts of common sense. It is against the Faith of Nature, which not having been *acquired* by experience can never be destroyed by argument. Now Q[y].—Do Are not these inexplicabilities of our making while we assumed that Perception is = passio, and mere self-modification?— Give the Soul Percipiency universally (genere) & let self-perception (= Sensation) be one[a] of its forms—and all is solved.—And why not? is to percipiency not supposed in self-percipiency?[3]

> [a] Here the note has reached the foot of the page; C has continued above 25 with "*(from the last line)*"

27[1] Separability. A use of the word is ascribed by *OED* to Henry More in 1682.

27[2] "Phenomenism" is a more usual form. C compounded ψίλος with other roots: see DONNE *Sermons* COPY B **8** n 3 and HOOKER *Works* **22**. The primary meaning is "mere, bare, naked" (as in "psilanthropy", for which see CHANNING **1** n 3). "Psilo-phænomenonism" evidently means "a theory of perception that rests *merely* upon the evidence of phenomena", as is implied by C's modification of Berkeley's *esse est percipi* to "to be, in terms of the senses, is to be perceived".

27[3] See *CN* IV 4540—quoted in *P*

Lects (1949) 60–1—in which C states that the contradictions inherent in the systems of idealism and materialism—"A position, which occurred to me 20 years ago as an objection to Idealism (as Berkley's &c)"—stem from the presupposition that "*Perception* is but a sort of, or at least an immediate derivative from, *Sensation*", whereas he assumes that "Percipiency in *genere* is an attribute of the Soul, and that sensation is nothing more than a species of Perception modified by the Object...". Cf *CN* III 3605 and n (c Aug–Sept 1809), and *Logic* (*CC*) 66. See also FICHTE *Bestimmung* **5** (at n 1).

28 p 214, pencil, cropped | ɪ § 244

Die Zirbel, in welche wir den geometrischen Ort der Gehirnthätig-
keit in ihrem Mittelpuncte sezen, ist endlich das merkwürdige
Organ, das einzig jene harte, feste Concremente enthält, die in
Gestalt kleiner, gelblicher, halbdurchsichtiger Sandkörnchen...
auch schon in Embryon sich finden...
Die Erscheinung dieser Sandkörnchen ist in der That sehr merk-
würdig. Wie werden sie als ein offenbar ganz inorganisches Produkt
im höchsten Organ gebildet, und zwar so, dass sie sich ganz losse um
die Basis jenes conischen Körperchens, das wir Zirbel nennen,
herlagern?

[The pineal gland, in which we place the geometrical location of brain-activity
in its central part, is finally that curious organ which alone contains those
hard, solid concretions which are already to be found...in the embryo in the
form of small, yellow, half-translucent grains of sand...
These grains of sand are indeed very curious phenomena. How are they
formed in the highest organ as an apparently quite inorganic product in such
a way that they group themselves quite loosely around the base of that small
conic structure which we call the pineal gland?]

The same Thought [i]n another form struck me more than 20 years
ago[1]—[v]iz. that these Sands afforded a sort of tactus constans[2]
realizing and steadying the mental products, as single Touch to the
Hand and external Skin.[3]

29 p 245, cropped | ɪ § 273

Noch sonderbarer ist das in der Geschichte des Strassburger
Mädchens bemerkte Phänomen, dass sie auf beträchtliche Ent-
fernungen ihrem Arzte und ihren Verwandten electrische Schläge
ertheilte.

[Still more curious is the phenomenon observed in the history of the girl from
Strasbourg, that at considerable distances she dealt electric shocks to her
physician and to her relatives.]

O Strassburg! Strassburg! Tow[n] endowed with the power of
creative Seein[g.][1]

28[1] I.e. in the early 1800s: see e.g. *CN*
ɪ 1039, 1827. Or in 1805: see *CN* ɪɪ 2399.
28[2] "Constant touch".
28[3] C considered the tactual sense of
great importance in any theory of
knowledge: see Böhme **24** n 9 and e.g. *P
Lects* Lect 3 (1949) 115. Cf **10** and **28** n 1,
above; see also **9** and n 1, above.
29[1] The Harmonics of Strasbourg,

directed by the Marquis de Puységur (see
Eichhorn *Alte Testament* **38** n 2), was
one of the many societies set up in France
by the followers of Mesmer. (Strasbourg
was a French city until 1871.) The aims
and methods of this and other societies
are discussed in Kluge *Versuch einer
Darstellung des animalischen Magnetis-
mus* pp 51–6.

30 p 247, pencil | I § 274

So gewiss der Organismus eine aus vielen mannigfaltigen Organen und Systemen bestehende Einheit ist, wovon jedes einem spezifischen Lebensgeseze gehorcht, so gewiss müssen diese spezifische Lebensgeseze, wenn ein Ganzes daraus werden soll, in einem allgemeinen Gesetz zusammenhängen. Aber dieses allgemeine Gesetz ist der unendlichen Formel des Analytikers gleich, die, weil das Unendliche nicht in der Erfahrung gegeben ist, auch nicht aus ihr abstrahirt seyn kann. Hier tritt das Bedürfniss der rein spekulativen Naturkenntniss ein, die ihre allgemeine Formeln oder Prinzipien aus der Idee selbst empfängt, und eben dadurch auch sich von allen getrübten Sinnenreflexen unabhängig macht. Um uns diss recht fühlbar zu machen, bedarf es eines so kräftigen Anstosses, wie der thierische Magnetismus ist, der unsern gewohnten Cyklus völlig durchbricht, und, da ihn keiner unter uns sich als Factum verhehlen kann, uns auf ein höheres Leben hinweisst, als das ist, was sich unsern Sinnen manifestirt.

[And as certainly as the organism is a unity consisting of manifold organs and systems, each of which obeys a specific vital law, just as certainly must these specific vital laws be linked in a universal law if they are to form a whole. But this universal law resembles the logician's formula of the infinite, which since the infinite is not given in experience cannot be abstracted from it. It is here that the necessity for a purely speculative natural philosophy becomes evident, which takes its general formulas or principles from the ideal itself, and by this very means emancipates itself from all sullied sensual reflexes. In order to bring this point home, such a powerful impulse as animal magnetism is necessary, which breaks through the customary internal circle and—since no one among us can deny it as a fact—suggests a higher life than that which manifests itself to our senses.]

Beautifully proved as a *Theory* of the Phænomena if these could be shewn to be *facts*[1]

31 pp 248–9, pencil | I §§ 275, 276

Da die Erscheinungen des Magnetismus theils im leiblichen, theils im geistigen Organismus sich äussern, so werden auch die Prinzipien, die zu seiner Erklärung dienen, theils aus der Physiologie, theils aus

30[1] For C's views on animal magnetism see *IS* 44–51, *P Lects* Lect 2 (1949) 104–5, 423–4 nn 16, 17, and e.g. *CN* IV 4512, 4908. See also BÖHME **26** n 3 and marginalia on JAHRBÜCHER *der Medicin* als *Wissenschaft*, JUNG *Theorie der Geister-kunde*, KLUGE *Versuch einer Darstellung des animalischen Magnetismus*, LOEWE *A Treatise of Animal Magnetism*, and MESMER.

der Psychologie genommen werden müssen. Zu dem physiologischen Prinzip rechne ich die Annahme *eines organischen Aethers mit bestimmten Eigenschaften*, zu dem psychischen Prinzip rechne ich *die Seele als unendliche Potenz*....

Man hat diese Potenz in unsern Physiologien bisher nur beiläufig erwähnt....Denn die *Qualitates occultae* seyen ohnehin aus jeder gesundern Logik verbannt, und nur das könne wahr und real seyn, *was* man sehe, höre, rieche, schmecke und betaste...aber sollte diss nicht eben so wahr und real seyn, *wodurch* man sieht, hört, schmeckt, riecht und betastet? Wenn diese Sinnfunctionen selbst zu den sinnlichen Qualitäten jenes organischen Aethers gehören, so scheint es lächerlich, zu erwarten, dass sie sich wie das Gesehene, Gehörte und Verochene verhalten sollen.

[Since the phenomena of magnetism manifest themselves partly in the physical, partly in the spiritual, organism, the principles that serve for its explanation must also derive partly from physiology, partly from psychology. I consider the hypothesis of *an organic aether with distinct characteristics* as belonging to the physiological principle, and I consider *the soul as infinite potential* as belonging to the psychic principle...

Until now this potential has received only passing mention in our physiologies.... For the *occult qualities* were at all events banned from every healthy logic and only what one saw, heard, smelled, tasted, and touched was supposed to be true and real...but should not that *whereby* one sees, hears, tastes, smells, and touches be equally true and real? Given that these sensory functions belong to the sensory qualities of the organic aether, it seems ridiculous to expect that they should behave like that which is seen, heard, or smelled.]

In the name of Common Sense, what can an *Organic* Aether mean? Not an organized Aether: for the terms are contradictory. What then? Answer. A *somewhat*. And then too the *cunning* logic by which this Somewhat is first taken for granted, without a word said— Mum!—then, how clearly the Author proves the unreasonableness of expecting to see, smell, or touch it—for why, by the very definition it is invisible, intangible &c!—[1]

32   p 250, pencil | I § 276

Unser ganzer peripherischer Sinnapparat scheint...dazu vorhanden, die unzählig viele Sensationen, die ihm eingedrücket werden, in

31[1] Cf **13**, above. C consistently attacked the animal magnetists for uncritically taking the magnetic agent (aether or the magnetic fluid) to be a fact rather than a mere hypothesis. C ex-

presses this opposition to the theory of the magnetic fluid in several annotations in KLUGE and MESMER and in a note on JUNG.

unendlich kleinen Abdrücken und Ziffern im Gehirn aufzubewahren, damit sie jederzeit als Gedächtnissspuren für die Seele in Bereitschaft stehen.... Die Wahrheit dieser Behauptung geht aus der Thatsache hervor, dass manche andere Nerven für die Sinnen vicariiren, wie bey den Nachtwandlern und den Magnetisirten; aber alle diese Eindrücke sind alsdann mit keiner Rükerinnerung verbunden.

[Our whole peripheral sense apparatus seems to exist so that the innumerable sensations that are impressed on it may be stored in the brain in infinitely small impressions and ciphers in order to be readily available to the soul as traces of memory.... The truth of this statement is evidenced by the fact that a number of other nerves perform the function of the senses, as in the case of sleep-walkers and mesmerised individuals; however, all these impressions are not subsequently connected with any recollections.]

False in fact. The Clairvoyant remembers on Tuesday all that had occurred during *the same* STATE on the day, or week, or month before.[1]

33 p 282, pencil | II Reine Psychologie § 290

Die Vermögen der *Gefühlsseite* sind *Einbildungskraft, Gefühlvermögen* und *Phantasie*.... Alle drey streben *zur Idee der Schönheit* zurück, und daraus bildet sich der Satz: *Das Schöne kann nur gefühlt werden.**

[The emotive faculties are *imagination, feeling*, and *fancy*.... All three seek to return *to the idea of beauty*, and from this derives the postulate: *the beautiful can only be felt*.]

* It would, ὡς ἐμοιγε δοκει, be far more just and appropriate to say: DAS SCHÖNE MUSS AUCH GEFÜHLT WERDEN.[1]

34 p 284, pencil | II § 291

Was der Philosoph als nothwendige Bedingung desselben, oder als ?*] nothwendige Folge davon erkennt, muss eben so gewiss seyn als es selbst.

[What the philosopher recognises as a necessary condition or consequence of this fact must be equally certain as the fact itself.]

32[1] C read critically the contemporary literature about clairvoyance: see e.g. *CN* IV 4908, in which he refers to J. C. Passavant *Untersuchung über den Lebens Magnetismus und das Hellsehen* (Frankfurt am Main 1821). See also *TT* 1 May 1823, AURELIUS **17** n 1, JUNG i 106–8

and nn, KANT *Vermischte Schriften* COPY C II 250–1. For C's clairvoyance see e.g. AURELIUS **17** n 3 and *CL* III 423–4.
33[1] "In my opinion, at least... Beauty must also be felt." For C on beauty see e.g. *CL* VI 811–13; and cf *Dejection* lines 37–8: *PW* (EHC) I 364.

* Will experience sanction this—that a *Fact* having been ascertained, there results the ⟨equal⟩ certainty of the only *theory* of the Fact, that I am able to conceive?—[1]

35 p 390, pencil | II § 387

Nach *Plato* sind die Ideen Urbilder, welche der Seele eingebohren sind....Nach *Aristoteles* hingegen ist die Seele eine *Tabula rasa*, die sich allmählig aus der Erfahrung fülle, und wobey uns nichts zukomme, als die Verarbeitung des Stoffs.

[According to *Plato*, the Ideas are primal images that are innate in the soul....According to *Aristotle*, however, the soul is a *tabula rasa*, which is gradually filled through experience, and leaves us nothing to do but to assimilate the material.]

I deem this a mistaken assertion. Aristotle in his Tabula rasa speaks merely of the mind relative to its distinct consciousness, and attributes to the outward things sometimes an impregnating, sometimes an obstetric power, but not a *sigillative* mechanism.[1]

It is too often overlooked, that the Tabula rasa is but a *Simile*, obiter, and no Simile quadrates.[2]

36 p 405 | II § 397

Das Selbstbewusstseyn ist schon für sich eine Trübung der Seele, in welcher das leibliche Prinzip seinen Antheil geltend gemacht hat....*Das Vermögen, dem er am meisten einverleibt ist das Gefühlvermögen, und zwar in diesem Ausdruck das Selbstgefühl.*

[Self-consciousness as such is always a dimming of the soul, in which the corporeal principle has asserted itself....*The faculty which it incorporates most of all is the faculty of feeling, that is to say, the consciousness of self.*]

Qy. A confounding of Self-consciousness with the consciousness of Self.

37 p 445, pencil | III Angewandte Psychologie § 426

Ueber dem Unendlichen steht das Ewige, über dem Menschlichen das Heilige; In ihm vollendet das Wesen sich, und die Ideen selbst erscheinen dann nur als Formen. So wird dann auch der Idealismus

---

34[1] That is, there may be other theories to explain the fact differently, but they have not yet come to mind.

35[1] Cf **19** and n 1, above.

35[2] A simile "incidentally" or "*en passant*". Cf "No simile goes on all fours" as in N Q f 7ᵛ. See also *C&S* (*CC*) 86 n 3 and *Logic* (*CC*) 132, 143, and CHALMERS **5** and n 1.

*] zulezt formal, das Wahre, Schöne und Gute sind sich nicht mehr genügend, sie weisen zurück auf die lezte Fülle der Vollendung *in Gott. Alle Dinge in Gott anschauen—das ist das System aller Systeme.*

[Above the infinite there is the eternal, above the human there is the holy; in it essence perfects itself and the ideas themselves appear then merely as forms. Thus idealism also ultimately becomes formal; the true, the beautiful, and the good are no longer self-sufficient but refer back to the ultimate plenitude of perfection *in God. To contemplate all things in God—that is the system of systems.*]

* But what does this prove but the absurdity of not beginning in God? Then the Ideas instead of going out into formalism would have kindled into, would have been the kindlings, in the original double sense of the word, the Scintillations and the Offspring, of Reality[1]— the Plenitude in the Absolute, the Sons of the Morn[2]

38   p 488, pencil | III § 458

Wer mit mir eine urbildliche und eine abbildliche Seele unterscheidet, und zugleich jenes Wechselverhältniss zwischen dem freyen und nothwendigen Prinzip annimmt, was freylich auf dem psychologischen Standpunct nur als Axiom erscheint, der wird auch einsehen, dass die Idee der Wahrheit, die der urbildlichen Seele innwohnt, wenn sie von jenem nothwendigen Prinzip differenziirt wird, in unendlichvielen Reflexen, d. h. Verhältnissen, Proportionen und Gesezen sich in der Objectivität darstellen müsse; Er wird einsehen, dass eben durch die Sollizitation des fremden Prinzips die urbildliche Seele in eine abbildliche sich verwandlen, und diese in zwey Hälften—in eine subjective und objective sich trennen werde.

[Whoever shares my distinction between an archetypal and a copy-soul and simultaneously assumes that interchange between the free and necessary principle (which, of course, appears only as an axiom from the physiological point of view) will also realise that the idea of truth inhabiting the archetypal soul, when differentiated from the necessary principle must express itself in the objective, in an infinite number of reflexes: i.e., relations, proportions, and laws. He will see that precisely through the attractive force of the foreign principle, the archetypal soul will be transformed into a copy-soul, which will divide itself into a subjective and an objective half.]

Was the transformation good or evil? If good, then the *Copy-Soul* must be better than the original Prototype Soul: & we have the

---

37[1] See the use of "Kindle-fuel" in *CL* II 680 (18 Feb 1801) and cf *CN* II 3136. Cf Aurelius **39** and n 1, particularly C's striking use of ἀναζωπυρεῖ in *CN* II 3136.

The image may have been called up by Eschenmayer's unexpected metaphor in **16** n 1 (*anzufachen*).

37[2] Isa 14.12 (var).

Schellingian Atheism.[1] If evil, how is the adulteration of a perfect free Essence by a blind and heterogeneous Inferior ₽ Conceivable? The more so, as the latter is a non-reality, and the former, the prototypal Soul (p. 23 et passim) remains unbetrübt,[2] impassive and transcendently one!—Esch. must either embrace my system, or suffer his own *Attempt* at a system to lie stifled in its own contradictions.[3]

S. T. C.

39   p 493, pencil | III § 462

Wenn alle Veränderungen der Seele, nemlich Gedanken, Gefühle und Handlungen für das Zeitleben vorherbestimmt sind, so fällt die Freiheit des Willens gänzlich weg. Denn setzen wir—die Seele wirke *] nach eigenem Willen ohne eine Prädisposition, so würde sie im Augenblick nicht mehr zu ihrer objectiven Welt passen.

[If all modifications of the soul, namely thoughts, feelings, and actions, are preordained for the temporal existence, then freedom of will is totally eliminated. For let us suppose that the soul would act according to its own will without a predisposition, from that moment on it would no longer correspond to its objective world.]

* This does not follow of necessity. Let a Boy stand in the midst of a Brook, and let both *have* and exert the most perfect Free Will in splashing the water in any conceivable direction—the course of the Brook remains as calculable as ever.

40   p 494, pencil | III §§ 462, 463

Er sagt, man stelle sich zwey Uhren vor, die vollkommen gleich gehen: diss kann nur auf dreyerley Weise geschehen, 1) durch einen

38[1] On the matter of Schelling's pantheism the marginalia on Schelling are unexpectedly silent; but an annotation of c 1815 notices passages in which "the *Spinozism* of Schelling's System first betrays itself". SCHELLING *System des transscendentalen Idealismus* (Tübingen 1800) p ⁻2, referring to p 54. The phrase "Schellingian Atheism" reflects a turning-point in C's admiration in early 1818—hence the ambiguous treatment of Schelling in the Philosophical Lectures: implications of Spinozism uttered in May 1818 (*CL* IV 863) had by Sept 1818 become a charge of "Hylozoic Atheism", and in Nov 1818 a judgement of "a mere Pantheism...this sort of Plotinised

Spinozism...this new hylozoism". *CL* IV 874, 883.

38[2] "Untroubled." For "p. 23" see **3** textus, above.

38[3] C often complained of "the impossibility [in the work of the *Naturphilosophen*] of connecting the Relative with the Absolute". STEFFENS *Grundzüge der philosophischen Naturwissenschaft* pp 46–7. C believed that his own system resolved the contradictions inherent in the *Naturphilosophie* by maintaining an original unity in the absolute (the Prothesis, God, or the absolute Identity of the Real and the Actual) prior to its division into polar entities. See e.g. *CN* III 4449 esp ff 25ᵛ, 30ᵛ and nn.

gegenseitigen Einfluss....2) Durch Beystand, indem beständig ein geschikter Künstler...sie stellet...oder 3) wenn die beyde Uhren so künstlich und richtig gemacht sind: dass man für alle Folgen von ihrer Uebereinstimmung versichert seyn kann (*systema harmoniae praestabilitae*). Das erste verwirft *Leibniz* aus dem Grunde, dass materielle Körper sich immateriellen und umgekehrt nicht mittheilen können; das zweite verwirft er, weil wir zur Erklärung einen beständigen *Deum ex machina* annehmen müssten. Es bleibe daher nur die Annahme des dritten Systems übrig....Aber es gibt eine andere schöne Bedeutung davon (*Harmonia praestabilita*) welche alle Schwierigkeiten löst....Die Seele ist an sich rein, immateriell und unsterblich, aber sie wird mit einem ihr entgegengesetzten Princip vereinigt, und jetzt entsteht erst ihr Zeitleben....Durch diese ursprüngliche Vereinigung mit dem nothwendigen Princip ist für das ganze Zeitleben das Aufeinanderwirken des materiellen und immateriellen, und der unmittelbare Einfluss beyder vermittelt ....Wie der Stein und die Seele einander sich mittheilen, wäre ganz unbegreiflich und gegen alles Gesetz der Stetigkeit, wenn nicht der Organismus als indifferenziirendes dazwischen träte...Zwischen Materie und Wesen liegt die Form...Zwischen Mechanismus und Spiritualismus der Organismus. Wie der Werth des Mittelgliedes gefasst wird, ist die Annahme des Systems des Einflusses keiner Schwierigkeit mehr angesetzt.

[He [Leibniz] says: imagine two clocks which keep precisely the same time; this can happen in only three ways: 1) by mutual influence...2) by outside assistance: a skilful craftsman constantly adjusts them...or 3) if both clocks are made so correctly and with such art that there can be a certitude of their agreement at all future times (a system of pre-established harmony). Leibniz rejects the first [possibility] on the grounds that material objects cannot communicate with immaterial objects, and vice versa; he rejects the second because, in order to explain it, we should have to postulate a constant *deus ex machina*. There remained therefore only the acceptance of the third system....It [the pre-established harmony] has, however, another lovely meaning, which solves all difficulties....The soul is in itself pure, immaterial, and immortal, but it becomes united with an opposite principle, and only now does its temporal life begin....This original union with the necessary principle mediates for the entire temporal life the interaction between the material and the immaterial, and the direct influence of both....How the stone and the soul communicate with each other would be totally incomprehensible and contrary to the entire law of continuity if the organism did not supervene as the unifying [lit. "undifferentiating"] power...Between matter and essence comes form...between mechanism and spiritualism [comes] organism. Once the value of the mediator is understood, the system of [mutual] influence will be accepted without further difficulty.]

§ 463. Precious Logic 'pon 'onor!—A beautiful View, or Scheme of Leib⁵ Pre-est. Harmony indeed![1] i.e. It asserts the first and implies the second of the two hypotheses, the impossibility of which is the sole ground of the third—viz. the Pre-est. Harm. itself!

41   p 548 | III § 497

Wir haben neun primitive Einheiten in unserem Decimalsystem, und diese Zahl, obgleich die Einheit in einem Zahlensystem eine willkührliche ist, scheint doch kein blinder Griff des menschlichen Verstandes gewesen zu seyn....*Neun* ist daher nicht nur die Grundzahl in einem Zahlensystem, sondern...auch die Grundzahl der Natur überhaupt.

[We have nine primary units in our decimal system and, even though the units in a numerical system are arbitrary, this number does not seem after all to have been a blind invention of the human mind....*Nine* is therefore not only the cardinal number in a given numeric system but...also the cardinal number of nature in general.]

9 and the whole 9 as an additional 1?[1]

42   p 558, pencil | III § 504

Beim Uranus hat die Abweichung wieder ein + Zeichen, und es kann daher gefragt werden, ob nicht noch ein entfernterer, der Stelle in der Progression 4 + 128.3 zugehöriger, Planet mit dem—Zeichen eine Konjunction mit dem Uranus eingehen werde.

[Since the divergence of Uranus has once again a plus sign, one could ask whether a still more remote planet with a minus sign and having a place in the progression 4 + 128.3 might not enter into a conjunction with Uranus.]

If so, what becomes of the tripolar magnet? + − +?[1]

40[1] C's fullest statement about Leibniz's "pre-established harmony" occurs in *BL* ch 8 (*CC*) I 130–1, repeated in *P Lects* Lect 8 (1949) 350; cf Lect 13, pp 383–4. For Leibniz's doctrine of pre-established harmony see *Theodicée*, especially the 1st, 2nd, and 3rd "Éclaircissement du Nouveau Système"—Pt I §§ 59, 61, 62, 66; Pt III §§ 291, 352, 353; and *Monadologie* §§ 51, 52 ff: in *Opera philosophica* ed J. E. Erdmann (1839–40) 131–6, 519–21, 590, 606, 709–12. Cf also MAASS *Versuch über die Einbildungskraft* (Halle & Leipzig 1797) pp ⁻2–⁻3.
41[1] See **42**, below.

42[1] In a preceding section (§ 503) Eschenmayer had outlined a plan of ordering the planets of the solar system according to three groups, each of which forms an independent system, and illustrates his meaning with a diagram of a "tripolar magnet" with two outer positive poles, the inner pole being negative. C questions Eschenmayer's postulation of a "still more remote planet with a minus sign", which would then yield, in the third system, an extra minus sign; in the tripolar scheme, Saturn and Jupiter acted as the two positive poles to the negative pole Uranus.

43 pp 558–9, pencil

It is curious at least, that his Philosophy obliged Pythagoras, to make the Solar System = 10, tho' his imperfect Astrognosy reduced him to the shift of including the Moon, ~~and~~ imagining an Antiχθων and taking the whole as a completory Unit[1]—Sun, Mer. Ven. Earth, Moon, Mars, Jupiter, Saturn, Antichthon = 9+Solar Syst = 1 = 10²

44 p 564, pencil | III §508

Und so fällt unter gleicher Voraussetzung die Hyperbel der Nebelsternordnung zu. Bey dieser ist aber der grosse früher bemerkte Unterschied, dass sie keine sphärische Einheit, sondern ein zusammenhängendes Gewebe von ganzen Systemen darstellt. Daran erinnert uns jenes milchweisse ChrystallLicht, das wie ein Gürtel um den ganzen Himmel gezogen ist. Ist es nicht etwa eine mit Systemen ausgefüllte Hyperbel?

[And thus according to the same hypothesis the hyperbola belongs to the category of nebulae. This is, however, the significant distinction pointed out earlier, that it does not represent a spheric entity, but a connected network of whole systems. We are reminded of this fact by that milk-white crystal light which engirdles the whole sky. Is this not a sort of hyperbola filled with systems?]

But it is *not* a girdle, but ends in a gaping Slit.[1]

43[1] This note can be glossed by *P Lects* Lect 2 (1949) 99: "Pythagoras held that there were ten bodies...in the universe...the planets then known, the moon, the sun, the comets, and so forth. These unfortunately made up but nine, in consequence of which he made up a tenth...which he called 'antichthon' or counter earth." For the Pythagorean tetractys—"the set of four", also the figure of ten, being "the source of all things"—see BÖHME 6 n 10.

43[2] In order to reach his ideal number 9 (see **41**, above) Eschenmayer had to resort to an arbitrary position, just as Pythagoras had to invent the antichthon to bring the number of planets to the perfect figure 10. Thus he asserts (pp 557–60) that although each of the three groups of planets has four planets the four asteroids then known must be regarded as forming one unit, thus making the total 9 rather than 12, including the hypothetical planet of **42** textus.

44[1] C's appeal is to his own direct observation. He challenged Kant on this point in KANT *Vermischte Schriften* COPY C **2**.

ETERNAL PUNISHMENT

Eternal Punishment Proved to Be Not Suffering, But Privation; and Immortality Dependent on Spiritual Regeneration: the whole argued on the words and harmony of Scripture, and embracing every text bearing on the subject.... By a member of the Church of England. In an appendix are given extracts from Jer. Taylor, Hooker, Barrow, Howe, Locke, Tillotson, Watts, & Leland, &c. London 1817. 8°.

British Museum C 126 g 3

"S. T. C." label on the title-page verso. John Duke Coleridge's monogram on p ⁻4. Pp 83–6 remained unopened in 1977, but C has written his notes to the end of the text (p 240) and one note on the 40-page Appendix.

MS TRANSCRIPT. (a) VCL MS 17: transcript by DC "copied from Dean Trench's manuscript". Richard Chevenix Trench (1807–86) was dean of Westminster 1856, abp of Dublin 1864; philologist, one of the proposers of *OED*. (b) University of Texas (Humanities Research Center): transcript by J. H. Green in a letter to EHC 13 May 1879.

DATE. Uncertain: possibly 1823–6 if notebook entries parallel to 1 and 4 (c Sept 1823) and 15 (Aug 1826) are indicative.

1   pp ⁻2–⁻1

The Writer of this Work, a Tinman of Hornsey,[1] has injured his own cause by his gross crass Materialism. The Faith, however, that best befits a Christian, and is ~~re~~ with least difficulty reconciled with Scripture, ~~is~~ may be thus expressed. The declarations of Christ ~~and of the Apostles~~ neither permit me to assert the utter *cessation* of ⟨the⟩

---

[1] The book itself gives little account of the anonymous author: only that he lived in a village (pp vi–vii), and that he had been from an early age employed in "learning and labouring truly to get his own living in a state of life" that was incompatible with polished refinements of language (p [v]); why "This learned Theban" (13), "whoever he was" (5), is associated with the next village to Highgate—Hornsey, where C later thought he would be buried (GREW 45)—does not appear. Snout, the tinker, and his companions in *A Midsummer Night's Dream* (who incidentally represented Thebans in their play) tempt consideration: a tinker is a tinman, a worker in tin, and Hornsey Wood could represent the wood near Athens in which the action of *A Midsummer Night's Dream* unfolds. But cf C's pun on the name of Tennemann (in TENNEMANN IX 12) "this Tinny Man"—i.e. a man who makes a thin or unreverberant sound when he purports to produce something more sonorous.

Man ~~with~~ in the dissolution of his visible material Body; nor authorize me to promise any determinate limit to the Consequences of Guilt. We are assured ⟨by our Lord,⟩ that there is a state above Time, consequently *timeless* (the only sense, in which Eternity can be predicated of a finite Being) which state is the greatest Good that Man can seek or possess; and that there is a State below Time, & therefore likewise timeless, which is the direst Evil, that Man can ~~be be warned to es~~ eschew or suffer. These are contrary States—the first being by our Lord ~~& by the Apostles~~ designated by the name, Eternal Life—the Second Eternal Death.[2] Now Reason & Common Sense inform us, that the mere Negation of a Thing is not the Contrary of that Thing. The Contrary of Love is Hate; not Indifference. The Death here threatened must therefore be a positive State.[3]—This is all we know from Scripture; & probably all, that in our present condition we are capable of knowing—~~Eternal~~ Everlasting Torment; ever-lasting Consciousness; &c are all arbitrary and illegitimate Consequences drawn by Divines—and supported only by texts transcribed from Parables, or by attracting literal ~~or~~ & proper senses to Terms necessarily and palpably metaphorical, or to epithets conjoined with these & therefore to be interpreted by the same rule—Ex. gr. Gehenna, or the Vale of Hinnom—likewise called Tophet, a vale near Jerusalem of a volcanic Soil.—[4]

1[2] For Christ's assurance of "eternal life" see e.g. Mark 10.30, John 3.15, 12.25. For "the second death" see Rev 21.8 and cf 2.11, 20.14, and *CN* III 4504 and n. Cf *CN* IV 4998 (c Sept 1823): "...here we have the abysmal Mystery of the Devil, the Evil One—the Contrary of God, absolute emptiness as God is the absolute Fullness, a mere Potence as God is a pure Act...a hidden Fire, for ever seeking a base in which it may actualize & finding it only to convert it into its own essences, which is necessarily baseless...For it is indeed an eternal Hunger, and the very *Sting* of Famine. Eternal because below all Time even as God is eternal by transcendency to all Time—and unintelligible, because an Outcast from intelligence even as God [is] incomprehensible as containing all intelligence. And lastly, Eternal Death as God is eternal Life." See also *CN* IV 5076 (c Dec 1823): "For pure Evil what is it but Will that would manifest itself as

Will, not in Being (ετεροτης), not in Intelligence (therefore *form*less) not in Union or Communion, the contrary therefore of Life, even eternal Death."

1[3] For a distinction between "negation" and "privation" in terms of limbo or purgatory see DONNE *Poems* 8 and n 1 and FIELD 32 and n 4.

The text of 1 from "must therefore be a positive State" was printed, from MS TRANSCRIPT, as App 3 to the Lectures on Revealed Religion in *Lects 1795* (*CC*) 341–2. See also C's notes of c 1807 on eternal punishment printed from the Harvard ms in *Lects 1795* (*CC*) 341–2 n 1 (also var from Cottle in *CL* III 467–9, conjecturally dated 1814).

1[4] Gehenna, Hebrew *Ge-Hinnom*, the Vale of Hinnom, in which a site was used in ancient times for human sacrifices and later as a refuse dump (the Tophet of 2 Kings 23.10, Isa 30.33, Jer 7.31); thought also to have been the name of a midden south of Jerusalem in Christ's time. See

It is an old and just rule of the Church, both of the elder or Jewish and of the younger or Christian Church—that God's Promises are to be understood to the entire extent of the terms in which they are conveyed; but his Threats conditionally.—So in this case of the Host of the Divine Mercies it has seemed good to the Divine Wisdom to reveal some and to leave others in the bosom of his own secret Decrees—To imagine & predict Mercies which God has not made known to us, is a breach of the command, Walk humbly with the Lord thy God.⁵ Now God has promised the grace of Penitence only during our sojourn *in* TIME—most wisely, most graciously! For so only can the two gigantic Evils of Procrastination, and of reckless Despair be efficiently counter-acted—and we may safely say—What interference He to whom all things are possible, may interpose between a sinful Creature & the naturally inevitable Consequences of Sin, we do not know; but assuredly, they who rely on unrevealed Mercies as encouragements to Continuance in Sin are the least likely to be the subjects of the same.

S. T. C.—

P.S.ᵃ The Writer no less than his Antagonists confound the terms Eternal, i.e. timeless, with ever-lasting Time—which is the same with infinite time, which is an impossible idea, a metaphysical Absurdity. Eternity & Time are ἕτερα γενῆ.⁶

2 pp viii–[xi] | Preface

...the author...has, as he best could, introduced himself to those most distinguished for rank, for talents, for zeal, in the Christian Ministry—he has solicited the objections of those who most warmly preach the doctrine he opposes, and—his conviction has been strengthened; to the word and to the sanctuary then he appeals, *] thinking he cannot better do his duty than by studying God's word, as in His presence.

* Alas! but a previous step was wanting—viz. the calm and dauntless tho' humble attempt to ascertain what God's Word is: and on what

---

ᵃ The postscript is written at the head of p ⁻2, crowded in above the beginning of the note

---

Lects 1795 (*CC*) 342n. In OT Gehenna is a place of iniquity; in NT the metaphorical reference is always to hell.

1⁵ Micah 6.8 (var). Incorporated into *The Eolian Harp* line 52: *PW* (EHC) I 102, II 1023 (line 53).

1⁶ "Different in kind[s]" or "essentially different". On time and eternity cf HOOKER **42** (at n 5) and see *AR* (1854) 256n (not in 1825). See also *CN* III 3973 f 24 and n.

Grounds He receives the 57 Books bound up in one or two Volumes, and called the Bible, as the Word ⟨of God⟩ or even as ~~the~~ Words dictated by God. This is confessedly no self-evident Proposition— Nay, in the present day and since Biblical Criticism has been raised into a distinct Study, the most Convinced and orthodox ~~D~~ Inquirers, even those who retain the hypothesis of ~~the~~ an especial inspiration of the sacred Penmen, confine this super human influence to the *Substance,* and reject as not only untenable but as dangerous, the notion of a verbal dictation or infusion. If then the purpose and the truths intended to be conveyed are ~~divine am~~ alone attributable to the Infallible Spirit, by what rules is our Search to be directed? What are the Canons of Interpretation? When I find four Wordings all in Greek of the same Saying of our Lord ⟨spoken⟩ in his vernacular language, viz. the Aramaic or Syro-Chaldaic, one only of which *can* be, and neither of which may be, a literal translation—which am I to take? Or rather is it not evident, that no logical deductions can be drawn from this or that word or phrase in either?—What is to be done?—Plainly, this! From the whole of the two Testaments draw forth all the passages, that are compatible & susceptible of being arranged in connection of dependency—and then seek from the Spirit of Truth that insight into the great Scheme of Revelation which will enable the Man of Faith to determine what the ~~Writers~~ words mean by a previous knowlege of what the Writers must have meant. Every Book worthy of being read at all must be read in and by the same Spirit, as that by which it was written. Who does not do this, reads a Dial by Moonshine.[1]

S. T. C.

P.S. It is but justice to admit, that this method the writer of this work has in the main adopted.

3   p xxi | Abstract of Contents

218. The narrow limits of Christianity are no objection, when it is
*] seen that a pleasurable animal existence is given to millions, from among whom some are conditionally to be advanced to a higher state of existence....

221. No spiritual life without sensual or without spiritual food.
*] Then the wicked will never put on immortality. The great bulk of

2[1] Cf "unmeaning they | As Moonlight on the Dial of the Day" in the draft of *Limbo* (referred to in **1** n 3, above). See   *CN* III 4073 f 146ᵛ; *PW* (EHC) I 430. Cf also *SM* (*CC*) 57.

mankind seek only meat, drink, and raiment; then they possess not immortality.

** Our Saints, the Elect in their own opinion, are proud enough already.[1] What would they be, as a privileged Class of Immortals, in a world of biped Beasts destined to become the dung among which they ~~were~~ are allowed a little while to crawl & delve!!—And yet the ⟨moral⟩ difference between the best of the Death-men and the least good of the Eternal Life-men—how disproportionate!—

4 pp 9–10

Should any one object that the existence of misery in any degree, contradicts the attribute of Goodness as infinite, I offer the following thoughts as sufficient to vindicate that attribute. Although we can fancy a state more perfect than the present, higher in intellectual and moral excellence, in which, being endowed with a stronger sense of right...we should be consequently less liable to misery; yet the goodness of God is manifested in giving existence even to the rank of beings to which we belong...for a chasm must otherwise have existed in the gradation which extends from the Deity to the dullest insect.

These are not satisfactory—[a]nay, inasmuch as they are grounded in a theory of emanation[1] with reality in the inverse ratio of the Distance from the Source, these thoughts pursued into their consequences would be subversive of Morality—The position that existence simply in itself is a good, is to my mind very doubtful.—The term, Good, as used in the first Chapter of Genesis must, I think, be used relatively—or as equivalent to *right*.[2] I know but one Scheme which is capable of satisfying the mind—that which contemplates Chaos as the Result & Phænomen of an Apostasis of the Spirits not-absolute—& the Formation of the World as the commencement of Redemption.[3]

---

a These four words are written in the outer margin beside the textus. C has then written " ∧ " below, and continued the note in the foot margin with " ∧ "

3[1] I.e. the Evangelicals.

4[1] See Böhme **110** n 2 and cf Eichhorn *Neue Testament* copy B **1** and Fleury **96**.

4[2] Cf *CN* iv 4998 (immediately preceding the quotation in **1** n 2, above): "The evil will has no power at all, except against itself, by its inherent self-frustration—much less can it exert any power over the Good.—It simply therefore *falls* from the Good, as a Precipitate." Cf *CN* iv 5076 (preceding the quotation in **1** n 2, above): "...the Evil Principle...therefore intrafluent instead of effluent, destructive of reality instead of causative and hence the Contrary of God...". On the meaning of "good" see Donne *Sermons* copy B **108–114** and nn.

4[3] See Donne *Sermons* copy B **115**. For Apostasis as the Fall see Böhme **153** n 8; cf Field **38** and n 1 and *CN* iii 4449 ff 28–29v.

5 pp 11–12

It is observed by one writer, that our works are finite, but our sins are infinite. If our sins are not our works, what are they?

Had this Writer, whoever he was, said, that tho' the Deeds—i.e. the ∗isensible motions and the changes and sensations of pain & pleasure occasioned thereby, are finite; but that the sin, i.e. the evil Will is infinite—the position might be vindicated.[1] But still there is an equivoque in the term, infinite. By infinite we may signify that than which there can be no greater; or that which is incapable of being thought of in any scheme of *extension*. In this sense all Qualities are infinite—Life, Thought, and Will by an especial right are infinite.— For this reason I could wish, that the term were applied exclusively to the Intuition of *Space*.—I distinctly apprehend what is meant by the Infinity of Space—in all other instances a some more appropriate term may be substituted.[2]

6 pp 32–4

That parting from life, or being deprived of existence, was the original curse, may be proved...above all, by...
The death of Christ:—also from
The words of the Apostle, "Without shedding of Blood, there is no remission of sins."

Heb. IX.22[a]

More probably, by Apollos. So Luther thought.[1] He *felt* the excellence of this Oration; but he felt with an assuring inward Tact,[2] that it was ⟨not⟩ the excellence of S[t] Paul, & not a Letter. The verse quoted is an argumentum ad hominem[3]—to those who made the violent death of Jesus an objection to his being the Messiah.—To a Roman who had made the same objection to our Lord's being our

---

[a] The reference is written in the margin beside the textus; the note is continued in the foot margin with the indicator "∗"

[5][1] Cf WW *The Borderers* III v 1539–44 (also epigraph to *The White Doe of Rylstone*): "Action is transitory... Suffering is permanent, obscure and dark, | And has the nature of infinity." *WPW* I 188, III 383.
[5][2] Cf C's concept of ἄπειρον ("infinite") as undifferentiated, longing to come into existence in e.g. BOHME **31** n 7.

[6][1] For the view that Hebrews was written by Apollos see BIBLE COPY B **134** n 1 and *TT* 6 Jan 1823.
[6][2] For this use of "tact" see DANTE COPY B **4** and n 1 and *Friend* (*CC*) I 419.
[6][3] An "argument addressed to a particular person", i.e. based on premisses acceptable to one's opponent, though not necessarily true. Cf CHILLINGWORTH COPY A **8** (at n 1).

Redeemer from Mortality, the Apostolic Advocate would have said, perhaps—Without Conflict there can be no Conquest—to Conquer Death Jesus must have met Death: for Disease is a mode of *Life*; and had he by his divine power healed himself of any the fiercest Sickness, he might have been said to have conquered Disease, but not to have been the Conqueror of Death. So too, he must have been a captive in Hades: or how could he have lead Captivity Captive?[4]— The truth itself, the heavenly Mystery, had been delivered by our Lord himself, (see John's Gospel) and repeated by St Paul, in *proper* terms, to the utmost extent of human language[5]—The object of the Sacred Writers in the texts here referred to, is to illustrate the Mystery by all the analogies & figures of Speech, most familiar to & best calculated to affect, those to whom they addressed themselves. Hence the typical & technical character of the Epist. to the Hebrews— compared with Paul's Epistles to the Corinthians, & with his Speech at Athens.[6]

7   p 42

On the same occasion that our Saviour warns his followers of the danger of hell fire, he addresses them in these remarkable words: St. Matt. v. 44. "But I say unto you, love your enemies, bless them that curse you, do good to them that hate you, and pray for them which despitefully use you, and persecute you: (45), That ye may be the children of your Father which is in heaven; for he maketh his sun to rise on the evil and on the good, and sendeth rain on the just and on the unjust;"—conduct and motives perfectly irreconcileable with dooming to Eternal Misery poor weak, blind, perishing sinners, for preferring the gratification of the senses, which God hath given them, to spiritual joys, which at length they have not even faculties to discern.

This is a very indiscreet Advocator/ With what overwhelming force might not an Atheist retort on him his own words, with regard to the dreadful penalties that attend the mistaken gratific. of the senses not seldom, even in this Life.—

8   p 59

[a complex argument centred upon John 5.29, to prove that sinners will not be damned eternally:] "They that have done good, unto the

6^4 Ps 68.18, Eph 4.8. 6^6 Acts 22.1–21.
6^5 Presumably John 10.25–6 and 1
Cor 15.21–3.

resurrection of life; and they that have done evil, unto the resurrection of damnation."

Still it is clear, that they that have done evil shall rise and come forth no less than they who have done good. Consequently, the Death which dissolves the sensible bodies of all alike, cannot have *destroyed* the Persons.[a] But if not this Death, what other physical force can be supposed capable of destroying ~~it~~ them? ⟨capable of destroying⟩ the Being, whatever it be, which remaineth after this death in order to rise again. From these texts therefore and from that of St Paul— "Thou Fool! not that which goeth into the Grave, riseth again."[1]—it is clear, that there is some Principle and Subject of Life distinct from and capable of existing separately from, the visible Body.[2]

9   p 60, perhaps an afterthought to **8**

What should prevent us from supposing, that what the ~~fleshly~~ testaceous Body of the Crab is to its ~~testaceous~~ fleshly Body, ~~or Shell~~, or the Butterfly to the Larva[b]—this our visible & ponderable Body may be to ~~an~~ an invisible, imponderable, yet nevertheless material, Body, the power of which may sink into a latent state?—

10   p 60

Now it is clear that a distinction is intended between "those that are dead" and "those that are in the graves," and to have been spiritually dead is common to all; whilst those only, who in this mortal life hear and believe, will rise to life:—the rest, when they come to judgment, are dead already, not having passed from death unto life.

how can they *rise*? how come forth? how be judged? The Judgement on them may be related as a *past* incident, but not be inflicted.

11   pp 62–3

Twenty-eight times in the first six chapters of St. John, does our Saviour declare mankind can only have life by believing in Him; yet in the face of this, a doctrine is maintained, which assumes, that men are naturally immortal.

[a] The note, begun in the foot margin of p 59, continues at the head of the page with "(*from the bottom of the page*)"
[b] Written "the Larva to the Butterfly"

    4   5   3 21   ~~12~~

8[1] A transformed conflation of 1 Cor 15.36 and Job 7.9.   **8**[2] See also **9** and **23**, below.

Nothing can be more evident than that by Life in all these places our Lord means something more than the animal Life/ for this is expressedly called *Death*. Who shall deliver me from the body of this Death.[1] *The Dead* shall hear my Voice[2]—Not—I will re-animate the Dead, and then the *Living* shall hear my voice[.] The true solution is this. Our Lord every where assumes that *the Man*, as the unity of which Soul and Body (i.e. the proper *dynamic* Body, or Corpus *Noumenon*)[3] are the two poles, or + and − states, is indestructible—save by God alone; but that by the Crisis, of which the dissolution of the visible organismus is the result, it is reduced from an actual to a merely potential State—in which it must remain till the Conditions are restored or supplied of its actuation. Now Christ is that actuating Condition./[4]

12　p 86

What is life? It is the enjoyment of all our faculties, in the highest possible degree: to perish must include the loss of all these faculties, and that of the very organization on which these depend. What then remains? will it be said the soul? that is the spirit of God united to the dust of the earth—the spirit is withdrawn—the body is cast out. *] Depart from me, ye cursed. Is it the spirit? that is imperishable, and returns to God who gave it: then man perishes, and the scripture is fulfilled.

* What? is God then a River, or a Reservoir—from which so many skins may be filled & left floating—till a rent is made in these "leathern Bottles"[1] & then what was a Man becomes a quart or gallon of Deity, according to the contents of the Vessel!!—

13　p 104

[On Rom 14.23:] "And he that doubteth is damned if he eat, because he eateth not of faith; for whatsoever is not of faith is sin."

11[1] From 7.24—a recurrent prayer of C's, especially in his closing years. See e.g. *CL* VI 909 (to Green, 18 May 1832).

11[2] John 5.25 (var).

11[3] On the "*Noumenal* Body" cf **8** and **9**, above, and **23** and n 3, below.

11[4] C's solution of the question to which the doctrine of purgatory was for him an unacceptable answer. See FIELD **60**.

12[1] "Maketh a rent" in Luke 5.36 provides part of the allusion, as does perhaps the pouring of new wine into old bottles in Luke 5.37–8; but the quotation draws attention to the song *The Leathern Bottel* and perhaps particularly to the lines: "And I wish his soul in heaven may dwell, | Who first invented the leathern bottel!"

Now is eating meat offered to idols, doubtfully, to cause Eternal Misery?—exclude from eternal happiness it may, because *that* is the consequence only of faith, which is inconsistent with doubt. Whatsoever is not of faith is sin, and the wages of sin is death, but it cannot be Eternal Misery.

This learned Theban[1] ~~comprehends~~ knows but of one sense of the word, *damned*—that in which it is used by the Orators of S[t] Giles's, Wapping, and other Schools of the damnatory class—,[2] in which Go to Hell! and "You be *damned*!" are synonimous phrases.—

S[t] Paul means, stands condemned in his own mind.[3]

14   pp 120–2

A gospel that threatens Eternal Misery, and one that does not, differ considerably. I am aware therefore, if the Apostle preached that doctrine, that I am under his condemnation...

S[t] Paul was an *orthodox* Jew, bred up in the ⟨creed⟩ ~~shul~~ as well as principles of the Pharisaic School—Now if it can be proved, as it may, that according to the Jewish Church the judgement after death was for every individual Soul final and admitting of no other change than from good to better, or from bad to worse—it would follow, not indeed that Paul after conversion should retain the same belief, but assuredly that had he received a new light he would have spoken of so very important a change. The negative evidence is in this case equipollent to a direct proof.

S. T. C.

15   pp 137–6

Here [2 Thess 1.6–12] the apostle gives a description of Eternal Punishment, which makes the common interpretation matter of astonishment to me, that those who hold the omnipresence of God, *] and that He must be present in hell to punish, should not see that those who are destroyed from His presence, and are beyond His power, must be non-existent.

* The writer has forgotten or overlooked the text, "God is a consuming Fire"[1]—and seems never to have reflected, that if God

13[1] See Shakespeare *King Lear* III iv 148: "I'll talk a word with this same learned Theban"—Thebes being the principal city of Boeotia, and the Boeotians proverbial for their stupidity (although Pindar was Theban by birth).

13[2] In the parish of St Giles in the Fields, which included the notorious Seven Dials district, and in Wapping on the riverside, a certain saltiness of idiom was to be expected.
13[3] *NEB* reads: "is guilty".
15[1] Deut 4.24, Heb 12.29.

be regarded as an exciting Cause, what may be Light, Glory, Bliss to Creatures confirmed and assimilated to the sustaining & exciting Element ⟨may, or⟩ must, be Fire, Blindness, Torment to Creatures of an opposite character. Behold yon light-inebriated Moth dashing madly at the Cone of Flame of the Candle! It is our Light—it is its Darkness.—[a2] Besides, the Writer confounds Omnipresence, i.e. the presence of all things to the Supreme Mind, with Ubiquity—the former being as certain an attribute of God as the latter is questionable.

S. T. C.

16   pp 140–1

[1 Tim 5] v. 11. "But the younger widows refuse: for when they have *] begun to wax wanton against Christ, they will marry; 12. Having damnation, because they have cast off their first faith."

* I entirely agree with Eichhorn and Schleiermacher in rejecting the first Epistle to Timothy from the list of the genuine Writings of S[t] Paul; and in more than doubting the Authenticity of all three of the so called Pastoral Epistles. They appear to me mere *Centos* of Pauline Phrases by some Bishop of the Age succeeding the Apostolic.—.[1] However this may be, "Damnation" cannot be here understood in its popular & most fearful acceptation.—The whole passage breathes the spirit of a Jerome or a S[t] Antony—and utterly alien from the Spirit of the great Apostolic Sage

17   pp 166–7, pencil

[I John 2:] 15. "Love not the world. 17. The world passeth away, and the lust thereof: but he that doeth the will of God, abideth for ever."

---

[a] Here the note has reached the foot of p 137, with " ∧ ∧ "; it is resumed in the foot margin of p 136 with " ∧ ∧ "

15[2] With this unusual rendering of the image of the moth and the candle-flame, cf a notebook entry of 2/3 Aug 1826: "...Of the large Moth with the immense proboscis that for half an hour had been with his back to the Candle trying every flower of 3 or four Scabiouses in my Flower-pot—and then turning round was struck with the Light & flew madly at the Candle scorched himself & fell—rose again, and dashed at it—I drove it off repeatedly—but in vain—again it dashed at the Light, till I succeeded in driving it about 3 yards off—& there the fascination seemed to cease—Well worth thinking of—". *CN* IV 5423. Cf *CN* I 1064.

16[1] For C's view, confirmed by modern biblical scholars, that the pastoral epistles were not written by Paul see also BIBLE COPY B **133** and n 1 and EICHHORN *Neue Testament* COPY B **32** and n 2.

15. My belief on this point is perhaps not more distant from the Author's than from the Everlasting Torment-Doctors; but tho' I perfectly agreed with the Author, yet candor would have compelled me to admit, that ~~from~~ in *such* texts *so* treated any point might be proved. St John was thinking not of the question in dispute, but merely of the permanency of a virtu~~ouse~~ compared with the transiency of worldly goods & pleasures. And this is the evil of *this* contraversy[1]—the meaning of the Writer is to be extorted from the words; whereas the right interpretation of the *words* depends on the knowlege of the Writer's *Meaning*.

18 179, pencil

It is said [in Rev 20.10], where the beast and false prophet *are;* what follows may mean, shall be tormented incessantly, as long as day and night continue.

May! Why? How?—Is not shall be for ever and ever[1] without any of those intermissions, as of Sleep &c, of which even the most wretched in the present state have the benefit—as strong expressions of continuous Futurity as Language can supply? Is it not = χρονος ανευ χρονου of Socrates—in Plato?[2]

19 pp 206–8

The operation of the fire here [Isa 66.17], is to consume...so the fire is not quenched, with respect to those cast into it at the day of judgment, until they are utterly destroyed: therefore, with respect to its subjects, it is literally that "their worm dieth not, and their fire is not quenched." [Isa 66.24, Mark 9.44, 46, 48.]

But wherein lies the distinction from the common Worm or Maggot in our church-yard Graves? from the common fire of the funereal

17[1] Upside-down-ery—not in *OED* in this sense, but cf "contraverse" and "contraversion". See ὕστερον πρότερον, "preposterous", "preposterize" in BöhME **112** n 1.

18[1] See Rev 20.10.

18[2] "Time without time"—elsewhere in the form χρονος ἄχρονος. C may be thinking of *Timaeus* 37C–39A and 47A (in which Timaeus, not Socrates, is speaking), but Plato does not use the phrase C uses here. The "father and creator", having created the world-soul in the "image of the eternal gods",

sought to "make the universe eternal, so far as might be"—"Wherefore he resolved to have a moving image of eternity, and when he set in order the heaven, he made this image eternal but moving according to number, while eternity rests in unity, and this image we call time". Tr Benjamin Jowett. Cf also **1** PS, above, and see FLEURY **62** and n 1. With χρόνος ἄχρονος cf other oxymorons that C liked—γλώσσαι ἀγλώσσαι, λόγος ἄλογος, βυσσὸς ἄβυσσος—all of which C seems to have invented. See also C on αἰώνιος in *Lects 1795* (*CC*) 341n.

pile in Greece or Rome?—which yet the epithets undying and unquenchable, for ever & ever must have been intended to convey?— What a ridiculous threat would it not have been, if the Assyrian Tyrant had told Shadrach, & his two Fire-mates,[1] that for them to punish them with a severity unprecedented, the Furnace which by being heated nine-fold (q? how, in the *then* state of chemical science?) beyond its average fierceness would reduce them to vapor and ashes in a few mominutes, should be kept up for a whole century after their death!—The threat of the "*ninefold* hotter" which would have been a remission not aggravation of the Punishment, is ridiculous enough as it is—/ But tho' we may make little scruple [to][a] attribute an Irish Bull to that a Chaldean Phalaris[2] in the drunkenness of his fury and perhaps the fury of drunkenness—or a blunderering oversight to the ignorant Jew who compiled the popular biographical traditions prefixed to the Visions of Daniel[3]—I would have give my own body to a Smelting Furnace rather than attribute the same to our blessed Saviour—& lose a finger or two rather than charge the Evangelists with so absurd a specimen of the Cambyses Vein!—[4]

S. T. C.

20 p 209

That there is an essential difference between those who have stood *] in the presence of God, who have seen God, (which no <u>man</u> hath done at any time, and which no man can do and live,) and mankind, no one can doubt...

* A writer on a subject like this, & who rests his argument on texts of Scripture, ought to have the originals before his eyes, and not an imperfect and not seldom erroneous Version.[1] God (says St John) God (the *Absolute* Will) hath *no one* seen at any time—not no *man*.[2]

a Word supplied by the editor

19[1] Shadrach, Meshach, and Abednego so enraged King Nebuchadnezzar by refusing to "worship the golden image" that he had them thrown into "a burning fiery furnace" heated "seven times more than it was wont to be heated". See Dan 3.8–30. C, however, uses not the biblical "seven times" but the Miltonic "Ninefold" of Satan's Hell in *Paradise Lost* II 434–6.

19[2] A tyrant of Acragas in Sicily in the first half of the sixth century B.C., said to have been a cruel ruler who roasted his victims in a brazen bull.

19[3] For the structure of the book of Daniel see EICHHORN *Alte Testament* 48 and n 1.

19[4] I.e. a mad ranting: see *1 Henry IV* II iv 430.

20[1] John 1.18, AV of which C finds unsatisfactory: "No man hath seen God at any time: the only begotten Son, which is in the bosom of the Father, he hath declared *him*." See n 3, below. See also CHILLINGWORTH COPY B 1 and 5.

20[2] The Greek reads οὐδείς, as C implies.

The force of the sentence is evidently—God *absolutely* is essentially immanifestable in himself—the Supreme BEING, eternally begotten, is his *Person.*—[3]

21 p 209, pencil

Now the quality of these organs [to which the spirit of God is united] doth not essentially depend on obedience or disobedience; since it would appear that man, by eating of the tree of life, would have lived for ever, after he had rebelled by tasting of the tree of knowledge of good and evil. But God having in mercy prevented him, this seems to be the distinction between our nature, and that of the fallen angels...

Strange Text of which the Church has never in her severest time required a *literal* interpretation, to found a doctrine on! Not to mention that the best Divines have supposed it *ironical*[1]

22 p 210, pencil

Here St. Jude [v 6] calls that everlasting* which is *unto* the judgment of the great day; and St. Peter says simply, chains of darkness, with no mention of everlasting.

* Aye, now! this *is* an argument—of much weight with all who understand the *Script*[s] by syllables and verses.[1]

23 ii 38–40 | Appendix No VII [extract from Sherlock's *Sermon on the Resurrection*]

"...whatever notions some may have of the soul in its state of *] separate existence, yet a *mere spirit* is not a *man*; for man is made of soul and body..."

* Sherlock was one of the *Blazes*, that every now & then acquire a prodigious celebrity, a vehement reputation that is any thing but reputable to the Age, that confermeds it.[1]—It would not be easy to

20[3] See n 1, above. C's "Supreme BEING" stands for ὁ ὤν (AV: "which is"): see BIBLE COPY B 119 n 1. His phrase "his *Person*" corresponds to "in the bosom of the Father".
21[1] Gen 3.22–4.
22[1] The two texts explain C's ironic tone. Jude 6: "And the angels which kept not their first estate, but left their own habitation, he hath reserved in everlasting chains under darkness unto the judgment of the great day." 2 Pet 2.4: "For if God spared not the angels that sinned, but cast them down to hell, and delivered them into chains of darkness, to be reserved unto judgment..."
23[1] For William SHERLOCK *A Vindication of the Doctrine of the...Trinity* (1690) see DONNE *Sermons* COPY B 8 n 5.

condense Nonsense more vigorously, than is done in this precious sentence!

Rust is a compound, of Iron and Oxygen—if Rust be any thing, Iron and Oxygen must each be *some* thing—& every *thing* must have cogitable qualities, properties or attributes/—*thinkg think*—ding denken—res reor—by which it may be distinguished from other things.[2] Now it would be edifying to hear from the *Soul + Body*-Divines,[3] 1. What the Soul is without the Body: 2. What the Body is without the Soul, & 3. What the Man is as = both; & whether the mere name of the two, as being together, just as a Pound Sterling is the *name* of 20 Shillings thought of collectively: or whether it expresses a tertium aliquid from the combination of the two, as a Neutral Salt is the tertium aliquid of an Acid and an Alkali—and if this latter, then what are its distinctive characters?—

23[2] For the relation of "think" to "thing", and the proposal that "to think" is "to thing", see esp *CN* ii 2784, iii 3587, 3968, and nn.

23[3] See also **8**, **9**, and **11**, above; and cf DONNE *Sermons* COPY B **76** and n 1. C attacked Edward Irving with particular vigour for this error in IRVING *Sermons* and LACUNZA *The Coming of Messiah*.

GEORGE STANLEY FABER

1773–1854

A Dissertation on the Mysteries of the Cabiri; or the great gods of Phenicia, Samothrace, Egypt, Troas, Greece, Italy, and Crete; being an attempt to deduce the several orgies of Isis, Ceres, Mithras, Bacchus, Rhea, Adonis, and Hecate, from an union of the rites commemorative of the deluge with the adoration of the host of heaven, &c. 2 vols. Oxford 1803. 8°.

New York Public Library (Berg Collection)

Leaves unopened from I 233 to the end of Vol I.

C's principal sources on the Greek mysteries, especially the Samothracian or Cabiric, were FABER and SCHELLING *Ueber die Gottheiten von Samothrace* (Stuttgart & Tübingen 1815). In his reading, C's speculative interest was guided by his belief in the spiritual priority of the OT. In the fragmentary "Lecture XI" of the literary lectures of Jan–Mar 1818, as printed in *LR* I 184–8 (but probably, on this subject, relating to Philosophical Lecture XI of 8 Mar 1819), the influence of Schelling is beyond question, the influence of Faber is submerged. (In a set of revisions to *LR* proposed to HNC, Edward Coleridge noted of "Lecture XI": "It should be explained, for it does not appear, how Asiatic and Greek Mythology, the Kabeiri, and the Samothracian mysteries came to be treated of in the same lecture with Robinson Crusoe!" VCL SMS F 11.2.)

In c Feb 1828 C looked back over his marginalia on FABER, transcribed and added to one note, and wrote a variant of another (see **1** n 1 and **11** n 2, below), and may at that time have added one or more new annotations.

C also had some acquaintance with Faber's *Dissertation on the Prophecies* (2 vols 1806): see EICHHORN *Apocalypse* COPY A **19** n 2, *CN* III 3793n, and *CL* VI 557.

DATE. c 1817–19, or earlier (but **1**, written "many years before" c Feb 1828, cannot be earlier than 1815, the date of publication of Schelling's *Samothrace*, and the first signs of C's use of this work appear in early 1817: see *CN* III 4335n and *Friend—CC*—I 370); also c Feb 1828 (see **1** n 1; and **13**, referring to *AR*, cannot be earlier than 1825).

1 I ⁻2, pencil

It would be a waste of time to attack a system built on arbitrary assertions and supported only by *Puns*.[1] But it may suffice to call on the Author for a proof of the possibility of a Religion founded on, and wholly consisting in, a past event—a Religion that has no Present and no Future.[2] Whence and why the tremendous Bond of Secrecy in the Mysteries? their purifying and redemptive influences?[3]

2 I 6–7, pencil | Ch 1 "Preliminary Observations"

Both these suppositions [that the Cabiric Triad alludes to the doctrine of the Trinity, and that it refers to a material Trinity of the heavens—Fire, Light, Air] evidently originate from the oriental etymology of the word *Cabiri*, and from the circumstances of those deities being occasionally described as *three*: but, unless their number be uniformly the same, and their history unincumbered with matters

[1] C transcribed this note, with small variations of spelling and punctuation, into N 36 f 79 (*CN* v) c Feb 1828, with the comment: "In the blank leaf of the first Volume [of 'Stanley's Faber's 2 Oct. Vols on the Cabiric Mysteries'] I find in black lead Pencil a remark of mine, written many years ago, which deserves, I think, a somewhat less perishable record." In the transcript he inserted after the word "*Puns*"—"*some of which remind me of Bob Allen, who said he never sees the Book of Common Prayer without thinking of the great King of Babylon, Nebuchadnezzar—i.e. propter duo syllabos priores* [because of the first two syllables], *Knee-Book*—". At the end of the transcript he drew a line and then continued: "Take an old Spelling Book—after the Alphabet, where the syllables are—Ab, Ba, Ca—/ or rather do what *ought to be done*. By the bye, instead of the worse than useless Alphabets/ make a syllabic Alphabet, of all the l̶e̶t̶t̶e̶r̶s̶ Consonants, as they are articulable—A̶b̶ Ba, ab, bab, be, eb, beb, bi, ib, bib; bo, ob, bob; bu, ub, bub; ca, ac, cac; &c &c/—And then look out in a Hebrew, Syro-Chaldaic, Arabic, Coptic, Welsh, Erse, Lexicons— for each, to see w̶h̶e̶t̶h̶e̶r̶ how many of these syllables are words in one or other of these—and I will undertake to prove

by etymologies to the full as plausible as the Rev^d St. Faber's, that t̶h̶e̶ H̶i̶s̶t̶o̶r̶y̶ Thucydides' Hist. of the Peloponnesian War is nothing more than a medley of mythological representations of the Story of Cain and Abel; or of the Passover thro' the Red-Sea—". N 36 ff 79–79^v. See also **11** n 2, below.

[2] Faber derives virtually the whole of Greek mythology from the corruption of the supposed annual celebrations of the escape from the flood, identifying all gods and heroes and symbolic animals with Noah, members of his family, the ark, the dove, and the raven. C's own interpretation includes the redemption by Christ.

[3] So well was secrecy observed that only hints have come down to us of the teaching of the mysteries. The attempts at reconstruction tend—even if not so jejune (like Faber's) or so commonplace that there would be no need for secrecy— to be so markedly at variance with overt religious beliefs as to make it improbable that two such systems could exist, as in fact they did, in harmony. C and Schelling in their theories, however over-imaginative (on which see also **13**, below), avoid both extremes.

C mentions the well-documented element of regeneration in the mysteries in *LS* (*CC*) 188.

directly hostile to such opinions, the systems at present under consideration will scarcely be found tenable. In the sequel however it will appear, that their number is by no means limited to *three*; and that their history comprehends such a singular combination of events, that we are almost compelled to refer their Mysteries to a totally different origin.

Reland supposes the Cabiri to be gods of the infernal regions, on account of their connection with Mercury, Ceres, Pluto, and Proserpine.

This hypothesis speaks the truth, but not the whole truth... [Valancey] maintains that Eon, Cronus, Saturn, and Dagon, are all one person, and all equally the patriarch Adam: and concludes... that the Mysteries of the Cabiri were founded upon the arkite worship.

The ancient Mystæ were so far Pantheists, that they made the lowest first, the highest posterior—primi quia inferiores, ultimi quia supremi. So Varro, himself the reformer of the Samothracian Rites.[1] If we however take the whole in the order of *manifestation* not of Power & Being, the system is then susceptible of a safe and orthodox interpretation—The 3 first Cabiri are physiological Deities, Gods of Chaos—then comes the caller forth, the *Word*, Hermes, Mercury— then appear the supreme Triad, in which the Hermes appears again as Apollo, or Minerva—& lastly, the mysterious 8th, in which he is

---

2[1] "First because lower, latest because highest"—the two phrases also occur (var) in an 1818 "lecture": see *LR* I 186. No exact source for the Latin is traced, but Augustine in *De civitate Dei* 7.9 quotes Varro as saying that "Jupiter is the god who has power over the causes of the existence of everything in the world. Janus is placed before him because Janus controls first things, Jupiter the highest things. Jupiter is rightly therefore called King of all. For first things are inferior to highest, because though the first things precede in time the highest surpass them in dignity." This is quoted in SCHELLING *Samothrace* p 104 (n 112). C may also be translating Schelling's German, as on p 23 and later. Schelling finds a chain of gods, revealed in the mysteries, beginning with the lowest and ascending to the highest.

Varro appears not so much the reformer as the explainer of the Samothracian rites (the rites of the Cabiri) in Augustine *De civitate Dei* 7.28, quoted in SCHELLING *Samothrace* pp 104–5 (n 112). (C quoted from this same passage in *CN* IV 4901, as cited in *Characteristick der alten Mysterien*.) Varro says there that the images of the three Cabiri —he does not recognise a "supreme Triad" (below), which seems to be C's invention—represent heaven, earth, and the patterns of things that Plato calls ideas. Of the more than fifty works of Marcus Terentius Varro (116–27 B.C.) three are quoted in connexion with Cabiri and Samothrace: *Antiquitates rerum divinarum et humanarum*, much used by Augustine (C lamented its loss in *CN* IV 5232); *De lingua latina*, of which bks 5–10 have survived; and *De re rustica*, his only surviving complete work. Cf *TT* 24 Sept 1830.

again to appear, as the infant Bacchus, the Son of a most high of a mortal Mother.[2] The *Ark* is absurd/[3]

3 I 46 | Ch 2 "An Analysis of the Phenician History of Sanchoniatho"

The generations of Cain enumerated in Scripture amount to eight: Adam, Cain, Enoch, Irad, Mehujael, Methusael, Lamech, and Tubal-Cain. If these be connected with the Phenician genealogy, the table of descents will stand as follows.

1. Protogonus, Eon	1. Adam and Eve
2. Genus, Genea.	2. Cain, and his wife.
3. Phos, Pyr, Phlox.	3. Enoch, and his brethren.
4. Cassius, Libanus.	4. Irad, and his brethren.
5. Memrumus, Usoüs.	5. Mehujael, and his brethren.
6. Agreus, Halieus.	6. Methusael, and his brethren.
7. Chrysor	7. Lamech.
8. Technites.	8. Tubal-Cain

But was *Greek* (τεχνιτης, γενος, πρωτογονος, αιων, φως, φλοξ, πῦρ, αγριος, ἁλιευς, χρυσωρ) the Ante-diluvian Language?[1]—Or were the Proper Names translated?[2] I confess, that from this latter singularity I should have mistaken them for a scheme of physiogony—[3]

2[2] The interpretation in this note derives in part from SCHELLING *Samothrace* pp 20–1, 74–5. See also 13, below, and *LR* I 186.

2[3] "The *Ark*" is short for Faber's whole scheme, for which see 1 n 2, above. See also 10, 12, below.

3[1] From Faber's left-hand column C has picked out a number of names that, except for the last, are identical with Greek common nouns: (8) *technites*—artificer, craftsman; (2) *genos*—kind; (1) *protogonos*—first-born; (1) *aiōn*—epoch; (3) *phōs*—light; (3) *pyr*—fire; (3) *phlox*—flame, fire; (6) *agrios* (wild)—for Faber's *Agreus*—hunter; (6) *halieus*—fisher; (7) *chrysor* (perhaps for *chrysaōr*, with a golden sword)—identified with Hephaestus (Vulcan) by Philo of Byblus, from Sanchuniathon (see n 2, below).

3[2] In the early pages of this chapter Faber shows that Eusebius of Caesarea in his *Praeparatio evangelica* 1.10 quotes from the Greek rendering by Philo of Byblus (A.D. 64–161) the account of the Phoenician religion given (in Phoenician) by Sanchuniathon, said to have lived before the Trojan war and now considered to have been a real person. Phoenician names would naturally be converted into the nearest Greek equivalents, in meaning or pronunciation. Cf the Greek names in 6 textus, below, and C's—and Faber's— constant use of Latin rather than Greek names of gods. In 13 (at n 10) C speaks of Cadmilus as the Mercury, rather than as the Hermes, of the Greeks.

3[3] See BLUMENBACH 1 n 3.

4 1 47

Agruerus was venerated by the Phenicians as the greatest of gods; such likewise were the honours universally paid to [Noah,] the second progenitor of mankind.

Vix credam.[1]

5 1 47–8

Agruerus is said to have been the father of Amynus the magician; Noah was the father of Ham, who is generally supposed to have been addicted to sorcery, and to have instructed his son Mizraim in the same nefarious practices.

Mizraim is literally Double-land[1]—the exact Description of Egypt. When then we find Mizraim the Progenitor of the Egyptians, can we avoid seeing the analogy between King Italus, the Christner of Italy (the Greek chronicler that Italic meant Pasture Land, whence Vitulus)[2]—Latium (the broad part of the Peninsula) a humanized into King Latinus, Britain into the Trojan, Brutus, another Celtic word into the Hero, Albion, &c &c?[3]

6 1 49

Eliun and Beruth dwelt in the neighbourhood of Byblus; and from them sprung Epigèus or Autochton, who was afterwards intitled *Uranus*, and a daughter, who was called *Ge*. In process of time, Uranus espoused his sister Ge, and became the father of Ilus, or Cronus, Betylus, Dagon, and Atlas.

Surely, these are Cosmogonical names! God the most High and the creative energy, ~~caused the~~ or rather (the feminine termination

---

4[1] "I can hardly believe it".

5[1] Samuel Bochart *Geographia sacra* (Frankfurt 1681) bk v ch 24—C's copy is described in *Green SC* (1880) 5 and was in the Highgate List in Wordsworth LC —says that Mizraim, a name for Egypt, is in the dual form in Hebrew (derived from *masor*, a fortified place), and that the name of the second son of Ham (Gen 10.6 and 13, 1 Chron 1.8 and 11) is taken from the name of the country. This etymology is no longer generally accepted.

5[2] *Vitulus* (calf)—the *v* standing for *digamma*.

5[3] Legends tell that countries took their names from the leader or progenitor of their inhabitants; C suggests that the geographical names may have come first and that the men were invented to account for them. If the man Mizraim is to be associated with the land "Mizraim", Egypt, the land has been humanised into the name of a "progenitor of Egypt". (Faber—pp 48n, 49—speaks of Mizraim as the father of the Egyptians.) C gives other examples of this onomastic process.

implying the negative or passive ⚹ positive or active) the creability,[1] i.e. Chaos, prima materia/[2] to bring forth the Heaven, or that which was over the Earth ἔπι γην,[3] and the Earth—and these gave birth to *Time*—[4]

7 I 63

There was likewise a city of Illyricum, upon which Cadmus...bestowed the appellation of *Buthoè* from the Egyptian *Buto*; and another town in Ionia, or *the land of the arkite dove*, which was called *Buthia*. Perhaps also the Scottish isle of *Bute* may once have been the seat of the same superstition, and may once, together with its sister island *Arran*, have beheld the wild rites...

Ιωᾶονες, evidently the descendant of Iavan, probably pronounced Yaowan/—Faber must have forgot the Scottish Iona/[1]

8 I 65

[Quoting Nonnus Dionys[iaca] 33.[338–40] on the anchoring of Delos by Apollo:]

εισοκεν αυτην
Αστατον ἱππευουσαν αμοιβαδι συνδρομον αυρῃ,
Κυμασιν αστυφελικτον ενερριζωσεν Απολλων.

6[1] Not in *OED*, but "creable" is recorded in *OED*, in two senses—believable and creatable.

6[2] "Primordial matter". On chaos see e.g. Böhme **146** and n 1; and for some of its approximate synonyms see e.g. Böhme **6, 10, 31, 52**, and nn.

6[3] Faber reports Sanchoniatho's mythology correctly. C, like Faber (cf **9**, below), finds it unsatisfactory that these cosmological names are given to a much later and quasi-human generation—four generations after Technites in the genealogy given in **3**, above. The first element of Eliun (to whom Faber gives the epithet *Hypsistus*, the most High) is (Hebrew) El—God. Cf, on Elohim (plural), Eichhorn *Alte Testament* **21** n 2. Beruth, as C says, has a feminine ending: see **9**, below. Ἐπὶ γῆν—"on or over (though touching) earth": C wants to explain Epigeus (ἐπίγειος, "on the earth", "terrestrial") as the equivalent,

not of Autochthon ("sprung from earth itself"), but of Uranus ("Heaven"). Gē means "Earth".

6[4] Cronus (approximately identified with Saturn in Latin myth) was traditionally explained as Chronus (Χρόνος), Time.

7[1] From Gen 10.2–5 it was deduced that Javan, son of Japhet, was the ancestor of the "Gentiles" of the "islands"; in Isa 66.19, Ezek 27.13, and Dan 10.20, 11.2 Javan in the Hebrew—and in AV—means Ionia or Greece, and is so translated in the Septuagint. See e.g. Samuel Bochart *Geographia sacra* (1681) I 174–5, of which C owned a copy: *Green SC* (1880) 248; cf *CN* IV 4839 f 122. C's idiosyncratic spelling *Ioaones* (also in *CN* III 4379, 4384) for *Iaones*, contracted to *Iones*, could be intended to show the connexion with the Greek form of Javan —Ἰωῦαν.

[[Asterie, the nymph of Delos]...riding restless before the changing wind, until Apollo rooted her in the waves immovable. (Tr W. H. D. Rouse LCL 1949–50.)]

Herman (bless his ears!) holds the hexameter to have first attained *perfection* in Nonnus's Dyonisiaca[1]—and D[r] Johnson would, I doubt not, have thought the same.[2] And doubtless, they are *stout well-timbered* Hexameters, that like the Dutch India-men, sail famously *right before the wind*—Indeed I can think of no apter illustration of Nonnus's Verses as compared with the Homeric, than a ~~D~~ stout Dutch Lugger compared with Dante's ~~Magic~~ gallant Bark, with magic virtue graced Deft at our will with[a] every breeze to fly—[3]

9 I 69

To Eliun the Phenician mythologist assigns a consort, whom he calls *Beruth*. For a satisfactory explanation of this part of the tradition, *] little more is necessary than barely to refer to the Hebrew scriptures.

"God spake to Noah, and to his sons with him, saying,—I will establish *my covenant* (in the Hebrew *Berithi*) with you; neither shall all flesh be cut off any more by the waters of a flood to destroy the earth." [Footnote:] Gen ix. 8, 11.

Hence it appears...that the inviolable *Berith* of God is personified by a female, who is described as his consort.

From this union...sprung Uranus and Ge...or...the Almighty, after the confusion of the deluge, created anew the heaven and the earth...

---

[a] The note having reached the limit of the foot-margin, the last four words are written above it

8[1] Nonnus (fl c 400), of Panoplis in Egypt, wrote an epic *Dionysiaca* in forty-eight books on the adventures of the god Dionysus (Bacchus), assembling all the legends relating to him. Its rather monotonous versification shows signs of the transition from quantitative to accentual metre. G. J. J. Hermann (1722–1848) in his *Elementa doctrinae metricae* (Leipzig 1816) 334 says of Nonnus and his metrical innovations that he so excelled his contemporaries that they took his heroic hexameters as their model, treating him as a new Homer. In a fragment of an introduction to a work on Greek prosody C speaks of Hermann as the "first systematic Analyst of Greek Prosody" and the defender (against Voss and Apel) of "the Prosody in present use". BM MS Egerton 2800 ff 56–57[v]; cf *TT* 23 Aug 1833. For C on Faber's frequent quotation of Nonnus see **13** (at n 4), below.

8[2] For C's judgement that Dr Samuel Johnson "had neither eye nor ear" see e.g. *TT* 16 Aug 1833. He found strong evidence of this in Johnson's "On Milton's Versification": see *CN* III 4190 and n and cf 3646.

8[3] If a quotation, not identified.

* forced in the extreme and utterly improbable. Far likelier is it, that ~~that~~ Beruth ìs a derivative from Bara, to make, create—/ turned into a Substantive of the feminine gender to express the − correlative of the + energy—or the creability ⚹ the creativity.[1]

10 ı 179 | Ch 4 "The Polyonymy of the Sun; and the Union of the Arkite and the Solar Worship"

The import however of *Theba*, in the Hebrew language, is *an ark*; and the only reason, why a heifer was designated by the same appellation, was the circumstance of its being used as an arkite emblem...Europa, who is the very same mythological character as Astartè, Venus, or the lunar Ark, notwithstanding she has borrowed her name from Eur-Op, *the Solar serpent*, is violently carried away from Phenicia upon *the arkite bull*....Cadmus, or Cadm-On, *the oriental solar deity*, comes in search of his sister, to Beotia, *the country of Buto*, or *the tauriform Ark*.

Because a Ship with the Image of a Bull at its Prow was named the Bull, *therefore* Noah's Vessel is the divine tauriform Ark!!—[1]

11 ı 181

All these variously perverted traditions relate equally to one event: Alistra is Al-Es-Tora, *the arkite heifer of the Sun*; Iodama is Io-da-Maia, *the great mother Io*, or *Isis*; Tithonus is Tit-On-Nus, *the helio-diluvian Noah*...

MORE probably Tom *Tit*, ⟨a Bird⟩ so notorious for its attachment to the Heliotrope or Sun Flower—It has a ring round its neck like the Ring-dove/ hence its name. Th' goine tit, i.e. The Dove of Chaos or of the Diluvial Colluvies,[1] on its first exposure to the Sun—/ of which the Sun-flower in full seeding is the appropriate Symbol.—I mean to found a new Heresy, as my Antagonists will call it, the distinguishing ⟨Tenet⟩ of which is, that *Ti*thonus, the Chaos–Sun–Noah, sent out a Sea-gull and a Tom Tit, not as is too commonly supposed, a Raven and a Pigeon.[a2]

a Some terminal letters have run over on to p 183

9[1] For Beruth see **6** and n 3, above. C's explanation of Beruth as deriving from Hebrew *bara* (create) is not implausible. See also **1** n 1, above.

10[1] C wilfully takes "arkite emblem" to be an emblem *on*, not *for*, a boat. Cf Faber's footnote *t*: "Buto is Bo-Do, *the divine tauriform ark*".

11[1] See EICHHORN *Alte Testament* **18** n 8, especially the definition quoted from *Rees's Cyclopaedia*, and cf "Colluvies Diluvii" quoted from N 36 in n 2, below.

11[2] See also **12**, below. When C read through these marginalia in 1828 he expanded this note. "The Sun-flower in its broadest Disk with the seedy area

12 I 185

According to Suidas, she [Diana] received this title [*Taurionè*], because she rode upon bulls; but, in reality, Taurionè is a mere compound of Tor-Ionah, *the tauric* or *arkite dove*.

Hence doubtless the Bull-finch, and in equal allusion to the G'Archa, or Illustrious Ark, the Horse Chesnut, in german *Nuss?*—i.e. the Ark (a Horse being ~~the~~ a common symbol ~~thereforeof~~) ch' es Nus—of the great Noah—/

13 I 193–203

And thus the author of the Orphic hymns styles him [Dionysus], *the deity with two horns, having the head of a bull, even Mars–Dionysus, reverenced in a double form, and adored in conjunction with a beautiful star.*

[He then quotes from *Orphic Hymn* 29:]

Κικλησκω Διονυσον, εριβρομον ευαστηρα,
Πρωτογονον, διφυη, τριγονον, Βακχειον ανακτα,
Αγριον, αρρητον, κρυφιον, δικερωτα, διμορφον,
Κισσοβρυον, ταυρωπον, Αρηϊον, ευϊον, αγνον.

[I invoke Dionysus, thundering shouter of Evoe, first-begotten, of two natures, thrice-begotten, Bacchic king, savage, not to be spoken, hidden, two-horned, two-formed, ivy-wreathed, bull-faced, associate of Mars, hurra-er, holy.]

I am almost afraid to divulge a suspicion, that has repeatedly during the perusal of this Work *lit* on my mind, and as often been hooted off; but still kept hovering—It is no less than that the Revd Stanley Faber's knowlege of the *Greek* Language is just sufficient to enable him after reading the *Latin* Column to guess at the correspondent Lines in the *Greek* one.—For is it conceivable, that a man even moderately conversant with the Greek should have construed ερι-βρομον ευαστηρα "*adored in conjunction with a* ~~double beautiful~~

within the circle of Florets a Symbol of Chaos in the moment of bring[ing] forth Light. At this time you will be sure almost of seeing a Tom Tit clinging to the Flower. In a large bed of Sun Flowers I have seen twenty of them thus hanging, each to some one Disk, with the pretty ring-dove circlet round their necks—/ How obvious then the true etymology of the Bird's name. T' goinah Tit, the Dove of Chaos!/ Or as Noah was the Sun, and the Ark the Heliotrope, and Mr Faber renders Tit Colluvies Diluvii [I 129n], the fat ooze & mud of the Retiring Flood—it is possible that it was the Tom Tit and not the Pigeon, that brought back the Olive Leaf—. Can any thing be more convincing?" N 36 ff 79^v–80 (*CN* v). On "a Raven and a Pigeon" cf 1 n 2, above.

beautiful star"?—which even if the word ευαστηρ had been derived from ευ and αστηρ, a star, could not have been even tortured into this sense?—But ~~even~~ no School-boy who had got into Xenophon could have blundered so egregiously, as to have mistaken αστηρα for αστερα—or to have been ignorant, that εὖ *bene*, ~~well~~ could not be prefixed to a primitive Noun Substantive, any more than our adverb, well—exempli gratiâ, well-star; and that if it had been a derivative whenther Subst. or Adjective, the word must have been εὐαστέριον. The Rev.^d St. Faber must have forgotten his Horace, or the Evoe, euan, would have informed him, that ευαστηρα is derived from ευαζειν, to shout Evoe, ευαν—the Bacchanal Hallelujah—and that the Greek Hexameter is—I invoke Dionysus, the thundering *Hurraer*— or Evōer/[1] the *valdisonant*[2] Shouter of Evoe.—But waiving Faber's numerous Blunders, in his interpretations of Greek, which in conjunction with the lawless combinations[3] of three or four *Substantives* in one Proper Name inclines me to suspect that his knowlege of the Semitic Languages does not extend very far beyond the ability of looking out for words in in a Hebrew Lexicon—I am sorry to say that he has *either* studied ⟨*consecutively*⟩ no mythological Work—not Nonnus, for instance, whom he quotes so frequently[4]—*or* that thise dense Medium of his Noetic theory has excluded or strangled all rays but those of one color—/ Had he actually construed the four lines from the Orphic Hymn,[5] he must have ~~seen~~ discovered the interesting fact, that the Cabiric Bacchus is the Second Person of the Celestial Trinity, who was to become incarnate & be born an Infant.[6] The correspondence of the epithets to those of the Logos of St John is awefully striking.[7] The true solution I have already hinted in my "Aids to Reflection."[8] The Samo-thracian Mysteries contained

---

13[1] See Horace *Odes* 2.19.5. C's exposition of the first line of the hymn is well founded, his translation (which makes the beginning of an English hexameter) correct and vivid. Neither "hurraer" nor "evoer" is in *OED*.

13[2] "Strongly sounding"—not in *OED*.

13[3] See 11 and 12, above, and the quotation from N 36 in 1 n 1, above.

13[4] See 8, above, and n 12, below.

13[5] In C's day it was already recognised that the collection of "Orphic" hymns— mainly consisting of strings of epithets— was probably written in the second century A.D., though drawing upon earlier sources, Fragments of much earlier poems have also survived, mainly in quotation by Neoplatonic philosophers. For another "Orphic" poem, entitled *Lithica*, see BROWNE *Works* 21 and n 1.

13[6] See textus, and n 12, below.

13[7] The epithets "first-begotten, two-natured, thrice-begotten" correspond rather to the teaching of John 1 about the Logos and to the teaching of Paul about Christ. Cf e.g. FLEURY 66 and n 2 and see n 14, below.

13[8] The "true solution" follows in C's annotation. In *AR* (1825) 276–8 the problem solved is the problem of original

the Patriarchal Faith & Expectations disfigured by their forced combination with Pantheism or the Worship of Nature—the eight Cabiri were as follows:—Axieros, Axiokersos, and Axiokersa, ~~were~~ the infernal Trinity—or dim Personëities of the Chaos in the throes of self-organization—corresponding according to Varro to Pluto, Vulcan and Proserpine[9]—4th the Camillus, or Cadmīlus, the Mercury of the Greeks, or Mediator between Hades and the World of Light/

> superis deorum
> Gratus et imis—/[a][10]

This same Cadmilus, however, is the same being who under other names fills the second place of the Superior and consequently later Trinity[11]—namely, Jove, Minerva (sometimes named Apollo, Helios, or the Sun) and Venus, or *the Spirit*, the Source of Life and Love—lastly, and as the eighth, but still ⟨to⟩ come, the same Cadmilus or Mercury, who in a higher function is Minerva, or Sol, will appear as the Mediator or Restorer of the fallen Souls—as the Conductor from Chaos to the κοσμος or World of Law, Order,[b]

---

[a] Here C has written "(turn over)"
[b] Written "Order, Law," and marked for transposition

sin; cf *LR* I 184–6 for another version of this solution. SCHELLING *Samothrace* pp 29–30 makes a similar suggestion about the survival of the patriarchal faith but only with reference to monotheism, not to the Trinity and the anticipation of the redemption by Christ.

13[9] The three names Axieros, Axiokersos, Axiokersa (see also *LR* I 186) are not from Varro; but see n 11, below. A scholiast on Apollonius Rhodius *Argonautica* 1.917 gives the names, quoting the antiquarian Mnaseas, and identifies them with Demeter (Ceres), Persephone (Proserpine), and Hades (Pluto); Schelling discusses this on pp 7ff. Hephaestus (Vulcan), according to some authorities, was the father of the Cabiri and so in some way one of them: SCHELLING *Samothrace* pp 26ff. Cf BÖHME **140** n 3, 4; and on chaos in general see **6** n 2, above. With this exposition of the Cabiri cf BÖHME **135**, **136**, **140**, **174**, and nn.

13[10] Cadmilus is also from the scholiast (see n 9, above). Varro (see **2** n 1, above) in *De lingua latina* 6 mentions that Camillus is the servant of the great gods in the Samothracian mysteries:

SCHELLING *Samothrace* pp 21, 75. The Latin— "welcome alike to gods above and those below"—Horace *Odes* 1.10.19–20 (also quoted in BÖHME **174** at n 2) is given by Schelling p 75 (n 85) to show that Cadmilus is above the lower triad of gods and in communication with the higher gods.

13[11] See "ultimi quia supremi" in **2** and n 1, above. Schelling (p 25) announces that he does not intend to go above Cadmilus in the ascending series of the seven or eight Cabiri. Mnaseas, he says, breaks off at Dionysus (p 82 n 84), though Zeus, Venus, and Apollo—in no order—are mentioned by others. In dealing with the higher trinity C goes much farther than Schelling. All the gods named as second in C's trinity can be taken as symbolic of the Word: Hermes (Mercury, Cadmilus) as messenger of Zeus; Minerva (Athena) as Wisdom; Apollo (Sol, Helios) as the "light of men" (John 1.4). Dionysus (see n 12, below) was also a sun-god, as Faber argues, and Hermes was also conductor of souls.

Beauty, so hereafter to be the reconductor from the Disorder or second Hades, the Redeemer—and in this function he is Bacchus, to be born on earth & worshipped (vide Nonnus)[12] as the Infant Bacchus—

Πρωτογονον, διφυη, τριγονον—ανακτα—αγνον, κρυφιον, διμορφον—i.e. First-begotten, of two Natures, thrice begotten, the King, the Holy One, the Disguised, of two forms[13]—N.b. The Christian Fathers, as Waterland justly remarks, considered Christ as τριγονον[14]—first, before the Creation of the Finite, or the Eternal Generation—secondly, in the manifestation, i.e. the Creation of the Finite/ He was *in* the World and the World knew him not. Gosp. John I.[15] lastly, in the incarnation. "This day have I begotten thee/"[16] How flat, how vapid, compared with this view doe is the endless Tautology of the Arkite Noetic Scheme! Of all these epithets what one is applicable to Noah or the Ark? s. t. c.

14 II 11–13 | Ch 7 "Concerning the Sacred Terms Hiph or Siph, and Cul or Col; and the Various Traditions Founded upon Them"

[note i:]...When we find the story of Edipus and Jocasta, the parents of Eteocles and Polynices, accurately preserved in the ancient books of the Hindoos, we shall not be easily persuaded to believe, that their tragical adventures ever really took place in Beotia....it is surely more probable, that the Greeks, through the medium of Egypt, borrowed the fable from the Hindoos, and adapted it to their own country, than that the Hindoos borrowed it from the Greeks.

According to Captain Wilford, one of the descendants of Palli "was Lubdhaca;—and from Lubdhaca descended the unfortunate Linasu—whose tragical adventures are told in the Rajaniti...". May we not reasonably conjecture, that Lubdhaca was the *Labdacus*, Linasu the *Laius*, and Yogacashta the *Jocasta* of the Greeks?

13[12] Faber (p 192) quotes Nonnus *Dionysiaca* 13.137, mentioning the infant Bacchus; but C is probably thinking of the story as told at length by Nonnus elsewhere in *Dionysiaca*, of Bacchus not only as an infant but as thrice-born. Zagreus, infant child of Zeus and Persephone, is killed by Titans, and given new birth as Dionysus (6.155ff); he is conceived again by the union of Zeus and Semele (7.308ff); is untimely born (8.396ff); is sewn into the thigh of Zeus and born again at full time (9.1ff). On κοσμος see also Böhme **52** n 12.

13[13] As C indicates, the infant Bacchus is also adumbrated in the textus, from which he quotes and translates.
13[14] "Thrice-begotten"—as C has just translated it. C is evidently basing his account of the threefold generation of Christ on WATERLAND *A Vindication of Christ's Divinity* (1720) 134–5 (not annotated). The NT quotations (nn 15, 16) are added by C.
13[15] John 1.10 (with an omission).
13[16] Acts 13.33, Heb 1.5, 5.5 (from Ps 2.7)—all var.

I am not ~~Brass~~ such a Front O' Brass[1] as to deny the primâ facie superior probability of this Position. Never the less so obstinately has the virus of scepticism relatively to the pretensions of the Chinese and the Hindoos ~~and who~~ combined with my *Habit* of Thought, that it would not petrify me with Surprize, tho' some future Wilford should make out a strong case of the Ante-dating of the Rajaniti,[2] or the Interpolation at least, even to the extent, that would be required in order to the vindication of the *Greek* Parentage of Oidipus & Jocasta. I freely admit, however, that till this has been done, the whole Mythus must be regarded as a derivative from Hindoo Literature.

14[1] Cf Shakespeare *Love's Labour's Lost* v ii 395; and Hacket *Century* 5 and n 3.

14[2] The "Captain Wilford" whose authority Faber cites from *Asiatic Re-*searches III 75 in the second paragraph of this same footnote—Lieut-Col Francis Wilford (d 1822), well-known orientalist. The *Rajaniti*—a Burmese Buddhist book on ethics and education.

WILLIAM FALCONER
1732–1769

The Shipreck. A poem in three cantos. By a sailor. [Edition not identified.]

First ed 1762, 1764 (enlarged), 1802 (11th ed; reprinted in CHALMERS XIV, 1810), &c. See G. W. Couchman "Editions of Falconer's *Shipwreck*" *N&Q* Oct 1953.

Not located. The version of C's poem *Written in a Blank Leaf of* FAULKNER's SHIPWRECK, printed in *Felix Farley's Bristol Journal* 21 Feb 1818 under the prefatory note "We believe we are correct in attributing the following Lines to the pen of Mr. COLERIDGE" is presumed to have been taken from the original ms, or from a transcript close to it, thus accounting for the marked variations it shows from the text that C published in *SL* (1817, compiled 1815).

A copy "presented to Miss K——" with the poem as a presentation inscription. Both JDC and EHC date the poem c 1814—see *PW* (JDC) 185 and *PW* (EHC) I 424–5; certainly a Bristol setting is strongly implied (see 1 n 1). The original inscribed copy is nowhere described; the "Note by G. E. Weare, Weston-super-Mare, January, 1905", to which EHC refers in *PW* I 424n, is in a small pamphlet citing the *Felix Farley* publication and reprinting the poem. The inscribed copy may also have been annotated by C, if it was the copy that F. T. Barnard described to HNC in a letter of 15 Oct 1834: "When Mʳ Coleridge left Bristol [c 10 Sept 1814: see FIELD 28 n 2], he presented me with Faulkners Poem of the Shipwreck, with his Marginal Notes". But Barnard had no distinct recollection of the book and supposed that it might have been destroyed when his warehouse was burned down in the Bristol Riots of c 1830–1. MS Leatherhead.

Self-educated and with an early taste for literature, Falconer spent his early manhood at sea, publishing occasional poems. The publication in 1762 of *The Shipwreck*—his account in verse of his ordeal as one of only three survivors from the wreck of a merchant ship on a voyage from Alexandria to Venice c 1750—with its dedication to the Duke of York (then rear-admiral) gained him a commission in the Royal Navy. Serving in a number of appointments as purser, he continued to write and publish. Shortly after he had published his widely recognised *Universal Marine Dictionary* (1769; 4 further eds to 1830) he was lost in the frigate *Aurora* when she burned at sea with the loss of all hands after making the Cape of Good Hope on a voyage to India.

For the possible contribution to *AM* of *The Shipwreck*—with the wealth of nautical terms to which some readers objected—see *RX* 51–2 (dolphins and porpoises) and 265 ("weft" defined in the *Marine Dictionary*).

DATE. c Oct 1813–Sept 1814.

1 "In a blank leaf"

> *Written in a Blank Leaf of* FAULKNER'S SHIPWRECK,
> *presented by a Friend to Miss K——.*[1]

Ah! not by Cam or Isis (famous streams!)
In cloyst'ring[2] groves, the youthful Poet's choice;
Nor while half list'ning midst delicious dreams
To harp and song from woman's[3] hand and voice;

Nor yet while gazing in diviner[4] mood
On torrent falls, on woody mountain dell,[5]
Nor in dim cave, with bladdery sea-weeds strew'd,
Attuning wild tales[6] to the ocean's swell,

Our SEA BARD sang *this* song! which still he sings,
And sings for *thee*, sweet friend!
                              Hark, Pity, hark!
It mounts, it totters[7] on the tempest's wings!
It groans, it quivers,[8] the replunging bark!

1[1] The Bristol setting suggests, not so late a date as the *Felix Farley* publication in 1818 or even the earlier publication in *SL*, but the year that C spent in Bristol from Oct 1813 to Sept 1814, when despite ill-health and a serious attempt to break his addiction to opium—or because of these—he spent much time with his old friends. For another ms poem, presented to the wife of one of these Bristol friends, Mrs William Hood, in 1814 see *A Hymn* in *PW* (JDC) 638(n) and *PW* (EHC) I 423–4 and n. The identity of "Miss K——" is not known. If Sarah King (sister of Tom Poole, the "Sally" of e.g. *CL* III 461) had a daughter, she would be a candidate for C's gift of a poem, not least because Sarah's husband was "an African merchant, trading in palm oil and ivory" (*Poole* II 164n; cf *CL* III 447), and because of the acquaintance with seafaring men that Poole's friendship with Clarkson involved. Another possible candidate would be Caroline Kiddell: according to tradition, J. J. Morgan was to have married her in 1798. *S Letters* (Curry) I 162. Her brother George Kiddell, a twenty-years' acquaintance of C's (*CL* III 457), was active with C in trying to rescue Morgan's financial affairs from ruin especially in Oct–Nov 1813. *CL* III 445, 452, 456–7, 461; cf 526. Both ascriptions, however, are entirely speculative.

1[2] *SL*—essentially the canonical version, *PW* (EHC) I 424–5—reads "archéd". In the following notes only substantive variants from *SL* are recorded.

1[3] *SL*: "lady's".
1[4] *SL*: "sublimer".
1[5] *SL*: "On cliff, or cataract, in Alpine dell".
1[6] *SL*: "Framing wild fancies".
1[7] *SL*: "Now mounts, now totters".
1[8] *SL*: "Now groans, and shivers".

"Cling to the shrouds" in vain, the breakers roar,
DEATH shrieks! With two alone of all his clan
The toil-worn Poet[9] pac'd the Grecian shore
No classic roamer, but a shipwreck'd man!

Say then, what power evok'd such genial strains,
And beckon'd godlike, to his trembling Muse?
The thought not pleasureless of suffer'd pains,
But *chiefly* friendship's voice, her holy dues;[10]

Demanding dear remembrances of friend[11]
Or absent or no more! Shades of the past,
Which love makes real! Thence[12] to thee I send
(O dear as long as love[13] and memory last.)

I send, with deep regards of heart and head,
Sweet Maid for friendship fram'd, this song[14] to thee!
And thou, the while thou canst not chuse but shed
A tear for FALKNER, wilt remember *Me*.

1[9] *SL*: "Forlorn the poet".
1[10] *SL*:

"Say then, what muse inspired these
    genial strains,
  And lit his spirit to so bright a
    flame?
The elevating thought of suffered pains,
  Which gentle hearts shall mourn; but
  chief, the name".

1[11] *SL*: "Of gratitude! remem-
brances".
1[12] *SL*: "makes substance! Hence".
1[13] *SL*: "life".
1[14] *SL*: "formed! this work".

HUGH FARMER
1714–1787

A Dissertation on Miracles, designed to show that they are arguments of a divine interposition, and absolute proofs of the mission and doctrine of a prophet.... Third edition. London 1810. 8°.

Not located; marginalia not recorded. *Gillman SC* (1843) 324: "with Note by Mr. Coleridge".

The same lot in the Gillman Sale included "Farmer on the Demoniacs. 1805."—i.e. *An Essay on the Demoniacs of the New Testament* (2nd ed 1805).

FRANÇOIS DE SALIGNAC DE LA MOTHE
FÉNELON

1651–1715

[An unidentified volume of "religious" extracts from the works of
Fénelon, tr into English.]

Not located. C's note is here reprinted from *LR* II 368–9.

Mrs Gillman's copy, which C refers to in LUTHER p 213: "See the MSS Note
written in the blank leaf at the end of a small volume translated from
Fenelon, belonging to my *all-dear-and-holy-Names-in-the-name-of-Friend*,
Mrs Gillman." HNC told Gillman in a PS to a letter of "Thursday 10" [?
Sept 1835] that "We can discover no traces of Fenelon." Ms letter in the
possession of Blackwell's c 1949. The long note that follows was printed in
LR without textus.

C's reference to "pages 196, 197" and the *LR* subtitle "Fénélon on
Charity" should make it possible to identify the book, but the actual book
is not known. What must be a similar book, however, provides the textus
printed below: *Extracts from the Religious Works of Monsr Francois Salignac
de la Mothe Fenelon, Archbishop of Cambray. Translated from the original
French by Miss [Louisa A.] Marshall* (London 1809). In the 1st ed (1809) the
textus here printed is on pp 181–6 "On Charity, and Peace with Society";
in subsequent eds—all 12°—the paging of this section is farther from C's
reference: 2nd (1815) and 3rd (1816) eds, pp 168–72; 4th ed (1822) pp 153–7.

What writings of Fénelon C read is not known. For *Aventures de
Télémaque* see BARCLAY COPY A 3 and n 4; for the possibility of the *Maxims
of the Saints Explored* (1698) see *CN* II 2540n. In Nov 1796 C cited as
Fénelon's the view that "*men* are degraded Intelligences, who had once all
existed...in a paradisiacal or perhaps heavenly state". *CL* I 246. In *AR*
(1825) 385–6 he chose Fénelon as the type of "a Mystic, an Enthusiast of
a nobler Breed". Cf *CN* II 2540, 2598, III 3560, 3922.

DATE. After Apr 1816, in Highgate; or as late as c 1829, a not-impossible
date for LUTHER p 213 (the earliest dated annotation in that book is 25 Sept
1819).

1   "blank leaf at the end", referring to pp 196–7 | "On Charity, and Peace with
    Society"

One of the greatest and most necessary virtues of this life is Charity;
it is also one of the most acceptable in the sight of God, on account
of its relation to our fellow-creatures. Charity, saith the Apostle, shall

cover a multitude of sins; if we desire to live at peace (even with the best people), we must bear a great deal, and ask little; the most perfect of human beings is still full of imperfections. Let us set our own faults against those of our neighbours, and we shall soon find the necessity of mutual forgiveness. Happy are they, who, in bearing each other's burthens, fulfil (as the Apostle says) the law of Christ....

...We must continually remember what God had done for the vilest sinner, and that admittance into heaven is promised to all such as truly repent and forsake their sins....

Note to pages 196, 197.

This chapter is plausible, shewy, insinuating, and (as indeed is the character of the whole work) "makes the amiable."[1] To many,—to myself formerly,—it has appeared a mere dispute about words: but it is by no means of so harmless a character, for it tends to give a false direction to our thoughts, by diverting the conscience from the ruined and corrupted state, in which we are without Christ. Sin is the disease.[2] What is the remedy? What is the antidote?—Charity?— Pshaw! Charity in the large apostolic sense of the term is the health, the state to be obtained by the use of the remedy, not the sovereign balm itself,—faith of grace,—faith in the God-manhood, the cross, the mediation, and perfected righteousness, of Jesus, to the utter rejection and abjuration of all righteousness, of Jesus, to the utter rejection and abjuration of all righteousness of our own! Faith alone is the restorative. The Romish scheme is preposterous;— it puts the rill before the spring.[3] Faith is the source,—charity, that is, the whole christian life, is the stream from it.[4] It is quite childish to talk of faith being imperfect without charity. As wisely might you say that a fire, however bright and strong, was imperfect without heat, or that the sun, however cloudless, was imperfect without beams. The true answer would be:—it is not faith,—but utter reprobate faith-lessness, which may indeed very possibly co-exist with a mere acquiescence of the understanding in certain facts recorded by the

1[1] Perhaps C's English version of some such French idiom as "se faire l'amiable".
1[2] For sin as a disease in the will see e.g. BAHRDT 2 (following n 7).
1[3] For "preposterous" as = back-to-front see BÖHME 112 n 1.
1[4] See also a marginal note on *Friend*

Copy H: "...not in St Paul's [interpret-ation], with whom Sola fides = fides quæ numquam sola *manet*, or ~~sola~~ unicaus *fons*, quæ nusquam sine flumine potest esse esse. [Faith alone = the faith that never *remains* alone, or the unique *spring*, which can nowhere be without a river.]" *Friend* (*CC*) I 283n.

Evangelists. But did John, or Paul, or Martin Luther, ever flatter this barren belief with the name of saving faith? No. Little ones! Be not deceived. Wear at your bosoms that precious amulet against all the spells of antichrist, the 20th verse of the 2nd chapter of Paul's Epistle to the Galatians:—*I am crucified with Christ, nevertheless, I live; yet not I, but Christ liveth in me: and the life, which I now live in the flesh, I live by the faith of the Son of God, who loved me and gave himself for me.*

Thus we see even our faith is not ours in its origin: but is the faith of the Son of God graciously communicated to us. Beware, therefore, that you do not frustrate the grace of God: for if righteousness come by the Law, then Christ is dead in vain.[5] If, therefore, we are saved by charity, we are saved by the keeping of the Law, which doctrine St. Paul declared to be an apostasy from Christ, and a bewitching of the soul from the truth.[6] But, you will perhaps say, can a man be saved without charity?—The answer is, a man without charity cannot be saved: the faith of the Son of God[7] is not in him.

---

[5] Gal 2.21.
[6] Gal 2.16–17, 3.1–12.

[7] Gal 2.20.

JOHANN SAMUEL FEST
1754–c 1797

LOST BOOK

Versuch über die Vortheile der Leiden und Widerwärtigkeiten des menschlichen Lebens zur Beruhigung meiner Brüder... Verbesserte und vermehrte Auflage, &c. 2 vols. Leipzig 1787. 8°.

Not located; marginalia not recorded. *Green SC* (1880) 196: "With autograph and MS. Note by S. T. Coleridge." The volumes also appeared as *Green SC* (1884) 14 and were sold by Bartlett & Welford in New York.

JOHANN GOTTLIEB FICHTE

1762–1814

According to a passage in his account of his visit to Germany 1798–9 C found that "not a single Professor... is not either a Kantean, or a disciple of Fichte whose system is built on the Kantean, and presupposes its truth...". *Friend* (*CC*) II 243 (not in the letters written from Germany). C evidently began to read both Kant and Fichte either in Germany or shortly after his return to England. Some of the works of Fichte that he annotated were probably—like some of the Kant editions—copies he had bought in Germany: all the eight annotated titles belonged to him, and of these only three were published too late for him to have brought them home from Germany.

Although C seldom referred to particular works of Fichte, it is evident that he read Fichte repeatedly over a period of at least twenty years; the number of Fichte titles annotated (8)—cf Steffens (7), Schelling (8), Kant (13)—is a mark of his serious interest. The first work of Fichte's that he mentioned by title was *Ueber den Begriff der Wissenschaftslehre*, from which he translated a long passage in a letter of 13 Feb 1801 (*CL* II 674); *CN* I 921 (of similar date) may have a source in Fichte (see Orsini 178–82). The one annotation on this book seems to be of this date, and some of the notes in *Versuch* and the one note on *Grundriss* may be as early as 1802. It is not possible to disentangle the order in which he read the various works, nor can many of the marginalia be dated with much precision. The small number of early marginalia (1802–4), written before C was in the habit of profuse annotation, do not indicate the extent or depth of his earliest reading of Fichte. In Dec 1804 he noted that it was in "Tetens, Kant, Fichte, &c" that "you will trace or if you are on the hunt, track me" (*CN* II 2375), and when in Feb 1808 he was considering the value of his library to his estate in the event of his "speedy death" he noticed how strong it was in "the critical Fichte & Wissenschaftslehre" (*CN* III 3276). Other annotations, especially those in *Bestimmung*, *Grundlage*, and *System*, were written in c 1815. The later notes (1820–2) seem to be those in *Anweisung* and *Der geschlossne Handelsstaat*. For a list of the works of Fichte that C owned in 1815–16 see *CN* III 4307 and n—eight titles, six of which are annotated and in the BM, the other two not otherwise reported as C's: *Einige Vorlesungen über die Bestimmung des Gelehrten* (Jena & Leipzig 1794) and *Appellation an das Publikum über die durch ein Kurf. Sächs. Confiscations-rescript ihm beigemessenenen atheistischen Aeusserungen* (Jena & Leipzig 1799). Cf *CN* III 3276n (at the end).

In Dec 1804 C said that he found it difficult to acknowledge particular obligations to Kant and the neo-Kantians because, though there were obvious "glaring resemblances", these were both more and less than they seemed because of his fellow-feeling with these philosophers. *CN* II 2375; cf

594

2382 and Orsini 183–91. In 1810 HCR recorded a conversation in which C said that "Fichte and Schelling... would be found at last to have erred where they deviated from Kant; but he considered Fichte a great logician, and Schelling perhaps a still greater man." *CRD* 15 Nov 1810 (not in *CRB*); cf *BL* (*CC*) I cxxvi–cxxvii. In *BL*, however, he wrote a summary judgement of Fichte that, with its "burlesque on the Fichtean Egoismus", includes both the grounds for his admiration and the defects that he pointed out repeatedly in marginalia, in conversation, and in correspondence: his Stoic ethics, his lack of method, his sophistic manipulation of the term *Ich*. *BL* ch 9 (*CC*) I 157–60 and n. In Dec 1817 he told Green that "Fichte in his moral system is but a caricature of Kant: or rather he is a Zeno with the Cowl, Rope, and Sackcloth of a Carthusian Monk. His metaphysics have gone by; but he has the merit of having prepared the ground for, and laid the first stone of, the *Dynamic* Philosophy by the substitution of Act for Thing". *CL* IV 792. Again, in Sept 1818, he said that "Fichte was far nearer the truth than Schelling—he had hold of the Horns of the Altar, but with nerve-palsied hand—and blind." *CL* IV 874–5; and cf *Friend* (*CC*) I 520 n 1 and 522 n 1 (ms). C's silence on Fichte—and his slight treatment of Kant and Schelling—is "to most readers perhaps [one of] the worst disappointments in the [philosophical] lectures" of 1818–19. *P Lects* (1949) 61. For a statement on Kant, Fichte, and Schelling in Apr 1825 see *CL* V 421.

Die Anweisung zum seeligen Leben, oder auch die Religionslehre. Berlin 1806. 8°.

British Museum C 43 a 15

For a possible quotation from p 50, or from KANT *Vermischte Schriften*, see *Logic* (*CC*) 151.

DATE. Perhaps in the 1820s; certainly after Jul 1815 (see **2** n 1). The list of desiderata for a holiday move in **5** may refer to 1824, but could refer to 1816, 1817, 1820, 1821, etc: see **5** n 2.

COEDITORS. Willem Schrickx, Raimonda Modiano.

1 p 3, pencil | Erste vorlesung

Wiederum *vereinigt* und *verbindet* innigst die Liebe das getheilte Ich, das ohne Liebe nur kalt, und ohne alles Interesse, sich anschauen würde.

[Then again love intimately *unites* and *combines* the divided "I", which without love would regard itself only coldly and without any interest.]

O woeful Love whose first act and offspring is *Self*![1] "I! and this not a present "I AM" but a poor *reflection* thereof![2]—In his better Days F. taught a nobler dogma—viz. the generation of the I from the Thou in all finite Minds.[3]

2 p +2, referring to pp 341–52 | Beilage zu der sechsten Vorlesung

Die Hauptlehre des Christenthums, als einer besondern Anstalt, Religion im Menschengeschlecht zu entwickeln: dass in Jesu zu allererst, und auf eine, keinem andern Menschen also zukommende Weise, das ewige Daseyn Gottes eine menschliche Persönlichkeit

1[1] For C's objection to the doctrine of self-love see e.g. *CN* III 3559 and *LS* (*CC*) 186–7n.

1[2] Cf *BL* ch 12 (*CC*) I 260, 275 and n.

1[3] Possibly a reference to *Versuch* §§ 3–4 (pp 40–81): "The moral law *alone* lies in God, and *without any limitation*.... There must therefore be an *eternal God*, and every moral being must continue to exist *eternally*, if the purpose of the moral law is not to become impossible.... We act according to the law of reason because it is *God's* law.... The idea of God, as lawgiver through the moral law in us, is grounded on a surrender of our own [being], on a transfer of a subjective [being] to a being outside us, and this surrender is the actual *principle of religion*... Thus God is the *creator*.... However, we are also, as physical beings—that is, beings who are under natural laws—parts of the creation.... Just as we recognise him [God] to be the creator of our nature, we must therefore also acknowledge him to be our moral lawgiver...".

For "I+He = Ye", which "enables *Man* to love his neighbour as himself", see *CN* IV 4636 (c 1819–25).

angenommen habe, dass alle übrigen nur durch ihn, und vermittelst
der Wiederholung seines ganzen Charakters in sich, zur Vereinigung
mit Gott kommen könnten; sey ein bloss historischer, keinesweges
aber ein metaphysischer Satz, heisst es im Texte (S. 166.)....Wer aber
noch zu wissen begehrt, durch welche—entweder willkührliche
Veranstaltung Gottes, oder, innere Nothwendigkeit in Gott—ein
solches Individuum möglich, und wirklich geworden, der überfliegt
das Faktum, und begehrt zu mctaphysiciren das nur historische. Für
Jesus war eine solche Transcendenz schlechtin unmöglich; denn für
diesen Behuf hätte er sich, in seiner Persönlichkeit, von Gott
unterscheiden, und sich abgesondert hinstellen...müssen. Aber es
ist ja der...wiederkommende Zug im Charakter des Johannischen
Jesus, dass er von einer solchen Absonderung seiner Person von
seinem Vater gar nichts wissen will...dass er immerfort annimmt,
wer ihn sehe, sehe den Vater, und wer ihn höre, höre den Vater, und
das sey alles Eins...

[The chief doctrine of Christianity, regarded as a special institution to
develop religion in the human race, is that in Jesus first of all, and in a way
that therefore befits no other human beings, the Eternal Being of God has
assumed a human personality, and that all others could achieve union with
God only through Him and by means of a re-enacting of His total character
in themselves; it is said in the text (p 166) that this is only a historical,
certainly not a metaphysical, proposition....Anyone, therefore, who wishes
to know still more about how—whether by God's arbitrary action or an inner
necessity in God—such an individual became possible and real, oversteps
what is merely a historical fact and concerns himself with metaphysics. For
Jesus such a transcendence was utterly impossible because for such a purpose
he would have had to differentiate his personality from God and present
himself as separate from God...But it is the...recurrent trait in the
character of the Johannine Jesus that he wants to know of no such separation
of his personality from his Father...that he always postulates that who sees
him, sees the Father, and who hears him, hears the Father, and it is all
one...]

p. 341–352.—

This is the theory and the language of the present Mystics in Persia
respecting Christ, according to Sir J. Malcolm.[1] The answer is given
in the fact, that Christ does not merely or simply affirm his identity
with the Father—*in* Fichte's words, that God was Jesus not that Jesus
was God[2]—but affirms it of himself *exclusively*, and promises it to
others as a privilege *communicated to them.* 2[ndly] He does not assert

2[1] Sir John Malcolm (1769–1833)
History of Persia ch 22 (1815, published
Jul) 382–415, esp 389, 415.

2[2] See 3 textus, below, last sentence.

his *identity* in Fichte's Sense of the Word—i.e. that the Father and he were the *same* Self or Person—but his union with the Father—and throughout attributes a distinct personality to himself—"My Father & I will come; and *we* will dwell in you"—[3]

3 p +2, referring to p 352

[continuing from **2** textus]...und dass er [der Johannische Jesus] ein Selbst an ihm...unbedingt abläugnet, und wegwirft. Ihm war nicht der Jesus Gott, denn einen selbstständigen Jesus gab er nicht zu; wohl aber war Gott Jesus, und erschien als Jesus.

[...and that he [the Jesus of John's Gospel] totally rejects and disclaims an individuality in himself. To him Jesus was not God, for he did not acknowledge a self-subsistent Jesus; but rather God was Jesus and was manifested as Jesus.]

352, l. 1. What is προς τον θεον, if [not][a] *an* ihm, or *am* Gotte?[1]—If there were no subsisting Jesus, consequently Jesus = O was not = God; but God *appeared* as Jesus, i.e. put on a phantom Body—in what sense could Christ even in his eternal Character be styled the Son of God, or speak of God as his Father?

4 p +3, referring to p 354, in ink, completed in pencil | Zweite Beilage

Wenige Ausnahmen abgerechnet, erhalten die Schriftsteller kein anderes Zeichen von dem Eindrucke, den sie auf das lesende Publikum machen, ausser durch das Medium der Recensionen. Durch dieses Medium bin ich nun, siet dem Beginne meiner schrift-stellerischen Laufbahn bis jetzt, in der Regel, misverstanden, ver-dreht, hämisch verlästert worden; liess ich nicht drucken, so wurde ich deswegen geschmäht, lasse ich drucken, so mache ich es nicht recht, und werde abermals geschmäht, und jedes neue Buch wird mir zu einem neuen Verbrechen. Ich muss sonach glauben, dass das lesende Publikum mich von der Mühe, für dasselbe zu arbeiten, entbinde...

[With few exceptions writers have no indication of the impression they make on the public mind except by reviews. In these, from the very beginning of my career as an author till the present time, I have been as a rule

a Word supplied by the editor

2[3] Cf John 14.23 (var).
3[1] On πρός in John 1.1 as "utmost possible *proximity*, without *confusion*; likeness, without sameness" see *TT* 6 Jan

1823. See also SHERLOCK p 222. But it is hardly feasible to be so precise about the meanings of prepositions in NT Greek.

misunderstood, distorted, and maliciously vilified. If I publish nothing, I am abused for not publishing; if I publish, things are no better—I am still abused, and every new book becomes a new crime. From this I must assume that the reading public has released me from the trouble of labouring further for it...]

354. How girlish! And because a Reviewer or two had attacked his Writings, therefore he must believe that the Reading Public have released him from the Task & Trouble of writing for them.[a] Besides, Fichtes vanity is downright outrageous—I at least should have considered such a Review of a work of mine highly complimentary, however much I might regret that the Reviewer had misconceived & thence misrepresented my meaning in certain passages.

S. T. C.

5   p +5, pencil[b]

2 Umb. and 1 Parasole
Henry's gr. Coat[1]
3 paper parcels + 2 Cake paperlets
1 Handkerchief Parcel
And this Book.[2]

[a] The rest of the note is in pencil, written in a different, larger hand
[b] Written with the book turned upside down, as though the back were the front

5[1] Henry Gillman (1814–58), the younger son of James Gillman. C took great interest in Henry's education, coaching him in Greek and Latin, procuring for him an admission to Eton through his nephew Edward and taking him to the college upon entry. For the reasons for his withdrawal and C's efforts on his behalf see *CL* vi 640–50, 652, 658. See also *CN* iv 5424 and n and 5456n.

5[2] This list suggests one of the many holiday visits from 1816 onward, usually to Ramsgate. For a possible clue to the date of this note—but not necessarily to the other notes in the volume—see the "mistake about the Umbrellas...One only was taken" in *CL* v 374 (6 Oct 1824). Cf also *CN* iv 5456 (26 Oct 1826), referring to receipt of a letter from Edward Coleridge about Henry Gillman's withdrawal from Eton (see n 1, above): "Alas! a fatality seems to follow our Ramsgate journey!.—"

Die Bestimmung des Menschen. Berlin 1800. 8°.

British Museum C 43 a 12

Binder's mark "1" in brown ink at the head of p ⁻1, and "2" at the head of the last printed page (p 338, facing p ⁺1 bearing 11). See also 18 n *a*, below. Cf *Der geschlossne Handelsstaat* headnote. On pp 289–90 two sentences are underlined in pencil, with what looks like a large check-mark with line above in the margin of both pages.

DATE. 1815 or later. See *CN* III 4307 and n, and cf II 2375n.

COEDITORS. Willem Schrickx, Raimonda Modiano.

1 title-page, pencil

= means equal to, the same as
+ more by, in addition to
− less by, subtracted
÷ divided by
⨯ in opposition to, in anthithesis[1]
$20 + 20 - 10 \div 3 = 10$
Will = I ⨯ Thing[2]

2 pp 6–7, pencil, cropped | Bk I "Zweifel"

Wenn ich nur dasjenige weiss, und von ihm überzeugt bin, was ich selbst gefunden,—nur dasjenige wirklich kenne, was ich selbst erfahren habe, so kann ich in der That nicht sagen dass ich über meine Bestimmung das geringste wisse; ich weiss blos, was andre darüber zu wissen behaupten; und das einzige, was ich hierinn wirklich versichern kann, ist dies, dass ich so oder so über diese Gegenstände sprechen gehört....

Was sie etwa wahres wissen, woher können sie es wissen, ausser durch eignes Nachdenken? Und warum sollte ich durch dasselbe Nachdenken nicht dieselbe Wahrheit finden, da ich eben so viel bin als sie? Wie sehr habe ich bisher mich selbst herabgesetzt und verachtet!

1[1] See EICHHORN *Apocrypha* 2. For a similar array of C's "abbreviations" or logical symbols see *CN* III 4241 and n (c 1814–18) and cf 4403 and n (c Apr 1818). C had used the sign ⨯, and a few others, as early as 1804 (see *CN* II 2384); but he seems not to have used his family of abbreviations consistently until 1814 at

earliest, and possibly not until c Apr 1818. The history of C's family of logical signs is considered in detail in JOANNES Scotus Erigena *De divisione naturae* (Oxford 1681) ii 88nn.

1[2] On the will as synonymous with "I" see *CN* I 1717.

[If I know and am convinced of only what I myself have discovered—if I really know only what I myself have experienced, then in fact I cannot say that I know even the slightest thing about my condition; all I know is what others maintain they know about it; and the only thing that I can really be sure of is that I have heard such and such a thing about these matters.... For instance, how can they know something to be true except by reflection? And why should I, who am their equal, not find the same truth in the same way? How I have degraded and despised myself hitherto!]

But is not this a contradiction to p. 3^d and 4^h?[1] The Author should at least have exprest his meaning less equivocally[2] which might have [b]een easily done, by saying in the [f]irst instance [tha]t my Te[acher?] [has] made me do this and *that.*[a] But this is a trifle. My main objection is that this [i]s not the [t]rue History [o]f the Process and Progress of a mind that instinctively feels and would fain, solve the Riddle of the World and of itself[3]—I would [? indite] an actual esoteric Biography from earliest rememberable Childhood—deduce the new Interest in watching Infants & Children/[4] the proof, that the Philosopher no less than the Poet, nascitur non fit/[5]—Before 6 months we may see in each infant, whether it is an Animal or a Mind/ From this state I would proceed to the Apostacy, produced by Custom & Authority,[6] passive Doctrine or Utility &c—and the Return/ in short, Pilgrim's Progress.—Hints for myself *rather than* Censures on Fichte

a Rubbed and scarcely legible

2[1] Fichte asserts (pp 3–4) that "I established my beliefs only in accordance with the testimony of my senses and of continuous experience; I touched what I saw, I analysed what I touched, I went over my observations...That is why I am as certain of the accuracy of this part of my knowledge as of my own existence...But—what am I myself, and what is my condition? Superfluous question—my teaching [*Belehrung*] about this subject was long ago completed, and it would take time to repeat all that I have heard, learned, believed about it."
2[2] Cf **13**, below.
2[3] For C's characterisation of "the minds that feel the Riddle of the World, and may help to unravel it" see *CN* I 1622 (c 28 Oct 1803), repeated in *Friend* (*CC*) II 73 (I 109), *BL* ch 4 (*CC*) I 80, and *SM*

(*CC*) 25. See Pope *An Essay on Man* II 18: "The glory, jest, and riddle of the world".
2[4] C and Tom Wedgwood ("forever...loving to look at Children" — *CN* I 1705[h]) took up "the new Interest" in observing children in order to understand perception and learning, their personal interest reinforced by new systems of education in which C—like the Wedgwoods—was much interested. See e.g. *CL* II 673, *CN* I 838, 923, and *Friend* (*CC*) II 8–9.
2[5] "A poet is born, not made"—a Latin proverb (possibly derived from Florus *De qualitate vitae* frag 8).
2[6] Possibly an echo of WW *Immortality Ode* lines 128–9: "And custom lie upon thee with a weight, | Heavy as frost, and deep almost as life." Cf also lines 67–76. *WPW* IV 283, 281.

3 pp 48–9

Nur die Begriffe, Verschuldung und Zurechnung haben keinen Sinn, *] ausser den für das äussere Recht. Verschuldet hat sich derjenige, und ihm wird sein Vergehen zugerechnet, der die Gesellschaft nöthigt, künstliche äussere Kräfte anzuwenden, um die Wirksamkeit seiner der allgemeinen Sicherheit nachtheiligen Triebe zu verhindern.... Von dieser Entdeckung Gebrauch für mein Handeln zu machen, †] kann mir nicht einfallen, denn ich handle ja überhaupt nicht, sondern in mir handelt die Natur...die Natur macht mich selbst, und alles was ich werde.

[The only meaning that the concepts of guilt and imputation have is in respect to the external law. A person is guilty, and he will be charged with his error, if he forces society to apply artificial external force in order to hinder the effect of those impulses of his that are disadvantageous to general security....It cannot occur to me to make use of this discovery in my action, for I do not act at all: nature acts in me...nature makes me what I am and everything that I become.]

* and † commences the Sophism—for "*I*" hitherto has been used as Natura naturans individua, per se determinata[1]—but now it stands for the result & total effect of the former. In the first case it is ego contemplans—in the second res contemplata, per quam quasi in speculo me contemplor.[2] I do not see any incompatibility of the first, i.e. of reformed Spinosism, with Freedom—ergo, not with Morals or Religion.—

4 p 50

Ich stehe unter der unerbittlichen Gewalt der strengen Nothwendigkeit; bestimmt sie mich zu einem Thoren und Lasterhaften, so

3[1] "The active individual Nature, self-determined". For *natura naturans* and *natura naturata* see BLUMENBACH 1 n 3 and *CN* III 4397 f 50ᵛ and n.

3[2] "I contemplating...the thing contemplated, through which I contemplate myself as in a glass". Cf *BL* ch 4 (*CC*) I 72–3n. Fichte, not as inconsistent as C claims here, had said earlier (pp 26–38) that in immediate self-consciousness the "I" appears to itself as free and self-subsistent, but upon reflection it realises that it is only a manifestation of an independent power of nature that makes each "I" what it is individually. "I did not originate from myself....I was brought into being by another force outside myself....However, I—what I call 'I', my own person—am not the power of nature that creates man, but only one of its manifestations; and I, *as my own self*, am only conscious of this manifestation, not of the power that I infer only through the necessity of explaining myself....This is why I find myself generally as an *independent* being....*In the immediate* self-consciousness I appear to myself as being free; through *reflection* on nature as a whole I find that freedom is utterly impossible; the former must be subordinated to the latter, for it can only be explained through the latter."

werde ich ohne Zweifel ein Thor und ein Lasterhafter werden; bestimmt sie mich zu einem Weisen und Guten, so werde ich ohne Zweifel ein Weiser und Guter werden.

[I stand under the inexorable power of strict necessity; if this power destined me to be a foolish and vicious person, I would no doubt become a foolish and vicious person; if it destined me to be a wise and good person, I would no doubt become a wise and good person.] In no other sense than that it is not an act of my own, that I am born a Man and not a Wolf or Sheep. As God, I should be above that wavering Choice, which we ~~know~~ learn our freedom from; as a beast, below it. But Wilkühr ist nicht der Wille;[1] and the highest Object of the Latter is to soar above the former—to leave it behind. Else, every perfect Habit of Virtue would be a Loss of Freedom.

5   pp 77–9 | Bk II "Wissen"

Der Geist....Also du hast ein unmittelbares Bewusstseyn deines Sehens und Fühlens?
   Ich. Ja.
   D. G. Deines Sehens und Fühlens, sagte ich. Du bist dir sonach
*] das Sehende im Sehen, das Fühlende im Fühlen; und indem du des Sehens dir bewusst bist, bist du dir einer Bestimmung, oder Modification *deiner selbst* bewusst?
   Ich. Ohne Zweifel.

[*The Spirit.*...Have you then an immediate consciousness of your seeing and feeling?
   I. Yes
   The Spirit. I said: of *your* seeing and feeling. Accordingly, you are the seeing subject in the act of seeing, the feeling subject in the act of feeling; and by being conscious of seeing are you conscious of a determination or modification in *yourself*?
   I. No doubt.]

* Here I make a stand: not so much as a philosopher, doubting the truth, as a logician dissatisfied with the reasoning. For here I come to the foundation-stone of Idealism, & this seems a gratuitous Assumption—viz—that no such power exists as that of Perception, but that ⟨what⟩ we so call, is only a self-consciousness of our being, as modified—i.e. a mere consciousness of self-modification: hereby identifying it with the ~~pai~~ sensation of Pleasure or Pain.[1] Now this

---

4[1] "Choice [in the sense of whim or caprice] is not will". Cf *BL* ch 12 (*CC*) I 293–4. On the difference between choice and freedom see *Versuch* 5.

5[1] For the grounds of C's attack on idealism see ESCHENMAYER 27 n 3.

is assuredly not the suggestion of the common sense of Mankind: we have no intuition of this, but rather a semblance at least of an intuitive persuasion of the contrary.[2] It ought therefore to be proved—& not ~~on~~ merely by physical Induction, as of Rays of light, Pulses of air, from the ~~or~~ bodies seen or heard: for this begins with admitting Realism, & so deduces its non-entity from its entity.

6 p 77

D. G. Du hast ein Bewusstseyn * deines Sehens, Fühlens, u. s. w. und dadurch nimmst du den Gegenstand wahr. Könntest du ihn nicht wahrnehmen auch ohne dieses Bewusstseyn? Könntest du nicht etwa einen gegenstand erkennen durch das Gesicht, oder durch das Gehör, ohne zu wissen, dass du sähest oder hörest?
Ich. Keinesweges.

[*The Spirit.* You have a consciousness of your seeing, feeling, etc, and in this way you perceive an object. Could you not perceive it without this consciousness? Could you not, for instance, recognise an object by sight or sound without knowing that you were seeing or hearing?
I. Certainly not.]

* No! I seem to myself to be conscious only [of][a] the object, not of my seeing:[1] unless from its glitter or from Disease, it makes my eyes *feel.*[2]

7 pp 112–13

D. G. Lass dich dadurch nicht irre machen. Der Akte deines Geistes wirst du dir nur bewusst, inwiefern du durch einen Zustand der Unbestimmtheit und Unentschlossenheit hindurchgehest, dessen du dir gleichfalls bewusst wirst, und welchem jene Akte ein Ende machen. Eine solche Unentschiedenheit findet in unserm Falle nicht statt: der Geist braucht nicht erst zu berathschlagen, welchen Gegenstand er zu seiner bestimmten Empfindung hinzu zu setzen habe, es kommt ihm von selbst. Man hat auch dafür eine Unterscheidung in der philosophischen Sprache. Ein Akt des Geistes, dessen wir uns als eines solchen bewusst werden, heisst *Freiheit*. Ein Akt, ohne Bewusstseyn des Handelns, blosse *Spontaneität*. Bemerke wohl, dass ich dir ein unmittelbares Bewusstseyn des Aktes, als eines

---

a Word supplied by the editor

5[2] I.e. we are persuaded that "there exist things without us": see *BL* ch 12 (*CC*) ɪ 259–62.

6[1] See **5** and n 1, above, and **8** and n 2, below.
6[2] Cf also ESCHENMAYER **10** and n 1.

solchen, keinesweges anmuthe, sondern nur dies, dass, wenn du hinterher darüber nachdenkst, du findest, es müsse ein Akt seyn.—Die höhere Frage, was es sey, das eine solche Unentschlossenheit, und das Bewusstseyn unsers Handelns nicht aufkommen lasse, wird sich ohne Zweifel tiefer unten von selbst lösen.

Man nennt diesen Akt deines Geistes *denken*, welches Worts ich mich auch bisher, mit deiner Beistimmung bedient habe; und man sagt, dass das Denken mit Spontaneität geschehe, zum Unterschiede von der Empfindung, welche blosse Recepticität sey.

[*The Spirit.* Do not be deceived by this. You only become aware of the acts of your mind in so far as you pass through a condition of indecision and indetermination, of which you also become aware and to which the aforesaid act puts an end. In our case such indecision does not occur: the mind does not first need to consider what object it has to bring into contact with a certain sensation it has: this comes to it of its own accord. For this too one finds a distinction in philosophical terms. An act of the mind of which we are aware as such is termed *freedom*. An act performed without consciousness of its performance is mere *spontaneity*. Notice in particular that I do not presume you to have immediate consciousness of the act as such, but of the fact that when you think about it afterwards you find that it must have been an act. The deeper question as to what it is that prevents such indetermination and the consciousness of our actions from coming about will undoubtedly be resolved below.

This act of your mind is called *thought*, a word I have used hitherto with your approval, and we say that thought occurs spontaneously, whereas sensation is mere receptivity.]

But this is clearly a desertion of the viæ (τῆς ⟨μεθοδοῦ⟩) argumenti prepositæ.[1] Here the direct path of Consciousness is interrupted: *and* I am referred to a (quoad *me*) ARBITRARY Distinction. Instead of a Fact I am drenched with an Hypothesis, a supposition—nay, that at the conclusion might be allowed. After all the Facts had been brought before the mind, some one Fact might have been selected as the Base and Supporter of the others. But this is (in the present stage of the argument) an ὑποποιῆσις, not an ὑποθεσις,[2] a *suffiction* not a *subposition*. N.B. I complain merely of a fault in method. The necessity of a self-conscious Being to climb beyond his recollected Consciousness, should have been first proved by Induction[3]—viz—If A, which is known to be real, be impossible with⟨out⟩ X, then X

7[1] Desertion "of the preferred way ('method'—the way through) of argument". *Via* and ὁδός are equivalent words.

7[2] A "hypopoiesis", not a "hypo-thesis". The distinction is clarified in *CN* III 3587 (Jul–Sept 1809) and much later in *CL* V 468. See also ARGENS 6 n 2, BÖHME 31 n 4, and GREW 8 n 4.

7[3] Cf 9 and 10, below.

must be real: or, That must itself ⟨be admitted as⟩ ~~be~~ real, which constitutes the sole possibility of that which is known to be real. But of all axioms this requires the most caution & insight in its application

8 p 138, pencil

Durch diese äussere Anschauung hindurch wird nun auch selbst die Wahrnehmung als eine äussere, und die Sinne, als äussere, erblickt. Es bleibt ewig wahr, denn es ist erwiesen: Ich sehe oder fühle *immer nimmer] die Fläche: wohl aber schaue ich an mein Sehen, oder Fühlen, als Sehen oder Fühlen einer Fläche.

[By means of this outward intuition perception itself is now seen to be something external as well, as are the senses. It remains eternally true, for it has been proved: that I always see or feel the surface: but I look upon my seeing or feeling as the seeing or feeling of a surface.]

* Should the emphasis be laid on "*die*" ⨉ "*einer*"? or ~~it~~ is not rather "*immer*" a misprint for "*nimmer*"?[1] See p. 88 et sequentes: & p. 146[2]

9 pp 140–1, pencil

Ich. Es muss ein doppeltes seyn. Die Empfindung ist selbst ein unmittelbares Bewusstseyn; ich *empfinde* mein Empfinden. Dadurch entsteht mir nun keinesweges irgend ein Erkenntniss eines Seyns, sondern nur *das Gefühl meines eignen Zustandes*. Aber ich bin ursprünglich nicht bloss empfindend, sondern auch anschauend; denn ich bin nicht bloss ein praktisches Wesen, sondern auch Intelligenz. Ich *schaue* mein Empfinden auch an; und so entsteht mir aus mir selbst und meinem Wesen *die Erkenntniss eines Seyns*. Die *Empfindung* verwandelt sich in ein *Empfindbares*; meine Affection,

---

8[1] Later editions do not support C's conjecture that "always" should be "never".

8[2] C wonders whether his difficulty could be resolved by emphasising the difference between "die Fläche" (*the* surface) in the first part of the statement and "einer Fläche" (*a* surface) at the end of it; or whether "I *always* see" could be a misprint for "I *never* see". In **5**, above, C had objected to Fichte's account of "seeing" and "feeling" as being properly the *consciousness* of objects seen and felt. At p 88 Fichte had said that "Every perception is a definite one. We never

merely see or feel or hear, but see, hear, or feel something definite, a red, green, or blue colour; cold, warmth, a smooth surface, a rough surface, the sound of a violin, the voice of a human being, etc." On p 146—as on pp 140–1 (see **8**, below)—Fichte discusses distance as an acquired concept and also introduces the problem of space. Cf p 148: "All consciousness of an object outside me is determined by the distinct and exact consciousness of my own state, and in the same consciousness contact is made between the object as it is grounded in me and as it exists outside me."

Roth, Glatt und dergleichen, in ein *Rothes, Glattes* u. s. w. ausser mir: welches—und dessen Empfindung, ich im Raume anschaue, weil mein Anschauen selbst der Raum ist. So wird auch klar, warum ich Flächen zu sehen oder zu fühlen glaube, die ich doch in der That weder sehe noch fühle. Ich schaue nur an mein Sehen oder Fühlen, als Sehen oder Fühlen einer Fläche.

[*I.* It must be a twofold consciousness. Sensation is itself an immediate consciousness; I *am sentient* of sensation. I can, however, acquire no knowledge of being by this means, but only the *feeling of my own condition.* But by nature I am not only a sentient being, but also an intuitive being; for I am not simply a practical being but also have intelligence. I also *intuit* my [act of] perceiving through the senses; and thus from myself and my being I derive the *cognition of a being. Sensation* changes into an *object of sensation,* how I feel it—red, smooth, etc.—into *something red, something smooth,* etc. outside me: a feeling that, and the feeling of which, I intuit in space, because my intuition is itself space. Thus it also becomes clear why I think I see or feel surfaces that I in fact neither see nor feel. I am merely intuiting my own seeing and feeling, as the seeing or feeling of a surface.]

Still I miss the inductive Proof of the *reality* of this marvellous Anshauung,[a] or conversion of sensation into Sense. The plain-minded Scholar might ask whether a faculty of perceiving Things separate from the Percipient, which all men by nature take for granted, & which is the ordinary state even of the Idealist himself, is a whit more wonderful, than this substituted Power of *seeing* Feelings, this instantaneous transmutation of Points into Lines, Lines into Surfaces, Time into Space?[1]—Here as elsewhere I complain not as so much of the *doctrine,* as of the Chasms in the Proof of it—.[2] For the actual existence of such a Faculty as that of *Anschauung* = Intuitio,[3] Fichte might refer to our Dreams: and then he would have to shew, why our Waking Perceptions are so different.[4] I *may* fancy myself awake when I am in sleep—but not asleep when awake.[5]

[a] A slip for *Anschauung*

9[1] See 5 and 6, above.
9[2] Cf 7, above, and 10, below. Cf C's admiration for the "austere beauty of Method" in Kant's work: HEINROTH 25.
9[3] In many notebook entries and marginalia C struggled with the concept of *Anschauung* (intuition): see 12, below, and e.g. KANT *Critik der reinen Vernunft* passim. One of his inventions for a self-evident English equivalent was

"Onlook" (*CN* III 3113); another was "Aspicience" (BM Add MS 34225 f 144). Cf 14 and n 4, below.
9[4] For a suitable line of reasoning, attributed to Pythagoras, see *P Lects* Lect 2 (1949) 106 and 402 n 40.
9[5] In *BL* ch 18 (*CC*) II 63–4 C uses, as an objection to idealism, the same example from dreams. Cf also *Versuch* 9.

10 pp 147–9, pencil, cropped

D. G. ...wonach magst du sie schätzen, diese Entfernung?
Ich. Ohne Zweifel nach der grössern Stärke oder Schwäche übrigens gleichartiger Eindrücke.—Ich erblicke vor mir zwei Gegenstände von demselben Roth. Der, dessen Farbe ich deutlicher sehe, ist mir näher; der dessen Farbe ich schwächer erblicke, entfernter, und um so viel entfernter, als ich sie schwächer erblicke....

...Ich habe durch lebenslängliche Uebung gelernt, schnell die Stärke des Eindrucks zu bemerken, und die Entfernung darnach zu beurtheilen. Es ist ein schon ehemals durch Arbeit Zusammengesetztes aus Empfindung, Anschauung, und ehemaligem Urtheil,— von welchem meine gegenwärtige Vorstellung ausgeht; welcher letztern allein ich mir bewusst werde. Ich fasse nicht mehr überhaupt das Roth, Grün und dergleichen ausser mir, sondern ein Roth oder Grün, *von dieser, und dieser, und dieser Entfernung* auf; dieser letzte Zusatz aber ist *blosse Erneuerung eines schon ehemals durch Ueberlegung zu Stande*.

[*The Spirit.* ...How can you estimate this distance?
I. Surely by the greater strength or weakness of otherwise homogeneous impressions. I see before me two objects of the same red colour. The one whose colour I see more distinctly is nearer to me; the one whose colour I see more weakly is farther away—the more weakly I perceive its colour, the more distant it is....

I have learned by lifelong practice to note quickly the strength of the impression and to judge the distance by that. It is something that has already, previously, been formed through sensation, intuition, and former judgement —from which my present conception of it originates; I become conscious of the latter only. I no longer perceive the red, green, etc outside me, but a red or green *from such and such a distance*; this latter adjunct is *the mere renewal of a judgement already made on the basis of consideration.*]

Gleichartig, i.e. homogeneous, is too broad a phrase for a strict Definition[.] Experiments (*here* in their proper place) are wanting. Two Wine Bottles, the one painted a full bright Red, the other, a dull faint Red, and equi-distant from the Eye—? will the former always appear nearer, the latter more distant? Relation, Position, positive as well as comparative, m[igh]t aid—& these are not Eindrücke. In short, let "der Geist" be as indignant as he can or will, das "Ich" will stay̶ill crave for a determining *Cause* of its individual Perceptions, and be rather silenced than convinced by their deduction from the infinite consequentiality of its (des Ich's) own Being—were this the case, would not the Perception follow at least a similar Laws with the Imagination & Memory?—See the sensible Treatise by the younger Reimarus, in answer to Jacobi, and the Supernaturalists.[1]— However, (I repeat) it is the method, I most complain of![2] Fichte ought in a work like this to have given a full and faithful Picture of a mind with the common Belief in the actual perception of Things really per se present: and then demonstrated—not that the Belief rests on a *Vorurtheil*[3] without *proof*—(which we admit—only remembering that what is believed without *Proof* is not of necessity or always believed without *reason*)—but that the Hypothesis or whatever the Assumption may be called does not solve the Problem/— See the Note *MS* at the end of the inside of the Cover.—[4]

11   p ⁺1,[a] referring to p 149, cropped

Note. to p 149.

I propose to myself to consider the philosophizing mind as gradually ascending not a Jacob's Ladder, but a sort of geometrical Stair-case with several Rests or Landing-Places[1]—each invisible to those below it, but commanding them and their Points of View—and on leaving any one to make it clear & lively why the mind in question could not but attempt to climb higher, and why so many remained there & believed nothing above but Clouds and the Sky. Now Fichte has not given us the pourtraiture either of the natural state of the mind previous to reflection ("It is there: for I *see* it") or of the second

---

a Inside back of original grey paper wrapper

10[1] Johann Albert Heinrich Reimarus (1729–1814). C is probably thinking of REIMARUS *Über die Gründe der menschlichen Erkenntniss und der natürlichen Religion* §§ 3–7 (not annotated), in which Reimarus, discussing the problem of human understanding, takes issue with the claim that revelation is a source of reliable knowledge about ourselves as well as about external objects (for reliability rests upon sensory evidence). He holds that belief in the disclosures of revelation is merely a form of personal believing or assuming that we have obtained true cognition; there is no immediate certainty of our conceptions being in accordance with the phenomena perceived. He denies the validity of such sensory evidence; our imagination can create things and situations at will; in a state of fever or in dreams our senses can

envisage objects and events without having been affected by actual impressions from outside. Mere feeling is unable to distinguish between reality and deception: to do this a cognitive power in man must be presupposed. "All cognition is a judgement of reason and can only be tested and corrected by the laws of reason, that is by the law of agreement or contradiction." Sense perceptions can never be more than the data to be submitted to the judgement of reason.

10[2] See 7 and 9, above.

10[3] "Prejudgement".

10[4] I.e. 11, below.

11[1] C used "Landing-Places" as a structural device in *The Friend* (1818) to interpose "small groups of essays...between the main divisions of the work". See *Friend* (*CC*) I 148–9. See also KANT *Vermischte Schriften* COPY C **10** n 5.

state, or that of *reflexion* and hypothesis[2]—Anima modificata suarum mutationum Conscia[3]—Locke, the Newtonian Opticians &c/[4] but hurries at once into the third state, Idealismus autoplasticus Defluence ab intra, ✳ Influence ab extra.[5]—And then [. . . . .]^{*a*} both.

12 pp 161–3, pencil, part overtraced, cropped

[The Spirit tries to persuade the "I" that we know nothing except ourselves, and that the manifold of intuition, and the connexion between the manifold of things, come into existence only in and through our consciousness. The "I" concedes that it understands and fully agrees with the Spirit's conclusions. The Spirit then "boasts", saying that the "I", now that it has gained this insight, will be free from any fear of that necessity which exists only in its thoughts, and will no longer be afraid of being oppressed by things that are after all only of its own creating and very different from its being.]

On my word, this is a most docile, easily contented Ich, and the Spirit a *rum* Spirit.—It is too evident, that Ich and Geist are but the Christian and Sirname of his weak Iness, J. G. Fichte. First, the natural assumption & assurance that we *see*, has not been shewn to be more incomprehensible than the Anschauung, & the precious mechanis[m] of Selbstbewusstsein[1] substituted for it/ and were this conceded, yet, secondly, Fichte has not proved, that by it & thro' it we may not know—i.e. perceive (capio *per* sensus)[2] even as a blind man perceives a wall by his Stick—and thirdly, whatever is proudly denied intellectually must all be smuggled in practically, under the name of Glaube, Faith.[3]—Just as if man were a Bundle of separate

^{*a*} One line of ms cropped

11[2] C refers to Fichte's distinction between primary and secondary consciousness (pp 110–11): "The first consciousness you find ready-made, therefore, just as you cannot find yourself without it; the second consciousness you produce as a result of the former.... When afterwards you reflect on that undivided consciousness of your self and of things, you distinguish between them, and inquire about their relationship to each other, you find then that the latter is conditioned by the former...I mean, *you produce* the second consciousness; you bring it forth through a true act of the mind."

11[3] "The Soul modified, Conscious of its own changes". Cf "consciousness of self-modification" in **5**, above.

11[4] See **15**, below.

11[5] "Self-shaping Idealism (is) a Flowing-down from inside, as contradistinguished from a Flowing-in from outside".

12[1] "Self-consciousness". This is the centre of C's objection to Fichte's doctrine of *Anschauung*: see **5, 9,** and **10,** above.

12[2] "I grasp *through* the senses".

12[3] Possibly a reference to §3 entitled "Glaube".

Essences.[4] How could Fichte have *made* these abstractions of Reason, Feeling, intuitive Space, but from some absolute Entity? and what entitled him to abstract?[5]—i.e. destroy the [.....][a] vital Copula, & then prove [b]Hair by Hair, that a Horse-tail ~~w~~could not be a Horse-tail?[c6] And the Boasting that follows inspires Disgust. Who does not see, that on Fichte's own distinction of Spontaneïty from Freedom, the "I" is equivocal and [b]if spontaneous "I" creates Brimstone and Fire; or the Stone and the operation of Lithotomy;[c] the poor [b]free "I" must tremble & shriek just as much and with the same good cause,[d] as if Nature had produced them[c7]

13 p 176, pencil, part overtraced, cropped

D. G.....Du wolltest wissen von deinem Wissen. Wunderst du dich, dass du auf diesem Wege auch nichts weiter erfuhrst, als—wovon du wissen wolltest; von deinem Wissen selbst; und möchtest du, dass es anders sey? Was durch das Wissen, und aus dem Wissen entsteht, ist nur ein Wissen. Alles Wissen aber ist nur Abbildung, und es wird in ihm immer etwas gefodert, das dem Bilde entspreche. Diese Foderung kann durch kein Wissen befriedigt werden; und ein System des Wissens ist nothwendig ein System blosser Bilder, ohne alle Realität, Bedeutung und Zweck. Hast du etwas anders erwartet? Willst du das innere Wesen deines Geistes ändern, und deinem Wissen anmuthen mehr zu seyn, denn ein Wissen?

[*The Spirit*....You wanted to know about your own knowledge. Are you surprised that on this track you came to know nothing more than what you wanted to know—your knowledge itself; and do you want the situation to be otherwise? What arises through and from knowledge is simply knowledge. All knowledge is merely illustration, and it demands something corresponding to a picture. This demand cannot be satisfied by any knowledge; and a system of knowledge is of necessity a system of mere pictures, without any reality, meaning, or purpose. Did you expect it to be otherwise? Do you want to change the inner essence of your mind and presume your knowledge to be more than knowledge?]

But where was the necessity or use of all this [e]Cap-and-Ball Conjuring[f] Why not have *begun*[g] with explaining the nature[g] and

---

[a] 3 or 4 words cropped   [b–c] Overtraced in ink, perhaps by C
[d] "cause" overtraced, and the word written above in ink
[e–f] Overtraced in ink, perhaps by C   [g] Words overtraced in ink, perhaps by C

12[4] C also challenges Kant for treating man as composed of separate entities: KANT *Logik* **7**.
12[5] On abstraction see **13**, below.

12[6] See A. FULLER **2** and n 2.
12[7] Cf **3** and **5**, above, and **17** and n 3, below.

uses^a of *Abstractions^a* as an ^{b}*Organon* Scientiæ?^{c1} Whence would ^{b}follow of itself an Insight into its sophistic *Abuse*, when the Instrument is, ⟨1st⟩ identified, with, and then substituted for, the Realities, which were to be understood^c by its Help?—Quære/ ^{b}whether a distinction between Knowing a Thing and knowing *of* a Thing,^{c} would not preclude this sophism

14 p 177, pencil, part overtraced, finished in ink, lightly cropped

Die Realität, die du schon erblickt zu haben glaubtest, eine unabhängig von dir vorhandene Sinnenwelt, * deren Sclav du zu werden fürchtetest, ist dir verschwunden; denn diese ganze Sinnenwelt entsteht nur durch das Wissen, und ist selbst unser Wissen; aber Wissen ist nicht Realität, eben darum, weil es Wissen ist.

[The reality that you believed you had already seen, a world of the senses existing independently from you, one of which you feared becoming the slave, had disappeared from you; for this whole world of the senses arises only through knowledge, and is itself our knowledge; but knowledge is not reality because of the very fact that it is knowledge.]

* Here recommences the Knot. Thus have I rid myself of the mundus sensibilis,^{1} but by the same legerdemain of *Abstractions^2 by* which I had evacuated *myself^a*? Still is t[he] ^{d}aweful Gift of *Sight^3* lef[t] uninvestigated:^{e} visio beatifica ⊰ Abspectio = abstractio a visu, *scientifica*,^{4} in the same sense in which a microscope a falso deducit verum^5

15 p 206, pencil | Bk III "Glaube" §1

Es schweben mir vor Erscheinungen im Raume, auf welche ich den Begriff meiner selbst übertrage: ich denke sie mir als Wesen meines gleichen. Eine durchgeführte Spekulation hat mich ja belehrt, oder wird mich belehren, dass diese vermeinte Vernunftwesen ausser mir

---

a Words overtraced in ink, perhaps by C   *b–c* Overtraced in ink, perhaps by C
d–e Overtraced in ink, perhaps by C; the rest of the note is in ink

13^1 "*Instrument* of Knowledge". See **12** and n 5, above. On the use and abuse of abstraction see e.g. *Friend (CC)* I 520–3 and n. For an analysis of abstraction as an instrument of knowing see KANT *Logik* **9** and *Logic (CC)* Index.

14^1 "The sensible world"—as in the title of Kant's inaugural dissertation, *De mundi sensibilis...forma* (Königsberg 1770).

14^2 See **12** and n 5 and **13**, above.

14^3 See **9**, above. The "Gift of Sight"

means presumably not only *Anschauung* (intuition) but also visual perception.

14^4 "The beatific vision [i.e. *Anschauung*, intuition, insight] in opposition to 'Abspection' [looking away] the same as abstraction from sight, *knowledge-making*". See also **9** n 3, above, For the meaning of the logical symbols see **1**, above.

14^5 "Brings out the true from the false"—i.e. corrects the false evidence given by the naked eye.

nichts sind, als Produkte meines eigen Vorstellens, dass ich nun
einmal, nach aufzuweisenden Gesetzen meines Denkens, genöthigt
bin, den Begriff meiner selbst ausser mir selbst darzustellen, und dass,
nach denselben Gesetzen, dieser Begriff nur auf gewisse bestimmte
Anschauungen übertragen werden kann. Aber die Stimme meines
Gewissens ruft mir zu: was diese Wesen auch an und für sich seyn,
du sollst sie behandeln, als für sich bestehende, freie, selbstständige,
von dir ganz und gar unabhängige Wesen.

[Appearances hover before me in space, to which I transmit the concept of
my self: I imagine them as beings like myself. A speculation already carried
out has taught me or will teach me that these presumably rational beings
outside me are nothing but products of my own power of representation,
that I now find it necessary, owing to demonstrable laws of my thinking,
to represent the concept of myself outside myself, and that according to the
same law this concept can be transferred only to certain definite intuitions.
Yet the voice of my conscience calls to me: whatever these beings may be
in and for themselves, you must treat them as beings existing in their own
right, completely independent of you.]

Truisms may be so disguised in high Words, that tho' the common
~~property~~ Stock of man, woman, & child, they seem to be the property
of an Individual.—If I adopt the Newtonian Optics, I take for
granted a picture in my Retina propagated, I know not how, thro'
my Brain into my Mind—& by *means* of this I see a *Chair*. Now
Conscience, aweful conscience, intervenes, & says/ tho' thou dost not
really See the *Chair*, but only a mode of thy own Being, yet I forbid
thee to run thy Shins against [it.]*a*1

16 p ⁻1,*b* referring to p 328, cropped

Zwar muss ich sie stets behandeln, und mit ihnen reden, als ob sie
wären, wovon ich sehr wohl weiss, dass sie es nicht sind; ich muss
ihnen gegenüber stets voraussetzen, wodurch allein ich ihnen gegen-
über zu stehen kommen, und mit ihnen zu handeln haben kann. Die
Pflicht gebietet mir einen Begriff von ihnen für das Handeln, dessen
Gegentheil mir durch die Betrachtung gegeben wird. Und so kann
es allerdings geschehen, dass ich mit einer edlen Entrüstung, als ob
sie frei wären, gegen sie mich kehre, um sie selbst mit dieser
Entrüstung gegen sich selbst zu entzünden; eine Entrüstung, die ich
selbst in meinem Innern vernünftiger Weise nie empfinden kann. Nur
der handelnde Mensch der Gesellschaft in mir ist es, der der

a Word supplied by the editor   *b* Inside front of original grey paper wrapper

15¹ A variant of Dr Johnson's gruff rejoinder to the subjective idealism of
Berkeley.

Unvernunft und dem Laster zürnt, nicht der auf sich selbst ruhende, und in sich selbst vollendete, betrachtende Mensch.

[Admittedly, I must treat them and talk to them as if they existed, but I know very well that it is not they that exist; in their presence I must always assume how I alone can come to be in their presence and to have dealings with them. Duty binds me to form a concept of them for my actions opposite to the one I form of them through contemplation. Thus, of course, it can happen that I behave towards them with noble indignation, as if they were free, to spark off this indignation in them against themselves; an indignation that I cannot rationally find in myself. It is only the active, social part of me that is angry with unreasonableness and vice, not the tranquil, complete, observing human being in me.]

In p. 328, Fichte plunges head over heels in the very same Whirlpool of deceiving ψευδοσοφy,[1] which he elsewhere calls aloud on all to avoid—the same contradiction between the Heart & the Reason— nay, worse than the Necessitarians! *They* preach the Wisdom of considering the Assassin = the Dagger;[2] but Fichte says, that *Duty* is or the Law of Conscience[3] is the Voice of God, for man the only Voice, the sole personality of God![4] that this is not only = Truth, but that for man there is no other Truth but this, & in this—! It is "Gewissen", Conscientia, the aggregate & Sum total of Truths! & yet this very Voice of Truth commands him to act & feel what he knows to be a Lie & Unjust—& all this by a Juggler's Trick of dividing his Individuality into the knowing & the acting (handalnde)[a] Man!

17 p 335

Aller Tod in der Natur ist Geburt, und gerade im Sterben erscheint sichtbar die Erhöhung des Lebens. Es ist kein tödtendes Princip in der Natur, denn die Natur ist durchaus lauter Leben; nicht der Tod tödtet, sondern das lebendigere Leben, welches, hinter dem alten verborgen, beginnt, und sich entwickelt. Tod und Geburt ist bloss das Ringen des Lebens mit sich selbst, um sich stets verklärter und ihm selbst ähnlicher darzustellen. Und *mein* Tod könnte etwas anders seyn—meiner, der ich überhaupt nicht eine blosse Darstellung und Abbildung des Lebens bin, sondern das ursprüngliche, allein wahre,

a A slip for "handelnde"

16[1] "Pseudosophy"—false wisdom. The earliest use recorded in *OED* is dated 1885.

16[2] An example used several times by C: see e.g. *Friend* (*CC*) II 72 (I 108), and *P Lects* Lect 12 (1949) 363.

16[3] For C on duty see *CN* I 1705–1711 and nn; cf II 2537. See also DE WETTE 15.

16[4] WW represented Duty as the "Stern Daughter of the Voice of God". *WPW* IV 83.

und wesentliche Leben in mir selbst trage?—Es ist gar kein möglicher Gedanke, dass die Natur ein Leben vernichten solle, das aus ihr nicht stammt; die Natur, um deren willen nicht ich, sondern die selbst nur um meinetwillen lebt.

[All death in nature is birth, and it is in death itself that the elevation of life is made manifest. There is no death-principle in nature, for the whole of nature is nothing but life; it is not death that kills, but more vital life, which, hidden behind the old, begins and develops. Death and birth are merely life's struggle with itself to represent itself as more and more glorified and true to itself. And could *my* death be something else—I, who carry within me by no means a mere representation and image of life, but the original, only true and essential life? It is just impossible to think that nature should annihilate a life that does not stem from it; for it is not I who live for nature's sake, but nature that lives for my sake.]

Mors ⟨ = vita vitalior[1] = viz.⟩ a few grains of Arsenic/ or the bloody Flux, or the Morbus Pediculosus![2] and this man yet deems himself a Critical Philosopher, who came not to destroy but to fulfil the Law[3] of his Master, Kant? This man, who page after page can rant away in the perfect silence of all human Consciousness! grounding all on an equivoque of the word "I"!—[4]

18 p +1, pencil

In other Words this [...]*a*

---

a The four words are in pencil, almost illegible; another word in pencil, illegible, has been overwritten by "4-2— —" in the same brown ink as the binder's marks on pp ⁻1 and 338

17[1] "Death is the same as more vital life"—picking up Fichte's phrase.

17[2] "Louse-disease", otherwise *Phthiriasis*, under which name the disease that killed Sulla and Herod is described in *Rees's Cyclopaedia*: an excessive and debilitating infestation to which aged persons are liable. Cf GREW 10 and n 1 for a less specific use of the term.

17[3] Matt 5.17 (var).

17[4] Cf 3, 5, and 12 (at n 4), above, and C's "burlesque on the Fichtean Egoismus" in *BL* ch 9 (*CC*) I 159–60n. A Coleridge ms that once belonged to Bertram Davis and is now at the University of Waterloo bears a statement by Edward Dowden that it was "now placed" in a copy of *PW* "side by side with the poem it glo[ss]es"—i.e. ΕΓΩ-ΕΝΚΑΙΠΑΝ in *PW* (EHC) II 981–2. It reads in part: "...both Fichte and Schelling with more than Scotist subtlety of

Logical Idea-splitting have evolved as their ground position the same doctrine, as Swedenborg, & Behmen: viz—that the I is identical with, and exclusively recognizes itself as, the Will; that the Self or Will *grounds* itself = setzt sich, and is the principle of its own Life or Existence; that therefore '*to be*' or '*I am*' is an ideal State, the product of the Self-constituting *Act*; thence the distinction between the primary and the empirical Self—and thence inevitably the identity of the former with God, and the final το Εν και Παν, the fatal Serbonian Bog of all Mysticism!..." The ms ends without answering the question: "What then is the πρωτον ψευδος, in which all those having joined have of necessity arrived at the same whirlpool of Chaos?—that transcends the ultimate [con]sciousness, i.e. the distinct. betw. *Sub. & Ob.*".

Der geschlossne Handelsstaat. Ein philosophischer Entwurf als Anhang zur Rechtslehre, und Probe einer künftig zu liefernden Politik. Tübingen 1800. 8°.

British Museum C 126 e 3

"S. T. C." label on title-page verso.

At the head of p ⁻1, and on the title-page, "1" is written; a corresponding "2" is written at the head of the last page (p 290) and at the head of p ⁺1 (facing p 290). These were probably keys for the binder to ensure the correct placing of the annotated leaves in rebinding.

DATE. After c 1815–16: see *CN* iii 4307.

COEDITORS. Willem Schrickx, Raimonda Modiano.

1   p ⁻1[a]

There have been, doubtless, eminent *Mathematicians* who have shewn themselves wretched Theologia[ns][b] and Philosophers; but it is not easy to have any confidence in a *Philosopher*, who has displayed such glaring Ignorance in the principles of State-organizati[on][b] of human Nature as it exists, nay even as it is essentially *is* and of course ought to be—souch ⟨a⟩ boorish inac-quaintance with contemporary Statistics, &c &c, as J. G. Fichte has exposed in this Work.[1] It is verily "UNTER ALLER KRITIK"!—[2]

S. T. Coleridge

2   p 32 | Bk i ch 2

Das entbehrliche ist überall den unentbehrlichen, oder schwer zu entbehrenden, nachzusetzen; eben so in der grossen Wirthschaft des

---

[a] Inside front of original grey paper wrapper   [b] Letters lost in the binding

1[1] For C's understanding of economic principles and his application of (undocumented) analyses and statistics of trade and commerce see *LS* (*CC*) passim, esp 215n, 211–21. He was well aware of the writings of Bentham and of David Ricardo (1772–1823) in this field. On 12 Dec 1826 C commented on Henry Colborne *A New System of Practical Domestic Economy* (1824), and scolded the author for "the absurd miscalculation" arising from failure to notice the variations of prices in different parts of the country. The purpose of his note was to remind himself to recommend to

Alaric Watts, editor of the *Amulet*, the publication of "Economic Journals for each of our Counties" based on the principle, not—as applied by Colborne— "how little such & such an establishment might be kept [for], under a confluence of wholesale purchases, inexorable System &c &c", but of "what in fact and on the average the several & total expences really are". *CN* iv 5469 (12 Dec 1826). Cf 9 and n 1, below. For C's interest in prices, e.g. in Germany in 1798–9, see *CN* i 338, 423, and cf *CL* i 463.

1[2] "Beneath all criticism".

Staates. Die Hände welche dem Ackerbaue entzogen, und den Künsten gewidmet werden können, müssen zunächst auf unentbehrliche Bearbeitungen, und nur so viele, als von diesen übrig bleiben, auf entbehrliche, auf Bedürfnisse des Luxus, gerichtet werden. Dies wäre die zweite klare Folge für den Staat. Er hat nicht nur die Zahl des Künstlerstandes überhaupt, sondern auch die Zahl derer, die sich einem besondern Zweige der Kunst widmen, zu bestimmen, und überall für die Nothdurft zuerst zu sorgen. Es sollen erst alle satt werden, und fest wohnen, ehe einer seine Wohnung verziert, erst alle bequem und warm gekleidet seyn, ehe einer sich prächtig kleidet.

[That which is dispensable should always take second place to that which is indispensable, or dispensable only with difficulty; equally so in the economy of the state. The hands which can be withdrawn from agriculture and devoted to the arts must be applied in the first instance to indispensable pieces of work, and only as many as are left after this be applied to dispensable items, the necessaries of luxury. This would be the second obvious course for the state [to pursue]. It must determine not only the size of the class of craftsmen in general, but also the number of those who devote themselves to a particular branch of craft, and must in every instance care primarily for necessities. All must eat their fill and dwell securely before someone decorates his dwelling; all be comfortably and warmly dressed before anyone dresses magnificently.]

Nonsense!—Where no one *dare* purchase the ornaments & dispensible Comforts of Life, what motive exists for the increased Industry & Talents of the Rest? Is it for the Comfort's sake or for the rank designated by it, that men wish & toil for fine furniture, fine Clothes, foreign Wines, &c?—Assuredly, for the latter. Fichte's Vanity strangely misled him in this Essay.[1] The style excepted, it possesses no one characteristic of his metaphysical Works: it is always shallow, & most often grossly erroneous.

S. T. C.

3   p [1] (fly-title to *Einleitung*), evidently referring to pp 115–16 | I 7

Ein Eigenthum des Bodens findet nach unserer Theorie gar nicht statt: wenigstens so lange nicht, bis diejenigen, die ein solches annehmen—wenn sich dieselben nur recht verstehen, und wirklich, so wie die Worte lauten, ein Eigenthum des *Bodens*, und nicht, wie wir es auch nehmen, das eigne und ausschliessende Recht auf einen gewissen *Gebrauch* des Bodens meinen—bis sie, sage ich, uns begreiflich machen, wie denn ein solches Eigenthumsrecht im wirklichen

2[1]   Cf *Anweisung* 4.

Leben *ausgeübt* werden solle. Die Erde ist des Herrn; des Menschen ist nur das Vermögen, sie zweckmässig anzubauen und zu benutzen.

[According to our theory, there is no such thing as ownership of land: at least not until those who assume such an ownership explain to us—if they really understand by this and mean literally an ownership of the *land*, and not, as we take it to mean, one's own and exclusive right to a certain *use* of land—until, I say, they make us understand how such property rights should be *exercised* in real life. The earth is the Lord's; mankind's is only the ability to cultivate it expediently, and to put it to good use.]

I am at a loss to conceive what Fichte can mean by his Theory of Property—or wherein it differs from that to which he opposes it.[1] The one says, I have an exclusive property in that field—no! answers Fichte—you have only an exclusive right to make use of it, for yourself & your posterity!—Good heavens! where is the difference! Who ever dreamt of *property* in the prima materia,[2] the mysterious substance of accidents?—I confess, this pretended distinction appears arrant Trifling to me—Indeed, the whole system of the Rechtslehre stands in no good odour with me: it supposes a sort of Justice without any reference to Virtue or Conscience, which passes my apprehension.[3] I can indeed *make* these *distinctions* as easily as Kant or Fichte; but I can never conceive a human Being acting upon them. All, that means any thing, in the system may be reduced to this simple fact—that it may be the Duty of A to award to B and not to C. what yet B. ought to have given to C.—i.e. cases of imperfect Obligation—but still it is A only (the civil Judge) that is in the *right*—B. is a rascal, spite of the Verdict./

4   p 144 | Bk ɪɪ ch 2

Ist das ganze christliche Europa, mit den hinzugekommenen Colonien, und Handelsplätzen in andern Welttheilen noch immer ein Ganzes, so muss freilich der Handel aller Theile mit allen frei bleiben, wie er ursprünglich war. Ist es im Gegentheil in mehrere, unter

---

3[1] On pp 111–13 Fichte writes: "In my opinion the basic flaw in the opposite theory of property, which is the prime source from which all other mistaken assumptions about property emerge... consists in regarding primary property as the *exclusive* possession of *a thing*....On the contrary, against this theory, our own regards primary property, the ground of

all others, as *an exclusive right to a given free activity*."
3[2] "Primal matter".
3[3] For C's early pantisocratic (God-winian) view of justice see e.g. *CL* ɪ 115 (Oct 1794). In C's mature view *Rechtslehre* (the law of rights) is a matter of legal definition of equity; justice is a human matter involving ethical discrimination. See e.g. *Friend (CC)* ɪ 194, 199, 208–9.

verschiedenen Regierungen stehende Staatsganze getrennt, so muss es eben so in mehrere geschlossene Handelsstaaten getrennt werden.

[If the whole of Christian Europe, with the additional colonies and points of trade in other parts of the world, is still a unity, then of course the trade of all its parts must remain free with all others, as it had been originally. If, on the contrary, it is divided into a number of unified states that are controlled by different governments, then it must be divided into equally numerous closed commercial states.]

Perchè?[1]

5 p 177 | II 5

Der Zweck bleibt immer derselbe, nemlich das Handelsverhältniss zu seinem Vortheil zu lenken; und es sind allenthalben so ziemlich die gleichen Mittel zur Erreichung des gleichen Zwecks gebraucht worden. Zuvörderst Vermehrung des Ausfuhr, und dadurch des Geldes, das man vom Ausländer zieht.... Dann Verhinderung oder Erschwerung der Einfuhr fremder *Fabrikate*, und die daraus erfolgende Verminderung des Geldes, das in das Ausland geht: entweder durch völliges Verbot dieser Waaren, oder durch beträchtliche Auflagen auf sie.

[The purpose remains the same always: i.e. to manage the terms of trade to its [the state's] advantage; and more or less the same means are employed on all sides to achieve the same purpose. First of all, the increase of the export and through it of the amount of money drawn from foreigners.... And second, the prevention or impediment of the import of foreign *manufactures* resulting in a reduction of the amount of money that goes abroad—either by complete prohibition of these goods or by considerable duties upon them.]

Fichte strangely passes over the necessity & the influences of Capital!—A nation may carry on a losing trade (i.e. in balance of gold) for many years—& yet a certain number of her citizens in each commercial Town acquiring a Capital, may be far more prosperous than before/ She has paid dear indeed; but she *has* however at length purchased the great *Machine* by which she may now set up, by degrees against her wealthier Neighbors.

6 p 183 | II 6

Endlich entstehen durch das HandelsInteresse politische Begriffe, die nicht abentheuerlicher seyn könnten, und aus diesen Begriffen

4[1] "Why?" C considered that Napoleon's unification of Europe into a "mighty and swarming empire, organized in all its parts for war" had reduced it to "the wretched state in which it was before the wide diffusion of Trade and Commerce". *Friend* (*CC*) I 231; cf *LS* (*CC*) 66 n 1.

Kriege, deren wahren Grund man nicht verhehlt, sondern ihn offen zur Schau trägt. Da entsteht eine Herrschaft der Meere, welche letztern doch, ausser der Schussweite vom Ufer der bewohnten Länder, ohne Zweifel frei seyn sollten, wie Luft und Licht. Da entsteht ein ausschliessendes Recht auf den Handel mit einem auswärtigen Volke, das keine der Handel treibenden Nationen mehr angeht, als eine andere: und über diese Herrschaft, und über dieses Recht entstehn blutige Kriege.

[Finally, political concepts arise through trade interests—concepts that could not be more adventurous; and from these arise wars, the true reason for which is not concealed but publicly exposed. Nations gain control of the sea, which, beyond gun-shot from the shores of the inhabited countries, should without doubt be as free as air and light. An exclusive right is established to trade with a foreign nation that is no more the business of any one trading nation than of another; and bloody wars arise because of this supremacy and this right.]

ausser der Schussweite[1]—well! but what part of the Sea is out of the gumn-shot of the British Navy? If by the possession of Cannon, a shore extends its dominion farther by a mile inland than formerly by bow & arrow, why not by mighty fleets, as far as they can conquer? Does not the whole rest on *power*? Else why the *Schussweite*?

7 p 223 | ш 4

Alle Möglichkeit des Welthandels beruht auf dem Besitze des in aller Welt geltenden Tauschmittels, und auf der Brauchbarkeit desselben für uns. Wer dasjenige Zeichen des Werths, welches der Ausländer annimmt, Geld- oder Silber-Geld, gar nicht hat, an den verkauft der Ausländer nichts. Für Wen dasjenige Geld, das ihm der Ausländer geben kann, von keinem Werthe ist, der kann an denselben nichts verkaufen. Ein Handel vermittelst des Geldes ist von nun an zwischen beiden nicht mehr möglich. Es bliebe nur noch der Tausch von Waare gegen Waare übrig.

[Every possibility of world trade is based on the possession of the universal means of making an exchange and its usefulness to us. The foreign power will not sell anything to a person who does not possess the currency that the former accepts, be it gold or silver. The person to whom the foreigner's money is of no value cannot sell anything to him. Trading that uses money is no longer possible between the two of them. All that remains is to make a mutual exchange of goods.]

? Strange assertion! What gold or silver does the Russian Nobleman bring to the English Ship-Captain? No! Furs, Tar, Tallow, Leather,

6[1] "Beyond gun-shot", "beyond artillery range".

Deal, &c &c—and the English give him Cutlery, a good Coat, Rum, &c &c—Does Fichte forget, that the *Balance* only requires *money*—and that this might be accomodated by bills of credit?[1]

8 p 230

Das neue Geld muss aus oben angeführten Gründen, durch keinen andern Menschen, noch irgend eine andere Regierung nachgemacht werden können.... Irgend ein wesentliches Bestandtheil der Zusammensetzung müsste ein Staatsgeheimniss seyn; in einem monarchischen Staate nur der regierenden Familie bekannt.

[For the reasons stated above, neither any other person nor any other government should be able to copy the new money.... Some essential component of its composition should be a state secret, known in a monarchical state only to the ruling family.]

There is nothing in the old Alchemists worse or more outrageous prattling than this!—If the essential Bestandtheil[1] is known to the King, the Stuff must be a compound—what one Chemist can compound, another cleverer or in a more advanced state may decompound—

9 p 266 | III 6

Die Regierung, von welcher wir reden, hat vermöge ihres Geld-Reichthums das Vermögen, sich so zu rüsten, von den Hülfsmitteln und Kräften des Auslandes auch zu diesem Zwecke soviel an sich zu kaufen, und zu dingen, dass ihr kein Widerstand geleistet werden könne; so, dass sie ihre Absicht ohne Blutvergiessen, und beinahe ohne Schwertschlag erreiche, und dass ihre Operation mehr ein Occupationszug sey, als ein Krieg.

[The government we are speaking about has, by reason of its financial wealth, the ability so to arm itself and to purchase and accumulate to this end so much of the means and power of a foreign nation that it cannot be opposed; so to arm itself that it may achieve its aims without bloodshed and almost without a sword-stroke, and that its operations may be more an occupation than a war.]

Good Heavens! how ignorant is this man—~~Does~~ Has he never heard that the whole currency in gold & silver of Great Britain, the richest country on earth, does not exceed 10,000,000£—and that her

---

7[1] Cf *CN* III 3455 and *Friend* (*CC*) I   8[1] "Component".
241 (II 167).

expences for *one* year often exceed 30,000,000![1] Why, all the money in Prussia would not pay half a year's War-costs in England! And yet F. talks as if the mere possession of all the gold & silver of a one country would make its government cock-a-hoop of the world!!—

10 p +1

Of all the silly Dreams, I have read, this is the silliest—as repulsive to the Imagination as it is absurd to the Reason![1] Fichte would have made a more pernicious & despicable Tyrant than Caligula or Eliogabalus.[2]—Indeed the whole of these Vernunft-gesetze[3] is but *Ego per me*—I by itself I[4]—and every body shall *obey me!*[5]

9[1] The exact source of C's figures is not identified; as a journalist he will have been familiar with ways of ready access to public accounts and statistics. His figures are close to those given in B. R. Mitchell's *Abstract of British Historical Statistics* (Cambridge 1962): Britain's total government expenditure in 1814 was £39 million; Britain's total gold and silver currency in 1817 was £7.2 million, increasing to £9.95 million in 1821.

10[1] C probably refers to ch 8 (pp 283–90), in which Fichte, after accusing his generation of breaking away from the earnest and temperate customs of their ancestors, attacks the popular belief that in international trade and travel nations will come together and their many-sided development be stimulated. He advocates, on the contrary, that, as a condition of co-operation, states should stand separate from each other and develop their national strength internally. When this separation had been perfected—and this is the "dream" that C refers to—nations would be interested in developing their own strength independently rather than in oppressing or subjugating one another; scientists and artists would freely exchange their ideas; wars would be eradicated.

10[2] Caligula and Elagabalus, Roman emperors (37–41 and 218–22), both notorious for their moral depravity and for their outrageous exercise of tyrannous powers.

10[3] In the "Einleitung" Fichte draws a distinction between *das wirkliche Staat*, the actual state, and the *Vernunftsstaat*, the concept by which the *wirkliche Staat* can be understood. He intends to analyse the concept of *Vernunftsstaat* and then apply it to the actual state by developing various rules and maxims of economy. For these rules and maxims C mockingly coins the word *Vernunft-gesetze*—laws of reason.

10[4] Cf *Bestimmung* 17 and n 3 and *BL* ch 9 (*CC*) I 157–60 and n.

10[5] For the proposition that egotism leads to tyranny see e.g. *Friend* (*CC*) I 320–3 and cf *EOT* (*CC*) I 63.

Grundlage der gesammten Wissenschaftslehre als Handschrift für *seine Zuhörer*. Leipzig 1794. 8°.
With half-title before the "Vorrede": *Zweite Lieferung der Grundlage der gesammten Wissenschaftslehre.*
Later bound, probably by Green, as first with *Grundriss des Eigenthümlichen der Wissenschaftslehre* and *Ueber den Begriff der Wissenschaftslehre* to make a second volume of *Das System der Sittenlehre*, and so identified on the spine.

British Museum C 126 f 13(1)

"S. T. C." label on the title-page verso.

DATE. Perhaps 1815. The notes seem to have been written after C had first annotated *Das System der Sittenlehre.*

COEDITORS. Willem Schrickx, Raimonda Modiano.

1 p ⁻2

Im. absolute<del>mn</del> Ich erkennt man Gott—nicht—im Gotte erkennt man das absolute Ich.[1] Ergo, Fichte und Schelling)(Malbranche. Aber = *Spinoza?*?[2]

2 pp ⁻2⁻⁻1

It may be, philosophically speaking, too early to ask the solution; but I own, it would have been a great, and for many, very many enquiring minds a necessary encouragement to commence the study of the Wissentschaftslehre,*[a1]* if the Author had but inserted any

a A slip for *Wissenschaftslehre*

1[1] "In the absolute I one knows God—not—in God one knows the absolute I." The sentence seems to be C's; cf, however, pp 235, 265. Cf also *Bestimmung* 12 and 16.

1[2] "Therefore Fichte and Schelling [are] disparate from Malebranche. But [are they] identical with *Spinoza?*" For C on Malebranche's idea that "we see all things in God" see *CN* III 3592 f 134 and 3974 and nn and *BL* ch 12 (*CC*) I 285–6. As C admitted that he had not read Malebranche (*CN* III 3974), the source for his reference is probably Kant, who in his Inaugural Dissertation quoted the Malebanche passage in Latin: *De mundi sensibilis atque intelligibilis forma et principiis* (1770) §4 Scholion, reprinted in

Vermischte Schriften II 474. The Schelling passage C probably has in mind is *System der transscendentalen Idealismus* pt III (Tübingen 1800) 319 (tr): "...and one would have to posit this *x* in an intelligence of some sort; as Malebranche did, who would have us see all things in God, or the sagacious Berkeley, who speaks of light as a converse of the soul with God...". See also *BL* ch 9 (*CC*) I 152–60, esp 158: "Fichte assuredly gave the first mortal blow to Spinozism, as taught by Spinoza himself"—i.e. the Spinozistic pantheism.

2[1] "Theory of Knowledge", specifically as evolved by Fichte and subsequent neo-Kantians. Cf *BL* ch 9 (*CC*) I 158 and n.

where, tho' in a note, or still better, in his preface, an explanation of the possibility of Sleep, or of the entrance & putting out of a Candle, on his System. Yet neither here nor in the Sittenlehre[2] do we find a word of Sleep or of Dreams or of Fatigue[3]—The first & last seemingly incompatible with the all-acting, always active "I", the Dreams on the other hand affording such striking exemplifications of the processes described in this work, that I some times imagine that I am reading a theory of *Dreams*—and that the philosophy is true and applicable to me only when I am asleep.[a]—To be sure, we may as well *assume* fatigue & remission as involved in the particular order of finiteness, as the finiteness itself—Some thing is clearly wanting here—possibly, the Author has omitted a whole class of reciprocal re-actions (Wechselwirkungen) between *Life* & *Intelligence/* and throughout the whole *Time* seems to tyrannize & antecede, instead of following—The *Ich* does but *one* thing at a time, & all things successively—now what if it did a 1000 things simultaneously—? = *Leben.*[4]

There seems too something very arbitrary in the generation of the Gefühl (Feeling) out of mere Activity: that is, to say that Feeling is only an activity, which exists in me but which I do not refer to myself, i.e. an activity under the form of inactivity,—is very ingenious;[5] but is not [this][b] a mere assertion? When I pinch myself, I am quite conscious of my activity at the moment; but clearly know, that the feeling, that accompanies it, is quite heterogeneous from it.[6]

---

[a] Change of hand; the rest of the note seems to be an afterthought
[b] Word supplied by the editor

[2] I.e. Fichte *Das System der Sittenlehre* (Jena & Leipzig 1798).

[3] On sleep and dreams in this context see *Bestimmung* 9.

[4] "*Life*". The notion of life as a multiple and constant inner dialectic is in *Grundlage* p 195: "The possibility of our consciousness, our life, our being for ourselves, i.e. our being as selves [*als Ich*], grounds itself on each act of imagination." Cf *BL* ch 12 (*CC*) I 280–1 (Thesis VIII).

[5] C refers to Fichte's discussion of the concept of "feeling" (*Gefühl*) in §§7–11 (pp 282–329). C might have taken the term *Wechselwirkung* (above) from §7 (pp 284–5): "The 'I' strives to fill the infinite; at the same time the 'I' contains the law and tendency to reflect about

itself. It cannot reflect about itself without being limited.... The 'I' then limits itself and is set in reciprocal reaction [*Wechselwirkung*] with itself: through the propensity [to fill the infinite] it continues to be driven outwards, through reflection it is stopped and stops itself. When both are united there appears a [sense of] coercion, [of] impotence.... This manifestation of impotence in the 'I' is called *a feeling.* In feeling, *activity*—I feel, I am the feeling [subject], and this activity is the reflection—[and] *limitation*—I *feel* that I am acted on and am not acting—are intimately united; there is coercion."

[6] For a similar distinction see *CN* III 3605 ff 119–18 (c Aug–Sept 1809).

3 p ⁻1, pencil

Is not a portion of the Obscurity of the Wissenschaftslehre attributable to the choice of the "Ich" instead of Soul, or Spirit? With the "I" we habitually connect the present Potence of Consciousness[1]

4 p 163 | Pt II § 4

Dic Totalität besteht in der Vollständigkeit eines *Verhältnisses*, nicht aber einer *Realität*.

(Die Glieder des Verhältnisses einzeln betrachtet, sind die *Accidenzen*, ihre Totalität ist *Substanz*, wie schon oben gesagt worden. ...) Die Accidenzen, synthetisch vereinigt, geben die Substanz; und es ist in derselben gar nichts weiter enthalten, als die Accidenzen: die Substanz analysirt, giebt die Accidenzen, und es bleibt nach einer vollständigen Analyse der Substanz gar nichts übrig, als Accidenzen. An ein daurendes Substrat, an einen etwanigen Träger der Accidenzen, ist nicht zu denken...

[The totality consists in the completeness of a *relation*, but not in that of a *reality*.

(The members of a relation, considered individually, are the *accidents*, their totality is the *substance*, as pointed out above. ...) The accidents, united synthetically, produce the substance, and there is nothing more contained in substance than the accidents: substance analysed gives accidents, and following a thorough analysis of substance there is nothing left except accidents. To imagine a permanent substrate, or some sort of carrier of the accidents, is a mistake...]

I ~~can~~ well remember with what delight I made out this idea of Substance while looking at a Rose 9 years ago.[1] S. T. C.

3[1] C points to the need for a word connoting a more permanent ground below the surface of consciousness. See also e.g. *BL* ch 12 (*CC*) ɪ 235; and cf his distinction between *Willkür* (choice) and *Wille* (will) in *Bestimmung* **4** and n 1.
4[1] No other account of this episode has been traced.

Grundriss des Eigenthümlichen der Wissenschaftslehre in Rücksicht auf das theoretische Vermögen als Handschrift für seine Zuhörer. Jena & Leipzig 1795. 8°.
Bound as second with *Grundlage* and *Ueber den Begriff*.
British Museum C 126 f 13(2)
DATE. Possibly c 1802.
COEDITOR. Willem Schrickx.

1 p ⁻1

wissentlich = sciential[1]
wissenschaftlich = scientific
Begriff = comprehension
ein begriff = a con-prehension, or notion, ~~that~~ i.e. the notio (= act of knowing) consists in comprehending. My notion of two lines is that they cannot inclose a space—that is, by combining any intuition of two lines I cannot comprehend, or circumscribe any space—. But Thought is composed of notions—therefore all thinking is circumscribing. What I cannot circumscribe can not be the Object of Thought—it is *incomprehensible*[2]

1[1] *Wissentlich* normally "knowing, deliberate, intentional, conscious".
1[2] On truths incomprehensible and

inconceivable see e.g. *LS (CC)* 99, 105, 113, and *Friend(CC)*1422. Cf *Empfindung* in KANT *Metaphysik der Sitten* **2** n 1.

Das System der Sittenlehre nach den Principien der Wissenschaftslehre. Jena & Leipzig 1798. 8°.

In a binding uniform with the volume comprising three works of the *Wissenschaftslehre*: see *Grundlage*.

British Museum C 126 f 12

Some of the annotations are so badly rubbed and offset as to be almost illegible.

MS TRANSCRIPT. VCL BT 22 (with omissions).

DATE. 1815. See *CN* III 4186.

COEDITORS. Willem Schrickx, Raimonda Modiano.

1 p ii, pencil, cropped | Einleitung §2

Das subjective, und objective wird vereinigt, oder als harmonirend angesehen, zuförderst so, dass das subjective aus dem objectiven erfolgen, das erstere sich nach dem letztern richten soll: *ich erkenne*.

[The subjective and objective are united, or are seen as being in harmony with each other, above all in that the subjective is supposed to follow from the objective and to be determined by it: *I know*.]

It seems to me, after long reflection, and some argument, that ⟨the meaning of⟩ the words *objective* & *subjective* as well as ⟨of⟩ our word (*from Hume*) *idea* as opposed to *impression*, may be in all Instances fully and appropriately expressed by ⟨A⟩ Thought & ⟨A⟩ Thing. NB *A Thought*, ⟨or Thoughts,⟩ not ~~the~~ Thought, ~~or Thoughts~~ even as a fancy, a labor is different from Fancy, and Labor.[1] A motion from [....] thro' our whole Language.

2 p iii, pencil[a]

Was den zweiten anbelangt, wie es möglich sey, einige unsrer Begriffe zu denken, als darstellbar, und zum Theil wirklich dargestellt in der ohne unser Zuthun bestehenden Natur, <u>darüber hat bisher die</u>

---

[a] The whole note is faint and rubbed

[1]1 For the difference implied here between substantive knowledge and abstract knowledge see the marginalia on the 1818 *Friend* recorded in *Friend* (*CC*) I 520–1 n 5; C had used exactly the same illustration in *CN* I 1077 (Dec 1801) and in *CL* II 1194–5 (13 Oct 1806). On the difference between "idea" and "impression" in Hume's use see e.g. *BL* ch 5 (*CC*) I 96–7n. On "Idea" generally see e.g. *Friend* (*CC*) I 467n and *C&S* (*CC*) 12–13 and n 1. On the difference between "Thought" and "a Thought" see *CN* III 3605 f 119 (and cf Plato *Meno* 73E–75C).

Philosophie sich auch nicht einmal gewundert. Man hat es ganz
natürlich gefunden, dass wir auf die Welt wirken können.
[With regard to the second [point]—i.e. how it is possible to think of some
of our concepts as representable and partly in fact represented in nature,
which exists without our involvement—*this is something that philosophy has
not even bothered to puzzle about hitherto. It has been found to be perfectly
natural that we can have an effect on the world.*]

Surely, this is not true. What was the ground of the whole Leibnitzian
Philosophy but the *wonder* & sense of the incomprehensib[le][1] and
consequent belief of the impossibility of the *Action* of any monad on
another?[2] What is the ground of Idealism but a wish to cut knots
it cannot untie—by denying "wirkung", & explainin[g] it by ideas
associated with certain feelings.—Lastly, who will read Berkley de
Motu & subscribe to the lines in the text underinscribed?[3]—But this
is one bad quality of the Kantian & Fichtean School—Their endless
P[...ing] to bran new originality in everything.

S. T. C.

3 p vii, pencil, lightly cropped | § 5

Ich weiss nicht, ohne *etwas* zu wissen; ich weiss nicht von mir, ohne
eben durch dieses Wissen mir zu Etwas zu werden; oder, welches
dasselbe heisst, ein subjectives in mir, und ein objectives zu trennen.
Ist ein Bewusstseyn gesetzt, so ist diese Trennung gesetzt: und es ist
ohne sie gar kein Bewusstseyn möglich.... Das Seyn ist durch sich
selbst, das Wissen aber hängt ab vom Seyn; so muss uns beides
erscheinen, so gewiss uns überhaupt etwas erscheint; so gewiss wir
Bewusstseyn haben.

[I do not know, without knowing *something*; I cannot know anything about
myself, without, precisely by means of this knowledge, becoming something
for myself; or—which is the same thing—distinguishing a subjective in
myself, and an objective. If a consciousness is postulated, then this distinction

2[1] See *Grundriss* 1.

2[2] In the *Monadologie* Leibniz states
that any change within a monad proceeds
from an internal principle and not from
an external cause; therefore no monad
can affect another externally. See esp §§ 7
(on "windowless monads") and 11.

2[3] C refers to Berkeley's *De motu sive
de motus principio et natura et de causa
motuum* (1721), in which Berkeley argues
that mind, not matter, is the principle of
motion, all matter being passive and
inert. He maintains that this view is

verified by personal experience (will), and
that it is supported by the most venerable
authorities (§§ 30, 31). Although bodies
are moved by mind, mind is itself
dependent upon a universal first principle
(§ 25), which is God, the "Almighty
Mind" (§ 32). He criticises Leibniz's
concept of motion as "abstract and
vague" (§§ 8, 17–19), and rejects New-
ton's concepts of absolute space and
absolute motion on the grounds that
space and motion are both relative
(§§ 16–17, 67).

is postulated; and without it no consciousness is possible at all....Being exists through itself; knowledge, however, depends on being; thus both must appear to us as surely as anything appears to us at all—as surely as we have consciousness.]

Cogito, *ergo* sum;[1] that is, in this way I am made to know that I am/ Having known this, I am then compelled to think my Being the Principle of my Thoughts, & to conclude Sum, ergo cogito.[2]—The first is a map of the Road, or Analysis; the second the nature and causative order of the Realities to which you have arrived by this road—i.e. Synthesis. In the same manner/ There exists a harmonious World: *ergo*, there is a God—i.e. by this mean[s] *I* know it[—]Knowing i[t,] I then sa[y:] There is a God: *ergo*, There is a harmonious ~~Universe~~ World.—

4 p viii, pencil

Wir finden hier eine unmittelbare Uebereinstimmung zwischen dem subjectiven und objectiven...Es wäre moglich, dass alle andere Uebereinstimmungen beider...nichts anderes wäre, als nur eine besondere Ansicht jener unmittelbaren Uebereinstimmung; und sollte sich dies wirklich nachweisen lassen, so wäre,—da diese unmittelbare Trennung und Uebereinstimmung die Form des Bewusstseyns selbst ist; jene andere Trennungen und Uebereinstimmungen aber den gesammten Inhalt alles möglichen Bewusstseyns erschöpfen,—zugleich erwiesen, dass alles, was im Bewusstseyn nur vorkommen kann, durch die blosse Form desselben gesetzt sey.

[We find here an immediate correspondence between the subjective and the objective....It is possible that all other correspondences of both are nothing but a special aspect of that immediate correspondence; and should this really be proved, then—since this immediate distinction and correspondence is the form of consciousness itself, while those other distinctions and correspondences exhaust the entire content of all possible consciousness—it would by the same token be proved that everything that can come to pass in consciousness is determined by the very form of that consciousness.]

I always fear an equivoque on the two meanings of this one word, *Consciousness*—. The first here given, the second synonimous with *Memory*.[1]

3[1] For C on Descartes's "cogito, *ergo* sum" ("I think, *therefore* I am") see e.g. **K**ant *Vermischte Schriften* copy b **10** and *BL* ch 12 (*CC*) i 276–7n. In a long note on the front and back flyleaves of Ernst **P**latner *Philosophische Aphorismen* (2 vols Leipzig 1793, 1800) C states that "the perfect co-incidence of Reality & Conception" is "realized in the two terms Sum, and Cogito".

3[2] "I am, therefore I think". Cf *BL* ch 9 (*CC*) i 145–6.

4[1] Cf *CL* vi 599–600 (27 Jul 1826), in which C distinguishes between memory

5   p xii | §§ 4–7

[Fichte says that the one inseparable "I" is active; it is the presence
of this objective "I" in me that influences the object. My activity
departs from the subjective and defines the objective. His argument
includes the following statements:] Ich finde mich, als wirkend in den
Sinnenwelt. Davon hebt alles Bewusstseyn an.... Wissen, und Seyn
sind nicht etwa ausserhalb des Bewusstseyns... getrennt, sondern nur
im Bewusstseyn werden sie getrennt... Um mir nur sagen zu konnen:
Ich; bin ich genöthigt, zu trennen... Nun soll *ich*, das Eine,
untheilbare Ich, thätig seyn; und das, was auf das Object wirkt, ist
ohne allen Zweifel dies objective in mir, die reele Kraft.

[I find that I am effectual in the material world. With this fact all
consciousness takes its rise... Knowing and being are not separated outside
of consciousness but only within consciousness... In order to be able to say
"I" at all, I am forced to separate... Now *I*, the single indivisible I, shall
be active; and that which acts on the object is without any doubt the
objective in me, the real force.]

There is an obscurity in this Deduction. Surely, the Ich finde mich,
is an act of Consciousness, and therefore of separation. How then
dare I assert, that das ungetheilte Ich ganz thätig sey?—[1]

6   p xvi | § 8

*] Nun soll aber doch der Wille Kausalität, und zwar eine unmit-
telbare Kausalität haben auf meinen Leib; und nur soweit, als diese
unmittelbare Kausalität des Willens geht, geht der Leib, als Werk-
zeug, oder die Articulation. (Bis zur Ansicht meines Leibes, als einer
Organisation, erstreckt sich diese vorläufige Uebersicht nicht.) Der
Wille wird daher vom Leibe auch unterschieden; erscheint daher
nicht als dasselbe. Aber diese Unterscheidung ist nichts anderes, denn
eine abermalige Trennung des subjectiven und objectiven, oder noch
bestimmter, eine besondere Ansicht dieser ursprünglichen Trennung.
Der Wille ist in diesem Verhältnisse das subjective, und der Leib das
objective.

[The will, however, should after all exert a causality, indeed an immediate
causality, on my body; and the body, as a tool, or the articulation, goes only
so far as this immediate causality of the will. (This preliminary survey does

---

as a "self-*re*taining" power of the mind
and a "self-*con*taining Power—a self-
conscious Being".
5[1] "The undivided I is wholly active".

The ego can find itself only by positing
itself as an object to itself; thus it cannot
remain undivided in the act of conscious-
ness. Cf *BL* ch 12 (*CC*) I 272–5.

not go so far as to view my body as an *organisation.*) The will is therefore distinguished from the body and consequently does not appear in the form of the body. This distinction is, however, no more than a reiterated separation of the subjective and the objective, or, to state it more accurately, a particular aspect of this original separation. In this relationship it is the will that is the subjective [element] and the body the objective.]

* This is Spinoza's Corpus = idea mentis.[1]

7 p ⁻2, referring to p xvi | 6 textus

Blindness—or A blows out the Candle—& all the *Objectivity* of B's Ichheit vanishes. How is this to be explained, if the Body itself as well as all objects external to it are no other than manifold Directions of the Active principle separated by the primary law of Consciousness, and becoming self-antithetic—the object being only ~~it~~*myself* self-contemplated, as Resistance.[1] The activity must remain—the will is not altered—or if it were, why should it suddenly alter in compliment to A's Caprice or an Accident?[a]

The only way of answering this must be by the old Εν και Παν,[2] into which all systems of Idealism must at length fall.[3]

Page xvi of the Introduction "nun soll"[4] is plainly the same with Spinoza's position that the Body is the Mind's Idea of itself, as an active power: mens se ipsam *objectiviter* ~~contemplans~~ intuens.[5] Idea is here used in its primitive material sense of a *total aspect* of any thing,[6] when the whole is seen without any distinct consciousness of attending to the Parts. Thus the word is used by Pindar & Aristophanes, (& by Sᵗ Matthew—) then Plato adopted it for the Zweckbegriff,

---

a The next paragraph, in a different hand and ink, continues at the line-break at the end of the first paragraph but slightly below it

6[1] "Body is the form (idea) of the mind": *Ethics* pt II props xix–xxx. See 7, below.

7[1] In pp 15–16 Fichte declares that since only matter can act on matter "I, regarded as principle of action in the physical world, am an articulated body; and the conception of my body is nothing but the conception of my own self, as cause in the physical world...as a given aspect of my absolute activity". For C on the definition of body see *CN* II 2402, esp ff 128ᵛ–129.

7[2] "One and All". See BAXTER *Reliquiae* COPY A 2 n 2 and cf *BL* ch 12 (*CC*) I 246–7.

7[3] Idealism resolves this problem by insisting that the natural world is a representation or manifestation of a single substance, spirit, and that the world owes its existence to the continuous willing of spirit. See e.g. Berkeley *Principles of Human Knowledge* §§6, 29.

7[4] Key-words for the beginning of 6 textus, above.

7[5] "The mind looking at itself *objectively*".

7[6] See esp DAVISON 14. The basic meaning of the root ϝιδ-, Latin *vid*-, is "see"—the sound basis for C's suggestion.

i.e. preconception with a causal power[7]—and lastly, it was used in one or other of two senses derived from the former—namely, as a mental exemplar, the mind's Ideal; or in opposition to all image, or sensual impression.[8] The mere *Idea* of Virtue.—[? all that] [. . . . .]*a*

8 p xvii | § 9

Das durch meine Wirksamkeit veränderliche Ding, oder die *Beschaffenheit* der Natur ist ganz dasselbe, was das unveränderliche, oder die blosse Materie ist; nur angesehen von einer andern Seite: eben so wie oben die Kausalität des Begriffs auf das objective, von zwei Seiten angesehen, als Wille und als Leib erschien. Das veränderliche ist die Natur, subjectiv, und mit mir, den thätigen in Verbindung, angesehen; das unveränderliche, dieselbe Natur, ganz und lediglich objectiv angesehen, und unveränderlich, aus den oben angezeigten Gründen.

[The thing that can be altered through my activity, or the *state* of nature, is exactly the same thing in essence as the unalterable or pure matter, except that it is seen from another perspective: just as (above) the causality of our concept of the objective appeared as will and body when seen from two different points of view. That which is alterable is nature, seen subjectively and in connexion with me as active; the unalterable is this same nature, seen completely and merely objectively, unalterable for the reasons shown above.]

i.e. from the necessity of Resistance to consciousness: but Resistance is the reflection, the echo, of Activity.—[1]

9 p 124 | Pt II Deduction der Realität, und Anwendbarkeit des Princips der Sittlichkeit § 7

Da hier schlechthin nicht weder Dinge an sich, noch Naturgesetze als Gesetze einer Natur ausser uns angenommen werden sollen, so

---

a Four or five words cropped at the foot of the page

7[7] On p xv Fichte says that *Zweckbegriff*, the idea of purpose, conceived objectively, is willing. For C's cluster of references—see Pindar *Olympian* 10.103, Aristophanes *Clouds* 289 and *Plutus* 559, Matt 28.3, and e.g. Plato *Republic* 507B—to uses of the word ἰδέα no source has been traced, but it may well spring from his own observation, for *BL* passim shows C quoting Pindar and Aristophanes in 1815–17 from *Poetae graeci veteres tragici, comici, lyrici, epigrammatarii* (Geneva 1606). See *BL* (*CC*) I 58

n 3 and Index: La Rovière. The source of the Pindar quotation in Böhme 22 (also used at the close of *BL*) was *Poetae graeci veteres*. (In Matt 28.3 the reading εἰδέα in some editions is merely a spelling variant for ἰδέα.) Cf *C on Sh* 38–9, from J. P. Collier's diary 21 Oct 1811.
7[8] For C on the meanings of "idea" see **1** n 1, above, and e.g. *CL* II 682, *SM* (*CC*) 100–14.
8[1] See **7** and n 1, above. Cf *CN* II 2402: "...all resistance presupposes action".

lässt diese Beschränktheit (unsrer Wirksamkeit auf den Gebrauch gewisser bestimmter Mittel, um einen bestimmten Zweck zu erreichen) sich nur so begreifen: dass das Ich selbst nun einmal sich so beschränke, und zwar nicht etwa mit Freiheit und Willkühr, denn dann *wäre* es nicht beschränkt, sondern zufolge eines immanenten Gesetzes seines eigenen Wesens; durch ein Naturgesetz seiner eigenen (endlichen) Natur.

[Since here neither a thing in itself, nor a law of nature as a law of nature outside us, should be assumed, the only way left to conceive of this limitation (a limitation of our effectiveness in the use of certain specified means to achieve a particular goal) is that the I itself limits itself; not indeed with freedom and choice, since then it would not *be* limited, but rather on account of an indwelling law of its own being; through a law of nature of its own finite nature.]

This is the *Achilles' Heel* of the System: for how is*^a this Nature compatible with pure Agility?[1]

* not determining itself becomes a *Thing*.

10   pp 163 and ⁻1, referring to p 163 | Anmerkung to § 9

Es liegt uns daran, dass man von dieser Absolutheit des Naturtriebes sich überzeuge. Jedes organisirte Naturproduckt ist *sein eigener* *] *Zweck*, d. h. es bildet, schlechthin um zu bilden,und bildet *so*, schlechthin um so zu bilden. Es soll damit nicht bloss gesagt werden, das vernunftlose Naturprodukt *denkt* sich selbst keinen Zweck ausser ihm; dies versteht sich ganz von selbst, indem es ja überhaupt nicht denkt: sondern auch, ein intelligenter Beobachter desselben kann ihm keinen äussern Zweck beilegen, ohne inkonsequent zu seyn, und völlig unrichtig zu erklären. Es giebt nur eine innere, keinesweges eine *relative* Zweckmässigkeit in der Natur. Die letztere entsteht erst durch die beliebigen Zwecke, die ein freies Wesen in den Naturobjecten sich zu setzen, und zum Theil auch auszuführen vermag.

[We are aiming to convince the reader of the absoluteness of the natural impulse. Every organised natural product is *its own end* in itself; i.e. it shapes merely in order to shape, and shapes *in a certain way* merely in order to do so in that way. By this we are not simply saying that the product of nature having no faculty of reasoning does not *think* of itself as having any purpose except itself [its own existence]; this is quite obvious—for it does not of course

---

^a C's pen has torn a small hole in the paper, removing most of his *

9[1] The "Achilles' heel" is the conflict between Fichte's *ursprüngliche Begränzung* (original limitation) and the *reine* *Thätigkeit* (pure activity—or, as C translates it, "pure agility") by which Fichte had defined intelligence in p 37.

think at all: we are also saying that an intelligent observer is unable to ascribe any external purpose to it without being inconsistent and giving a completely wrong explanation. There is only an internal, not a *relative*, purposiveness in nature. The latter arises only as a result of the desired purposes that a free being is capable of setting itself in natural objects and, partly, of carrying out.]

* Blank Leaf, p. 2.[a]

   p. 2.

   p. 163.—But in order to reconcile with ⟨Facts & good Sense⟩ this denial of a "*relativer* Zweckmässigkeit" in ⟨the products of⟩ Nature we must admit the unity of all Nature, ⟨as one Product:⟩ and doubtless, where is there is but one act constituting one Integer, there can be no *extrinsic* relation. But such relation, as the one wing of a Bird has to its other wing, the Bird itself has to its Mate—& so on. So little do these terrible ~~new~~ wild Truths become when they are analysed—even very tame and harmless Truisms!—[1]

11 p 173, pencil | § 10

Kein Gegner der Behauptung einer Freiheit kann läugnen, dass er solcher Zustände sich bewusst sey, für die er keinen Grund ausser ihnen angeben kann. Wir sind uns dann keinesweges bewusst, dass diese Zustände keinen äussern Grund haben, sagen die Scharfsinnigern, sondern nur, dass wir uns dieser Gründe nicht bewusst sind....Sie schliessen weiter: daraus, dass wir uns dieser Gründe nicht bewusst sind, folgt nicht, dass jene Zustände keine Ursachen haben....Da nun aber alles seine Ursache hat, fahren sie fort, so haben auch unsre freigeglaubten Entschliessungen die ihrigen, ohnerachtet wir derselben nicht bewusst sind. Hier nun *setzen* sie offenbar *voraus*, dass das Ich in die Reihe des Naturgesetzes gehöre, was sie doch *beweisen* zu können vorgaben. Ihr Beweis ist ein greiflicher Cirkel....Sie sind nur discursive Denker, und es fehlt ihnen gänzlich eine Intuition.

[No opponent of the assertion of a freedom can deny that he is conscious of conditions for which he can state no reason beyond the conditions themselves. We are then by no means conscious that these conditions have no external reason, say the more ingenious critics, but only that we are not conscious of these reasons....They deduce further: the fact that we are not conscious of these reasons does not signify that these conditions have no cause....Since everything has a cause, they continue, so also do our

                   [a] I.e. verso of the only front flyleaf

10[1] On "*Truisms*...disguised in high Words" see *Bestimmung* **15**.

decisions, which we consider free, regardless of our not being aware of them.
Now they obviously *assume* here that the ego partakes of the order of natural law, which indeed they maintained themselves able *to prove*. Their proof is a palpable circle [of argument]....They are merely discursive thinkers, and suffer from a total lack of intuition.]

Surely, this is rash Arguing. The degree and extent of consciousness depend on the Habit of Self-watchfullness joined to original power & sensibility. I have been able to anticipate what a Man would say by observing the Train of his associations, of which he himself was wholly *unconscious*

11A   p 426, marked in the margin | Pt III sec 3 § 25

Man enthalte sich sonach endlich jener eben so unbestimmten und seichten, als schädlichen und alle wahre Moralität von Grund aus vertilgenden Ausflüchte...

[Let us then avoid all the pretexts, as indefinite and shallow as injurious, that eradicate all true morality...]

12   pp 432–3, pencil, cropped

So sage man z. B. denen, welche die Möglichkeit eines uneigennützigen Triebes im Menschen schlechthin läugnen; einem *Helvetius* und seines gleichen: Ihr habt entdeckt, wie ihr uns berichtet, dass die Menschen nur durch Eigennützigkeit getrieben werden, und dass sie sich gröblich täuschen, wenn sie anderer Antriebe sich für fähig halten. Nun wohl, das ist gut für euch; benutzt diese Entdeckung, so gut ihr könnt....Aber warum theilt ihr denn eure Entdeckung uns mit; was mögt ihr, da alle Menschen, und also auch ihr, nur aus Eigennutz handeln können, durch diese Mittheilung gewinnen, oder welchen Verlust durch sie von euch abwenden?...Kurz, da ihr gar keinen Gewinn von der Mittheilung eurer Entdeckung haben könnt, so widerspricht eure Aussage, eurer Aussage selbst.—

[Let us say, for example, to those who completely deny the possibility of a selfless drive in man—a *Helvétius* and his kind: You have discovered, as you tell us, that men are driven only by selfishness and that they deceive themselves grossly if they consider themselves capable of other motives. Very well; this is fine for you; make what best you can of this discovery....But why do you communicate this matter to us? what do you gain? since all men, and you amongst them, can only act from selfish motives by communicating it to us?...In short, since you can gain nothing by communicating your discovery, your assertion contradicts itself.]

Eigennutz[1] has no meaning but the desire of pleasure; or of the empowering *means*; or the mood of mind consequent on these Habits. Now in this Case, (& there is other just as apt) I fear that these arguments would have little weight with the Hobbists & Mandevillians.[2] They would answer, there is a pleasure attached by Nature to the Communication of such Ideas, & to the knowlege knowlege[a] or belief that our Ideas influence those of others. It is *power*—and with all acts of Power we associate pleasure, because the greater number of our keenest pleasures are procure[d] & retained by acts of power—But if all actions were disinte[r]ested that were not done for *Profit*—in its most limit[ed] sense—the debauching a woman would be [a] disinterested action.[3]—The[re] is in this instance a pleasure attached to a certain act; and a restlessness implie[d] to the action/ & Fichte does not shew that the eagerness to frivolity is a whit more disinterested than the eager[ness to en]joy a woman, or to eat venison.

13 pp +1–+2, pencil, cropped

X = a man by nature acute, but not comprehensiv[e—]this would aid the circumstances that may [be][b] imagined as fostering Vanity/ take him away from all *benignant influences* of domestic affection, so that dear & tender Names convey to his Heart no remembrances & consequent[ly] no feelings, but of struggles, jealousies, intrigues & resentme[nts/] let him be from youth a Lad *of his own will*, in spite [of] this, & of let Vanity by nature & aid of accidents ripen into the love of Power—& every thing be done for some definite end—and from nature & bad education you will have already had *passionateness* which joined with *Vanity*, intense *Egoism*, & a mind naturally narrowed th[o'] acute will produce perpetual Impatience, both to oral teachers & to books, more to the former than ⟨to⟩ the latter; but then restlessness & vanity & want of Love for [? any/every] thing in itself will not permit him to remain long with the Latter/—Deduce

12[1] "Self-interest".

12[2] Those who subscribe to the view of Bernard Mandeville (1670–1733) in his *The Fable of the Bees* (for which see MANDEVILLE). Inquiring into the "Origin of Moral Virtues", Mandeville claimed that human desires are essentially evil and produce "private vices", whereas wealth was a "public benefit"; hence civilisation depends upon the development of vicious propensities. Mandeville argued with Hobbes that the origin of virtue is to be found in selfish and savage instincts.

12[3] For C on self-interest see e.g. *Friend* (*CC*) I 424–5 and n 5; and cf *CN* III 3559 and n.

all the morals & intellectuals of this ~~miand~~/ his Impatie[nce] will strip
[him][a] of all knowlege that does not palpably & instant[an]eously
come to him so as to appear the Growth of his mind, so as to feed
his self-adulation/ it will attach him to all errors, that can cloath
themselves in these forms/ it will mak[e] him abhor abstractions
because they are toilsom[e,] all poetic feeling because it is built on
the love of things for themselves & implies generalizatio[n &]
tranquillity—his impatience, passionateness, Vanity, Disappoint-
ment always rankling too, & finally, Envy & Hauntings of Rivalry
will make him *disputatious*—for he is too restless to remain either
spectator or auditor—misconceptions making bulls of passion &
taking hold of every subject [in] that relation which makes it a tool
of anger rather than [. . . . .][b] his natural acuteness dwindles—&
truly to a vast number of Objects he becomes to the last degree *blunt*
& dull.—On the other hand take another mind naturally compre-
hensive because assimilative; with feelings appropriate & reactive (i.e.
loving because he assimilates, & assimilating because he loves)—but
not *acute*—nay, rather dull to the difference, pronc to dream-like
mistakes, awkward &c/ and yet you shall see how the Spirit of Love
will [ap]pear by itself—and in the result you shall find among his
other Qualities a second Birth of Acuteness & Accuracy, not exactly
the same with the former perhaps, but answering the same ends more
perfectly & free from its defects.—

Ueber den Begriff der Wissenschaftslehre oder der sogenannten Philosophie. Zweite verbesserte und vermehrte Ausgabe. Jena & Leipzig 1798. 8⁰.

Bound as third with *Grundlage* and *Grundriss*.

British Museum C 126 f 13(3)

DATE. Probably Feb 1801. In a letter of 9 Feb 1801, C translated a long passage from this work: *CL* II 673–4.

COEDITOR. Willem Schrickx.

1 p 33, lightly cropped | Pt II § 4

[Footnote:] Auf einen möglichen Einwurf—Die eigentlichen Aufgaben des menschlichen Geistes sind freilich, so wohl ihrer Anzahl, als ihrer Ausdehnung nach, unendlich; ihre Auflösung wäre nur durch eine vollendete Annäherung zum Unendlichen möglich, welche an sich unmöglich ist: aber sie sind es nur darum, weil sie gleich *als* unendlich gegeben werden. Es sind unendlich viele Radien eines unendlichen Zirkels, dessen Mittelpunkt gegeben ist; und so wie der Mittelpunkt gegeben ist, ist ja wohl der ganze unendliche Zirkel, und die unendlich vielen Radien desselben gegeben. Der eine Endpunkt derselben liegt freilich in der Unendlichkeit; aber der andre liegt im Mittelpunkte, und derselbe ist allen gemein.

[The proper problems that the human mind sets itself are indeed infinite, in number as well as in extent; their solution would be possible only by a perfect approximation to the infinite, which is impossible in itself: but these problems are so only because they are given *as* infinite. There are an infiniite number of radii of an infinite circle the centre of which is given; and just as the centre is given, so is the whole infinite circle, as are the infinitely numerous radii of it. One end point of each radius lies indeed in the infinite, but the other extreme lies in the centre that is the same for all the radii.]

an infinite circle—i.e.—a circle without a circumferen[ce—]i.e. a circle = n[ot] a circle. Hm[!] ~~theo center of~~ bisect a[n] infinite Line[—]*hm*! a stran[ge] postulate.—Der Endpunc[t] eines unendlichen Radius!—*Hm*[!][1]

1[1] For a statement taken from p 46 of this book that in a child abstraction does not necessarily involve self-consciousness see *Logic* (*CC*) 14 and n 1.

Versuch einer Kritik aller Offenbarung. Zweite, vermehrte, und verbesserte Auflage. Königsberg 1793. 8°.

British Museum C 43 a 6

DATE. Unknown. Possibly 1801 and 1811. For this work as a possible source for a notebook entry, *CN* I 921 (c Feb–Mar 1801), see Orsini 182–3. See also **8**: "To this note I add *10 years* after the above was written...".

COEDITORS. Willem Schrickx, Raimonda Modiano.

1 pp ⁻2–⁻1, pencil

Mem. to state the use and utility of generalizing, or making some one name the representative of a group—& thence to shew its inapplicability & uselessness to inward & indescribable experiences, except as far as nature herself has generalized them for us by making them either distinguishable only by means more or less of intensity, (or for Locality, and apparent difference in extension are probably products of visual association) or by differences ⟨of sort⟩ so subtle as to permit (especially being things in their own nature rememberable only by as they are recognizable) no other discrimination—And all the only distinction*a* conception we have of them, is that they all alike are sensations, which, whether desired or undesired, make the Mind passive[1]—for tho' we in common usage we appropriate suffering to that, which we suffer unwillingly (or considered in itself) yet it in fact we suffer pleasure even as we suffer pain.—They are within us as if yet they were without—& stand as the supporting stratum of the Perceptions, which there too are properly within us or rather on the surface, yet represent themselves as without/—

Perceptions = sensations so minute as to excite the *activity* of the mind by its re-action on the momentary passion—[2]

2 p 3 | Einleitung §2 "Theorie des Willens..."

Sich mit dem Bewusstseyn eigner Thätigkeit zur Hervorbringung einer Vorstellung bestimmen, heisst *Wollen*; das Vermögen sich mit

a A slip for "distinctive"

[1] Cf *AR*(1825)267n: "Generalisation is a Substitute for Intuition, and for the Power of *intuitive* (that is, immediate) knowledge." See also *Bestimmung* **13** and n 1. For C on the inadequacy of language see e.g. *CN* II 2998 ff 27ᵛ–28, III 4350.

[2] On the difference between perception and sensation see ESCHENMAYER **27** n 3 and e.g. *CN* I 634 and *SM* (*CC*) 113–14.

diesem Bewusstseyn der Selbstthätigkeit zu bestimmen, heisst *das Begehrungsvermögen*: beides in der weitesten Bedeutung. Das Wollen unterscheidet sich vom Begehrungsvermögen, wie das Wirkliche vom Möglichen.—Ob das im Wollen vorkommende Bewusstseyn der Selbstthätigkeit uns nicht vielleicht täuschen möge, bleibt vor der Hand ununtersucht, und unentschieden.

[[The act] of self-positing [conceived as] consciousness of one's own activity in the production of a concept is called *volition*; the faculty by which one posits oneself through this consciousness of self-activity is called *the faculty of desire*: both are understood in their broadest sense. Volition differs from the faculty of desire as the real differs from the possible.—Whether the consciousness of self-activity occurring in willing may not perhaps deceive us remains for the present unexamined and undecided.]

Warum nicht der Wille? Surely, to the highest Wollen, viz. the *Creative* act, it would be contradictory as well as irreverend to attribute ein Begehrungsvermögen?[1] This is no trifling error; but a vice in the first concoction, according to which there would be no *will* at all, but a mere impulse, differing from the total mechanism of the mind only as a the Current of a River from the River:[2] in direct oppugnancy to the Author's own faith and purpose.

3 p 7 | § 2 1

Zwar geben alle obern Gemüthsvermögen durch ihre Geschäfte reichlichen Stoff *für* den sinnlichen Trieb, aber sie geben ihn nicht *dem* Triebe; ihm giebt sie die Empfindung. Die Thätigkeit des Verstandes bei'm Denken, die hohen Aussichten, die uns die Vernunft eröfnet, gegenseitige Mittheilung der Gedanken unter vernünftigen Wesen u. dergl. sind allerdings ergiebige Quellen des Vergnügens; aber wir schöpfen aus diesen Quellen gerade so, wie wir uns vom Küzzel des Gaumens afficiren lassen—durch die Empfindung.

[Admittedly all the higher faculties of the mind are engaged in providing abundant material *for* the sensuous impulse, but they do not give this material *to* the impulse; it is sensation that does that. The activity of the understanding in thinking, the lofty prospects that reason opens up before us, reciprocal communication of thoughts amongst rational beings—these, and the like, are certainly rich sources of pleasure; but we draw from these sources in exactly the same way as we allow ourselves to be affected by the titillation of the palate—through sensation.]

[1] "Why not the Will? Surely, to the highest willing...it would be contradictory...to attribute a faculty of desire?"

[2] On will as more than the current of a river see *AR* (1825) 74. Cf *LR* IV 437–8 ("Essay on Faith").

I hold in much suspicion, I own, this *hypostasis* or *quasi-person*, yclept Der Trieb, = Impulse: & in still greater this *one*, every where the same, *some thing*, called die Empfindung[1]—And these my doubts are hugely strengthened by the consequences here deduced, namely, that "the activity of the Understanding in Thinking, the high Views & Prospects which the Reason opens out to us" occasion the same *kind* of gratification as Apple-pie & Custard!—I[n][a] short, I hold the whole tribe of Vermögens graviter suspectum.[2]

4 p 13, pencil | § 2 II

Alles, was blosser Stoff ist, und nichts anders seyn kann, wird durch
*] die Empfindung gegeben; die Spontaneität bringt nur Formen hervor...

[All that is mere matter, and can be nothing else, is given through sensation; spontaneity produces only forms...]

* But this is a mere assertion—& one that is not easily reconciled with *production* (hervorbrin[g]en)[b1] in any sense.

5 pp 14–15, pencil

Formen kündigen sich dem Bewusstseyn nur in ihrer Anwendung auf
*] Objecte an. Nun werden die in der reinen Vernunft ursprünglich liegenden Formen der Anschauung, der Begriffe und der Ideen auf ihre Objecte mit dem Gefühl der Notwendigkeit angewendet; sie
*] kündigen sich demnach dem Bewusstseyn *mit Zwang*, und *nicht mit Freiheit* an, und heissen daher auch *gegeben*, *nicht hervorgebracht*.

[Forms make themselves known to the consciousness only in their application to objects. Now the forms of intuition, of concepts, and of ideas originally residing in pure reason are applied to their objects with the feeling of necessity; they therefore become known to the consciousness *under compulsion* and *not freely*, and thus are said to be *given, not produced*.]

* All this again is most erroneous. Zwang or Compulsion is not the same as Necessity, nor Choice (Willkühr) the same as Freedom. On the contrary, Necessity and absolute Freedom are one.[1] And of this

---

a Letter supplied by the editor   *b* Letter supplied by the editor

3[1] "The sensation".
3[2] "Faculties seriously suspect". For C's view that Fichte, as well as Kant, tends to confuse intellectual desires with physical desires see *CN* III 3558 ff 27–8. Cf **6**, below.

4[1] See *bringt...hervor* in textus.
5[1] Cf Schelling "Philosophische Briefe über Dogmatismus und Kriticismus" Letter 9: "To many who find Spinoza's teaching objectionable on the ground that he thought of God as a being with-

Identity the Assent of the Mind to a Mathematical Demonstration is a Foretaste and Analogon.[2]

6 pp 32–3, pencil | § 2 III

Nemlich der Glückseeligkeitstrieb wird vors erste durch das Sittengesetz nach Regeln eingeschränkt; ich *darf* nicht alles wollen, wozu dieser Trieb mich bestimmen könnte. Durch diese vors erste blos negative Gesetzmässigkeit nun kommt der Trieb, der vorher gesetzlos und blind vom Ohngefähr oder der blinden Naturnothwendigkeit abhing, überhaupt unter ein Gesetz, und wird auch da, wo das Gesetz nicht redet, wenn dieses Gesetz nur für ihn *alleingültig* ist, eben durch das Stillschweigen des Gesetzes, *positiv* gesetzmässig, (gesetzlich noch nicht).

[It is precisely the instinct for happiness that is limited by the moral code, according to rules; I *must* not desire everything that this instinct could lead me to desire. Because of this at first merely negative conformity to the law, the instinct that previously depended lawlessly and blindly upon chance or blind natural necessity now comes to be subject to a law, and comes *positively* to conform with the law (but has not yet become statutory) by reason of the silence of the law—even in cases where the law does not dictate, and where this law is valid *solely for it*.]

I do not feel satisfied as to the *phrase* "Glückseligkeitstrieb".[1] Each Stimulable asks to be stimulated; but to average and reconcile their often discordant Claims, subordinating the transient to the more permanent, & all to the one absolutely permanent, in which Self becomes evanescent, or transfigured—this is no Instinct (Trieb) but the work of the Free Will aided by Grace, i.e. a Will ~~more~~ perfectly free.[2]

7 p 80 | § 4

Der eine deducirt die Möglichkeit der Religion überhaupt richtig, entwickelt ihren Inhalt, stellt ihre Kriterien fest; und gelangt nun durch drei ungeheure Sprünge 1) indem er Religion in der weitersten, und die in der engsten Bedeutung verwechselt, 2) indem er natürliche

---

out freedom, it may not be superfluous to point out that Spinoza himself also conceived of absolute necessity and absolute freedom as identical." In SCHELLING *Philosophische Schriften* (Landshut 1809): C wrote eight annotations on these letters but none on this passage.

5[2] Cf *CN* I 1717: "In all inevitable

Truths...I feel my will active: I seem to *will* the Truth, as well as to perceive it." See also *Bestimmung* **4**.

6[1] "Instinct for happiness"—in textus.

6[2] C detects another instance of confusion between intellectual and physical faculties: see **3** and n 2, above.

und geoffenbarte Religion verwechselt, 3) indem er geoffenbarte überhaupt und christliche verwechselt...Ein andrer, dem es sich freilich nicht verbergen konnte, dass diese noch etwas mehr sey, setzt dieses Mehrere blos in grossere Versinnlichung der abstracten Ideen jener....Jeder, auch der schärfste Denker, meine ich, denkt sie sich, wenn er sie in praktischer Absicht auf sich anwendet, mit einiger Beimischung von Sinnlichkeit, und so geht es bis zu dem rohsinnlichsten Menschen in unmerkbaren Abstufungen fort. Ganz rein von Sinnlichkeit ist *in concreto* keine Religion; denn die Religion überhaupt gründet sich auf das Bedürfniss der Sinnlichkeit. Das Mehr oder Weniger aber berechtigt zu keiner Eintheilung.

[The one deduces the possibility of religion correctly on the whole, develops its content, and establishes its criteria; yet he makes three appalling leaps: 1) in that he confuses religion in its broadest sense with religion in its narrowest sense, 2) in that he confuses natural with revealed religion, 3) in that he confuses revealed religion in general with the Christian religion...Another, from whom undoubtedly the fact cannot be concealed that there must be more to religion [than the former makes of it], places this additional meaning solely in the greater sensory embodiment of the former's abstract idea [of religion]....Everyone—even the most acute thinker, I believe—conceives of it, when he makes a practical application of it to himself, with some admixture of sensuousness; and so the matter proceeds in imperceptible gradations up to the most coarsely sensuous man. No religion is *in the concrete sense* completely free from sensuousness; for religion as such is based on the need for sensuous feeling. The extent of this need, however, does not justify any division.]

True! But surely that the one is conscious, that it is an illusion, and that the other thinks the illusion (not ⟨as⟩ the vehicle or inward metaphor of the Truth, but) the true Reality itself,—surely this makes a distinction, und berechtigt[a] zu einer Eintheilung.[1]

8 p 81

Alle Religionsstifter haben sich zum Beweise der Wahrheit ihrer Lehren nicht auf die Beistimmung unsrer Vernunft, noch auf theoretische Beweise, sondern auf eine übernatürliche Autorität berufen, *] und den Glauben an diese, als den <u>einzigen</u> rechtmässigen Weg der Überzeugung, gefordert.

[All founders of religion refer to supernatural authority, not to the assent of our reason or to theoretical evidence, to prove the truth of their doctrines, and they have demanded belief in this supernatural authority as the *sole* rightful way towards religious conviction.]

[a] A slip for "berechtigt"

7[1] "And does justify a division"—an inversion of the last clause of textus.

* not true: for Christ refers to the practische Vernunft as the highest Evidence. "Do the will of my Father: and ye shall know whether I am of God"—[1] To this note I add *10 years* after the above was written, nay! Fichte is in the right: for Christians appeal even to the practical Reason in the authority, & by the command of Christ.

S. T. C.

9 pp 218–19, pencil | §14

Wollte man etwa noch zuletzt als den einzigen Weg, wie wir hierüber belehrt werden könnten, annehmen, Gott selbst könne es uns mittheilen, so wäre dies eine neue Offenbarung, über deren objektive Realität die vorige Unwissenheit entstehen würde, und bei der wir wieder da seyn würden, wo wir vorher waren.—Da es aus allem gesagten völlig sicher ist, dass über diesen Punkt keine Überführung des Irrthums, d. i. dass *für uns* überhaupt kein Irrthum darüber möglich sey, eine Bestimmung des Begehrungsvermögens aber uns treibt, uns für das bejahende Urtheil zu erklären, so können wir mit völliger Sicherheit dieser Bestimmung nachgeben.

[If perhaps we still wished to consider the way [presented above] as the only way in which we could be informed [about the validity of revelation], God himself could impart it to us, but this would be a new revelation itself and this would give rise to the previous uncertainty about its objective reality; we would find ourselves again where we had started. As it is completely certain from everything we have said that, as regards this point, no error might possibly be committed—that is, *for us* in general there is no possibility of error—but that a determination of the faculty of desire drives us to choose a positive judgement, we can therefore yield to this determination with complete assurance.]

To all but the man thus made certain. But surely there is no impossibility (however improbable it may be) that the Holy Spirit may give the Soul an intellectual Intuition, equal to—"I see." How do you know that? Because I see—conjoined with a *positive* or waking Faith.—The Objection from Dreams rests on a Sophism—the negation of *denial* is assumed as = the position of Assent.[1]

8[1] Conflation of e.g. Matt 7.20 (12.50 etc) and John 7.17 (but cf John 5.30, 6.39).

9[1] Cf *Friend* (*CC*) I 515–18. For another reply to the "Objection from Dreams" see *BL* ch 18 (CC) II 63–4.

10   p 244, pencil | Schlussanmerkung

Dass von der Realität aller Ideen vom Übersinnlichen keine objektive Gewissheit, sondern nur ein Glaube an sie stattfinde, ist nun zur Genüge erwiesen. Aller bisher entwickelte Glaube gründet sich auf eine Bestimmung des Begehrungsvermögens.... Es ist nemlich an sich gar nicht zu läugnen, dass man oft andre, und eben so oft sich selbst überredet, man glaube etwas, wenn man blos nichts dagegen hat, und es ruhig an seinen Ort gestellt seyn lässt. Von dieser Art ist fast aller historischer Glaube.... Über Meinungen... findet dennoch zu jeder Zeit ein Experiment statt, dass man sich nemlich aufs Gewissen frage, ob man wohl für die Richtigkeit einer gewissen Meinung einen Theil seines Vermögens oder das ganze, oder sein Leben, oder seine Freiheit verwetten wolle, wenn etwas gewisses darüber auszumachen seyn sollte.

[That there is no objective certainty about the reality of all ideas of the supersensible, but only a belief in them, has now been satisfactorily proved. All belief developed up to now is based on a disposition of our faculty of desire.... It is of itself not to be denied that one often convinces others, and just as often oneself, that one believes something when one merely has nothing against it, and quietly accepts it. Practically all historical belief is of this kind.... As for opinions... there is nevertheless at any time a test worth trying: let one ask oneself conscientiously if one would wish to stake a part of one's fortune, or the whole of it, or one's life, or one's freedom, on the correctness of a particular opinion if anything certain could be ascertained about it.]

Acquiescence: Belief: : Certainty. Fichte has rightly distinguished the second from the First; but in this page seems to confound the second with the Third.[1]

11   p +2

> the two Lovers hu[n]g over each other
> as fearfully, as lovingly,
> as the half-open'd & yet opening Leaves
> of the moss Rose—/

> Stole over her heart
> Soft as the pearly-fleecyes ~~Cloud~~ of ⟨the⟩ Noon
> over the Islets of the Sky in Autumn/

10[1] For the distinction between belief and certainty see e.g. HOOKER 49 and see *LS* (*CC*) 175, *SM* (*CC*) 20–1, and *Friend* (*CC*) II 76 n 4, the first two of which include a distinction between certainty and positiveness, as in *CN* II 3095. See also *CN* III 3592, esp f 136ᵛ and n, and *C&S* (*CC*) 21 n 1.

Fancy or a Fancy-ette
    On a Dragon-fly—Libellula—herself seemed like the Image
doubled to the eye by the whiz-mist of the little Hippogryph's
[? crossing/tossing] [?its/her] wings.[1]

12 p $^{+2a}$

Intensity & Extensity combinable only by blessed Spirits[1]—Hence it
is, that Lovers in their finite state incapable of ~~measuring~~ fathoming
the intensity of their feelings *help* the thought *out* by extension,
commute as it were—& thus think the passion as wide in *time* as it
is deep in essence—Hence—*auf ewig* dein![2]

---

^{a} This note, written immediately below **11**, may have been part of the same draft

11[1] Not recorded in *PW* (EHC). The title-page of this book has a vignette of a grasshopper or locust; any connexion with dragonfly or hippogryph would seem to be coincidence. *Libellula*—Linnaean name for the family of dragonflies, of which C noted in *CN* IV 4892 (c 2–9 Apr 1822): "The Libellulidæ fly all ways without needing to turn their bodies—onward, backward, right and left—with more than Swallow-rivalling rapidity of wing, readiness of evolution, and indefatigable continuance." The *hippogryph*—a griffin (having the head and wings of an eagle) with the body of a horse instead of the body of a lion.

12[1] Possibly informed by §2 (p 19), in which Fichte, in defining the feeling of respect ("das Gefühl der Achtung") in terms of quantity and quality, uses the words *Intension* and *Extension* ("intensity" and "extension").

12[2] "Yours *forever*". Cf *CN* III 4061 (2 Apr 1811). For the phrase "auf ewig dein" used as a noun referring to a male lover in an abortive suicide pact see *CN* IV 4552 (c 14 Jun 1819).

MARSILIO FICINO

1433–99

Platonica theologia de imortalitate animorum: accuratius noviter impressa: et cum exemplaribus eiusdem authoris collata, etc. [Florence] 1525. 4º.

British Museum C 126 e 2

Autograph inscription on p ⁻2: "S. T. Coleridge Messina, 9 Octʳ 1805". Below this, in pencil in an unidentified hand: "Preserve this leaf". "S. T. C." label at the foot of p ⁻2. John Duke Coleridge's monogram on p ⁻4. A few short marginal notes are written throughout in an earlier hand, e.g. ff 1, 2, 2ᵛ, 3, 8, 41, 66ᵛ, 73, 90, etc, and marginal marks in a scalloped shape especially in the "Repertorium".
For C on Ficino generally see *CN* III 3861. See also *BL* ch 9 (*CC*) I 144 and *P Lects* Lect 10 (1949) 295.

MS TRANSCRIPT. VCL BT 21: EHC transcript.

DATE. After 9 Oct 1805. C left this book behind at Allan Bank in 1810: Wordsworth LC 383, 1179.

1   ff 1ᵛ–2 | Bk I ch 2 *Corpus natura sua nihil agit*

Virtus vero sicut unione augetur, ita dispersione minuitur. Idcirco siccitas vim tum caloris tum frigoris auget, quia unit: Humiditas vero debilitat, quia dispergit. Deinde quo maius corpus est, eo secundum seipsum pigrius, incptiusque ad motum. Igitur quanto magis augetur corpus, tanto magis retardat motum: ac differt diutius actionem. Nempe vis levitatis sursum tollit scintillam velocius quam flammam. Vis gravitatis celerius deorsum trahit lignum si acutum fuerit quam si latum. Postremo cum corpus quodlibet suum impleat locum ac locus unus duobus corporibus nequaquam sufficiat: commigrare in unum corpora nequeunt: ac etiam soliditate densitateque sua penetrationem mutuam prohibent.

[*Body does not act at all by its own nature.* Indeed virtue is increased by union as it is decreased by dispersion. So dryness increases the force of heat and cold because it unites, but humidity weakens them because it disperses. Then, the bigger a body is the more inert it is in relation to its own nature and the less apt to motion. Therefore the more a body is increased in size, the more it retards its motion and the longer it takes to act. Indeed the force

647

of levity lifts a spark faster than a flame. The force of gravity pulls down a piece of wood faster if it is sharp than if it is thick. Lastly, since any body fills its own space and one space is not enough for two bodies, bodies cannot coalesce into one, and they prohibit mutual penetration by their very solidity and density.]

The gross errors of the Platonists in Physics, wch tho' they do not affect the essential meaning, yet seem to do so to impatient minds: & are the secondary *cause* of the present *supercilium* toward Platonism/ the primary cause is that Impatience itself which characterizes Europe, & in a growing ratio from the days of Verulam to Condilliac—occasioning, & occasioned by, the passion for merely sensuous phænomena.[1] Finger-active, brain-lazy we ~~grin~~ look with the same arch scorn at ancient philosophy, with which a shrewd Rustic grins at an Astronomer's assertions of the motion & size of the Earth relatively to the Sun, the poor Sage having previously mistaken Oats for Barley, or a Plough for a Harrow.—Common sense, cry the one! Mother-wit, cries the other.

S. T. C.

---

[1] I.e. the march of "rationalism", from the end of the sixteenth century to the latter part of the eighteenth. (Francis Bacon's *Advancement of Learning* was published in 1605; Condillac died in 1780.) Bacon and Condillac appear as crucial figures in the Jun 1803 outline for C's "Organum verè Organum": see *CL* II 947 §§ 9–11. Cf *CN* II 2193 (5 Oct 1804), III 3244, 3281.

RICHARD FIELD

1561–1616

Of the Church, five bookes.... The third edition. Oxford 1635. F°.

Victoria College Library (Coleridge Collection)

C's copy, acquired 15 Nov 1814 at Ashley, Box, Bath (**61**); presented to DC on 28 Mar 1819 (**1**) but evidently left with C in Feb 1824 and given to DC on C's death in 1834.

Inscribed on p $^+$1: "Hannak Scoltock Her Book February 10 1787"; and on p $^+$2: "Hannah Scoltock Her Book Febr^{ry} 10 1787", both inscriptions ceremoniously written in a large copybook hand, as though by a child, between guidelines traced in pencil. Leaf $^+$1/$^+$2 consists of two leaves pasted together: these appear to have been originally front flyleaves transferred by mistake to the back of the volume in rebinding or repairing, thus displacing both Hannah Scoltock's inscriptions and C's note of acquisition (**61**). Inscribed by DC on p $^-$2: "This Book was left by S. T. Coleridge, at his death, to his younger Son. Derwent Coleridge.—1834." (DC has written, and initialled, a note in pencil on p 472; on p 65 "* qu?—D.C.—"; a marginal pencil mark on p 488 beside a sentence on two orders of the ministry seems also to be his.) A note by EHC in a pocket attached to p $^+$9 (p–d): "I desire that this book be preserved in my family after my death, and that if ⟨my⟩ sons should marry & have sons of their own that this book be the property of the eldest surviving male descendant of S. T. Coleridge—E. H. Coleridge Nov. 18. 1896". In the top right-hand corner of the title-page a succession of notes of ownership, each in autograph, with separating lines between the first four signatures:

E. T. Mag. Coll: Cant.
S. T. C. Jes. Coll. Cant.
D. C. Helleston, Corn.
E. H. C. Weybridge, Surrey
G. H. B. C. Christ Church Erith.
A. H. B. C. Epsom Surrey

At the upper left-hand corner of the title-page, a black wax seal that may have been used to attach a sheet of paper. To the right of the device, some lightly pencilled numbers, the last of which is "129"; at the foot of p *2, "149" in pencil; and on p 14 an asterisk underlined in the margin.

C's note on the word "harberous", in *CN* III 4043, if written c 1810–11, is the only sign of his knowing Field *Of the Church* before he acquired this copy on 15 Nov 1814; a marginal note on that word is written in Field's text (**58**), and the corresponding note in *CN* III 4191 seems to have been written after Nov 1814. As soon as he had acquired this copy, C began to write marginalia in it. By early May 1815 he had lent the book to Brabant and was trying to recover it so that he could lend it to Bowles (*CL* IV 566, 567); c Apr 1818 he told a Mr Pryce: "If you meet with 'The Church', by Field, a folio of James Ist's time, do not let it pass by you. For 7 to 12 Shillings it's common price.—" *CL* IV 849. Later words of approval appeared in public: see *SM* (*CC*) 107 and *AR* (1825) 304–5.

When C addressed this volume to DC in Mar 1819 (**1**)—and it is not clear whether he was presenting it to him or simply commending it to him—he was tacitly expressing his hopes for his younger son: that he should go to Cambridge, become a strong Anglican, and take Holy Orders, DC then being not yet nineteen. DC cannot have taken the book away in Mar 1819, for C wrote a note in it again on 4 May 1819 (**12**). DC went up to St John's in the autumn of 1820 and in Jan 1824 took a pass degree. See *CN* IV 5113 and cf *CL* V 336. He passed through Highgate in Feb 1824 on his way to take up a post as schoolmaster in Plymouth. The book remained in Highgate, however, for C wrote a note in it on 12 Mar 1824 (**36**); and in Highgate it remained until C's death, as DC's inscription attests.

MS TRANSCRIPTS. (*a*) BM Ashley 4771. Inscribed on p ‾2: "The Revd James Gillman the Gift of his Father." MS facsimile in a copy of the Oxford 1635 ed, made for the Gillman family, the transcriber's hand not identified. *Ashley LC* VIII 95–7 describes this copy in some detail, as though the notes in it were written in C's autograph, remarking that the writing (shown in a reproduction) was "in Coleridge's neatest hand (which could be clerkly, in spite of Lamb's remarks)".

(*b*) Rev A. D. Coleridge: *Green LC* 215. MS facsimile made in a copy of the Oxford 1635 ed, for the Green family, the transcriber's hand not identified. This copy was bequeathed, as an inscription in it shows, by Mrs Ann Green to DC and was "presented to St Mark's Coll. Chelsea by Ernest Hartley Coleridge. 1902". Perhaps through oversight, EHC's wish to leave a memorial in the college of which his father was Principal 1841–64 was not fulfilled; the book remained in the library of his son GHBC and so passed to EHC's second grandson, Antony.

DATE. 15 Nov 1814–c 1815; Mar–May 1819; Mar 1824. Five notes are dated in ms: 15 Nov 1814 (**61**), 4 Dec 1814 (**28**), 28 Mar 1819 (**1**), 4 May 1819 (**12**), 12 Mar 1824 (**36**).

1   title-page verso and sig 2 (facing), pencil, overtraced

My dear Derwent   28 March, 1819

This one Volume thoroughly understood and appropriated will place you in the highest rank of *doctrinal* Church of England Divines (of such as now are) and in no mean rank as a true doctrinal Church Historian.

Next to this I recommend Baxter's own Life edited by Sylvester, with my Marginal MSS notes.[1] Here (more than in any of the

---

1[1] Almost certainly BAXTER *Reliquiae* COPY A. For C's enthusiastic commenda- tion of Baxter to Morgan on 23 May 1814 see *CL* III 497–8.

Prelatical and Arminian Divines, from Laud to the death of Charles the Second)[2] you will see the strength, and beauty of the Church of England—i.e. its Liturgy, Homilies,[3] and Articles. By contrasting too its present state with that which such excellent men as Baxter, Callamy, and the so-called Presbyterian or Puritan Divines,[4] would have made it, you will bless it as the bulwark of Toleration.—

Thirdly, Eichhorn's introductions to the O. & N. Testament, and to the Apocrypha, and his Comment on the Apoc[al]ypse[a] (to all which my Notes and your own previous studies will supply whatever antidote is wanting)[5]—these will suffice for your *Biblical* Learning, and teach you to attach no more than the supportable weight to these and such like outward evidences of our holy and spiritual Religion.—

So having done, you will be in point of professional knowlege such a Clergyman as will make glad the heart of your loving

Father   S. T. Coleridge[6]

N.B.—See Book IV. Chap. 7. p. 353, both for a masterly confutation of the Paleyo-Grotian Evidences of the Gospel[7] & a decisive proof in what light it was regarded by the Church of England in its

a Letters supplied by the editor

[1][2] I.e. from 1633, when Laud became abp of Canterbury, to 1685, the death of Charles II. But C refers less to a chronological period than to an attitude of mind that he often stigmatised, which he found even in his favourite writer of that period, Jeremy Taylor. For Arminianism see BUNYAN COPY B 7 n 3. In seventeenth-century England the anti-Calvinist movement, especially as represented by Abp Laud, was often called by its opponents "Arminian".

[1][3] The Homilies were often bound into the Book of Common Prayer rather than printed as an integral part of it, as was the case for the Thirty-nine Articles, the metrical Psalms, and the *Companion to the Altar* (see BOOK OF COMMON PRAYER headnote). For C's copy see SERMONS OR HOMILIES. and for his including the Homilies in his definition of the Church of England see *C 17th C* 266 (from the *Christian Observer* Jun 1845).

[1][4] Richard Baxter and his friend Edward Calamy (see BAXTER *Reliquiae* COPY B 83 n 1) were Presbyterians within the Church of England until driven out by the Act of Uniformity in 1662.

[1][5] See EICHHORN, and the dates of marginalia as given in the headnotes to the separate titles.

[1][6] DC, after doing poorly at Cambridge and going through a period of "Atheism", was eventually ordained in Jul 1827. See also **40**, below.

[1][7] See BAHRDT **2** and n 1 and DONNE *Sermons* COPY B **110**. See also **46**, below, the textus to which immediately precedes the passage C refers to: "For wee should beleeve the Articles of our faith, because they were revealed, and beleeve they were revealed, because our Auncestors soe delivered unto us, and the Church soe beleeveth. And from hence it would farther follow, that seeing the assent yeelded to the conclusion, can bee noe greater, nor more certaine, then that which is yeelded to the premisses, whence it is deduced and inferred, wee should have no greater certainty of things Divine and revealed, then such as humane meanes and causes can yeeld.... The Apostles builded themselves upon the sure and unmooveable rocke of Divine truth, and authority: therefore we must doe so likewise."

best age—like Grotius himself, it is half-way between Popery and Socinianism

2 p 5, lightly cropped | Bk 1*ᵃ* ch 3

[Six reasons given by the Schoolmen why, although "The Fall of Angels was irrecoverable", God looked with compassionate mercy upon man's sin.] Thirdly, the Angels in the height of their pride, sought to be like unto God in omnipotencie, which is an incommunicable property of divine beeing, & cannot be imparted to any creature. But men desired onely to be like unto God in omniscience and the generall knowledg of all things which may * be communicated to a creature, as in Christ it is to his humane soule...

* Surely this is more than doubtful; and even the instance given irreconcileable with Christ's own Assertion concerning the last Day,[1] which must be understood of his human Soul, by all who hold the faith delivered from the foundation—namely, his Deity. Field seems to have excerpted this incautiously from the Schoolmen, who on this premise could justify the communicability of Adoration as of the Saints. Omniscience[, it]*ᵇ* may be [proved,]*ᵇ* implies omnipotence.

3 p 6

Fourthly, the Angels were immateriall and intellectuall spirits, dwelling in heavenly palaces, in the presence of God and the light of his countenance, and therefore could not sinne by error of misperswasion, but of purposed malice which is the sinne against the holy Ghost, and is irremissible. But man fell by misperswasion, and by being deceived by the lying suggestion of the spirit of errour.

The fourth argument, and as closely connected with it the first[1] (only somewhat differently stated) seem the strongest—or rather the only

---

ᵃ In the running headline, C has corrected "Booke III" to "I"
ᵇ Cropped text restored from *LR*

2[1] John 6.39, 40, 44; 11.24; 12.48.

3[1] "First, for that the Angels are not by propagation one from another, but were created all at once, so that of Angels some might fall and others stand: But men descend by generation from one stocke or roote, and therefore the first man falling and corrupting his nature, derived to all his posterity a corrupted and sinfull nature: if therefore God had not appointed a redemption for man, he had beene wholly deprived of one of the most excellent creatures that ever hee made; whereas among the Angells, notwithstanding the Apostasie of some, hee held still innumerable in their first estate."

ones. For the ~~third~~ second[2] is a mere anticipation of the fourth—and all that is true in the third is involved in it.

S. T. Coleridge

4 p 9 | 15

...& *they were all* [at the Pentecost] *filled with the holy Ghost, and began to speake with other tongues, as the spirit gave them utterance...*

i.e. other than the Hebrew and Syro-chaldaic, which (with rare and reluctant exceptions in favor of the Greek) were appropriated to public Prayer and Exhortation: just as the Latin in the Romish Church.—The new Converts preached and prayed, each to his Companions in his and their dialect—they were all Jews but had assembled from all the different Provinces of the Roman and Parthian Empires, as the Quakers among us to the Yearly Meeting in London.[1]—This was a *Sign* not a Miracle. The Miracle consisted in the ⟨visible and audible⟩ descent of the Holy Ghost, and in the fulfilment of the Prophecy of Joel, as explained by Peter himself.[2]

5 p 10 | shoulder-note *k* to **6** textus

Aliud est Etymologia nominis, et aliud significatio nominis. Etymologia attenditur secundùm id à quo imponitur nomen ad significandum: Nominis verò significatio secundùm id ad quod significandum imponitur [Aquinas] 2.2. q. 92 art. 1

[The etymology of a word (name) is one thing, the meaning another. The etymology is considered according to what the word meaningfully derives from: the meaning of a word, however, is considered according to what the word is applied to.]

An apt motto for a Critique on Horne Tooke's επεα πτεροεντα.[a1]
    The best service of Etymology is when the sense of a word is still

---

[a] This sentence, prefixed by "*", is written beside the shoulder-note, and ends "See *above*." The second paragraph, prefixed with "*", fills the head-margin and runs down the outer margin

3[2] "Secondly, the Angels fell of themselves, but man by the suggestion of another." For the third "reason" see **2** textus, above.

4[1] The democratic organisation of the Society of Friends allows for preparative meetings (of a single congregation), and for monthly, quarterly, and yearly meetings of increasingly wide constituency, the yearly meeting drawing from the whole of Britain, except Ireland.

4[2] The prophecy of Pentecost is in Joel 2.28–32, repeated in Acts 2.16–21. Peter refers to the "promise" of "the gift of the Holy Ghost" in Acts 2.39. For C's sceptical attitude to the "gift of tongues" see e.g. FLEURY **6**, T. FULLER *Church History* **3**, and HERBERT **24**.

5[1] For Horne TOOKE Έπεα πτερόεντα, *or The Diversions of Purley* see also BÖHME **57** n 2; and cf e.g. *CN* III 3587 f 43ᵛn, 4237n.

unsettled, and especially when two words have each two meanings, A = a b, and B = a b, instead of A = a and B = b.[2] Thus Reason and Understanding, as at present popularly confounded—Here the etyma, Ratio, the relative proportion of Thoughts and Things, and Understanding, as the power which substantiates phænomena (*substat* iis)[3] determines the proper sense. But most often, the etyma being equivalent, we must proceed ex arbitrio—as Law *compels*, Religion *obliges*: or take up what had been begun in some one derivative. Thus fanciful and imaginative *are* discriminated—& thus supplies the ground of choice for giving to Fancy and Imagination, to each its own sense. Cowley a *fanciful* Writer; Milton an *imaginative* Poet.[4]—Then I proceed with the distinction—How ill *Fancy* assorts with *Imagination*, is instanced in Milton's Limbo.[5]

6   pp 10–11

Neither doth any of our Divines...call this societie of Christians a *Synagogue*, though...wee use the word congregation, which is the Latine of συναγωγὴ, & feare not to say that the people of God, in the state of the new Testament, are the Congregation of Christ, and are congregated in his faith and name: even as, though ἐκκλησία, *Ecclesia, convocatio, caetus evocatus*, a multitude called out, or called together, both Greeke, Latine, and English words, doe originally signifie one and the same thing....It followeth not therefore that wee call the companie and societie of Christians a *Synagogue*...[1]

[a]I should rather express the difference between the Faithful of the Synagogue and those of the Church thus: that the former hoped ⟨generally⟩ by an *implicit* faith—"It shall ⟨in all things⟩ be well with ⟨all,⟩, ~~that~~ that love the Lord—therefore it cannot but be good for

a "3", not in C's hand, at the head of the entry indicates the third ms element on p 10

5[2] This note provides a central statement, unusually analytical, of C's principle of "desynonimisation", for which see BAXTER *Reliquiae* COPY A **40** n 1. For another aspect of this discrimination see **37**, below.

5[3] Lit. "*under-stands* them". See BIBLE COPY B **136** n 2 and *AR* (1825) 6 and n. For the reason/understanding distinction see e.g. BAXTER *Catholick Theologie* **14** n 3, and esp *AR* (1825) 208–28. On "confounding" reason and understanding see e.g. HOOKER **28** (at n 4) and ِń.

5[4] This appears to be the first version of C's well-known statement in *BL* ch 4 (*CC*) I 84 that "Milton had a highly imaginative, Cowley a very *fanciful* mind". The central discussion of the distinction between imagination and fancy is in *BL* chs 4, 13, 14.

5[5] See *Paradise Lost* III 487ff.

6[1] This passage is also related to BLOMFIELD **4** n 1 and may well be the source for C's derivation of ἐκκλησία in *C&S* (*CC*) 45 and 125, in HOOKER **10**, and in notebooks.

us, and well· with us, to rest" with our forefathers"/[2] But the Christian hath an *assured* Hope by an explicit and particular Faith—a *Hope* because its object is *future* not because it is *uncertain*. The one was on the road, journeying towards a friend of his Father's who had promised that he would be kind to him even to the 3rd & 4th generation. He comforts himself on the road, first, by means of the various places of Refreshment which that Freuniend had built for Travellers & continued to supply—& 2ndly by anticipation of a kind reception at the Friend's own Mansion-House.[3] But the other has received an express invitation to a Banquet, beholds the preparations & has only to wash & put on the proper Robes, in order to sit down

7   p 11

The reason why our translators, in the beginning, did choose rather to use the word *Congregation* than *Church*, was not as the adversarie malitiously imagineth, for that they feared the very name of the Church; but because, as by the name of religion and religious men, ordinarily in former times, men understood nothing but *factitias religiones*, as *Gerson* out of *Anselme* calleth them, that is, the professions of Monkes and Fryers.

For the same reason the word *Religion* for θρησκεια in St James ought *now* to be altered to—Ceremony or Ritual.[1] The old Version has by change of language become a dangerous mistranslation, and furnished a favorite Text to our *moral* Preachers, Church Socinians, and other *christened* Pagans now so rife among us. What was the *substance* of the Ceremonial Law, is but the *Ceremonial* Part of the Christian Religion; and but it is *its* solemn Ceremonial *Law*, and tho' not the *same*, yet *one* with it and inseparable, even as Form and Substance.[2] Such is St James's Doctrine, destroying at one blow Antinomianism[3] and the Popish Doctrine of good works.

8   p 27,[1] pencil, overtraced | I 18

But if the Church of God remained in *Corinth*, where there were *divisions, sects, emulations, contentions, and quarrels, and going to law*

6[2] See e.g. Deut 4.40, 12.25, and Eccles 8.12.

6[3] See e.g. Jer 6.16.

7[1] θρησκεία is translated "religion" in AV of James 1.26, 27. Cf *AR* (1825) 15–16.

7[2] On the relation between the ceremonial law and Christian religion see *AR* (1825) 15–16 and n.

7[3] The doctrine that Christians, being under the law of grace, need not observe the moral laws. Cf EICHHORN *Neue Testament* COPY B **24** n 2.

8[1] On this page appears the passage quoted from Augustine in *C&S* (*CC*) 160 (not noted there).

one with an other for every trifle, and that under the infidels; where that
wickednesse was tolerated and winked at, which is execrable to the very
heathens; where *Paules* name & credit was despitefully called in
question...where *the resurrection of the dead* (which is the life of
Christianity) *was* with great scorne *denied*; who dare deny those
societies to be the Churches of God, wherein the tenth part of these
horrible evils and abuses is not to be found?

It is rare to meet with sophistry in this sound Divine; but here he
seems to border on it. For first, the Corinthian Church upon
admonition repented of its negligence; and 2. the objection of the
Puritans was, that the institution of the Church precluded Discipline.

9   p +1, referring to p 31 | Bk ii 2

This profession of the faith of Christ, though it distinguish the
Christian Church from the *Jewes* and Pagans...yet doth it not
separate the multitude of right beleeving *Christians*...from seduced
miscreants, being common to both.
...These [notes of difference] are...such as doe perpetually, and
ever sever the true Church from all conventicles of erring and seduced
miscreants.

P. 31. Miscreant used twice in its original Sense of Misbeliever.[1]

10   p +1, referring to pp 34–5 | ii.4

What a thing is, wee desire to know, either by our owne discourse,
or by the instructions or directions of an other...

P. 35. Discourse for the discursive Acts of the Understanding: even
as discursive is opposed to intuitive as by Milton.[1] Thus understand
Shakespear's "Discourse of Reason"—i.e. those discursions of mind
which are peculiar to rational Beings.—[2]

11   p 53 | Bk iii 1

The first publishers of the Gospel of Christ delivered a rule of Faith
to the Christian Churches which they founded, comprehending all

---

9[1] "Miscreant"—unbeliever, from
Latin *credere* (believe), or more directly
from French *croire*.

10[1] C makes the same point, with the
reference to Milton and a quotation from

Paradise Lost v 490, in *SM* (*CC*) 69. See
also e.g. *Friend* (*CC*) i 156.

10[2] *Hamlet* i ii 150–1. See also *SM*
(*CC*) 69 and *AR* (1825) 327–8 and cf
BÖHME 33 n 3.

those Articles that are found in that *epitome* of Christian Religion, which wee call the Apostles Creede. This needs proof. I rather believe, that the so called Apostles' Creed was really the Creed of the Roman or Western Church (& possibly, in its present fortm, the Catechismal rather than the Baptismal Creed) and that other Churches in the East had creeds equally ancient, and from their being earlier troubled with anti-trinitarian Heresies, more *express* on the divinity of Christ than the Roman.—[1]

12 pp 58–69, pencil, overtraced; PS in ink

But they that are Orthodoxe teach...Fourthly, That it is no lesse absurd to say, as the Papists doe, that our satisfaction is required as a condition, without which Christs satisfaction is not applicable unto us; then to say, *Peter* hath paid the debt of *John*, and hee to whom it was due accepteth of the same payment, conditionally if hee pay it himselfe also.[1]

This *propriation* of a *metaphor*, viz. forgiveness of Sin and abolition of guilt thro' the redemptive Power of Christ's Love and ⟨of his⟩[a] perfect Obedience during his voluntary assumption of Humanity expressed, on account of the sameness of the ~~effect~~ consequences[a] in both cases by the payment of a *Debt* for another, which ⟨Debt⟩ the Payer had not himself incurred—the *propriation* of this, I say, by transferring the *sameness* from the ~~effect~~ consequents[a] to the ~~Causes~~, Antecedents,[a] is the one point of Orthodoxy (so held, I mean) in which I still remain at Issue it seems to me so evidently a μεταβασις εις αλλο γενος.[2] A metaphor is an illustration of something less known by ~~some~~ a[a] more or less *partial* identification of it with something better understood.[3] Thus St Paul illustrates the *consequences* of the act of Redemption by four different metaphors drawn from things most familiar to those, for whom, it was to be illustrated— viz. Sin-offerings or ~~E~~ sacrificial expiations 2. Reconciliation. 3. Ransom from Slavery. 4. Satisfaction of a first Creditor

---

a Words in pencil not overtraced

11[1] See also BAXTER *Catholick Theologie* 9 and n 1.

12[1] Quoted, with more text before and after, and C's interpolations, in *AR* (1825) 309–11.

12[2] "Transition to another kind". See BAXTER *Reliquiae* COPY A **29** n 1.

12[3] A "logical" account of metaphor, as found in Aristotle. In DONNE *Sermons* COPY B **33** C referred to metaphor as the "conventional exponent of a Thing"; in *AR* (1825) 198–200 he associates "Analogies" with "Conviction", "Metaphors" with "Illustration". See also C. BUTLER *Vindication* **1** n 3.

by vicarious payment of^a the Debt.[4]—These all refer to the ~~effect~~ consequences of Redemption. Now St John without any metaphor declares the mode by and in which it is effected—for he identified it with a *fact*, not ~~an effect~~, with a Consequence,^{b} and a fact too not better understood in the one case than in the other—namely, by generation and birth[5]—There remains therefore only the Redemptive *Act* itself—and this is transcendent, ineffable, and a fortiori therefore inexplicable—here the act of primal Apostacy, it is in its own nature a *Mystery*, known only thro' faith in the Spirit.

James owes John a 100£, which (to prevent James from being sent to prison) Henry pays for him, & John has no longer any claim. But James is a cruel and ungrateful [son]^c to Mary, his tender Mother. ~~James~~ Henry, tho' no relation, acts the part of a loving & dutiful Son to Mary. But will this satisfy the Mother's claims on James, or entitle him to her Esteem, Approbation and Blessing?—If indeed by force of Henry's example, or persuasion, or any other more mysterious Influence James repents and becomes himself a good and dutiful Child, then indeed Mary is wholly satisfied—but then the ~~mat~~ case is no longer a question of Debt in that sense in which it can be payed by another, tho'^{d} the effect, of which alone St Paul was speaking, is the same in both cases, to James, as the Debtor, and to James as the undutiful Son. He is in both cases liberated from the burthen, and in both cases he has to attribute his exoneration to the act of another as cause, simply, = the payment of the Debt, or as *likewise* causa causæ[6] = James's reformation.[7]—Such is my present opinion. God grant me increase of Light, either to renounce or confirm it.

S. T. Coleridge
4 May, 1819./

^{e}P.S. Perhaps, the different Terms of the above position may be found more clearly stated, on the margin overleaf:

1. Agens causator?
2. Actus causativus?

^{a} Word in pencil not overtraced
^{b} Insertion, deletion, and substitution are in ink in the same "later" hand as the PS
^{c} Word supplied by the editor
^{d} The overtracer has written "the", but the apostrophe in "tho'" is clear in pencil
^{e} The PS is written in ink, evidently at a later date

12[4] On "this Debtor and Creditor Scheme" see also DONNE *Sermons* COPY B 6 and esp BAHRDT 2 n 5.
12[5] Cf *AR* (1825) 315.
12[6] "The cause of the cause".
12[7] This discussion of the metaphors of redemption, which is parallel to BAHRDT 2, could have served as draft for the detailed discussion in *AR* (1825) 311–27; even the illustration of "James and John" is repeated in refined form.

3. Effectum causatum?

4. Consequentia ab Effecto?[8]

1. The co-eternal Son of the Living God, incarnate, tempted, 2 crucified, resurgent, communicant of his Spirit, ascendent, and obtaining for his Church the descent of the Holy Ghost.

2. A spiritual and transcendent Mystery.

3. The being born anew, as before in the flesh to the World, so now in the Spirit to Christ: where the differences are, the Spirit ⚹ the Flesh, and Christ ⚹ to the World, the punctum indifferentiæ,[9] or combining term remaining the same in both, is a *Birth*. (Rain Water ⚹ River Water. We might as rationally call the term, Water, a *metaphor* here, as call the term, Birth, a metaphor in St John.)[10]

4. Sanctification from Sin and liberation ~~of~~ from the consequences of Sin, with all the means and process of Sanctification, being the same for the Sinner relatively to God and his own Soul, as the satisfaction of a Creditor for a Debt⟨or;⟩ as the Offering of a atoning Sacrifices for a Transgressor of the Law; as ~~the~~ a reconciliation, ~~of~~ for a rebellious Son or Subject to his alienated Parent or offended Sovereign; and as a ransom is for a Slave in a heavy Captivity.—/ Now my complaint is, that our systematic Divines transfer the §4 to the §[s] 2nd and 3rd interpreting proprio sensu et ad totum what is affirmed sensu metaphorico et ad partem—i.e. ad *consequentia* a regeneratione effectâ, per actum causativum primio Agentis, nempe, Λογου redemptoris[11]—and ~~the~~ by this interpretation substituting an identification absolute for an equation proportional.

13   p 62, pencil, overtraced

For they [the Nestorians] are said to affirme, that the nature of man is imperfect without personalitie, and therefore that the Sonne of GOD who assumed not an imperfect humane nature, assumed the nature of man, together with the personality of the same. Whence it seemeth to follow, that there are two persons in Christ. For the clearing of this point it is to bee noted, that *personality is nothing*

12[8] Following C's version in *AR* (1825) 326–7: "The Agent and Personal Cause...The Causative Act...The Effect caused...The Consequents from the Effect".

12[9] "The point of indifference"—the *Nullpunct* or node. See BÖHME **173** n 1.

12[10] The substance of this paragraph is also printed in *AR* (1825) 330.

12[11] Interpreting "in a literal sense and as applying to the whole" what is affirmed "in a metaphorical sense and applying to the part—i.e. to the *consequents* from the effected regeneration, through the causative act of the first Agent—that is, of the Word as redeemer". See also *AR* (1825) 327–8.

but the existence of nature in it selfe; which is in two sorts, potentially, or actually.

* God alone has his nature in him self—i.e. God alone contains in him self the ground of his own existence.[1]

⟨But⟩ Were this ⟨*definition of F's⟩ right, we might predicate *personality* of a worm, or where ever we find Life. Better say: Personality is Individuality existing *for* itself, but with a nature as its Ground

14 p 67, pencil, overtraced

Nicetas saith, the *Armenians* are *Monophysits*, and that *Immanuel* the Emperour, in the yeare 1170 sent *Theorianus* to conferre with their Catholick or chiefe Bishop, & to reclaime them if it might bee, from that heresie.

It puzzles me to understand what sense Field gave to the word, Heresy. Surely, every slight error even tho' unpersevered in is not to [be][a] held a Heresy, or its Assertors accursed. The Error ought at least to respect some point of Faith essential to the great ends of the Gospel. Thus the phrase "*Cursed* Eutyches"[1] is to me *shockingly* unchristian. I could not dare call even the opinion *cursed* till I saw how it injured the faith in Christ, weakened our confidence in him or lessened our love & gratitude.

15 p 71

Fourthly, they [the Habassines] are baptized in the name of the Father, Sonne, & Holy Ghost, in such sort as other Christians are, but they are also circumcised both Male and Female, which may seeme to cut them off from the fellowship of true Christians, and the *][b] hope of salvation: according to that of the Apostle, *If yee be circumcised yee are fallen from grace, and Christ shall profit you nothing.*

* It seems impossible but that these words had a relation to the particular state of feeling and belief, out of which the anxiety to be

---

a Word supplied by the editor   *b* C's * in pencil

13[1] For God as "at once the Ground and the Cause" see *SM* (*CC*) 32 and BöHME **31**.

14[1] Cis quoting from p 66: "*Leonardus* Bishop of *Sidonia* reporteth, that when he

conferred with the Patriarch of the *Jacobites* to this purpose, hee cleerely accursed *Eutyches* confounding the natures of God and man in Christ...".

circumcizedcised did in those particular persons proceed—and not absolutely and at all times to the Act itself—seeing that St Paul himself circumcised Timothy, from motives of charity & prudence.[1]

16 pp 76–7, pencil, overtraced | III 3

The things that pertaine to the Christian faith and religion, are of two sorts: for there are some things *explicitè*, some things *implicitè credenda*; that is, there are some things that must be particularly and expressly knowne and beleeved, as that the Father is God, the Sonne is God, and the Holy Ghost God, and that yet they are not three Gods, but one God; And some other, which though all men, at all times bee not bound upon the perill of damnation to know and beleeve expressely, yet whosoever will be saved must beleeve them !!!!!] at least *implicitè*, and in generality, as that *Joseph*, *Marie*, and *Jesus* fled into *Egypt*. [Ascribed to Occam in shoulder-note.]

Merciful God! Eternal Misery and the immitigable Wrath of God and the inextinguishable Fire of Hell amid Devils, Parricides, and Haters of God and all goodness—this is the Verdict which a Protestant Divine passes against the man who tho' sincerely believing the whole Nicene Creed, and every Doctrine and Precept taught in the New Testament and living accordingly, should yet have convinced him that the first Chapters of Matthew & Luke were not parts of the Original Gospels!—[1]

17 p 77

*] So in the beginning *Nestorius* did not erre, touching the unitie of Christs person in the diversitie of the natures of God and man: but only disliked, that *Mary* should be called the Mother of God: which forme of speaking, when some demonstrated to bee very fitting and unavoidable, if Christ were God and Man in the unity of the same person, he chose rather to deny the unity of Christs person, than to acknowledge his temeritie and rashnesse, in reproving that forme of speech which the use of the Church had anciently received and ·allowed.

* A false charge grounded on a misconception of the Syriac Terms. Nestorius was perfectly justifiable in his rejection of the epithet,

---

15[1] See Acts 16.3.

16[1] This represents C's settled view of the *evangelia infantiae* or *Christopaedia* interpolated at the beginning of Matt and

Luke: see CHILLINGWORTH COPY B 2 and n 2, DONNE *Sermons* COPY B 9 and n 1.

Θεοτοκος,[1] as applied to the Mother of Jesus. The Church was even then only too ripe for the idolatrous hyper-dulia of the Virgin.[2] Not less weak is Field's defence of the propriety of the term. Let the ~~closeness~~ exactness of the *logical* parity excuse the apparent irreverence, if I say, that by the same logic a She-Ass big with a Mule might be called ἱπποτοκος,[3] because the Horse and Ass were united in one and same Subject. The difference in ⟨the⟩ "*perfect* God and *perfect* man",[4] does not remove the objection: for an epithet, which conceals half of a Truth, the power and special *Concerningness* of which, relatively to our redemption by Christ depends on our knowlege of the whole, is a deceptive, and ~~da~~ dangerously deceptive, Epithet. S. T. C.

18   p 110 | m 20

Thus then, though the Fathers did sometimes, when they had particular occasion to remember the Saints, and to speake of them, by way of *Apostrophe* turne themselves unto them, and use words of doubtfull compellation, praying them, if they have any sense of these inferiour things to be remembrancers to God for them, yet shall our adversaries never prove, that they did prostrate their bodies, bow their knees, or make prayers to them, in a set course of devotion, but this both adoration and invocation of Saints and Angels, was directly condemned by them. Wee honour the Saints, saith *Ierome*, but do not worship or adore any creature, neither Angels, Archangels, nor any name that is named in this world, or that which is to come.

The distinct gradations of the process, by which Commemoration and rhetorical Apostrophes passed finally into Idolatry, supply an analogy of mighty force against the heretical Hypothesis of the modern Unitarians. Were it true, *they* would have been able to have traced the progress of the Christo*latry* from the lowest sort of Christo-*dúly* with the same historical Distinctness, asgainst the

---

17[1] θεότοκος—"God-bearer" or "Mother of God"—not in NT, was used as an epithet for the Virgin Mary by the Greek Fathers from Origen onwards. Nestorius attacked the term in 429 as incompatible with the full humanity of Christ, but the use of it was formally upheld by the councils of Ephesus (431) and Chalcedon (451), whereafter its orthodoxy remained virtually unchallenged.

17[2] Superior veneration due to the Virgin Mary, of an order above *dulia* and below *latria*: see **18** n 1, below. See also BLANCO WHITE *Practical Evidence* **10** n 2.

17[3] "Mother of a horse".

17[4] Eph 4.13.

universal Church, as the Protestants that of Hierolatry against the Romanists.[1]

19 p 110, pencil, overtraced[a] | 18 textus

The gentle and soft censures which our Divines during the reign of the Stuarts pass on the Roman Saint Worship, or Hiero-duly, as an inconvenient superstition, must needs have alarmed the faithful Adherents to the Protestantism of Edward VIth, and the surviving Exiles of bloody Queen Mary's times, and their disciples.

20 pp 111–12, pencil, overtraced

But the *Romanists* say...that they [the Saints] know all things that concerne us, that they watch over us with a carefull and vigilant eye, *] that they carrie us in their hands, and by their mediation procure our good from God, the fountaine of all good; and therefore they worship them with spirituall worship. The miracles that God wrought in times past by them made many to attribute more to them then was fit, as if they had a generalitie of presence, knowledge, & working: but the wisest and best advised never durst attribute any such thing unto them.

* To a truly pious mind awefully impressed with the surpassing excellency of God's ineffable love to fallen Man in the revelation of himself to inner man thro' the Reason & Conscience, by the spiritual Light and Substantiality (for the Conscience is to the Spirit or Reason what the Understanding is to the Sense, a substantiative power)[1] this consequence of Miracles is so fearful, that it cannot but redouble his Zeal against that fashion of modern Theologists which would convert Miracles from a Motive to attention and soliciting examination, & at best from a negative Condition of Revelation into the positive foundation of Christian Faith.[2]

a Written in the foot-margin before **18** was written

18[1] "Christ-*worship* from...Christ-*veneration*...Saint-worship" (see also "Hiero-duly" in **19** and "hierolatria" in **35**, below). In Roman Catholic theological use *dulia* (veneration) is offered to the saints, *latria* (worship) is due only to God. C's -latry compounds, however, often carry with them something of the implications of idolatry—cf Εἰδωλολατρεῖα (*Idololatry*) in *CN* III 4410 § 9—and his -duly compounds tend to recall the radical meaning of enslavement. For C's family of compounds formed with -latry and -duly see also **BAXTER** *Reliquiae* COPY A **38** n 1.

20[1] For an expanded version of this distinction between conscience and understanding, and an account of conscience as "a *spiritual sensation*", see *SM* (*CC*) 66–8.

20[2] Paley and Priestley particularly: see **HERDER** *Briefe* **11** and **12** and nn. For C's definition of miracle see *CN* III 4452 (var in *LR* I 370–2, *CIS* 159–61); cf **DEFOE 6** n 1. For C's rejection of miracle as the "foundation of Christian Faith" see e.g. **DE WETTE 18** and **33**.

21 p 116 | III 22

...others, whom *Augustine* refuteth...were of opinion, that all Christians how damnably soever they live, holding the truth of Christian profession, may and shall be saved. This, hee [Bellarmine] saith, is the doctrine of the Protestants. If any of us ever wrote, spake, or thought any such thing, let God forget ever to do good unto us, and let our prayers be rejected from his presence: but if this be as vile a slander, as ever Satanist devised, the Lord reward* them that have beene the Authours and devisers of it, according to their workes.

* O no! no!—this the good man did not utter from his Heart; but from his Passion. A vile, a wicked Slander it was, and is! O may God have turned the Hearts of those who uttered it—or may it be among their unknown Sins done in Ignorance for which the infinite merits of Christ may satisfy!—I am most assured that if Dean Field were now alive, or if any one had but said this to him, he would have replied—I thank thee, Brother! for thy Christian Admonition—join in thy prayer—& pray God to forgive *me* my inconsiderate Zeal! S

22 p 119 | III 23

For what rectitude is due to the specificall act of hating God? or what rectitude is it capable of?

Is this a possible act, the man understanding by the word God what we mean by God?

23 pp 129–33

And this is agreable to that of S. *Augustine* that God enclineth or moveth no man to evill, but that he enclineth such as are evill, to this or that evill. With whom *Anselme*...agreeth, where he saith, That God may be said to deliver men up to their own hearts desires when being prone to evill, he stayeth them not: and addeth, that it is also manifest, that God doth worke in the hearts of men, to incline their wills whithersoever he pleaseth, either to choose things that are good out of his mercy, or to choose things that are evill according to their deserts the reasons of his judgement being sometimes manifest, sometimes hid, but alwaies just.

It is this complicated Dispute, which supplies to Atheism its most plausible because its only moral arguments; but more especially to that species of Atheism which existed in Greece in the Form of

Polytheism, admitting moral and intelligent Shapers and Governors of the World, but denying an intelligent Ground, or self-conscious Creator, of the Universe: their Gods being themselves the offspring of Chaos and Necessity (Χαοῦς καὶ Ἀνάγκης) i.e. of Matter and its essential Laws or Properties.[1] The Leibdnitzian Distinction of the eternal Reason or Nature of God (= τό Θεῖον· Νοῦς καὶ Αναγκη of Timæus Locrus)[2] from the Will or Personal Attributes of God, (= θέλημα καὶ βουλησιν, ἀγαθοῦ Πατρὸς ἀγαθὸν βούλημα)[3] planted the Germ of the only possible Solution[4]—or rather perhaps in words less exceptionable, and more likely to be endured in the Schools of orthodox Theology brought forward the Truth involved in J. Behmen's too bold Distinction of God and the Ground of God—who yet in this is to be excused not only for his good aim and his ignorance of scholastic terms, but likewise because some of the Fathers ~~Lactantius, ex. gr.~~, exprest themselves no less crudely in

23[1] C's translation of the Greek phrase precedes the parenthesis. That "the pantheism of the sage necessarily engenders polytheism as the popular creed" is a central theme in "*Prometheus*": see *LR* II 326–7, 332–4, 338. See also *Friend* (*CC*) I 503–4 (much of which is quoted in "*Prometheus*") and *CN* III 3824. For C on chaos see e.g. Böhme 52 and 146.

23[2] "The Divine: Mind and Necessity." For τὸ Θεῖον see Böhme 6 and n 5, 68 and n 1. Although C was already quoting Timaeus Locrus in Greek in *CN* III 3824 f 111ᵛ–12 (May 1810), this is the first of a series of quotations and paraphrases from Daniel Waterland *A Second Vindication of Christ's Divinity* (1723); here from pp 251–2: "None of the *Antients* durst have said, that God exists by *Necessity*, because it would have been the same as to say, that He was compelled by a superior Force, and against his Will (such was their Sense of the Word *Necessity*) to exist. Ἀνάγκη had been much used among Philosophers in This hard Sense. Some had made νοῦς and Ἀνάγκη, *Mind* and *Necessity*, the Two *Causes*, or *Sources* of all Things." Here Waterland cites Timaeus Locrus de Anim. Mund. p. 543. *Amst*, i.e. *Opuscula mythologia, physica et ethica* ed Thomas Gale (Amsterdam 1688) 543.

23[3] "Will and intention, the good intention of the good father". From Waterland again, pp 281–2. To the question "What think you of Those that gave the Name of *Will*, or the *Father's Will*, to the *Person* of the Son?" Waterland provides a number of quotations from the Fathers, including "Ἀγαθοῦ πατρὸς ἀγαθὸν βούλημα. Clem. Alex. p. 309." and "Βουλὴ καὶ θέλημα τοῦ πατρός. Athanas. p. 613." In classical Greek ἐθέλω implies preference or wish, βούλομαι implies will; but since this distinction would hardly obtain in the mind of God, neither NT nor the Fathers recognise a consistent difference. θέλημα is consistently tr "will" in AV; βούλημα (βούλησις does not occur in NT) is tr "intention" in Acts 27.43 and the "will [of God]" in e.g. Rom 9.19.

23[4] By adding to the Aristotelean precept that "there is nothing in the mind which was not before in the senses" the rider "except the mind itself", Leibniz taught "that the deity, as the great Mind, not merely *modified into* thoughts as our minds do, but *gave* each thought a reality, and that the deity was really different from all creatures by that thing—the pre-conception of things conceived". *P Lects* Lect 13 (1949) 383, 386.

the other extreme: tho' it is not improbable, that the meaning was the same in both. At least, Behmen constantly makes Self-existence a positive act, so as ⟨that⟩ by an eternal περιχωρησις, or mysterious intercirculation,[5] God wills himself out of *the Ground* (τὸ θεῖον, τὸ ἓν καὶ πᾶν, Indifferentia absoluta ⟨realitatis infinitæ et⟩ infinitæ potentialitatis)[6] and again by his will, as God existing, gives Being to the *Ground*. Αὐτογενὴς; αυτοφυης; Υιος Εαυτου; Solus Deus est, itaque principium, qui ex seipso dedit sibi ipse principium[;] Deus ipse sui origo est; suæque causa substantiæ; Id quod est, ex se et in se continens; Ex seipso procreatus ipse se fecit;[7] &c, of Synesius, Zen: Veron:, Jerom, Hilary, Lactanti[us,] and others, involve the same Conception.

S. T. Coleridge.

24 p 140 | iii 27

The seventh is the heresie of *Sabellius*, which he [i.e. Calvin] saith was revived by *Servetus*. So it was indeede, that *Servetus* revived in our time, the damnable heresie of *Sabellius*, long since condemned in the first ages of the Church. But what is that to us? How little approbation hee found amongst us, the just and honourable proceeding against him at *Geneva* will witness to all posterity.

Shocking as this Act must and ought to be to all Protestant Christians at present; yet this passage, & a 100 still stronger from

---

23[5] See BÖHME **103** and n 1.

23[6] "The divine, the one and all, absolute Indifference of infinite reality and infinite potentiality". For Ἐν καὶ πᾶν—the basis of pantheism—see BAXTER *Reliquiae* COPY A 2 n 2.. On "the Ground" generally, see BÖHME **98–103**.

23[7] This passage too is from Waterland's footnote to the statement (p 428): "the Question upon which the learned have differed, is This; whether when we say any Thing exists *of it self*, or is *self-existent*, the Words *a se*, or *of self*, have any *positive* Meaning, or mean only that it does *not exist of another*. Some have carried the Notion of its being *positive*, so far as to say God is the *Cause of Himself*, or even *made Himself*, as *Lactantius* expresseth it...". The footnote then reads: "The Expressions of αὐτο-γενής, and αὐτοφυής ["self-generated" and "self-existent"], if strictly taken, lead

to such a Meaning: As also *ex se ortus*, *ex seipso* ["originating from self, out of himself"], and the like. *Petavius* cites several Testimonies of this kind. De Trin. 1. 5. c. 5. p. 294. | υἱὸν ἑαυτοῦ ["son of himself"]. Synes. | Solus Deus est, itaque Principium; qui ex Seipso dedit sibi ipse principium ["He alone is God, therefore the Beginning, who himself from Himself gave himself his beginning"]. Zen. Veron. [Zeno of Verona] | Deus—ipse sui Origo est, suaeque Causa Substantiae ["God is his own Origin and Cause of his own Substance"]. Hieron. [Jerome] in Ephes. 3. | Id quod est, ex se, atque in se continens ["containing that which is, both outside himself and inside himself"]. *Hilar*. [Hilary] | ... | Ex seipso procreatus —ipse se fecit ["Begotten of himself he created himself"]. *Lactant*." Cf *CN* iii 4189 = *BL* ch 12 (*CC*) i 246–7n.

Divines, & Church Letters, contemporary with Calvin, prove Servetus's death not to be Calvin's Guilt especially, but the common opprobrium of all European Christendom/ Of the Romanists, whose Laws the Senate of Geneva & followed, and from fear of whose reproaches (as if Prot^nts favored Heresy) they executed them—& the Protestant Churches who applauded the act, & returned thanks to Calvin & the Senate for it./[1] *S. T. C.*—

25   p 143 | iii 30

The twelfth heresie imputed to us is the heresie of *Jovinian*, concerning whom wee must observe, that *Augustine* ascribeth unto him two opinions, which *Hierome* mentioneth not, who yet was not likely to spare him, if he might truely have beene charged with them.

The first, that *Mary* ceased to be a Virgine, when shee had borne *] Christ; the second, that all sinnes are equall. If these were the opinions of *Jovinian*, as it may very well bee doubted, wee condemne them, and his errour therein, as much as the *Romanists* doe.

* Neither this or that is worthy the name of Opinion. It is mere unscriptural, nay anti-scriptural *Gossiping*.

26   p 143 | **25** textus par 2

Are we to blame, or not rather to praise the anxiety, manifested by the great Divines of the C. of E. under the Stuarts, not to remove farther than necessary from the Romish Doctrines?—Yet one wishes a bolder method (ex. gr. As to Mary's private history after the conception & birth of Christ, we neither know, nor care about it).[1]

27   pp 146–7 | iii 31

For the opinions wherewith *Hierome* chargeth him [Vigilantius], this we briefly answer. First, if hee absolutely denyed that the Saints departed doe pray for us, as it seemeth he did by *Hieromes* reprehension, wee thinke* he erred. For wee hold they do pray in *genere*.

* Yet not heretically; and if he meant only that we being wholly ignorant whether ~~they did or~~ they do or no, ought to act as if we knew, they did not, he is perfectly right: for "whatever ye do, do it

---

24[1] Calvin *was* responsible for Michael Servetus' death: see BIBLE NT *Gospels* 2 n 1.

26[1] See also DONNE *Sermons* COPY B 16 (at n 6) and 27.

in faith."[1] As to the ubiquity of Saints, it is Hierom who is the Heretic—nay, Idolater, if he reduced his opinion to practice. It perplexes me, that Field speaks so doubtingly on a matter so plain as the incommunicability of omnipresence.[2]

28 p 147 | iii 32

Touching the second objection that *Bucer*, and *Calvin* deny originall sinne, though not generally, as did *Zuinglius*, yet at least in the children of the faithfull: if hee had said that these men, affirme the earth doth move, and the heavens stand, hee might have as soone justified it against them, as this hee now saith.

very noticeable! a similar passage occurs even so late as Sir T. Brown, just at the Dawn of the Newtonian System, & after Kepler[1]—What a Lesson of Diffidence! S. T. C. 4th Decr 1814. Ashley, Box, Bath.[2]

29 p 148

For wee do not deny the distinction of veniall and mortall sinnes: but do thinke, that some sinnes are rightly said to be mortall and some veniall; not for that some are worthy of eternall punishment, and therefore named mortall, others of temporall onely, and therefore judged veniall, as the Papists imagine: but for that some exclude

27[1] Not a biblical phrase, but cf 1 Cor 10.31: "...do all to the glory of God", and Col 3.17: "...do all in the name of the Lord Jesus". Cf also Col 3.23 and 3 John 5.

27[2] See also **35**, below.

28[1] C made this point several times about Sir Thomas Browne: see e.g. *IS* 46 (c Jul 1817), *CL* iv 864 (Jun 1818), *P Lects* Lect 6 (1949) 200–1 (25 Jan 1819), *Logic* (*CC*) 148n. For Browne's offending statements see *Pseudodoxia Epidemica* bk i ch 3, ch 5 (quoted in *Logic*—*CC*—148 n 2), *Religio Medici* pt ii §13: in BROWNE *Works* i 7, 13, ii 28. Elsewhere, however, Browne speaks respectfully of Copernicus; in "repudiating" the Copernican system he seems simply to be affirming his allegiance to the motions of the sun as he saw them—the same order that governs the sun and the moon in *AM*—the poet's eye finding the astronomer's abstract truth less real. In the *Pseudodoxia Epidemica*, in the sentence immediately

preceding BROWNE *Works* **6** textus, Browne wrote: "...if any affirm that the earth doth move, and will not believe with us, it standeth still; because he hath probable reasons for it, and no infallible sense, nor reason against it, I will not quarrel with his assertion". Johann Kepler (1571–1630) published in 1609 his First and Second Laws, which provided the foundation for Newton's discoveries. Browne's *Religio Medici* was written c 1635, the *Pseudodoxia Epidemica* was first published 1646.

28[2] On c 10 Sept 1814 C joined the Morgans at Ashley Cottage (property of Mrs E. Smith, Grocer) "about 4 miles from Bath, & ½ a mile from Box" and lived with them there until in Dec 1814 they all moved to Calne in Wiltshire. If the Morgans followed the plans that C reported to Daniel Stuart on c 23 Nov 1814 (*CL* iii 542), this note was written the day before they left Ashley for Calne.

grace out of that man in which they are found and so leave him in
a state wherein hee hath nothing in himselfe that can or will procure
him pardon: and other, which though in themselves considered, and
*] never remitted, they be worthy of eternall punishment, yet do not
so farre prevaile, as to banish grace, the fountaine of remission of
all misdoings.

* Would not the necessary consequence of this be, that there are no
actions than*a* can be pronounced mortal Sins by Mortals? And that
what *we* might fancy venial might in individual cases be mortal, &
vice versâ?

30   p 148 | **29** textus continued

All sinnes then in themselves considered are mortall.... First because
every offence against God may justly be punished by him in the
strictnesse of his righteous judgements with eternall death, yea with
annihilation; which appeareth to be most true, for that there is no
punishment so evill, and so much to be avoided, as the least sin that
may be imagined: so that a man should rather choose eternall death,
yea utter annihilation, than commit the least offence in the world.

But this (which *I* admit to be scriptural) is what is wanted: clearly
to state the difference between eternal Death and Annihilation. For
who would not prefer the latter, if the former were ~~eternal~~ everlasting
misery?

30A   p 149 | III 33

The assumption we deny, and he doth not so much as endeavour to
prove it...

31   pp 162–3 | III 41

[Shoulder-note *f*:] *But hee will say, Cyprian calleth the Roman Church
the principall Church whence sacerdotall unitie hath her spring:
hereunto we answer, that the Roman Church not in power of over-ruling
all, but in order is the first and principall: and that therefore while she
continueth to hold the trueth, and incroacheth not upon the right of
other Churches, shee is to have the priority: but that in either of these
cases shee may be forsaken, without breach of that unity, which is
essentially required in the parts of the Church.*

---

a A slip for "that". DC has corrected the -n to -t

f. This is too large a concession. The real Ground of the Priority of the Roman See was that Rome for the first 3 or perhaps four Centuries was the Metropolis of the Christian World. Afterwards for the very same reason the Patriarch of New Rome, i.e. Constantinople claimed it—& never ceased to assert at least a co-equality.[1] Had the Apostolic Foundation been the Cause, Jerusalem & Antioch must have had priority—not to add, that the Roman Church was not founded by either Paul or Peter—as is evident from the Ep. to the Romans.[2]—*S. T. Coleridge*

32   pp 205–7 | Appendix to Bk III "An Answer to Mr Brerelies Objection Concerning the Masse..."

After this there followeth an other prayer in the Canon, wherein as humble suppliants, they that come to celebrate, and to communicate, beseech Almighty God to command the oblations which they offer, to bee carried by the hands of his holy Angel unto his Altar that is on high, and into the view and sight of his divine Majestie; that so many as shall by partaking of the Altar, receive the sacred body and blood of his Sonne, may bee filled with all heavenly benediction and grace thorough the same Lord JESUS CHRIST.

That Transubst.[n] is absolute no-meaning, I think demonstrable: and yet I do not hold this the most successful Point of the orthodox Protestant Controversialists. The Question is, what is meant in Scripture, as in John VI. by Christ's Body, or Flesh, and Blood.[1] Surely, not the visible tangible accidental Body, i.e. a cycle of images and sensations in the Imagination of the Beholders; but his supersensual Body, the Noumenon of his Human Nature, which was united to his divine nature. In this sense I understand the Lutheran Ubiquity—But in this passage may not the Oblations have meant the alms-offerings always given at the Eucharist?—*a*

a The PS continues without a paragraph break

31[1] For C's version of the history of the priority of the Roman See see e.g. *C&S* (*CC*) 140–1n. Cf also *CN* III 3872.

31[2] When St Paul wrote his Epistle to the Romans (c A.D. 58) a large Christian community already existed at Rome. For the idea of the Church of Christ see Rom 12.5, 1 Cor 12.13–18, Eph 1.19–23—implicitly not a human institution founded by one person (e.g. Paul or Peter), though individual communities were. The claim for St Peter as founder of the Church rests upon Matt 16.18—"upon this rock I will build my church"—the interpretation of which has been matter of strong controversy. The early tradition that St Peter reached Rome in A.D. 42 is not well substantiated.

32[1] John 6.35, 47–51, 53–8; esp 6.53: "Except ye eat the flesh of the Son of man, and drink his blood, ye have no life in you."

P.S. If by Substance be meant id quod verè est, and if the divine Nature be the sole ens verè ens,[2] then it is possible to give a philosophicalally ~~and~~ intelligible Sense to Luther's doctrine of Consubstantiation—at least, to a doctrine that might bear the same name.[3] At all events, the Mystery is not greater ⟨than,⟩ if it be not rather the same as, the assumption of the Human by Divine Nature. Now to the possible Conception of this we must accurately discriminate the incompossibile negativum from the incompatibile privativum[4]—Of the latter are all positive Imperfections, ~~Ignorance~~ as Error, Vice, &c—of the former simple Limitation. Thus if, (*per impossibile*) Human Nature could make itself sinless and perfect, it would become, or pass into, God—and if God should abstract from Human Nature all imperfections, it might without impropriety be affirmed, even as Scripture doth affirm; that God assumed or took up into himself, the Human Nature. Thus ~~by~~ to use a dim similitude & merely as a faint illustration, all materiality abstracted from a circle, it would become Space—and tho' not infinite, yet one with infinite Space.[5] The mystery of omnipresence greatly aids this conception—totus in omni parte:[6] and in truth this is the divine character of all the Christian Mysteries, that they aid each other, and many Incomprehensibles render each of them, in a certain qualified sense, less incomprehensible. *S. T. Coleridge*

33   p 208

But first it is impious to thinke of destroying CHRIST in any sort. For though it bee true, that in sacrificing of CHRIST on the Altar of the Crosse, the destroying and killing of him was implied, and this his death was the life of the world; yet all that concurred to the killing of him: as the *Jewes*, the *Roman* Souldiers, *Pilate* and *Judas* sinned damnably, and so had done, though they had shed his blood, with an

---

32² "What really is... being [which is] really being". See Böhme 20 (at n 6).

32³ For Luther's doctrine of consubstantiation see Blanco White *Practical Evidence* 12, and esp C. Butler *Vindication* 1 n 2; see also Fleury 32 n 3.

32⁴ "Incompossible by negation... incompatible by privation". "Incompossible" (cf. e.g. Baxter *Reliquiae* copy a 32 at n 1, Blanco White *Letters* 7 at n 2) applies to what cannot exist together or be true in combination. For the distinction between negation and priva-

tion see the draft of *Limbo* in *CN* iii 4073, 4074 (c Apr–May 1811). Cf Donne *Poems* 8 and n 1, Eternal Punishment 1 and n 3.

32⁵ On God in terms of the circle and space see Böhme 6 and n 9 and cf Fichte *Ueber den Begriff* 1.

32⁶ For the distinction between omnipresence and ubiquity see Eternal Punishment; on *totus in omni parte* see e.g. Blanco White *Practical Evidence* 13 n 7.

intention and desire, that by it the world might bee redeemed. So in like sort, let the *Romish* Priests have what intention they will, it is hellish and damnable once to thinke of the destroying of Christ in any sort.

Is not this going too far? Would it not imply almost, that Christ himself could not righteously sacrifice himself? Especially considering, ~~that~~ as the Romanists would have a right to say, that Christ himself had commanded it. But Bellarmine's Conceit is so absurd, that it scarce deserves the compliment of a serious Confutation.[1] For if sacramental Being be opposed to natural or material, as Νουμενον to Φαινομενον,[2] Place is no attribute or possible accident of it, in se—consequently, no alteration of Place relatively to us, can affect, much less destroy, it. And even were it otherwise, yet Translocation is not Destruction[3]—for the Body of Christ, according to themselves, doth indeed nourish our Souls, even as a Fish eaten sustains another Fish, but yet with this essential difference, that it ceases not to be & remain itself—and instead of being converted converts. So that truly the only things *sacrificed* in the strict sense are all the evil qualities or Deficiencies which divide our Souls from Christ. S. T. C.

34 p 218

Algerus excellently expresseth the same thing in these words. "...That which we doe is done in remembrance of that which was then done, for he saith, doe this in remembrance of me. We do not therefore offer another sacrifice, but we alwayes offer the same, or rather that wee doe, is a remembrance of that sacrifice, which was once offered."

This is a metastasis[1] of Scripture/ Do *this* in rem. of me[2]—i.e. that which Christ was *then* doing. But Christ was not then suffering, or dying on the cross.[3]

33[1] See FIELD p 207: "*Bellarmine...* hath an other [conceit] of his owne. For hee saith, that Christ hath a two-fold beeing; the one naturall, the other sacramentall. The *Jewes* had him present among them visibly, in his naturall beeing; this beeing they destroyed, and so killed and sacrificed him. The *Romish* Priests have him not so present, neither can they destroy his naturall beeing, and so kill him; but they have him present in a sacramentall presence, and in a sacramentall beeing, this beeing they destroy."

33[2] "As Noumenon to Phaenomenon".

33[3] *OED* cites this use by C of a seventeenth-century word. For others of his compounds with the prefix *trans-* see DONNE *Sermons* COPY A 4 n 6.

34[1] Metastasis—(here) a shift from one place to another. Cf **38** n 1, below.

34[2] Luke 22.19, and in the office of Holy Communion.

34[3] For the Eucharist as *anamnesis* see BLANCO WHITE *Poor Man's Preservative* **2** n 3.

35 pp 223–4

...let us come to the other objection touching the commemoration of the blessed Apostles, and other Saints and holy Martyrs, by and through whose intercession, and for whose merits, the priest and people desireth God to grant that they may in all things be kept safe and strongly defended, by the helpe of divine protection. That the Saints doe pray for us *in genere,* desiring God to be mercifull to us, and to do unto us whatsoever in any kinde he knoweth needfull for our good, there is no question made by us; and therefore this prayer wherein the Church desireth God to be gratious to her, and to grant the things shee desireth, the rather for that the Saints in heaven also are suppliants for her, will not be found to containe any point of Romish doctrine disliked by us.

To have placed this question in its true light so as to have allowed their full force to the Scriptures asserting the communion of Saints and the efficacy of their intercession without undue concessions to the hierolatria[1] of the Romish Church, would have implied an acquaintance with the Science of Transcendental Analysis and an Insight into the philosophy of Ideas not to be expected in FIELD, and which was then only dawning in the mind of Lord Bacon. The proper Reply to Brerely[2] would be this—the communion and intercession of Saints is an Idea, and must be *kept* such. But the Romish Church has *changed* it *away* into the detail of particular and individual Conceptions, and Imaginations—into Names and Fancies.[3]

36 p 223

N.B. Instead of the Roman Catholic *read* throughout, in this and all other works; & every where and on all occasions unless where the duties of personal courtesy forbid, *say* the Rom*ish* Anti-catholic Church—Rom*ish* to mark that the corruptions in Discipline, Doctrine and Practice ~~have~~ do for the worst and far larger part owe both

---

35[1] "Saint-worship": see **18** n 1, above. On the mediation of saints see also **27**, above.

35[2] Lawrence Anderton (1575/6–1643), Roman Catholic controversialist, to whose *Protestants Apologie for the Roman Church* by "John Brerely, Priest" (2nd ed 1608)—incorrectly ascribed to James Anderton in *DNB*—Field was replying. Bk III App is subtitled "An Answer to Mr Brerelies Objection concerning the Masse, publickly used in all Churches at Luthers appearing".

35[3] C here distinguishes between ideas or "Truths of the pure Reason" and conceptions or "Truths of the pure Understanding". See his "letter" to the Rev James Gillman in *C&S* (*CC*) 233; and for the distinction see ibid 12–13 and esp 13 n 1.

their origin & their perpetuation to the Court and local Tribunals of the City of Rome, & are not & never have been the catholic (i.e. universal) Faith of the Roman Empire or even of the whole Latin or Western Church[1]—and Anti-catholic because no other Church acts on so narrow and excommunicative a principle, or is characterized by ~~so~~ such a jealous Spirit of Monopoly and Particularism,[2] counterfeiting ~~the Universal~~ Catholicity by a negative Totality, and heretical Self-circumscription—cutting off, or cutting herself off from, all the other members of Christ's Body.

S. T. C.
12 March 1824.

37   pp 224–5, referring to p 223

So God said to *Abraham,* if there were but fifty righteous in the city, hee would spare the whole city for their sakes. Neither onely doth hee good for their sakes whose workes hee thus rewardeth, while they live, but even after they are dead also. And therefore God promiseth that hee will protect *Hierusalem* for his owne sake, and for *David* his servant.... This *David,* saith *Chrysostome,* did not only please God while he was in the body but he is found to have yeelded great comfort after his death, to such as hee left behinde him alive. The Prophet *Esay* commeth to *Hezekiah* and saith unto him, I will defend this City for mine own sake, and for *David* my servants sake. *David* is dead, but his vertues that pleased God do still live.

NOTE on the last 16 lines of p. 223.

It is of the utmost importance, where ever clear and distinct conceptions are of importance, to make out in the first instance whether the Term in question (or the main Terms of the question in dispute) represents a *fact* or class of facts simply, or some self-established or previously known Idea of Principle, of which the Facts are instances & realizations, or which is introduced in order to explain and account for the facts.—Now merit, as applied to Abraham, the Saints, &c belongs to the former—It is a mere nomen appellativum of the *Facts.*[1]

36[1] Cf *C&S* (*CC*) 122n. See also the quotation from N Q in ibid 139 n 2.

36[2] In *OED* this is the earliest use recorded of " particularism " in this sense.

37[1] An " appellative name "—i.e. it designates a class of facts, thereby evoking not an idea but a generalisation upon the facts; perhaps referring to the distinction between ideas and concepts in **35** and n 3, above.

38   p 252 | App to III 5

The Papists and wee agree that originall sin is the privation of originall righteousnesse; but they suppose there was in nature without that addition of grace, a power to doe good, and that it was not given simply to make man able to do good, but constantly, and so as to merit heaven... But wee say there neither was nor could be any power in nature as of it selfe, to doe any act morally good, or not sinfull...

Nothing seems wanting to this argument but a previous definition and explanation of the term, Nature. Field appears to have seen the truth, viz. that Nature itself is a peccant (I had almost said, an unnatural) State—or rather, no *State* at all, οὐ στασις, αλλα ἀπόστασις—[1]

39   p 269, pencil, overtraced in part | App to III 6

*] And surely the wordes of *Augustin*, doe not import that shee [the Virgin Mary] had no sinne, but that shee overcame it, which argueth a conflict: neither doth he say, he will acknowledge shee was without sinne, but that hee will not move any question touching her, in this dispute of sinnes and sinners.

* Why not say at once, that this anti-scriptural superstition had already begun?[1] I scarcely know[a] whether to be pleased or grieved[b] with that *edging on* toward the Roman-catholic Creed, that exceeding almost scriptural tenderness for the Divines of the 4th, 5th, & 6th Century, which distinguishes the Church of England Dignitaries from Elizabeth (inclusive) to our Revolution in 1688, from other Protestants.

40   p 279, pencil | App to III 10

Derwent! Should this page chance to fall under your eye, for my sake read, *fag*, subdue and take up into your proper mind, this Chap. 10. Of Free Will.[1]

S. T. Coleridge

_a Mistakenly overtraced as "knew"
_b Here the overtracing stops

[a] Mistakenly overtraced as "knew"
[b] Here the overtracing stops

38[1] The play on the Greek root στάσις cannot be directly rendered into English: "not a state (*stasis*) but a fall from a state (*apostasis*)". Cf ETERNAL PUNISHMENT **4** n 3. Ἀπόστασις, which often for C (as for Milton) is a word for "the Fall",

seems to stand for "the Creature"—i.e. created thing—in **42**, below.
39[1] I.e. the immaculate conception of the Virgin Mary.
40[1] See **1** and n 6, above.

41 p 281, pencil, overtraced

Of these five kindes of liberty, the two first agree only to God, so that in the highest degree τὸ αυτεξούσιον, that is, freedome, of will, is proper to God only; and in this sense *Calvin* and *Luther* rightly deny, that the will of any creature is, or ever was free.*

* I add: except as in God, and God in us. Now the latter alone is Will, for it alone is ens superens.[1] And here lies the mystery, which I dare not openly and promiscuously reveal.[2]

42 pp 281–2, pencil, overtraced

...God indeed worketh the will to determine it selfe; neither is it possible, that he should so worke it, and it should not determine it selfe accordingly; yet doth not Gods working upon the will take from it the power of dissenting, and doing the contrary; but so inclineth it, that having liberty to doe otherwise, yet shee will actually determine so.

This will not do!—were it true, then ⟨either⟩ my Understanding would be free in a math. proposition: or the whole position amounts only to this, that the Will tho' compelled is still the Will. Be it so! yet not a free Will.—In short, Luther and Calvin are right so far—N̶o̶ A *creaturely will* can ⟨not⟩ be free, but the Will in a rational creature may cease to be creaturely, and the Creature (= αποστασις) finally cease, in consequence, and this neither Luther or Calvin seem to have seen.[1] In short, where Omnipotence is on one side, what but utter[a] impotence can remain for the other?—To make freedom possible the antithesis must be removed. The removal of this *Antithesis* ⟨of the creature to God⟩ is the object of the Redemption—and forms the glorious Liberty of the Gospel. More than this I am not permitted to expose.[2]

43 pp 283–4, pencil, overtraced

It is not given nor is it wanting to all men to have an insight into the mystery of the Human Will and its mode of inherence in the Will which is God, as the ineffable CAUSA SUI;[1] but this Chapter will

[a] Mistraced as "either"

41[1] "Being above being".
41[2] With this unusual appeal to esoteric knowledge as too dangerous to disclose cf **42**, last sentence, below.

42[1] See **38** n 1, above.
42[2] Cf **41**, above.
43[1] "Self-cause". See **23**, above.

suffice to convince you, that the doctrines of Calvin were those of Luther in this point—that they are *intensely* metaphysical—and that they are diverse toto genere from the merely moral & psychological tenets of the modern Calvinists. Calvin would have exclaimed, Fire and Faggot! before he had got thro' a 100 pages of D[r] Williams's "Modern Calvinism."[2]

44 pp 296–7 | App to III 11

Neither can *Vega* avoyde the evidence of the testimonies of the Fathers, and the Decree of the Councell of *Trent*, so that hee must be forced to confesse, that no man can so collectively fulfill the Law as not to sinne, and consequently, that no man can performe that the Law requireth.

The Paralogism of Vega,[1] as to this perplexing question, seems to lurk in the position that God *gives* a Law which it is impossible we should obey collectively. But the truth is, that the Law, which God *gave* and which from the essential Holiness of his Nature it is impossible he should not have given, Man deprived himself of the ability to obey. And was the Law of God therefore to be annulled? Must the Sun ceased to shine because the Earth hath become a Morass, and so that even that very glory of the Sun hath become a new cause of its steaming up ~~the dense~~ clouds & vapors that strangle the rays?—God forbid!—"But for the Law I had not sinned."[2] But had I not been sinful, the Law would not ⟨have⟩ occasioned me to sin, but would have cloathed me with righteousness, by the transmission of its splendor.—Let God be just: and every man a Liar[3]

45 p 346, pencil, overtraced | Bk IV 4

The Church of God is named the *Pillar of trueth*; not, as if the truth did depend on the Church... but because it doth strongly hold and maintaine the saving profession of the trueth, notwithstanding all the violence of wicked and cruell enemies... it strengtheneth, stayeth, and supporteth such as otherwise would fall...

43[2] Edward Williams (1750–1813) *Defence of Modern Calvinism* (1812). Cf C's letter to Brabant [10 Mar 1815]: *CL* IV 547–9. On modern Calvinism see also *AR* (1825) 153–4, *C&S* (*CC*) 135 and n, and A. FULLER **4**.

44[1] Andreas Vega *De justificatione doctrina universa*...(1st ed 1548), quoted and discussed by Field.

44[2] The quoted statement is not biblical. See, however, Rom ch 7, esp 7.7, and Rom 6. 14–15.

44[3] Rom 3.4 (var).

Field might have strengthened his argument by the custom of not only affixing records and testimonials to the Pillars but of the Books &c. See Horace.[1]

46   p 353, pencil, overtraced | IV 7

Others, therefore, to avoide this absurdity [that "we beleeve the Articles of our Christian faith, and whatsoever is contayned in the bookes of the Prophets and Apostles, because wee are perswaded, that they were revealed by Almighty God"], run into that other *] before mentioned, that wee beleeve the things that are divine, by the meere and absolute command of our will, not finding any sufficient motives and reasons of perswasion; & hereupon they define faith in this sort: *Fides est assensus firmus inevidens*; that is, faith is a firme, certaine & full assent of the minde, beleeving those things, the truth whereof no way appeareth unto us.

* Field nor Count Mirandula has penetrated to the *heart* of this *most* fundamental question.[1] In all proper *Faith* the *Will* is the prime agent, but not therefore the *Choice*. You may *call* it Reason if you will; but then carefully distinguish the speculative from the practical Reason, and the Reason itself from the Understanding.[2]

45[1] Not Horace, but Martial 1.117.9ff: "There is a shop opposite Caesar's forum with writings hung all over the columns on both sides, so that you can quickly run through all the poets...." Most editors and translators take this to mean advertisements or titles of books hung on the door-posts; C, not inappropriately, supposes copies of books (i.e. scrolls).

46[1] C refers to the next page, i.e. 354: "...they hold that a man may beleeve a thing meerely because hee will, without any motives or reason of perswasion at all: the contrary whereof when *Picus Mirandula* proposed, among other his conclusions to bee disputed in *Rome*, hee was charged with heresie for it. But hee sufficiently cleared himselfe from all such imputation, and improved their fantasie that so thinke, by unanswerable reasons,

which I have thought good to lay downe in this place.

"It is not, saith hee [*Apologia* q. 8 de libertate credendi], in the power of man, to thinke a thing to bee, or not to bee, meerely because hee will; therefore much lesse firmely to beleeve it. The trueth of the antecedent wee finde by experience, and it evidently appeareth unto us, because if a doubtfull proposition bee proposed, concerning which the understanding and minde of man resolveth nothing, seeing no reason to leade to resolve one way or other, the minde thus doubtfull cannot incline any way, till there bee some inducement, either of reason, sight of the eye, or testimony or authority of them wee are well conceipted of, to settle our perswasion...."

46[2] For C on faith and reason cf **43**, above, and **48**, below. See also DONNE *Sermons* COPY B **30** and n 2.

47 p 356, pencil, overtraced | IV 8

Wee hold therefore, that every true Christian doth most evidently discerne and know, that it is God that speaketh in the Scriptures; which *Calvin* excellently expresseth.

Illius virtute (saith he) *illuminati, jam non aut nostro, aut aliorum judicio credimus a Deo esse Scripturam, sed supra humanum judicium certo certius constituimus, non secus, ac* *] *si ipsius Dei numen illic intueremur, hominum ministerio ab ipsissimo Dei ore fluxisse.* After we are enlightened by the spirit, we do no longer trust, either our owne judgement, or the judgment of other men, that the Scriptures are of God; but above all certainety of humane judgment, we most certainely resolve, as if in them we saw the Majesty and glory of God, as Moses saw it in the Mount, that by the ministery of men, they came unto us from Gods owne most sacred mouth.

* Greatly doth this fine passage need explanation, that knowing what it doth mean the Reader may understand what it doth *not* mean, nor of necessity imply. Without this Insight our Faith may be terribly shaken by Difficulties & Objections—ex. gr.—If all the Scripture, then each component part—thence every faithful Christian infallible &c.[1]

48 p 357

Hugo de Sancto Victore maketh three sorts of beleevers.... In the second the light of divine reason causeth approbation of that they beleeve: In the third sort, the purity of divine understanding, apprehendeth most certainely, the things beleeved, and causeth a foretasting of those things, that hereafter more fully shall be enjoyed.

Here too Field distinguishes the Understanding from the Reason, as *experience* following *perception* of *sense*.[1] But as perception thro' the mere presence of the object perceived whether to the outward or inner sense is not *insight* which belongs to the "Light of Reason",[2] therefore Field marks it by "purity", i.e. *unmixed* with fleshly sensations, or the idola of the bodily eye.[3]

47[1] See **51**, below, and ETERNAL PUNISHMENT 2.
48[1] Field is, however, paraphrasing quite freely his quotation from Hugh of St Victor (omitted from textus). See also **49** (at n 1).
48[2] Cf ASGILL 2 and DONNE *Sermons* COPY B **64**.

48[3] For C's recurrent distinction between εἴδωλον and ἴδεα (idol and idea) —Baconian in support if not in origin (see e.g. *Friend—CC*—I 492-3)—see *SM* (*CC*) 61n (marginal note), and cf "*Prometheus*" in *LR* II 345. See also **60** (at n 1), below.

49   p 357

[Calvin:] "We find a greater light of understanding shining unto us in this doctrine of faith, then is found within the compasse of nature: a satisfaction touching many things, in which humane reason could not satisfie us in…"

Tho' Field is by no means consistent in his *epitheta* of the Understanding, he seldom confounds the word itself.[1] In theological Latin, the Underst. as influenced by and combined with the affections and desires is most frequently expressed by "cor",[2] the Heart.— Doubtless, the most convenient form of appropriating the terms would be to consider the Understanding as *the man's* intelligengtial faculty, whatever be its object—the sensible or the intelligible world—while Reason is the ~~spiritual~~ tri-unity, as it were, of ~~Ey~~ the spiritual Eye, Light, and Object

50   p 358

Thus then it is true, that the authority of Gods Church, prepareth us unto the faith, and serveth as an introduction, to bring us to the discerning and perfect apprehension of divine things, but is not the ground of our faith, and reason of beleeving. And that doubtlesse is the meaning of those wordes of *Augustine, that hee would not beleeve the Gospell, if the authority of the Church did not move him thereunto.*

Field from the nature and special purpose of his Controversy is reluctant to admit any error in the Fathers—too much so indeed. And this is an instance. We all know what ~~m~~we mean by the Scriptures; but who knows what he means by the Church, which is neither Thing nor Person/.[1]

51   p 359, pencil | iv 10

Stapleton sayth, the comparison may be made, and the Church preferred before the Scriptures, foure wayes. First, so as if the Church *]* might define contrary to the Scriptures, as shee may contrary to the writings of particular men, how great soever.

49[1] Field is paraphrasing Calvin very freely and himself introduces understanding and reason, which are not in the Latin of Calvin that he quotes.

49[2] The word Field translates as "understanding" in **48** textus. And in Hebrew *leb* (heart) is "the seat of the

intellect", as C noticed in LEIGHTON COPY B III 194 (*LR* IV 175–6). See HEINROTH **40** n 1.

50[1] On the meaning of "Church" see **6** and n 1, and cf **31** n 2, above. See also e.g. *CN* III 3872 and *AR* (1825) 166n.

* Verbally, the more sober Divines of the C. of Rome do not assert this; but practically and by consequence they do. For if the Church assign a sense contradictory to the true sense of the Scripture, none dare gainsay.[1]

52 p +1, referring to p 359

...but this wee deny, and will in due place improve their errour herein.

P. 359. Improve for to prove against, or detect & confute.[1]

53 p 360, pencil, overtraced | IV 11

If the comparison be made betweene the Church, consisting of all the beleevers, that are and have beene, since Christ appeared in the flesh, so including the Apostles, and their blessed assistants the Evangelists: we deny not, but that the Church is of greater authority, antiquity, and excellencie than the Scripture of the new Testament, as the witnesse is better than his testimony, and the Law-giver greater than the Lawes made by him, as *Stapleton* alleageth.

The SS[1] may be and are an intelligible and real One, but the Church *on Earth* can in no sense be such, in and through itself—i.e. its component parts; but only by their common adherence to the body of Truth made present in the Scripture. Surely, you would not distinguish the Scripture from its contents? $S - C = 0$.[2]

54 p 361 | IV 12

For the better understanding whereof wee must observe, as *Occam* fitly noteth, that an Article of faith is sometimes strictly taken, onely for one of those divine verities, which are contained in the creede of the Apostles: sometimes generally for any Catholike verity. This question is not meant of articles of faith in the first sense, but in the second; and so the meaning of the question is, whether one Church that now is, may by her approbation make those assertions and propositions to bee Catholike verities, that were not before, or those hereticall that were not.

51[1] On "the infallibility of Scripture" see BLANCO WHITE *Practical Evidence* 11. See also **47**, above, and **53**, below. *CN* III 4143 is a central discussion of this point.

52[1] *OED* notes this sense of "improve"

—obs. "to disprove, refute, confute"— quoting this passage from Field.

53[1] I.e. "Scriptures".

53[2] Hence the pungency of BLANCO WHITE *Practical Evidence* 11 (cited in **51** n 1, above). See also BAXTER *Reliquiae* COPY B **63** and n 2.

I am persuaded, that this Division will not bear to be expanded into all its legitimate Consequences, sine periculo vel Fidei vel Charitatis.[1] I should substitute the following—I. The Essentials of ⟨that⟩ Saving Faith, ~~that having their~~ which having its root and its proper and primary seat in the Moral Will, i.e. in the Heart and Affections, ~~as~~ is necessary for each and every individual Member of the Church of Christ: 2. Those Truths, which are essential and necessary in order to the logical and rational possibility of the former, and the Belief & Assertion of which is indispensable to the Church at large, as those ⟨Truths⟩ without which the *Body* of Believers, the Christian *World*, could not have been, & cannot be continued/ tho' it be possible that in this body this or that Individual may be saved without the conscious knowlege of, or an *explicit* Belief in them.—

55   p 361

But wee thinke, that it is not the authority of the Church, but the cleare deduction from the things which we are bound expressely to beleeve, that maketh things of that sort, that they must bee particularly and distinctly knowne and beleeved that were not necessarily so to bee beleeved before: and therefore before, and without such determination, men seeing cleerely the deduction of things of this nature from the former, and refusing to beleeve them, *] are condemned of hereticall pertinacy; and men not seeing that deduction, after the decree of a Councell hath passed upon them, may still doubt and refuse to beleeve, without hereticall pertinacy.

* rather, I should think, of a non-descript Lunacy than of heretical pravity. A child may explicitly know that $5 + 5 = 10$, yet not see that therefore $\mathbf{5}$ $10 - 5 = 5$; but when he has, how he can refrain from believing the latter as much as the former, I have no conception.[1]

56   p 367 | iv 16

...wee make three kindes of interpretation; the first private...the second of publike direction, and so the Pastors of the Church may publikely propose what they conceive of it; and the third of jurisdiction, and so they that have supreme power, that is the Bishops assembled in generall Councell, may interpret the Scripture, and by their authority suppresse all them that shall gainesay such

54[1] "Without danger to either Faith or Charity".

55[1] C quoted from p 365 in LEIGHTON COPY B IV 214 (not in *LR* IV).

interpretations, and subject every man that shall disobey such determinations as they consent upon, to excommunication and censures of like nature.

This would be satisfactory: if only Field had cleared the point of the Communion in the Lord's Supper—whether taken spiritually tho' in consequence of excommunication not ritually, it yet sufficeth to Salvation. If so, Exc. is merely declarative: and the evil follows not the declaration but that which is truly declared—as when Richard says, that Francis deserves the Gallows, as a Robber. The Gallows depends on the *fact* of the Robbery, not on Richard's saying.

57 p 391 | IV 29

In the 1. *Cor.* 15. the *Greeke* that now is, hath in all Copies, *The first man was of the earth, earthly, the second man is the Lord from heaven*: the later part of this Sentence, *Tertullian* supposeth to have beene corrupted, and altered by the *Marcionites*, in stead of that the *Latine* Text hath, *The second man was from heaven, heavenly*, as *Ambrose, Hierome*, and many of the Fathers reade also. Touching this place wee answer, that not onely the *Greeke* Copies now extant have it, as we reade and translate, but the *Syriack* and *Arabick* also, and that *Damascene de orthodoxa Fide* readeth in the same sort.

Notwithstanding, because many of the Fathers both *Greeke* and *]*a Latine*, follow the other reading, wee think it very doubtfull which is the originall veritie.

* There ought ~~not~~ to be and with any Man of Taste there can be no doubt that our version is the true one. That of Ambrose, Hierome &c is worthy of these flashy rhetoricians—a flat formal play of Antithesis instead of the weight and solemnity of the other. According to the former, the Scales are even—in the latter the Scale of Christ drops down at once, and the other flies to the Beam like a Feather weighed against a mass of Gold.—And then the wretched creeping "*was*" of the Latin Text!!—[1]

58 pp 704–5 | V 57

If any man (saith the Apostle) *desire the office of a Bishop, he desireth a worthy worke: A Bishop therefore must be unreproveable, the*

a C's asterisk in pencil

57[1] 1 Cor 15.47 (AV): "The first man *is* of the earth, earthy: the second man *is* the Lord from heaven". No verb is expressed in either the Greek or the Vulgate version, or in Tertullian. The "creeping *was*" is apparently supplied by Field.

husband of one wife, watching, sober, modest, harberous *, *apt to teach, not given to wine, no striker, not given to filthy lucre: but gentle, no fighter, not covetous, no young scholler, but well reported of, even of those that are without.*

* a *beautiful* word which ought not to have become obsolete—"given to hospitality" (our present versions,) or hospitable does not so affectingly express the φιλοξενος of Sᵗ Paul—. Κοσμιος should be rendered, *courteous*—it is not easy to give the full force of either the Greek κοσμιος, or the Latin, mundus—from the double feeling of ornate and *world*. In his *manners* & in innocent indifferent things he is a Man of the *world*, we say: but our "wor[l]dly"ᵃ has quite a different meaning—Gentlemanly in dress and ~~demeanor~~ address, is the full meaning of κοσμιος.[1]

59 p 705

The Canons of the Church require . . . that no man may be chosen and ordained a Minister of the Word and Sacraments till he be 30 yeares of age. . . . Wherefore, letting passe the things the Apostle prescribeth, and those other which the Canons adde, of which there is no * question, let us come to the marriage of them that are to be admitted into the holy Ministery of the Church.

* How so? Does the C. of E. admit no Priests under 30 years of age?—The great fault of the early Divines of our Church was the too great Reverence of the first 4 Centuries[1]—This Milton saw and reprobated.[2]

ᵃ Letter supplied by the editor

58[1] C remarked on the words φιλό-ξενος and κόσμιος in *CN* III 4043 (c 1810–11), apparently before acquiring this copy of FIELD. In *CN* III 4191 (c 1814–15), probably after acquiring this copy, he noted "φιλοξενος rendered *harbourous* in the version of 1. Tim. 3. cited by Field, of the Church, B. V. p. 704"—i.e. Tyndale's translation ("harberous"), which Field quotes without giving the Greek. κόσμιος immediately precedes φιλόξενος in 1 Tim 3.2; Tyndale renders it "modest", AV "of good behaviour". For "the double feeling" of κόσμιος and *mundus* as "ornate" and "of the world" see *CN* III 4043.

59[1] See e.g. HACKET *Century* 24 and HERBERT 16.

59[2] Milton's "reprobation" of the "Antiquarians"—the first of the three sorts of "hinderers of the Reformation", against whom most of Bk I of *Of Reformation Touching Church-Discipline in England* (1641)—reaches its climax in the paragraph from which C quoted "a paroxysm of citations" in 1796 (*CN* I 108; cf 106, 110): "But let the Scriptures be hard; are they more hard, more crabbed, more abstruse than the Fathers? He that cannot understand the sober, plain, and unaffected stile of the Scriptures, will be ten times more puzzled with the knotty Africanisms, the pamper'd Metaphors; the intricate and involv'd Sentences of the Fathers, besides the fantastick and declamatory flashes, the cross-jingling Periods which cannot but

60 p 752 | An Appendix Containing a Defence of...the Former Foure Bookes Pt i § 4

And againe hee [Tertullian] saith, That every soule immediately upon the departure hence, is in this appointed invisible place, having there either paine, or ease, and refreshing: that there the rich man is in paine, and the poore in a comfortable estate: for, saith hee, why should wee not thinke, that the soules are tormented, or refreshed in this invisible place appointed for them in expectation of the future Judgement?

This may be adduced as an instance, *specially*, of the evil consequences of introducing the εἴδωλον of Time as an ens reale into spiritual doctrines,[1] thus understanding literally what St Paul had expressed by figure and adaptation[2]—Hence the doctrine of a middle state, & hence Purgatory with all its abominations[3]—and *generally*, of the incalculable ⟨possible⟩ Importance of speculative Errors on the happiness & virtue of mankind.[4] *S. T. C.*

60A p 756, pencil

Gulielmus Antistodorensis thinketh, that prayers be availeable and helpefull to the damned, not to diminish or interrupt their torments, or but to strengthen the sufferers, that so the burden...may be borne by them with the lesse paine...

61 p $^{+1}$,^{a} referring to the inscription "Hannak Scoltock Her Book February 10 1787"

This, Hannah Scollock!^{b} may have been the case.
Your writing therefore I will not erase.
But now this Book, once yours, belongs to me,
The Morning Post's & Courier's s. t. c.ol

^{a} For displacement of this leaf, see headnote
^{b} The signature clearly reads "Scoltock" in both cases, and C clearly reads "Scollock". Cf "Hannak" for "Hannah" in headnote

disturb, and come thwart a settled Devotion, worse than the din of Bells and Rattles." *Works* ed Birch (2 vols 1738) I 13.

60[1] For εἴδωλον (*idolon*) see **48** n 3, above; *ens reale*—"a real entity". On the reification of time see e.g. ETERNAL PUNISHMENT 1.
60[2] 1 Cor 15.51–2.
60[3] Of the doctrine of purgatory C noted that "The silence...of the New

Testament is more than negative evidence against it." JUNG 33. Cf *CN* III 3473, ETERNAL PUNISHMENT 11, BLANCO WHITE *Practical Evidence* 2. Purgatory is a central theme in the draft of *Limbo* in *CN* III 4073; cf **32** n 4, above.
60[4] For C on "speculative errors" in morals see *Friend* (*CC*) I 338; in religion, see *AR* (1825) 160–3, *SM* (*CC*) 59, but cf *Friend* (*CC*) I 227; in politics, see *Friend* (*CC*) I 183–4.

Elsewhere in College, Knowlege, ~~Joy~~ Wit and Scholerage
To Friends & Public known, as S. T. Coleridge.
Witness hereto my Hand, on Ashley Green,
One thousand, twice four Hundred, & fourteen
Year of our Lord—and of the Month November,
The fifteenth Day, if right I do remember.[1]
15 Nov.[r] 1814. Ashley, Box, Bath.

61[1] Printed var in *LR* III 57–8, *PW* (EHC) II 981 (10). Cf *PW* (EHC) II 972 (70), in which "Coleridge" is rhymed with "Polar ridge". The matter of correct pronunciation is settled definitively in a playful footnote to a letter addressed to the Morgans on 7 Jul 1814: "...it is one of the vilest Belzebubberies of Detraction to pronounce it Col-ridge, or Cŏllĕridge, or even Cole-ridge. It is & must be to all honest and honorable men, a trisyllabic Amphimacer, - ᴜ -!" *CL* III 518.

HENRY FIELDING
1707–1754

The Life of Mr Jonathan Wild the Great. [Edition not identified.]

Not located.

The one surviving note, preserved in *LR* II 376–7, was "Communicated by Mr Gillman."

DATE. 27 Feb 1832.

1 on a flyleaf?

Jonathan Wild is assuredly the best of all the fictions in which a villain is throughout the prominent character. But how impossible it is by any force of genius to create a sustained attractive interest for such a ground-work,[1] and how the mind wearies of, and shrinks from, the more than painful interest, the μισητὸν,[2] of utter depravity, —Fielding himself felt and endeavoured to mitigate and remedy by the (on all other principles) far too large a proportion, and too quick recurrence, of the interposed chapters of moral reflection, like the chorus in the Greek tragedy,—admirable specimens as these chapters are of profound irony and philosophic satire. Chap. VI. Book 2, on Hats,[3]—brief as it is, exceeds any thing even in Swift's Lilliput, or

[1] One of C's most concentrated examinations of the dramatic problem of presenting a villain as a prominent figure in the action is to be found in a long annotation on *Lear* in SHAKESPEARE *Dramatic Works* (2 vols 1807) [COPY D] II 928–32, also in *Sh C* I 52 (var).

[2] "Hateful". The word is from Longinus: see BEAUMONT & FLETCHER COPY A 10—in which C contrasts μισητέον to φόβερον ("terrible, terrifying, frightening")—and n 1; see also COPY B 58, and *CL* III 428 (25 Jun 1813).

[3] "Wild had now got together a very considerable gang, composed of undone gamesters, ruined bailiffs, broken tradesmen, idle apprentices, attorneys clerks, and loose and disorderly youth, who being born to no fortune, nor bred to any trade or profession, were willing to live luxuriously without labour. As these persons wore different *principles*, i.e. *hats*, frequent dissentions grew among them. There were particularly two parties, viz. those who wore hats *fiercely* cocked, and those who preferred the *nab* or trencher-hat, with the brim flapping over their eyes. The former were called *Cavaliers* and *Tory rory Ranter Boys*, &c. the latter went by the several names of *Wags*, *Round-heads*, *Shake-bags*, *Old-Nolls*, and several others. Between these continual jars arose; insomuch that they grew in time to think there was something essential in their differences, and that their interests were incompatible with each other; whereas, in truth, the differences lay only in the fashion of their hats."

Tale of the Tub. How forcibly it applies to the Whigs, Tories, and Radicals of our own times. Whether the transposition of Fielding's scorching wit (as B. III. c. xiv.) to the mouth of his hero be objectionable on the ground of *incredulus odi*,[4] or is to be admired as answering the author's purpose by unrealizing the story, in order to give a deeper reality to the truths intended,—I must leave doubtful, yet myself inclining to the latter judgment. 27th Feb. 1832.

1[4] Horace *Ars poetica* 188: "I disbelieve and detest". See e.g. in III xiv: "...'You are greatly mistaken, Sir,' answered Wild [to Blueskin]; 'you are talking of a legal society, where the chief magistrate is always chosen for the publick good, which, as we see in all the legal societies of the world, he constantly consults, daily contributing, by his superior skill, to their prosperity, and not sacrificing their good to his own wealth, or pleasure, or humour: but in an illegal society, or gang, as this of ours, it is otherwise; for who would be at the head of a gang, unless for his own interest? and without a head, you know, you cannot subsist. Nothing but a head, and obedience to that head, can preserve a gang a moment from destruction. It is absolutely better for you to content yourselves with a moderate reward, and enjoy it in safety at the disposal of your chief, than to engross the whole with the hazard to which you will be liable without his protection....'"

The History of the Adventures of Joseph Andrews and his friend Mr Abraham Adams, written in imitation of the manner of Cervantes. [Edition not identified.] 1st ed 2 vols London 1742. The annotated copy was apparently in 1 vol, e.g. Novelists Magazine (1780), or perhaps 2 vols bound in 1. Not located.

A copy belonging to Isaac Bage, Highgate bookseller from 1817 (at latest) to (at least) 1824, from whom C bought three "red pocket-books" (i.e. N 27, 28, and another now lost): N 28 ff 2, 2ᵛ. In this copy C wrote at least one note, to which he referred on 17 Oct 1830 and of which J. H. Green had by then made a transcript (now lost). See ANNEX to this entry.

For references to *Joseph Andrews* see e.g. *BL* chs 11, 22 (*CC*) I 227, II 133.

DATE. Before 17 Oct 1830

1 "Blank Leaf at the end"

[A note "on the χ (= disparity) of the Terms Faith and Belief",[1] ending:]

"the *substance* of the things hoped for",[2] the stem that is to become the Flower and the Fruit.—

Annex

N 47 ff 16ᵛ–17ᵛ (*CN* v). "Postscript to the Note...written in the blank Leaf at the end of Bage's Jos. Andrews.—which Mʳ Green had thought worth the trouble of transcribing, & for that purpose taken the volume home with him..."

Note the propriety of the Apostolic term, the *Seed* of Christ—& all the other metaphors or rather symbols all taken from VEGETABLE Life—the Rock—the Branches—the *engrafted* Word &c—Mem. My remark long ago made as to the systematic application of the attributes and accidents of Vegetable Life to the incidents, states and functions of our spiritual Being, while those from Insects and animals are with few exceptions applied in malum usum, to the evil passions and appetites—& where otherwise, as in the instance of the Ant & Bee, yet not to the Affections, but to the prudential obligations, to the exercises of the Understanding as the potentiated Adaptive Faculty, the intelligent *Instincts* in the Animals—this being the Flower & culmination of the 2ⁿᵈ Form of Life, the Insectivity, most inadequately called Irritability—

Life⁽¹ = Vegetive or phytozöic
Life⁽² = Insectile or entomozoic
Life⁽³ = Animal or idiozöic.[1]

1¹ See *Tom Jones* 9 n 2.
1² Heb 11.1 (var)

ANNEX¹ For the identity and establishment of these terms by c 1822 see HEINROTH 38 n 2.

Hence too, as soon as the Seed of Christ is awakened & begins to expand, the regenerate Man strives to transfer his "I" thereto, and to identify it with his proper and spiritual Self—and contemplates his animal Self as an hostile Alien, an evil *ground out* of which he is to grow & growing to loosen & extricate his roots preparatively to a final transplantation into a divine Ground—. He no longer ~~calls~~ endures to think of it, as *him*, but as his *Nature*—tho' with sincerest humiliation and groans that can have no *utterance*,[2] no outward expression, he knows it to be *his*, and cries out to be delivered from "the body of this Death."—[3]

ANNEX[2] For utterance as "outerance" see BÖHME **100** n 2.

ANNEX[3] Rom 7.24: cf BIBLE COPY B **137** n 2.

The History of Tom Jones, a Foundling. In four volumes. 4 vols. London 1773. 12º.

British Museum C 28 c 5–8 (acquired 9 Mar 1853)

Inscribed on the title-page of Vols I, II, III: "J Williams 1. Jany 1795"; and on the title-page of Vol. IV: "J Williams F G S". Inscribed in pencil on I ⁻3: "Louisa Williams". Bookplate of the Rev James Gillman on p ⁻4 of Vols I, II, III, and on IV ⁻2. A note in an unidentified hand in ink on III 24 refers to a binder's error in placing IV sig C in Vol III.

Contrary to the implied evidence of *LR* II 373–6 and *NLS* II 244–6, only this one annotated edition provided the early editors with marginalia on *Tom Jones*: the "first set" of notes "Communicated by Mr. Gillman" and printed in *LR* was supplemented in *NLS* with three more notes from the same copy. The leaf IV ⁻3/⁻2, with more than half of **4**, is missing.

C considered Fielding a great "master of composition" and reckoned "the Œdipus Tyrannus, the Alchemist, and Tom Jones, the three most perfect plots ever planned". *TT* 5 Jul 1834. See also *Sh C* I 101. For traces of *Tom Jones* see e.g. *Friend (CC)* I 90, 110, and nn. See also **4** n 6, below.

MS TRANSCRIPT. VCL BT 37.2: SC transcript of **1, 3, 8**, evidently for *NLS*.

DATE. c Sept 1816–17, or perhaps within the compass of the literary lectures of 1818–19. An earlier date might be suggested by AURELIUS **59A** n 1, *Friend (CC)* II 47, and by **4** nn 5–6, **8** nn 1 and 3, below; but the Williams association is decisive.

1   I 13 | Bk I ch 4

Beyond this the Country gradually rose into a Ridge of wild Mountains, the Tops of which were above the Clouds.

As this is layed in Somersetshire, the Clouds must have been unusually *low*. One would be more apt to think of Skiddaw or Ben nevis,[1] than of Quantock or Mendip Hills.—

1A   III 12, pencil | x 2

...but the Lady [Mrs *Waters*] stopped her short, and having itted] absolutely acquaintted her of not having had any Share in the past Disturbance...

1[1] Skiddaw, 3054 feet (cf Scafell Pike, 3210 feet, the highest in the Lake District), standing behind Greta Hall "not half a mile distant—indeed just distant enough, to enable us to view it as a Whole", was the most spectacular feature of the setting, "entering into all our views". *CL* I 619, 610. For cloud on Skiddaw see *CN* I 781, 783, 788, 789, 1627 f 19, 1701. Ben Nevis, 4406 feet, in Invernesshire, the highest mountain in Great Britain, which C saw on the Scottish tour: see *CN* I 1489 esp ff 51ᵛ–52, 57–57ᵛ.

2   iii 61, pencil | xi 1

Vice hath not, I believe, a more abject Slave; Society produces not
*] a more odious Vermin; nor can the Devil receive a Guest more
worthy of him, nor possibly more welcome to him, than a Slanderer.

* The very word Devil, Diabolos, means a Slanderer.[1]

3   iii 202–3, pencil | xii 12

And here we will make a Concession, which would not perhaps have
been expected from us: That no limited Form of Government is
capable of rising to the same Degree of Perfection, or of producing
the same Benefits to Society with this. Mankind have never been so
happy, as when the greatest Part of the then known World was under
the Dominion of a single Master; and this State of their Felicity
continued during the Reign of five successive Princes.*

[Footnote:] * *Nerva, Trajan, Adrian,* and the two *Antonini.*

Strange, that ~~he~~ so bold a lover of polit. Liberty as Fielding should
have forgotten, that the glaring infamy of the Roman Morals and
Manners immediately on the Ascent of Commodus prove, that even
five excellent Despots in succession were but a mere temporary
Palliative of the evils inherent in Despotism, and its Causes. Think
you, that all the Sub-Despots were Trajans and Antonines?[1] No!
Rome was left as it was found by them—incapable of Freedom—

4   iv −3−−2 (missing), continued on p −1 and frontispiece (recto)

[a]Manners change from generation to generation, and with manners
morals appear to change,—actually change with some, but appear
to change with all but the abandoned.[1] A young man of the present
day who should act as Tom Jones is supposed to act at Upton, with
Lady Bellaston, &c. would not be a Tom Jones; and a Tom Jones
of the present day, without perhaps being in the ground a better man,
would have perished rather than submit to be kept by a harridan of
fortune.[2] Therefore this novel is, and, indeed, pretends to be, no

---

[a] Text on the missing leaf iv −3/−2, not included in MS TRANSCRIPT, is supplied from *NLS*

2[1] For a spirited play on the word
διάβολος (from which "devil") see *EOT*
(*CC*) ii 454 (18 Mar 1817) and n 3.

3[1] The reign of the five emperors
named by Fielding was preceded by the
reign of Domitian (81–96), the last of the
Flavians, which ended in seven years of
terror and murder. As soon as Com-
modus succeeded Marcus Aurelius, the
second of the Antonines (161–80), dis-
order and licence quickly spread through
Rome and the empire. Cf *LS* (*CC*) 208.

4[1] Cf *Friend* (*CC*) i 444.

4[2] See also **6**, below.

exemplar of conduct. But, notwithstanding all this, I do loathe the cant which can recommend Pamela and Clarissa Harlowe as strictly moral, though they poison the imagination of the young with continued doses of *tinct. lyttae*,[3] while Tom Jones is prohibited as loose. I do not speak of young women;—but a young man whose heart or feelings can be injured, or even his passions excited, by aught in this novel, is already thoroughly corrupt. There is a cheerful, sun-shiny, breezy spirit that prevails everywhere, strongly contrasted with the close, hot, day-dreamy continuity of Richardson.[4] Every indiscretion, every immoral act, of Tom Jones, (and it must be remembered that he is in every one taken by surprise—his inward principles remaining firm—) is so instantly punished by embarrassment and unanticipated evil consequences of his folly, that the reader's mind is not left for a moment to ᵃdwell or run riot on the criminal indulgence itself. In short, let the requisite allowance be made for the increased refinement of our manners—and then I dare believe, that no young man who consulted his heart & Conscience only, without adverting to *what the World* would say—could rise from the perusal of Fielding's Tom Jones, Joseph Andrews, And Amelia, without feeling himself a better man—at least, without an intense conviction that he *could* not be guilty of a *base* Act.—

If I want a servant or mechanic, I wish to know what *he does*—but of a Friend, I must know what he *is*.[5] And in no Writer is this momentous distinction so finely brought forward as by Fielding. We do not care what Blifil *does*—the *deed*, as separate from the ᵍeagent, may be good or ill—but Blifil *is* a villain—and we feel him to be so, from the very moment he, ⟨the Boy Blifil,⟩ restored Sophia's poor captive Bird to its native & rightful Liberty![6]

S. T. C.

5 ɪᴠ 45, pencil, overtraced | xɪᴠ 8

*] Notwithstanding the Sentiment of the *Roman* Satirist, which denies the Divinity of *Fortune*, and the Opinion of *Seneca* to the same Purpose; *Cicero*, who was, I believe, a wiser Man than either of them,

ᵃ Ms begins here

4[3] Tincture of *Lytta vesicatoria*, known as cantharides or Spanish fly, supposed to be an aphrodisiac.

4[4] For another comparison of Richardson and Fielding see *CN* ɪɪ 2471 (Mar 1805). Cf *TT* 5 Jul 1834.

4[5] For the difference between what a person is and what he does or knows see *CN* ɪɪ 2077, *CL* ɪɪɪ 216, and Aᴜʀᴇʟɪᴜs 59A n 1. See also n 6, below.

4[6] C used the same illustration of Blifil, but citing a different detail, in *Friend* (*CC*) ɪɪ 47 (10 Aug 1809) (= ɪ 49).

expresly holds the contrary; and certain it is, there are some
Incidents in Life so very strange and unaccountable, that it seems
to require more than human Skill and Foresight in producing them.

* Surely Juvenal, Seneca and Cicero, all meant the same thing—
namely, that there was no *chance*, but instead of it Providence, either
human or divine.[1]

6 IV 115–17 | xv 9

[Tom Jones's letter to Lady Bellaston:] "...O lady *Bellaston*, what
a Terror have I been in, for fear your Reputation should be exposed
by these perverse Accidents. There is one only Way to secure it. I
need not name what that is. Only permit me to say, that as your
Honour is as dear to me as my own; so my sole Ambition is to have
the Glory of laying my Liberty at your Feet; and believe me when
I assure you, I can never be made completely happy, without you
generously bestow on me a legal Right of calling you mine for ever."

Even in the most questionable part of Tom Jones, I cannot but think
after frequent reflection on it, that an additional paragraph, more
fully & forcibly unfolding Tom Jones's sense of self-degradation on
the discovery of the true character of the relation, in which he had
stood to Lady Bellaston—& his awakened feeling of the dignity &
manliness of Chastity—would have removed in great measure any
just objection/ at all events, relatively to Fielding himself, & taking
in the state of manners in *his* time.

7 IV 161, pencil, overtraced | XVI 5

...I very much question whether he could have heard a more
afflicting Piece of News, than that *Sophia* was married to another,
though the Match had been never so great, and never so likely to
end in making her completely happy. That refined Degree of
*] *Platonic* Affection which is absolutely detached from the Flesh,
and is indeed entirely and purely spiritual, is a Gift confined to the
female Part of the Creation; many of whom I have heard declare,
(and doubtless with great Truth) that they would, with the utmost
Readiness, resign a Lover to a Rival, when such Resignation was
proved to be necessary for the temporal Interest of such Lover.

* I firmly believe that there are *men* capable of such a sacrifice, &

5[1] Cf e.g. *C&S* (*CC*) 32, *SM* (*CC*) 83.

this without pretending to or even admiring, or seeing any virtue in, this "absolute detachment from the flesh."[1]

S. T. C.

8 IV 266–7 | XVIII 4

Many of that Sect [i.e. Philosophers], as well ancient as modern, have, from the Light of Reason, discovered some Hopes of a future State; but, in Reality, that Light was so faint and glimmering, and the Hopes were so uncertain and precarious, that it may be justly doubted on which Side their Belief turned.

No greater proof can be conceived of the strength of the instinctive anticipation of a future state in man, than that it was believed at all by the Greek Philosophers, with their vaguel & (Plato excepted) pantheistic conception of the First Cause.[1]

9 IV 266–8, pencil, overtraced

"...*Plato* himself concludes his *Phaedon* with declaring, that * his best Arguments amounts only to raise a Probability; and *Cicero* himself seems rather to profess an Inclination to believe, than any actual Belief in the Doctrines of Immortality. As to myself, to be very sincere with you, I never was much in earnest in this Faith, till I was in earnest a Christian."

* No! Plato does not say so, but speaks as a philosophic Christian would do. The best arguments of the scientifical Intellect, the assurance is derived from a higher principle. If this be Methodism, Plato and Socrates were arrant Methodists and *New Light* men;[1] but I would ask Fielding, what ratiocinations[a] [...] [would?] not[b] do more than raise a high degree of *Probability*? But assuredly, an historic *Belief* is far different from Christian *Faith*.[2]

a–b This phrase, not overtraced, is very faint and almost illegible

7[1] Whatever examples C could have had in mind, he may have thought of his own ability to resign SH to John Wordsworth when he went to Malta in 1804. See e.g. *CN* II 2861; cf 2517 ff 47–47ᵛ, 2531, 2537.

8[1] On the immortality of the soul see *Friend* (*CC*) I 428 and the Plato references cited in I 428 n 2.

9[1] Many sects, of rather free theological beliefs and practices, were from the mid-eighteenth century called "New Lights".

9[2] Cf *Joseph Andrews* 1. C repeatedly affirmed, especially in his examination of Socinianism and Unitarianism, that there was an important difference between the "belief" that depended upon verifying "facts of history" and a true "Christian *Faith*". Insisting upon the reality of the death and resurrection of Christ, he held that "*Unless ye believe...ye cannot understand.*" See e.g. *AR* (1825) 79, 201, 207, 210–28, and the "Essay on Faith" in *LR* IV 425–38. On faith see BLANCO WHITE *Letters* 1.

JOHN FITZGIBBON
FIRST EARL OF CLARE
1749–1802

The Speech of the Right Honourable John Lord Baron Fitzgibbon, Lord High Chancellor of Ireland, delivered in the House of Peers on the second reading of the Bill for the Relief of His Majesty's Roman Catholic Subjects, March 13, 1793. Dublin [1793]. 8°.
BMC gives a conjectural date [1793]. The first London ed was 1798. Cf the reprint "for J. J. Stockdale", with unsigned preface added, London 1813.
Bound as fourth with DYER *Poems* and GODWIN *Spital Sermon*.

British Museum C 45 f 18(4)

Charles Lamb's copy "brought over from Dublin by Rickman & given to Lamb". *CL* III 539. John Rickman (1771–1840), statistician, a friend of Tom Poole, was secretary to Charles Abbot, Chief Secretary for Ireland, at the time that C first mentioned him to RS in Oct 1801 (*CL* II 768), and continued as Abbot's secretary when Abbot became speaker in Feb 1802. In Jul 1814 he became a clerk at the table of the House of Commons.

On p 1 the phrase "that grave and Reverend Bench" is glossed "Law. Bishop of Killala"; on p 6 "Ireland" is corrected to "England"; and a large pencilled "R"—cf "R" (for *recollige*) in DONNE *Sermons* COPY B; but the form of C's "R" is less florid—is written beside the gloss on p 1, and on pp 5, 19, 23; on p 5 words are underlined. These marks may not be C's; but two passages marked in ink on pp 17 and 25, which may have been noted by C, are printed in the ANNEX to this entry. Corrections of "Gongales" to "Gonzales" on pp 17–19 appear to be press or author corrections.

In late Oct 1814, when C was planning, with Daniel Stuart's help, to have his "8 Letters to Mr Justice Fletcher" reprinted by Ridgway as a pamphlet, he told Stuart that he would like to append the text of this "admirable Speech [of Fitzgibbon's], worthy of Demosthenes", which "might be deservedly called, the Philosophy of the past and present History of Ireland". *CL* III 539; cf 543. The "Letters" were printed in the *Courier* over the signature "An Irish Protestant"—six letters in eight parts 20 Sept–10 Dec 1814—but were not reprinted. See *EOT* (*CC*) II 375–417.

DATE. Possibly 1803, when C was in London with Lamb and seems to have met Rickman for the first time. See *CL* II 768, 941. The early date is suggested by the other items in Lamb's made-up volume.

1 p 2

It is my firm and decided conviction, that in the private intercourse between man and man, it matters not to what particular sect he belongs, if he adheres conscientiously to the principles and precepts of the Christian Religion.

if? if?—what *Xtn* doubts that? The ? is, whether the principles & precepts, to which the Romanist adheres, *are* those of Christianity[1]— the right of burning dissentients, for instance/[2] the claim of forming a spiritual Magistracy of unlimited influence independent of the civil government—the known *consequences* of Excommunication, &c &c &c.—[3]

Annex

Two passages are marked with an ink line in the margin: these may be C's marks.

(*a*) p 17

The corner stone of her policy has been to promulgate articles of religious faith, which necessarily gave to the Pope a very great degree of secular power in every State acknowledging his spiritual supremacy; and having laid this foundation, the laws of their church proceed to denounce as hereticks and schismatics, every sect of Christians who presume to dissent from any one article of religious faith promulgated by the Holy Fathers.

(*b*) p 25

If it is to produce a popular assembly detached altogether from the influence of the other estates, influenced only by the people and implicitly obeying their instructions, this alternative becomes inevitable; either the machine of Government must be at a stand, and the nation sink into a state of anarchy, or if a government should exist, it must necessarily become a pure democracy.

[1] See FIELD 36.

[2] On the Inquisition and the burning of heretics see BAXTER *Reliquiae* COPY A 15 n 1, COPY B 1 n 6. See also ANNEX (*a*) and *Friend* (*CC*) I 95.

[3] For C's rejection of every *imperium in imperio* see e.g. *EOT* (*CC*) II 381 (cf 276) and *C&S* (*CC*) 149 and n 2. On the effects of excommunication in Ireland see also FLEURY 100 and n 1.

CLAUDE FLEURY

1640-1725

The Ecclesiastical History of M. L.'Abbé Fleury, with the Chronology of M. Tillemont. Vol. I. Containing the three first centuries. (Vol. II. Containing the fourth century. Vol. III. Containing the fifth century.) [Translated by H. Herbert and G. Adams.] Vols I–III (of 5). London 1727, 1728. 4º.

Two states of at least Vol I of this translation have been found, showing considerable variations in the text, though with the same date and imprint in the title-page.

Harvard University (Houghton Library)

A printed leaf pasted to the front paste-down of each volume suggests that C may have acquired these volumes under duress: the notice that "This book is the property of W. A. Hunt, Subscription Library, Market Place, Ramsgate..." (the volumes are numbered 210, 211, 212) is accompanied by an "Extract from the Library Rules" including "5. If any book is written in...while in the possession of a Subscriber, the same (or, if it belongs to a set, that set of books) to be paid for."

On the first page of "A List of the Encouragers of this Undertaking...", a section tipped in between "The Names of the Subscribers" and "The Author's Preface", someone has written: "Translation of M Fleury's Ecclesiast History". A bookseller's inscription in pencil on I ⁻1 (p–d): "(imperfect) with *many Autograph* MS notes of S. T. Coleridge (unpublished) Coleridge's copy 3 vols £21—0—0".

Through Vols I and II a large number of passages have been marked and words underlined, few of which can be definitely identified as C's; the marked passages are not reprinted here. On I 327, above C's **45**, "Gibbon's sixteenth chapter" written in pencil in an unidentified hand. Most of Vol III is unopened; most of the title-page of that volume has been torn out.

Early in Nov 1827 (see DATE, below) C noted: "...with all Fleury's obsequious submission to the decisions of the Church his Eccles. Hist. is incomparably more delightful, aye, and more instructive too, than Mosheim's which has gained a reputation far above its deserts". N 35 f 38ᵛ (*CN* v).

DATE. 27 Oct–c 15 Nov 1827, at Ramsgate, and probably later. Much of N 35, esp ff 26ᵛ–46, is taken up with comments on the matter presented in these volumes, often with page references to Fleury's text, the latest of which is to II 376 (on which C has written **95**).

1 I xi, pencil | Author's Preface

They represented to me that religion wou'd cease to be, if we gave it any other foundation than a belief in supernatural actions; and that *] the sensible proofs of the divine power have more effectually converted the idolatrous, than reason or disputation.

* An assertion ~~often~~ easily made & readily admitted; & yet neither probable a priori, nor borne out by authentic history. Idolatrous nations believe miracles too readily to receive them as proofs of any *one* religion as *exclusively* true.

2 I xi, pencil

A good Christian then ought to be under no constraint, as to a faith in miracles in general; we may only doubt concerning some particular incident. Those which are recorded in the holy Scripture are above all authority; but those related by grave authors are also proportionably authentick: St. IRENEUS ought to be believed, when he asserts the cure of diseases, the other miracles and gift of prophecy in the catholic church in his time. St. CYPRIAN...HERMAS... St. PERPETUUS...TERTULLIAN...St. AUGUSTIN; and I believe the rest in proportion to the authority of those who have deliver'd them.

Was Fleury in earnest? A precious faith verily that is capable of fractions! Ex. gr.

Scripture Miracles = 1
Irenæan   = $\frac{7}{10}$ of 1.
Hermas   = $\frac{6}{10}$
St Perpet.   = $\frac{4}{10}$
Metaphrastian   = $\frac{1}{10}$ of 1
Jac. de Voragine[1] = $1 - 1\frac{1}{4}$—i.e. Belief = 0, + Disbelief
                 = $\frac{1}{4}$ of 1.—and N.B. each of these after the first

consisting of a larger or lesser fraction, ad libitum Credentis!!—[2]
A belief in proportion!! Good! very good!—
Most holy Perpetuus![3] I can not say, I actually *believe* you; but pray, do not think, I mean to give you the Lie!—This is like

2[1] Simeon Metaphrastes ("Metaphrastus" in printed text), or Logothetes (fl c 960) compiled a pious and uncritical *Menologion* or collection of lives of saints. The *Golden Legend* of Jacobus de Voragine (c 1230–98), also pious and uncritical, was very popular and influential; translated and printed by Caxton 1484.

2[2] "According to the desire (whim) of the Believer".

2[3] Properly "Perpetua".

Addison's Ghost-faith—who professed to believe Ghosts in general, tho' he had never heard of any one particular that he credited!—[4]

3 I 52 | I xxxiii

[Summarising Gal 2.] St. *Paul* then seeing, that they walked not right according to the truth of the Gospel...said to him [i.e. St Peter] in the presence of all: If you, who are a *Jew*, live like the *Gentiles*, and not like the *Jews*; why will you force the *Gentiles* to judaize?... St. *Peter* had just before declared in the council, that the *Gentiles* were not obliged to the observances of the law; and besides, St. *Paul*...lived as a *Jew* amongst the *Jews*; for fear lest he should seem to condemn those ceremonies as bad, which were good during the time for which GOD had ordained them.

See Jakob Rhenferd's admirable Disquisition of the Ebionites & Christians of Palestine.[1]

4 I 53 | I xxxv

*] As they were going to the oratory, a girl who divined by an evil spirit, of which she was possessed, cried out after them: These men are the servants of the most high GOD, who teach you the way of salvation. She continued thus several days; St. *Paul* was troubled at it, and turning, he said to the spirit: I command thee in the name of JESUS CHRIST to depart from this damsel; and he went out in the same hour.

* It is difficult for us who are conversant only with the powers of vital excitability under the conditions of a bracing Climate and hereditary Hardihood of Nerves to credit the influence of the Zoo-magnetic process on young females in the Southern Climates & in states of relaxed Morality.[1] Magnetic Crises were among the

---

2[4] See e.g. *Spectator* no 12 (14 Mar 1711), no 110 (6 Jul 1711), no 419 (1 Jul 1712)—none of which, however, matches C's summary statement exactly.

3[1] Jacob Rhenferd (1654–1712) "De fictis Judaeorum haeresibus" and esp "De fictis Judaeorum et Judaizantium haeresibus" in RHENFERD *Opera philologica* (Utrecht 1722), which C annotated in Jul 1827. Rhenferd discusses Gal 2.10 on p 130 (in the second title cited), two pages before C's first annotation on the

second tract. C is remarking upon the existence of a separate group of Jewish Christians.

4[1] On zoomagnetism (animal magnetism) see CHILLINGWORTH COPY B **11** n 2; and cf "mesmerism" in **11**, below. For C on the effect of climate on morality see e.g. BLANCO WHITE *Letters* **5** and cf *Practical Evidence* **9** and HOFFBAUER **2** n 1. C was well aware of certain of the characteristics of female neurosis.

common wonders exhibited in the Temple of Venus at Corinth—
Females so affected were called Pythonesses.

5 1 57, pencil | 1 xxix

He calls to their remembrance what he had said to them, and adds,
Hold to the traditions which you have heard, whether by word of
mouth, or by my letter. From whence it is evident, that the Apostles
taught a great many things by word of mouth, which were as worthy
of credit as their writings...

No doubt: *if* only we knew what they were. It is on this subject that
the Protestant Divines are most triumphant, and their confutation
of the Romish Pretences total and conclusive./

The *probability* is that what the Apostles commanded as Managers
of particular Churches requisite for the particular time, place, and
exigences, they trusted to Oral Instructions: while their Ordinances,
as Apostles, of permanent obligation & for the Church Universal in
all ages, were committed to Writing.

6 1 59, pencil | 1 xlii

He [Paul] caused them to be baptized in the name of the LORD JESUS;
then he laid his hands upon them, and they received the Holy Ghost;
so that they spoke <u>divers</u> languages, and prophesied.

n.b.—This word is *added*—Luke says only, ελαλουν γλωσσαις/[1]
which had nothing to do with *foreign* languages, but means, that they
spake *ecstatically*, the Spirit speaking with their tongues/ had the
former been meant, the construction must have been ελαλουν τε
γλωσσ<u>ας</u>.[2]

6[1] Fleury is describing the events of
Acts 19.1–9—C's phrase in Greek, "they
spake with tongues", is from Acts
19.6—but has introduced "divers" from
the account of Pentecost (Acts 2.4),
λαλεῖν ἑτεραῖς γλώσσαις ("to speak
with other tongues"). C is here in accord
with the view widely held, and supported
by 1 Cor 14.1–6, that "speaking with
tongues" is the broken speech of persons
in religious ecstasy. Cf FIELD **4** for an
earlier opinion.

6[2] "And they spoke tongues (i.e.
languages)"—using the accusative case.
In Acts 2.4, as in 10.46, 19.6, and 1
Cor 14.1–6, the dative is used ("with
tongues"), which C takes to be an
idiomatic use referring specifically to
ecstatic speech. He would then render
ἑτεραῖς γλώσσαις as they spoke "with
tongues other than their own—i.e. of the
Spirit". See also **11**, below. Cf BAXTER
Reliquiae COPY B **64** n 3.

7 I 59, pencil

Many of the Faithful [at Ephesus]…who had studied unprofitable arts, brought their books and <u>burnt them</u> in the face of the world. The price of them, being computed, was found to amount to fifteen thousand livres of our money.

The more the pity! The greater part were, no doubt, miserable Trash—but probably with facts interspersed that would have furnished valuable Materials on the state of chemical & physical science in Asia at that time—& yet more, illustrative of manners, and customs./

Suspirium Roxburghiense—or the Sigh of a Member of the Roxburg Club.[1]

8 I 61–2, pencil | I xliv

…we are all one in JESUS CHRIST: all the children of *Abraham*, and the inheritors of the promises; circumcision no longer availeth any *] thing, but faith which worketh by charity; for the love of our neighbour takes in all the law.

* All enlightened men, Catholic and Protestant, ⟨now⟩ hold the same doctrine respecting Faith and Charity/—and find it hard even to keep up the appearance of a *verbal* difference, the Protestant using Faith, as the Principle *inclusive* of Charity, and the Catholic mentally distinguishing the Fountain from the Stream. The one would hold accursed the doctrine of a Faith separated from Charity, and the other anathematize the Heresy of Charity separated from Faith, as its Source. So it is now. But it was far otherwise in the time of Luther.

The Roxburghe Club, an exclusive association of bibliophiles formed in Jun 1812—with Lord Spencer as president and T. F. Dibdin as vice-president—to commemorate the sale of the library of John Ker, 3rd Duke of Roxburghe (1740–1804). The sale aroused great excitement, especially at the competition between the Marquis of Blandford (later Duke of Marlborough) and Lord Spencer for a Venice 1471 Boccaccio (which sold to Blandford for £2260—the highest price hitherto paid for a book—and which Spencer seven years later bought from the Marlborough estate for a third of that price). At the first meeting of the club eighteen men dined together; six more members were elected at the dinner, and seven more were elected in the following year. Each member was to reprint some scarce piece of ancient lore, with one copy on vellum for the president and as many other copies as there were members. C's friend Francis Wrangham became a member in 1812; by 1832 there were forty-one members. See Clive Bigham *The Roxburghe Club* (Oxford 1928). C could hardly fail to recall how a certain Mr Hare had refused to allow him to consult the "unique collection" of Giordano Bruno "purchased for a trifle at the Roxburgh Sale". *CL* IV 656; cf 926.

Then the popish doctrine of *Works* had curdled the very Life-blood of Religion & true Morality throughout the whole Latin Church.[1]

9 I 64, pencil | I xlvi

He advises virginity and continence to those who are free, rather than *] marriage, because those who are unmarried are only employed in pleasing GOD...contrary to the condition of married persons, who are obliged to endeavour to please one another, and are divided between GOD and the world...

* This can only be understood as applicable to the then disturbed and persecuted Condition of the Christian Church—not to add that every Christian at that time might be considered as exercising the functions of a Missionary.

10 I 64, pencil, marked with a line in the margin

He proves this maxim by his own example. I might, says he, demand the necessaries of life, and cause myself to be served. I might carry with me a woman from amongst the sisters, as the other Apostles do...

an evasion of Fleury's to keep the marriage of the Apostles out of Sight—. The Sister was Peter's *Wife*.[1]

11 I 66-7, pencil | I xlvii

*] Here the Apostle enters into a detail of the supernatural graces, giving the gift of languages the last place, because it was too much esteemed by the *Corinthians*...

* Erasmus alone, tho *he* would not presume to determine, what the Gift of Tongues was, shewed clearly what it was *not*—viz. *not* a power of speaking or understanding foreign languages *unlearnt*. He did not choose to *utter* the truth *positive*; but he insinuates it by referring to a Passage in Plato, describing those who prophecied with *the tongue alone*, the mind of the Speaker unconscious.—[1]

8[1] On the doctrine of works see e.g. DONNE *Sermons* COPY B 63, *CN* II 2434, and HOOKER **43**.
10[1] See 1 Cor 9.5: "Have we not power to lead about a sister, a wife, as well as other apostles, and as the brethren of the Lord, and Cephas [i.e. Peter]?"

For Peter's wife see Luke 4.38–9. In EICHHORN *Neue Testament* COPY A **55–58** C dismisses the conjecture that in 1 Pet 5.13 St Peter refers to his wife.
11[1] Plato *Timaeus* 72AB, untraced in Erasmus, who in the *Paraphrasis in Acta Apostolorum* on Acts 2 speaks of the new

A more delicate but at the same time a more interesting subject does not exist than this of the effusion of the H. Spirit in sensible operations. Let the myriads who would be scandalized by any reference to τῷ μεσμερισμῳ,[2] remember that operations in the nerves must be qualified by the laws of the Nervous System, let the Spirit operating be holy or unholy.[3]

12 ɪ 67, pencil

It plainly appears, that these supernatural gifts were very common, since there was occasion for these regulations...

a just observation!

13 ɪ 67, pencil

... these holy assemblies... were held on *Sunday*... and men were not to fail of coming. There [in a hall in some particular house] they read the Holy Scriptures, not only the Old Testament, but also the *] epistles of the Apostles.

* Where else could they have been read? But were they read after they had been once publicly read to the whole Church? After a time, & when they had been collected into an Ἐπιστολικον,[1] they were—

14 ɪ 70–1, pencil | ɪ xlix

[Fleury draws upon Philostratus' story of Apollonius curing a plague among the Ephesians by causing them to stone an old beggar until his body was buried in a pile of stones. Apollonius ordered the stones to be removed, and "They found only a great dog."] We may believe, *] if we will, that the Devil caused a phantom to appear, to favour his Prophet. But it is probable enough that there was nothing in it but boldness and industry; and that in removing the stones he had caused a dead dog to be conveyed thither, which being found, they looked no farther...

* What an outcry would Fl. have made, had an Infidel offered such a bald and *improbable* solution of a Monkish Miracle!—He had

---

tongues needed to convey the new message, and of the various dialects of Hebrew and Greek spoken by both the disciples and their auditors. *Opera* (Leyden 1703) vɪɪ 667. In a note on Acts 10.33 he comments on the inadequacies of the Apostles' Greek and remarks that

the gift of tongues was not permanent. *Opera* vɪ 476–7. On the gift of tongues see **6** and nn, above.

11[2] "To mesmerism"—i.e. animal magnetism. See **4** n 1, above.

11[3] Cf ESCHENMAYER **9** and n 1.

13[1] "A book of letters".

caused!—as if a Cairn of Stones thus raised and for such a purpose would not have had a thousand Eyes upon it!—And as if it were not incomparably more likely, that the whole Story is as pure as it is ridiculous a Lie.—

15 1 71, pencil

Apollonius commanded the Devil to go out of him, and as a sign of his exit, to overset a statue. This he did, and the young man became so grave, that he took upon him the habit of a Philosopher, and lived after the manner of *Apollonius.*

Methinks I hear a Voltaire exclaim—Noscitur a socio![1]

16 1 72, pencil, | 1 l

*] [Paraphrasing 2 Cor 10.10:] They despised St. *Paul*, as speaking in a vulgar manner, and said, His letters indeed have strength and power, and by them he endeavours to affright you; but his presence and his discourse have nothing but what is low and despicable.

* From entire absence of needful documents we cannot even form a conjecture of the connection between the Greek Churches & that of Jerusalem. We only know, that there was an attempt to set off Peter against Paul.[1]

17 1 73, pencil

[Summarising 2 Cor 12:] At length he proceeds to his visions and revelations...and in order to humble himself, he returns to his weaknesses, and says, For fear lest the greatness of the revelations should raise me up, a thorn in the flesh has been given me, a messenger of *Satan* who buffets me; by which he signifies either the adversaries which persecuted him, or some corporal inconvenience, or a violent temptation...

The tradition was that the Apostle was subject to a species of Epilepsy, which exposed his mission to odious detractions: as if he had mistaken the trances of Disease for divine Revelations.—A shaprper or more envenomed Thorn we can scarcely imagine to a

---

15[1] "He is known by his companion" —proverbial. "Voltaire" here stands for any witty sceptic.
16[1] In Gal 2.7–21 Paul rebukes Peter for allowing a party of Judaising Chris-

tians, who claimed to be building on the foundation of Paul's work, to disparage Paul by representing themselves as supporters of Peter. See also 1 Cor 1.12, 3.10, 7.1.

noble mind,[1] whose whole Affections were in the Spread of the Gospel!/

18   I 74, pencil | I li

[St Paul] wrote to the *Romans*; that is, chiefly to the converted *Gentiles*; for there was a great number of them, whether it was St. *Peter*, or some others, that had instructed them.

Had it been Peter, surely Luke would have mentioned it[1]

19   I 96, pencil | II vii

The tradition of the Church informs us, that this epistle [to the Hebrews] is his... but the stile... gives reason to think, with some of the ancients, that either St. *Paul* did not dictate it word by word; or that some of his Disciples, whether St. *Luke*, St. *Clement*, or St. *Barnabas*, wrote it by his orders... or... that St. *Paul*, having wrote it in *Syriac*, some Disciple translated it into *Greek*.

Luther with better tact thought it to have been written by Apollos.[1]

20   I 112 | II xxiii

[§22 describes, from Philostratus, Apollonius of Tyana's visit to Rome and his restoring a dead woman to life.] And at another time he [Nero] caused an *Icarus* flying to be represented on the theatre; but, at his first starting, he fell just near the Emperor's seat, and all besparkled him with blood. *Simon* [on the evidence of Arnobius and others] likewise promised to fly, and ascend the skies, which he effectually did, being carried up by evil spirits: But St. *Peter* and St. *Paul* kneeling, prayed together, and invoked the name of JESUS; which, having terrified the Devils, they abandoned *Simon*, who fell down to the ground, and remained stretched out, with his legs broken; he then was carried away to another place; where, not being able to endure his pains, nor the shame he felt, he cast himself down a precipice: And thus perished *Simon* the Sorcerer, by the power of the Apostles.

By the odd admixture of the stories of Apollonius &c, one is almost tempted to think, that M. L'Abbé Fleury was laughing in his Sleeve,

17[1] The interpretation of "a thorn in the flesh" in 2 Cor 12.7 is not certain. C seems to take it to be Paul's tendency to epilepsy.

18[1] Cf FIELD **31** and n 2.

19[1] For Luther's view that Apollos was the author of Hebrews see BIBLE COPY B **134** and n 1 and *TT* 6 Jan 1823.

at the no less odd stories (this of Simon, for instance) related by ~~thesee~~ ~~solemn~~ Christian Fathers,[1] "for profound

And solid Lying so renown'd."—[2]

21   I 117 | II xxix

But the *Idumeans*, not satisfied with this slaughter, fell upon the city, plundered the houses, and killed all that they met with, especially of the Priests; amongst whom, ~~were~~ *Ananus* and *Jesus*, whose dead bodies they abused, and left without burial. The death of *Ananus* was looked upon as the first step towards the taking of *Jerusalem* . . .

Herder, followed by Eichhorn, supposes Jesus and Ananus to be the two Witnesses of the Apocalypse.[1]

22   I 145–6 | II xlvi

Speaking of fasting, he [Hermas] says, that a man must begin by observing the commandments of GOD; that if afterwards he is willing to add any other good work, as fasting, he will receive a greater reward.

It is sad to observe, at how early a period and under sanction of what good and sincere Christians many of the most dangerous Corruptions of the Papal ~~Church~~ Apostacy stole into the Church of Christ! Here we have the inflating doctrine of Supererogation and Merit. I have often thought that we wrong the Roman Catholics and injure our own cause by the too late dates which our protestant episcopal Divines assign to the doctrinal errors and superstitious practices of the R. Catholics.[1] But far sadder is it to see, how little the blessed doctrine of John and Paul of Salvation by the Cross and the Spiritual Blood of Christ appears in these earliest post-apostolic Fathers— what a monkish unctionless scheme of Ascetic Ethics their Religion for the greater part is!

20[1] For the "solid Lying" of the Fathers see **26** and n 2, below.

20[2] Samuel Butler *Hudibras* I i 539–40 (var).

21[1] In BIBLE *NT Revelation* I 257n (not annotated) Heinrichs mentions Herder and Eichhorn as holding this belief. See EICHHORN *Apocalypse* COPY A **19** and n 1.

22[1] For C on the early origin—both Greek and Roman—of the errors retained by the Roman Church after the Reformation see also **52**, below, and FIELD **59**. The errors occurred, he says, in the Catholic—i.e. the whole—Church, for the definition of which see *CN* III 3872.

23　ɪ 155 | ɪɪ liii

The life of *Apollonius*, which is delivered to us, was written by *Philostratus* the sophist, above one hundred and twenty years after his death; but his manner of writing hath not gained him much credit.

There is one point of difference between Oour Lord, and this Ape of his Character & Miracles, Apollonius, which I do not recollect to have seen noticed—that of Apollonius we do not ~~even~~ know what was actually even believed by his Contemporaries, however credulous, or for a 100 years after his death. We have merely a *romance* founded on certain Traditions—which Philostratus has mixed up with many others, some from the reports of Pythagoras, others palpably from the Christian Gospels, both the true and the Apocryphal.—/[1]

24　ɪ 156 | ɪɪ liv

[St John, in old age, deliberately sought out the young captain of a band of robbers.] The young man, who was their commander, waited ready armed; but when he perceived the Apostle, his confusion was so great, that he ran away. St. *John* pursued him at full speed, without considering his great age, crying out, My son, why doest thou fly from thy father, from an old man who beareth no arms.... Stay, my son, and believe that our LORD JESUS CHRIST hath sent me hither. At these words the young man stopt, and looking downwards, flung his arms on the ground, then began to tremble, and weep bitterly. When the holy Apostle was come up to him, the young man embraced him with expressions of grief, but hid his right hand; whilst St. *John*, on the other side, was comforting him, and declaring to him that he had obtained pardon for him from the LORD; and thus after having kneeled, prayed, and kissed his right hand, which was, as it were, *] washed with his tears; he brought him back to the Church, and continued instant in prayer, and fasted with him, giving him daily such wholesome admonitions as were proper to soften his disposition, till at last he restored him to the Church, as a remarkable example of repentance.

* This is so beautiful a story that one wishes it to be true.

23[1] For Apollonius of Tyana see BIBLE COPY B **98** n 1. Flavius Philostratus (c 170–c 250), Greek sophist, wrote (c 220) an idealised life of Apollonius. Later writers drew a parallel between the life of Apollonius and the life of Christ. See **13–15** and **20**, above.

25 I 166, pencil*a* | III ii

Nevertheless, he [Elxai] condemned sacrifices, as not being agreeable to GOD; and having been offered unto him, neither by the Fathers nor by the intention of the law: He was against eating flesh as was the custom of the *Jews*, and rejected the altar and holy fire as *strange* to GOD. He inserted these words in his book: Children walk not according to the form of fire lest you should be bewildered, it is altogether erroneous; it seems to you very near, and yet it is far off: walk not therefore according to the form thereof, but rather according to the voice of water; for he affirmed that water was good. He described CHRIST like a certain Virtue, of which he gave the measure, *viz.* twenty schenae, *i.e.* ninety-six thousand paces in length, six schenae or twenty-four thousand paces in breadth, and proportionably in thickness. These measures seem to have been invented from a passage of St. *Paul* [Eph 3.18], taken according to the letter. By a like error he makes the Holy Ghost of the female sex, probably because the *Hebrew* word *Rouah*, which signifieth the *Spirit*, is of the feminine gender: He supposeth him to be like CHRIST, and to be set before him in an erect posture, like a statue upon a cloud, between two mountains but however invisible; he assigned the same measure to them both, saying, that he came to the knowledge of it by the heighth of the mountains, because their heads reached thither. He in his book taught a prayer in barbarous terms, the meaning of which he forbad enquiring after; but it is thus translated by St. *Epiphanius*, "The unworthiness, the condemnation, the oppression, and the trouble of my ancestors is past, through the perfect mission which is come." The disciples of *Elxai* joined themselves to those of *Ebion*; they observed circumcision and the sabbath, and contin[u]ed several ages.

all so many gross Blunders of Irenæus and Epiphanius, arising from their utter ignorance of the Hebrew Language joined to their Gentile Prejudices.[1] No such Sects existed. The "Ebionim" are litterally, the Poor, the Mendicants, a name which the Churches of Palestine received & indeed assumed in the time of St Paul. See *Acts* of the

a Textus marked with a brace in pencil in the margin

25[1] See **32**, below.

Apostles.[2] If any one man in particular was entitled Ebion, it must have been the Apostle Barnabas.[3]

[a]For the confutation of all this Trash respecting the Elxaites (a Hebrew word signifying Renegados or Apostates, and applied by them to the Jewish Christians collectively,/ and by the gross ignorance of the Gentile Fathers personified into a Man, Elxai by name, and the founder of a Christian Heresy!) see Jac. Rhenferd.[4]

26 i 169, pencil | iii v

The epistle [of St Ignatius] to the *Ephesians* begins thus: *Ignatius* or *Theophorus* to the Church, blessed with the greatness and fulness of GOD the father...

assuredly, rarely hath any resolve or declaration been more a ~~pf~~ Mal a propós, than the worthy Abbe's ⟨(see his Preface)⟩[1] to eschew all *criticism*, i.e. all examination on principles of reason and experience of the claims to credibility in the narratives of eccles. history, and to authenticity in the writings extant under the names of Apostles & primitive Fathers.[2] The only means of checking Credulity, and thereby preventing groundless Scepticism, is strangely denounced by Fleury as the opposite *Extreme* of Credulity.—This remark is eminently applicable to the Ignatian Epistles.—[3]

---

a This paragraph is written above the first, apparently after the first had been written

25² On the assumed poverty of the Palestinian Christians see Acts 4.34–7, in which Barnabas is also mentioned. For the Ebionites, *pauperes* and *mendicos*, see RHENFERD (cf **3** n 1, above) pp 130, 134 (not annotated) and EICHHORN *Neue Testament* COPY A **1** n 4.

25³ For Barnabas as *Ebion* see RHENFERD p 139.

25⁴ See RHENFERD pp 151–5 (not annotated).

26¹ See i ix. Fleury saw two extremes to be avoided, credulity and criticism: "...the pernicious emulation of appearing learned has ensnar'd some Catholicks into the same excess [i.e. overstretch'd Criticism]. There are those who dare not give credit either to miracles or visions, for fear of appearing too ignorant; and if I wou'd have follow'd the advice which some gave me, I shou'd have suppress'd several which I have mentioned; but I found persons of a superior genius to

those who call themselves Free-Thinkers, who confirm'd me." i x–xi. 1 textus (on i xi) follows directly.

26² See **20**, above. Cf N 35 f 33ᵛ (*CN* v): "...But how to trace and to account for the Rage of LYING, so disgraceful[ly] characteristic of the Ecclesiastic Fathers & Memoir-writers! It makes it a path of thorns to read their works—when you are only certain that a great deal is false and don't know what to receive as true!"

26³ Seven letters now extant are accepted as written by St Ignatius (c 35–c 107), bp of Antioch, during his journey from Antioch to his martyrdom in Rome: for the titles see BIBLE *Apocryphal NT* CONTENTS. In the "traditional" version of Ignatius' letters there were several spurious letters and the genuine letters were much interpolated. Cotelier (see below) gives the text of seven true letters, seven interpolated, five supposititious, and two spurious (the letters to

27 ɪ 171, pencil

[From Ignatius' (genuine) *Letter to the Ephesians* ch 19:] The Prince of this world was ignorant of the virginity of *Mary*, and her bringing forth a child, and of the death of our LORD; three extraordinary mysteries which were performed by GOD in silence.

a difficult passage! That the Evil Principle was ignorant of Joseph's Bride remaining a Virgin, is intelligible, but how is he said to have been ignorant of ours Lord's Birth, and Death? He who prompted Herod to attempt the murder of the Holy Child, and entereding into Judas Iscariot betrayed our Lord to his Death?—I suspect a false translation/ viz. that ηγνοιησεν or some equivalent word in the first aorist has been mistaken for a past tense, instead of being rendered, *continues ignorant* or *"is incapable of knowing"*; and that Ignatius speaks of a mystic conception, Birth and Death of the Spiritual Christ.—[1]

28 ɪ 173, pencil | ɪɪɪ vii

[From Ignatius' *Epistle to the Trallians* ch 3:] And again: It is *] therefore necessary, as you make it evident by your practice, not only to do nothing without the Bishop, but to be even subject to the Priest as unto the Apostles.

spurious?[1]

29 ɪ 175, pencil | ɪɪɪ viii

[From Ignatius' *Epistle to the Romans* ch 5:] GOD grant that I may meet with the wild beasts that are prepared for me. I hope to find

---

Christ and to the Virgin Mary). Fleury refers to Jean Cotelier (1627–86) and his edition of the Apostolic Fathers, *SS Patrum qui temporibus apostolicis floruerunt* (2 vols Paris 1672; 2nd ed 1698), and it is on Cotelier's authority that Hone gives (in tr) the text of the seven genuine letters in BIBLE *Apocryphal NT*. Cotelier's first edition clearly separates the categories of letters; the 2nd ed includes the dissertation by James Ussher (1644) that first gave the evidence for the shorter recension. See also **28** and **29** and nn, below.

27[1] The Greek word is ἔλαθεν (second

aorist). Kirksopp Lake's tr in *Apostolic Fathers* (LCL) ɪ 193 differs in no significant respect from Fleury's. The aorist tense in Greek could be used, as the present tense is often used in English, to make a statement true at all times, past, present, and future. In C's day some grammarians thought this to be a function only of the first (or weak) aorist.

28[1] In a shoulder-note Fleury refers to a note in which Cotelier holds that this passage is genuine. Ignatius' view that the best safeguard of the Christian faith lay in the authority of the bishop is a distinctive feature of his position.

them in readiness, and I will sooth them, that they may devour me
the more speedily; and that it may not happen to me as to some
others, whom they would not meddle with; but if they are unwilling
I will force them.

S[t] Paul and S[t] Peter did not talk thus of their expected Martyrdom.
I confess, that these passages in ⟨the⟩ Ignatian Letters, if genuine,[1]
seem to me to betray the boastfulness of Fear—like the Bully who
with pale face & chattering ʈeeth exclaimed—What a d—— passion
I *am* in!

30 ɪ 181, pencil | ɪɪɪ xiii

[From Polycarp's *Epistle to the Philippians* ch 4:]...That the
widows...should be moderate in whatever concerns the faith, *i.e.*
that they should not desire to know too much of it...

N.b. the first faint Dawning of the doctrine of meritorious Ignorance.[1]
How contrary to the exhortations of the Apostles, Paul, John, and
Peter!

31 ɪ 183, pencil | ɪɪɪ xv

PAPIAS...taught, that after the resurrection of the dead, JESUS
CHRIST would reign in the body, upon earth, for the space of a
thousand years.

I am perfectly convinced that the Apocalypse does not sanction the
fiction of the Millennium/[1] tho' it makes use of it, as of other Jewish
Cabbalas, *symbolically*, in order to destroy the carnal hope by
substituting the truth—i.e. the establishment of Christianity as the
Religion of the Roman Empire for an *indefinitely long time*—⟨i.e.⟩
in the symbolical language of the Jews, a thousand years—[2]

29[1] His forthcoming martyrdom was a
pervasive theme in Ignatius' letters. This
passage is considered genuine. For C's
doubts about the motives of martyrs see
38 (at n 2), below.

30[1] The gloss—from "i.e."—is
Fleury's not Polycarp's.

31[1] See Rev ch 20. The "fiction of the
Millennium"—the late pre-Christian
Jewish apocalyptic speculation (based on
Dan, 2 Esdras, and Enoch) combined
with a literal reading of Rev 20 especially

among the Gnostics and Montanists—
had been revived in C's day by Irving and
others. For a larger discussion of this
issue, and C's objection to a literal
interpretation of millennium as 1000
years, see LACUNZA **2** and **47** (Vol ɪ front
flyleaves); see also C. BUTLER *Vindi-
cation* **1** n 7.

31[2] For the Jewish use of *millennium*
as an indefinitely long time see e.g. Ps
90.4, quoted in 2 Pet 3.8.

32   I 185, pencil | III xix

BASILIDES... said, that the Father, who hath no beginning, produced *Nous*, that is, the Understanding, who begot *Logos*, that is, the Word, who brought forth *Phronesis*, that is, Prudence, who brought forth *Sophia* and *Dynamis*, that is, Wisdom and Power, who brought forth the Virtues, Princes, and Angels, who made the first heaven...

It is much to be regretted, that none of the Writings of the Gnostic Christians have been suffered to survive/[1] & that we can only refer to such convicted ~~Bigots~~ Bigots & Blunderers as Epiphanius & Irenæus!—[2]

[a]N.B. Nous = the pure Reason: Logos = the intelligential Imagination, or Reason manifesting itself in *forms*; Phronesis = the Understanding[3]

33   I 185, pencil

He [Basilides] taught, that in each man there was a number of Spirits surrounding the reasonable Soul, which excited the different passions; that far from opposing these, we ought to obey them; that is, give our selves up to all sorts of impurity.

incredible

34   I 186, pencil | III xx

From this principle it followed, that all lasciviousness was not only permitted but commanded; and indeed, there was none but what was practised by the *Gnosticks*; for the followers of *Carpocras* assumed that fine name as well as those of *Basilides*, which signifieth knowing

[a] This paragraph is written at the head of the page

32[1] Basilides, of Gnostic tendencies and claiming to draw upon a secret tradition transmitted from St Peter, taught at Alexandria c 125–50, denying the doctrine of the resurrection. For C's view that "the extinction of all the Writings of the Gnostics [is] among the heaviest losses of ecclesiastical Literature" see Jeremy TAYLOR *Polemicall Discourses* i 949 and EICHHORN *Neue Testament* COPY B 5 n 4.

32[2] Cf **25**, above. Fleury gives his sources for this section as Eusebius (of Caesarea), Irenaeus, Clement (of Alex-

andria), and Epiphanius. St Epiphanius (c 315–403), bp of Salamis, attempted in his *Panarion* to refute all heresies then known; St Irenaeus (c 130–c 200), bp of Lyons, in his *Adversus omnes haereses* directed his attack particularly against the Gnostics and the millennarian Montanists. See also **34** and **37**, below. For C on Gnosticism generally see CHILLINGWORTH COPY B 1 n 2.

32[3] On Νοῦς see textus and **36**, below. For another version of C's distinction between Νοῦς and Λόγος see BÖHME **122**.

or illuminated, which the Catholicks never apply but to the most perfect Christians.

palpable Slanders, sufficiently detected by the vast multitude of Gnostic Christians.*—A few Fanatics, like the Ranters among us,[2] might profess such blasphemous Frenzies—but large Churches? —impossible!

* the very perversion of our Lord's words proves the fact, that they received the Gospels. On what metaphoric or catachrestic phrases & enigmas the fathers grounded these Charges against the Gnostics,[1] the loss of all the writings of the latter makes it impossible to determine.

35 I 190, pencil | III xxv

He [Aquila] then applied himself to learn the *Hebrew* language; and becoming master of it, he made a new version of the Scripture, making it his business to correct the Septuagint, and lessen the force of such passages as make mention of JESUS CHRIST.

The fact is simply this: that Aquila made a servilely and almost superstitiously literal translation of the Hebrew, even to the disregard of Syntax.—thus he uses συν expletively before the accusative Case, as answering to the Objective *eth* of the Hebrew.[1]

36 I 191, pencil, marked with a line in the margin | III xxvii

Valentinus refining upon those who preceeded him, deduced a long genealogy of several *Aeons* or *Aiones*, as he called them, abusing a

34[1] Cf EICHHORN *Neue Testament* COPY B **24** n 3.

34[2] A "fanatical antinomian and pantheistic sect of the mid-17th century" (*ODCC*), mistakenly confused for a time with the Quakers. See BAXTER *Reliquiae* COPY B **27**. In the nineteenth century, nonconformist preachers—especially Primitive Methodists—were colloquially called "Ranters".

35[1] After the Septuagint had been rejected from the synagogue as too far removed from the Hebrew text, Greek-speaking orthodox Jews needed a Greek text of OT that would be subservient enough to the Hebrew original to be acceptable to the scribes and rabbis. The

first of these—the first of four Greek versions in Origen's *Hexapla* (c 230–250)—was prepared by Aquila (fl c 130); it adhered rigidly and minutely to the Hebrew text in defiance of Greek grammar and idiom. C gives as one instance Aquila's rendering of אֵת (*eth*) by a non-functional use of σύν. The Hebrew suffix -*eth* means "with", but is also the sign of the object. Aquila therefore introduced the Greek preposition σύν (with), which takes the dative case, superfluously and ungrammatically before direct objects. This point is made by EICHHORN *Alte Testament* I 322 (to which see **10**).

name which is often found in Scripture, and signifieth no more than ages; but he made persons of them. The first and most perfect was in an inexplicable and invisible profundity, and he called him *Proon* pre-existent, and by several other names; but most commonly *Bythos,* *a*that is, depth. He continued many ages unknown, in silence and in rest, having only *Ennoia* with him, that is, Thought, whom *Valentinus* likewise called *Charis* grace, or *Sigè* silence, whom he made use of as his wife. At last *Bythos* was inclined to produce the principle of all things, and with *Sigè* he begot *Nous* his only son, like unto and equal with himself, who alone was able to comprehend him. This son was the father and first principle of all things. *Nous* in *Greek* signifieth Understanding; but it is of the masculine gender: he, therefore, made a son of him, and although he was an only child, he gave him a sister *Aletheia,* that is, Truth. These two first matches *Bythos* and *Sigè,* and *Nous* and *Aletheia,* formed a square, which was as the root and foundation of all the system; for *Nous* begot two other persons, or *Aeons, Logos* and *Zoè,* the Word and Life, and these two produced still two others *Anthropos* and *Ecclesia,* Man and the Church. These eight *Aeons* were the chiefs of all. *Valentinus* pretended to find them in the beginning of the gospel of St. *John;* God was *Bythos,* Grace *Sigè,* the Beginning *Nous;* the Truth, Word, Life, and Man, are there found in their proper terms; but unfortunately there is no mention made of the Church...

No! Νους = *Reason. Logos* is *understanding.* *b*1

Evidently a Poem, like Henry More's Song of the Soul/[2] The Allegory seems very well imagined.

37   ɪ 193, pencil | ɪɪɪ xxviii

Such was the whole fable of the divinity of the *Valentinians.* I have related it somewhat at length, because many famous heresies have

---

a Marginal line begins here
b Written in the margin beside the marked word "*understanding*"; the second part of the note is written in the head-margin associated with the marginal line for the whole textus

36[1] Cf **32** and n 3, above. In this context C is thinking of the Platonic and Gnostic usage in relation to his own desynonymisation of reason and understanding. Cf EICHHORN *Apocrypha* 18.

36[2] I.e. *A Platonick Song of the Soul* in Henry MORE *Philosophical Poems* (Cambridge 1647). C did not annotate this poem, but in "*Prometheus*" (*LR* ɪɪ 356–7) he quoted from a longer extract that he had copied into N 29 in c Jul 1822, beginning with the statement that WW's *Immortality Ode* v–vɪ is "pre-figured in coarser Clay, by a less mastering hand & with a less lofty Spirit, yet excellent in its own kind by Henry More...[in] his Poem on The Pre-existence of the Soul". *CN* ɪv 4910. See also EICHHORN *Apocrypha* **22** n 1.

since retained or renewed the greatest part of it; and I thought it would not be amiss to shew, for once, how far the greatest genius's have gone astray, when they have followed their own imaginations in explaining the Scripture, contemning the infallible rule of Apostolical tradition and the authority of the Church. But it was not an easy matter to refute the *Valentinians*, because it was almost impossible to come to a perfect knowledge of their doctrine. It was carefully concealed from the prophane, that is, from those who were not of their sect.

The Sum of the Matter, ὡς ἐμοίγε δοκεῖ,[1] is this: Valentinus was a Platonist and a man of Genius—who attempted a sort of translation of the Christian Faith into a poetico–metaphysical System by prefixing all the *ideas* requisite to the intelligibility of its first Principles, viz. the Fall, and Redemption.[2]

38 I 194–5, pencil | III xxix

...Some [Valentinians] gave themselves up to the most infamous pleasures, without restraint, saying, that they were to give that to the flesh which is of the flesh, and that to the spirit which is of the spirit; and many women, who were converted to the Catholick faith, confessed that they had corrupted them. They derided the Catholicks, who feared the sin of words, and even of thoughts, calling them simple and ignorant. Above all, they condemned martyrdom, and said, that it was a folly to die for GOD.

The very quotations from Scripture shew the improbability of these Charges/[1] and it is not difficult to conceive the occasion of these Slander. The same language which Luther used in depreciation of the Scourgings, fastings, endowings of Monasteries, and such like "*good Works*" of his Contemporaries,[2] Valentine in all likelihood employed

---

37[1] "In my opinion, at least".

37[2] Valentinus (fl c 136–165), probably the most influential of the Gnostics and founder of a Gnostic sect that took his name, evolved a system from the Platonic conception of a parallel between the world of ideas and the world of phenomena. See **36** textus, above.

38[1] The Valentinians, in Fleury's account (pp 191–2), quote Matt 20, Col 2.9, Col 1.19, and Matt 9.20.

38[2] Cf LUTHER *Colloquia Mensalia* ch 24 p 329 (not annotated). "The Popish Fasting is a right cave of Murther,

whereby many people have been utterly spoiled, in observing the times without all differences...insomuch that nature's strength thereby is wholly weakned." "St. Barnard...was 36 years of age, in which time hee built and erected one hundred and threescore Monasteries, and richly provided for them with Annual Revenue. Let us but consider what might belong to the maintening of 160 Monasteries. In such sort Superstition arose in a short time to the highest, insomuch that in the mean time the Gospel went on begging for bread."

on respecting the extravagant estimation of the Confessors & Martyrs by the Catholics of his times, and denied any merit in the wanton rushing into Dragon's Jaws, so fashionable in that age. See the Epistle to the Romans of Ignatius.[3]—A few high-colored phrases in the Writings of Valentinus or his Disciples, and a few acts of crazy men or women who had called themselves by the name of the last new Sect, are sufficient to explain the rest. Only read the accounts given by Divines, both presbyterian & episcopal, of the first Quakers —& later still, of the Moravians—& then think, what the Quakers & Moravians really are/[4] so judge of Epiphanius' Charges.

39 I 194 | III xxx

There were afterwards several sorts of *Valentinians*, amongst whom were reckoned three sects, somewhat obscure, but very singular for their extravagant notions; The *Sethians*; who particularly honoured *Seth*, and alledged that JESUS CHRIST was only *Seth* himself; the *Cainists* who held those to be Saints, and perfect, whom the Scripture condemns, *viz. Cain, Core,* the *Sodomites*; and above all the traitor *Judas*; The *Ophites*, who said, that Wisdom had turned itself into a Serpent, and worshipped a Serpent for JESUS CHRIST.

38[3] In his *Epistle to the Romans,* Ignatius urged his associates in Rome not to plead with the pagan authorities to deny him his witness unto death. See **29** and n 1, above. The high honour accorded to martyrs by the early Church was informed by certain passages in the Gospels: by e.g. 2 Cor 4.11 and Rev 14.13, by the deaths of Stephen, James, Paul and Peter, and by the dignified impassivity of the early martyrs. About Ignatius' sincerity in going deliberately to his death in Rome there can be no doubt; but under successive persecutions martyrdom became almost an obsessive vogue among Christians, especially in Phrygia and Africa. See also **55** and n 1, below. In N 35 ff 33–33ᵛ (*CN* v) C remarked upon the "grievous Snare" presented by "the enthusiastic admiration for Martyrs & Confessors, and the over-wrought appreciation of the Merit of Martyrdom".

38[4] George Fox (1624–91), founder in 1668 of the Quakers, suffered a succession of insults, persecutions, and imprisonments; his followers suffered constant persecution until the Toleration Act (1689) and intermittently thereafter into C's time esp for their rejection of oaths and refusal to bear arms. See AURELIUS **47** n 1. Fox was a candidate for C's projected "Vindiciae Heterodoxae". For the Moravians see BROOKE **25** n 2; they too rejected oaths and military service. C expresses approval for them in e.g. *CN* IV 4909, N 35 f 38ᵛ (*CN* v); and see George LAVINGTON *The Moravians Compared and Detected* (1755), annotated c 1807–8. The scandalous charges brought against both groups were strongly at variance with the dignity and quietness of their lives. For C's view of "modern" Quakers, however, see *TT* 12 Jan 1834 and cf AURELIUS **47** n 1. For C's rejection of the charge that in his early years he was "a hot-headed Moravian" see *TT* 23 Jul 1832.

Rhenferd has so ~~unanswerably~~ disproved the existence of any such Heresies.[1]

40   i 195 | iii xxxi

Adrian the Emperor built a country house...Having finished this palace, he intended to dedicate it by heathen ceremonies, and began to offer sacrifice, in order to make the idols oracles speak: But the demons answered: The widow *Simphorosa* and her seven sons daily torment us, by invoking her god; if she sacrificeth with her sons, we promise to perform what you require. *Adrian* ordered her and her sons to be seized, and at first in mild terms exhorted them to sacrifice. *Symphorosa* answered: My husband *Getulius*, and his brother *Amantius*, being your Tribunes, have suffered divers torments for the name of JESUS CHRIST, rather than sacrifice to idols, and have vanquished your demons by their death, chusing to be beheaded rather than to be overcome: the death they suffered drew upon them ignominy amongst men, but glory amongst the Angels, and they now enjoy eternal life in heaven. [Refusing to sacrifice, she was tortured and then drowned.]

The Hint for this Romance is found in the Maccabees—[1]

41   i 204, pencil, marked with a line in the margin | iii xli

[§ xli summarises and quotes extracts from Justin Martyr's *First Apology*.] ...But as by the word of GOD JESUS CHRIST was made flesh, and took upon him flesh and blood for our salvation; so the food which would become our flesh and blood by the change our nourishment receiveth, being sanctified by the prayer of his word, becometh the flesh and blood of the same JESUS CHRIST incarnate.

I have not a Justin Martyr near me to consult, so cannot determine whether this precious Sentence is chargeable on Justin, or on Fleury or on the English Translator. I suspect a bad translation by the Frenchman made intolerable by the Englishman.[1]

39[1] See "De Sethianis" in RHENFERD pp 165–93: on the Cainites esp pp 190–1, 193; on the Ophites p 193.

40[1] See 2 Macc ch 7. The "Romance" given by Fleury is from *Acta martyrum sincera*: see **42** n 1, below.

41[1] In modern editions of Justin Martyr, § 66; Migne *PG* vi 428–9. Cf tr E. B. Pusey *Works...of Justin the*

Martyr (1861) 51 (in Library of the Fathers): "For we do not receive them as ordinary food or ordinary drink, but as by the Word of God Jesus Christ our Saviour was made flesh, and had both flesh and blood for our salvation; so also, the food which was blessed by the prayer of the Word which proceeded from Him and from which our flesh and blood, by

42 I 205, pencil | III xlii

[The martyrdom of St Felicitas:] ...The Prefect caused her to be brought by her self, and endeavoured to persuade her, both by mildness and threats, exhorting her at least to preserve her children; but she continued steadfast. [After punishing her seven sons one by one, the authorities had them killed, and finally beheaded the mother.]

Strange! that a man of Fleury's sense should insert trash of this kind from the Acta Mart.—as of equal authority with Eusebius.[1]

43 I 213, pencil | III xlviii

[St Polycarp's prayer before being burned alive:] LORD GOD Almighty, the Father of JESUS CHRIST, thy blessed and well-beloved Son, by whom we have receiv'd grace to know thee: GOD of Angels and Powers, GOD of all creatures, and of all the nation of the just who live in thy presence; I give thee thanks that thou hast vouchsafed to bring me to this day and to this hour, wherein I shall be number'd amongst the martyrs, and partake of the cup of thy CHRIST, to rise again to the eternal life of soul and body in the incorruption of the Holy Ghost. That I am this day admitted into thy presence with them as a fat and acceptable offering, according as thou hast prepared it, foretold, and brought it to pass; thou, who art the true GOD, incapable of falshood: therefore, I praise thee for all things, I praise thee and glorify thee through the eternal and heavenly Priest JESUS CHRIST thy dear Son, with whom glory be to thee and to the Holy Ghost, now and for evermore, *Amen.*

This Prayer (and indeed the whole Proceeding)[1] worthy of the

---

assimilation, receive nourishment, is, we are taught, both the flesh and blood of that Jesus Who was made flesh." C's hesitation arises from his not believing that the Fathers taught the doctrine of transubstantiation. Cf C. BUTLER *Vindication* 1 and n 2, *CN* III 3847 f 125ᵛ, and FIELD **32**.

42[1] Fleury, in his shoulder-note, cites "Acta. Mart. Sincera, p. 21"—viz. Thierry Ruinart (1657–1709) *Acta primorum martyrum sincera et selecta* (Paris 1689), frequently reissued. Cf **40** and n 1, above, and **61** (at n 1), below.

43[1] When Roman "archers and horsemen" came to arrest St Polycarp in Smyrna, he refused to try to escape. Brought before two justices of the peace, he declined to acknowledge the divinity of Caesar and was impassive in face of their abuse. He similarly rejected the proconsul's attempts to make him deny the sovereignty of Christ, and was unmoved by threats of being thrown to wild beasts or of being burned alive, replying "with a countenance full of grace": "But why do you delay? bring what you please." The heathens and Jews clamoured for his death by fire. He was, by his own statement, eighty-six years old.

Disciple of St John.[2] I would have ⟨it⟩ transferred to our Liturgy, among the Prayers on possible Occasions, as a model and a support to our Missionaries.—[3]

44 I 221, marked with a line in the margin | III liv

In uttering a word we beget it, but not by separation, so as to diminish our reason.

a fine & just Thought.

45 I 327, pencil | V xlii

...*Tertullian* adds: All this we can certify to you by your own officers and counsellors...The secretary of one of them had a devil cast out of him, who was just going to throw him headlong; there was another cast out of one of his relations, and another out of a little boy...

In that extreme corruption of manners, it is probable that mania, epilepsy, hysterical & hypochondriacal Disorders, were frequent and in multiplied forms—So only can I explain the so frequent reference to Dæmons in the first 3 Centuries.[1]

46 I 338, pencil, marked with a broken line in the margin | V liv

He [Origen] also held the stars to be animated, and to be nothing but a stately sort of prisons for such spirits as were less culpable than those of this lower world..:.[He said] that the devil himself should, in time, cease being an enemy to GOD...but that this will not happen till after a long series of ages, because, after this world there will be another, and several others after that, as there have been many before it...

Origen had blended these notions with *Plato*'s Philosophy, of which he was a perfect master; amongst the rest, he had from thence taken this specious principle: That all punishments are medicinal, and are designed only to correct him who suffers them, which seemed

---

43[2] Fleury reports (p 211) that among those martyred at Smyrna in 155/6 was "St. *Polycarp* [c 69–c 155] their Bishop, who had governed that Church about seventy years, having been put in it by St. *John* the Apostle".

43[3] C did not usually approve of the attitude of missionaries: see e.g. BAXTER

Reliquiae COPY B **43** and n 1. But he was well aware, from his reading, of the tribulations they suffered, often to the death, and admired their fortitude.

45[1] For C on epileptic and hysterical disorders see also **17**, above, and **60** and **81**, below.

to him the more likely way of reconciling GOD's justice with his mercy, than the notion of eternal torments: Nevertheless, he asserts nothing which he does not support by some passage of Scripture; but very often in a wrong sense.

The Short of the Matter seems to be this: that all the errors, which the envy of ignorant Priests detected or fancied in Origen's Metaphysics they charged against him, as a Christian, without any proof, that Origen was aware of the consequences to be drawn from this or that position, or that he was not ready to retract them as soon as they should be proved irreconcilable with his Creed.—He was too great a man for his Age—.[1] The Church vehemently rejected the *principles* of Manes, before Manes was born; but alas! their morality was tinged with Manichæism throughout.[2]

47   1 341 | v lvii

[Origen's instruction of his disciples:] Having thus prepared and excited them to instruct themselves by a chain of agreeable discourse which they could not resist, he began to give them more solid instructions in true Philosophy, first in Logick...He afterwards made them apply themselves to physics...

He besides taught them the Mathematicks, particularly Geometry and Astronomy, and last of all Ethicks...

After they had gone through their studies, he led them to Theology...He made them read all the writings of the ancients, whether Poets or Philosophers, *Greeks* or *Barbarians*, excepting those only which professedly taught Atheism...At last he explained the

---

46[1] For C's admiration for Origen (c 185–c 254) see DONNE *Sermons* COPY B **97** n 1. Fleury is summarising Origen's metaphysical work, Περὶ ἀρχῶν, which, apart from fragments, has survived only in a "corrected" translation by Rufinus. Fleury's rather confused account follows the tradition that Origen was excommunicated for heresy, but the attacks on his doctrines were made mainly after his death; the deprivation of his bishopric was, rather, on the grounds of irregularity at his ordination. See *ODCC* under "Origenism".

46[2] Manes (also called Manichaeus) (c 216–276) devised a system on the principle of a primordial conflict between good and evil, light and darkness, thereby seeking to harmonise the doctrines of Zoroastrianism with Christianity. Because the Manichaeans considered that matter was evil they practised severe asceticism. Origen himself (Περὶ ἀρχῶν 1.8) attacked the anticipation of Manichaeanism in Valentinian and Marcion: according to Rufinus, "...Origen, on the contrary, makes it evident, that there is none but GOD, who is of his own nature good and immutable...that the cause of evil is the imperfection of the reasonable creature, who, making an ill use of his liberty, fell from his original perfection merely by his own fault." Fleury 1 337.

holy Scriptures to them, of which he was the most skilful instructor of his time. A noble scheme of Education. 1. Belles Lettres. 2. Logic & Mathematics. 3. Natural History and Astronomy. 4. Ethics & Psychology. 5. Theology. 6. The whole exemplified, applied, & turned to their true ends & profit in the study and interpretation of the Scriptures—and an Origen for the Tutor![1]

48 I 393 | VI xlv

[From the letter of the Clergy of Rome to Cyprian, concerning Apostates:] GOD knows what he will do with them, and how he will determine his sentence; but it behoves us to be very careful, not to give reason to the wicked to commend our excessive lenity, and to true penitents to accuse us of harshness and cruelty.

This is a valuable passage respecting the actual power assigned by the earlier Fathers to Church Absolution.[1] I have long thought, that the famous Text on which the Pretence is grounded,[2] refers to the miraculous Cure of Diseases given to the 70.[3]

49 I 427, pencil | VII xix

[Origen on the divinity of Christ, against Celsus:] None can form a *] worthy conception of him that is uncreated and the first born of all created nature [Col 1.15 (var)], but the Father only, who hath begotten him...

* an improper & even erroneous rendering of πρωτογενής:[1] and yet

47[1] For a few parallels to this scheme of education see e.g. *CL* I 320–1 (1797: self-preparation for writing an epic on the Origin of Evil), I 361–2 (1797), IV 552 (1815), V 219–20 (1822). On the principles of education that continuously inform C's thinking—which *SM* and *AR* both embody, and of which the *Logosophia* was to be a comprehensive declaration —see e.g. *SM* (*CC*) 40–2 and the "Essays on Method" in *Friend* (*CC*) esp I 473–81, 500–1.
48[1] That is, no power. C quotes from this same letter in *EOT* (*CC*) II 279–80 (13 Sept 1811), *CN* III 3773 (c Apr–Jun 1810).
48[2] See Matt 16.19, 18.18, in which St Peter is given the power to bind and loose—the alleged authority for the

papal "Pretence" to that power. Cf John 20.22–3.
48[3] Only in Luke 10.1–20 is the commission to heal given to "other seventy". Cf Matt ch 12, Mark 6.7–13.
49[1] A slip—the word in Col 1.15 is πρωτότοκος, for which see BIBLE COPY B 131 and n 4; cf CHILLINGWORTH COPY B 1 and n 5. The word πρωτογενής, found in Plato and in Septuagint, does not occur in NT Greek, but the meanings of πρωτογενής and πρωτότοκος are indistinguishable. AV translates πρωτότοκος as "firstborn" in Rom 8.29, Col 1.15, but as "first begotten" in Heb 1.6, Rev 1.5. For C's rendering as "-begotten" see *TT* 17 Aug 1833 (HNC's note). See C's footnote, below, and **66** n 2, below.

it is difficult' to find a substitute—the pregĕnite² ⟨of⟩ (*begotten before*)³ all created being—gives the sense.†

† Some of the Greek Fathers seem to have held that the Son was *eternally* begotten ἐν κόλπῳ πατρος;⁴ but *born before*, because *in order to*, the Creation—he being the Almighty *Word*, the antecedent Creative Energy, the first as giving rise to the Series, yet not the first but the superlatively-before, as not being a part of it.⁵

50 1 427, pencil | vii xx
In this treatise of prayer, he [Origen] says, that it is not JESUS CHRIST only who prays for us, but the angels also.

who ever doubted it? But Origen does not infer, that we should pray to the Angels, or thro' them—& *this* is the ? between Prot. and Romanists.¹

51 1 429, pencil | vii xxii

St. *Cyprian*, who presided in this council, sent the decrees of it in writing to *Fidus*, both in his own name and in that of his Brethren; and these words are very remarkable in his epistle: Since, says he, the greatest sinners coming to the faith, receive remission of sins and Baptism; how much less ought we to refuse an infant, who is but just born, and hath been guilty of no sin, save only his being born of *Adam*, according to the flesh, and that at his first birth he contracted the old contagion of death? He ought to be the more easily admitted to forgiveness of sins, inasmuch as they are not his own sins, but those of another which are remitted. Thus St. *Cyprian* acknowledges original sin.

49² *Pre* (before)+*genite* (born)—not in *OED*. For the meaning of *pre/prae* as distinguished from *ante* see BÖHME 6 and n 8. See also n 5, below.
49³ For the terms "created", "begotten", and "proceeding" see 66 and nn 2 and 3 and the tetrad given in 91, below.
49⁴ "In the bosom of the father"—John 1.18, a verse that C found inexhaustible to contemplation. The phrase is immediately preceded by the word μονογενής and by the phrase ὁ ὤν, which C interpreted in a special way: see 56 n 4, below. Cf BÖHME 20 n 12.
49⁵ See 63 n 2, below, and cf *SM (CC)*

44n; sec also SHERLOCK p 156, "*infinitely before*".
50¹ But see 27, above. C doubted the existence of angels: see e.g. HOOKER 19 and n 3. He seems here to have drawn angels into his usually vehement dismissal of the Roman Catholic custom of praying to saints, for which see e.g. FIELD 35. Cf N 35 f 39 (c 8 Nov 1827) (*CN* V): "A most powerful argument...against the Romish invocation of Saints may be derived in Origen's Command—to pray to the *Father only*, but *thro'* the Son, according to the universal faith & practice of the whole Catholic Church from the first foundation by the Apostles". Cf FLÖGEL 13 and n 1.

—Alas! at once acknowleges it and his utter ignorance of its true character.*

   * It seems a necessary conclusion, however, that there were serious Scruples in this age respecting the Baptism of Infants, tho' they were over-ruled—Scruples, that appear incompatible with the notion, that Infant Baptism had been previously the *general* Practice of the Church—[1]

52   I 430, pencil | VII xxiii note

[Translator's note:] Tho' prayers for the dead were very early in use, they were very different from those now used by the Romanists; since it was then usual to pray not only for the virgin *Mary*, but the Apostles and Martyrs themselves.

True! but not less true, that it *was* a mistaken, and *is* a cowardly, attempt on the part of Protestant Divines to fix the beginnings of the Corruptions of the Church after the 5th, or even the 4th, yea, or even the 3rd Century[1]—or to make them corruptions of the Romish Bishops/. The most practically important Corruptions were truly corruptions of the Catholic Church, East & West—in any *historic* sense of Catholic.

53   I 443, pencil | VII xxxv

[Epistle of Dionysius of Alexandria to Philemon:] . . . I heard a voice which commanded me plainly in these words: Read whatever cometh into thine hands, for thou art able to reform and prove any thing; thou hast had this advantage from the beginning, and it hath led you unto faith.

Extract this.[1]

51[1] For C on the question whether infant baptism was an ancient Christian practice see e.g. BAXTER *Reliquiae* COPY A **8** and n 2 and ANDERSON COPY A **1** and n 4. Cf *CL* IV 581 and *AR* (1825) 361n.

52[1] See **22** and n 1, above.

53[1] In N 35 f 38 (*CN* v) C did "extract" this passage, underlining the words "*to reform and prove*", with the memorandum: "I must consult the original". He thought the quotation

from St Dionysius would make "a good motto for my Theological Novel".

   In N 35 f 38[v] C referred to I 461, the "beautiful Tale" of Sapricius and Nicephorus, thinking that "an affecting dramatic Poem might be founded on it —I must think of it"; he then continued with the comment on Fleury's book as delightful and instructive (quoted in headnote, above).

54 I 465, pencil | VII lii

[Asturius exposes an imposture of the devil—sacrificial victims thrown into a certain fountain were seen no more.] As soon as he had ended his prayer, the victim returned to the surface of the water of the fountain, and there was no more mention made of this pretended miracle.

Nay! Miracle on Miracle, if there be truth in the Story at all.

55 I 466, pencil | VII liii

[Epistle of Dionysius to the Alexandrians on the plague:] The greatest part of our Brethren, through an excess of charity, have not secured themselves: They have gone in their turns to visit the sick, without any precaution...The best of our Brethren are departed after this manner...and it is thought that this kind of death is in nothing different from martyrdom.

suicide, rather![1] But Superstition of all sorts was now at its Springtide, in the Church, and Fantasts and Fanatics[2] took the place of Saints and Sages!

56 I 466-7, pencil | VII liv

[Dionysius:] ...I proved the accusation which was formed against me to be false; as if I had said that JESUS CHRIST is not *] *Consubstantial* with GOD.

* How many good men in this & the next Century were disquieted by this unhappy, ill-chosen Word—but yet I was not aware, that it had been introduced so early.[1] P.S. One fatal objection to the word,

55[1] For the danger of not distinguishing between martyrdom and virtual suicide see e.g. AURELIUS **28** n 1.

55[2] On superstition cf **97** and n 1, below. For "fantast" (visionary) *OED* records C's use in BROWNE *Works* **1** (between n 2 and n 3). See HACKET *Century* **16** n 1. On fanaticism see e.g. BIRCH **1** n 1.

56[1] Fleury is recounting the successful defence of Dionysius the Great (d c 264), bp of Alexandria from 247, against a charge of tritheism brought by Dionysius, bp of Rome (d c 268). "Consubstantial" is Fleury's word here, translating Dio-

nysius' ὁμοούσιος. The first use of *consubstantialis* is ascribed to Tertullian (c 155/160–after 220) as a central idea when he is defending the unity of God against Gnostic dualism and finding a basis for the doctrine of the "Trinity" (which term he was also the first to use). *Consubstantialis* is often assumed to be derived from it (see n 2, below). But since there seems to be no record of ὁμοούσιος until after Tertullian's death, it is possible that ὁμοούσιος was coined as the Greek equivalent of *consubstantialis* rather than—as C evidently supposed—the

had there been this only, is—that it is no proper translation of ὁμοουσιος/[2] & this again occasioned the introduction of the still more unhappy term, *Person*—in order to distinguish in Latin ὑποστασις from ουσια/[3] and how can either be right, when S[t] John assures us, that the Father is ὑπερουσιος—the only-begotten being ο ων.[4] See below the scheme of S[t] John—

The Absolute Will, the Cause of all reality = Θεος[5]

1. The I AM = Ο πατηρ.   2 The Supreme Being = Υιος
    3 Life proceeding = το πνευμα[6]
And ο πατηρ, ο υιος, το πνευμα εισι Θεος.[7]

57 I 474, pencil | VII lix

...for these Philosophers [the Neoplatonists], according to the doctrine of *Plato*, acknowledged a sovereign being, but without any prejudice to the gods and demons whom they placed under him in divers orders: thus they ∧ followed and authorised all the superstitions of idolatry, and even of magick.

other way around. Although ὁμοούσιος had become suspect from its use by Neoplatonists and Gnostics, and had first become a centre of controversy in the proceedings that led to the deposition of Paul of Samosata in 268, the term was introduced at the Council of Nicaea in 325 with the apparent intent of restoring the original meaning of *consubstantialis* and the implications that Tertullian had attached to the word. See **66** textus and e.g. *ODCC* under "Homoousion".

56² Ὁμοούσιος ("of the same essence/ substance") is literally "same-being", whereas *substantia* is "understanding". Although οὐσία (as "being, essence") can be translated exactly as *essentia*, there is no possibility of coining an exact Latin equivalent to ὁμοούσιος or an exact Greek equivalent to *consubstantialis*. See also **70**, below.

56³ The exact etymological equivalent to ὑπόστασις (hypostasis) is *substantia*; but because *substantia* was already in use as the equivalent to οὐσία ("being, essence"), another word was needed in talking in Latin about God as one substance comprising three hypostases—

that word was *persona* (person). For C on the use of "Person" in trinitarian theology see Böhme **161** n 3, Channing **1** n 2, Donne *Sermons* COPY A **4** (at n 3). See also **100** and n 1, below.

56⁴ According to John 1.8—in C's interpretation, for which see BIBLE COPY B **119** and n 1—the Son only is ὁ ὤν ("the being"): therefore οὐσία cannot be applied to the Father. But the remaining term ὑπόστασις ("standing-under") cannot apply to the Father, who is "above" the Son, ὑπερούσιος ("above being")—a word not in NT Greek, but often in Proclus and in the Fathers. See also **70** (at n 2), below, and cf Böhme **140** and n 2.

56⁵ "God".

56⁶ "1. The I AM is the same as The father. 2. The Supreme Being is the same as the Son. 3. Life proceeding is the same as the spirit". See also **66**, and the tetrad in **91**, below. For "I AM" as the name of God see e.g. Baxter *Catholick Theologie* **14** and n 2.

56⁷ "The father, the son, the spirit are God". See also **66**, below.

∧ Plotinus himself excepted*

* Plotinus by magic intends and sanctions only Natural Philosophy, and experimental Dynamics.[1] Of his disciples it is too true. ⟨Even⟩ Porphyry was a strange Compound of Priest, Juggler, Scholar & Philosopher—in short, a profoundly learned Old Woman.[2]

58   1 475, pencil

After his [Plotinus'] death *Aurelius*[a] consulted the oracle of *Apollo*, to know what became of his soul; and the oracle answered, by making an encomium upon *Plotinus*, after a more pompous than solid manner, and placing him in the *Elesian fields* with *Plato* and *Pythagoras*; which any Poet whatsoever might have said, and yet *Porphyry* pretended to make a mighty advantage by this oracle.

and a vile Poetaster the Oracle must have kept. The Lines are valuable from their very worthlessness, as shewing the low state, to which all polite literature had already sunk—[1]

59   1 484 | VIII vii

[How St Anthony shut himself up in a sepulchre in Egypt, leaving word for his friends to bring him bread from time to time.] The devil came thither and attacked him in the night, and beat him in such a manner, that he left him stretched upon the ground, and speechless, and feeling excessive pains.

a Bedouin Arab, no doubt.

60   1 484

[Continuing the story of St Anthony:] Then he heard a great noise, by which the whole building was shaken; the devils as if they had

[a] Misprinted for "*Amelius*"

57[1] For Plotinus and magic see *P Lects* Lect 7 (1949) 242–3, Lect 10, 296. For alchemy as the source of chemistry see ibid 440 n 41, and cf Böhme **128** and n 1.

57[2] In *CN* IV 5081 f 38ᵛ C discusses Porphyry at some length and finds in "his own Theosophy...good and evil Dæmons, Dreams, Prophecies, ceremonial and theurgic Rites &c"; in his works against the Christians "an eager & industrious detection of contradic-tions & inconsistencies" and "acute and enlightened Remarks on Magic".

58[1] For another estimate of the Greek of this period see ACTA **2**. C had the text of the oracle in his PLOTINUS (Basle 1580) f γ 2. Though full of reminiscences of Homer, it is not a distinguished piece of versification. For a translation see Plotinus tr A. H. Armstrong (LCL 1966–) I 65–9.

opened the four walls of the room, seemed to enter it in great numbers, under the forms of divers terrible beasts, *viz.* lions, bears, and leopards; bulls, wolves, scorpions, asps, and other kinds of *] serpents; each of them making a great noise, and furiously flying upon him.

* A manifest case of febrile hypochondriasis from inanition, in conjunction perhaps with the effect of Contusions on the nervous system.[1] The credulity shewn by so great a man, as St Athanasius in his Life of St Anthony, is one of the many facts, that cast a cloud of doubt on the miracles of this Century.[2]

61 ɪ 497 | vɪɪɪ xx

[The martyrdom of St Victor of Marseilles:] Being seized, he was *] immediately brought before the Priests, who exhorted him not to resign his expectations and the favour of the Prince, for the worship of a dead man; such they took Jesus Christ to be.

* I suspect, that the Abbè interpolated his history with these absurd Romances from the notorious Acta Sincera[1] to make his Book sell: Nuts for the Devotees.

62 ɪɪ 41, pencil | x xxx

[From the letter of Alexander of Alexandria to Eustathius, attacking Arius:] For these words: *He was, Always, And before all worlds,* do not signify the same thing as *unbegotten*: they seem to signify, as it were, an extension of time; but they cannot properly express the Divinity; and, if we may so speak, the antiquity of the only Son.

The improper words "*before* all time" instead of αχρονως, i.e. eternity negatively expressed,[1] occasioned much confusion.

I believe Christ to be the Jehovah of the Old Testament.[2]

60[1] On the psychopathology of religious enthusiasm and the effects of ascetic deprivation see **4, 17, 45,** above, and **81,** below.

60[2] St Antony of Egypt (c 251–356), hermit and founder of monasticism, was closely associated with Athanasius in the Arian controversy. Athanasius, to whom the *Vita Antonii* is traditionally (but not certainly) ascribed, encouraged the ascetic movement in Egypt and was the first to introduce a knowledge of monasticism to the West.

61[1] Fleury cites "Act. Sinc. 300" in a shoulder-note. See **42** and n 1.

62[1] Lit. "timelessly, outside time". The "improper words" are not Alexander's—he used ἄχρονος, as did Arius—nor indeed Fleury's, but the English translators'. See also **63** n 2, **73,** and **84,** below. Cf Bӧhme **165** and n 2.

62[2] For C's view of Christ as the "Jehovah-Word" see Bible copy b **11** and n 1, **55** and n 3, and **119** n 1. Cf **87** (at n 1), below.

63 II 46–7 | x xxxv

[Letter of Eusebius of Nicomedia to Paulinus:] We have never heard that there are two Beings *unbegotten*, or divided into two, after the manner of bodies... But we believe that there is an *unbegotten* Being, and a Being which he hath really produced; but without taking him from his substance... We believe that his beginning is not to be expressed by words, or even comprehended by thought... If he was taken from him as a part, or an emanation of his substance, it would no longer be said that he was created or founded; he would have been unbegotten from the beginning, like him from whom he proceeded. ...He is GOD, all things else were made according to his good pleasure, by his Word, in order to become like him...

Eusebius's error consisted in his applying Rules, Notions and Conceptions of the Understanding abstracted and generalized from Sensible Objects under the Forms of Sense (i.e. the Intuitions of Space and Time) to spiritual Subjects whose Being transcends Space and Time, and concerning which even the Pure Intellect can only form negative judgements.[1] Hence he involves himself in the absurdity of a time before Time/ for such is the contradiction implied in his Position, that the Son *had* begun before all time—instead of the sublime Truth, that the Suon is eternally begotten of the Father[2]—a truth perfectly intelligible, tho' inconceivable—for this plain reason that it is *not* a Conception to be conceived but an *Idea* to be contemplated.[3]

64 II 52 | x xlii

Thus spake the Emperor Constantine, or rather the secretary who drew up this letter by his order, and perhaps it was composed by

63[1] The basis of the Kantian critique, and also the basis of C's persistent distinction between concepts and ideas (for which see e.g. DAVISON **14** and nn). On the transcendence of the idea of God see DE WETTE **2**.

In N 35 f 42ᵛ (*CN* v) C wrote a longer version of this note, including an additional passage at this point: "Whatever is more than this, must be discerned by a higher light: the Spirit alone knoweth the things of the Spirit. From inadvertence to this, or rather from a want of a previous analysis or assay (δοκιμασία) of the constitution and limits of the Understanding (Λογος) and its difference *in kind* from Reason (Νους), Eusebius involves himself...".

63[2] For C's interpretation of "before", and for the Son as eternally begotten—ἀχρονῶς γέννητος in N 35 f 42ᵛ (cited in n 1, above)—see e.g. BUNYAN COPY B **16** and n 3 and ETERNAL PUNISHMENT **1** and **18**; cf also "*Prometheus*": *LR* II 337. For C's change of "Sun" to "Son" see AURELIUS **35** n 2.

63[3] On things intelligible but inconceivable see DE WETTE **34**.

In N 35 ff 40–40ᵛ (*CN* v) C summarises II 49—an anecdote about Constantine's first entry into Byzantium.

Eusebius of Nicomedia. Besides, the question which they were treating as trifling was nothing less than to determine whether JESUS CHRIST was GOD or a creature, and whether all those martyrs and other saints who had adored him ever since the publication of the Gospel were idolators, by adoring a creature; or whether they had adored two Gods, that is, supposing that being GOD he was not the same GOD as the Father.

a very just remark of the Abbe's. No one has shewn the vital importance of this controversy with more force & evidence than our own D[r] Waterland.[1]

65   II 60–1 | XI ix

...This was saying, that JESUS CHRIST was not true GOD, but GOD only by participation, like all those to whom that name is attributed. He [Arius] added, that he was not the Word substantial of the Father and his very Wisdom, by which he made all things; but that he himself was made by the eternal Wisdom; that in every respect he is a stranger to the Father's substance; that we were not made for him, but he for us; when GOD who was before by himself had a mind to create us. That he was made by the will of GOD, like others, having no existence before: For he is not a proper and natural production of the Father, but an effect of his grace; he is not the natural and real virtue of GOD; but the Scripture ascribes virtue to him in the same manner as to cater-pillars and other insects...Such were the blasphemies of Arius, abominable even to mention.

It is incredible that if Arius had openly avowed these convictions, and in this broad language, he should have been countenanced by the Men who at this time & after this time, it is well known, *did* countenance him/[1] Eusebius of Nicomedia, Hosius of Corduba, and Constantine himself. Where could have been the difficulty of finding precise terms, to distinguish the Orthodox from the Arian Belief —what ground for the exulting acclamation in the discovery of this Criterion in the word, homoousios, casually introduced by the

64[1] See Daniel WATERLAND *A Vindication of Christ's Divinity* (Cambridge 1719) 279–413 (**24–34**).

In N 35 ff 40[v]–41 (*CN* v) C refers, from II 59 , to "the truly beautiful story of the Conversion of the Philosopher at the famous Council of Nice [i.e. Nicaea]" : "I do not wonder, at the Philosopher's having been converted by the simple Creed of the illiterate old Man rather than by all the Subtleties of the learned Athanasius...".

65[1] There is no doubt that these words, for which Fleury cites Athanasius *Oratio in Arium* as his source, express the doctrine of Arius. See also n 3, below.

Advocates of Arius[2]—if Arius had openly taught what is now called Arianism?[3] That the Faith of the Church in the co-eternity and true deity of the Son should be placed beyond all pretence of doubt, was a point of infinite importance; but that this desideratum was happily supplied by the term, ὁμοούσιος, subject to the objection of its untranslateableness into Latin (for *substantia* answers to ὑποστασις not to ουσια, and persona for ὑποστασις is no translation at all)[4] is far from being clear.

66   II 62–3 | XI xii

Then the Bishops perceiving their dissimulation and unfair dealing, were obliged, in order to explain themselves more clearly, to include the sense of the Scriptures in one word, and to say that the Son is

65[2] Various sources attribute the introduction of the word ὁμοούσιος (*homoousios*)—on which see **56** nn 1 and 2, above—at the Council of Nicaea (325) to Eusebius of Nicomedia (pro-Arian), Hosius of Cordova (anti-Arian conservative), and the emperor Constantine (indifferent); all three were concerned to achieve a compromise. Eusebius is reported (Fleury XI xii) to have said when stating his position at the beginning of the proceedings that the Son was not of one substance (*homoousios*) with the Father, Hosius to have agreed beforehand with Arius' bishop, Alexander (see **62**, above), that *homoousios* would be a good test word (not in Fleury), and Constantine to have instructed the bishops to use Eusebius of Caesarea's confession of faith with the word *homoousios* added (Eusebius' letter to Caesarea explaining why he signed this formula: see also **67**, below). According to Athanasius, the bishops first tried to formulate their beliefs in the words of the NT, but the Arians always succeeded in turning these to fit their own doctrine. The unscriptural word *homoousios* was introduced as a pivotal term that might be acceptable to both orthodox and Arian. Once they found it necessary to go beyond the words of NT for an important element in the Creed, the "difficulty of finding precise terms" was extreme: see **56** and nn 1, 3, and 4, above. The Arians rejected the word; the orthodox bishops, wary at first, eventually accepted it and after the Council used it as a rallying point.

65[3] There can be no reasonable doubt that Arius did indeed stress the unity and perfection of God, and objected to the division (as he saw it) of the one substance into Father and Son; the Son must be a perfect creature, the firstborn of all creation; "there was when he was not," even though he might have been eternally begotten. For this he found ample support in Holy Scripture, as did his opponents. His works—popular songs embodying his doctrines, and letters—copiously quoted by his enemies, show despite much slander and abuse attempts at serious discussion. As time went on, Arius seems to have expressed himself less grossly in order to meet the arguments brought against him. (Fleury shows e.g. that Arius repudiated the teaching of Manes that the Son was a consubstantial part of the Father.) The fact that Arius' doctrines prevailed in the Eastern Church between the Councils of Nicaea (325) and Constantinople (381), and for much longer among the barbarians of the West, shows that they had to be taken seriously and engaged philosophically. Cf **74** and see **87** (at n 2), below.

65[4] For ὑπόστασις, οὐσία, and *persona* see **56** nn 3 and 4, above. For C's misgivings about all four terms see e.g. *CL* v 87–8 (16 Jul 1820).

CONSUBSTANTIAL with the Father, making use of the Greek word ὁμοούσιος, which has since become so famous by this dispute.

Without the *Idea* present to the mind of the Speaker or Hearer, what can *words* be but articulated Sound? Vox et præterea Nihil?[1] And with the Idea, the words, begotten, proceeding & created[2]—atchieve all that human Language is capable—. All Beings are *Created*, save the Father, from whom are all, and the Son, eternally begotten of the Father, and the ⟨uncreated⟩ Spirit eternally proceeding[3]—and thesee Father, the Son and the Spirit are the one only God.[4] This was the confession of the Great Council at Rimini:[5] and how the mere omission of the word, ομοουσιος, for Peace' sake, could render it heretical, only the Madness of Party can explain![6]

66[1] "A sound and Nothing more"—said by a Spartan after eating a nightingale: Plutarch *Moralia* 233A ("Sayings of Spartans").

66[2] This whole annotation is also written, with slight variation, in N 35 f 43 (*CN* v), immediately following the version of 63 (see 63 n 1, above). At this point C has added: "severally and exclusively applied to the Son, the Spirit, and the Sum of infinite Beings". See also n 6, below.

In the NT (AV) "begotten" occurs in five places to render parts of the verb γεννάω (1 Cor 4.15, Philem 10, 1 Pet 1.3, 1 John 5.1 and 18); otherwise it occurs only as rendering the second element in μονογενής ("only-begotten": in John 1.14 and 18, 3.16 and 18, but in no other gospel, also in Heb 11.17, 1 John 4.9) or πρωτότοκος ("first-begotten": in Heb 1.6, Rev 1.5). For these last two words see 49 nn 1 and 4, above. "Proceeding", in the sense here intended, occurs only in John 8.42 (Christ of himself) and John 15.26 (of "the Spirit of truth"), the verbs being ἐξῆλθεν and ἐκπορεύεται (went out). "Created" is used sparingly: see Eph 2.10 and cf 3.9. Cf 98 and n 4, below.

66[3] Cf 56 (at n 6), above, and 91, below.

66[4] See also 56 (at n 7).

66[5] See Jeremy TAYLOR *Polemicall Discourses* ii 989–90, in *LR* III 265 (var). In 359 the emperor Constantius called a synod of the Western bishops at Ariminum (Rimini), and of the Eastern

bishops at Seleucia, to try to resolve the Arian controversy, which had not been settled by the Council of Nicaea and the banishment of Arius in 325. The synod of Rimini, strongly orthodox, reached a firm anti-Arian decision, refused to accept the Arianising creed formulated at Sirmium in May 359, and insisted on approving the Nicene Creed of 325; but they were eventually browbeaten by the emperor into subscribing, at Nice in Thrace—a place said to have been chosen by the Arians to confuse the two "Nicene" creeds—to an Arianising creed in which ὁμοούσιος was replaced by ὅμοιος (like). The victory of Arianism, however, did not survive the death of Constantius. The West was soon restored to orthodoxy under the emperor Valentinian I (321–375), the final victory of orthodoxy coming at the Council of Constantinople in 381. See 83 n 2, below.

66[6] The N 35 version of this annotation (see n 2, above) ends: "...and how the mere omission for peace-sake of the unscriptural term, ὁμοουσιος, could cause it to be denounced as heretical, only the Fever-heat of Party can account for.—Give up ὁμοουσιος, the dear lucky ὁμοουσιος, that had set all Christendom by the ears? It was not to be thought of!"

The formula C gives here may be of his own constructing; it can be seen as a cento of elements found in the creed of Sirmium (May 359), the Constantinopolitan Creed (381), and the "Pseudo-Athanasian" Creed (see 76).

67 II 64 | XI xiii

Eusebius of Caesarea approved* the word *Consubstantial*, though he had opposed it the day before. Of these five there were three who yielded for fear of being deposed and banished; for the Emperour had threatned to banish those who would not subscribe.

* rather *acquiesced in*. It was new, he said, and not scriptural;[1] but as he approved of the meaning, it was intended to convey, still more, was hostile to that, it was ~~meant~~ intended to exclude, he would no longer oppose it.

68 II 83 | XI xxxiii

[Destruction of the temple of the oracle of Apollo Pythias in Cilicia:] Then a great number of Pagans opened their eyes, acknowledging the vanity of their religion; several became christians, and many at least despised what they had before respected, seeing what was hid under the fine appearance of temples and idols. They found there, either bones or sculs hidden for magical operations, or filthy rags or heaps of hay or straw; for with such stuff were the hollow parts of the idols filled up. There was neither god, who rendred oracles, as had been believed, nor demon, nor gloomy fantome, in the most secret parts of the temple. There was no cavern so obscure and deep, nor sanctuary so close, into which those whom the Emperor sent, and even the soldiers did not penetrate unhurt; and they discovered the blindness which reigned for so many Ages.

our Henry 8.th[1]

69 II 93 | XI xli

Two Pagan philosophers went one day to find him [St Anthony] there: he...said to them, why do you weary yourselves so much to

---

67[1] C is taking his summary of Eusebius from Eusebius' letter to the Caesareans describing the proceedings: Migne *PG* xx 1535–44. What details we have of the proceedings are from Eusebius' letter and from Athanasius' various works. It was Athanasius, not Eusebius, who remarked that ὁμοούσιος was not in the Bible.

68[1] Henry VIII sacked and pillaged the monasteries under the pretext of eradicating a lax and immoral way of life

harmful to the newly established Church of England.

In N 35 ff 41ᵛ–42 (*CN* v), citing Fleury II 91, C wrote a note on the "impudent Improbability" of "The story of the Three Crosses found in the Holy Sepulchre", ending with a lament upon the "passion of *Lying*" as "the most mischievous Weed that ever the Devil was permitted to sow in the Wheat-field of Christ's Visible Church!"

seek after a mad man. They answered, that they believed he was very wise. And he added; if you come to seek a mad man, your labour is vain; and if you think me wise, become such as I am; for if I went to seek after you, I should imitate you; but I am a Christian: upon this, they went away astonished....Others coming to mock him because he was not a Scholar, he said to them, What think ye? Which is to be preferred, good sense or learning? Which is the cause of the other? Good sense, say they, is the chief, and from it learning proceeds, Then, replied Anthony, learning is not necessary to him who has good sense.

How often has this Sophism been repeated! Even Milton (Par. Reg.) puts it into the mouth of our Lord![1] What if a man should ask—which is to be preferred, a blunt Ax or a Grind-stone?—

70 II 111, pencil | XI lv

Constantine was satisfied with this profession of faith [by Arius at the Council of Jerusalem, 335], not being aware that neither the word *Consubstantial*, nor any thing like it was there; and that on the contrary it was rejected under the name of Useless Terms...

The single circumstance, that consubstantial is neither the proper Rendition nor the identical Idea, of ομοουσιος,[1] ought to have determined against the *expedience of both*: and even the original Greek Term (the Latins were poor Crass Metaphysicians, even in pagan times) is inapplicable; ⟨at least,⟩ in the sense of the Homoousians themselves. *I* can use it, with *less* offence: tho' the Ipseity is rather the *mid term* between the ῾Υπερ Ουσιαν and the Ουσια, than distinctly it.[2]

71 II 119, pencil, marked with a line in the margin | XI lx

It is probable, that Baptism washed away all the stains of his [Constantine's] life, in which we find several very considerable faults, even after he had seen the miraculous cross, and had declared for the Christian Religion.

69[1] See Milton *Paradise Regained* IV 321–30, esp 325: "(And what he brings, what needs he elsewhere seek?)"—"a sophism which...is unworthy of Milton; how much more so of the awful person in whose mouth he has placed it?" *BL* ch 9 (*CC*) I 151. Cf ANDERSON COPY A 5 and n 1 and HAYLEY 1 n 5.

70[1] See **56** and nn 1, 2, and 4, above. Cf **65** and n 3, above.

70[2] The "Ipseity is...the *mid term* between the 'Above Being' and the 'Being'". In **56** (at n 4) C attributes ουσία to the Son alone; in the tetrad of **91**, below, the "Ipseity" is "The Self-originated = the Father".

FAULTS! good! very good!—Q[y] Whether *foibles*, peccadilloes, would not have been the more delicate word—for some score Murders, ex. gr. of his own Son, his Wife & so forth.[1]

72 II 125–6, pencil | XII vi

...he [Eusebius of Caesarea] accuses Marcellus of sabellianism, because he said, that before the creation of the world there was none but GOD alone; and that GOD and his Word were one and the same thing; which <u>every Catholick says at this day.</u>

Indeed?—but the good Abbé is out of his depth.[a]

As long as it shall be deemed necessary that *all* Christians should be obliged to *say* something or other respecting this mystery; and as long as it shall be the *fact*, that *all* Christians, or even the greater number of those so called, are not possessed of the *Idea*, so long will the Nicene Form be the safer Doctrine.[1] For under *this* state of the Church, the point to be considered is, not so much what truth the Words will convey, as what errors they will exclude.[2] Otherwise I would say (& pledge my existence on its being the doctrine of John and of Paul) that the Logos is the Son and God (Θεος) but that the Father with the Son and the Spirit is alone to be named O Θεος.[3]

73 II 125, pencil

He [Eusebius of Caesarea] says that the Father exists and subsists <u>before</u> the generation of the Son; so that he alone is unbegotten.

i.e. in order of thought, not in time.[1]

74 II 126–7, pencil

In relating the laws of Constantine against Hereticks, he [Eusebius of Caesarea] makes no mention of that which condemned the *] writings of Arius to be burnt. Speaking of the council of Tyre, he

---

[a] This sentence is written separately beside the underlined words; the rest is written in the head- and foot-margins

71[1] Constantine was baptised in 337 on his deathbed. Fleury goes on to tell how, in 326, he had put to death his son and his second wife.

72[1] The opening formula of the Nicaean Creed of 325 (Fleury II 63) reads: "I believe in one God [i.e. (positively) *one*, not (negatively) *many*]...and in one Lord Jesus Christ, the only-begotten Son

of God, begotten of the Father i.e. of the substance of the Father...".

72[2] I.e. as glossed in n 1, above: by positively affirming belief in *one* God the error of tritheism is excluded.

72[3] On "God" and "The God" see **84** and n 3, below.

73[1] For this interpretation of "before" see **62** and n 1, **63** (at n 2), above, and **84** (at n 1), below.

says not a word of the process of St. Athanasius, who was the subject of it.

* All these facts are so many proofs to me that Arius could not have avowed the gross Heresy attributed to him.[1] But it was no uncommon thing at this time to describe *that* as a Man's Doctrine, which his Enemies believed to be the necessary *Consequence* of the Doctrine, without proof that the Man ⟨himself⟩ either saw or admitted it: or even *against* proof.[2]

75 II 131, pencil | XII xi

[A "form of Faith" approved at the Council of Antioch (341):]...As our LORD JESUS CHRIST commanded his Disciples, saying, Go, teach all nations, baptizing them in the name of the Father, and of the Son, and of the Holy Ghost.

This text[1] has been urged by the German Neologists[2] as a proof of the *non-apostolicity* of our first Gospel—on the pretext, that it ~~isn~~ is irre⟨co⟩ncilable with the Fact as recorded in the Acts of the Apostles—viz. that the Apostles baptized simply in the name of Jesus[3]

76 II 132, pencil

Nevertheless as the length of this form rendred it a little obscure, Theophronius Bishop of Tyana proposed another which was shorter; it was conceived in these words, GOD knows, and I take him to witness, that upon my soul I believe thus: In GOD the Father Almighty, Creator of the Universe, of whom are all things; and in his only Son GOD the Word, Power, and Wisdom, our LORD JESUS CHRIST, by whom every thing exists, begotten of the Father before all ages, perfect GOD of perfect GOD, who is hypostatically in GOD; and who descended in the latter days, and was born of a virgin, and whatever else relates to the incarnation. Then he adds: And in the

---

74[1] See **65** and n 3, above, and **87** (at n 2), below.

74[2] Arius' opponents, according to C, were reasoning by consequences. On the undesirability of deciding the orthodoxy of a position by its imagined consequences see T. FULLER *Appeal* **1** and n 3.

75[1] Matt 28.19.

75[2] For the identity of the "German Neologists"—by which C usually meant Eichhorn, Paulus, and Schleiermacher—see BAXTER *Reliquiae* COPY B **45** and n 1.

75[3] See Acts 2.38: "in the name of Jesus Christ"; 8.16: "in the name of the Lord Jesus"; 10.48: "in the name of the Lord". Cf BAXTER *Catholick Theologie* **7** n 1.

Holy Ghost the Comforter; the Spirit of truth; whom GOD by his prophets promised to spread upon his servants, whom the LORD promised to send unto his disciples, and has actually sent him. An excellent Creed! Would to God, it were in our Church substituted for the Pseudo-Athanasian![1]

77　II 140, pencil | XII xvi

[St Paul the Hermit and St Anthony:] After the holy kiss they sate down, and Paul began thus, This is he whom you have taken so much pains to search for; a body consumed with old age; covered with white dishevelled hair; a man who must soon be reduced to dust. But, tell me, how does mankind proceed? Do they still make new buildings in ancient cities? How is the world governed? Do they still adore demons? As they discoursed in this manner, they saw a Raven perch upon a tree, which flying gently, came and laid a whole loaf before them, then flew away. Ha! says St. Paul, see the goodness of the LORD, who has sent us food; for these sixty years have I received half a loaf daily; but upon your coming JESUS CHRIST has doubled the portion.

Is the Raven an Egyptian Bird? I much doubt it.[1]

P.S. How many stupendous miracles must be supposed in order to acquit Paul & Anthony of being Receivers of stolen goods!

78　II 140, pencil

[How the 90-year-old hermit St Anthony sought out the cave "where St. Paul the first Hermit had retired ninety years before"; how they supped miraculously (**77** textus), and how St Paul died (**80** textus) and St Anthony buried him.]

Tho' the Septuagint and the New Testament were read in the Churches, it is too evident that the Scriptures were neither in the Hands or the Hearts of the People—they were at the utmost but the Spice, not the Food. Or such ghastly Mummeries could not have been so generally and superstitiously honored.

76[1] For the "Pseudo-Athanasian" Creed (*Quicunque vult*) see BÖHME 33 n 1 and *CL* VI 684 (25/6 May 1827).

77[1] It appears from ornithological records that *Corvus corax*, the common raven, though widely distributed, is not found in Egypt, but *Corvus ruficollis*, the brown-necked raven, is. Some translators of this fable call the bird a crow.

79 ɪɪ 140

It would be of great use in these times to write a Work on the merits and demerits of the Christians, of the second, of the third, and of the 4ᵗʰ Century.—Of the first we know too little to speak of their character—[1]

80 ɪɪ 141, pencil | xɪɪ xvii

...and when he came to the cave, [he] found the body [of St Paul] kneeling, with the head upright, and the hands extended on high. He thought at first that he was alive and still prayed, and began to pray likewise; but not hearing him sigh according to custom, in praye[r]s, he embraced him, weeping, and found that he was only in the posture of prayer. He wrapped up the body, drawing it out, and singing hymns and psalms according to the tradition of the Church: But he was afflicted when he could find no instrument to dig the earth; and was in doubt whether to return to the monastery, or stay, when two lyons ran from the bottom of the desart, with their hair erect. At first he groaned; but the thoughts of GOD strengthned him; they came directly to the body of St. Paul, and fawning upon him with their tails, lay down at his feet roaring, as a testimony of their grief. Then they began near it to dig the earth with their paws, and throwing out the sand, they made a grave big enough to hold a man. Then as demanding their reward, they came couching and hanging their ears to St. Anthony, who knew that they demanded his blessing, and said, LORD, without whose will a sparrow does not fall to the ground, give them what thou knowest agreeable to them; then making a sign with his hand, he commanded them to depart.

It would be a relief to the mind to think, that these narrations were intended by their writers as pious *Romances*—Heroic Poems, or Idylls.[1]

81 ɪɪ 143, pencil

The reputation of St. Hilario spread so far, that one of the guards of Constantius the Emperor...came also to him, that he might be delivered from a devil which had tormented him from his childhood....He understood no other language but the latin, and his

79[1] See also **16**, above, and C's lament, in **32**, above, for the loss of the Gnostic writings.

80[1] For the romance-like quality of many of the stories Fleury repeats see e.g. **24, 36, 40, 54, 61**, above.

mother tongue, which was the German. The saint spoke to him in Syriack; he was immediately lifted up, so that he hardly touched the ground with his feet; and crying out in a frightful manner, he replied in Syriack, according to the idiom of Palestine, pronouncing it exactly with the accent and aspirations. The saint examined him likewise in Greek, that his interpreters might understand him, who understood none but That and the Latin tongue. The devil declared how he entred into him, and pretended that he was forced by magical operations. St. Hilario said, I care not how thou has entred; but in the name of our LORD JESUS CHRIST, I command thee to come out.

I know no disease applicable to cases of this kind but Epilepsy, or St Vitus's Dance—i.e. Chorea *invita*.[1]

81A II 143, pencil | XII xviii

In one of these visits he came to Eleusa in Idumea, on the day when all the people were assembled in the temple of Venus to celebrate her !] festival; for the <u>Sarazens</u> adored this goddess, because of the planet which bears her name.[1]

82 II 156, pencil | XII xxviii–xxix

[§ xxviii (II 154) begins:] In the mean time [A.D. 342] Sapor king of Persia grievously persecuted the Christians who were very numerous in his kingdom....Sapor...began to load the Christians with excessive taxes, that he might reduce them to insupportable poverty... and he committed the exaction of these taxes to unmerciful men. Afterwards he ordered the Priests and Ministers of GOD to be put to the sword, their churches to be destroyed, and their treasures

---

81^1 On epilepsy see **17** and **45**, above. *"Involuntary* Dance"—i.e. *Chorea Sancti Viti*, St Vitus's Dance. In the fifteenth century an epidemic of dancing madness, probably hysterical, which spread from Germany throughout Europe, was associated with St Vitus (d c 303) because of his gift of curing sickness and demonic possession, his name later being invoked against sudden death, hydrophobia, and convulsive disorders. Burton repeats the legend that those stricken with St Vitus's Dance "can do nothing but dance till they are dead, or cured". *Anatomy of Melancholy* I i 1 (4). The disease *chorea*, in the seventeenth

century, was medically associated with involuntary movements of the muscles, especially in young persons. RS is recorded as saying that C's mind "is in a perpetual St Vitus's dance—eternal activity without action". Quoted by H. D. Traill *Life of Coleridge* (1884) 106.

81A^1 If the "!" is C's, and if he implies by it that Fleury is anachronistic in using the name "Sarazen" at this date, he is mistaken. The name had been used to describe the Arabs or Syrians long before it was used by the crusaders as a synonym for Mohammedans: see *OED* under "Saracen".

confiscated, and that Simeon should be brought to him as a traytor against religion and the state. [Fleury then gives a detailed account of the martyring of St Simeon and St Usthazadius, and of many indiscriminate mass executions.] [§ xxix] The following year likewise... Sapor published an edict throughout Persia, which condemned to death, not only Ecclesiastical persons, but all such as confessed themselves to be Christians. [The account of executions and martyrdoms then continues.]

The fortune of christianity in Persia is not unlike that of the Reformation in Spain./[1]

83   II 164, pencil | XII xxxv

They came afterwards [in the Council of Sardica (Sofia)] to the third question which they were to decide, and which was undoubtedly the most considerable, viz. the complaints formed on all sides against the Eusebians. The most capital was... that they communicated with the Arians condemned at the council of Nice... and that they had not only received them into the Church, but also raised the Deacons to be Priests, and the Priests to be Bishops. In every particular their design of re-establishing that heresy plainly appeared; for all the cruelties which they had committed at Alexandria, or elsewhere, were against those only who refused to communicate with the Arians. They were convicted of calumny by the justification of these whom they would have destroyed.... Then the council pronounced sentence against the heads of these factions... [They] were deposed and excommunicated.

The extreme moral corruption of the Church (of the Churchmen at least), at this time[1] is evident in the ~~comparatively~~ trifling criminality attached to the Cruelties perpetrated by the Anti-athanasian Party, compared with the crime of favoring Arians.[2]

82[1] Unable to defeat the Romans decisively, Shapir II (309–379), king of Persia, began a general persecution of Christians. Shapir also forcibly converted Christians into Zoroastrians, as the Spaniards forcibly converted Jews and Muslims into Christians.

83[1] I.e. c 347, according to Fleury's running headline.

83[2] Athanasius (c 296–373), bp of Alexandria from 328, was driven into exile or hiding several times (336–66) by the Arians with the support of Arianising emperors. The triumph of Athanasian orthodoxy came at the Council of Constantinople (381), eight years after Athanasius' death; the creed then approved is that which—under the title "Nicene Creed"—is used at Holy Communion in the C of E and in the Roman Eucharist. At the Council of Sardica (c 343), called to decide Athanasius' orthodoxy, Athanasius was declared innocent on evidence examined in the absence of

84 II 178–80 | XII xlvii

...Aetius could never comprehend...how an eternal generation could be brought about.... He boasted that he knew GOD as clearly as he knew himself; and abusing the passage of the Gospel, where it is said, That eternal life is to know GOD and JESUS CHRIST, he reduced all religion to this speculative knowledge... Besides, the doctrine of Aetius was pure Arianism; and he differed in nothing from the rest, only that he had followed their principle better, carrying his consequences to a greater length; maintaining, that the Word was not only not equal to the Father, but was not even like him.

If there were no other reason for confining the public Confession of the Mystery of the Tri-unity to the simplest terms & those strictly Scriptural, this would suffice: that the Mass of Christians cannot be supposed to have attained that power over their own imagination, as to exclude from their thoughts the alien form of *Time*, which the imperfection of all human language will not fail to obtrude—.[1]

Even the most orthodox are in their reasonings against the Eusebians[2] guilty of unfairness in attributing to their opponents a separability of the Son from the Father which they expressly disclaimed. The Eusebians professed that the Father with the Son & the Spirit is the one only God = ο Θεος, & the Son therefore (as Sᵗ John asserts) Θεος.—But—exclaim the orthodox/ is not the Son in himself ο θεος?—.[3] We do not understand you, reply the

---

the Eastern bishops. No punishment was inflicted on those who had given false evidence, but eight bishops leading a faction that had espoused the Arian cause were deposed and excommunicated. In N 35 f 43ᵛ (*CN* v) (11 Nov 1827) C noted: "The rapid spreading Corruption of the Church and the frightful increase of crimes among Christians under Constantine, both cause and effect of the mania for settling the speculative modes of conceiving and wording Articles of Faith, and of raising these logical formulæ into Art. of Faith themselves... which first took firm root in the proceedings of the Council of Nice [i.e. Nicaea], & grew with the rapidity of a Weed till in the reign of Constantine it spread its Upas arms over the whole Garden of the Church...."

84[1] For "the alien form of *Time*" see 62 and n 1, 63 (at n 2), and 73, above.

84[2] Arians were often called—and are regularly so called by Fleury—"Eusebians", after Eusebius of Nicomedia, Arius' most influential supporter at the Council of Nicaea.

84[3] What "Sᵗ John asserts" is (John 1.1): ὁ Λόγος ἦν πρὸς τὸν Θεόν, καὶ Θεὸς ἦν ὁ Λόγος (AV: "the Word was with God, and the Word was God"; word-for-word: "the Word was with *the* God, and God was the Word"). C's attempt to distinguish between ὁ Θεός (lit. "the God") as the Trinity and Θεός (lit. "God") as the Son (for which see also 72, above) is not transferable into English idiom; nor is it valid. Θεός, like any proper noun in Greek, is normally preceded by the definite article, but is

Eusebi[a]ns*ᵃ*—You ask what *would* be if that which is impossible, *were*. Such a question does not deserve an answer.

85 ɪɪ 183 | xɪɪ liii

Several young virgins, who before this, were designed for the married
*] state, consecrated their virginity to JESUS CHRIST, and several
young men embraced a monastick life, being prevailed upon by the
example of others.

* a melancholy proof, how far from the wisdom of the Gospel
Athanasius's Views of Religion were.¹ In part, his admiration of the
Monk, Anthony; and in part, the engrossment of his thoughts by
controversial and speculative notions; had blown him above the
humility of the Truth in Jesus!²

86 ɪɪ 188 | xɪɪɪ ii

When they [the Persians] made their approach [in 350], they were
greatly surprized to find a new wall behind the other; and it was St.
James Bishop of that city [Nisibis], so famous for his virtue and
*] miracles, who had encouraged the garrison and the inhabitants
to raise this work with so much expedition; he continuing at prayer
in the mean time in the church.

<hr>

ᵃ Letter supplied by the editor

<hr>

used without the article when a predicate
or epithet. Of the crucial texts (which also
involve another problem with the article)
over which Arians, Socinians, and Uni-
tarians have disagreed with trinitarians
on the attribution of divinity to Christ (cf
CN ɪɪɪ 3275 and n), Eph 5.5 has no article
before Θεός, whereas 2 Thess 1.12 (on
which see BIBLE COPY B **132**) and Titus
2.13 have the article.

85¹ Fleury, however, nowhere sug-
gests that Athanasius incited these young
persons to embrace celibacy. On C's dis-
taste for celibacy see also e.g. HACKET
Scrinia **21** and n 1, HEAD **6**, and *TT* 18
Apr 1833. In N 35 ff 41–41ᵛ (*CN* v) C
noted: "Never was there a more impres-
sive instance or on so large a scale of the
mischief of seeing one half of the Truth
only, as in the gradual introduction of the
constrained Celibacy of the Clergy in the

Christian Church. It was not perfected
indeed till the Bishops of Rome formed
their dark and too successful Scheme of
reducing the whole Body of the Priest-
hood to a Mameluke Guard of the
Papacy; but the Popes could not have
succeeded in this, had they not had the
Jeromes and Sᵗ Antonies for their Pio-
neers—Doubtless, Concupiscence and
Generation are the Generic Nature ✶
Princip Individualitatis; but the latter
needed its ✶ to manifest itself in. As Lust
is the most ~~prominent~~ extensively
Generic = *animal*, so is *Love* the most
intensely individual = *human*. Hence Sᵗ
Paul so profoundly calls Marriage a great
mystery, or sacramental Symbol."

85² For "the Monk, Anthony" see **59**
and **60**, above. For "the Truth in Jesus"
see Eph 4.21.

* How easily and without any intent to deceive might this Incident have passed into a stupendous Miracle! In the language of piety St James would have been said to have raised the wall by his prayers in one night—and if no historian had added the co-operation of the Soldiers—we should have had a miracle!—

87   ɪɪ 191 | xɪɪɪ vi

It [the creed formulated at Sirmium A.D. 351] neither affirms, that the Son is consubstantial with the Father, nor even that he is like him; but expressly says, We do not make the Son equal to the Father, but conceive that he is subject to him. It pronounces anathema's against those who assert, that it was not the Son who appeared unto Abraham, or who wrestled with Jacob; and it is certain that several of the antients have been of opinion, that it was at that time that the Son of man first began to be sent unto men. Photinus denied it, because he would not acknowledge that GOD had a Son before JESUS was born of the Virgin Mary; but then the Arians made an ill use of it, pretending thereby to prove, that the Father alone was of his own nature invisible and incomprehensible. However, St. Augustine has since fully proved, that these kinds of operations have been performed by angels; that frequently there's no manner of reason for ascribing them to any one of the Divine Persons, more than the other; and that the Trinity itself is manifested to men upon these occasions.

I would not detract from the ~~mert~~ merit of the Post-Nicene Fathers of the 4th and 5th Centuries in guarding the Church from Creature-worship in all its subtlest disguises; but it is doubtful whether this merit was not counter-balanced by the too great separation of the Old from the New Testament ~~by~~ in their refusal to recognize Christ as the Jehovah and the adored Angel of the Patriarchs & of Moses.[1] The name of *Arians* given to all who did not approve of the unscriptural term, consubstantial, was a mischievous tho' too common Slander of Party Intolerance. Indeed whether Arius himself was an Arian, is doubtful.[2]

87[1] For C's view of Christ as the "Jehovah-Word" see **62** and n 2, above. For the Angel as the Logos see also EICHHORN *Apocrypha* **17** and n 2. The "Angel of God" or "Angel of the Lord" often proclaims the word of God in OT, especially in the Pentateuch.

87[2] For "consubstantial" see **56** n 1, above. For the Arianism of Arius see **65** (at n 3) and **74** n 1, above.

88 II 240, pencil | XIII xlv

This is the principal poyson of this formulary [published in Latin by the Council of Sirmium A.D. 357]; for by forbidding them to say, that *] the Son is *Consubstantial*, they are given to understand that the is of *another Substance*, or made out of nothing, like creatures.

Why so? Might they not, nay, *were* they not given to understand that they ought neither to think one or the other, but confess it to be above their comprehension, and "walk humbly with the Lord their God"?[1]

89 II 240–1, pencil | **88** textus

* Melancholy instance of Folly in attempting an the impracticable— i.e. the securing the presence of an unique Idea in the minds of all men by forcing them to utter this or that set of *words*![1] If the express declarations of the Apostles on the *Unity* of the Godhead, and their equally express assertions of the *Deity* of Christ, leave some possible error unguarded against—where & whence is the *proof*, that it *is* an error? Or that there is any *need* of guarding against it? But above all, where is the proof, that any expressions not scriptural, such as consubstantial, but invented by fallible men will not be still less efficient? that they will not lead to some new error?—

90 II 241, pencil | XIII xlvi

Thus did Liberius Bishop of Rome abandon St. Athanasius, whose cause was then inseparable from that of the faith.

So much for Papal *Infallibility*![1] & yet how plausibly might the conduct of Liberius be defended! But all is *PREJUDICE.[a]*

91 II 242 (misprinted 342), pencil | XIII xlvii

...[Athanasius] writes them [the Monks] an account of his own sufferings, and of those of the Church; and that he undertakes to confute the heresy of the Arians: But, adds he, the more I endeavoured to write, the more I strove to consider the Divinity of the Word, and

---

a Word in swash capitals

88[1] Micah 6.8 (var).

89[1] On the impossibility of imposing an idea through a form of words see **66** and n 1 and **72** (at n 2), above. The Creed of Sirmium was presented, slightly altered, to the Council of Rimini in 359: see **66** and n 5, above.

90[1] On papal infallibility see e.g. *C&S* (*CC*) 126, 137, and cf FIELD **51** and n 1. The doctrine was not officially established until 1870.

the knowledge of it withdrew still farther from me, and I found that I was so much the farther off, by as much as I imagined myself to comprehend it; for I could not even write what I thought I understood, and that which I wrote was still above the faint shadow of truth which I had in my mind.... Though it is impossible to comprehend what GOD is, it is possible to say what he is not.[1] Thus is it with respect to the Son of GOD; it is easy to condemn what hereticks advance, and to say, The Son of GOD is not this or that; it is not even lawful to entertain such thoughts, much less to utter them with the tongue.

1 Identity
The Absolute Originless

2 Ipseity   3 Alterity
The Self-originated = the Father   The Originated of Another, the
Eternally Begotten, the Son.

4 Community
The originated of another, not begotten but proceeding
= Spirit.[2]

---

92   II 243, pencil

~~The~~ Every error, ~~from~~ that consists in the ignorance of a necessary Truth, may generate two contrary errors. So was it with Athanasius and Eusebius—or with the Consubstantialists and the rejectors of the Term.—They both omitted and were ignorant of the αει προπρωτον[1] —and of the truth, that the Trias must be contemplated in the Light of the Tetractys[2]—both forget the absolute Affirmant.[3]

91[1] In N 35 f 43ᵛ (*CN* v) C noted: "Mem. Fine passage in Athanasius...in that the extreme difficulty of comprehending ~~the~~ a mystery is perfectly compatible with its being possible & even easy to confute all heresy concerning it. We can not comprehend what God is; but we can clearly demonstrate what he is not." (11 Nov 1827).

91[2] With this version of "the adorable tetractys" (see **92** n 2, below) cf the formula in GREW **1** and in *TT* 8 Jul 1827, and cf *TT* 15 May 1830.

92[1] "Eternally *before-the-first*". προπρωτον—not in Liddell & Scott, or *NT Gk Lex*; perhaps C's coinage. In the "Formula fidei" (1830) "The adorable

"πρόπρωτον" is that "which whatever is assumed as the first, must be presumed as its antecedent." *LR* III 1.

92[2] The "Trias" (Father, Son, and Holy Spirit) must be contemplated as four—i.e. with the αει προπρωτον as the first of all. See **91**, above; and e.g. *TT* 24 Apr 1832: "The adorable tetractys, or tetrad, is the formula of God; which...is reducible into, and is, in reality, the same with the Trinity." On the tetractys as identical with the trias see esp BÖHME **6** n 10.

92[3] I.e. the αει προπρῶτον—before the Father—"The Absolute Originless" of **91**, above.

93 II 348–9 | xv xliii

[The attempt to rebuild the temple:] As Alypius earnestly pressed on
the work... such terrible balls of fire were frequently shot out of the
earth near the foundation, that it was impossible to come near the
place, they having several times scorched the workmen; so that being
continually repulsed by this element, they gave over the enterprize.
These are the words of Ammianus Marcellinus a pagan historian who
lived in those times, who as much hated the Christians as he admired
Julian. This is likewise recorded by the Christian authors, who add
the following particulars: This prodigy happened on the night
preceding the day on which they intended to begin the work, having
before prepared and cleared the place. They were surprized with a
great earthquake, which scattered all the stones of the
foundation... and overturned almost all the buildings of the
place.... Prodigious heaps of lime, sand, and other materials, were
suddenly carried away by whirl-winds.... No miracle that we know
of is better attested than this...

That the incident might have been related to Ammianus Marcellinus
with great exaggeration, is not improbable; that it was ~~an act~~ Miracle
worked by divine interference, I will not ~~pretend~~ venture to affirm,
and find it difficult to believe Warburton to have been in earnest in
his pretended proofs,[1] which have a most suspicious air of having
been designed to shew, that the phænomena were produced by a local
earthquake occasioned by what we call coal-blasts in our mine
pits.[2]—but to reject it altogether on account of Nazianzen's silence,
with Lardner & Gibbon seems to me scepticism in excess.[3]

93[1] C's response is coloured—as the
last sentence might suggest—by Gibbon
Decline and Fall ch 23 (12 vols 1802)
IV 106–9. Cf p 107n: "...the bishop
[Warburton] has ingeniously explained
the miraculous crosses which appeared
on the garments of the spectators...[as]
the natural effects of lightning"; p 108n:
"Warburton labours...to extort a con-
fession of the miracle from the mouths of
Julian and Libanius, and to employ the
evidence of a rabbi who lived in the
fifteenth century. Such witnesses can only
be received by a very favourable judge."
For C's reading of Warburton's *Julian.
Or a Discourse Concerning the Earth-
quake and Fiery Eruption which Defeated
That Emperor's Attempt to Rebuild the
Temple at Jerusalem* (1750) see *CN* III
3805–8.

93[2] Firedamp (a mixture of methane
and air), ignited at the flame of an open
lamp. Humphry Davy invented the
safety-lamp in 1815, at the request of the
mining industry, to prevent such ac-
cidental explosions.

93[3] C has confused Gibbon's argu-
ment. Gibbon (p 108) states that
Gregory Nazianzen published an account
of the miracle; at 109n he says that "Dr.
Lardner, perhaps alone of the Christian
critics, presumes to doubt the truth of this

94 II 351 | xv xliv

After having extolled the mighty acts which he pretends to have been performed by his gods and heroes many ages before, he [Julian] adds: JESUS has been famous these three hundred years past, for having persuaded people that he wrought miracles, without doing any thing worthy of notice during his life, unless the curing the blind and the lame, and exorcising those that were possessed with the devil in the little towns of Bethsaida and Bethany, be reckoned great actions. He *] plainly acknowledges the truth of these facts, after which it is of little importance whether he thinks them wonderful or contemptible.

* Unluckily both parties, Pagans & Christians, admitted the fact of each others' miracles—& the Pagans thought (& on their premises consequently enough) that they proved nothing on other side. M̶ Too much stress therefore must not be layed on these admissions. Men trouble themselves to seek for proofs only when the assumed facts appear impossible or wholly unaccountable—at least, highly improbable.

95 II 376 | xvi iii

[St Hilary, exiled by Valentinian,] published a treatise in writing, directed to all the Catholicks, both Bishops and people, wherein he displays all the artificies of Auxenius. He proves at first, that they ought not to be deceived by the specious title of union, and that the Church doth not stand in need of any temporal support...

Sᵗ Hilary like many other good men did not reflect, that ⟨when⟩ the inhabitants of a whole Empire took the name of christians, there must arise a National Church, which it is perhaps possible, indeed, to *conceive* so constructed, as that it might *contain* the church of Christ as a concentric Circle ⊚ —but cannot *be* that Church. It is this church, the Offspring of Human Law, that needs the support of human Powers.[1]

---

famous miracle.... The silence of Jerom would lead to a suspicion that the same story, which was celebrated at a distance, might be despised on the spot." Gibbon declines to believe "the specious and splendid miracle".

95[1] For a detailed exposition of the distinction between a National Church

and the Church of Christ see *C&S* (*CC*) esp 114–28 ("The Idea of the Christian Church"). In N 35 ff 44–44ᵛ (c 11 Nov 1827) (*CN* v) C wrote a note referring to "Fleury, Vol. II p. 376", the first paragraph of which is similar in wording to this annotation. See also **96** n 1, below.

96 II 377–8, pencil

You say JESUS CHRIST was born before the beginning of time; the
*] devil also was created before the beginning of time and ages.

* Hilary's angry zeal has here hurried him into very hazardous
theology. It may be true; but it requires ample exposition and very
subtle limitations in order not to convey falsehood. If the Devil was
created before all time, then not in time; then eternally—and an
eternal *creation* must either be generation, or emanation.[1] It did not
fall to the lot of all the ~~Orthodox~~ sainted Doctors to possess the
metaphysical depth and acumen of Dionysius of Alexandria, and
Athanasius. That some of the Fathers were Tritheists against their
Will, and spite of their most vehement disclaimings, it would be easy
to demonstrate.[2]

97 II 395, pencil | XVI XV

[St Gregory Nazianzen's funeral oration on St Caesarius and St
Gorgonia] St. Gregory his brother spoke his funeral oration, his
father and mother being present....St. Gorgonia their sister died
some time after, St. Gregory likewise made her funeral oration, where
describing her virtues, he sets a patern of Christian perfection to
married women. She was so extreamly reserved and modest, that she
thought much of the least smile; she mortified her eyes, her ears, and
all her senses....She prayed with fervour and attention, frequently
shed tears, was frequently upon her knees, fasted and watched often,

96[1] On the origin of evil, and the
"Devil...before all time", see BÖHME
165 and DONNE *Sermons* COPY A **2**. In N
35 f 44ᵛ (cited in **95** n 1, above) C said:
"...Hilary's Zeal against the disguised
Arianism of Auxentius has hurried him
into some hazardous positions—ex. gr.—
Auxentius had admitted that Christ was
begotten *before all time*—So was the
Devil, replies Hilary, created *before all
time*—then eternally—but an eternal
creation can only be generation or
emanation...." On emanation see
BÖHME **110** n 2.
96[2] In N 35 ff 44ᵛ–45 (*CN* v),
following directly upon the passage
quoted in n 1, above, C wrote a slightly
modified version of this annotation,
adding "our Sherlock" to those Fathers

who (unlike Dionysius and Athanasius)
were "Tritheists against their Will", and
concluding: "I affirm that the Man is a
Tritheist, who *in such a way* thinks of
Jesus Christ as true and entire God, that
his mind is not under the necessity.of
thinking at the same time of the Father
and of the H. Spirit. The Tri-unity is
intelligently confessed only where the
Idea, God, contains *distinct* ideas of the
Father, of the Son, and of the Spirit, yet
such that being distinct they are at the
same time inseparable, and after a
determinate and immutable Order.—But
alas! how can such a faith be expected,
when the mind is still ~~entangled~~ birdlimed
in the conception of negative Unity, and
mistakes this for *The One*...".

and was as constant in singing of Psalms.... Another time in a
distemper which the physicians judged desperate, she laid her head
upon the altar, and began to pray, crying out, and pouring forth a
flood of tears, of which mixt with what she could preserve of the
Antitypes of precious body or blood, that is of the Eucharist, she
made an ointment, and forthwith returned perfectly cured; this could
not have happened till after her baptism, since the Eucharist was only
administred to the faithful who had bccn baptized. Such was the
character of St. Gorgonia, who is commemorated by the Church on
the ninth of December.*

* These funeral Orations are valuable, and it would be worth while
to make a collections of those, that are extant, of different Fathers
ch[r]onologically*a* arranged. They supply important Data for a
History of the Progress of Superstition in the Christian Church. It
must have already reached to a fearful height, when a Man like Greg.
Naz. could relate of this Sacr. *Salve*-ation.[1]

98 II 403–4, pencil | XVI xxii

There had been at Corinth a dispute concerning the mystery of the
incarnation. Some said that the body of JESUS CHRIST was
consubstantial to the Word, pretending, that if it were not so, they
must admit of a quaternity instead of a Trinity. Whence it followed,
that the body of JESUS CHRIST was not taken from Mary, since it
was eternal as well as the Divine nature; or that the Divinity of the
Word had changed its nature in becoming flesh. Others fell into the
contrary extreme, and affirmed that JESUS CHRIST was a man
adopted to be the Son of GOD, and consequently like the other
prophets. That the Word of GOD was different from the CHRIST the
Son of Mary, who suffered. They who disputed upon these questions
were the disciples of Appollinarius; but he was not yet known to be
the author of these errors.

The misfortune of the Church has been, that none of the eminent
Nicene and Post-nicene Fathers, who treat of the Incarnation,

a Letter supplied by the editor

97[1] In N 35 f 45ᵛ (*CN* v) C noted:
"...a large portion of the ⟨Blame
respecting the⟩ superstitions & immor-
alities of the Christians from the third to
the 6ᵗʰ Century should be assigned to the
rapid and promiscuous Conversion of
the Empire, instead of the whole being
burthened on the Hierarchy...." On the
"causes of Superstition" see *CN* III 3372.
Cf **55** (at n 2), above.

explain what they mean by the *Body* of Christ. They uniformly speak of it, as a one fixed identity, in like manner as we speak of a Statue, the same in the component particles as well as in their relative position, this Year as in the year before. But how can this apply to the sensible *Body*, all the particles of which are in a continual flux, and the very arrangement different, in different periods of Life—in infancy, Childhood, Youth, &c!/[1]

Bp. Horsley seems to me (*Posthumous Sermons*) to have approached nearest to the truth;[2] and yet I questioned, whether his opinion would not be regarded by our Divines generally, as a dangerous Approximation to the Error of the *Docetæ*.[3]—By the bye, our "was made", is not a happy or a precise translation of εγενετο.[4]

---

99 II 405, pencil | XVI xxiii

...St. Athanasius inflicted the most severe penalties the Church could enjoin, on the governour of Libya, a man of a brutish temper, and wholly given up to cruelty and debauchery. St. Athanasius excommunicated him...to the end that the whole world might shun his communion. St. Basil answered...that this wretch would be cursed by all the faithful, and that no body would share with him, either as to fire or water, or be under the same roof with him....We see by this instance what were the consequences of excommunication at that time, even with regard to civil society.

98[1] On the identity of the body see BROOKE **24** and n 1.

98[2] Samuel Horsley *Nine Sermons* (1815) Sermon IV, which C had cited in C. BUTLER *Vindication* **1** at n 9, referring to the status of Christ's body after the resurrection. In pp 198–200 Horsley maintains that before the crucifixion Christ's body "was plainly the body of a mortal man".

98[3] Horsley, in the same sermon (p 198), remarks that "had his [Christ's] previous habits been as studiously observed" as in his appearances after the resurrection, "the error of the Docetae, who taught that he was a man in appearance only, might have been universal". Δοκηταί from δοκεῖν ("seem,

appear"), a name first applied by Serapion, bp of Antioch (190–203), to those who regarded the humanity and sufferings of Christ as apparent rather than real, largely on the basis of 1 John 4.1–3 and 2 John 7.

98[4] I.e. John 1.14: ὁ Λόγος σὰρξ ἐγένετο, the AV translation of which— "the Word was made flesh"—C said in *AR*, "is perhaps the best, that our language admits, but is still an inadequate translation." C then referred to an earlier comment in *AR*: "The Greek word ἐγένετο, unites in itself the two senses of *began to exist* and *was made to exist*. It exemplified the force of the *middle voice*, in distinction from the verb reflex." *AR* (1825) 380n, 16n. Cf **66** n 2, above.

Yes! and a fearful Precedent it hath proved: as Ireland can bear witness at this day[1]

100 II 406–8, pencil | XVI xxiv

[St Basil] required nothing more of the Macedonians, who were desirous of returning to the Church, than to confess the Nicene Creed, and to declare that they did not believe the Holy Ghost to be a creature; without obliging them expressly to affirm, that he is GOD. And himself in his writings and sermons forbore to call him formally GOD: although he used terms of the like signification, and proved his Divinity by unanswerable evidence....He saw that the Hereticks being protected by Valens, wanted only a pretence to turn the Bishops who were most zealous for the truth out of their Sees, himself more especially; and that the Eastern Church was full of *] division and faction; so that he reckoned that the most effectual method to preserve religion, was to procure unity and concord, using the weak with all possible indulgence...

*Q.y Had S[t] Basil secret doubts respecting the *personality* of the H. Spirit?[1] It looks very like it.—Thus he might safely deny the Holy Ghost to be a creature, and safely affirm the consubstantiality of the H. G. with the Father.[2] I myself entertain no doubt; but I confess, that after separating these texts in which the Holy Ghost is equivalent, in some to the divine influence, in others to the miraculous Gifts (Δυναμεῖς),[3] I cannot find any *decisive* passage in the New Testament, any text which *must* be so interpreted; tho' I find many, from which

99[1] For C on the effects of excommunication in Ireland see FITZGIBBON 1 and n 3.

100[1] In *CN* IV 5078 C noted: "...the Church itself by the distinction between the *begetting* of the Logos, the filial Deity, the Son, and the *Proceeding* of the Spirit from the Father and from the Son implies & as it were insinuates a *diff*erence, which Language did not supply the means of expressing—a difference, which might be *marked* by the term, the *personality* of the Son, and the *personëity* of the Holy Ghost...."

100[2] St Basil was dealing with the conservative section of the "Macedonian" sect who accepted the consubstantiality of the Son but rejected the divinity of the Holy Ghost, holding that the godhead was a dyad, and the Holy Ghost a creature. It was as a result of this controversy and the hesitation of most theologians, including St Basil, that the "Nicene Creed" of BCP affirms of the Holy Ghost "...who proceedeth from the Father and the Son, who with the Father and the Son together is worshipped and glorified...." as compared to the certainty of the Athanasian Creed "and these three are one" (cf **65**, above) and the brevity and inexplicitness of the original Nicene Creed of 325, "And [I believe] in the Holy Spirit".

100[3] Lit. "Powers". See e.g. John 20.22–3; Acts 2.4, 10.38; 1 Cor 12.8–11; Heb 2.4; 1 Thess 1.5.

the doctrine may, I think, be legitimately inferred.[4] Be this as it may, S[t] Basil's *Conduct* makes it evident, that the Church at large was not as clear on this point or as unanimous as on the distinct yet equal Divinity of the Son.

101   II 410, pencil | XVI xxviii

[The story of a rich woman whose son fell into a well while she was serving St Julian as a guest. She covered the well and showed no concern. When Julian ordered the well to be uncovered, they saw the child sitting on the water unhurt.]

The Mother's cool and easy behaviour is the greatest miracle (*?thumper?*) of this miraculous incident. Strange, that they *dared* parody the acts of our blessed Saviour in this way!

102   II 411, pencil

*] Theodoret, who records these wonders, had learnt them from Acatius, one of the saint's disciples.

* In the page before, Fleury asserts that Theodoret was *himself* an eye-witness of these Miracles!—

100[4] Perhaps Matt 28.19 (see BAXTER *Catholick Theologie* 7, EICHHORN *Neue Testament* COPY A 21, and cf 75 n 3, above); John 14.26 (which C considered "The strongest scripture argument for the personëity, and *distinct* personëity of the Holy Ghost. Yet there are difficulties...": N 48 f 45[v], c 19 Dec 1830); 15.26 (cf 66 n 2, above); or Rom 8.26. C rejected as an interpolation the overt trinitarian statement in 1 John 5.7: see H. COLERIDGE 3 and n 3.

CARL FRIEDRICH FLÖGEL
1729–1788

Geschichte der komischen Litteratur. 4 vols. Liegnitz & Leipzig 1784, 1785, 1786, 1787. 8°.

Harvard University (Houghton Library)

C's copy, taken from his library by RS, at Mrs C's suggestion in Dec 1813, for £1.8s. See *S Letters* (Curry) II 89. Autograph signature "Robert Southey" on the title-page of Vol I, and his Bewick bookplate on the title-page verso of Vol I. Bookplate of Harry Buxton Forman in all four volumes.

RS has written a series of page references and two short notes in pencil on a slip of paper now pasted to I ‾2; he has also written notes in pencil on II 387 and IV 173.

DATE. By 1813: dated in 37.

If this date is indeed in C's hand—and there is no palaeographical reason for doubting it—it is necessary to consider how the volumes could have been at Greta Hall in Dec 1813, yet bearing at least one note written by C in 1813 after he had paid his last visit to the Lakes in Feb–Mar 1812. C was lecturing on the drama in London in May–Aug 1812, and again in Nov 1812–Jan 1813 at a time when he was consorting with actors in the production of *Remorse* (see 37 and n 1, below); in Sept 1813 he was talking about comic drama (*CL* III 441). RS was in London from late Aug until mid-Nov 1813, intermittently in C's company, though with increasing irritation and disapproval. *S Letters* (Curry) II 77–9, 81–2, 85–6, 88. C had said that he intended to return with RS to Keswick, bringing the Morgans with him, as soon as he had settled the Morgans' financial and domestic affairs. *S Letters* (Curry) II 65, 86; *WL* (*M* 2) II 127, 143. But in late Oct 1813 C moved the Morgans to Bristol and nothing more was said about his going to Keswick. On 25 Sept 1813 C had told Daniel Stuart that he was "compelled to sell my Library", and did in fact pawn a few books and other items at this time. *CL* III 442, 455. It appears then that RS took these 4 vols back to Greta Hall with him, and that his purchase of FLÖGEL and others of C's books in Dec 1813 may have been by agreement with C in London in fulfilling part of his need to realise some ready cash from his books.

COEDITOR. Hans Eichner. Textus translation is adapted and corrected from Buxton Forman's version in *Cosmopolis* IX (1898) 635–48, X (1898) 52–67, with editorial additions.

1 I 261 | Zweyte Abhandlung II

Johann Moritz Schwager...liess in den dritten Theil der Berlinischen Monathschrift (1783.) eine Erzählung einrücken, in welcher zwey Schuster eine neue Messiasgeschichte anspinnen. Dabey fiel Herrn *Gedicken* die Frage ein: woher kommt es, dass bey keinem Gewerbe so viele über ihre Sphäre hinausvernünftelnde Köpfe sich finden, als unter den *Schustern*?...Es ist nicht leicht eine Wissenschaft oder Fakultät, in der sich nicht von Zeit zu Zeit ein Schuster berühmt gemacht. Der Hang zum Speculiren kann nicht blos aus der sitzenden Lebensart der Schuster erklärt werden, denn diese haben sie mit vielen andern Gewerben gemein, wo dergleichen Erscheinungen doch seltner sind. Doch macht sie diese Lebensart besonders zur Schwärmerey empfänglich....Die besondre Manier der Arbeit beym Handwerk der Schuster scheint diese Leute zum düstern Nachdenken und hypochondrischen Grübeleyen zu stimmen.

[Johann Moritz Schwager...had a story inserted in the Third Part of the *Berlinische Monathschrift* (1783), in which two shoemakers made up a story of a new Messiah. At this the question occurred to Herr *Gedicke*—why is it that in no other trade as among shoemakers are so many people found engaged in a [kind of] thinking that is above their *station*?...It is not easy to find a faculty or science in which from time to time a shoemaker has not made himself famous. This tendency to speculation cannot be explained merely by the shoemakers' sedentary mode of life, for they have this in common with many other trades in which yet such a thing is rarer. Yet this mode of life makes them prone to enthusiasm....The particular nature of the work in the craft of shoemakers seems to dispose these people towards gloomy speculations and hypochondriac broodings.]

To this may be added, that there are more Shoemakers than any other Handicraftsmen.[1] Next in number are the Taylors: and these have been, perhaps, proportionately prolific of Geniuses, Enthusiasts, Fanatics, &c[2]

[1] For C on shoemakers and genius see BÖHME 9 n 2. See also 2 and nn, below.

[2] C seems not to have left any list of tailor-geniuses. A few English instances that might have come to his mind are: James Carter (1792–1853), author of *Lectures on Taste* and *A Lecture on the Primitive State of Man*; Robert Hill (1699–1777), the first Hebraist of his time, author of *Christianity the True Religion* (1775); Francis Place (1771–1854), radical reformer, author of tracts and newspaper articles and of *The Principles of Population* (1822)—see LS (*CC*) xl; Benjamin Robins (1707–51), author of *New Principles of Geometry* (1742) and compiler of Anson's *Voyage* (1748); John Speed (c 1552–1629), historian, antiquary, and geographer, author of *Theatre of the Empire of Great Britaine* and *The History of Great Britaine* (both 1611), *Asia* and *America* (both 1626)—see CN III 4395n; John Stow (c

2 I 262

Derjenige, welcher den Ewigen Juden zum erstenmal in die Welt geschickt, hat ihn vielleicht nicht ohne Ursache zu einem Schumacher gemacht. Wie viel Lermen der bekannte Jakob Böhm erreget, braucht allhier nicht erst erzählt zu werden... so waren die vornehmsten in der Quakerischen Gemeine zu Danzig zwey Schuster.

[He who first sent the Wandering Jew into the world made him, perhaps, not unreasonably, a shoemaker. Of the stir made by the well-known Jakob Böhme we need not make mention here... two shoemakers were the most eminent men of the Quaker community in Danzig.]

Hans Sachs.[1]
George Fox, the Founder of the Quakers.[2]
Bloomfield.[3]
Gifford.[4]

3 II 4 | Erstes Hauptstück "Von der Satire" x

Der Kaiser Augustus spottete in solchen Versen des Pollio; der aber weiter nichts antwortete, als: ich mag gegen den nicht schreiben, *] der mich verbannen Kann. [Footnote:] *Macrob. Saturnal. Lib. II. c. 4. Non est facile in eum scribere, qui potest proscribere.*

1525–1605), chronicler and antiquary, editor of Chaucer (1561), author of *Summarie of Englyshe Chronicles* (1565), *The Anneles of England* (1592); John Woolman (1720–72), Quaker abolitionist, whose *Journal* both C and Lamb admired.

For C on the peculiar contribution made to "speculative science" by "the illiterate" and the simple"—including Böhme, Johann Tauler, and George Fox—and the reason why "All without distinction were branded as fanatics and phantasts", see *BL* ch 9 (*CC*) I 146–51, esp 149–50.

2[1] Hans Sachs (1494–1576), shoemaker of Nuremberg, wrote many *Meistergesänge*, *Spruchgedichte*, and *Swänke* (Merry Tales), and some 200 plays in verse. For C's reading of Sachs's *Die ungleichen Kinder Eva* see **46** and n 1, below. See also SACHS *Gedichte Fabeln und gute Schwenk* (Nuremberg 1781).

2[2] George Fox (1624–91), apprenticed to a cobbler, became a candidate for C's projected "Vindiciae Heterodoxae": see e.g. *CN* II 2269 and BÖHME headnote.

2[3] Robert Bloomfield (1766–1823), shoemaker, author of *The Farmer's Boy* (1800), of which poem some 26,000 copies are said to have sold in less than three years. C and WW saw extracts of the poem in Sept 1800 and were "pleased very much" with what they had read. *CL* I 623; cf II 716. By Jul 1802 C had chosen Bloomfield as one of the figures to be presented in his proposed 2-volume collection of essays and selections. *CL* II 829, 847; see also *CL* II 913, *CRB* I 28.

2[4] William Gifford (1756–1826), shoemaker's apprentice for a time, satirist— *Baviad* (1794), *Maeviad* (1795), editor of the *Anti-Jacobin* (1797–8)—first editor of *Quarterly Review* (1809–24), whom John Taylor Coleridge succeeded for less than a year.

[In verses of this kind [i.e. Fescennine] the Emperor Augustus ridiculed Pollio, to which his only reply was: "I must not write anything against a man who can banish me." [Footnote:] Macrobius *Saturnalia* 2.4. "It is not easy to write against a man who can write you off."]

* N.B. a model, un morceau precieuse,[1] of flat Translation, or rather an instructive example how to *traduce* an Author—as the Dutch would say, the meaning is *overset* in Teutch![2]—der mich (oder, mein Leben) verschreiben kann.—[3]

4 II 12

Horaz tadelt auch die Prahlerei an ihm [Lucil], dass er sich gerühmt *] bald aus dem Stegereif und ohn ein Bein zu strecken, Zween Bogen voller Nichts mit Jauchzen auszuhecken. [Footnote:] *Horat. Lib. I. Sat. 4.*

Nam fuit hoc vitiosus: in hora saepe ducentos,
Ut magnum, versus dictabat, stans pede in uno.

[Horace also berates him [Lucilius] for his conceit in maintaining that, extempore and without stretching a leg, he could exultantly hatch two sheets full of nothing. [Footnote:] Horace *Satires* 1.4.[9–10]. "Herein lay his fault: often in an hour, as though a great exploit he would dictate 200 lines while standing, as they say, on one foot." (Tr H. R. Fairclough, LCL 1926)]

* another specimen of *Traduction!*[1] And mark the exquisite Congruity of the Metaphor in the German " ⟨Bald⟩ *aus dem Stegereifes*, und ohn ein *Bein zu strecken, Zween Bogen* voller Nichts mit Jauchzen auszuhecken."[2] Bravo!—Verse too: yea, Rhymes!

5 II 16–17

Hatten denn die Griechen sonst keine Satire ausser der dramatischen im Satyrspiele, die mit der Römischen mehr Aehnlichkeit hatte? doch

3[1] A slip for *un morceau précieux*—"a prize bit".

3[2] "Teutch" = *Deutsch*, German. C ascribes this multilingual pun on *traduire* and *übersetzen* (to translate) to RS in RITSON *Select Collection of English Songs* (3 vols 1783) I x: "...M[ilton] had been *overset* ("overgeset") into Dutch, and traduced (traduit) in French." The pun is well-known to Italian schoolchildren: *traduttore/traditore*—translator/ traitor. See also **4**, below, and cf AURELIUS 29.

3[3] By substituting *verschreiben* for Flögel's *verbannen* C has restored the Latin pun (as given in textus tr).

4[1] " Traducing/Translation " — but see **3** n 2, above.

4[2] The incongruities identified by C's underlining are: "straight *from the stirrup*" for Horace's *in hora* (in an hour); "*without stretching one leg*" for *stans pede in uno* (standing on one foot); "*Zween Bogen*" (two sheets) for *ducentos...versus* (200 lines); *auszuhecken* (hatch out, contrive) for *dictabat* (dictated). Also Flögel transforms Horace's criticism of Lucilius into Lucilius' own boast, adding gratuitously the words "full of nothing".

ehe ich die Frage beantworte, will ich die Beweisgründe der gegenseitigen Meinung anführen. Man sagt nämlich:
1) Die Satyrspiele waren dramatisch, und die lateinischen Satiren nicht.

2) Die Griechen nennten diese Schauspiele *Satyrica*, nämlich *dramata* oder *Satyri*, von den darin vorkommenden Satyrn; die Lateiner aber ihre Spottgedichte *Satiras* von *Satur*.

3) Die Griechen brauchten in ihren satyrischen Schauspielen gemeiniglich jambische oder trochäische Verse, die Lateiner aber heroische, ausgenommen Ennius und (zuweilen)* Lucilius.

[Did the Greeks then have, apart from their satyr-plays, no satire more like the Roman? Yet before I answer this question, I wish to present the arguments for the opposing view. It is said that:
1) The satyr-plays were dramatic, and the Latin satires were not.

2) The Greeks called these plays *satyrica*—that is, *dramata* or *satyri*, after the satyrs appearing in them—but the Latins called their mocking poems *satirae*, from *satur*.

3) The Greeks commonly used iambic or trochaic verses in their satyric plays, but the Latins—except for Ennius and ⟨(sometimes)⟩ Lucilius—used heroic verse.]

* for out of 30 Books of Satires by Lucilius 21 were in heroic, i.e. hexameter, Verse.[1] But the whole Controversy is too silly to deserve a Critique. Who in his senses ever doubted that the Greeks, or indeed that any other nation, had satirical Poems, both dramatic & undramatic?[2] Surely, neither Horace or Quintilian.[3]—And what Scholar will not rest satisfied with their joint assertion, that the

5[1] Flögel gives the information that Lucilius wrote thirty books, the first twenty-one entirely in hexameters, in II 9–10, adding that about 1500 lines of Lucilius "have survived, quoted mainly by the grammarian Nonius". The characteristic metre of Roman satire is dactylic hexameter. See **8** and n 3, below.

5[2] Later satyr-plays—only Euripides *Cyclops* has survived—seem to have been cheerful and amusing, not dominantly satirical except when making fun of the mythology that tragedians took seriously. Horace explicitly states (*Satires* 1.4.1–7) that the element of invective in old comedy—Eupolis, Cratinus, Aristophanes, and others—was imitated by Lucilius, with only the metre changed (Flögel II 14); but see n 3, below. The

undramatic Greek satirical poems are listed in **8** textus, below.

5[3] Horace says that Lucilius (or Ennius) was the "originator of a poetry unknown to the Greeks" (*Satires* 1.10.66) and that Lucilius was "first to compose verses in this manner" (*Satires* 2.1.63). See Flögel II 13, 10. The source of the controversy that C treats quizzically is rather Quintilian's statement: "Satira quidem tota nostra est" (Satire indeed is all ours). *Institutio oratoria* 10.1.93 (Flögel II 13). C here outlines a common-sense solution that is consistent with (e.g.) Dryden's interpretation of Quintilian, in his "Dedication" to his tr of Juvenal (C had it e.g. in ANDERSON XII 650): "satire was wholly of Latin growth, and not transplanted from Athens to Rome".

particular *Form* of Poetry, called Satire, did not exist among the Greeks. Lampoons in abundance; but no Poem formed on the same plan as Juvenal's, &c.[4]

6 II 17

[Footnote *f*:] *Diomedes col.* 483. *Satyra autem dicta, sive a Satyris, quod similiter in hoc carmine ridiculos* [for *ridiculae*] *res pudendaeque dicuntur, quae velut a Satyris proferuntur et fiunt; sive a Satyra lance, quae referta variis multisque primitiis, in sacro apud priscos diis inferebat; vel a copia et saturitate, res Satyra vocabatur.*

[*Diomedes* col 483. "But it is called Satire either from the Satyrs, because in this sort of verse ridiculous and immodest things are said, spoken, and acted as though by Satyrs; or from the Satyric dish that was carried, full of many and varied first-fruits, in the worship of the ancient gods; or it was called 'sated', from plenty and satiety."]

Perhaps, post-prandial, or after-dinner Verses—perhaps, *intentionally* a title equivalent or rather multivocal was given: because the Poem comprized all three, & the word might mean all 3.—[1]

7 II 18–19

Vielleicht wäre man dem Zweck und der Beantwortung der Frage näher kommen, wenn man alle Arten der griechischen Satire mit den Römischen arten verglichen, und daraus die Sache entschieden hätte.... Die Griechen hatten

1) *Epische Satiren*, wohin der *Margites* des Homers gehört.... Denn dass *Müller* sagt, der Margites des Homers wäre mehr einem Pasquille als einer Satire gleich, weil er nicht Laster, sondern eine Person mit Namen heftig angriffe; entscheidet zum Ursprunge der Satire von den Römern gar nichts....

5[4] The difficulty of defining satire, whether Roman or modern, tends to intensify the problem. It can be said that satire now mostly holds up to ridicule folly or wickedness, whether personal, social, or political; but Roman satire had a wider scope, ranging from lampoon (personal invective) to light-hearted snatches of autobiography. Roman satire developed in two streams: Lucilius, Horace, Persius, and Juvenal, as discussed here by C; and in a form consisting of prose interspersed with verse, confessedly modelled on the Greek Menippus, handed on through Varro, Seneca, Petronius, and the emperor Julian. What the Romans undeniably had, which the Greeks did not have, was both a word to include these miscellaneous writings under a single term and a considerable surviving corpus of such writings. Since Quintilian's account of satire also applies to Varro, his dictum cannot be taken as referring to "form" in a narrow sense.

6[1] The original meaning is now thought to be "miscellany", but the concept of satire in later Roman times was perhaps influenced by all three interpretations. For "multivocal" see also HOOKER **26** and n 1.

2) Die *lyrische Satire des Archilochus* hat Horatz in einigen seiner Oden und Epoden unstreitig nachgeahmt.

3) *Dramatische Satire* hatten die Griechen vor den Römern in ihren satyrischen Schauspielen, der alten und mittlern Komödie...

4) Hatten die Griechen auch *didaktische Satire?* die *Sillen* waren nichts anders, nach den wenigen Nachrichten zu urtheilen, welche uns die Alten davon hinterlassen haben.

[Perhaps we should approach our purpose and answer the question more closely, if we compared all the kinds of Greek satire with the Roman kinds, and decided the matter from that.... The Greeks had

1) *Epic satires*, to which Homer's *Margites* belongs.... For Müller's assertion that Homer's *Margites* is more like a lampoon than a satire—on the grounds that he attacked, not a vice but a person by name—decides nothing at all with regard to the origin of Roman satire....

2) It is indisputable that Horace in some of his Odes and Epodes imitated the *lyric satire of Archilochus*.

3) The Greeks had *dramatic satire* before the Romans in their satyric plays, old and middle comedy...

4) Did the Greeks also have *didactic satire?* The Silloi were nothing other than this, to judge by the few accounts of it that the ancients have bequeathed to us.]

We have in our own language a case in point, & compleatly conclusive of the Question.—Chaucer is full of exquisite Satyr— Pierce Plowman is a didactic Satire = Σιλλος[1]—Dramatic Satires, as the four Ps,[2] & 50 others—Lampoons of all kinds in old Skelton[3]—& yet, notwithstanding ⟨all⟩ this, Donne & Hall called

7[1] Σίλλοι (lit. "squinting [verses]") were mocking poems, mainly in dactylic hexameters, written first by Xenophanes, who gives good-humoured glimpses of social life and attacks such abuses as excessive veneration of athletes. His admirer, Timon of Phlius, known as the Sillographer, parodied Homer in his criticism of philosophers and his contemporaries in general, and took Xenophanes as his guide to the underworld.

C's description of *Piers Plowman* would be an accurate account based on the selective version of the B text current in C's day, consisting of the Prologue and the first seven *Passus* ("The Vision"), which deals with social matters. Not until Skeat's parallel edition of all three texts (or versions) in 1886 was the whole of the three versions, with the treatment of religious matters, available to scholars. Authorship is now confidently, but not definitively, ascribed to William Langland (c 1330–c 1400).

7[2] John Heywood (c 1497–c 1578) *The Playe called foure PP; a newe and a very merry interlude of a Palmer, a Pardoner, a Potycary, a Pedlar* (1544). This play was included in R. Dodsley *A Select Collection of Old Plays* (12 vols 1744) Vol I: cf DONNE *Poems* 3 n 1. See also **38**, below.

7[3] John Skelton (c 1460–1529), who used a distinctive irregular metre in short rhyming lines now called "Skeltonics", the force of which is best seen in his political and clerical satires, especially *Colyn Cloute* (1522), *Speke Parrot* (1521), and *Why Come Ye Nat to Court?* (1522). For C's "Skeltoniad (to be read in the Recitative *Lilt*)"—later entitled *The Two Round Spaces on the Tombstone*—attack-

themselves and are admitted by all their Posterity to have be⟨en⟩, the first Writers of *Satires* in English.[4]—

S. T. C.

8 II 24–5

Er [Horatz] hat die Satire des Lucils verfeinert und veredelt; seine wesentliche Veränderung bestand darinn, dass er der Satire ein gewisses bestimmtes Sylbenmaass, nämlich das heroische gab. ...Seine Manier ist nicht so heftig und beisend als des Lucils, der gleichsam mit blossen Schwerdt auf das Laster losgieng...Ja wenn er von Lastern spricht, so zeigt er sie gemeiniglich nur von der lächlerlichen Seite; also ganz anders als Juvenal...Diesen Charakter hat auch Persius der Horatzischen Satire schon in alten Zeiten beigelegt.

[Horace polished and ennobled the satire of Lucilius; his real change was that he gave to satire a positive and definite metre, viz. the heroic....His manner is not so virulent and biting as that of Lucilius, who attacked vice, as it were, with a naked sword...When Horace speaks about vice he generally exposes only its ludicrous side—quite unlike Juvenal in this...In ancient times Persius had already attributed this character to the Horatian satire.]

Whoo! had not Lucilius done this in 21 books out of 30?[1]—And are not many of Horace's Epodes Iambic & Lyric Satires?[2] No! Horace *invented* a style & metre, "sermoni propiora", of which no Imitation is extant.[3] The style of Persius is half sophistic, i.e. abrupt, jagged,

---

ing Sir James Mackintosh, see *CL* I 632 (9 Oct 1800), *PW* (EHC) I 353–5. In SHAKESPEARE *The Works* (8 vols 1773) [COPY A] III 353–5 C spoke of Skelton's *Philip Sparrow* as "an exquisite & original Poem" (also in *Sh C* I 128). Skelton's poems were not included in *B Poets* but were in CHALMERS (1810) Vol II.

7[4] Joseph Hall (1574–1656), in his Prologue to Bk I (lines 1–4) of *Virgidemiarum, sixe bookes...of satyrs* (1597), claimed to be the first English versifier to attempt systematic imitations of the formal Roman satirists (though the claim was challenged by his contemporaries); he is acknowledged to have introduced Juvenalian satire into English. Donne's *Satyres*, showing the influence of Horace, Persius, and Juvenal, were greatly admired by Ben Jonson and aroused C's

enthusiasm when he first encountered them in c 1796. See also DONNE *Poems* **36** n 2.

8[1] See **5** and n 1, above.

8[2] Horace's *Epodes*, esp 3–6, 8, 10, 12, 17, involve personal invective. But C seems to be going back on what he says in **5** and **7**, above: these *Epodes* could be described as lampoons, and in a Greek—not a Roman—kind. See **7** textus.

8[3] For Horace's description of his style in the *Satires* as "closer to [common] speech (or to prose)" see **10** textus, below. This phrase had earlier provided Lamb with a pun to mock some of C's solemn early poetry: see DYER *Poems* **1** n 1. For Horace's metre in the *Satires* see also **10**, below. C has here shifted his attention from Horace's *Epodes* (iambic and lyric) to the *Satires* (in dactylic hexameter).

thorny; & half declamatory—: & the metre corresponds. Juvenal again is altogether rhetorical, a flow of impassioned Declamation: and the correspondent metre is as unlike Persius, and Horace, as their Schemes of metre are unlike each other.[4] All three wrote Hexameters, it is true; & so did Shakespear, Milton, & Young all three write *blank Verse* in Lines of ten syllables![5] But o the asinine luxuriance of Ear that does not perceive that they are 3 perfectly distinct & different forms of metre & rhythm. Perhaps, the Horatian Hexameter may be compared to the blank Verse of Massinger, the Persian to that of Young, the Juvenalian to Cowper's.—[6]

9 ii 25

Seine [Horatzes] Sittenlehre ist lauter und rein, und aus der besten Quelle geschöpft; doch sind auch unreine Dinge hier und da mit untergemischt, welche schon Quintilian zu seiner Zeit nich erklären mochte. [Footnote:] *Quintil. Lib. I. c. 13. Horatium in quibusdam nolim interpretari.*

[Horace's moral teaching is pure and unsullied, and drawn from the best source; yet improprieties are intermixed here and there, which Quintilian even in his time did not care to explain. [Footnote:] Quintilian 1.13: "In certain passages I should prefer not to explain Horace."]

But does Q. here refer to the *Satyrs* of Horace? Why, not to his Epodes?[1]

10 ii 26–7

Der Ausdruck in seinen [Horatzes] Satiren ist nicht hoch, wie in den Oden, sondern deutlich und natürlich, wie man im gemeinen Leben

8[4] C's comparison of the style of three great Roman satirists, which does not follow Flögel, is entirely just and not unconventional. As his annotations on Donne, Jonson, and Beaumont and Fletcher show, C was much aware of the interaction between metrics and the strong meaningful delivery of verse. See **10**, below. For C's copy of the Casaubon ed of Persius see PERSIUS *Satirarum liber* (1647).

8[5] For C on varieties of English blank verse see BEAUMONT & FLETCHER COPY B **10** and cf **28, 41**; see also n 6, below. On Young's blank verse see ANDERSON COPY A **11** n 1. There is an important long

note on English prosody in TEGNÉR and in N Q ff 77–75 (*CN* v).

8[6] For C on the blank verse of Massinger see BEAUMONT & FLETCHER COPY B **10, 28, 41**, DONNE *Poems* 2 n 2; of Young, see n 5, above; of Cowper, see ANDERSON COPY B **34** n 1, BARCLAY COPY A 1 n 4.

9[1] The *Epodes*, which include lampoons (see **8** n 2, above), are often coarse and bitter in tone—see esp 8 and 12; the *Satires* (see esp 1.4, 10 and 2.1) discuss the *nature* of satire. Quintilian (1.8.6) is indeed speaking not of the *Satires*, but of the *Epodes* and what lyric poems are suitable for boys to read in school.

redet.... Daher will er auch in dieser Absicht nicht einmal unter die Dichter gezählt werden. [Footnote:] *Horat. Lib. I. Sat. 4. v. 39.*

> *Primum ego me illorum dederim quibus esse poetas*
> *Excerpam numero; neque enim concludere versum*
> *Dixeris esse satis; neque si quis scribat, uti nos,*
> *Sermoni propiora, putes hunc esse poetam.*

...Seine Hexameter sind lange nicht so wohlklingend als die Versarten in seinen Oden...

[The expression in Horace's *Satires* is not elevated, as in the *Odes*, but clear and natural, as one speaks in ordinary life....It is therefore also in this respect that he refuses even to allow himself to be counted among the poets. [Footnote:] Horace *Satires* 1.4.39–42: "First of all I shall except myself from the list of those whom I would grant to be poets: for you would not say that it is enough to confine a verse within (metrical) limits, nor would you consider any one a poet if, like myself, he were to write in a manner closer to prose."...His hexameters are not nearly so melodious as the verse in his *Odes*.]

Horace's Satires alone would suffice to prove, that the Romans did not recite Verses by scansion—else, how could they be distinguished so widely from the more poetic Hexameter. Read scanningly; & you will find it difficulty*a* to distinguish Virgil from Ovid—not to speak of the destruction of all appropriate emphasis. But this is a most obscure Subject. I incline to the opinion, that the mode of reading varied with the nature of the Poem: & that in some, as the Lyric, for instance, the metre was more *humoured* than in others (even as in the Anapestic & the Hudibrastic)[1] but in none *wholly* per scansionem.[2]

11 II 29

Noch seltsamer ist der Einfall des sonst so gelehrten *Erasmus von Rotterdam*, wenn er an dem Horatz auszusetzen scheint, es habe seine Schreibart gar nicht die Gestalt und das Ansehn der Schreibart des Cicero.

a A slip for "difficult"

10[1] I.e. in the manner of Butler's *Hudibras*, for which see **11** and n 2, below.
10[2] "According to scansion." Cf e.g. DONNE *Poems* 1 and n 1. This whole matter is still an obscure subject. The metrical ictus and the word-accent tend to conflict at the beginnings of lines and to coincide at the ends of lines—at least in dactylic hexameters.

[Still stranger is the notion of the otherwise so learned *Erasmus of Rotterdam*, when he appears to find fault with Horace because his style had not at all the form and appearance of Cicero's.]

But was not this Irony? Surely. It was the very purpose of Erasmus to ridicule the Pedants, who would admit no style as good which was not *Ciceronian*.[1] Even as if I should with mock gravity, & in the character of a modern Reviewer, speak of Butler as altogether *un Miltonic* in his metre & diction.[2]

S. T. C.

11A II 37

[Footnote:] *Erasmus Ep. 1010 . . . Est omino liberale quoddam jocandi genus; est et perpetua quaedam orationis jucunditas, quae virum bonum at] non dedeceat, si in loco adhibeatur; et in Seneca saepe cachinnos sentias potius, quam risum.*[1]

[There is such a thing as a well-bred kind of pleasantry, and also a continuously witty style of writing not unfitting to a gentleman on appropriate occasions; *and* ["but"] one feels that Seneca calls forth guffaws rather than laughter.]

11B II 113 | XI

[Flögel quotes from the *Zodiacus vitae* ascribed to Marcellus Palingenius Stellatus; Virgo [Lyons 1566] p 164 v 4:]

quæque?][1] *Et rura et silvae infames, urbs quoque lupanar.*

[Both country and woods are vicious, *also* the city is a brothel.]

12 II 147

Lelio Capilupi. Ein lateinischer Dichter aus Mantua, der sich besonders wegen seiner virgilianischen Centonen berühmt gemacht hat. . . . Sein *Cento* über den Ursprung, das Leben und den Gottesdienst der Mönche und der gegen das Frauenzimmer sind

11[1] The Erasmus passage is not traced: Flögel refers, apparently incorrectly, to *Dialogus Ciceronianus* p 147. C, however, is correct in his account of Erasmus' attack on the Renaissance idol, Cicero.
11[2] But Butler and Milton do not provide an exact parallel. Horace was a great poet; Cicero was a great orator and prose writer, but a lamentable poet— as indeed Erasmus reminds us in *Dialogus Ciceronianus*. Nevertheless, Butler's

Hudibras is written in tetrameter couplets, uses unadorned diction, and is *sui generis*.
11A[1] Both the Leyden 1703 ed of Erasmus' letters cited by Flögel and the *Opus epistolarum Erasmi Roterodami* ed P. S. and H. M. Allen (Oxford 1906–) VIII 34 read "at", as C recommends. In Flögel's text "et" is probably a misprint.
11B[1] C's correction restores the integrity of the hexameter. The revision reads "and every city a brothel".

bittre Satiren.... Die Satire auf die Frauenzimmer gehört unter die anzüglichsten und ist dabei sehr schmutzig. Daher weiss ich nicht, wie *Toscanus*, der diese Satire drucken liess, sagen kann, er hätte alles unzüchtige herausgeworfen, und nichts darinn gelassen, was frommen und ehrbaren Ohren unanständig wäre. [Footnote:] Nur eine Probe, ob mein Urtheil falsch ist:

> *Sed fugite, o miseri, fugite hinc, latet anguis in herba.*
> *Viperam inspirans animam, lasciva puella*
> *Cum dabit amplexus, atque oscula dulcia figet*
> *Nuda genu, nodoque sinus collecta fluentes*
> *Vos agitate fugam: direptis crura cothurnis*
> *Attrectare nefas, talis se se halitus atris*
> *Faucibus effundens nares contingit odore.*
> *Turbidus hic coeno vastaque voragine gurges*
> *Pestiferas aperit fauces, furor impius intus*
> *Pallentesque habitant morbi sub rupe cavata,*
> *Quo lati ducunt aditus, nemus imminet umbra*
> *Desuper horrenti....*

[*Lelio Capilupi*. A Latin poet from Mantua, who made himself famous especially for his Virgilian *Centos*.... His *Cento* on the origin, life, and worship of the monks, and the one against women are bitter satires.... The *Satire on Women* belongs among the most charming, and is at the same time very obscene. Hence I do not know how *Toscanus*, who printed this satire, can say he had rejected everything indecent and left in nothing that was disgusting to pious and virtuous ears. [Footnote:] Just one sample, to test whether my judgement is false: "But flee, unhappy men, flee from here; a snake lurks in the grass. When the lustful woman, breathing viperous breath, embraces you and presses sweet kisses upon you, bare-kneed, her flowing robes girded in a knot, haste then to flee: to take off her buskins and fondle her legs is forbidden, such an exhalation pours from the dark gulf and offends the nostrils with its odour. Here an abyss turbid with filth and vast whirlpool opens the noxious defile; a foul fury and pale diseases dwell within the hollow rock, to which broad ways lead; a grove looms above with horrid shade...."]

It is plain, that Flögel would not have done, what Toscanus did, however imperfectly; for he has taken care to give as much & wide Publicity, as in him lay, to the precious Gleanings of the Filth-harvest. The truth is, that such passages can injure no one's morals. If the Reader's mind is tolerably pure, they can only affect his Stomach: if capable of deriving pleasure from the Perusal, why what harm does a Dung-yard do the Hog, already coated with filth?[1]—S. T. C.—

12[1] For C on the moral effect of reading Richardson and Fielding see FIELDING *Tom Jones* 4.

13 II 161

[*Pietro Paolo*] *Vergerio* hat eine Menge satirischer Schriften gegen die römische Hierarchie geschrieben, nachdem er von dieser Kirche abgetreten.... Ich will nur eine einzige Stelle in der Anmerkung anführen, woraus man die Heftigkeit seiner Schreibart beurtheilen kann. [Footnote:] In dem *Postremus Catalogus Haereticorum. p. 2. 3. Vix ulla fuit unquam crassior fabula, et nocentior Ecclesiae Dei impostura, quam quae de stigmatibus Franciscanis Papistae, ut adimerent Christo gloriam confinxerunt.—Quis vero dicendus fuerit intolerabilis error, quae haeresis infanda, si ea non est, quae Filii Dei, Domini nostri Iesu Christi praeciosissima vulnera habet eodem numero et loco, quo fabulosa et male dicta Francisci stigmata? Proh, inauditam blasphemiam ac scelus!*

[[Pietro Paolo] *Vergerio*... wrote a mass of satirical works against the Roman hierarchy, after he left this Church.... I will quote in the note only one single passage, from which one can judge his violent style of writing. [Footnote:] In the *Latest Catalogue of Heretics* pp 2–3: "There has scarcely ever been a grosser fiction nor an imposture more harmful to the Church of God than that about the stigmata of St Francis, concocted by the Papists in order to detract from the glory of Christ. What error shall we be able to call intolerable, what heresy abominable, if not that which makes the most precious wounds of the Son of God, our Lord Jesus Christ, the same in number and position as the fabled and accursed stigmata of St Francis? Shame on the unheard-of blasphemy and wickedness!"]

Surely, no true *Christian*, among the Protestants at least, will deem this passage vehement beyond the occasion. The Liber Conformitatum in its original form was indeed "inaudita Blasphemia ac Scelus."[1]

14 II 189

Metu seditionum terrendos esse principes. Melanch. Epist. CVII. p. 134. Bayle Diction. Illyricus. [Flögel continues: "It was very wrong of Flacius Illyricus to maintain the dangerous principle that princes must be kept in a state of apprehension by the fear of insurrection."]

13[1] The "occasion", not explained by Flögel, was the publication of the *Flosculi* (*Little Flowers of St Francis*). C reasonably assumes that it was the *Liber conformitatum* [*vitae beati Francisci ad vitam Jesu Christi*] (1510 and later eds) by de' Rinonichi of Pisa. This was assailed by Erasmus Alber in *Der*

Barfüsser Münche Eulenspiegel und Alcoran (1st ed 1542). Both these and associated works are discussed by Flögel (III 275–93). For a similar example of Protestant objection to the raising of saints too near to equality with Christ see FLEURY **50** and n 1.

["By the fear of insurrection princes should be frightened (i.e. kept in a state of apprehension)." Melanchthon Letter 107 in Bayle's *Dictionary* p 134 sv Illyricus.]

Did Fl. Ill. mean more by this than the Legislature of G. Britain when it made it treason to the State to assert ~~the~~ *unconditionally* the criminality of all resistance, or the duty of passive Obedience, to the first magistrate: let him tyrannize as he would?—[1]

15 II 336–7, pencil | xiv

...allein er [Sir Thomas More] beschrieb einen Staat, der nirgends existirte, welches auch der Name *Utopia* anzeigt, welches eigentlich *] *Nirgendsheim* (von griechischen οὐδεὶς) bedeutet.

[...Sir Thomas More described a state that nowhere existed, as the name itself, *Utopia*, indicates—which (from the Greek οὐδεὶς) really means *Nowhereland*.]

* I have suspected that Flögel quotes Greek without understanding it. Β for ουδεις, I guess, ου τοπος (no place) must have been intend[ed];[a] but surely ευτοπια (regio beata) is the obvious etymology.[1]

S. T. C.

16 II 346, pencil

[Flögel lists and describes the works of John Donne, including:] 2) *Ignatius his Conclave*: or, his Inthronisation in a late Election in Hell: wherin many things are mingled by way of Satyr. Concerning the Disposition of Iesuites. The Creation of a new Hell, the establishing of a Church in the Moone.... I believe, that ~~is~~ this work is falsely attributed to Donne.[1]

a Letters supplied by the editor

14[1] Cf 27 and n 3, below. See *Watchman (CC)* 387 n 4.

15[1] C berates Flögel for treating οὐδείς—"nobody" or "no" (adj)—as though it meant "nowhere" (οὐ τόπος, "no place"—unidiomatic as a compound word but the derivation intended by More, the Greek ου- regularly transliterated as u- in Latin). But the usual pronunciation of the U-, sounding like εὐ- (well), together with the opulence of More's title—"A fruteful and pleasaunt worke of the beste state of a publyque weale, and of the new yle called Utopia"—combine to make the second meaning "obvious" to C and to many others. Thomas More himself—or his friend Peter Giles—in the *Hexastichon Anemolii Poetae Laureati* prefixed to *Utopia*—acknowledged, or quizzically acceded to, the second sense: (in a literal translation) "Once called Utopia for my unfrequentedness...I now, rivalling Plato's commonwealth, deserve the name Eutopia."

16[1] *Ignatius His Conclave* (Latin [1611], English 1611) was certainly written by Donne, as a virtuoso companion-piece to *Pseudo-martyr* (1610) and the posthumously published *Biathanatos*.

17 ıı 372

Dieses ausserordentliche Frauenzimmer [Miss Manley] wurde auf der Insel Hampshire gebohren, wo ihr Vater *Roger Manley* Gouverneur war.

[This remarkable woman [Miss Manley] was born in the island of Hampshire, where her father, *Roger Manley*, was Governor.]

Ods bods! where may the Island of Hampshire lie?—[1]

18 ıı 375

Er [Defoe] starb in seinem Hause zu Issigton 1731. nachdem er beständig ein gutes Auskommen genossen, welches ihn selten in die gewöhnliche Dürftigkeit der feilen Schriftsteller versetzte.

[Defoe died in his house at Islington in 1731, after he had steadily enjoyed a good competency, which seldom exposed him to the want that afflicts trivial authors.]

altogether mistaken. He was in needy circumstances, a bankrupt, & wrote for his Bread.—[1]

19 ıı 376[a]

Zuletzt schrieb er [Defoe] sich an den Pranger in der Schrift, betitelt: *Der kürzeste Weg mit den Nonconformisten.*...Dem *Tutchin*, der an der Empörung des *Monmouths* gegen den König Jacob II. Antheil genommen, und desswegen eine politische Schrift herausgegeben hatte, wurde das Urtheil gesprochen, durch verschiedne Städte in dem westlichen Theile Englands, und zwar so scharf gepeitscht zu werden, dass er auch den König hat, man möchte ihn lieber aufhenken lassen. Sie sind beide in der Dunciade des *Pope* in folgenden Versen verewigt worden:

Ohne Ohren stand hoch unverschämt *de Foe*, und unten *Tutchin* mit entblössten Rücken, der noch von der Geissel roth war.

[Finally Defoe wrote himself into the pillory, with his work entitled *The Shortest Way with the Nonconformists.*...*Tutchin*, who had taken part in the rebellion of *Monmouth* against King James ıı and had therefore published

---

[a] C's note is written beside the footnote with its reference to *Dunciad* ıı

17[1] Sir Roger Manley (c 1626–88) was for a time (1667–74) Lieutenant-Governor and Commander-in-Chief (not Governor) of the island of Jersey, where his daughter was born. Flögel's error may arise from Manley's later governorship of Landguard Fort.

18[1] Defoe's fortunes up to the time when he finally abandoned journalism and turned to fiction with *Robinson Crusoe* (1719) are as C describes them.

a political work, was sentenced to be whipped through various towns in the western part of England—and whipped so hard that he even asked the king to let him be hanged instead. They are both immortalised in the following verses of Pope's *Dunciad*:

> Earless on high, stood unabashed De Foe,
> And Tutchin flagrant from the scourge below.]

Mean Brute was Pope!—[1]

20 II 399, pencil[a] | Jonathan Swift

13) *Das Fragment, oder die Abhandlung von der mechanischen Wirkung der Seele*, ist eine Satire wider die Schwärmerei, und die vorgeblichen Begeisterungen, die gemeinschaftlich mit Thorheit anfangen und mit Laster sich endigen. In diesem Tractat sind die Spöttereien des Verfassers gar zu ausgelassen, viele von seinen Vorstellungen sind eckelhaft, einige sind unanständig, und andre scheinen der *] Religion zu spotten.

[13) *The Fragment, or a Discourse Concerning the Mechanical Operation of the Spirit* is a satire against enthusiasm and that supposed inspiration which always begins with folly and ends in vice. In this tract the mockery of the author is all too untrammelled, many of his conceptions are disgusting, some are indecent, and others seem to mock religion.]

* all religion seated in the fancy or the nervous System; no where in that Religion which through the Reason or Conscience acts on the Will.[1]

21 II 402 | Karl Churchill

Churchill ist einer von den heftigsten und bittersten Satirenschreibern der Engländer.... Er hat oft ein burleskes Metrum.

[*Churchill* is one of the most violent and bitter satirical writers among the English.... He often uses a burlesque metre.]

What can Flögel mean by Churchill's "burlesque metre?" Surely, not that in *one* poem, & that his very worst, he employed the 8 syllable (tetrameter) Iambic, instead of the common heroic or pentameter (10 Syllable) Iambic?[1]

---

[a] Some of the short words, and parts of words, overrunning the edge of p 399, are written on p 401

19[1] Cf *CN* III 3696, adapting an epigram on Voltaire by Jean Paul: "Pope like an old Lark who tho' he leaves off soaring & singing in the heights, yet has his *Spurs* grow longer & sharper, the older he grows." Cf e.g. *CN* II 2826.

20[1] Cf e.g. *Friend* (*CC*) I 192, *C&S* (*CC*) 105, *AR* (1825) 168.

21[1] Charles Churchill (1731–64) in *The Ghost* (1762–3) attacked Dr Johnson and his circle in octosyllabics; he also used that measure in *The Duel-*

22 II 406 | Paul Withead

Es kommen in seinen Werken von 1774. einige mittelmässige *Satiren* vor, als die *Sitten der Zeit*, die *Staatsdunse.*

[Among his works of 1774 appear some mediocre *satires*, such as *The Customs of the Times* [and] the *State-Dunces*.]

The Charge to the Poets is an incomparable Satirical Poem; but this was by W. Whitehead, here omitted.[1]

23 II 460, pencil | xv

[Flögel discusses Rabelais' *Pantagruel.*] Die Einwohner der Insel *Ruach* (wahrscheinlich das deutsche Wort Rauch) leben vom Winde. Hier wird der Hof geschildert, wo alles Eitelkeit ist. Die vornehmsten essen parfurmirte Winde, die zarten Personen... speisen Zugwinde.

[The inhabitants of the island of *Ruach* (probably the German word *Rauch* [smoke]) live on wind. Here the court, where all is vanity, is depicted. The highest-born eat perfumed winds, delicate people... dine on draughts.]

Strange! that Flögel should not know that Ruach is Hebrew for Wind, or Spirit—as Tohu and Bohu is for Chaos, or Waste & void.[1]

S. T. C.

24 II 474

Darauf gieng er [Étienne Dolet] und *Marot*, der auch der Religion wegen vebannt war, nach Italien. Dieses bezeugt *Jean Vouté* in einem seiner Sinngedichte im vierten Buche, wo die Stadt Lyon die Verbannung dieser zwei Männer beklagt. In einem Sinngedichte des ersten Buchs betitelt *de Doleto, Brixio, Macrino*, hatte der Dichter schon gesagt:

> *Hunc Genabum atque Liger, Charitesque novemque Sorores*
> *Et Stephanum expulsum Gallia tota dolet.*

Aus dem Zeugnisse dieses Zeitgenossen des Dolets, sieht man doch, dass Dolet nicht der verächtliche Mann in Frankreich war, wie einige glauben...

---

list. Churchill's poems are included in *B Poets* x. Cf C's mention of the Hudibrastic metre in **10** (at n 1), above.

22[1] William Whitehead (1715–85), poet laureate in succession to Colley Cibber, wrote *A Charge to the Poets* (1762) in reply to severe attacks on his official productions as laureate. His poems are in *B Poets* x.

23[1] *Ruach*—spirit, wind, breath—in OT normally the instrument of divine action. For *tohu bohu* see Böhme **53** and n 4, **146** n 1.

[Thereupon *Dolet* and *Marot*, who had also been banished for his religion, went to Italy. *Jean Vouté* notices this in one of his epigrams in the Fourth Book, in which the town of Lyon laments the banishment of these two men. In an epigram entitled *On Doletus, Brixius, and Macrinus*, in the First Book, the poet had already said: "As for him, Orléans and the Loire, the Graces and the nine Sisters, the whole of France grieves (*dolet*) for *Stephen* [Dolet] in exile."

From the evidence of this contemporary of Dolet's one can yet see that Dolet was not the contemptible man in France that some believe him to have been...]

Indeed? I should have thought, that it *proved* no more than the opinion of the Epigrammatist; or rather that the Lines were written by a Friend of Stephen Dolet.—

25 II 477

[Flögel quotes an epigram by Dolet:]

Ad Nicolaum Fabricium Valesium.
De Cucullatis.

Incurvicervicum Cucullatorum habet
Grex id subinde in ore, se esse mortuum
Mundo; tamen edit eximie pecus, bibit
Non pessime, stertit sepultum crapula,
Operam veneri dat, et voluptatum assecla
Est omnium. Id ne est mortuum esse mundo?
Aliter interpretare. Mortui sunt hercule
Mundo Cucullati, quod iners terrae sunt onus,
Ad rem utiles nullam, nisi ad scelus et vitium.

[*To Nicolas Fabrice Valese. On Monks.* The flock of monks, with their heads bowed, say repeatedly that they are dead to this world; yet they eat the best beef, drink not the worst wine, snore buried in deep drunkenness, make love, pursue every pleasure. Is that being dead to the world? Interpret it another way. The monks are dead to the world because they are a dead weight on the earth, useful for nothing except for sin and vice.]

an admirable Epigram; however licentious the Iambic metre may be.

26 II 483 | Hubert Languet

[Flögel ascribes to Hubert Languet the book entitled:] Stephani Iunii Bruti *Vindiciae contra Tyrannos, sive De Principis in Populum, Populique in Principem legitima potestate. Edimburgi* 1579. 8.

But this must be a mistake; it was written by an English Bishop—[1]

26[1] Whether *Stephani Junii Bruti vin-*   Basle] 1579) was written by Hubert
diciae contra tyrannos (Edinburgh [i.e.   Languet (1518–81) or by Philippe de

27 II 484–5

Dieses Buch [*Vindiciae contra tyrannos*] machte anfänglich im bürgerlichen und gelehrten Staate wegen seiner gefährlichen Grundsätze viel Lermen.... Es enthält unter andern den gottlosen Satz, dass man einen Tyrannen tödten könne.

[This book at first caused a great stir in bourgeois and scholarly society by its dangerous principles.... It contains among others the godless doctrine that one may kill a tyrant.]

lege, *gott-gebotnen* vide Ehudi exemplum, &c[1]—or rather, consult common sense. A Tyrant's Crime consists in suspending Law/ he therefore make[s][a] himself "*exlex*"; but whoever is exlex, is ipsâ lege vögelfrey,[2] that is, he stands in the relation of a Vulture, Adder, or Mad dog—Ergo, a Tyrant may be rightfully killed, whenever it is *prudent* to kill him. As to the Sophism, that fanatics might deem a lawful King a Tyrant, it suffices to answer—What may not Fanatics & Mad men think? and who expects to controll their actions by moral reason?[3] If this objection were valid, a Surgeon dared not amputate a leg, because (if that be allowed) some madman might think himself justified in hamstringing every man, who in his opinion required it.—

S. T. C.

27A III title-page, pencil

Mit einer Kupfertafel.[1]

p. 350

28 III 39, pencil | XVI

[Discussing the history of different versions of *Reineke Fuchs*, Flögel refers to "an old French [verse] romance in ms" entitled *Le Renaud*

---

a Letter supplied by the editor

Mornay (1549–1623) is still in dispute: see Flögel II 483–4. Bayle suggests Robert Parsons (1546–1610) as author (not in Flögel); but Parsons was a Jesuit missionary, not a bishop.

27[1] "Read *gott-gebotnen* [god-commanded]: see the example of Ehud"—referring to Ju 3.15–30, the brutal and bold-faced murder of Ehud of Eglon, King of Moab, who had enslaved the children of Israel for eighteen years. Ju 3.15 reads: "the Lord raised them up a

deliverer... a man lefthanded". Cf *CN* IV 5371 f 4[v].

27[2] "Whoever is *exlex* [i.e. outside the law, and therefore having no civil or judicial rights] is by the same law 'outlawed'".

27[3] For C on the legality of killing a tyrant see *Friend* (*CC*) I 322–4 and *EOT* (*CC*) II 210, 211, 218–21.

27A[1] Facing III 350 a wood-engraving (not a copperplate engraving) illustrates an allegorical tale by Johann Fischart showing various animals attending Mass.

contrefait, and in a long footnote (III 38–40) gives some account of it with quotations.]

this is an Oriental tale[1]

29 III 40

[Continuing his account of *Le Renard contrefait* in the footnote:] Seite 376. wird das Wunder des *heiligen Jangou* erzählt. Seine Frau hatte mit einem Priester ein Liebes-Verständniss, und tödtete ihren Mann im Schlafe. Als man die Leiche zum Grabe trug, wurden viele Kranken geheilt, die sie anrührten. Da die Frau dieses von ihrem Kammermädchen erzählen hörte, sagte sie: *Je le crois tout ainsi comme mon cul chante*, was geschah? ihr A—— fieng alsbald an zu singen, und laut und hässlich zu tönen, und so oft, *que c'etoit une fine merveille*. Am ärgsten war es alle Freitage, als an welchem Tage der Heilige war getödtet worden; denn bie jedem Worte, welches aus *] ihrem Munde gieng, hörte man zugleich von hinten grässliche Töne.

[On p 376 the miracle of St. Gengulphus is told. His wife had a love-affair with a priest, and killed her husband in his sleep. As the body was being carried to the grave, many sick people who touched it were healed. When the woman heard her maid recount this, she said: "I believe that as much as I believe that my arse sings." What happened? Her a[rse] began immediately to sing and resound with loud and ugly noises, and so often, "that it was a fine marvel". Fridays were the most dreadful, that being the day on which the saint had been killed; for at every word that came out of her mouth, horrible noises were to be heard at the same time from behind.

* miraculum foret plenius, si et vulvæ dentes accrevissent, mentulam monachi adulteram emorsuræ.—[1]

30 III 77

*] [Flögel lists printed editions of *Reineke Fuchs*, including:] 1592. *Reyneke voss de olde* mit sidlyckem Vorstande unde schönen Figuren erluchtet und verbetert. 4. Am Ende steht: MDXCII. Rostock bey

28[1] Beast epics centred on the figure of Reynard the Fox, sharply criticising the upper classes and the clergy, were popular through western Europe from the mid-twelfth century; they seem to have originated in Germany in the region of Alsace. The suggestion of an oriental origin may come from an assumption that the Reynard epics derived from the Indian fables known as *Panchatantra* or *The Fables of Bidpai*, collected before A.D. 500 and said to have come into Latin through Persian and Arabic versions.

29[1] "The miracle would have been more complete if teeth had grown on her vulva, to bite off the monk's adulterous penis."

Stephan Möllemann, in Verlegginge Laurentz Albrechts, Boek-
händlers in Lübeck. 1592. mit Holzschnitten.

* It is remarkable, that in my Copy of this very edition of 1592, as
the date at the last page is, yet in the Title Page stands M.DC.X.—
1610.—Was it printed first & published 1592? and then a new Title
page in 1610, to pass it off for a new Book?[1]

S. T. C.

31 III **96**

[Flögel discusses the satirical drama *Apotheosis Johannis VIII
Pontificis Romani*, attributed to Theodoricus Schernberk.] Ich will
nur den Anfang davon hersetzen, wo Lucifer sein höllisches Gesinde
in <u>*Sheakspears* Ton</u> zu Hause ruft:

> Wolher, wolher, wolher,
> Alles Teufelisches Heer,
> Aus bechen und aus brüchich,
> Aus wiesen und aus rohrich,
> Nu kompt her aus holtze und aus Felden,
> Eher denn ich euch beginn zu schelden...

[I shall reproduce only the beginning of it, in which Lucifer calls home his
hellish followers in a *Shakespearean* tone: "Hither, hither, hither, | All thou
hellish army, | From streams and bracken, | From fields and reeds, | Now
come hither from forest and meadow | Before I start to scold you..."]

!!! Whoo!!

32 III 224–5, pencil | Martin Luther

Die *Tischreden*, die er nicht geschrieben, auch niemals gesehn hat,
giebt man für den Codex seines Glaubens aus; da doch Niemand
unter den Protestanten den geringsten Beweis daraus anzunehmen
kan genöthigt werden. Unter andern will man daraus beweisen, was
Luther vor ungeheure Begriffe von dem ewigen Leben gehabt habe.
Es kommt unter andern folgende Stelle darinn vor: Im ewigen Leben
werden alle Creaturen lieblich seyn.... Da werden Ameisen, Wanzen,

30[1] The 1610 ed appears, as C de-
scribes it, in C. Borchling and B.
Claussen *Niederdeutsche Bibliographie* II
1244; only one copy is recorded (at Greifs-
wald), as compared to twenty-seven
locations for the 1592 ed (I 1066–7), of
which the BM has two copies. The 1610
ed differs from the 1592 ed only in the
title-page. C treasured his copy, and
noted in SIDNEY *Arcadia* (front flyleaf):
"Would I were rich enough to procure a
handsome *authentic* Russia-leather Bind-
ing for this, and the Renard the Fox, &
a few other Jewels."

und alle unflätige und stinkende Thiere eitel Lust seyn, und aufs beste riechen.

[The *Table Talk*, which he did not write down and never even saw, is presented as his code of faith; whereas no one among the Protestants can be obliged to accept the least proof from it. People claim to prove from it, among other things, what grotesque concepts *Luther* had of eternal life. There occurs, among others, the following passage: "In the eternal life all creatures will be pleasing.... There the ants and bugs and all foul and stinking animals will be pure joy and will smell most beautifully."]

It is highly probable, that the Table Talk was taken down, ⟨not only⟩ most incorrectly, but by some thick-witted Bozzy, who mistook Irony for Earnest.[1] Ex. gr. This Description seems to me to have been an ironical Satire on the ludicrous Consequences of conceiving Heaven as the gratification of our worldly whim & wishes instead of the perfect emancipation from them.

S. T. C.

33 IV 58 | Zweites Haupstück "Von der Komödie" III

[Flögel quotes J. G. Sulzer on Aristophanes:] Sein ist der unerschöpfliche und alles durchdringende Witz, die höchste Gabe zu spotten, darinn ihm weder *Lucian*, noch unter den Neuern *Swift*, noch irgend jemand gleich kommt...

[He possesses inexhaustible and all-penetrating wit, the highest gift for ridicule, in respect of which neither *Lucian*, nor—among the moderns—*Swift*, nor anyone else is his equal.]

With all due respect for Aristophanes, & with the keenest admiration of his most exquisite Attic Graces, I venture to assert, that there is more everlasting *Wit* in Shakespear's Trilogy of Hen. 4 & 5th, than in the whole Works of Aristophanes extant.[1]

S. T. C.

32[1] "Bozzy"—Boswell. Conrad Cordatus, in 1531, was the first of Luther's circle to take down his table-talk; Veit Dietrich, Luther's amanuensis, was the next; Antony Lauterbach took notes on two visits, Sept 1531–Feb 1533 and Oct 1536–Jul 1539. Of this older group there were altogether six note-takers; five of a younger group, including Aurifaber, the first editor of Luther's letters and table-talk, took notes from 1540 onward. All these actually sat at Luther's table,

notebooks in hand, recording everything they heard. In Feb 1826 C said that Luther's *Colloquia Mensalia*, which he annotated extensively, "is next to the Scriptures my main book of meditation, deep, seminative, pauline, beyond all other works in my possession, it *potenziates* both my Thoughts and my Will". *CL* VI 561.

33[1] For C on Shakespeare's wit see e.g. *Sh C* I 214, II 90–1, 237. See also **42**, below, and CHALMERS 4 and n 1.

34 IV 72 | IV

Die ersten Dichter der lateinischen Komödie durch die republikanische Freiheit beherzt gemacht, folgten dem Aristophanes, als *Plautus*.

[The earliest writers of Latin comedy, heartened by republican freedom, followed Aristophanes, as *Plautus* did.]

In what sense can this be said? Surely, in no other but that there are dirty and smutty passages in Plautus. Not only are all his Fables & Characters, ~~Greek~~ now extant, from the later Comedy, but I do not recollect that Plautus ⟨is SAID to have⟩ borrowed any one piece from Aristophanes.[1]
His resemblance to Epicharmus I suppose to consist in style & hardness of manner—.[2]

35 IV 73

Die Ursache, warum die *Komödie* bei den Römern eher eingeführt und vervollkommnet worden, als die Tragödie, lässt sich nicht leicht ausfindig machen, man müsste denn diese annehmen, dass die jungen Leute in Rom, welche natürlicher Weise an der Komödie mehr Vergnügen hatten als an der Tragödie, an der Einführung der Schauspiele grossen Antheil hatten.

[The reason why *comedy* was introduced and perfected among the Romans earlier than tragedy is not easy to ascertain; we have, then, one supposes, to assume this as the reason—the fact that the young men in Rome, who naturally found comedy more enjoyable than tragedy, contributed greatly to the introduction of the plays.]

The merciless Sport of the Gladiators must have had no little Share in rendering legitimate Tragedy insipid to the Romans—To obviate

---

34[1] Twenty-one plays of Plautus are now extant (one very fragmentary); presumably these are the ones selected by Varro as genuine out of 130 attributed to Plautus (Flögel IV 110). All these are apparently—and in many cases are acknowledged by Plautus himself to be—adaptations of Greek comedies of the late fourth and early third centuries B.C., principally by Philemon, Diphilus, and Menander.
34[2] The comparison with Epicharmus is from Horace *Epistles* 2.1.58, quoted by Flögel (IV 76): "Plautus hurries along like his model, Epicharmus of Sicily" (tr H. R. Fairclough LCL). Flögel (IV 110) says that Plautus imitated Epicharmus and Diphilus, and describes his style: "All is action, movement, and fire. His light, rich, natural genius provided him with all he needed, impulses to tie and untie knots...naïve, powerful (*starke*), and robust (*körnichte*) expressions." This last phrase could account for C's "hardness of manner", otherwise hardly appropriate to the fragments of this great comic poet of the sixth-fifth centuries or to Plautus.

this the few Roman Tragic Writers out-heroded Herod,[1] or deformed the dialogue into the epigrammatic yet bloated Rhetoric of the Sophists.[2]

36 IV 75

...*Quintilian* sagt, man könne den *Thyestes* des *Varius* mit der besten Griechischen Tragödie vergleichen...

[...*Quintilian* says, we may compare the *Thyestes* of *Varius* with the best of Greek tragedies...]

Credat Romanus, Amator Nominis ipse sui:—haud ego![1]

37 IV 79, pencil

Nach einigen Jahren soll es *Livius* [*Andronicus*] zuerst gewagt haben, ein regelmässiges Drama statt der Mischspiele [*saturarum*] vorzustellen, so dass er selbst agirte, wie alle dramatische Dichter in diesen Zeiten thaten.

[Some years later *Livius* [*Andronicus*] is supposed to have been the first to venture to present a regular drama instead of the medleys [*saturae*], so that he acted himself, as all dramatic writers did in these times.]

Who but must remember Shakespear? painful as to *us* it is to think of him, as (not being; but as) having been an ACTOR![1] *1813.*

37A IV 201, pencil | IX

Man sieht hieraus, dass *Every-Man* ein ernsthaftes, feierliches Stück, und nicht ohne einige rohe Versuche ist, Schrecken und Mitleiden zu erregen, so dass man ihn also nicht unfüglich unter die Classe der Κ̆ομ̆ο̈Tragödie rechnen kann.

35[1] Shakespeare *Hamlet* III ii 16. Cf AURELIUS **59** n 1, quoting *CN* II 2077.
35[2] Flögel is alluding to Livy 2.7 on the origins of Roman drama (c 361 B.C.), which he discusses more fully in IV 77–84. Young Romans imitated the (wordless) scenic performances of Etruscan actors, adding jests in rough verse. The first real play was presented by Livius Andronicus in 240 B.C.; he wrote tragedies as well as comedies. The only surviving tragedies are Seneca's, probably written for reading aloud rather than for acting; but fragments of earlier Roman tragedy, and the

subjects from Greek myth (e.g. *Thyestes* in **36**, below), bear out C's judgement.
36[1] "Let the Roman, a true Lover of his own Name, believe it: not I!" A play on Horace *Satires* 1.5.100–1: "credat Iudaeus Apella, non ego" ("Apella the Jew may believe it—not I"). Cf e.g. *Lects 1795* (*CC*) 309, *AR* (1825) 309n.
37[1] Although C was much with actors when *Remorse* was being produced in 1813, and on the whole admired them, he found it disgraceful that a great writer should have had to make his living for a time as an actor.

[From this one sees that *Everyman* is a serious, grave piece, not without a certain rough attempt to arouse terror and pity, so that one can also not inappropriately consider it under the class of C̶o̶m̶e̶⟨Trage⟩dy.]

38 iv 207, pencil

Unter seinen [John Heywood's] Zwischenspielen findet sich eins, in welchen er die Mönche und Ablasskrämer lächerlich macht, welches den Titel führt: *A marry play between the pardoner and the Frere, the Curate and Neybourpratte.* gedruckt 1533.

[Among John Heywood's interludes is one in which he ridicules the monks and pardoners, called: *A Merry Play Between the Pardoner and the Frere, the Curate and Neybour Pratte*, printed in 1533.]

It is strange, that Floegel should have pass'd over Heywood's Four Ps—that masterpiece of rude Comedy—or is it the same Play?[1]

39 iv 212, pencil

...*die erste Englische Komödie*...die den Titel hat: *Gammer* pithy] *Gurton's Needle, a right <u>pity</u> pleasant and merry Comedy.*
...Der Inhalt ist ohngefehr dieser: die Frau *Gammer Gurton*, als sie ihres Bedienten *Hodge* Beinkleider stickte, hat ihre Nadel dabei verlohren, und ihre Nachbarin Dame *Chot* fällt bei ihr in den Verdacht, als ob sie ihr diese Nadel entwendet habe. Sie lässt sie sogar durch den Pfarrer des Orts von ihr wider abfordern, und bei einem Haare wäre ein greulicher Zank darüber entstanden. Doch *Hodge* findet die Nadel noch zu rechter Zeit in seinen Beinkleidern, und macht der Komödie dadurch ein Ende.

[*The first English comedy*...is entitled *Gammer Gurton's Needle, a right pithy, pleasant and merry Comedy.*....The plot is approximately this: Mrs *Gammer Gurton*, as she sewed her servant *Hodge's* breeches, lost her needle during her work, and her neighbour Dame *Chat* incurs her suspicion of having stolen the needle from her. She even gets the parish priest to demand it back from her, and they were within a hair's breadth of a ghastly quarrel over the matter. But *Hodge* at the crucial moment finds the needle in his breeches, and so makes an end of the comedy.]

A very lame and most meagre account of this exquisite Piece of low Humor![1]

38[1] For "The Four Ps" see 7 and n 2, above. "*A Merry Play*"—Flögel's citation of the title is substantially correct— is a different play; C may not

have been familiar with it because it was not included in Dodsley.
39[1] In Dodsley Vol ii.

40 iv 214, pencil

Die lustigen Weiber zu Windsor sind sein [Shakespeares] Meisterstück im komischen...

[*The Merry Wives of Windsor* is Shakespeare's comic masterpiece...]

No! No! No![1]

41 iv 215, pencil

Sie [Beaumont and Fletcher] fanden so viel Beifall, dass man sie zu ihrer Zeit dem *Shakespear* vorzog, welches aber ietzt nicht mehr geschieht; ob sie gleich correcter sind als er.

[Beaumont and Fletcher enjoyed such acclaim that they were preferred to *Shakespeare* in their time—which, however, no longer happens, *albeit they are more correct than he.*]

Whoo!!

42 iv 215, pencil

Unter den Engländern scheint er [Ben Jonson] fast den meisten Humor zu haben....

[Among the English Ben Jonson seems almost to have had the most *humour*....]

who scarcely can be said to have any *Humor* at all.—[1]

Philipp Massinger (st. 1639.) hat gute Plane und zeigt viel Menschenkenntniss und Humor...

[*Philip Massinger* (d 1639) has good plots and shows much knowledge of human nature and much *humour*...]

And then Massinger's *Humor*! But this is the mistake frequent with Foreigners—they confound Humor with *Character*, a species with its Genus.[2]

40[1] *Twelfth Night* and *As You Like It* were C's favourite comedies; he seems seldom to have mentioned *The Merry Wives of Windsor*.

42[1] C refers to Ben Jonson. C said that, compared with Shakespeare, "Ben Jonson gave wit as salt instead of meat". *Sh C* II 237; cf I 213.

42[2] C admired Massinger's command of verse but regarded him as a dramatist greatly inferior to Shakespeare. See e.g. *LR* I 111–12.

43 IV 219, pencil

*] [At the end of the discussion of Congreve, Fielding, Gay, and before the discussion of Cibber]

* Among 20 other Omissions that of *Farqhar* is the strangest—[1]

44 IV 221, pencil

[Of Garrick:] Sein Meisterstück war *Fieldingskopf*, den er nach der täuschendsten Aehnlichkeit so treflich in allen Mienen und Zügen nachzuahmen wusste, dass jeder, der Fieldingen gekannt hatte, bekennen musste, er sähe den leibhaften Fielding.

[His masterpiece was *Fielding's Head*, which he knew how to imitate so exquisitely in every expression and lineament as to produce the most illusory likeness, insomuch that all who had known Fielding were obliged to own that they beheld the real Fielding.]

What can Flögel allude to here?—*Fielding's Head!!*[1]

45 IV 226, pencil | x

Die alten Provenzalischen Dichter, die unter dem Namen der *Troubadors* bekannt sind, heissen auch *Trombadours, Trouveors, Trouveours, Trouverses* und *Trouveurs.*

[The old Provençal poets, who are known under the name of *Troubadours,* are also called *Trombadours, Trouveors, Trouveours, Trouverses,* and *Trouveurs.*]

The Troubadours & the Trouveurs, were two distinct & different classes—the former in the S, the latter in the N. of France/ the former wrote Love-songs, &c, the latter metrical Romances.[1] The Trouveurs were the *Homerides* of Europe.[2]

43[1] The comedies of George Farquhar (1678–1707), esp *The Recruiting Officer* (1706) and *The Beaux' Stratagem* (1707), are written in a tone of genial realism in marked contrast to the artificiality of much of the comedy of the period.

44[1] Flögel alludes to an anecdote that a pen-drawing made after Fielding's death for the frontispiece to an edition of his *Works* was taken by Hogarth from Garrick made up and dressed as Fielding. John Nichols and George Steevens *The Genuine Works of William Hogarth* (3 vols 1808–17) I 350–1 denies the story; Hogarth is said to have drawn the portrait from memory.

45[1] C also makes this distinction between Troubadours and Trouveurs in the 1818 literary lectures: *LR* I 80–1, *Misc C* 19–20, 21.

45[2] The Homeridae, a clan at Chios who claimed descent from Homer and as minstrels preserved the Homeric tradition. In the same way that, according to some authorities, the Homeridae spun together the *Iliad* and *Odyssey* into their present form, so the Trouveurs interwove the romances of Arthur, Charlemagne, and others. On *Homereumenoi*—the name invented by C as a variant on *Homeridae*—see HOMERIC HYMNS 1 n 1.

46 IV 306–7, pencil | XI

[Of Hans Sachs:] Unter seinen Komödien will ich nur einer einzigen gedenken... *Comödia die ungleichen Kinder Evä, wie sie Gott der Herr anredt.* 1553.[a]... Diese Komödie enthält nun viel Lächerliches, und ungeheure Anachronismen.... Es examinirt nämlich unser Herr Gott Adams Kinder aus dem Katechismus Lutheri, und hält sich genau an die fünf Hauptstücke desselben. Abel besteht in dem Katechismusexamen mit seinen Brüdern sehr wohl, aber Kain und seine Brüder mischen alles durch einander.

[Of his comedies I will mention only one... *How the Lord Addressed the Unequal Children of Eve*, 1553.... This comedy contains much that is amusing, and enormous anachronisms.... Our Lord examines Adam's children on the Lutheran Catechism, and insists precisely on the five sections of it. Abel with his brothers passes the examination on the catechism very well, but Cain and his brothers mix everything up.]

I have read this Comedy of Hans Sachs,[1] & can truly say, that Flögel has given a most lame and pitiful account of it.—In short, the whole Work is a mere Collectanea, a certain small quantity of *memorandum Papers* toward a History of Comic Literature—a sort of Vantage-Ground from which an author might *start*—and wretchedly imperfect. Of all 4 Volumes, the last is far the worst. Had Flögel confined himself to German Comic Literature, he might have made an interesting book; but the outline was too vast for any man to fill up.

47 IV 308, pencil, overtraced

Der Eifer Schauspiele zu schreiben, war in diesem Jahrhunderte [XVI] in Deutschland so allgemein, dass auch grosse Herren sich damit beschäftigten; so schrieb *Herzog Julius* von Braunschweig und Lüneburg zwei Schauspiele, eins von Vincentio Ladislao Satrapa von Mantua... das andre hat diesen Titel: *Tragoedia H. I. B. A. L. D. E. H. A. von geschwinder Weiberlist einer Ehebrecherin...*

[The enthusiasm for playwriting in this [sixteenth] century was so general in Germany that even great men took a hand at it; thus *Duke Julius* of Brunswick and Lüneburg wrote two plays, one about Vincentio Ladislav Satrapa of Mantua... the other entitled: *The Tragedy H. I. B. A. L. D. E. H. A. of the Quick Feminine Guile of an Adulteress...*

Surely, one might expect the interpretation of these letters, H. I. &c.[1]

---

[a] This phrase on IV 303 is at the beginning of an account that runs to IV 306, where C has written his note

46[1] For C's acquaintance with Sachs's *Die ungleichen Kinder Eva*, especially in Germany in 1799, see *CN* I 453 and n, III 4384 and n.

47[1] The letters identify the author as "Henricus Iulius Brunsvicensis Atque Luneburgensis Dux Episcopatus Halberstadensis Antistes" (K. Goedecke *Grund-*

48 IV 309

[Of *Radtschlag des allerheiligsten Vaters Bapsts Pauli des dritten*...
wie das angesetzte Concilium zu Trient fürzunehmen sey (*The Holy
Father Pope Paul III's Suggestion*...*How the Council Convened at
Trent Should be Conducted*):] Ich würde von diesem seltnen, sehr
komischen und satirischen Stück einen Auszug mittheilen...wenn
es nicht *Riederer* schon gethan hätte.
[I would...give an extract from this scarce and very comic and satirical
piece...if *Riederer* had not already done so.]

absurd! as if every man were expected to possess every book.[1] The
Duty of a Writer is to make *his* Book as perfect as possible & to avail
himself of, nay, to supersede, the historical collections of his
predecessors—even as every judicious Encyclopædia supersedes the
former.—The Works of Genius alone, the Individualities of mighty
minds, must not, because they cannot, be superseded!—

49 IV 313

[Of Andreas Gryphius:]...man kann behaupten, dass er dem Drama
in Deutschland zuerst die Bahn gebrochen habe; und wenn er in
einem bessern Zeitalter gelebt hätte, so würde er unter den komischen
Dichtern einen hohen Rang erlangt haben.
[...it can be said that he first paved the way for the drama in Germany;
and if he had lived in a better age he would have reached a high rank
among comic poets.]

Take the immediate Predecessors of Shakespear—note the general
Taste of Milton's age—& then deduce the *ungroundedness* of the
supposition, that a great Genius produced dull works on account of
the *Age*, in which he lived. It is the royal prerogative of Genius to
outrun, & to form the Taste of the Age.—[1]

---

*riss zur Geschichte der deutschen
Dichtung*—Dresden 1886—II 520): i.e.
Julius, Duke of Brunswick and Lüneburg
(1528–89), who kept a troop of English
players at his court and wrote plays for
them.
48[1] C objects to the assumption that
he, as a reader of Flögel, would naturally
have at hand a copy of Johann Batholo-
maus Riederer *Nachrichten zur Kirchen-,
Gelehrten- und Bücher-Geschichte* (Alt-
dorf 1764–8). He made a similar, but

much more highly elaborated, objection
to Niebuhr's *History of Rome* in N 37 f
75ᵛ (*CN* v) (25 May 1828), upbraiding the
author for "forgetting that THE
PUBLIC might not chance to be sitting
in a Library...".
49[1] That works of original genius
form the taste of those who appreciate
them is a truth that both C and WW
declared. See e.g. *CN* II 3225 (from
Propyläen), *WL* (*M* 2) I 150.

50 IV 315

[Of Gryphius' *Peter Squenz*:] Die Erfindung ist aus *Shakespears* Johannisnachtstraum, wo ein Zwischenspiel eingeschaltet ist, wo ein Schulmeister *Quince* vorkommt; oder vielmehr aus einer aus dem französischen übersetzten Novelle von Pyramus und Thisbe.

[The plot is from Shakespeare's *Midsummer Night's Dream*, in which an interlude is introduced in which a schoolmaster *Quince* appears; or, rather, from a story of Pyramus and Thisbe translated from the French.]

What means this "*vielmehr*"? Surely, not that the French Novel of P. & T. afforded the character of Peter Quince & Comrades, prior to Shakespear? And if not this, what can it mean? Answer— C. F. Flögel ~~wrote~~ or rather C. F. Flögel's *Pen*, wrote without any distinct meaning—a case of more frequent Occurrence in the Literary World, than the majority of Readers are aware of/

S. T. C.

51 IV 316

Daniel Caspar von Lohenstein... gehört zwar nicht hieher, weil er nur Trauerspiele geschrieben hat; ist aber des Zusammenhangs wegen nicht zu übergehn, weil er eine eigne Art des Geschmacks in Deutschland eingeführt hat, und viele Nachfolger unter den Dichtern gehabt hat. Er war ein frühzeitiger und sehr fähiger Kopf, dabei besass er eine weitläufige Gelehrsamkeit, sein Unglück war, dass er dem falschen und ausschweifenden Witze der neuern Italiener...zu sehr bildete; darüber verfiel er in Schwulst, und brachte seine Gelehrsamkeit am unschicklichen Orte auf eine pedantische Weise....Uebrigens war *Lohenstein* gar nicht der schlechte Mann, wozu ihn einige Kunstrichter haben herabwürdigen wollen. Es kommen besonders in seiner Prosa im *Arminius* wahrhaftig erhabne Stellen...vor....So sehr *Lohenstein* auch ist verschrieen worden, so haben doch einige unsrer besten Dichter ihm ihre erste Bildung zu verdanken...

[*Daniel Caspar Lohenstein*...admittedly does not belong here, because he wrote only tragedies; but his connexion [with comedy] is not to be neglected because he introduced into Germany a special kind of taste, and he had many imitators among the poets. He was an early and very clever thinker, and, besides, amassed vast erudition, his misfortune being that he cultivated too much the false and eccentric wit of the new Italians...besides, he lapsed into bombast and displayed his learning in the wrong places in a pedantic manner....After all, *Lohenstein* was not the entirely bad man that certain critics would make him. There are to be found, especially in his prose in

Arminius, really sublime passages.... However much *Lohenstein* has been abused, certain of our best poets nevertheless have him to thank for their first development.]

I remember reading, of this Lohenstein, an ode or address to Fortune, of more than a 1000 Lines, which the Hero of the Romance in melancholy mood did one morning engrave on Mount Caucasus![1]

S. T. C.

and I agree, however, fully with Flögel's remarks, both generally, & in relation to Lohenstein in particular: who with all the extravagances & absurdities common to his age possessed likewise the nerve, the sinew, & the marrow of Intellect.

51[1] Daniel Casper von Lohenstein (1635–83)—perhaps his *Eitelkeit des Glückens und des Hofes*.

DUNCAN FORBES
1685–1747

The Whole Works of the Right Honourable Duncan Forbes, late Lord President of the Court of Session. Now first collected, &c. 2 vols (in 1). Edinburgh [? 1755]. 8°.

British Museum C 60 e 4

Inscribed on the title-page of both volumes: "Geo. Frere 1801"; and on II ⁻2 "G. Frere". For George Frere see BAXTER *Reliquiae* COPY B headnote. Pencil notes in an unidentified hand on I 144–6, 150, 155, and two words in ink on I 254.

The address of **6**—"Dear Sir"—suggests that C annotated the volumes at Frere's request. The two volumes were bound into one after C had written his notes in them. Pencil note on p ⁻4: "2 Vols in 1   With autograph notes of Samuel T Coleridge ⟨at end of first vol⟩ Vol. I   very rare as well as curious"—insertion in another hand.

CONTENTS. I *Thoughts Concerning Religion, Natural and Revealed* (**1–6**). II *A Letter to a Bishop, Concerning Some Important Discoveries in Philosophy and Theology* (**7–9**); *Reflexions on the Sources of Incredulity with Regard to Religion* (**10**).

DATE. Aug 1817 (**6**).

COEDITOR. James D. Boulger.

1   I 37–8, pencil | *Thoughts Concerning Religion*

*] Of the many Nations and Kindreds famous for Prowess, for Laws, for religious Opinions, is there any that remained, that preserved their Name after a Conquest? Did not all mix and blend themselves with the Conqueror? Of all the Religions that ever have been, did any stick so close to the profession of it [as the Jews did], that, for a series of Ages, they did not forsake it for the Religion of the Country they became subjects of...?

* Hindostan under the Tatar, Mahometan, and Christian Conquerors?[1]—If the Gypsies had carried with them *a Book* of their Laws

1[1] Details of the history and religion of Hindustan had been brought to public attention by the impeachment and seven-years' trial of Warren Hastings 1788–95: see *Lects 1795* (*CC*) 58 and n, 225. For C's reading on India see DUBOIS headnote and passim.

and Oracles?—we must not press *too much* on the fact, ⌐as if it⌐*a* were wholly *miraculous*—Enough for the argument, that it is strikingly *providential*.

2 I 60, pencil

...before their Records were disturbed by the Captivity, it could not well be otherwise, but that every body of any note amongst the *Jews* could tell you the name of his Ancestor, who first had the Family-possession, in the days of *Joshua*, and how many degrees, and by what descent, he was removed from him. And yet 9 in 10. became Idolators/[1] a strong argument in support of the Catholic Faith; but an Enigma for such as rely *exclusively* on outward historical evidence.

3 I 61, pencil

The appointment and observance of the *Sabbatical* year, and, after the seventh *Sabbatical* year, a year of JUBILEE...made inquiry into TITLES, and consequently genealogy, necessary every fiftieth year; *] and as the cessation from culture, every seventh year, gave continual occasions for the Deity's displaying his power in increasing the Crop of the sixth, pursuant to his promise.

* But is it not strange, that this miraculous Increase of the Crops, *every seventh year*, should not be mentioned in the Histories, and alluded to & dwelt on in the Hymns and Prophecies?

3A I 66, pencil

And yet the time between the entry of *Israel* into the *Land*, and the reign of *David*, being but about four hundred years, is too short a ?] space for forgetting the real manner of that Entry, and forging another, to be received by a People, whose genealogy was so fixed, and whose time was reckoned by such PERIODS.

4 I 74–5, pencil

What then must the religious *Jews*, who believed that sacrifice was of divine Institution, who believed at the same time that it was of

---

a Three words at the foot of the page erased but faintly legible

2[1] On the need of teachers to keep the Jews from idolatry see *Lects 1795* (*CC*) 136–7 and cf *SM* (*CC*) 9.

no effect towards pardoning no sin and procuring favour, and who
*] were bound to meditate on the depths, the hidden things of the
Law, conclude?

* I cannot imagine even a plausible Answer to this, on the part of
the Unitarians. The Deist may deny the wisdom of the Legislator,
but what shall *he* say, who admits the inspiration of Moses yet denies
the redemption of by Christ? Answer. He can lie and shuffle, and
declaim as if the Sacrifices had been all of them Thanks Offerings/
and about *dark* ages.

5   1 77, pencil

...*and his name was to be called*... *The Mighty God, The everlasting
Father, The Prince of Peace.*

Πατηρ τῶν αἰώνων[1]

6   1 +1-+2, referring to 1 99

MR. *TINDAL* would avoid this difficulty, by supposing that the *light
of* NATURE teaches man that God is merciful, and that he will pardon,
upon repentance, and a purpose of amendment: and, if this was true,
his argument would go pretty far. But this is most certainly not true:
the *Deist* borrows, in this, an article from REVEALED RELIGION,
which, by ascribing to *the light of* NATURE, he would make use of
to overthrow that very Religion that discovered it.

Dear Sir   August. 1817.
    It is much to be regretted, that so good and wise a man, as Duncan
Forbes, and so calm and solid a reasoner, should not have explained
himself more at large, concerning the position, p. 99, that by the Light
of Nature[1] men might have learnt the benignity and mercifulness of

---

5[1] "Father of the ages". As in BIBLE
COPY B 52, C renders into Greek the AV
phrase "everlasting Father" of Isa 9.6,
on the assumption—which is incorrect—
that Septuagint has a phrase correspon-
ding to AV "the everlasting Father".
Elsewhere, in Septuagint and NT,
the word for "everlasting, eternal" is
αἰώνιος; but C may well have in mind
βασιλεὺς τῶν αἰώνων (AV "King
eternal") of 1 Tim 1.17, in which
splendid verse the word αἴων is three

times repeated. Cf Θεὸς αἰώνιος (God
eternal) in Septuagint Isa 40.28, AV "the
everlasting God".
    6[1] The "Light of Nature", as the
capacity to discern divine truths without
the help of revelation, is first noted in
OED for 1599. For C's objection to the
phrase see DONNE *Sermons* COPY B 64.
Abraham Tucker (under the pseudonym
Edward Search) *The Light of Nature
Pursued* (8 pts 1768, 1778) had given wide
currency to the term. C owned a copy of

the God of Nature, but could not have deduced that he would pardon ~~the~~ a Sinner sincerely and effectively penitent—μετανοοῦντα.[2] Doubtless, he had weighty grounds for this affirmation, of the importance of which he himself seems to have been fully sensible. The desire to record this regret of mine has tempted me to the liberty of disfiguring this Leaf in a Book of yours. You or your Brothers may perhaps be led to some solution of this problem, the assertion contradicted by Duncan Forbes being one of the main foundation-stones of the Deists, whether simply Deists simply, or Unitarians.— For my own part, I feel inclined to agree with D. F. in the second or negative position, but doubt the first—viz. that by the Light of Nature, as contra-distinguished from all Revelation, Man could have learnt any of the moral attributes of God.

S. T. Coleridge

P.S. In the second Volume (the Sketch of the Hutchinsonian System)[3] in which is a *model* of its kind, in clearness and candor, in sobriety of Judgement and[a]

---

7 II ⁻1, referring to II 17 | *A Letter to a Bishop*

Our Author [Hutchinson] thinks that, by the light of nature only, men could not possibly have discovered whether this material system, which, he says, is so framed, as to be a self-moving machine, existed from eternity, and was the cause and support of itself, and of every

a The note breaks off

---

the book—it was a favourite of Beddoes and Davy by 1798—and in 1803 urged Hazlitt to prepare an abridged edition for which he himself would write a prefatory essay. *CL* II 949. Hazlitt's *Abridgment of the Light of Nature Pursued* was published anonymously in 1807, without an essay by C. C left his copy of Tucker at Allan Bank in Oct 1810; it is now in VCL.

6[2] "Repenting"—probably echoing Luke 15.7, the joy in heaven ἐπὶ ἑνὶ ἁμαρτωλῷ μετανοοῦντι ("over one sinner that repenteth"). The whole statement may be reinforced by the "Comfortable Words" in the office of Holy Communion.

6[3] I.e. Forbes's *A Letter to a Bishop* (see CONTENTS), on which C wrote 7–9. John Hutchinson (1674–1737), who in

Moses's Principia (1724) attacked Newton's theory of gravitation with pseudo-scientific arguments and sought to establish the Mosaic cosmogony and the infallibility of Scripture as containing all the elements of philosophy as well as of true religion, founded a pietistic cult to which Forbes belonged. Although C referred to "the Cabbala of the Hutchinsonian School" as "the dotage of a few weak-minded individuals" (*CIS* 51), he recommended Forbes's *Letter* as containing "the most important points of the Hutchinsonian doctrine in the most favorable form, and in the shortest possible space". *Friend* (*CC*) I 502n; in 502–3 C draws upon FORBES II 41 and 76–7 (not annotated).

thing in it; or whether it was contrived, and the parts of it put together, by an higher hand.

It is seldom, that the most original Minds, and who oppose themselves most diametrically to the opinions in vogue, ~~are~~ rise above the temptation of procuring a hearing for their own opinions by flattering some dogma then in the ascendant. Thus it was that Hutchinson, Des Cartes, Boyle, and Newton, ~~and~~ with Locke, had conspired with the spirit of their times in setting up the idol of Mechanism,[1] as the presiding Genius not only of Common sense against the substantial forms of the Scholastic Aristotelians, and the Hylarchs, anima mundi s, &c of the Alchemists;[2] ~~and~~ but likewise against the later Antinomians and New-Light Men,[3] ~~but~~ as the Safeguard of rational Religion.—To this Idol Hutchinson sacrificed the consistency of his System—and gave us the old Death out of Life, and fumum de Luce/[4]—in short, the πρῶτον ψεῦδος[5] of deducing from mechanism all that mechanism presupposes, in each atom as much ⟨as⟩ in a world.[a6]

See p. 17.—Most assuredly, Man could not: for if the World can *be* and *exist* without God for a moment, it might for an eternity. The Sophism of the contrary in a Watch or other human Arte-fact[7] proceeds on the forgetting that the *powers* of attraction, repulsion, and the synthetic tertium aliud et majus,[8] Gravitation, are pre-

---

[a] Here C has written ‡‡ and resumed the note with ‡‡ at the head of II ⁻1 above the first part of 7, which he had begun more than halfway down the page

[7][1] See n 6, below. For the "differences between mechanic and vital philosophy" see e.g. *SM* (*CC*) 89.

[7][2] Hylarchs—"rulers of matter"—an alchemical term for postulated principles commanding the shaping of matter, also used by Paracelsus, Cudworth, and Henry More. Cf *CN* III 4136. "Souls of the world" (C adding an -s to the normal phrase *anima mundi*)—another alchemical term, for which see AURELIUS 58 and n 1. For C's view of prescientific attempts to understand and control the physical universe, and the contribution of alchemists to the development of scientific chemistry, see e.g. *P Lects* Lect 9 (1949) 283 and T. FULLER *Holy State* 7.

[7][3] Antinomians—those who reject the moral law. See FIELD 7 and n 3; cf EICHHORN *Neue Testament* COPY B 24 n 2. For "New-Light Men" see FIELDING *Tom Jones* 9 and n 1.

[7][4] "Smoke from Light"—a play on *lux e luce* ("Light of Light") in the Nicene Creed. See BOOK OF COMMON PRAYER COPY B 29 and n 3; cf BÖHME 169 and n 1.

[7][5] "Fundamental error". See BAXTER *Reliquiae* COPY B 92 n 1.

[7][6] Cf C's attack on atomic chemistry—which he considered one facet of "the idol of Mechanism"—as having "dearly purchased a few brilliant inventions at the loss of all communion with life and the spirit of nature" in *SM* (*CC*) 76–7; cf *CL* IV 760–1.

[7][7] The figure of the universe as "a polished and accurate watch or timepiece" was given widest currency by William Paley's *Natural Theology* (1802) but was current earlier. See *Lects 1795* (*CC*) 98n.

[7][8] The "third, other and greater". Cf *SM* (*CC*) 89 and n 3.

supposed in all mechanics—which can ~~nev~~ not explain the *motion*, but only the *mode* in this particular instance.[9] The Statue of a Boxer ✶ a Boxer.

8 ii 55

He [Hutchinson] imagines that *Adam* was not deceived as *Eve* was; but that seeing her lost, his passion for her made him desperately resolve to share the same fortune with her...

Par. Lost.[1]

9 ii 56

He [Hutchinson] says that the עוֹן *aven*, which properly signifies the act of cohabitation with a woman, is in the *Hebrew* language made the root for iniquity or wickedness. And that פתח *Petah*, which principally signifies that part of the body that *Eve* is supposed to have hid, in the same language is made expressive of seducing, overpersuading, deceiving.

ngaven; then the ע was softened gn, kn, n, g, ch, u, w, the Hebrew *gnaiin* being the Greek Digamma, retained in αγγελος.[1] In German knaben, a boy & a Knave—from *Pethah*, πειθη.[2]

10 ii ⁺2, referring to ii 154 | *Reflexions on the Sources of Incredulity*

The words *Trinity*, and *Person*, or *Hypostasis*, are terms not to be met with in the sacred book: and yet to these terms, and the application of them, the revolt against the doctrine [of the Trinity] is chiefly owing.

What the Scripture acquaints us with, is this, and no more: That what it characterises the FATHER, the avenger of wrong, and

---

7[9] The basic terms of C's dynamic scheme of attraction (thesis), repulsion (antithesis), and gravitation (synthesis): see e.g. BÖHME passim. On the failure to explain motion by the divisibility of space see e.g. KANT *Vermischte Schriften* COPY c 29 and n 6.

8[1] *Paradise Lost* IX 997–9:

He scrupl'd not to eat
Against his better knowledge, not deceav'd,
But fondly overcome with Femal charm.

9[1] See also H. COLERIDGE 4 and n 1.
9[2] C derives Greek πειθή (fem adj) "persuasive" from Hebrew *petah* (in textus). πειθός occurs only once in NT Greek: in 1 Cor 2.4 (AV "enticing", *gloss* "persuasible").

rewarder of right, is GOD; that what it characterises the SON, the WORD, the Creator of the world, the Redeemer of mankind, sent for that purpose by the Father, is GOD; that the HOLY SPIRIT, the correspondent with, and Comforter of the spirits of men, is GOD; and that nevertheless the DEITY, the SELF-EXISTENT BEING, is but ONE.

P. 154. It surprizes me that so truly good and sensible a Man, as D. F. should make such a childish objection to the words, Trinity and Person. In the name of Common Sense, is there any advantage that the word "what" or "somewhat" can have over the word "Person"? A somewhat, that is named the Father, and that is not the same as the Son or Holy Ghost, (nay, according to Forbes, having distinct attributes which I do not believe to be the Catholic or the Scriptural Faith with the one necessary exception of Self-origination) is God; that a somewhat, called the Son, that is not the same as the Father or Holy Ghost, is God; and that a somewhat, characteristzed as the Holy Ghost, that is not the same as the Father and or as the Son, is God; and that these three "Whats" are nevertheless but one God—/

What is this but an expansion of the words, Trinity of Distinction and Unity of Godhead?—And what does "Person" mean, but an intelligent, moral "What"?[1]—S. T. C.—

10[1] For C's objection to the use of "person" in credal formulations of the doctrine of the Trinity, however, see DONNE *Sermons* COPY B 7 and n 1, FLEURY **56** and n 3 (and on "Trinity" and "Hypostasis" see nn 1, 3, and 4).

JAMES FOSTER

1697–1753

LOST BOOK

The Usefulness, Truth, and Excellency of the Christian Revelation defended against the objections contain'd in a late book, intitled, Christianity as old as the Creation [by Matthew Tindal]...The third edition, corrected, &c. London 1734. 8⁰.

Not located; marginalia not recorded. *Green SC* (1880) 205: "With autograph Note by S. T. Coleridge." This book also appeared as *Green SC* (1884) 15 and was sold by Bartlett & Welford in New York.

ST FRANCIS OF SALES
1567–1622

Il Teotima o sia il trattato dell' amor di Dio...Nuovamente con ogni diligenza tradotto ed illustrato da Carlo Barbieri, &c. 2 vols. Padua 1790, 1791. 8°.

Victoria College Library (Coleridge Collection)

Inscribed by C in ink on I ⁻2, II ⁻2: "S. T. Coleridge 4 Jan. 1806". He acquired the book, then, after arriving in Rome c 31 Dec 1805 and before withdrawing to Washington Allston's house at Olevano Romano. See *CN* II 2759, 2784–2786.

C several times referred to the phrase "il più nell' uno" as St Francis's "brief and happy definition of the Beautiful" (*CL* VI 799, N 50 f 31) and parallel to his own definition "multëity in unity" or "unity in multëity". See *CL* V 100 (c Aug 1820); cf *TT* 27 Dec 1831, 1 Jan and 23 Jun 1834.

DATE. Possibly c Jan 1806 (near the time of acquisition), but perhaps c Jul 1809–Jul 1810 (see *CN* III 3560, 3907, 3922, 3925).

1   I 20–1, pencil | Bk I ch 5

3. Gli Stoici, al riferir di S. Agostino (*de Civ. Die lib. XIV. c. 8. n. 1.*), ancorchè negassero che l'uomo saggio aver potesse passioni, mostravano tuttavia di confessar ch'egli avesse degli affetti, cui davan nome d' *Eupathie*, cioè di buone passioni, o come Cicerone (*Tuscul. quaest. lib. IV.*) le chiama, costanze: imperciocchè dicevano, il saggio non desiderar, ma volere; non allegrarsi, ma godere; non temer cosa alcuna, ma prevedere e guardarsi: dimodochè non per altro si muova egli mai che per la ragione e secondo essa.

[The Stoics, according to St Augustine (*de Civ. Dei* 14.8 n 1), although they denied that the wise man could have passions, appeared nonetheless to confess that he had emotions, to which they gave the name of *Eupathie*, i.e. good passions, or as Cicero calls them (*Tuscul. quaest.* 4) conditions of constancy: for they used to say that the wise man did not desire, but that he willed; that he was not joyful, but that he enjoyed; that he did not fear anything, but that he looked ahead and took care: so it is that he is never moved except by reason and in accordance with it.]

The good Saint always forgets that the wise man of the Stoics was an *Ideal*, to which no real existence in any Individual had been given. The wise man is a mathematical Circle[1]

---

[1] I.e. the idea of the wise man, bearing to any individual wise man the same relation that the mathematical idea ("not image" or concept) of a circle bears to any actual and particular circular form. See *Friend* (*CC*) I 177, 459, and nn (in which C wondered whether in the context of geometry "theorem" might be a more appropriate term than "idea"). Cf *P Lects* Lect 6 (1949) 218–19, on the Stoics and on wisdom as the attainment of an ideal.

JOHN HOOKHAM FRERE

1769–1846

Prospectus and Specimen of an Intended National Work, by William and Robert Whistlecraft, of Stow-market, in Suffolk, harness and collar-makers [i.e. John Hookham Frere]. Intended to comprise the most interesting particulars relating to King Arthur and his Round Table. Cantos I, II. London 1817. 8°.

Cantos III, IV were issued together in 1818.

Not located. *Gillman SC* (1843) 436: "With curious MS. Note by S. T. Coleridge". *Maggs SC* 350 (1916) lot 239.

In the possession of J. T. Brown in 1863–4, from whose transcript in *North British Review* XL (Feb–May 1864) 80 the note is here reprinted.

As an undergraduate at Cambridge C had some slight acquaintance with Frere but as a scholarly rival rather than as a friend. *CN* I 1656. It is not known whether C knew who had written the lampoons on himself, RS, and Erasmus Darwin in the *Anti-Jacobin* (1799). Later, C will have known of him as minister plenipotentiary to the Central Junta in Spain, severely criticised for the advice he had given to Sir John Moore in his campaign against the French and in the events that led to the Convention to Cintra. Cf *EOT* II 45–6 n 5. Some time not long before May 1816 C met Frere and "the day, when I first saw Mr Frere, [was] among the most memorable Red Letter Days of my Literary Life". *CL* IV 637. In May 1816 C borrowed from John Murray printed sheets of Frere's verse translations of Aristophanes *Frogs* (*CL* IV 637; the translations, four plays in all, were not completed and published in full until 1839–40) and at the same time sent Frere the sheets of *BL* and *SL*, evidently in the hope that Murray might be persuaded to become C's publisher. Murray declined the offer of *BL* and in the following year Frere failed to establish C as a regular contributor to *QR*.

C found Frere a brilliant and sensitive foil to his own concern for the craft of poetry, and over the years a friend discreetly generous. In c Jan 1817 C copied into N 25 a long extract from Frere's verse translation of Aristophanes *Frogs* and used a four-line motto from the translation of the *Frogs* in *The Friend* (1818). See *CN* III 4331, 4332, 4336; *Friend* (*CC*) I 18. Frere "*at a heavy expence* (I was astonished to learn thro' Mr Gillman from the Scribe himself, at how heavy an expence!) has had my [Philosophical] Lectures taken down in short-hand". *CL* VI 917. He also made a substantial contribution to the expense of sending DC to Cambridge 1820–3. *CL* V 193.

Several of C's letters to Frere are preserved, showing *inter alia* the care with which C arranged for Frere to meet his friends—Green, the Beaumonts, the Gillmans, Ludwig Tieck. In 1818 Frere, who had given up his diplomatic career, retired to Malta because of his wife's ill-health, but occasionally returned to England for visits of limited duration. N 26 records a meeting with Frere in Highgate in Sept 1826 a few days before he left for Malta, including "Mementos in the handwriting of the Right Honorable John Hookham Frere—" and an inscription of affection, respect, and gratitude written partly in Greek. *CN* IV 4440, 4441. It may have been at this time that Frere left with C the ms of his *Acharnians*, *Knights*, and *Birds* that C bequeathed to James Gillman "as an Heir-loom in the Gillman Family". *CL* VI 559n, 999.

DATE. Probably 1817.

1   p 30, PS in pencil | Canto II st x

> He found a Valley, closed on every side,
>   Resembling that which Rasselas describes;
> Six miles in length, and half as many wide,
>   Where the descendants of the Giant tribes
> Liv'd in their ancient Fortress undescried:
>   (Invaders tread upon each others kibes)
> First came the Britons, afterwards the Roman,
> Our patrimonial lands belong to no man:

I have ever found an unpleasant effect where the consonances A, C, and E are assonant to the consonances B, D, and F.
⟨What can I have meant by this?⟩[1]

1[1] C may have lost the thread of his own analysis from treating the first six lines in a sequence of letters A–F instead of using letters to show the rhyme-scheme —*ababacc*. His complaint is that the *a*-rhyme consonances (side, wide, undescried) and the *b*-rhyme consonances (describes, tribes, kibes) are assonant, have the same vowel-sound and a similar consonant after the vowel. In any case Frere's intention in his use of *ottava rima* is facetious, in the manner of Pulci, Berni, and Casti—a tune that Byron at once picked up from "Whistlecraft" and turned to his own unique uses first in *Beppo* and then in *Don Juan*. See also BARCLAY COPY A 1 n 1.

DAVID FRIEDLÄNDER

1750–1834

Sendschreiben an seine Hochwürden, Herrn Oberconsistorialrath und Probst Teller [i.e. Wilhelm Abraham Teller (1734–1804)] zu Berlin, von einigen Hausvätern jüdischer Religion, &c. [Anonymous.] Second edition. Berlin 1799. 8º.

"Bound up with three other German pamphlets of later date"—*Blackwell SC* 531 (1948); "...German pamphlets dated 1820 and 1829"—*Blackwell SC* 513 [1945].

Not located. *Green SC* (1880) 713: "With several other German Tracts, &c. some with marginal notes in the same [i.e. C's] handwriting". The annotation is reprinted from *Blackwell SC* 531.

Inscribed by C on the title-page: "S. T. Coleridge June 3rd 1799". C did not leave Göttingen on his way home to England until 24 Jun 1799. "Three marginal notes by S. T. C. in his handwriting. These have been transcribed by Ernest Hartley Coleridge on a sheet of note-paper which is inserted": *Blackwell SC* 513. "Two notes in the margin, and one on the end-paper": *Blackwell SC* 531.

The BM copy of Friedländer's anonymous pamphlet is bound with W. A. Teller *Beantwortung des an Herrn Probst Teller erlassenen Sendschreibens einiger Hausväter jüdischer Nation* (Berlin 1799).

DATE. Presumably shortly after 3 Jun 1799.

1, 2

["two notes in the margin", location and text not recorded]

3 "on the end-paper"

This seems a strange muddle-headed application—neither more nor less than whether the Christian Church will consider and call a Jew a Christian, because instead of believing the Old Testament only he believes neither. This is two negatives make an affirmative with a vengeance.

ANDREW FULLER

1754–1815

The Calvinistic and Socinian Systems Examined and Compared, as to their moral tendency, in a series of letters addressed to the friends of vital and practical religion, especially those amongst Protestant Dissenters, &c. Market-Harborough 1793. 8°.

Not located. Probably Thomas Poole's copy. The text of C's annotations is here reprinted from *LR* IV 289–95, from which the page-references for the annotations are also taken, even though the limited margins in this volume suggest that the long notes 1 and 4 were probably written on flyleaves or in the blank spaces at the ends of letters.

DATE. 1807: *LR*, possibly on Poole's statement, if this was one of the group of books that C annotated on his last visit to Poole in Nether Stowey in 1807: see ADAM, and HAYLEY headnote.

---

1 pp 38ff | Letter III "The Systems Compared as to Their Tendency to Convert Professed Unbelievers"

If the Jews in the time of Christ had thought it impossible, or, which is the same thing, inconsistent with the unity of God, that God the Father should have a Son equal to himself, how came they to attach the idea of *equality* to that of Sonship?... They did not deny that to be God's *own Son* was to be equal with the Father, nor did they alledge that such an equality would destroy the divine unity: a thought of this kind never seems to have occurred to their minds. The idea to which they objected was, *that Jesus of Nazareth was the Son of God*; and hence, it is probable, the profession of this great article was considered in the apostolic age as the criterion of christianity.

In so truly excellent a book as this is, I regret that this position should rest on an assertion. The equality of Christ would not, indeed, destroy the unity of God the Father, considered as one Person: but, unless we presume the Jews in question acquainted with the great truth of the Tri-unity, we must admit that it would be considered as implying Ditheism. Now that some among the Jews had made very near approaches, though blended with errors, to the doctrine taught

797

in John, c. i., we can prove from the writings of Philo;[1]—and the Socinians can never prove that these Jews did not know at least of the doctrine of their schools concerning the only-begotten Word—Λόγος μονογενής[2]—not as an attribute, much less as an abstraction or personification—but as a distinct *Hypostasis* συμφυσική:[3]—and hence it might be shown that their offence was that the carpenter's son, the Galilean, should call himself the Θεὸς φανερός.[4] This might have been rendered more than probable by the concluding sentence of Christ's answer to the disciples of John;—*and blessed is he, whosoever shall not be offended in me* (Luke vii. 23.); which appears to have no adequate or even tolerable meaning, unless in reference to the passage in Isaiah, (lxi. 1, 2.) prophesying that Jehovah himself would come among them, and do the things which our Saviour states himself to have done. Thus, too, I regret that the answer of our Lord, (John x. 34–36) being one of the imagined strong-holds of the Socinians, should not have been more fully cleared up.[5] I doubt not that Fuller's is a true interpretation; and that no other is consistent with our Lord's various other declarations. But the words in and by themselves admit a more plausible misinterpretation than is elsewhere the case of Socinian displanations.[6] In short, I think both passages would have been better deferred to a further part of the work.

Let me add that a mighty and comparatively new argument against the Socinians may be most unanswerably deduced from this reply of our Lord's, even were it considered as a mere *argumentum ad homines*:[7]—namely, that it was not his Messiahship that so offended

---

[1] See EICHHORN *Neue Testament* COPY A **32** and n 1.

[2] See John 1.1–18, esp 14; and again, EICHHORN *Neue Testament* COPY A **32** and n 1. The Socinians by recognising God the Father as the one God denied the divinity of Christ. See BAHRDT **1** n 1 and *LS* (*CC*) 181–4n. On μονογενής see e.g. FLEURY **49** nn 1, 4.

[3] "A *person* [or *substance*?] of conjoint nature". C appears to be inventing συμφυσικός because the later word ὁμοούσιος would be an anachronism in this context. On ὁμοούσιος see FLEURY **56** and n 3. On Philo as holding this belief see EICHHORN *Apocrypha* **23** and n 3.

[4] "God manifest"—a phrase formed from John 1.31 on the evidence of John 1.1 and 1.14. Jesus' statement to which the Jews objected (John 5.18) was that "I

and my Father are one" (John 10.30). Fuller refers to the first of these passages in the textus and cites the second on the next page.

[5] John 10.34–6: "Jesus answered them, Is it not written in your law, I said, Ye are gods [Ps 82.6]? If he called them gods, unto whom the word of God came, and the scripture cannot be broken; Say ye of him, whom the Father hath sanctified, and sent into the world, Thou blasphemest; because I said, I am the Son of God?"

[6] Not in *OED*. Either directly from Latin *displanare*, "flattenings"; or a contemptuous variant of "explanations" implying diffuseness—explainings away.

[7] For *argumentum ad hominem* see ETERNAL PUNISHMENT **6** n 3. C here suggests that Christ is saying: "Suppose

the Jews, but his Sonship; otherwise, our Saviour's language would have neither force, motive, or object. "Even were I no more than the Messiah, in your meanest conceptions of that character, yet after what I have done before your eyes, nothing but malignant hearts could have prevented you from adopting a milder interpretation of my words, when in your own Scriptures there exists a precedent that so much more than merely justifies me." And this I believe to be the meaning of the words as intended to be understood by the Jews in question; though, doubtless, Fuller's sense exists *implicite*. No candid person would ever call it an evasion, to prove the injustice and malignity of an accuser even from his own grounds:—"You charge me falsely; but even were your charge true, namely, that I am a mere man, and yet call myself the Son of God, still it would not follow that I have been guilty of blasphemy."[8] But as understood by the modern Unicists,[9] it would verily, verily, be an evasive ambiguity, most unworthy of Christian belief concerning his Saviour. Common charity would have demanded of him to have said:—"I am a mere man: I do not pretend to be more; but I used the words in analogy to the words, *Ye are as Gods*;[10] and I have a right to do so: for though a mere man, I am the great Prophet and Messenger which Moses promised you."[11]

2   p 72 | Letter v "On the Standard of Morality"

If Dr. Priestley had formed his estimate of human virtue by that great standard which requires love to God with all the heart, soul, mind, and strength, and to our neighbour as ourselves; instead of representing men by nature as having "more virtue than vice,"—he must have acknowledged with the scriptures, that *the whole world lieth in wickedness—that every thought, and imagination of their heart*

I *were* no more than the Messiah (but I *am* more than that), you would still be wrong."

1[8] It followed from the Socinians' denial of Christ's divinity that he was a "mere man". On the meaning of the title "Son of God" in relation to "Son of Man" see BIBLE COPY B 71 and n 1.

1[9] *OED* cites this note as the first use of "Unicist". C held that the modern Socinians in maintaining that God was *unicus* (one and one only) were wrong to

call themselves "Unitarians" because "Unity or Union, and indistinguishable *Unicity* or Oneness, are incompatible terms". *LS (CC)* 176; see also pp 249–60, App C "Coleridge and the Unitarians", and cf 182n. Cf GREW 5 (at n 1) and *TT* 4 Apr 1832.

1[10] Ps 82.6, in John 10.34, quoted in n 5, above.

1[11] In Deut 18.15; quoted in Acts 3.22, 17.37.

is only evil, continually—and that *there is none* of them *that doeth good, no not one.*

To this the Unicists would answer, that by *the whole world* is meant all the worldly-minded;—no matter in how direct opposition to half a score other texts! "One text at a time!" sufficient for the day is the evil thereof![1]—and in this way they go on pulling out hair by hair from the horse's tail, (say rather, dreaming that they do so,) and then conclude with a shout that the horse never had a tail! For why? This hair is not a tail, nor that, nor the third, and so on to the very last; and how can all do what none of all does?[2]—Ridiculous as this is, it is a fair image of Socinian logic. Thank God, their plucking out is a mere fancy;—and the sole miserable reality is the bare rump which they call their religion;—but that is the ape's own growth.

3   p 77

First, That all punishments are designed for the good of the whole, and less, or corrective punishments for the good of the offender, is admitted. Every instance of divine punishment will be not only proportioned to the laws of equity, but adapted to promote the good of the universe at large. God never inflicts punishment for the sake of punishing....It does not appear from any thing we know of governments, either human or divine, that the good of the offender is necessarily, and in all cases the end of punishment.

This is not, ὡς ἔμοιγε δοκεῖ,[1] sufficiently guarded. That all punishments work for the good of the whole, and that the good of the whole is included in God's design, I admit: but that this is the sole cause, and the sole justification of divine punishment, I cannot, I dare not, concede;—because I should thus deny the essential evil of guilt, and its inherent incompatibility with the presence of a Being of infinite holiness. Now, exclusion from God implies the sum and utmost of punishment; and this would follow from the very essence of guilt and holiness, independently of example, consequence, or circumstance.[2]

[2]1 Matt 6.34 (var). For "Unicists" see 1 n 9, above.

[2]2 In *CN* IV 4822 (c Apr 1821) C made memorandum to illustrate this "Sophism a gradibus continuis, or the Horse-Tail Conundrum" as an argument against resisting the king in an unjust act, or against resisting a usurper. In ancient times this sophism was called *sorites*

("heap"), from the figure of taking away one grain at a time from a heap of corn or adding one grain at a time: see e.g. Cicero *Academicae quaestiones* 2.16.49. The figure of plucking a hair at a time from a horse's tail is mediaeval.

[3]1 "As it seems to me, at least".

[3]2 On argument from consequences (generally) see T. FULLER *Appeal* 1

4 pp 90ff | Letter vɪ "The Systems Compared, as to Their Tendency to Promote Morality in General"

As to our being *passive* in regeneration, if Dr. Priestley would only admit that any one character could be found that is so depraved as to be destitute of all true virtue, the same thing would follow from his own Necessarian principles. According to those principles, every man that is under the dominion of a vicious habit of mind, will continue to chuse vice, till such time as that habit is changed, and that by some influence from without himself. "If says he, I make any particular choice to day, I should have done the same yesterday, and should do the same to morrow, provided there be no change in the state of my mind respecting the object of the choice." [*On Necessity*] p. 7. Nor can any person in such a state of mind be supposed to be active in the changing of it; for such activity must imply an inclination to have it changed, which is a contradiction; as it supposes him at the same time under the dominion of evil, and yet inclined to goodness.

I have hitherto made no objection to, no remark on, any one part of this Letter; for I object to the whole—not as Calvinism, but—as what Calvin would have recoiled from. How was it that so good and shrewd a man as Andrew Fuller[1] should not have seen, that the difference between a Calvinist and a Priestleyan Materialist-Necessitarian consists in this:—The former not only believes a will, but that it is equivalent to the *ego ipse*, to the actual self, in every moral agent; though he believes that in human nature it is an enslaved, because a corrupt, will. In denying free will to the unregenerated he no more denies will, than in asserting the poor negroes in the West Indies to be slaves I deny them to be men. Now the latter, the Priestleyan, uses the word will,—not for any real, distinct, correspondent power, but,—for the mere result and aggregate of fibres, motions, and sensations; in short, it is a mere generic term with him, just as when we say, the main current in a river.[2]

---

n 3. For the Socinian position on guilt see *LS* (*CC*) 182n § 2. On punishment as an aspect of human discipline see *SM* (*CC*) 40n and *Friend* (*CC*) ɪɪ 99–101 (ɪ 169–72).

4[1] C could have heard about Andrew Fuller as a leading Baptist and one of the founders of the Baptist Missionary Society from his friend the Rev John

Ryland (1753–1825), minister of Broadmead Chapel and president of the Baptist college in Bristol from 1793 until his death, a fellow-founder of the Baptist Missionary Society and secretary of the Society from 1815 to 1825.

4[2] With this central comment on the "new Calvinism" cf FIELD **43** and n 2 and *AR* (1825) 153–5.

Now by not adverting to this, and alas! misled by Jonathan Edward's book,[3] Fuller has hidden from himself and his readers the damnable nature of the doctrine—not of necessity (for that in its highest sense is identical with perfect freedom; they are definitions each of the other); but—of extraneous compulsion. O! even this is not adequate to the monstrosity of the thought. A denial of all agency;—or an assertion of a world of agents that never act, but are always acted upon, and yet without any one being that acts;—this is the hybrid of Death and Sin, which throughout this letter is treated so amicably![4] Another fearful mistake, and which is the ground of the former, lies in conceding to the Materialist, *explicite et implicite*, that the νούμενον, the *intelligibile*, the *ipseitas supersensibilis*,[5] of guilt is in time, and of time, and, consequently, a mechanism of cause and effect;—in other words, in confounding the φαινόμενα, τὰ ῥέοντα, τὰ μὴ ὄντως ὄντα,[6]—all which belong to time, and cannot be even thought of except as effects necessarily predetermined by the precedent causes, (themselves in their turn effects of other causes),—with the transsensual ground or actual power.[7]

After such admissions, no other possible defence can be made for Calvinism or any other *ism* than the wretched recrimination: "Why, yours, Dr. Priestley, is just as bad!"—Yea, and no wonder:—for in essentials both are the same. But there was no reason for Fuller's meddling with the subject at all,—metaphysically, I mean.

5   p 95

Secondly, If the unconditionality of election render it unfriendly to virtue, it must be upon the supposition of that view of things, "which

---

[4][3] Jonathan Edwards (1703–58), American theologian and president of the College of New Jersey (later named Princeton University), *A Careful and Strict Enquiry into the Modern Prevailing Notions of that Freedom of Will which is supposed to be Essential to Moral Agency, Vertue and Vice, Reward and Punishment, Praise and Blame* (1754). In a letter to John Ryland (see n 1, above) on 3 Nov 1807 C discussed "President Edwards's Works" (*CL* iii 35), and in a notebook entry of c Dec 1823 made an unsympathetic comment on "Edwards' Book on Necessity" (*CN* iv 5077).

[4][4] For C on the integrity of action as the basis of morality see e.g. *Friend* (*CC*) i 313–19 and cf *AR* (1825) 329. On sin and the devil as in (or out of) time see FLEURY 96 and n 1.

[4][5] "Conceding 'explicitly and implicitly' that the '*noumenon*, the intelligible, the supersensible selfness' of guilt is in time...".

[4][6] "Phenomena, the things in flux, the things that have no real being".

[4][7] *OED* cites only this note for the use of "transsensual"—"Lying beyond or transcending the senses". For C's view that guilt is not "in time" see ETERNAL PUNISHMENT 1 and FIELD 60.

ascribes more to God, and less to man," having such a tendency; which is the very reverse of what Dr. Priestley elsewhere teaches, and that in the same performance.

But in both systems, as Fuller has erroneously stated his own, man is annihilated.[1] There is neither more nor less; it is all God; all, all are but *Deus infinite modificatus*:[2]—in brief, both systems are not Spinosism, for no other reason than that the logic and logical consequency of 10 Fullers + 10 × 10 Dr. Priestleys, piled on each other, would not reach the calf of Spinoza's leg.[3] Both systems of necessity lead to Spinosism, nay, to all the horrible consequences attributed to it by Spinoza's enemies. O, why did Andrew Fuller quit the high vantage ground of notorious facts, plain durable common sense, and express Scripture, to delve in the dark in order to countermine mines under a spot, on which he had no business to have wall, tent, temple, or even standing-ground!

5[1] Fuller had written pp 94–5: "If there be any difference between that election which is involved in Dr. Priestley's own scheme, and that of the Calvinists, it must consist, not in the original appointment, or in the certainty of the event; but in the immediate causes or reasons which induced the Deity to fix things in the manner that he has done."

5[2] "God infinitely modified".

5[3] For C's admiration for Spinoza see e.g. *P Lects* Lect 13 (1949) 384–6.

THOMAS FULLER
1608–1661

C's earliest acquaintance with Fuller's writings is not clearly recorded. RS borrowed the *History of the Worthies of England* (1662 f°) from the Bristol Library Society May–Jun 1795 (*Bristol LB* 54) and quoted Fuller in his notes, to *Joan of Arc* (1796). If C read the book then, when he was contributing to that poem, it left no recognisable trace; but in Nov 1801 he referred to the *Worthies*. *CN* I 1006; 1012 and 1013 are at second hand. He seems to have been reading the *Worthies* and *Holy State* in c 1809–10 (*CN* III 3596, 3656, 3660), whether inspired by the mature enthusiasm that Lamb was to express in his "Specimens from the Writings of Fuller" (1811), being mainly a selection of epigrams and anecdotes, or simply drawing upon RS's library, or WW's, is not known. In Jul 1816 he proposed to John Murray "a Review of old Books" to include "Paracelsus, Cardan, old Fuller" (*CL* IV 648), but that scheme did not prosper.

In Jul 1829 C said that "Next to Shakspeare I am not certain whether Thomas Fuller ⟨beyond all other Writers⟩ does not excite in me the sense and emotion of the Marvellous" (*Church-History* 1), and in c Oct–Dec 1829 he established as one of the two classes of men of genius those "in whom the virtue is over all, in root, stem, leaves, & flower—Jer. Taylor, Fuller, Shakespear" (N 41 f 78: *CN* v); yet of those three Fuller is by far the least annotated, with a total of less than fifty marginalia in seven titles, and of these only two are dated by C—*Church-History* 6, on 30 Aug 1824, and 1 (cited above). Except for the joint volume comprising *A Triple Reconciler* and *Life Out of Death*, all the known annotated copies are located and show on examination that the marginalia in them are in a hand "late" rather than "early". It may be that C had been acquainted with Fuller's work for so long that, as with other early favourites, he did not much annotate his copies, and that the surviving marginalia were written at the times those particular volumes came into his hands, all by chance at a rather late date.

Of the seven annotated works of Fuller, all are seventeenth-century editions except for the *History of the Worthies* (2 vols 1811). On c 30 Nov 1833 C was given a copy of *A Triple Reconciler* and esteemed it "a prized addition to my assemblage of Fuller's Works". N Q: see *Triple Reconciler* headnote. But Basil Montagu's gift of the *Church-History* (1655) on 24 Aug 1824 was to Gillman, not C; and it was from Gillman, not C, that Lamb in Nov 1829 borrowed a copy of the *Church-History* and the *History of the Worthies* (*LL* III 234, 263). *Gillman SC* (1843) includes seven Fuller titles, four of which were probably annotated by C. By comparison, *Green SC* (1880) includes four Fuller titles, none of which is shown as C's or annotated by him.

In c Nov 1830 C made a note about "T. Fuller's first Publication, in

1631—a divine Poem, entitled David's Heinous Sin, Heartie Repentances and Heavie Punishment in a thin Octavo. Mem. to remember not to forget to ask Mr Cary whether it is in the Br. Museum—". N 47 f 47 (*CN* v); C had the information from Nichols's "Memoir" in the *History of the Worthies* (1811) I vii. The BM had acquired a copy of *David's Hainous Sinne, Heartie Repentance, Heavie Punishment* (1630) in 1807, but it is not known that C borrowed it.

The Appeal of Iniured Innocence: unto the religious learned and ingenuous reader. In a controversie betwixt the animadvertor Dr. Peter Heylyn and the author Thomas Fuller, &c. 3 pts in 1 vol. London 1659. F°.

Bound as second with Thomas FULLER *The Church-History of Britain* (1655).

British Museum Ashley 4774

For a description of the composite volume, and for Lamb's borrowing in 1829–30, see *Church-History* headnote.

DATE. c 1824–9, if annotated at the same time as the *Church-History*.

1 i 5 | Pt I ch 5

Yea, there want not *learned Writers* (whom I need not name) of the Opinion that even the *Instrumental Pen-men* of the *Scripture* might commit ἁμαρτήματα μνημόνικα [memory-mistakes]; though *open* that *window* to *profaneness*, and it will be in vain to *shut* any *dores*; *Let God be true, and every man a lyer*: However, I mention their judgments to this purpose, to shew that *Memory-mistakes* have not been counted such *hainous* matters, but *venial* in their own *nature*, as not only *finding* but *deserving pardon*.

It has been matter of complaint with hundreds, yea, it is an old Cuckoo Song of grim Saints, that the Reformation came to its close long before it came to its Completion/ But the cause of this imperfection has been fully laid open by no party—scilicet, that in Divines of both Parties of the Reformers, the Protestants and the Detestants there was the same Relic of the Roman Lues,[1] the habit of deciding ⟨for or against⟩ the orthodoxy of a Position, not according to its truth or falsehood, not on grounds of Reason or of History, but by the imagined *Consequences* of the Position.[a] The very same principles, on which the Pontificial Polemics vindicate the papal infallibility, Fuller et sexcentum alii[2] apply to the (if possible) still

---

[a] The note, written in the head and outer margin, was stopped by the shoulder-note; C wrote " ∨ ∨ " and resumed the note in the foot-margin with " ∨ ∨ "

[1]1 Generally, a disfiguring disease (see e.g. EDINBURGH MEDICAL JOURNAL 2–4); here used metaphorically of any spreading or contagious evil, political or social.

[1]2 Lit. "and 600 others", idiomatically "a large number".

more extravagant Notion of the absolute truth and divinity of every syllable of the O. and N. Testament.[3]

2 i 21

[Fuller's challenge to Heylyn's preface to *Examen Historicum*] Sure I am, that one of as much *Meekness*, as some are of *Morosness*, even upright *Moses* himself, in his Service of the *Essential*, and *Increated Truth* (of higher consequence than the *Historical Truth* controverted *] betwixt us) had notwithstanding *a respect to the recompence of Reward.* [shoulder-note:] Heb. 11. 26.

* In *Religion*, the Faith pre-supposed in the *respect*, and as its condition, gives to the motive a purity and an elevation, which of itself, and where the recompence is looked for in temporal and carnal pleasures or profits, it would not have.

1[3] Fuller's argument "by the imagined *Consequences* of the Position", to which C objects, is in effect: the Bible is God's word; if we say that there is any error in the Bible, however unimportant, the *consequence* is that God's word is not true; but it is impossible that God should tell a lie, therefore every word in the Bible is literally true. Roman Catholics also use the same argument for the complete infallibility of the Pope and of the Church. See *CN* III 4143 and e.g. FITZGIBBON ANNEX [*a*]. For other kinds of arguments from consequences see e.g. FLEURY **24** textus, Andrew FULLER **3**. For a discussion of the conditions necessary for an argument by consequences to be valid see *CN* IV 5117 and cf 5134.

The Church-History of Britain; from the birth of Jesus Christ, untill
the year M.DC.XLVIII. Endeavoured by Thomas Fuller. [Together
with:] The History of the University of Cambridge, since the
Conquest. 1655. [and] The History of Waltham-Abby in Essex,
founded by King Harold. 1655. 4+2 pts in 1 volume. London 1655.
Fº.

Bound as first in a volume with Thomas FULLER *Appeal of Iniured Innocence*
(1659). The *Church-History* is normally bound to include the histories of
Cambridge and Waltham Abbey.

British Museum Ashley 4774

Bookplate of Basil Montagu on p ⁻5 (p–d). Inscribed on p ⁻2: "With Basil
Montagu's love to his friend James Gillman August 24. 1824." On 20 Dec
1827 C apologised to Montagu for failure, through Gillman's illness, to fulfil
some obligation with regard to "the *Fullers*". *CL* vi 718–19. On p ⁻1 a note
by Gillman: "In July 1828, he ⟨S. T. C.⟩ made a short tour up the Rhine
with Wordsworth, and returned in August, when I was in Paris with the Duke
of Sᵗ Albans—James Gillman". Pencil marks in the margins on many pages,
e.g. 4, 8, etc. A passage on ii 170–1 is marked; in the Index at KETTS the
reference to p 339 is corrected to 393. None of these marks is C's.

Lamb borrowed this composite volume, with Thomas FULLER *History of
Worthies*, in Nov 1829, reckoning "on having massy reading till Christmas".
He returned them in the spring of 1830, writing to Gillman: "Pray do you,
or S. T. C., immediately write to say you have received back the golden
works of the dear, fine, silly old angel, which I part from, bleeding." *LL* iii
234, 237, 263.

C chose from *Church-History* i 199 an epigraph for the section of *C&S*
"On the Third Possible Church, or the Church of Antichrist". *C&S (CC)*
130.

DATE. 30 Aug 1824 (**6**), Jul 1829 (**1**).

1   pp ⁻2–⁻1, in pencil, overtraced*ᵃ*

Next to Shakspeare I am not certain whether Thomas Fuller
⟨beyond all other Writers⟩ does not excite in me the sense and
emotion of ~~Wonder~~ the Marvellous; the *degree*, in which any given
faculty or combination of faculties is possessed and manifested, so
far surpassing what one would have thought *possible* in a single Mind
as to give one's Admiration the flavor and quality of Wonder![1] Wit
was the Stuff and Substance of Fuller's Intellect—it was the Element
⟨the earthen base,⟩[2] the material which he worked in—& this very

---

ᵃ The first 7 lines were overtraced apparently by HNC, the rest by Gillman

[1] See also *History of Worthies* 1 and   [2] For the pun "*Fuller's* Earth" see
2 and 2 n 2.   *History of Worthies* 1 and n 3.

circumstance has defrauded him of his due praise for the practical wisdom of the Thoughts, for the beauty and variety of the Truths, he ~~changed it~~ shaped the Stuff into—T. Fuller was incomparably the most *sensible*, the *least* prejudiced, great Man of an Age that boasted a Galaxy of Great Men.

He is a very voluminous writer, and yet in all his numerous Volumes on so many different Subjects, it is scarcely too much to say, that you will hardly find a page in which, ⟨some⟩ one Sentence out of ⟨every⟩ three does not deserve to be quoted for itself, as motto or as maxim,[3]—GOD BLESS THEE, dear Old Man!! May I meet with thee! ⟨which is tantamount to—May I go to Heaven!.⟩[4]

July 1829   S. T. Coleridge
Grove, Highgate.

2   i 27 | Bk i 5th Century §1

This *Pelagius* was a *Britan* by Birth...as some say called *Morgan*, that is in Welsh, *near the Sea.*...Let no Foreiner insult on the infelicity of our Land in bearing this Monster: But consider, first, if his excellent natural Parts, and eminent acquired Learning might be separated from his dangerous Doctrine, no Nation need be ashamed to acknowledge him. Secondly, *Britain* did but breed *Pelagius*, Pelagius himself bred his Heresy, and in forein Parts where he travelled; *France, Syria, Aegypt, Rome* it self, if not first invented, much improved his pestilent *Opinions*. Lastly, as our Island is to be pittied for breeding the Person, so she is to be praised for opposing the Errours of *Pelagius*.

It raises or ought to raise our estimation of Fuller's good sense & the general Temperance of his Judgement when we see the heavy

1[3] C used a sentence from *Church-History* as a motto to a section of *C&S*: see headnote. This, however, seems to be the only motto C drew from Fuller. None of the aphorisms in *AR* is taken from Fuller, although aphorisms are taken from a dozen authors other than Leighton. In 1811 Lamb published "Specimens from the Writings of Fuller, the Church Historian", mainly a selection of Fuller's epigrams and anecdotes.
1[4] In N Q f 38 (*CN* v) in a series of notes on *A Triple Reconciler*, C wrote a doggerel "Monument to the Memory of Dr Thomas Fuller":

A Lutheran stout, I hop'd for *Goose*
   and *Gandry*.
Both the Pope's Limbo, and his fiery
   Laundry.
No wit e'er saw I in Original Sin,
⟨And no Sin find I in Original Wit;⟩
But if I'm all in the wrong; and Grin
   for Grin,
Scorch'd Souls must pay for each too
   lucky Hit....
Oh! Thomas Fuller! Oh!—so vast thy
   Debt,
Thou art not out of Purgatory yet!

weight of prejudices, the universal code of his Age, incumbent on his Judgement—and which nevertheless left ~~his nature him~~ a sanity of opinion the general Character of his Writings.[1] This remark was suggested by the term, Monster, attached to the worthy Cambrian, Pelagius—the Teacher Arminianismi ante Arminium.[2]

3 i 54 | ii 6th Century § 5

Whereas in Holy Writ, when the Apostles (and Papists commonly call *Augustine* the *English Apostle*, how properly we shall see hereafter) went to a Forreign Nation, God gave them the Language thereof, least otherwise their Preaching should have the Vigour thereof abated, taken at the second Hand, or rather at the second *] Mouth, as *Augustine's* was; who used an Interpreter (not as *Ioseph* to his brethren, out of State and Policie, but) out of mere Necessity.

* What a loss, that Fuller had not made a reference to his *authorities* for this assertion—I am sure, he could have found none in the New Testament—but facts that imply, & in ansence[a] of all such proof, *prove*, the contrary.

4 p ‾2, referring to i 55 | ii § 6

Thus we see the whole Week bescattered with *Saxon* Idols, whose Pagan-Gods were the God-fathers of the Dayes, and gave them their Names. This some Zealot may behold as the Object of a necessary Reformation, desiring to have the Dayes of the Week new dipt, and called after other Names. Though indeed this Supposed Scandall will not offend the wise, as beneath their Notice, and cannot offend the Ignorant, as above their Knowledge. Wherefore none need so hastily to hurry to the Top of the Main Mast, thence to pluck down the Badge of *Castor* and *Pollux*: but rather let them be carefull, steadily to steere their Ship to the Heaven, for which it is bound; *and let us redeem the Time, for the Dayes are evill*: not because in their Name they bear the Cognizance of the Pagan-Gods; but because swarming with the Sins of Prophane men, which all should labour to reprove in others, and amend in themselves.

Book II. p. 55. §6 ad finem. A curious prediction fulfilled a few years after in the *Quakers*; and well worthy of being extracted and

[a] A slip for "absence"

[2[1]] See also *History of Worthies* 3.
[2[2]] The Teacher "of Arminianism before Arminius". For Arminius see

BAXTER *Reliquiae* COPY A **49** n 2; for Pelagianism BUNYAN COPY A **24** n 1.

addressed to the present FRIENDS.[1] Mem. Error of the Friends, but natural & common to almost all sects, the perversion of the Wisdom of the first Establishers of their Sect into their own Follingy by not distinguishing between the conditionally right and the permanently and essentially so.[2]—Ex. gr. It was *right* conditionally in the Apostles to forbid black puddings even to the Gentile Christians, and it was wisdom in them—but to continue the prohibition would be folly & Judaism in us.—The elder Church very sensibly distinguished Episcopal from Apostolic Inspiration—the Episcopal Spirit, i.e. that which dictated what was fit and profitable for a particular Community or Church at a particular period from the Apostolic & Catholic Spirit, which dictated Truth and Duties of permanent and universal Obligation.

S. T. C.

5   p ⁻2, referring to i 59 | II 7th Century. Latin Dedication

Socrates *interrogatus, quo* Philtro *Natura* Sympathias *conciliaret, quidve esset incausa, ut alii hominum* primo occursu *ament medullitus, alii sibi mutuò sint insensi; hanc rationem reddidit.*

Deus, *inquit, ab aeterno quicquid futurum esset animarum creavit; creatas, per immensum temporis spatium in uno cumulo collocavit; collocatas, corporibus, prout indies generantur, infundit. Hinc est, si contingat vel fortuitum consortium inter eos homines, quorum animae in hoc acervo propinquiores, quod* primo visu (*quasi veteris vicinitatis memores*) *se invicem diligant; dum isti,* primo intuitu, *antipathiae stimulis urgeantur, quorum animae adversantes diametricè opponebantur.*

4[1] See Thomas Clarkson *A Portraiture of Quakerism* (2nd ed 3 vols 1807) I 317–19: "Another alteration, which took place in the language of the Society [of Friends], was the disuse of the common names of the days of the week, and of those of the months of the year. The names of the days were considered to be of heathen origin. Sunday had been so called by the Saxons, because it was the day, on which they sacrificed to the Sun...Now when the Quakers considered that Jehovah had forbidden the Israelites to make mention even of the names of other gods, they thought it inconsistent in Christians to continue to use the names of heathen idols for the common division of their time...Hence they determined upon the disuse of these words, and to put other names in their stead. The numerical way of naming the days seemed to them to be the most rational, and the most innocent. They called, therefore, Sunday, the First day; Monday, the Second...and so on to Saturday, which was of course the Seventh. They used no other names but these, either in their conversation or in their letters." The injunction against using the heathen names of days and months was retained in the official "advices in discipline" of the Society of Friends until 1883.

4[2] On the Quakers generally and the changes in their views from primitive to "modern" see AURELIUS 47 n 1.

Fateor commentum hoc Socraticum *à* Theologia *abhorrere; et in* Philosophia *plurimis asystatis laborare.*

Quod si ei subesset tantum veritatis, quantum ingenii, *sanctissimè voverem, in hoc* animarum cumulo Tuam et Meam *continguas olim jacuisse: cum* Te *primum conspectum et animitus amarem, et à* Te *redamarer.*

[Socrates was once asked by what *magic* Nature produced *affinities*, and what was the reason why some people fall head over heels in love *at their first meeting* while others are indifferent to each other. He gave this explanation:

God, he said, created the whole sum of souls to be at the beginning of eternity and put them all together in one heap for a measureless space of time; and now, every day, as the time comes for their birth, he pours them into their bodies. So it is, that if even a chance association should arise between people whose souls were close together in the heap they love one another *at first sight* as though they remembered their former proximity, while those whose souls were diametrically opposite are *at first sight* pricked by the spurs of antipathy.

I admit that this fabrication of *Socrates* is quite at odds with *Theology* and suffers from many inconsistencies as *Philosophy*; but if it contained as much *truth* as *ingenuity* I would swear by the most solemn pledges that in that *heap of souls Your soul and Mine* once lay side by side, since I loved *You* with all my heart and at first sight and was loved by *You* in return.]

P. 59. Latin Dedication—remarkably pleasing and elegant—Milton in his classical youth, the æra of his *Lycidas*, might have written it—only he would have given it in Latin Verse.[1]

6   p +1, referring to iv 11 | x 17th Century

[Account of the Hampton Court Conference of 1603/4] BP. of Lond. *May your Majesty be pleased, that the ancient Canon may be remembred*, Schismatici contra Episcopos non sunt audiendi. *And, there is another Decree of a very ancient Council, That no man should be admitted to speak against that whereunto he hath formerly subscribed.*

And as for you Doctor Reynolds, *and your Sociates, how much are ye bound to his Majestie's Clemency, permitting you, contrary to the Statute* primo Elizabethae, *so freely to speak against the Liturgie, and Discipline established. Faine would I know the end you aime at, and whether you be not of Mr.* Cartwright's *minde, who affirmed, That we ought in Ceremonies rather to conforme to the* Turke

5[1]   Milton, born in Dec 1608, published *Lycidas* in 1638. His verse compositions in Latin (with those in Greek and Italian) were published in 1645 under a title announcing that most of them had been composed by the age of twenty—*Poemata quorum pleraque intra annum aetatis vigesimum conscripsit.* For C's praise of an English dedication of Fuller's see *Triple Reconciler* headnote.

than to the Papists. *I doubt you approve his Position, because here appearing before his Majesty in Turky-Gownes, not in your Scholastick habits, according to the order of the Universities.*

If any man, who like myself hath attentively read the Church History of the reign of Elizabeth, and the Conference before and with her pedant Successor (see Bish. of London's reply to or rather interruption of Dr Reynolds, X Book p. 11) can shew me any essential difference between Whitgift and Bancroft, during their rule, and Bonner and Gardner in the reign of Mary, I will be thankful to him in my heart and for him in my prayers.[1] One difference I see, viz. that the former professing the New Testament to be their rule & guide, & making the fallibility of all Churches and Individuals an article of faith, were more inconsistent and therefore less excusable, than the Popish Persecutors.

S. T. C.

30 Aug. 1824.

N.B. The crimes, murderous as they were, were the vice and delusion of the *Age*—and it is ignorance to lack charity towards the persons, Papist or Protestant; but the *tone*, the *spirit*, characterizes, and belongs to, the Individual—ex. gr. the bursting spleen of this Bancroft, not so satisfied with the precious Arbitrator for having precondemned ⟨his opponents⟩ as fierce and surly with him for not hanging them up unheard!—

7 iv 136 | xi 17th Century § 3

During the sitting of the last *Parliament*, one *Leighton* a *Scotish-man* presented a Book unto them; had he been an *English man*, we durst call him *furious*, and now will terme him a *fiery* (whence *kindled* let other ghess) *Writer*. His Book consisted of a continued railing, from the beginning to the end; exciting the Parliament and People to kil *] all the Bishops, and to smite them under the *fifth Rib*. He bitterly enveyed against the *Queen*, calling her a *Daughter* of *Heth*, a

6[1] At the Hampton Court Conference held in Jan 1604, James I presiding, to consider Puritan demands for church reform, the Puritans were led by John Rainolds (1549–1607)—Fuller's "Reynolds"—the bishops by Richard Bancroft (1544–1610), who succeeded John Whitgift (c 1530–1604) as abp of Canterbury and leader of the anti-Puritan forces. The Puritans achieved little at the Conference. For C's view of the brutality of Edmund Bonner (c 1500–69) and Stephen Gardiner (c 1483–1555) see BAXTER *Reliquiae* COPY B **65** and n 1, *Reliquiae* COPY A **35** and n 1.

Canaanite and *Idolatress*, and *ZIONS PLEA was* the specious Title of his *Pamphlet*; for which he was sentenced in the *Star*-chamber, to be whipt and stigmatized, to have his eares cropt and nose slit. But betwixt *pronouncing* and *inflicting* this *Censure*, he makes his escape into *Bedford-shire*.

* Qᵞ Did Fuller copy this Lie from Heylin or H. from F.?[1] For a wicked *Lie* it is. Leighton recommending some act of Reform adds that this would be the way to smite Prelacy under the 5ᵗʰ Rib.[2] He had before expressly and affectionately disclaimed every evil wish against the Persons whose Learning & Virtue as Individuals he extols.[3]

7[1] Fuller's *Church-History* was first published in 1655, Heylyn's account of Alexander Leighton's trial in 1668. HEYLYN *Cyprianus Anglicus* (C's ed 1671) 187 tells the same story as Fuller: "*Leighton*...a fiery *Puritan* in Faction, dedicated a most pestilent Book unto them, called *Sions Plea*. In this Book he incited them *to kill all the Bishops, and to smite them under the fifth Rib*...".

7[2] Alexander Leighton (1568–1649) in *An Appeal to the Parliament; or Sions Plea Against the Prelacie* (1629) used strong language against the episcopacy ("those *men of bloode*, the Prelacie") and called the queen (see textus) a "*Daughter of Heth*" (p 172), and wrote (p 240): "Smite that *Hazaell* in the fifth ribbe: Yea if Father or Mother stand in the way, away with them; (we beseech you,)...Make rather a *rotten Tree* fall, then that the rotting droppes thereof should kill the Sheep." The "act of

Reform" that Leighton had in mind was the abolition of the episcopacy, not the actual killing of the bishops.

7[3] Cf *Sions Plea* p 81: "...it is the evills of their callings, and not persons, which we oppose"; and on the last page (p 344): "We feare they are like *pleuritickes patients* that cannot *spitt*, whom nothing but *inscision* will cure (we meane of their callinges, not of their persons,) to whom we have no quarrell, but wish them better than they either wish to us, or to themselves." Robert Leighton, whose work was the starting-point for *AR*, was the son of Alexander Leighton and one of the most saintly bishops in the history of the Church. On 16 Aug 1823 C asked Taylor & Hessey to procure him a copy of *Sion's Plea. CL* v 294. Green's library included a copy of it, not shown as C's: *Green SC* (1880) 551. See LEIGHTON general note.

The History of the Worthies of England: endeavoured by Thomas Fuller, D.D. First printed in 1662. A new edition, with a few explanatory notes, by John Nichols... In two volumes. 2 vols. London 1811. 4º.

Indiana University (Lilley Library)

Inscribed on I ⁻2 in ink by a bookseller: "2 Vols: 5.. 5..—With Notes by Samuel Taylor Coleridge." Also incribed on I ⁻2 and II ⁻2: "Stephen Coleridge—7 Egerton Mansions SW—February—1893", and with the bookplate of Stephen Coleridge on the half-title of Vol I. "Cat. 233" in ink on the front paste-down of Vol I.

Lamb borrowed this volume from C in 1829–30: see *Church-History* headnote.

MS TRANSCRIPT. VCL BT 37: SC transcript, from which the *NTP* version was printed.

DATE. c 1823–9. Cf the Fuller extracts in *CN* IV 4944, 4960–4963 (c Jul 1823).

1   I v | Preface by the Editor

Even Bishop Nicolson, fastidious as in this instance he is, admits that the Work at least "*pretends* to give an account of the Native Commodities, Manufactures, Buildings, Proverbs, &c. of all the Counties of England and Wales, as well as of the Great men in Church and State, though the latter looks like the principal design, and makes up the greatest part of the volume...."

Much might be said, if it were necessary, in vindication of the language of Dr. FULLER, and even in palliation of occasional mistakes. In his early years, quaintness was the characteristick of almost every Writer of eminence; and if he has followed their example, he has certainly refined upon it, and rarely, if ever, degenerates into vulgarity. The style which he had acquired in the Reign of the Pedant James was not likely to be improved amidst the horrors of Civil Commotion; and he did not long enough survive the Restoration, to correct the erroneous taste in which he had so long indulged.

Fuller's Language!—Grant me patience, Heaven!—A *tythe* of His Beauties would be sold cheap for a whole Library of our classical Writers from Addison to Johnson and Junius inclusive.[1]—And Bishop Nicholson—a painstaking old Charewoman in the Anti-

[1] For C's uncomplimentary view of "our classical Writers" see AURELIUS 1 n 3.

quarian and Rubbish Concern[2]—The Venerable Rust and Dust of the whole Firm are not worth an ounce of *Fuller*'s Earth![3]

2 I vii

Shakespear! Milton! Fuller! De Foe! Hogarth![1]—As to the remaining mighty Host of our great Men, other Countries have produced something like them—but these are uniques—England may challenge the World to shew a correspondent name to either of the Five—I do not say, that with exception of the First, Names of equal glory may not be produced, in *a different kind*. But these are Genera, containing each only one Individual.[2] *S. T. C.*

3 I vii–viii | Memoirs of the Author

He continued at the Savoy, to the great Satisfaction of his people, and the neighbouring nobility and gentry, labouring all the while in private and in publick to serve the King...He soon found that he must expect to be silenced and ejected, as others had been; yet desisted not till he was, or thought himself, unsettled....

In April 1643, he conveyed himself to the King at Oxford, who received him gladly. As his Majesty had heard of his extraordinary abilities in the pulpit, he was now desirous of knowing them personally; and accordingly Fuller preached before him at St. Mary's church. His fortune upon this occasion was very singular. He had before preached and published a sermon in London, upon "the

1[2] William Nicolson (1655–1727), bp of Carlisle, then of Derry, antiquary, whose great work, among many other antiquarian studies, was the *Historical Library* (English 1696–9, Scottish 1702, Irish 1724); the quotation in textus is from I 14.

1[3] A hydrous silicate of alumina, like potter's clay, formerly used in fulling (cleansing) cloth, now used as a filtering agent and a catalyst. In the seventeenth and eighteenth centuries the term was used figuratively of purifying or cleansing the conscience or intelligence. C, in punning on Fuller's name, refers to Fuller's wit particularly. In *Church-History* **1** wit is "the Stuff and Substance of Fuller's Intellect...the Element ⟨the earthen base,⟩ the material which he worked in"; in N Q f 36 (*CN* v) C refers

to the "incomparable FULLER, that great intellectual Potter, whose Clay was wit, whose ~~shaping~~ Wheel was sound ~~Common~~ Good Sense, with Learning and Charity for the moulding Hands". On Fuller's wit see also **4** and n 1, below.

2[1] Cf *Church-History* **1**. For C on Hogarth see BEAUMONT & FLETCHER COPY A **1** n 1.

2[2] C also noted in c Oct–Dec 1829: "Men of Genius—of two classes—I. Those who secrete their virtuous or odoriferous [? Realism] in some distinct product—the seed, the fruit, the blossom, this or that gland—and II. those, in whom the virtue is over all, in root, stem, leaves, & flower—Jer. Taylor, Fuller, Shakespear, are of this latter class—". N 41 f 78 (*CN* v).

new-moulding Church-reformation," which caused him to be censured as too hot a Royalist; and now, from his sermon at Oxford, he was thought to be too lukewarm: which can only be ascribed to his moderation, which he would sincerely have inculcated in each party, as the only means of reconciling both.

Poor Fuller! with too strong a leaven of University Prejudice not to be warped in favor of the worser of the two Factions! Of Too ~~superior sense~~ enlightened not to see ~~the~~ its abuses and errors! ~~of THIS oun of any~~ And ~~of~~ too ~~much~~ honesty, not to admit the truth and force of sundry complaints urged by the ~~Antagonist Party~~ other party!—nothing but a Miracle of attraction & amiableness in his personal Disposition and Demeanor could have saved him, in such a conflux, from being stoned by both Factions!—To have been abused and slandered—this was merely an ~~overdusted~~ powdered Coat from the dust and dirt thrown up by the Shot that had passed him—and may be fairly accounted as part and sign of his wonderful preservation.[1]

3A   i 24 | Ch 9 "Of Writers of the Canon and Civil Law..."

...seeing they "enjoyed all things in common," what use they had of Lawyers; seeing no propriety, ~~on~~ no pleading...

3B   i 29 | Ch 10 "Writers"

In recounting up of Musitians, I have only insisted on such who made it their profession, and either have written books of that faculty, ~~and~~ or have attained to such an eminence therein as is generally acknowledged.

3C   i 109 | Bark-shire. Henry VIII

8th] 24. HUMPHRY FORSTER, Knight. He...confessed to King Henry the <u>Third</u>, that never any thing went so much against his conscience...as his attending the execution of *three poor men* martyred at Windsor.

4   i 285 | Devon-shire. Souldiers

GEORGE MONCK. Some will say he *being* (and long may he *be*) alive belongs not to your *Pen*, according to your *premised Rules*. But,

---

3[1] See also *Pisgah-Sight* **10**.

know, he is too *high* to come under the *Roof* of my *Regulations*, whose *merit* may make Laws for me to observe. Besides, it is better that I should be *censured*, then he not *commended*.

I remember no other instance of flattery in this not less wise than witty,[1] and (for one speck in a Luminary does not forfeit the name) not less honest than liberal, ⟨Writer:⟩ tho' liberal and *sensible* to a degree unprecedented in his age, and unparalleled.—These §phs, however, form a glaring exception. The flattery is rancid.[2] A No more thoroughly worthless Wretch ⟨than Monk,⟩ or of meaner talents, could be History furnish wherewith to exemplify the caprice of Fortune.[3] Or shall I not rather say, the Judgement of Providence—in righteous scorn & Chastisement of a thankless & corrupt Nation, bringing in one reptile by the instrumentality of another, a lewd lazy mean Tyrant by a brainless avaricious perjured Traitor—and to this hateful Ingrate alone Charles II. shewed himself not an Ingrate!—See Clarendon—last Oxford Edition.[4]

5   ɪ 287 | Sea-men

Sir WALTER RAWLEIGH.... He was bred in Oriel Colledg in Oxford; and thence comming to Court, found some hopes of the Queen's favours reflecting upon him. This made him write in a glasse window, obvious to the Queen's eye,

"Fain would I climb, yet fear I to fall."

Her Majesty, either espying or being shown it, did under-write,

"If thy heart fails thee, climb not at all."

4[1] Cf 1 n 3, above, and *Church-History* 1 (at n 1). In a note of c Jul 1823 C borrowed a simile "from the witty-wise, tho' not always wisely witty, Fuller". *CN* ɪv 4963; for the simile see *Holy State* headnote. Also, in a note of c Nov 1833 referring to *A Triple Reconciler*, he spoke of "the *ever-witty*, but tho' ⟨a⟩ less acknowleged yet not less distinguishing quality ⟨of the man,⟩ eminently, yea in that age of political and theological party-passions, *pre*-eminently *Judicious*, FULLER." N Q f 35ᵛ (*CN* v). See also *Holy State* 7 and *Pisgah-Sight* 8.
4[2] See also *Holy State* 10.
4[3] See also BAXTER *Reliquiae* COPY B 83 and n 4.

4[4] C seems to be thinking of how George Monck (1608–70) after capture and imprisonment in 1644 in the service of Charles ɪ held positions of trust and authority under Cromwell; and how, through his parliamentary influence and his power as a military commander, he became the instrument for the return of Charles ɪɪ to England, and how he was rewarded at the Restoration with the Order of the Garter and elevation to the peerage, and afterwards with a succession of military appointments. The passage C refers to in Clarendon has not been identified, though the "last Oxford Edition" of the *History of the Rebellion* would have been that of 1807 (3 vols), the next Oxford edition being 1839 (7 vols).

more commonly written—

> Fain would I climb but o! I fear to fall—
> If thy heart fail thee, climb not then at all.—[1]

But I prefer Fuller's, as more quippish and *adagy*.[2]

6 i 288 | Writers

ROGER the CISTERTIAN lived (neer the place of his birth) at Ford Abbey in this County. Here the judicious Reader will please himself to *climb* up the two *following Mountains* of extreams (onely with his eye), and then descend into the Vale of *Truth*, which lieth betwixt them.

Lela'nd:	Bale, Cent. iii. num. 23.
"Doctis artibus et pietati, insolito quodam animi ardore, noctes atque dies invigilavit."	"Invigilavit fallaciis atque imposturis diabolicis, ut Christi gloriam obscuraret."
[He devoted himself night and day to the learned arts and to devoutness, with a certain unusual zeal of spirit.]	[He devoted himself to fallacies and diabolical impostures, so as to obscure the glory of Christ.]

I believe that *bilious Bale* would have been sick of the *yellow Jaundies*, *] if not venting his *choller* in such expressions.

* How happened it, that Fuller is so bitter against Bale? Bale's restless and calamitous Life (driven as he was from Dan to Barsheba) which renders his voluminous labors a marvel, ought to have shielded him from anyll severity of Censure. And in this instance & I think in some others frowned at by Fuller, Bale was clearly right.[1]

7 i 376 | Gloucester-shire. Wonders

THE HIGRE. Men as little know the cause of the name, as the thing thereby signified. Some pronounce it the *Eagre*, as so called from the

---

5[1] Scott in *Kenilworth* ch 17 has another variant: "Fain would I climb but that I fear to fall".

5[2] "Adagy" was commonly used in the seventeenth century as a form of the noun "adage", but *OED* does not record the adjective as used here by C.

6[1] John Bale (1495–1563), educated in a Carmelite monastery and at Jesus College, Cambridge, turned Protestant and thereafter engaged in savage controversy with the Roman Catholics. Twice

driven from the country for the virulence of his invective, he also received influential appointments, as bp of Ossory by Edward VI and as prebendary of Canterbury by Elizabeth. Fuller quotes here from *Illustrium Majoris Britanniae scriptorum...summarium* (Wesel 1548), Bale's chief work. Roger the Cistercian, or Roger of Ford (fl 1170–80), was a recorder of pious fictions of the kind C abhorred. Cf *Pisgah-Sight* 3 and FLEURY **26** and n 2.

keenesse and fiercenesse thereof. It is the confluence or encounter (as supposed) of the salt and fresh water in *Severne*, equally terrible with its flashings and noise to the seers and hearers; and oh how much more then to the feelers thereof! If any demand why the *Thames* hath not an *Higre* as well as the *Severne*, where we find the same cause, and therefore why meet we not with the same effects? I re-demand of them why is there not an *Euripus* with the same reciprocation of Tides, as well about the other *Cyclides*, as *Euboea* alone? Thus, in cases of this kind, it is easier to ask *ten*, than answer *one* question with satisfaction.

A single Look on two good County Maps, in which the course of the Severn from the mouth, and of the width & then the reaches of the Thames, would have explained the existence of the Higre or Boar in the Severn, the Trent, and the Parrot,[1] and its absence in the Thames, without a voyage to the Eubœan Cyclides.[2]

7A II 291 | Somerset-shire

caring] Thomas Coriat.... drave on no design, ~~carrying~~ for Coin and Counters alike...

8 II 419 | Warwick-shire. Benefactors to the Publick

[Footnote by Nichols on "the *three English Schools* of the *first Magnitude*":] Eton, Westminster, and the Charter-house.

Winchester?[1]

7[1] When a tide of exceptional range flows into a constricted channel a wave forms like a wall of water, in extreme cases as much as ten or twelve feet in height. The most spectacular instance of this in Britain is in the Severn, the Trent bore being of smaller amplitude. The river Parret, flowing into the Bristol Channel at Burnham-on-Sea, develops a bore almost as high as that of the neighbouring Severn, and was well known to C because Bridgwater, the port on the river Parret, was the nearest town to Nether Stowey and on the most direct route between Stowey and Bristol. C used the bore as a figure in an *MP* article of 14 Oct 1800: "they returned, as the tide does in our rivers, Trent and Parrot, not by any gradual growth, but *in a head*, and like a wall of waters". *EOT (CC)* I 360; cf I 255, *CL* IV 830n. He also punned on the name of the river, regularly so spelling it: "I have wandered too by the River Parrot, which looks as filthy as if all the Parrots in the House of Commons had been washing their Consciences therein." *CL* I 217; cf *CN* I 296.

7[2] The Euripus, the long narrow channel between Euboea and the mainland of Greece, has very fast and dangerous alternating currents that change direction from six to fourteen times a day. The cause is not yet completely understood. The other islands in the Cyclades being more widely spaced develop no such marked tidal peculiarities.

8[1] Winchester College, founded 1382,

8A II 448 | Wilt-shire. Writers

"Leland...informs us, that, during the flourishing of the glory of the Britains, before the University of Oxford was founded, two Scholarsools were famous both for Eloquence and Learning, the one called *Greeklade*, where the Greek; the other *Latinlade*, where the Latine tongue was professed; since corruptly called *Cricklade* and *Lechlade* at this day."

was larger and much older than Charterhouse (founded 1611); it is generally considered the oldest public school in England. Charterhouse, like Winchester and Westminster, had an earlier but discontinuous history as a centre of monastic education.

The Holy State.... The fourth edition. London 1663. F°.

Fly-title at p [341]: The Profane State [being "Book V"], &c. London 1663. The first title-leaf (typographical) is followed by an engraved title-page for *The Holy State*, Cambridge 1648.

British Museum Ashley 4775

Heraldic bookplate of Lord Berwick on p ⁻3 (p–d). A seventeenth-century memorandum on honey etc is written at the foot of the typographical title-page. Autograph signature "—Anne Gillman—" on p ⁻2. Six calculations of money, perhaps in C's hand, are written in ink on the verso of the typographical title-page. Distinctive ink marks—rather like a lower-case q in geometrical form—on sig A2 (contents), pp 457, 461, 465; these are not by C.

In a notebook entry of c Jul 1823 C illustrated "M^r [Edward] Irving's error" of using "Declamation (high & passionate Rhetoric not introduced & pioneered by calm and clear Logic)" with an image from *Holy State* IV ch 9 (p 267): "to knock a nail into a board without wimbling a hole for it, which then either not enters, or turns crooked, or splits the wood it pierceth". *CN* IV 4963; cf *History of Worthies* 4 n 1.

DATE. 1825 or later. A date of c Jul 1823 would be suggested if the annotations were associated with the notebook entry quoted above; but C had been familiar with *The Holy State* long before then, and marginalia on Scott's *The Fortunes of Nigel* are written in a set of the Waverley novels published in 1825: see **8** n 1, below.

1 sig A3^v, pencil | "To the Reader"

And I conjure thee by all Christian ingenuity, that if lighting here on some passages, rather harsh-sounding then ill-intended, to construe the same by the general drift and main scope which is aimed at.

It was long before "ingenuous" and "ingenious", ingenuousness and ingenuity, were currently desynonimized.[1] Fuller meant "ingenuousness"/—

2 p 3, pencil | *The Holy State* Bk I ch 1 "The Good Wife"

Her maids follow the president of their mistresse, live modestly at home.

1[1] For the use of "ingenuous" as a synonym of "ingenious" see also *Appeal to Iniured Innocence* title-page; cf *Life Out of Death* **4**. See also BAXTER *Reliquiae* COPY A **40** and n 1. For another instance of failure to desynonymise terms see **2**, below.

As ingenious and ingenuous, so did our elder writers confound president and precedent.[1] F. meant the latter.

3 p 4, pencil | I 2 "The Life of Monica"

[Engraved portrait of "Monica Wife of Patricius, Mother to St Augustine..."]

O what a temptation to wed!

4 p 21, pencil | I 9 "The Life of Eliezer"

He will not truant it now in the afternoon, but with convenient speed returns to Abraham, who onely was worthy of such a Servant, who onely was worthy of such a Master.

On my word, Eliezer did his business in an orderly and sensible manner; but what there is to call forth this super-encomiastic "who only"—I cannot see. S. T. C.

5 p 21, pencil | I 10 "The Good Widow"

She is a woman whose head hath been quite cut off, and yet she liveth, and hath the second part of virginity.

What? was the former in her *head*?

6 p 22, pencil

Her grief for her Husband though real, is moderate. Excessive was the sorrow of King Richard the second, beseeming him neither as a King, man, or Christian, who so fervently loved Anna of Bohemia his *] Queen, that when she dyed at Shean in Surrey, he both cursed the place, and also out of madnesse overthrew the whole house.

* I do not remember whether Shakespear hath availed himself of this trait in Rich. II[nd's] Character.[1]

2[1] *OED* notes that, especially in the sixteenth and seventeenth centuries, "president" and "precedent" were confused in meaning through the virtual identity of pronunciation; Cromwell, Milton, and Charles II are cited as examples.

6[1] Grief is a prominent motif in Richard's self-disclosure in Shakespeare's play, reaching a climax in IV i 181–93; but this is not grief at the loss of his wife, nor is it overmastering. The Queen in *Richard II* is not the first queen—Anne of Bohemia (1366–94), who died of the plague at Sheen, as Fuller records—but the child-queen Isabella of France (1389–1409), whom Richard married in 1396 at least two years before the events in Shakespeare's play and who outlived Richard by nine years.

7 p ⁻1, referring to p 51 | ɪɪ 3 "The Life of Paracelsus"

P. 51. It is matter of regret with me, that Fuller (whose wit, ~~both~~ alike in quantity, quality and perpetuity surpassing that of the wittiest in a witty Age, robbed him of the praise not less due to him for an equal superiority in sound shrewd Good Sense and freedom of intellect)[1] had not looked thro' the two Latin Folios of Paracelsus's Works.[2] It is not to be doubted, that a rich and delightful Article would have been the result./ For ~~what could he select of~~ who, like Fuller, could have brought out, and set forth, this singular Compound of true philosophic Genius with the morals of a Quack and the manners of a King of the Gypsies?[3] Nevertheless, Paracelsus belonged to his Age, viz. the Dawn of Experimental Science; and a well-written ~~Life of~~ Critique on his Life & Writings would present thro' the magnifying glass of a Caricature the distinguishing features of the Helmonts, Kircher, & in ~~a~~ short, of the host of Naturalists of the 16ᵗʰ Century—/[4] The Period might begin with Paracelsus and end with Sir Ke~~lm~~nelm Digby.[5]

S. T. C.

N.b. The Potential (= Λογος θεανθρωπος),[6] the ground of the Prophetic, directed the first *Thinkers* (= Mystæ) to the metallic bodies, as the Key of all natural Science. The *then* Actual blended with this instinct all the fancies, and fond desires, and false *perspective*, of the Childhood of Intellect. The *essence* was truth, the *form* was

7[1] For "Judicious FULLER" see *History of Worthies* 4 n 1.

7[2] For a copy of Paracelsus *Omnia opera* (3 vols Geneva 1658 f°) from Green's library with a few notes incorrectly ascribed to C, now in the Royal College of Surgeons, see BAXTER *Reliquiae* COPY B 28 n 2. For C's intention of including Paracelsus in "a Review of old Books" see n 5, below.

7[3] For C on Paracelsus generally, and as "a braggart and a quack", see BÖHME 96 n 2.

7[4] C's chronology is confused: Helmont and Kircher both flourished in the seventeenth century, and Kenelm Digby (see n 5, below) died fifteen years before Kircher died. For a long note on the early chemists and "Chrysopoets", partly extracted from BOERHAAVE, see *CN* ɪɪɪ 4414. In it attention is paid to the Flemish physician, physiologist, and chemist,

Jean Baptiste van Helmont (1577–1644). See also *CL* v 326. C owned two works of the German scholar and mathematician who wrote on a wide variety of subjects, Athanasius Kircher (1601–80): *Mundus subterraneus* (2 vols Amsterdam 1678 f°) and *Prodromus Coptus sive Aegyptiacus* (Rome 1636); both are in Wordsworth LC twice marked as C's. The *Mundus subterraneus*, included in the list of books WW sent from Rydal to Highgate, was later in DC's possession but is now lost; the other, in VCL, is not annotated.

7[5] For Sir Kenelm Digby (1603–65) see BROWNE *Religio* 33 and n 2. In Jul 1816 C proposed to John Murray, unsuccessfully, "a Review of old Books" in every number of which "there should be a fair proportion of positively *amusing* matter—such as a Review of Paracelsus, Cardan, old Fuller...". *CL* ɪv 648.

7[6] "The god-man Word".

folly: and this is the definition of Alchemy.[7]—Nevertheless, the very terms bear witness to the veracity of the original Instinct/ The World of Sensible Experience cannot be more luminously divided than into the modifying powers, το αλλον—that which *differences*, makes this *other* than that: and the μετ᾿ αλλον, that which is beyond or deeper than the modifications.[8] Metallon is strictly "the *Base* of the Mode:" and such ~~are~~ have the Metals been determined to be by modern Chemistry.—And what are now the great problems of Chemistry? The difference of the Metals themselves, their origin, the causes of their locations, of their co-existence in the same ore (ex. gr. of Iridium, Osmium, Palladium, Rhodium, and Iron with Platinum).[9]— Were these problems solved, the results who dare limit? In addition to the Celeste Mechanique we might have a new department of Astronomy, the Celeste Chemique, i.e. a philosophic Astrology.[10]— And to this I do not hestitate to refer the old connection between Alchemy and Astrology—the same divinity in the idea, the same childishness in the attempt to realize it. Nay, the very invocations of Spirits were not without a ground of truth/ The Light was for the greater part suffocated, and the rest fantastically refracted; but still it was a Light struggling in the darkness—And I am persuaded, that to the full triumph of Science, it will be necessary that Nature should be commanded more *spiritually* than hitherto—i.e. more directly in the power of THE WILL.—

[7] In the Philosophical Lectures C said that Bacon had strongly contrasted "experiment" with "the 'gossiping with nature', as he calls it, of the Alchymists, the putting one thing to another in order to see if anything would come out of it". *P Lects* Lect 11 (1949) 331. See also FORBES 7 and n 2. For a note (which includes part of *CN* III 4414) added by Green to the fragmentary record of Literary Lecture 12 (Mar 1818), in which C declines to accept uncritically that the "very strange and incredible stories told of and by the alchemists" are assignable to "a specific form of mania", or that the alchemists should be accused "generally of dabbling with attempts at magic", see *LR* I 208–10, in *Misc C* 202–3.

[8] "The other"..."*beyond other*". This etymology was suggested by P. C. Buttmann in *Lexilogus* (2 vols Berlin 1818–25) I 139–40.

[9] The metals iridium and osmium were discovered and named by Smythson Tennant (1761–1815) in 1803. William Hyde Wollaston (1766–1828) discovered palladium in the same year, and rhodium in 1804. Platinum ore, brought to Europe from South America in the mid-eighteenth century and first described in 1754, was noted by Davy in his *Chemical Philosophy* (1812) as "very rare". In 1803 or 1804 W. H. Wollaston discovered a process for fashioning metal into wire and components for laboratory use, thereby giving some currency to a hitherto almost unknown metal. In *CN* III 4309 f 39ᵛ C remarked upon it as an instance of "new words... for new Metals".

[10] For the "Celeste Mechanique" see BROWNE *Works* 52 n 1. In BÖHME 106 C noted: "Astrology/ that is, the Celeste *Chemique*, is a Science in POSSE."

8 p +1, referring to p 323 | IV 19 "The Prince or Heir Apparent to the Crown"

He sympathizeth with him that by a Proxy is corrected for his offence: yea, sometimes goeth further, and (above his age) considereth, that it is but an Embleme, how hereafter his people may be punished for his own fault.

P. 323.—by a Proxy. See Sir W. Scott's Fortunes of Nigel.[1] In an oriental Despotism one would not have been surprized in finding such a custom—but in a Christian Court, and under the light of Protestantism, it is marvellous. It would be well to ascertain, if possible, the earliest date of this contrivance—whether it existed under the Plantagenets—or whether first under the Tudors—or lastly whether it was a precious import from Scotch-land with gentle King Jamie.—

9 p 334 | IV 20 "The Life of Edward the Black Prince"

And what a worthy woman must she needs be her self, whose very *garter* hath given so much honour to Kings and Princes?

great mistake[1]

10 p +1, referring to pp 334–5 | IV 21 "The King"

He is a mortal God. This world at the first had no other Charter for its being, then Gods *Fiat*: Kings have the same in the Present tense, *I have said ye are Gods.* We will describe him, first as a good man (so was Henry the third) then as a good King (so was Richard the third) both which meeting together make a King compleat. For he

[8][1] There is no instance of punishment by proxy in *The Fortunes of Nigel.* See, however, *Waverley* ch 68: Evan Dhu Maccombich addresses the judge who is about to pass sentence. "I was only ganging to say, my Lord...that if your excellent honour, and the honourable Court, would let Vich Ian Vohr go free just this once, and let him gae back to France, and no to trouble King George's government again, that ony six o' the very best of his clan will be willing to be justified in his stead; and if you'll just let me gae down to Glennaquoich, I'll fetch them up to ye mysell, to head or hang, and you may begin wi' me the very first man." C owned and annotated a set of all seventeen of the Waverley novels, in 13 vols (published in 25) in uniform binding (Edinburgh 1823–5). *The Fortunes of Nigel* (with 3 marginalia) is in the *Novels and Romances* (1825); *Waverley* (with 9 marginalia) is in the *Novels and Tales* (1823).

[9][1] The Order of the Garter, the most ancient and exalted order of knighthood, was instituted by Edward III c 1346. The story that the Order arose from an amorous encounter between Edward and the Countess of Salisbury is fictitious. Even if the anecdote were accepted as reliable the identity of "the Countess of Salisbury" is in question.

that is not a *good man*, or *but a good man*, can never be a good Sovereign.

334. 35 &c. Compare the fulsome flattery of these and other passages in this volume (tho' modest to the common language of James's Priests & Courtiers) with the loyal but free and manly tone of Fuller's later works, towards the close of Charles Ist's reign & under the Common-wealth & Protectorate.[1] And doubtless this ~~is not~~ was not peculiar to Fuller; but a great and lasting change was effected in the mind of the Country generally. The Bishops and ⟨other⟩ Church Dignitaries tried for a while to renew the old king-godding Mumpsimus[2]—But the Second Charles laughed at them; and they quarreled with his Successor, and hated the Hero who delivered them from him too thoroughly to have flattered with any unction, even if William's Dutch Phlegm had not precluded the attempt by making its failure certain.[3]

11 p +1, referring to p 387 | *The Profane State* v 11 "The Rigid Donatists"

Seventh Position. That Magistrates have a power to compel people to serve God by outward punishment: which is also the distilled position of our Anabaptists, thus blinding the Ministers, and binding the Magistrate, what work they do make?

387—and elsewhere.—The only serious Macula in Fuller's mind is his uniform support of the right and duty of the Civil Magistrate to punish errors in belief. ~~this would~~ Fullers would indeed recommend *moderation* in ~~this~~ practice; but of Upas, Woorara, and Persecution there are no *moderate* doses possible.—[1]

10[1] Of the works of Fuller that C annotated, *The Holy State* was the earliest published (1642). Ordained in 1630 at the age of twenty-two, Fuller received rapid preferment, leaving his Dorset parish in c 1640 to take up a lectureship to the Savoy. Once in London —C suggests—he became something of a courtier. Cf *A Triple Reconciler* headnote. As a strong royalist he lost his preferment in the Commonwealth (see *History of Worthies* 3), but was reinstated by Charles II . Cf *History of Worthies* 4.

10[2] For "Mumpsimus" see BAXTER *Reliquiae* COPY A 44 n 6.

10[3] James II succeeded Charles II, reigning 1685–8; William of Orange came to the throne in Feb 1689 after an interregnum of two months.

11[1] For the upas tree and its baleful effects see EICHHORN *Apocalypse* COPY A 4 n 3. Woorara = the plant woorali, from which is extracted curare, a resinous substance that induces motor paralysis, used on the tips of arrows by Amazon natives for hunting game. The use of it in surgical procedures in St Thomas's Hospital after World War II made open-heart surgery possible. C's source may well have been that cited by *OED*: J. G. Stedman *Narrative...of Surinam* (2 vols 1776) I xv 395; cf DONNE *Sermons* COPY B 60 n 5.

Life Out of Death. A sermon preached at Chelsey, on the recovery of an honourable person. London 1655. 8°.

Probably bound as second with T. FULLER *A Triple Reconciler*, which see.

Not located.

MS TRANSCRIPTS. (*a*) VCL BT 37: SC transcript, from which the annotations are here printed. (*b*) University of Texas (Humanities Research Center): a second transcript by SC.

DATE. c Nov 1833–Mar 1834, if annotated at the same time as *A Triple Reconciler*.

1   p 4

And Hezekiah wept sore. Strange, what made him take on so bitterly at the tidings of death...Was not *Hezekiah* assured that the setting of his Sun here in a mortal life, should be the rising thereof in a blessed immortality.

Noticeable even in the sensible Fuller this disposition to consider the Bible from Genesis to the Apocalypse *one* book so as to antedate the Gospel and attribute to the good men under the Law not only the *Faith* but the clear and distinct Belief and Assurance of Christians.[1] Bp. Warburton fell into the contrary extreme.[2]

2   p 6

Well the Prophet *Isaiah* is sent with a welcom Counter Message, that *Hezekiahs* prayer was heard, and a longer lease of life indulged unto him, confirmed with miracle from Heaven of the going back of the Sun.

Was not the recovery itself a sufficient sign? The sun of his life had gone backward, if at sixty he was carried back and reimplaced in the

[1] The OT passages give no hint that Hezekiah had any idea of the immortality of his soul. Fuller, as C points out, is anticipating later Christian beliefs.

[2] William Warburton (1698–1779) in his *Divine Legation of Moses* (1737–41) argues that the Jews had no idea of an after-life. In Jul–Nov 1820 C provided "the complete answer to & Confutation of Warburton's Fancies in his 'Divine Legation of Moses'", including the following statement: "The unity & monotheism of God & all his attributes were everywhere *taught*, and kept present and prominent before their eyes—. How is it conceivable that these attributes should not be brought to bear on the nature of the Future State? That they *were* so, we know...." *CN* IV 4708. Cf *Friend* (*CC*) II 34 (I 29–30).

strength and health of fifty.[1] Query. A figurative *expression* of a fact interpreted by the hearers for a distinct fact in itself?[a]

3 p 11

Sicknesse is a time to suffer, not to do in; Patients are like Bees in winter, no flying abroad to finde fresh flowers, either they must starve, or live on that stock of honey which they have provided in the summer time.

A beautiful improvement might be made of this—viz. that God's mercy through Christ *does* supply to his wisest Bees a power of making fresh honey by patience and acknowledgment.

4 p 14

David therefore alledgeth this as an Argument to be continued in the Land of the living, *shall the dust prayse thee O Lord,* that Gods service might still be preserved so in him, that his body might not be altogether uselesse, as in dead folke, but have a portion of praysing of God, conjoyned with his soul (as the opposite part of the Quire) in lauding the Lord.

With an ingenuity worthy of Fuller; but more ingenious than ingenuous.[1] Better say: it was a question to which sinful man might thro' God's mercy hope but could not of his own merits expect, an affirmative answer. Compare with Ezekiel, *Can these dry bones live?*—[2]

---

[a] In MS TRANSCRIPT (*a*) **2–4** end with "S. T. C.". This is probably SC's usual mark for identifying C's annotations in her transcripts

2[1] See Isa 38, and cf 2 Kings 20.1–11, esp 8–11. The sign given to Hezekiah, of the sun turning back, is involved in the early development of C's identification of sun with Son: see *CN* I 349.

4[1] See *Holy State* 1 and n 1.
4[2] Ezek 37.3, the word "dry" being carried forward from v 2.

A Pisgah-Sight of Palestine and the Confines Thereof, with the history of the Old and New Testament acted thereon, &c. 2 pts in 1 vol. London 1650. F°.

Printed title-page cited. The volume is provided with maps.

London University (School of Oriental and African Studies)

Inscribed on p ⁻2: "J. T. Coleridge Montague Place 30/– May 20ᵗʰ 1843. This book belonged to my Uncle S. T. Coleridge—and contains several marginal notes in his handwriting. J T C. It was sold at a Sale by Mʳˢ Gillman of books, part of her late husband's library, which contained many of S. T. C.'s books—in April. 1843—" (Record of the Gillman sale shows that the book was bought by J. Bohn for 25s.) Beside JTC's inscription the monogram "C" is written; whether this is John Duke Coleridge's mark, as is usually the case in books from the Ottery Collection, is doubtful. The label of E. Baer, Old & New Books, 134 Ashford Ct, London NW2 on p ⁻5 (p–d) provides one clue to the route by which the book reached its present location.

On i 191 C has corrected "We must not forget the people near *Samaria*, wherein *Ahabs* chariot was washed..." to "forget the poole" (noted in Errata); on i 245 he has corrected shoulder-note *k* from "1 Sam. 6.14" to "11.14" (not in Errata).

DATE. Uncertain; c 1824–9, possibly at the same time as the *Holy State* was annotated. See **8** n 2 (1824 or later). The marginalia on RHENFERD (see **6** and n 1) were written in c Jul 1827.

On 28 Aug 1830, in N 46 f 7ᵛ (*CN* v), C seems to refer to this book: "I know [not] whether such a map is in existence—but a map of the journeys of the Israelites from Rameses to the Jordan, accomodated as far as possible to the present names and divisions of Arabia, would be no trifling benefaction to the Biblial Student.—Mem. Consult Fuller's Holy Land."

---

1   i 16–17 | Bk ɪ ch 6 "Objections Against the Fruitfulnesse of Judea Answered" § 9

As therefore the cleare and lovely complexions, the handsome and *] proper persons, the bold and valiant Spirits, the comely and courtly behaviour of the ancient *Jews*, are not to be measured by the suspicious and louring looks, the low and crooked statures, the slavish and servil conditions, the base and sordid demeanour of the *Jews* now adays; no more are our judgments to contract the former fruitfulness of their soil to the present sterility thereof.

* It seems, primâ facie at least, somewhat difficult to reconcile the Aversion, and Contempt, ⟨with⟩ which the Jews are spoken of by the Greek and Roman Writers, with this handsome portrait of worthy Master Fuller. The misanthropic, and supercilious demeanour of the

Jews will, I admit, go a good way toward accounting for it. By the bye, handsome & even beautiful Jewesses are not uncommon; but I do not recollect to have ever seen a very handsome Jew.

⟨S. T. C.⟩[a]

2 i 17 | i 7 "Of the Ancient Division of the Land Betwixt the Seven Canaanitish Nations"

The first difficulty we meet with, is the number of these [Canaanitish] nations, so variously reckoned up. They are counted up thus: two, *Gen.* 13. 7. three, *Exod.* 23. 28. five, *Exod.* 13. 5. sixe, *Exod.* 3. 8. 17. seven, *Josh.* 3. 10. ten, *Gen.* 15. 19. eleven, *Gen.* 10. 15. & 1 *Chron.* 1. 13 and seventeen, if a collective number of them all be cast up. *] Now how come they to be so differently computed where one and the same Spirit is the Auditour to state their account?

* What wild work we should have, were this theory carried into Ancient Records universally! If for instance the Volumes of Herodotus, Thucydides, Xenophon, Dyonisius Halic. &c were all gravely assumed to have been written by the Historic Muse!—

3 i 30–1 | i 9 "The Third Division of the Land into Twelve Tribes…" § 3

Nor is the testimony of *Josephus* to be slighted herein, though *Jos. Scaliger* causlessly condemns it, affirming that the King of *Egypt* employed seventy two *Jews* to translate the Bible into Greek, taking six out of every Tribe, which compleat that number.

One great evil from the early perusal of ecclesiastical history, when the Student has been trained up to take for grave truths whatever he finds gravely narrated, is the Obtunding the natural sense of probability—. This takes place to such a degree, that the Rule & Measure of Judgement is actually inverted—the anticipation of marvellous stories from the frequency of their occurrence in ~~the~~ our previous Reading supplies the place of probability—for we cannot but find that probable, which we had expected to meet with—In this way I account for Fuller's adhesion to the absurd Legend, which Josephus had borrowed from Aristeas, & his censuring Joseph Scaliger's animadversion (i.e. detection of Aristeas's mendacity) as causeless.[1]—N.B. Joseph Scaliger was among the earliest En-

a Possibly not in C's hand

3[1] Legends about the writing of the Septuagint are discussed in several works known to C, especially EICHHORN *Alte*

Testament I 313–57, where the earliest account, that in the "Letter of Aristeas", is criticised. The "Letter" is known

lighteners, and Asserters of fearless *Thinking*—a Free-thinker, in the best sense.—[2]

4   i 31 | § 5

That in the time of Christ, and his Apostles, some pious people of all tribes, were extant in *Judea*, plainly appears…
*] 3. By the superscription of S. *James*, his Epistle, *To the Twelve Tribes which are scattered abroad, greeting*. Being Christian *Jews* probably, dispersed from *Ierusalem*, after the martyrdome of Saint *Stephen*.

* It is remarkable that Fuller should not have learnt from his Rabbinical Reading that "the 12 Tribes" was a common idiom for the Jews universally—without any intended reference to Tribes.[1] Thus the 12 Tribes looked for the Res[n] = the Resurrection was the universal belief among the Jews./

5   i 33 | i 10 "Of Palestine rent into two kingdomes…" § 12

…For, whilst the *Babylonish* captivity did onely snuffe *Iudah*, for seventy years, (blazing * the brighter when they returned from banishment) the *Assyrian* conquest utterly extinguished *Israel*, from ever appearing again, in a formed Common-wealth, in their own Countrey.

* Egregious falsification of History! Consult Ezra and Nehemiah—especially the prayer at the opening of the Temple.[1] What could Fuller be thinking of?—The metaphor, "snuffe"—and that joke required an Antithesis for its completion.

---

mostly from long quotations in Eusebius, quoted in part in Josephus *Antiquitates judaicae* 10.12.48, 49, 56, and here summarised by Fuller. Aristaeas represents himself as a Greek courtier to Ptolemy II Philadelphus (283–247 B.C.), and in the rôle of an eye-witness and assistant recounts the events leading to the first Greek version of the Pentateuch. The "Letter", long recognised as a fiction, has been assigned to various dates between 200 B.C. and A.D. 50. See also GREW **24** and n 1.

3[2] Joseph Justus Scaliger (1540–1609), one of whose poems—*Iambi gnomici*

21—C copied out in 1809 (*CN* III 3621). C's "old Gr. Test. cum Lexico, apud Joannem Billium, Londini, 1612 [actually 1622]" (see BIBLE COPY B headnote I 416) contained "a long and somewhat miscellaneous Note of great value and interest", which also left on C's mind "a strong impression of Joseph Scaliger's freedom as well as strength of intellect". N 34 f 24[v], 35 f 8 (*CN* v) (c Jul 1827); another description of this Greek NT, with the correct imprint 1622, is given in N 37 f 51[v] (*CN* v) (c Mar 1828).

4[1] See Acts 26.7 and James 1.1.
5[1] Ezra 9.6–15; cf Nehem chs 9–10.

6   i 94 | ii 3 "Manasseh beyond Jordan" §10

Pella seems to be hereabouts, whither many Christians warned by many prodigies fled for shelter from *Jerusalem*, before the Romans besieged it. As we congratulate their thus preventing persecution according to Christ's precept [Matt 24.16], so we cannot but condole, that the same persons [footnote: Epiphanius [*Contra*] *haer*[*eses*] 29] were afterwards poisoned with hereticall opinions, contrary to the *] express word of God, and became Apostate *Nazarites*.

See Rhenferd's masterly vindication of these Nazarites, and his detection of the calumnious Lies and Blunders of Epiphanius, Irenæus & Co.[1]

7   i 95 | §11

Here Divines both for number and learning are almost equally divided [in the matter of Jephthah's daughter], some avouching her really sacrificed...whereof some footsteps in the Fable of *Agamemnon* sacrificing *Iphigenia* (haply corrupted for *Jephthagenia* *] or *Jephtha's* daughter) others maintaining that she was onely sequestred to perpetuall virginity.

* My own judgement inclines to that of our Translators as implied in their marginal reference to I. Sam. I.[1]—And yet I must acknowlege

---

6[1] Jacob **RHENFERD** (1654–1712) *Opera philologica* (Utrecht 1772); C refers to the chapters cited in **FLEURY 3** n 1. Rhenferd's main attack on Epiphanius comes in the *Dissertatio de fictis judaeorum haeresibus* in *Opera* 76–124, the discussion of this passage in Epiphanius on p 98. Cf ÉICHHORN *Apocalypse* 1 and 2 n 1, and *Neue Testament* COPY A 1 n 4. As the revolt against Rome gathered momentum, the Jewish Christians in Jerusalem, after the martyrdom of James and out of sympathy with the extreme militarism of the Zealots, obeyed a revelation and took refuge in Pella in c A.D. 68. Their reasons for the move were not, as alleged by the Zealots, indifference to the fate of Jerusalem or an exclusive desire to preserve the purity of their Nazarite vows and ritual. Rhenferd's vindication of them against the charge that, in isolation from the mainstream of

Christianity, they lapsed into gross heresy has been supported by later scholarship.

7[1] The story of Jephthah and his daughter is in Judges 11.29–40. Jephthah made a vow to the Lord: "If thou shalt without fail deliver the children of Ammon into mine hands, Then it shall be, that whatsoever cometh forth of the doors of my house to meet me, when I return in peace from the children of Ammon, shall surely be the Lord's, and I will offer it up for a burnt offering." Jephthah was victorious, and when he came home "behold, his daughter came out to meet him with timbrels and with dances: and she was his only child; beside her he had neither son nor daughter". The marginal reference is from Judges 11.31 and 1 Sam 1.11 and 28—the story of Hannah, childless, who vowed that if the Lord would give her a man child "then I will give him unto the Lord all the days of his life, and there shall no razor

that the Euphemism in v. 39, as if the Historian shrunk from the direct naming of the Action (—"her father, who *did with her according to his Vow*")—The silence of the Bible respecting any body of Vestals dedicated to the Service of the Tabernacle—and the seeming inadequateness of a mere dedication to a single life to account for the yearly lamentation of the Daughters of Israel[2]—to which may be added as an inclining tho' small weight, the parallel fact of Iphigenia—are arguments of no trifling force in favor of the actual sacrifice, tho' not, I think, sufficient to counter-balance the argument drawn from the main stress being layed on her "knowing no man"/—& her Virginity not her Death lamented.[3]

8 i 110 | II 4 "The Tribe of Naphtali" §16

[Fuller comments upon the account of the taxation of Christ in Matthew 17.37:] Hence *Peter* was sent to sea, where a fish, which *] probably had plundered a peece of money out of the Pocket of some shipwracked fisherman, lost his life for the fact, and the felons goods found in him were justly forfeited to *Christ*, Lord Paramount both of sea and soil.

* Fuller lived in Wit, as a Fish in Water.[1] It was his Element—Or as in ~~frozen Lan~~ sundry places of the Frozen Zone the Esquimaux fabricates their Houses, Windows, Furniture, of Snow, because it is utter Snow-land[2]—so & much more might Fuller's Brain be termed Wit-land. ~~In a~~Any other Man this §ph would convict of Profaneness: in him it was the n[e]cessity*a* of his Material.

a Letter supplied by the editor

come upon his head". When she had received a man child she said: "the Lord hath given me my petition which I asked of him: Therefore also I have lent him to the Lord; as long as he liveth he shall be lent to the Lord".

7[2] Judges 11.39–40: "And it was a custom in Israel, That the daughters of Israel went yearly to lament the daughter of Jephthah the Gileadite four days in a year."

7[3] See Judges 11.37–9.

8[1] See also *Holy State* 7 and cf *History of Worthies* 4 (at n 1).

8[2] Possibly a recollection of George Francis Lyon (1795–1832) *The Private Journal of Captain G. F. Lyon, of H.M.S. Hecla, during the Recent Voyage of Discovery under Captain Parry* (1824), to which C refers in *The Delinquent Travellers* lines 3–4—*PW* (EHC) I 444 —and again in detail in HILLHOUSE 1 (at n 11). For C's interest in William Edward Parry through his early acquaintance with two of his brothers see BAINES 3 n 1.

9   i 111–12 | § 20

[Fuller reflects upon the delay in the healing of the blind man in Mark 8.25:] But how came it to pass that he, who otherwhiles healed at *] distance by the Proxie of his word...should here be so long, not to say tedious, in working a miracle?...Let us not raise cavills where we should rather return thanks, seeing Christ, that our dull meditations might keep pace with his actions, did not onely goe slowly on set purpose, but even stayed in the mid way of a miracle, doing it first by halves, that our conceptions might the better overtake him.

* This whimsical confusion of slowness in an Act and a slow and distinct manner in the exposition of the Act, in accomodation to the slow apprehensions of the persons to be instructed, is truly characteristic of Fuller—and much the moretive, for rationale, of Christ's action in this instance having been premised as *inconceivable.* —i.e. Ch. performed acted in an inconceivable way in order to help us to conceive it! But Fuller would mount an Irish BULL rather than lose a witty turn.[1]

10   i 114–15 | § 28

[Fuller refers to the city of Meroz, which "after *Deborah's* execration so dwindled by degrees, that nothing is left of *Meroz*, but *Meroz*, nothing surviving of the thing but the name."] For the exact position *] whereof we refer the reader to those our learned Divines, which in these unhappy dissensions have made that Text [Judges 5.23] so often the subject of their Sermons.

* A good hit. It is amusing to see the Cavalier *peep* out, every now and then—but Fuller was no bigot—and wisely considered that by shewing a full face he should do more harm to Thomas Fuller than good to Charles Stuart.—By parading his Loyalty, and popping Head and Shoulders out of his Hiding Hole, he might occasion a Schism between them, a separation and falling off—which he was too good a Churchman to hazard[1]

9[1] A "bull"—a self-contradictory proposition (*OED*)—by C's day commonly received the epithet "Irish". C was fond of detecting instances of this: see e.g. *Omniana* No 113 (1812) 220–1,

CN III 3255 and n, and *BL* ch 4 (*CC*) I 72n.
     10[1] See also *Holy State* 10 and *History of Worthies* 4.

11   i 161 | ii 7 "The Tribe of Issachar" §17

But, this accident was onely the *hilt* or handle, for *Solomon* to take
hold on; *Adonijah's* former fault was the edge, to cut off his life. Thus,
*] let those, who once have been desperately sick of a Princes
displeasure, and recovered, know, that the least relapse will prove
deadly unto them.

* How thankful to divine Providence ought we to be, that remarks
like these so frequent in our Writers before the Revolution are now
foreign to us, and read like translations from Russian or Arabic!

12   i 271 | ii 13 "The Tribe of Judah" § 10

Lot with his wife was enjoined onely not to look back, wherein
she disobeyed the commandement, either out of

  1 High contempt: Yet seeing for the main she had been a good
    woman...our charity believes her fact proceeding rather from

*] 2 Carelessness, or incogitancy, having for that instant forgotten
    the command; or

  3 Curiosity...or

  4 Infidelity...or

  5 Covetousness...or

  6 Compassion...

Were they any, or all of these, back she looked, and was turned into
a pillar of salt, which, St. *Hierome* saith, was extant in his age.

* Curious instance of a metaphor turned into a Miracle! The sacred
Historian simply says, that she became a pillar of Salt—i.e. in that
Shower of fire in which she was overtaken, She dissolved as a pillar
of Salt would do in an ordinary Shower.

12A   p 297 | ii 14 "The Land of Moriah" § 10

——] ...he [David] politickly resolved not to be pent in *Jerusalem*
(where the land-flood of a popular mutiny, might presently drown
him) but to retire to the uttermost bounds of his kingdome, mean
time giving his subjects leasure and liberty to review what they had
done, dislike what they reviewed, revoke what they disliked; that so
on second debates they might seriously undoe, what on first thoughts
they had furiously attempted: knowing full well that Rebellion
——] though running so at hand is quickly tyred, as having rotten
lungs, whilest well breathed Loyalty is best at a long course....

    *] But, ô the Bran in that Bread, rottenness in those Raisons,
dregs in that wine he brought, joining with them a false accusation
of his Master *Mephibosheth* to be a Traitour...

A Triple Reconciler, stating the controversies whether Ministers have an exclusive power of communicants from the sacrament. Any persons unordained may lawfully preach. The Lords Prayer ought not to be used by all Christians. London 1654. 8°.

Probably bound as first with T. FULLER *Life Out of Death*: see below. C describes his copy as imprinted "London: Printed by Will. Bentley, for Will, Sheers at the Bible in St Paul's Church Yard. Anno Dom. 1654." N Q f 36 (*CN* v). No copy matching this description examined. The copy here cited—BM E 1441 (2)—is "Printed by Will. Bently, for John Williams at the Crown in S. Pauls Church-yard. Anno Dom. 1654."

Not located.

On c 30 Nov 1833, after copying out the title-page and dedication of this book, C noted: "Mem. The [. . .] is sent to me/ and a prized addition to my assemblage of Fuller's Works." He then wrote an extended but discontinuous series of notes, dating to c 27 Mar 1834, referring to pp 3–107 (of 144): these consist of variatim extracts from Fuller's text, memoranda for passages to be extracted, and comments in the form of quasi-marginalia. N Q ff 35^v–45^v, 51^v–52, 71^v (*CN* v); an incomplete version is given in *C 17th C* 232–30. For extracts from these notes see *Church-History* 1 n 4, *History of Worthies* 1 n 3 and 4 n 1, and *Holy State* 10 n 1; see also 1 n 1 and 3 n 1, below. In N Q 36^v he noted of the dedication of *A Triple Reconciler*: "Could the most accomplished Gentleman in the Drawing-Room of Elizabeth, in the days of Leicester and Sir Philip Sidney, have addressed a high-born Dame with more courtly elegance?"

An early note of the editor's, now mislaid, describes *A Triple Reconciler* and *Life Out of Death* as bound together but does not record the authority for that statement. It is supported, however, though not proved, by the fact that in VCL BT 37 the transcript of *A Triple Reconciler* is immediately followed by the transcript of *Life Out of Death*, whereas the transcript of the *History of Worthies* appears twenty pages earlier in the volume. Again, *Gillman SC* (1843) 320 enters *A Triple Reconciler* and two other Fuller titles, but not *Life Out of Death*; the cataloguer might easily have missed, or may deliberately have ignored, the brief sermon (pp iv + 37) added to *A Triple Reconciler* (pp viii + 144)—indeed C himself, when he described the book in N Q, may not have been aware that it included the sermon.

MS TRANSCRIPTS. (*a*) VCL BT 37: SC transcript, from which the annotations are here printed. (*b*) University of Texas (Humanities Research Center): a second transcript by SC.

DATE. c Nov 1833–Mar 1834, on the assumption that the marginalia were written at about the same time as the notes in N Q.

1   p 7 | "The First Reconciler"

Doctrine. God's ministers ought without fear or favour to perform their office, neither to be frighted nor flattered. It is observed that *Moses* first hanselled this Law on his Sister *Myriam, Numb.* 12.15.
Secondly, we finde it served by Subjects on their Soveraign in the case of *King Uzziah,* 2 Chron. 26.20.

Five years later this would have cost Fuller a rap on his knuckles from his Bishop.*ᵃ*¹

2   p 8

Sad and sorrowfull the condition of a sequestred Leper. Indeed some of us have been sequestred, and blessed be God we have born our yoke in our youth, hopeing that more freedom is reserved for our old age, but our sequestration is not to be named with that of a leper...

A hope amounting to an anticipation of the fast approaching Restoration, while Cromwell was yet alive.¹ But there were men who hoped for a restoration of the Established Church under a moderate Episcopacy from Cromwell himself, and had he dared take the name of King, he probably would not have disappointed them.²

3   pp 63–4

[The grounds of Paul's authority:] First... by his *extraction,* being a *Levite*... to whom it belonged by their Profession to teach the *people.*
Secondly, he had an *extraordinarie call* from God... besides, at this time a *civil invitation* from the *Masters* of the *synagogue.* Thus his three-fold cable cannot be broken, nor any unlawfull invading of the *Ministeriall office* be charged upon him. Thirdly, St. *Pauls Commission* to preach, doth appear both by his *abilitie* and *authoritie* for the same.

ᵃ In MS TRANSCRIPT (*a*) all three annotations end with "S. T. C.". This is probably SC's usual mark for identifying C's annotations in her transcripts.

1¹ Two instances of being striken with leprosy as God's punishment for presumption: Miriam for speaking against Moses "because of the Ethiopian woman he had married", Uzziah for improperly assuming a priest's function.

In N Q f 37 (*CN* v), perhaps coincidentally, C transcribed variatim from p 3: "The Leprosy of the Jews, as we have not, so [we] have a disease the Jews had not..." and wrote above the extract "Leprosy ϰ Syphilis". Cf *Appeal* 1 and n 1.

2¹ See **1**, above. *A Triple Reconciler* was first published 1654; Cromwell died in 1658.

2² See FIELD **1** n 4.

Fuller is here trying to support a plain truth on a false or very questionable Pediment. What wonder that he fails? For those, who admitted that Miracles had ceased in the Church convincing arguments might have been brought. For those who believed in immediate Calls, no arguments could have been convincing.[1]

3[1] Cf N Q f 52 (*CN* v), referring to p 105: "I have often noticed among the lower and more enthusiastic Calvinists, Separatists, [. . .] &c the Tenacity, the Badger, Bull-dog Teeth, with which they will cling to this or that Text on an argumentative Chapter of St Paul's ⟨neither the ground, occasion, object or Logical connection of which they understand;⟩ contrasted with their nonchalance and [? vast] indifference to all the numerous & express Texts in all the N.T. Writings, the very strongest being in St Paul himself, respecting the relative Duties of Pastor and Flock, and the guilt of assuming the ministerial office without a lawful Authority.... See the last page of the last Leaf but five in this Book. But whence flows this evil? O most beautifully has Fuller answered in the 4 last §phs. of his Second Reconciler, p. 105–7. Nos sacerdotes, dico aperto, nos desumus [we priests—I say it openly —have failed]—".

JOHN GALT

1779–1839

The Provost, or, Memoirs of His Own Times. By the author of Annals of the Parish; Ayrshire Legatees; and Sir Andrew Wylie [i.e. John Galt]. Edinburgh 1822. 12º.

Not located. Annotation here reprinted from *TLS* 25 Sept 1930.

A. J. Ashley, who transcribed and published the note in *TLS*, reported that this copy "was among the books in the poet's possession when he died at Mr Gillman's house in Highgate". There appear to have been inscriptions showing the successive owners of the volume: Ashley states that the volume had been "rebound to the order of the third owner, the Rev. William Poulton", curate of St Martin's-in-the-Fields 1855–62.

DATE. Between Dec 1822 (after publication of *The Entail*) and 1825 (see *CL* v 439 of c 8 May 1825).

1 p [iii], "the dedication page", cropped at the end

This work is not for the Many; but in the unconscious, perfectly natural, Irony of Self-delusion, in all parts intelligible to the intelligent Reader, without the slightest suspicion on the part of the Autobiographer, I know of no equal in our Literature. The governing Trait in the Provost's character is no where caricatured. In the character of Betty, John's wife, or the Beggar Girl intense Selfishness without malignity, as a *Nature*, and with all the innocence of a Nature, is admirably pourtrayed. In the provost a similar *Self*ness is united with a *Slyness* and a plausibility eminently successful in cheating the man himself into a happy state of constant Self-applause.[1] This and "The Entail"[2] would alone suffice to place Galt in the first rank of contemporary Novelists—and second only to Sir W. Scot in te[. . .]ᵃ

ᵃ Ashley states that the "last word was almost cut away when the book was rebound...the word is almost certainly 'technique'"

[1] On c 8 May 1825 C wrote to J. T. Coleridge asking him to give Murray his letter proposing "the republication of the 'Specimens of Rabbinical Wisdom'", but without much hope of Murray accepting the proposition. He added: "P.S. My unfavourable Opinions or rather feelings, of μυρραι [Murray] originated in sundry anecdotes which Wordsworth told me, in addition to a conversation of M. himself with Wordsworth. Did you ever read Galt's *Provost*? If you have, you will understand me." *CL* v 439.

[2] *The Entail* was published in Dec 1822: *EC*.

LOST BOOK

Sir Andrew Wylie, of that Ilk. By the author of "Annals of the Parish" [i.e. John Galt]. 3 vols. Edinburgh 1822. 12⁰.

Not located; marginalia not recorded. *Green SC* (1880) 211: "Notes by S. T. Coleridge, presentation copy from the Author".

CHRISTIAN GARVE
1742–1798

Fragmente zur Schilderung des Geistes, des Charakters, und der Regierung Friedrichs des zweyten. 2 vols. Breslau 1798. 8°.

Uebersicht der vornehmsten Principien der Sittenlehre, von dem Zeitalter des Aristoteles an bis auf unsre Zeiten... Eine zu dem ersten Theile der übersetzten Ethik des Aristoteles gehörende und aus ihm besonders abgedruckte Abhandlung. 2 vols. Breslau 1798. 8°.

Vermischte Aufsätze welche einzeln oder in Zeitschriften erschienen sind. 2 vols. Breslau 1796, 1800. 8°.

Versuche über verschiedene Gegenstände aus der Moral, der Litteratur, und dem gesellschaftlichen Leben, &c. 4 vols. Breslau 1792–1802. 8°.

Green SC does not cite the editions, giving only "Breslau 1792, &c". The titles cited above are first editions.

Not located; marginalia not recorded. *Green SC* (1880) 212: "Together 10 vol. some of the vols. with MS. Notes by S. T. Coleridge". Bought by Stibbs and presumably taken to New York for sale by Bartlett & Welford.

For C's recognition of Garve's writing on landscape and the picturesque see *CN* I 1675, 1676. In *BL* ch 19 (*CC*) II 90–1 he quoted from "Vermischten Anmerkungen über Gellerts Moral, dessen Schriften überhaupt, und Charakter".

EDWARD GIBBON
1737–1794

The History of the Decline and Fall of the Roman Empire. Vol. III (of 12). [Probably] London 1818. 8°.

Not located. The annotation is here reprinted from *C at H* pp 126–7.

Lucy Watson, daughter of James Gillman the younger, reports that "In one of my father's school prizes, a volume of Gibbon's 'Roman Empire', I discovered a scrap of paper, bearing the date...1827, on which, in the Poet's hand, was written the following:".

For other editions of Gibbon that C may have read or consulted see *CN* III 3814–3816, in which C comments on Gibbon III 314–15 and 322. For C's examination of Gibbon's faults see *TT* 15 Aug 1833; but cf *CN* III 3823: "with all these faults he is our greatest Historian".

DATE. 1827.

1 on "a scrap of paper" inserted, apparently referring to III 324 | Ch 21 [Shoulder-note:] Mysterious nature of the Trinity

The same subtle and profound questions concerning the nature, the generation, the distinction, and the equality of the three divine persons of the mysterious *Triad*, or Trinity, were agitated in the philosophical, and in the Christian, schools of Alexandria. An eager spirit of curiosity urged them to explore the secrets of the abyss; and the pride of the professors and of their disciples was satisfied with the science of words. But the most sagacious of the Christian theologians, the great Athanasius himself, has candidly confessed that, whenever he forced his understanding to meditate on the divinity of the *Logos*, his toilsome and unavailing efforts recoiled on themselves; that the more he thought, the less he comprehended; and the more he wrote, the less capable was he of expressing his thoughts. In every step of the enquiry, we are compelled to feel and acknowledge the immeasurable disproportion between the size of the object and the capacity of the human mind. We may strive to abstract the notions of time, of space, and of matter, which so closely adhere to all perceptions of our experimental knowledge. But, as soon as we presume to reason of infinite substance, of spiritual generation; as often as we deduce any positive conclusions from a negative idea, we are involved in darkness, perplexity, and inevitable contradiction.

Vol. III. p. 234[a]

I trust James, that before you have read this work, you will have so far mastered the true nature and constitution of the understanding or the faculty by which we think of things and their apparent relations by their common characters, in distinction from the sense, which presents to us the things individually or as concretes[1]—as to be prepared for the perplexities and contradictions that must of necessity arise when a faculty which depends for all its materials on the sense, the object of which it generalises, *i.e.*, reduces to genera or kinds, is employed on truths that have no connection with the senses, nor are capable of being generalised from sensible objects. This absurd misapplication of the understanding, Gibbon makes in order to expose these truths to ridicule—and the same misapplication thousands of Divines make in order to explain and support them, and the blunder is far more mischievous in the latter than in the former instance.

I have never heard an argument against the Trinity that did not apply with equal force against the existence of a Supreme Being in any form.

S. T. COLERIDGE

---

[a] Apparently a slip for "324"

1[1] See e.g. *Friend(CC)* i 177n and *Logic (CC)* 153–4.

WILLIAM GODWIN
1756–1836

Thoughts Occasioned by the Perusal of Dr. Parr's Spital Sermon, preached at Christ Church, April 15, 1800: being a reply to the attacks of Dr. Parr, Mr. Mackintosh, the author of An Essay on Population [i.e. T. R. Malthus] and others. London 1801. 8°.

Bound as second with DYER *Poems* (1801) and FITZGIBBON *Speech... on...the Relief of His Majesty's Roman Catholic Subjects* (Dublin [1796]).

British Museum C 45 f 18 (3)

Lamb's copy. For a description of the composite volume and the date and circumstances of C's annotating it see DYER *Poems* headnote.

Passages marked on pp 24 (in blue ink), on 35 and 36 (pencil), and on each of the seven pages 63–9 (in ink). C's last note is written on p 62.

On 23 Jun 1801 C told Godwin that he had not yet received this pamphlet, but that Daniel Stuart had sent him "Fenwick's Review of it in a paper called the Albion", and that he had heard from Longman that he had at his house a copy for C that Godwin had ordered. The extracts that C had heard had pleased him, but he found the introduction "incorrectly & clumsily worded" and added—"But indeed I have before observed that whatever you write, the first Page is always the worst in the Book." *CL* II 736. By 11 Aug, as he told RS, he had "met with [the pamphlet] by accident" while staying with the Hutchinsons at Bishop's Middleham; like RS, he was "delighted" with it, except for a "loathsome & damnable passage", which RS identifies as "at the end one loathsome cursed passage for which I could in right vexation root up his nose. His folly in thus eternally making himself a mark for abuse is inconceivable. Come kick me—is his eternal language." *CL* II 751; *S Letters* (Curry) I 246. For C's final assessment of the eighty-two-page pamphlet, expressing to Godwin his "unmingled delight & admiration" except for "that one hateful Paragraph" see *CL* II 761.

It is not clear whether the annotated copy, which eventually belonged to Lamb, was originally C's or Lamb's; and if C's, whether it was the copy ordered by Godwin or the copy C "met with" by accident at Middleham.

DATE. Late 1802, after the Peace of Amiens: see 3 and n 2. C read the pamphlet in Aug 1801: see above.

---

1   pp 1–2

Where was the ingenuous heart which did not beat with exultation, ?] at seeing a great and cultivated people [i.e. the French] shake off ?] the chains of <u>one</u> of the <u>most</u> oppressive political systems in the

?] world, the most replenished with abuses, the least mollified and
?] relieved by any infusion of liberty?

Had this been the fact, which the whole History of the French
Revolution in its first workings disproves a posteriori, it would have
been *a priori* impossible that such a revolution could have taken
place. No! it was the discord & contradictory ferment of old abuses
& recent indulgences or connivances—the heat & light of Freedom
let in on a half-cleared, rank Soil, made twilight by the black fierce
Reek, which this Dawn did itself draw up.[1]—Still, however, taking
the sentence *dramatically*, i.e. as the then notion of good men in
general, it is well—& just.

2 pp 6–7

All the great points embraced by the revolution remain entire:
hereditary government is gone; hereditary nobility is extinguished;
the hierarchy of the Gallican church is no more; the feudal rights,
the oppressive immunities of a mighty aristocracy, are banished never
!!] to return. Every thing promises that the future Government of
France will be popular, and her people free.

Let not these !! be deemed the Sneer of after-wit—but see the
Morning Post, then the sturdy adherent of Liberty, from the very
day, Buonaparte entered the Seat of Legislature to the promulgation
of ~~its~~ his constitution.[1] In those essays it was demonstrated that the
reign of pure despotism, (the worst of all pure despotism, military
despotism)[2] had commenced—& that all the preceding victories of
Humanity ("all the great points embraced by the revolution &c")[a3]
remained only to be transmuted into the most direful means or
facilitations of a bloody Ambition, a limitless Tyranny.—[4]

---

[a] C has closed the quotation after both "revolution" and "&c"

[1] For C on the origins of the French
Revolution see the three essays "Com-
parison of...France with...Rome" (21
Sept–2 Oct 1802) in the *M Post*: *EOT*
(*CC*) I 311–39, and with this annotation
cf esp 315–18. These essays were in effect
a sequel to the essays of 1799 cited in **2**
n 1, below.
[1] I.e. the four essays "On the French
Constitution" (7–31 Dec 1799) in the *M
Post*: *EOT* (*CC*) I 31–6, 46–57, and cf

63–4. For the change in C's attitude to
Napoleon between the 1799 and 1802
essays see *EOT* (*CC*) I 318 n 17 (in which
2 is also quoted).
[2] See *EOT* (*CC*) I 53, and cf 155, 314.
[3] In textus.
[4] See the three essays on "Bona-
parte" (11–15 Mar 1800) in the *M Post*:
EOT (*CC*) I 207–16, esp "Bonaparte. In
His Relations to France" (207–11).

3 p 7

The revolutionary societies in this metropolis were once numerous; they had spread their ramifications through almost every county in England; revolutionary lectures were publicly read here and elsewhere with tumults of applause, almost every alehouse had its artisans haranguing in favour of republicanism and equality...

This acco⟨unt⟩ is likewise erroneous—Jacobinism was then the weakest, when it excited the whole hullo-bulloo of alarm/[1] & sinking from men of letters down to the labouring Classes it has increased in strength & danger in exact proportion as the alarm has decreased. It is with Jacobinism—as with the French Empire, we made peace just at the very time, that war *first* became just & necessary.[2]

4 p 8

[These pages (8–12) relate to the attack by Mackintosh, Parr, Mathias, and others on the attitude of mind displayed by Godwin when he wrote his *Enquiry Concerning Political Justice* in "the innocence of my heart". See ANNEX.]

I remember few passages in ancient or modern Authors that contained more just philosophy in appropriate, chaste, & beautiful diction than the five following pages. They reflect equal Honor on Godwin's Head & Heart.[1] Tho' I did it only in the Zenith of his Reputation, yet I feel remorse *ever* to have spoken unkindly of such a Man.[2]

S. T. C.

3[1] C noted in "Letter I to Mr. Fox" (*M Post* 4 Nov 1802) how the Jacobins, though numerically weak, had so effectively spread rumours of their strength as to strike "a universal panic of property". See *EOT* (*CC*) I 380–2.

3[2] See also *EOT* (*CC*) I 384 at n 22. The Revolutionary War was declared on 1 Feb 1793, when Pitt was prime minister; the Peace of Amiens, signed on 27 Mar 1802 under Addington's premiership, lasted until 16 May 1803. For C's analysis of Jacobinism see "Once a Jacobin Always a Jacobin" (*M Post* 21 Oct 1802) in *EOT* (*CC*) I 367–73. His affirmation of the position implied in this annotation is to be seen in his sharp attack on Fox's position in the two

"Letter[s] to Mr. Fox" (*M Post* 4, 9 Nov 1802) in *EOT* (*CC*) I 367–400. C's early association with English Jacobins was to cause him embarrassment by association when the ms of RS's youthful and impetuous *Wat Tyler* was published without authority in 1817: see C's response in the *Courier* of 17 Mar–2 Apr 1817: *EOT* (*CC*) II 449–60, 466–78.

4[1] See ANNEX to this entry.

4[2] When C first read Godwin's *Political Justice* (1793) he thought it harmonious with the principles of pantisocracy and addressed a complimentary sonnet to Godwin in *M Chron* 10 Jan 1795. See *CL* I 115, *PW* (EHC) I 86. He soon regretted the sonnet, and in *The Watchman* V (2 Apr 1796) published a

5 p 42

[Parr has accused Godwin of using Fénelon as an example: If we both were drowning, would you rescue Fénelon or his valet? Godwin adds:]...if I had put the case of Bonaparte, upon the assumption that his existence was necessary to avert the restoration of despotism on the one hand, or the revival of all the horrors of anarchy on the other, few persons, I believe, would have felt any difficulty in deciding.

A striking Instance of the Danger, philosophers expose themselves to, who take, tho' even suppositively, contemporary Examples, as Illustrations. The practice is beneath them. The Philosopher is *always*, not *now*, except as the *now* is *always*.

6 p 62

...the safety of the world can no otherwise be maintained, but by a constant and powerful check upon this principle [of unlimited population]. This idea demands at once many maxims which have been long and unsuspectedly received into the vulgar code of morality, such as, that it is the first duty of princes to watch for the multiplication of their subjects, and that a man or woman, who passes the term of life in a condition of celibacy, is to be considered as having failed to discharge one of the principal obligations they owe to the community. On the contrary it now appears to be rather the !!!] man who rears a numerous family, that has in some degree trangressed the consideration he owes to the public welfare.

Strange, that G. should so hastily admit principles so doubtful in themselves, and so undoubtedly dreadful in their consequences.

rejection of "Mr. Godwin's Principles as vicious; and his book as a Pandar to Sensuality". *Watchman* (*CC*) 194–8; see esp 196, and 197 n 1 (which quotes this annotation), and cf 98–100. His "examination" of *Political Justice*, announced in *The Watchman* and described in several letters as nearing completion, had been quietly abandoned by the summer of 1797. Before May 1796 C had met Godwin once, apparently through the group of literary friends Godwin had gathered around him, including WW, William Frend, and George Dyer. *CL* I 215, *W Life* (M) I 262–3. He was not impressed by Godwin's intellect or by his conversation—"futile sophisms in jejune language"; nor was he more impressed when Godwin renewed the acquaintance through the Wedgwoods. *CL* I 214–15, 413, 549. Yet by Jan 1800 C had accepted him as a friend, and introduced Davy and Lamb to him. In an uneasy and ambiguous relationship, renewed until c 1812 whenever C was in London, C was drawn into correcting Godwin's mss in support of a succession of desperate literary ventures—the fate of many of Godwin's friends. See also BROWNE *Religio* 7 n 1 and AURELIUS **43** n 1.

There exists no proof, & no ~~improbability~~ has been evinced by Malthus, that an excess of population arising from *physical* necessity has introduced *Immorality*/ or that Morality would not, ~~of~~ in itself have contained the true, easy, & effectual Limitation.[1] The whole ? is a business of "*which is the Cause? wch the effect?*" Good heavens! it is proved, that no Country yet exists, not capable under a moral government of sustaining more than its Inhabitants—not even China, whose population is yet the effect of wicked & foolish Laws preventing Emigration.[2]

Annex

In 4, above, C praises "the five following pages"—i.e. pp 8–12.

But it is not my disposition to see the characters and actions of men in the worst point of view. I can discern other human weaknesses concerned in this conversion of my neighbours, less offensive to the moral feelings than bare worldly wisdom and personal interest. It is not in the nature of man to like to stand alone in his sentiments or his creed. We ought not to be too much surprised, when we perceive our neighbours watching the seasons, and floating with the tide. Nor is this fickleness by which they are influenced, altogether an affair of design. It is seldom that we are persuaded to adopt opinions, or repersuaded to abandon them, by the mere force of arguments. The change is generally produced silently, and unperceived except in its ultimate result, by him who suffers it. Our creed is, ninety-nine times in a hundred, the pure growth of our temper and social feelings. The human intellect is a sort of barometer, directed in its variations by the atmosphere which surrounds it. Add to this, that the opinion which has its principle in passion (and this was generally the case with the opinions of men on the topic of the French revolution) includes in its essense the cause of its destruction. "Hope deferred makes the heart sick." Zeal, though it be as hot as Nebuchadnezzer's furnace, without a continual supply of fuel will speedily cool.

I feel little resentment against those persons who, without any fresh reasons to justify their change, think it now necessary to plead for establishments, and express their horror at theories and innovation, though

6[1] Thomas Robert Malthus (1766–1834) *An Essay on the Principle of Population, as it Affects the Future Improvement of Society; with Remarks on the Speculations of W. Godwin, M. Condorcet, and Other Writers* (1798). C owned, and had read, a copy of this pamphlet before he left for Germany in Sept 1798, and found it "exceedingly illogical". See *CL* I 417, 517. That copy has not survived. Malthus published a much-expanded version—*An Essay on the Principle of Population* (1803)—a copy of which, given him by Daniel Stuart, C annotated to assist RS in reviewing it in the *Annual Review*. See MALTHUS: C's notes, especially that on p vii, deal largely with Malthus's failure to establish any relation between morality and population.

6[2] Godwin proceeds to "prove" it on pp 63–77, in which passages are marked in ink on pp 63, 64, 65, 66–7.

I recollect the time when they took an opposite part. But this I must say, that they act against all nature and reason when, instead of modestly confessing their frailty and the transformation of their sentiments, they rail at me because I have not equally changed. If I had expressed a certain degree of displeasure at their conduct, I should have had a very forcible excuse. But I was not prepared with a word of reproach: I would have been silent, if they would have permitted me to be so.

Down to about the middle of the year 1797, as I have said, the champions of the French revolution remained unattacked. About that time a forlorn hope of two little skirmishing pamphlets began the war. But the writers of these pamphlets appear to have been uninstructed in the school of the new converts I have attempted to describe, and their productions were without scurrility. The next and grand attack was opened in Mr. Mackintosh's Lectures. A book was published about the same time, professing to contain remarks upon some speculations of mine, entitled an Essay upon Population. Of this book and the spirit in which it is written I can never speak but with unfeigned respect. Soon after followed a much vaunted Sermon by Mr. Hall of Cambridge, in which every notion of toleration or decorum was treated with infuriated contempt. I disdain to dwell on the rabble of scurrilities which followed: the vulgar contumelies of the author of the Pursuits of Literature, novels of buffoonery and scandal to the amount of half a score, and British Critics, Anti-Jacobin Newspapers, and Anti-Jacobin Magazines without number. Last of all, for the present at least, for I am not idle enough to flatter myself that the tide is gone by, Dr. Parr, with his Spital Sermon before the Lord Mayor, brings up the rear of my assailants. I take occasion from this first avowed and respectable publication*, to offer the little I think it necessary to offer in my defence.

But, before I enter upon particulars, let me stop a moment to observe upon the singular and perverse destiny which has attended me on this occasion. I wrote my Enquiry Concerning Political Justice in the innocence of my heart. I sought no overt effects; I abhorred all tumult; I entered my protest against revolutions. Every impartial person who knows me, or has attentively considered my writings, will acknowledge that it is the fault of my character, rather to be too sceptical, than to incline too much to play the dogmatist. I was by no means assured of the truth of my own system. I wrote indeed with ardour; but I published with diffidence. I knew that my speculations had led me out of the beaten track; and I waited to be instructed by the comment of others as to the degree of value which should be stamped upon them. That comment in the first instance was highly flattering; yet I was not satisfied. I did not cease to revise, to reconsider, or to enquire.

I had learned indeed that enquiry was the pilot who might be expected to steer me into the haven of truth. I had heard a thousand times, and I believed, that whoever gave his speculations on general questions to the public with fairness and temper, was a public benefactor: and I must add, that I have never yet heard the fairness or temper of my publication called into doubt. If my doctrines were formed to abide the test of scrutiny, it was

* The main attack of the Essay on Population is not directed against the principles of my book, but its conclusions.

well: if they were refuted, I should still have occasion to rejoice, in having procured to the public the benefit of that refutation, of so much additional disquisition and knowledge. Unprophetic as I was, I rested in perfect tranquillity, and suspected not that I should be dragged to public odium, and made an example to deter all future enquirers from the practice of unshackled speculation. I was no man of the world; I was a mere student, connected with no party, elected into no club, exempt from every imputation of political conspiracy or cabal. I therefore believed that, if my speculations were opposed, and if my opponent were a man of the least pretension to character and decorum, I should be at least opposed in that style of fairness and respect which is so eminently due from one literary enquirer to another.

My attention was not much excited by what I have already called the preliminaries of the combat. Mr. Mackintosh was the first person who awakened me to any strictness of attention. How much then was I surprised at finding his printed preliminary Discourse written, in such parts as had any allusion to my doctrines, in a spirit lofty, overbearing and scornful, such as that I scarcely recollected its parallel in the publications of the eighteenth century! I had been for some years in habits of friendly intercourse with Mr. Mackintosh; the frankness of my disposition led me therefore immediately to address him with a letter of expostulation.

GEORG AUGUST GOLDFUSS
1782–1848

Handbuch der Zoologie, &c. 2 vols. Nürnberg 1820. 8°.
With collective title-page facing the title-page of each vol, identifying the
work as Vol III (2 pts) of G. H. Schubert *Handbuch der Naturgeschichte* (4
vols of 5, all published [i.e. I–III, v] Nürnberg 1813–23).

Victoria College Library (Coleridge Collection)

At the foot of the title-page of Vol I in pencil, possibly in EHC's hand: "——
Green 1/14/0". Description by EHC in a pocket attached to II +3 (p–d).
Marked "Green Bequest". Part of the original dark blue wrapper has been
bound at the back of Vol I (i.e. I +2/+3) in order to preserve C's note 6
written on the back of it.

DATE. c Apr 1827, if N F° f 64ᵛ (*CN* v) referring to **14** (see **14** n 3) was written
soon after the marginalia were written. There are references to Goldfuss in
N 59 (see e.g. **10** n 1, below) also in c 1827. Later references in c Sept 1833—in
N 29 and N 59 (*CN* v)—are less circumstantial. See also HEINROTH **12** and
n 1, of Aug 1826.

COEDITORS. Hans Eichner, Raimonda Modiano.

1 p⁻³

And what if X and Y themselves be but one and the same
Ousia¹ = Z?—Thus:

Z unpolarized = Chaos, the dynamic Prothesis of Body.

Z polarized = X. i.e. Pondus,² ponderable Body, and Y, Light.

Nitrogen = X in the tendency of transition into Y.

Oxygen = Y in tendency of transition into X.

or Light becoming Body is Oxygen:

Body striving to become Light is Nitrogen.³

1¹ Οὐσία—essence, substance.
1² "Weight, gravity"—C's special
term applied in his distinction between
matter and body, *pondus* being essential
to body but not to matter. See **2** § 2,
below.
1³ C's system of the four chemical
elements (the "four chemical Stuffs")—
oxygen, hydrogen, carbon, and nitrogen
(Lavoisier's "azote")—in relation to the

polar powers as "Syntheses of Light and
Weight" is given or implied in some
detail in **2**, below. For central formula-
tions see esp *CN* III 4226, 4418 (esp ff
14ᵛ–15ᵛ), 4420; *CL* IV 772–3, 807–9; *TL*
57; *Friend* (*CC*) I 94n. Marginalia on
this subject are to be seen particularly
in BÖHME, KANT *Metaphysische An-
fangsgründe*, OERSTED *Ansicht der chemi-
schen Naturgesetze*, OKEN *Lehrbuch der*

2 1 ⁻3-⁻1, concluded in pencil

The great mistakes of the Natur-philosopher[1] are—1. that they confound the Ideal Polar Powers with the Bodies entitled to represent them, each by the *predominance* of the particular Power, not by the exclusion of the others. 2. That their N. and S., as the Poles of Magnetism are made in fact the only distinct Powers, viz. Attractive and Repulsive—while the E. and W. as the Poles of Light, in the form of Electricity, are represented as nothing more than the **A** same Attractivity and Repulsivity in separation. Whereas the North and South being Attraction and Repulsion, the East and West are *Con*traction· and Dilation.[2] Hence they fall in with the Herd of mechanico-corpuscular Psilosophers in calling Air a Fluid & an elastic Fluid—which is for *me* not much better than a square Circle.[3]

Naturgeschichte, RUNGE *Neueste phytochemische Entdeckungen,* STEFFENS *Beyträge zur innern Naturgeschichte der Erde,* and ZEITSCHRIFT *für speculative Physik.* C regarded as "a memoria technica" rather than as a descriptive stylisation the schema or diagram in which he usually explicated his theory—the "bi-lineal quadri-polar Antithesis" of **2** (at n 7), below: see *CL* IV 773–5 (Sept 1817), in which he also discusses the advantages of such a device.

2[1] For the philosophers included generally under the title of *Naturphilosophen* see ESCHENMAYER **13** and n 1, and cf **14** and n 1, below. For a history of the *Naturphilosophie* and its beginnings in Kant's *Metaphysische Anfangsgründe* see Barry Gower "Speculations in Physics: The History and Practice of 'Naturphilosophie'" *Studies in the History and Philosophy of Science* IV (1972–3) 301–56, esp 303–11.

2[2] For C's assessment of the *Naturphilosophie* in Dec 1817 see *CL* IV 792–3. His most frequent and vigorous attacks on the *Naturphilosophen* dealt with these first two errors: (*a*) they regarded the four "Stuffs" as actual physical bodies rather than as symbols of the ideal powers of attraction, repulsion, contraction, and dilation; and (*b*) they either confused the substantive powers (attraction and repulsion, the polar powers of magnetism and gravitation represented by carbon at the North pole and nitrogen at the South pole) and the modifying powers (contraction and dilation, the polar powers of electricity and light represented by oxygen at the East pole and hydrogen at the West pole), or else they entirely neglected the modifying powers. Examples of C's detection of these errors can be seen in OERSTED generally, in OKEN *Lehrbuch der Naturphilosophie* pp 22–3, in STEFFENS *Beyträge zur innern Naturgeschichte der Erde* pp ⁺11–⁺12, and in ZEITSCHRIFT *für speclative Physik* (Jena & Leipzig) I i 48–9.

2[3] For "psilosophy" see DONNE *Sermons* COPY B **8** n 3. For variants of the phrase "mechanico-corpuscular Psilosophers" see e.g. *Friend* (*CC*) I 94n ("mechanical atomistic Psilosophy"), *CL* IV 792 ("the mechanic corpuscular system"), *AR* (1825) 398 ("the Mechanico-corpuscular Philosophy"), ZEITSCHRIFT pp ⁻2–⁻1 (Schelling's "dynamico-atomistic Assumption"), *TL* 57 ("the absurdity of the corpuscularian or mechanic system").

In STEFFENS *Grundzüge der philosophischen Naturwissenschaft* p 87 C noted that "the Air is not the Symbol of Fluidity; but this most productive Error is common to all the Natur-philosophen"—the error arising from the

3. They make the Metals combinations of *chemical* Carbon &
Nitrogen, in different proportions—whereas they are not even
reducible into Products of the ~~two~~ Ideal or Dynamic Carbon &
Nitrogen/ not to object what yet is obvious, that the chemical Carbon
& Nitrogen are themselves two Metals, and consequently themselves
Compounds.[4]—4. Warmth, tho' well characterized by Steffens,[5]
remains only an Accident not an ingredient of their four *Stuffs*.[6]

Now I retain the bi-lineal quadri-polar Antithesis,[7] in respect of
the *Powers*; but I make the Powers of the same *kind*, North and
South, ~~being opp~~ and East & West, being Opposites; while N. and
E., S. and West, are Disparates.—

Opposites.

Attraction ⚹ Repulsion
Contraction χ Dilation

---

general confusion of substantive and
modifying powers (as noted in n 2,
above). In ZEITSCHRIFT I i 45–6 he noted
further: "It seems strange to me that
Schelling and Steffens should so often—
indeed almost always—overlook the
essential differences of the Fluid and the
Aeriform. Nay, more than overlook—
they destroy it and refer both alike to the
absolutely fluid...."

2[4] In STEFFENS *Beyträge* pp 262–3 C
noted: "It is an error...and an inconsis-
tency in Steffens to speak of Metals as
composed of Carbon and Nitrogen—
unless these are taken as the Power
predominant in each. And even so, yet
not as composed *of* them, but as
constituted *by* them." C regarded the
metals as "different proportions of
Carbon and Azote indifferenced by the
minimum of Hydrogen or Oxygen" (*CN*
III 4420 ff 19ᵛ–20)—i.e. as constituted by
the interaction between substantive and
modifying powers. The error of regarding
metals as "combinations of *chemical*
Carbon & Nitrogen" is an instance of the
confusion of bodies and ideal bodies—
error (*a*) in n 2, above. For C on metals
see also BÖHME 17 and *TL* 69. See also
n 13, below.

2[5] Steffens had defined warmth as the
indifference of light and gravity: *Grund-
züge* p 64 (not annotated): cf pp 48–9,

134–5 (not annotated). Cf *CL* IV 773
(Sept 1817): "Warmth is the Indifference
...of Light and Gravitation, partaking of
both; an idea which fully explains...it's
various mysterious Properties." At p 48
Steffens had written (tr): "...therefore,
there must also be an indifference of the
whole tetrad through which that which
reveals itself as the Absolute through the
identity of light and gravitation, mani-
fests itself as indifference in nature....
This takes place through warmth. Hence
the strange mystical, never fully fathomed
essence of warmth, hence its affinity with
gravitation and light simultaneously."
See also **2** (at n 10), below.

2[6] I.e. the four chemical elements—
oxygen, hydrogen, carbon, nitrogen. See
1 n 3, above.

2[7] The interaction between the North–
South line of magnetism and the East–
West line of electricity marked by the
four chemical elements, as in the diagram
given in e.g. *CN* III 4226 and *CL* IV 772;
cf *TL* 56. For the diagram as "a memoria
technica" see **1** n 3, above. For the
"quadri-polar" scheme C may have
owed something to STEFFENS *Grundzüge*,
esp ch 3 pp 36–65; but not uncritically,
for he raises a number of objections to
Steffens's theory in annotations at pp 38,
43, 46–7, 48. See *CN* IV 4555 for C's
"Compass of Nature".

Disparates

Attraction // Contraction
Repulsion // Dilation.[8]

Secondly, I suppose all four chemical Stuffs to be Syntheses of Light and Weight[9]—that Carbon is the latter with a minimum of the former; that Nitrogen is Weight or Body striving to be luciform, Oxygen = Light in its transition to Body; while lastly, Hydrogen corresponds to the *Indiff[er]ence[a]* of Light and Body, i.e. Warmth.[10]— Hydrogen I would state as embodied Warmth, or Warmth with the minimum of Body. Likewise, in the production of the Metals, Hydrogen in my scheme, plays as the *Negative* of Carbon, or the power of which Cohesion is the Product.[11]

Hydrogen, as ⟨()⟩ the principle of Continuity as the analogous Different of Cohesion:⟨)⟩[b] when giving out a portion of its warmth thro' the Antagonism of the contracting Oxygen (the principle of Particularity) but with the remaining portion universalizing (continuifying) the Oxygen, becomes the Base of Water.

Hydrogen, retaining its Warmth, but coerced by the predominence of Carbon, and its Continuity made to Cohesion, but at the same time rendering the Cohesion of the Carbon more continuous, is in combination with Carbon Metal—and κατ' εξοχην[12] Gold.

The greater or lesser Action of the Nitrogen, as the *Negative* of

---

[a] Letters supplied by the editor
[b] The inserted parentheses are in pencil, as is the continuation of the note, except the *w* in "when"

2[8] C insisted upon distinguishing between "opposite", "disparate", and "contrary", and consistently used (as here) special signs to secure the distinctions. Opposites "are always of the same kind, and tend to union.... Thus the + and − poles of the magnet, thus positive and negative electricity are opposites." *C&S (CC)* 24n; cf *Friend (CC)* 1 94n. See also Böhme 139, 158 n 2. In C's scheme the powers of attraction and repulsion (the line of magnetism) and the powers of contraction and dilation (the line of electricity) are opposite, but powers that occupy the poles of different lines—such as attraction (marked by carbon at the North pole of the line of magnetism) and contraction (marked by oxygen at the East pole of the line of electricity)— are disparate.

2[9] The powers of light and of weight (or gravitation) correspond to the lines of electricity (East–West) and of magnetism (North–South). In *CN* III 4420 f 19 C gave the difference between these powers: "...there are two not only imponderable but immaterial *Powers*, Gravitation and Light. There is one imponderable yet material Power, with two opposite forces = Electricity + and −. And lastly, there is one imponderable Power, phaenomenic by *motion* but not visible as a matter per se = Magnetism + and minus...." For a different view of the powers of nature see Böhme 137.

2[10] See n 5, above.

2[11] For C on cohesion see *CN* III 4223 and cf Boerhaave 7. For the distinction between cohesion and coherence see *CN* III 4433.

2[12] "Eminently".

Carbon, constitutes the more or less incoherent Metals.[13] Under what condition Nitrogen may exercise the functions of a Positive Principle (i.e. Volatility) as in Arsenic [becomes the question.][a][14]

3 1 4, pencil | 1 Naturgeschichte des Thieres § 7

Das Thier wurzelt im All, trennt sich egoistisch von demselben, und setzt sich reflectirend auf die Aussenwelt, und auf sich selbst. Die organischen Systeme seines Leibes sind daher das *Generationssystem*, das *Verdauungssystem*, das *Gefäss-* und *Respirationssystem* und das *System der* nach innen und aussen gerichteten *Bewegung*.

[The animal has its roots in the universe, egoistically separates itself from this, and, reflecting, bases itself on the external world, and on itself. The organic systems of its body are therefore [*daher*] the *system of generation*, the *digestive system*, the *vascular* and *respiratory system*, and the *system of motion* directed inwards and outwards.]

The smooth, easy, matter-of-course, use of the *Daher* amuses me.[1]

4 1 ⁺2, referring to 1 19 | §14

Bis zur Zeit seiner vollkommenen Entwickelung strebt es [das Thier] nach zwei entgegengesetzten Polen hin sich auszubilden, und diese polare Entzweiung spricht sich zunächst in der Differenz der männlichen und weiblichen Geschlechtsorgane aus. Im Acte der Begattung wird diese Differenz auf einen Augenblick aufgehoben, und die getrennten Geschlechtsthiere werden wieder ein Ganzes, wobei jedoch das erregende, männliche, im basischen, weiblichen, aufs neue den Gegensatz hervorrufet, welcher sich nun in demselben als Frucht entwickelt.

[Until the time of its complete development it [the animal] strives to evolve in two opposite polar directions, and this polar division is first expressed in the difference between the male and the female sexual organs. In coitus this difference is suspended for a moment, and the separate sexual animals again become a whole; in such a way, however, that the stimulating male animal

---

a Three words at the rough bottom edge of the leaf are rubbed and almost illegible

2[13] C's concept of metals seems to have been affected by Steffens's division of the metals into a coherent series and a non-coherent series—the first represented by carbon (the pole of utmost coherence), the second by nitrogen (the pole of least coherence). See STEFFENS *Grundzüge* ch 6 pp 88–133 (of which only p 110 is annotated). For C on metals generally see n 4, above.

2[14] For C on arsenic see BOERHAAVE 11 and n 1.

3[1] For another complaint against the use of an illogical *daher* (therefore) in the arguments of the *Naturphilosophen* see e.g. STEFFENS *Grundzüge* p 87: "the logical force of the *Daher* is right curious!"

again calls forth in the basic female the opposite, which now develops in the female as the foetus.]

P. 19. Better say nothing than nothings that pretend to say every thing—ex. gr. this "polar Gegensätz",[a1] these polar Halves that in the orgasm of coitus become a Whole—but yet so that male exciting Half excites in the basish female Half the Gegensätz[a] anew which then developes itself in the female Half as the Fœtus.[2]—And pray what *is* this new Gegensatz? What determines its sex? How comes this to be contingent—sometimes a b[o]y,[b] sometimes girl, sometimes a succession of Boys, sometimes a succession of Girls![3]—In short, I do not understand a word of the §ph.

5 ɪ 26–7, pencil | §16

Allein nicht bloss die chemische Absonderung des Sauerstoffes aus *] der Luft und der Uebertritt desselben in das Blut, und Ausscheidung von Kohlensäure aus dem Blute und Uebertritt desselben in die Luft ist das Wesen der Veränderung, die mit der Luft und dem Blute in der Lunge vorgeht. Blut, Luft und Lunge sind vielmehr in eine lebendige Metamorphose verflochten, deren Resultate geröthetes Blut und gekohlte Luft sind.

[But the chemical separation of the oxygen from the air and its passing into the blood, and the removal of carbon dioxide from the blood and its passing into the air, is not the sole change that the air and the blood undergo in the lung. Rather, blood, air, and lung are involved in a living metamorphosis resulting in reddened blood and carbonised air.]

* It is singliar that the Continental Physiologists seem ignorant of Allen & Pepys's Experiments proving that in Breathing the Blood is decarbonateds itself by an exudation of Carbon on the surfaces of the Air-vessels, without any Oxygen *entering* the Vessels or combining with the Blood.[1] See *MSS in the Cover*[2]

---

a A slip for *Gegensatz*
b Letter supplied by the editor

4[1] "Polar opposite"—from textus (var).

4[2] For similar erotic imagery see ESCHENMAYER 17.

4[3] C offers an answer to this question in KANT *Vermischte Schriften* COPY B ɪɪ 161–160: "...I think it probable, that the sex depends in part at least on the excitement of the Imagination at the moment and that a woman intensely pleased + [i.e. conceives] a girl."

5[1] William Allen (1770–1843)— Quaker, friend of Humphry Davy, associate of Clarkson and Wilberforce in their campaign against slavery, supporter (unlike C) of Joseph Lancaster in the educational controversy with Andrew Bell—refined the work of Priestley, Lavoisier, and Séguin on respiration, with the help of instruments ingeniously contrived by William Haseldine Pepys (1775–1856), by showing that "the

6 1 +3,[a] referring to 1 26

Die letzten Verzweigungen der Pulmonararterien und der Luftröhre, und mit ihnen Blut und Luft, lösen sich in die Substanz der Lunge auf, wodurch momentan ein Zustand der Indifferenz eintritt, der sich aber sogleich wieder in Lungenvenen und Arterien, in rothes und dunkelfarbiges Blut polarisch gestaltet, und zugleich Lungensubstanz auf der einen und gekohlte Luft auf der andern Seite bildet.

[The last branchings-out of the pulmonary arteries and of the bronchial tubes, and with them blood and air, dissolve into the substance of the lung, so that a momentary state of indifference results; this state, however, is at once transformed into the polarities of pulmonary veins and arteries, into red and dark blood, and simultaneously forms lung-substance on the one side and carbonated air on the other.]

P. 26.—The last ramifications of the Pulmonary Arteries and of the Air-pipes (Luftröhre? Air-tubes? What are they? What we call cells?) and with them ~~the~~ Blood and Air dissolve or decompose into the *Substance* of the Lungs—
(What can this mean?)
and thus a momentary *Indifference* takes place—
(Why? how does this follow?)
The whole § ph is unintelligible to me[1]—and I cannot help doubting whether Golden-foot attached any distinct conception to the term, Indifference.

[a] Inside of original blue paper wrapper

volume of carbonic acid gas expired from the lungs is almost exactly equal to the volume of oxygen abstracted from the inspired air" (as summarised in *DNB* under W. H. Pepys). The results of these experiments were reported in *Phil Trans RS* xcvii (1808) 249–81, xcix (1809) 404–9. The process of diffusion by which oxygen enters the blood and carbon dioxide is returned to the atmosphere was not yet understood. In a note preserved in BM Add MS 34225 f 148[v] C quotes from "Goldfuss' Handbuch der Zoologie P. 25. §. 2."—(tr) "The venous blood has a red-black colour and contains more carbon than the bright red arterial blood, which has a greater proportion of oxygen"—and remarks: "The not yet thoroughly ascertained part which Oxygen plays in Respiration, and the mode of its operation on the Surfaces of the Lungs in removing the exuded— whether Carbon simply...or Carbonic Acid...ought to be carefully distinguished from its Operation *in* the ~~Body~~ System, as a constituent part [of] the Body." In a note on the blood of Christ, *CN* iv 4854 c Jan 1822, C repeated the incorrect view given here: "(*Allen & Pepys* versus *Priestley & Lavoisier* de Oxygene non in sanguinem permaente)" —i.e. the view of *Allen & Pepys*, contrary to that of Priestley & Lavoisier, of Oxygen as not penetrating into the blood. See also **6**, below.
5^2 I.e. **6** on 1 +3.
6^1 For other objections to Goldfuss's method of deduction see **3**, above, and **7**, below.

Likewise I complain of the *Jack of all trades* use of the term, polarisch—.[2] Where is the proof that red and dark-colored Blood are the polar opposites? What is the Identity, of which they are the Poles? Air and Air-vessels, Blood and Blood-vessels dissolved into the Substance of the Lungs?—But this Quartette are the Indifference— And Indifference supposes an Identity, no less than the Thesis and Antithesis[3]

Id.

T. ⟋⟍ An.

In.

Polarisch? Carbonated & decarbonated Blood! As well might you call Curds and Curds & Cream polarish[a] gestaltet.[b][4]

7   I [+]1, referring to I 29 | §17

Doch kann letztere [die Bewegungsthätigkeit des Gangliensystems] im magnetischen Schlafe so gesteigert werden, dass sie sich bis zu geistigen Actionen erhebt, und die Function des Kopfgehirnes übernimmt.

[But the latter [i.e. the motional activity of the ganglionic system] can be so intensified in magnetic sleep that it attains to mental actions and takes on the functions of the brain.]

P. 29. first three Lines.—
Sweet Fairy Foot-of-Gold! O for the *Proof* of this!—It is one way of rendering the possibility of the assumed facts of the recorded Cases intelligible—of seeming to do so at least. But even as this, it appears to me ⟨a⟩ far less probable hypothesis, than that the magnetic treatment, like Opium, may throw the nerves of the outward Senses into a state of Torpor while the Brain remains in a waking state—or rather a more intense state of excitement.[1] That knots of Nerves intended for the purpose of involuntary Motion should in a moment

---

a A slip for *polarisch*
b C seems first to have written *gestalten*, then altered it to *gestaltet*

6[2] For C's concept of polarity see e.g. *Friend* (*CC*) I 94n. Cf also **2** nn 7, 8, above. See also Owen Barfield *What Coleridge Thought* Appendix.
6[3] Cf the diagram and statement by Green in *Spiritual Philosophy* (2 vols 1865) quoted by Barfield ibid p 261 n 9.
6[4] "Polarly...polarly patterned (disposed)"—"polarly", C's word in e.g.

N 59 f 8 (*CN* v), not in *OED*. The German phrase is in textus, there rendered "transformed into the polarities".
7[1] C is evidently describing his own condition under the influence of opium, as attested by many witnesses. Cf his account of the dream in which he composed *Kubla Khan*: *PW* (EHC) I 296. See also KLUGE **1** and n 4 and **45**.

put on the functions of perception, memory, combination of thoughts, &c &c is hugely anomalous, to say the least.

S. T. C.

8 I +1,[a] referring to I 29

Das Gangliensystem ist demnach das Gehirn, welches das materielle Leben vermittelt; das Nervensystem des Rückenmarks belebt das irritable System, und das Gehirn selbst entspricht der Sensibilität.

[Hence the ganglionic system is the brain that facilitates the material life; the nervous system of the spinal cord animates the irritable system, and the brain itself corresponds to sensibility.]

The following short §ph—the first sentence at least—is one of a hundred instances of the abuse of analogy among the later German Naturalists.[1] What fair analogy is there between the Ganglia (there are many) and the Brain?

9 I 45 | § 22

Die Pflanzen bedürfen mehr des Lichtes, die Thiere mehr der Wärme, und überall, wo die Temperatur auf einen gewissen Grad erhöhet, die Stärke des Lichtes aber geschwächt ist, findet sich eine Tendenz zu animalischen Bildungen.

[Plants have greater need of light, animals of warmth, and wherever the temperature has risen to a certain degree while the intensity of the light is diminished, a tendency towards animal organisation is found.]

Is it not the presence of Moisture with Heat ⟨& consequent abundance of vegetable Nourishment⟩ rather than the diminished Light, that favors the formation and developement of Animals?

10 II 3 | [Introduction to 8th Class *Pisces*] § 2

Die Natur verfolgt, bei der Bildung der höhern Thierreihe, einen ähnlichen stufenweisen Bildungsgang, wie bei den niedern Classen.... Die niederste Stelle nehmen die Fische ein, die höchste die Säugthiere. Zur Seite stehen die Reptilien und Vögel, einander gegen über.

---

a Written immediately below 7

8[1] For C's account of analogy see *CN* II 2319 and n, and 2320. For analogy and symbol see *CN* II 2274 and *AR* (1825) 254. For the misuse of analogy by the *Naturphilosophen* see e.g. BÖHME **74**, ESCHENMAYER **18** and **24**.

[In the formation of the higher series of animals nature follows a progressive course similar to that in the formation of the lower animals.... The lowest position is occupied by fish, the highest by mammals. At the two opposite sides there are the reptiles and birds.]

Did that spirit-awing Anomaly of an Understanding apparently next to human in the VIth Class (Insecta) never take hold of Goldfuss's Attention?[1]

11 ɪɪ 203, pencil | 10th Class *Aves*. Ist Order *Natatores* 3rd Family *Anserides*. 4 *Cygnus*

How is it, that the Black Swan of Botany Bay is omitted?[1]

12 ɪɪ 291, pencil | 8th Order *Oscines Singvögel* § 148

...Ihre Stimme ist Gesang, oder sie lernen wenigstens Worte nachsprechen.

[...Their voice is song, or they learn at least to repeat words.]

10[1] See ɪ 243–50, Introduction to VIth Class, esp § 161 (tr): "Few [insects] are directly useful to man; on the contrary, many are very bothersome and harmful to him." But on ɪ 513 § 253 (which C did not annotate) Goldfuss does say (tr): "This sociability towards a communal goal...from the ant to the bee, is a most remarkable phenomenon, and undoubtedly the most spiritual manifestation of life in the insect world." For C, insectivity represented an advanced stage in the development and differentiation of consciousness, with the highest insects being endowed with "a faculty for which there is no other word but *Understanding*". *SM* (*CC*) 19 n 1 (marginal note); see also *AR* (1825) 210–14 and *TL* 75–9 (beginning with the statement that " THE INSECT WORLD IS THE EXPONENT OF IRRITABILITY..."); cf *CN* ɪɪɪ 4418 f 16.

11[1] The black swan (*Chenopis atrata*) was first sighted on 6 Jan 1697 on the southwest coast of Australia at what is now named Swan River. The black swan became the armorial device of the colony of Western Australia because the bird was first sighted in that region, but James Cook and other voyagers found that it ranged over most of Australia and was abundant in many districts. C could have found a description in William Dampier (see DEFOE **15** n 1) or in the detailed descriptions appended to the account of

Cook's voyage in *Endeavour* (1768–71), for in Botany Bay, so named for the profusion of new varieties discovered there by Joseph Banks and Daniel Solander, black swans were sighted and the first kangaroo. A more likely source than Cook's printed account, however, would be Lamb's friend Barron Field (1786–1846), judge of the supreme court of New South Wales from 1817, whose privately printed *First Fruits of Australian Poetry* (Sydney 1819: pp 12)—the first volume of verse to be printed in Australia—Lamb reviewed in the *Examiner* 16 Jan 1820. He told Field (16 Aug 1820: *LL* ɪɪ 282) that he, C, WW, and Charles Lloyd were "hugely taken with your [poem] Kangaroo"—which with *Botany-Bay Flowers* made up the whole content of the first edition. Field presented a copy of the second edition of the *First Fruits* (Sydney 1823: pp 19) to C and RS when he returned to England in 1824. C's occasional poem *The Delinquent Travellers* (c 1824) matches the cheerful, even facetious, tone of Field's *Botany-Bay Flowers*. Field had included in his celebration of the curiosities set down at Botany Bay to perplex the taxonomist "sooty swans" and "duck-moles"; and C writes in lines 108–9: "I'll go with you, | Hunt the black swan and kangaroo". *PW* (*EHC*) ɪ 443–7.

I should guess, that Goldfuss is no Musician. *Gepfeif* nicht Gesang
—Vögel *singen* nur in Dichter-gesang.[1]

13 ɪɪ 406 | 11th Class *Mammalia*. 6th Order *Chelopoda*. 4th Family *Canina* § 203

Die Erde belebte sich anfangs mit gigantischen Wallen, mit Sirenen,
Robben, mit Nashörnern... ungeheuern Elephanten, Büffeln, Hir-
schen und mit Pferden.... Allein alle diese Bildungen konnten nicht
*] zum Ziele, zur Menschenähnlichkeit hinführen. Es trat ein Winter-
sturm ein, der sie vernichtete, so dass sich nur noch ihre Knochen-
reste vorfinden.

[The earth was first populated by gigantic whales, sea-cows, seals, rhino-
ceroses... enormous elephants, buffalo, deer, and horses.... But all these
creatures could not lead to the goal, to the approximation of man. A "winter
storm" occurred, which destroyed them, so that only their bones remain.]

* I should like to know whether Goldfuss really meant any thing by
this Winter-storm/ i.e. whether he meant to have any meaning![1]

14 ɪɪ 488–9 | Der Mensch § 280

Bei ihm [dem Jüngling] sind körperliches und geistiges Leben noch
im Streit begriffen. Der vollendete Mann strebt das körperliche
Daseyn dem geistigen unterzuordnen, und wird, wenn es ihm gelingt,
ein Ebenbild der Gottheit auf Erden.... Endlich reisst sich der Geist
von den Fesseln des müden Körpers los, er gibt sein irdisches Daseyn
*] auf und lebt in seinen Nachkommen körperlich und in der ganzen
Menschheit geistig fort.

[With him [the youth], physical and spiritual life are still in conflict. The adult
strives to subordinate his physical to his spiritual existence and, if he
succeeds in so doing, becomes an image of the Godhead on earth.... Finally
his spirit casts off the fetters of his tired body, he gives up his earthly
existence, and lives on physically in his descendants and spiritually in the
whole of mankind.]

12[1] "Piping, not song—Birds *sing*
only in the songs of poets." Cf *TL* p 84:
"That all languages designate the melody
of birds as singing (though according to
Blumenbach man only sings, while birds
do but whistle), demonstrates that it had
been felt as, what indeed it is, a tentative
and prophetic prelude of something yet
to come." Cf also *CN* ɪɪɪ 4022: "Man the
only animal who can *sing*...".

13[1] Goldfuss, following Cuvier's
theory that the epochal extinction of
species of organisms was delineated by a
sequence of natural catastrophes—rather
than, as we now suppose, by a sequence
of glacial interventions—refers here to a
catastrophic blizzard that would be
followed by the "spring" of the next
epoch.

* The influence of the Natur-philosophy; and still more perhaps of the Circumstance that the Nat. Phil. won over ⟨to⟩ itself all the youthful Genius of Germany and used poesy tho' not metre, as its form; shews itself in the higher and better Spirit of this and the three or four preceding §phs.[1] But if there had been no other proof that this spirit was from without, a stratum of electricity on the surface, not a Life evolving, that it was *caught* not born,[2] in Goldfuss, the last 7 words of §ph 280 would suffice.[3]

*a*What? Individuality the *aim* thro' all, and dissipation into universality the *crown*ing, o no! the mocking *fool's cap*ping End![4]

---

a Written at the head of p 489, introduced by "*continued from below*"

14[1] The *Naturphilosophie*, developing in the intellectual context of German romanticism, was coloured and shaped by the romantic conception of nature as an active, dynamic, and organic whole. Fichte having failed to find a philosophical body for that concept of nature, Schelling with the encouragement of Goethe and the founders of German romanticism made the first attempt to "portray a Romantic conception of nature using methods and ideas familiar in classical philosophical thought". Barry Gower (as cited in **2** n 1, above) p 310 and n 40. See also ESCHENMAYER **13**

n 1. For C's view that "poetry of the highest kind may exist without metre" see *BL* ch 14 (*CC*) ii 14, and cf ch 18 (*CC*) ii 66–72.

14[2] The concept of a surface power became a significant metaphor for C.

14[3] C refers to the last seven words of the textus: "and spiritually in the whole of mankind". Cf *CL* iv 875.

14[4] In N F⁰ f 64ᵛ (*CN* v) (c Apr 1827) C refers to "my Note on the penultimate page of Goldfuss"—i.e. this annotation. For C on individuation see **10** n 1, above, and e.g. *CL* iv 690 and *TL* 42.

THOMAS GRAY
1716–1771

The Works of Thomas Gray with memoirs of his life and writings by William Mason to which are subjoined extracts philological poetical and critical from the author's original manuscripts selected and arranged by Thomas Mathias, &c. 2 vols. London 1814. 4⁰.

Not located. Annotations here reprinted from *NLS* ii 265–71.

In a ms note dated 12 May 1820 C referred to "Gray's Anal. of the BIRDS of Aristophanes, in 2nd Volume of Matthias's Edition of Gray's Works" as "a delicious model" of "an analysis of [the] Work from Scene to Scene". *CL* v 43n. SC, in her comments on Henry Reed's *Memoir of Thomas Gray* (1851), said: "I was a little disappointed that you did not notice here my Father's notes on Gray's *Platonica*"; she quoted part of **5** and repeated C's adverse comments on the *Ode on a Distant Prospect of Eton College* from **2–3**. L. N. Broughton *Sara Coleridge and Henry Reed* (Ithaca NY 1937) 69.

C was early taught to admire Gray's verse (see e.g. *CL* i 18, 27–8), as a young man quoted freely from the small canon of his poetry (e.g. *Misc C* 355, *Watchman—CC*—40), and in early 1796 intended to prepare an "Edition of Collins & Gray with a preliminary Dissertation" (*CN* i 161[i], 174 §15). By c Jan–May 1799, however, he noticed how his turning away from Gray's poetry marked a turning-point in his poetic taste: "When no criticism is pretended to...Poetry gives most pleasure when only generally & not perfectly understood. It was so by me with Gray's *Bard*, & Collins's odes—*The Bard* once intoxicated me, & now I read it without pleasure. From this cause it is that what *I* call metaphysical Poetry gives me so much delight.—" *CN* i 383. Later he objected to Gray's typographical exaltation of abstractions, but recorded his delight in the *Elegy*, even though he had "long before detected the defects in 'the Bard'". *BL* ch 1, 2 (*CC*) i 20, 40–1n; cf *TT* 21 Apr 1811, *CL* i 153, *CN* iii 4313 f 151, DAVISON **19**. Much later, finding Gray's Installation Ode "very majestic" he found *The Bard* "and the rest of [Gray's] lyrics...frigid and artificial" and said that there was "more real lyric feeling in Cotton's Ode on Winter". *TT* 23 Oct 1833. He gives an even harsher view in a notebook entry of c Apr 1829; in praising the power of the Hebrew poets of the OT he says that they "reasoned with the organ of Imagination" and did not set themselves "to work out a cold-blooded carpentry of ~~Dreams~~ Furors, like ~~Grays~~ the Bard or [Southey's] the Vision of Judgment". N 41 f 18ᵛ. For C's high opinion of Gray as a classical scholar see **5** n 2, below.

CONTENTS. i Poems (**1–4**); Notes Imitations and Variations; Memoirs of the Life and Writings of Thomas Gray by William Mason; Miscellaneous tributes to Gray, verse translations, etc; Appendix: Letters from Thomas Gray to Horace Walpole. II Extracts Philological Poetical and Critical 1. Metrum; 2. Poetical—Miscellaneous—Classical [Aristophanes]; 3. Geographical: relating to some parts of India and Persia; 4. Some Account of the Dialogues and of the Epistles of Plato (5–9); Appendix: A Specimen of Some Illustrations of the "Systema Naturae" of Linnaeus; Postscript by the Editor.

DATE. Probably 1819: after publication of *The Friend* (1818) in c mid–Nov 1818 (cf *CL* IV 881 and n)—see 9. Note 5 is dated "1819" in *NLS*, but no evidence is cited; the date could be C's, written (as printed) as part of his annotation. In a lecture of 11 Jan 1819 C quoted at length from "A General View of the Works of Plato" by Floyer Sydenham (1710–87), who translated nine of the dialogues under the title of *Works of Plato* (4 vols 1759–80). *P Lects* Lect 4 (1949) 160–3. C probably found it in this edition of Gray, in which Mathias has inserted it as prefix to "Some Account of the Dialogues... of Plato", C's long quotation being from the bibliographically anomalous II 290*–292*. Cf also *P Lects* (1949) 165.

1   1 9 | *Ode on a Distant Prospect of Eton College* lines 9–10

> Wanders the hoary Thames along
> His silver-winding way.

We want, methinks, a little treatise from some man of flexible good sense, and well versed in the Greek poets, especially Homer, the choral, and other lyrics, containing first a history of compound epithets, and then the laws and licenses.[1] I am not so much disposed as I used to be to quarrel with such an epithet as "silver-winding;" ungrammatical as the hyphen is, it is not wholly *illogical*, for the phrase conveys more than silvery and winding. It gives, namely, the unity of the impression, the co-inherence of the brightness, the motion, and the line of motion.

2   1 10 | lines 21–30

> Say, Father THAMES, for thou hast seen
> Full many a sprightly race
> Desporting on thy margent green
> The paths of pleasure trace,
> Who foremost now delight to cleave
> With pliant arm thy glassy wave?

1[1] See HOMER 1 n 8. Cf C's condemnation of his own use of "double-epithets" in the Preface to *Poems* (1797): *PW* (EHC) II 1145.

The captive linnet which enthrall?
What idle progeny succeed
To chase the rolling circle's speed,
Or urge the flying ball?

This is the only stanza that appears to me very objectionable in point of diction. This, I must confess, is not only *falsetto* throughout, but is at once harsh and feeble, and very far the worst ten lines in all the works of Mr. Gray, English or Latin, prose or verse.

3 I 12 | lines 68–70

     * And envy wan, and faded care,
     † Grim-visaged comfortless despair,
     ‡ And sorrow's piercing dart.

* Bad in the first, † in the second, ‡ in the last degree.[a]

4 I 15 | *Ode to Adversity* line 6

The proud are taught to <u>taste of pain</u>;[b]

There is a want of dignity—a sort of irony in this phrase to my feeling that would be more proper in dramatic than in lyric composition.

5 II [298] (fly-title verso)[c] | "Some Account of the Dialogues of Plato and of His Epistles with Notes"

Whatever might be expected from a scholar, a gentleman, a man of exquisite taste, as the quintessence of sane and sound good sense, Mr. Gray appears to me to have performed.[1] The poet Plato, the orator Plato, Plato the exquisite dramatist of conversation, the seer and the painter of character, Plato the high-bred, highly-educated, aristocratic republican, the man and the gentleman of quality stands full before us from behind the curtain as Gray has drawn it back. Even so does Socrates, the social wise old man, the *practical* moralist. But Plato the philosopher, but the divine Plato, was not to be comprehended

---

a C's more usual footnote sigla are substituted for "1, 2, 3" of *NLS*
b This phrase, not italicised in the printed text of 1814, is taken to be underlined by C
c Or on II [290], facing the fly-title "Extracts", or on a flyleaf

5[1] Gray's "Some Account of the Dialogues...of Plato" opens with "Brief Notices of Socrates and of his Friends"; he then provides for each of the dialogues he treats (though not for *Gorgias*) a summary account, with notes on the Greek text. He does not present *Parmenides, Epinomis, Timaeus, Critias, Menexenus,* or *Laws* 5–10.

within the field of vision, or be commanded by the fixed immoveable telescope of Mr. Locke's human understanding.[2] The whole sweep of the best philosophic reflections of French or English fabric in the age of our scholarly bard, was not commensurate with the mighty orb. The little, according to *my* convictions at least, the very little of proper Platonism contained in the *written* books of Plato,[3] who himself, in an epistle, the authenticity of which there is no tenable ground for doubting, as I was rejoiced to find Mr. Gray acknowledge, has declared all he had written to be substantially Socratic, and not a fair exponent of his own tenets, even this little, Mr. Gray has either misconceived or honestly confessed that, as he was not one of the initiated, it was utterly beyond his comprehension.[4] Finally, to

5[2] The most concentrated evidence for Gray's admiration for Locke is to be seen in the incomplete *De principiis cogitandi*, first published by William Mason in *Life and Letters of Gray* (1774): the poem contains interesting observations on the senses, particularly the sense of touch, and on pain (cf **4** textus, above). The text of it is at I 277–85 in C's edition of the *Works*, and with tr in *The Poems of Thomas Gray...* ed Roger Lonsdale (1969) 321–32. Gray also refers to Locke quite often in his notes on the Greek text. In an annotation of c Oct 1820 C noticed how "many who retaining their love and veneration of the ancients were anxious to combine it with the new Orthodoxy by explaining Aristotle and even Plato *down* into John Locke. Such was that excellent man, and genuine *Classic* Scholar, the Poet Gray." John Petvin *Letters Concerning Mind* (1750) p ⁻1. Henry Reed, in the *Memoir of Gray* that he sent to SC for her comments, said of Gray's *De principiis cogitandi* that "It was meant to stand in much the same relation to Locke's 'Essay on the Human Understanding' as Lucretius's poem 'De Natura Rerum' did to the system of Epicurus." Broughton *Sara Coleridge and Henry Reed* 87 n 1.

5[3] For the "proper Platonism" found not in Plato's own writings but in the writings of his successors the Neoplatonists, see *P Lects* Lects 4, 5 (1949) 156, 163–6 (at 165 C refers to this note of Gray's), 174–7.

5[4] Gray's note on Letter 2 at 312D (II

492) reads: "φραστεον δη σοι δι' αινιγμων [I must expound it to you in riddles]. We see here that Plato, as well as the Pythagoreans whom he imitated in many respects, made a mystery of his art; for none but adepts were to understand him. It was by conversation only that he cared to communicate himself on these subjects.[4] In the seventh epistle he professes never to have written any thing on philosophy; and all that has been published in his name he attributes to Socrates. As I am not an initiate it is no wonder if this passage is still a riddle to me, as it was designed to be. Thus much one may divine indeed; namely, that it is a description of the Supreme Being, who is the cause and end of all things...[footnote:] [4] And in the end of this very epistle p. 314 [C] οὐδ᾽ εστι συγγραμμα Πλατωνος ουδεν...["and no treatise by Plato exists, or will exist, but those which now bear his name belong to a Socrates become fair and young". Tr R. G. Bury (LCL Plato VII 417)]." Cf also Gray on the *Sophist* (II 412): "...that part [of this dialogue] which is intended to explain the nature of existence and of non-existence" he found "obscure beyond comprehension".

The authenticity of Letter 2 is not certain. C was convinced that "Plato's *writings*...were intended as *preparations* for Platonism, and by no means containing the same". Valckenaer *Diatribe de Aristobulo Judaeo* (Leyden 1806) p 65. See also *Friend* (*CC*) I 460–2 and *P Lects* as cited in n 3, above.

repeat the explanation*a* with which I closed the last page of these notes and extracts,

> Volsimi————e vidi Plato
> (ma non quel Plato)[5]
> Che'n quella schiera andò più presso al segno,
> Al qual' aggiunge, a chì dal Cielo è dato.[6]
>
> S. T. COLERIDGE, 1819.

6 II 385 | *Hippias Major*

We learn from this dialogue in how poor a condition the art of reasoning on moral and abstracted subjects was, before the time of Socrates; for it is impossible that Plato should introduce a sophist of the first reputation for eloquence and knowledge in several kinds, talking in a manner below the absurdity and weakness of a child; unless he had really drawn after the life. No less than twenty-four pages are here spent in vain, only to force it into the head of Hippias, that there is such a thing as a general idea; and that, before we can dispute on any subject, we should give a definition of it.

Is not this, its improbability out of the question, contradicted by the *Protagoras* of Plato's own drawing?[1] Are there no authors, no physicians in London at the present moment, of "the first reputation," i.e. whom a certain class cry up: for in no other sense is the phrase *historically* applicable to Hippias, whom a Sydenham redivivus or a new Stahl might not exhibit as pompous ignoramuses?[2] no *one*

a Perhaps a slip or mistranscript for "exclamation"

5[5] These words, not in Petrarch or in GRAY, are C's interjection.

5[6] Petrarch *Trionfo della fama* III 4–6, following the text of *Rime* (2 vols 1778) [COPY B] II 194.

I turned...and Plato there I saw
(but not that Plato)
Who of them all came closest to the goal
Whereto by Heaven's grace men may attain.

Tr E. G. Williams (Chicago 1962).

6[1] Protagoras (c 490–c 420), one of the earliest of the Sophists, and one of the most successful and respected. In Plato's *Protagoras* he gives a much more distinguished performance than most of Socrates' interlocutors and receives more sympathetic treatment. His famous dictum "Man is the measure of all things" is discussed in *Theaetetus* 152Aff.

6[2] Little is known about Hippias of Elis other than from Plato's dialogues. He was about the same age as Socrates but much younger than Protagoras, a polymath, and very conceited. He is easily outwitted by Socrates in both *Hippias Major* and *Hippias Minor* but appears in a better light in *Protagoras* 337C and more so in Xenophon *Memorabilia* 4.4.14ff.

A "Sydenham reborn" refers to Thomas Sydenham (1624–89), one of the most famous English physicians of his day, who for his accurate descriptions of certain diseases is reckoned a founder of modern clinical medicine. C copied a paragraph from his *Opera universa* (1726) in *CN* IV 5201. For Georg Ernst Stahl (1660–1734), physician and co-propounder of the phlogiston theory, see ANDERSON COPY B **19** n 2, and as

Hippias amongst them? But we need not flee to conjectures. The ratiocination assigned by Aristotle and Plato himself to Gorgias and then to the Eleatic school,[3] are positive proofs that Mr. Gray has mistaken the satire of an individual for a characteristic of an age or class. May I dare whisper to the reeds without proclaiming that I am in the state of Midas,[4]—may I dare to hint that Mr. Gray himself had not, and through the spectacles of Mr. Locke and his followers,[5] could not have seen the difficulties which Hippias found in a *general* idea, *secundum Platonem?*[6] S. T. C.

7   II 386 | *Hippias Major* 289A, B

Passages of Heraclitus: Πιθηκων ὁ καλλιστος αισχρος αλλω γενει συμβαλειν.—Ανθρωπων ὁ σοφωτατος προς Θεον πιθηκος φανειται. [The most beautiful of apes is ugly compared with another race.—The wisest of men, when compared to a God, will appear but an ape.] This latter passage is undoubtedly the original of that famous thought in Pope's Essay on Man, B. 2;

"And shewed a Newton, as we shew an ape,"

contributing to the progressive advance of natural science see *Friend* (*CC*) I 494n and 512.

6[3] Tennemann *Geschichte der Philosophie* II 362–73 describes the pseudo-Aristotelian *De Xenophane, Zenone et Gorgia* which may (as he says) preserve matter from Aristotle's own work on Gorgias. The work summarises Gorgias' Περὶ φύσεως ἢ μὴ ὄντος (*On Nature, or the Non-existent*), in which he purports to prove—whether seriously as an exercise in logic or to make fun of the Eleatics—that nothing exists, that if it does exist it is unknowable, and that if it is knowable we cannot communicate that knowledge. Cf *Friend* (*CC*) I 437–8; in TENNEMANN I 366–8 C praises this work of Gorgias and comments at length upon it, saying *inter alia* that "These Paradoxes...are worth a thousand of Zeno's." In Plato's dialogue named for him Gorgias appears in person and is represented as a rhetorician rather than as ratiocinator; some of his teaching can be seen in *Meno* 76C–D and *Phaedrus* 267A–B, his insistence that he teaches rhetoric, not "virtue", in *Meno* 95C. Of the "ratiocinations" of the

Eleatics (for whom see DUBOIS 1 and n 1) Plato gives account especially in the *Sophist, Parmenides, Phaedrus, Theaetetus*; Aristotle's account of them is mostly in the *Physics* and *Metaphysics*.

6[4] Midas, King of Phrygia, as punishment for claiming that he was a better singer and flute-player than Apollo, had his ears turned into an ass's ears. He tried to conceal from his people this mark of his stupidity, but one of his servants, noticing what had happened and unable to keep it to himself, made a hole in the ground, spoke his secret into the earth, and filled the hole to bury his words. Reeds grew up there and when stirred by the wind repeated the buried secret. Ovid *Metamorphoses* 11.146ff. C used "the ears of King Midas" as a simile in a poem of Jan 1800: *EOT* (*CC*) I 95, *PW* (EHC) I 342 line 48.

6[5] Cf 5 and n 1, above.

6[6] "According to Plato". *Hippias Major* does not go beyond an attempt to establish the concept of "beauty in itself" as distinguished from this or that beautiful object; it contains nothing of what C calls "proper Platonism".

which some persons have imagined that he borrowed from one
Palingenius, an obscure author, who wrote a poem called "Zodiacus
Vitae."
I remember to have met nearly the same words in one of our elder
Poets.[1]

8   II 390 | *Protagoras* 312A

[Gray's note on the discussion of Sophists by Socrates and Hipparchus
while they wait until the right time to visit Protagoras:] Ἐρυθριάσας
[blushing]. For the bad morals of the professors (see the Gorgias, p.
520...and the Meno, p 91...) had brought the name [sophist] into
general disrepute; though it was once an honourable appellation, and
given afterwards to all such as called themselves Φιλόσοφοι
[Philosophers]. Solon was the person who first bore the name of ὁ
Σοφιστης [the Sophist]. (See Isocrat. Περι Ἀντιδωσεως, p. 344.)
Socrates defines a sophist, such as the character was in his time,
Ἔμπορος τις, η καπηλος των αγωγιμων, αφ' ὧν ἡ ψυχη τρεφεται
["a kind of merchant or rather a retailer of food for the soul" tr
Gray]. Protag. p. 313.

Query, if Socrates,[a] himself a scholar of the sophists, is accurate, did
not the change of ὁ σοφός into ὁ Σοφιστης, in the single case of
Solon, refer to the wisdom-causing influences of his legislation?[1]

a Evidently a transcriber's or printer's slip for "Isocrates" (see textus)

7[1] Gray refers to the translation of the
Zodiacus vitae of Palingenius—i.e. Pier
Angelo Manzoli de la Stellata (c 1500–c
43)—by Barnabe Googe (1540–94), VI
167–9 of which reads:

An Ape (quoth shee) and jesting stock
is Man to God in skye,
As oft as he doth trust his wit to much,
presuming hye,
Dare search the things of nature hid...

Thomas Warton the younger (1728–90)
gives the lines (with the Latin original) in
his *History of English Poetry* (4 vols 1824:
IV 286–7) saying that "Pope has copied"
them, adding that "as Pope was a great
reader of the old English poets, it is most
probable that he took it immediately
from our translator [Googe]". Another
possible trace is in Thomas Dekker (c
1570–1632), though here—in *The Seven*

Deadlie Sinns of London, chapter on
"Apishnesse"—writing in prose: "Man
is Gods Ape, and an Ape is *Zani* to a
man, doing over those trickes...which he
sees done before him...". Cf also
Measure for Measure II ii 117–22.

8[1] Σοφός (wise) was in earlier, though
post-Homeric, times an appropriate
word to apply to a good statesman, poet,
artist, or craftsman as well as to a
philosopher. Σοφιστής first appears in
extant literature in the fifth century B.C.
with much the same meaning. This
statement of Isocrates' is the only
evidence that the word existed as early as
Solon, the Athenian lawgiver and poet (c
639–c 559 B.C.). In the late fifth century
the word became attached to the itinerant
teachers—some of them honourable,
learned, and very prosperous—who
undertook for a fee to teach "virtue"
and "wisdom" in the civic, social,

Mem:—to examine whether Φροντιστής was, or was not, more generally used at first *in malum sensum*,² or rather the proper force originally of the termination -ιστής, -αστής—whether (as it is evidently verbal) it imply a reflex or a transitive act.³

9 ɪɪ 399 | *Protagoras* 357ᴅ

῞Οτι Ἀμαθια.] This is the true key and great moral of the dialogue, that knowledge alone is the source of virtue, and ignorance the source of vice: it was Plato's own principle, (see Plato. Epist. 7. p. 336. Ἀμαθια, εξ ἧς παντα κακα πᾶσι ερριζωται και βλαστανει, και ὑστερον αποτελει καρπον τοις γεννησασι πικροτατον. ["...ignorance, which is the root whence all evils for all men spring and which will bear hereafter most bitter fruit for those who have planted it..." tr R. G. Bury (LCL).] See also Sophist. p. 228 and 229. and Euthydemus. from p. 278 to 281. and De Legib. L. 3. p. 688.) and probably it was also the principle of Socrates: the consequence of it is, that virtue may be taught, and may be acquired; and that philosophy alone can point us out the way to it.

More than our word, Ignorance, is contained in the Ἀμαθία of Plato.¹ I, however, freely acknowledge, that this was the point of

---

and practical sense those words then had. See also "On the Origin and Progress of the Sect of Sophists in Greece"—and on sophists as "wisdom-mongers"—in *Friend* (*CC*) ɪ 436–47; *P Lects* Lects 3, 4 (1949) 133–6, 147; and on the history of the two words cf *Logic* (*CC*) 30.

8² "In a bad sense".

8³ C suggests that σοφός (wise) may be converted by the suffix -ιστής into "one who makes people wise". Similarly φροντιστής (thinker)—a nickname given to Socrates (see Gray ɪɪ 299, referring to Xenophon *Memorabilia* [4.6.7] and Aristophanes *Clouds* 266)—would mean "one who makes people think". But from their first appearance these nouns in -ιστής and -αστής, and the verbs in -ζω from which they are derived, seem usually to imply tendency towards, or exercise of, the quality or activity indicated by the first element in the compound, whether reflexively or directed on some external object. Thus φροντίζω means "I exercise mind, I think, I engage in

thinking, I think about something"; σοφίζομαι means "I am clever about something". Only as late as the Septuagint does σοφίζω appear as an active verb meaning "I make [somebody] wise", the suffix -ζω showing this causative force in later Greek as it often does—in the form -ize—in modern English.

9¹ Cf N 25 f 46 (among notes for the Philosophical Lectures, not included in *P Lects* 1949): "—Socrates's amathia, or ignorance ~~from~~ with unteachableness— All Vice from it—all virtue from Knowlege—& Philosophy the only Teacher thereof.—" Cf *P Lects* Lect 4 (1949) 149ff, in which C argues against the hedonistic view expressed by Socrates (as in *Protagoras* at this point, and as summarised later by Gray at ɪɪ 401), that given adequate knowledge we cannot fail to choose the morally good because it leads to the greatest pleasure in the end. C continues (pp 150–1): "But if on the other hand Socrates meant that vice was not possible, was not compatible with the view, from which Socrates did *for the most part* contemplate moral good and evil. Now and then he seems to have taken a higher station, but soon quitted it for the lower, more generally intelligible. Hence the vacillation of Socrates himself: hence, too, the immediate opposition of his disciples, Antisthenes and Aristippus.[2] But that this was Plato's own principle I exceedingly doubt. That it was not the principle of Platonism, as taught by the first Academy under Speusippus, I do *not* doubt at all.[3] See the xivth Essay, p. 129–39 of *The Friend*, vol. i.[4] In the sense in which ἀμαθίας πάντα κακὰ ἐρρίζωνται, κ.τ.λ.[5] is maintained in that Essay, so and no otherwise can it be truly asserted, and so and no otherwise did ὡς εμοίγε δοκεῖ,[6] Plato teach it.[7]

---

clear perfect insight into the very nature of the action of the soul...how is this to be given? For his great doctrine was that it could be taught. The only answer to be made was: it must be given to a mind predisposed to it. And hence he uses the word *amathia*, not *agnoia*, for ignorance." (*P Lects* (1949) reads "*apatheia*" and "*ignoria*".) In his annotation on GRAY C may be correcting his error of attribution in *P Lects*, for Plato put this distinction between ἀμαθία and ἀγνοία into the mouth not of Socrates but of an "Eleatic stranger" in the *Sophist* 229 (cf textus). Cf also Gray at II 412: "The most remarkable things in [the *Sophist*] seem to me to be, his description of that disorder and want of symmetry in the soul, produced by ignorance, which puts it off its bias on its way to happiness, the great end of human actions: the distinction he makes between Αγνοια and Αμαθια; the first of which, Αγνοια, is simply our ignorance of a thing, the latter, Αμαθια, an ignorance which mistakes itself for knowledge, and which (as long as this sentiment attend it) is without hope of remedy: the explanation of the Socratic mode of instruction (adapted to this particular kind of ignorance) by drawing a person's errors gradually from his own mouth...and exposing to his own eyes their inconsistency and weakness."

9[2] For C's account of Socrates' vacillation between asceticism and an enlightened hedonism, and how An-

tisthenes—devoted disciple of Socrates, and present at his death, according to *Phaedo* 59B—adopted asceticism and founded Cynicism, and how Aristippus— an older companion of Socrates, wealthy and luxurious—adopted hedonism and founded the Cyrenaic School, see *P Lects* Lects 3, 4 (1949) 141–2, 153–5.

9[3] On Speusippus, son of Plato's sister and Plato's successor as head of the Academy (347–339 B.C.), see *P Lects* Lect 5 (1949) 174–7.

9[4] SC was citing the 1837 ed. See *Friend* (*CC*) I 100–6.

9[5] "All the evils of ignorance take root, etc"—in textus (var).

9[6] "As it seems to me, at least".

9[7] Although in this essay in *The Friend* C also stresses the importance of religion, his argument on pp 105–6 nevertheless closely follows that of Socrates in *Protagoras* and seems to exclude the Platonic ideas as irrelevant to the question. For C's attack on Socrates that "he left to every man to determine whether virtue or vice would be likely to be most agreeable in the long run" see *P Lects* Lect 4 (1949) 154; but in an annotation in TENNEMANN II ⁻1–⁻2 (referring to II 50–5) he compared Socrates with Christ as prescribing the same ultimate end—the approach to God; and declared that happiness and virtue are the same. Yet cf *CN* I 1705 and n.

FULKE GREVILLE
BARON BROOKE
1554–1628

Certaine Learned and Elegant Workes of the Right Honorable Fulke
Lord Brooke, written in his youth, and familiar exercise with Sir
Philip Sidney. The severall names of which workes the following page
doth declare. 2 pts in 1 vol. London 1633. 4º.
The text of all copies of this edition begins with p 23; pp 1–22 contained
a poem suppressed by Archbishop Laud.

Not located. Sotheby Sale 20 Apr 1903. Annotations here reprinted from
Athenaeum No 3436 (Sept 1893) 322.

Charles Lamb's copy, described in *Lamb SC* (1848) 16 as containing "Long
extracts relative to Ld. Brooke, marginal corrections, and note on the
suppression of one of his works". Lamb mentioned in "The Two
Races of Men" (Dec 1820) "those abstrusest cogitations of Greville, now,
alas! wandering in Pagan lands", but it is not clear what he meant by that
or even whether he referred to this annotated copy (cf *CN* II 2918n). When
H. S. Young described Lamb's copy in 1893 and transcribed some of the
annotations —the book was then with a "firm of booksellers in Liverpool"
—he seems not to have recognised that some of the notes could have been
in Lamb's hand: "...the numerous MS. notes on the margins of its pages,
and bracketed...passages are evidence of the careful and critical manner in
which he [C] read books of this class"; "The volume is full of interesting
notes, which show not only the attention with which Coleridge read, but also
something of his kindly nature and artistic ideal."
   In *Courier* 12 Sept 1806 C published a variant of *Caelica* Sonnet XCIV under
the title "Lines on a King and Emperor-Making Emperor and King, altered
from the 93d sonnet of Fulke Greville...". *EOT* (*CC*) III 298 (text not given),
PW (EHC) II 1116 (inaccurate transcript). In *Courier* 27 Sept 1806 he
published a personal "adaptation" of *Caelica* Sonnet LXXXIV, entitled
Farewell to Love. *EOT* (*CC*) III 298 (text not given); see also **5** and nn 1, 2.
See also *CN* II 2918 (c Oct–Nov 1806).
   In c Mar 1810 C made a series of transcripts variatim from Greville and
copied out the motto from Cowper given in **8**, below. *CN* III 3709–3719
(except 3713). C quoted from *A Treatise of Humane Learning* when he
annotated James SEDGWICK (see DATE, below); from *A Treatie of Warres*
as an epigraph in *LS* (*CC*) 120 (from *CN* III 3717), cf *AR* (1825) 93, *PW*
(EHC) II 1115; and from *Alaham* in *CN* II 2918–2931, in *LS* (*CC*) 144 (from
CN III 3718), and in *CN* III 3719. The reference to Greville's *The Nature of
Truth* in *CN* I 1040 is not to this edition of *Workes*.

873

CONTENTS. i *A Treatise of Humane Learning*; *An Inquisition upon Fame and Honour* (**1**); *A Treatie of Warres*; ii *The Tragedie of Alaham*; *The Tragedie of Mustapha*; *Caelica, containing CIX. Sonnets* (**2–5**); "A Letter to an Honorable Lady" (**6, 7**); "A Letter of Travell".

DATE. c Sept–Oct 1806. EHC, in a note in the *Athenaeum* No 3939 (25 Apr 1903) 531, said that C was reading Lamb's copy of *Certaine Learned... Workes* in Aug–Sept 1806 on his return to London from the Mediterranean. Although EHC does not cite the evidence for his statement, it may be in some way confirmed by a notebook reference of c Oct–Nov 1806 to "my own note in the waste Leaf of his [Greville's] works" apparently discussing a line in *Alaham*. CN II 2918. This and the series of references to *Alaham* ending in *CN* II 2931, however, were written after C had arrived in Keswick on 30 Oct 1806 (*CN* II 2905) and could have referred to Lamb's copy if C had taken it from London with him, or to RS's copy of the same edition at Greta Hall (see *CN* II 2918n, III 3709n); in either case "the waste Leaf" could have been a loose sheet of paper inserted in the volume and later lost or overlooked. Young's transcript does not include any note on *Alaham* or on *Fame*; it might have been part of the "long note" (**1**) now lost (see **1** nn *a* and 1, below), except that neither i 69 nor ii 69 could properly be described as "a waste Leaf".

Farewell to Love (**5**), the "Asra poem" adapted from Grenville, seems to refer to C's loss of SH when she withdrew from Allan Bank to Wales in Mar 1810, and seems therefore to coincide with the cluster of quotations from Greville in *CN* III 3709–3719 at that same date; but C had already published that poem in Sept 1806. RS's copy of Greville could have provided the source for the notebook extracts both in 1806 and in 1810 and for the six lines from the *Treatise of Humane Learning* written on the half-title of RS's copy of James SEDGWICK *Hints to the Public... on the Nature and Effect of Evangelical Preaching* (4 pts 1808–10) by 13 Jun 1810. There is no evidence that C had Lamb's copy of GREVILLE in the Lakes in late 1806 or in the spring of 1810.

1 i 69*a*

["A long note on p 69 states the meaning and value of spondee, trochee, iambic, and other metrical measures, giving examples of each."][1]

a It is not clear whether Young's "p 69" was in Pt i or Pt ii. At ii 69 there is no room for "a long note", nor does there seem enough prosodic interest thereabout to incite a long note on metre. Of i 69, however, about one-third is blank; below 10 lines of verse and a printer's device there is space for a ms note of some length

1[1] If C's note were written on ii 69, it would be close to *Alaham* IV (part of Chorus Quartus); if on i 69, at the end of *An Inquisition upon Fame and Fortune*; the note, however, need not have referred to either work. Greville was one of the first poets to introduce classical metres to English verse: this may have provided C with a starting-point for his note. Young suggested, when he published his transcript in 1893, that "it was probably after working out the subject [of metre] in this way [i.e. by defining the values of metrical measures] that Coleridge wrote the verse 'Metrical Feet: Lesson for a Boy...'"—for which see *PW* (EHC) I 401. EHC dates lines 1–7 of that nineteen-line poem in 1806 as addressed

2 ii 192 | *Caelica* Sonnet XLIV

> *Absence*, the noble truce
> Of *Cupids* warre:
> Where though desires want use,
> They honoured are.
> Thou art the just protection,
> Of prodigall affection,
> Have thou the praise;
> When bankrupt *Cupid* braveth,
> Thy mines his credit saveth,
> With sweet delayes.
>
> Of wounds which presence makes
> With Beauties shot,
> Absence the anguish slakes,
> But healeth not:
> Absence records the Stories,
> Wherein Desire glories,
> Although she burne,
> She cherisheth the spirits
> Where Constancy inherits
> And Passions mourne.
>
> Absence, like dainty Clouds,
> On glorious-bright,
> Natures weake senses shrowds,
> From harming light.
> Absence maintaines the treasure
> Of pleasure unto pleasure,
> Sparing with praise;
> Absence doth nurse the fire,
> Which starves and feeds desire
> With sweet delayes.

A sweet poem supposing it to end with the third stanza; and but that
I make it part of conscience never to mutilate a book, even tho' an

---

to HC, on the evidence of a ms then in
his possession; he states further that the
verses were later extended and adapted
for DC to use. For C's interest in metrics
see generally "Metrical Experiments" in
PW (EHC) II 1014–19; but more par-
ticularly see *CN* II 2224 (41) and (47),
2881, 3180. See also e.g. HERBERT **13**.

immorality were the honest motive [. . .]*a* I should have been tempted
to have torn out the next leaf[1]

3   ii 200 | Sonnet LV lines 1–11

> All my senses, like Beacons flame,
> Gave *Alarum* to desire
> To take armes in *Cynthia's* name,
> And set all my thoughts on fire:
> Furies wit perswaded me,
> Happy love was hazards hire,
> *Cupid* did best shoot and see
> In the night where smooth is faire;
> Up I start beleeving well
> To see if *Cynthia* were awake;
> Wonders I saw, who can tell?

A poem this not to be written but by men of *some* genius. Would
to Heaven that men of *any* genius would never write such poems.

4   ii 201, cropped | lines 49–54

> Let no Love-desiring heart,
> In the Starres goe seeke his fate,
> Love is onely Natures art,
> Wonder hinders Love and Hate.
> *None can well behold with eyes,*
> *But what underneath him lies.*

Truly lyric as are all the lines incrotcheted, it is a comfort to observe
that in general the thoughts most innocent are the most poetical in
themselves, and bring with them the most poetical [. . .]*b1*

---

a The elision is in Young's text
b According to Young, "the last word is partly cut off by the binder". *Misc C* reads "poetical [images?]"

2[1] The last two stanzas read:

Presence to every part
Of Beauty tyes,
Where Wonder rules the heart
There Pleasure dyes:
Pleasures plagues minde and senses
With modesties defences,
Absence is free:
Thoughts doe in absence venter
On *Cupids* shadowed center,
They winke and see.

But Thoughts be not so brave,
With absent ioy;
For you with that you have
Your selfe destroy:
The absence which you glory,
Is that which makes you sory,
And burne in vaine:
For Thought is not the weapon,
Wherewith *thoughts-ease* men cheapon,
Absence is paine.

4[1] Young says that C's note was
written "against some later lines" but
he does not identify the lines "in-
crotcheted".

5   ii 234 | Sonnet LXXXIV

> *Farewell* sweet Boy, complaine not of my truth;
> Thy Mother lov'd thee not with more devotion;
> For to thy Boyes play I gave all my youth,
> Yong Master, I did hope for your promotion.
>
> While some sought Honours, Princes thoughts observing,
> Many woo'd *Fame, the child of paine and anguish,*
> Others judg'd inward good a chiefe deserving,
> I in thy wanton Visions joy'd to languish.
>
> I bow'd not to thy image for succession,
> Nor bound thy bow to shoot reformed kindnesse,
> Thy playes of hope and feare were my confession,
> The spectacles to my life was thy blindnesse:
>> But *Cupid* now farewell, I will goe play me,
>> With thoughts that please me lesse, & lesse betray me.

> Farewell my Love! yet blame ye not my Truth.
> More fondly never mother eyed her child
> Than I your form: Your's were my hopes of youth,
> And as you wove the dream I sigh'd or smil'd.
> While some sought wealth; others to pleasure swerving,
> Many woo'd fame; and some stood firm apart
> In joy of pride, self-conscious of deserving,
> To you I gave my whole weak wishing heart.
> And when I met the maid that realized
> Your fair creations, and had won her kindness,
> Say but for *her*[1] if aught on earth I priz'd?
> Your dreams alone I dreamt and caught your blindness.
> O grief!—but farewell Love. I will go play me
> With thoughts that please me less and less betray me.[2]

S. T. C.

5[1] Young prints "[?]" against the word. The poem, entitled *Farewell to Love,* refers to SH: see *C & SH* 171.
5[2] The poem was first published in the *Courier* 27 Sept 1806: *EOT (CC)* III 298.

See also *PW* (EHC) I 402–3 (recording the variants in this ms, but giving the number of the sonnet as "LXXIV" and the page as 284).

6 ii 282, referring to ii 285–6 | *A Letter to an Honourable Lady* ch 5

If you desire an example of this *Obedience*, which I urge you to; It may please you, in that arch-story of love, to read the licentious affection of *Antonie* toward *Cleopatra*. Where you shall see, that if his vertuous wife *Octavia* had striven to master his dissolutenesse; *Augustus* was her Brother, and his Competitor in the Empire; whereby Right, and Strength, might with some possibility have lifted up her ambition, and revenge from the barren grounds of Duty. If shee had striven to please him with change, whom she could not keepe from it; the pride of *Rome* did then minister variety of delights, and the servile instruments of Time, and Greatnesse, would soone have had an eye to their Gaine, and her Fortune. If she would have rowled the stone of *Sysiphus*, and studied with merit to call backe his love; she was as yong, equall in beauty, stronger in honour; but ever the same, which (she knew) was not so pleasing to him, as the same in others. Besides, she had the colour of Estate to enammell all revenges upon his ungratefulnesse. Notwithstanding this worthy *Lady* would never yeeld to adventure her Honour upon the dice of Chance, nor vainly seeke to have power over him, that had none over himselfe; but dividing her innocency from his errors with the middle wall of a *severe life*, she remained still his good Angell with *Octavius*; temper'd publike jealousies, and all advantages of private wrongs; and to be short, was content, when she could not doe the workes of a well-beloved Wife, yet to *doe well*, as *becomes all excellent Women*. In which course of moderation shee neither made the World her Judge, nor the Market her Theater, but contented her sweet minde with the triumphs of Patience, and made solitarinesse the tombe of her Fame: which Fame, as true to her Worth, and envious to his Lasciviousnesse, hath multiplied her Honour, and his Shame, to live (as you see) many ages after them both.

The whole letter is excellent, but the passage marked[1] is almost divine.

7 i 23, referring to ii 285–6 | **6** textus

Assuredly few authors yield a passage of such compleat excellence as that in 285th–286th [pages][a] of this volume.

a Word supplied by the editor

6[1] According to Young, "a long passage" is "marked in pencil" but he does not identify it. For C's praise of this "beautiful piece of prose" see also *TT* 5 Jul 1834.

8   ii 298, written after the word "Finis"

Motto for the Whole Volume
A quarry of stout spurs and knotted fangs
That, crook'd into a thousand whimsies, clasp
The stubborn soil.

Cowper's "Yardley Oak."[1]

8[1] William Cowper *Yardley Oak* lines 117–19, first printed in William Hayley's *The Life, and Posthumous Writings, of William Cowper* (2 vols Chichester 1803), of which Sir George Beaumont presented a copy to C. C also copied these lines into *CN* III 3713, and wrote them on a piece of paper now tipped into KANT *Critik der Urtheilskraft*. For C's "sort of allegory, or connected simile and metaphor of Wordsworth's intellect and genius" as a gigantic deep-rooted tree see *BL* ch 22 (*CC*) II 155.

NEHEMIAH GREW

1641–1712

Cosmologia Sacra: or A Discourse of the universe as it is the creature and kingdom of God. Chiefly written, to demonstrate the truth and excellency of the Bible; which contains the laws of his kingdom in this lower world. In five books. London 1701. F°. Engraved portrait of the author facing the title-page.

British Museum C 44 g 1

Autograph signature "JOSEPH HENRY GREEN" on p ⁻5. Heraldic bookplate of John Pearson on p ⁻6 (original p–d).

Annotations, mostly corrections made according to the Errata on p xviii, are written on pp xviii, 18, 34, 35, 36, 37, 58, 61, 69, 72, 77, 81, 87, 110, 123, 152, 155, 161, 180, 196, 199, 212, 216, 280, 299, 316, 322, 349, 364; those on pp 34 and 77 might be C's. On p 196 Green has written out C's definition of miracle: see **26** n 1, below.

DATE. Oct–Nov 1833. One note (**4**) dated 1833. For close connexions between these marginalia and entries in N 53 (*CN* v) of c Oct 1833 see **1** n 2, **26** n 1, **27** n 1, **35** n 3; and for connexions with entries in N 52 (*CN* v) of c Nov 1833 see **1** nn 1, 4, **44** n 1 (*f*). The drafts of C's *Epitaph* on two back flyleaves (**44** and **45**) were written c 26 Oct 1833: see **44** n 1.

1 p ⁻3

$$[\text{Τετ}[\text{ρ}]\text{ακτυς}]^{a}$$

$$\text{Θεος}$$

Ο Θεος   τον Θεον, ὁ μονογ⧽ενης.

$$\text{Θεοτης, αυτη Θεος.}^{1}$$

a Not in C's hand—presumably Green's

1¹ "Tet[r]actys" written in Green's hand above C's first diagram: "God | The God...God [acted upon], the only begotten | Godhood, itself God." For μονογενής see e.g. FLEURY 49 and nn 1, 4. Here Θεός without the definite article (ὁ, τόν) is God as the Absolute, the "Super-relative" of the third tetractys; ὁ Θεός as God the Father, the begetter, and τὸν Θεόν as God the son, the begotten, the "Jehovah-Word", are given relativity by the definite article. Cf C's implied explanation of "θεὸς, without an article and yet not an adjective" in the "Formula Fidei" of 1830 (*LR* III 1), and cf a different application of Θεός and ὁ θεός in FLEURY **84**. This first tetractys in exactly this same wording is also written in N 52 f 25 (*CN* v) (c 5 Nov 1833), one leaf before draft (*f*) of C's *Epitaph* (see **44** n 1, below); see also n 4, below.

N.B. Ἡ Σύνταξις; μὴ ῥηματικὴ, ἀλλα κάτα νοῦν καὶ λόγον—
Grammatice *interior*; *verborum*, non vocum seu vocabulorum—/
Platonis quamvis non Priscianio arridens.[a2]

	1	
Identity	Super-relative	
	2	3
Isteity	Alterity Relatively Objective—	Rel. Subj.
	4	
Community.[3]	Relatively Objective to the Subjective,	
	relatively Subjective to the Objective/[b4]	

[a] This passage follows immediately on "αυτη Θεος", but is enclosed with a line in ms
[b] This tetractys is inserted in a compact cluster of words in the space below the enclosed passage (n *a*, above) and beside the other English version of the tetractys

1[2] "The Syntax? not rhematical, but according to reason and logic—*interior* grammar of *words* [as ideas], not of words and vocables/ agreeable to Plato, though not to Priscian." C is commenting on the accusative τὸν Θεόν with nominative μονογενής in apposition. (Cf the "false grammar but sound philosophy" of "Deus...est Fili*um*" in HEGEL 3 at n 9.) He establishes an opposition between Σύνταξις ῥημάτων or ῥηματικὴ ("rhematic"), the art of joining words into sentences, and γραμματικὴ ("grammar"), which in its derivation from γράμμα (a letter, written character) is the art of joining letters together, spelling. Or, cf *CN* IV 4771: "Grammar [is] the scheme & instrument of connecting words significantly, the Meta-grammatic ⟨Rhematic⟩, the Doctrine of arranging words perspicuously"; see also *Logic* (*CC*) 23. When νοῦς is opposed to λόγος in the context of human knowledge, the corresponding meanings are "reason" and "understanding, or logic"; in a theological context Νοῦς is the divine Reason, God the Father, and Λόγος is the divine Word, God the Son. The opposition between *verbum* ("word", sometimes "verb", sometimes "the Logos, the divine Word") and *vox* ("voice, word") or *vocabulum* ("word", sometimes "noun") is the opposition between an idea and a grammatical unit, between a meaningful word and a mere sound, between the spirit and the letter, between λόγος and ῥῆμα (as in BÖHME

145 n 1). Priscian, Latin grammarian of the sixth century A.D., would not have approved of C's liberties with "rhematic", but Plato— whose philosophy deals with the Word in the higher sense of the divine Reason, of Ideas as "Truth-powers" (in e.g. HOOKER 22 and nn 3 and 4)—would have approved. In N 53 f 22 (*CN* v) (c Oct 1833) C similarly wished, "despite Priscian and Lilly", to "make the verb substantive [i.e. "to be"] govern an accusative case" in the context of human self-discipline.

1[3] "Isteity" (from the demonstrative pronoun of the second person, "that of yours") must be a slip for C's usual word "Ipseity", Selfness, as in e.g. the tetractys in FLEURY 91. A note of special force on "The *inexhaustible* import and importance of the Ipsëity, as a *distinct* hypostasis, the first of the hypostatic Triad" occurs in N 55 ff 22ᵛ–19ᵛ (*CN* v) (c Mar 1834).

1[4] In the "relativity" tetractys C has made another slip, reversing the position of "Relatively Objective" and "Rel. Subj."; he may have introduced the numerals to correct the error, but numbered "Relatively Objective" 2 instead of 3. These two tetractyses are combined, and explicated at some length, in the "Formula Fidei de Sanctissima Trinitate" of 1830: *LR* III 1· They are combined in diagrammatic fo͘ in e.g. N 48 f 32ᵛ (*CN* v) (c Dec 1830) ͺ ͗d N 52 f 25 (*CN* v) (c 4 Nov 1833).

(N.B. Hence by the ⟨Latin⟩ Fathers the Holy Ghost is named—Vinculum Deitatis—Concordia—Love.[5]—The Supreme self-affirming WILL, and the Supreme MIND, the Only-begetter, ~~in~~ with the Supreme LIFE; ⟨the⟩ LOVE, ⟨the⟩ Wisdom, the eternal Procession and Perichoresis.)
Will, the I AM, Reason, Life, *are*⟨!⟩ ~~the~~ Not *properties*, not faculties, not attributes![a] ⟨We do not predicate them of God; but affirm them as God.—⟩ But God IS—Will, the I AM, the ~~Mind~~ Reason (or Being), the Life.—And as these can never be, even in thought, *separated*, so neither can they be *confounded*. The disturbing of the ORDER, ~~or~~ and the attempt to sustain it by the CONCEPTION of an ANTERIORITY, are equally ~~total~~ extinctions of the IDEA—total Eclipses of The Truth.—

2 p ⁻3, following immediately on note 1

The Catholic Faith is essentially Realist,[1] πέρι τῶν ὄντως ὄντων—/[2] the prevailing Theology characteristically Nominalist, & inversive/[3] the Substances it half-conceives, half-imagines, as SHADOWS.—the Shadows its[b] worships as the Substances. It *makes* the Idol: and the *Idol* is its God.—[4]

3 p ⁻2

Of the modern Divines:
~~Its C~~ The very essence of ~~its~~ their Conception consists in a continued Striving now to conceive Shadows ~~as~~ into Substance, and now to *imagine* Substance ~~as~~ into Shadows—to trans-*conceive* what cannot be imagined, and to transimagine what cannot be conceived[1]—and baffled in both, yet forget their defeat in the one by renewing their

---

[a] Here C has written " ∧ ", and repeated " ∧ " at the beginning of the inserted sentence, written at the end of the note   [b] A slip for "it"

1[5] "Bond of Deity—Concord". For this idea, but not the wording, see Augustine *De fide et symbolo* 9.19.
2[1] I.e. the universal Christian Faith.
2[2] "About things that really *are*".
2[3] For the Realist/Nominalist distinction see EICHHORN *Apocrypha* 18 n 4.
2[4] "Idol" in two senses: as image-for-worship and as εἴδωλον, an appearance, often tenuous and deceptive, the radical sense a shadow—as in BÖHME 7 (at n 3); and see 3, below. The use is Baconian: see *Friend (CC)* I 492–5. Cf the

annotation on IRVING *Sermons* quoted in *C&S (CC)* 143–4 n 4.
3[1] For the incomprehensible as "the ground of all comprehension"—a notion that also occurs in BÖHME—see e.g. *Friend (CC)* I 519 and cf *SM (CC)* 105. Cf also 18 (at n 4), below. Neither "trans-conceive" nor "transimagine" is in *OED*; cf "transimaginate" in JACOBI *Ueber...Spinoza* 20 (at n 1). For other compounds with the prefix "trans-" see DONNE *Sermons* COPY A 4 n 6.

attempt with the other, and thus *always* fighting (i.e. dreaming that they are fighting) they are never *conquered*: for the Dream continues. Who shall *awake* them? In what Sacred Temple is the Trumpet of Luther uphung? Whose Arm shall reach it? Whose Breath shall fill it and make it utter the blast?—

4 p 1 | Bk I ch 1 "Of God"

This Chapt. I—it is not all, I could wish it—it does not grapple with the only, for men who attach a distinct meaning to their words, the only possible Question—Autotheism? or Pantheism? Deus, quamvis Mundus non esset? or Deus Mundus?¹—for Atheism in any other interpretation is a mere blasphemy of a babbling Bravado!—yet o how it does not to the shame of our theology of 1833, weigh down the Bridgewater 8000£ Treatises!² *S. T. C.*

5 pp 1–2 | § 2

For if there could have been an Instant, wherein there was Nothing: then, either Nothing, made Something: or Something made it self: and so, was, and acted, before it was. But if there never could be Nothing: then, there is, and was, a Being of necessity without any Beginning.

4¹ Autotheism—"God [is], even though the World were not"; Pantheism—"God [is] the World". With this stylised definition of pantheism cf e.g. HILLHOUSE 1 (C's footnote) and BAXTER *Reliquiae* COPY A 2 n 2.

4² Francis Henry Egerton, 8th Earl of Bridgwater (1756–1829), eccentric and scholar, left a bequest of £8000 as a prize for the best work "On the Power, Wisdom, and Goodness of God as manifested in the Creation", the disposal of the fund to be at the discretion of the President of the Royal Society, then Davies Gilbert (formerly Giddy) (1767–1839), friend of Humphry Davy and old acquaintance of C's (see *CL* VI 1016). (Egerton also bequeathed to the BM his collection of mss and autographs with funds to extend the collection, now identified as Egerton MSS.) In 1832 Gilbert appointed eight persons to write treatises on the assigned topic; they were published as the "Bridgwater Treatises".

Of the first four, published in 1833, (I) Thomas Chalmers wrote *On the Adaptation of External Nature to the Moral and Intellectual Constitution of Man*; (II) John Kidd *On the Adaptation of External Nature to the Physical Condition of Man*; (III) William Whewell *On Astronomy...Considered with Reference to Natural Theology*; (IV) Sir Charles Bell *The Hand: Its Mechanism and Vital Endowments as Evincing Design...*Two more treatises followed in 1834: (V) Peter Mark Roget *On Animal and Vegetable Physiology...*; (VIII) William Prout *On Chemistry, Meteorology, and the Function of Digestion...*Two writers whose work C had previously found interesting did not publish their treatises until after his death: (VI) William Buckland *On Geology and Mineralogy...*and (VII) William Kirby *On the Power, Wisdom, and Goodness of God as Manifested in the Creation of Animals and in Their History, Habits, and Instincts*—both in 1835.

BEING, assuredly! but *a* Being? *that* is the point to be *proved*. Nay, even if unity could be proved = Being; yet Unicity?[1] Yet a distinction in kind between the Unum and the sum total of the Many?[2] Not only Being, but *a* Being, even *the* Being, and yet not the World—not the *Universe* of *Beings*.—O vain is it to seek a proof of the Idea, out of the Idea! an antecedent in reason to the Supreme Reason! O ~~va~~ idle to look at the Son by the light of a farthing Candle![3] Father of Lights![4] let me see Light in *thy* Light!

S. T. Coleridge.

6 p 3 | § 14

Again; He that is Self-existent, existeth without a Cause. But if it be possible, for some one Being to exist without a Cause; then it is possible, and much more conceivable, for all other Beings, to exist with one. And therefore, for that One, to give Existence to all other Beings; that is, to be Omnipotent.

This is an attempted Unfolding, or evolution of the ideas, contemplable in the IDEA, God—but the question is, whether ⟨the Unity⟩ the IDEA be not lost in the multiplicity of the CONCEPTIONS?[1]

7 p 6 | I 2 "Of the Corporeal World" § 2

We can never come to its utmost Extent: We see enough to admire in the Vast, and to us, Unlimited Distance of the Fixed Stars, which are Visible. The *Parallax* of the *Pole-Star* subtended by the *Diameter* of the *Orbis Magnus*, is not above a Minute: Therefore its Distance from the Sun not less than 3400 Diameters of the *Orbis Magnus*; or from the Earth, when nearest, 3399.

And even this Minute now admitted to be a delusion. The existence of *any* sensible parallax of any body out of our System is still sub lite.[1]—But tho' this might evidence the *universality* extensivè of the

5[1] For "Unicity"—or "Oneness"— see *LS* (*CC*) 176 and A. FULLER **1** n 9.

5[2] For the distinction between the One and the Many see e.g. "On the Principles of Genial Criticism" (1814) in *BL* (1907) II 230, BÖHME **46** and n 3, and ATHENAEUM **31** n 3.

5[3] Though the phrase is proverbial, cf Edward Young *Love of Fame* sat 7 lines 96–7: "How commentaries each dark passage shun, | And hold their farthing candles to the sun." As commonly, C puns on Sun and Son.

5[4] James 1.17.

6[1] On ideas and conceptions see DAVISON **14** and n 3 and FIELD **35** n 3.

7[1] "In dispute"—debate on this question having continued through the preceding decades, the practical difficulty depending upon the lack of sufficiently

Cause, whether *independent*, or *contained*; yet I do not see how it proves that *all*-perfection which we must mean in order to name the Cause, GOD. That ⟨a known⟩ B is *not* X is surely no proof of an *unknown* A = X.—But such must be the sophistic results of every pretence to understand God by the World, instead of the World by God. It is an attempt to see the Soun by Moonlight.[2]

8   pp 8–10 | §§16, 18, 21, 22

16. Yet there are remaining Difficulties: For tho' the Sun be allowed a Power to move the Planets, yet the Co-operation of some other Cause, seemeth necessary to direct this Motion into a Circle, and this Circle always the same. For why else should not all Bodies within the Compass of the Gravitating Power of the Earth, also move in a Circle about it, instead of descending towards its Centre?

18. It therefore seemeth probable, that for the better stating of the Distances of the Planets one from another, and from the Sun, there are as many several Spheres, and therefore kinds of *Aether*, as there are Planets which swim therein.

21. ... Thus much is plain; That the several Species of Moving Powers are all of kin to the Magnetick. So is Gravitation it self....

22. The Magnetick Poles are also a great Secret; especially now they are found to be distinct from the Poles of the Earth: As also not to be fix'd, as the Poles of the Earth are, but to be moveable, varying with us, about a Degree in six Years, but with much Regularity.

16.—This might have been urged against Buffon's hypothesis or rather fancy of the projection, quasi explosion, of the Planets from the Body of the Sun[1]—viz. that in order to solve the orbital motion of the Planets, the projectile Power of the Sun must be supposed equally continual & active as the attractive or gravitating power—i.e. ⟨opposite Forces of one Power,⟩ ever co-present, and co-operative. But if this be assumed, the hypothetical Fact of a Projection is superfluous, and answers no purpose—unless the Sun itself had been projected out of a Sun's sun, and this out [of]*a* a third or grand *Sun*—

a Word supplied by the editor

accurate instruments of measurement. See e.g. J. F. W. Herschel in *Phil Trans RS* CXVI (1826) iii 266: "the merit of the discovery of parallax must rest with him...who shall first point out the star in which it exists".

7[2] See ETERNAL PUNISHMENT **2** n 1.
8[1] For Buffon's scheme of the birth of the planets, as compared with Böhme's, see BÖHME **81** n 1.

& so on ad infinitum a minori ad majus[2]—an endless series of multiplication by ⟨subtraction &⟩ Division—each grand Sun being a Sun's Grandfather, in linguâ *Punicâ*[3]—S. T. C.[a]

Now an inherent projectile is but another & less proper word for a repulsive Force; and the Orbital Motion the Common product of the two antagonist forces of attraction & repulsion; & the exponent of their proportionality—which again is inconsistent with a pr supposed priority of Sun to Planet. For this would suppose & imply an excess of the repulsive over the attractive Force, then acting as a *retentive* force—and thus converting the repulsive into a projectile or explosive *power* destroy the its supposed inherent *proportionality*, as a Co-*force* and resolve it, not into an essential Attribute of the Son, but into a *property* of some one or more of the solar ingredients, ex. gr—gaseous matter, & the result of an *accidental* excess of the same. That is, the pretended Solution of a known Fact would resolve itself into an assertion of an *imagined* Fact, i.e. Fiction, which, if imagined, would itself & more hopelessly, need to be solved. Now such mock-solutions I call *suffictions*, not sup*positions*, hypopoiēses (or hyponeiroses) not hypo*theses*.[4]—And to this class belongs the Cartesian Fancy in § 18, p. 8. of this interesting work:[5] but I believe § 21, 22, are of a far other & worthier kind.[6]

9   p 10 | § 26

For as a Mist is a Multitude of Small, but Solid Globules, which therefore descend; so a Vapour, and therefore a Watery Cloud, is nothing else but a *Congeries* of very Small and Concave Globules, which therefore ascend, *viz.* to that Heighth, in which they are of equal Weight with the Air, where they remain suspended, till by some Motion in the air, being broken, they descend in Solid Drops...

[a] After "S. T. C." the note continues without a break in the line

8[2] "To infinity, from the smaller to the greater".

8[3] "In *Punning* language". For C's use of "Punic" as "punning" see e.g. *CL* II 867 (in ANNUAL ANTHOLOGY **10** n 3); cf *OED* "pun" 1: "Punnic fame" (1713).

8[4] C defined a "hypothesis" or "supposition" as "the placing of one known fact under others as their *ground* or foundation. Not the fact itself but only its position is imagined." In a "hypopoiesis" or "suffiction" "both the position and the fact are imagined". See *CN* III 3587 f 1ᵛ and n, *BL* ch 5 (*CC*) I 102, and ARGENS **6** (at n 2). Here C adds "hyponeirosis"—from ὄνειρος (dream) —to mean "the dreaming [up] a fact [and placing it] under others as their *ground*" in much the same way that "hypopoiesis" is making up (contriving) a fact and placing it under others as their foundation. See also FICHTE *Bestimmung* **7** and n 2.

8[5] In textus.

8[6] In textus.

§ 26.—If "some Motion" be taken as = y, i.e. *some* unknown cause, or agency—Grew seems to have had as good a theory of Clouds & Rain, as our present Meteorologists.

10 p 10 | § 29

It is also very reasonably suppos'd by some of late...that it [the Moon] is another Terraqueous Orb, having its Atmosphere, Winds, Seas, and Tides; and herewithal a suitable tho' perhaps a different Furniture of Animals, Plants and Mines.

But why, of necessity, any? Must *all* possible Planets be lousy? None exempt from the Morbus pedicularis[1] of our verminous man-becrawled Earth?

11 p 11 | 1 3 "Of the Principles of Bodies"

This Chapter has an interest for my mind from the ⟨utter⟩ ~~its~~ confusion of Subjective and Objective, and consequent inadvertence to the essential *Subjectivity* of all abstract (or *formal*) Science, ex. gr. Logic, Geometry, &c.[1]

12 p 11, redrafted and continued on p ⁻5 | § 1

As there is no *Maximum* whereunto we can go, but God only; so there is no *Minimum*, but a Point: which hath no Dimensions, but only a Whereness, and is next to Nothing. For as far as the Whole is Extensible, so far the Parts are also Divisible, both Indefinitely; or as Mathematicians speak, Infinitely: that is, beyond any Human Observation or Conception.

Well and happily expressed! But I should like to see the Partition-Wall between Nothing & *Next to* Nothing.[1] *No* Thing, and his next neighbor, Whereness, a ⟨strange⟩ Gentleman who *is* his own empty House—not admitting even his neighbor Nothing's next of Kin, Any Thing. Neither of the two, however, the Thisbe nor the Pyramus,[2]

10[1] "Louse disease". In FICHTE *Bestimmung* **17** (at n 2) C recognises that "Morbus Pediculosus" (as he calls it there) can be a fatal disease; here he probably means nothing more specific than "Vagabond's disease", infestation by lice.

11[1] Cf *Logic* (*CC*) 118–22.

12[1] On the fiction of "nothing" cf

ARGENS **18** and n 1. Cf HOOKER **31**: the "Unit is diluted to evanescence".

12[2] Two lovers, forbidden to marry by their parents, "regularly received each other's addresses through the chink of a wall, which separated their houses" (Lemprière). Cf the version in *Midsummer Night's Dream* v i. The sad outcome of the affair is not the point here.

~~are~~ is left *anonymous*—*Then* indeed we might question the *authenticity* of the Narrative.—But no! the Name of the One, is Nothing; & the other was called *Point*—whether as Sirname, or by baptism, is not ascertained.—It is clear, however, & abundantly descriptive.—the first being, ~~a~~ No Thing *any where*; & the second, *any* ~~Thing~~ where that is no thing—or No Thing that is nowhere & ~~no~~ where that is Nothing*a*

Hue & Cry, the accused accomplices being—A Nothing that is any where, and an ~~any~~ Any where that is Nothing.!—N.B. They are next door Neighbour[s],*b* the one *being* the other's House.

c~~a~~ A Nothing that is No where: and a *Where* only, that is Nothing. Ch. III. p. *11*.

Mem.—The Gentleman last mentioned is called *Point*; whether as Sirname, or by individual Christening, I have not learnt—only, that ~~they~~ NOTHING and POINT ~~we~~are next door neighbours: and strange to say, the Latter ~~was~~ *is* the other's empty house, (Bedless, however—& therefore, ⟨even if the *Spelling* had been less irreconcilable,⟩ not to be confounded with the ⟨WARE so celebrated for its⟩ great Bed.)[3] ~~of Ware, even if the *Spelling* had not precluded it.—⟩~~ This House, which *is* Nothing, ⟨tho' *punctual* in the extreme⟩ is so inhospitable as not even to admit the next-door Neighbor, Nothing's next of Kin, Any Thing!—

P.S. WHERE-ONLY is *Nothing's* Landlord—inasmuch as He *is* at once his own, & his ~~nei~~ Neighbour's, house—Tenementum *merum*, quod nihil tenet.[4]

Mere WHERE-RENESS! NOTHING's Landlord & next Neighbor,
Who *art* thy own and NOTHING's empty house—
Tenantless Tenement!—& pinch-gut ~~ever~~ *only* WHERE!
Would, thou wert No Where! & that thy neighbor, Nothing,
Were any Thing but what He is and is not!—
From a MSS Poem, ανεκδοτου,[5] of
ATHANASIUS SPHINX.

a The note continues in the head-margin without an indicator
b Letter supplied by the editor
c The redraft begins

12[3] The Great Bed of Ware, noticed in *Twelfth Night* III ii 48, a four-poster twelve feet square capable of holding twelve people (later shortened), dates from the late sixteenth century, was originally at the Saracen's Head, an inn in Ware, near Hertford, then at Rye House, Hertfordshire, and since 1931 in the V & A. Whether C's short sojourn at Christ's Hospital in Hertford acquainted him with it is not known.

12[4] "A *mere* tenement, that contains nothing".

12[5] "Unpublished".

13 p ⁻5 referring to the version on p ⁻4

Mem.—Intended as a Retort, or Tit for Tiat courteous,[1] ~~of if the~~ any of the Doctors of the Mechanic corpuscularian Philosophy, the caloric and choloric Atomists of the Daltonial School[2] should, ⟨as most probably they will,⟩ crow and cachinnate over my Ens super Ens, Ens verè Ens, and Ens ferè non ens.[3]

S. T. C.

14 p 11 | § 5

...tho' some have very well shewn the Rectification of Curve Lines, and the Squaring of some Curve Figures; yet this cannot be done to a Point, by an immediate Comparison between a Strait Line, or Rectilinear Figure and a Curve; but requireth the mediate help of Motion; from the Velosity whereof, as I have heard the Learned Mr. *Newton* affirm, the Length of the Curve may be calculated.... But the Equality can never be brought to a Point. For as the smallest Part of a Line, is a Line; so the smallest Part of a Curve Line, though divided Infinitely, is a Curve.

as if the same objection would not apply to the last *Moment* of the Time, by which the Motion must be measured!

15 p ⁻6, referring to p 11 | **14** textus

p. 11. velo*c*ity spelt velo*s*ity.—On a clumsy Dutch Schooner heavily rigged, and wabbling on three knots per hour under crowded Sails[1]

13[1] Cf *As You Like It* v iv 76, 96.

13[2] "Heated and bilious"—"choloric" being a variant of "choleric". John Dalton (1766–1844), chemist and natural philosopher, laid the foundation for modern atomic chemistry with his approximate determination of twenty-one atomic weights in Oct 1803 (later extended and refined), and brought about that triumph of the theory of atomism over the theory of affinity which C—with his abhorrence for "the Mechanic corpuscularian Philosophy"—was reluctant to accept. For his distress that Davy had become "an Atomist" see BÖHME **17** (at n 3).

13[3] "Being above Being, Being [that is] really Being, and Being [that is] almost non-being"—Scholastic phrases, or variations on them, that derive from Plato's οὐσία ὄντως οὐσία (*Phaedrus* 247c, E)

and the Neoplatonists. Cf the use of them by Pico della Mirandola quoted in *CN* I 374. See also BÖHME **20** n 6 and cf **7** and n 3; cf also *CN* III 3575, 3861.

15[1] C's imprecise usage, now regarded as a solecism, was not unknown among seafaring men of his day. Strictly speaking, a knot is a measure of speed = one nautical mile an hour, as determined (in sailing ships) by counting the number of knots passed in a measured time (usually a minute) on a log-line streamed astern. In view of C's fascinated attention to nautical language on the voyage to Malta, and his acquaintance with seamen in Bristol, with John Wordsworth and Alexander Ball, one is nevertheless surprised to find "knots an hour" in e.g. *CN* II 1993, 2002, 2087 (Apr–May 1804); cf 2086, a breeze of "between 3 & 4 miles an hour".

—"Ift ~~we may judge~~ is clear from the quantity of Canvas, that that Vessel possesses great velosity.—"[2]

16 p 12, pencil | § 9

These Instances may also shew how very conceivable it is, That the Qualities of Bodies, whereby they Operate one upon another, may so properly belong to some one Corporeal Principle, as not to subsist primarily in any other. That Heat, for Example, tho' communicable, to any sort of Bodies; yet there is some Subtile Body, which is the primary Subject hereof.

9. unsatisfactory for an anticipation of Electricity.

17 p 13, pencil | § 13

It is plain that the Atoms of Water, are Hard, and Unalterable in their Figure...

The culpa communis[1] of Grew & his Contemporaries was to assume as the measure of every truth its reduction to Geometric Imaginability. They first postulated Atoms, i.e. *absolutely hard* ultimate particles; and then proved the existence from the Postulate.

18 p ⁻4, referring to pp 11–17

It is from admiration of Dr N. Grew, and my high Estimate of his Powers, that I am almost tempted to say, that the Reasonings in Chapt. III. *ought* to have led him to the perception of the essential *phænomenality* of Matter. Its *Esse* is Videri. = Materia = ipsa Visio: id quod merè videtur; & thus ✗ Spirit—i.e. ~~Esse~~ Est = Agit.[1] Agere is its Esse.—Est et *in* se non videri potest.[2]

Matter.
Videtur, non est.

15[2] C jokingly derives "velosity" (not in *OED*, and with no Latin equivalent) from *velum* (sail). Cf "felisity" from *felis* (cat) in N 26 f 150, in *SW&F (CC)*: "Lingua...Catterwauliana—a felisity in speech though no great felicity".

17[1] "Common fault".

18[1] The "*Being* (existence) [of Matter] is in being seen/appearing [or, For Matter, to be is to be seen/appear]; Matter is itself Vision [or, Vision itself]— that which is merely seen/appears; and

thus it is distinguished from Spirit—that is, 'It is' is 'it acts'." *Phaenomenon* is present participle middle and passive of φαίνω, "I make appear"; phaenomena are things appearing to the senses. For similar interaction between the meanings of the passive voice of *videre*—to be seen, or to seem—see e.g. *SM (CC)* 81n and *C&S (CC)* 143–4 n 4.

18[2] "To Act is its Being.—It is and it cannot be seen/appear *in* itself."

Spirit

Agit, ergo est: Est, et, nisi per alterum, non videtur.[3]

It is evident therefore, that both contemplated dividually and in Antithesis are abstract Terms, Universalia Logica. M = the Phænomena of the Substance. S = the Substance of the Phænomenon.

Matter may be *imagined* without Spirit: Spirit may be *conceived* without Matter; but Matter cannot be *conceived* without Spirit, nor Spirit be *imagined* without Matter. [4]

Again, Matter *implies* Spirit, for Spirit is *the* Substance; but Spirit does not necessaryily imply (or rather *supersume*) Matter: for Matter is only *an* Accident of Spirit.

All is *Spirit*: but Spirit must be contemplated as −Sp. & +Sp. and the ascent from − to + as follows—

−Sp. = Materia præsumptionalis—Materia Hades i.e. αειδης, contradictio sui, Chaos, the Mystery of Darkness.[5]

Powers, Forces: Life, ~~Lives~~ Organization: Lives, Bodies, Functions.

Souls, ~~Minds~~ or *Subjects*: *Minds*, or a Subject that is its own Object—

Ɨ Ειμιδες, Eimids, *I* I *I*, *I ams*—.[6]

Here leave pro tempore an intervacuum, quasi intermundium[7]—and then—

+Spirit: GOD = Love & Life life-giving; the Supreme Mind, the Reason and Being: the I AM.—The Absolute Will, ~~whose~~ the superessential GOOD.[a]—The interspace between ~~the~~ non-absolute *I* and the Absolute Life & Love, the Holy Spirit, becomes by participation ~~of~~, of the Holy Spirit the *Sanctified* Spirit

19 p 133, continued on p [132], pencil | ɪᴠ 1 "Of the Integrity of the Hebrew Code"
§ 2

The Poems supposed to be Homer's, were collected either by Pisistratus... or by Lycurgus... after the Interval of a long time, from

---

[a] This word is written in upper-and-lower characters but much larger than the other writing around it

18[3] Matter "*is seen*/appears, but does not exist." Spirit "Acts, and therefore exists: It exists, and cannot be seen/appear, except through something else."
18[4] Cf n 3, and **3** and n 1, above.
18[5] Negative Spirit is "presumptional Matter—Matter [as] Hades (i.e. 'unseen'), a self-contradiction". "Hades" (ἀείδης) is the Septuagint version of Sheol, "the unseen state" (cf e.g. Isa 38.18), but the etymology α-

ιδης = unseen may be fanciful: see IRVING *Sermons* ɪ 200–4 n 6. Cf *C&S* (*CC*) 113.
18[6] Greek and English forms of a coinage from εἴμι (I am)—neither in *OED*.
18[7] Here leave "temporarily an intervening empty space like the space between worlds"—the "interspace" that becomes (below) the "*Sanctified* Spirit".

we know not whose Hands and Keeping. Yet upon the current
*] Testimony of Antiquity, no body doubts, but that he was the
Author of them.

* Grew must have been contemporary with *Vico*, tho' perhaps
somewhat senior. Could he have read the Nuova Scienza of the
Italian Philosopher,[1] or *foreseen* the lucubrations of the German
Philologer (Wolfius)[2] he would have paused at this, "nobody
doubts."[a]

That there was an Author, or that there were Authors, of the Iliad,
no body can doubt, who does not mistake it for a Plant, or a
Chrystallization. ~~of~~ But whether there was a one man, called Homer,
who composed the 24 books called collectively the Iliad, as parts of
one Poem, many *may* doubt: & S. T. Coleridge disbelieves.[3]

20 p [132][b] | continuing textus **19**

* And the like may be said, with respect to the Authority of many
other Books.

* A defect of *indistinction* lurks in this sentence. Homer, Eschylus,
Pindar are for us the *names* of the Iliad & Odyssey; of the Prometheus

----

a The note continues at the foot of p [132]
b Written at the head of p [132], above the second paragraph of **19**, beginning "* Note on the last line of p.
133."

19[1] Grew was twenty-seven years
older than Giambattista Vico (1668–
1744) and did not live to see the third
edition of the *Scienza nuova* (1744), the
first to contain the "Discovery of the
True Homer". C's earliest detailed
acquaintance with the *Scienza nuova*—the
Milan edition, with *Vita* prefixed—was
through Giocchino de' Prati in May
1825, though he may have picked up
information about Vico at second hand
rather earlier (see *CN* III 3656 and n). By
the date of these marginalia (late 1833)
HNC may have completed his translation
of Vico on Homer for his *Introductions
to the Study of the Greek Classic Poets*
(2nd ed 1834). Vico's "Discovery of the
True Homer" was incidental to a study
of the state of Greek society in the heroic
age—mythological in thought, barbaric
in manners, ignorant in "recondite
wisdom"—thereby raising the question
whether the *Iliad* and *Odyssey*, as we have
them, could have been written by a
member of that society.

19[2] On Friedrich August Wolf and
his *Prolegomena ad Homerum* (1795) see
EICHHORN *Alte Testament* **31** and n 1.
HNC added a note to *TT* 12 May 1830:
"Mr. Coleridge was a decided Wolfian in
the Homeric question, but he had never
read a word of the famous Prolegomena,
and knew nothing of Wolf's reasoning
but what I told him of it in conversation.
Mr. C. informed me, that he adopted the
conclusion contained in the text [see *TT*
9 Jul 1832] upon the first perusal of Vico's
'Scienza Nuova;' 'not,' he said, 'that
Vico has reasoned it out with such
learning and accuracy as you report of
Wolf, but Vico struck out all the leading
hints, and I soon filled up the rest out of
my own head.'"

19[3] For pronouncements by C on
the authorship of Homeric poems,
beyond those referred to in nn 1, 2,
above, see e.g. HOMERIC HYMNS **1** and
n 1. See also **20**, below.

&c; and of the Prize-Odes. The works give the meaning and the interest to the Names—they are in fact what we mean by the Authors.—But this dare not be applied to a charter or code, where the Author gives the authority to the Work—Whoever wrote the Iliad, was Homer; but it must have been *Matthew* who wrote the Gospel attributed to him—The work derives its Authority from the Author.[1]

21   p 134, pencil | continuing **20** textus

Whereas the Ten great Commands, commonly called, the *Moral Law*, contained in the Two Tables of Stone: so soon as received by *Moses*, were immediately put into the Ark, *Deut*. 10. 5. and with the Ark preserved in the Tabernacle and the Temple, above 800 Years, *viz.* until the Temple was robb'd and burnt by *Nebuchadnezzar*'s Army. When, as *Polyhistor*, cited by *Eusebius*, Pr. Ev. 9. 39. as a very Learned and Famous Author, and who gives a large Account of the *Jewish* Affairs, saith expresly, "The *Babylonians* nevertheless left the Ark, with the Tables which were kept in it, in the hands of the Prophet *Jeremy*.... And the Judicial and Ceremonial Laws, contained in the Five Books of *Moses*, were by him also written in a Book: And this Book was laid, and kept by the Priests, in the Tabernacle, and in the most Holy Place within the Veil...

If the 10 Commands were ingraved on two Stones; & *if* these two Stones were put into an Ark, and *if* the Ark, &c &c—Why, *then*—so and so—I believe the whole of this; but do not take the whole as proof of the Parts

This is an odd way of proving the veracity of an assertion by another assertion of the same Assertor! *Consistency*, it may prove; & hence the *possibility* of its actual truth it may prove/

Left in the hands of Jeremiah to what purpose? What became of them? As far as we know, the Babylonians might as well have taken them away.

22   pp 134–5, pencil

None but a sincere Believer in the truth can feel the pain, I feel, at these weak defences of it!—A single fair historic testimony, that the two Stone-tables were in the Ark, when the Temple was robbed by

---

20[1] See Herder *Von der Auferstehung* **11** n 1. For a similar discussion of the   names and authority of texts see *CN* iv 5071.

Nebuchadnezzar would have been invaluable; & in proportion, any historic proof of their existence in the intermediate periods from Moses. Do I doubt it? No!—But I doubt the validity of these arguments.

23   p 135, pencil | § 5

It is also evident, that from this Original, many Copies, and from these, many more, were taken through all succeeding Times. For first, their Kings were expressly required to take a Copy of it...Nor can we think, that the good Kings, particularly *David, Asa, Jehoshaphat, Hezekiah, Josiah*, did any of them fail to do as they were required. Or that any of the aforesaid Elders, were without a Copy for their private Use; besides that they kept, as it's most likely, among the Publick Records, for their Use in common.

The impression made by the discovery of the Sacred Roll under Josiah may be a difficulty/[1] but it cannot, I think be rationally doubted, that the Pentateuch in its *present form* was in existence from the age of *Solomon*/[2] I have no doubt of its existence from *Moses*—/ what I mean is, that there is no need of proof for any period posterior to Rehoboam/[3]

24   p 136, pencil | § 6

Now may we doubt, but that as the Original Books of the Prophets, and the rest compriz'd under one Name of the *Hagiographa*, were kept among the Publick Records: So were they also copy'd into many Hands....But 'tis likely, there were not many who had compleat Copies, till after the Captivity: when by *Ezra, Ezekiel, Daniel, Mordecai, Zerubbabel, Nehemiah, Haggai, Zachary, Malachi*... most of them Contemporaries, they were collected into one Volume. Who being many of them Prophets, and foreseeing, that after themselves, no more would be sent...could not but conclude it

23[1] See 2 Chron 34.8–35.19. Josiah, King of Judah c 640–609 B.C. (one of "the good kings", according to Grew), in the course of other reforms undertook restoration of the neglected Temple. There "Hilkiah the priest found a book of the law of the Lord given by Moses" (34.14).

23[2] The Pentateuch was, by tradition, written by Moses: see EICHHORN *Alte Testament* **31** textus, and on Eichhorn's analysis of OT as forerunner of resolutions of the Homeric question see **31** n 1. Solomon, king of Israel, reigned from c 970 B.C. (*ODCC*).

23[3] Rehoboam, son of Solomon and successor to him as king of Judah (in the divided kingdom), reigned 922–915 B.C. Modern scholars assign the finished form of the Pentateuch to the period sixth–fifth century B.C.

necessary, to fix the Books of the Sacred Canon. Which Books were the same, as were ever after received by the *Jews*, and the whole Christian Church unto this Day.

§6—Lame & halt syllogisms!—But the excellent Writer lived in the infancy of historical Criticism. Still, it is painful to meet in so sensible a Book such faith in such palpable fables, as those of *Aristæas*.[1]

25   p 166 | IV 3 "Of the Truth and Excellency of the Hebrew Code..." §12

That... the Prophet *Isaiah* [wrote] the Book of *Job* [is not unlikely]. *] The Author's alluding to the Sun's standing still in the time of *Joshua*, Ch. 9. 7. shews, it could not be writ by *Moses*. And his making use of the *Chaldean* Astronomy; that it was writ after *Solomon* had introduced that Learning.

A most arbitrary, and utterly improbable, interpretation of Job IX.7. –The very words chosen are such as preclude the notion of any allusion to Joshua.[1]—But throughout the Book of Job it is evident that the Poet must have been a Patriarch, before the Law, or not under it.[2]

24[1] For Aristeas' account of the composing of the Septuagint see T. FULLER *Pisgah-Sight* 3 n 1. Grew tells how Ptolemy Philadelphus, not long after 300 B.C., commissioned seventy-two learned Jews chosen by the high priest Eleazar, six from each tribe, to translate the entire Hebrew canon into Greek (p 136 §8). He notices that "some additions [to the story] are certainly fabulous" and—rather less credulous than C suggests acknowledges that "Some particulars of this Account, taken chiefly from *Aristaeas*, have been doubted of ..." (foot of p 136).

25[1] Job 9.7: of God "Which commandeth the sun, and it riseth not; and sealeth up the stars." This is evidently, as C notes, an item in the delineation of God's infinite power, not a reference to a presumed historical event—the miracle in Josh 10.12–14, in which the setting of the sun was delayed. See also **27**, below.

25[2] In EICHHORN *Alte Testament* 52 (referring to III 513) C said that he found in Job "nothing...that might not have been written by a contemporary of

Abraham", and that if asked to date the poem he would place it "between the times of Joseph and Moses". Eichhorn maintained that Job is the oldest poem of the whole of antiquity, a theodicy that has been admired for four thousand years (III 472). (Cf "this most precious as most ancient Poem": BIBLE COPY B **28**.) For Eichhorn the absence of any reference to Mosaic law or to any circumstances of later than patriarchal times proves such an early date, or at least establishes that the author had no knowledge of the Law. Although the setting is in an Arab nomad culture, the language proves that Job was a Jew, not an Arab. The poem could have been written by Moses before the giving of the Law. See also *TT* 29 May 1830. The patriarchal background of the poem is authentic in detail, embodying material that goes back to the second millennium B.C. In its present form, however, Job is post-exilic; nineteenth-century critics assigned it to the seventh century, present scholarship to a period between the sixth and fourth centuries.

The misinterpretation of "Satan", in the Προλογος to this great Epic Drama, in a sense which it bore not till perhaps a 1000 years after Job could alone have given rise to any doubt respecting its antiquity—[3]

                                                                    S. T. C.

26 p 175 | § 34

The Book of *Job*, I take to be, neither a History, as some do, nor a Parable, as some others: But a Divine Vision, made to the Prophet *Isaiah*; and grounded upon the real Story of *Job*.

The Doctor has not explained the grounds of this odd fancy of his.[1]

25[3] Job 1–2, a prose Prologue (Προλογος), contains details inconsistent with the poem itself, not least the unusual term "the Satan". C agrees with Eichhorn that these inconsistencies are deliberate, that the author is writing in a different character in order to distance himself from the action of the poem (*Alte Testament* III 522–3). Eichhorn doubts whether the authenticity and date of the prologue would ever have been suspect if readers had not come to the book informed with later Chaldean ideas about Satan. He argues that the conception of Satan in the prologue is of great antiquity: he is God's angel of judgement, his envoy for investigation, correction, and punishment. In *TT* 29 May 1830, commenting on Job 2.1, C distinguishes between Satan and διάβολος (from which our word "devil"), saying that the Satan in Job is "the *circuitor*, the accusing spirit, a dramatic attorney general". In SWEDENBORG *De coelo* 242 he points to the source of confusion between the ancient and later senses of Satan: "Διαβολος, Diabolus, is a mere translation of the Hebrew Satan...". Septuagint regularly translates the Hebrew word Satan as διάβολος, the word not being a proper name but the word for an accuser; although in NT the primitive sense of accuser, slanderer (cf FIELDING *Tom Jones* 2, LACUNZA II 30–1) occurs in at least five places, Satan or the Devil has become a supernatural adversary of God, a tempter or seducer who could be thought of as having a

proper name; and Greek NT, without any recognisable consistency, uses διάβολος in thirty-two places and σατανᾶς in thirty-three.

26[1] On Eichhorn's opinion that Job was justly called a "drama" inasmuch as it is "a dialogue", C commented that Milton considered it "a didactic Epic Poem" (for which see *The Reason of Church Government* bk 2). EICHHORN *Alte Testament* **51**. Elsewhere C stated that "the poetic Dialogue of Job was his [Milton's] model" for *Paradise Regained*. HAYLEY **1**. Cf HERDER *Briefe* **4** (at n 1).

On p 196 Green has marked: "12. A Miracle [Green's underlining] then, is the extraordinary Effect, of some unknown Power in Nature, limited by Divine Ordination and Authority, to its Circumstances, for a suitable End." He then wrote: "In other words a Miracle is the phaenomenon of an intelligent *Will* in the Law as the ground of the Law. The course of Nature is the Will in the Law i.e. the W̶i̶l̶l̶ Law is the Form of the Will. A Miracle is the Law in the Will[:] the Will itself appears as the form of the Law. S T C". This note is almost identical with a notebook entry of c 13 Oct 1833 headed "Dr Nehemiah Grew's Cosmologia... p. 196". C begins by stating that "...Dr Grew's is incomparably better than the routine definition of the Paleyan Divines —[that a Miracle is] ["]the Suspension of the Laws of Nature by divine interference", quotes the passage that Green has marked in Grew's text (the chief difference being the alteration of Grew's "some

27 p 203 | § 38

[Spinoza explains the standing still of the Sun (Josh 10.12) as an illusion produced by optical diffraction.]

The learned *Grotius*, as well as Spinosa explain the incident described in a quotation from a triumphant War-Ode by a refraction of the Solar Image—/and indeed the Context, ex. gr. the Hail storm &c favor the interpretation.[1]

28 p 210 | IV 6 "Of the Prophecies" | § 8

When *Abraham* was commanded to sacrifice *Isaac*, his dutiful, and his only Son; the Son of his best beloved Wife, of his Old Age, and of the Promise; and in contradiction to a Law, solemnly given to the World, against the shedding of Innocent Blood; yet resolved to obey. Which so pious and wise a Man would never have done, had he not been sure... that this Command was not a Phantasm, but Divinely given.

But is not this something like *proving* the wisdom of the Act by *presuming* it?

29 p 224, pencil | § 37

He [Isaiah] singles out the very person for this Service [i.e. "The Return of this Peoples Captivity"], and gives him the Name of *Cyrus*. Which so far prevailed... That if he had any other, as Grotius, from Herodotus, says he had, it was soon utterly lost, and unknown. As *Persian*, it is supposed... to signify the Sun. As *Hebraick*, and written with a *Caph*, may not improperly be derived of *Cherub* and *Rus*: As

---

unknown Power" to "an undetermined ascertained power"), and continues: "In other words, a Miracle is the phænomenon & revelation of an intelligent *Will* in the Law—as the ground of *the Law*. The Course of Nature is the Will in the Law—i.e. the Law is the Form of the Will. A Miracle is the Law in the Will: the Will itself appears as the Form of the Law." N 53 ff 3ᵛ–4 (*CN* v).

27[1] Grotius' explanation of Josh 10.13, given in his *Annotata ad Vetus Testamentum* (Paris 1644) I 183–4, also appears e.g. in HACKET *Scrinia* i 2 Proem

§5: "*The Learned* Grotius (*Who can stop his Conjectures?*) *thinks it not improbable, but that the Sun went down,* Josh. 10. 13, when Joshua *pursued the Kings of* Canaan *in the Valley of* Ajalon: Sed post Solis occasum speciem ejus in nube supra horizontem extanti per repercussum ostendere: *That is, a kind of Sun, that made a great Lustre, shined sufficiently to make it Day, not in his Presence, but in the repercussion of his Beams upon a Cloud.*" C refers to this explanation again in another note on miracles in N 53 ff 8–9ᵛ (*CN* v) (c mid–Oct 1833).

much as to say, a Prince of a Right Noble, and Angelical Mind, without great Riches. Which is very agreeable to his Character.

The affinity of the Gothic, the Latin, the Persian and the Sanscrit is now generally acknowleged—and it may be no irrational conjecture, that Kyrus of the Person[a] answered to the *Quirinus* of the Romans/ the Root still extant in *Ger*, (man), Guerre, *War*—& thus Cyrus be The Warrior/ & ⟨from⟩ Herodotus we learn, that this was an Agnomen.[1]

30   p 230, pencil | iv 7 "Of the Divine Law…" §16

Much less could the Offering of a Burnt Sacrifice, be indicated by the Light of Nature. And still less, the burning of Flesh and Bones, which make so egregious a stink. Could he [Abel] have thought the burning of any thing, acceptable; why not rather, of some Fragrant Wood or Gum?

16. Very just. And therefore I am the more confirmed in my Opinion, that a *Church* Contribution is here allegorized.

31   p 231, pencil | § 18

To suppose then, that *Abel* offer'd a Lamb, as the best sort of Meat, when it was unlawful to eat Flesh; or that he burnt it…as a devised Homage to his Lord and Benefactor, when nothing hereof could be indicated by the Light of Nature, is a Phantastick Conceit. *] But to say, he did it, because he was commanded; is agreeable unto good Sense, and the Scriptures.

* 18. ad finem. Is not this almost tantamount to saying, that a very absurd and ridiculous act was dictated by the Supreme Reason?

32   p 238, pencil | iv 8 "Of the Mosaick Law" § 9

…when his [a servant's] Years were expired, he was put to his Choice, Whether he would go out free, without his Wife and Children; or continue a Servant, with them, *Exodus* 21. 4, 5, 6. And very justly: in that he knew his Choice, when he took his Wife.

More just, than generous.

[a] A slip for "Persians"

29[1] Modern etymologists do not suggest a common origin for these words. The Herodotus reference, not given by Grew, is 1.113. The term *agnomen* was loosely used in English of any additional name or nickname (see *OED*); C does not imply that he thinks the Persians had a system of naming that corresponded to the Roman custom.

33 p 239, pencil | § 17

Of a Purchased Servant, the Rule was given, *Exod.* 21. 21. That if he dy'd under the Rod, the Master should be punish'd: But not *if he continued a day or two; because he was the Master's Money.*

a Sort of Spartan Law, permitted, perhaps, to keep alive the love of Freedom/ which in that age could scarcely have been effected without a very marked diffcrence in the Legal rights of Slave & Freeman—

34 p 243, pencil | § 29

The Laws for securing every one's Property, were very exact. *If an Ox, Ass, or Sheep, being stoln, was found alive in the hand of the Thief; he was to restore double, Exodus* 22.4....If he could not do this, he was to be Sold, *Exodus* 22.3....We have learned indeed, Since the growth of our Plantations to Transport them [Felons]. But no Satisfaction is hereby given to the Party Robb'd, as by God's Law, is done.

Why, the *being sold* for a Slave is the same as, or worse than our transportation; and surely God's Law did not either confine the guilt of Theft to Persons of some Property, or give a Property, i.e. the means of restitution, to all Thieves.

35 pp 244–5, pencil | § 34

The *Levites* also, though being under *Jacob's* Prophetick Curse, they had no Original Lot: yet that Curse being turned into a Blessing, they had a Secondary Lot, of 48 Cities, with their Suburbs, out of the other Tribes....Together with the Tithe of the Product of the Country....And the Tithe of this Tithe, was to be the Priests...

The hatred of Tythes, under the present form and appropriation, is a mixt feeling—right and wrong, good and evil.[1]—But if Tythes were duly appropriated, and faithfully applied—*then*, I say, that the *impatiency* of Tythes would be an infallible Criterion of the national Decline—of Apostacy from God to Mammon, from *Country* to *Self*, and thus from *Nation* to that sand desart of Selves, the *People*—and

35[1] For C on tithes see e.g. *LS (CC)* 167 and n 2, 212–13n and n 1; *C&S (CC)* 161 n 2 and the notebook entry quoted in 90 n 2. For C's early intention, unfulfilled, of writing "a Book—Concerning Tythes & Church Establishment" see *CL* ɪɪ 829 (Jul 1802).

for its punishment, from People to *Populace*²—i.e. the sands
constructed for destruction by an Eddy–blast—with Cobbets, O
Connels, and Tom Moores, for the Eolian puft-cheeked Cherubs,
the brainless Heads of the headless Democracy.³—Ah! that the
wings attached to the Heads were prophetic, of flying off from
their owners' Neck & Shoulders!⁴

S. T. C.

36 p 245 | § 38

It seemeth therefore, that as the Rich never used to Borrow, so
neither were they concerned in this Precept. Nor any now, where the
lending of Money, upon Use, is not an Oppression, but a Kindness.

Aye! when it is lent *from* Kindness—and at least for mutual ad-
vantage.

37 p 247 | § 47

If then there was one God, Superior to them all; they could not but
conclude, That this One, had all Perfections in himself.

35² For the distinction between people
and populace see *LS* (*CC*) 164 and n 3.

35³ Another version of this note
appears in N 53 ff 16–17 (*CN* v), ending:
"...and thus [a Decline] from a NATION
to that multitudinous Sand Desart of
Selves, and PEOPLE—and, ⟨finally,⟩ as
the punitive consequence, from People to
Populace—i.e. the Sands constructed for
destruction by every Eddy-blast!—the
corrupt Nature being the unseen Eolus,
with Tom Moore, O Connel, Cobbett, &c
&c for the Eolian trumpet-cheeked
Cherub-Heads, the brainless heads which
(as the duck-wings seem to imply) have
flown off from the Trunk of the beastly
Hydra. Would, they were prophetic of
their flying off from the Neck &
Shoulders of their nominal Owners—if
so, there might be Peace & Common-
sense on Earth!—" At this time Daniel
O'Connell (1775–1847) was engaged in a
long-drawn-out attempt to secure the
dissolution of the Act of Union between
England and Ireland through parliamen-
tary reform, his chief way of rallying
popular sentiment in Ireland lying in his
ability systematically to arouse agitation

through mass meetings. See *CL* vi 885:
"O'Connel, & the gang of Agitators"; cf
898, 903, and the doggerel verses,
naming O'Connell and Cobbett, in 918,
925. In this annotation C may simply
be sketching out the spectrum of de-
magoguery, using the type-figures of
O'Connell as orator and parliamen-
tarian, Moore as Irish poet-historian,
and Cobbett as radical journalist. In *TT*
Feb 1833 C speaks of O'Connell with
respect, giving as reason why he is "tri-
umphant in debate and in action" that—
unlike the English ministers who oppose
him—"he asserts a broad principle, and
acts up to it, rests all his body on it, and
has faith in it".

35⁴ For the original of this symbol of
demagoguery, drawn from Revelation,
see *LS* (*CC*) 146–7n and cf 143 and nn.
The apocalyptic imagery may here be
cross-fertilised with a memory of the
puff-cheeked cherubs, which C called
"No-bodies", "looking up the Virgin's
petticoats as roguishly as may be" on the
front of the cathedral church in Syracuse:
see *CN* iii 2244, 2370 and nn.

I A M.—the LORD/ including all other Being, & governing all—*thy* God—acting for and on ~~each~~ every man, yet entire for each—in these thou knowest *me*: & thou shalt have no other God but *me*, i.e. The Father, the Son, and the Spirit of the Father and the Son/ the one living only God.—[1]

38   p 247 | § 49

The *Third Command, Not to take the Name of God in vain*; was given, To shew the Sacracy of this Most Excellent Majesty.

Surely, the *primary* sense of this Command was the prohibition of using the Name of God in magical incantatations.

39   p 257 | §105

In the Tabernacle, the *Jews* likewise saw something of Heaven. By the Charge which *Moses* so often received, *Exod.* 25, 26, and 27. To make it with all its Furniture, *after the Patterns shewed him in the Mount*: they might understand, what St. *Stephen* also tells us, *That all was given to him, by the Ministry of Angels.* And by the Cherubims on the Throne, That the Communication, which God at any time had with *Moses* afterwards, was also by their Mediation.

D[r] Grew's conception of the Scriptures—and if I thought, it could add in the least to my love, and reverence for them, I would pray fervently that it might be my own!—did not permit him to make any allowance for the fact, that the New Testament references are for the most part to the *Septuagint* and that *this* was one of the instances in which the Jewish Translators *accomodated* the Original to the anticipated Objections of the Greek Philosophers—/viz. an *anthropomorphism* in their religion, analogous to that of Greeks— as Jupiter on Ida or Olympus, so Jehovah on Sinai &c/—To avoid this, they substituted *Angels.*[1]

37[1] Cf Deut 5.6–7.

39[1] Grew refers to Acts 6.30, 38, in which an angel rather than the Lord himself speaks to Moses. Cf Hastings *Dictionary of Religion and Ethics* under "Demons", in which it is stated that all the pre-exilic references to "angels" represent "sendings" or "manifestations" of Jehovah. The "sons of God" in Job would appear to be angels in the sense C objects to. Cf DONNE *Sermons* COPY B 12, HACKET *Century* 16 and nn, and HOOKER 19–21.

40   p 298, pencil, and marked in the margin | v 2 "Of the Truth and Excellency of the New Testament..." § 22

*] *Matthew* wrote his Gospel, about the 8th year after our Saviour's Ascension; *Mark*, about the 10th; *Luke*, the 15th, *John*, the 32*d*. *Theoph. Pref.* in *Matth.*

* Bold Assertions! grounded on precarious Chronology, Master Grew![1]

41   p 314, pencil | v 3 "Of the Contents of the New Testament..." §13

?—?—] St. *Luke* tells us of several, who before himself, had published the History of the Gospel: declaring those Things, which they had from Eye-Witnesses, and *were most surely believed by the Churches.*

As Evangelists in the Churches—but as Writers of the whole Memorabilia of Christ? Luke seems to me to say the very contrary.[1]

42   p 315, pencil | §14

The great Darkness, is described by the forementioned *Phlegon*... saying... *That it happened in the 4th Year of the* 202 *Olympiad, the Year of our Saviour's Passion. That it began at the Sixth Hour of the Day,* that is, *at Noon,* as the Scriptures also say: *and was the greatest Eclipse of the Sun,* as he calls it, *as was ever beheld, the Stars being then seen.*

How comes it then, that with our present Astronomical Science there can remain any doubt respecting the Chronology of our Lord's Death?[1]

40[1] C himself was not of settled opinion about the dates of the Gospels. Cf BAXTER *Catholick Theologie* 7 and n 1 and DONNE *Sermons* COPY B 16 and n 3. C's objection here is not to the particular dates proposed but to the air of precision. Eichhorn argued that there is no evidence that the four Gospels existed in the form we have them before the third century.

41[1] See Luke 1.1–4. Cf BIBLE *NT Gospels* 1.

42[1] The darkness from the sixth to the ninth hour is probably to be associated with the earthquake that followed the crucifixion (Matt 28.45, 51–4; also Mark and Luke). The evidence of the Gospels is that the crucifixion took place at the time of Passover (Matt 26.17, 19; Mark 14.12, 16; Luke 22.8, 11, 13; John 19.14)—that is, at the full moon, when an eclipse of the sun would be a miracle beyond the scope of astronomical calculation. The various evidences suggest three possible dates: in A.D. 27, 29, 32–3, the last of these being the fourth year of the 202nd Olympiad (in textus).

43 p +1

Almighty ~~all good, all wise~~, God—our Father, who art in Heaven!
who fillest Heaven and Earth, yea, Heaven & the Heaven of Heavens
cannot contain—who eminently art, when Spirits conformed to thy
will live in the beatific vision of thy presence—Hallowed—and by us,
who look toward thee thro' the Veil of the flesh with fear & with
thanksgiving—hallowed be thy NAME/ even the Name which above
all names THOU hast glorified even ~~with~~ as thyself, Jehovah, the Word
Incarnate, JESUS! that living Name, in which alone (we believe in our
Hearts & profess with our Lips) there is salvation on earth—the
gracious Name, by adoption into which we, poor Sinners, are
privileged to call thee, the almighty God, Father, OUR Father!—
Father of our Lord Jesus Christ: and ~~thro'~~ in him Father of all
Mercies! Lord of Lords, and King of Kings!—Thy Kingdom
come—thy Kingdom & the Kingdom of thy Christ—O let it be
established in our Hearts,[a] ~~that we may be one before thee quelling
every rebellious thought, & scourging out all every impure desire~~ as
who now call ⟨to⟩ thee! by the power of thy Spirit ~~scourging out
every rebellious thought, every unclean impure subduing the will of
the flesh, and scourging out~~ O cleanse our Hearts, and by the power
of thy Spirit Scourge out every impure, every profane desire, ~~that~~
every thought that trafficks with the Flesh and this World—that ~~th~~
we may be one before thee, even thy Church which thou beholdest
& lovest in the dear Son of thy Love! O build up thy Throne
therein—as in a living Temple dedicated to thy Service—and fill it
with thy Glory, that thy Will may be done *on earth* as it is in
Heaven/[1]

44 p +4, pencil[b]

ETESIS'S[c] Epitaph[1]
⟨Stop, Christian Visitor! stop, Child of God⟩[d]

[a] The words "our Hearts", cancelled in error, are here printed in clear
[b] Because the draft on p +4 is an earlier version than the draft on p +3, the normal order of transcription is here reversed. EHC printed them in the order in which they appear in the volume, numbering **45** as "1" and **44** as "2": *PW* (EHC) II 1088–9
[c] A slip for "ESTESI'S"
[d] This line, an afterthought, is inserted between the title and the line "Here lies a Poet..."

43[1] With this extended meditation upon the Lord's Prayer cf BROOKE **14**.

44[1] Of eight versions of C's *Epitaph*, all but two in ms, this draft and the draft following (**45**) are the earliest surviving mss, and the second and third earliest in order of composition: written c 26 or 27 Oct 1833—see (*d*), below; they represent a crucial phase in the transformation of the poems from four lines to eight. The eight versions, in apparent order of composition, are: (*a*) Written in Poole's copy of an unidentified edition of the TODTENTANZ—printed in *Poole* II 301 as

[a]⟨And read with gentle heart! Beneath this Sod
There lies a Poet—&c⟩[b]
Here lies a Poet: or what once was He![2]
⟨O⟩Pause, Traveller pause and pray for S. T. C.
That he who many a year with toil of Breath
Found Death in Life, may here find Life in Death.

Inscription on the Tomb-stone of one not unknown; yet more commonly known by the Initials of his Name, than by the Name itself.[3]

45 p +3, pencil[c]

Epitaph
In Hornsey Church-yard[1]

[a-b] This line-and-a-half is written, after a small space, below the line "Found Death..." prefixed with " ∧ ", the point of insertion in the text marked with " ∧ ".

[c] At pp +2/+3 and +4/+5 a folio sheet of ruled laid paper is guarded in, containing (in ink) a transcript of each draft, one facing p +3 (EHC's version "1"), the other facing p +4 (EHC's version "2"); the hand is not identified

a six-line version, but reprinted in *PW* (JDC) as of four lines: see n 2, below. (*b*) GREW **44**—a four-line version expanded by the insertion of two lines at the beginning. (*c*) GREW **45**—a variant of the revised (*b*) with a couplet added to bring the poem to the substance and extent of the final version. (*d*) Letter to Green 28 Oct 1833 (*CL* VI 963)—except for changes in lines 3 and 4, and italicising "*to be forgiven*" in line 5, this follows (*c*); C says: "the Epitaph, I rewrote last night, or rather re-*thought* (for I am now first to re-*write* it)...". (*e*) Letter to Eliza Aders, nd [c 5 Nov 1833] (*CL* VI 969–70). (*f*) N 52 f 26 (inside back cover) (*CN* v) [c 5 Nov 1833]. (*g*) Letter to John Gibson Lockhart 5 Nov 1833 (*CL* VI 973). (*h*) The final version—printed in *PW* (1834), from a ms dated 9 Nov 1833, presumably lost—for the first time has in line 2 "And read with gentle breast". (The version printed in *QR* LII—Aug 1834—292, similar to (*h*) but reading "lift a thought" for "lift one thought", was probably contributed by HNC.) See *PW* (EHC) I 491.

44[2] The ms clearly shows that this was the first line of verse that C wrote on p +4, corresponding to the first line of version (*a*), and confirming JDC's judgement in printing in *PW* (JDC) 645–6 only the first four lines of the *Poole* version; he probably recognised, on the evidence of the GREW versions, which he also printed, that the closing couplet had been added from the final version in *PW* (1834). In (*a*) line 3 reads: "That he who threescore years, with toilsome breath"—the only other occurrence of "toilsome" is in (*e*)—and line 2 reads: "Pray, gentle Reader, pray for S. T. C.". The new opening couplet, in which "Visitor" is an undesirable anticipation of "Traveller" in the original second line, resolved into the "Passer-by" of the next draft (**45**, and all later versions), clarified the function of the line on prayer, and initiated a syntactical momentum that would overrun the rhetorical unity of the couplets.

44[3] The prominence of the initials "S. T. C."—"fondly Graecized" (*CL* VI 963)—in various forms in the text and in some titles is reinforced by C's repeating this "Inscription" variatim in (*d*)–(*g*). See **45** n 2, below, and cf ANNUAL ANTHOLOGY **10** n 3.

45[1] Hornsey, lying a short distance down the easterly slope of Highgate Hill, was then the parish church for Highgate.

Hic Jacet S. T. C.[2]
Stop, Christian Passer-by! Stop, Child of God!
And read with gentle heart. Beneath this Sod
There lies a Poet: or what once was He.
~~Up~~ O lift thy soul in prayer for S. T. C:
That He who many a year with toil of breath
Found death in life, may here find life in death.

C may have expected to be buried there because the old cemetery at the top of Highgate Hill west of the Grammar School had been closed some time before this date; although C was well aware of the long-drawn-out controversy over a new chapel for Highgate, he may not have been familiar enough with the detailed resolution of that issue to know that the old Highgate cemetery was to be extended to include the adjoining site of the old Grammar School chapel as soon as that chapel was demolished. For the controversy over the use of funds from the charity of Cholmeley's Free Grammar School (later Highgate Grammar School) to build a new chapel in Highgate, which began in 1821 and was finally settled by act of parliament in Jun 1830, see e.g. *CL* v 189 n 3, 241–2 n 1, vi 883–4 n 2. A new chapel built on the south side of Pond Square—now St Michael's Church—was consecrated on 8 Nov 1832, C attending (*CL* vi 995 n 1). When the old chapel of the Grammar School was torn down in 1833 the site became an extension of the old graveyard and was assigned to the use of the new chapel. Here, inside the western boundary of the new cemetery, in—as it seemed to SC's eye—"the old church-yard, by the road side", C was to be buried in Aug 1834 in a tomb in which (later enlarged) he was joined in succession by HNC, Mrs C, SC, and Herbert Coleridge. The new graveyard was closed in 1857; when a new chapel for the Grammar School was built over the site in 1866 the Coleridge tomb was preserved in a sort of open crypt under the west end of the chapel, and there, for lack of clearly defined responsibility for looking after it, suffered neglect. The contents of the tomb were removed to the nave of St Michael's Church in Mar 1961, and a memorial of Cumberland slate was placed in the pavement with the text of the *Epitaph* incised by Reynolds Stone in a beautiful cursive letter.

Highgate Old Cemetery, lying west of Swain's Lane and now enveloping the whole hillside directly below St Michael's Church, was laid out in 1838 as the third of the new London inter-denominational commercial cemeteries. Here George Wombwell the menagerist was buried in 1850 with a tame lion on his monument, and later Michael Faraday was buried near the east wall, and in 1863 Joseph Henry Green was entombed below the columbarium—the double ring of sepulchral vaults disposed like the cells of a dovecote belowground around a huge cedar tree—and here his widow Ann Eliza joined him at her desire sixteen years later.

The letter to Eliza Aders accompanying (*e*) shows that C intended to have commissioned an engraved vignette of a tombstone with the *Epitaph* on it; according to EHC, this was to have been printed on the last page of the "Miscellaneous Poems" in *PW* (1834) Vol II: see *PW* (EHC) I 491n.

45[2] In a prefatory remark to version (*d*) C made further play upon his initials, in Greek and Latin, as an extension of the HIC JACET inscription: "ἔστησε: κεῖται· ἀναστήσει [he hath stood; he lies at rest; he will rise again]—Hic Jacet, qui stetit, restat, resurget [Here Lies one who hath stood, awaits, will rise again].— ΕΣΤΗΣΕ". In (*f*) and (*g*) variants of this are set at the end of the poem like a formal lapidary inscription. See also ANNUAL ANTHOLOGY **10** n 3.

Mercy for praise, to be forgiven for fame[3]
He ask'd, and hoped thro' Christ. Do thou the same.

45[3] In version (g) C added a note to "for" in "Mercy for Praise": "N.b.— 'for' in the sense of 'instead of'.—" *CL* VI 973. The italicised words in "*to be forgiven* for Fame" in versions (d) and (e)—and (a)—were probably meant, by parallel construction, to convey the same meaning of "for"—"to be forgiven, *instead of* being accorded fame". Cf *OED* under "for" II 5.

SIR HENRY GEORGE GREY
VISCOUNT HOWICK,
LATER THIRD EARL GREY
1802–1894

Corrected Report of the Speech of Viscount Howick, in the House of Commons, May 14, 1833, on Colonial Slavery, with an appendix, containing a plan for the abolition of slavery. London 1833. 8°.

Bound as third in "PAMPHLETS ON THE SLAVE TRADE", a made-up volume of three reports on the slave-trade 1821–33, the second of which is ANALYSIS *of the Report of a Committee of the House of Commons on the Extinction of Slavery* (1833).

British Museum C 126 h 14 (3)

On pp 13 and 32, ink brackets in the text, possibly C's. At the head of p 1 a pencil note, the hand unidentified, has been erased and is no longer legible.

It was the 2nd Earl Grey, father of Henry George Grey, who as first lord of the Treasury arranged in 1831 that C be offered a grant of £200 in lieu of the lapsed Royal bounty as a Fellow of the Royal Society of Literature—an offer that C declined. *CL* vi 854–7n.

DATE. 1833.

1   p 5, pencil

...It appears by the evidence last year...that the annual value of all supplies, of every description, usually furnished by a Jamaica Planter, to each Negro, is highly estimated at 45 shillings....But allow that it is even higher than Mr. Shand has stated, and assume that 52 shillings is not more than the value of the supplies now furnished to the Negroes, it will follow that...a shilling a week, or two pence a day, is to be the remuneration for which the Negro is, during three-fourths of his time, to be compelled to labour.

But were not the Planters' Supplies, = 45ˢ or 52ˢ, exclusive of the Garden & the Provision Grounds? I dare not suspect Lord Howick of so gross a blunder, but yet his statement is so very improbable.

2 p 42

At least, Sir, there is nothing in the state of things I have described which is calculated to lead to bloodshed; the slaves would have obtained all they can desire, why, therefore, should they be guilty of any acts of violence?...Why, Sir, slavery depends for its existence, from hour to hour, on the support of the military power of this country: this is the very breath of its being, which, if withdrawn, it would perish at the instant; no active interference on our part is necessary in order to put down slavery; we have but to refuse to uphold it, and from that moment it is at an end.

P. 41–43. Could Lord H. have been in his sober senses when he delivered to Parliament & to the Public these opinions? In the supposed Case the Colonists may have brought the consequences on themselves; but as sure as there is truth in history, the consequences would be the Massacre of every *Male* White, and the brutal violation of every female not murdered. A Licence by the King of G. Brit. for Spoliation & seizure of the Land could not but be interpreted by the furious and triumphant Slaves as a Licence for Murder. And in fact, it would be a clear Permission. If A be the known sole Preventive of B, the intentional Withdrawing of A is the perpetration of B. Causa Causæ causa causati[1]—*S. T. C.*

3 p 45

[An outline of what Grey calls (p 51) "the proposed measure for converting the Slaves in the British Colonies into apprenticed labourers" had been given on p 4: "...the Negro is to be apprenticed to a master not of his own choice, and is to be compelled to enter into a contract, the terms of which he is not at liberty to alter or to reject. For that master he is to be compelled to labour three-fourths of his day, and in return he is to receive the same supplies, the same necessaries, which the Planter is at present in the habit of furnishing."]
It is true, that during one-fourth of the day, the Negroes are to labour on their own account; but what they earn, even in this portion of their time, is not to be at their own disposal; it is to be taken from them in order to accumulate, for the payment of a debt which they will feel they do not justly owe; and till the expiration of 12 years, they will derive no advantage whatever from it.

2[1] "The Cause of a Cause is the cause of the effect". Cf DONNE *Sermons* COPY
B **65** n 1.

This apprentice-scheme, which he still clings to, with the appropriation of the poor Slaves wages to pay the Master, which he has consented to abandon, ha~~ve~~s much lowered my estimation of Mr Stanley's *intellect*, at least as a Statesman[1]—And how could Lord Brougham assent to so crude a Scheme?[2]

4 p 48

I have heard the conduct of Russia condemned in no measured terms for having by military force put down and punished the [Polish] insurgents. But if the cause of the Poles was just, what shall we say of that of the Negroes in the case I have supposed....

Sir, I ask what Hon. Gentleman is there in this House, who has joined in the general condemnation of the conduct of Russia, who could vote supplies for carrying on such a contest with the Negroes?

The cases are not ejusdem generis.[1] Those, who voted "supplies for &c"– might conscientiously vote in the conviction that the safety of the civilized world ⟨would be endangered,⟩ and the moral welfare of the Negroes themselves would be sacrificed by such a contest. Our indignation against Russia is grounded on the *fitness* of the Poles for Freedom—/[2] I am jealous of all arguments of this kind.

3[1] Edward George Geoffrey Smith Stanley (1799–1869), 14th Earl of Derby, as colonial secretary carried the act for the abolition of slavery in British possessions in 1833, but had resigned before it became law in 1834. His original resolution was modified by reducing the period of apprenticeship and increasing the compensation to the slave-owners.

3[2] Brougham, who had made widely applauded speeches in the House against the slave-trade in 1824 and 1830, was appointed Lord Chancellor in Grey's ministry in Nov 1830, devoting his energies to law reform and education. Superseded in office in Nov 1834, and no longer popular, he continued with intermittent brilliance to take a part in public

life, and in 1838 returned to his attack on slavery.

4[1] "Of the same kind/order".

4[2] The strong revival of nationalist spirit in Poland led to general insurrection in Nov 1830, the Diet proclaiming in Jan 1831 that Poland was independent of Russia. As the war with Russia continued, successfully at first, the Poles appealed to the West for support, but the appeals went unheeded and Britain declined to support the Polish claim to independence. In Sept 1831 the Russians captured Warsaw; 10,000 leaders and soldiers were exiled, and the Polish constitution was abolished in Feb 1832. Not until the First World War did an opportunity arise for the Poles to regain their independence.

HUGO DE GROOT (GROTIUS)
1582–1645

LOST BOOK

De jure belli et pacis. Accedunt annotata in epistolam Pauli ad Philemonem. Amsterdam 1763. 8°.

No copy of this edition has been traced.

Not located; marginalia not recorded. *DC SC* (1891) 899: "autograph notes of S. T. Coleridge, with autograph of H. N. Coleridge on title".

JOHN HACKET

1592–1670

A Century of Sermons upon several remarkable subjects: preached by the Right Reverend Father in God, John Hacket, late Lord Bishop of Lichfield and Coventry. Published [and with An Account of the Life and Death of the Author] by Thomas Plume, D.D. London 1675. F°.

British Museum Ashley 4778

Bookplate of James Gillman the younger on p ⁻5 (p–d). Passages are marked with an ink line in the margin on pp 527, 530, 531, 685, 687, 689, 691, 978, 979, 980; these seem not to be C's marks. Three notes in pencil on p ⁻4 (**1, 9, 10**) have been overtraced, perhaps by HNC.

DATE. c late 1823. In *CN* IV 5073 (c 12 Dec 1823) C refers to "Hackett's Sermons on the Incarnation, the Temptation and the Transfiguration"—the sermons annotated in **7–19**. In late Aug or early Sept 1823, when preparing materials for the Life of Leighton, one of the books C submitted to "laborious Collation" was "Hacket"—i.e. not this *Century of Sermons* but the biography of John Williams, HACKET *Scrinia Reserata: CL* v 300 (9 Sept 1828). According to **13** and **24** C had read *Scrinia Reserata* before he wrote those two notes.

In a notebook entry of c 13–21 May 1828—N 37 ff 62–3 (*CN* v)—C referred to Hacket's "Sermons on the Advent" (not annotated) to support his argument that "dim romantic notions...about the ⟨Primitive⟩ Christians", the "*sensualizing* [of] the Christian history" as seen in "This Foolery" of the Cherry Tree Carol, had "received a knock-down Blow at the Reformation", but was "only stunned, not killed, and was on the point of resuscitation by the tender care of Laud and the High Church Divines of his faction". Such an argument can also be seen in **8, 11–13, 15, 16**, below, but it does not appear that any of the annotations in this volume are of so late a date.

1   p ⁻4, pencil, overtraced

Sermons

    p. 4. Latter part of last §ph. but one.¹

    – 5 a valuable Remark...²

    – 5 X a very different §ph!...³

1¹ See **9**, below.   1³ See **12**, below.
1² See **10**, below.

2 p ⁻4

Sermons—noticeable passages of.
    Part I. P. 5 § ph. 1¹—24.3. a pretty piece of Poetry, and as prettily
worded./² P 27.³

3 p viii | An Account of the Life and Death of the Author

[Hacket had two livings—] *Holbourn* for *wealth* and *Cheam* for
health; these two Livings being within a small distance, of ten
miles...Yet he would often dispute the necessity of a *Country Living*
for a *London Minister* to retire to in hot Summer time, out of the
Sepulchral air of a *Church-yard*, where most of them are housed in
the City, and found for his own part that by *Whitsuntide* he did *rus
anhelare*, and unless he took fresh air in the Vacation, he was stopt
in his Lungs and could not speak clear after *Michaelmas*: But upon
one of these he was constantly resident, making as few excursions for
pleasure or recreation, as any man living, scarce ever absent from
both, nor long from *either*; in so much that his friend *Dr. Holdsworth*
said, *Dr. Hacket* resided more upon *two* Livings, than any *Puritan*
(that ever he knew) did upon *one*...

A plausible Reason certainly why A. and B. should change Posts
occasionally; but a very weak one for A's having both Livings all
the year thro'.—

4 p ⁻4, referring to p xliii

The *Bishop* was an enemy of all separation from the *Church* of
England, of whatsoever *Faction* or *Sect*...and he would challenge *any*
to shew him in all Antiquity for 1500 years where any *Christian*
withdrew from the *Churches Communion*...for their imposition of
indifferent matters or *Ceremonies?* though in ancient times they
imposed *more* than *we* do now.... These things were only spoken to
make *our Church* odious to ignorant people, and being permitted
must needs in time destroy *our Foundations* again;ᵃ and therefore *he*
wished that as of old, all *Kings* and other Christians subscribed to
the *Conciliary Decrees*, so now a *Law* might pass that all *Justices* of
Peace should do so in *England*, and then *they* would be more careful
to punish the depravers of *Church Orders*.

    ᵃ From here to the end of textus marked with a pencil line in the margin

2¹ I.e. **10** textus, below.   2³ See **17A**, below.
2² See **17**, below.

P. 43. The little or no ef[fect of recent experience and][a] Sufferings still more recent, in curing the [mania of persecution! How] was it possible that a man, like Bishop Hacket, [should not have seen] that if Separation on account of the imposition of [things by himself] admitted to be indifferent & as such justified was criminal [in those] who did not think them indifferent, how doubly criminal mu[st the] Imposition have been, how tenfold criminal the perseverance in occasioning Separation, how guilty the imprisoning, impoverishing, driving into wildernesses their Christian Brethren—for admitted Indifferentials—in direct contempt of St Paul's positive Command to the Contrary![1]

5   p ⁻4, referring to pp xliii–xliv

In the *Quinquarticular* Controversie he was ever very moderate, but being bred under *Bishop Davenant*, and *Dr. Ward* in *Cambridge*, was addicted to *their Sentiments. Bishop Usher* would say *Davenant* understood those Controversies better than ever any man did since *St. Austin*; but He used to say, he was sure he had *three* excellent men of his mind in *this Controversie.* 1. *Padre Paulo*... 2. *Thomas Aquinas.* 3. *St. Austin....* He disliked no *Arminian*, but such a one as reviled and defamed every one that was *not so*, and would often commend *Arminius* himself for his excellent wit and parts, but only tax his want of reading and knowledg in Antiquity, and ever held it was the foolishest thing in the world to say the *Arminians* were *Papists*...

p 43. two last lines & 44—Could Bishop Marsh ever have read this striking §ph?[1] As to Bishop Tomline, alias Pitt Prettyman, it would

---

[a] The top right hand corner of the leaf is torn off. The following restorations in [ ] are supplied from *LR*, which seems, however, to be a conjectural emendation rather than a transcript made before the leaf was damaged

4[1] Rom 9.34–9. Cf HOOKER 8.

5[1] At the Synod of Dort (1618–19) the Calvinists of the Dutch Reformed Church condemned Arminian doctrine in five sets of articles. These articles were then formulated into ninety-three canonical rules, through the application of which some two hundred Arminian clergy were deprived, Grotius was sentenced to perpetual imprisonment (but escaped after three years), and a friend of Grotius' was beheaded on a charge of high treason. See also BAHRDT 2 n 2. Herbert Marsh (1757–1839), professor of

theology at Cambridge (1807–39), bp of Llandaff (1816), then of Peterborough (from 1819), unrepentant defender of William Frend at his Cambridge "trial" in 1793 (which C attended), editor and translator of Michaelis's *Introduction to the New Testament* (which C drew upon for his theological lectures in 1795: see DAVISON 5 n 1), became notorious for his high-handed attempt to root out Evangelicals from his diocese by insisting that his clergy answer his "eighty-seven questions", known as "a trap to catch Calvinists". This aroused violent op-be useless[2]—Plausible Dullness answers the same purpose for him, that the Goliah Armour of Impudence, the Panoply of Brass, did for his ultra-arminian Predecessor, Heylin.—[3]

6   p xlv, pencil

While living He would urge for the indissolubleness of Wedlock....
    We plight our faith in the face of the *Church* to hold *till death us do part*, not till *Adultery* or any other scandalous cause, which promise ought to be alter'd if we do not think meet to perform it. Upon these and many like considerations...*he* held it more safe to bear with a private inconvenience than alter the antient strictness according to the looseness of our later times...

Hacket was twice married, and each time happily and to the Woman of his Choice.[1] It is easy for such men to talk thus rigidly—Poor Hooker would have held a different Language.[2]

---

position, and led to a small war of pamphlets and two petitions to the House of Lords from those who refused to answer Marsh's "questions". After Sydney Smith had denounced Marsh's policies in a brilliant essay in the *Ed Rev* in Nov 1822, Marsh gradually relaxed the rigour of his rule. In *AR* (1825) 156–7n C quoted **5** textus (extending the last sentence to its completion) as an ideal of moderation that might enlighten the conflict between the evangelical literalists on one side and, on the other, the men of "popish principles"—Marsh and Christopher Wordsworth (1775–1839) (who as master of Trinity College, Cambridge, had become unpopular for his stern discipline).
    5[2] George Pretyman, later Tomline (1750–1827), here called "Pitt Prettyman" because he was tutor to the younger Pitt. See BAXTER *Reliquiae* COPY A **44** [*i*] and n 1, in which C notices Tomline's anti-Calvinism and his Arminianism (for which see also BUNYAN COPY B **7** n 3).
    5[3] For C's adverse view of Heylin as a "bitter factionary" see HEYLYN **4** and n 1. With the "Panoply of Brass" cf "Front o' Brass" in FABER **14** (at n 1).

For "Arminian" as a name for the anti-Calvinist party see FIELD **1** n 2.
    6[1] An account of Hacket's marriages is given at p x. He and his second wife "lived to see 32 Children and Grandchildren before his death".
    6[2] Izaak Walton gives the story in his "Life" of Hooker. Having been well looked after by John Churchman and his wife when he went from Oxford to preach in London, and being "perswaded by her...*that it was best for him to have a Wife*", Hooker asked Mrs Churchman to choose him one, "Promising upon a fair Summons to return to *London*, and accept of her choice". "Now, the Wife provided for him, was her Daughter *Joan*, who brought him neither Beauty nor Portion; and for her Conditions, they were too like that Wife's, which is by *Solomon* compared to a Dripping House: So that he had no reason to *rejoyce in the Wife of his Youth*...And by this means the good man was drawn from the tranquillity of his Colledge: From that Garden of Piety, of Pleasure, of Peace, and a sweet Conversation, into the Thorny Wilderness of a busie World; into those corroding cares that attend a Married Priest, and a Countrey Parsonage...". HOOKER pp 6–7.

7   p 1, pencil | The First Sermon upon the Incarnation

I am in love with my Text [Luke 2.7]; but how shall I open and dilate my joy upon it? No, that most venerable name *Mary*, the *blessed Mother* of our *Lord*, knew not how to do it.

Name = νουμενον, numen.[1]

8   p 3

Moreover as the Woman *Mary* did bring forth the Son who bruised the *Serpents* head, which brought sin into the world by the woman *Eve*, so the *Virgin Mary* was the occasion of Grace, as the *Virgin Eve* was the cause of Damnation: *Eve* had not known *Adam* as yet when she was beguiled, and seduced the man; so *Mary* had not known *Joseph*...and she brought forth her *first born Son*. And thus you see...wisdom did build her self an house.

A Rabbinical Fable or Gloss on Gen. 3.1.[1] Hacket is offensively fond of these worse than silly Vanities.

9   p ⁻4, referring to p 4, pencil, overtraced, marked with a pencil line in the margin

...and why then was he [the Holy Ghost] not called his *Father?* because to be the *father* of another thing is not enough to be the active principle of it: for even the Sun is the active cause that produceth Worms and Flies, and all those which are called *insecta animalia*, and yet it is not called the *father* of those creatures; a *father* must beget a thing according to his own kind and species; and therefore Christ was born after the species and nature of the Woman, whereby he is called not the Son of the *Holy Ghost* but the Son of *Mary*.

p. 4. Latter part of last §ph. but one.

10   p ⁻4, referring to p 5, pencil, overtraced, marked with a pencil line in the margin

The more to illustrate this, you must know that there was a twofold root or foundation of the *Children of Israel* for their temporal being:

7[1] For C's sense of a possible identity between *nomen* (name) and *numen* (divine power, deity), and between *numen* and *noumenon*, see BROWNE *Works* **42** and n 1; cf BIBLE COPY B **33** n 1.

8[1] Gen 3.1, introducing the serpent as "more subtle than any beast of the field which the Lord God had made", does not seem the most apt place for the hypothetical gloss. C may have meant to provide as reference-point the passage that Hacket echoes—Gen 1.15, in which the Lord God said to the serpent: "And I will put enmity between thee and the woman, and between thy seed and her seed; it shall bruise thy head, and thou shalt bruise his heel."

Abraham was the root of the people; the Kingdom was rent from *Saul*, and therefore *David* was the root of the Kingdom....So...as *Abraham* and *David* are roots of the People and Kingdom, especially Christ is called the Son of *David*, the Son of *Abraham*; and to say no more, their Faith in the *Incarnation of Christ* is of some moment in this point.

– 5 a valuable Remark & confirmative of my Convictions respecting the Conversion of the Jews—viz. that whatever was ordained for them, as Abrahamidæ[1] is not repealed by Christianity—but only what appertained to the Republic, Kingdom or State. ~~Ex gr~~. The modern Conversions are in the face of God's Commands.[2]

11 p 5[a]

I come to the third strange condition of the Birth, it was without travel, or the pangs of woman...says St. *Cyprian, Mary* was both the *Mother* and the *Midwife* of the *Child*; far be it from us to think that the weak hand of the woman could facilitate the work which was guided only by the miraculous hand of *God*. The *Virgin* conceived our *Lord* without the Lusts of the flesh, and therefore she had not the pangs and travel of women upon her, she brought him forth without the curse of the flesh. These be the Fathers comparisons, As Bees draw honey from the flower without offending it, as *Eve* was taken out of *Adams* side without any grief to him, as a sprig issues out of the bark of the tree, as the sparkling light from the brightness of the Star, such ease was it to *Mary* to bring forth her first-born Son...

Can we wonder that the strict Protestants were jealous of the Back-sliding of the Arminian Prelatical Clergy & of Laud their Leader,[1] when so strict a Calvinist as B. Hackett could trick himself up in such fantastic rags and lappets of popish Monkery? Could skewer ~~should~~uch frippery patches, cribbed from the Tyring-room of Romish Parthenolatry,[2] on the sober gown and cassock of a Reformed ⟨and Scriptural⟩ Church?

[a] C marked **11** textus with a large **X** in pencil, then wrote his annotation over the pencil mark

10[1] "Sons of Abraham".

10[2] For C on the conversion of the Jews see *CL* v 1–7 (4 Jan 1820) and *TT* 14 Apr 1830.

11[1] See LAUD *The History of the Troubles* (1695) and *The Second Volume of the Remains* (1700). For C on Laud as prelatical and papistic see e.g. DONNE *Sermons* COPY B **1** and n 1 and HEYLYN 17; in *CN* IV 5042 (Oct–Nov 1823) C spoke of Laud as sharing certain views with "the papistic divines", who introduced "Pseudo-Catholicism" with its "spirit-blighting liberticidal effects".

11[2] "Virgin-worship". *OED* notes C's use of "parthenolatry" in this note. See BLANCO WHITE *Practical Evidence* **10** n 2.

12   p ⁻4, referring to p 5, pencil, overtraced | 11 textus

– 5 X a very different §ph![1] and quite on the *Cross* Road to Rome.
It really makes me melancholy—but one of 1000 instances of the
influence of Patristic Learning by which the Reformers of the Latin
Church were distinguished from the Renovators of the Christian
Religion.[2]

13 ˜ pp 7–8

But to say the truth, was he not safer among the beasts than he could
be elsewhere in all the town of *Bethlem*? His enemies perchance would
say unto him as *Jael* did *to Sisera, Turn in, turn in my Lord*, when
she purposed to kill him; as the men of *Keilah* made a fair shew to
give *David* all courteous hospitality, but the issue would prove, if
God had not blessed him, that they mean to deliver him into the
hands of *Saul* that sought his bloud. So there was no trusting of the
Bethlemites, who knows but that they would have prevented *Judas*,
and betrayed him for thirty pieces of Silver unto *Herod*? More
humanity is to be expected from the beasts than from some men, and
therefore she *laid him in a Manger*.

Did not the "Life of Archb. Williams" prove otherwise,[1] I should
have inferred from these Sermons, that H. from his first Boyhood
had been used to make themes, epigrams, copies of verses, &c. on
all the Sundays, Feasts and Festivals of the Church; had found
abundant nourishment for this humour of Points, Quirks, and
Quiddities in the study of the Fathers and Glossers; and remained
an Under-soph all his life long.

I scarcely know what to say. On the one hand, there is a
triflingness, a Shewman or Relique-hawker's Gossip, that stands in
offensive Contrast with the momentous nature of the Subject, and
the dignity of of the ministerial Office, as if a Preacher, having chosen
the Prophets for his theme should entertain his Congregation by
exhibiting a traditional Shaving Rag of Isaiah's with the Prophet's
stubble hair on the dried Soap-sud. And yet on the other hand there
is an innocency in it, a security of Faith, a fullness evinced in the play

---

12[1] I.e. very different from 10 textus—
12 being written immediately below 10.
12[2] For C's view that "patristic
leaven" was a fault see e.g. DONNE
Sermons COPY B 1 and n 3 and HERBERT
16 and n 1. See also 13, below.

13[1] I.e. HACKET *Scrinia Reserata*,
which, according to 24, below, C had
read before writing at least some of these
annotations. In *CIS* p 52n HNC printed
the first paragraph of this note, adding 24
to it.

and plash of its overflowing that at other times give me the same sort
of pleasure as the sight of Blackber⟨r⟩y Bushes and Children's
Handkerchief Gardens on the slopes of a rampart, the Promenade
of some peaceful old town, that stood its last siege in the 30 Years'
War.

14　p 14 | The Second Sermon upon the Incarnation [Luke 2.8]

Tiberius propounded his mind to the Senate of *Rome*, that Christ,
the great Prophet in *Jury*, should be had in the same *honour* with the
other *Gods* which they worship in the *Capitol*. The motion did not
please them, says *Eusebius*, and this was all the fault, because he was
a *God*, not of their own, but of *Tiberius* invention...

Here, I own, the negative evidence of the Silence of Seneca, and
Suetonius, above all of Tacitus and Pliny outweighs in my mind the
positive testimony of Eusebius—which rested, I suspect, on the same
Ground with the Letters of Pontius Pilate so boldly appealed to by
Tertullian.—[1]

15　p 22 | The Third Sermon upon the Incarnation [Luke 2.9]

Finally, their bodies after they had appear'd to discharge their
embassage, vanisht into elements never to return again into that
composition, but our bodies shall revive out of that dust into which
they were dissolv'd, and live for ever in the resurrection of the
righteous.

I never could satisfy myself as to the continuance and catholicity of
this strange Egyptian Tenet in the very face of S[t] Paul's indignant,
"Thou fool! *not* that &c."[1]

I have at times almost been tempted to conjecture that Paul taught
a different doctrine from the ~~other~~ ~~Apostles~~ Palestine Disciples on
this point/ and that the Church preferred the sensuous and therefore
more popular Belief of the Evangelists κατα σαρκα[2] to the ⟨more⟩

14[1] C has evidently no detailed
memory of the numerous discussions of
this question. Hacket's reference (un-
stated) is to Eusebius *Ecclesiastica his-
toria* 2.2, quoting Tertullian *Apologeticus*
5. Earlier in 2.2, in much the same words
as Tertullian *Apologeticus* 21, Eusebius
mentions that Pontius Pilate reported to
Tiberius on the death of Christ. Such a
report might well have been made, but

only late forgeries of the correspondence
between Pilate and Tiberius exist.

15[1] 1 Cor 15.36: "Thou fool, that
which thou sowest is not quickened,
except it die". Cf **22** (at n 2), below.

15[2] The Gospels "according to the
flesh"—the gospels that record the life of
Jesus from a human point of view—i.e.
Matthew, Mark, and Luke. See BLANCO
WHITE *Practical Evidence* **1** n 2.

intelligible faith of the spiritual Sage of "the other Athens". (For so Tarsus was called.)[3]

16 pp 23–4

As an evil *Angel* did co-operate to bring death into the world, so a good *Angel* was a choice instrument to bring the tidings of salvation: for why did the Son of *God* take flesh? to repair the fall of man.... *Paul* enforceth modesty to the *Corinthian* women in the house of Prayer because of the *Angels*, 1 Cor. 11. 10. *Angelos testes habent honesti pudoris aut impudentiae*, as the most expound, the Angels make one congregation with us, and therefore they are witnesses of their modesty or impudence.

And was there no symptom of a commencing relapse to the errors of that Church which had equalled the traditions of men, yea, the dreams of Phantasts,[1] with the Revelations of God, when a chosen Elder with the Law of Truth before him, and professing to divide & distribute the Bread of Life, could §ph after §ph, ~~could~~ place such unwholsome Vanities before his Flock, without even a hint, which might apprize them that they gew-gaw Comfits were not part of the Manna from Heaven! All this superstitious trash about Angels, which the Jews learnt from the Persian Legends, asserted as confidently as if Hacket had translated it, word for word, from one of the 4 Gospels![2]

[a]Salmasius (if I mistake not) supposes the original word to have been = Bachelors, young unmarried Men.[3] Others interpret Angels

---

[a] This paragraph, which begins at the head of p 24 without any space being left at the end of the first paragraph (at the foot of p 23), could be a separate annotation referring to the second paragraph of textus

15[3] I.e. Paul of Tarsus, who referred to his birthplace as "no mean city" (Acts 21.39). The earliest records of Tarsus, at the mouth of the river Cydnus on the south-east coast of Asia Minor, the scene of Antony's meeting with Cleopatra, are of the ninth century B.C. After the founding of a celebrated philosophical school there, Tarsus became under Augustus (63 B.C.–A.D. 14) a centre of intellectual life—according to Lemprière, "the rival of Alexandria and Athens in literature and the study of the polite arts".

16[1] By a "Phantast" C means a visionary or dreamer, and usually spelled the word as here (but cf "Fantast" in BROWNE *Works* 1) in order to recall the Greek origin of the word in φαντάζειν,

thereby avoiding the sense of fantastical, eccentric. See e.g. FLEURY **55**, HEINROTH **37** n 1 ("phantastery"), *BL* ch 9 (*CC*) I 149, *Friend* (*CC*) I 494n.

16[2] For C's distaste for the doctrine of angels see e.g. BIBLE COPY B **135** n 1, GREW **39** and n 1, HOOKER **19–21**, and cf FIELD **3** (at n 1). The two paragraphs following comprise a key discussion of the subject.

16[3] C's source is untraced. In *Epistola ad Andream Colvium: super cap. XI. Primae ad Corinth. Epist. de caesarie virorum et mulierum coma* (Leyden 1644) 698–701 Salmasius argues against those who thought that "angels" here meant bishops, that St Paul would certainly not have debased the word by using it of men.

as meaning the Bishop and Elders of the Church.[4] More probably it was a proverbial expression, derived from the Cherubim in the Temple: as the country-folks used to say to Children—Take care! the Fairies will hear you. It was a common notion among the Jews in the time of St Paul, that these Angels were employed in carrying up the⟨ir⟩ Prayers to the Throne of God. See the Apocalypse.[5] Of course, they must have been in ⟨special⟩ attendance in ~~the~~ a House of Prayer.

After much search and much thought on the subject of Angels, as a diverse *Kind* of finite Beings, I find no sufficing reason to hold it for a revealed doctrine. And if not revealed, it is assuredly no truth of Philosophy, which can conceive but three kinds. 1. The Infinite Reason: 2. the Finite rational: & 3. the finite irrational—i.e. God, Man, and Beast.[6] What indeed even for the Vulgar is or can an Archangel be, but a Man with wings, better or worse than the wingless Species according as the Feathers are white or black? I would that the word had been translated instead of Anglicized in our English Bible!—

17^a p ⁻4, referring to p 24

The *Incarnation* of Christ is, I may say, the perfection of all things in the world; and therefore good reason that all creatures should have some participation and interest in it. Men did share in him in his own sex and person, women in the Womb that bare him: poor men in the Shepherds, great ones in the sages of the East: the Beasts by the stable wherein he was born: the Earth in the Gold that was offered: the Trees in the Myrrhe and Frankincense; and to reckon up no more, the Heavens in the Star that blaz'd: all the works of God, even they which by natural obedience bless him and magnifie him for ever, did claim some office to make one in the solemnity when their *Creator* was born. Why surely some room was left for the *Angels*, it was fit they should be in the train at the *Inauguration* of this *mighty Prince*,

^{a} Continuing from 2, above

16[4] See n 3, above.

16[5] Rev 1.20: "...The seven stars are the angels [messengers] of the seven churches...". For "the angel of the church" see Rev. 2.1, 12. For the angels carrying prayers see Rev 8.3, 4.

16[6] For this threefold division see HOOKER **21** and cf HEINROTH **3**. In *CN* IV 4633 (c 1819–20) C noted: "The Inhabitants [of Jupiter and Sirius] must be either Men or Beasts—. For we might as well attempt to conceive more than three Dimensions of Space as to imagine more than three kinds of living Existence, God, Man, and Beast—& even of these the last is obscure...passing into an unripe or degenerate species of humanity". See also e.g. BÖHME **84** and DE WETTE **28**; and cf *Scrinia* **24** n 1.

and their place, according to their dignity was very honourable; they were *Gods Embassadors*: and as if they had a *Patent* to use their office frequently, they had many errands from Heaven, to *Mary*, to *Joseph*, to the *Shepherds*...

24. 3. a pretty piece of Poetry, and as prettily worded./

17A   p 27, marked with an ink line in the margin (the page noted in **2**)

By this it appears how suitably a beam of admirable light did concur in the *Angels* message to set out the *Majesty* of the *Son* of *God*; and I beseech you observe, all you that would keep a good *Christmas* as you ought, that the glory of *God* is the best celebration of his *Sons Nativity*; and all your pastimes and mirth (which I disallow not, but rather commend in moderate use) must so be manag'd, without riot, without surfeiting, without excessive gaming, without pride and vain pomp, in harmlessness, in sobriety as if the glory of the *Lord* were round about us. *Christ* was born to save them that were lost, but frequently you abuse his Nativity with so many vices, such disordered outrages; so that you make this happy time an occasion for your loss rather than for your salvation. Praise him in the congregation of the people, praise him in your inward heart, praise him with the sanctity of your life, praise him in your charity to them that need and are in want. This is the glory of *God* shining round, and the most *Christian* solemnizing of the *Birth* of *Jesus*.[1]

18   p 339[a] | The Fourteenth Sermon upon Our Saviours Tentation [Matt 4.8]

As the Temptation is found in all three Gospels, and in all that the Fathers of the first and second Century used, it must have formed part of the Proto-evangellion or Original Gospel[1] From the Apostles therefore and from some or all who had heard the account from our Lord himself. How then are we [to][b] understand it? To confute the whims and superstitious nugacities of these Sermons, and the hundred other comments & interpretations ejusdem farinæ[2] would be a sad waste of Time. Yet some meaning and that worthy of Christ it must have had—The struggle with the Suggestions of the evil principle, first, to force his way & compel belief by a succession

---

a Written in the blank space at the end of the sermon   *b* Word supplied by the editor

17A[1] In *LR* III 178 HNC supplied a comment of C's not present in the ms: "The following paragraph is one of Hacket's sweetest passages. It is really a beautiful little hymn."

18[1] Mark 1.12–13; Matt 4.1–11; Luke 4.1–13.
18[2] "Of the same stuff".

of Miracles, disjoined from moral & spiritual purpose, Miracles for Miracles' sake—2ᵈ. Doubts of his Messianic Character & Divinity & temptations to try it by some *Ordeal* at the risk of certain Death—3. To interpret his Mission as his Countrymen generally did, that of Conquest & Royalty.

19   p 449ᵃ | The Fourth Sermon upon the Transfiguration [Luke 9.33]

I could wish that my self were accursed from Christ for my brethren, my kinsmen according to the flesh, Rom. ix.3.

Paul does not say—I *would* decide; nor does he speak of any deliberated *Result* of his Considerations; but representings the a transient passion of his Soul,* ⟨an actual, but *undetermined, Impulse,*⟩ as a striking proof of the *exceeding* Interest, which he continued to feel in the welfare of his Countrymen. His heart so swelled with Love and Compassion for them, that if it were possible, if Reason & Conscience permitted it, Methinks (says he) I *could* wish that myself were accursed if so they might be saved—Might not a mother figuring to herself *as* possible & existing an impossible or *not* existing remedy for a dying child, [have]ᵇ exclaimed—O I *could fly* to the ends of the Earth to procure it!—Let it not be irreverent, if I refer to the fine passage in Shakespear, Hotspur's rapture-like Reverie, so often ridiculed by shallow wits[1]—In great Passion Man the *Crust Opake* of present & existing weakness and boundedness is, as it were, fused & vitrified for the moment—and thro' the transparency Man the Soul catches a gleam of the infinity of the Potential in the will ⟨of Man—⟩ reads the future for the present. Percy[2] is rapt in the contemplation of the physical might inherent in the concentrated Will, the inspired Apostle in the sudden sense of the depth of its moral Strength.—

    * An impulse in and for itself, in the moment of its ebullience, and not completed by an Act & Confirmation of the Will.

ᵃ The textus is on p 448, with C's " * "; the annotation is written in the blank space at the end of the sermon, directly opposite the textus
ᵇ Word supplied by the editor

19[1] *1 Henry IV* II iii 1–35.
19[2] I.e. Hotspur, the sobriquet of Henry Percy, son of the Earl of Northumberland.

Aphorism VI of the Aphorisms on Spiritual Religion in *AR* (1825) 146–7 is taken from this p 449, on which C wrote this annotation.

20 p 550, pencil, overtraced | The First Sermon upon the Resurrection [Acts 2.24]

...St. *Austin* and *Epiphanius* in their Catalogues of Hereticks rehearse more Adversaries against the Resurrection of Christ than any other doctrinal Point that concerns our Salvation. *Simon Magus* wrote many books against it. *Basilides*, a venemous *Dogmatist*, taught that Christ as he was led to be crucified vanished away by Art and Praestigiation, and that *Simon* of *Cyrene*, who bore his Cross some part of the way, was put to death in his stead, but that *Jesus* did never die, and therefore was never raised from the dead. The dross of so many Heresies was strained through these wicked wits, that the *Church* might enjoy truth more triumphantly after such great resistance.

One great Error of Textual Divines is their inadvertence to the dates, occasion, object, and circumstances, at & under which the words were written or spoken. Thus the simple assertion of one or two *Facts introductory to* the Teaching of the X^{tn} Religion, is taken as comprizing or constituting the Xtian Religion. Hence the disproportionate weight laid on the simple fact of the Resurrection of Jesus, detached from the mysteries of the Incarnation & Redemption.

21 p 551, pencil, overtraced

St. *Austin* says that *Tully* in his 3. *lib. de Repub.* disputed against the reuniting of soul and body. His Argument was, To what end? Where should they remain together? For a body cannot be assumed into heaven. I believe *God* caused those famous monuments of his Wit to perish, because of such impious opinions wherewith they were farced.

I believe, however, that these books have ~~been~~ recently themselves enjoyed a resurrection by the labor of Angelo Mai.[1]

22 p 553, pencil, overtraced

And let any equal Auditor judge if *Job* were not an *Anti-Socinian*, *Job* xix. 26. *Though after my skin worms destroy this body, yet in my*

21[1] Angelo Mai (1782–1854) published in 1822 in Rome the first edition of the surviving books of Cicero's *De republica* from a ms of c fifth or sixth century A.D. that he discovered in 1820 in the Vatican Library. C quotes from another of Mai's sensational discoveries in *EOT* (*CC*) III 260 (c 1820). This passage—*De republica* 3.28—has been preserved only by its being quoted by St Augustine in *De civitate dei* 22.4, and by Lactantius, the ms of bk 3 being faulty.

flesh shall I see God, whom I shall behold for my self, and mine eyes shall see, and not another. And is it not equity, that the righteous in the same body wherein they have worshipped *God* they shall be glorified, that the wicked in the same body wherein they have lusted after evil things they shall be punished?...as *God* raised up Christ, so he will raise us up in our own bodies.

This text rightly rendered is nothing to the purpose, but refers to the dire cutaneous disease, with which Job was afflicted. It is merely an expression of Job's Confidence of his being justified in the eyes of *men* and in this life./[1]

P.S. In the whole wide Range of theological Mirabilia I know of none stranger than the general Agreement of Orthodoxists to forget to ask themselves, *what* they precisely meant by the Body. Christ's & Paul's meaning is evident enough—i.e. Personality[2]

23 p 553, pencil, overtraced

First, St. *Chrysostomes* judgment upon it ["having loosed the pains of death"] is, that when Christ came out of the Grave death it self !!—] was delivered from pain and anxiety...death knew it held him captive whom it ought not to have seized upon, and therefore it suffered torments like a woman in travel, till it had given him up again. Thus he. But the Scripture elsewhere testifies that death was put to sorrow, because it had lost its sting, rather than released from sorrow by our *Saviours* Resurrection.

Most noticeable!

Mem. The influence of the surrounding Myriotheism—*Dea Mors*—/[1]

22[1] For C's version of this passage in Job 19 see BIBLE COPY B **27** and n 1 and DONNE *Sermons* COPY B **88**.

22[2] Cf **15**, above. C is thinking of Paul's doctrine in 1 Cor 15, in which there is some tension between the Greek view that the body is a handicap to the soul and the Hebrew view (which Paul espouses) that a man is incomplete without a body. Paul's solution, less forthright than C suggests, is that a mortal body (ψυχικόν, of the soul, or "natural" in AV) is buried, and that an immortal body (πνευματικόν, of the spirit) is raised up. See, however, DONNE *Sermons* COPY B **79** and n 1, **83**, **88** and n 2. Cf the statement that "*Spirits* are not necessarily Souls or I's" in HILLHOUSE **1** (at n 13); see also HUGHES **1** and n 6 and *CN* IV 4935.

23[1] "Surrounding"—i.e. in the lifetime of St Chrysostom, c 347–407. "Belief in a myriad of gods"—*OED* cites this note from *LR* III 183—accounts for the implied "*Goddess* Death". Here Hacket is referring to Acts 2.24 (the text of the sermon), in which St Peter is speaking.

24 p 557

Let any competent Judge read Hackett's Life of Archbishop Williams,[1] and then these Sermons—and so measure the stultifying nugifying[2] effect of the Study of the Fathers, and the prepossession in favor of Patristic Authorities, on the Minds of our Church Dignitaries in general, in the reign of Charles I.—[3]

24[1] I.e. HACKET *Scrinia Reserata*, as in **13** (at n 1), above.

24[2] *OED* cites this use of "nugifying"

from *LR* III 183; cf C's use of "nugacities" in **18**, above.

24[3] On "patristic" influence see **12** and n 2, above. See also FIELD **59**.

Scrinia Reserata: a memorial offer'd to the great deservings of John Williams, D.D. who some time held the places of Ld Keeper of the Great Seal of England, Ld Bishop of Lincoln, and Ld Archbishop of York. Containing a series of the most remarkable occurrences and transactions of his life, in relation both to Church and State, &c. 2 pts in 1 vol. London 1693. F°.

British Museum Ashley 4779

Bookplate of James Gillman the younger on p ⁻4 (p–d). On p ⁻3 Gillman's initials "JG" are written in pencil in the space between **40** and **8**.

Passages are marked with a pencil line or an X in the margin on i 12, 14, 15, 54, 75, 79, 85, 87, 152, 216, 223; ii 27, 30, 34, 35, 36, 37, 39, 40, 165, 166, 167, 183, 209, 226, 227. On ii 210 a date has been corrected in ink.

Tipped into this copy at the end: Edmund Gosse's review of *Ashley LC* VIII in the *Sunday Times* 15 May 1927 and two proof copies of both the reproductions in *Ashley LC* VIII 111–12.

DATE. c 1823, before 9 Sept, to 1833 (the date of **4** and **33**).

By 9 Sept 1823 C had made, for his Life of Leighton, "my laborious Collation" of several books including "Hacket"—i.e. *Scrinia Reserata. CL* v 300; and see Gilbert BURNET *Memoires* for C's reading of some of these books in the Sion College Library. Three references to *Scrinia* in N 30 point to a reading in 1823. A reliable division of notes into the two dates does not seem possible; **5** and **12** were written in 1824 or later, **17** in 1829 or later, and **47** is associated with 1833 through a parallel in N 52 (see n 4).

1   p ⁻2

Prudence installed *as* Virtue, instead of being *employed* as one of her indispensable Handmaids/[1] *this* the character of the Divines & Statesmen from Henry VIIIth to the Civil War—& the products of this exemplified & illustrated in the Life of Archbishop Williams—is a Work, I could warmly recommend to my dearest Hartley Coleridge. A man bred up to the determination of being *righteous*, both honorablbly striving, and selfishly ambitious, but all within the bounds & permission of the LAW (even the reigning System of Casuistry)—in short, a ~~World~~ *Legalist* in Morals, and a Worldling in impulses & motives—and yet by pride and by innate nobleness of Nature munificent, and benevolent—With all the negative virtues of temperance, chastity &c—take this man on his road to his own worldly aggrandizement, thridding his way thro' a crowd of powerful Rogues, by flattery, professions of devoted attachment, and by actual & zealous as well as able Services, till at length he has in fact been

[1] See **4** and n 2, below.

as great a knave, as the Knaves (Duke of Buckingham ex. gr.)[2] whose favor & support he had been conciliating—till at last in some dilemma, some strait between Conscience & Fear, and p increased confidence in his own political strength, he opposes or hesitates to further some too foolish or wicked project of his Patron Knave, or affronts his pride by counselling a different course, (*not* as less wicked but as more profitable & conducive to his Grace's Elevation), and is floored or crushed by him, & falls unknown & unpitied—. Such that truly wonderful School[a] & Statesman, Arch[b] Williams.—

S. T. C.

2 p ⁻2, referring to p 50, pencil | I § 61

" Before I proceed, though Anger be an Enemy to Counsel, I confess I cannot refrain to be angry; O hearken not to *Rhehoboams* Ear-Wigs, drive them away to the Gibbet, which they deserve, that would incite the King to Collections of Aid, without concurrence of his Parliament. God bless us from those Scorpions, which certainly would beget a popular Rage. An English mans Tribute comes not from the King's Exaction, but by the peoples free Oblation, out of the Mouth of their Representatives. Indeed our Ancient Kings from the beginning did not receive, but impose Subsidies.... And God forbid that any other Course should be Attempted. For this Liberty was settled on the Subject, with such Imprecations upon the Infringers, that if they should remove these great Land-Marks, they must look for Vengeance, as if Entail'd by publick Vows on them and their Posterity." These were the *Deans* Instructions...

P. 50
What a damning Contrast to the despotic Philo-despot, Laud!—[b1]

3 p ⁻3, referring to p 63,[c] pencil, marked with a pencil line in the margin | I § 73

That in the instability of humane things, every man must look for a Dissolution of his Fortunes, as well as for the Dissolution of his

---

[a] A slip for "Scholar"
[b] *LR* reads: "He deserves great credit for them. They put him in strong contrast with Laud."
[c] See 39 n *b*, below

1[2] George Villiers, 1st Duke of Buckingham (1592–1628), court favourite first of James I, then of Charles I, exerting a potent and sinister influence upon public affairs. See **32** and n 2, below. In **6**, below, C speaks of him as the "*beslobbered* Minion" of James. In BM Egerton MS 2800 f 170ᵛ C summarises the views of Hacket and of Walter Scott in *Nigel*

which make him "The completest & most fascinating Man & Courtier in Europe". 2[1] *OED* cites C's use of "Philodespot" in a letter of 1796: see *CL* I 208. Cf also "Philo-despotist" in BARCLAY COPY B **2**. For C on Laud see also *Century* **11** and n 1, BAXTER *Reliquiae* COPY B **76** n 1, and LAUD.

Body; the latter, of sure Things is most sure; the former, of usual Things is most usual. Common Men are in doubtful Places; great men of slippery Places; but Sacrilege, being a Raven that continually croaks over the Church-Patrimony, Clergy-men were in most obnoxious Places. Many have paid dear for this Experience, That Fortune will fly quite away, when she is well fledge. Then let such as are upon the highest Stairs of those Preferments, have this Forecast, To keep a little Room behind their Back-door, to which they may retreat.

p 63

4 i 69 | 1 § 80

What true Applause and Admiration the King and your Honour have gained for that gracious, and most Christian-like Remorse shewed the E. of *Southampton*, a Delinquent by his own Confession, I refer to the Relation of others, lest I might be suspected to amplifie any thing, which my self had propounded.... Now poor Mr. *Selden* flies to the same Altar of Mercy, and humbly Petitioneth your Lordship's Mediation and Furtherance. He, and the World, take knowledge of that Favour your Lordship hath ever afforded my motions, and my self without the motion of any, and so draweth me along to Entreat for him.... I presume therefore to leave him to your Lordship's Mercy and Charity.

All this WE (1833) should call abject, base; but was it so in Bp. Williams? In the History of the Morality of a People, Prudence, yea, Cunning, *is* the ⟨earlier⟩ *Form* of Virtue.—Jacob, Ulysses—.[1] Then. All the most ancient Fables.

It will require the true philosophic Calm and Serenity to distinguish and appreciate the Character of the Morality, of our great men, from Henry 8th to the close of James I—(the motto, nullum numen abest, si sit *Prudentia*)[2] and of that of Charles I to the Restoration/—The difference almost amounts to Contrast.

4[1] Although it was known by divine oracle that Jacob would triumph over his elder brother (Gen 25.23), Jacob nevertheless by treacherous guile first stole Esau's birthright (Gen 25.29–34) and then his blessing (Gen 27). In Homer, Ulysses is represented as cunning and a fluent liar.

4[2] "No god is missing from our side, if only *Prudence* is there". Cf Juvenal *Satires* 10.365–6, which reads (tr): "You have no divine power, Fortune, if we have prudence; it is we that make you a divinity." See also **29** (at n 1) and **31** (at n 2), below.

5 i 70–1 | 1 § 81

The Lord-Keeper being so great a Dealer in the Golden Trade of Mercy, and so successful, he followed his Fortune, and tried the King and the Lord Marquess further in the behalf of some, whom their dear Friends had given over in Despair to the Destiny of Restraint. ...The Earl of *Northumberland* had been a Prisoner in the *Tower* above 15 years.

How is it that so deeply read [a]*[a]* Historian, as Southey is,*[b]* should not have seen, how imperfect and precarious the rights of personal Liberty were, during this period? or seeing it, do such scanty Justice to the Patriots under Charles I?[1]—The truth is, that from the reign of Edward I. (to go no farther backward) there was a Spirit of freedom in the people at large, which all our Kings in their senses were cautious not to awaken by too rudely treading on it; but for Individuals, as such, there was none till the conflict with the Stuarts—[2]

6 i 72 | 1 § 84 Speech of Williams to "a mighty Confluence" at the Court of Chancery

For my Calling unto this Office, it was...not the Cause, but the Effect of a Resolution in the State, to Change or Reduce the Governour of this Court from a Professor of our municipal Laws to some one of the Nobility, Gentry, or Clergy of this Kingdom. Of such a Conclusion of State (quae aliquando incognita, semper justa) *as I dare not take upon me to discover the Cause, so I hope I shall not endure the Envy....*

This perversion of words respecting the decrees of Providence to the caprices of James and his *beslobbered* Minion, the D. of b.,[1] is somewhat nearer to Blasphemy, than even the *Euphuisms* of the Age can excuse.

7 i 73, marked with an ink line in the margin | 1 § 85

It was (without the least Inclination or thought of mine own) the immediate work of God and the King: And their Actions are no ordinary Effects, but extraordinary Miracles. What then? Should I beyond the Limits and Duty of Obedience despond, and refuse to

[a] Word supplied by the editor
[b] This clause omitted in *LR*

5[1] See **12** and n 1, below, and cf **49** (at n 1), below.

5[2] In BM Egerton MS 2800 f 170 C quotes *Scrinia* i 112 (var): "What a world of Love and Bee-like Loyalty and Heart-adherence did the Stuarts trick and tyrannize away.—/"

6[1] For C on the Duke of Buckingham see **1** n 2, above.

*] make some few years Tryal in this place? Nor,—*Tuus, O Jacobe, quod optas Explorare labor, mihi jussa capessere fas est* ["Your task it is, O James, to decide what are your wishes; for me it is proper to execute your commands": *Aeneid* 1.77 (var)]. I will therefore conclude this Point with the Excuse of that Poet, whom the Emperor *Gratian* would needs enforce to set out his Poem, whether he would or no...*I am no way fit for this great Place, but because God and the King will have it so, I will endeavour, as much as I can, to make my self fit, and put my whole confidence in his Grace and Mercy...*

* In our times this would be pedantic Wit: in the days of James I. & in the mouth of Archb.P Williams it was witty Pedantry.[1] *S. T. C.*

8 i 75 | 1 § 89

...Our time is but a Span long, but he that doth much in a short Life products his Mortality. To this he had such a Velocity of mind, that out of a few Words discreetly spoken, he could apprehend the Strength and Sirrup of that which would follow. This is that Ingeny which is so much commended. [Cicero] 4. *Tuscul. Multarum rerum* percursio[a]] *brevi tempore percussio*...[1]

Mem.—"products" for "produces"—i.e. lengthens out—ut *apud geometros*./[2] but why B.P Hacket did not say "prolongs", I know not—

9 i 75 and p −3[b]

See what a Globe of Light there is in natural Reason, which is the same in every Man; but when it takes well, and riseth to perfection, it is call'd Wisdom in a few.

The GOOD affirming itself (the WILL = I AM) begetteth the TRUE: and Wisdom is the Spirit proceeding. But in the popular acceptation, ~~of the word,~~ Common sense in an uncommon degree is ~~not~~ what Men mean by Wisdom—

p. 75.

Common Sense in an uncommon degree is what the World calls Wisdom.[1]

[a] In pencil
[b] The annotations on p −3 are written in the order 39, 3, 22, 41, 9 (par 2), 20

7[1] In the passage that Hacket quotes from Virgil in textus Aeneas is addressing Dido.

8[1] "The review of many things in a short time". C's emendation is correct.

8[2] "As *with geometricians*". In giving examples of "product" (verb) in all three main senses of "produce" *OED* quotes this particular use by Hacket.

9[1] Cf *AR* (1825) 252–3n: "The Common Sense of a People is the moveable *index* of its average judgment and information." See also e.g. *BL* ch 4 (*CC*) I 86–7n and *SM* (*CC*) 110.

10   i 79 | 1 § 92

A well-spirited Clause, and agreeable to Holy Assurance, that Truth is more like to win, than lose. Could the Light of such a Gospel as we profess, be eclips'd with the Interposition of a single Marriage? And yet Hacket must have lived to see the practical confutation of this shallow Gnathonism[1] in the results of the marriage with the papist, Henrietta of France!—[2]

10A   i 81 | 1 § 94

...Both these Assertions, if men were peaceably disposed, and affected, the Dispatch of the common Business, might easily be reconciled.

11   i 83 | 1 § 96

Among other passages of his Reviling Throat, it was proved against him, that he had said, that our Bishops were no Bishops, but were *]Lay-men, and Usurpers of that Title. *Floud,* says the Lord Keeper, *Since I am no Bishop in your Opinion, I will be no Bishop to you.* I concur with my Lords (the like I never did before) in your Corporal punishment.

* I see the *wit* of this speech; but the WISDOM, the *Christianity,* the *beseemingness in a Judge and a Bishop?*—HEM![1]

12   i 83

The Officers that are yet alive will say as much...that the Fines of the Court were never shorn down so near before: And after the

10[1] Sycophancy, parasitism; from Gnatho, name of a parasite in Terence *Eunuchus. OED* gives examples of various cognates naturalised in English, but for "gnathonism" cites only this use of C's (from *LR* III 187).

10[2] Henrietta Maria (1609–69), youngest child of Henry IV of France, married Charles I in 1625 after attempts to achieve the "Spanish Match" had been abandoned: see **19** and n 1, below. Although Charles promptly disregarded the undertaking given in the marriage treaty to relieve the English Catholics, Henrietta was allowed openly to practise her religion and to maintain influen-

tial relations with Church authorities in France and Rome. Her politically naïve intrigues to raise military and financial support for her husband after the dissolution of the Short Parliament (May 1640) played an important part, in the end, in ensuring Charles's execution.

11[1] Williams, according to Hacket, had previously stated that he "never condemn'd an Offender to be Branded, to be Scourg'd, to have his Ears cut", accepting the opinion of Lord Coke that "the Canons of Councils had forbidden Bishops to Act any thing, to the drawing of blood in a judicial Form".

Period of his Presidency [of the Star Chamber], it is too well known how far the Enhancements were stretch'd. *But the wringing of the Nose bringeth forth Blood*, Prov. 30. 33.

Southey[a] might have learnt from this and 50 other passages, that it did not require the factious prejudices of Prynne or Burton to look with aversion on the proceedings of Laud.[1] Bp. Hacket was as hot a *royalist* as a *loyal* Englishman could be./ yet Laud was allii nimis.[2]

13 i 84–5 | I § 97

New Stars have appeard and vanish'd; the ancient Asterisms remain, there's not an old Star missing.

[a] Southey's name omitted in *LR*

12[1] C refers to "A Speech Delivered in the Star-Chamber...at the Censure of J. Bastwick, H. Burton, and W. Prinn" in LAUD *The Second Volume of the Remains* (1700), which C read in the Sion College copy in autumn 1823. He is probably not thinking here of any particular statement by RS in e.g. *The Book of the Church*; an example of the "50 other passages" in Hacket would be *Scrinia* ii 86 (II §85) on the severity of the attack by Williams on Laud. In several notebook entries of 1823 C criticised RS and the *QR* reviewers, not least for manipulating biographical and documentary evidence according to principles of "prejudice & Partiality". See e.g. *CN* IV 4985, in H. COLERIDGE **23** n 1. In *CN* IV 5026 (c 15 Oct 1823) he rejected the proposition advanced by "your modern Impartialist" that Hacket as "the Zealous Friend of Archbishop Williams" could be no reliable witness against Laud "when no other perhaps could have come at the information". Cf *CN* IV 5057. See also *CN* IV 5042 (c Oct–Nov 1823): "Let ὕΣΣε [RS] ask himself whether the spirit-blighting liberticidal Effects of Pseudo-Catholicism can rationally be attributed to those particulars, dogmatic or ceremonial, which Arch. bishop Laud continued to reject, and disown? Or not rather to the points, as to which he was one with the papistic Divines, and their Competitor in the race of Persecution?" For ΥΣΣΕ as a name for RS, occurring variatim in all the references except *CN* IV 5057, see H. COLERIDGE **23** n 1.

William Prynne (1600–69), barrister and Puritan pamphleteer, after a year's imprisonment for alleged attacks on the King's honour, was in 1634 condemned to life imprisonment, degraded and fined, and brutally pilloried. From the Tower he continued to write and publish, and in 1637, with Henry Burton (1578–1648), Puritan divine, was charged with sedition. Both were condemned to life imprisonment, to be fined and degraded, and pilloried; their punishment was carried out with notable inhumanity. In these proceedings Laud had played a commanding rôle. As soon as the first Long Parliament was in session petitions were presented on behalf of both Prynne and Burton. In Mar 1641 their sentences were declared illegal and both were released. By then Laud had been impeached and imprisoned by the same Parliament. In the trial that followed in 1644 Prynne prosecuted Laud with intense animosity, manipulating evidence in a way that altered the charges to the capital offence of sedition. Laud was beheaded on Tower Hill on 10 Jan 1645.

12[2] Literally "too much garlic", i.e. too severe; or, with a double slip—C perhaps attracted towards the spelling of ἄλλος (other)—"too much the other way". I.e. whereas Hacket's true loyalty could be held in question because of his great leniency (the subject of i 82–3), Laud's genuine loyalty could be disregarded because of his punitive severity.

If they had, they would not have been old.—This therefore, like many of Lord Bacon's Illustrations, have more wit than meaning.[1] But it is a good trick of Rhetoric—The vividness of the Image ~~makes the~~ per se makes men overlook the imperfection of the Simile: "You see my *Hand*—the hand of a poor puny fellow-mortal: and will you pretend not to see the hand of Providence in this business? He who sees a mouse, must be wilfully blind if he does not see an Elephant."—

14 i 87–8 | I §100

A few things more… were thought meet to be Castigated in Preachers at that time.… To *Be subject to the Higher Powers*, is a constant and a general Rule; and Reason can discern, that the Supreme Majesty, which unquestionably is in our King, is inviolable.

The Error of the first James,[1] an ever well-intending, well-resolving but alas! ill-performing Monarch, a kind-hearted, affectionate and fondling old Man, really and extensively learned yea, and as far as quick Wit, and a shrewd Judgement go to the making up of Wisdom, wise in his generation,[2] and ⟨a⟩ pedant by the right of pedantry conceded at that time to all Men of Learning—(Bacon, for example) his Error, I say, consisted in the notion, that because the Stalk and Foliage were originally contained in the Seed, and were derived from it, that therefore they remained so in point of right after their Evolution.[3] The Kingly Power was the Seed: the H. of Commons and the municipal Charters and Privileges the Stalk & Foliage. The Unity of the Realm, or what we mean by the Constitution, is the Root—. Mean while the Seed is gone, and reappears as the Crown and glorious Flower of the Plant.—But James was an Angel compared with his Son and Grandsons/[4] as Williams to Laud, so James I to Charles I./

S. T. C.

13[1] For Bacon's "fondness for point and antithesis…where we must often disturb the sound in order to arrive at the sense", and his "faulty *verbal* antitheses", see *Friend* (*CC*) I 487, 489 and n.

14[1] James I (1566–1625), King of Scotland from 24 Jul 1567, became King of England on 24 Mar 1603 on the death of Elizabeth.

14[2] Cf Ecclus 44.7.

14[3] For a similar statement about James I see *TT* 15 May 1833.

14[4] For C on Charles I see e.g. **45** and n 1, below; on Charles II see HOOKER **1**; on James II see **49** and n 1, below. Cf *CN* IV 5055 (c Oct–Nov 1823): "A wise & rightly feeling Historian will find it hard to decide which on the whole was the more despicable & worthless character, of the four Stuart kings—all cruel, all liars, all morally cowards, and two loathsome…".

15 i 90, marked with an ink line in the margin | 1 §102

Restraint is not a Medicine to cure epidemical Diseases; for Sin becomes more sinful by the Occasion of the Law.

A most judicious Remark.

16 i 92–3 | 1 § 104

Concerning that Offence, taken by many people, both this side the Borders, and in *Scotland,* from that Clemency, which his Majesty was pleased to extend to the Imprisoned Lay-Recusants of this Kingdom...In the general, as the Sun in the Firmament appears unto us no bigger then a Platter, and the Stars but as so many Nails in the Pomel of a Saddle, because of that Esloignment and Disproportion between our Eyes and the Object: So there is such an un-measurable distance betwixt the deep Resolution of a Prince, and the shallow Apprehension of Common and Ordinary people; that as they will be ever Judging and Censuring, so they must be Obnoxious to Error and Mistaking....I was not called to Counsel by his Royal Majesty, when the Resolution of this Clemency to the Lay-Recusants was first concluded: But if I had been asked my Opinion, I should have advised it without the least Hesitation. His Majesty was so Popishly addicted at this time, that (to the incredible exhaustments of his Treasury) he was a most Zealous Interceder for some Ease and Refreshment to all the Protestants in *Europe....*I would therefore see the most subtle State-monger in the World, chalk out a way for his Majesty, to mediate for Grace and Favour for the Protestants, by Executing (at this time) the Severity of his Laws upon the Papists. And that this Favour should mount to a Toleration is a most dull, and yet a most devilish, misconstruction. A Toleration looks forward to the time to come: This favour backward to the Offences past.

It is clear to us, that this illegal or præter legal & desultory toleration by connivance at particular cases; ~~and~~ this precarious ~~grace~~ Clemency depending on the momentary mood of the King, and this in a stretch of a questioned Prerogative, Could neither satisfy nor conciliate the Catholic Potentates abroad but was sure to offend, and alarm the Protestants at home. But on the other hand, it is unfair as well as unwise to censure the men of an age for want of that which was above their age.[1] The true principles, much more the practicable

16[1] Cf **4**, above, and **26** and **28**, below.

Rules of Toleration, were in James's time obscure to the wisest—but to the Many, Laity as no less than Clergy, would have been denounced as Soul-murder and disguised Atheism.[2] In fact, and a melancholy fact it is, *Toleration* is then first becomes practicable, when *Indifference* has deprived it of all merit.

S. T. C.

N.B. In the same spirit I excuse the opposite party, the Puritans & *Papophobists*.[3]

17 i 93 | 1 § 105

For because he was principally employ'd by his Office to distribute the King's Favours to some of the adverse Sect, he was Traduc'd for a Well-willer to the Church of *Rome*, nay so far by a ranting fellow about the Town, that he was near to receive a chief promotion from that Court, no less than a Cardinals Hat.

It was scarcely to be expected that the passions of James's Age would allow of this wise distinction between *Papists*, the intriguing restless Partizans of a foreign Potentate, and simple *Catholics*,[1] who preferred the Mumpsimus of their Grandsire to the correct Sumpsimus of the Reformation![2] But that in our age this Distinction should have been neglected, in the calamitous Catholic Bill![3]

18 i 94 and p ⁻3

"...But this invisible Consistory shall be confusedly diffused over all the Kingdom, that many of the Subjects shall to the intolerable exhausting of the Wealth of the Realm, pay double Tithes, double Offerings, and double Fees, in regard of their double Consistory. And *Mem.*—] if *Ireland* be so poor, as it is suggested, I hold, under Correction, that this invisible Consistory is the principal cause of the exhausting thereof."

16[2] For a similar linking of "Soul-murder" with toleration see BAXTER *Reliquiae* COPY B **92** and n 3. C may also remember Baxter's discussion of toleration in *A Holy Commonwealth* (1659), which Lamb bought for him in Nov 1802 (*LL* I 325) and from which C chose an epigraph for the 1809–10 *Friend* (*CC*) II 197 (I 245).
16[3] "Pope-fearers". *OED* cites this use from *LR* III 189, repeating the *LR* spelling "Papaphobists".

17[1] For the distinction between Papists and Catholics see e.g. *C&S* (*CC*) 120–1n, 131–2.
17[2] For *mumpsimus/sumpsimus* see BAXTER *Reliquiae* COPY A **44[b]** n 1.
17[3] I.e. the Catholic Emancipation Act, which became law on 13 Apr 1829, the controversy over which was the immediate occasion of *C&S*. See *C&S* (*CC*) esp 5–8 and nn; for the text of the Act see 203–9.

p. 94.

—Memorable remark on the evil of a double Priesthood in Ireland—

19   i 94, marked with an ink line in the margin

"Doctor *Bishop*, the New Bishop of *Chalcedon*, is come to *London* privately, and I am much troubled at it, not knowing what to Advise his Majesty, as things stand at this present. If you were Shipped with the *Infanta*, the only Counsel were to let the Judges proceed with him presently; Hang him out of the way, and the King to blame my Lord of *Canterbury*, or my self for it." Surely this doth not savour of addiction to the Purple-Hat, or the Purple-Harlot.

Poor King James's main errors arose out of his superstitious notions of a Sovereignty inherent in the Person—hence, a *sacred* Person, tho' in all other respects a very Devil. Hence his yearning for the SPANISH Match, & the ill-effects of his Toleration became rightly attributed by his Subjects to *foreign* influence—a Tol. against his own acknowleged Principle, not ON a Principle.[1]

20   p ‾3, referring to i 94 | **19** textus

p. 94.

Striking instance & illustration of the *tricky* policy which in the 16th Century passed for State-wisdom even with the comparatively wise. But there must be a *Ulysses* before there can be an Aristides or a Phocion.[1]

[19][1] The negotiations between James I and Philip of Spain for a marriage between Charles and the Infanta, in 1617–18, and again in 1623–4, earlier entertained for the elder son Henry (d 1612). James hoped for a rich marriage settlement, a balance of political and religious forces in Europe, and support for his dwindling authority at home; the Spaniards' condition was that James take a positive step towards the return of England to Catholicism. The negotiations, intensely unpopular at home, foundered over the religious issue and led to a declaration of war. In 1625 Charles married Henrietta Maria of France, also a Roman Catholic: see **10** n 2, above. In BM Egerton MS 2800 f 169 C wrote: "What shall we say of the intended Spanish Match? Perhaps this.
—It was most unwise in James to have sought either Spain or France—The true Policy would have been to have sought a Daughter-in-law with Sweden, or Saxony, or Brandenburgh—& to have gone heart & soul into the offensive & defensive Cause of Protestantism/ It would have enabled him to quench popish Recusancy in his Dominions, & by thus satisfying the Nation have taken the Teeth, yea, the Fang, out of Presbyterianism/ But alas! he was always dreaming of a Reconciliation not indeed with Romans but of the Roman & Protestant Churches who F. and S. supposed the alternative...."
[20][1] For Ulysses as a mixture of prudence and cunning see **4**, above.

21 i 96 | 1 §107

Four Scholars he Added to the 40 *Alumni* in the College of *Westminster*. For their Advancement he provided and endowed four Scholarships in St. *John's* College, upon their Maturity and Vacancy of those places to be Translated to them. Two Fellowships he Newly Erected in that House, into which only out of those four the best were to be chosen.

I have at times played with the thought, that our Bishoprics, like our Fellowships, might advantageously be confined to Single Men—if only it were openly declared to be on grounds of public Expediency; & on no supposed moral superiority of the Single State/.[1]

22 p ⁻3, referring to i 97 pencil | 1 §108

When he was Dean of *Westminster* he had a Voice in the High Commission Court....He appear'd but once at *Lambeth*, when that Court sat, while he was Dean. A sign that he had no Maw to it.

97. High Commission Court—[1]

23 i 98

I have heard the Lord Keeper (who was no Advocate for Sin, but for Grace and Compassion to Offenders) dis-relish that way, for this Reason. That a Rector, or Vicar, had not only an Office in the Church, but a Free-hold for Life by the Common Law, in his Benefice.

O if Archbishop W. had but seen in clear view what he indistinctly saw, viz. the essential distinction of the Nationalty, and its Trustees and Holders—& the Christian Church and its Ministers![1]

Aristides the Just (c 520–c 468 B.C.) and Phocion (c 402–318 B.C.), both Athenian soldiers and statesmen, became proverbial—through the influence of Plutarch's lives of them—for their honesty, steadiness of purpose, and responsible judgement.

21[1] C considered that the pastoral clergy could be "each in his sphere the germ and nucleus of the progressive civilization" only if they were "*in the rule* married men and heads of families". *C&S (CC)* 53n; see also n 2. For C's rejection of "compulsory celibacy in connection with, and in dependence on, a foreign and extra-national head" see e.g. *C&S (CC)* 81.

22[1] In i 97 Hacket writes that Williams "was not satisfied in two things [about the High Commission Court]: Neither in the Multiplicity of Causes, that were pluck't into it, nor in the Severity of Censures....He knew that a Pastoral Staff was made to reduce a wandering Sheep, not to knock it down."

23[1] For this distinction see e.g. *C&S (CC)* 77–81.

24   i 103, pencil | I §111

I will represent him [the Archbishop of Spalato] in a Line or two, that he was as indifferent, or rather dissolute in Practice, as in Opinion. For in the same *Cap. Ar.* 35. this is his Nicolaitan Doctrine, *A pluralitate uxorum natura humana non abhorret; imò fortasse neque ab earum communitate.* [Human nature does not abhor a plurality of wives; perhaps not even a community of them.] [a]Thus leaving all Differences of Religion *indeterminat, & in vago...*

How so? The words mean only, that the human animal this not withheld by any natural instinct from plurality or even community of females. It is not asserted, that Reason & Revelation do not forbid both the one and the other: or that Man unwithheld would not be a Yahoo, morally inferior to the Swallow. The Emphasis is to [be][b] layed, on "natura", not on "humana"/ i.e. *Humanity* forbids plural and promiscuous intercourse, not however by the *animal* nature of man but by his the Reason and Religion that constitute his moral and spiritual Nature.[1]

S T C

25   i 104 | I §112

But [the Pope Liberius] being thrown out into Banishment, and hunted to be destroy'd as a Partridge in the Mountain, he subscrib'd against his own Hand, which yet did not prejudice *Athanasius* his Innocency.

I have ever said this of Sir John Cheke. I regard his recantation, as one of the *cruelties* suffered by him/ & later the guilt flying off from him & settling on his Persecutors.[1]

---

[a] From here to the end of textus marked with a pencil line in the margin
[b] Word supplied by the editor

24[1] At the end of a notebook entry on "the gradual introduction of the constrained Celibacy of the Clergy" C writes: "As lust is the most extensively Generic = *animal*, so is *Love* the most intensely individual = *human*. Hence St Paul so profoundly calls Marriage a great mystery, or sacramental Symbol." N 35 f 41[v] (*CN* v) (c Nov 1827). See also *Century* **16** n 6 and HOOKER **21**.

25[1] Sir John Cheke (1514–57), one of the most learned men of his age, tutor to Edward IV, and a principal restorer of Greek learning to England. Although he was not in holy orders and played no influential part in political affairs, his zeal for the protestant faith, his office as secretary of state in Lady Jane Grey's brief reign (10–19 Jul 1553), and Queen Mary's desire to associate a man of his eminence with the Roman faith all led to his being charged with treason (Jul 1553), imprisoned in the Tower, and then released (Sept 1554) with a licence to travel abroad. Travelling from Brussels to Antwerp, he was treacherously seized (May 1556), carried clandestinely to

26 i 143 | ɪ §151

...but should conclude your Sacred Majesty to have often offended against your Conscience...because your Papists are not suppressed, and your Penal Statutes have been so often intended and remitted. These things you may well do, this Point continuing but a matter of State; but you may not do it, without committing a vast Sin, if now you should strein it up to a matter of Conscience and Religion, against the Opinion of all moderate Divines, and the Practice of most states in Christendom. I conclude therefore, that his Highness having admitted nothing in these Oaths or Articles, either to the prejudice of the true, or the Equalizing, or Authorizing of the other Religion, but contained himself wholly within the Limits of Penal Statutes, and connivences, wherein the Estate hath ever Challenged and Usurped a directing Power, hath Subscribed no one Paper of all these against his own, nor (I profess it openly) against the Dictamen of my Conscience.

Three points wanting to render the L. K.'s argument air-tight—First, the proof that a King of E. even then had a right to dispense, not with the execution of individual cases of the Laws, but with the Laws themselves in omne futurum[1]—i.e. to repeal Laws by his own act. 2. The proof, that such a Tooth & Talon-drawing of the Laws did not endanger the equalizing & final Mastery of the unlawful Religion—3. The utter want of all reciprocity on the part of the Spanish Monarch—In short, it is pardonable in Hacket, but would be contemptible in any other person, not to see this advice of the Lord Keeper's as a black Blotch on his character both as a Protestant Bishop and as a Councillor of State in a free & protestant country.—

S. T. C.

27 i 144 | ɪ §152

And I dare say the Tydings of that Letter, had followed the News of the Sermon, if it had been a Chicken of the same Brood. Finally, There was nothing done that needed a Recantation. Yet Opinions

---

England, and again imprisoned in the Tower. Under threat of the stake he finally agreed to profess belief in Roman doctrines, and was obliged to make a humiliating recantation (Oct 1556) before the Queen and publicly before the whole court. "Pining away with shame and regret for his abjuration of protest-

antism" (*DNB*), he died within less than a year, at the age of forty-three. C quotes briefly from Cheke in *Friend* (*CC*) ɪ 282, but no such compassionate comment as this has come to light elsewhere in C's writing.

26[1] "For the whole future".

were so various, that some spread it for a Fame, That the Prince himself gave the Lord Keeper no Thanks for his Labour.

Q.y Was it not required of, at all events usual, for all present at a Council to subscribe their names to the Act of the Majority? There is a modern case in point—that of Sir Arthur Wellesley's (now Duke of Wellington's) signature to the infamous Convention of Cintra.[1]

28　i 157 | 1 §164

This is the lively Character of him that wrote it, Policy mixt with Innocency.... Cunning enough, yet not divided from Conscience: For Wit, when it is not sheathed, as it were, in the fear of God, will cut like a sharp Razor.

What a fine india-rubber Conscience Hackett as well as his Patron must have had! "Policy with Innocency, Cunning with Conscience", lead up the Dance to the tune of Tantara! Rogues all!

29　i 192 | 1 §§ 197–8

I can scarcely conceive a greater difficulty, than for one honest, warm-hearted man of *Principle*, of the present day, so to discipline his mind by reflection on the circumstances, and received moral system of the Stewartorian Age (from Eliz. to the Death of Charles I), and its *place* in the spiral line of Ascension, as to be able to regard the D. of B. & Charles the 1st as not *Villains*: and to resolve their acts into passions, consciences-warp'd and hardened by half-truths, and the secular creed of Prudence, as *being* Virtue, instead of one of her handmaids,[1] when interpreted by minds constitutionally & by their accidental circumstances, imprudent, rash yet fearful and

---

27[1] Arthur Wellesley (later Duke of Wellington) in Aug 1808 was prevented by his senior officer, Sir Harry Burrard, from following up his victory over Junot at Vimiera; the French were allowed to retreat to Torres Vedras. Sir Hew Dalrymple then took command and negotiated the "infamous" Convention of Cintra, allowing the French army freedom to move out of the area of combat. At Dalrymple's request Wellesley—foreseeing no military disadvantage—signed the armistice in spite of his disapproval of some details. Thereafter his advice was ignored; he returned to

England in protest and had to face the storm of indignation aroused there by publication of the Convention. Accused of having negotiated the agreement, he presented to the court of inquiry dignified and authoritative evidence that absolved him of all blame. For C's admiration for Wellesley as a commander in the Peninsular War see e.g. *EOT (CC)* II 157–8. For WW's pamphlet attacking the Convention of Cintra (1809), and C's and De Q's part in the printing of it, see *W Prose* I 219–343, with Introduction, Appendixes, and Commentary.

29[1] See **4** (at n 2), above.

suspicious; & with Casuists and Codes of Casuistry as their
Conscience-Leaders!—One of the favorite works of Charles the I,
who died a martyr to his vice of Lying, & Perfidy, was Sanderson
de Juramento![2]

S. T. Coleridge—

30   i 194–5, pencil[a] | I § 200

Wherefore he waves the strong and full defence he had made upon
the stopping of an Original Writ, and deprecates all offence by that
Maxim of the Law, which admits of a mischief rather than an
inconvenience. Which was as much as to say, That he thought it a
far less Evil, to do the Lady the probability of an Injury, (in her own
sense) than to suffer those two Courts to clash together again, and
fall into a new Dispute about their Jurisdiction, which might have
produc'd a publick inconvenience, which is most carefully to be
avoided.

A tangle of *Sophisms*.[b]
   The assumption is—It is better to inflict a private wrong, than a
public one—we ought to wrong one rather than many. But even then
it is badly stated. The principle is true, only when the tolerating of
the private wrong is the *only* means of preventing a greater public
wrong.—But in this case it was the *certainty* of the Wrong of one
to avoid the *chance* of an *inconvenience* that MIGHT, perchance, be
the occasion of wrong to many, ~~and~~ which inconvenience both easily
might and ~~we~~ should, have been remedied by rightful means—by
mutual agreement between the Bishop & Chancellor, or by the King,
or by an Act of Parliament.

31   i 198–9 | I § 203

"I have discover'd him to be a Wanton, and a Servant to some of
our English Beauties, but above all to one of that gentle Craft in
Mark-Lane....I have a Friend that hath brib'd her in my Name, to
send me a faithful conveyance of such Tidings as her *Paramour
Carondelet* brings to her. All that I instructed the Duke in, came out
of her Chamber....Truly, Sir, this is my Dark Lanthorn, and I am
not asham'd to inquire of a *Dalilah* to Resolve a Riddle; for in my

---

   a A few words overtraced in ink, and much of the first part overtraced in pencil
   b This phrase is written in the margin opposite the textus. The note is then written in the foot-margin of I 194
and the head-margin of I 195

   29[2] For Robert Sanderson *De juramento* (Latin 1647, English 1655) see
EIKON BASILIKE 1 n 4.

Studies of Divinity I have glean'd up this Maxim, *Licet uti alieno peccato*; though the Devil make her a Sinner, I may make good use of her Sin. *Yea*, says the Prince *Merrily, do you deal in such Ware?* 'In good Faith, Sir, *says the Keeper*, I never saw her Face.'"

And Hacket's evident *admiration* and not merely approbation of this base Jesuitry! His *Divinity* had taught the Arch[bp], Licet uti alieno peccato!.[1] But Charles himself was a student of *such* Divinity—& yet (as Rogues of a higher rank comfort the *pride* of their Conscience by despising inferior Knaves) I suspect, that the "merrily", was the Sardonic mirth of bitter Contempt—but only because he *disliked* Williams—who was a̶ simply a man of his Age—w̶i̶t̶h̶ his *base* ness for us, not for his Contemporaries or even for his own mind— S. T. C.[a2]—But the worst of all is the Archbishop's heartless disingenuousness, and m̶o̶r̶e̶oon-like *Nodes*, towards his kind old Master, the King. How much of *truth* was there in the Spaniard's information respecting the intrigues of the Prince & the Duke of Buckingham? If none, if they were mere Slanders, if the Prince had acted the filial part, towards his Father & King, and the Duke the faithful part towards his Master & only too fond and affectionate Benefactor, what more was needed, than to expose the falsehoods? But if Williams knew, that there was too great a mixture of truth in the charges, what a cowardly Ingrate to his old Friend to have thus curried favor with the Rising Sun by this base jugglery!!—[3]

32   i 203 | I § 209

He [the Duke of Buckingham] was the Top-sail of the Nobility, and in Power and Trust of Offices far above all the Nobility.

James I. was no Fool; and tho' thro' weakness of character an unwise Master, yet not an unthinking Statesman,[1] and I still want a satisfactory solution of the accumulation of Offices on the D. of B.[2]

***

a C originally ended his note here, then continued

31[1] From textus, where it is freely translated.

31[2] See also **1** (at n 1) and **26**, above.

31[3] See **1**, towards the end.

32[1] See also **14**, above.

32[2] George Villiers, coming to London from Leicestershire in 1614— impoverished and in search of a rich marriage and a court appointment—was introduced to James I, who immediately

made him his favourite. In spite of the hostility of Somerset, Villiers was first appointed cupbearer to the King (Nov 1614), then gentleman of the bedchamber; in Apr 1615 was knighted and given a pension of £1000; in 1616 was made Master of the Horse, given the Order of the Garter, and created Viscount Villiers and Baron Waddon with a grant of land valued at £80,000; in 1617 was

33 i 206 | 1 §212

Prudent Men will continue the Oblations of their Forefathers Piety. They were ever readier to supply the publick need in the Custody of the Church, than in the Maws of Cormorants.

The danger and mischief of going far back, & yet not half far enough! Thus Williams refers to the Piety of ~~our~~ Individuals, our Forefathers, as the origin of Church Property! Had he gone further back & traced to the Source, he would have found these partial Benefactions to have been mere restitutions of Rights co-original with their own Property, and ~~as~~ a *National ~~Reservae~~serve* for the purposes of *National* Existence the conditio sine quâ non[1] of the equity of their *Proprieties*: for without Civilization a People cannot be or continue to be a Nation. But alas! the ignorance of the essential distinction of ~~a~~ National Clerisy, the Enclesia, from the *Christian* Church, the Ecclesia, has been the *Eclipse* in the ~~ins~~ intellect of both churchmen & Sectarians, even from Elizabeth to the present day. 1833.[2]

34 i 208 | 1 §214

It is certain that all Grants at the Court went with the Current of my Lord Dukes Favour. None had Power to oppose it, nor the King the Will. For he Rul'd all his Majesties Designs: I may not say his Affections: Yet the L. Keeper declin'd him sometimes in the Dispatches of his Office, upon great and just Cause.... [But the King] did procure, that his own Beneficence should be unprevented.... He would believe his own Judgment, and his own Ears, what they heard out of Depositions.... And being threatned, his best Mitigation was,

---

created Earl of Buckingham and Lord High Admiral, in 1618 Marquis of Buckingham, in 1623 Duke of Buckingham, and in 1625 made Chancellor of Cambridge University. Although at first he had no political ambitions and sought only to be a dispenser of patronage, his influence became increasingly surreptitious and pervasive. In the last years of James's reign he was virtually prime minister; and after Charles i acceded to the throne (1625) Charles followed his advice so meekly that for three years Buckingham was virtually king of England. He was assassinated. See also **1** n 2 and **6**, above, and **38**, below.

33[1] "Essential condition".

33[2] For the distinction between the National Church and the Christian Church see *C&S (CC)* 113–28, esp 117 and n 4, 139 n 2. For the distinction between the clerisy, *enclesia*, "an order of men, chosen in and of the realm, and constituting an estate of that realm", and the clergy, *ecclesia*, "the communion of such as are called out of the world", see *C&S (CC)* 45–9. See also **23**, above. For the terms *ecclesia/enclesia* see BLOMFIELD 4 n 1, and for the term "clerisy" see BLOMFIELD 3 n 1. See also HOOKER 10.

That perhaps it was not safe for him to deny so great a Lord, yet it was safest for his Lordship to be Denied....Of two Evils the less was to be chosen by the Keeper, rather to provoke one Man, then all Men; nay, rather provoke Man than GOD: That some will be provok'd it cannot be avoided.

Strange it must seem to us. Yet it is evident, that Hackett thought it necessary to make a mid something, half apology & half eulogy, for the Lord Keeper's timid half resistance to the insolence & iniquitous interference of the Minion Duke![1] What a portrait of the Times!

35 i 208

The King heard the noise of these Crashes; and was so pleas'd, that he Thank'd God before many Witnesses, that he had put the Keeper into that Place: For, says he, *He that will not wrest Justice for* Buckingham's *Sake, whom I know he Loves, will never be corrupted with Money, which he never Lov'd.*...And because the Lord Keeper had Husbanded that Stock Three years and half, and lived fairly upon it, and was not the Richer by the Sale of one Cursitors Place in all that time, His Majesty Granted him a Suit, by the Name of a New-Years-Gift, after the size of the Liberality of that Good Master, which was enough to keep a Bountiful *Christmas* twice over.

But the dotage of the King in his maintenance of the Man whose insolence in wresting justice he himself admits! But how many points both of the Times, and of the King's personal character, must be brought together before we can fairly solve the intensity of James's Minionism[1]—his kingly Egotism, his weak kind-heartedness, his vulgar coarseness of temper, his systematic jealousy of the ancient Nobles, his timidity, &c, &c./.[2]

36 i 209

His Majesty bewailed that his Grand-Children, then Young and Tender, would be very Chargeable to *England* when they grew to be Men. It was their Sole Refuge....*Sir*, says the Lord Keeper...*Breed them up for Scholars in Academial Discipline; keep them strictly to their Books, with such Tutors as will Teach them, not to abuse*

34[1] Cf **31** (at n 3), above.
35[1] *OED* cites two uses of "mini-

onism" in 1611, but includes this use by C, from *LR* III 198.
35[2] Cf **14** and **19**, above.

themselves with vain Hopes upon the Greatness of their Birth. . . . If they fall to their Studies, design them to the Bishopricks of Durham and Winchester, *when they become void. . . . The office of a Bishop, imprudently by many Malign'd . . . will be the more Inviolable, when the Branches of Your Royal Stock have so great an Interest in it. And such Provision is Needful against Schismatical Attempts, both for Religions Sake, and the Publick Weal.*

Williams could not have been in earnest, in this villainous Counsel; but he knew his man. This conceit of dignifying Dignities by the simoniacal prostitution of them to Blood Royal was just suited to James's Fool-Cunningness!

37 ii 75 | II § 74

The body of the Doctrin is worst of all, that it concerns us upon our Loyalty, nay, upon our Salvation, (for else Damnation is threatned) to yield not only Passive Obedience (which is due) but Active also, if the King's Will and Pleasure be notified in any thing not opposite to the Law of God and Nature...

What in the name of common Sense can this mean—i.e. speculatively? *Practically*, the meaning is clear enough, viz. that we should do what we can, so as to escape hanging.—But the distinction is for Decorum/ so let it pass.—

38 ii 76 | II § 75

This is the Venom of this new Doctrine, that by making us the King's Creatures, and in the state of Minors, or Children, to take away all our Propriety: Which would leave us nothing of our own, and lead us (but that God hath given us just and gracious Princes) into Slavery.

And yet this just and gracious Prince prompts, sanctions, supports and openly rewards this Envenomer, in flat Contempt of both Houses of Parliament—protects and prefers him and others of the same principles and professions on account of these professions![1] And yet the Parliament and Nation were inexcusable, forsooth, for not trusting in this man's Assurances, or rather the assurances put in his Mouth by Hyde, Falkland, &c,[2] that he had always abhorred these principles!

38[1] See **32** n 2, above.
38[2] For Clarendon and Falkland as advisers and mouthpieces to the King see DYMOCK **2** and n 1.

39 p ⁻3, referring to ii 144ᵃ, marked with a pencil line in the margin | II §136

When they saw he was not Selfish (it is a word of their own new Mint) some of their Ministers, that were softened with the dewy drops of his Tongue, eased their Stomachs with Complaints against the Courts Ecclesiastical, and the rugged Carriage of certain Prelates.

Part II. p. 144.—Singular!—From this passage I learn that our so very common word "selfish" is no older than the latter part of the reign of Ch. I.ᵇ¹

40 ii 145 | II §137

Their [the Presbyterians'] politick Aphorisms are far more dangerous, That His Majesty is not the highest Power in his Realms; That he hath not absolute Soveraignty; That a Parliament sitting is co-ordinate with him in it: He may have the Title of only Supreme, yet a Senate have an essential part without the Name. The Soveraignty was mixt, and distributed into the Hands of King, Lords, and Commons. Though a Nation war against a King, and they on the Merit of the Cause have the worser side, yet may he not war against the Publick Good on that account, nor any help him in such a War.

H. himself repeatedly implies as much: for would he deny that the King with the Lords and Commons is not more than the King without them? or that an act of Parliament is more than a Proclamation?

41 p ⁻3, referring to ii 161, pencil | II §154

What a venomous Spirit is in that Serpent *Milton*, that black-mouth'd *Zoilus*, that blows his Vipers Breath upon those immortal Devotions, from the beginning to the end! This is he that wrote with all Irreverence against the Fathers of our Church, and shew'd as little Duty to his Father that begat him: The same that wrote for the Pharisees, That it was lawful for a man to put away his Wife for every cause; and against Christ, for not allowing Divorces: The same, O horrid! that defended the lawfulness of the greatest Crime that ever was committed, to put our thrice-excellent King to death: A petty School-boy Scribler, that durst graple in such a Cause with the Prince of the learned men of his Age, *Salmasius*.

ᵃ Above **39** a pencil note almost rubbed away, at the end of which can be read "...16ᵗʰ [centu]ry"
ᵇ This annotation written over the pencilled "p. 63", i.e. **3**, above

39¹ *OED* devotes a separate note to Hacket's statement about the origin of "selfish", ascribing the coinage to the events of the year 1641.

Vide p. 161, Part II.—A contemporary of Bishop Hackett's designates Milton as the Author of a profane and *lascivious* Poem, entitled Paradise Lost.[1] The Biographers of our divine Bard ought to have made a collection of such passages. A German Biographer in a Life of Salmasius acknowleges that Milton had the better in the conflict in these words: *Hans* (i.e. Jack) von Milton, not to be compared in Learning and *Genius* with the incomparable Salmasius, yet a shrewd and cunning Lawyer &c.[2]—O sana Posteritas![3]

42   ii 188, pencil | ii §174

Upon mature Judgment, he [King Charles] travels by easie Journeys, with his Houshold, into the *North*, where he finds the Parliament professing Hostility against him by their Command and Overt Act, denying him way into the Town of *Hull*, and the use of his Magazine; a Confront no less outragious than if they had given him Battel.... Subjection being quite disclaimed, and that with a Martial Defiance, it was in vain to dispute what Redress there was for it, when there was none, but to look to the Array, and to muster stout and loyal Souldiers: Yet with what unwillingness did his Wise and Pious Heart go about it? How many Offers of Accordance did he make in that very Instant? How many Messengers were posted to *London*? which was no better than to dry-ditch the business; for every Offer of Grace made his Enemies haughty, the King's Reputation less, his Friends suspicious, that he could sooner entreat for, than defend, his Cause. Paper Mercuries, well worded, are fine things, but not forcible...

certainly not for a man who had & was known to have, the incurable vice of Lying[1]

43   ii 188, pencil

And to speak to common Reason and Charity, a man whose Paths were Piety,[*] his Governance Mercy,[†] his Bed Chastity,[‡] his

41[1] Cf *CL* iv 918–19 (Feb 1819), esp "At Sir George Beaumont's at Coleorton I found a Tract in which Milton is described as 'the blind monster who has newly dared put in print an *obscene* poem, called Paradise Lost'." C seems to have made this up as a defence against the charge of obscenity brought against *Christabel* by the anonymous pamphlet *Hypocrisy Unveiled* (1818).

41[2] Source untraced. This may also be an invention of C's. Cf *CN* iv 4610 (c Oct 1819): "Milton versus Salmasius—hic latrat, ille *rugit* [Salmasius barks, Milton roars]."
41[3] "O sound Posterity!"
42[1] Charles i. See **45** n 1, below; and cf **14**, **29**, above, and **43**, below.

Repast Sobriety, his Addresses Humility,[**] how could he set a Ditty to any other Prick'd-Song, but the Tune of Peace?

[*] Q.^y Jesuitry?
[†] Nose-slitting & Ear-cropping?
[‡] uxorious dotage?[1]
[**] Duplicity?

44   ii 188, pencil | II § 175

What Pardon can we expect from the Censure of a better Age, that we did not stop the Fury of Malecontents, before any drop of Blood was shed? I appeal to Fidelity, Homage, Duty, why did we not instantly raise an Host of Horse and Foot, which Rebels would not dare to encounter?

We! i.e. the Bishops, ~~and~~ about a third of the Clergy, & about ~~one~~ a third of the Gentry—these decided Kingsmen; add another third of the Gentry, desirous to impose even terms on both parties—THEY! i.e. $\frac{9}{10}$ths of all the rest of the Island. *Why* did not *we*? Why, because THEY would not let *We*.

45   ii 191, pencil | II § 178

Dare they not trust him that never broke with them? And I have heard his nearest Servants say, That no man could ever challenge him of the least Lye?

The impudence of this Assertion after the publication of Charles's Letters to his Wife![1] Not a month before his Execution he signed three contradictory treaties with three different parties, meaning to keep neither/ and at length died with a Lie—viz. the making himself the Author of Gauden's Icon Basil.[2]

43[1] C speaks of Charles I in N 38 f 7^v (*CN* v) as "the poor uxorious Slave of a lewd Virago..."; cf "the He-queen's She-King" in H. COLERIDGE **23**. Henrietta Maria styled herself on occasion "Her She Majesty Generalissima". C. V. Wedgwood *The King's War* (1958) 225.

45[1] Cf N 38 f 7^v (*CN* v): "...Charles the first, Martyr to the inveterate Vice of Lying...and the perjured Accomplice in the atrocity of the Irish Massacre...." Cf H. COLERIDGE **19**. After the battle of Naseby (14 Jun 1645) copies of Charles's correspondence with his wife fell into the hands of the parliamentary forces, disclosing details of Henrietta Maria's untiring secret negotiations to secure military support for him. C. V. Wedgwood *The Trial of Charles I* (1964) 18 reminds us that "The duplicity for which [Charles] has often been blamed was, in the last years of his life, the only weapon left to him for the defence of the things in which he believed"—his sovereign authority, a sacred trust delivered to him by God. See also H. COLERIDGE **23**, HUTCHINSON **15**.

45[2] See EIKON BASILIKE, esp **2** and n 2.

46   ii 193 | ii §180

If an Undersheriff had arrested *Harry Martin* for Debt, and pleaded that he did not imprison his Membership, but his *Martin*-ship, would the Committee for Priviledges be fob'd off with that distinction?

To make this good in analogy, we must suppose that Harry Martin had notoriously neglected all the duties while he perverted and abused all the privileges of Membership: and then I answer, that the Committee of Privileges would have done well and wisely in accepting the Undersheriff's Distinction, and out of respect for the Membership consigning the *Martin*-ship to the due course of Law.

47   ii 193

St. *Paul instructs the Christians at* Rome, *That every Soul should be subject to the higher Powers.* The higher Power under which they lived, was the meer Power and Will of *Caesar*, bridled in by no Law.

False, if meant *de jure*; and if *de facto*,[1] the plural "powers" would apply to the Parliament far better ⟨than,⟩ and to Cromwell as well as, to Nero.—Every even decently good Emperor professed himself the Servant of the Roman Senate/ the very term, Imperateror as Granavina observes, implies it—for it expresses a delegated and instrumental power.[2] Before the assumption of the Tribunitial character by Augustus, by which he became the representative of the Majority of the People—majestatem indutus est[3]—"Senatus consulit, Populus jubet, imperent Consules" was the constitutional language.[4]

47[1] "According to the law" and "according to the fact". Hacket applies his argument to Charles I; C points out that it would apply as well to Parliament and to Cromwell.

47[2] Giovanni Vincenzo Gravina (1664–1718) *De romano imperio* (1712) §19; C's edition has not been identified. In Oct–Dec 1804 C copied out a long passage, including the detailed argument upon which C's general statement stands. *CN* II 2225 and n (citing *Opera* Leipzig 1737). C used, or recalled, this passage when making notes on Brougham's *Inquiry into the Colonial Policy of the European Powers* (1803) for Alexander Ball, and turned Gravina's arguments against Brougham. See *IS* 292–3 and n.

47[3] "He put on majesty". On majesty and majority see *C&S* (*CC*) 20 and n 1 (which includes KANT *Anthropologie* COPY B 2), *EOT* (*CC*) I 136, and C. BUTLER *Vindication* 4 and n 1. Cf also (on majesty and unity) HUTCHINSON 17 and n 3.

47[4] "The Senate counsels, the People order, let the Consuls command". Source untraced; the epigram may be C's. A variant occurs in a note on *majestas* in N 52 ff 18ᵛ–19 (c Sept 1833), with "imperator executus est" as the third element in the triad. In JOHNSON *Works* p 81 it appears again, also associated with the name of Gravina.

48 ii 204 | II § 190

Yet so much dissonancy there was between his Tongue and his Heart, that he [Cicero] triumpht in the murder of *Caesar*, the only *Roman* that exceeded all their Race in nobleness, and was next to *Tully* in eloquence. Boast not therefore in Success, which is an advantage to make Infidels proud: but the abtruse ways of God's Providence, which setteth up one, and pulleth down another, as he pleaseth, should make us Christians humble.

There is something so shameless in this self-contradiction, as of itself to extinguish the charitable Belief, that the Prelatic Royalists were mistaken Reasoners but yet conscientious in their Conclusions. For if the Senate of Rome were not a lawful Power, what could be? And if Cæsar, the thrice perjured Traitor,[1] was neither perjured nor traitor only because he by his Gaulish troops turned a Republic into an arbitrary Monarchy—with what face, under what pretext, could Hacket abuse "Sultan Cromwell"?—[2]

49 ii 205 | II § 191

Treasurers of the Army, Excise-men, Collectors of Taxes, Victuallers of the Navy, Committee-men, with their Scribes, Officers of all sorts, abundance of decayed Fortunes, nay Scoundrels, not worth a Groat before, are swell'd into vast Estates, progging and prowling every way in purveyance for themselves. Will not these choose war rather than Peace against Foe or Friend? For the Wheel will run easily into any mischief when it is well greased. *Who are they*, says *Polybius*, *that prefer a Soldiers life before any?...They that loved to eat upon other mens cost, and to live upon their Countrymen.* So sensible are all men of this fatal and general empoverishing, because we are so far from having the wound healed, that the Arrow is not pluckt out, but sticks still in our side.

What childish womanish Contradictions! A Kingdom consists of A B C X Y Z—Yesterday A B C were rich—to day X Y Z/. Ergo, the Kingdom is impoverished!!—Of all the Benefactors *for* whom

---

48[1] Cf Shakespeare *Julius Caesar* III ii 95–7, referring to Caesar's thrice refusing the crown.

48[2] See ii 200, pt II § 187: "Now...a Prisoner is tryed at the Bar, neither by the Law for Reason, nor by Jury upon Matter of Fact, but by the Conscience of some that are commissioned to judge upon Law, Reason, Right, and Fact. Suppose that the Conscience of Sultan *Cromwel*, and his Visier *Bashaw*, alias *Bradshaw*, sit among them, that Court must prove a Rock, against which an Innocent cannot chuse but split...".

G. Britain ought to thank God, James the Second stands foremost—
Had not his bigotry made free with the property and exclusive priv-
ileges of these Priests, nothing could [have]*ᵃ* saved us from Despotism
—The Church of England detested every form of Freedom.[1]

49[1] C is perhaps thinking of the
Catholic James's leniency towards his
fellow religionists, the harsh rectification
of which after James's abdication, es-
pecially in Ireland, C notices in *C&S*
(*CC*) 152 (and n 3), 153 (and nn 1, 2).
For James II as a "furious & bigotted
tyrant" see *EOT* (*CC*) III 246n and cf
239; as "a Traitor to the British Consti-
tution" see *IS* 128; and cf **14** (at n 4),
above. On the Church of England as
an enemy of freedom at this period see
also HUTCHINSON **13** (at n 5) and
BAXTER *Reliquiae* COPY B **115** (esp at
nn 7–15).

NATHAN HALE
1784–1863

The American System, or the effects of high duties on imports designed for the encouragement of domestic industry; with remarks on the late annual Treasury Report. [Anonymous.] Boston 1828. 8°.
In paper wrappers, issued "from Nathan Hale's Press, Congress-Street".

Harvard University (Houghton Library)

Inscribed on p ⁻2 (outside of original paper wrapper): "Joshua Bates, Esqre".
    On p 10 C has corrected "duties...has" to "duties...have", and on p 18 "inadequate remuneration" to "adequate remuneration"; a textual correction on p 34 is not in C's hand. Passages are marked on pp 23, 25, 67, 68, 69, 77, not by C.

DATE. 2 Sept 1828 (dated in 1).

1 title-page recto and verso, pencil, overtraced, revised, and concluded in ink[a]

This pamphlet is the Work of a very reflecting and very able Man, whoever he may be.[1] I do not hesitate to affirm, ⟨as my individual but impartial & deliberate Judgement,⟩[b] that these 86 pages contain more wisdom with less alloy, than any half dozen Octavos or ~~on the fashionable~~[c] even Quartos ofn[d] the ⟨fashionable⟩[b] Subject of Political Economy, that have fallen under my Reading. S. ~~T. Coleridge~~[e] The Writer is not only thoroughly Master of the Facts, but one of the Few who can track a great and operative PRINCIPLE thro' all its consequences with that quiet persistency of Intellect which enables

---

[a] The overtracing is by C   [b] Inserted in ink
[c] Cancelled in pencil   [d] "on" written over the pencilled "of"
[e] The signature is cancelled in ink; the note continues in ink to the end, the ink of the same colour as the inserts above

[1] The author of this anonymous pamphlet was trained as a lawyer but became a journalist, edited the *Boston Daily Advertiser* (1814–54) and was one of the founders of the *North American Review* and of the *Christian Examiner*. A member of the Massachusetts House of Representatives (1820–2) and of the Senate (1829–30), he became president of the Boston and Worcester Railroad (1831–49) and wrote an *Epitome of Universal Geography* (1830) as well as a number of pamphlets on canals, water supply, railroads, and banking. His uncle was the famous Nathan Hale (1755–76) who, as a soldier of the Continental army, was caught by the British trying to penetrate the lines to gain intelligence for Washington and was hanged as a spy.

him to place the Facts under their proper causes, and to dissipate the illusion created by accidental and temporary Influences[2]—and thus secures him from the too general Error, the *Queen-Bee* in the whole Hive of Errors[3]—*Cum hôc*: ergo, *propter hôc*.[4]

2 Septr 1828.   S. T. Coleridge
                                                                              Grove, Highgate/

2 pp 6–7, pencil

Similar effects [of depreciation of value] are also produced, by the various schemes for forcing into circulation an unsound paper currency. The ultimate effects are acknowledged by all men of sense to be injurious to the public. These expedients, nevertheless, serve to produce a nominal increase of prices, both of labour and of commodities, and the nominal value of all property; but such an increase of the nominal price of labour, cannot be considered an increased reward of industry.

As a general Rule, true; but there are cases, in which a paper money wholly baseless may create a base for itself by its influence as a stimulus to Labor—Say, I had, no matter how, caused it to be generally believed, in one of the rude but easily improveable districts of Ireland, that I possessed 20,000£—in 20 Bank notes of a 1000£ each/ & on the pretext of the impossibility of immediate change had issued notes from 5 Shillings to a Pound, which the little chandlers, ale-houses &c would take—& thus influenced the Hovellers to bring a thousand acres into cultivation in the course of two or three years/ it is very conceivable, that at the close of this period I might be fairly worth 60, or even 100,000£—and the Country enriched to a yet greater amount[1]

1[2] I.e. he is an exemplar of method, working from ideas rather than from conceptions (for which see HOOKER **3** and n 3). For C's conviction that a law cannot emerge from generalisation on "facts" see e.g. *Friend (CC)* I 472–87.

1[3] See BAINES **1** n 2.

1[4] " *With* this; therefore, *because of*

this." See BAXTER *Reliquiae* COPY B **31** n 1 and cf BÖHME **175** and n 3.

2[1] An innocent prophetic glimpse of the Keynesian economics. For C on paper money see *EOT (CC)* III 56–7 (C's collaboration with Poole). On Britain's "*system* of credit" as a stimulus to labour and wealth see *Friend (CC)* I 233–4.

JOHN HALL

1627–1656

An Humble Motion to the Parliament of England concerning the advancement of learning: and reformation of the universities. By J. H. [i.e. John Hall]. London 1650. 4º.
Bound in "CROMWELLIAN TRACTS II".

Not located. *Gillman SC* 500.

MS TRANSCRIPT. VCL BT 37: SC transcript evidently used for *NTP*. The annotations are here printed from MS TRANSCRIPT.

DATE. 1828 (see 1), or later. The date "1828"—the year London University opened—may have been supplied by SC.

1 [p 1 ?]

This third Tract[1] is a truly admirable memorial, opusculum verè *Baconicum*.[2] J. H. is, I believe, John Hall, a young man of highest promise, who died in the 22nd year of his age.[3] It would be desirable to reprint this "Motion" dedicated to the Founders of the London University.[4] *1828.—*

1[1] I.e. in the made-up volume, the constitution of which is in question. See CROMWELLIAN TRACTS.

1[2] "A little opus truly *Baconian*": that is, that would bring to education the principles—of Platonic and Baconian origin—evolved in the "Essays on the Principles of Method", in which "every principle is actualized by an idea; and every idea is living, productive, partaketh of infinity, and (as Bacon has sublimely observed) containeth an endless power of semination". *SM (CC)* I 23–4. For a central statement on the process of right education see *Friend (CC)* I 499–500.

1[3] Actually in the 29th or 30th year of his age; the source of the error—which may have been the transcriber's and not C's—has not been detected. Hall's first book, published at the age of nineteen in his first year at St John's College, Cambridge, "amazed not only the Uni-versity but the more serious part of men in the three nations" (John Davies' biographical memoir prefixed to the posthumous edition of Hall's *Hierocles* in 1657). Poet and pamphleteer, he published several political pamphlets of substance, served Cromwell as adviser in Scotland in 1650 and was rewarded for his services. Hobbes, Hartlib, and Henry More were his friends; when he died, having published half a dozen elegant and learned works, he left behind the mss of several other writings.

1[4] In order to consolidate the efforts made by Thomas Campbell, Jeremy Bentham (whose skeleton and embalmed head are still preserved at University College), and Lord Lansdowne to found a University of London, Lord Brougham in 1825 formed a joint-stock company to establish a university that would provide a literary and scientific education to

2 pp 16–17

...it will not be hard to inferre, that other Universities of a later standing and poorer substance, have both in extent of knowledge, and multiplicity of excellent persons, been able to equall, if not out-doe them. Nay that those present Revenues whereupon they now surfeit, have choaked abundance of active Industries, nay beene a meanes to thrust into Ecclesiasticall or Litterary offices a many*ᵃ* of persons, who had they been suffered to obey their owne inclinations, and followed some Trade or Handicraft, might have ranked themselves amongst the ablest of their Profession...

Menie whence menial, the set or whole number of slaves or inferior servants, attached to a menial Estate, Farm or *Lordship*. Q*ʸ* a Meniè?*ᵇ* i.e. a menial set, a set of menial souls, who &c.[1]

3 pp 25–7

For the first: I could never yet make so bad an *Idaea* of a true University, as that it should serve for no nobler end, then to nurture a few raw striplings, come out of some miserable Country-school,

ᵃ This word, not italicised in the printed text, is taken to be underlined by C
ᵇ MS TRANSCRIPT reads "Meniè"

students of all denominations at a nominal cost. By May 1825 C was "reflecting earnestly and actively on the subject" (*CL* v 445) and in 1828 HCR bought a £100 share in the university "as a sort of debt to the cause of civil and religious liberty" (*CRD* 3 May 1828; in 1852 he said "Never were £100 better spent"). Because of the support the proposal received from dissenters it was attacked as irreligious and satirised as Cockney College. The foundation stone was laid by the Duke of Sussex in 1827, but before the College opened in Oct 1828 a Church of England group under the patronage of George IV—Wellington, the bp of London, and others—set up a scheme to found King's College as a rival to the secular University of London (later University College). Cf a verse of 1828:

But above all, O, bless this Royal
  College;
Make it a *Hot-bed* of such heavenly
  knowledge

As will suffice to guard the Church
  from evil,
And frustrate Brougham, Bentham,
  and the Devil.

King's College, founded by royal charter in Aug 1829, opened in Oct 1831. When the University of London was incorporated in 1836 University College and King's College were designated "teaching bodies", the power of granting degrees, which had not previously been assigned to either college, being assigned to the University. For C's successful recommendation (1827) of his friend Hyman Hurwitz as first Professor of Hebrew at University College see HURWITZ headnote.

2[1] *OED* records "many" as a confused spelling of *menie* (*meinie*) as early as 1569 and as late as Dryden, meaning a household, suite or retinue, company (as of soldiers), but usually referring to servants.

with a few shreds of Latine, that is as immusicall to a polite ear as the gruntling of a Sow, or the noise of a Saw can be to one that is acquainted with the Laws of harmony. And then possibly before they have survayed the Greeke Alphabet, to be racked and tortured with a sort of harsh abstracted logicall notions, which their wits are no more able to endure, then their bodies the Strapado, and to be delivered over to a jejune barren Peripatetick Philosophy, suited onely, (as *Mounsieur Des-Cartes* sayes) to wits that are seated below Mediocrity, which will furnish them with those rare imaginations of *Materia prima*, *Privation*, *Universalia*, and such Trumpery, which they understand no more then their Tutors, and can no more make use of in the affaires of life, then if 3000. yeares since they had run through all the Hieroglyphicall learning of the *Egyptians*, and had since that time slept in their *Mummy*, and were now awaken. And then as soone as they have done licking of this file, to be turned to graze in poor *Ethicks*, which perhaps tell them as much in harder words, as they had heard their Mothers talke by the fire-side at home. Then are they turned loose, and with their paper-barks committed to the great Ocean of Learning; where if they be not torne, they returne back so full of desperation and contempt of their profession, and sad remembrance of their youth so trivially spent, that they hate all towardly engagements that way, and suffer themselves either to sinke in a quagmire of idlenesse, or to be snatched away in a whirlepool of vice. But in case some with much adoe get a shore (for a long or a far voyage upon these termes they cannot make) and by the foresaid means stilt themselves into some profession; what deplorable things (unlesse it be those few which Nature makes for ostentation to be jewells in this earth) prove they, in filling the world with detestable quacking Empericks, lewd, and contentious, Gown-men, or ignorant mercenary Divines?

It would be thought unjust and calumnious to offer this paragraph to line 3rd p. 27 as a portrait of either of our two universities in their present state. Yet within three Decennia last past, a true Exposè of Oxford tuition would have differed from this only by substituting nothing for nothing's worth, *nihil vicè nihilorum*.[1] But at this very

---

3[1] C's translation precedes the Latin. RS as an undergraduate was contemptuous of the condition of Oxford, C less so of Cambridge. In fact, both universities had shown a general improvement in the level of studies towards the end of the eighteenth century: written examinations gradually replaced perfunctory oral examinations and the range of studies was extended. For C's glimpse of "young men ... be-tutored, be-lectured, any thing but *educated* ... varnished rather than

moment I will consent to take a hard student, and an average or οἱ πολλοι[2] man of the Oxford of 1640—and of 1820, and on a detailed statement of the schemes of study and the kinds and quantum of knowledge of the former two, and those of the latter two, after a fair comparison of the first with the first, and of the second with the second, in respect of intrinsic worth and of (not adventitious and conventional, but) actual utility, to maintain the superiority of the Oxford of A.D. 1640.[3]

S. T. C.

---

polished; perilously over-civilized, and most pitiably uncultivated" see *Friend* (*CC*) I 500.

3[2] "The many"—ordinary.

3[3] C has chosen the date 1640 probably because the statutes of the University of Oxford codified in 1636 (by Abp Laud when chancellor) were still in force, with certain modifications, in C's day. D. A. Winstanley in *Unreformed Cambridge* (Cambridge 1935) records that particularly in the last decade of the eighteenth century there was a good deal of "idleness and extravagance" among the undergraduates (p 212), and "not a little actual vice" (p 210), and that "throughout the eighteenth century rioting and disorder were very frequent both inside and outside the colleges" (pp 212–13). All historians refer to the iniquitous privileges given to idle rich undergraduates at that time: they were not expected to attend lectures or even to write examinations, were charged higher fees, and paid in various monetary ways for their privileges.

In 1816, however, C had said publicly that "the late and present condition of manners and intellect among the young men at Oxford and Cambridge, the manly sobriety of demeanor, the submission to the routine of study in almost all, and the zeal in the pursuit of knowledge and academic distinction in a large and increasing number, afford a cheering testimony to such as were familiar with the state of the two Universities forty or even thirty years ago...". *EOT* (*CC*) II 433. Cf *CL* VI 1054 (May 1825): "Oxford and Cambridge [are] national blessings; but not true universities".

FRIEDRICH LUDWIG VON HARDENBERG
"NOVALIS"
1772-1801

Novalis Schriften. Herausgegeben von Ludwig Tieck und Fr. Schlegel.
Dritte Auflage. Vol I (of 2). Berlin 1815. 8°.

British Museum C 43 a 18

In a letter to Green on c 3 Jul 1818 C discussed "*the Form*" in which he
might cast "my system of constructive Philosophy"; "A novel or romance"
might be well "adapted to the analytical elucidation of a system so abstruse"
but of that kind "assuredly, Heinrich von Ofterdingen is no tempting or
encouraging example". He added parenthetically that "Your short critique
on which [i.e. *Heinrich von Ofterdingen*] pencilled at the end of the IInd Vol.
contains my full judgement & convictions thereon". *CL* IV 870. Perhaps by
"the IInd Vol." C meant the now-missing Vol II of this ed of *Novalis
Schriften*, although the whole text of the novel is in Vol I. Even the
provenance of this Vol I is obscure: although it bears the same date of
acquisition (10 AU 1880) as the first and larger group of books acquired from
the Green sale through John Wilson, the title does not appear either in *Green
SC* (1880) or in the invoice for the books purchased from Wilson.

CONTENTS. *Heinrich von Ofterdingen* (the whole text), and editorial matter.

DATE. Before 3 Jul 1818 and after the first meeting with Joseph Henry Green
on 13 Jun 1817 (see ATHENAEUM headnote). In c May 1818 C translated
an aphorism from *Novalis Schriften* II 140. *CN* III 4410; cf 4497n.

1   I 115 | *Heinrich von Ofterdingen* pt I ch 5

[The hero meets a hermit in a cave, who talks at length about
problems of historiography and the relationship between history and
poetry.]

St[r]angely out of place. Why in a Cavern? and by a ghostly old
Hermit?[1]

1[1] In Jul 1818, in the discussion of the
form for his "constructive Philosophy"
(cited in headnote), C said that "My
present thought is to give it in part the
Dialogue, in part the Lecture, Form—so
as to divide the Work into 3 parts...the

second [of which would be], conversations
in the Cavern by the Sea Shore—
containing the theosophical [part]...".
CL IV 870. For C's projected "Weather-
bound Travellers" see *CN* IV 4549 (c 10
Jun 1819) and n.

DAVID HARTLEY
1705–1757

Observations on Man, His Frame, His Duty, and His Expectations. In two parts. Part the first: containing observations on the frame of the human body and mind, and on their natural connexions and influences. (Part the second: containing observations on the duty and expectations of mankind.) [To which is added a third volume:] Notes and Additions to Dr. Hartley's Observations on Man; by Herman Andrew Pistorius... translated from the German original... to which is prefixed, a sketch of the life and character of Dr. Hartley [by his son David Hartley]. 3 vols. London 1791. 8°.

British Museum C 126 i 2

The initials "S T C", not in C's hand, are written on the title-page of each volume. "S. T. C." label on the title-page verso of each volume. John Duke Coleridge's monogram on I ⁻2 and II ⁻2.

DATE. After C's visit to Germany 1798–9 and before 1802.

1   I ⁺1, referring to I 81, pencil | Pt I ch 1 Sec ii "Of Ideas..." prop xiv, cor 3

...the intellectual pleasures and pains may be greater, equal, or less, than the sensible ones, according as each person unites more or fewer, more vivid or more languid miniature vibrations, in the formation of his intellectual pleasures and pains, &c.

P. 81.—Ideas may become so as vivid & distinct, & the feelings accompanying them as vivid, as original Impressions—And this may finally make a man independent of his Senses.—one use of poetry.[1]

1[1] For the proposition that "deep feeling has a tendency to combine with obscure ideas" see *Friend (CC)* I 106 and n; and for the connexion of this with poetry see *CN* I 383 and entries cited in 383n. See also *Sh C* II 103–4 and *CN* IV 4714 (in *C 17th C* 556–7); and cf BAXTER *Reliquiae* COPY A **51**. Cf also WW's account of the way "successful composition generally begins": "the emotion is contemplated till, by a species of re-action, the tranquillity gradually disappears, and an emotion, kindred to that which was before the subject of contemplation is gradually produced, and does itself actually exist in the mind". *W Prose* I 149.

2 I 82, cropped | I 1 ii prop xiv cor 6

If beings of the same nature, but whose affections and passions are, at present, in different proportions to each other, be exposed for an indefinite time to the same impressions and associations...they will become perfectly similar, or even equal.

~~What~~ a very [? ap]t phrase, this!—[*the*] *same nature?* Is [the]re no difference [in] the organs, or a [pr]iori causes of [*I*]*deas?*—[1]

2A I 105, two passages marked with a pencil line in the margin

After a sufficient repetition of the motory vibrations which concur in this action, their vibratiuncles are generated, and associated strongly with other vibrations or vibratiuncles, the most common of which, I suppose, are those excited by the sight of a favourite play thing which the child uses to grasp, and hold in his hand....By pursuing the same method of reasoning, we may see how, after a sufficient repetition of the proper associations, the sound of the words *grasp, take hold,* &c. the sight of the nurse's hand in a state of contraction, the idea of a hand, and particularly of a child's own hand, in that state, and innumerable other associated circumstances, *i.e.* sensations, ideas, and motions, will put the child upon grasping, till, at last, that idea, or state of mind which we may call the will to grasp, is generated...

3 I +3, referring to I 273[a] | I 3 i "Of Words..." prop lxxx

Fifthly, The words denoting sensible qualities, whether substantive or adjective, such as *whiteness, white,* &c. get their ideas in a manner which will be easily understood from what has already been delivered. [b]Thus the word *white,* being associated with the visible appearances of milk, linen, paper, gets a stable power of exciting the idea of what is common to all, and a variable one in respect of the particularities, circumstances, and adjuncts. And so of other sensible qualities.

273. a fair instance of the art of humdrumming—at the par: Fifthly, &c—

---

[a] 3, 4, and 5, written as one annotation, have been divided to indicate the textus to which each refers
[b] From here to the end of textus, marked with an ink line in the margin

2[1] See *CN* I 1723 and n (c 6–13 Dec 1803)—a marked passage in KANT *Grundlegung zur Metaphysik der Sitten* (1785).

4   I $^+$3, referring to I 276

Eleventhly, The names of intellectual and moral qualities and operations, such as fancy, memory, wit, dulness, virtue, vice, conscience, approbation, disapprobation, &c. stand for a description of these qualities and operations; and therefore, if dwelt upon, excite such ideas as these descriptions in all their particular circumstances do. But the common sentences, which these words enter, pass over the mind too quick, for the most part, to allow of such a delay. They are acknowledged as familiar and true,^{a} and suggest certain associated visible ideas, and nascent internal feelings, taken from the descriptions of these names, or from the words, which are usually joined with them in discourses or writings.

a still more glorious instance of hum-druming over the only difficult part of the question in page 276.—^{1}

5   I $^+$3, referring to I 277, lightly cropped

This is by no means a full or satisfactory account of the ideas which adhere to words by association. For the author perceives himself to be still a mere novice in these speculations; and ^{b}it is difficult to explain words to the bottom by words; perhaps impossible. The reader will receive some addition of light and evidence in the course of this section...

But then how the *moral* character of Hartley ever comes in, & makes atonement for any deficiencies of reasoning! Vide 277—a paragraph of genuine beauty & dignity of Feeling!^{1}

6   I $^+$3, lightly cropped

It might be said, I think, that Hartley himself must have *felt* that association was not of itself capable of explaining all the phænomen[a] of the human mind—in several parts he (*unconsciously* perhaps) presupposes the power of abstraction always acting—ex. gr. when he talk[s] of the "stable part of ideas" in his explanation of such

---

^{a} The underlined words are also marked with an ink line in the margin
^{b} Marked with two ink lines in the margin

4^1 See the underlined words in textus.
5^1 From the end of textus the paragraph concludes: "For our assent to propositions, and the influence which they have over our affections and actions, make part of the ideas that adhere to words by association; which part, however, could not properly be considered in this section."

words a[s]*ᵃ* White, whiteness, sweet, &c¹—the whole of p. 279²
presents almost a *humorous* instance (if in the works of so good &
great a man one could permit oneself that sort of feeling) of
explaining the obscurum per obscurius.³—It is singular, that Hartley,
a good algebraist, & who so clearly saw the analogy of Language
in its effects on the mind to the operations of algebra,⁴ did not set
himself about explaining by an accurate analysis what those
operations are—

7   1 279

*] Lastly, the particles *the, of, to, for, but,* &c. have neither definitions
nor ideas.

*   ! ! !   *ᵃ* Letter supplied by the editor

6¹ "The names of simple sensible
qualities are of the first class [i.e. "Such
as have ideas only"]. Thus *white, sweet,*
&c. excite ideas; but cannot be defined.
It is to be observed here, that this class
of words stands only for the stable part
of the ideas respectively, not for the
several variable particularities, circum-
stances, and adjuncts, which inter-mix
themselves here." This is from the
illustrative section following the formula-
tion of four classes of words, as given
parenthetically in n 2, below.
  6² "Cor. II. This matter [of the four
classes of words] may be illustrated by
comparing language to geometry and
algebra, the two general methods of
expounding quantity, and investigating
all its varieties from previous *data.*
  "Words of the first class ["Such as
have ideas only...The names of simple
sensible qualities"] answer to proposi-
tions purely geometrical, *i.e.* to such as
are too simple to admit of algebra; of
which kind we may reckon that concern-
ing the equality of the angles at the basis
of an Isosceles triangle.
  "Words of the second class ["Such as
have both ideas and definitions...The
names of natural bodies, animal, vege-
table, mineral"] answer to that part of
geometry, which may be demonstrated
either synthetically or analytically; either
so that the learner's imagination shall go
along with every step of the process
pointing out each line, angle, &c. accord-
ing to the method of demonstration used

by the ancient mathematicians; or so that
he shall operate entirely by algebraic
quantities and methods, and only repre-
sent the conclusion to his imagination,
when he is arrived at it, by examining
then what geometrical quantities the
ultimately resulting algebraic ones de-
note. The first method is in both cases
the most satisfactory and affecting, the
last the most expeditious, and not less
certain, where due care is taken. A blind
mathematician must use words in the last
of these methods, when he reasons upon
colours.
  "Words of the third class ["Such as
have definitions only...Algebraic quan-
tities, such as roots, powers, surds, &c."]
answer to such problems concerning
quadratures, and rectifications of curves,
chances, equations of the higher orders,
&c. as are too perplexed to be treated
geometrically.
  "Lastly, Words of the fourth class
["Such as have neither ideas nor defini-
tions...the particles *the, of, for, but,*
&c."] answer to the algebraic signs for
addition, subtraction, &c. to indexes,
coefficients, &c. These are not algebraic
quantities themselves; but they alter the
import of the letters that are; just as par-
ticles vary the sense of the principal
words of a sentence, and yet signify
nothing of themselves."
  6³ "The obscure through the more
obscure".
  6⁴ See Hooker **41** and n 2.

THOMAS HARWOOD
1767–1842

LOST BOOK

Annotations, Ecclesiastical and Devotional: intended to illustrate the liturgy and the XXXIX Articles of the United Church of England and Ireland; with an historical introduction. London 1826. 8°.

Not located; marginalia not recorded. Clemens SC (Parke Bernet 8 Jan 1945) 202: "With manuscript corrections believed to be in Coleridge's autograph."

SELINA HASTINGS
COUNTESS OF HUNTINGDON
1707–1791

A Select Collection of Hymns to be universally sung in all the Countess of Huntingdon's chapels, collected by her Ladyship, &c. [lacking title-leaf.] [c 1790]. [12°.] [Edition not identified.]

Title of the London 1780 ed, the last authorised in the Countess's lifetime, cited. That edition contained 298 items, to which supplements were added in 1796 and 1808. It is unlikely that the Countess wrote any hymns herself. In the compilation she was assisted by her sometime chaplain, the Rev Walter Shirley (1725–86), Methodist preacher and hymn-writer.

Not located; marginalia not recorded.

Described in Sotheby SC 12–13 Dec 1893, lot 444: "This copy belonged to S. T. Coleridge, and on the inside of the cover and on the fly-leaf is an original unpublished Hymn, entitled *Divine Consolation*, in his autograph, concluding:—

> Is that a Death-bed where the Christian lies;
> Yes! but not his—tis Death itself that dies!

and signed 'S. T. Coleridge.' Again Hymn LXIX has an entire new verse interpolated in Coleridge's autograph, and to Hymn LIX are notes and interlineations, which clearly indicate the fervour of his religious feelings at the period. Altogether the volume is one of the most unusual interest. It afterwards passed into the possession of 'Leigh Hunt, Church Street, Stoke Newington, 1822.' In addition to the items already specified, Coleridge has in some instances added the names of the authors of the hymns." This copy is mentioned by W. C. Hazlitt in *Bookworm* VII (1894) 69.

In the auctioneer's annotated copy of the catalogue, in the BM, lot 444 is marked "withdrawn", the reason for withdrawal not stated. The ascription of the notes and interpolations to C is to be accepted with reserve. The poem quoted was not composed until c 1832, and in 1822 Leigh Hunt was, until May, held up in Portsmouth on his way to Italy, finally arrived in Leghorn in Jul, and did not return to England until Sept 1825.

The quoted lines of verse are lines 13–14 (var) of *My Baptismal Birth-day*, first collected (with that title) in *PW* (1834), first published in *Friendship's Offering* for 1834 as "Lines Composed on a Sick-bed, under Severe Bodily Suffering, on my Spiritual Birthday, October 28th". *PW* (EHC) I 490–1; see also *CL* VI 950, sent to Thomas Pringle 6 Aug 1833. When Emerson visited C on 5 Aug 1833 C recited the whole of this poem to him (*C Talker* 209);

if the poem was composed on or near the date of his birthday, it could not have been composed later than Oct 1832 (though it may have been composed earlier).

Hymns 59 and 69 cannot be identified with certainty. In ten of twelve editions examined in the BM Hymn 59 is *Perseverance*, "Stand fast in the gospel; 'tis Christ makes you free", and Hymn 69 is *Let thy presence go with me*, "Death cannot make my soul afraid". In the other two editions Hymn 59, without title, is "Lo! He comes with Clouds descending" and Hymn 69, also without title, is "Nothing in this World I want".

WILLIAM HAYLEY
1745–1820

The Life of Milton, in three parts. To which are added, conjectures on the origin of Paradise Lost: with an appendix, &c. ("Second edition, considerably enlarged.") London 1796. 4⁰.

Henry E. Huntington Library

Thomas Poole's copy, inscribed by him in ink on the title-page: "Marginal Notes ~~by and~~ written by: *S: T: C:*". Poole communicated the notes to J. H. Green; they were printed in *LR* ɪ 179–84. On the front p–d, in an unidentified hand: "Beautiful copy with rare mezzotints inserted and numerous annotations and marginalia by Samuel Taylor Coleridge the poet", and, facing p 236, a pencilled note in an unknown hand.

Two inscribed sheets of paper among the MSS Leatherhead in the Humanities Research Center, University of Texas, accompanied at some time a group of transcripts (of undetermined extent) of Coleridge marginalia taken from Tom Poole's books. One sheet reads: "Marginal Notes by S. T. Coleridge inserted in various books belonging to Mʳ Poole—"; the other reads:

> Mʳ Poole's Notes of S T C
>
> Hayly's Milton
> Parnell's Apol
> Alg. Sydney
> Hobbes Leviathan
> Copied S. D.

("S. D." was a transcriber of marginalia referred to by EHC, but whether a transcriber who worked for him or a copyist whose transcripts he had inherited does not appear: see VCL BT 37 f 21, in which, however, none of the seven titles ascribed to "S. D." is the same as any of these four.) The Texas papers include a transcript of two of these four sets of notes—this copy of HAYLEY and Thomas HOBBES *Leviathan* (1651). HNC published only the HAYLEY annotations—the only set of marginalia acknowledged by the early editors as written in a book of Poole's. DC printed in *NTP* without acknowledgment to Poole two notes from HOBBES and notes from Algernon SIDNEY's *Works* (1772). The one long note in Thomas PARNELL *An Historical Apology for the Irish Catholics* (Dublin 1807) was printed in 1935 in *TLS*, showing that the book had Poole's signature in it but giving no evidence that Poole had communicated the annotations to Green. The Texas list not only indentifies four of the books from which Poole sent transcripts to Green; it also shows that these transcripts were in the editors' possession in 1835–6 (if HAYLEY was to be included in *LR* ɪ) and identifies as Poole's two books not otherwise known to have been his—the HOBBES (not located) and the SIDNEY (now in the University of Indiana library, but without Poole's signature).

Whether Poole sent transcripts for more than these four books is not known. Immediately after C's death Poole had written to HNC offering the editors whatever "papers and information" he had, and on 21 Aug 1834 Green asked Poole to send any marginalia from his books. HNC replied on 3 Sept 1834, asking that "such materials—written materials I mean—as you possess and are willing to communicate, should either by originals or copies, entire or selected, be sent to Mr. Green" (as literary executor); and on 17 Sept he recommended Poole to "number each page in order, & put your initials on them". On 4 Jun 1835 Poole sent "what I possess...letters and other M.S. of which the accompanying Sheets contain a Catalogue with occasional explanatory remarks"—including "The Sermon and the Remarks which he had made in the margins of some of my Books, which latter Mr Ward has been so good as to copy". BM Add MS 35344 ff 200–1. (Along a route that need not here be traced, most of these papers came to the BM—to form the three bound volumes Add MS 35343–35345—as a gift from bp Charles Waldgrave Sandford (b 1828), second son of bp John Sandford (1801–73), whose first wife was a niece of Thomas Poole; and the "Thomas Ward copy-book" of correspondence between C and Poole, once EHC's—the "MS (P)" that in 1949 Antony Coleridge placed in my safekeeping for a time—is now in the Berg Collection of the NYPL.) Poole's "Catalogue" has not survived with the papers in the BM. When HNC wrote to Poole again on 16 Apr 1836 to say that *LR* I and II were "now printed" and remarked how the preparation of them had been "a task of considerable difficulty, in consequence of the exceedingly scattered state of my materials, and especially of my not having them all before me at once", he may have been ensuring that Poole had sent him all he had: he also asked him "to say to Mr Wade"—i.e. Josiah Wade, Launcelot having died c 1830—that he would be glad to have "any communications...of MS. or marginal notes". BM Add MS 35344 ff 110–11, 112–13, 127.

The dispersal of Poole's library without any record having been made of its contents or of books with C's annotations in them is a grievous loss. Beyond the four books already noticed, only five other annotated books are known to have been Poole's: ADAM, COLQUHOUN, TODTENTANZ, Edward STILLINGFLEET *Origines Sacrae* (1675), and the lost set of the *Philosophical Transactions of the Royal Society* (see *CM* I lxxvi–lxxvii). The annotated Andrew FULLER now in HEHL may have been Poole's. See also *CM* I lxxxiv–lxxxv.

MS TRANSCRIPT. University of Texas (Humanities Research Center): a complete transcript in an unidentified hand, possibly printer's copy for *LR*.

DATE. Jun–Sept 1807, at the time of C's last visit to Poole in Nether Stowey.

1   pp 70–1, a few letters illegible in tightly bound gutter

[Hayley quotes from *The Reason of Church Government* as illustrating] the mental character of Milton, with a mild energy, a solemn splendor of sentiment and expression peculiar to himself.

"Time serves not now, and, perhaps, I might seem too profuse to give any certain account of what the mind at home, in the spacious circuits of her musing, hath liberty to propose to herself, though of highest hope and hardest attempting; whether that epic form, whereof the two poems of Homer, and those other two of Virgil and Tasso, are a diffuse, and the book of Job a brief, model; or whether the rules of Aristotle herein are strictly to be kept, or nature to be followed..."

These words deserve particular notice. I do not doubt, that Milton intended his Paradise lost as an Epic of the first class, and that the poetic Dialogue of Job was his model for the general Scheme of his Paradise Regained.[1]

Readers would not have been disappointed in this latter poem, if they had proceeded to it with a proper preconception of *the kind* of interest intended to be excited in that admirable work. In its kind it is the most *perfect* poem extant; tho' its *kind* may be [of][a] inferior Interest, being in its essence didactic, to that other sort, in which Instruction is conveyed more effectively because more indirectly, in connection with stronger & more pleasurable Emotions, & thereby in a closer affinity with *action*.[2] But might we not as rationally object to an accomplished Woman's conversing, however agreeably, because it has happened that we have received a keener pleasure from her singing to the Harp?[3] Si genus sit probo et sapienti homine haud indignum, et si poema sit in suo genere perfectum, satis est![b] quod si hoc autor[c] idem altioribus numeris et carmini diviniori ipsum pene divinum superadderit,[d] mehercule, satis est, et plusquam satis.[4] I

---

[a] Word supplied by the editor
[b] Punctuation point first written as a comma then changed to!
[c] A slip for "auctor"
[d] A slip for "superaddiderit"

1[1] For Job as a model of epic see EICHHORN *Alte Testament* 51 and GREW 26 n 1. For other references to this passage in *The Reason of Church Government* see H. COLERIDGE 7 n 1.

1[2] Cf C's statement that "it is far, far better to distinguish Poetry into different Classes; & instead of *fault*-finding to say, this belongs to such or such a class—thus noting inferiority in the *sort* rather than censure in the particular poem or poet". MILTON *Poems* 1.

1[3] C may be thinking of Basil Montagu's second wife, Laura Rush (d 1806); cf his remarks on the "*Power*" by Practice" exhibited in Laura Montagu's "fair white arms" playing the pedal harp. *CN* III 3361.

1[4] "If the kind be not unworthy of a good and wise man, and if the poem be perfect in its kind, that is enough. But if the same author shall have superadded this, itself almost divine, to heightened numbers and still more divine song, that by heaven is enough and more than enough." The rather awkward Latin of "this noble quotation" seems to be C's.

cannot however but wish, that the answer of Jesus to Satan in the fourth book, 1. 285 et sequentia,[5] had ~~not~~ breathed the spirit of this noble quotation rather than the narrow bigotry of Gregory the Great.[6] The passage indeed is excellent, & is partially true;[7] but partial Truths is the worse mode of conveying falsehood.[8]

S. T. C.

2   p 75

The sincerest friends of Milton may here agree with Johnson, who speaks of his <u>controversial merriment as disgusting</u>...

The man who reads a work meant for immediate effect on one age, with the notions & feelings of another, may be a refined gentleman, but must be a sorry Critic.[1] ~~To have~~ He who possesses imagination enough to *live* with his forefathers, and leaving comparative reflection for an after moment, to give himself *up* during the first perusal to the feelings of a contemporary if not a partizan, will, I dare aver, rarely find any part of M.'s prose works *disgusting*.

3   pp 101–2

The odium which the president <u>justly</u> incurred in the trial of Charles seems to have prevented even our liberal historians from recording with candour the great qualities he possessed: he was undoubtedly not only an intrepid but a sincere enthusiast in the cause of the commonwealth.

1[5] *Paradise Regained* IV 285–92:

To whom our Saviour sagely thus
    repli'd.
Think not but that I know these things,
    or think
I know them not; not therefore am I
    short
Of knowing what I ought: he who
    receives
Light from above, from the fountain of
    light,
No other doctrin needs, though granted
    true;
But these are false, or little else but
    dreams,
Conjectures, fancies, built on nothing
    firm.

See also the continuation, to line 364; in lines 321ff Christ dismisses all shallow and injudicious reading (for which see ANDERSON COPY A **5** and n 1, COPY B **29**, and FLEURY **69** and n 1).

1[6] For Gregory's bigotry in condemning secular literature see his prologue to his life of St Benedict *Dialogue* 2 (a passage from this work is quoted in *CN* III 3899), and more strikingly in his letter to Desiderius, *Letters* XI 54. Migne *PL* LXVI 126 and LXXVII 1171–2. A later tradition says that he burned the works of Livy and Cicero whenever he could get hold of them. Gregory's *Magna moralia* is a commentary on the book of Job.

1[7] I.e. the passage in *Paradise Regained* in n 5, above.

1[8] For C's view that "half-truths are whole errors" see e.g. *SM (CC)* 59, *LS (CC)* 228, *C&S (CC)* 7; see also HOOKER **10** (at n 2).

2[1] See also **6**, below.

Why *justly*? What would the contemptible Martyr-worshippers, (who yearly apply to this fraudulent would-be-despot the most aweful phrases of holy writ concerning the Saviour of Mankind, concerning the Incarnate *Word* that is with *God* & *is God*,[1] in a cento of ingenious blasphemy, that has no parallel in the annals of impious Adulation)[2] what would even these men have? Can they, as men, expect that Bradshaw & his Peers *should* give sentence against the Parliament & Armies of England, as guilty of all the blood that had been shed—as Rebels and Murderers![3] Yet there was no other alternative. That he or his peers were influenced by Cromwell is a gross Calumny, sufficiently confuted by their after lives & by their death-hour[4]—& has been amply falsified by M[rs] Hutchinson in her incomparable Life of her Incomparable Husband, Colonel Hutchinson.[5] O that I might have such an action to remember on my Death-bed![6] The only enviable part of Charles's Fate & Life is

---

3[1] John 1.1 (var).

3[2] In BCP from 1662 to 1859 a special form of prayer was provided for Charles the Martyr on 30 Jan; it includes many messianic passages but not John 1.1. Cf *CN* II 2908 and n. Even more extreme proposals were put before Convocation at the Savoy Conference (1661), as reported by e.g. Gilbert Burnet. Cf N 38 f 7[v] (*CN* v) (quoted in part in HACKET *Scrinia* 45 n 1): "O Heavens! What a Leash of Patron Saints have the Tory Clergy fixed on for the Anglican Church!—I. Charles the first, Martyr to the inveterate Vice of Lying, the poor uxorious Slave of a lewd Virago, and the perjured Accomplice in the atrocity of the Irish Massacre...."

3[3] John Bradshaw (1602–59), president of the parliamentary commission established to try Charles I in 1649. Milton, his friend, praised him in the *Defensio secunda pro populo Anglicano* (1654)—as Hayley noted with approval, quoting and translating from Milton (pp 98–100)—and defended him against the calumny of being subservient to Cromwell.

3[4] There is little doubt that Bradshaw's overbearing and undignified conduct of the trial of Charles, and his merciless condemnation of the leading royalists after the execution of Charles, expressed his own conviction rather than Cromwell's

instructions. He is reported to have said shortly before he died that "If the King were to be tried and condemned again, he would be the first man that would do it." Of the forty-one regicides still alive at the Restoration, three were allowed to leave the country and eight escaped. The rest were brought to trial, at which only a few behaved cravenly; most affirmed their faith "in a cause not to be repented of"; the nine who suffered the barbarous extremity of punishment reserved for traitors behaved with great dignity.

3[5] HUTCHINSON ii 303, and see esp 12 and n 1. According to Lucy Hutchinson, those who later claimed that they had served the High Court "under the awe of the armie, and overperswaded by Cromwell, and the like" were lying: "it is certeine that all men herein were left to their free liberty of acting, neither perswaded nor compelled; and as there were some [forty-seven] nominated in the commission who never sate, and others who sate at first, but durst not hold on [eight left before the trial, and twenty-one attended the trial but did not sign the death-warrant], so all the rest might have declin'd it if they would, when it is apparent they should have suffer'd nothing by so doing."

3[6] Cf the transcript of an annotation on BAXTER *Reliquiae* COPY A i 373 (not

that his name is connected with the greatest names of ancient or modern times—Qui cum victus erat, *tantis* certâsse feretur.[7]

S. T. Coleridge.

4 p 104

[Referring to Milton's answer to *Eikon Basilike*:] Milton himself may be also urged as an example to enforce the same caution [against prejudice]; for although he was certainly no impostor in imputing the prayer in question to the king, yet his considering the king's use of it as an offence against heaven, is a pitiable absurdity; an absurdity as glaring as it would be to affirm, that the divine poet is himself profane in assigning to a speech of the Almighty, in his poem, the two following verses:

> Son of my bosom, son who art alone
> My word, my wisdom, and effectual might—

Because they are partly borrowed from a line in Virgil, addressed by a heathen goddess to her child:

> "Nate, meae vires, mea magna potentia solus."
> [Son, my strength, my great power alone.]

Assuredly, I regret that Milton should have written the passage alluded to/[1] and yet the adoption of a prayer from a Romance on such an occasion does not evince a delicate or deeply sincere Mind.[2] We are the creatures of association—there are some excellent moral & even serious Lines in Hudibras/ but what if a Clergyman should

---

in *CM* I): "...I believe, that the majority of Charles's judges acted from conscience. How he was brought before such judges is another case. I confess, that had I been sworn in a judge, I should have given my verdict, as Martin & Colonel Hutchinson did...". For Colonel Hutchinson, regicide, see n 5, above. Henry Marten (1602–80), very active in bringing Charles to trial, signed the death-warrant but later became hostile to Cromwell and Bradshaw; he surrendered at the Restoration, conducted his trial ably and with great courage, and was sentenced to life imprisonment rather than to death.

3[7] Ovid *Metamorphoses* 13.20 (var). Tr: "Who, when conquered, will be famed for having fought against *such great men*". The original reads: "quod, cum victus erit, mecum certasse feretur" —"because, when conquered, he will be famed for having fought with me".

4[1] Hayley quotes *Paradise Lost* III 169–70 and *Aeneid* 1.664–5. In patristic and mediaeval times *Aeneid* 1.664–5, like the well-known *Eclogue* 4, was thought to show that Virgil was a Christian before Christ.

4[2] In *Eikonoclastes* ch 1 Milton accused Charles, with great severity, of taking his "prayer in captivity" from Pamela's prayer in Sidney's *Arcadia* bk 3. In fact, a copy of this prayer was appended to only a few copies of *Eikon Basilike*.

adorn his Sermon with a quotation from that Poem?[3] Would the
abstract propriety of the Lines leave him "*honorably acquitted*?"[4]
The Xtian Baptism of a Line of Virgil is so far from being a parallel,
that [it]*[a]* is ridiculously inappropriate—"an absurdity as glaring" as
that of the bigotted puritans, who objected to some of the noblest
& most scriptural prayers ever dictated by wisdom & piety simply
because the Catholics had used them. S. T. C.

5 p 107

The ambition of Milton was as pure as his Genius was sublime; his
first object on every occasion was to merit the approbation of his
conscience and his God; when this most important point was
secured, he seems to have indulged the predominant passion of great
minds, and to have exulted, with a triumph proportioned to his toil,
in the celebrity he acquired...

I do not approve the so frequent use of this word relatively to Milton.
Indeed, the fondness of ingrafting a good sense on the word
"ambition" is not a Christian Impulse in general.[1]

6 p 110

It was the opinion of Johnson, and Milton himself seems to have
entertained the same idea, that it is allowable in literary contention
to ridicule, vilify, and depreciate as much as possible the character
of an opponent. Surely this doctrine is unworthy of the great names
who have endeavoured to support it, both in theory and practice;
a doctrine not only morally wrong, but prudentially defective; for
a malevolent spirit in eloquence is like a dangerous varnish in
painting...

If ever it were allowable, in this case it was especially so.[1] But these
General Observations, without meditation on the particular times &
Genius of the times, are most often as unjust as they are always
superficial.[2]

[a] Word supplied by the editor

4[3] Cf Anderson copy a **10**,
Chalmers **4** (at n 1), and Flögel **10**
(at n 1).

4[4] Hayley wrote (p 103) that Birch
"honourably united with another candid
biographer of the poet, the learned
bishop of Bristol" in denying "such
contemptible evidence".

5[1] See e.g. Matt 18.1–4, 20.20–2; Luke
22.24–7.

6[1] In the reply to Salmasius, *Pro
populo Anglicano defensio* (1650).

6[2] Cf **2**, above.

7 p 133

With a mind full of fervid admiration for his [Cromwell's] marvellous atchievements, and generally disposed to give him credit for every upright intention, Milton hailed him as the father of his country, and delineated his character: if there were some particles of flattery in this panegyric...it was completely purified from every cloud or speck of servility by the most splendid and sublime admonition that was ever given to a man possessed of great talents and great power...

Besides, however Milton might, & did regret the immediate necessity, yet what alternative was there? Was it not better that Cromwell should usurp power to protect religious freedom at least, than that the Presbyterians should usurp it to introduce an accursed religious persecution; extending indeed the notion of spiritual concerns so far, as to leave no freedom even to a man's bed-chamber?—

8 p 250 | "Conjectures on the Origin of the *Paradise Lost*"

In the course of this discussion we may find, perhaps, a mode of accounting for the inconsistency both of Dryden and Voltaire; let us attend at present to what the latter has said of Andreini!—If the *Adamo* of this author really gave birth to the divine poem of Milton, the Italian dramatist, whatever rank he might hold in his own country, has a singular claim to our attention and regard.

If Milton borrowed a hint from any writer, it was more probably from Strada's Prolusiones, in which the fall of the Angels &c is pointed out as the noblest subject for a Christian Poet.[1] The more

8[1] Famiano Strada (1572–1649) *Prolusiones academicae, oratoriae, historicae, poeticae* (Cologne 1617; also e.g. Oxford 1631, 1745). In Feb 1808 C made note to transcribe a passage from this book at Cuthell & Martin's bookshop: *CN* III 3276 f 72ᵛ (8). He left his own copy behind at Allan Bank in 1810; the edition is not identified. See Wordsworth LC 107 (twice marked as C's), 1279 (Highgate List). In *LR* I 183n HNC comments on this annotation by citing "the 5th Prolusion of the 1st Book", from which he quotes in Latin. In Bk I Prolusio 5, entitled (tr) "Whether subjects taken from sacred literature are as suitable for poetic treatment as those from profane literature", Strada says that classical poets—Orpheus, Homer, Hesiod, Virgil, Ovid—have taken from sacred literature such themes as their descriptions of Chaos and the Flood (pp 99–101, 1745 ed). He then (pp 103ff) "adumbrates" a description of the courts of God peopled by symbolic characters—e.g. Providence, Peace, Liberty, Arts, Graces—and an account of a high tower, with which HNC's quotation begins (tr): "Here let the bow and the weapons be kept with which in that great tumult of the angels Michael leader of battle struck down the author of treachery; here the thunders that terrify the mind of man....I shall marshal armed legions for war in the

dissimilar the detailed images are, the more likely it is that a great genius should catch the general idea.[2] S. T. C.

9 p 295 | "Appendix, Containing Extracts from the *Adamo* of Andreini"[a]

[*Adamo* I ii 1–24:]

LUCIFERO.

Chi dal mio centro oscuro,
Mi chiama a rimirar cotanta luce?...
Dimmi architetto vile,
Che di fango opre festi,
Ch' avverra di quest' huom povero, ignudo...
Tessa pur stella à stella,
V' aggiunga e luna, e sole,
S' affatichi pur Dio,
Per far di novo il ciel lucido adorno,
Ch' al fin, con biasmo e scorno,
Vana l'opra sara, vana il sudore,
Fu Lucifero sol quell' ampia luce,
Per cui splendeva in mille raggi il cielo;

LUCIFER.

Who from my dark abyss
Calls me to gaze on this excess of light?

This is unfair: & may suggest that Milton really had read & did imitate this Drama. The Original is "on so great Light". Indeed the whole translation is affectedly & inaccurately Miltonic[1]

[a] Italian and English texts on facing pages

clouds, and then call out appropriate auxiliary forces on earth...The Coelites (Sky Spirits), who are said to be the guardians of the elements, will mingle for me those first bodies, collect them into clouds, and let down such storm of rain...as will scatter the armies...".

8[2] Cf C's remark about the dismay of the "commentators [who] only hunt out verbal Parallelisms" when confronted by the puzzle of "Haemony" in *Comus* 629–41: "They thought little of Milton's platonizing Spirit—who wrote nothing without an interior meaning. 'Where more is meant, than meets the ear' is true of himself beyond all writers. He was so great a Man, that he seems to have considered Fiction profane, unless where it is consecrated by being emblematic of some Truth/". To Sotheby 10 Sept 1802: *CL* II 866.

9[1] The translation is William Cowper's. On the "Miltonism" of Cowper's tr of Homer see HOMER **1** n 11.

Say, thou vile architect,
Forming thy works <u>of dust,</u>   of *dirt*
What will befal this naked helpless man...
Let him unite above
Star upon star, moon, sun,

Let him weave star ~~on~~ to star,
There join both moon & sun,

And let his Godhead toil
To re-adorn and re-illume his heav'n;
Since in the end derision
Shall prove his works, and all his efforts,
    vain;

Since finally with censure and disdain
Vain shall the work be, & his Toil be vain—   *word* for *word*

For Lucifer alone was that full light,
Which scatter'd radiance o'er the plains
    of Heav'n.

Thro' whom in thousand rays the Heaven was used to shine.—

NICOLA FRANCESCO HAYM
1679–1729

Notizia de' libri rari nella lingua italiana divisa in quattro parti principali; cio è, istoria, poesia, prose, arti e scienze. Anessovi tutto il libro della Eloquenza Italiana di Mons. Giusto Fontanini, con il suo Ragionamento intorno la detta materia. Con tavole copiosissime, e necessarie. [Compiled by N. F. Haym.] London 1726. 8°.

Victoria College Library (Coleridge Collection)

"S T C" in ink on the title-page, not in C's hand. Description by EHC in pocket attached to p +4 (p–d).

DATE. Before Oct 1810, when the book was left behind with the Wordsworths, to be included later in Wordsworth LC.

1   p 184, pencil

GIORDANO BRUNO Nolano, spaccio della Bestia Trionfante. In *] Parigi 1584. in 8vo. *Libro Ateistico, ma rarissimo; l'Autore di esso fu bruciato in effegie.*

[GIORDANO BRUNO of Nola, *The Expulsion of the Triumphant Beast.* Paris 1584. 8°. *An atheistical book, but very rare; the author of it was burned in effigy.*]

ne rarissimo, ne ateistico.
  * Catalogus quam maxime imperfectus.
  Spaccio d. B. T. può trovarsi senza gran difficoltá; l'autore di esso, e di quell' opera profundissima, e quasi "divina", "del Monade; e ~~de~~ De Infinito et Immenso " fu bruciato sì ~~nelli~~ quella *effigie* della gran anima sua, vuoldirsi, in *corpo suo*,—in Roma, anno 1600. Giord: Bruno annoverò fra gli amici suoi Sir Philip Sidney, et Fulk Greville, osia Lord Brooke.[1]

1[1] Bruno's book is "neither very rare, nor atheistical". And this is "A Catalogue imperfect in the highest degree."
"*The Expulsion of the Triumphant Beast* can be found without much difficulty; the author of it, and of that most profound—even 'divine'—work 'On the Monad: and On Infinity and Immensity', was burned in that *effigy* of his great spirit, namely, *his body*—in Rome, in the year 1600. Giordano Bruno numbered among his friends Sir Philip Sidney and Fulk Greville, Lord Brooke." C has confused two similar titles: *De monade...De numeris, immenso et infigurabili* (Frankfurt 1591) and *De l'infinito universo et mondi* (Venice 1584).

For C's reading of Bruno's works see BAXTER *Reliquiae* COPY B 103 n 1 and cf *CN* II 2264n, III 3825 f 114 and n. For his projected life of Bruno see *Friend (CC)* II 81–2n (I 117–18n).

976

FRANCIS BOND HEAD

1793–1875

Bubbles from the Brunnens of Nassau. By an old man [i.e. Francis Bond Head]. London 1834. 8º.

Victoria College Library (Coleridge Collection)

Inscribed on the half-title: "Mrs H. N. Coleridge From the Publisher"; and by HNC on the title-page: "Sara Coleridge from J. Murray. Hampstead 1834." and above this, the signature of "Edith Coleridge". Original dark-red paper wrappers bound in, preserving the opening of 1 on the inside of the front cover. On p 43 "one class of cold iron water" is corrected to "glass" with a pencilled "g" in the margin.

A pocket pasted to p $^+$7 (p–d) contains a letter from Head to HNC, dated 29 Aug 1835, part of which is published in *CL* vi 978n, objecting to the version of C's annotation published by HNC in *TT* (1835): see 1 n 1, below. The pocket also contains HNC's draft reply to Head:

"Sir—

"I have received your letter of this date calling my attention to an extract from a note written by Mr S. T. C. on a copy of the Bubbles &c. & published by me in &c [i.e. *Table Talk*] vol. 2 p — & in which you request an apology from me for publishing the ~~passage~~—

"If it had occurred to me that the expressions of w͞ch you complain, could be taken in a personally offensive sense, I certainly would not have published them—knowing that nothing could have been further from Mr S. T. C.'s intention than to impute want of veracity to the author of the Bubbles &c—much less slander or blasphemy in the ordinary meaning & application of those words. I thought the context of the passage very plainly showed that nothing of that sort was intended, & I think so still. But as you, who have a right to feel the most concerned, conceive these expressions in question to be personally injurious, it is my duty to express to you, as I willingly do, my regret at having given you pain & to tender to you the apology w͞ch you request for publishing this passage, w͞ch at the earliest opportunity in my power, I will—so far as those expressions are concerned —withdraw.

"With regard to giving your name to a work published anonymously, I acknowledge the impropriety, & can only plead general notoriety as an excuse—I am—"

For the cancellation made by HNC in the text of *TT* in harmony with his letter to Head see 1 nn 5 and 7, below. When Head wrote to HNC in Aug 1835 he was poor-law commissioner in Kent; not until Nov of that year was he offered the post of Lieutenant-Governor of Upper Canada, in which he served until he resigned in 1838. After his return to England he became a regular contributor to the *Quarterly Review*. Cf 1 n 6, below.

DATE. 18 Mar 1834 (1).

1   pp ⁻3−−1,ᵃ continued on the half-title

18 March, 1834. Grove, Highgate

My dear Henry,

    I, the most incurious of all sensitive animals, do feel very curious
to know ⟨who is⟩ the Writer of this Book.[1]—The strange discrepancy
of his account of the *Maltese* with my own recollections startled me.
Had he been speaking of the *Messinese*, I should have recognized the
truth to the Hair of a Cheek-Mole![2]—But this ~~contrast of fact is a
trifle compared with~~ variation of mine & the other "Old Man's"
recollections, is a trifle. But how can I account for the Anglo-
gentlemanly, the sensible & kindly, mind breaking forth every where
in the first half of the Volume, ⟨as contrasted⟩ with the strange,
one-sided representation of our public Schools—which, with full
admission on *my* part of their Defects, or rather *Deficiencies*, or
still better, their *Paucities*, ~~can~~ amounts to a *double* Lie, a Lie by
exaggeration, and a Lie by *Omission*/ And the Universities—even
relatively to Oxford 30 years ago it would have been Slander—to
Cambridge, as it now is, blasphemy![3]—And then his absurd attrib-

a p ⁻3 is the inside of the original red paper wrapper

1[1] When C wrote his annotations he
had not identified the author: see n 6,
below. HNC gave offence by naming the
author in *TT* (1835) 16 Apr 1834 as
though C himself knew who the author
was (see n 2, below): "But what can Sir
Francis Head, in the *Bubbles*, mean by
talking of the musical turn of the
Maltese?..." As a footnote to this
remark HNC printed C's note 1 (var),
beginning "How can I account for
the Anglo-gentlemanly...mind", and
added: "Perhaps, if the author of the
Bubbles had not *finished his classical
studies at fourteen* [as Head states in p
224n], he might have seen reason to
modify his heavy censure on Greek and
Latin. As it is, it must be borne with
patience." For Head's reaction to the
breach of anonymity and to HNC's quip
see *CL* vi 978n. Before going to the Royal
Military Academy, Woolwich, Head had
attended Rochester Grammar School;
the anonymous "old man" who wrote
this book was forty-one years old when it
was published.

1[2] Head had served in the Mediterra-
nean 1811–15, based on Malta; in his
book he gives an account of the Knights
of Malta (pp 161–78) and a detailed
account of the trial and public execution
of a Turkish assassin in Malta (pp 179–91)
and of the turbulent and vociferous
behaviour of the Maltese crowd as the
condemned man was being paraded to
the gallows. The contrast C makes in his
annotation between the Maltese and
Messinese is elucidated by *Friend* (*CC*) i
566, in which C compares "the religious
processions in honor of the favorite
saints, both at Vallette and at Messina or
Palermo", suggesting that any observer
"must have been struck with the contrast
between the apparent apathy, or at least
the perfect sobriety, of the Maltese, and
the fanatical agitations of the Sicilian
populace".

    C's objection to "the musical turn of
the Maltese"—in *TT* but not in the
marginalia—may have been initiated by
Head's reference to the sound of the
cow's horn that was the signal for the
march to the gallows: "...at Malta,
where the ear has been constantly
accustomed to good Italian music, and to
listen to nothing more discordant than

ution of the National Debt of 800, Millions, to the predominance of *Classical* Taste, and Academic Talent![4] And his strange ignorance that without the rapidly increasing National Debt Great Britain could never have become that monstrous Mammon-bloated *Dives*, or ~~Synod~~ Woden-Idol of stuffed Pursemen, *part* of whose un-⟨r⟩ighteous Wealth ~~it~~ this Debt constitutes!!

In short, at one moment I imagine that Mr Frere, or you, or any other Etonian, or Alumnus of Westminster or Winchester, might be the Author/ at another, fall back to Joseph Hume, Dr Birkbeck, Edingburgh or Aberdeen.[5]

Do ask Lockhart, if it may be dared./[6]   S. T. C.—

One[7] constant blunder of these New-broomers (or Broughamers)[8]—

the lovely and love-making notes of the guitar, this savage whoop was indescribably offensive...". For C's account of the noise in Malta see *CN* ii 2614, esp ff 94^v–95^v, and cf 2114.

1[3] In his letter of protest to HNC Head expressed his "astonishment that your Uncle should have discovered Slander and blasphemy in my bubbles, that he should have affixed the same to me by name, altho' *my* work was published anonymously...". *CL* vi 978n. For HNC's reply to this charge see par 2 of his draft letter in the headnote, above.

1[4] Head wrote (pp 236–7) of "the luxury of reading Greek and Latin poetry" that "the price of its statesmen studying ancient poets instead of modern discoveries—of mistaking the 'orbis veteribus cognitus' for the figure of the world, amounts to neither more nor less than a national debt of EIGHT HUNDRED MILLIONS of English pounds sterling!...". For C's indignation at the national debt see e.g. *LS(CC)* 195, 204–5, and cf DONNE *Sermons* COPY B **81** n 2.

1[5] Here HNC's quotation in the footnote to *TT* 16 Apr 1834 ends. In the 1836 ed he cancelled both the footnote and the opening paragraph in which Head is named.

John Hookham Frere and HNC were both Etonians; the style that established *Bubbles* as Head's best book suggests the urbane classicism of such a training. Joseph Hume (1777–1855), from humble beginnings and poor schooling, studied medicine at Aberdeen and Edinburgh, then in London, and after ten years' medical service with the East India Company was a radical MP 1818–55. George Birkbeck (1776–1841) studied medicine at Edinburgh, became a friend of Brougham (whose birthplace and university were also Edinburgh) and of Jeffrey, became a leader in popular education, and founded the mechanics' institutes; he was also associated with Brougham in founding the University of London. See n 16, below, and *C&S (CC)* 61–2 and nn 3, 5. See also n 8, below.

1[6] John Gibson Lockhart (1794–1854), editor of *QR* 1825–53, would probably know who had written an anonymous book published by John Murray. For C's early acquaintance with Lockhart see e.g. *CL* v 123–4n.

1[7] HNC printed this postscript, without its footnote, as a footnote to *TT* (1835) 8 Jul 1833 by way of comment on C's remark that neither elementary mathematics nor the modern languages German and French should be included in the curriculum of "the great schools". In the 1835 ed HNC described the note as "pencilled by Mr. C. on a blank page of my copy of the 'Bubbles from the Brunnens'"; in the 1836 ed he altered this to read: "pencilled by Mr. C. on a margin".

1[8] Head argues (pp 223–39) for the study of modern history and current affairs, in both school and university,

these Penny Magazine Sages and Philanthropists,* in reference to our Public Schools, is to compare their view to what the School-Masters teach the Boys, with entire oversight of all, that the Boys are excited to learn from each other, and of themselves—with more geniality, even *because* ~~they~~ it is *not* a part of their compelled school Knowlege.

—An Etonian of 15's knowlege of the St Lawrence, Mississippi, Missouri, Orellana &c &c will be, generally, found in exact proportion to his knowlege of Issus, Ilissus, Hebrus, &c[15]—as modern Travels & Voyages are more entertaining & fascinating than Cellarius—or Robinson Crusoe, & Dampier, & Captn Cook than the Periegesis.[16] Compare the *Lads* themselves from Eton &c with the alumni of the New-broom Institutions, & not the lists of School-lessons: & be that the Criterion![17]—*S. T. C.*

* That variety who prescribe solitary imprisonment for Burglary, Highway-robbery &c might be distinguished as Felon-trappists:[9] & these again distinguished from the humane Philheautists,[10] who plant Man-gins, spring-guns &c in their grounds,[11] by nameing the latter *Villain-trapists*—the "Villain" interpreted midway between the original *villanus*, = peasant,[12] & the modern *product* or hominifact[13] of our peasantry—ex. gr. Poachers, or Cottage Boys a nutting or Orchard-robbing—which latter, any where within 10 miles of the Metropolis, & 5 of any large Town, is to be excepted from the 8th Commandment for all Males & females not 14 years old.[14] *S. T. C.*

rather than of classical history and literature, as preparation for public life. Brougham's name is here invoked by C not only for his association with popular education and the founding of the University of London (see HALL 1 n 4) but also for his championing (1808 onwards), with the Whigs, Quakers, and *Ed Rev*, of the school system established by Joseph Lancaster as against the system of Andrew Bell supported by the Church of England, the *QR*, and C. See *IS* 82–9. In an undated ms note C intended to write as one of "A series" a letter "on the Lancastrian Faction for National Heady-cation—i.e. a process for rendering the populace heady, leaving them as brainless as before". VCL ms.

1[9] Cf "Villain-trapists", below.
1[10] Exponents of the principle of self-love. Cf *OED* "philauty".

1[11] Cf Boswell *Johnson* 20 Mar 1776: "...he should have warned us of our danger...by advertising, 'Spring-guns and man-traps set here'". *Boswell's Life of Johnson* ed G. B. Hill rev L. F. Powell (Oxford 1964) II 448.
1[12] *Villanus*—vulgar Latin, from *villa*—"rustic".
1[13] On the analogy of "artefact", [an object] made by man. Cf *OED* "hominify" (to render human).
1[14] For C's indignation at the oppressive criminal code of his time see e.g. *IS* 312–14. Cf also BAXTER *Reliquiae* COPY B 3 on the sins of "nutting or Orchard-robbing".
1[15] This arises from Head's statement (p 224n): "At this age [fourteen] I myself left my...classical school, scarcely knowing the name of a single river in the new world—tired almost to death of the

2 pp 61–2, referring to pp 59–60 | The Bath

[An account of taking the baths of Langen-Schwalbach:]...so, descending the steps, I got into stuff so deeply coloured with the red oxide of iron, that the body, when a couple of inches below the surface, was invisible....I was no sooner immersed in it, than I felt it was evidently of a strengthening, bracing nature, and I could almost have fancied myself lying with a set of hides in a tan-pit....

These baths are said to be very apt to produce head-ach, sleepiness, and other slightly apoplectic symptoms; but surely such effects proceed from the silly habit of not immersing the head?...Even the common pressure of water on the portion of the body which is

---

history of Ilissus. In after life I entered a river of America more than five times as broad as from Dover to Calais [i.e. the Rio de la Plata]—and with respect to the Ilissus, which had received in my mind such distorted importance, I will only say, that I have repeatedly walked across it in about 20 seconds, without wetting my ancles." Children of fourteen, he continued (p 224), "in this degraded state, with the energy and curiosity of their young minds blunted...[were] released from their schools to...sail from their country ignorant of almost everything that has happened to it since the days of the Romans...". The Ilissus, sacred to the Muses, flowed past the walls of Athens, and provided the idyllic setting of Plato's *Phaedrus* (229A–230C). Issus was the name of a town—did C mean to write "Hyssus", a river of Cappadocia that flows into the Euxine Sea? Hebrus— the river of Thrace into which the severed head of Orpheus was thrown.

1[16] Christoph Cellarius (1638–1707), classical scholar of Halle University, wrote numerous books on ancient history and geography as well as on grammar and style. *Robinson Crusoe* was a favourite book of C's: see DEFOE. C's copy of William Dampier (1652–1715) was *The Voyages and Adventures of Capt. William Dampier* (2 vols 1776), a series of C's quasi-marginalia on which is preserved in BM Egerton MS 2800 f 105: see DEFOE 15 n 1. C was familiar with James Cook's voyages, but the editions are not identified; for his acquaintance with William Wales, Cook's astronomer on the second voyage around the world, then director of the navigation school at Christ's Hospital, see BÖHME **66** n 1. C refers finally to the Περιήγησις τῆς οἰκουμένης (Figure of the Known World), a geographical treatise in 1185 Greek hexameters by Dionysius "Periegetes" c A.D. 300 (editio princeps Ferrara 1512).

1[17] I.e. the mechanics' institutes established by the work of George Birkbeck (see n 5, above). After studying medicine at Edinburgh University, he was appointed professor of natural philosophy at Andersonian College, Glasgow, when he was twenty-three; there in 1800 he began within the university low-fee courses in scientific subjects for working-class men. In 1804 he moved to London to practice medicine, but the courses he had established so flourished that they led to the founding of the Glasgow Mechanics' Institution in 1823. Birkbeck, encouraged by friends to form a similar establishment in London, contributed money for a lecture-hall and in 1824 became the first president of the London Mechanics' Institution, associated in this—as in the first council of the new University College, London (1827)—with Brougham, who had been a fellow-student and friend at Edinburgh University. Birkbeck continued to be active for the Institution, despite ridicule and varying fortunes, until his death in 1841. See also *C&S* (*CC*) 61–2 and 62 nn 3 and 5.

immersed in it, tends mechanically to push or force the blood towards that part (the head) enjoying a rarer medium; but when it is taken into calculation that the mineral mixture of Schwalbach acts on the body, not only mechanically, by pressure, but medicinally, being a very strong astringent, there needs no wizard to account for the unpleasant sensations so often complained of.

...I resolved that my head should fare alike with the rest of my system: in short, that it deserved to be strengthened as much as my limbs.

This *seems* very sensible; but how, if the Patient's Body from Neck to Sole remain submerged in the metallic Tan-pit for *Half an Hour*, can he contrive to keep his head *submerged*? and if only for a few seconds, how are these to prevent the after rush of the blood to the Brain, thro' the remaining $29'\frac{1}{1,51}$ of the $30'$? It *may*, nay, I believe, does *lessen*; but surely cannot preclude, the effect of the disparity— S. T. C.

N.B. besides, I am very sceptical respecting the whole theory. It is far, far too mechanical and hydraulic

3   pp 278–9 | The Monastery of Eberbach

In the year 1131, St. Bernhard, the famous preacher of the crusade, (whose followers eventually possessed, merely in the Rhine-gau, six monastic establishments—namely, Tiefenthal, Gottesthal, Eberbach, *] Eibinger, Nothgottes, and Marienhausen,) was attacked by a holy itch, or irresistible determination to erect a monastery; but not knowing where to drop the foundation stone, he consulted, it is said, a wild boar, on this important subject. The creature shrewdly listened to the human being who addressed it; and a mysterious meeting was agreed upon, he silently grubbed with his snout, in the valley of Eberbach, lines marking out the foundation of the building; and certainly such a lovely stye, for men basking in sunshine, to snore away their existence, no animal but a pig would ever have thought of!

* Only imagine to yourself the state and condition of the Country and Soil, and the almost *nullity* of the Population, at the time of the erection of these Cœnobite Establishments! Think of their *immediate* Results, all unqualified *Good*—of the Good, that still accompanied the evils from their own corruption, & the blighting influence of the Papacy—and how little shall we ⟨be⟩ disposed to ridicule their

sainted Founders, or to depreciate them—because St Ælfric in the 6th or 7th, or St Bernhard in the 11th Century[1] had not the Lights or Predilections of the 18th or 19th Century!—Holy *Itch*—? *Jeffray* should have written these words.[2]

4 p 278

It is not improbable, that the *Boar* (or Pig, as the Southeyizing Writer chooses to call it)[1] was the Symbol of the first attempt towards cultivation—the living Turner-up of the sluggish Earth! Nature's *Hint* of the Spade and the Plough!—

5 p 279

...when all was completed, monks were brought to the abode, and the holy hive, for many centuries, was heard buzzing the wild mountains which surrounded it: however, in the year 1803, the Duke of Nassau took violent possession of its honey, and its inmates were thus rudely shaken from their cells. Three or four of the monks, of this once wealthy establishment, are all that now remain in existence, and their abode has ever since been used partly as a government prison, and partly as a public asylum for lunatics.

And is this matter for a Christian's Triumph! It almost tempts a good man to become a R. Catholic!

If the monks had become Wasps, why not substitute Bees?

6 p 281

...I felt within me a strong emotion of pity for those poor, forlorn misguided beings, whose existence had been uselessly squandered in such mistaken seclusion; and I could not help fancying how acutely, from the spot on which I stood, they might have compared the moral loneliness of their mansion, with the natural joy and loveliness of that river scenery, from which their relentless mountain had severed

---

3[1'] St Aelfric (c 955–c 1020), Benedictine abbot of Eynsham; St Bernard (1090–1153), Cistercian abbot of Clairvaux. St Aelfric is not mentioned by Head; the grounds for C's misdating are not known.

3[2] Francis Jeffrey (1773–1850) (whose name C regularly spelled "Jeffray"), one of the founders of the *Ed Rev* (1802) and editor 1803–29. C felt deep resentment for his attacks on *Lyrical Ballads* and for

associating his name with WW's alleged "silliness" (see e.g. *CL* v 421, 475, 734, 1023–4), for mangling his review of Clarkson's *History of the Abolition of the Slave Trade* in 1808 (*CL* III 116–19, 124–5), and for arranging for a hostile review of *Christabel* and of *SM* and *BL*.

4[1] For the qualities of a "Southeyizing Writer" see e.g. H. COLERIDGE 5 and n 1. Here he is accused of democratic levelling?

them: indeed, I hope my reader will not think an old man too Anacreontic for saying, that if any thing in this world could penetrate the sack-cloth garment of a monk, "and wring his bosom," it would be the sight of what I had just turned my back upon—namely, a vineyard full of women! That the fermentation of the grape was intended to cheer decrepitude, and that affections of a softer sex were made to brighten the zenith of mid-day life, are truths which, within the walls of a convent or a monastery, it must have been most exquisite torture to reflect upon.

No man can contemplate with deeper reprobation than I do, all constrained Vows of Abstinence or of Celibacy.[1] But too many Protestants have carried their *protestations* into absolute *Sensuality*: as if there could be *none*, who could virtuously live ~~single~~ unmarried for the Kingdom of Heaven.—[2]

7 p 292

The madman is now soundly sleeping where the fanatic had in vain sought for repose—and the knave unwillingly suffering for theft *] where the hypocrite had voluntarily confined himself!

* But why, necessarily, hypocrite?—Why always *fanatic*? Was Bede either? Or Benedict?—[1]

6[1] For C on "constrained...Celibacy" of the clergy see FLEURY 85 and n 1.

6[2] See Matt 19.12, and cf 1 Cor 7 passim, esp 8–9 and 32.

7[1] The illustrations are C's: Head does not mention Bede or Benedict. The Venerable Bede (c 673–735), biblical scholar and "Father of English History", St Benedict (c 480–c 550), founder of Western monasticism.

SAMUEL HEARNE
1745–1792

A Journey from Prince of Wales's Fort, in Hudson's Bay, to the Northern Ocean. Undertaken by order of the Hudson's Bay Company. For the discovery of copper mines, a North West Passage, &c. In the years 1769, 1770, 1771, & 1772. Dublin 1796. 8°.

Harvard University (Houghton Library)

Pencil checks, not by C, on pp 343, 345. The volume was described by Lowes in *RX* 493 n 7; see also H. F. Watson "A Note on The Ancient Mariner" *PQ* xiii (1934).

C refers obliquely to this work in a note of 3–4 Nov 1803 (*CN* i 2297 f 81). If *The Three Graves* was composed during the *annus mirabilis*, and if the poem was from the beginning as much affected by Hearne's account of witchcraft among the Copper Indians as C suggests in his prefatory note to the poem in *SL*, his first acquaintance with Hearne's *Journey* may have been as early as his reading of the other book he associates with *The Three Graves*—Bryan Edwards's *History...of the British Colonies in the West Indies* (2 vols 1793), which he borrowed from the Bristol Library 14 Jul–7 Aug 1795 (*Bristol LB* 64). See *Friend* No 6 of 21 Sept 1809 (*CC*) ii 89 (the reference to Hearne and Edwards preserved in i 431n); see also the prefatory note to *The Three Graves*, revised from *The Friend*, in *SL* and later, with its appeal to ballad-language and to "merits...exclusively psychological"— *PW* (EHC) i 267–9. The passage on witchcraft (pp 214–22) is not marked or annotated in this copy.

William Wales (for whom see Böhme **66** n 1) was instrumental in the publication of Hearne's *Journey* in Oct 1792, a month before Hearne's death: see Samuel Hearne *A Journey...* ed Richard Glover (Toronto 1958) xli–xliii.

Kant mentions Hearne's *Journey* in *Die Religion innerhalb der Grenzen der blossen Vernunft* (Königsberg 1795) 28–9, 28n (not annotated), saying that there is a natural bias to evil in man, as is proved—contrary to the assertions of those philosophers who believe that primitive man is good—by the ceaseless wars and murders of the Indians in northwest America.

DATE. Unknown. Perhaps as late as 1824 (see **1** n 4, below).

1   p ⁻2, referring to pp 344–5 | Ch 9 "A Short Description of the Northern Indians..."

RELIGION has not as yet begun to dawn among the Northern Indians; for though their conjurors do indeed sing songs, and make long speeches, to some beasts and birds of prey, as also to imaginary beings, which they say assist them in performing cures on the sick, yet they, as well as their credulous neighbours, are utterly destitute of every idea of practical religion. It is true, some of them will reprimand their youth for talking disrespectfully of particular beasts and birds; but it is done with so little energy, as to be often retorted back in derision. Neither is this, nor their custom of not killing wolves and quiquehatches, universally observed, and those who do it can only be viewed with more pity and contempt than the others... and I never found any of them that had the least idea of futurity. Matonabbee, without one exception, was a man of as clear ideas in other matters as any that I ever saw; he was not only a perfect master of the Southern Indian language, and their belief, but could tell a better story of our Saviour's birth and life, than one half of those who call themselves Christians; yet he always declared to me, that neither he, nor any of his countrymen, had an idea of a future state. Though he had been taught to look on things of this kind as useless, his own good sense had taught him to be an advocate for universal toleration; and I have seen him several times assist at some of the most sacred rites performed by the Southern Indians, apparently with as much zeal, as if he had given as much credit to them as they did...

Being thus destitute of all religious controul, these people have, to use Matonabbee's words, "nothing to do but consult their own interest, inclinations, and passions; and to pass through this world with as much ease and contentment as possible, without any hopes of reward, or painful fear of punishment in the next."

The most doubtful part of this excellent work is that (p. 344, 345) respecting the utter irreligion of the Northern C. Indians.[1] An instance of speculative Religion occurs in the very page preceding, 343—as respectable a cosmogony, ands that of the E. Indians, and the allegory more intelligible.[2]—I should suspect strongly,

---

[1] Northern C[anadian] Indians—the Chipewyans.

[2] This is the "cosmogony" recounted by Hearne (p 343). The first person on earth was a woman. Searching for berries, she came upon "an animal like a dog", which followed her about and lived with her so that they became great friends. The dog had the art of transforming himself into a handsome young man, which he did only at night: in this guise he visited the woman, who thought that what occurred between them was a dream. But "these transformations were soon productive of the consequences which at present generally follow such intimate connexions between the two sexes, and the mother of the world began to advance in her pregnancy.

"Not long after this happened, a man of such a surprising height that his head reached up to the clouds, came to level the land, which at that time was a very rude mass; and after he had done this, by

that Motanabbee represented his own *Fort-esprit* rather than gave the true account of his fellow countrymen.[3] Hearn should have questioned the old men, and the women.[4]

---

the help of his walking-stick he marked out all the lakes, ponds, and rivers, and immediately caused them to be filled with water. He then took the dog, and tore it to pieces; the guts he threw into the lakes and rivers, commanding them to become the different kinds of fish; the flesh he dispersed over the land, commanding it to become different kinds of beasts and land-animals; the skin he also tore in small pieces, and threw it into the air, commanding it to become all kinds of birds; after which he gave the woman and her offspring full power to kill, eat, and never spare, for that he had commanded them to multiply for her use in abundance. After this injunction, he returned to the place whence he came, and has not been heard of since."

[3] That is, Matonabbee was a free-thinker. A "famous Leader" of the "Northern Indians", known for some years to the Hudson's Bay Company officials at Prince of Wales's Fort, he was named in the "Orders and Instructions" of 6 Nov 1769 given to Hearne to direct him on his first, and abortive, journey to find the Coppermine River. Nobody knows where Matonabbee was when the "Orders" were written, but Hearne first met him on 20 Sept 1770, on his second journey, after he had turned back from Dubawnt Lake because of damage to his quadrant. Matonabbee told Hearne that his troubles were due to "the misconduct of my guides" and the lack of women, and undertook to guide him to the Coppermine after he had refitted at Prince of Wales's Fort; he then became Hearne's guide and principal adviser. Matonabbee died in 1782.

[4] C rewrote and expanded this note in *AR* (1825) 346–7n as a comment upon the following statement in his text: "I am persuaded, that as the belief [in the immortality of the soul] of all mankind, of all tribes, and nations, and languages, in all ages and in all states of social union, it must be referred to far deeper grounds [than Jeremy Taylor found in the misallotment of worldly goods and fortunes], common to man as man: and that its fibres are to be traced to the *tap-root* of Humanity."

GEORG WILHELM FRIEDRICH HEGEL
1770–1831

Wissenschaft der Logik, &c. 3 pts (in 2 vols). Nürnberg 1812, 1813, 1816. 8°.

British Museum C 43 a 13

Bookplate of "Josʰ Henry Green" on ɪ ⁻5 (p–d) and ɪɪ ⁻5 (p–d). Heavy straight pencil marks, typical of Green, in the margins of ɪ i pp iii, xiii–xiv, xix–xx, xxii, xxiii–xxiv, xxvii. Athough the volumes were rebound by Green, some gatherings of ɪ i, ɪ ii, and ɪɪ remain unopened.

In view of the apparently Hegelian colour of some of C's terms and logical schemata the evidence of a cursory and unsympathetic reading—seen in the small number of marginalia (some 928 pages of text remain unannotated), the unopened gatherings, and the terse dismissive remark in *CN* ɪɪɪ 4445 (see 3 n 5, below)—is striking.

DATE. c 1818, perhaps Aug–Sept. *CN* ɪɪɪ 4445, a rare reference to Hegel by name, implies that C had read the book by Oct 1818; other notebook entries that have a bearing on these annotations—*CN* ɪᴠ 4418, 4427, 4429, 4436 (as cited in **3** nn 1, 6, and 7, **7** n 1, below) cluster in Aug–Sept.

COEDITORS. Willem Schrickx, Raimonda Modiano.

1   ɪ i 31 | Bk ɪ Das Seyn pt i ch 1 "Das Seyn" C 1 Anmerkung 1

[Hegel deals with the universally held view that Being is the opposite to Nothing. In fact, he holds, both are the same and their unity produces Becoming. We *think* that Being is the opposite to Nothing and this seems evident. The unity of Being and Nothing, that is, Becoming, also retains this opposition, not as a real opposition, however, but as one constructed in the mind ("einen gemeynten Unterschied").] Das Resultat behauptet also den Unterschied des Seyns und des Nichts eben so sehr, aber als einen nur *gemeynten.*— Man meynt, das Seyn sey vielmehr das schlechthin Andre, als das Nichts ist. . . . Ihr Unterschied ist daher völlig leer . . . er besteht daher nicht an ihnen selbst, sondern nur in einem Dritten, im Meynen. Aber das Meynen ist eine Form des Subjectiven, das nicht in diese Reihe der Darstellung gehört.

[Thus the outcome maintains the disparity of Being and Nothing, but only as a *construct* (a distinction construed). We construe Being as completely different from Nothing....Their difference is therefore completely empty...consequently, it does not lie in themselves but in a third [entity], in the construed notion. But this notion (construct) is a form of the subjective, which does not belong to this order or presentation.]

Strange! Before the distinctions of Objective and Subjective have been noticed, we have a modification of the latter brought forward, as forming a class of primary Notions. Gemeynten![1]

2 ı i 41–3, pencil | Anmerkung 4

Wenn die Welt oder Etwas angefangen haben sollte, so hätte sie im Nichts angefangen, aber im Nichts oder das Nichts ist nicht Anfang; denn Anfang schliesst ein Seyn in sich, aber das Nichts enthält kein Seyn.—Aus demselben Grunde kann auch Etwas nicht aufhören. Denn so müsste das Seyn das Nichts enthalten, Seyn aber ist nur Seyn, nicht das Gegentheil seiner selbst....Indem die absolute Geschiedenheit des Seyns vom Nichts vorausgesetzt wird, so ist— was man so oft hört—der Anfang oder das Werden allerdings etwas unbegreifliches; denn man macht eine Voraussetzung, welche den Anfang oder das Werden aufhebt, das man doch auch wieder zugibt....Da das angeführte Räsonnement die falsche Voraussetzung der absoluten Getrenntheit des Seyns und Nichtseyns macht, ist es auch nicht *Dialektik*, sondern *Sophisterey* zu nennen...

[If the world or Something were to have begun, then it would have begun in Nothing, but in Nothing is no beginning, or Nothing [is no beginning], as beginning includes a Being within itself, whereas Nothing contains no Being. This is also why Something can never end, since, accordingly, Being would contain Nothing, whereas Being is only Being, not its own opposite....As long as the absolute diversity of Being and Nothing is assumed, then—as we so often hear—Beginning or Becoming is of course something incomprehensible; for an assumption is made that suspends Beginning or Becoming—a factor that, however, is then admitted again.... Since the argument cited makes a false assumption of the absolute disparity of Being and Not-being, it cannot be called *dialectic* but *sophistry*...]

I seem to perceive a logical informality in this reasoning—viz. that the "*To be*" (Seyn, το ειναι) is opposed to the "Nothing" (Nichts) whereas the true Opposite of "To be" is "Not to be". Thing, is the opposite to Nothing: for even Something or Somewhat (Etwas) implies more than Being and belongs to predicable *E*xistence, having as its proper opposite no what or not-any-thing.[1] Therefore, I would

1[1] "Construed"—i.e. a distinction construed by the mind rather than inherent in the thing itself. See 3, below.

2[1] On the relation between being and existence cf *Friend* (*CC*) ı 94n: "The *Identity* of Thesis and Antithesis is the

not say Das Seyn ist Nichts; *but* Das Nichts ist das reine Seyn in der
Existenz—or das *reine* Seyn in und mit dem *existirendem* Seyn[2]—the
Potential of Existence, as it were.—It follows then, that in Hegel
himself "ist es nicht Dialectik, sondern Sophisterey*a* zu nennen"[3]—
and that it is an equivocation to affirm, simply, Nichts ist das Seyn
im Werden, whence doubtless it might be inferred, that das Werden
ein die Einheit des Nichts und des Seyn ist—and so, ⟨again:⟩ that
Nichts dem Seyn gleich sey. The true position is: das Nichts ist das
Seyn im werden zur Existenz.[4] s. t. c.

See the blank page, at the beginning of the Volume.—[5]

3   1 ⁻4⁻1, pencil, referring to 1 i 1–50

The Einleitung not free from a confusion of Thought; but the first
40 or 50 pages of the First Book seem to me bewilderment throughout
from confusion of Terms—originating in the πρωτον ψευδος of
overbuilding the Προθεσις by the Thesis, Antithesis and Synthesis.[1]

a Written "Sophisterey sondern" and marked for transposition

---

substance of all *Being*; their *Opposition*
the condition of all *Existence*, or Being
manifested". For the distinction between
being and existence in relation to God see
Friend (CC) I 514–15, *P Lects* Lect 9
(1949) 276–7, and BÖHME **20** and **31**.

2[2] "I would not say 'Being is Nothing',
but 'Nothing is pure Being in Existence'—
or '[Nothing is] *pure* Being in and with
existing Being'."

2[3] "It is not not to be called dialectic, but
rather sophistry"—from textus, in which
Hegel is attacking Kant.

2[4] "It is an equivocation to affirm,
simply, [that] 'Nothing is Being in
Becoming', whence…it might be inferred
that 'Becoming is the Unity of Nothing
and Being' and so…that 'Nothing is the
same as Being'. The true position is [that]
'Nothing is Being coming into Exist-
ence'." Cf Hegel at p 23 (tr): "*Pure Being
and pure Nothing* are one and the
same…".

2[5] I.e. **3**, below.

3[1] On p 40 Hegel writes (tr): "Becom-
ing…is that kind of unity of Being and
Nothing which lies in the nature of each;
Being in and for itself is Nothing, and
Nothing in and for itself is Being." The
"fundamental error", in C's view, is

Hegel's "overbuilding" the "Prothesis"
and so eliding a four-term relation into
three terms. See also **1**, above, and n 6,
below. (For the term πρῶτον ψεῦδος see
BAXTER *Reliquiae* COPY B **92** n 1.)

"Prothesis", as a logical term, is a term
introduced by C: *OED* enters only two
examples of this use, both by C, one from
DONNE *Sermons* COPY B **49** (c 1831–2),
the other from the "Essay on Faith":
"…as a *synthesis* is a unity that results
from the unity of two things, so a
prothesis is a primary unity that gives
itself forth into two things"—from *LR* III
92, IV 429n. C's earliest uses of the term,
however, are in Aug–Sept 1818, among
which the uses in HEGEL may well be
placed: in *CN* III 4418 f 12ᵛ the Prothesis
is described as "*not* Synthesis" of two
terms but the "potential Identity of
both" (cf "the Presuppositum", below),
and the term is used again in ff 13, 14, 14ᵛ;
see also *CN* III 4427 ("the Prothesis or
Unground of both [terms]") and 4436 f
28ᵛ. For later uses see e.g. *AR* (1825)
172–4n and the definition in *CL* VI 816–17
(Sept 1829). See also n 7, below. For C's
use of "prothesis" in the context of the
philosophy of grammar see e.g. *TT* 18
Mar 1827.

The Presuppositum is confounded with the Position and Counter-position—and thus that which is exclusively Subjective (ex. gr. Nichts) assumed in that which is neither Sub. or Obj. because it is the Identity of Both.

According to ~~me~~ my insight, the following is the truer Genesis of our primary notions

Prothesis
= The*
Identity of Sub: and Ob:ject
= Reines Seyn.

Thesis		Antithesis
=		=
Subject	⚹	Object
=		=
~~Nichts~~		
Seyn	⚹	Existenz
=		=
Nichts	⚹	Etwas
=		=
Denken	⚹	Ding

Synthesis
Das Werden. Anschauung.[2]

See p. 41, 42[3] | Thus too,

Seyn + Nichts = Existenz
Nichts + Denken = Etwas
Denken + Etwas = Ding, i.e. etwas *gedacht*.[4]

Nichts is at all times *subjective*—that is, a *word*, expressing the relation of Being not manifested, relatively to the Subject, *to whom*

---

[*] I use. = for equal to, or the same as
⚹ for contra-distinguished to
+ for in combination with, or added to.

[3][2] The German terms in the schema may be summarised thus: *Prothesis*— "Pure Being"; *Thesis*—"Being, Nothing, Thought"; *Antithesis*—"Existence, Something, Thing"; *Synthesis*—"Becoming, Intuition".
[3][3] I.e. **2**, above.

[3][4] "Being + Nothing = Existence |
Nothing + Thought = Something |
Thought + Something = Thing, i.e. something *thought*." For the connexion between "thing" and "think" (as in the fourth pair of terms before n 2, above) see ETERNAL PUNISHMENT **23** n 2. An elaboration of this tetractic scheme appears in *CN* IV 4784.

it is not manifested—In plain English *Nothing* = nothing *to you*. An Objective nothing is not so truly *non-ens* as *non-sens*[5]—it is an absurdity = *Ob* jacet quod omnino non jacet[6]

N.B. It is a general rule, that the Prothesis in its self-duplication, or polar divolution communicates its name to the Thesis, Protheseōs Dignitas remanet in Thesi.[7] Thus

$$\text{το ον self-manifested in the Trinity}$$

$$= \text{το ον} \text{————} \text{ο Λογος}$$

$$=$$

$$\text{το αγιον Πνευμα.}[8]$$

The Word is the Son of God, in the co-eternal filiation of whom God is the Father. It would be false Grammar but sound Philosophy to say, Deus est Pater, dum est Fili*um*[9]—namely, est as a verb transitive, = izzes or is-es—by being gives being to.[10]

Whether the primary error of opposing Seyn to Nichts, instead of nicht seyn affects the work throughout, I have not yet read enough of it to discover. But I hope, that much may be retained by substituting for Nichts das relative · Seyn, relative, I mean, to Existence—the omneity in Each, the Infinity in the Finite.—Ουδε υιος, ει μη ὁ πατηρ says the Scripture in the Text so misinterpreted by Arians and Socinians[11]—the true meaning being of this day

[3][5] Not "*non-being*" but "*non-sense*". Cf *CN* III 4445 ff 21ᵛ, 23ᵛ.

[3][6] "Object", from *obicio* (I throw in the way of), when it is opposed to "subject" in this context means literally "a thing thrown before the mind". *Obiaceo* (I lie in the way of) is almost the equivalent of a perfect passive of *obicio*. C's comment means, approximately, "That is an object (it lies in the way, it is a stumbling-block) which is not an [obj]ect at all (it does not lie anywhere)". See also "object or *quicquid objicitur menti*" in *BL* ch 12 (*CC*) I 254.

[3][7] "The Dignity (Value) of the Prothesis persists in the Thesis." Cf below at n 12.

[3][8] Being = "being ———— the Word = the holy Spirit". Cf *CN* III 4427.

[3][9] "God is the Father, as long as he 'is-es' the Son". C's point is made by his underlining the accusative ending of "Fili*um*". Cf *CN* IV 4697: "Ipse Deus sum res omnis et *sum* omnem rem ["I, God, am everything (nominative, pre-

dicate) and *am* everything (accusative, direct object)"]. I *am* it or by an act of my being given being, transitively cause it to be."

[3][10] See *CN* III 4223 f 86 on "the Ideal as interior to the Real, and as Possibility": "...what it *izzes* (facit esse) [makes to be], *is* as a verb substantiant, i.e. immanence *transitive*)". In GREW 1 (at n 2) there is an instance of what C describes elsewhere as making "the verb substantive [i.e. to be] govern an accusative case". See also IRVING 1 and n 2.

[3][11] Mark 13.32 (AV): "But of that day and that hour knoweth no man, no, not the angels which are in heaven, *neither the Son, but the Father*." The literal meaning of the Greek phrase— "...nor (not even) the Son, if not the father"—is consistent with C's interpretation. C discussed this verse often: see e.g. SHERLOCK p 177, WATERLAND *Vindication* p 416 (*LR* IV 219–20, 238). The Arians and Socinians, denying the true divinity of Christ, used this text as

knoweth no man, no not the Angels, no not even the Son, except as = the Father—i.e. not as the Antithesis, except as far as the Antithesis is one with the Thesis in the Prothesis, the dignity of which remanet in Thesis.[12]

Availing myself of the same construction, I ~~should~~ would have inscribed on my Tomb-stone:

Ουκ ην ει μη ὁ αει εστι· και εγενομην. Ουκ ειμι· αλλ' εσομαι.[13]

Now the ουκ ειμι, ει μη ὁ αει εστι· αλλ' εσομαι γινομενος[14] is the true sense of the Nihil Philosophorum—viz. the *posse* of the Future...[15]

In this sense only should the Nihil be used, subjectively to wit and as the Nihil limitatum—and it cannot without erroneous consequences be confounded with the Nihil limitativum—which indeed is ~~mo~~ in *no* sense Nihil, but on the contrary a Vis apparens[16]—for who would confound the outline of a ~~Daf~~ Leaf with the Fall of an Arrow, or the extreme point, to which I can reach, with the outline of my Hand and Arm?—

4 I i 47 | I i ch 2 "Das Daseyn" A 1 Daseyn überhaupt

*] Daseyn ist das *einfache* Einsseyn des Seyns und Nichts.

[Existence is the *simple* unity of Being and Nothing.]

* Substitute for this strange phrase the simple words "partial manifestation": & what would the Reader lose but a *stare*?

5 I i 54, pencil

A treatise concerning Synonymes &c in any language, if accurate, is highly valuable to those who speak that language. But Philosophy

---

authority for an essential difference between an all-knowing Father and a not-all-knowing Son.

3[12] C repeats the formula (var) given above at n 7.

3[13] "I had not been, were it not that the eternal [Person] is [*or* eternal being (*neuter*) existed]; and I did come into being (did become). I am not, but I shall be."

3[14] "I 'am not, unless the eternal [Person] is [*or* the eternal being (*neuter*) is], but I shall be coming into being (becoming)".

3[15] The "Nothing of the Philosophers—namely, the *potentiality* (the *can be*) of the Future".

3[16] The "Nothing"...the "limited Nothing"...the "limitative Nothing"..."an apparent Force".

ought to be translatable into all languages. But here the definitions are not accurate, even as German/ and yet as German Idioms, they are *plausible* to Germans only.[1]

6　ı i 54–5, pencil | ı i ch 2 A 2 Realität Anmerkung

Realität kann ein vieldeutiges Wort zu seyn scheinen, weil es von sehr verschiedenen, ja entgegengesetzten Bestimmungen gebraucht wird. Wenn von Gedanken, Begriffen, Theorien gesagt wird, *sie haben keine Realität,* so heisst dies hier, dass ihnen kein äusserliches Daseyn, keine *Wirklichkeit* zukomme; *an sich* oder im Begriffe könne die Idee einer platonischen Republik z. B., wohl wahr seyn.—Umgekehrt *]* wenn z. B. nur der Schein des Reichthums im Aufwand vorhanden ist, wird gleichfalls gesagt, *es fehle die Realität,* es wird verstanden, dass jener Aufwand nur ein äusserliches Daseyn sey, das keinen innern Grund hat. Von gewissen Beschäftigungen wird gesagt, sie seyen keine *reelle* Beschäftigungen, nemlich keine solche, die Werth an sich haben;—oder von Gründen, sie seyen nicht reell, insofern sie nicht aus dem Wesen der Sache geschöpft sind.

[*Reality* may appear to be a word of many meanings, since it is used for different, even opposed, definitions. When thoughts, concepts, and theories are said *to have no reality,* this means that they have no external existence, no *actuality*; but *in itself* or conceptually the idea of a Platonic republic, for example, may well be [real and] true.—Conversely, when, for example, the mere appearance and display of wealth is present, *it is said likewise to lack reality* and [the display of wealth] is understood to exist only externally, with no internal basis. Certain occupations are said to be *unreal,* namely such as have no value in themselves. Certain principles are likewise said to be unreal, because they are not drawn from the essence of the thing.]

* Even this is a proof (one among many) of the neglect of sound Logic by the disciples of der neueste Philosophie,[1] and that the Rückfall von Kant[2] has avenged itself. There is no *reverse* (umgekehrt) in this—The Platonic Republic is an Idea: ohne Erscheinungskraft[3]— the Prodigal's Expenditure ist eine erscheinung, or outward reality, which cannot *last* because it is its own root—He spends 2000£ in a one year—this ought to be the *fruit* of 50,000£, in order *to last*—but it is the whole Tree. Still the 2000£ is as much a reality as the 50000£.

5[1] C may be thinking of Hegel's "Daseyn", "Seyn-für-Anderes", etc at the top of this page. He similarly complained about the use by the *Naturphilosophen* of "strange new-minted words" in German in OKEN *Lehrbuch der Naturgeschichte* v back flyleaves.

6[1] "The newest philosophy".
6[2] "Back-sliding from Kant", of which in C's view Fichte was first guilty. See FICHTE *Bestimmung* esp 16.
6[3] "Without power of outward reality (manifestation)".

7 1 i 56, pencil

Das Ding-an-sich ist dasselbe, was jenes Absolute, von dem man nichts weiss, als dass Alles eins in ihm ist.

[The thing-in-itself is the same as that Absolute of which nothing is known, except that All is one in it.]

No! not the *same* as the *absolute*; but as its Idea in *God*. In the mere Absolute (i.e. the *Almight*) there is neither Division nor Distinction; but in God, *whose* is the Almight, there is *each* as well as *all*, perfect unity, but yet *distinction*/[1]

8 1 i 65, pencil | 1 i 2 B Bestimmtheit 2

Die Grenze gehört dem Etwas selbst an; es hat kein Daseyn ausser ihr; sie ist das Ansichseyn des Etwas selbst....Etwas *hat* eine Bestimmtheit. In diesem Ausdrucke wird das Etwas und seine Bestimmtheit von einander unterschieden. Dieser Unterschied gehört aber der äussern Reflexion an.

[Limitation belongs to the Something itself; it has no existence beyond [limitation]: [limitation] is the Being-of-itself of the Something....Something *has* a determinateness. In this expression the Something is distinguished from its determinateness. However, this distinction belongs to outer reflexion.]

This is Spinosism in its most superficial form = Ocean and Waves:[1] the utter insufficiency of which to solve the problem of the World has been shewn by Leibnitz and Kant.[2] It may explain a wave; but not a Leaf or an Insect.

9 1 i 75, pencil | 1 i 2 B 3 c Negation Anmerkung

Die Bestimmtheit überhaupt ist Negation, (Determinatio est negatio) sagte Spinoza...

[*Determinateness in general means negation,* (Determinatio est negatio) Spinoza said...]

7[1] For C the Absolute is equivalent to "Prothesis", for which see **3** n 1, above. C often attacked the *Naturphilosophen* for placing division in the absolute. See OKEN *Lehrbuch der Naturphilosophie* pp 4–6, 22–3; STEFFENS *Grundzüge* pp 46–7. See also *CN* III 4449 (c Oct 1818) and n, *CL* VI 874 (30 Sept 1818). Cf "Christ...is the Idea Idearum...the Unity in the form of the Distinctity, as the Father is the fulness of the Distinctity in the form of Unity". N F° f 86 (*CN* v).

8[1] I.e. naïve pantheism incapable of expressing the inner determination exemplified by organic nature. In C's illustration, the Ocean (the "Something"), in order to have Waves ("determinateness"), would have to be wavy by nature.

8[2] See KANT *Vermischte Schriften* COPY C **5** n 1, which includes Leibniz's solution.

True! and even this position is το πρωτον ψεῦδος of Spinoza's Ethice.[1] He attributes to Determination (= determina*re*) what belongs exclusively to the being determined (= determina*ri*)[2]

10   I i 89, pencil | I i 2 C Qualitative Unendlichkeit 3 Anmerkung

Wenn statt des Unendlichen das Seyn überhaupt genommen wird, so scheint das Bestimmen des Seyns, eine Negation an ihm, leichter begreiflich. Denn Seyn ist zwar selbst das Unbestimmte; insofern es also bestimmt ist, ist es das bestimmte Unbestimmte, Einheit der Bestimmtheit und Unbestimmtheit. Aber es ist nicht unmittelbar an ihm ausgedrückt, dass es das Gegentheil des Bestimmten sey. Das Unendliche hingegen enthält diss ausgedrückt; es ist das *Nicht-endliche*. Die Einheit des Endlichen und Unendlichen scheint somit unmittelbar ausgeschlossen; die unvollendete, vorstellende Reflexion ist daher am hartnäckigsten gegen diese Einheit.

[If instead of taking the infinite we take Being, the determination of Being—a negation to itself—seems easier to understand. For Being is itself the undetermined; so, in so far as it is determined, it is the determinate undeterminate, the unity of determinateness and indeterminateness. But it is not immediately expressed that Being is the opposite of the determinate. In the infinite, however, this is found expressed: the *non* finite. The unity of the finite and the infinite appears immediately to be excluded: the uncompleted, representing reflexion, is therefore most resolutely against this unity.]

This is the first sensible Remark, I have met with. It occurs in Plato, who forbids us to call God the Infinite—God being more truly the common measure of the Infinite and the Finite.[1]

11   I 91, pencil | I i ch 3 "Das Fürsichseyn"

Wie nun das Daseyn sich zum Daseyenden bestimmt oder macht, so bestimmt *erstens* das Fürsichseyn sich zum Fürsichseyenden, oder zum *Eins*.

Zweytens ist das Eins *Repulsion* und geht in *Vielheit der Eins* über.

Drittens aber hebt sich diss Andersseyn des Eins durch die

9[1] For the phrase "the fundamental error" see 3 n 1, above. For Spinoza's error see e.g. *CN* III 4445.

9[2] On the error of attributing to the power itself the limitations resulting from its manifestation see **3**, above, and GOLDFUSS **2**.

10[1] C is recalling Jacobi's account of

Plato, as he had in BÖHME **31** (and see n 7). God is "the measure of all things" in Plato *Laws* 716C, but in the context of ethics. C's source is JACOBI *Werke* III 211–12 (not annotated). Cf *C&S* (*CC*) 168 n 6 (referring, however, to *Theaetetus*). There is a similar passage in *CN* IV 5087 (c Dec 1823).

Attraction auf, und die Qualität, die sich im Fürsichseyn auf ihre Spitze trieb, geht in *Quantität* über.

[Just as Existence determines itself or makes itself into Being, so Being-for-itself *first* determines itself into Being-for-itself-in-process-of-being, or the *One*.

Secondly, the One is *Repulsion* and is converted into a *multiplicity of Ones*.

Thirdly, this Being-other of the One is annihilated by *attraction*, and quality, which in Being-for-self reached a peak, turns into *quantity*.]

My Stars! now we *pop* upon it all at once! *The* To *self*-subsist determinates itself into the Self-subsisting, oder zum Eins[1]—&c &c!!—And so comes Repulsion, Attraction, and Quantity. What christian Heart could desire a clearer account—a more luminous elucidation?

11[1] "Or to the One". Considering the efforts that Kant went to in the *Himmelssystem* and *Metaphysische Anfangsgründe der Naturwissenschaft* to deal with repulsion, attraction, and quantity, and C's effort to master Kant's position, Hegel's peremptory treatment of the subject could be expected to arouse C's contempt. For a long passage on the forces of repulsion, attraction, and quantity see *TL* 55–6. See also *CN* III 4449.

JOHANN CHRISTIAN HEINROTH

1773–1843

Lehrbuch der Anthropologie. Zum Behuf academischer Vorträge, und zum Privatstudium. Nebst einem Anhange erläuternder und beweisführender Aufsätze, &c. Leipzig 1822. 8°.
Original mud-coloured wrappers bound in.

British Museum C 43 b 18

Autograph signature on p ⁻1: "JOSEPH HENRY GREEN". At the head of p 233, in ink: "se v".

DATE. Aug 1826: dated by C—4 Aug 1826 (3), 19 Aug 1826 (43). These dates are reinforced by entries in N F° referring to Heinroth's *Anthropologie* variously dated c 2–14 Aug 1826, *CN* IV 5425–5432: see **4** n 1, **22** n 1, **28** n 1, **29** n 1. *CN* IV shows C reading the book after midnight: "14 Aug. 1826.—i.e. Tomorrow. And what if I died during the two remaining Hours of to Night!..." He was then at, or near, the end of this reading, commenting on pp 414–21 (cf **42**, **43**).

COEDITORS. Willem Schrickx, Raimonda Modiano.

1 p ⁻1, pencil[a]

Christians who content themselves with the *Headings* of the Chapters of Christian Belief [? live][b] a life of Grace by Faith till we pass into a life of Glory! What is this if not the other world *now* preparative to the other world *to come*? And the Eucharist—are you *in earnest*? do you deliberately *mean* what your words mean, in the administration and participation of the Flesh and Blood of Christ? If so, is not *this* an *other* world?—¹

---

[a] Written at the outer edge with the book turned sideways, leaving a narrow vertical space in which **25** was later written
[b] Word rubbed and illegible

1¹ On 7 Aug 1826, looking at a "beautiful Sunset", C meditated on "the impossibility that a Mind in this sensual trance should attach any practical lively meaning to the Gospel Designation of a Christian as living *a life of Grace by Faith*, in the present state, and to pass to a life of Glory; as opposed to those, who *live* without God in the World; and...of the unmeaningness or dark superstition of the Eucharist to such men, and the consequent necessity of knowing and communing with an *other* world that now is, in order to an actual and lively Belief of another world *to come*...". *CN* IV 5428. For C on the eucharist see *CN* III 3847 and SC's letter quoted in 3847n. C carried over the theme of "an *other*

2 title-page, pencil

Self-conceit, that christens itself Selb-ständigkeit,[a][1] and ~~Die~~ Vanity that will be an original Thinker and a Head-master, and tries to establish its claim by CRITICISM, i.e. picking holes in the Coat of the Philosopher last in fashion; and lastly, the Professorial Auditorensucht[2]—these are the ~~two~~ Factors, to which the exhausted effortshunning yet excitement-craving State of Men's Minds; the vast increase in the number of drest people from Shop, Factory and Counting House, who must know something *about* every thing; and the multisciolous *Reviewing ~~Mind~~* Spirit of Literature generally;[3] are the Co-efficients.—The Effects = Detraction—mixty maxty/[4] Still ~~the~~ Cold-meat of Sunday, Mon. Tues. Wednes. Thurs. Fri. but warmed up in the Saturday Squab-pie of new terms & new schematisms/ Add the terribly pietistic cant of the Schliermacher School[5] —& you have the present state of philosophizing in Germany![6] Every [? man looks] with [. . . . .][b]

3 pp 36–7 | Pt I § 20

Wie sich vom Menschen abwärts die Lebendigkeit in immer weiteren Kreisen verliert, so erhebt sich das Menschenleben noch über das animalische und steigert sich zum Bewusstseyn. Im menschlichen

---

[a] A slip for "Selbst-ständigkeit"   [b] The rest of the sentence is rubbed and illegible

---

world" into his Appendix to *C&S*, a letter of 27 Jul 1826 to Edward Coleridge: (*CC*) 173–85 (= *CL* VI 593–601 var); see 117, 174, 177–8, 183.

2[1] "Self-reliance".

2[2] "Craving for an audience".

2[3] "Multisciolous" (not in *OED*)— having a superficial knowledge of many subjects; cf "multiscience" in *SM* (*CC*) 26. In **20**, below, C remarks upon Heinroth's "flea-skip philosophical histories". For "sciolism, sciolist" see KANT *Logic* **3** and n 1. On the "*Reviewing* Spirit" see e.g. *BL* ch 2 (*CC*) I 38–44.

2[4] This term, used e.g. by Robert Burns, seems generally to be a Scottish usage.

2[5] Friedrich Daniel Ernst Schleiermacher (1768–1834), brought up and trained in a community of the Herrnhuter, finding his intellectual horizon enlarged by his study of Aristotle and the Kantian philosophy in the University of Halle, and by his acquaintance with the romanticism of the Schlegels, made a sustained attempt in writing and in his ministry to attract educated Germans away from the prevailing rationalism back to religion. Romantic in the sense that he regarded religion as "a sense and taste for the infinite", he was also "sentimental" in holding that religion is based on intuition and feeling and is independent of all dogma. Generally grouped with the "Neologic Divines" (for whom see *CN* III 4401 and n, and cf BAXTER *Reliquiae* COPY B **45** n 1), he adopted a distinctive position that had a strong influence in Protestant circles. In DE WETTE **38** C refers to "the sentimental Theologians of Herder's and Schleiermacher's School"; he annotated Schleiermacher's studies of Luke and of 1 Timothy.

2[6] Cf **3**, **6**, and **24**, below; and see FICHTE *Bestimmung* **17**.

Bewusstseyn geht ein neues Reich des Lebens auf: das Reich des Geistes und der Freiheit. Im Bewusstseyn des Menschen lebt das sich selbst erzeugende Licht des Gedankens, und das Licht als Gedanke nennt sich Geist. Der denkende Geist besitzt die Kraft der Selbstbestimmung und findet sich frei.

[Just as animation fades away to nothingness from man downwards, so human life lifts itself above animal life and rises to consciousness. In human consciousness a new realm of life comes into being: the realm of the mind and of freedom. In the consciousness of man there lives the self-generating light of thought, and as thought, this light is called "mind". The thinking mind possesses the power of self-determination and finds itself free.]

That the Vis vitæ[1] sublimes itself into mind is incomparably more difficult to conceive, thatn the reverse. viz. that Mind reflects itself & has, as it were, its confused echo, in Life. The going contrary to the old principle, A Iove principium[2] is the characteristic of the Naturphilosophy, and the cause of its failure.[3] But neither theory solves the problem of the chasm, the difference in kind, between Man and the noblest mere animal.[4] Nay, that there is no nobl*est* animal, no one that we can decisively rank above all others, is an objection to Heinroth's Assumptions

S. T. Coleridge 4 Aug. 1826

Besides, Heinroth, *according to the reigning fashion* in the German School of the newest philosophy, professes himself a Christian. As such, he might have learnt a very different scheme from this self-sublimation (sich-steigern) of Life into ⟨seif-conscious⟩ Mind; and Spirit, from St John, Ch. I. v. 4, 5...[5] The Darkness did not contain the *Light*—i.e. the Light *of Reason* had not its potential

---

3[1] "Life-force"—a Leibnizian term.

3[2] "Begin with Jove"—Virgil *Eclogues* 3.60.

3[3] According to C, the vital powers of organic nature—its "life"—are unintelligible unless "mind" is presupposed as a "self-*retaining*" power; this leads to the idea of a "self-conscious being" and ultimately to the "Absolute Will" of "the Supreme *Being*". As in "every living form...the grounds of its *intelligibility*" must be sought "in that which is *above* it", it follows that the existence of "mind" must be referred to God just as the "life" of organic nature must be

referred to "mind". See *C&S* (*CC*) 179–83 (= *CL* VI 597–601 var) and 66 n 2. For other errors of the *Naturphilosophen* see e.g. GOLDFUSS **2** and nn 2–4, *CN* III 4449, and *CL* IV 874.

3[4] In *SM* (*CC*) 19 C states that man and animal differ, not in degree, but in kind: animals possess some form of understanding, but only man is privileged with the God-given faculty of reason. See also *Friend* (*CC*) I 15–17, 160, II 75–8.

3[5] "In him was life; and the life was the light of men. And the light shineth in darkness; and the darkness comprehended it not." The three dots are C's.

existence in the not-self-conscious Principle, i.e. the Animal Life, but the Light, but the Light shon[e] into it./[6]

4   p 44 | I § 30

Zuvörderst haben wir den Zeugungsmoment als den ersten Schöpfungsact anzusehen, wiefern die zeugenden Kräfte, als Reiz von Seiten des Vaters, als Reaction von Seiten der Mutter, mit einander in das Verhältniss von Wechsel-Erregung, oder in polarisches Verhältniss treten. Beide zeugende Kräfte, als Erregungspole, begegnen sich, ausgestrahlt oder ergossen als Flüssigkeiten, die männliche mit dem Charakter der bildenden, formgebenden Kraft, die weibliche mit dem Charakter der formempfangenden, oder des zu bildenden Stoffs. Die weibliche Flüssigkeit als Bildungsstoff, als flüssiger Keim der zu bildenden Gestalt, wird von der männlichen, als dem Erregungsprinzip der Bildung räumlich umfasst und eingeschlossen, indem die männliche Flüssigkeit zur Form der Erhülle gerinnt. Das *ovulum* entsteht, dessen Reizpol die väterliche Hülle, dessen Reactionspol das von der Hülle eingeschlossene mütterliche plastische Tröpfchen ist. Beide erregen sich gegenseitig.

[First of all we must regard the moment of procreation as the first productive act, and consider the extent to which the procreating forces—acting as stimulus on the part of the father and as response on the part of the mother—enter into a relationship of reciprocal excitation, or a polar relationship. The two procreating forces, as poles of excitation, meet each other by emanating or gushing forth as fluids, the male fluid taking on the character of a shaping, form-giving power, and the female fluid that of a receptacle of form, or of formative matter. The female fluid, as form-building matter, as liquid seed of the shaping form, is surrounded spatially and enclosed by the male fluid which acts as principle of excitation, so that the male fluid coagulates into the form of the egg membrane. [Thus] the ovule comes into being; its pole of excitation is the male sheath, its pole of response the female formative drop closed in by the sheath. Both stimulate each other reciprocally.]

I have my doubts of this whole theory; but particularly de feminæ humore seminali effuso,[1] as a *co-factor*. There is no proof that it is an indispensable Agent, or a formative Agent at all.[2]

3[6] For a similar use of these images see e.g. *SM (CC)* 97 and *Friend (CC)* I 156–7. For C on the origin of light and its relation to "the Mosaic darkness" see *CN* III 4418 ff 14ᵛ–15, *CL* IV 770–2, 805–7.

4[1] "About the discharge of the woman's seminal fluid". Cf *CN* IV 5425

(c 2–6 Aug 1826): "...The power & function which the seminal Contagion exercises on the ovulum of the female, that same p. and f. the Brain exercises on the lower organisms./"

4[2] Cf GOLDFUSS 4.

5   p 65 | 1 i § 41

*] Die Sinne fassen den äusseren Weltstoff auf, damit er sich zu innerer Form gestalte; und die Glieder tragen diese innere Form auf die äussere Welt über und prägen in ihr den Charakter des inneren Lebens aus. Die Sinnenthätigkeit ist der Eingangs- und Anfangspunkt des inneren Lebens... Kurz, die Empfindungs- und Bewegungsorgane sind die Uebergangspunkte des Raumlebens in das Zeitleben und umgekehrt.

[The senses take in the substance of the external world so that it may shape itself into an internal form, and the limbs transfer this internal form to the external world and imprint on it the character of inner life. The activity of the senses is the point of entry and the beginning of inner life...In short, the organs of sensation and movement are the crossing points of existence-in-space into existence-in-time, and vice versa.]

* Query. Did Dr J. C. A. Heinroth mean any thing by this sentence? And if so, what did he mean? The Organs of Sense take up the outward World-stuff, in order that (or therewith) it ⟨i.e. the Stuff⟩ may form itself to inward Form!! and what is er? it? An The Natur-Phil^n are apt to mistake the new-naming of a thing per antithesim ex. gr. Raum-leben ⧓ Zeit-leben, for additional Insight.[1]

6   pp 65–6

The Followers of Fichte, Baader,[1] Schelling and Steffens, like those of Plotinus, affect to be Eclectic Philosophers—but as you truly remarked,[2] they neglect *Logic*—or rather do not understand what Logic is. Thus, what Kant asserted as an assumption for the purposes of a formal Science, Heinroth asserts as matter of fact.[3] It is a necessary fiction of *pure* Logic; just as the very contrary is a necessary fiction of pure Somatology.[4]

5[1] "By antithesis: for example, 'space-life' in contradistinction to 'time-life'". With the trick of "new-naming" cf C's remark, in FICHTE *System der Sittenlehre* 2, on the claim of the *Naturphilosophen* to "bran new originality". See also 2 (at n 4), above.

6[1] Franz Baader (1765–1841) contributed two articles to *Jahrbücher der Medicin als Wissenschaft* (3 vols Tübingen 1805–8). C annotated one of these and referred to the other in *SM (CC)* 24, 29, 83. See also *CL* iv 792, 874–6.

6[2] Joseph Henry Green, who owned this book.

6[3] For Kant space and time are pure forms of *a priori* intuition. Heinroth seems to regard space and time not as formal conditions of perception but as having actual "crossing-points" (*Uebergangspunkte*) in sensibility: see 5 textus, above.

6[4] The science of the properties of bodies. Cf "somatosphere" in KLUGE 1.

7 p 71 | 1 i § 43

Beweis aus der mathematischen Gesetzlichkeit des Lichts in der äussern Natur, dass die Körperlichkeit überhaupt nur eine Hülle des Geistes ist.

[Proof from the mathematical lawfulness of light in external nature that corporality in general is but a husk of the spirit.]

And what then *is* a Hülle? If it be the Husk of the Spirit, it is *not* the Spiri[t]*a* but a Husk. And wherein does this differ from saying, that the Body is not body, but merely the Soul's Body? or our Bodies are not body because they are the Bodies of our Souls? Why not say at once, that Spirit condenses & shapes itself into an Eolian Harp, on which the*b* unindividualized Spirit as the + Power plays and that the resulting *Tune* is what we call *body*, or phænomenal existence/ the living Harp being at once the Mother & the Auditress of the Music?[1]

8 p 73 | 1 i § 45

Wenn sich einerseits in der Gliederung der Muskeln eine Zweck-mässigkeit ausspricht, welche nur vom Standpunkte des psychischen Lebens aus begriffen werden kann, und wenn auf diese Weise die Muskeln offenbar als Organe, Träger und Hüllen des nach aussen gewendeten psychischen Lebens erscheinen; ja, wenn sogar der Grad der Muskelkraft den Grad der geistigen Thatkraft, oder der *] Willensstarke, bezeichnet: so stehen anderer Seits das Gefäss- und Nervensystem in nicht geringerer Berührung mit der inneren Seite des psychischen Lebens, als Organe, Träger und Hüllen desselben.

[If, on the one hand, an expediency is expressed in the formation of the muscles that is only to be comprehended from the point of view of psychic life, and if in this way the muscles appear obviously as organs, carriers, and husks of the outward-turned psychic life, if indeed even the degree of muscular power signifies the degree of mental agility or strength of will: on the other hand the system of vessels and nerves stands in no less a connexion with the inner side of the psychic life, as its organs, carriers, and husks.]

---

a Cropped
b The note having reached the foot of the page, C wrote "(turn to the top)" and continued at the head of the page

7[1] Cf *The Eolian Harp* lines 26–9: *PW* (EHC) I 101. Cf Böhme **59** and n 3 and   Kant *Critique der reinen Vernunft* **4** and n 3.

Indeed??*a*
* What a poor creature in respect of ~~the~~ spiritual Power (That-kraft) must Shakespear or Leibnitz have been, compared with a Flea or a Caterpillar![1]
§ 45. I venture to denounce as TRASH.*b*

9 p 76 | 1 ii § 46

Die erste Entfaltung des verschlossenen Inneren, gleichsam des Seelenkeimes ist das Gefühl...Das Gefühl ist gleichsam der Brennpunkt des gesammten Seelenlebens, und bleibt es auch das ganze Zeitleben hindurch....So erwacht also das Seelenleben zur Stunde der Geburt gleichsam mit einem Schlage auf drei Punkten: auf dem des Sinnes, des Gefühls und des Triebes, von denen aber der des Gefühls der Mittelpunkt ist, an den sich der Erregungspunkt des Sinnes, und der Reactionspunkt des Triebes, gleichsam wie Arme, anschliessen...

[The first unfolding of the enclosed inner life or, so to speak, of the germ of the soul is feeling...Feeling is, as it were, the focus of the whole life of the soul, and such it remains throughout the whole lifetime....Thus the life of the soul awakes at the moment of birth as if with one stroke, as it were, in three different points: in the sense, in the feeling, and in the instinct, and of these three feeling is at the centre where the stimulating point of the senses and the reaction point of the impulses join the feelings, as it were, like arms...]

N.B.
Three gleichsams in one §.ph.—a suspicious symptom.[1]

10 p 86 | 1 ii §51

Die erste Entwickelung des Seelenlebens schliesst mit dem Glauben, und wird von dem Glauben getragen. Auf diesen Grund soll sich nun, der Naturbestimmung des Menschen gemäss, das Seelenleben weiter fortbauen....Vom Band des Glaubens zusammengehalten wirken Gemüth, Geist und Wille fördernd in einander ein, und entwickeln im Menschen das höchste Leben, dessen er sich erfreuen soll. Der Geist soll das Höchste erkennen, das Gemüth es lieben, und der Wille es erstreben.

a This word, followed by *, is written in the margin beside the textus; the second paragraph is written in the foot margin, beginning with *
b Written as a separate interjection

8[1] Cf 3 and n 3, above.

9[1] *Gleichsam*—"as it were", "so to speak"—occurs four times in this textus.

[The first development in the life of the soul terminates in belief, and is supported by belief. On this foundation, in conformity with the natural destiny of man, the life of the soul should continue to make its way.... Held together by the bond of belief, mind, spirit, and will work upon and reinforce each other, and develop in man the highest life that he should enjoy. The spirit should discern the highest, the mind love it, and the will strive for it.]

What find we here but a series of bold *Assertions* meant to correspond to the commonly received epochs of Man's developement; but even these, the motive rather than the ground of the assertions, are doubtful/.[1]

11   pp 102–3 | I ii §§ 58–9

Der Glaube, die ursprüngliche, innere Gewissheit, trägt und festiget die Thätigkeiten des Geistes und des Willens; und ohne ihn schwankt und zerfällt das ganze Gebäude der inneren Lebensentwickelung. Und so ist denn auch der Glaube die innere Bedingung des Gemüths zu seiner Vollendung in der Seligkeit....

Die geoffenbarte Religion, wiefern sie nicht durch menschliche Missverständnisse oder Zusätze verfälscht ist, ist als die echte und vollständige Kunstschule zur Entwickelung und Vollendung des Seelenlebens anzusehen/...

[Belief, the original, inner certainty, supports and strengthens the activities of the spirit and the will; and without it the whole edifice of the development of inner life totters and crumbles to pieces. And thus belief is also the inner condition of the spirit for its perfection in bliss.... Revealed religion, insofar as it is not falsified through human misunderstandings or additions, is to be regarded as the genuine and perfect art-school for the development and perfection of the life of the soul...]

Glauben!

Surely, there has not often occurred a more impudent Juggle, and Trick of Hand, than this shifting of "Belief in the mission & miracles of Jesus" to "die ursprüngliche Gewissheit unsers Seyns und Lebens".[1] *Trick of Hand* did I call it? 'Twas a sad misnomer! As well might I have called crepitum tonitruosum mephitissimum bombardinare a Trick of BVM.[2]

10[1] In §§ 46–50 (pp 75–86) Heinroth describes the development of various faculties in man from the awakening of feelings and instincts in early childhood to the full growth of self-consciousness and reason.

11[1] "The original certainty of our being and life"—quoted selectively and variatim from textus.

11[2] "To let fly with a thunderous and most evil-smelling fart"—C's Latin. The point of "BVM"—a usual abbreviation for the Blessed Virgin Mary—appears when "V" is read as a roman "U".

Joy = Boiled Mutton: for we cut capers for both![3] The two senses jammed into the word, Glauben, are not much less disparate.

S. T. C.

P.S. I too distinguish Faith and Belief, as Major and Minor.[4]

12   p 105 | I iii § 61 "Allgemeiner Naturbegriff des Geschlechts"

Positiver Pol.	Negativer Pol.

a
Reich der Kräfte.

| Contractionskraft | Expansionskraft. |
| (Lichtkraft.) | (Schwerkraft.) |

b.
Elementarreich.

| Lebensluft. | Stickluft. |

c.
Reich der Stoffe.

| Säurenbasis. | Kalienbasis. |
| (Sauerstoff.) | (Wasserstoff.) |

Reich der Körper.

Sonne.	Planeten.
Starre Körper.	Flüssige Körper.
(Erde.)	(Wasser.)
Kieselerde.	Kalkerde.
Sprode Metalle.	Dehnbare Metalle.
(Eisen.)	(Gold.)

| [Positive Pole | Negative Pole |

a.
Forces.

| Force of Contraction | Force of Expansion |
| (Force of Light) | (Force of Gravity) |

b.
Elements.

| Vital Air | Suffocating Air |

c.
Substances.

| Acid Basis | Alkali Basis |
| (Oxygen) | (Hydrogen) |

11[3] Shakespeare had used the pun on caper and mutton in *Twelfth Night* I iii 139.

11[4] For the distinction between faith and belief see FICHTE *Versuch* **10** n 1.

	Bodies.	
	Sun	Planets
	Solid Bodies	Fluid Bodies
	(Earth)	(Water)
	Silicious Earth	Calcareous Earth
	Brittle Metals	Ductile Metals
	(Iron)	(Gold)]

If I do not flatter myself, the Scheme, which I constructed 6 or 7 years ago, is both more true to Nature and more complete.[1] * is unintelligible to me.

13   p 125, pencil | I iv § 73

Wie im Magnetismus die Electricität verborgen liegt, so im Schlafe *] das Wachen. Die magnetische Urkraft erzeugt sich in sich selbst und aus sich selbst. Sie ist die Nahrungsquelle der electrischen Kraft. Ist diese demnach erschöpft, so muss sie zu der ersteren zurückkehren und sich in ihr zu neuer Erscheinung und Thätigkeit erquicken.

[Just as electricity is latent in magnetism, so the waking state is latent in sleep. The original magnetic force produces itself in itself and out of itself. It is the source of nourishment for the electrical power. Consequently, if this power is exhausted, it must return to the first [the magnetic force] and there reanimate itself in it in order to appear and become active again.]

Ergo, God—[a]

* What a strange mixture, dear Friend! does this Heinroth make of the crudest Okenism and the Popular Christianity?[1]

14   pp 126–7, postscript in pencil

Auch im Tode wird das wachende Leben aufgehoben, aber mit ihm zugleich die Basis, auf welcher es ruht: das vegetative Leben. An

[a] These words are written in the margin; the second paragraph is written in the head margin

12[1] With this fourfold scheme cf GOLDFUSS 1 and 2, *CN* III 4226, 4420, and *TL* 55–6. The "Scheme" of "6 or 7 years ago" is found in his detailed examination and reconstruction of the *Naturphilosophie* c Jun 1819 (or earlier) to c Oct 1820 in a series of three notebooks—a lost notebook, N 27 (entitled XHMIKO-Φιλοσοφικον), and N 28. See *CN* IV 4645n, 4646n, and General Notes on N 27 (*CN* III) and N 28 (*CN* IV).

13[1] Okenism—the view of Lorenz Oken (1779–1851) that nature is the conversion of the All into the world or man. Oken, whose *Erste Ideen zur Theorie des Lichts* (Jena 1808), *Lehrbuch*

der Naturgeschichte (3 vols Jena 1813–26), and *Lehrbuch der Naturphilosophie* (Jena 1809) C annotated, sought to determine the relation of light to matter and the philosophical and religious implications of that relation. Oken's view of magnetism and electricity is to be seen in e.g. OKEN *Lehrbuch der Naturphilosophie* pp 111–19, 188–96, 226–7, on which C wrote a total of three notes. C criticised Oken for his Schellingian dualism and for the irreligious pantheism that resulted from it. For C on Oken see esp *CN* III 4427–4429, 4445 f 21ᵛ (c Aug–Oct 1818). The "dear Friend" is Green: see **6** n 2, above.

dieses Leben ist aber der Zauber des Lebensmagnetismus gebunden. Ist dieser durch die Auflösung der Kette des vegetativen Lebens *]gleichfalls gelöset: so findet kein Erwachen mehr Statt: Bewusstseyn, Empfindung und Bewegung, oder das Zeitleben, ist aufgehoben, weil das Raumleben aufgehoben ist, von welchem jenes abhängt.

[In death also waking life is suspended, but so, simultaneously with it, is the foundation on which it rests: vegetative life. To this life, however, the spell of the vital magnetism is (closely) bound. If this magnetism is also suspended because of the breaking of the chain of vegetative life, then no awakening is possible: consciousness, sensation, and motion, in other words life-in-time is suspended, because of the suspension of life-in-space, the former being dependent upon the latter.]

* Here lurks, thank God! a sophism, a Quid pro quo.[1] The *function* is put for the *Principle*. And this may constitute the difference between Sleep and Death—that in Sleep the restoration of the exhausted irritability and sensibility is found in the functions of Vegetive Life[2]—in Death by a deeper retraction into the common Principle of all 3 Powers.[3]

[a]But in what proportion of cases does Death take place from the exhaustion or dissolution of the Magnetic Power of Life? This might perhaps account for Death by extreme Old Age; but not for 20 more common cases.

15 p +1, referring to pp 127–8, pencil | I iv §§ 73–4

Und hierin unterscheidet sich der Tod vom Schlafe.... Der Tod ist, wie ein Dichter sich ausdrückt, das Zerfallen des Lebens in

[a] This paragraph, in pencil, is written at the head of p 127, the completion of the previous paragraph (in ink) having filled the whole foot margin; but reference is to "Lebensmagnetismus" at the beginning of the textus

14[1] Lit "something for something [else]"; here, a false substitution. See *AR* (1825) 35–7: "...the juggle of sophistry consists, for the greater part, in using a word in one sense in the premise, and in another sense in the conclusion....Make it a rule to ask yourself the precise meaning of the word, on which the point in question appears to turn; and if it may be...used in several senses, then ask which of these the word is at present intended to convey. By this mean, and scarcely without it, you will at length acquire a facility in detecting the *quid pro quo*....the *quid pro quo* is at once the rock and quarry, on and with which the strong-holds of disbelief, materialism, and (more pernicious still) epicurean morality, are built."

14[2] See **38** and n 2, below. The word "vegetive" was commonly used before C as a variant of "vegetative"; but C uses the word in a special sense, which he attributed to Bichat, to mean growth or productivity; see *C&S* (*CC*) 179 and n 2.

14[3] The three powers—vegetivity, irritability, and sensibility—correspond, as in **38**, below, to the powers of magnetism, electricity, and galvanism and determine the development of the plant, the insect, and the animal world. See e.g. *CL* IV 769–75, VI 597–9, *CN* III 4226, and *TL* 70–1.

gleichgültigen Staub, nur durch den Odem des Ewiglebenden zu erquicken.... Die Fortdauer des in Raum und Zeit erscheinenden Lebens nach dem Tode [ist], erwiesener Massen (§ 73.) unmöglich. Sollte demnach eine Fortdauer des Lebens nach dem Tode Statt finden, so könnte sie nur ausserhalb des Raumes und der Zeit als möglich gedacht werden... Dieses höhere Seyn offenbart sich uns in der Vernunft... Die Vernunft muss Gott denken, sie ist nur dadurch Vernunft, dass sie Gott denkt.... Unser Geist erkennt in dem Leben ausser der Vernunft nur ein Nachtwandeln, einen Traum, der vor dem Tageslichte der Vernunft verschwindet... Dem Vernunft- und Offenbarungsgläubigen erscheint der Tod nur als die Auflösung irdischer Fesseln, als der Befreier den Raum und Zeit, worin das Unsterbliche in uns nur noch wie in der Raupenhülle lebt... Mag also das magnetisch-electrische Leben der Erde aufgelöset werden, mögen die Formen des Raumes und der Zeit zerfallen... der Keim des ewigen Leben in uns wird, wenn dieser Ausdruck erlaubt ist, von dem Magnetismus der ewigen Liebe festgehalten...

[And in this, death is distinguished from sleep... Death, as a poet expresses it, is the crumbling of life into indifferent dust, only to be reanimated by the breath of Him who has eternal life.... The continuance of life after death, manifesting itself in time and space, [is] impossible, as has been proved (§ 73). If accordingly there is to be a continuance of life after death, it can only be conceived of as possible beyond space and time... This higher Being reveals itself to us in Reason... Reason has to conceive of God; it is reason only in that it conceives of God.... Our spirit perceives the life outside reason only as sleep-walking, as a dream that is dispelled before the daylight of reason... To the man who believes in reason and revelation death appears only as the dissolution of earthly fetters, as the liberation from space and time in which our immortal spirit still lives as in the skin of a caterpillar... Therefore, let the magnetic-electrical life of the earth be destroyed, and let the forms of space and time crumble to pieces... the germ of eternal life in us is, if I may say so, maintained by the magnetism of eternal love...]

P. 127 §. 74

Either §. 73 teaches a grievous Error, viz. that the Productivity, or first Force of Life = Life₁,[a] *is* Life—not merely a Force, but the *Grund-kraft*, the grounding Power itself:[1]

a Written "Life$^{(1)}$"; printed "Life₁" to avoid confusion with footnote indicators

15[1] In **14** textus, above, Heinroth states that the foundation of life is vegetative life or the power of magnetism; if the power of magnetism were suspended, all life would become extinct. According to C, life is "but the copula of all three [of the constituent forces]... Life itself is not a *thing*—a self-subsistent *hypostasis*—but an *act* and *process*". *TL* 93–4.

or §. 74 talks of *a non-entity*, a Life that remains after the whole Life is gone! of a more glorious Bubble that survives the Soap-film and the air, it had imprisoned!—I venture to assert, that Immortality is a contradiction on Heinroth's Scheme, which with all its parade and palaver of Biblical and Liturgical Phrases and Dogmas is essentially Atheistic—Atheism in a Gown & Surplice![2]

God *is* Reason[3]—What is that, which communes with the Light?

The common Notion is erroneous by affirming of the Soul what is only affirmable of the Spirit; but ⟨with this rectification⟩ to the old System of Soul (= Spirit) and Body these Men must revert, if they are sincere in their Belief of a Hereafter.

16   p 127, pencil

Unsere Vernunft aber, obwohl in der Zeit erscheinend, ist dennoch weder an die Zeit, noch an den Raum gebunden.... Unsere Vernunft führt uns in eine Welt der Freiheit, in eine moralische, heilige Ordnung und Gesetzlichkeit... Durch die Vernunft werden wir der Erscheinungswelt entrückt...

[But our reason, although appearing in time, is not bound by either time or space.... Our reason leads us into a world of freedom, into a moral holy order and code of laws... Through reason we become removed from the world of appearances...]

Vernunft! Vernunft! aye! aye! but UNSERE! what is *unsere* Vernunft?[1]

17   p 128, pencil

Jeder Moment, wo wir uns diesem Gesetz fügen, wo wir in der Vernunft leben, ist ein Moment des ewigen Lebens selbst... Wir

15[2] The only "*sufficient cause, quae et facit, et subest*" that can account for life is, in C's view, God. *TL* 35. Heinroth in §73 traces the "grounding Power itself" to magnetism, a force of nature, not the divine will; his system is therefore inevitably atheistic and his concept of immortality self-contradictory. See also **24**, below.

15[3] For the proposition that "God *is* Reason" see *C&S* (*CC*) 182 (= *CL* VI 600) and e.g. *AR* (1825) 144.

This clause and the rest of the note may be a separate annotation referring to **24** textus.

16[1] For *unsere* see also **17** and **18**, below. In *SM* (*CC*) 68 n 3, C states that reason "in the highest sense" is "the Supreme Being contemplated objectively"; "the Word or Logos is life, and communicates light"—reason. Human reason is "the capability with which God had endowed man of beholding...the divine light"; the "capability is itself that light...as the life or indwelling of the living Word, which is our light". The Reason in man (p 70) "cannot in strict language be called a faculty, much less a personal property, of any human mind", for "Each individual must bear witness of it to his own mind, even as he describes life and light".

können solche Momente nicht fortsetzen, ohne die Spur, die klare Erkenntniss, die Gewissheit des ewigen Lebens zu erfahren...

[Each moment that we conform to this law and live in reason is a moment of eternal life itself... We cannot pursue such moments without experiencing at the same time the trace, the clear knowledge, the certainty of eternal life...]

We! we! we! but what *is* WE?[1]

18   p 129, pencil

*] Die Vernunft verbindet, einiget uns mit Gott, und wir erfahren immer mehr von Gott, je mehr wir die Vernunft in uns walten lassen.... Wir finden Gott, er wird uns gegenwärtig, wenn wir uns von der Vernunft leiten lassen.... In diesem Geiste erkennen wir, dass unser freies, der Vernunft verbundenes Wesen unsterblich... ist.

[Reason joins and unites us with God, and we learn more and more about God, the more we let reason govern us.... We find God, he becomes present for us, when we allow ourselves to be guided by reason.... In this spirit we perceive that our free nature, which is joined with reason, is... immortal.]

* As well almost might I say of a Looking-glass every moment, the Light falls on it, it is in commune & union with an infragile element, and discovers its ⟨own⟩ infragility and independence of its constituent Glass and Quicksilver!/[1]

19   p 186, pencil | ɪ vi § 107

[Heinroth criticises Gall's craniological theories on the following grounds: they are too generalised; they do not account for qualities such as religion and virtue; if based on animal physiology, they do not apply to man; they are inferred from too few cases; the cranium develops gradually; and, lastly, once abilities have developed and grown, the knowledge derivable from the organs is superfluous.]

This Critique like that on Zoo-magnetism[1] is conducted in a poor

---

17[1] See **16** and n 1, above.

18[1] See **16** and n 1, above, and cf **29** and **42**, below.

19[1] I.e. §§131–3 (pp 233–47), esp §131 (pp 233–9), "Erster Blick auf den sogenannten Lebensmagnetismus—Polemische Excursion" (on which C wrote **23**, below), which includes such unfavourable remarks on animal magnetism as the following (pp 236–7, tr):

"However, to us animal magnetism itself does not appear to have the great importance attributed to it by its opponents no less than by its advocates: by the former in that they regard it as some kind of plague that had to be suppressed and eradicated as soon as possible; by the latter in that they found in it the source of all physical well-being, if not of all spiritual happiness."

ungenial utilitarian Spirit. Is it *true*? If Gall has given us a new *Truth*, trust to God for its *utility*.[2]

20 p 218, pencil | Pt II i §128

[Heinroth gives a rapid survey of the history of human endeavour in understanding nature, starting from biblical times through Indian, Persian, and Egyptian mythology to the Greek philosophers.]

I do detest these flea-skip philosophical histories![1] and this is diabolically shallow and coxcombly.

21 pp 222–3, pencil

Materie ist noch bis auf den heutigen Tag die Basis der Natur bei den Physikern und Chemikern von Profession, obschon die neuest Chemie durch ihre subtilsten Experimente die Stoffe unter ihren Händen verschwinden, und in das Reich gesetzlicher Kräfte über-treten sieht, und obschon die aus der Schule der Idealphilosophie ausgehenden Stimmen immer lauter werden, die es aussprechen, dass die Kraft der Träger der Dinge ist, die Dinge selbst nur Erscheinungen der gesetzlich gebundenen Kraft sind, die Erscheinungen unserer *] Sinne aber darum das Gepräge der Körperlichkeit an sich tragen, weil unsere Vorstell-Kraft alle den Raum erfüllende Kraft nur unter den Formen des Starren und Flüssigen erscheinen sieht.

[To this day matter is still the basis of nature among professional physicists and chemists, even though the newest chemistry by means of its most subtle experiments can make substance vanish under their own hands and pass into the realm of forces governed by laws, and even though idealist philosophers are increasingly clamouring that force is the vehicle of things and that the

19[2] Heinroth says in the second sentence of this section (tr): "But, even admitting that this system is true in its whole field, it is not useful on all sides for the purposes of our investigation; because the cranium grows slowly cranioscopy cannot be used in paedagogic theory [*Erziehungslehre*]."

Franz Joseph Gall (1759–1828), with his associate Johann Gaspar Spurzheim (1776–1832), was famous in his day for developing the pseudo-science of phrenology (or physiognomy, or craniology). (Spurzheim read C's bumps and delivered a set of laughably wrong answers: see *CL* v 460 and n, and cf *TT* 29 Jul 1830.) The

fact that both Gall and Spurzheim descended in the end to popularising quackery does not diminish the importance of their anatomical discovery of the spatial location of faculties in the brain. C deplored the quackery (e.g. *CL* VI 812) but was aware of "the undoubted splendor and originality of [their] Anatomical Discoveries as to the structure of the Brain". *CN* III 4355 f 26[v]; cf *TT* 24 Jun 1827. John Abernethy presented C with a copy of his *Reflections on Gall and Spurzheim's System of Physiognomy and Phrenology* (1821).

20[1] Cf **2**, above.

things themselves are only the manifestations of force controlled by their own laws; our sense-perceptions are, however, marked by the imprint of corporality, precisely because our representational faculty reads all space-filling force only as manifested in the form of solid and fluid states.]

* Well! but (an Hobbesian or Lockian might retort) why does our Vorstell-kraft present the space-filling Power only in these two *forms*, the fluid and the rigid?—Is it not the most natural solution of this question, to reply—Because these *are* the two modes &c?[1]

22 p 223, pencil

Die Dinge sind nichts anderes, als die nothwendigen Erzeugnisse äusserer individueller Kräfte, die unser Empfindungsvermögen auf *] bestimmte Weise afficiren. Hiermit ist ausserordentlich viel gewonnen: denn die Welt löset sich so in ein Reich von Kräften auf, die unter bestimmten Gesetzen stehen und unserer Vorstellkraft und den Gesetzen unserer Vorstellung homogen sind.

[Things are nothing but the indispensable products of external individual forces, which affect our faculty of perception in a definite way. By this means a great deal is gained: for the world is thus broken up into a realm of forces that obey certain laws; they are forces homogeneous with our faculty of representation and its laws.]

* *This* I *cannot* see for the Life of me! In order to affect me with a moss rose there must ⟨be⟩ that identical moss-rose Power—a precisely determined Unit—u.a.[1]

23 p 237 | ɪɪ i § 131

Wie wir aber diese Kräfte, oder diese Richtungen der psychischen Kraft des Menschen, aus der täglichen Erfahrung kennen, geben sie uns keine Hoffnung, zu Begründung lebens-magnetischer, heilbringender, Einwirkungen Eines Individuums auf Andere.

21[1] C's "Hobbesian or Lockian" retort exposes the weakness of Heinroth's subjectivism by making an alternative assertion from the position of naïve realism. C finds Heinroth's method wanting in comparison with Kant's "austere beauty of Method" (**25**, below). Cf **6**, above.

22[1] *u*[nd] *a*[ndere]—et cetera. In a notebook entry of 13 Aug 1826 C commented on this annotation, ending:

"A Power of Vegetation will not explain to me any one Vegetable in particular. It must be a Moss-rose Power that produces a Moss-rose.—Nota bene—I do not intend this as an argument of settled validity; but merely as a clearing up of the question—which well deserves, and God permitting shall receive an orderly enucleation." *CN* ɪᴠ 5431 (13 Aug 1826).

*] Denn Einbildungskraft, Wille und Glaube bleibt immer nur an das Individuum selbst gebunden, welches diese Kräfte, wenn auch in noch so hohem Masse besitzt.

[The way in which these forces or these directions of psychic force in man are known from daily experience gives us no hope of finding proof that one individual can heal another by the influence of magnetism. For imagination, will-power, and belief remain always exclusively tied to the individual possessing these faculties, however highly they may be developed.]

* Curious Logic!—to ~~deny~~isprove the fact by an assertion, the truth of which is called in question by this very fact! Does the Will of necessity have[a]

24   pp 252–5 | II i §§133–4

Die Natur ohne die ihr gegenüber stehenden Geist ist eben so wenig denkbar, als es die Planeten ohne die ihr gegenüber stehende Sonne sind.... Die Offenbarung durch Wunder leugnen, heisst das Wirken des Geistes und seiner Kraft leugnen; und die Wunder natürlich erklären, heisst den Geist aus der Natur, das Licht aus der Finsterniss ableiten. Es folgt aber hieraus, dass der Kreis der Wunder in den Kreis des Heiligen eingeschlossen ist: denn Heiligkeit ist das Wesen des Geistes, der sich in der Natur offenbart.... Nur die heilige Hand thut Wunder: denn durch sie wirkt der Geist; und der Geist ist die Kraft, die die Natur beherrscht.... Jetzt... der Mensch ist grossentheils zum Zugthier geworden... Zerstörende Leidenschaften und Triebe haben sich seiner bemächtliget, und sein ursprünglich edles Wesen verunreiniget, verderbt, und zu Boden gedrückt. Wir wissen nicht mehr, welche Gestalt der über die Natur gesetzte Mensch hat und haben soll... Wir sind in eine grobe Abhängigkeit von der Natur versunken, die alle reinen Lebensverhältnisse des Menschen gestört, verwischt hat. Der Mensch mache sich wieder frei, erscheine wieder frei, was er nur vom Standpunkt der Vernunft aus kann, und er ist wieder Herr der ihn zunächst umgebenden Natur. Eine Idee, die nicht so leicht realisrt werden möchte, aber dennoch ausgesprochen werden muss, da sie in der Tiefe des menschlichen Wesens liegt. Auf jeden Fall sagt die Vernunft, dass für den Menschen das freie Leben allein ein gesundes Leben ist; und die Erfahrung fügt hinzu: in dem Masse wie der Mensch gesund ist, wächst seine erregende Kraft.

[Nature without a spirit standing opposite to her is as inconceivable as the planets without their corresponding sun....To deny revelation through miracles is to deny the operation of spirit and its powers, while to explain

_____
[a] The note is incomplete

miracles naturally is to derive spirit out of nature, or light out of darkness. It follows from this, however, that the circle of miracles is enclosed by the circle of holiness: for holiness is the essence of spirit that reveals itself in nature.... Only the holy hand does miracles: for through it spirit works; and spirit is the power that rules nature.... Nowadays...man has to a large extent turned into a draught animal...Destructive passions and instincts have gained control over him, defiling, corrupting, and crushing down his originally noble being. We no longer know what stature man, who has been set above nature, has or should have...We have degenerated into a state of gross dependence on nature that has destroyed and obliterated all man's pure living conditions. Man should make himself free, appear free again, and this he can do only by adopting the view of reason, and he is again lord over the surrounding [world of] nature. An idea that might not be realised so easily, although it must nevertheless be expressed, since it lies in the depth of man's being. In any event, reason dictates that only free life is for man a healthy life; and experience confirms this: to the extent that man is healthy, his activating power grows accordingly.]

I beseech you,[1] advert to the tone of this §. 134. It is quite characteristic of that mischmasch of Spinosism, Evangelicalism, and abstract Dynamics generalized from the recent experiments of Electro-magnetic Chemistry, which make up the newest German Eclecticism, and pietistic Philosophy.[2] Heinroth is a Philosopher, and must not talk altogether like a common Christian: or rather, I think, his Conscience twits him—and so it is Geist, that works true miracles: and Geist is *gegenüber*[3] Nature, as the positive Pole. But Poles are, of course, antitheta ejusdem essentiæ:[4] and Geist therefore is the positive Pole of Natur-Geist.

Natur-geist

+ Geist $\not\!+$ Natur −

And it is this Positive Pole that performed the miracles of the O. and N. Testament, turned Water into excellent Wine at Cana in Galilee, and into undrinkable Blood in Egypt.[5] But Positive Pole is a positive sort of cheat, that deals in the negative, and won't work (*tho' we were before informed that he or it is the only Jack of* ALL *work*) except where it meets—with Saints? No! with Heiligkeit[6]—and Heiligkeit *is*

24[1] I.e. Green: see **6** n 2 and **13** n 1, above.

24[2] Referring to e.g. Schleiermacher (see **2** and n 5, above), Oken (see **13** and n 1, above), Goldfuss (see **15** and nn 1–2, above), and Christian von Wolff (see **25** and n 1, below).

24[3] "*Opposite to*".

24[4] "Opposites of the same essence". See also **41** (at n 4), below.

24[5] John 2.1–11; Exod 7.17–20. Heinroth's conception of spirit as a mere pole of nature is incompatible with Christian belief in a transcendent God. Cf **3** and n 3 and **15** and n 2, above.

24[6] "Sanctity".

Geist—and Geist is no Animal Magnetist, and only works Miracles when it happens to be Geist!—Philosophy!!—

25 p ⁻1, referring to p 252, corrected in pencil

See Mss Note p. 252.*ᵃ*

All that staid and sober Dignity of logical Arrangement, which Wolf had introduced,[1] all that austere beauty of Method, which Kant added, seem to have deserted the present German Philosophers— who are sinking back rapidly into Miscellany, popular Opinionism, at once superficial and arbitrary; ⟨&⟩ in short, into the style of oratorical Lectures to ⟨~~sentimental~~ *blue*⟩ Ladies[2] and grown up Gentlemen, who have not time for reading.—This degeneracy is, I grieve to say, too apparent in this work, *on anthropology/* which might more fitly have been entitled—Sketches of all manner of things about men, women & children, Greeks & Romans & Dʳ Gall[3] & the New Testament, with fag ends of sentimental Sermons!—

26 p 255, marked with an ink line in margin | ɪɪ ii §136

Gut geschaffen, wie der Mensch ist (§. 124.), trägt er und sein ganzes Geschlecht den Keim oder den Samen des Guten in sich, als Prinzip *] der Freiheit, des Lichts: die Vernunft.

[Well fashioned as man is (§124), he and his race bear within themselves the germ or seed of the Good—the principle of freedom, of light: Reason.]

* Surely, Heinroth could never have asked himself, what he meant by Vernunft!—or he must have reversed this position.[1]

ᵃ In pencil

25[1] Baron Christian von Wolff (1679–1754), "admirer and illustrious systematizer of the Leibnitzian doctrine" (*BL* ch 8—*CC*—ɪ 131; cf *CN* ɪɪɪ 4151), born in Breslau, studied in Jena and lectured in Leipzig before taking the chair of mathematics and natural philosophy in Halle. His work, which in the end dealt systematically with almost the whole field of speculative philosophy, won early popularity, but he was driven from Halle by his pietistic colleagues in 1732 and remained in exile in Marburg until he was recalled and reinstated at Halle by Frederick the Great in 1740. In the second half of the eighteenth century his work provided the staple of philosophical study in most German universities and provided the background against which Kant developed his critical philosophy. Cf *Friend* (*CC*) ɪɪ 246. C annotated an English translation of the *Logic* (1770) and was also familiar with the German original (1712): see *CN* ɪ 891, 902.

25[2] Learned or pedantic females.

25[3] See **19** textus, and **19** and n 2, above.

26[1] See **16** and n 1 and **18**, above, and **39** (last par), below.

27   p 261 | ɪɪ ii § 139

Die Völker selbst erschufen ihre Herrscher: denn sie bedurften ihrer; und sie stellten dieselben unübersehlich hoch, damit sie sich desto tiefer vor ihnen, als Repräsentanten der Gottheit, beugen konnten: denn anbetende Verehrung ist der Charakter und das Bedürfniss des Orients. Seine Völker wurden Sklaven, nicht aus Sklavensinn, sondern aus schrankenloser, von Phantasie durchdrungener Religiosität. Und nur in späterer Zeit artete die freie Unterwürfigkeit in Sklaverei aus, weil auch die Herrscher ihre Gewalt in das Schrankenlose ausdehnten: denn Despotie und Sklaverei bedingen sich gegenseitig.

[The [oriental] people themselves produced their rulers: for they needed them and they raised them to an unchecked height, in order that they themselves might bow down that much lower to those representatives of the Deity. For worshipping veneration is the character of the Orient and their need. Its people became slaves, not from a slave mentality, but from an unlimited religiosity drenched in fantasy. Only in later times did this free subservience turn into slavery, because the rulers also extended their power to unlimited proportions; for despotism and slavery condition each other.]

Polygamy; and the vast extent of fertile Plains and the equal continuity of the Mountain Districts, in Asia, occasioning a succession of Conquerors, with the greatest possible temptations to, and facilities of, Conquest: these two characteristics of Asia furnish ὡς ἐμοίγε δοκεῖ,[1] a far more satisfactory solution of Asiatic Despotism. Where they did not find place, as in Asia Minor, and Palestine, Asia was the Birth-place of Republic and free Cities—[2]

S. T. C.

N.B. Early existence of Arab and Tartar Marauders—a Slave-trade the consequence/ Polygamy the consequence of the Slave-Trade—and *perhaps* the unequal number of male & female Births an effect, and then an supporting Cause of Polygamy.

28   p 264, marked with an ink line in margin | ɪɪ ii § 141

Rom konnte nur besitzen und herrschen; was es in sich aufnahm, nahm es nicht in sein Wesen, sondern nur in seinen Dienst auf: des Auslandes Götter nicht minder, als die Künste desselben.

27[1] "In my opinion, at least".   27[2] Cf, however, *Friend* (*CC*) ɪ 167, 438.

[Rome could only possess and dominate; whatever it absorbed did not become an essential part of its life, but was merely taken into its service: foreign gods no less than foreign arts.]

an excellent Remark: an Oasis in this sandy Wilderness.[1]

29 pp 280–1 | ii ii §144

Der Sinn, wie der Verstand, fordern gleichsam die Vernunft heraus, sich an sie anzuketten, und ihre Lücken zu ergänzen...ihre offenen Schranken zu schliessen.... Die Vernunft knüpft den Anfang und das Ende aller Dinge und Zeiten an die höchste Einheit, an Gott, das ewig-heilige Wesen, und wirft von diesem, als ihrem Stand- und Haltungspunkt aus, einen Lichtstrahl reingeistiger oder heiliger Zweckbeziehung auf Alles was da ist, war und wird. Des heiligen, und in seiner Heiligkeit seligen, Wesens theilhaftig zu werden, ist, nach dem Ausspruch der Alles ausgleichenden Vernunft, der Zweck der Welt.

[Sense, as well as understanding, challenges reason, so to speak, to connect them to itself and supplement their deficiencies...close their open boundaries....Reason binds the beginning and end of all things and times to the highest unity, to God, the eternally holy Being, and from this, as from its basis and foundation, it casts a ray of light of pure spiritual or holy intention upon everything that is, was, and will be there. To partake of the holy Being—blessed in its holiness—is, according to the dictum of all-harmonising reason, the purpose of the world.]

A Reason that begins to work and yet is represented (as by Heinroth) as having no Antecedent—a Reason, that proposes means in order to a not yet existing End—is a misnomer.[1] But in fact it is demonstrably impossible, that the Riddle of the World should be solved by a Philosophy, which commences by drawing a circle, that

28[1] Cf *Friend (CC)* i 505: "It was the Roman instinct to appropriate by conquest and to give fixture by legislation." See also *C&S (CC)* 150–1 and cf *CN* iv 5430 (12 Aug 1826): "Rome took the ideas of Greece not into her Being but into her *Service: She made use of them.*—Rome was the proper Type of the PATRON. Pericles to Phidias & his Compeers was one Man of Genius befriending another; but Mæcænas and Augustus Cæsar were PATRONS of the Fine Arts".

29[1] In *SM (CC)* 19 n 1 C stated that understanding is "A power of selecting and adapting fit means to proximate ends" and that "Reason knows nothing of means for ends". Cf *CN* iv 5429 (12 Aug 1826): "...Reason = Identity or Cöinherence of Means and End. Understanding = Separation of Means and Ends. Hence in the present state both of Man and of Nature, the materials being heterogeneous and imperfect, the highest possible State is a *State* of Understanding, τὸ ἄμεινον [the better]. The greater number of the component parts of the resulting Whole must be *Means* where they are not Ends...."

can never open, around it; and which therefore must for ever stagger to and fro between two intolerable Positions—first, an absolute Identity, that monopolizing all *very* Being leaves only a Universe of mere Relations without focuses, to which they refer—i.e. when the Looking-glasses are themselves only Reflections. 2. A real Nature, in which Potential Being is a the bona fide Antecedent to all actual Being, and every higher Power is the Creature and Product of the lower—all therefore of the lowest.[2]

30   p 283

[Heinroth draws a contrast between the law of selfness ("das Gesetz der Selbstheit") in nature and the law governing the life of the spirit:] ...das Princip des Geistes dem der Natur eben so entgegengesetzt ist, wie in die Natur selbst das des Lichts dem der Schwere. Das Princip des Geistes ist Einheit, Ungetrenntheit...denn Zwiespalt mit sich selbst zerstört den Geist. Das Leben und die Erhaltung des Geistes demnach ist an Bedingungen gebunden, welche denen der Erhaltung des Naturlebens gerade entgegengesetzt sind, wie Einheit und Friede der Trennung und dem Kampfe....Leben ist Thätigkeit; die Thätigkeit des Geistes aber ist auf ganz andere Weise bedingt als die der Natur; wie das Licht nach einem ganz andern Gesetz thätig ist als die Schwere; und der Geist ist allezeit nur dem Licht vergleichbar, wie die Schwere oder Selbstheit den eigentlichen Kern der Natur ausmacht, oder dasjenige, was man Stoffheit oder Materie zu nennen pflegt....Auch das Naturleben besteht zum Theil durch diese Kraft der Einheit, oder Einheit der Kraft, welche, als eigentliche Lebenskraft, als die Seele der Dinge, das aus einander Stebende bändiget und zusammenhält, das aus einander fallende Reich der Schwere in die Schranken des Lichts einfasst, und so Form und Gestalt und das ganze schöne Entwickenlungsleben hervorruft...Ohne Geist kein Leben; aber nicht umgekehrt ohne Leben kein Geist: denn das Leben der ganzen Natur ist Erzeugniss des Geistes, und wird vom Geiste getragen.

[...the principle of the spirit is opposed to that of nature just as in nature itself the principle of light is opposed to that of gravity. The principle of the

---

29[2] If the priority of the absolute, "the Self-affirmant and self-affirmed", is denied as the ground of all things, all relations in the universe lose their reality and become "either mere *logical Entities*, or mere Umbrae apparentiae"; and any

system that does not proceed from an original unity prior to all polarity becomes a circular, closed system. *CL* IV 767–8 (c Sept 1817). Cf **3** and n 3 and **8**, above. For the "looking-glass" illustration see **18**, above.

spirit is unity, undividedness... for inner discord destroys the spirit. The life and preservation of the spirit depend therefore on conditions that are directly opposed to those governing the preservation of life in nature, as unity and peace are opposed to division and strife.... Life is activity; the activity of the spirit is, however, conditioned in a completely different way from the activity of nature; just as light acts according to a completely different law from gravity; and the spirit is at all times comparable to light alone, just as gravity or selfness constitutes the actual kernel of nature, or that which one used to call substance or matter.... Even natural life exists partly by virtue of this power of unity, or unity of power, which, as actual vital power, as the soul of things, binds and fastens disparity, envelops the disintegrating world of gravity in the boundaries of light, and thus calls forth form and contour and the whole beautiful development of life; without spirit, no life; but not vice versa, without life no spirit; for the whole life of nature is a creation of the spirit, and is supported by the spirit.]

I thought, we should come to this! which is in fact an unsaying of all the former. If Nature cannot exist without Geist, neither can Geist exist without Nature—i.e. on Schelling's and Heinroth's principles, Spirit = Light; Selfness = Gravity.—Does not the Light presuppose the Gravity? Nay, is not Gravity the principle of the *unity*, and Light of Plurarity*a* in Unity?—As well therefore might we make Light the Representative of Selfness.[1]

31 p 284

*] Das geistige Licht ist, wie das physische, ein erregendes Prinzip, welches, je intensiver, energischer, concentrirter es ist, folglich, je mehr es den Charakter der Ungetrenntheit, der Einheit der Kraft an sich trägt, desto mehr, und mit desto grösserem Erfolg, bestrebt ist sich auszubreiten, den Kreis seines Wirkens, des Erhellens, des Tagbringens, zu erweitern.

[Spiritual light is, like physical light, an activating principle that will strive to expand itself and to widen the range of its influence and its brightness more fully and with greater success in proportion to its intensity, energy, and concentration and, therefore, in proportion to its coherence and unity of force.]

* not true! Ex. gr. the Lens. By convergence Light becomes a

a A slip for "Plurality"

30[1] Since, according to "Heinroth's principles", nature and spirit are opposites (see **24** and n 4, above), neither can exist without the other: hence light and gravity must "presuppose" each other. For C on light and gravity see e.g. *CL* IV 771–4 (Sept 1817), 806–8 (Jan 1818), *CN*

III 4418, 4420 (c Aug–Sept 1818). Schelling's discussion of light and gravity is mainly in SCHELLING *Einleitung zu seinen erster Entwurf eines Systems der Naturphilosophie* (Jena & Leipzig 1799) i 99–122, 139–46 (not annotated).

consuming Fire. But what but confusion can arise out of these endless metaphors, that are evermore shifting their meaning?[1]

32 p 285

...das Lichtleben der Menschheit—und diess ist das Leben nach dem Gesetz der Vernunft...kann nur seine geistige Vollendung... herbeiführen, nur die gesammten Kräfte des Menschengeschlechts, die sich jetzt noch zum Theil bekämpfen...durch Vereinigung und Zusammenstimmung steigern, und ein allgemeiner Hebel höherer Erkenntniss und höheren Wirkens werden. Also: möge die Aussenwelt, die Welt der Natur, die noch unter dem Gesetz der Schwere befangen liegt...nicht ohne Zwiespalt und Kampf bestehen können...in der Welt des Geistes, zu welcher das Leben der Menschheit...herauferzogen wird, ist es nicht also.

[...mankind's life-in-light—and this is life according to the law of reason...can only bring about his spiritual perfection; only intensify through union and harmony the entire powers of the human race, which are still now in partial conflict with one another, and become a general lever of higher perception and higher activity. Thus, even if the outer world, the world of nature, which is still imprisoned in the law of gravity...cannot exist without discord and conflict...this is not the case in the world of the spirit towards which the growth of mankind...is directed.]

Give us a clear Idea of an intelligible World without an imperfect World of Nature—then shew the possibility and thereby the Origin of the Latter—& *so* there may arise some Hope of shewing its possible *Desinence*[1]—and the means, by which this is feasible.

If *all*—i.e. each and every—has never been perfect: if the only perfection consists in a resolution of Discords into a Concord, that exists only for an infinite Ear—a perfect Whole, that has no existence for any one of its innumerable integral Parts—how should we discover that any other Perfection ever will exist? or ever can?[2]

33 pp 288–9

Hierauf ist zu erwiedern...dass...das Prinzip der Herrschaft, in der Vernunft, und nicht in der Natur liegt, dass diese zum Gehorchen angewiesen, und ihr Bestehen nur im Gehorsam gegen die Vernunft gesichert ist, dass in diesem Verhältniss von Naturgehorsam und

---

[31][1] On the German naturalists' abuse of analogy see e.g. GOLDFUSS 8.

[32][1] I.e. coming to an ending.

[32][2] Cf **29** and n 2, above, and *SM* (*CC*) 68–9 n 3. C is here objecting to the consideration of people as means to an end, and—disregarding the happiness or misery of the individual—as parts of a (social) whole.

Vernunftherrschaft das richtige Ebenmass des Lebens besteht, dass nur in ihm das Leben sich frei und in voller Gesundheit bewegt.... Das Wachstum des Guten kann nur in der Reife der Vernunft endigen. Geht nun das Böse im Menschengeschlecht endlich unter, so muss das Gute in demselben endlich siegen.... Die Entwickelung, wie sich Herder ausdrückt, in einer Asymptote von Erdpunkt zu Erdpunkt fortschreitet, und die folgende Generation sich... den Reichthum der früheren assimilirt. So verführen die Griechen mit dem Orient, die Römer mit den Griechen, die Neu-Europäer mit den Römern...

[To this we may reply... that... the principle of control appertains to reason, not to nature; that the latter is allotted the function of being obedient, and its continued existence is assumed only by virtue of its continuing obedience to reason; that it is in this relation between natural obedience and rational control that the correct balance of life consists; that it is only in this relation that life moves freely and in complete health.... The growth of Good can only culminate in the maturity of reason. If then evil in the human race is finally destroyed, the Good in it must finally be victorious.... This development, as Herder put it, progresses in the form of an asymptote from one point of the earth to the other, and the next generation assimilates the riches of the previous one. This is how the Greeks proceeded with the Orient, the Romans with the Greeks, the neo-Europeans with the Romans...]

The only imaginable scheme of a Paradisiacal World is that which several of the Greek Fathers entertained—viz. that at a certain period a pre-determined numbers of redeemed and perfected human Spirits will have been completed—that then the Planet will undergo a complete Revolution and a new Heaven & a new Earth will arise, in harmony with the regenerate natures of the new Inhabitants, who will neither marry nor die any more.—Alas! quoth a French Wit/ I should be an exception: I should certainly die of Ennui.[1]

34   p 305 | II ii §148

Wie das physische Feuer unter der Erde sich durch galvanische Ketten über Welttheile hinzieht, warum sollte das geistige Feuer nicht Aehnliches auf ähnliche Weise über der Erde vermögen?

[As physical fire traverses parts of the world under the surface of the earth by means of galvanic reactions, why should spiritual fire not be able to operate similarly on the surface of the earth?]

Quite delicious! had a Flash of Lightning knocked the Devil down from the Top of Lincoln Spire,[1] why should not a Syllogism knock

---

33[1] Source not identified—possibly fictitious.

34[1] C alludes to the phrase "He looks as the devil over Lincoln", which

down the God Fo, and the Lama or Babe-God of Thibet?[2] Warum,
I say! Warum sollt' es nicht?[3]

35   pp 382–3 | Appendix i par iii

Geologische, ja cosmogenische Betrachtungen gehen also hier denen
über den Menschen voraus; worauf denn dieselben Kräfte, die im
Grossen und Ganzen walten, im Kleinen und Einzelnen aufgezeigt,
die Kräfte und Gesetze der allgemeinen Natur in denen der indivi-
duellen Menschennatur nachgewiesen werden, jedoch eben so wieder
in dieser die Strahlen und die Abglanz des höchsten Ideellen. Ein
grosses Unternehmen, welches die Vorarbeiten nicht blos von Indi-
viduen, sondern von Generationen verlangt, und welches, genau
betrachtet, dennoch nicht anders als entweder nur fragmentarisch
oder poetisch zu Stande kommen kann. Denn was und wie viel wissen
wir von der grossen und allgemeinen Natur, von ihren Erscheinungen,
Kräften und Gesetzen... Schon das Leben... der Thiere begreifen
wir immer weniger... kennen wir denn unsere eigene? Unser eigenes
leibliches Leben... ist uns in seiner inneren Wesenheit noch ein
Geheimniss... Legen wir also im Betreff des grossen Ganzen, dessen
geringer Theil wir sind... lieber das Bekenntniss unserer Unwissen-
heit ab, als dass wir uns der Gefahr aussetzen, eben so eitle
als vermessene gigantische Versuche, die Tiefen und Höhen des
Unermesslichen zu umfassen, zu unserer grössten Demüthigung
scheitern und durch sich selbst vernichtet zu sehen.

[Geological, indeed cosmogonical, considerations thus precede those re-
garding man. Thereupon the same forces that operate on a large scale are also
exhibited in small individual things. The forces and laws of universal nature
are established in those of individual human nature; similarly it is in this
human nature that the rays and reflection of the highest ideal are manifested.
A great undertaking, which demands preparation not merely by individuals
but by generations, and which on precise examination cannot be implemented
other than fragmentarily or poetically. For what and how much do we know
of great nature in general, its phenomena, forces, and laws?... Already we

---

Thomas Fuller explains in his *Worthies*:
"Lincoln Minister is one of the state-
liest structures in Christendom.... The
devil... is supposed to have overlooked
this church... with a torve and tetrick
countenance".
34² Fo or Foh—the Chinese name of
Buddha, Buddhism having been intro-
duced into China in c A.D. 67. C men-
tions the "Chinese God Fo" in LRR:

Lects 1795 (CC) 183; cf *EOT (CC)* ii 344.
The Dalai Lama, whom C mentions in
EOT (CC) i 70, iii 133, *CN* iii 3288, was
and is believed to be an incarnation of
Buddha; on the death of a Dalai Lama a
search immediately begins for the baby in
whom he is to be reincarnated.
34³ "Why... Why should it not be?"
See also **35**, below.

comprehend less and less about the life...of animals...do we understand our own? The inner essence of our own corporeal life is still a mystery to us...With regard to this great Whole of which we are the least part...let us then rather admit our ignorance than expose ourselves to the danger and greatest humiliation of seeing our gigantic attempts to grasp the heights of the immeasurable, which are as conceited as they are impertinent, founder and destroy themselves.]

This is what Bacon describes as pusillanimitas non sine arrogantiâ.[1]

The same Determents might as fitly have been urged against Kepler when he proposed to himself to render the innumerable Host of the starry Heavens comprehensible, by evolving their motions out of the eternal Forms of Reason. How can you tell, O Kepler![2] that none of the innumerable Bodies of the material universe are weightless, attractionless?—Wait, Friend! till you find one.

So it ever is with unfountainous *canal*-like Intellects, such as Heinroth's.[3] The Natur-philosophy had foundered. Instead of revising the *Make* of the Vessel, in order to discover where the Leak was, he shrugs his shoulders and denounces the Voyage.

36　p 387 | par iv

Sollen wir diesen Standpunkt des Forschers, welcher uns der des reifsten Denkens zu seyn scheint, mit einem Namen Bezeichnen...so ist es der des *gegenständlichen Denkens*, den wir zugleich mit der Methode selbst, einem Genius verdanken, welcher von den meisten nur für einen Dichter, nicht auch für einen Denker gehalten wird. Es ist *Göthe*. Man muss in ihm, bei näherer Betrachtung, den Denker ganz vom Dichter sondern, und in ihm ein hohes Denkvermögen anerkennen, welches aber freilich nicht auf die gewöhnliche, philosophische, abstracte, sondern auf ganz eigenthümliche Weise, nehmlich eben *gegenständlich* thätig ist. Hiermit soll nicht gesagt seyn, dass sich sein Denken mit Gegenständen beschäftiget—was besonders zu bemerken lächerlich wäre, da alles Denken seinen Gegenstand haben muss—: sondern diess soll damit gesagt seyn, dass sein Denken nicht von den Gegenständen abgesondert ist, dass die

35[1] "Small-mindedness not without arrogance". Bacon *Novum Organum* I 88. In Jan–Feb 1801 C copied out from this aphorism the sentence including this phrase (*CN* I 913), quoted it in Latin in *BL* ch 12, and telescoped it into the phrase "the arrogance of pusillanimity" in ch 8: *BL* (*CC*) I 293, 138.

35[2] For C on Johann Kepler (1571–1630) see e.g. *SM* (*CC*) 51, *Friend* (*CC*) I 485–6, and *TT* 8 Oct 1830. For a comparison of Kepler and Bacon see *P Lects* Lect 11, esp (1949) 331, 336–7.

35[3] Cf C's distinction between "two Kinds of Heads in the world of Literature...SPRINGS...[and] TANKS". *CL* III 355 (c Dec 1811).

Elemente der Gegenstände, die Anschauungen, in dasselbe eingehen und von ihm auf das innigste durchdrungen werden, so dass sein Anschauen selbst ein Denken, sein Denken ein Anschauen ist...

[If we have to supply a name to this attitude of the researcher, which seems to us to be the most mature in thought... then it is that of *objective thinking*: a name which, together with the method itself, we owe to a genius who is taken by the majority to be only a poet rather than a thinker also. It is *Goethe*. On closer examination one must distinguish completely the thinker in him from the poet, and recognise in the man a high intellectual capacity, which indeed is not active in the usual philosophical abstract way, but in a quite special way. That is to say, it is *objectively* active. This does not signify that his thought concerns itself with objects—which, as a particular observation, would be absurd, since all thought must have an object—but it denotes the fact that his thought is not divorced from objects; that the elements of the objects—the contemplative intuitions given—proceed into the thought and are permeated by it most thoroughly, so that his intuition itself is thought, and his thought intuition...]

The oddity of finding any thing new in bringing the results of meditation to bear on the notices of Observation, and vice versâ—so as to combine thinking with th Seeing, or rather to unite activ[e]*[a]* and passive Seeing in ⟨reference to⟩ the same A̶c̶t̶ Object—and the adulatory reference to Göthe, as the Inventor—and the modest statement of himself, as the Ali of the philosophic Mahomet[1]—amuses me!

What in the name of common sense is the meaning of the word, Contemplation, but this so quaintly called gegenständliche Thatigkeit?*[b2]*

---

37 p 393 | Appendix II

[After discussing the genesis of the embryo and the human foetus Heinroth outlines a number of views that he considers erroneous.]
...ist es auffallend, wie die Beobachter, ohne Ausnahme kann man sagen, einen Embryo im Ey annehmen, ehe er gebildet ist, wie sie das Rudiment des Embryo voraussetzen, ehe sie es mit Augen erblicken ...Von bildende Kräften, die den Typus der Gestaltung in sich *]* tragen, ahnen sie nichts, weil sie dieselben nicht mit Augen sehen: Wie kommt denn aber die Gestalt in das ursprünglich Ungestaltete?

[...it is a striking fact that the observers, one might say without exception, presuppose an embryo in the egg before it is formed, just as they take for

---

a Cropped   *b* A slip for "Thätigkeit"

36[1] Mohammad's son-in-law and most faithful follower.   **36**[2] "Objective activity"—adapted from textus.

granted the rudiment of the embryo before they have seen it with their own eyes...They have no notion of the creative forces that carry the prototype of the form within themselves, because they cannot perceive them with their eyes. But how does form appear in that which was originally formless?]

* This would throw the doors wide open to every species of Phantastery.[1]—Mem.—proves the importance of our principle,[2] that the inseparability of the product from the productivity in the idea of Life is essential to the Idea.[3] H. makes Life *creative*.

38 p 395

[Heinroth outlines (adversely) the view that the human embryo and foetus pass through all animal states, each according to its specific animal structure.]

I cannot say what Meckel and others have intended;[1] but I know, that I never understood more than a progressive metamorphosis by successive evolution of the three forms or forces of the Vital Principle, α. Vis φυτοειδης: β. εντομοειδης: γ. ιδιοζωικη.[2]— i.e. that the human Fœtus exists as a Plant, an Insect, and an Animal; but in each state specifically in reference to *the Man*.

39 pp 400–1

Aber man *soll* denken, nicht in das Blaue hinein, sondern gegenständlich...Schon hat man zugestanden und anerkannt, dass das

37[1] "Fancy": perhaps *Phantasterei* anglicised. Not in *OED*. Cf "phantast" in Hacket *Century* **16** n 1.

37[2] I.e. the principles of C and Green in their theory of life.

37[3] See e.g. *C&S* (*CC*) 180–4 (= *CL* vi 598–601), *CL* iv 775.

38[1] Johann Friedrich Meckel (1781–1833) in his *System der vergleichenden Anatomie* (6 vols Halle 1821–33) i, Vorrede xv–xvi, discusses the importance of comparative anatomy to the understanding of human anatomy and physiology. He quotes the view of Haller and Dütrochet that the formation of the human foetus cannot be explained without reference to the development of membranes in various animals, including amphibia, birds, and mammals. According to Dütrochet, the neglect of such comparisons between the membranes of vertebrate animals and the human

embryo accounts for the inadequate knowledge of human embryology. C annotated a copy of Meckel's *System*, most of his notes concentrating on the Vorrede to Vol i. In a letter of 8 Dec 1821 C mentioned two articles in *Allgemeine Encyclopädie der Wissenschaften und Künste* in which Meckel collaborated. *CL* v 191.

38[2] "a. plant-like force; b. insect-like [force]; c. individual-animal [force]." See *CN* iv 4886 (2 Apr 1822): "Instead of the vague terms Reproduction, Irritability, Sensibility, I would substitute, 1: το φυτοειδες: 2. το εντομοειδες: 3 το ιδιοζωικον..."; in the same note C identifies these terms with "Life[(1], Life[(2], Life[(3]", for which see also e.g. Fielding *Joseph Andrews* annex (i.e. N 47 ff 16^v–17^v: *CN* v). See also **14** n 3, above, and *CN* iv 4890, 4892, 4895 (all c Apr 1822), and 4929 (? 1822/1827).

erste Rudiment aus der Wechselwirkung des Eyhäutchens und der ursprünglichen Flüssigkeit entsteht. Also: thätige Kräfte! nach Gesetzen wirksame Kräfte! gesetzlich bildende Kräfte! Nun diese Gesetze müssen diesen Kräften vorgeschrieben seyn, der ganze Typus der Bildungsgesetze muss sich nach und nach in den immer mehr auf äusseren Reiz von innen sich entfaltenden Kräften entwickeln, in mannichfaltigen Metamorphosen allerdings; aber diese Metamorphosen sind nicht die des Gebildes selbst...sondern sie sind Umwandlungen der bildenden Organe. Das erste bildende Organ ist das Eyhaut....Dieses erste Organ erzeugt—nicht den Menschen, sondern neue bildende Organe: Kopf-Rumpf-Darm-Bläschen. Nichts natürlicher, als dass diese auf die in ihnen enthaltenen Flüssigkeiten wirken. Diese verdichten sich allerdings zu neuen Rudimenten, überall mit Gefässbildung: jedes werdende Organ erhält sein besonderes Gefässsystem. Woher nun die Nahrung?... Aus dem allgemeinen Gefässsystem durch das Herz und sein Blut....So, vorwärts und ruckwärts, gehe man nur Schritt vor Schritt von Bedingungen zu Bedingungen fort, erkläre das Vorhandene nicht aus dem was noch nicht da ist, sondern umgekehrt, das was da wird aus dem schon Vorhandenen, und man kommt wenigstens zu der Vorstellung...einer Einheit, die allerdings zuletzt an die Idee eines unsichtbaren Grund-Typus geknüpft ist, welcher aber...in der gesetzlich bildenden Kraft als Totalität von BildungsGesetzen liegt, die sich allmählich in der Zeit entwickeln.

[But we *shall* think, not in a pointless vacuity, but objectively...It has already been admitted and recognised that the first rudiment arises from the interaction of the ovular membrane and the original fluid. Here are forces! forces acting according to laws, forces forming according to laws. Now, these laws must be prescribed to these forces, the whole typology of the laws of form must develop gradually in the forces unfolding themselves from within in ever greater response to external stimulus—in manifold metamorphoses, of course; but these metamorphoses are not those of the structural entity itself...but are changes in the forming organs. The first forming organ is the ovular membrane....This first organ begets—not the human being, but new forming organs: head—trunk—intestine—vesicle. It is entirely natural for these to act upon the liquids contained in them. These latter solidify, of course, into new rudiments, with the formation of vessels at all points: each developing organ receives its own system of vessels. From where, then, does the nourishment come?...From the general system of vessels through the heart and its blood....So, backwards and forwards, let us proceed step by step from one condition to another, explain what is present not with reference to what is not there yet, but vice versa, explain what is coming into being by what is already present, and we shall arrive at the representation... of a unity, which indeed is ultimately bound to the idea of an invisible basic type: a basic type, however, which...exists in the lawfully operating force of form, as a totality of laws of formation that develop gradually in time.]

All well and smoothly till we come to the Plastic Powers, the dynamic Polarities.[1] What are these?—They have a Law implanted in them.— *Them*?—and *a* Law?—That is not enough! It must be *the* Law—i.e. not a Law in any accepted sense of the word; but an individual pre-existing spiritual Fac Simile of that particular numerical Product. And to what does this lead us?—I *fear*, to a mere repetition of the Effect in connection with the obscure Notion of *Cause*—a retro- instead of pro-jected Image, disimaged[2] into the ens logicum[3] of simply *Being*.—Or if not to this—then to an intelligent Creative Soul—yet finite & liable to err?[a]

All these bewilderments arise out of the πρωτον κοινον τε ψευδος[4] of the German Philosophers—the not seeing that there is a deeper than Reason, and that what is deeper than Reason cannot be an object of Reason, and consequently not of distinct knowlege.[5]

---

40   pp 403–4 | Appendix III

Nicht um hier einen Beweis durch Spiele der Analogie zu führen, sondern blos um auf die wirklich bemerkbaren inneren Unterschiede aufmerksam zu machen, stehe hier die Parallele der psychischen, der organischen, und der äusseren Natur-Kraft.

Gemüth,	Geist,	Wille.
Herz,	Hirn,	Muskel.
Wärme,	Licht,	Schwere...

Kurz, wir haben ein für Freude und Leid empfängliches Herz, einen der Erkenntniss fähigen Geist, und einen thatkräftigen Willen, ohne den keine, such die geringste unserer Handlungen zu Stande kommt.

[It is not to present proofs by way of analogy, but to draw attention to the easily discernible essential differences, that the following parallels between psychological, organic, and external natural forces are drawn up.

Temperament,	Mind,	Will-power.
Heart,	Brain,	Muscle,
Warmth,	Light,	Weight...

[a] Here C has written "(Turn to the top of P. 400)."

39[1] The phrase "dynamic Polarities" comes a little later in Heinroth's text.
39[2] Not in *OED*.
39[3] A "logical entity".
39[4] The "first and common error".

On the "fundamental error" of German philosophers cf HEGEL **3** and n 1.
39[5] On the question "what is deeper than Reason" see *Friend (CC)* I 515–16 and n 3, *SM (CC)* 67 n 2, and *P Lects* Lect 13 (1949) 390.

In short, we possess a heart receptive to joy and sorrow, a mind capable of knowledge, and an energetic will without which not even our slightest action could take place.]

This "Heart" as contra-distinguished from Muscle, is an arbitrary Hypothesis connected with the no less arbitrary assertion of the Feelings, Sentiments and Affections having their source & seat in the Heart. Even in language, it is but an Idiom of this & that Language. In the Semitic Tongues the Heart was made the Seat & used as the Symbol of the Intellect. Where we should say, Head or Brain, the Hebrews said, Heart. Thus "to say in the heart" is the Hebrew Idiom for "to think". The Fool (or more faithfully, the worthless Man, Vaurien) hath said in his heart, There is no God.[1] i.e. The worthless Man reasons with himself, &c.

41 pp 406–7

Wir aber, die wir uns im vollen, lebendigen Bewusstseyn auffassen, nennen annoch unser inneres, unsichtbares, Eines, in dem Namen Ich zusammengefasstes, Freude und Leid fühlendes, denkendes, dichtendes, Thaten beschliessendes und ausführendes Wesen: *] Seele, im Gegensatz gegen unser äusserliches, räumliches, leibliches Ich und Leben.

[We, however, who are aware of ourselves in full active consciousness, give the name of "soul" to our internal, invisible being which is contained in the word "I" and which feels joy and sorrow, thinks, produces poetry, makes decisions and carries them out: the "soul" as opposed to our external, spatial, corporeal ego and life.]

*Mercy on us! And is it come to this?—The distinction of the intuitions, Space and Time, *corpus-mortuum*ed[1] into two heterogeneous Somewhats! With the exception of one doubtful text,[2] the

40[1] AV translates the Hebrew words *leb* and *lebab* usually—i.e. in hundreds of places—as "heart". *Peake* 268g notes on Judges 16.15: "'Heart': in Hebrew [*leb*] the seat of the intellect rather than the emotions; the same word is translated 'mind' in 16.17." See also 313a, 459a on *leb* in 1 Chron 17.18, Isa 57.15. AV translates *leb* as "mind" in twelve places, and the related *lebab* as "mind" in four places. In C's quotation —Ps 14.1, 53.1—the Hebrew word for "heart" is *leb*. The sense of *nabal* (AV "fool") is, according to Gesenius, "impious, ungodly, abandoned", but "empty" is a possible sense consorting

with C's recommendation. Knox reads "reckless heart", *NEB* "impious fool". Isaac D'Israeli had used *Vaurien* (literally "worthless", cf American "noaccount") as the title of a book in 1797. The earliest entry in *OED* for *vaut-rien* is for 1825, for *vaurien* 1868.

41[1] Turned into a dead body, or into the worthless residues left at the end of a chemical process. For *corpus mortuum* see BÖHME **71** n 2.

41[2] Cf 1 Cor 15, as in HACKET *Century* **22**. Tertullian had used Luke 16.19–31 as evidence for the corporeality of the soul.

Scriptures teach nothing of a *Soul* included in a Body; but of the *Man*. I, Thou, He, or She, the Person—supersede the use, much more the necessity, of the word, Soul, employed as the *Contrary* to Body. For *Opposite* would subvert the whole dogma[3]—inasmuch as opposites are necessarily ejusdem essentiæ.[4]—If a philosophical distinction were needed, we might distinguish the Many in the One from the Many under the coercion of the Many-in-the-One—the first = *I*, the second = *mene* momentarié et in transitu.—[5]

42 p 419

Dass mein Bewusstseyn durch mein Denken nicht zu Stande kommt, ist mir ganz klar: denn ich denke *im* Bewusstseyn, wie der Vogel in der Luft fliegt...Ich *bin* überhaupt, auch wollend, auch empfindend, im Bewusstseyn: kurz, es ist das Element, in dem ich als Seelenwesen lebe. Blicken wir das Bewusstseyn recht genau an!...Es hat gar keine Gestalt oder Form; es ist nichts als eine Klarheit, ein Licht, wobei und in welchem wir uns selbst sehen, Wie wir durch das äussere Licht die Gegenstände erkennen.

[It is quite obvious to me that my consciousness is not created by virtue of my thought; for I think *in* consciousness, just as the bird flies in the air...I *am*, purely and simply, whether willing or experiencing, in consciousness: in short, it is the element in which I live as a being with a soul. Let us examine consciousness precisely!...It has no feature or form; it is nothing but a clarity, a light by which and in which we see ourselves, just as we recognise objects through outer light.]

This seems to me very like talking of a Light to see the Light by. The very word Bewüsst-seyn should have saved H. from this absurd Caricature of Malbranche![1]

43 p 474, pencil

1. Against Spinoza and Schelling.[1]
    Shall he that made the Eye, not see? he that made the Ear not hear?[2]

41[3] For the crucial distinction between opposite and contrary see GOLDFUSS **2** n 8 and *Friend (CC)* I 94n.

41[4] "Of the same essence". Cf **24** and n 4, above.

41[5] "Me, perhaps, momentarily and in passing". On 14 Aug 1826 C noted that Heinroth in pp 414ff "seems to me to have given a confused account of Sensa-tion & Feeling, in contra-distinction from Will and Thought". *CN* IV 5432.

42[1] For C on Malebranche see FICHTE *Grundlage* **1** n 2.

43[1] I.e. in general against the pantheism of Spinoza and Schelling.

43[2] Ps 49.9 (var). See also JACOBI *Ueber...Spinoza* **16**.

2. Against Stahl and H. Steffens[3]

If that, which made the eye and ear, can hear and see, why did it make eyes and ears? Lynceus ~~never~~ as little thought of inventing Spectacles, as the Lynx of wearing them.[4]

S. T. C. 19 Aug. 1826

43[3] Georg Ernst Stahl (1660–1734), physician and professor of medicine, propounded a doctrine of animism in his *Theoria medica vera* (1707); see also GRAY 6 n 2. C annotated seven works of Heinrich Steffens (1773–1843).

43[4] Lynceus, one of the Argonauts, famed (as is the lynx) for his keen eyesight.

GEORGE HERBERT
1593–1633

The Temple. Sacred poems and private ejaculations. By Mr George Herbert, late Oratour of the University of Cambridge. Together with his life [by Izaak Walton]. With several additions.... The tenth edition, with an alphabetical table for ready finding out the chief places. London 1674. 12°. [Together with] The Synagogue: or the shadow of the temple. Sacred poems, and private ejaculations. In imitation of Mr. George Herbert [by Christopher Harvey (1597–1663)]. The sixth edition, corrected and enlarged. London 1673. 12°.

New York Public Library (Berg Collection)

Inscribed in an unidentified early hand on p ⁻2: "this Book was given me by Susanna Trosse the 3 of october 1711"; C has written **2** around the inscription. On p ⁻4 four lines of verse are written in a civility hand; C's **16** is written above. Inscribed on the lower half of p ⁻5 in a twentieth-century hand in pencil: "A. L. Chetwode to R. H. Grille & E A Grille 7.7.03." Also inscribed in pencil on p ⁻1 in an unidentified hand: "S. T. Coleridges Copy with many notes by him". The title-page of *The Synagogue* is inscribed: "H. Grove Kiddell. 1781. Christus meus mihi in Omnia."

C has made a mark (§) in ink on ii 50 beside the poem *Vows Broken and Renewed*. A pencil brace around the verses quoted on iii 59:

—All must to their cold Graves;
But, the religious actions of the just,
Smell sweet in death, and blossom in the dust.

Pencil ticks, possibly by C, on iii 14, 15, 17, 18, 19, 20, 29, 30, 33, 34, 35, 36, 43, 44, 47, 48, 49, 50, 51, 52, 53, 57.

Wordsworth LC includes a copy of Herbert's *Remains* twice marked as C's and included in the "Highgate List" (996, 1225), edition not identified: this may have been the copy C was reading in 1809–10 (see below), but it can hardly have been the copy of the 1652 edition with C's autograph and his inscription "To Thomas De Quincey Esq." unless De Q had left it behind with the Wordsworths before 1823 (see I Introduction pp cxi–cxii). (WW also owned a copy of the 1652 ed: see *SC* 180, LC 995.) The earliest direct reference to this annotated copy is in *CN* IV 5327, in which C identifies the 10th ed of 1674. W. C. Hazlitt, in *Book-Worm* VII (1894) 69, describes another copy as "Herbert (George), 'Temple', an early edition, wanting title, with part of a page of MS. in Coleridge's hand. 12mo." but there is no other record of such a copy, and it may have been a facsimile of part of this annotated copy. Green's library included a copy of *The Temple* 12th ed 1703, not shown as C's: *Green SC* (1880) 348. The number of copies of Herbert associated with C may be accounted for by the absence of Herbert's poems from both ANDERSON and CHALMERS.

C's earliest references to George Herbert are extracts from five poems set down in Jul–Sept 1809 and in Mar 1810. *CN* III 3532, 3533, 3579, 3580, 3735. Extracts from a poem by Harvey, normally printed with Herbert's *Temple*, appeared in *The Friend* No 3 (10 Aug 1809) with a remark on Herbert as "that model of a man, a Gentleman, and a Clergyman" and the statement that "the quaintness of some of his thoughts (not of his diction, than which nothing can be more pure, manly, and unaffected,) has blinded modern readers to the great general merit of his Poems, which are for the most part exquisite in their kind". *Friend* (*CC*) II 44n (I 45n). In *BL* again C said that Herbert's work was "too little known" and quoted three poems, one of which he later quoted in *AR*. *BL* ch 19 (*CC*) II 93–7, *AR* (1825) 12n; see **5** n 1, below. In a letter of Dec 1818 he admitted that he had previously read Herbert "to amuse myself with his quaintness—in short, only to laugh at", but now found in his poems "more substantial comfort...than in all the poetry, since the poems of Milton". *CL* IV 893. Perhaps it was in the matter of "quaintness" that C and Lamb differed—"a rare Occurrence"—for C reported in Mar 1826 that Lamb "greatly prefers Quarles—nay, he *dis*likes Herbert". *CL* VI 573. By then C was annotating this copy for the second time, with deep and steady admiration: see DATE and **10** n 1, below. The associations of Herbert's poems with LUTHER *Colloquia mensalia* (see **10** n 1, below) may be explained in part by a notebook entry of 1826: "When I read these poems [of Herbert], and compare my feelings & judgements respecting them at different periods of my own life—I cannot avoid drawing the Conclusion, that as the *Readers* did at that time comprize the most thinking & competent Members of the Community, there must have been more religious *experience*, more serious interest in the Christian Faith as a business-like Concern of each Individual, than there is at present—". *CN* IV 5327 (16–18 Feb 1826). Notes of admiration are also found for Jun and Oct 1830: N 45 f 12^v (*CN* v), 47 f 13^v (*CN* v).

DATE. Jun 1824 (dated in **3**) and Feb–Jun 1826 (see **5** n 1, **9** n 1, **10** n 1). The composition of *Work Without Hope*, 21 Feb 1825, was composed to a "Strain in the manner of G. HERBERT": see *CN* IV 5192, *PW* (EHC) I 447 n 2, II 1110–11.

1   p $^-$5

37 & 38....[1]

40[2]

p. 182...[3]

1[1] See **5**, below.   1[3] See **15**, below.
1[2] I.e. *Repentance* ("Lord, I confess my sin is great").

Synagogue, 9. 13–17[4]
50, 51. 52. 53.[5]

2 pp ⁻2–⁻1, pencil, overtraced by C, continued in ink

G. Herbert is a true Poet; but a Poet sui generis;[1] the merits of whose Poems will never be felt without a sympathy with the mind and character of the Man. To appreciate this volume it is not enough that the Reader possesses a cultivated judgement, classical Taste or even poetic sensibility—unless he be likewise a CHRISTIAN, [a]and both a zealous and an orthodox, both a devout and a *devotional*, Christian. But even this will not quite suffice. He must be an affectionate and dutiful Child of the Church, and from Habit, Conviction and a constitutional Predisposition to Ceremoniousness, in piety as in manners, find her Forms and Ordinances Aids of Religion, not sources of Formality. For Religion is the Element in which he lives, and the Region in which he moves—./

THE TEMPLE

2A i 2 | *The Church-Porch*: *Perirrhanterium* st 7

> Shall I, to please anothers wine-sprung mind,
> Lose all mine own? God hath giv'n me a measure
> Short of his Can and body: Must I find
> A pain in that, wherein he finds a pleasure?
>   Stay at the third glass: If thou lose thy hold,
>   Then thou art modest, and the winde grows bold.[b1]

[a] From here the note is continued in ink
[b] Sts 6–8 are enclosed in a pencil box for omission: see ANNEX

1[4] In Harvey's *Synagogue: The Church-Porch* (ii 9–10), which C had quoted in *The Friend* (see headnote); *The Reading Pue*, *The Book of Common-Prayer*, *The Bible*, and—if meant to be included (ii 17–19)—*The Pulpit*.

1[5] If, as the sequence of the list seems to imply, C refers to Pt ii *The Synagogue*, the poems are *Vows Broken and Renewed*, *Confusion* (from which C quoted st 1 in *BL* ch 19—*CC*—II 95 as a "burlesque passage" expressing a "ludicrous tone of feeling"), *A Paradox*, and—if ii 53–6 was meant to be included—*Inmates*. If the reference is to Pt i, Herbert's *The Temple*, the poems are *The Holy Scriptures* I and II (cf **8** and **9**, below), *Whitsunday*, *Grace*, and *Praise*.

2[1] "In a class of his own".

2A[1] For C's proposed revision of *Perirrhanterium* see ANNEX. In *CN* IV 5327 C commented on st 20 ("When thou dost purport aught..."), adding that he would like to offer a prize ("Had I £10 to spare") "for the Eton Boy who should send in the best Translation of Herbert's Church-porch [i.e. *Perirrhanterium*], with about ¼th of the Stanzas omitted, in Elegiac Latin Verse./"

3   i 10, pencil | st 48

> If thou be single, all thy good and ground
> * Submit to love; but yet not more than all.
> Give one estate, as one life. None is bound
> To work for two, who brought himself to thrall.
>   God made me one man; love makes me no more,
>   Till labour come, and make my weakness score.

* I do not understand this Stanza.[1] S. T. C. June 1824.

4   i 29, pencil | *The Church: The Reprisal* st 4

> Yet by confession will I come
> Into the conquest. Though I can do nought
> Against thee, in thee I / will overcome
> The man, who once against thee fought./

A *good Alexandrine.*

5   p ⁻5, referring to i 37–8 | *Sin*

> Lord, with what care hast thou begirt us round!
> Parents first season us: then School-masters
> Deliver us to laws; they send us bound
> To rules of reason, holy messengers,
>
> Pulpits and Sundays, sorrow dogging sin,
> Afflictions sorted, anguish of all sizes,
> Fine nets and stratagems to catch us in,
> Bibles laid open, millions of surprizes,
>
> Blessings beforehand, ties of gratefulness,
> The sound of Glory ringing in our ears:
> Without, our shame; within, our consciences;
> Angels and Grace, eternal hopes and fears.
>
> Yet all these sences and their whole array
> One cunning bosom-sin blows quite away.

37 & 38. a good sonnet.[1]

3[1] C marked this stanza for deletion: see ANNEX.

5[1] In KANT *Religion innerhalb der Grenzen der blossen Vernunft* 4 (at n 5) C noted: "(See that fine Sonnet, entitled Sin, p. 37 of Herbert's Temple)". This is one of the three Herbert poems that C quoted in *BL* ch 19 (*CC*) ɪɪ 93–7, saying

6 i 39, pencil | *Affliction* st 5 lines 1–2

<blockquote>
* My flesh began unto my soul in pain,   ? *
  Sicknesses cleave my bones,
</blockquote>

* either a misprint, or a noticeable idiom of the word "began"? Yes! and a very beautiful idiom it is = the first colloquy or address of the Flesh—[1]

7 i 42, pencil | *Faith* st 11

<blockquote>
*   What though my body run to dust?
     Faith cleaves unto it, counting ev'ry grain,
* With an exact and most particular trust,
     Reserving all for flesh again.
</blockquote>

* I find few historical facts so difficult of solution as the continuance in Protestantism of this anti-scriptural superstition.[1]

8 i 50, pencil | *The H. Scriptures.* II st 2

<blockquote>
     This verse marks that, and both do make a motion
     Unto a third, that ten leaves off doth lie:
*   Then, as dispersed herbs do <u>watch</u> a potion,
     These three make up some Christians destinie.
</blockquote>

* Some misprint?[1]

9 p +2, referring to i 50, pencil, overtraced by C | **8** textus

Important—

The Spiritual Unity of the Bible = the order & connection of organic forms in which the[a] unity of Life is shewn, tho' as widely

---

[a] A second "the" not overtraced

---

that it is "equally admirable for the weight, number, and expression of the thoughts, and for the simple dignity of the language. (Unless indeed a fastidious taste should object to the latter half of the sixth line.)" He quoted it again in full in *AR* (1825) 12n.

6[1] *OED* cites three instances of this use—begin [to speak]—from the six-

teenth, seventeenth, and eighteenth centuries.

7[1] For C's rejection of a literal interpretation of "the resurrection of the body" see e.g. DE WETTE **4** and n 1.

8[1] The mss and 1st ed (1633) read "watch": i.e. "turn green". See *OED* "watchet" B c. See also **9**, below.

dispersed in the world of the mere Sight—as the Text—(p. 50) II.*ᵃ¹*
"This verse marks that?"²

9A   i 80 | *Virtue*

> Sweet day, so cool, so calm, so bright,
> The bridal of the earth and sky:
> The dew shall weep thy fall to night;
>   For thou must dye.
>
> Sweet Rose, whose hue angry and brave
> Bids the rash gazer wipe his eye:
> Thy root is ever in its grave,
>   And thou must dye.
>
> Sweet spring, full of sweet days and roses,
> A b̶o̶x̶ Nest, where sweets compacted lie;
> My musick shews, ye have your closes,
>   And all must die/!
>   _____¹

10   i 84–5, pencil | *Man* st 7

> Each thing is full of duty:
> Waters united are our navigation;
> *   Distinguished, our habitation;
> Below, our drink; above, our meat:
> Both are our cleanlinesse. Hath one such beauty?
> Then how are all things neat!

* I understand this but imperfectly. Dist. they form an Island? And
the next lines refer perhaps to the then belief, that all fruits grow and

ᵃ Not overtraced

9¹ *CN* ɪᴠ 5399 (10–14 Jun 1826) cites
"p. 50—. II.—" and notes: "The
Spiritual Unity in the Bible = the *Idea* of
the Organic World, as the product of one
Spirit of Life but (N.B.) + 1, a pregnant
inclusive not a negative exclusive One-
ness—such as is the Unity of Light,
comprehending the Colors, and infinite
shades or intensities of each Color...".
9² In **8** textus.

9A¹ C's line marks for omission the
last stanza:

Only a sweet and virtuous soul,
Like season'd timber, never gives;
But though the whole world turn to
    coal,
    Then chiefly lives.

When C quoted this poem in *BL* ch 19
(*CC*) ɪɪ 95 he omitted this last stanza and
also read "nest" for "box" in the third
stanza.

are nourished by water?? but then how is the ascending Sap "our cleanliness"? Perhaps therefore, the Rains/[1]

11   i 128–9 | *Divinity* st 6

> * But he doth bid us take his blood for wine.
> Bid what he please; yet I am sure,
> To take and taste what he doth there design,
> Is all that saves, and not obscure.

* nay! the contrary—take Wine to be Blood—and *the* Blood of a Man, who died 1800 years ago. This is the Faith which even the C. of E. demands: for Consub. only *adds* a mystery to that of Transub. which it implies.—[1]

12   i 160, pencil, overtraced | *The Flower*

> How fresh, O Lord, how sweet and clean
> Are thy returns! ev'n as the flow'rs in spring;
> To which, besides their own demean,
> The late-past frosts tributes of pleasure bring.

10[1] The meaning is: waters united (continuous) provide us with the medium for seafaring; water divided (into continents and islands) provides us with places to live (cf Gen 1.9–10); water below (i.e. springs and wells) provides us with drink; water (from) above—rain and dew—nourishes our food; both (i.e. wells and rain) keep us (physically and ritually) clean. In any case "cleanliness" implies a moral habit.

In *CN* IV 5401 (14 Jun 1826) C wrote out in detail the scansion of *Antiphon* ("Praised be the God of Love"), the poem next after *Man*, his note beginning: "Prayer = A sort of Tune which all things hear and fear.—Herbert. ~~The more~~ Every time I read Herbert anew, the more he grows in my likeing. I admire him greatly...".

In *CN* IV 5327 (cf **2A** n 1, above) C refers to "The Dialogue, p. 107" ("Sweetest Saviour, if my soul..."—the twelfth poem before *Love Unknown*) and reflects upon stanzas 1 and 2, modifying the text to his meditation. In *CL* VI 573 (c 18 Mar 1826) he refers to the same poem, and again in LUTHER *Colloquia mensalia* (1652) p 403 (c Aug 1826). C again

associates LUTHER and HERBERT in *CN* IV 5327 and N 47 f 13ᵛ (*CN* v), referring in both cases to Luther's ch 12 "Of the Law and the Gospel" (pp 187–207).

In *BL* ch 19 C printed the whole of *Love Unknown* ("Dear friend, sit down, the tale is long and sad"—the fifth poem before *Divinity*, i.e. **11**) as exemplifying—in contrast to *Sin* (see **5**, above)—"the most fantastic thoughts in the most correct and natural language".

11[1] For C on consubstantiation and transubstantiation see FIELD **32** and n 3. On 29 Nov 1843 HCR referred to this annotation as published in an appendix to the Aldine edition of Herbert (1836): "I had a long interesting chat with Mrs. Henry Coleridge on Puseyism and her father's note in Pickering's Herbert on the Sacrament, which reads like a sneer at the Church of England...." *CRB* II 636. SC, convinced that C would have rephrased his note if he had written it out again, provided an explication "not...by way of *argument*, but because I cannot re-print such a note of my father's, which has excited surprise in some of his studious readers, without a protest." *NLS* II 258n.

Grief melts away
Like snow in *May*,
As if there were no such cold thing.
   had been no such thing!*ª*

Who would have thought my shrivel'd heart
Could have recover'd greenness? It was gone
Quite under ground, as flow'rs depart
To see their Mother-root, when they have blown;
   Where they together
   All the hard weather
Dead to the world, keep house unknown.

.   .   .   .

And now in age I bud again,
After so many deaths I live and write,
I once more smell the dew and rain,
And relish versing. O my only light,
   It cannot be
   That I am he
On whom thy tempests fell all night.

.   .   .   .

a delicious poem.*ᵇ¹*

13 i 160/1, a slip of paper tipped in,*ᶜ* referring to line 4, pencil | **12** textus

Ĕpītrītūs primus + Dāctўl + Trōchĕe + a long word-syllable which together with the pause intervening between it and the word-trochee, equals ᴗ ᴗ ᴗ—form a pleasing variety in the Pentameter Iambic with rhymes—Ex. gr.

   Thĕ lātē-pāst Frōsts | Trībŭtes ŏf | Plĕasŭre | brīng.

N.B. First, the Difference between – ᴗ | – and an Amphimacer – ᴗ – | and this not always or necessarily arising out of the latter being one ⟨word.⟩ It may even consist of three words: & yet the effect be the same. It is the pause that makes the difference—Secondly, the

---

ª C's revision in pencil is not overtraced   *ᵇ* The comment is written below the title of the poem
ᶜ C has written on both sides of the slip of unwatermarked paper

12¹ A special favourite of C's, with deep personal import particularly in the second and third stanzas given in textus. See *CL* IV 893 (6 Dec 1818). For C's use of the word "delicious" cf BARTRAM **1** and n 1.

expediency if not necessity that the first syll. both of the Dactyl &
the Trochee should be short by quantity, and only = - by force of
Accent or Position—the Epitrite being true *Length*.—Whether the
last Syllable be - or = -, the force of the Rhyme renders indifferent.
—Thus ∪ ∪ ∪[1]

13A   i 165, pencil | *Self-condemnation* st 1

> Thou who condemnest Jewish hate,
> For choosing *Barabbas* a murderer
>   Before the Lord of glory;
> Look back upon thine own estate,
> Call home thine eye (that busie wanderer)
>   Thateir choice may be thy story.

14   i 165, pencil | sts 3, 4

> He that hath made a sorry wedding
> Between his soul and gold, and hath preferr'd
>   False gain before the true,
> Hath done what he condemns in reading:
> For he hath sold for mony his dear Lord,
>   And is a *Judas-Jew*.
>   √√ L'Envoy ——
> Thus we prevent the last great day,
> And judge our selves. That light which sin and passion
>   Did before dim and choak,
> When once those snuffs are ta'en away,
> Shines bright and clear, ev'n unto condemnation,
>   Without excuse or cloak.

√√ either omitted or divided as L'Envoy.[1]

14A   i 167, pencil | *The 23. Psalm* st 5

> Nay, thou dost make me sit and dine,
>   Ev'n in my en'mies sight: *foemens'*

13[1] For other evidence of C's subtle
and accurate metrical sensibility see e.g.
his comments in DONNE *Poems*. See also
GREVILLE 1 n 1 and *CL* VI 944–6 (26 Jul

1833). Cf *CN* IV 5401, cited in **10** n 1,
above.
14[1] Cf **9A**, above, in which C has
drawn a line to indicate omission of the
last stanza.

15 p ⁻5, referring to i 182 | *Judgment* st 2

> What others mean to do, I know not well,
>   Yet I here tell,
> That some will turn thee to some leaves therein
>   So void of sin,
> That they in merit shall excel.

p. 182, Stanza 2ᵘᵈ—I should not have expected from Herbert so open an avowal of Romanism in the article of *Merit*. In the same spirit is "*holy* Macarius and great Anthony" p. 185.—¹

16 p ⁺1, referring to i 185 | *The Church Militant* lines 37–42

> To *Egypt* first she came, where they did prove
> Wonders of anger once, but now of love.
> The ten Commandments there did flourish more
> Then the ten bitter Plagues had done before.
> Holy *Macarius* and great *Anthony*
> Made *Pharoah Moses*, changing th' history.

p. 185

The Church—say rather, the Churchmen—of England d under the two first Stuarts, has been charged with a yearning after the Romish Fopperies & Ch even the papistic Usurpations/ but we shall decide more Correctly as well as more charitably if for Romish & Papistic we substitute the *patristic* leaven./¹ Their error was (natural enough from their distinguished Learning, & knowlege of ecclesiastical Antiquities) an over-rating of the Church & of the Fathers, for the first 5 or even 6 Centuries = These Lines on the Egyptian Monks, "Holy Macarius and *great* Anthony" supply a striking instance & illustration of this.

S. T. Coleridge—

15¹ See **16** textus and annotation, below.

16¹ For the "patristic leaven" that C detected in Donne, Hacket, and Jeremy Taylor see DONNE *Sermons* COPY B 1 and

cf 70, HACKET *Century* **24**, and HEYLYN **12** and n 1. For C's disapproval of Antony's asceticism see e.g. FLEURY **60** and **85** and HACKET *Scrinia* **21** n 1.

THE SYNAGOGUE

17 ii 20, pencil | *The Communion-Table* st 3

And for the matter whereof it was made,
The matter is not much,
* Although it be of tuch,
Or wood, or metal, what will last, or fade;
So vanity,
And superstition avoided be.

* Tuch, German for Cloth. I never met with it before, as an English word.[1]

18 p ⁻4, referring to ii 20, pencil, overtraced by C, continued in ink | **17** textus

Synagogue, p. 20. *Tuch* rhyming to *Much* from the German Tuch, Cloth. I never met with it before, as an English word/[1]
  *a*So I find Blatt for foliage in Stanley's Hist. of Philos. p. 22.[2]

19 ii 33 | *The Bishop* st 3

But who can shew of old that ever any
Presbyteries without their Bishops were:
* Though Bishops without Presbyteries many,
At first must needs be, almost every where?

* an instance of *proving too much*. If Bish. without Presb., B = Presb. i.e. no Bishop.[1]

a From here the note is continued in ink

17[1] See **18** and n 1, below.

18[1] *Tuch* does indeed mean "cloth" in German, but cloth is not a very practical material to make an altar of—even in the conceit of a metaphysical poet. For "tuch" = touchstone, a black marble or similar material used in monumental work, see *OED* "touch" *sb* 6.

18[2] Thomas STANLEY *The History of Philosophy* (1701) i 22: Solon's regulation that no fig-trees or olive-trees be planted closer than nine feet to a neighbour's trees because "to some [trees] their blatt is prejudiciall". Not in *OED*. Stanley does not give the reference to Plutarch *Life of Solon* 24.5, in which the Greek word means, not foliage, but effluvium.

19[1] "Presbyter", literally "elder", is the source of the word "priest". Under the earliest organisation of the Christian churches in Palestine each church was administered by a group of elders, a presbytery: see Acts 11.30, 14.23, 15.22. At first, πρεσβύτεροι ("elders") and ἐπισκόποι ("overseers, bishops") were interchangeable terms: see Acts 20.17, 20.28, Tit 1.5, 7. From the second century the title "bishop" was given to the president of a council of presbyters. Episcopalians and Presbyterians both claimed that their practice was that of the primitive church; Episcopalians arguing that ἐπισκόποι were superior to πρεσβύτεροι, the Presbyterians arguing that because "elder" and "overseer" were interchangeable terms bishops were not

20 ii 33 | st 6

> To rule and to be ruled are distinct,
> And sev'ral duties, sev'rally belong
> To sev'ral <u>persons</u>, can no more be link't
> In altogether, than amidst the throng
>> Of rude unruly passions, in the heart,
>> Reason can see to act her soveraign part.

functions, & times; but not persons, of necessity? Ex: Bish. to Archb.[1]

21 ii 35–6 | *Church Festivals* lines 9–20

> The Florilegia of celestial stories,
> Spirits of joys, the relishes and closes
> As Angels musick, pearls dissolved, roses
> Perfumed, sugar'd honey-combs, delights
>> Never too highly priz'd
>> The marriage rites,
>> Which duly solemniz'd
> Usher espoused souls to bridal nights
> Gilded Sun beams, refined Elixars,
> And quintessential extracts of stars:
> Who loves not you, doth but in vain profess
> * That he loves God, or Heaven, or happiness.

* Equally unthinking & uncharitable. I approve of them; but yet remember Rom. Cath. Idolatry—and that it originated in such high flown Metaphors as these. S. T. C.

22 ii 35, pencil |* *The Sabbath. Or Lord's Day*

Hail	Vail
Holy	Wholly
King of dayes,	To thy praise,

superior to presbyters. Although Harvey's appeal is to the practice "of old", he is writing in the context of the Caroline conflict between the Church of England and the Presbyterian Church, and also of the conflict between the episcopal purists and those unordained presbyters who, like Richard Baxter, ministered within the Church of England until the Act of Uniformity (1662) deprived them of that privilege: see FIELD **1** n 4, HEYLYN **3**, and HUTCHINSON **13** n 4.

20[1] An archbishop, who holds authority to consecrate bishops, is not precluded from the functions of a bishop: the same person can both rule and be ruled. C's comment is parallel to his distinction (in various verbal forms) between the king and the crown: see HUTCHINSON **17** n 3. For the connexion between "person" and "parson" see *C&S* (*CC*) 53n.

The Emperour,   For evermore
Or Universal   Must the rehersal
Monarch of time, the weeks   Of all, that honour seeks,
Perpetual Dictatour.   Under the worlds Creator,
Thy   My
Beauty   Duty
Far exceeds   Yet must needs
The reach of art,   Yield thee mine heart,
To blazon fully,   And that not dully:
And I thy light eclipse,   Spirits of souls, not lips
When I most strive to raise thee Alone, are fit to praise thee

What   That
Nothing   Slow things
Else can be,   Time by thee
Thou only art   Hath got the start,
Th' extracted spirit   And doth inherit
Of all Eternity   That immortality
By favour antidated.   Which sin anticipated.

              O
              That I
              Could lay by
              This body so,
              That my soul might be
              Incorporate with thee,
              And no more to six days owe.

* Make it sense, and lose the rhyme; or make it rhyme, and lose the
Sense.

23 i 37–8 | *The Nativity, or Christmas-day* * lines 1–10

              Unfold thy face, unmask thy ray,
              Shine forth bright sun, double the day.
              Let no malignant misty fume,
              Nor foggy vapour, once presume
              To interpose thy perfect sight
              This day, which makes us love thy light
              For ever better, that we could
              That blessed object once behold.
              Which is both the circumference,
              And centre of all excellence:

* The only Poem in this Synagogue which possesses *poetic* Merit.
With a few changes & additions this would be a striking Poem.

> *a*To sheath or blunt thy one happy Ray
> That wins new splendor from the Day.
> This Day that gives thee power to rise
> And shine on Hearts as well as Eyes,
> This Birth-day of all Souls when first
> On Eyes of Flesh & Blood did burst—
> That primal, great lucific Light
> That Rays to thee, to us gave Sight.

24 ii 44–5 | *Whitsunday.**

> Nay, startle not to hear the rushing wind,
>   Wherewith this place is shaken:
> Attend a while, and thou shalt quickly find
>   How much thou art mistaken,
>   If thou think here
>   Is any cause to fear.

> See'st thou not how on those twelve rev'rend heads
>   Sit cloven tongues of fire?
> And as the rumour of that wonder spreads,
>   The multitude admire
>   To see it: and
>   Yet more amazed stand

> To hear at once so great variety
>   Of language from them come,
> Of whom they dare be bold to say they be
>   Bred no where but at home,

* The spiritual Miracle was the descent of the H. Ghost: the outward
the wind and the Tongues. And—so S[t] Peter himself explains it.[1] That
each Individual obtained the power of speaking all languages is
neither contained in, nor fairly deducible from, S[t] Luke's account.[2]

---

a C has written his version beside lines 5–9

24[1] Acts 2.14–18.
24[2] I.e. Acts 2.4, 6–11. For C's
interpretation of speaking with tongues

see e.g. BAXTER *Reliquiae* COPY B **64**,
FLEURY **6** and nn 1, 2.

25 ii 47, pencil | *Trinity Sunday* st 2

> Stay, busie soul, presume not to enquire
> Too much of what Angels can but admire,
> And never comprehend:
> The Trinity
> In Unity,
> And Unity
> In Trinity,
> All reason doth transcend.*

`*] most true; but no *contradict*. Reason is to Faith, as the Eye to
the Telescope.[1]

26 iii 32 | Izaak Walton "The Life of Mr. George Herbert"

The third day after he was made Rector of *Bemerton*, and had
*] chang'd his sword and silk Cloaths into a Canonical Coat; he
return'd so habited with his friend Mr. *Woodnot* to *Bainton*...

* Curious—for he had been a Deacon & Prebendary for 3 years.[1]

Annex

C has marked *Perirrhanterium* (i 1–15) in a special way for revision. In addition to
his correction of a printer's error in st 7 (see **2A**) and the addition of a short note
to st 48 (see **3**), he has marked the whole poem for the omission of seventeen of the
seventy-seven (unnumbered) stanzas, providing in pencil the stanza-numbers for his
revised version (except for st 33, which is numbered "23" in ink); sts 6–8 are enclosed

25[1] Cf *P Lects* Lect 9 (1949) 269:
"Now what the telescope is to the
eye...faith (that is the energies of our
moral feelings) is to the reason. Reason
is the eye, and faith (all the moral
anticipation) the telescope."

26[1] When Herbert accepted the pre-
bend of Layton Ecclesia in 1626 he had
not committed himself to a clerical life;
although he was made deacon at that
time he seems not to have undertaken any
pastoral duties. Having withdrawn first
from court, then in 1627 for reasons of
health from the post of orator at
Cambridge and from the prebendary, he
had married the daughter of his late

friend Charles Danvers of Baynton,
Wiltshire, and was living a secular life
there. When he received the offer of
Bemerton, therefore, there was every
reason why he would be wearing court
dress. He was strongly disposed to
decline the offer, but Laud, then bp of
London, summoned him to Salisbury
and persuaded him to accept. Herbert's
arrival home in Baynton in clerical dress
was his first dramatic signal to his wife,
and to everybody else, that he had at last
made up his mind to become a priest. For
these details Walton's Life is a principal
authority.

in a pencilled box; the other cancelled stanzas are marked with a pencil line in the margin. The revision is as follows:

C's Number	Original Stanzas	Cancelled Stanzas
1–5	1–5	
		6–8
6–12	9–15	
		16, 17
13	18	
		19
14–17	20–23	
		24
18–21	25–28	
		29
22	30	
		31, 32
23	33	
		34
24	35	
		36
25	37	
		38
26–28	39–41	
		42
29–33	43–47	
		48
34–49	49–64	
		65, 66
50–60	67–77	

JOHANN GOTTFRIED HERDER
1744–1803

C's first acquaintance with Herder's work came with his purchase in Hamburg on 28 Sept 1798 of the *Volkslieder* (2 pts Leipzig 1778–9). *CN* I 346; the copy is now in the BM. From this collection of "Popular Songs" he had, by 23 Apr 1799, made a verse translation of *Der Flug der Liebe*. *CN* I 625 (32), *CL* I 488–9, *PW* (EHC) I 313, II 1129. Soon after returning from Germany, he wrote to RS on 30 Sept 1799 saying that there were "two works which I particularly want"—perhaps William Taylor could lend them—Zimmermann's *Geographische Geschichte des Menschen* and Herder's *Ideen zur Philosophie der Geschichte der Menschheit. CL* I 535. In a later letter, 2 Sept 1802, he recalled to RS a discussion at Keswick about the historicity of the Resurrection in which he had repeated an argument from Herder's *Von der Auferstehung*—"the book now before me". *CL* II 861–2. Whether C had brought this book home with him from Germany is not known, but by 19 Dec 1804—according to *Kalligone* 1—he had read Herder's *Metakritik*, the *Briefe, Zerstreute Blätter*, and *Ideen* (as cited above), as well as *Kalligone* and *Von der Auferstehung*. His annotated copies of *Briefe, Kalligone*, and *Von der Auferstehung* are preserved; whether he owned or annotated other Herder titles does not appear. In spite of this evidence of early reading of Herder only one note—*Kalligone* 1—can be reliably dated as early as Dec 1804; the large untidy writing in *Briefe* and *Von der Auferstehung*, at first sight similar to some of the writing in *Kalligone*, is probably so because of the poor paper and offers only a deceptive hint of an early date. It is not certain that any other annotation on Herder is earlier than 1811, and most are probably later than that.

In Apr 1823 De Q published in the *London Magazine* an article on Herder that included the statement that "Upon the whole, the best notion I can give of Herder to the English reader is to say that he is the German Coleridge; having the same all-grasping erudition, the same spirit of universal research, the same disfiguring superficiality and inaccuracy, the same indeterminateness of object, the same obscure and fanciful mysticism (*schwärmerey*), the same plethoric fulness of thought, the same fine sense of the beautiful, and (I think) the same incapacity for dealing with simple and austere grandeur. I must add, however, that in fineness and compass of understanding our English philosopher appears to me to have greatly the advantage...."

In 1826–7, when he was studying the Apocalypse, C knew what Herder had written on the subject, but had reservations about his conclusions, for he regarded Herder, like Schleiermacher, as the leader of a school of "sentimental Theologians". DE WETTE **38**; see also EICHHORN *Apocalypse* COPY A **19** n 1 and FLEURY **21**, supported by N 35 f 17ᵛ (*CN* v). Whether at that time he was reading Herder's theological writings or merely reacting to references and quotations by other commentators does not appear. But in Oct–Nov 1833 it was Heinrichs's citation of Herder that called forth an adverse comment on "the sad historic prosaisms" of Herder's interpretation (BIBLE *NT Revelation* 1); and this overflowed into a notebook entry closing with the judgement that "*Herder's* Genius was of this unlucky sort—as to be discovered with equal vehemence of repulsion by the Poet and the Philosopher". N 53 f 23ᵛ (*CN* v). He was using *Von der Auferstehung* in Mar 1826; see *Von der Auferstehung* headnote.

Briefe, das Studium der Theologie betreffend. 2 vols (in 1). Frankfurt & Leipzig 1790. 8°.

This copy, rebound by the BM in 1949, had previously been rebound (? by Green) to form a set with C's copy of *Kalligone*.

British Museum C 43 a 4

Before rebinding in the BM this volume bore on the front paste-down the pencil notation "Lot 349", identifying it as from the same lot in *Green SC* (1880) as *Kalligone* and *Von der Auferstehung*. Since the BM invoice shows lot 349 as 4 vols, the 2 vols of *Briefe* were already bound in one in 1880.

DATE. c 1811–14. The large handwriting, much like that in *Von der Auferstehung*, might suggest as early a date as *Kalligone* 1—c Dec 1804; but the earliest reading did not always produce the marginalia that have survived, and in any case the large writing is unreliable evidence for dating. According to **13**, C read this book after he had read *Von der Auferstehung*, a book that he had read as early as 1799; but the earliest possible date for **11** would be 1811, and **7** could not be earlier than 1814. In c May 1814 C copied into a notebook from one of the letters not annotated in this copy a passage that he quoted (var) and translated in *BL* ch 11 (*CC*) ɪ 231. *CN* ɪɪɪ 4192 and n.

COEDITORS. Lore Metzger, Raimonda Modiano.

1　ɪ [1]–2 | Letter ɪ

Menschlich muss man die Bibel lesen: denn sie ist ein Buch durch Menschen für Menschen geschrieben: menschlich ist die Sprache, menschlich die äussern Hülfsmittel, mit denen sie geschrieben und aufbehalten ist; menschlich endlich ist ja der Sinn, mit dem sie gefasst werden kann, jedes Hülfsmittel, das sie erläutert, so wie der ganze Zweck und Nutzen, zu dem sie angewandt werden soll. Sie können also sicher glauben, je humaner (im besten Sinne des Worts) Sie das Wort Gottes lesen, desto näher kommen Sie dem Zweck seines Urhebers, der Menschen zu seinem Bilde schuf, und in allen Werken und Wohltaten, wo er sich uns als Gott zeigt, für uns menschlich handelt.

[The Bible must be read in a human way; for it is a book written by men for men. The language is human, so also the external means by which it was written and preserved; finally the sense in which it can be comprehended is human, and so is every means of explicating it, and the whole purpose and use to which it should be put. You may therefore truly believe that the more humanly (in the best sense of the word) you read the word of God, the closer you come to the purpose of its author, who created men in his image and who acts humanly for us in all works and benefactions in which he reveals himself to us as God.]

In other words the Bible or Word of God is not the Word of God.
Truth is Truth—Falsehood is Falsehood—the only medium is Fable.
But this is kindisch, not menschlich.[1]

S. T. C.

2 I ⁻3, evidently referring to I 1 | **1** textus

A famous word, a serviceable and accomodating word is that
menschlich/ human, or rather human-natural!—It is the cousin
german of Charity, and employed by Herder to cover as many Follies
(according to himself, not to *me*) as the latter does Sins.—
See the first Page of the first Letter.[1] Menschlich ad infinitum.—how
can man reason otherwise? Can he reason göttlich[2]—If he can, ought
he not? If he cannot, Herder can only mean that there are zwey
mögliche Weisen der menschlich-denken/[3] how can [w]e*a* determine
the better of these two, t[i]ll*a* they are contra-distingui[shed.]*a*
Kindisch is what Herder should have said—& this is the true
Dispute, whether the Bible is capable of being interpreted as we
would interpret Plato, Kant, Leibnitz—or only as Esop's Fables
for Children.

3 I 15 | Letter II

Daher die manchmal unpassende Fragen und Gesichtspunkte: ob
das Buch Hiob ein wahres Drama? das Höhe Lied ein wahres
theokritisches Hirtengedicht sey? und unter welche Classe von Oden
und Gedichten jeder Psalm, jeder Prophet gehöre? Sammt und
sonders gehören sie unter keine dieser Classen und Arten: nicht blos,
weil (Regeln nach,) keine dieser Classen und Arten noch erfunden
war, sondern weil überhaupt kein biblischer Scribent (im Sinn der
Griechen und Römer, geschweige der Neuern) Dichter seyn wollte.
Seine Poesie war nicht Kunst, sondern *Natur, Beschaffenheit der
Sprache, Nothgedrungenheit des Zwecks, der Wirkung.*

[Hence the sometimes inappropriate questions and points of view: whether
the Book of Job is a true drama? whether the Song of Songs is a true
Theocritan pastoral? and to which class of odes and poems each psalm, each

---

a The paper was at some time torn and crumpled (now repaired), leaving a hole with the loss of a few letters
in the ms

1[1] "Childish, not human". C expands
and explicates this comment in **2**, below.
In challenging the word *menschlich* in the
textus C reminds us that Herder elsewhere
(see e.g. **4** textus) characterises the
mentality of the age of Christ and his
Apostles as *kindisch*. C would perhaps
prefer "child-like" to "childish": see e.g.
Sh C II 112.

2[1] I.e. **1** textus, above.

2[2] "Divinely".

2[3] "Two possible modes of human
thought".

prophet belongs? One and all belong to none of these classes and kinds: not only because (according to the rules), none of these classes and kinds had yet been invented but also because no biblical scribe whatsoever wished to be a poet (in the Greek or Roman sense, let alone in that of the modern poets). His poetry was not art but rather *nature, the condition of language, the restriction of purpose, of effect.*]

This the Psalms themselves contradict. Doubtless, the Hebrews had Poetry, intentional Poetry: for such Art is the first Step of progressive Nature.[1]

4 I ⁻2, referring to I 17, lightly cropped

Die Geschichte des Paradieses und *der ersten* Sünde soll z. E. nichts als ein *allegorisches Lied*, eine *moralische Fabel* seyn. Paradies, Baum der Versuchung, Schlange habe es nie gegeben...Ich lese und lese wieder: kein Ton des Liedes kommt in mein Ohr...wo fängt das Lied an, wo endigts? wo fängt die Fabel an, wo endigt sie? Ist kein Paradies, kein Baum, keine Schlange da gewesen, sind sie nur Geschöpfe der Fabel, warum nicht auch Sünde, Adam und Eva? ...Adam und Eva sind also historische Wesen und ihre *Schöpfung*, *ihre Zusammenführung, die Lenkung ihrer ersten Kenntnisse und Empfindungen* konnte für kindliche Zuhörer der ältesten Zeit nicht simpler, wahrer, begreiflicher, historisch-treuer erzählt *werden*, als hier erzählt wird.

[[Let us suppose,] for example, that *the story of paradise* and of *the first* sin were nothing but an *allegorical song*, a *moral fable*. Paradise, tree of knowledge, serpent never existed...I read and read again: no sound of such song comes into my ear...Where does this song begin, where does it end? Where does the fable begin, where does it end? Was there no paradise, no tree, no serpent? If they were mere fictions, why not also sin and Adam and Eve?...Adam and Eve are therefore historical beings, and the story of how *they were created, brought together, and guided in acquiring their first notions and perceptions* (feelings) could not *be* told to the childish auditors of ancient times in a form that was any simpler, more genuine, more intelligible, and truer from a historical standpoint than the one related here.]

3[1] That the Psalms, called "Songs of Praise", were meant to be sung and are often provided with musical directions— e.g. 4, 6, 54, 55, 67, 76 "On Neginoth [stringed instruments]"; 5 "Upon Nehiloth [wind instruments]"—shows that they were by their nature poetry, and that they were composed with conscious art, probably according to certain formal traditions. For poetry as "the first Step of progressive Nature" see e.g. "On Poesy or Art" in *BL* (1907) II 253–4, *Sh C* II 111–12. For C's view, contrary to Herder, that "The earliest Greeks took up the religious and lyrical poetry of the Hebrews" see *Friend* (*CC*) I 503; and for C's early praise of Hebrew poetry see *CL* II 865–6 (10 Sept 1802). Cf EICHHORN *Alte Testament* **50**.

P. 17. How can Herder have had the effrontery to assert that there is no Tone of ALLEGORY in the Tree *of Life*, and the Tree of the Knowlege of Good and Evil—& a talking Serpent—&c &c. If these do not possess all the marks of Eastern Allegory, of allegory indee[d] in genere, what *does*? And why should not Moses introduce historical Persons in an allegory, as well as the Author of the Book of Job?[1]—History was for instruction—no such cold Divisions then existed, as *Matter of fact* Chronicles, & genial Gleanings of the Past, such as those of Herodotus

5 I 19, pencil

So giebt er ihm *eine Gattin*, die sein Herz aufschliesst, und ihm eine neue Welt geselliger Freuden, ein Band der Liebe zeigt, die (wie er an Thieren bemerkt hatte, und jetzt selbst empfand,) über jede andre Liebe gehet.

[Thus God gives him [Adam] *a mate* who opens his heart and shows him a new world of more sociable joys, a bond of love that (as he observed in animals, and now experienced in himself) surpasses every other kind of love.]

And thus according to this demi-semi-quavering[1] Philosoph-Christian, Adam in the state of perfection acquired his first notion of Love from He-Goats & Ram-Cats in their Orgasms.—

6 I ‾2–‾1, referring to I 21–2

Eine Schlange musste die Verführerin seyn, die wahrscheinlich von der Frucht maschte, und dem Weibe zuerst die grosse Möglichkeit zeigte, das man davon essen *könne*, ob-sogleich des Todes zu sterben. Da die Menschen alles von Thieren lernten und absahen;

4[1] For C's mature but incomplete account of allegory, as distinct from symbol, see *SM* (*CC*) 30. There, however, he recognises symbol as the characteristic language of the Bible, and sharpens the difference by adding (p 79) that "by a symbol I mean, not a metaphor or allegory or any other figure of speech or form of fancy, but an actual and essential part of that, the whole of which it represents." For C on Job generally see GREW **25** and HAYLEY **1**. On the relation between allegory and history see e.g. *AR* (1825)

250–4n, and particularly 250–2n on the oriental figures of tree and serpent.

5[1] Demi-semi-quaver—a sixty-fourth of a semi-breve, or (in American notation) a thirty-second note: see BAXTER *Reliquiae* COPY B **101** n 2 (where, however, the term is incorrectly given as "semi-demi-quaver"). This use, as an extreme diminution of "quavering", is not recorded in *OED*, but "demi-semi" (and "semi-demi") is noted as a contemptuous diminutive. See also *Von der Auferstehung* **18**.

warum sollten sie auch dies nicht lernen und ahmen? Die Schlange, dachten sie, ist so *klug* vor allen Thieren; vielleicht wird sies eben daher?...Dazu nannte ihn der Schöpfer so sonderbar: *Baum der Erkenntniss.* Der Erkenntniss? und verbot ihn uns? sollte er ihn nicht etwa für sich behalten? sollte er nicht unsichtbar davon geniessen und deshalb die *Weisheit der Elohim* haben? Verbot er ihn etwa aus Missgunst? Die kluge Schlange isst und bleibt gesund: er reizt: er lockt; herab sank die schöne Zauberfrucht dem lüsternden Munde entgegen: das Weib ass, der Mann ass und es folgte, was natürlich folgen musste. Wir wissen nicht, was es für eine Frucht gewesen.... Sie regt Lüste auf, sie sehn sich nackt; die sonderbare, unangenehme Regung erinnert sie an das Verbot, sie stehn beschämt da, sie wissen nicht, was zu thun sey, sie machen sich kindische Decken. Der Vater kommt....Der Vater, (über dessen Vaterverhör an schöner Wahrheit der Erzählung nichts gehet,) thut, was er zu thun hat, wozu er auch diesen frühen Fall *zuliess*; er macht ihnen ihr Versehen zur *Pforte eines andern schwerern* und doch auch *nöthigen* Zustandes, ihre Strafe ist nicht Tod, wie er sie zu schrecken gedrohet hatte, sondern *eine neue, nur ihnen herbere Wohlthat.*

[The temptress had to be *a serpent,* who probably tasted the fruit secretly and first showed the woman the great possibility of eating it without instantly dying from it. Since men imitated and learned everything from animals, why should they not also learn and copy this? "The serpent," they thought, "is so much more *clever* than other animals; perhaps that is the reason for it?"...Moreover, the creator named [the tree] so strangely: *tree of knowledge.* Of knowledge? And forbade it to us? Was he perhaps not to keep it for himself? Was he not to eat of it invisibly and therefore have the *wisdom of Elohim?* Did he perhaps forbid it out of ill will? The clever serpent eats of it, and remains healthy: [the tree] attracts: [the tree] lures; the beautiful magic-fruit descended into the lustful mouth; the woman ate, the man ate, and then followed what naturally had to follow. We do not know what kind of fruit it was....It arouses lust; they see themselves naked; the strange disagreeable sensations remind them of the prohibition; they stand ashamed and do not know what to do, childishly they make coverings for themselves. The Father comes...The Father (whose paternal interrogation is unsurpassed in beautiful truth of narration) does what he has to do: an action in whose interest he *allowed* this early fall—he makes their crime an *entrance into another severe* yet *necessary* condition; their punishment is not death, as He had threatened, to terrify them; but *a new benefaction, harsher only to them.*]

p. 21. 22.—I scarcely know—whether I am reading intentional Blasphemies or mere Follies?—Is this Herder's Lord God Eternal, & Infinite?—What was this fruit-caused Lust? Wherein could it have differed from what Adam (according to Herder) had seen & envied in the Brutes? Why were they ashamed of this, more th[an][a] Hunger?[1]

7 I ii,[b] pencil, lightly cropped

N.b. to observe in my great Work[1] on the painfulness of being oblige[d][c] to speak contemptuously of—*Truths* when taken as subordinate parts of a Whole, but absurdities when assumed as forming *the whole*—Socinians[2]—&c.—Yet what offence & scandal to the feelings of weak minds—/ King of England, Scotland, & Berwick upon Twee[d—] What if a man should declare George the III[d] to be King only of Berwick upon Tweed—/ If I shew the absurdities of this taken as a *whole*, do I deny that he is King of Berwick together with England, Scotland, Ireland &c &c—

8 I 214–15, pencil, lightly cropped | Letter XIII

Gnug, Matthäi griechisches Evangelium war uns allein bestimmt und wir haben an ihm, verglichen mit den andern dreyen, unstreitig die älteste, schlichteste *Volksnachricht* vom Leben Jesu. Er folgt ihm Schritt vor Schritt auf seinen Reisen, Zügen, Wundern: bey ihm ist kein Plan, keine Anordnung etwa zum Resultat eines allgemeinen Satzes, wie bey Johannes, oder zu einer strengen Zeitbemerkung. Er schreibt, wie er gehört oder gesehen hat, Reisen, Wunder, Sprüche, Gleichnisse, so dass er nur vielleicht einige derselben, wenn sie einander nahe lagen, zusammen bindet, manchmal viele Wunder in Eins fasst, offenbar aber nur *Epitomen*, Summarien des Lebens Christi schreibet.

[Enough that Matthew's Greek Gospel was alone destined for us and that it is, compared with the other three, undoubtedly the oldest, simplest *popular narrative* of the life of Jesus. He follows him step by step on his journeys, movements, miracles: he uses no plan, no ordering for the sake perhaps of

---

[a] Smudged and cropped
[b] Recto of blank leaf between half-title and title-page of Vol I pt ii. Possibly this was originally a back flyleaf of I i, or a front flyleaf to I ii, misplaced by the binder. The heavy offsetting of the pencil note on the half-title verso shows that the leaf was placed where it now is whenever the volumes were first bound, perhaps soon after C's death
[c] Letter supplied by the editor

6[1] On Adam's fall see e.g. *SM* (*CC*) 61–2 and *AR* (1825) 251–6 (with 250–4n cited in **4** n 1, above).

7[1] I.e. presumably the "Logosophia", first mentioned in Apr 1814 (*CL* III 480) but never completed; for the progressive changes in plans for it see *CN* III 4265n, 4300n, 4440n, and

J. A. Appleyard *Coleridge's Philosophy of Literature* (Cambridge Mass 1965) 151– 6. Cf *CL* III 534 for the purpose of the work.

7[2] C is alluding to the Trinity, affirming the status of Christ as one of three as opposed to Christ as—according to Socinian doctrine—mere man.

a universal maxim, as in John, or for a stern topical comment. He writes what he has heard or seen—journeys, miracles, maxims, parables—only that he perhaps connects some that touched on each other, sometimes combining many miracles into one, but evidently he writes only *epitomes*, summaries of the life of Christ.]

All this runs [g]lib as cream; [bu]t, most noble [H]erder! was not [th]is Gospel writ [by] Matthew? And [w]as not Matthew [an] Eyewitness?[1] [An]d is it natural [i]n a plain [m]an, who had seen three Miracles at [t]hree different times under different [ci]rcumstances to confound them into [*o*]*ne*? And this too when After events had unspeakably elevated the importance of the Worker of these Miracles? Surely, far more natural were it for such a man to multiply Miracles. *S. T. C.*

9 I 216–17, pencil

Je schlichter, wenn ich so sagen darf, d.i. je weniger angestrengt und kritiksüchtig, je aufrichtiger, freyer, liberaler, Volksmässiger man diese Bücher [Evangelien] lieset; desto mehr ist man in ihrem Sinn, im Geist ihres Ursprunges, und Inhalts. Sie hatten gleichsam kein Arg, in dem, was sie auf treuen Glauben und gut Gewissen erzählten; sie bauten also auch Kabalen feindseliger Kritik nicht vor, so wenig sie eigentlich für solche schrieben. Ihre Rede war Milch der Wahrheit, Honig einer frölichen Botschaft für Kinder, Jünger, Christen, einfache, arglose Leser....Lesen Sie jeden Evangelisten allein und messen ihn nach seiner Absicht: wenn [S]ie nachher die drei ersten zusammenstellen, so geschehe es noch frey, nicht Sylben- sondern Sektionenweise, wie etwa der und jener dieselbe oder eine ähnliche Rede und Handlung beschreibet....Ich bin überzeugt, Sie werden sehen, es habe nur Ein Christus gelebet und so verschieden man auch von ihm erzählt hat: so sey das Zeugniss aller, gerade im Wesentlichsten und Wunderbarsten, nur Ein Zeugniss.

[The more simply, if I may say so, i.e. the less strenuously and critically, the more honestly, freely, liberally, popularly, one reads these books [the Gospels], the closer one comes to their intention, the sense of their origin and meaning. They saw no harm, as it were, in what they related in true faith and good conscience; they therefore took no precautions against intrigues of hostile criticism any more than they actually wrote for such. Their words were the milk of truth, the honey of a happy message for children, disciples,

8[1] This rhetorical question is not consistent with the doubt C expresses in *Von der Auferstehung* **11**. For C on the authorship of the "first" Gospel, i.e. Matthew, see e.g. BIBLE COPY B **80–82** and EICHHORN *Neue Testament* COPY A **1** and nn.

Christians, simple, innocent readers.... Read every evangelist individually, and measure him according to his intention: if afterwards you match the first three, then let it be done freely, not by syllables, but by sections, to compare how the one or the other describes the same speech or action, or a similar one.... I am convinced you will see only *one* Christ lived; and however disparately He has been reported, the testimony of all is—precisely in the most essential and miraculous points—*one* testimony only.]

Cream! or at least Charcoal so exquisitely levigated, that it *tastes* to the Palate smooth as Cream.[1]—But, alas! what Story by what Fanatic might not be so supported? Heaven forbid! that the Gospels should need such Defence! Alas! might not some sturdy Infidel reply—The Four Evangelists do indeed agree *in the main*: just as in common Life we find a number of men all agreeing & disagreeing in a story, which all had heard cursorily, but no one had seen.—[2]

10   I 218–19, pencil

Ich begreife nicht, wie der Verfasser des Fragments über den Zweck Jesu und seiner Jünger, den letzten einen Plan, die Geschichte ihres Meisters wissentlich zu verkehren, hat beymessen können; in ihrer Erzählung, wie wir sie jetzt haben, ist nichts von diesem Doppelsinn, von dieser später hin ihrem Meister geliehenen Endabsicht merkbar. Entweder wissen wir nichts von Christus, falls wir diesen seinen Zeugen nicht glauben dörfen; wohl, so wissen wir nichts von ihm, weder böses noch gutes, und so mag die Sache ruhen. Oder wir wissen etwas durch sie und dörfen sie lesen... wohlan, so müssen wir sie lesen, *wie sie sind*; nicht sagen, "das schreiben sie, das will ich glauben, jenes schreiben sie zwar auch, das glaube ich ihnen aber nicht, das haben sie erdichtet und erlogen" denn ich sehe gar nicht, wo hier die Grenze zwischen Wahrheit und Lüge sey?

[I cannot comprehend how the author of the fragment on the purpose of Jesus and his disciples could attribute to the latter a plan knowingly to misrepresent the story of their master. There is nothing of this ambiguity observable in their narrative as we now have it, nothing of this intention later foisted upon their master. Either we know nothing of Christ, if it is the case that we may not believe these witnesses; very well, then we know nothing of him, neither good nor bad, and there the matter can rest. Or we know something through them and may read them—well then, we must read them *as they are*; we may not say "they write this; I shall believe it; it is true they also write that, but I cannot credit them; they have invented and falsified it", because I utterly fail to see where the border between truth and falsehood lies here.]

9[1] See also **8**, above, and *Kalligone* **2**.
9[2] For the grounds for the credibility and authenticity of the Gospels see e.g. EICHHORN *Neue Testament* COPY A **4**.

Now apply this to Wesley's Journal,[1] or 20 other Books of the same kind—especially, the Lives of R. Catholic Saints.[2] What? are there no rules of discrimination?—Am I to disbelieve all that Quintus Curtius relates of Alexander, because some parts contradict themselves, & other parts contradict Common Sense?[3]—The Tract alluded to might be easily rendered as ridiculous to a sound Understanding, as it is hateful to a good Heart, without this undermining of all wholesome Criticism.[4]

11   I 220–1, pencil

Vielleicht wenden Sie ein, dass alle das wohl angienge, wenn sie [die Evangelisten] nur nicht so *wunderbare* d. i. unwahrscheinliche Sachen erzählten...[aber]...das Wahrscheinliche ist gerade nicht immer, wenigstens nicht ausschliessend und unbedingt, das Kennzeichen der Wahrheit: sonst müsste jener Indianische König recht gehabt haben, der das Eis läugnete, weils *ihm* unwahrscheinlich war. Jede neue Naturentdeckung müste so lange falsch seyn, bis sie uns *a priori* wahrscheinlich würde, und alle individuellen Umstände einer Lebensgeschichte, die für uns oft unwahrscheinlich genug, in ihrem Zusammenhange aber eben dadurch vielleicht desto eigenthümlicher und charakteristisch wahrer sind, müsten durch dies Maas zu unserm Gedankenkreise oder gar zu unsrer Willkühr die unwidersprechlichsten Lügen werden.

[Perhaps you will object that this would all be in order, if only [the evangelists] did not narrate such *miraculous*, i.e. improbable things....[But] it is not always the case that probability is the distinguishing characteristic of truth—at least not exclusively and absolutely; otherwise the Indian king, who denied the existence of ice because it seemed improbable to *him*, would have to have been in the right. Every new natural discovery would have to be false until it became probable *a priori*, and all the individual circumstances of a life-history, which often seem to us improbable enough—but which, in their context, are by virtue of this perhaps all the more characteristic and

10[1] Cf BIBLE *Apocryphal NT* **3**. In considering the effect upon believers of "the supernatural gifts of the founder, or the miracles by which his preaching had been accredited" in *Friend* (*CC*) I 430–1 C also cited Wesley's *Journal*. See also *Von der Auferstehung* **8** and n 1.

10[2] Alban Butler (1711–73) *The Lives of the Fathers, Martyrs, and Other Principal Saints* (1756–9; 2nd ed 1779–80; 3rd 1798–1800; still in print today). For C on the incredibilities to be found in

such "Lives" see e.g. FLEURY **77** and **86**, and Thomas FULLER *History* **6**.

10[3] Quintus Curtius Rufus (1st century A.D.) *De rebus gestis Alexandri Magni*, in ten books, the first two of which do not survive. Some historical inaccuracy does not negate the historical value of the whole or diminish its dramatic and rhetorical interest.

10[4] Herder does not identify the "fragment"; it does not appear that C had read it or knew its title.

peculiarly true—would, by this standard, become the most incontrovertible lies in the face of our intellectual capacity, or indeed of our arbitrary pleasure.]

O! Kant has answered this in a way, that no *Meta-critik* of 20 Herders will effectually rejoin to![1] After 16 years meditation[2] I dare affirm, that no miracle is susceptible of full proof, unless it derive the greater part of its evidence A PRIORI: i.e. unless the Religion prove it, even more than it proves the Religion. On this ground I believe that Christ wrought Miracles.[3]

12 I 225, pencil, lightly cropped | Letter XIV

Wäre Eine falsche Spur in ihren Apostels Schriften, oder in ihrem Leben: wäre Einer aus ihrem Mittel z. E. abtreten, hätte ihre Betrugerey, ihre Verabredung, die Geschichte Jesu zu verstellen, auch nur *feindselig* entdeckt; hätte Judas, der Verräther, es auch nur in der Stunde entdeckt, da sein Bauch barst—so wäre *Indicium* gegen sie und nun müsste man schwanken, prüfen, rechtlich, richterlich, erzkritisch untersuchen...Nun ist von allen gerade das Gegentheil. Keiner wird seinem Zeugniss und der Sache desselben untreu; sie leben, leiden, sterben darüber; der Verräther büsst seinen Pöbelgeiz mit dem Leben und konnte *nichts* verrathen, als—den Garten, wo Christus war, wo ihn die nächtlichen Diebe fangen konnten.

[If there were any sign of falsehood in the writings and lives of the Apostles; had one withdrawn from their midst, for example, and if only out of pure hostility disclosed their deceitfulness, and their agreement to falsify the history of Jesus; had Judas, the traitor, made such a disclosure in the very hour that his stomach burst—this would be *evidence* against them and therefore one would have to waver (ponder), prove, and examine their writings honestly, judiciously, and with utmost critical perspicacity...But quite the contrary is the case. None of the disciples disavows his testimony and his cause; they live, suffer, die for them; the traitor pays with his life for his vulgar greed and could not betray *anything more* than the garden where Christ was, where the thieves could seize him in the dark.]

11[1] See also *Kalligone* 1 and n 1. In his *Metakritik* (1799) Herder attacked the *Critique of Pure Reason* as dangerously misleading, as a linguistic monstrosity, and as perpetuating the obsolete faculty psychology. For C's notice of Kant's devastating review of Herder see KANT *Vermischte Schriften* COPY C 32. The Kant essay that C refers to is "Der einzig mögliche Beweisgrund zur Demonstra-

tion des Daseyns Gottes"; for C's annotations on it see KANT *Vermischte Schriften* COPY B 6–14 and COPY C 8–15.

11[2] If referring back to his reflections on miracles in LRR of Sept 1795—see e.g. *Lects 1795* (*CC*) 112ff—this will have been written in 1811. Cf 12, below.

11[3] On the relation between miracles and faith see e.g. *Friend* (*CC*) I 431 and n 2, *CN* I 1010, II 3022.

Yet still, this Treachery of Judas[1]—It was the first Scruple that my
own Though[*t*] elaborated in my earliest Manhood.[2] And the only
Answ[er] to it/ only [O!] that Mirac[les] were not to the Jews *all* that
[they] are to us—that they perpetually confoun[d] not only the
marvellous with the miraculo[us,] but the Unusual with the
marvellous—[O!] what a thick-set Hedge of Difficulties for the Paleys
& Priestlys—[3]

13 I 227, pencil, lightly cropped

...überhaupt sind grosse Bände von Beweisen der Wahrheit der
Christlichen Religion keine Speise für mich...ja endlich nach Allem
will ich noch kein Wort für die Wahrheit der Christlichen *Religion*
(so verflochten, als man das Wort Religion nimmt) gesagt haben;
allein für die Wahrheit dieser kleinen *Geschichte*, wie sie in ihrem
ersten Zusammenhange dort erscheint, konnte und kann ich nicht
anders reden, bis man mich eines andern überzeuget.

[I have no taste generally for large volumes proving the truth of the Christian
religion...indeed, after all I do not wish to have spoken one word for the
truth of the Christian *religion* (however entangled one may take the word
"religion" to be); but I could not and cannot do other than speak for the
truth of this short *history*, as it first appeared there in its earliest context,
until I am otherwise persuaded.]

Who could fancy that this same Herder had written "Ueber die
Auferstehung"[1]—the result of which is evidently to explain away all
the Miracul[ous] of this little, simple, honest HISTORY![2]

12[1] According to Herder, Judas still
believed in Christ and his miracles and
did not accuse him of imposture (p 224);
the "treachery" consisted simply of
saying where Christ was to be found. For
a later consideration of Judas's motives
see *IS* 163–5 (N 41 ff 70ᵛ–72ᵛ: *CN* v) of
28 Sept 1829.

12[2] Cf 11 and n 2, above. But there are
few early references to Judas, and then as
a figure of hypocrisy in political contexts:
see *Lects 1795* (*CC*) 64 (and cf 217 n 1),
Watchman (*CC*) 167.

12[3] Cf *Friend* no 19 (28 Dec 1809), in
which C remarks upon "our tendency to
exaggerate all effects, that seem dispro-
portionate to their visible cause, and all

circumstances that are in any way
strongly contrasted with our notions of
the Persons under them" as accounting
for the "love of the marvellous" scarcely
less general than the "religious feeling of
Mankind". *Friend* (*CC*) II 249 (I 527).
The "Difficulties for the Paleys &
Priestlys" arise from their finding "evi-
dences" in miracles, and so mistakenly
making faith depend upon miracles. See
CL II 1189–90 [4 Oct 1806]. For C's
outline of the articles of faith of the
"modern Socinian creed" see *SM* (*CC*)
181–4n.

13[1] See *Von der Auferstehung*, below.

13[2] Herder refers to the history of
Jesus as told by the evangelists.

14 I 230–1, pencil, lightly cropped

Ihre Freudigkeit im Leben und im Tode, kam nur davon, dass sie nothgedrungen und von Gott bestellt, eine *wahre, selbstgesehene* Geschichte, insonderheit der *Auferstehung* predigen mussten. Gerade die Simplicität dieser Lehre, als eines *gewissen, selbsterlebten Facti* trug am meisten zu der Revolution bey, die das Christenthum machte. Der blossen Lehren, Zweifel, philosophischen Fragen und Scrupel über Dienst und Verehrung Gottes, über Unsterblichkeit und ewiges Leben, war man müde: Jahrhunderte hin war man durch Disputiren nicht weiter gekommen, als man Anfangs war und die menschliche Seele will *Gewissheit,* sie dürstet nach *Factis.*

[Their [the Apostles'] joy in life and in death derived solely from their having to preach necessarily and on God's command a *true, eye-witnessed* history, in particular of the *resurrection.* Precisely the simplicity of this teaching as of a *certain, personally experienced fact* contributed most to the revolution that Christianity brought about. People were tired of mere dogmas, doubts, philosophical inquiries and scruples about the service and worship of God, about immortality and everlasting life; for centuries no progress had been made through disputes; while the human soul desires *certainty,* it thirsts for *facts.*]

Merciful Heaven!—and is a tale, how a man that was thought dead on Friday Night—[a]ppeared [a]live again [o]n Sunday Morning/ [t]hat *certainty* [of] the [i]mmortality [of] all men, which the human Soul thirsts after? And is it fact, that the *History* of Christ was the [c]hief means of establishing Xtny? Do not the Scriptures themselves attribute it to the Holy Ghost, to a supernatural Influence, to a *gift* of Faith to the Hearts tha[t] sincerely yearned after it?[1] I be[lieve:] Lord! help my Unbelief![2]—Tha[t,] then, is the state of a young Xtian!

15 I 231, pencil, lightly cropped

Der grösseste, nützlichste, glückseligste Theil der Menschen braucht *Facta,* weil er sich an selbsterdachte Hypothesen nicht halten kann, weil jeder Wind sie umreisst...Ein Christ, der an Christum *thätlich* glaubt, d. i. das *Factum* des Lebens desselben durch sein Leben still und wirksam ausdrückt, hat an diesem thätigen Glauben mehr, als der grösste Theoretiker, der allgemeine Moral im Buchstaben aufputzt.

14[1] See Eph 2.1–8; and cf Isa 61.1–6, 2 Tim 3.16–17.   **14**[2] Mark 9.24 (var). On faith and belief see e.g. *CN* III 3888 (Jun 1810).

[The greatest, most useful, and happiest part of mankind needs *facts* because they cannot stick to self-fabricated hypotheses, as such hypotheses are blown down by every wind... A Christian who *actively* believes in Christ, that is, through his own life expresses calmly and effectively the *fact* of the life of Christ, possesses more through this active faith than the greatest philosopher who adorns his writings with glamorous universal morals.]

In *my* experience at least, this too is false. The best & warmest Xtians of the lower & middle Classes dwell almost exclusively on the Dogmata fidei[1]—namely, *Grace & Redemptio[n.]*

16 I 232, pencil

Mir ists immer rührend, wenn eine Christliche Gemeine mit Herz und Ueberzeugung Auferstehungs- Geburts- Passionslieder, als *Facta* und Entschlüsse über *Facta* singet; in ihrer grösten Simplicität ist eine Kraft, die manches neuere Machwerk von gereimtem oder ungereimtem Raisonnement weder nachahmen, noch ersetzen kann. Auch hier gilts: "Wasser thuts nicht, sondern Wort Gottes und Glaube" um welches sich die besten Raisonnemens der Menschen nur wie Kränze um den Stamm flechten.

[I always find it moving when with feeling and conviction a Christian congregation sings hymns of resurrection, birth, and passion as *facts* and deductions about *facts*; in their greatest simplicity resides a power that a good many modern works, whether with or without rhyme or reason, can neither imitate nor replace. Here too the following applies: "Water effects nothing but only God's word and faith" around which men's best arguments only twine themselves like garlands around the tree-trunk [i.e. Maypole].]

I doubt it not; but then these references to Facts were only Mementos of the sublime mysteries, of which they were the *Symbols*, rather than the Evidences—tho' doubtless *both*.[1]

17 II 308 | Letter XLVII

...so lesen Sie Klopstocks Prose. Nichts ist bescheidner, sanfter, und... Lammesfrommere als sie! sie fliegt nicht, sie geht einfältig an der Erde. Ein gleiches ist mit der Prose Miltons und beiden grossen Schriftstellern, die in beiderlei Styl Muster seyn können, geschieht das empfindlichliste Unrecht, wenn unverständige Jünglinge die

---

15[1] "Dogmas of faith". The meaning of the term *dogma* is a crux in *Von der Auferstehung* **16**.

16[1] As in C's doctrine that a symbol "always partakes of the Reality which it renders intelligible; and while it enunciates the whole, abides itself as a living part in that Unity, of which it is the representative". *SM (CC)* 30.

neugeschaffne, hohe Götter- und Empfindungssprache derselben zu einer Pandorenbüchse machen, aus der Sie Schildereien, lyrische Gedichte, geradbrechte Lieder und Empfindungen schütteln.

[...then read Klopstock's prose. Nothing is more modest, gentle, and...lamb-like in piety! It does not take wing, but walks in simplicity upon the earth. *The same is the case with Milton's prose* [C's emphasis], and both great authors, who can be exemplary in both styles, suffer the harshest injustice, when uncomprehending youths turn their newly-created language of gods and feeling into a Pandora's box out of which they shake descriptions, lyrical poems, marvellous songs and sentiments.]

Whoo!!¹

17¹ For Klopstock as "the German Milton—a very *German* Milton indeed!" see *CL* I 445 (20 Nov 1798). In *BL* ch 11 (*CC*) I 231 C quoted from Letter XXIII (I 371) a passage he had copied into *CN* III 4192.

Kalligone. Vom Angenehmen und Schönen. (II: Von Kunst und Kunstrichterei. III: Vom Erhabnen und vom Ideal.) 3 vols (in 2). Leipzig 1800. 8°.

Vols I–II bound together, in mottled calf; Vol III rebound after C's death, preserving the original marbled paper boards but with gold-tooled calf spine matching that of *Von der Auferstehung.*

British Museum C 43 a 11

Inscribed in pencil on I ⁻5 (p–d) and III ⁻7 (p–d): "Lot 349"—i.e. in *Green SC* (1880)—which lot included the annotated copies of *Briefe* and *Von der Auferstehung.*

Vol III (i.e. the second bound volume) was heavily cropped in rebinding, with the loss of about $\frac{1}{2}''$ in height and $\frac{3}{8}''$ in width. Some leaves were folded in to preserve C's notes, but others have been severely cropped, with loss to the notes written on them.

Helen Zimmern (*Blackwood's* CXXXI 120) and Shawcross (*N&Q* 28 Oct 1905) both described the first bound volume as containing a single note "written on a sheet of note-paper, and bound into the volume". This sheet was made up of the original grey wrappers of the two volumes, pasted together to form a single thick leaf with C's writing on both sides of it. When the volume was repaired in the BM the composite leaf was separated, making it clear that C's ms consists not of one note but of two, each referring to the volume in which it was originally written. See **1** and **2**, below, and textual notes.

DATE. Dec 1804 (**1** dated 19 Dec 1804) to c 1815 (perhaps only **2** and **6**). *CN* II 2351 (c 18 Dec 1804) has recently been discovered to be an adaptation of a passage from *Kalligone* pt II ch 1.

COEDITORS. Lore Metzger, Raimonda Modiano. The translations of Kant in **2, 6, 8** are J. C. Meredith's.

1 I ⁺2ᵃ

Dec. 19. 1804. Malta.—And thus the Book impressed me, to wit, as being Rant, abuse, drunken Self-conceit that kicking and sprawling in the 6 inch-deep Gutter of muddy Philosophism from ⟨the drainings⟩ [of]ᵇ a hundred Sculleryies dreams that he is swimming in an ocean of the Translucent & the Profound/—I never read a more disgusting Work, scarcely so disgusting an one except the Meta-critik of the same Author.[1] I always even in the perusal of his better works, the Verm. Blätter, the Briefe das Stud. Theol. betreffends and the

---

ᵃ Inside back of original grey paper wrapper of Vol I   ᵇ Word supplied by the editor

1[1] For Herder's *Metakritik* (1799) see *Briefe* **11** and n 1. For "philosophism" the earliest *OED* entry is for 1792; C's use of the word in a letter of 15 Oct 1799 (*CL* I 538) is also noticed.

Ideen zur Gesch. der Mensch.[2] thought him a painted Mist with no sharp outline—but this is mere Steam from a Heap of Mans dung.—[3]

2 II ⁻1,[a] referring to II 14 et passim

Mithin sind *Kunst* und *Handwerk* nicht dadurch unterschieden, dass "jene frei, diese eine *Lohnkunst* heissen möchte, indem jene nur als *Spiel*, d. i. als eine Beschäftigung, die für sich selbst angenehm ist, zweckmässig ausfallen, diese als *Arbeit*, d. i. als eine für sich unangenehme und beschwerliche Beschäftigung nur durch ihre Wirkung, z. B. den *Lohn* anlockend ist, mithin *Zwangmässig aufgelegt* werden kann;" eine Abtheilung polizirter Staaten, von der die Natur nicht weiss. Sie kennet ursprünglich nicht gebohrne Patricier, die allein Künste des *Spiels*, und gebohrne Knechte, die nur Sklavenkünste (*artes illiberales s. serviles*) treiben müssten. Sie kennet keine Kunst, die blos Spiel seyn dürfe, wenn sie gelingen soll...

[Consequently *art* and *handicraft* are not distinguished by the fact that "the first is called free, the other may be called *industrial art*. [We look on] the former as something which could only prove final (be a success) as *play*—i.e. an occupation which is agreeable on its own account; but on the second as *labour*, i.e. a business, which on its own account is disagreeable (drudgery), and is only attractive by means of what it results in (e.g. the *pay*), and which is consequently capable of being a *compulsory imposition.*" This is a division made by civilised states, of which Nature knows nothing. Originally she knows no born patricians who practise only the arts of *play*, nor born slaves who must engage only in slave arts ("illiberal or servile arts"). She knows no art that, if it is to succeed, must be pure play...]

It disturbs my patience to see a man transform the thoughts of a profound Philosopher into poetic Whip-Syllabub:[1] and then by affixing a different meaning to the same words give himself the air of confutation & Insult. Vide p. 14 et passim.[2] So important is Kant's

[a] Inside front of original grey paper wrapper of Vol II

[1][2] C refers to *Zerstreute Blätter* (1785–97), *Briefe, das Studium der Theologie betreffend* (1790), and *Ideen zur Philosophie der Geschichte der Menschheit* (1784–91), for Kant's review of which see KANT *Vermischte Schriften* COPY C 32. Of these, C is known to have annotated only the *Briefe*, but he wanted to borrow a copy of *Ideen* in Sept 1799 (*CL* I 535).

[1][3] See also the passage from N F⁰ quoted in *Von der Auferstehung* 13 n 1.

[2][1] Curdled milk or cream; figuratively—(like C's "Whip-Syllabub") light and frothy, esp if floridly vapid discourse

or writings: see *OED* "sillabub". Cf *Briefe* **8** and **9**.

[2][2] Herder is quoting from, commenting on, Kant's *Critique of Judgement* pt I bk II "Analytic of the Sublime" § 43 par 3, the distinction between art and nature, and between art and handicraft. According to Kant, no product of nature can be properly called a work of art since "it is only production through freedom, i.e. through an act of the will that places reason at the basis of its action, that should be termed art". Tr J. C. Meredith (Oxford 1911). Cf **8**, below.

distinction, that one of the surest Characteristics of Genius, as compared with Talent, rests upon it.[3] Ex. gr. Alston & Jack Dawe are both employed, each on a picture[4]—The latter constantly meditates on the arbitrary Consequence of his *Handlung*, or Business—the 300£ promised—The former cannot work at all except as far as he removes this from his mind, & finds the end in the means, the true delight *in* the very Labor.[5]

[a]If ever there was a = first syllable of the Latin for Thrush[6] in a Bandbox, or meanness in ⟨musk &⟩ millanery, it is realized in this Diatribe of Herder's!!—

3   III ⁻1,[b] lightly cropped

The sad mistake of the Idea-ists in Germany, since the appearance of the Natúr-philosophie has been in making it supersede the *logical* discipline.[1] First, let firm footing have been obtained on the central

---

[a] This sentence comprising three lines of writing is crushed into the head of the page above the first line of 2, the lower part of the page having been completely filled, and is evidently an afterthought, not a separate note
[b] Inside front of original grey paper wrapper

2³ C several times refers to the distinction between genius and talent—one of his favourite adoptions from Kant (see *The Critique of Judgement* pt I bk II §§ 46–9). In *BL* ch 11 (*CC*) I 224 he points to the distinction as it applies here: "it is one contradistinction of genius from talent, that its predominant end is always comprized in the means; and this is one of the many points, which establish an analogy between genius and virtue". See also *BL* chs 2, 4 (*CC*) I 31–2, 81; "On the Principles of Genial Criticism" in *BL* (1907) II 224; *Friend* (*CC*) I 110, 415, 419; and cf e.g. *CL* IV 667.

2⁴ Washington Allston (1779–1843), American landscape painter, whom C first met in Rome in 1806 (see *CN* II 2794n) and on whose behalf C wrote the series of essays "On the Principles of Genial Criticism" that appeared in *Felix Farley's Bristol Journal* in Aug and Sept 1814 when "poor Allston...[was] exhibiting his Pictures at Bristol". *CL* III 520, 534; for the text of the essays see *BL* (1907) II 219–46. For an unfinished portrait of C painted by Allston in Rome in 1806 see *CL* III frontispiece.

George Dawe (1781–1829), English portrait painter, made in 1811 "a chalk drawing of my face, which I think far more like than any former attempt, excepting Allston's full length Portrait of me" (*CL* III 351; for the chalk drawing see *CL* III 351 facing plate, *CN* III 4142 and facing plate; for the Allston portrait see *CN* III plate facing 4197, and *CL* III facing 509), and in 1812 exhibited at the Royal Academy a bust of C and a painting entitled *Genevieve* based on C's poem *Love*. *CL* III 351, 386. C here calls him "Jack" Dawe perhaps to imply either that he collects and hoards bright objects perhaps or that he imitates the voices of others.

2⁵ By May 1815, as C complained to WW, Allston was still in some distress, while Dawe, obsessed with money, was thriving: "Good God! to think of such a Grub as *Daw* with more than he can do—and such a Genius as Allston, without a single Patron!" *CL* IV 576. C refers to Dawe as "Grub" in an uncharitable note and mock epitaph written on the occasion of his burial in 1829: see *CN* III 4142n.

2⁶ *Turdus*. Cf the end of **1**, above.

3¹ For the *Naturphilosophen* see ESCHENMAYER **13** n 1 and GOLDFUSS **14**

point of Reflection, and the whole Sphere have been measured out
& filled—the Functions inferred from the *given* Products, then the
possible Products deduced from the presumed Functions—& the
truth of both tested by the correspondence or rather the identity of
both.—When this has been effected, then proceed to *Ideas*—i.e. when
you know ⟨*that*,⟩ why you want them.—

4   III 7, pencil | I "Geschichte des Erhabnen in der menschlichen Empfindung"

A. Und *Longins* Erhabnes (το υψος) darf es dem Schönen oder der
Schönheit entgegengesetzt werden?
   B. Nichts weniger. Auch ihm ists die höchste Höhe, Fülle oder
Stärke der Rede...
   [A. And may *Longinus'* sublime (το υψος) be opposed to the beautiful or
to beauty?
   B. To nothing less. For him too it is the highest height, fullness, and force
of discourse...]

It appears to me, that the title of Longinus' work is, on the Language
of Excitement, on the highly Impassioned. How else could Sappho's
ode have been given as the akmè of the υψος? of the highly
impassioned it is indeed the akmè.[1]

5   III 48–9, cropped | I 2 "Kritische Analyse des Erhabnen"

Frage 2. Darf man sagen: "dass das eigentliche Erhabene in keiner
sinnlichen Form *enthalten seyn könne*, sondern *nur Ideen der Vernunft
treffe*, welche, obgleich keine ihnen angemessene Darstellung möglich
ist, eben durch diese *Unangemessenheit, welche sich sinnlich darstellen
lässt*, rege gemacht und ins Gemüth gerufen werden."
   Antwort. Enthalten kann das Erhabne eben so wenig in einer Form
seyn, als das Schöne; beide werden an Gegenständen *empfunden*.
Trift das Erhabne blos Ideen der Vernunft, so kann es (nach den
Grundsätzen der Kritik selbst) kein Gefühl regen. Und, wenn sich
Ideen der Vernunft (nach eben dieser Kritik) nicht darstellen lassen,
wie lässt sich ihre *Unangemessenheit darstellen*?
   [*Question 2.* Is it possible to say that "the sublime, in the strict sense of the
word, *cannot be contained* in any sensuous form, but rather *concerns ideas*

---

n 1. For their failure to recognise the true
nature of ideas see esp KLUGE **2** and n 2
and cf JUNG **19** and n 1 and *CL* IV 875–6.
See also GOLDFUSS **2** on "The great
mistakes of the Natur-philosophen".

4[1] See DYER *Poems* **3** and nn. C's
discussion of the sublime continues in **6**,
below.

of reason, which, although no adequate presentation of them is possible, may be excited and called into the mind by that very *inadequacy itself which does admit of sensuous presentation*"?

Answer. The sublime is as little capable of being *contained* in a form as the beautiful; both are *felt* through objects. If the sublime concerns only ideas of the reason, it can (according to the principles of the Critique [*of Judgment*] itself) arouse no feeling. And if ideas of the reason (according to the same Critique) cannot be represented, how can their *inadequacy be represented*?]

Long before Herder's glossy-green and gold-flesh-fly Sting[1] was protruded against the Cuticle of the Konigsburg Sage, I had formed the same opinion of his mind, the Falsetto [.....][a] found no other proof, this Frage 2 with the Antwort would have satisfied me that Herder never possessed an *Idea*[2]—but used & underst[ood] the term now [? as applied] [.....][a]

6   III 59–62, cropped

Frage 7. "Erhaben nennen wir das, was *schlechthin* gross ist."[*]

Antwort. Schlechthin gross ist nichts; jedes Grosse hat und gewährt Maas....

Frage 8. "Wenn wir etwas nicht allein gross, sondern schlechthin-absolut-in aller Absicht-über alle Vergleichung gross, d. i. erhaben nennen, so siehet man bald ein, dass wir für dasselbe keinen ihm angemessenen Maasstab ausser ihm, sondern blos in ihm zu suchen *verstatten*. Es ist eine Grösse, die blos sich selber gleich ist..."

[*Question 7.* "We call that sublime which is *absolutely great*."

Answer. Nothing is absolutely great; every greatness has and allows for degrees....

Question 8. "If we call something not only great but absolutely in every respect great beyond comparison, i.e. sublime, then we soon comprehend that it is not *permissible* to seek any adequate standard for the sublime outside it but only within it. It is a greatness that is comparable only to itself..."]

[In answer Herder utterly rejects Kant's proposition, claiming that standards of comparison are a component, albeit unnoticed, of our

[a] At least one line of ms cropped

5[1] One of a large family of flies, esp the genus *Sarcophaga*, that lay their larvae in the flesh of dead animals and in open wounds. William Kirby and William Spence *Introduction to Entomology* (1815–26)—from which C quotes in the *Logic*, in *CN* IV 4879–4896 (c Apr 1822), and in *AR* (1825) 210, 235n: see GOLDFUSS **10** n 1—cites Linnaeus' claim that three flesh-flies and their progeny could consume a horse faster than a lion

could. Cf *CN* II 1970 and n. C also has in mind the same figurative use as e.g. Cowper in *The Progress of Error*: flesh-flies "Who fasten without mercy on the fair".

5[2] Herder quotes from the *Critique of Judgement* pt I bk II §25. For C's reaction to Herder's misunderstanding and unfair criticism of Kant see **1** and **2**, above, and **9**, below.

feelings of sublimity. By removing the sublime from nature Kant also removed all measures whereby something can be regarded as high or low, big or small, and so succeeded in robbing the sublime of its own foundation. The person who agrees with Kant that the sublime is that in comparison with which all else is small will either have to admit that nothing he experiences through his senses and feelings is sublime or else reach a suspect position of self-aggrandisement by declaring himself as the only absolute and all-encompassing sublime.]

*[a] We call an object sublime, in relation to which the exercise of Comparison is suspended; while, ⟨on the contrary,⟩ that object is most beautiful, which in the highest perfection sustains while it satisfies the Comparing Power.[1] The subjective Result is C[.....][b] when a wheel turns so smoothly and swiftly as to present a stationary image to the eye—or as a Fountain (such as either of the two in the Colonnade of S[t] Peter's at Rome) Fons omni fonti formosior!/[2] It is impossible, that the same Object should be sublime & beautiful at the same moment to the same Manind[3]—tho' a beautiful Object may excite & be made the Symbol of an Idea that is truly [.....][c] Serpent in a wreath of folds basking in the Sun is beautiful to Aspasia,[4] whose attention is confined to the visual impression, but excites an emotion of Sublimity in Plato who contemplates under that symbol the Idea of Eternity.[d5]

[a] C did not put "*" in the textus—he evidently refers back to the "*" printed at the end of *Frage 7*
[b] Cropped, with the loss of two or three lines of ms
[c] Shawcross's conjectural reading is "[sublime, A...]"
[d] Here C has written "†" and continued the note at the foot of the page beginning with "†". Note 7 is written within the type-area of III 61 below the end of *Frage 8*

[6][1] On the sublime as "suspending the power of comparison", but in a sense closer to Burke's *Philosophical Inquiry into...the Sublime and the Beautiful* (ii §1) than to Kant, see *Friend (CC)* II 257. In this annotation C is attacking Herder's position, not Kant's. In a series of notes on Solger *Erwin* C wrote: "...No object of Sense is sublime in itself; but only as far as I make it a symbol of some Idea.... The Beautiful is the perfection, of the Sublime the suspension, of the Comparing Power...." BM MS Egerton 2800 f 71. Cf *Critique of Judgement* pt I bk II §23.

[6][2] Perhaps suggested by Kant's reference to St Peter's in the *Critique of Judgement* pt I bk II §25: cf **5** n 2, above.

"Fountain more beautiful than any fountain" is untraced.

[6][3] Cf WW's fragmentary essay "The Sublime and the Beautiful" (1811–12) in *W Prose* II, esp 349 lines 21–6, 353–4, 356.

[6][4] A brilliant and cultivated figure in fifth-century Athenian society, and Pericles' mistress. The pseudo-Platonic dialogue *Menexenus* consists largely of Socrates' repeating a long memorial speech composed by Aspasia; there is in it no sign of her admiring a serpent basking in the sun, but C's point is secure without documentary support.

[6][5] Plato does not use the snake as a symbol of immortality; to him, snakes figuratively represent the bite and pangs of love. For some account of the

Herder mistakes for the SUBLIME sometimes the GRAND, some-times the MAJESTIC, and sometimes the INTENSE:[6] in which last sense we must render a [.....]*a* or magnificent, but as a *Whole*, (a visual Whole, I mean) it cannot be sublime. A mountain in a cloudless sky, its summit smit with the Sunset is a beautiful, a magnificent Object—the same with its Summit hidden by Clouds, & seemingly blended with the Sky, while mists & floating Vapors of [.....]*a7*

7 III 61, marked with a line in the margin | "Frage 8"

"...Die obige Erklärung kann auch so ausgedrückt werden: *Erhaben ist das, mit welchem in Vergleichung alles andre klein ist.*"

["...The above definition may also be expressed in this way: *that is sublime in comparison with which all else is small.*"]

Here Kant *has* layed himself open to just censure.[1]

8 III 224, pencil, cropped | III "Von schönen Wissenschaften und Künsten"

"Schöne Kunst ist eine Kunst, sofern sie zugleich Natur zu seyn scheint. Die Natur war schön, wenn sie *zugleich* als Kunst *aussahe*; und die Kunst kann *nur* schön genannt werden, wenn wir uns bewusst sind, sie sey Kunst, und sie uns doch als Natur aussieht." Und doch arbeitet in allen Künsten, die fortschreitend wirken, der Künstler darauf, dass man seine Kunst vergesse...

["A product of the fine arts is art insofar as it appears like nature at the same time. Nature proved beautiful when it wore the appearance of art *at the same time*; and art can *only* be termed beautiful, where we are conscious of its being art, while yet it has the appearance of nature." And yet in all arts that function progressively, the artist labors to make us forget his art...]

a Cropped, with the loss of two or three lines of ms

symbolic importance of snakes to C see John Beer *Coleridge the Visionary* (1959) 69–71.

6[6] For C's definition of the sublime, the grand, the majestic, and other aesthetic categories see Allsop I 197–9, in *BL* (1907) II 309. See also *CN* II 2012 ff 41–2.

6[7] Cf "The grandest efforts of poetry are where the imagination is called forth, not to produce a distinct form, but a strong working of the mind, still offering what is still repelled, and again creating what is again rejected; the result being

what the poet wishes to impress, namely, the substitution of a sublime feeling of the unimaginable for a mere image." *Sh C* II 103–4 (Dec 1811). Kant had written in pt I bk II §26: "Who would apply the term 'sublime' even to shapeless mountain masses towering one above the other in wild disorder, with their pyramids of ice...? But in the contemplation of them...the mind abandons itself to the imagination...". Tr J. C. Meredith.

7[1] Herder quotes from the *Critique of Judgement* pt I bk II § 25.

[N]othing [to?] my [fe]eling [wa]s ever [m]ore [clea]rly & [ha]ppily expressed than this Quotation [fr]om Kant.[1]—The objection to a [s]ingle sentence out of a large Work [f]or not *explicating* the whole is [.....]*a*

9   iii +1*b*

This and the former Volume are much less disgusting than the first, and contain some splendid Commonplaces, tho' I think, no new lights, but every where he grossly misunderstands Kant, confounding all that the great man had said of that in each which is common to all, or should be so, with the individual meum and tuum/[1] & then that endless Rant about the Greeks, & Homer, with no love of Truth, no feeling of Reality, no collation of these Fineries with the real *History* of these eulogized Greeks—their manners, ignorance, cruelty, treatment of Women, &c &c/[2]—Besides, all is vague generality or guess work of [per]verse etymology—no *fine* [.....]*c*

---

a Cropped, with the loss of one or two lines of ms
b Inside back of orginal grey paper wrapper
c Cropped, with the loss of one or two lines of ms

8[1] *Critique of Judgement* pt i bk ii § 45. Cf *Sh C* i 181 §7 at n 3 (from BM MS Egerton 2800 ff 21–2), which cites this passage as a parallel.

9[1] "Mine and yours".

9[2] Throughout *Kalligone* Herder shows partiality to the Greeks and often resorts to aesthetic and moral norms formulated by the Greeks in order to refute Kant's arguments. See e.g. *Kalligone* iii pp 5–12 and **4** textus, above.

Von der Auferstehung, als Glauben, Geschichte und Lehre. Frankfurt & Leipzig 1794. 8°.

Rebound after C's death to match his copies of *Briefe* and *Kalligone*.

British Museum C 43 a 7

Inscribed in pencil on p ⁻5 (p–d): "Lot 349"—i.e. in *Green SC* (1880)—which lot included the annotated copies of *Briefe* and *Kalligone*.

A reminiscence, in a letter of 2 Sept 1802 to RS, of an occasion when C cited evidence from this book in Keswick suggests that he had read the book by c mid-Sept 1799. *CL* II 861–2, and for the earlier occasion *CL* I 528, 540; see also general note, above.

DATE. Perhaps 1816 and later. See **23** n 2 for a date not earlier than 1819. A sequence of entries in N F°, including a transcript of **15** and reflections parallel to **13–16**, show that C reread and considered the annotations in Mar 1826: see **13** n 1, **14** n 3, **15** n 1, **16** n 3.

COEDITORS. Lore Metzger, Raimonda Modiano.

1	p [5], pencil, first word in ink | Pt I § 1

Das älteste Gesetz über Leben und Tod schien den Menschen wohl lange Zeit das natürlichste: *Du bist Erde und sollt zur Erde werden.* (1 Mos. 3, 19.) Hiebei beruhigte sich der sinnliche Mensch, und wie viele Nationen gibt es noch jetzo, die sich dabei beruhigt finden!

[For a long time the oldest law regarding life and death seemed to men the most natural: *dust thou art, and unto dust shalt thou return* (Gen 3.19). Hereby the sensualist set his mind at rest, and even now how many nations are there that thus find comfort!]

False! At least H. should have stated some 3 or 4 of these *wie viele Nationen!*[1]—The contrary is notoriously the fact.

2	p 7, pencil | I § 3

Der einzige Elias ward weggenommen im Ungewitter, im feurigen Streitwagen Jehovahs; *sonst*, sagt Sirach, *war ni[e]mand auf Erden geschaffen, dass er dem Henoch gliche, der weggenommen ward von der Erde.* (Sirach 49, 16.) Eine Henoch-gleiche Aufnahme zu Jehovah blieb den Ebräern also das Ideal des menschlichen Hinganges.

[Only Elijah was taken up in the thunderstorm, in Jehovah's war-chariot of fire; *there was no other creature on earth*, says Sirach, *who was like Enoch, who was taken up from earth* (Ecclus 49.16). Thus an Enoch-like ascension to Jehovah remained for the Hebrews the ideal of man's demise.]

1[1] "How many nations"—in textus.

Is not this a contradiction?—No one in future time had the same honor as Enoch/ then der einzige Elias[1] had the same and more *conspicuously* and *therefore (also)*[2] Enoch remained the Jewish Ideal. Precious Logic![a]

3   p 7, pencil | I § 4

Für die gemeine Anzahl der Menschen blieb das *Begräbniss*, die *Versammlung zum bleibenden Wohnhause der Väter unter der Erde* das Ziel ihres Lebens, woraus sich denn bald die Vorstellung eines *unterirrdischen Schattenreiches* bilden musste.

[For a great number of people, *the burial, the gathering into the abiding subterranean dwelling of the fathers*, remained the goal of their lives, from which the notion of a subterraneous realm of shadows was bound to take shape.]

Does not this very phrase "gathered to the Dwelling of their Fathers" prove their Belief in some form or other of future Being? Undoubtedly, it does: and their great anxiety about the place of their Sepulchres is inexplicable on any other ground.

4   p 9, pencil | I § 6

Die Vorstellung des *Schattenreiches* ward bei den Ebräern, wie bei andern Völkern, durch Dichter fortgebildet. Diesen war es ein *geräumiges Land*, weil alles dahinkehrt, der König und Knecht, der Dränger und der Gedrängte, der Reiche und Arme.... Fürchterlich ist sein Eingang und keine Rückkehr aus demselben. Bald ward es ein *Dunkler Pallast mit Pforten und Riegeln, in welchem der Tod als ein Tyrann herrschte*. Unbestechlich, unbezwingbar ist sein Gewalt; kein Freund kann von ihr erlösen, kein Bruder loskaufen; das Lösegeld ist zu hoch; er muss es in Ewigkeit aufgeben.

[The Hebrews' conception of a realm of shadows, like that of other peoples, was advanced by the poets. For them it was a *spacious land* since all go there, king and vassal, oppressor and oppressed, rich and poor.... Its entrance is terrible, and there is no return from it. Soon it became a *dark palace with gates and bars where death ruled as a tyrant*. His power is incorruptible, unconquerable; no friend can be redeemed from it, no brother can be ransomed from it; the ransom is too high; he must abandon it for ever.]

How could Herder explain the singular fact of a Death-realm[1]

---

[a] C has drawn a line at the end of his note; this looks as though he had italicised "Precious Logic"

2[1] "Only Elijah"—in textus.   4[1] I.e. "the realm of shades" in 3 and
2[2] German *also* (therefore)—in textus.   4 textus.

without an Elysium among the Jews, if not from some revelation concerning the spiritual Death, till the coming of the Redeemer?[2]

4A p 13 | I § 11

"...*Aus dem Schattenreiche will ich sie erlösen; Vom Tyrannen, dem Tode, will ich sie erretten. Ein Gift will ich dir seyn, o Tod, Verheerung deinem Reiche.*" Ezech. 37. Hos. 6, 1. 2. 13th Cap. ~~13~~ 10, 14.)[1]

[(AV:) "...*I will ransom them from the power of the grave; I will redeem them from death: O death, I will be thy plagues; O grave, I will be thy destruction*"...]

5 p 17, pencil | I § 16

Den frühzeitigen Tod der Lieblinge Gottes betrachtet der Verfasser dieses Buchs, als ob er die Aufnahme Henochs commentirte: "*Der Gerechte, ob er wohl gestorben zu seyn scheinet; er ist in Ruhe. Denn er gefiel Gott wohl und war ihm lieb, und ward hinweggenommen aus dem Leben unter Verbrechern.*"

[The author of the book [The Book of Wisdom] deals with the early death of God's favourites as if he were commenting on Enoch's ascension: "*The upright man, although he may appear to have died, is at rest. Because he pleased God and was loved by him and was taken away from his life among sinners.*"]

What has Enoch to do with "unter Verbrechern?"[1]

6 pp 24–5, pencil | I §§ 19–20

Gleichergestalt trieb unter Tyrannen, wie Antiochus war, die Noth der äussersten Unterdrückung das Gemüth des Menschen dahin, *einen Richter der Tyrannen zu suchen, und ein künftiges Weltgericht zu glauben.*

Dahin hatten Propheten und Psalmen vorbereitet; diese Zuversicht entwickelt die Rede gegen Tyrannen, das *Buch der Weisheit.* Denn

[4][2] Cf **3**, above. The Jews, for whom death was represented by the desolate places of Sheol and Gehenna, did not believe in eternal life after death, heaven being the abode of God to be entered only by a rare Ezekiel or Enoch. Cf e.g. T. FULLER *Life Out of Death* 1. Even Isa 25.6–8, important to the Christians as prefiguring Christ's triumph over "the last enemy", is silent about resurrection and heaven. The notion of a heavenly Paradise, as a restored Eden in which the souls of the dead await the Judgement, enters with the pseudepigraphical 1 Enoch.

4A[1] The passage quoted by Herder is, as he notes (though perhaps ambiguously), Hosea 13.14. C's correction to Hosea 13.10 is not understood. Ezek 37.12 reads (AV): "Behold, O my people, I will open your graves, and cause you to come up out of your graves, and bring you into the land of Israel."

5[1] "Among sinners"—in textus. Yet Enoch "walked with God" (Gen 5.22).

das Gemüth der Menschen ist unbezwinglich: nehme man ihm den Trost, seine Freude in diesem Leben; es stärkt sich mit Hoffnungen eines zukünftigen, eines andern Lebens....

Mithin sehen wir auch die Keime der verschiedenen Secten, denen bei ruhigern Zeiten nachher diese oder jene Lehre vorzüglich lieb seyn musste. Der epikuräische Sadducäer... läugnete Auferstehung und ein andres Leben, weil er sie weder bedurfte noch wollte. Der Pharisäer, der an der Ehre seines Landesgesetzes in allen Gebräuchen und Satzungen hing, cultivirte insonderheit die Lehre von Auferstehung der Todten, knüpfte sie an sein gehofftes Reich des Messias, und zierete sie mit tausend Andeutungen der Propheten in sinnreichen oder albernen Fragen aus.

[Similarly under Tyrants like Antiochus the distress caused by utmost repression impelled the heart of man *to seek a judge of tyrants, and to believe in a future day of judgement*. Prophets and psalms had prepared for this; the oration against tyrants, the *Book of Wisdom* develops this conviction. For the mind of man is invincible: to take away man's comfort, his joy in this life, is to strengthen his hope in a future, another life....

Thus we also observe the germ of the different sects, who in later, calmer times had to prefer this or that doctrine. The epicurean Sadducee...denied the resurrection and after-life because he neither needed nor desired them. The Pharisee, who clung to the honour of the law of the land in all customs and statutes, cultivated especially the doctrine of the resurrection of the dead, connected it to his hoped-for kingdom of the Messiah, and embellished it with a thouand allusions to the prophets in sensible or foolish questions.]

What vile Trash! That such a Faith as that portrayed in the Maccabees[1] should have been the sudden Growth of the Day! Is there a word implying that it was a new Faith? Is it not on the contrary declared, in the Book of Wisdom, that none but the most hardened and cruel Sensualists disbelieved a future state?[2] And even in the Prophets, how much more natural to suppose that what they took for granted concerning each Individual, they should apply metaphorically to the *State* and its fortunes, than ⟨that what⟩ was only metaphorical of as to the State, th should be applied in solemn and literal reality to the Individual! Besides, had this been the case, the

6[1] I.e. the apocryphal 2 Maccabees. For the Maccabaean dynasty see DAVISON 22 n 1.

6[2] See Wisd 1.16–2.24. 1 Macc (early first century B.C.) gives a strictly historical account of the first forty years of the Maccabaean rule, with no allusion to the immortality of the soul or the resurrection of the dead, and with little colour of Messianic hope. 2 Macc (c A.D. 40), dealing with the same historical period, combines the doctrines of resurrection and the immortality of the soul in a blend of Jewish and Greek eschatology. 2 Macc, included in the Vulgate, has provided support for RC teaching on prayers to the dead and on purgatory.

Jews would have appropriated the resurrection to themselves, and not have extended it at once to the whole human Race.

7   p 26, pencil | I § 21

...der Pharisäismus mit seiner Auferstehungslehre ward aber die Hauptsecte. Was einst das menschliche Gemüth in Zeiten des grössesten Druckes von aussen, oder in Augenblicken des freiesten Aufschwunges von innen an zukünftigen Hoffnungen erspähet hatte, ordnete dieser stolz und kalt in Ein System vom *Reich des Messias und der mit ihm verbundenen Palingenesie der Dinge*, wozu das Weltgericht und die Auferstehung der Todten mit gehörte. Lasset uns sehen, wie dieser Glaube zur Zeit der Ankunft Christi beschaffen war, und was die Gottheit wunderbar auf solchen Glauben gebauet habe.

[... but Pharisaism with its doctrine of resurrection became the principal sect. What the human spirit had glimpsed of future hopes in time of greatest external pressure or in moments of the most uninhibited inward inspiration, this sect organised proudly and coldly into a system of the *Kingdom of the Messiah and the related palingenesis of things*, including the last judgement and the resurrection of the dead. Let us see how this faith was constituted at the time of the advent of Christ and what the deity marvellously built upon such faith.]

So God sent his own Son from Heaven, in order that the Fictions of Hypocrites and the Phantasms of Dreamers "might be fulfilled"[1]— O blasphemy!

8   p 39, pencil | Pt III § 5

Der folgende Tag, der Sabbat, verstrich, und Tages darauf frühe kommen einige Freundinnen des Verstorbenen, den Leichnam zu salben. Sie sehen die Grabhöle offen und hören die Nachricht: "euer Verstorbener ist nicht hier; er ist *auferstanden und hinweggegangen.* In Galiläa will er seine Freunde wiedersehen, und *vor* ihnen daseyn; saget es ihnen." So urkundlich und glaubwürdig die Nachricht vom Tode des Gekreuzigten ist, so glaubwürdig muss unter solchen Umständen auch diese von seiner Wiederauflebung im Grabe seyn: denn sie beruhet auf dem Glauben derselben Geschichtschreiber.

[The following day, the sabbath, passed and early the day after some women came, friends of the deceased, in order the embalm the body. They saw the

7[1] "Hypocrites", i.e. Pharisees, a lay sect who gave currency to beliefs in the future life, angels, and demons. The phrase "might be fulfilled" occurs in Matt 1.22 (and eight other places), in John 12.38 (and six other places), and in Rom 8.4, usually of the fulfilment of prophecy or "the scriptures".

open sepulchre and heard this message: "Your departed one is not here, he is *risen and passed hence*. In Galilee he shall see his friends again and he shall go *before* them; tell them." As authentic and credible as is the news of the crucified's death, as credible must also be that of his resurrection from the grave: for it rests on the credence of the same historians.]

Curious Logic! So if a Biographer of Wesley after a minute account of his Death should add a story of his apparition as seen by several of his Followers, the latter is to be as trust-worthy as the former—as being written by the same Man![1]

9 p 40, pencil

Hier hatte *Er* also nichts mehr zu schaffen: denn seinen Feinden, oder gar öffentlich sich zu zeigen, (wie so manche es <u>unbesonnen</u> verlangt haben,) wäre die unbesonnenste Sache der <u>Welt</u> gewesen. Zum zweitenmal sollte und wollte er nicht <u>ergriffen</u>, <u>gebunden</u>, <u>verhöhnet</u>, <u>verspeiet</u>, mit <u>Fäusten geschlagen</u>, <u>gegeisselt</u> und <u>gekreuzigt</u> werden; für *diese* Welt hatte Er vollendet.

[*He* had nothing more to do here: for to show himself to his enemies, or even to the public (as many so *heedlessly* demanded), would have been the most imprudent thing in the world. He should not and would not a second time be taken, *bound, despised, spat upon*, beaten *with fists*, scourged and crucified; He had done with *this* world.]

And he would have commanded ten Legions (60,000) of Angels! And could pass thro' closed Doors!/[1]

10 p 41, pencil | III § 6

Der Auferstandene liess es indess bei dieser Nachricht an seine Freunde nicht bewenden; er zeigte sich dem Ersten, dem er sich zeigen konnte. Eine Maria ersah er nahe dem Grabe; sie sah ihn für den Gärtner an: denn seine Kleider hatten die Kriegsknechte getheilt, die Leinen waren im Grabe zurückgeblieben, und er war mit dem, dessen er habhaft werden konnte, bekleidet.

[The risen Lord meanwhile did not rest satisfied with this message to his friends; he showed himself to the first to whom he could show himself. He saw a certain Mary near the grave; she took him for the gardener, for the soldiers had divided his clothes among themselves, his linen remained in the grave, and he was clothed in whatever he could obtain.]

8[1] Cf *Briefe* 8 and n 1 and see **10** n 1. On the trustworthiness of observations of supernatural events see also e.g. KANT *Vermischte Schriften* COPY C **16** and **17**.

9[1] Matt 26.53 (twelve legions) and John 20.19, 26.

An infidel would ask where Jesus procured the Gardner's Dress—or whatever it was, in which Mary met him?[1] It is plain, he would say, that Jesus must have had friends & confederates, unknown to, or unnoticed by the Apostles.[a]

11   p 42, pencil | III § 8

Dem ungläubigen Thomas, der seinen Glauben in der Hand haben wollte, zeiget er, acht Tage nachher, sich nochmals also; daher es wundersam und fast unbegreiflich ist, wie die spätere Zeit diese körperliche, leibhafte Person, die sich *handgreiflich als Denselben Jesus von Nazareth* zeigte, zu einem geistigen Phantasma habe machen wollen, und machen dörfen. In den drei Geschichtschreibern, Matthäus, Markus und Johannes, deren zwei Augenzeugen waren, ist hievon nicht die mindeste Spur.

[Eight days later he showed himself again to the doubting Thomas, who wished to hold his faith in his hands; it is therefore marvellous and almost incredible how later generations have wished to and have been allowed to make into an immaterial chimera this physical, incarnate person who *palpably showed himself as the same Jesus of Nazareth*. There is not the slightest trace of this in the three historians, Matthew, Mark, and John, of whom two were eye-witnesses.]

Is it then quite certain that κατα Ματθαιον meant written by Matthew?[1]

12   p 43, pencil | III § 9

Lukas allein, der kein Augenzeuge war...mag etwa dazu Anlass gegeben haben, inden er bei einem Mitgange des Auferweckten mit zweien Schüler zuletzt den Ausdruck braucht: "*er entzog sich ihrem Anblick;*" woraus man denn ein unkörperliches Verschwinden abnehmen konnte....

[Luke alone, who was no eye-witness...may possibly have given rise to this report by ultimately using the following expression about the risen Christ's walk with two of his disciples: "*he vanished from their sight*", from which one could infer that he vanished spiritually....]

But pray what does Herder make of the *closed doors?*[1]

[a] The note is written in the head-margin of p 41 and around §7 on p 41, but clearly refers to §6, which ends on p 40

10[1] See John 20.15.

11[1] "*According to* Matthew". The phrase embraces a family of possibilities: e.g. the Gospel as written by, or as told by, Matthew; or put together by somebody else from what Matthew told him, or from various reports of what Matthew had said. See EICHHORN *Neue Testament* COPY A 1 and **19**. Cf *CN* III 3879 and 4402. See also *Briefe* **8** and GREW **20**.

12[1] See **9** and n 1, above.

13   pp 44–5 | III §11

...Den Jüngern waren alle Schuppen von den Augen gefallen; jetzt und hier war an ein weltliches Reich nicht mehr zu gedenken. Ihr erwarteter König der Welt war am Pfahle gestorben, und dorfte sich micht mehr zeigen.

[...The eyes of the disciples were opened; a kingdom on earth was no longer conceivable here and now. Their expected ruler of the world had died at the stake and must not show himself any more.]

Are we to understand from this Arch-Jesuit,[1] that Christ's former declarations[2] were all delusions? Verily, broad strait-forward Disbelief is religion & Christianity compared with this Assassin-like Stab at the character of our Lord![3]

14   pp 92–3, pencil | Pt v § 24

Mithin verbietet es keinem denkenden Menschen, in den Tiefen der menschlichen Seele, im Natur- und im Weltlaufe nach Wahrscheinlichkeiten oder nach Gründen zu spähen, die eine Fortdauer nach dem Tode glaubhaft machen oder diesen Glauben befestigen mögen; vielmehr haben alle Verständige sich um diese Wahrscheinlichkeiten auch im Christenthum bemühet. Nur das Christenthum selbst ist nicht auf diese Wahrscheinlichkeiten, es ist auf den *Glauben** an eine Geschichte gebauet, die den grössesten Theil dieser Gründe mit sich führet.

[Thus no thoughtful man is forbidden to search in the depths of the human soul, in the course of nature or of the world, for probabilities or grounds that make an existence after death credible or that may confirm this belief; on the contrary, all wise men, even in Christendom, concerned themselves about these probabilities. Only Christianity itself is not founded on these probabilities but rather on the *faith in a history* that contains the greater part of these grounds.]

* A strange inconsistency does this appear to me. We are to found our trust in a future state on *a History*: and yet according to Herder a History so disguised in Symbols, allusions, and short and long

13[1] Cf "Herder is a paltry Juggler, a tricksy gaudy Sophist, a rain-bow in the Steam of a Dunghill—". *CN* IV 5334 (13 Mar 1826), preceding the reference in **14** n 3, below. Cf **28**, below, and see *Kalligone* **1**.

13[2] See **24** n 3 and **27** n 1.

13[3] Cf N F° f 35ᵛ (*CN* v): "The supposition that the greater part of Christ's declarations and promises respecting himself... before his Crucifixion were Messianic Prejudices of his Education, Delusions which melted away after his re-animation... is, I think, quite new—a morceau of the Herderian Sterne–Marivaux–Richardsonian psilanthropic Christianity!"

Allegories, that of the two main Facts, which give their value to all the others, Herder believes in the *literal sense* neither the one or the other/[1] and does not supply even a Hint, what we are to believe, i.e. historically, instead of it/—If we are to understand any thing, Christ neither really *died* ⟨on the Cross,⟩ nor really ascended to Heaven.[2]—What then became of Him?—If it be replied, we neither ⟨know⟩ nor care *biographically*, then how can your Faith be founded on a History.—[3]

15 pp +1–+2, apparently referring to pp 92–3

It is hard under one name to designate Herder's Faith—"*if Faith it may be call'd, which Faith is none*".[1] It is, or seems to be, composed of contrary Elements in the act of balancing each other, but not yet balanced, & thence substantial; but still glowing in restless vibrations.—A *sensibility*, a certain refined Epicurism of moral Sense, a desire to possess the sympathies of the Mass of Christians & to govern them thereby—and yet an equal desire to be respected by the Philosophers, *the Intellectuals./* He will linger in and about the Camp of the *Religious*, but then he will have, or will forge for himself, a Ticket, a Certificat from the Philosophists, authorizing him so to do!—Alas! but is not this very like *a Spy?*—The most amusing thing in all Herder's Theological Tracts is the cool (*vornehm*) "*quality*-like"[2] looking down upon all the Founders of Christianity—!! Poor simple Creatures!—excuse them, Gentlemen! —they had very good hearts—& tho' they were somewhat silly, yet really put ourselves in their place, suppose that instead of our rank, education, & various immeasurable Superiority, we had been vulgar ignorant Jew-blackguards, like Peter, John, &c, we should have thought & acted much the same!—And this is a Defence of Christianity!!!—

14[1] The "two main Facts", as C states them at n 2, below—that Jesus died, and that he rose from the dead and ascended into heaven; another, as in **16**, below, is that Jesus was the son of God.

14[2] See DONNE *Sermons* COPY B **124** and n 3 and HEYLYN **8**.

14[3] An extension of this note in *CN* IV 5334, referring to "Von der Auferstehung, p. 92." and quoting from the textus given above, attacks vigorously and in detail Herder's examination of the

"probabilities or evidences" for the resurrection.

15[1] C transcribed this annotation with little variation in *CN* IV 5334 (13 Feb 1826), immediately following the passage cited in **14** n 3, above. Cf Milton *Paradise Lost* II 667: "If shape it might be calld that shape had none...".

15[2] For C's use of the word *vornehm* see KANT *Vermischte Schriften* COPY C **24** n 4. See also **17**, below, and EICHHORN *Alte Testament* **9** n 1.

16   pp 106–7,[a] pencil | Pt vi §§ 4–12

[Herder states that the Apostles and Church Fathers distinguished between the Christian "Rule and canon of faith and hope" ("Regel und Norm des Glaubens und der Hoffnung"), which was based on the historical facts, teachings, and promises of Christ (such as the fact that Christ was the son of God and that he rose from the dead), and Christian dogmas and prescripts, which arose out of various opinions and interpretations of these facts. The latter, which varied according to the different ways the Apostles narrated the same events, were never accepted, like the former, as articles of faith. In two footnotes (to pp 97–8) he establishes the Greek terms that he needs to clarify his distinction: δόξαι, "opinions"; δόγματα or δοξήματα, "dogmas" or "settled tenets"; κηρύγματα, "rules of faith". He also quotes St Basil: ἄλλο γὰρ δόγμα, ἄλλο κήρυγμα, "*dogma* is one thing, *kerugma* another".]

Well! this is indeed a Lullaby Lie! Eia, Puleia! Kindchen, geschweigen/[1] 1. First, it is utterly false, that the Resurrection of Christ, as a mere *proof* of a future state and ⟨of⟩ retribution ever did produce the effects of Christianity, either of Belief or of Persecution. Good Heavens! who, except perhaps Jews, would ever have persecuted innocent men for helping out their Belief in rewards and punishments after this Life by an account of an apparition distinguished from the common sort by being tangible/ 2. Still more false is it, that the Apostles teach different Dogmata/[2] 3.[b] And falser still that they distinguished *their* Dogmata from their κηρυγμα.[3] 4.

---

[a] The textus runs through pp 95–106; C's note is written in the blank space (more than half a page) at the end of pt vi and continues in all the available space in the first page of pt vii

[b] C has written "3." at the end of a line, and repeated it at the beginning of the next line

16[1] "Hush-a-by! Baby, be quiet!", to embody the "Lullaby Lie". C's departure from the usual *Eia popeia!* is not understood.

16[2] In §§ 4–7 (pp 95–8) Herder had pointed out that the Apostles and Church Fathers distinguished between the Christian "Rule and canon of faith and hope", which was based on historical facts, teachings, and promises of Christ (e.g. that Christ was the son of God and that he rose from the dead), and subsequent dogmas that varied according to the different ways the Apostles interpreted the same events. "Dogmas originated from opinions; opinions,

however, could never—according to the first Church—provide articles of faith. Paul and John, James and Peter, often expressed the same thing differently; yet, notwithstanding their individual way of presenting things, they all shared the Christian rule of faith as fact, promise, and practical teaching" (p 97).

16[3] "Pronouncements". In two footnotes to pp 97–8 Herder clarifies his distinction between δόγματα and κηρύγματα by using Greek rather than German terms, and quotes St Basil: ἄλλο γὰρ δόγμα, ἄλλο κήρυγμα—"*dogma* is one thing, *kerugma* another". In N F⁰ C discusses especially p 98, in which Herder

But falsest of all, that they subordinated articles of Faith to acquiescence in Historic Facts[4]—St Paul would no longer know Christ himself after the Flesh[5]—i.e. in mere reference to historic Phænomena/ In short, the one great ~~Fact~~ continuous Fact of 1800 years has demonstrated, that such opinions as these of Herder's were never held, & never could hold together, any promiscuous Congregation.

17   p 109 | Pt vii § 2

...denn bei jedem sinnlichen, rohen Volk müssen Aufschlüsse über die Zukunft, die ihrer Fassungskraft voreilen, in kurzem nothwendig die gröbsten Träume werden. Ueberhaupt ist das, was der menschliche Verstand sich selbst erarbeitet, worauf er nur durch eignes Bedürfniss kam und kommen konnte, ihm auch das gelegenste und liebste....Die erziehende Gottheit that das Ihrige, indem sie ihm Begebenheiten vorlegte, oder ihn in Umstände setzte, wobei er sich einen solchen Trost nicht anders als zueignen konnte. Dies geschah durch die Aufnahme Henochs, Elias und auf eine so vorzügliche Weise durch die *Wiederbelebung Christi*.

[...for with every sensual, primitive people, disclosures about the future that exceed their power of comprehension will necessarily become the crudest dreams in a short time. The human understanding generally finds that the gain obtained through its own effort, at which it has arrived and could have arrived only according to its own necessity, is also its most appropriate and precious one....The instructing deity did its share by presenting such events to the human understanding or by placing it in such circumstances that it had no other choice than to adopt such comfort, as in the case of the ascension of Enoch, Elijah, and so eminently of the *resurrection of Christ*.]

And why not of all the other, collected by Huet, Zuinglii Theat.

gives as an example that the article of faith, the *symbolon* (which he equates with the κήρυγμα), is that Christ rose from the dead, whereas the meaning of this, whether he was truly dead or in a trance, is a mere δόξα (opinion); the hardening into dogma, Herder seems to imply, belongs to a later age. But C writes: "I think, I might safely defy a Polyhistor to produce a more amazingly impudent piece of Sophistry than in this antithesis of κηρυγμα = Rule or Canon of Faith, and Δοξα = opinion of Divines, which Δοξαι when many consented became Dogmata = determined or Settled

Opinions, or Tenets...". *CN* iv 5336 (14–18 Mar 1826). For C's own use of the term κήρυγμα see e.g. EICHHORN *Neue Testament* COPY A **1**.

16[4] In § 6 (p 97) Herder writes: "This rule of faith and hope did not actually contain any dogmas; rather, it contained *History and Teaching*, that is, the *facts*, *prescripts*, and *promises of Christ*."

16[5] I.e. κατὰ σάρκα. See 2 Cor 5.16 and cf DONNE *Sermons* COPY B **16** n 5. For the κηρύγματα common to "the three Gospels τὰ κατὰ σάρκα" see IRVING *For Missionaries* **11**.

Hum. Vit., and the Humane Society?[1] And is this *the* Religion, this the name, to which Heaven and Earth is to bow, & Hell to tremble?[2] A Religion founded on as Gross a calumny of the human Soul, which no where but as monstrous exceptions has doubted its own amenability & perpetuity, as it is, an affected "vornhemhm"[3] perversion of the God's holy Word.

18   p 113, pencil, marked with a line in the margin | VII § 5

So haben alle Völker gefühlt: sie haben Strafe und Belohnung nach diesem Leben geglaubt, wenn sie die gute Sache bis zur Unterdrückung leiden, und edle Menschen ungehört unterdrückt sahen. Nicht nur in diesem Leben glaubten sie eine verborgne, gerechte Nemesis, die den trotzigen Underdrücker beuge, den frechen Tyrannen stürze, die Laster der Vorfahren noch an späten Geschlecht strafe; in der Unterwelt selbst dachten sie sich unerbittlichstrenge gerechte Richter.

[All peoples have felt thus: they have believed in punishment and reward in a life hereafter when they have suffered oppression for the just cause and have seen noble men unduly oppressed. Not only in this life did they believe in a concealed, equitable nemesis, which bows the proud repressor, overturns the insolent tyrant, visits the sins of the fathers even on a later generation; in the underworld itself they conceived of inexorably strict judges.]

Most true! & a compleat confutation of $\frac{9}{10}$ths of this semi-demi-quavering Book[1]

19   p 117 | VII § 6

Ihr weint mit Admetus zärtliche Thränen, wenn sein geliebtes Weib, die sich für ihn in den Tod gab, durch seinen Gastfreund ihm ungehofft zurückgeführt wird...und fühlet mit einem Vater, der seinen Sohn, mit einem Freunde, der seinen Freund wiederfindet: "Er war todt, und siehe, er ist lebendig. Er war verlohren, und ist wiederfunden."...Sähen wir die Evangelien, die Schriften Petrus und insonderheit Johannes auch nur als liebevolle Denkmale

---

17[1] C refers, in a general way, to the evidence of actual resurrections, or returns to life after death, collected by Pierre Daniel Huet (1630–1721), scholar, apologist for Christianity in his *Demonstratio evangelica* (1679); by Theodorus Zwingler (1533–88) in his *Theatrum vitae humanae* (1571); and by the Society for the Recovery of Persons Apparently Drowned (formed 1774, renamed the Humane Society in 1776 and a little later the Royal Humane Society), which published anecdotal *Transactions* from 1784 onward.

17[2] See Phil 2.10 and Jas 2.19.

17[3] See **15** n 2, above.

18[1] Properly "demi-semi-quavering", for which see *Briefe* **5** n 1.

der Erinnerung eines abgeschiedenen Freundes an, sollten wir nicht jeden Zug der Achtung, Zärtlichkeit und Verehrung in ihnen hochschätzen und lieben?

[You weep tender tears with Admetus when his beloved wife who died for him is unexpectedly restored to him through his guest...and you feel with a father who finds his son once more and with a friend who finds his friend: "He was dead and behold he is alive. He was lost and is restored."...If we regarded the Gospels, the Scriptures of Peter and especially of John also merely as beloved memorials commemorating a departed friend, should we not love and esteem in them every line of respect, tenderness, and reverence?]

Merciful Saviour! and this is to pass for a *defence* of, no, an apology/ a mendicant canting Excuse for this everlasting Gospel! We must read Peter and John, as we read a Novel—& compare it with the fable of Admetus!

20   p 117 | vii § 7

Also auch das süsse *Zutrauen auf das Wort ihres abgeschiedenen* * *Freundes*, dass er bei ihnen seyn, dass sie bald mit ihm seyn, dass er wiederkommen und sie auf immer zu sich holen werde, wollen wir ihnen gönnen und sie desshalb nicht verspotten.

[Thus let us also grant them and not mock them for their sweet *faith in the word of their departed friend* that he shall be with them, that they shall soon be with him, that he shall return and take them unto him forever.]

* What one of the New Testament writers ever presumed to use this familiar Language, or any answering to it, in any other sense than they used it of Almighty God?—Lord & Savior—God blessed over all![1] God incarnate—the substantial adequate Idea of the Father!

21   p 119, pencil | vii § 9

Ueberhaupt ist ja der christliche Glaube *Glaube*. Er dringt sich niemand weder als Wissenschaft noch als Zwang und <u>Gebot</u> auf; er ist Hoffnung und Zuversicht des Zukünftigen, des Unsichtbaren.

[In general, the Christian faith is indeed *faith*. It does not force itself upon anyone as either science or as compulsion or *commandment*; it is hope and trust in the future, in the invisible.]

No?—And yet Herder had read the VIth Cap. of the Gospel according to St John?[1] If to declare that not to do so is to forfeit

20[1] It is possible to translate Rom 9.5 "Christ who is God blessed above all for ever". See also BIBLE COPY B 119 and n 1.

21[1] John 6.31–58—Christ's disclosure of himself as "the bread of life", with the promise of the sacrament and eternal life.

Salvation, and to have the Lot of accursed Spirits,[2] be not a command so to do, I know not what is—[3]

22 pp 122–3, pencil | Nachschrift § 1

Möge sodann der Naturalist sagen: "sonderbar gnug, aber unter den Umständen war es doch kein Wunder," möge er manche Folgen, die die Apostel daraus zogen, manche Beweise, die sie darauf bauten, absondern; ist das Factum als Geschichte gerettet, so mache Jeder daraus, was er will. Evangelien, Apostelgeschichte, apostolische Briefe werden damit auf einmal wenigstens lesbare Schriften, deren Erzählung und Lehren der Aufmerksamkeit werth sind, statt dass sie, auf einen dunkeln Betrug gegründet, solche kaum anzusprechen wagen.

[Well, then, let the naturalist say: "strange enough, but under the circumstances it was for all that no miracle"; let him exclude many conclusions that the Apostles drew therefrom, many proofs, as long as the fact is preserved as history, everyone may make of them what he will. Gospels, Acts of the Apostles, apostolic Epistles thus suddenly become at least readable documents, the narrations and doctrines of which are worthy of attention instead of being based on a dark deception and scarcely daring to claim attention.]

Not in the least would it explain the writings of Paul or John? Did they, or any of the Jews ever pray to Enoch or Elias—or declare them the Creator of the World? Did they join their names industriously with God the Father—What should we think of God and Enoch and God acting? For so they Herderists interpret the Holy Ghost.—

23 p 124, pencil | § 2

Geschiehet im Naturreich Gottes Etwas ohne seine Kraft und Allmacht? geschähe Etwas dergleichen in seinem physisch-moralischen Reiche?

[Does anything happen in God's natural creation without his power and omnipotence? could anything comparable happen in his physical-moral realm?]

21[2] See Gal 1.6–9.

21[3] In a letter of 2 Sept 1802 to RS C translated "one sentence" from "p. 120": "They held that to be a miracle which probably was no miracle; they believed that this Resurrection was effected by the omnipotence of God, when perhaps it was merely a natural resuscitation in consequence of the powerful Perfume of Nicodemus." *CL* II 862.

Mahomet's Pigeon, for instance,[1] and Prince Hohenlohe's Cures?[2]

24   pp 124–5 | § 3

Ist, nach der Behauptung der Physiologen, das Kriterion des Todes so ungewiss, dass es nur in der äussersten Folge desselben, der wirklichen Auflösung des Körpers sich unwidersprechlich zeiget; so mögen die Physiologen das unter sich ausmachen. Uns sagen die Apostel deutlich: *Christus habe die Verwesung nicht gesehen; Gott könnte es nicht zugeben, dass seinen Auserwählten die Verwesung nur berühre.*

[If, as the physiologists maintain, the criterion of death is so doubtful that it is unequivocally evident only in its most extreme consequence, in the actual dissolution of the body, then let the physiologists settle the question among themselves. The Apostles tell us clearly: *Christ was untouched by any decay; God could not permit his elect to be even touched by decay.*]

Besides, turn back to p. 39, line 12–17.[1] and then ask, are the Resurrection & Ascension the only Wonders related by these Historians, in the character of Eye-witnesses? Or only the conclusion of a long series? Does not the same John solemnly attest the resuscitation of the already putrid Lazarus:[2] & the twice feeding of 3 & 4000 men with a few Loaves & small Fishes?/[3]

25   p 125, pencil | § 3

[Footnote:] Es wäre also auch sehr unpassend, wenn man den gehässigen Namen "*Scheintod*" hier anbrächte. Vor göttlichen und menschlichem Gericht war Christus gestorben; er hatte vollbracht, was er vollbringen sollte, und seinen Geist den Händen Gottes

23[1] A pigeon or dove that Muhammad taught to pick seed placed in his ear and so persuaded his followers that he received communication from the Holy Ghost in the form of a dove. C could have found this story in e.g. Ralegh's *History of the World* bk I ch 1 §6.

23[2] Alexander Leopold Franz Emmerich, Prince of Hohenlohe-Waldenburg-Schillingsfürst (1794–1849), an RC priest who practised cure by prayer, had acquired by 1819 a large reputation as a miracle-worker at Munich and Bamberg and drew great crowds there until the authorities intervened. He moved to Vienna in 1821, and then to Hungary. C referred to him contemptuously in c Dec 1823, (*CN* IV 5081), to his "thaumaturgic operations" in a letter of 18 Mar 1826 (*CL* VI 572), and— in a note of Nov 1827 on Fleury—to his "passion for *Lying*" (N 35 f 42: *CN* V).

24[1] See **8** textus, above.

24[2] John 11.38–44.

24[3] Matt 14.21, 15.38; Mark 6.44, 8.9; first miraculous feeding only, Luke 9.14; John 6.10. The number given for the first incident (all four Gospels) is "about 5000"; for the second (Matt and Mark), 4000 and "about 4000".

übergeben; sein Leichnam ward begraben. Mich dünkt an diesem *Consummatum est* können wir uns begnügen, und es der Vorsehung überlassen, wie sie ihn erweckt habe. Ohne Zuthun der Menschen geschahe es gewiss.

[It would thus be also very unsuitable to apply here the odious term, "*semblance of death*".[a] Christ died before divine and human judgement; he had fulfilled what he was intended to fulfil and had delivered his spirit into God's hands; his body was buried. It seems to me that this "it is finished" should suffice us and that we should leave to providence the manner in which he was awakened. It certainly happened without human assistance.]

This is too, too bad!—What? is it of no consequence, whether Christ's resurrection were a miracle or an accident? If the latter, must not all his predictions have been forgeries?[1]

26 p 126, pencil

Er verschied, er athmete aus; todt ward er vom Kreuz genommen, mit Specereien und Leinen umhüllt, begraben. Nach Einem Tage und zweien Nächten, am Anbruch des dritten Tages war er erstanden und zeigte sich lebend. Äusserst kindisch wäre es, den Aposteln Vorwürfe zu machen, dass sie die Semiotik nicht besser verstanden, oder dem Nikodemus, dass er statt seiner Myrrhen und Aloen bei hundert Pfunden, nicht lieber die Rettungsmittel der heutigen Medicinischen Policei angewandt habe.

[He died, he expired; he was taken dead from the cross, wrapped in spices and linen, and buried. After one day and two nights, at dawn of the third day he rose and showed himself alive. It would be extremely childish to reproach the Apostles for not better understanding the symptomatology or Nicodemus for not applying the resuscitation methods of the present-day medical officers instead of his hundred pounds of myrrh and aloes.]

All this Trash might be silenced by one Question. Whatever Christ's state was, when taken from the Cross, real Death or only suspended animation,[1] was it for brought back again by such means, as he foreknew, could and did foretell?

27 p 127, pencil | § 4

Von Jenem [Nikodemus] war es edel, dass er sich dieses Todten nicht schämte und ihm eine so auszeichnende Bestattung gönnte; von diesen, den Weibern, wars ein Zeichen der Liebe, dass sie, Trotz der

---

[a] Or "*suspended animation*", the term C uses in **26**, below

25[1] Cf **23**, above, and **27**, below. textus, above. See also **14** and n 2, above,
26[1] Cf Herder's use of *Scheintod* in **25** and **28**, below.

Gesetze und der Gefahr der Verunreinigung, mitten in Tagen des grössesten Festes sich in das Grab des Todten wagten. Das Alles geschah, nicht in der mindesten Hoffnung einen Gestorbenen lebend zu finden.

[It was noble of the former [Nicodemus] that he was not ashamed of the deceased and bestowed on him such an excellent burial; for the women it was a sign of their love that despite the law and the danger of pollution, they dared enter the grave of the dead in the middle of the highest holiday. All this occurred without the least hope of finding a dead man alive.]

and yet Christ had told them of it repeatedly![1]

28　p 132, pencil | §10

Auf also! (gebietet uns die Geschichte der Auferstehung,) auf aus der Herzensträgheit, die dem Glaubwürdigsten zuweilen den Glauben weigert. *Der Heilige ist wirklich auferstanden*, und dadurch, eben nur dadurch ward das Christenthum gegründet. Ηγερθη ὁ Κυριος οντως.

[Onward! (the history of the resurrection commands us) arise from the heart-weariness that sometimes denies belief even in that which is most worthy of belief. *The Lord is risen indeed*, and thereby, only thereby, was Christianity founded. "The Lord is risen indeed".]

Impudent Sophistry! when it is clear that in Herder's System the whole burthen of the Proof, that Christ really *died* & rose again from Death to Life, rests on the visible Ascension.—

29　p +3

What is the great nostrum of Unitarianist[a]?[1]

To persuade (an easy Task) wealthy half-educated Tradesmen, and youths in the first Processes of Thinking, ~~when~~ that their Ignorance is sound Sense—Consequently those natural Doubts which meeting with the presumptuousness incident to youth and prosperity, which can only be counteracted by Docility and Reverence of ~~th~~ Great Men departed, are ripened at once into insolent *Positiveness*.[2] To such men Infidelity is a comparative Blessing—even as much as the giving up a quack Medicine to a sick man, even tho' he should not yet have called in a regular Physician.—He is more likely to do so.

[a] A slip for "Unitarianism"

27[1] Matt 12.40, 16.21, 17.23; Mark 9.31, 14.28; John 2.19.

29[1] For C on Unitarianism or modern Socinianism see *LS* (*CC*) 176–7, 181–4n, 254–8.

29[2] On the difference between positiveness and certainty see BLANCO WHITE *Practical Evidence* 11 n 2. Cf also HOOKER **48** and **49**.

Denique mihi quidem litterae ν paragogicae
ufus eo usque patere videtur, eam ut omnino ibi,
ubi vox loquentis requiefcit, addendam exiftimem.
Atque in poetis quidem, quorum omnis oratio ad
aurium aeftimationem compofita eft, non dubito,
quin in fine cuiusque verfus, qui quidem ultimam
fyllabam ancipitem habeat, addendum fit ν, quo
facilius in ea fyllaba vox confiftere et paufam face-
re poffit, antequam ad fequentem verfum pergat.
Id in iis verfibus faciendum effe, quorum ultima
fyllaba metri lege longa effe debet, vix, puto, erit,
qui neget. Ita quis eft, quin fentiat, longe afpe-
rius ad aures accidere illud, quod vulgo legitur
in Aefchyli Prometheo,

σήμηνον, ὅστις ἐν Φάραγγί σ' ὤχμασε,

quam quod fcribi debebat,

σήμηνον, ὅστις ἐν Φάραγγί σ' ὤχμασεν.

Ad hanc quoque rem advocari ea poterunt, quae
fupra dixi de fimili cautione Latinorum poetarum,
fyllabas, quas nulla ratione producere liceat, aegre
in fine pentametri elegiaci collocantium. Illud au-
tem difficilius fortaffe a multis concedetur, etiam
ubi in thefin, eamque brevem, dummodo non fit
ab ancipitis fyllabae ufu aliena, verfus exeat, ad-
dendum effe ν paragogicum. Dicent enim con-
fentaneum effe, ut, fi metri ratio ultimam fylla-
bam brevem effe iubeat, nihil morae obiiciatur,
quominus corripi ea fyllaba poffit. Nihilo tamen
minus, fi quis aures confuluerit, fateatur neceffe
eft, in cuiusque verfus extrema fyllaba diutius mo-
rari vocem debere, quo is verfus ab fequente ver-
fu iufto intervallo dirimatur. Nam fi quis non
pateretur in ifta fyllaba vocem parumper confifte-
re, fubito intercipienda foret, ne duorum verfuum

5. A page of J. G. J. Hermann *De emendenda ratione graecae grammaticae pars
prima* (Leipzig 1801) annotated by Coleridge in Latin. See HERMANN **1**
The British Library; reproduced by kind permission

JOHANN GOTTFRIED JAKOB HERMANN
1772–1848

De emendenda ratione graccae grammaticae pars prima. Accedunt Herodiani aliorumque libelli nunc primum editi. Leipzig 1801. 8°.

British Museum C 126 e 8

Inscribed "S T C" on the title-page, not in C's hand.

On c 25 Jan 1808 C wrote to De Q: "If you should meet with Hermann de Emendatione &c, in the course of a month or two (for I shall certainly not want it for two or three months...) and it be procurable at any decent price, be so good as to secure it for me." At the same time he asked for "Hermann's Hymns"; he came to own and annotated a copy of that too: see HOMERIC HYMNS. For De Q fulfilling a similar book-buying commission in Feb 1808 see BÖHME headnote. C also had some acquaintance with Hermann's "Commentatio de metris Pindari" included in Pindar *Carmina* ed C. G. Heyne (4 vols Göttingen 1798–9): see *CN* III 3721 and n (c Mar 1810). The reference to "Hermann's De Emend. Rat. Gramm. Gr. p. 319" in *CN* IV 4831 f 57ᵛ (c Sept 1821) is from Creuzer.

DATE. Unknown; possibly 1808, near the time of acquisition.

1   pp 22–3, cropped | Bk I ch 5 "De littera ν paragogica"

Ita quis est, quin sentiat, longe asperius ad aures accidere illud, quod vulgo legitur in Aeschyli Prometheo,

σήμηνον, ὅστις ἐν φάραγγί σ᾽ ὤχμασε,

quam quod scribi debebat,

σήμηνον, ὅστις ἐν φάραγγί σ᾽ ὤχμασεν.

[So who can fail to sense that what is commonly read in Aeschylus *Prometheus* as σήμηνον, ὅστις ἐν φάραγγί σ᾽ ὤχμασε falls much more harshly on the ears than what ought to be written...σ᾽ ὤχμασεν.]

Mihi quidem[1] το ν omittendum videtur in fine hujus versûs ob

[1] "It seems to me, however, that the ν (*n*) ought to be omitted at the end of the line because of the excessive accumulation of *n* sounds (-on, -en, -ang) and perhaps because at the end of the line the ν (*n*), since the word is dactylic, does not consort so well with the initial and medial *s* because of a sort of ti*ntinn*abulation of sound, and because of the double rise and stress of the voice in ὤχμασέν. Also, the *s* sound is extended through the whole word more than it should be; to my ear at least it sounds stronger than is pleasant. Indeed sometimes a certain

nimietatem Νυισμου (ον, εν, αγγ) et forsan quod sub fine versûs to[a] v, cum verbum dactylicum sit, non tam be⟨ne⟩ cum "σ" initiali & medio consentit, propter quiddam quasi tintinnabulum soni, et propter duplicatam arsin et emphasim vocis—σ' ὤχμασέν[b2] Sigmatismus ⟨quoque⟩ per totum verbum[c] plus justo profertur; & fortius quam dulce sonat—meis saltem auribus. Quin et infirmitas quædam in versûs conclusione aliquando [. . . . .][d] suas veneres habet, varietatis causâ, [. . . . .][d] hanc [? plane/vilant] [. . . . .][e] tintinnans.[3]

S. T. C.

Hanc regulam potius in Sophocle quam in Eschylo vel Euripide admittere[m] ut ex. gr. liberty, majesty, reverence, vix in Popio nostro, et Popi imitatoribus—sæpissime in Spensero, et seculo robustiorum poetaru[m] [. . . . .][f]

2 p 39 | 1 8 "De muta ι"

Id vocabulum [μορφή] nusquam in Iliade occurrit; composita autem ex eo in neutro carmine. Quo minus probo Ruhnkenii coniecturam πολύμορφοι in hymno Cereris v. 23. Iste locus, nisi fallor, ita scribendus est:

οὐδέ τις ἀθανάτων, οὔτε θνητῶν ἀνθρώπων
ἤκουσεν φωνῆς, τῶν τ' ἀγλαόκαρποι ἀλωαί.[1]

[This word [μορφή—form] occurs nowhere in the *Iliad*; and its compounds occur in neither poem [*Iliad* and *Odyssey*]. Therefore I think less of Ruhnken's conjecture πολύμορφοι in the *Hymn to Ceres* line 23. That passage, if I am not mistaken, should read: [as given above].]

[a] A slip for το
[b] Stress marks, not Greek accents, intended
[c] A slip for "versum"
[d] Cropped—about two or three words lost
[e] Cropped, with loss of perhaps one line of ms. The next legible word is on p 23
[f] A line lost in cropping

weakness at the end of a line has its own charms for the sake of variety...this... [? simply / they bleat]...tinkling...

"I would recognise this rule in Sophocles rather than in Aeschylus or Euripides, as for example liberty, majesty, reverence seldom occur in our Pope and his imitators, but very often in Spenser and in the age of more muscular poets".

1[2] The first stress-mark is stronger than the second.

1[3] Cis defending the generally accepted practice of his contemporaries: all Blomfield's editions (C annotated an early ed of his AESCHYLUS *Prometheus*, in which this is line 639) read ὤχμασε, as do Brunck, Porson, Dindorf, Schütz, Stanley, and others. Hermann states his new rule (p 20) that ν should be added (to the words that take it) whenever the voice pauses, including the ends of lines of verse, and was the first to apply the rule to this line of Aeschylus; both are accepted by modern editors. MATTHIAE *Copious Greek Grammar* (2 vols 1824) accepted the rule, acknowledging Hermann as its author.

2[1] "And not one of the immortals, nor of mortal men, and their fair-fruited fields, heard her voice."

Ipse² hanc conjecturam feceram, quod ad αλωαι refert: sed duram ελλειψιν του "ουδε", et mutationem periodi abruptam, nec homerici seculi, quis no†n sentit?

Personam dat Poeta terræ frugiferæ/ sunt in istis Hymnis antiquis multa, quæ hebraicùm spirant. Quid si Νυσιον πεδιον oliveti[s] celebre?³—Et MSS. Moscov. veram et vivam lectionem habeat?.— Sine dubio, grammaticaster quidam ελαιαι in margine scripsisse crcdatur; cum et hoc unǝus sensus του "αλωᾳ" est—at corruptio per se facillima.—⁴

3   pp 54–7 | ı xii "De consonantibus"

Ex his [ζ, θ, σχ] θ nullam habet controversiam. Id hodierni Graeci, pariter ac Britanni suum *th*, lingua ad dentes appellente pronunciant, ut medium sit inter *t* et *s*. Eumdemque huius litterae sonum etiam apud antiquos obtinuisse, multa documenta sunt, Dorica mutatio huius litterae in cognatam σ, ut Ἀσανάτα, σεῖος...

[Of these [consonants *z*, *th*, *sch*] θ causes no disagreement. Present-day Greeks, just like the British with their *th*, pronounce it by putting the tongue to the teeth, so that the sound is midway between *t* and *s*. There are many proofs that the same sound of this letter was used among the ancients, the

2² Translating the entire 2: "I had already made this conjecture as far as αλωαι [cultivated fields] is concerned: but who can fail to notice the harsh omission of the ουδε and the abrupt change of syntax, not characteristic of the Homeric age? The poet is personifying the fruitful Earth/ there are many things in these ancient Hymns that breathe a Hebraic tone. What if the 'Nysian plain [was] rich in olive-groves'?—And the Moscow MS has the true and vital reading? Undoubtedly some would-be grammarian can be supposed to have written ελεαι [olive trees] in the margin because this is one meaning of αλωαι, but the corruption is easy in itself."
2³ The Greek phrase is from line 17: Νύσιον ἄμ πεδίον—"on the Nysian plain", known only from this line, as the scene of the rape of Persephone.
2⁴ On this subject C has evidently been reading more than the work he is here annotating and the HOMERIC HYMNS ed Hermann (which see for his projected translation). The only ms of the *Hymn to*

Ceres is in the Moscow ms discovered in 1777 by C. F. Matthiae; thc hymn was first edited by David Ruhnken (Leyden 1780). In ms, lines 22–3 read: οὐδὲ... οὐδὲ...οὐδ' ἀγλαόκαρποι ἐλαῖαι. This text was found objectionable because the olive-trees were thought irrelevant and because of contradiction with lines 38–9, in which the mountains, the sea, and Demeter her mother did hear Persephone's cries. Ruhnken printed the ms reading as his text but (in 2nd ed 1782) suggested in a footnote the emendation οὐδ' ἀγλαόμορφοι (not πολύμορφοι) ἑταῖραι—"nor her fair-formed companions". In HOMERIC HYMNS Hermann read οὔτε... οὐδ' ἀγλαόκαρποι, acknowledging the change from οὐδέ to οὔτε but refraining from comment either on that or on his reading ἑταῖραι (companions) for ἐλαῖαι (olive-trees). After Ruhnken's 2nd ed, conjectural emendations increased with the next three editors—Mitscherlich (1787), Ilgen (1796), A. Matthiae (1800, 1805)—and then subsided.

Doric change of this letter into the cognate *s*, as in 'Ασανάτα [for Attic 'Αθανάτα], σεῖος [for Attic θεῖος]...]

Et hodie parvuli et qui balbutiant,[1] mutant apud nos Anglos th in s.— S quasi Consonans, σύμφωνον, esse videtur, et mediam naturam inter vocalem et spiritum habet. Est igitur pronunciationis prope automaticæ—quot Parvululos audivi proferre hansissiz pro hand-kerchief, &c—/ 'ΕΞ dialecto Romano sex—επτα septem/ post s m fortasse spiritui proximum, quod eliditur ante vocales, ut et s apud ~~an~~ veteres Latinos—& quod in Lingua Italica, Hispana, et~~semperc~~, ubique periit—et in Sicelicâ, qui u Romanum retinent—multu, vice molto, &c.

Nostr~~o~~is th et dipthongis addantur *ch* Germanicum (quin et Scotorum) et vocales de more Italorum et ore rotundo,[2] Græcè loquemur, haud quidem omnino ut prisci Græci loquebantur sed satis bene. Hoc Miltonus suadet[3]—hoc modo exceptis 2 vel 3 dipthongis impropiis*a* qui vix, et ⟨non⟩ nisi subtillimis Organis, apte distingui possint, omnis litera Græca suam propriam vim habebit.

a A slip for "impropriis"

3[1] "And today children and lispers, in English, change *th* to *s*.—*S* seems to be a quasi-Consonant (in Greek σύμφωνον), and stands midway between a vowel and a breathed sound. The pronunciation of it therefore is almost automatic—how many Small Children have I heard say *hansissiz* for *handkerchief*, &c.—/ Greek HEX is *sex* in Roman dialect—*hepta septem/* after *s*, *m* is perhaps closest to an aspirate, because it is elided before vowels, as was *s* also in old Latin, and because in Italian, Spanish, &c it disappears everywhere—even in the Sicilian language, in which they keep the Roman *u*—*multu* instead of *molto*, &c.

"To our *th* and our diphthongs let there be added German *ch* (which the Scots have too) and vowels in the Italian manner, with rounded mouth [and] we shall speak Greek not indeed exactly as the ancient Greeks spoke, but well enough. This is Milton's advice—and in this way, except for two or three improper diphthongs which could hardly be distinguished except by the most subtle Organs, every Greek letter will have its own value. We speak Greek, or rather ungreek, with a barbarous, indeed a most sound-murdering confusion of vowels. When I read a Greek writer in the manner of my countrymen I seem to myself to slaughter both the harmony of an almost divine language and my own ears."

Cf Vico on stammering and singing, which C quoted in May 1825 from *Scienza nuova* ch 5 § 451. *CL* v 465.

3[2] The phrase is familiar from Horace *Ars poetica* 323: "Graiis dedit ore rotundo Musa loqui" ("the Muse gave the Greeks...speech in well-rounded phrases"), but Horace is not referring to Greek pronunciation. C is thinking of the shape of the mouth while voicing the vowels.

3[3] Milton spoke of Latin pronunciation in "Of Education": "Their Speech is to be fashion'd to a distinct and clear pronunciation, as near as may be to the *Italian*, especially in the Vowels" if they are not "to smatter *Latin* with an *English* mouth". *Works* ed Birch (2 vols 1738) I 137. He seems not to have said anything about Greek pronunciation, however.

A Barbaruma, immo, φωνοφονοτατῳ, confusione vocalium Græce, vel potius ingræce,[a] loquimur angli. Dum lego scriptorem græcum de more patrio ipse mihi videor et linguæ prope divinæ harmoniam, et proprias aures jugulare.[4]

---

[a] The first two letters are written in larger characters

3[4] More detailed evidence of C's pronunciation of Greek appears in N Q ff 70–69 (*CN* v), summarised in H. COLERIDGE **29** n 1. Cf *CN* III 3792.

JOHN HEWITT
1614–1658

[Conjectural identification.]

Nine Select Sermons, preached upon special occasions in the parish church of St. Gregories by St. Pauls.... Together with his publick prayers before and after sermon. London [c 1655].

Not located; marginalia not recorded. Watson List 17: "Hewitts Sermons (one note)". *Lost List.*

PETER HEYLYN
1600–1662

Cyprianus Anglicus: or, the history of the life and death, of the most reverend and renowned prelate William [Laud]...Lord Archbishop of Canterbury, Primate of all England...and one of the Lords of the Privy Council to his late most sacred majesty King Charles the First...containing also the ecclesiastical history of the three kingdoms of England, Scotland, and Ireland, from his first rising till his death, &c. London 1671. F°.

British Museum Ashley 4776

Inscribed on p ⁻1 "Wᵐ Arundell his book 1691"; and on the title-page "J Watkins". In addition to C's annotations there are two sets of notes: (A) one set evidently by William Arundel, (B) the other unidentified but perhaps J. Watkins's: (A) pp 3, 11, 13, 14, 102, 111, 153, 158, 355, 373, 375, 380; (B) pp 50, 54, 69 (misprinted 67), 80, 136 (misprinted 146), 143, 171, 183, 187, 199, 203, 217, 243, 251, 253, 255, 320, 379, 383, 395, 422, 445, 481, 497, 502, 503. Corrections and marginal marks in pencil and in ink, not C's, on pp 96, 118, 124, 129, 238, 256, 341, 344, 347, 374, 453, 456.

C also owned a copy of Heylyn's *The History of the Sabbath* (1636)—BM C 126 c 2—but it is not annotated.

DATE. Autumn 1823–25; in association with the projected "Life of Leighton" (an early stage of *AR*), for which C had made a "laborious Collation of Spottiswood, Heylin" *et al* by 9 Sept 1823. *CL* v 300. At the same time he borrowed HOWIE from Allan Cunningham for the same purpose, and had annotated the two volumes of LAUD in Sion College Library. As part of an outline and notes for *AR* C transcribed the title-page of *Cyprianus Anglicus* and wrote a lively note on its typographical style. BM MS Egerton 2801 f 194 (in *IS* 198–9). Also, in c Feb–May 1825 he wrote, under the heading "Heylin's 'Necessary Introd. to his Life of Laud'.— " notes referring to pp 3 and 4 (cf 5, below). *CN* IV 5202.

1 p 5, pencil | "A Necessary Introduction to the Following History" § 6

But though the *Presbyters* or *Priests*, were both in *Order* and *Degree* beneath the *Bishops*, and consequently not enabled to exercise any publick Jurisdiction in *Foro judicii*, in the Courts of Judicature: yet they retained their native and original power in *Foro Conscientiae*, in the Court of Conscience, by hearing the confession of a sorrowful and afflicted *Penitent*, and giving him the comfort of *Absolution*, a power conferred upon them in their *Ordination*; in the Form whereof, it is prescribed that the *Bishop*, and the assisting *Presbyters*, shall lay their Hands upon the Head of the Party who is to be *Ordained Priest*, the Bishop only saying these words, *viz. Receive the* *] *Holy Ghost, whose sins thou doest forgive they are forgiven, and whose sins thou doest retain, they are retained; In the name of the Father, and the Son, and of the Holy Ghost, Amen.*

* I profess, I do not see any injurious or superstitious consequence of this. Either it *is*, or is *not*, a Sin in the Sight of God—if it is, and the Sinner is impenitent, assuredly his resistance to the admonition of God's appointed Minister, is an aggravation: if not, then there is no Sin to be retained. It is merely a mistaken, or uncharitable opinion of the Priest—for which He alone must answer.

S. T. C.

2 p 6, pencil | § 7

Confession made upon such security will be as saving to the *Fame* of the Penitent, as the *Absolution* to his Soul. In which respect it was neither untruly nor unfitly said by a learned Writer, *Dominus sequitur servum*, &c. Heaven (saith he) waits and expects the Priests Sentence here on Earth; for the Priest sits Judge on Earth, the Lord follows the Servant; and what the Servant binds or looseth here on Earth (*Clave non errante*) that the Lord confirms in Heaven.

Clave non errante.[1] If this have any meaning, it means, I presume, that if the Lord was of the same opinion before, this opinion would not be altered by the Priest's expressing the same. Has Christ entrusted every thing to a Bishop, *needful for Salvation*, which any & Christian is not permitted, nay, which every Christian is not bound, to *profess*?

3 pp 6–7, pencil | § 8

The like Authority is vested in the Priest or Presbyter at his *Ordination* for officiating the Divine Service of the Church, offering the Peoples Prayers to God, Preaching the Word, and Ministring the Holy Sacraments in the Congregation; Which *Offices*, though they

---

2[1] "The priest (or bishop) not being in error"—the key (*clavis*) being the sign of authority, with "power of binding and loosing", as granted to Peter (Matt 16.19).

may be performed by the *Bishops*, as well as the *Presbyters*: yet they perform them not as *Bishops*, but as *Presbyters* only.

How instantly all this High-priest Mummery would be dissipated by a simple consecutive History of a single Christian Church, Rome for example, from its first planting. In the most, the first Planter or Collector of the Church would be its Overseer, Episcopus or Bishop: and the Presbyters would follow. In others, the Elders or Presbyters would exist at and *as* the beginning; and a President, or Chairman, would follow.—[1]

4 p 7, pencil

Who, being a Christian, can avoid feeling the worldly, harsh, *unspiritual* Spirit of this bitter Factionary! I scarcely know a more unamiable Churchman, as a Writer, than Dr Heylin.[1]

S. T. C.

5 p 13 | §15

Thirdly, That *Images* are still used in the *Lutheran* Churches, upon which our first Reformers had a special eye; and that *Luther* much reproved *Carolostadius* for taking them out of such Churches, where before they had been suffered to stand, letting him know...that the worship of Images, was rather to be taken out of mens minds by diligent and painful preaching, then the Images themselves to be so rashly, and unadvisedly cast out of the Churches.

Vide. p. 3. "No regard paid to Luther"!—& yet too according to this High-Church Fanatic, Melancthon was called by Royal Letters!—[1]

3[1] For *Episcopus* and *Presbyter* see HERBERT **19** n 1.

4[1] See also **14** (at n 2), below, and HACKET *Century* **5** (at n 3).

5[1] "In the managing of which great business[i.e. the Reformation in England], they took the Scripture for their ground, according to the general explication of the ancient Fathers...No regard had to *Luther* or *Calvin*, in the procedure of their work, but only to the Writings of the Prophets and Apostles, *Christ Jesus* being the *Corner-stone* of that excellent Structure. *Melancthons* coming was expected (*Regiis Literis in* Angliam *vocatus* [called to England by Royal Letters], as he affirms in an Epistle to *Camerarius*)

but he came not over. And *Calvin* made an offer of his service to Arch-Bishop *Cranmer*...but the Arch-Bishop knew the man, and refused the other [? *misprint for* offer]; so it cannot be affirmed, that the *Reformation* of this Church, was either *Lutheran* or *Calvinian* in its first original." C discusses this passage in detail in *CN* IV 5202. As early as 1627 Heylyn, in a deliberately contentious debate with the regius professor of divinity in Oxford, had asserted (with learned evidence) that the Church of England had derived directly from the Church of Rome and not from the influence of the leading Protestant dissenters. This argument first drew Heylyn

6   pp 18–19, pencil | § 21

The *Pope* they deprived of that unlimited Supremacy, and the Church of *Rome* of that exorbitant power, which they formerly challenged over them; yet did they neither think it fit to leave the Church without her lawful and just Authority; nor safe to put her out of the protection of the Supream Governour. Touching the first, it was resolved in the 20. Article, *"That the Church hath power not only to decree Rites and Ceremonies, but also in Controversies of Faith"*, as the English, *Ecclesia habet Ritus et Ceremonias Statuendi jus, et in fidei controversiis Authoritatem*, as it is in the Latin.

Surely, Dr H. was not so mean a Scholar, as not to know, he was falsely translating the Latin words. He could not have overlooked the so obvious, so prominent Antithesis of *Jus* and *Authoritatem*. The Church had full power, original *right*, in the one; and a reverend *Authority* in the other.[1]

S. T. C.

7   p 19, pencil

For in the 34. Article it is thus declared, "That whosoever through his private judgment willingly and purposely doth openly break the Traditions and Ceremonies of the Church, which be not repugnant unto the word of God, and be ordained and approved by common Authority, ought to be rebuked openly...". More power then this, as the See of *Rome* did never challenge; so less then this, was not reserved unto it self by the Church of *England*.

a Lie! resting on a lying translation and perversion of the 20th Article[1]

---

to Laud's attention and commended him as a useful colleague. Cf **17**, below, and for Heylyn's record as a malicious controversialist see **14** n 2, below.

6[1] The "Latin words", with Heylyn's translation, are in the textus; see also **7**, below. Heylyn's version, by ignoring the word *Authoritatem*, places "Controversies of Faith" on an equal footing with "Rites and Ceremonies" under the power of decree. C would translate it literally as: "The Church hath the right/power...and [hath] authority...".

7[1] For the 20th Article of the Acts of Convocation 1562 (i.e. the "Thirty-nine Articles"), with Heylyn's translation, see **6** textus, above. In BCP this article reads: "The Church hath power to decree Rites or Ceremonies, and authority in Controversies of Faith: And yet it is not lawful for the Church to ordain any thing that is contrary to God's Word written, neither may it so expound one place of Scripture, that it be repugnant to another...."

8 p 24, pencil | § 27

Many of the *Calvinian* party understand nothing by Christs *Descent* into Hell, but his *Descending* into the Grave; and then his descending into Hell will be the same with his being buried.

Was H. ignorant, that this clause did not exist in the Creed till after the 6ᵗʰ Century? It seems to have been levelled against some heretical or infidel assertion, that Christ's Death on the Cross was merely a Trance, or state of suspended animation.[1]

9 p 32, pencil | § 35

It was the Heresie of *Pelagius* to ascribe so much power to the will of man, in laying hold upon the means of his Salvation, *Ut gratiam Dei necessariam non putaret*, that he thought the Grace of God to be unnecessary, of no use at all. And *Luther* on the other side ascribed *]* so little thereunto, that he published a Book entituled, *De servo Arbitrio*, touching the servitude of the will; in which he held that there was no such thing as *Free-Will...*

* I do not believe, that H. understood or has rightly stated Luther's opinion. If there be a Servum *Arbitrium*, then there must be an Arbitrium.[1] Luther was zealous against the pretence of a *free* will in unregenerate Man.

10 p 58, pencil | Pt ɪ bk 1

And knowing how much the Peace of this Church did depend upon it, he managed a secret Correspondency with King *James* in *Scotland*, insinuating unto him the necessity of conforming the Churches of both Kingdoms in Government and Forms of Worship, and laying down a plot for restoring *Episcopacy* to that kirk, without noise or trouble: Which counsel being advisedly followed by King *James* before his coming into *England*, was afterwards so well pursued (though not without some violent strugling of the *Presbyterians* of that Kingdom) that on the 21. day of *October* in the year 1609. the designed Bishops of *Glascow*, *Brechen*, and *Gallo-Way* received Episcopal Consecration in the Chappel of *London*-house...

8[1] See DONNE *Sermons* COPY B **125** and nn 2, 3.

9[1] If a "Slavish *Will*", then a "Will"— i.e. a "Free-Will"—both terms being in textus.

And what was the final Result of all this neat priestly plot? Sullen Faction thro' James's reign, & the Scaffold of his Successor, with Laud for his Avant Courier![1]

11   p 59, pencil

[Bancroft] being dead, there was a Consultation amongst some of the Bishops and other Great men of the Court, whom to commend unto King *James* for his Successor in that *see* [as Chancellor of Oxford]. They knew that *Montague* and *Abbot* would be venturing at it, but they had not confidence enough in either of them, both of them being extremely popular, and such as would ingratiate themselves with the *Puritan* Faction... And thereupon it was resolved to fix on *Andrews* for the man.... The Motion was no sooner made, but it was embraced, and they departed from the King with as good assurance as if the business had been done.... In confidence whereof... others lessened their accustomed diligence about the King, and thereby gave an opportunity to the Earl of *Dunbar*... to put in for *Abbot*... and he... carried it, and had the Kings Hand to the passing of the publick Instruments, before the other Bishops ever heard of the Plot: But when they heard of it, there was no *Remedy* but Patience;[a] but it was *Patience perforce*, as the Proverb hath it: For much they feared that *Abbot* would unravel all the Web which *Bancroft* with such pains had weaved...

The strange manner, in which the Churchmen of this age unite ascetic rigor of Life with all the wiles, intrigues, & inquietudes of worldly Ambition, & thirst of preferment, is highly characteristic.

12   p 157, pencil | Bk 3

For on that very day which gives date to the said *Instructions*, the most Learned and Reverend Bishop *Andrews*, Bishop of *Winton*, and Dean of his Majesties Chappel-Royal, departed this Life at his *Episcopal* House in *Southwark*.... A man he was of such extraordinary Abilities, that I shall rather chuse to express his Character by the Pen of others, than my own. Thus then says own of our late Historians: *] "This year we lost the stupendiously profound Prelate Doctor *Andrews*... an excellent Disputant, in the Oriental Tongues surpassing knowing; so studiously devoted to the Doctrine of the Ancient

------

[a] From here to end of textus marked with a line in the margin

10[1] Laud was executed in 1645, Charles I in 1649.

Fathers, as his extant Works breathe nothing but their Faith...so venerable in his Presence, so grave in his Motions, so pious in his Conversation, so primitive in all."

* Bishop Andrews is one & a prominent instance of the difference between the men of their age, and the men of after Ages, or rather of all ages. A wise, pious & right learned Man he was; but who could *now* from the perusal of his works have guessed at these stupendous Attributions?[1]

S. T. C.

13 pp 158–9, pencil

...some of the Preachers did their parts according as they were required by the said *Instructions*, amongst whom *Sibthorp*, Vicar of *Brackly* in *Northamptonshire*, advanced the Service, in a Sermon *] Preached by him at the Assizes for that County. *The scope of which Sermon was to justifie the Lawfulness of the general Loan, and of the Kings imposing Taxes by his own Regal Power, without consent in Parliament, and to prove, that the people in point of Conscience and Religion ought chearfully to submit to such Loans and Taxes without any opposition.*

* What more can we need, to justify the jealousy, the remonstrances, & finally the active resistance of our Ancestors? The Licensing of this treasonable Sermon, against the will of the Arch-bishop, was, doubtless, a grievous misdemeanor on the part of Laud, & merited punishment. But unhappily for the Church of England—the consequences are felt even at this day—the Bishops generally, as well as Laud, saw no difference between the French & Spanish Monarchs, & the limited King of G. B./

14 pp 160–1, pencil

The Fleet and Forces before mentioned being in a readiness, and the Duke [of Buckingham] provided for the Voyage, it was not thought

---

12[1] For Lancelot Andrewes see ANDERSON COPY B **32** and n 2. C considered that Andrewes—like Donne, Hacket, and Jeremy Taylor—showed in his work "a strong *patristic* leaven" that placed him below the order of "Apostolic" divines. See DONNE *Sermons* COPY B **1**. Although C had a high regard for Andrewes's learning, and for his spiritual and intellectual power (see DONNE *Sermons* COPY B **132** and *TT* 12 Jan 1834), there are few direct traces of C reading his works. He owned a copy of the *XCVI. Sermons* (1661 f°)—it is now in VCL, not annotated—and two other works of Andrewes in folio in Green's library may have been C's.

either safe or fit that the Duke himself should be so long absent, without leaving some assured Friend about his Majesty, by whom all practices against him might be either prevented or suppressed, and by whose means the Kings affections might be alwaies inflamed towards him; To which end *Laud* is first desired to attend his Majesty to *Portsmouth*, before which the Navy lay at Anchor, and afterwards to await the whole Progress also...

And Heylin coolly and complacently relates these damning proofs of Laud's base creatureship to Buckingham!! And then what must not both he & the Duke have thought of the King, who needed so much watching![1] But above all floats the baseness & true priestly bitterness & worldly-mindedness of Heylin himself. And what an appetite for persecution the Fellow had![2]

14[1] In BM MS Egerton 2800 f 170^v C noted "Laud's practical Servility to the Duke of Buckingham". On Laud generally see **17**, below, and HACKET *Century* **11** and n 1. See also LAUD.

14[2] Brilliant, learned, combative, and intensely ambitious to attain a position of ecclesiastical and political power, Heylyn at the beginning of his career deliberately courted attention by acrimonious debate and controversial writing. In 1630 Laud made him one of the King's chaplains and then manoeuvred him into the prebendary of Westminster Cathedral with the express purpose of harassing John Williams, then dean of Westminster (later abp of York, the subject of Hacket's *Scrinia*), principal opponent of Laud, who was then in disgrace at Court. Heylyn pursued Williams by every possible means, not least in print, until Williams was suspended by the Star Chamber in Jul 1637. Heylyn had also, in 1633, prepared the first case against Prynne (see HACKET *Scrinia* **11** n 1). At the dissolution of the Short Parliament in 1640 he was instrumental in introducing to Convocation seventeen new canons asserting the divine right of kings, but these did not prevail and Charles had to call the Long Parliament. By that time—early 1641—with the impeachment of Laud, the release of Williams, and the

reinstatement of Prynne, the tide had turned against Heylyn. Forced to withdraw into retirement, he was declared delinquent in 1642, his house and library were stripped of their contents, and he was left to wander destitute at the mercy of his friends. Nevertheless, although he had been blind since 1651, he continued to publish controversial books and pamphlets, and in his last years completed his most important work, comprising a history of the ecclesiastical issues of his time and a vindication of Laud: *Ecclesia vindicata* (1657), *Ecclesia restaurata* (1661); and after his death, *Cyprianus anglicus* (1668) and *Aerius redivivus, or the history of Presbyterianism* (1670) were published. After the Restoration he was treated with respect but was too infirm to assume the offices that might otherwise have been assigned to him. See also **4** and n 1, above.

In the first part of his *Examen historicum, or a Discovery...of the Mistakes...in Some Modern Histories* (1658–9) he attacked Thomas Fuller's *Church-History*; to Heylyn's attack on William Sanderson's *History of Charles I* in the second part Fuller replied in *The Appeal of Iniured Innocence*—a response that led to friendship between the two men.

15 p 170, pencil

For his Majesty looking on him [Manwaring] in that conjuncture as one that suffered in his cause, preferred him first to the Parsonage of *Stamford-Rivers* in *Essex*, (void not long after by the promotion of *Mountague* to the See of *Chichester*) afterwards to the Deanery of *Worcester*; and finally to the Bishoprick of St. *Davids*.

And yet after all this the Royalists, & (o shame!) still existing Partizans of the Martyr blame the Parliament for not *trusting* the King!!—the Martyr?—Yea, verily; but it was to the vice of Lying.[1]

16 p 176, pencil

Taken upon suspicion, and questioned about the Murder [of Buckingham], he [i.e. John Felton] made no scruple to avow it as a meritorious Act, of which he had more cause to glory than to be ashamed: And being afterwards more cunningly handled by one of his Majesties Chaplains (sent to him from the Court of purpose to work him to it) he confessed plainly and resolvedly, That he had no other motive to commit that Murder, but the late *Remonstrance*, in which the Duke had been accused for being the Cause of all the Grievances and Mischiefs in the Common-wealth.

The naivtè, with which Heylin relates this, is exquisite—the more, that he had before assigned the true cause, that Felton brooded over the wrong he had suffered from the Duke, in being passed over in the Service.—But the Chaplain, the cunning Isaac![1] & sent for this very purpose!!—

17 p 177, pencil

... Which being perceived by those of the Town, who had placed their last hopes in this Attempt, they presently set open their Gates, casting themselves upon the Mercy of their Natural Prince, whose Government and Authority they had for so many years before both opposed and slighted. And on the other side, being well assured of that infinite anguish and disconsolation which *Laud* (his now most trusty Servant) must needs suffer under, by the most barbarous Assassination of so dear a Friend [the Duke of Buckingham], he [the

15[1] See HACKET *Scrinia* **45** n 1 and cf **41** and n 1. See also **18**, below.
16[1] I.e. Isaac Mendoza in Sheridan's *The Duenna*—a Portuguese Jew who prided himself that "I'm cunning, I fancy; a very cunning dog, ain't I?", and claims that he can't be duped, yet is duped by everyone.

King] dispatched *Elphiston* his Cup-bearer with a *gracious* Message to comfort him in those disquiets of his Soul; and on the neck of that, a Letter of his own hand-writing to the same effect.

And this creature called himself a Protestant! Judge by him of his Master and Patron! It is idle to pretend that Laud's *Affections* were not towards the Papists & the papistic Governments, however in some speculative points he might protestantize.[1]

18   p 178, pencil

He knew, that by the Laws of the Land all Ministers were to read the Book of Articles audibly and distinctly, in the hearing of their Parishioners, when they first entred on their Cures; and that by the Canons of the Church, all that took Orders or Degrees were publickly to subscribe unto them. A Declaration to the same effect before those Articles must needs give such a general signification of his Majesties pleasure, that no body could from thenceforth pretend ignorance of it.... Upon which prudent considerations he moved his Majesty that the Book of Articles might be reprinted; and such a Declaration placed before them as might preserve them from such misconstructions as had of late been put upon them, and keep them to their native literal and *Grammatical* sense.

Laud's first Act, as "*the sage*" Premier,[1] to indulge the passions of his Faction by rekindling the theological discords!—and under what circumstances both of the King & Country! One's pity for Charles's fate is lost in one's contempt for his narrow-mindedness, and one's Astonishment at his folly and infatuation.[2]

S. T. C.

17[1]   See DONNE *Sermons* COPY B **1** and esp BAXTER *Reliquiae* COPY B **76** n 1. Cf HACKET *Century* **11** and n 1.

18[1]   On the previous page (p 177) Heylyn has written: "He [Charles I] looks upon him [Laud] now as his Principal Minister well practised in the Course of his Business, of whose fidelity to his Person, and perspicacity of Judgment in Affairs of State, he had found such good proof...".

18[2]   See also **15**, above.

JAMES ABRAHAM HILLHOUSE
1789–1841

Hadad a dramatic poem. New York 1825. 8°.

A fragmentary unbound copy of the preliminaries: pp [iii–xii], comprising title-page (verso with New York copyright notice), dedication leaf (verso blank), Introduction (pp [vii]–x), Dramatis Personae (verso blank).

Yale University (Beinecke Library)

MS TRANSCRIPT. Cornell University (Wordsworth Collection) *Healey* 2613: Anne Gillman transcript of c 1825.

DATE. Probably Mar–Jun 1827: dated Jun 1827 in *LR* I 210. HNC printed C's footnote (†) to 1 as *TT* 10 Mar 1827, but in the *TT* ms this was crowded in without a date. 1 §3 was also printed in *TT* variatim under date 1 May 1825, but in the ms it appears under date 10 Mar 1827. In a notebook entry of Jan 1828 C refers to the subject of n 11.

1   pp [vi]–xi, 2nd footnote in pencil | Introduction

The belief in a former intercourse between mankind, and the good and evil beings of the Spiritual world, harmonizes with the solemn twilight of the scriptural ages, and is sustained by many declarations *] of Holy Writ. The passages involving that part of the doctrine which relates to the Fallen Spirits—for example, those reciting the necromantic power of the Egyptian Magicians, or the Sorceress of Endor...and the Demonian possessions of a later period—are explained, by some paraphrasts, in a manner which precludes spiritual agency; but by most commentators, supported by the common faith of the Christian world, they are understood as simple narrations of actual occurrences....Dr. Gray, in his observations on the Book of Tobit, which he considers as entitled to the credit of an authentic historical narrative, remarks: "With respect to the agency of Angels, there is nothing inconsistent with reason, received opinions, or Scripture, in supposing a limited superintendence of Superior Beings. We know, indeed, that under the peculiar circumstances of the Jewish economy, the ministry of Angels was manifestly employed in subserviency to God's designs; and that particular personages were occasionally favoured with their familiar intercourse. It is likewise unquestionable, that before the power and

1105

malevolence of Evil Spirits were checked and restricted by the control of our Saviour, their open influence was experienced."

Thus understood, the Scriptures offer scenes of unrivalled wildness and sublimity...

* The apocryphal Book of Tobit consists of a very simple but beautiful and interesting Family Memoir, into which some ⟨later⟩ Jewish Poet or Fabulists of Alexandria wove the ridiculous and frigid Machinery, borrowed from the popular superstitions of the Greeks (tho' probably of Egyptian Origin) and accommodated, clumsily enough, to the purer Monotheism of ⟨the⟩ Mosaic Law.[1]—N.B. The Rape of the Lock is another instance of a simple Tale, thus inlayed at a ~~lat~~later period—tho' in this by the same author, and with a very different result[2]—Now unless M[r] Hillhouse is Romanist enough to receive this Nursery-tale Garnish of a domestic Incident as grave History and Holy Writ (*for which even from learned Catholics he would gain more credit as a very obedient Child of the Church than as a Biblical Critic—*) he will find it no easy matter to support this assertion of his, by ~~any~~ the passages of Scripture, ~~interpreted~~ here referred to, consistently with any sane interpretation of their import and purpose.

First—"the Fallen Spirits". This is the mythological Form (or, if you will, the Symbolical Representation) of a profound Idea necessary as the *Pre-suppositum*[3] of the Christian Scheme,†[a] or a Postulate of Reason ⟨indispensable⟩ if we would render the existence of a World of Finites compatible with the assumption of a super-mundane God not one with the World. In short, t~~h~~eis IDEA is the *Condition*, under which alone ⟨the Reason of Man⟩ ~~we~~ can

† The Idea, to which reference is here made, is the possibility of a birth of Evil, originating in a pure Act of the Will, exclusive of all motive or temptation ab extra[4]

a C's footnote indicator and his corresponding footnote are both in pencil

1[1] *Tobit*, originally written in Aramaic or Hebrew in c 200 B.C., is now considered to have a historical centre enriched by legendary and folklore materials. Persian influences to be seen in the demonology are confirmed by the Dead Sea scrolls.

1[2] Pope's *The Rape of the Lock*, composed in 1711, was first printed in Lintott's *Miscellany* anonymously as a poem of 334 lines in two cantos. In 1713 Pope added to it and published it separately in five cantos. Thereafter a few verbal changes were made, in 1717 a speech of thirty lines was added, and verbal changes were again made in 1736. In its final form the poem was 794 lines long.

1[3] The first premiss or Prothesis. See HEGEL 3 and n 1.

1[4] "From the outside". On the relation between the "Devil" and the origin of evil see n 17, below.

retain the doctrine of an Infinite and Absolute Being & yet keep clear of Pantheism, as exhibited by Benedict Spinoza*[a]

2nd the Egyptian Magicians.—This whole narrative is, a probabley, ⟨a⟩ Relic of the old diplomatic Lingua Arcana,[6] or State-symbolique —in which the prediction of Events is expressed as the immediate Causing of them. Thus the Prophet is said to destroy the city, the destruction of which he predicts. Εἰργασται.[b7]—The word which our version renders by "enchantments" signifies ᶜMetallic Plates— astrological Almanachs.[d8]

* Pantheism; or the Scheme of Spinosa. (G = God. W = World.)

$W - G = 0$. i.e. the World without God is an impossible Idea

$G - W = 0$ i.e. God without the World is $d.°$

Christian Theism

$W - G = 0$—i.e, as in the Spinosistic Scheme

$G - W = G$. i.e. But God without the World is God, the Self-sufficing.[5]

---

[a] Here C has written "*See* † above, †", the footnote being crowded into the head of p [vi] above the beginning of 1 [b] Cancelled in pencil

[c-d] Here *LR* I 211 continues with an attempt at correction: "...'flames or burnings,' by which it is probable that the Egyptians were able to deceive the spectators, and substitute serpents for staves. See [John] Parkhurst [*An Hebrew and English Lexicon* (1762)] *in voce*." *LR* then omits § 3, and resumes at "And with regard to the possessions in the Gospels..."

1[5] For other versions of this scheme see "*Prometheus*" (*LR* II 328–9) and *TT* 10 Mar 1827.

1[6] "Secret Language". *Arcana* is the word in Vulgate of Exod 7.11 corresponding to AV "enchantments": see n 8, below.

1[7] C found much significance in the word εἰργασται (here cancelled)—"it is done" or "it has been done"; cf *CN* IV 5394. He sometimes seems to think that the word occurs in the Bible, although it does not, and sometimes in Euripides *Medea*; see *CL* IV 214. The word actually occurs in Euripides *Orestes* (line 284), which play C was reading with James Gillman Jr in c Mar 1826. See *CN* IV 5136. The word that AV translates "it is done" in e.g. Luke 14.22, Rev 16.17 is γέγονε; "it is finished" in John 19.30 is τετέλεσται; the verb for "they did" (with their enchantments) in Exod 7.11, 22 and 8.7, 18 is (in Septuagint) ἐποιήσαν. See also C's annotation on WEBSTER quoted in n 8, below.

1[8] Cf John WEBSTER *The Displaying of Supposed Witchcraft* (1677) p 134 (not annotated): "There is also the word לאט involvit, velavit, arcanum, and the like, which the vulgar Latin do attribute to *Pharoahs* Magicians, when our translation saith, *and they did in like manner with their inchantments*: It is *et fecerunt similiter per sua arcana*, thinking the word had been derived from לאט *arcanum*, when it is really from להט flamma, lamina; a polisht and bright piece of metal...". See also p 155: "...the word being *Belahatem* ought to have been rendered, *suis laminis*...that is, with their bright plates of metal, for the word doth not signifie Inchantments in any one place in all the Old Testament....Metalline bright plates framed under certain fit constellations, and insculped with certain figures by which naturally (and without any Diabolical assistance) they did perform strange things, and made the shapes of some things appear to the eye." Webster goes on to discuss (p 158) "the certain efficacy of Planetary Seals", and (pp 159ff) the effects of metals. Webster is discussing Exod 7.11; cf 7.22 and 8.7, 18. C similarly

3. The Witch (Hebrew Ob, i.e. Bladder a or Ventriloquist)[9] of Endor is a simple record of the Facts, the solution of which the sacred Historian leaves to the Reader. It was evidently a g trick of Ventriloquism *got up* by the Courtiers & Friends of Saul to prevent him, if possible, from hazarding an engagement with an army as so despondent and oppressed with Bodings of Defeat.[10] Saul did not *see* Samuel—The Woman only pretends to see him—(Compare Capt[n] Lyon's account of the Scene in the Cabin with the Esquimaux *Bladder* or Conjurer. It is scarcely possible not to be reminded of the *Bladder*-Witch of Endor.)[11]—And then what does this Samuel do?—Merely repeat the Prophecy known to all Israel which the true Samuel had given some years before.—For the true sense of the

suggests in WEBSTER pp 84–5, obviously alluding to these same passages in Exod, that "we may throughout render the words—& this the Priests had likewise predicted in their Almanachs, or meteoro- and astro-logical Reports to the Government". Cf BIBLE COPY B 7 and nn 1–3.

1[9] See 1 Sam 28.7ff. C must again have WEBSTER in mind, pp 120–31, 165–6; esp p 120, in which Webster, discussing Deut 18.10–14, explains that the Hebrew *Ob* means either (*a*) a bottle (Job 32.19) or—quoting for the philological evidence V. Schindler (who also gives the Vulgate equivalent *Pytho*)—(*b*) an evil spirit so called "because those that had it...being pufft up with wind, did swell like blown bladders, and the unclean spirit, being interrogated did forth of their bellies give answers of things past, present and to come, whence also they were called ἐγγαστρίμυθοι, *ventriloqui*, speakers in the belly, or out of the belly". The word is also used, as C correctly implies, of the person possessed, the witch. Cf also e.g. BIBLE COPY B 10 and n 1, H. COLERIDGE 8, *TT* 1 May 1823, *CN* III 3753, 4409.

1[10] See again 1 Sam 28.7ff, discussed in WEBSTER (pp 165–77), which favours the view that the Witch was an impostor.

1[11] George Francis Lyon (1795–1832)—C also refers to him in *The Delinquent Travellers* lines 3–4: *PW* (EHC) I 444—in *The Private Journal of Captain G. F. Lyon, of H.M.S. Hecla, during the Recent Voyage of Discovery* [in 1821–3] *under Captain Parry* (1824) gives two accounts of Toolemak, the principal male wizard or conjuror of Igloolik, calling up his patron spirit Tornga (female) from the sea: pp 358–61, 365–7. In view of N 36 ff 76ᵛ–77 (17 Jan 1828)—"(*Ob*—Ventriloquist, ignorantly rendered *Witch*. See Captain Lyon's most interesting Account of the Esquimaux *Bladder* & the Scene that took place in his Cabin)"—C evidently has the first of these in mind. The ceremony was conducted in total darkness, the wizard's old wife singing throughout. Toolemak for some time "chanting to his wife with great vehemence", began "turning himself rapidly round, and in a loud powerful voice vociferated for Tornga with great impatience, at the same time blowing and snorting like a walrus". Presently "His wife...informed me very seriously that he had dived, and that he would send up Tornga. Accordingly, in about half a minute...the old woman informed me that Tornga was come to answer my questions. I accordingly asked several questions...to each of which inquiries I received an answer by two loud slaps on the deck, which I was given to understand were favourable. A very hollow, yet powerful voice, certainly much different from the tones of Toolemak, now chanted for some time, and a strange jumble of hisses, groans, shouts, and gabblings like a turkey, succeeded in rapid order." At length the spirit, exhausted, "asked leave to retire".

passages in the Laws of Moses Consult Webster's admirable Treatise on Witchcraft[12]—and with regard to the *Possessions* in the Gospels, bear in mind first of all, the *Spirits* are not necessaryily Souls or *I*'s (Ichheiten or Self-consciousness*a*)[13] and that the most ludicrous absurdities would follow from taking them as such in the Gospel Instances.—Secondly, that the Evangelist who has recorded the most of these incidents, himself says—"who are likewise called *moon-struck* or Lunatics."[14]—while St John names them simply, diseased or deranged Persons.[15] That Madness may result from Spiritual Causes, and not only or principally from physical ailments, may readily be admitted/. Is not our Will itself a *Spiritual* Power? Is it not the *Spirit* of the Man? The *mind* of a rational & responsible Being (i.e. of a Free-agent) is a Spirit: tho' it does not follow that all Spirits are *minds*. Who shall dare determine what spiritual Influences may not arise out of the collective evil Wills of wicked Men? Even the bestial Life, sinless in animals and *their* Nature, may when awakened in the Man & by his own act admitted into his Will, become Spiritual Influences—He receives a a Nature with his Will, which by this very act becomes a Corrupt Will: and Vice versâ, this Will becomes his Nature, & thus a *corrupt* Nature.—All this may be conceded—and this is all, that the recorded Words of our Saviour[16] absolutely require in order to receive an appropriate sense—but this is altogether different from making Spirits to be Devils, and Devils self-conscious Individuals—[17]

a LR reads "self-consciousnesses"

1[12] For **WEBSTER** see n 8, above. C here refers to Deut 1.14–18, which Webster discusses with related passages in his ch 6 (pp 106–36), maintaining that "there is not one word [in Scripture] that signifieth a familiar Spirit or a Witch".

1[13] See also **HACKET** *Century* **22** and n 2.

1[14] Matt 4.24: "they brought unto him...those which were lunatick"; cf 17.15—in both cases the word for "lunatic" being from σεληνιάζεσθαι, "to be moon-struck".

1[15] St John does not recognise "possessions". See e.g. the cases of disease and infirmity in John 5.3–14.

1[16] E.g. Matt 7.17–18.

1[17] Cf above, at n 4. In c Sept 1823 C noted: "...And here we have the abysmal Mystery of the Devil, the Evil One—the Contrary of God, absolute emptiness as God is the absolute Fullness, a mere Potence as God is a pure Act, wherein all is that actually is—a hidden Fire, for ever seeking a base in which it may actualize & finding it only to convert it into its own essence, which is necessarily baseless...and still...roaming about, like an hungry Lion, seeking whom it may devour. For it is indeed an eternal Hunger, and the very *Sting* of Famine. Eternal because below all Time even as God is eternal by transcendency of all Time—and unintelligible, because an Outcast from the intelligence even as God [is] incomprehensible as containing all intelligence. And lastly, Eternal Death as God is eternal Life....The unbelief, the unconsciousness of the Devil is the characteristic of our Age—and a perilous symptom of the spread of his Dominion...." *CN* IV 4998. See also *CN* II 2320, III 3866.

THOMAS HOBBES
1588–1679

Leviathan, or the Matter, Forme, and Power of a Common-wealth Ecclesiasticall and Civil. London 1651. F°.

Not located.

Thomas Poole's copy.

MS TRANSCRIPT. University of Texas (Humanities Research Center): copy used for *NTP*; on p 11 of "Marginal Notes of S. T. Coleridge inserted in various books belonging to Mr Poole—", for which group of transcripts see HAYLEY headnote. The annotations are here printed from MS TRANSCRIPT.

DATE. Probably 1807, at Nether Stowey.

1 p 4 | Pt I "Of Man" ch 1 "Of Sense"

But the Philosophy-Schools, through all the Universities of Christendom, grounded upon certain Texts of *Aristotle*, teach another doctrine; and say, For the cause of *Vision*, that the thing seen, sendeth forth on every side a *visible species* (in English) a *visible shew*, *apparition*, or *aspect*, or *a being seen*; the receiving whereof into the Eye, is *Seeing*.

The Schoolmen taught in other words the very same doctrines that are now taught.—They gave to the external a power of calling the sense into action,—some affirming that they did so *formaliter*, i.e. as a dog impresses reflection on a mirror,—others *eminenter*, as the Painter's brush impresses the figure of the dog, on a canvas, or rather as a magnet will arrange steel filings into a circle.—[1]

2 p 197 | Pt III "Of a Christian Common-wealth" ch 32 "Of the Principles of Christian Politiques"

…how great soever the miracle be, yet if it tend to stir up revolt against the King, or him that governeth by the Kings authority, he that doth such miracle, is not to be considered otherwise than as sent to make triall of their allegiance. For those words, *revolt from the*

---

[1] [1] C's most brilliant illustration of the Scholastic distinction between *eminenter* and *formaliter*. Cf BÖHME 12 n 1.

Lord your God, are in this place equivalent to *revolt from your King*. For they had made God their King by pact at the foot of Mount *Sinai*...

If by King, be meant God only, or such as teach & do the will of the true God, this is not only true, but a mere truism. But if by King be meant any constituted Authority, as the Emperor of Japan, or Domitian, it is a *wicked lie*; and all the Miracles of the Prophets & Apostles must have been sent by God not to be believed, but merely to try the allegiance of Subjects to their Tyrant.[1]

2[1] The argument here is parallel—perhaps intentionally—to the argument of anti-evolutionists who held that God had placed the fossils in the rocks to tantalise sceptical rationalists and test the faithful. Cf C's belief, stated in various forms, that "thank Heaven, it is still our possession, as well as birth-right, that we have a KING, and no *Monarch*!" *EOT* (*CC*) I 136–7 and n 5.

JOHANN HEINRICH HOFFBAUER

b 1796

Der Mensch in allen Zonen der Erde. Leipzig 1832. 12°.

Harvard University (Houghton Library)

From J. H. Green's library. Bookplate of Henry W. Poor on the front paste-down. A leaf is inserted at pp ⁻3/⁻2 with notes 2–4 written on it. Most of the gatherings are unopened after p 61.

DATE. 1832–3.

COEDITOR. Hans Eichner.

1 half-title verso, referring to p 3 | I "Die Polarvölker"

Wir kennen das alte und unabänderliche Naturgesetz, dass die Kälte...nicht nur die todten Körper kürzt und ihre Materie gleichsam zusammendrückt, sondern auch die festen thierischen Theile zusammenzieht....Daher hauptsächlich die niedere Gestalt, der gedrungene Bau und die verkürzten Extremitäten dieser Polarmenschen...

[We know the old and unalterable law of nature, that cold...not only shortens lifeless objects and as it were compresses their matter, but also contracts the solid parts of the animals....Hence, in the main, the low stature, the squat build, and the shortened extremities of these polar men...]

N.B. The Cold of the Polar Zone naturally *dwarfs* Men—for which *reason*, I presume, the same Zone is famous for *Whales*, White Bears, Sea Lions, Sea Leopards &c!! But perhaps the Whales of the Arctic Seas are only Dwarf Crakens,[1] whose Ancestors existed when the

1[1] The kraken, a fabulous sea-monster of enormous size to be seen off Norway from time to time, first achieved wide notoriety through Pontoppidan's *History of Norway* (1752), in which it is stated that the kraken is "the largest and most surprizing of all the animal creation". "Monsters—the Kraken—Mermaids" were part of the substance of C's discourse during the memorable walk with Keats over Hampstead Heath on 15 Apr 1819. See *The Letters of John Keats* ed. H. E. Rollins (Cambridge, Mass. 1958) I 88–9. For C's report of an eye-witness account of a huge serpent seen in the open sea off the Cape of Good Hope by a naval lieutenant of his acquaintance see G. H. von SCHUBERT *Ansichten von der Nachtseite der Naturwissenschaft* (Dresden 1808) p 296—C's comment (dated Mar 1821) on Schubert's discussion of large animals including the kraken. C's belief in the "Sea-Snake" and RS's belief in the kraken are recorded in Walter SCOTT *Waverley* COPY C I 30 (on *The Pirate* ch 2).

North enjoyed a tropical Climate—& "there were Giants in the Land."[2] S. T. C.

2 inserted leaf, referring to p 5

...der Geschlechtstrieb...dessen Reize mit der zunehmenden Wärme andrer Erdstriche so ungeheuer wachsen...

[...the sexual drive...the stimulations of which increase so immensely with the increasing heat of other regions of the world...]

P. 5.

Not because the Weather is hot—for the Heat produces Languor and Relaxation—no! the Natives of the South are lewd, because they are lazy, ignorant, improvident, superstitious, and enslaved—& without Ideas, and Affections—lewd because they are loveless.[1]

3 inserted leaf, referring to p 6

Wie alle grobfühlende Nationen in einem rohen Zustande, so leben auch diese Menschen gefrässig...sie essen auch mit wildem Geschmack, was ihnen vorkömmt...

[Like all insensitive nations in a state of crudity, these men live greedily...they eat with savage taste whatever is available...]

P. 6

Not a whit grosser feeders than yourself, Dr Hoffbauer! The poor Greenlanders eat what they can get—and so do you.—Were you wrecked on the Coast, I will answer for it, you would find Seal & Seal Oil, as good daintyies, as Beef Steaks & Porter.

4 inserted leaf, referring to p 18 | II "Schön gebildete Völker" 1 "Die Araber"

Ueberhaupt hat die Lehre des Propheten von Arabien aus, nach allen Richtungen hin, einem grossen Theile der Menschheit in Betreff der Civilisation einen unschätzbaren Dienst geleistet.

[Generally, the teaching of the Prophet, spreading from Arabia in all directions, has done an incalculable service to a large part of mankind with respect to civilisation.]

1[2] Gen 6.4.   2[1] Cf FLEURY **4** n 1 and BLANCO WHITE *Letters* **5**.

P. 18.

Mercy! mercy! mercy! on the Man—"the incalculable service above all value, that Mahometanism has done for civilization!!"[1]—Nay, I can read no more—Goodbye, D[r] Hoffbauer/

4[1] For Mahomet as responsible for "the establishment of the most extensive and complete despotism, that ever warred against civilization and the interests of humanity" see *C&S* (*CC*) 138–9. One of C's sources on Mahometism was John Malcolm's *History of Persia* (1815): see FICHTE *Anweisung* 2.

ERNST THEODOR AMADEUS HOFFMANN
1776–1822

Fantasiestücke in Callot's Manier. Blätter aus dem Tagebuche eines reisenden Enthusiasten. Mit einer Vorrede von Jean Paul. Zweite durchgesehene Auflage. 2 vols. Bamberg 1819. 8°.

British Museum C 104 e 15

On Vol II title-page in ink in an unidentified hand: "Spassky [or Spafky] 1819" (perhaps the name of a bookseller, or the engraver of the portrait of Hoffmann); and on II +4 some pencil notes not in C's hand.

Possibly HCR's copy. HCR owned a copy of *Fantasiestücke* by 1825–6, when Carlyle was preparing to make his translations from German and sought advice and books from him. See *CRB* III 824–8. There may be a reference to *Fantasiestücke* in *Logic* (*CC*) 200.

When C wrote to HCR on 12 Feb 1830, "Do not forget Hoffman's Tales", he may have been referring to *Die Serapions-Brüder*, the first two vols of which had appeared in 1819–21, the others posthumously to 1825: there was a copy of this (4 vols in 2, Berlin 1827) in Green's library. *Green SC* (1880) 355.

DATE. After c 1820. C's "Historie and Gests of Maxilian" *Blackwood's* XI (Jan 1822) was inspired by "Der goldene Topf" in the *Fantasiestücke*: see Heather Jackson *Comparative Literature* XXXIII (1981) 38–49.

1 II 368–9, pencil | IV Kreisleriana 7 "Johannes Kreislers Lehrbrief"

Es ist kein leeres Bild, keine Allegorie, wenn der Musiker sagt, dass ihm Farben, Düfte, Strahlen, als Töne erscheinen...So wie, nach *] dem Ausspruch eines geistreichen Physikers, Hören ein Sehen von innen ist, so wird dem Musiker das Sehen ein Hören von innen...

[It is no empty image, no allegory, when the musician says that colours, fragrances, rays, appear to him as sounds...Just as hearing is, as an ingenious physicist expressed it, a seeing from within, thus seeing becomes for the musician a hearing from within...]

* I suspect, that this is a mere ting tang, meaning nothing or a truism. But I have often thought, that Hearing might be called a Seeing of the Inward, *of* (not merely *from*) the *within*. Only *from* within can we either see or hear. But a Seeing *of* the Within is necessarily ✷ the seeing of the Surface, i.e. of the passive Shape, Massive Colors, & negative outlines.

✷ means "opposed to," "contra-distinguished from". Thus Sweet ✷ Sour: Outward ✷ Inward. &c.

1115

LUDWIG HEINRICH CHRISTOPH HÖLTY

1748–1776

LOST BOOK

Gedichte, &c. Frankfurt 1792. 8°.

[No copy examined.]

Not located; marginalia not recorded. *Green SC* (1880) 326 (entered as by "Hölth"): "With MS. Notes by S. T. Coleridge."

Bought by Wilson at the Green Sale, this book was offered to the BM with the description "Long MS Note by S. T. Coleridge", but declined; it appeared again in the Wilson Catalogue of 1880 as item 194. HCR recorded on 13 Mar 1811 that he called on C and discussed German poetry and literature, and that C "read me extracts from Holty, whom he praised, and lent me". *CRB* I 25–6, which, however, reads "Holtz". In a letter to William Blackwood 19 Sept 1821 C undertook to send in "a second packet" certain items for publication including "4. The Life of Hölty, with specimens of his poems, translated into English Verse.—" *CL* v 166 and n. This proposal may have been the result of the visit to C in Aug 1821 (recorded in an inscribed copy of *LS*) of John Anster, the putative Dublin author of the "Life of Hölty" in *London Magazine* IV (Nov 1821) 518–26. C's only surviving translation from Hölty is Fragment 64 in *PW* (EHC) II 1013, from *Adelstan und Röschen* (without title in ms), the composition of which J. C. C. Mays places in c Aug–Sept 1821, despite De Q's claim for composition in 1807–12.

HOMER
CHAPMAN'S TRANSLATION

The Whole Works of Homer; Prince of Poetts in his Iliads, and Odysses. Translated according to the Greeke, by Geo: Chapman, &c. London [1616]. [and in the same volume] The Crowne of all Homer's Workes, Batraχomyomaχia; or the battaile of frogs and mise. His Hymnes and Epigrams, &c. 3 pts in 1 vol. London [1624]. F°

Washington University, St Louis, Missouri

Inscribed at the head of the dedication leaf: "Johannes Boys". Below this, "S. T. Coleridge—⟨given by him to his friend S. Hutchinson⟩", the signature in C's hand, the addition apparently by SH. At the head of the dedicatory poems, in an earlier hand: "Constit. Tres Folio—" and a phrase, apparently in the same hand, at the end of *Iliad* xi (i 158). The catalogue of the W. H. Arnold sale reported a pencil note in an unidentified hand, "This book belonged to the Poet Wordsworth...", but this note is no longer in the volume.

Wordsworth LC shows two copies of Chapman's Homer: 1045 twice marked as C's, and 1044, presumably WW's copy. *Wordsworth SC* (1849) also shows two copies: 491, which is clearly the C–SH copy, and 490, another copy nd, presumably WW's copy. SH wrote to Green on 10 Jan 1835: "You will observe by one Ex^t from a Letter [i.e. 1, below] to me that Chapman's *Homer* was a gift of our dear Friend to me—& therefore will not wonder that I am desirous of re-possessing it—His Books were sent from Rydal when I was absent—& I do not know whether it was sent to Highgate or to Helston—Should you meet with it among the books I shall be greatly obliged if you will retain it for me." *SHL* 439; cf *CM* i Introduction clviii–clix n 1.

Part of a letter sent by C to SH with this book in c Apr 1808 was inserted in the volume. This letter, present in the volume when it was received by Washington University, was "inserted" in the volume when it was sold in the Arnold sale in 1901, and had evidently been in the book ever since SH had received it from C in 1808. Because part of the incomplete letter was printed in *LR* i with a selection of C's annotations in this volume, the whole surviving text of the letter (not in *CL*) is here printed as 1.

Lamb may first have drawn Chapman's Homer to C's attention, writing enthusiastically, and with quotations, on 23 Oct 1802:"it has *most* the continuous power of interesting you all along, like a rapid original, of any: & in the uncommon excellence of the more finish'd parts goes beyond Fairfax or any of 'em". He promised to tell C "more about Chapman & his peculiarities in my next", but if he did so the letter has not survived. *LL* (M) II 82–3; cf **1** n 11, below. Lamb's *Adventures of Ulysses* (1808) was paraphrased from Chapman. For the relation between Lamb and C's marginalia see also *CM* I Introduction lxxxviii–xcii.

CONTENTS. i *Iliad*; ii *Odyssey*; iii *Batrachomyomachia*, Hymns, Certain Epigrams and Other Poems.

MS TRANSCRIPTS. BM Add MS 47553 f 187: a transcript headed "Extract from a Letter sent with ~~Chapman's Homer~~ to S. H. the volume* 1807. ⟨1808⟩ * communicated through Mr Wordsworth." Literal changes identify this as the copy for *LR* I 259–61.

DATE. 12 Feb 1808 (**2**), and a little earlier. The accompanying letter (**1**) was written 2 or 9 Apr 1808, i.e. the Saturday before or after WW left London on 3 Apr. See **1** n 1, below.

1 Letter from C to SH accompanying the book[1]

[. . . . .]
In the Box containing the Piranesi Folios for William,[2] ⟨there petition you to accept them⟩ a little but very neat N. Testament,[3]

1[1] Addressed: "Miss S. Hutchinson | Mʳ Monkhouse's | Penrith | Cumberland | SATURDAY." In the upper right corner of the address-fold "2" is written, perhaps indicating that this was the second of two separate parts of the letter; the first part is neither preserved nor recorded. Griggs dated his version of the letter (*CL* III 67–8) at [12 Feb 1808] from the date of **2**, and associated the letter with the gowns sent to the Wordsworth household and acknowledged by C on 29 Mar 1808 (*CL* III 81). But the gowns were sent by the Morgans to Grasmere, and C's letter—whether or not it accompanied the box of books—was addressed to Penrith. Although WW did not leave London until 3 Apr (Sunday), he went to Dunmow to stay with the Beaumonts on 23 Mar (Wednesday). *WL* (*M2*) I 202. If this had been WW's effective departure from C, and he had decided that he could not take the books with him, C could have sent them off on 26 Mar or 2 Apr, or on the Saturday following WW's departure from London. In any case, the letter was addressed to Penrith, not to Grasmere.

1[2] Giambattista Piranesi (1720–78), architect, engraver of Roman buildings and antiquities, and of emotionally charged, often nightmarish, imaginary architectural constructions, especially of prisons. Whether the "Folios" were bound volumes or separate prints, whether they belonged to WW or were lent to him, is not known; they are not mentioned elsewhere. After Piranesi's death, his sons, trying to escape in 1798 from Italy to France with their father's copperplates, were captured at sea by a British ship. As a result, many prints, usually of bad quality, were made from the original plates—as many as 4000 impressions were made from each of his 991 plates—and were sold in curiosity shops, so that Piranesi's prints flooded Europe like travel posters. In Nov 1814 C drew Kenyon's attention to "Piranesi's astounding Engravings from Rome and the Campus Martius" and "*a Ghost in Marble*", C's description of which informed an annotation on Jeremy TAYLOR (*LR* III 328) that he quoted in *AR* (1825) 275. *CL* III 541. C invoked "the Spirits of Rembrandt and Piranesi" c Sept 1826, when he was imagining a historical painting on the subject of Nehem 2.12–15. *CN* IV 5162.

1[3] This copy has not been identified.

Chapman's Homer/ which is become very scarce & valuable, & a new work—Huber's History of Bees.[4] This is inde[e]d a wonder-tale, ⟨of *reality*,⟩ a true romance, of *Nature*—& to me as entertaining as ever was the Arabian Nights.[5] [a]Chapman I have sent in order that you might read the Odyssey/ the Iliad is a fine but less equal in the Translation as well as less interesting in itself.[6] What is stupidly said of Shakspere is really true & appropriate of Chapman—"mighty faults counterpoised by mighty Beauties."[7] Excepting his quaint epithets which he affects to render literally from the Greek, a language above all others "blest in the happy marriage of sweet words",[8] and which in our language are mere Printer's compound Epithets—such as—quaff'd divine *Joy-in-the-heart-of-man-infusing* Wine/ the undermark'd is to be one word, because one sweet mellifluous Word expresses it in Homer[9]—excepting this, it has no

[a] MS TRANSCRIPT begins

1[4] François Huber (1750–1831), blind Swiss naturalist; *New Observations on the Natural History of Bees* tr Sir John Graham Dalyell (Edinburgh 1806). C's copy remained at Allan Bank in Oct 1810 and is twice marked as C's in Wordsworth LC 920. His continuing interest in Huber is noted in LEIGHTON COPY C I 71–86n.

1[5] The *Arabian Nights' Entertainments* cast a peculiar spell upon C as a child: see *CL* I 347, *Friend* (*CC*) I 148 and n 2, *Sh C* II 72 (1811–12 lectures). In a notebook entry of c Apr–May 1816 he remarked upon the story in the *Arabian Nights* with which he tried to explain to Mrs Barbauld the "moral" of *AM. CN* III 4317, cf *TT* 31 May 1830. Lecture 11 of the first 1818 literary series (3 Mar 1818) was announced as "On the Arabian Nights Entertainments, and on the *romantic* Use of the Supernatural in Poetry". *Sh C* II 242; see also *CN* III 4500.

1[6] Lamb shared this view: "I shall die in the belief that he [Chapman] has improved upon Homer, in the Odyssey in particular". *LL* II 304 (c Aug 1821).

1[7] Cf "I have often thought that the vulgar misconception of Shakspeare as a wild irregular genius 'in whom great faults are compensated by great beauties' would be really true applied to Chapman." Lamb *Specimens of English Dramatic*

Poets (1808) 99n. For Shakespeare as a *lusus naturae* or "a sort of irregular genius", and C's objections to that view, see e.g. *Sh C* I 194–5, II 44, 105. See also *BL* ch 2 (*CC*) I 34n.

1[8] Quotation untraced. For C on the virtues of the Greek language see e.g. *CN* III 3365, *Friend* (*CC*) II 241 and n, 244; cf *CN* I 1613.

1[9] Cf GRAY 1. In the Preface to *Poems* (1797), responding to a charge that his earlier volume was marred "with a profusion of double-epithets", C said that he had "pruned the double-epithets with no sparing hand". *PW* (EHC) II 1145; see also *BL* ch 1 (*CC*) I 6 and n. There are plenty of double epithets in Chapman's translation, as there are in Milton; but Chapman uses a number of hyphenated compounds of three elements, and some of four, five, six, and even seven words. The epithet C has in mind, citing from memory, is in *Odyssey* 7.256 (of Chapman's text; line 182 of the Greek text): "And hony-sweetnesse-giving-minds wine filld", to which, in a shoulder-note, Chapman comments upon "this long Epithete", identifying μελίφρονα as (what C calls) "the one sweet mellifluous Word". The word μελίφρων—which Chapman here translates "honey-sweet-to-the-mind"—

look, no air, of a translation. It is as truly an original poem as the Faery Queen[10]—it will give you small Idea of Homer; tho' yet a far truer one than from Pope's *Epigrams* or Cowper's cumbersome most anti-homeric *Miltoniad*[11]—for Chapman writes & feels a Poet—as Homer might have written had he lived in England in the reign of Queen Elizabeth/. In short, it is an exquisite Poem, spite of its frequent & perverse quaintnesses and harshnesses, which are however amply repaid by almost unexampled sweetness & beauty of language, all over spirit & feeling, in the main/ it is an English Heroic poem, the *tale* of which is borrowed from the Greek—& I anticipate pleasure in your enjoyment of it.—The dedication to the Iliad is a noble Copy of Verses, especially those sublime Lines, ɨon the second page, beginning at the 5ᵗʰ line, and ending at the word "raigning"— the last but one/[12]—and likewise ⟨read⟩ the 1ˢᵗ, the 11ᵗʰ, and the last but one, of the prefatory Sonnets to the Odyssey.[13]

Could I have foreseen any other speedy opportunity, it should ⟨have⟩ begged your acceptance in a somewhat *handsomer Coat*; but as it is it will represent the Sender, to quote from myself

> A man disherited, in form and face,
> By Nature and Mishap, of outward Grace.[a][14]

a MS TRANSCRIPT ends

occurs about twelve times in Homer; elsewhere Chapman translates it "sweet" and once as "luscious". For C's use of extended compounds see e.g. BIBLE COPY B **134** (Jul 1829) and BAXTER *Reliquiae* COPY B **107** and n 2.

1[10] For C on Spenser's *Faerie Queene* cf *CN* III 4501. Lamb considered Chapman's Homer "not so properly a translation as the stories of Achilles and Ulysses re-written". *Specimens* (1808) 98–9 n 41.

1[11] For C on Pope's *Homer* see e.g. *BL* ch 2 (*CC*) I 34n, 39–40n; cf *CRB* I 62 (27 Jan 1812). In Oct 1802 Lamb had condemned to C "Cowper's damn'd blank verse [which] detains you every step with some heavy Miltonism [while] Chapman gallops off with you his own free pace." *LL* (M) II 82; cf III 23 (31 Jul 1809). Despite C's admiration for Cow-

per's blank verse and the fruitful influence it had on his own poetry (see BARCLAY COPY A **1** and n 4), it does not appear that he would disagree with Lamb about Cowper's *Homer*.

1[12] For the text of this passage, marked by C, see ANNEX (*a*).

1[13] For the text of these three sonnets, the first and third of which are also noticed in **8**, below, see ANNEX (*b*).

1[14] *To Two Sisters* lines 8–9 (var): *PW* (EHC) I 411 (the variant not noted). The first publication of the poem (62 lines) in the *Courier* 10 Dec 1807 over the thinly disguised signature SIESTI, gave offence to the Wordsworths through the comparison of Mary Morgan and Charlotte Brent with MW and SH, and the implied transfer of C's affections from the Wordsworths to the Morgans.

A Lady, a poetess & handsome, Laura Temple,[15] having been enraptured with my Poem "Love" in the L.B. [. . . . .]*ª*[16] Miss B.[17] he *might* have been, I dare say, if—if— —"what?"—why, I don't know—why, *in short if he had not been quite otherwise*. When her Brother's[18] letter informed me of this, which she *begged* him not to do, I was in great pain; but there was a funny simplicity in the words, that made me laugh till I moaned fretfully at the pain at my navel, which my Laughing occasioned[.] Morgan to teize her told her, he had assured me, that she had said this out of jealousy to prevent *more people from* being in love with me, *in case of an accident*.—Of all the families I have known, that you do not know, this is the only one that I wish, you did—because I [am]*ᵇ* sure, you would more than merely like them. Mʳˢ Morgan is quite a Duplicate of Mary—at least, would have been if she had been bred up in the country, and had had a Dorothy for her friend, and a Wordsworth for her Lover & Husband—and her Sister is almost as much like you—in size & form exactly. But Mʳˢ M. is what the world calls very beautiful; tho' the feature that alone prevents her face from resembling Mary's as much as her stature, thinness, & the manner of putting her Limbs is to my feeling the only unpleasant part in it— a pair of large brilliant black Eyes, which seldom fail to eat up or *put out* the mild & true beauties of a female face.[19]—I have gossiped

ª At least one line of ms cropped from the foot of the sheet, and correspondingly from the continuation on the reverse side of the sheet
ᵇ Word supplied by the editor

1[15] Laura Sophia Temple of Bristol, whom, despite his playful description here, C had not met. Josiah Wade had sent some of her verses to WW, with copies of his *Mercantile Gazette*, in Sept 1806. *WL* (*M*2) I 81 and n 3. She published *Poems* (1805) and *Lyric and Other Poems* (1808), but C wanted to find out from the editor of the *M Post* "who this Miss Laura *Temple is*". *CL* III 50, 67. See also n 16, below.

1[16] She sent Morgan, shortly before 1 Feb 1808, a "blush-compelling note" about C's poem *Love*, to which C instructed Morgan to return an answer, suspecting that a joke was being played upon him by somebody concealing her identity. See *CL* III 50, 67. C is here retelling the story against himself in order to endear the Morgans to SH. The poem "All thoughts, all passions, all delights",

included in *LB* 1800–5 under the title *Love*, was first published, with four additional stanzas at the beginning and three at the end, in *M Post* 21 Dec 1799 as *Introduction to the Tale of the Dark Ladie*. *PW* (EHC) I 330–5, *EOT* (*CC*) I 42–3, III 290. An "Asra poem", *Love* was one of the most widely admired of C's poems during his lifetime and throughout the nineteenth century.

1[17] Charlotte Brent (b 1783), sister of Mary Morgan (b 1782).

1[18] John James Morgan, Charlotte Brent's brother-in-law. See ANDERSON COPY B headnote.

1[19] This is one of the most vivid impressions we have of the physical appearance of MW, Charlotte Brent, and Mary Morgan. For Lamb's comparison of SH with Charlotte Brent in a letter of 22 May 1815 see *LL* (M) III 162.

thus in order to turn from gloomy thoughts, & to show you that I endeavour to do so whenever I can.—ᵃI found yesterday an unopened Letter of yours. (O dearest it went like [. . . . .]ᵇ once by my hope, & vowed to the Almighty, that never hereafter would receive a Letter from you which I would not immediately read thro' in whatever state of mind imaginable.[20]—and after this I seriously added that now there were not coming any Letters from Grasmere.—So dearest do forgive [. . .] Iliad,ᶜ if I find that [. . . . .]ᵈ

2   dedication leaf verso

Chapman in his moral heroic verse, as in this Dedication and the prefatory Sonnets to his Odyssey stands above Jonson, more dignity, more lustre, and equal strength; but not *midway* QUITE between him and the sonnets of Milton.[1] I do not know, whether I give him the higher praise, ~~when~~ in that he he reminds of meᵉ B. Jonson ~~by~~ with a sense of his superior excellence, or that he brings Milton [to]ᶠ memory notwithstanding his Inferiority. His moral Poems are not quite out of Books, like Jonson's;[2] nor yet do the sentiments so wholly grow up out of his own native habit & grandeur of Thought as in Milton. The sentiments ~~are~~ have been attracted to him by a natural affinity of his Intellect, & so combined—but Jonson has taken them by individual and successive acts of Choice. S. T. Coleridge

The Translations I have not yet read. Feb. 12, 1808./

3   ii sig [A5] | *Epistle Dedicatorie* to the *Odyssey*

Of the divine Furie (*my Lord*) *your* Homer *hath ever bene, both first and last* Instance; being *pronounced absolutely*, τον σοφωτατον. και

ᵃ⁻ᵇ Seven lines of ms heavily obliterated in ink, not by C. Only fragments are now legible. Cropped at the end
ᶜ This word written over the word originally written, to disguise it
ᵈ About 5 words illegible, the last possibly "sentence"
ᵉ A slip for "me of"
ᶠ Word supplied by the editor

[1] [20] A symptom of C's state of mind (see e.g. *CN* II 3075, 3146, 3147, 3182, 3215, 3228), which at the nadir of his addiction to opium became for a time a distressing paralysis of initiative. For WW's anxiety at receiving from C no reply to three letters he had written within a few days of returning to the Lakes in Apr 1808 see *WL* (*M* 2) I 217.
[2] [1] C had Milton's sonnets well enough in mind to quote from them from time to time, probably from memory, especially in *The Friend*. But he does not mention them in his "Sheet of Sonnets" [1796], nor did he make any general critical comment upon them in ANDERSON, HAYLEY, or MILTON.
[2] For C on Jonson the poet see ANDERSON COPY B 16 and JONSON in *CM* (*CC*) III.

τον θειοτατον ποιητην; *the most wise and most divine Poet. Against whom, whosoever shall open his prophane mouth, may worthily receive answer, with this of his divine defender;* (Empedocles, Heraclitus, Protagoras, Epichar: &c. *being of* Homers *part*)...*who against such an Armie, and the Generall* Homer *dares attempt the assault, but he must be reputed ridiculous? And yet against this hoast, and this invincible Commander, shall we have every* Besogne *and foole a Leader. The common herd (I assure my self) readie to receive it on their hornes. Their infected Leaders,*

> Such men, as sideling ride the ambling *Muse*;
> Whose saddle is as frequent as the stuse.
> Whose Raptures are in every Pageant seene;
> In every Wassall rime, and Dancing greene:
> When he that writes by any beame of Truth,
> Must dive as deepe as he; past shallow youth.

All this and the preceding is well felt and vigorously tho' harshly expressed, respecting sublime poetry, in genere; but in reading Homer I look about me, and ask—how does all this apply *here*? For surely never was their[a] plainer Writing—there are [a][b] thousand charms, of Sun & moonbeam, Ripple and wave & stormy Billow— ; but all on the *Surface*. Had Chapman read Proclus and Porphyry? and did he really believe them? or even that they believed themselves?[1] They felt the immense power of a *Bible*, a Shaster,[2] a Koran/ there was none in Greece or Rome/ & they tried therefore by subtle allegorical accomodations to conjure the poems of Homer into the βιβλιον θεοπαραδοτον[3] of Greek Faith.

4   ii 1 | The Argument of *Odyssey* I

Observe, that Heroe and Heroes in this poem are pronounced in 3 syllables—Hē rō ē, (e as a) Hē rō ēs.

[a] A slip for "there"   [b] Word supplied by the editor

3[1] Whether or not Chapman had read Proclus and Porphyry we do not know. But Porphyry and Proclus—as C knew well—found in Homer theological instruction in more mundane passages as well as in those accounts of the gods which they also allegorised; and both wrote separate works on the subject. C had Thomas Taylor's translation of Porphyry's "Concerning the Cave of the Nymphs in the Odyssey" in

PROCLUS *The Philosophical and Mathematical Commentaries...on...Euclid's Elements* (1792) Vol II, and Proclus' "An Apology for the Fables of Homer" is translated in Taylor's introduction to Plato's *Republic* bks I and II, in Plato *Works* (1804) I.
3[2] Any sacred writing of the Hindus.
3[3] The "book handed down from God". Cf *CN* II 2445 and *SM* (*CC*) 95.

5　ii 53 | *Odyssey* IV 335–8

> And thus through every streete
> He crept discovering: of no one man knowne.
> And yet through all this difference, I alone
> * Smok't his true person.

* I do not remember to have seen this word elsewhere, except in some modern novels, in print. Possibly, it might originally have been a metaphor of poetic origin, & a word of dignity, in Chapman's age.[1]

6　ii 54 | *Odyssey* IV 382ff

[Shoulder-note:] *Hellen counterfetted the wives voices of those Kings of Greece, that were in the woodden horse, and calls their husbands.*

> When all the voices of their Wives in it
> You tooke on you; with voice so like, and fit;
> And every man by name, so visited...

How, in Jove's name, could their Wives have been supposed to have come there? Or is this one of the Passages, which justify the suspicion that the Iliad & Odyssey were not of the same Author or (perhaps) Age?[1]

6A　ii 55 | IV 423

> Speake truth; Some publicke? *need?* or onely thine?

7　ii 193 | *Odyssey* XII, inscription at the end

Opus novem dierum.

[The work of nine days.]

Something more than "a nine day's wonder", if it refer to the whole 12 Books! I should rather ~~apply~~ confine it to the last Book; which without pressing too hard on our Faith will yet be honorable to the Translator's Industry, and fluent Vein of Thought & Verse.[1] S. T. Coleridge.

5[1] To "smoke"—to get an inkling, or idea, of—now archaic, was common usage c 1600–1850, according to *OED*.

6[1] See **9** and n 2, below.

7[1] In the "Preface to the Reader" in the *Iliad* Chapman said that "lesse than fifteene weekes was the time in which all the last twelve books were entirely new translated", and that he then intended with "all uncheckt alacritie [to] dive through his *Odysses*". Most critics, like C, think that Chapman meant bk 12; the

The Whole Works

8 verso of blank leaf following the end of *Odyssey* XXIV

Odyssey. Instances του βελτιονος, ωσ*ᵃ* μοι δοκει.¹
1 Sonnet to the D. of Lennox.²
Last but one. to the Lord Walden.³
(several intervening *Lines*)⁴

9 iii sig ¶4 | "The Occasion of This Impos'd Crowne"

After this not onely Prime of Poets, but Philosophers, had written his two great Poems, of *Iliads* & *Odysses*...(finding no compensation) he writ, in contempt of Men, this ridiculous Poem of Vermin, giving them Nobility of Birth, valorous elocution not inferior to his Heroes. At which the Gods themselves put in amaze, call'd Counsailes about their assistance of either Armie, and the justice of their Quarrels, even to the mounting of Joves Artillery against them, and discharge of his three-forckt flashes: and all for the devouring of a Mouse. After which sleight and onely recreative touch, hee betooke him seriously to the honor of the Gods; in Hymn's resounding all their peculiar Titles, Jurisdiction, and Dignities....Al his observance and honor of the Gods, rather mov'd their envies against him, then their rewards, or respects of his endeavours. And so like a Man *verecundi ingenii* [of respectable genius] (which he witnesseth of himselfe) he liv'd unhonord and needie till his death; yet notwithstanding all mens servile and manacled Miseries, to his most absolute and never-equall'd Merite; yea even bursten profusion to *Imposture* and *Impiety*; heare our-ever-the Same intranced and never-sleeping, Master of the Muses, to his last accents, incomparablie singing.

Chapman's Identification of his fate with Homer's is interesting¹—and his compleat forgetfulness of the distinction between Xstianaity & Idolatry, under the general feeling of *some* Religion, very in-

ᵃ A slip for ως

1st ed of the *Iliad* (1614) comprises only bks 1–12 and ends with the words quoted. Allardyce Nicoll *Chapman's Homer* (2 vols 1956) II xiii notes that Chapman may have been following the practice of Thomas Phaer, who in his tr of the *Aeneid* set down the number of days he had taken to translate each book; Nicoll notes further that in a copy of the 1st ed of the *Iliad* presented by Chapman to Sir Henry Fanshawe the words "Opus novem dierum" were heavily inked out, presumably by Chapman.

8¹ Instances "of the better [sort], in my opinion".

8² The first of the three sonnets noted in **1** (at n 13): see ANNEX (*b*).

8³ The last of the three sonnets noted in **1** (at n 13): see ANNEX (*b*).

8⁴ Lines unspecified in Sonnets 12–14.

9¹ Many references in Chapman's works show that he suffered poverty and neglect.

teresting. It is amusing to observe, how familiar Chapman's Fancy has become with *Homer*—his Life & its Circumstances—tho' the very existence of such an, ⟨or of any,⟩ *Individual* at least with regard to Iliad & the Hymns, is more than problematic.[2]

N.B. The rude Engraving in thi[s] page was designed by no vulgar Hand, It is full of Spirit & Passion.—[3]

10　iii 17 | at the end of the *Batrachomyomachia*

I am so dull that neither in the original or in any translation could I ever find any wit or wise purpose in this Poem. The whole Humor seems to lie in the names[1]—the Frogs & Mice are not F. or M., but men/ & yet they do nothing that conveys any satire. In the Greek there is much beauty of language—but the joke is very flat. But this is always the case in rude ages—their serious Vein is inimitable—their comic low & low indeed—The psychological cause[a] is easily stated & copiously exemplifiable.—

Annex

(*a*) In **1** (at n 12) C wrote: "The dedication to the Iliad is a noble Copy of Verses, especially those sublime Lines, on the second page, beginning at the 5th line, and ending at the word 'raigning'—the last but one/—" i.e. lines 29–60. He marked the passage with a line in the margin and cancelled the line after "...raigning", i.e. "And proves, how firme Truth builds in Poets faining".

　　　　　　　　　　　O! tis wondrous much
(Though nothing prisde) that the right vertuous touch
Of a well written soule, to vertue moves.
Nor have we soules to purpose, if their loves
Of fitting objects be not so inflam'd.
How much then, were this kingdomes maine soule maim'd,
To want this great inflamer of all powers
That move in humane soules? All Realmes but yours,
Are honor'd with him; and hold blest that State
That have his workes to reade and contemplate.
In which, Humanitie to her height is raisde;
Which all the world (yet, none enough) hath praisde.

　　　　a C wrote "cause psychological" and marked the words for transposition

9[2] For C on the authorship of "Homer" see HOMERIC HYMNS **1** n 1 and GREW **19** nn 1–3; cf also *TT* 12 May 1830.

9[3] The device, printed wider than full measure above the title "The Occasion of This Impos'd Crowne", includes four figures mounted on horseback under a rayed sun.

10[1] Chapman provides his comic translations of the names in the margins: e.g. Psycharpax "Gather-crum", Pternotroctes "Bacon-flitch-devourer", Embasichytrus "Enter-pot", Tyroglyphus "Cheese-miner", &c &c.

Seas, earth, and heaven, he did in verse comprise;
Out-sung the Muses, and did equalise
Their king *Apollo*; being so farre from cause
Of Princes light thoughts, that their gravest lawes
May finde stuffe to be fashioned by his lines.
Through all the pompe of kingdomes still he shines,
And graceth all his gracers. Then let lie
Your Lutes, and Viols, and more loftily
Make the Heroiques of your *Homer* sung,
To Drums and Trumpets set his Angels tongue:
And with the Princely sport of Haukes you use,
Behold the kingly flight of his high Muse:
And see how like the Phoenix she renues
Her age, and starrie feathers in your sunne;
Thousands of yeares attending; everie one
Blowing the holy fire, and throwing in
Their seasons, kingdomes, nations that have bin
Subverted in them; lawes, religions, all
Offerd to Change, and greedie Funerall;
Yet still your *Homer* lasting, living, raigning;

(*b*) In **1** (at n 13) C commended three of the "prefatory Sonnets to the Odyssey"—the first, eleventh, and fifteenth of the sixteen; in **8**, he listed the first and fifteenth as "Instances of the better sort".

Sonnet 1: "To the right gracious and worthy, the Duke of Lennox"

Amongst th' Heroes of the Worlds prime years,
    Stand here, great Duke, & see them shine about you:
Informe your princely minde and spirit by theirs,
    And then, like them, live ever; looke without you,
For subiects fit to use your place, and grace:
    Which throw about you, as the Sunne, his Raies;
In quickning, with their power, the dying Race
    Of friendlesse *Vertue*; since they thus can raise
Their honor'd Raisers, to *Eternitie*.
    None ever liv'd by *Selfe-love*: Others good
In th' obiect of our owne. They (living) die,
    That burie in themselves their fortunes brood.
To this soule, then, your gracious count'nance give;
    That gave, to such as you, such meanes to live.

Sonnet 11: "To the happy Starre, discovered in our Sydneian Asterisme; comfort of learning, Sphere of all the vertues, the Lady Wrothe"

When all our other Starres set (in their skies)
    To Vertue, and all honor of her kind;
That you (rare Lady) should so clearly rise,
    Makes all the vertuous glorifie your mind.
All let true Reason, and Religion trie,
    If it be Fancie, not judiciall Right,

If you t' oppose the times Apostasie,
  To take the soules part, and her saving Light,
While others blinde and burie both in Sense;
  When, tis the onely end, for which all live.
And, could those soules, in whom it dies, dispense
  As much with their Religion; they would give
That as small grace. Then shun their course, faire Starre;
  And still keepe your way, pure, and circular.

Sonnet 15: "To the right noble and Heroicall, my Singular good Lord, the Lord of Walden"

Nor let the vulgar sway *Opinion* beares
  (Rare Lord) that Poesies favor shewes men vaine,
Ranke you amongst her sterne disfavourers;
  She all things worthy favour doth maintaine.
Vertue, in all things else, at best she betters;
  Honour she heightens, and gives Life in Death;
She is the ornament, and soule of letters:
  The worlds deceipt before her vanisheth.
Simple she is as Doves, like Serpents wise;
  Sharpe, grave, and sacred: nought but things divine,
And things divining, fit her faculties;
  (Accepting her as she is genuine.)
  If she be vaine then, all things else are vile;
  If vertuous, still be Patrone of her stile.

HOMERIC HYMNS

Homeri hymni et epigrammata. Edidit Godofredus Hermannus. Leipzig 1806. 8°.

Cornell University (Wordsworth Collection)

DC's bookplate, and on p ⁻5 the Helston Grammar School library press-mark "No. 202. H. G. S. L."

A transcript and translation of C's note made by EHC, dated 24 Mar 1894, is tipped in at pp ⁻3/⁻2.

In c Nov–Dec 1809, when he was planning the extension of his collection of books, C thought that "It would be a pleasing employment, had I health, to translate the Hymns of Homer from Hermann's edition, with a disquisitional attempt to settle the question concerning the *personality* of Homer...." *CN* III 3656. In Jan 1808 C had asked De Q to secure him a copy of this edition, together with HERMANN *De emendenda* (*CL* III 48), and "Hermann's Edition of the Hymns of Homer" is one of two titles under the heading "Libri desiderati" in a notebook entry of apparently similar date. *CN* III 3279.

DATE. Possibly early 1808, if acquired by De Q as requested and associated with HERMANN *De emendenda* (see above); but associations with EICHHORN *Alte Testament* and with N 29 suggest a later date, possibly 1812–19.

1 pp vi–vii | Hermann's Introduction

Ex quo vir summus, Fr. Aug. Wolfius, Homerum nobis non uno modo restituit, quum de aliis rebus multis rectius iudicari coeptum est, tum rhapsodorum ars et disciplina in clariorem lucem poterit protrahi.

[Since that great man Friedrich Augustus Wolf in more than one sense restored Homer to us we have begun to judge more correctly on many other matters, and it will now be possible to bring out into a clearer light the art and training of the rhapsodes.]

Quid si*a* titulus Iliadis fuisset in primâ poematum istium*b*
feruminatione—Ραψωδια Ομηρευμενων &c—Rapsodia (sive con-
sutio) Poetarum qui de rebus Iliacis unâ cecinerunt? Et inde ortum
esset nomen Homeri?[1]

---

a Or "Quodsi" ("But if")   *b* Perhaps "istorum"

[1] "What if the title of the *Iliad* at the
first welding together of those poems had
been Ραψωδία Ὁμηρευ[ο]μένων &c—
the Rhapsody (or stitching together) of
the Poets who sang together about the
affairs of Troy? And [what if] the name
of Homer had originated from this?"

The derivation of ὁμηρ- from ὁμο-
(together) +ἀρ- (join) goes back to
Hesychius and Eustathius and is given by
Stephanus, Scapula, and others. Karl
David Ilgen, in his *Homeri hymni* (Halle
1796) x, applied this meaning, saying that
Ὅμηρος was originally a common
noun—one who sang verse to the
accompaniment of music—and that a
succession of ὅμηροι were involved in the
production of the poems that we now
know as the *Iliad* and *Odyssey*. C makes

the same suggestion that he does in this
annotation more briefly in EICHHORN
Alte Testament 31 (possibly 1810–12) and
at greater length in *CN* IV 4832 f 61 (c
1821). On the authorship of the Homeric
poems see also HOMER 9 and n 2 and
GREW 19 nn 1–3.

With C's invention, the *Homereuomeni*,
cf the *Homeridae*, who in the various
ancient accounts seem to become indis-
tinguishable from the rhapsodes, from
the authors of the poems in the epic cycle,
from the bards who composed the lays
that later were incorporated in the *Iliad*
and *Odyssey*, and from the reciters of the
poems at public festivals. See FLÖGEL 45
and cf H. N. COLERIDGE "Hesiod" 8
and n 2.

RICHARD HOOKER

c 1554–1600

The Works of that Learned and Judicious Divine, Mr. Richard Hooker, in eight books of Ecclesiastical Polity, compleated out of his own manuscripts. With several other treatises by the same author, and an account of his life and death [by Izaak Walton]. Dedicated to the King's most excellent majesty, Charles II. by whose royal father (near his martyrdom) the former five books (then only extant) were commended to his dear children, as an excellent means to satisfie private scruples, and settle the publick peace of this Church and Kingdom, &c. London 1682. F°.

Engraved title-page facing portrait reads: *Of the Lawes of Ecclesiastical Politie Eight Bookes*, &c.

British Museum Ashley 5175

Bookplate of James Gillman Jr on p ⁻4 (p–d). C referred to this book as "Mʳ Gillman's Hooker" in N 36 f 33ᵛ (*CN* v), cited in **10** n 3.

C's first reading of Hooker is not recorded; there are signs of it by the end of 1801 in the admiration C expressed for Hooker's prose style as well as for his theology. *CN* I 1052, 1655. Although Hooker is not named in C's earliest account of his projected "Examination of the Style of our English Prose Writers under Charles I. & the Commonwealth" (*CL* II 870: 21 Sept 1802), by the time the book of selections was published by Basil Montagu in 1805 Hooker's name, with Hall and Bacon, appeared in the title with Jeremy Taylor, and Milton had disappeared. In Jul 1803 C recommended Hooker, as a theologian, as a prominent figure for inclusion in Vol v of RS's projected "Bibliotheca Britannica". *CL* II 956. Hooker began to appear noticeably in the 1809–10 *Friend* (WW and RS both owned a copy of *Ecclesiastical Polity* at some time) and was carried forward, sometimes by repetition, sometimes by fresh quotation, into the 1818 *Friend* (see **21** n 1), into *BL* (see **17** n 1), and the early 1818 literary lectures (see **27** n 1). In Jan 1824 C provided an aphorism from Hooker for *AR* (*CL* v 324): this seems to be the first direct reference to this annotated copy. Thereafter several notebook entries, especially for Sept 1826, overlap the marginalia written in this copy (see e.g. **11**, **21**, **31**, **43**). In the last *TT* entry made by HNC before C's death, dated 10 Jul 1834, C said that as Hooker wished to complete his *Ecclesiastical Polity* he too hoped to live to complete his "*Philosophy*".

CONTENTS. Dedication: An Epistle to the King (**1**); To the Reader; The Copy of a Letter Writ to Mr Walton, by Dr King; The Life of Mr Richard Hooker (**2–4**); George Cranmer's Letter unto Mr Richard Hooker; Epitaph, by Sir

1131

William Cooper; *Of the Lawes of Ecclesiastical Politie* (**5–39**); "Several Other Treatises": A Supplication made to the Council by Master Walter Travers (**40**); Master Hooker's Answer to... Master Travers (**41**); A Learned Discourse of Justification, Works, and How the Foundation of Faith Is Overthrown (**42, 43**); A Learned Sermon of the Nature of Pride; A Remedy Against Sorrow and Fear, Delivered in a Funeral Sermon (**44–46**); A Learned... Sermon of the Certainty and Perpetuity of Faith in the Elect (**47–52**); Two Sermons upon Part of St Jude's Epistle.

DATE. c Jan 1824 to autumn 1826: dated 12 Aug 1826 (**37, 40, 41**), 8 Sept 1826 (**15**), and 15 Sept 1826 (**26**). In a letter of Jan 1824 C sent an extract from this book—presumably this copy—for *AR*: see **43** n 1, below. In **41** C says that he is writing "a year or more after the preceding", the PS being dated 12 Aug 1826; and **31** was written after C had written marginalia in SKELTON *Works* (6 vols 1824), which he was reading in late Nov 1825.

1 sig A2 | Dedication to Charles II

*a*Although I know how little leasure *Great Kings* have to read large Books, or indeed any, save only *Gods*... Yet having lived to see the wonderful and happy *Restauration* of *Your Majesty* to *Your* Rightful Kingdoms, and of this *Reformed Church* to its just Rights, Primitive Order, and Pristine Constitution, by *Your Majesties* prudent care, and unparallel'd bounty, I know not what to present more worthy of *Your Majesties* acceptance, and my duty, than these *Elaborate* and *Seasonable Works* of the Famous and Prudent Mr. *Richard Hooker*... to add a further lustre to *Your Majesties* glorious Name, and *happy Reign*, whose transcendent favour, justice, merit, and munificence to the *long afflicted Church* of *England*, is a subject no less worthy of *admiration* than *gratitude* to all Posterity.

? Little Kings, I presume, are better off! O how hateful yet alas! how common, is adulation *in the mouth* of a protestant Bishop[1]—which even Dogs, from whom the metaphor is derived, perpetrate with their Tail![2]—Read the first paragraph, so worthy of of a Christian Minister—then what follows of "prudent care, unparalleled bounty, transcendent Merit," &c. &c—& reflect on the even then generally

---

a Here, as at the beginning and end of most textus in this book, a small X is written in ink as an identifying mark for a copyist, whether HNC, SC, or some other. See **25** n *a* and **27** n *a*

1[1] John Gauden (1605–62), bp of Winchester, wrote the dedication to Charles II for his edition of Hooker's *Works* (1662), of which this 1682 ed is the 4th ed. With the tone of the dedication cf HACKET *Scrinia* 4. Gauden was probably the writer of *Eikon Basilike* in the name of Charles I.

1[2] C may have in mind that the Latin verb *adulo* is often used of dogs and other animals wagging their tails or fawning, and that the root *-ul-* may mean "tail".

suspected papistry and *known* NOTORIOUS profaneness and profligacy of the heartless Brotheller, Charles II!!—[3]

2　pp 15–16 | The Life of Mr Richard Hooker

Mr. *Travers* excepted against Mr. *Hooker*, for that in one of his *] Sermons he declared, *That the assurance of what we believe by the Word of God, is not to us so certain as that which we perceive by Sense.* And Mr. *Hooker* confesseth he said so, and endeavours to justifie it by the Reasons following.

* There is, I confess, a shade of doubt on my mind as to this position of Hooker's. Yet I do not deny that it expresses a truth. ~~My dou~~ The Question in my mind is only, whether it adequately expresses *the* truth. The Ground of my doubt lies in my inability to compare two things that differ in *kind.* It is impossi~~bility~~le that any conviction of the Reason, even where no act of the Will advenes as a co-efficient, should possesses[a] the vividness of an immediate Object of the *Senses*: for this vividness is given by Sensation. Equally impossible is it, that any truth of the super-sensuous Reason should possess the *evidence* of the pure Sense. ~~Al~~ Even the Mathematician does not find the same *evidence* in the results of the transcendental Algebra, as in the demonstrations of simple Geometry.[1] But has he less assurance?—In answer to Hooker's argument I say, that God refers to our sensible experience to aid our will by the vividness of sensible impressions, and 2nd to aid our understanding of the truths revealed—not to increase the conviction of their certainty, when they have been understood.　　*S. T. C.*

3　p 27, concluded in pencil | An Appendix to the Life of Mr Richard Hooker

[An addition to passages restored by Dr Barnard to the text of posthumous Bks VI–VIII:] First, *As there could be in Natural Bodies no motion of any thing, unless there were some first which moved all things, and continued Unmoveable; even so in Politick Societies, there must be some unpunishable, or else no Men shall suffer punishment*...

It is most painful to connect the venerable, almost sacred, name of R. HOOKER with such a specimen of puerile sophistry—scarce worthy of a Court-Bishop's Trencher-chaplain in the slavering times

---

[a] A slip for "possess"

1[3] See also HACKET *Scrinia* **14** (at n 4).　　2[1] See **31** (at n 3) and **41** n 2, below.

of our Scotch Solomon![1]—[a]It is, however, of some value, some *interest* at least, as a striking example of the Confusion of an *Idea* without a *Conception*. Every Conception has its sole reality in its being referable to a Thing or Class of Things, of which it is or of the common characters of which it is a *reflection*. An Idea is a POWER (δυναμις νοερα)[2] that constitutes its own Reality—and is, in order of Thought, necessarily antecedent to the Things, in which it is, more or less adequately, realized—while a Conception is as necessarily posterior.[3]

4 p 28, evidently referring to pp 26–8

I have declared in his Life... that he lived to finish the remaining three of the proposed eight; but, whether we have the last three [books] as finisht by himself, is a Just and Material Question; concerning which I do declare, That I have been told almost forty years past, by one that very well knew Mr. *Hooker*, and the affairs of his Family, that about a month after the death of Mr. *Hooker*, Bishop *Whitgift*, then Arch-Bishop of *Canterbury*, sent one of his Chaplains to enquire of Mrs. *Hooker*, for the three remaining Books of Polity, writ by her Husband; of which, she would not, or could not give any account; and I have been told, that about three months after the Bishop procured her to be sent for to *London*, and then by his procurement she was to be examined...concerning the disposal of those Books...the Bishop invited her to *Lambeth*, and, after some friendly questions, she confessed to him, *that one Mr.* Chark *and another Minister that dwelt near* Canterbury, *came to her, and desired that they might go into her Husbands Study, and look upon some of his Writings; and that there they two burnt and tore many of them, assuring her that they were writings not fit to be seen, and that she knew nothing more concerning them.* Her lodging was then in *King-street* in *Westminster*, where she was found next morning dead in her Bed, and her new Husband suspected and questioned for it, but was declared innocent of her Death....

In this Relation concerning these three doubtful Books of Mr. *Hooker*'s, my purpose was to enquire, then set down what I observed and know, which I have done, not as an engaged Person, but

[a] From here the note is continued in pencil without a break in the line

[3][1] James VI, King of Scotland, afterwards James I of England (1566–1625).
[3][2] An "intellectual power". See BÖHME **122** n 4.

[3][3] See **18** and **23**, below. For the distinction between ideas and conceptions see also DAVISON **14** and n 3 and cf DONNE *Sermons* COPY B **60**.

indifferently, and now leave my Reader to give sentence, for their Legitimation, as to himself, but so, as to leave others the same Liberty of believing, or disbelieving them to be Mr. *Hooker*'s. . .

It is a strange blind story, this of the 3 last books, and of Hooker's live Relict, the Beast without Beauty, instead of Beauty and the Beast.[1] But Saravia?? if honest Isaac's[2] account of the tender, confidential, even confessorial Friendship of Hooker and Saravia be not accurate—how chanced it, that H. did not entrust the MSS to his friend who stood [be]side[a] him in his last moments? At all events, Saravia must have known whether they had or had not received the Author's last hand. Why were not M[r] *Chark* and *the other* Canterbury parson called to account—questioned at least as to the truth of M[rs] Joan's story. Verily, I cannot help suspecting that the doubts cast on the authenticity of the latter books by the High Church Party originated in their dislike of the Contents.

In short, tis a blind story, a true Canterbury Tale,[3] dear Isaac!

S. T. C.

OF THE LAWS OF ECCLESIASTICAL POLITIE

5   p 48 | Preface § 2

Here were the seeds sown of that controversie which sprang up between Beza *and* Erastus, *about the Matter of Excommunication, Whether*

a Letters supplied by the editor

4[1] About Hooker's allegedly unhappy marriage there is doubt: he named his "wel-beloved wife" (*née* Joan Church-man) sole executrix and residuary legatee.

4[2] I.e. Izaak Walton, the "dear Isaac" at the end of the annotation, C assuming correctly that Walton was author of the Appendix to the Life as well as of the Life. (The revised version of Walton's Life was first prefixed to the 1666 ed of Hooker's *Works*, then to 1676, and to 1682—C's ed.) Cf a letter "writ to Mr. Walton, by Dr. King, Lord Bishop of Chichester", which begins "Honest Isaac...". HOOKER sig B.

4[3] "Blind" because it leads to no clear conclusion. The first edition of *Ecclesiastical Politie* (?1594) announced "Eyght Bookes" and listed a summary of the contents of eight books, but included the text of only four. Bk v was published in 1597, but no more appeared during Hooker's lifetime. Bks vi and viii were published in 1648, Bk vii appeared in 1662 in Gauden's ed of Hooker's *Works*. The genuineness of the posthumous Bks vi–viii has been much disputed. John Spencer stated in his ed of 1604 that the last three books had been completed by Hooker, that they had been destroyed by "some evil disposed minds", leaving "nothing but the old imperfect mangled draughts dismembred into pieces", but that "it is intended that the world shall see them as they are". HOOKER p 26 (not annotated). Critical examination of Hooker's surviving papers and of the many transcripts made from his notes shows that Bks vii and viii are, though imperfect, drawn from Hooker's working papers for *Ecclesiastical Politie*, but that Bk vi, though drawn from genuine notes of Hooker's, is based on material not pertinent to the *Politie*. The account of the fate of Hooker's mss as given in Walton's Appendix has been generally accepted by biographers.

there ought to be in all Churches an Eldership having power to Excommunicate, and a part of that Eldership to be of necessity certain, chosen out from amongst the Laity for that purpose. In which Disputation, they have, as to me it seemeth, divided very equally the Truth between them...

How readily would this and indeed all the disputes respecting the powers and constitution of Church-government have been settled, or perhaps prevented, had there been a insight into the distinct nature & origin of the National Church and the Church under Christ! To the ignorance of this, all the fierce contentions between the Puritans and the Episcopalians under Eliz. and the Stuarts; all the errors and exorbitant Pretentions of the Church of Scotland; and the Heats and Antipathies of our present Dissenters, may be demonstrably traced.[1]

S. T. C.

6   p 49 | § 3

Pythagoras, by bringing up his Scholars in speculative knowledge of numbers, made their conceits therein so strong, that when they came to the contemplation of things natural, they imagined that in every particular thing, they even beheld, as it were with their eyes, how the Elements of Number gave essence and Being to the Works of Nature: A thing in reason impossible, which notwithstanding through their mis-fashioned pre-conceit, appeared unto them no less certain, than if Nature had written it in the very Foreheads of all the Creatures of God.

I am too little conversant with the Volumes of Duns Scotus, to know whether he is an *exception*; but ~~it~~ I can think of no other instance of *metaphysical Genius* in an Englishman.[1] Judgement, solid Sense, Invention in Spec~~ail~~tialies[a], fortunate Anticipations, and instinctive *Fore-tact* of Truth, in these we can shew *Giants*.—It is evident from this example from the Pythagorean School, that ⟨not⟩ even our incomparable Hooker could raise himself to the idea:[2] so rich in truth

---

a Presumably for "Specialties"

5[1] For C's distinction between the National Church and the Church of Christ see HACKET *Scrinia* 33 and n 2.

6[1] See also DE WETTE 2. For C's acquaintance with Duns Scotus' works see BLANCO WHITE *Practical Evidence* 13 n 5. In Apr 1801 he had visited Durham Cathedral Library in search of (*inter alia*) Duns Scotus' books, but could find only his *De sententiis*. See also BAXTER *Reliquiae* COPY A 34 n 1.

6[2] For Hooker as "a Giant of the Race, Aristotle" see 19, below. C seems to be reacting to Hooker's failure to understand that Pythagoras was dealing in *ideas*, not *pre-conceits* (hypothetical premisses). Cf 3, above. It is surprising to find here among the gifts by which C characterises the English metaphysical giants—abilities that he considers inferior to the power to apprehend ideas directly—"the instinctive *Fore-tact* of

which is contained in the words, Numero, Pondere, et Mensurâ generantur Cœli et Terra.—[3] + O, αριθμος ὑπεραριθμιος Had Hooker asked himself concerning WILL, ABSOLUTE WILL = numerus omnes numeros ponens, numquam positus!—[4]

7 p 50 | continuing **6** textus

When they of the Family of Love *have it once in their heads, that Christ doth not signifie any one Person, but a Quality whereof many are partakers...How plainly do they imagine, that the Scripture every where speaketh in the favour of that Sect?*

If the Familists thought of Christ, as a *Quality*, it was a grievous error indeed![1] But I have my doubts whether this was not rather an *inference* drawn by their Persecutors.

8 p 51

When Instruction doth them no good, let them feel but the least degree of most mercifully tempered Severity, they fasten on the head of the *] *Lord's Vicegerents here on Earth, whatsoever they any where find uttered against the cruelty of Blood-thirsty men; and to themselves they draw all the Sentences which Scripture hath in the favour of Innocency persecuted for the Truth; yea, they are of their due and deserved sufferings, no less proud than those ancient distributors, to whom St.* Augustine *writeth saying,* Martyrs, rightly so named, are they not which suffer for their disorder, and for the ungodly breach they have made of Christian Unity; but which, for Righteousness sake are persecuted: For *Agar* also suffered persecution at the hands of *Sarah*; wherein, she which did impose, was holy, and she unrighteous which did bear the burthen....If that must needs be the true Church which

---

Truth": elsewhere he places a high value upon the (metaphorically) tactual capacities of the mind and its ability to touch "the Tact-nerve of Truth". See e.g. *CL* III 541 (3 Nov 1814). "Foretact" is not in *OED*.

6[3] "By Number, Weight, and Measure the Heavens and Earth are brought into being". Cf "Omnia in mensura, et numero, et pondere disposuisti" ("Thou hast ordered all things in measure, number, and weight") in Wisd 11.20. C similarly varies this passage in *CN* IV 5406 (see also n 4, below).

6[4] "Positive zero, number above number...number positing all number, never [itself] posited!" See also *CN* III 4418 f 14. What is here symbolised by "+0" C considered in N 26 in c Jun 1826: *CN* IV 5406 ff 88^{v}–91^{v}, a note that continues with a longer and more impassioned answer to Hooker on Pythagoras in ff 93^{v}–94^{v}, continued in *CN* IV 5442 ff 95^{v}–96^{v}. For ἀριθμοἰ (numbers) as ideas see BÖHME **6** n 10 and cf **171** n 2, **172** n 1; see also *C&S* (*CC*) 166, 184.

7[1] For the Familists see DONNE *Sermons* COPY B **117** n 1.

doth endure persecution, and not that which persecuteth, let them ask of the Apostle, what Church *Sarah* did represent, when she held her Maid in affliction...even...The true Church of God.

* How great*a* the influence of the Age on the strongest Minds, when so eminently wise a man as Richard Hooker could overlook the obvious impolicy of inflicting punishments which the Sufferer himself will regard as Merits, and all who ~~are~~ have any need to be deterred, will extol as Martyrdom. Even where the *necessity* can be plausibly pretended, it is *war*, not punitive Law.[1] (And Augustin's argument from Sarah!)—[2]

9   p 52 | § 4

We require you to find out but one Church upon the face of the whole Earth, that hath been ordered by your Discipline, or hath not been ordered by ours, that is to say, By Episcopal Regiment, sithence the time that the Blessed Apostles were here conversant.

Hooker was so good a man that it would be wicked ~~him~~ to suspect him of knowingly playing the Sophist. And yet strange it is, that he should not have been aware that it was Prelacy, not primitive Episcopacy, the *thing* not the name that the Reformers contended against/ and if the Catholic Church & the National Clerisy ħ were (as both parties unhappily took for granted) one and the same, contended with good reason.[1] Knox's Ecclesiastic Polity[2] (worthy of a Lycurgus!)[3] adopted Bishops under a different name; or rather under a translation instead of a corruption of the name, Episcopus.— He would have had Superintendents.[4]

9A   p 53

...every Christian Church standeth bound by the Law of God to put elect] *down Bishops, and in their room to* reject *an Eldership so authorized...for the Government of each Parish.*

a The * and two first words, and * alongside textus, in pencil

8[1] Cf HACKET *Century* **4**.

8[2] In textus.

9[1] See **5** n 1, above, and **10** (at n 2), below.

9[2] I.e. the so-called *First Book of Discipline* of the Church of Scotland (1560), drawn up by John Knox and other ministers in response to a commission from the Scottish Parliament that they prepare a statement of "the policy and discipline of the kirk as well as they had done the doctrine". In this book Knox's opinions were dominant. For Knox generally see BLOMFIELD **6** and n 3 and cf DONNE *Sermons* COPY A **7** and n 2.

9[3] Lawgiver to the Spartans, perhaps legendary. See DAVISON **6** n 1.

9[4] For the dispute about the meaning of *episcopus* see HERBERT **19** and n 1 and e.g. HEYLYN **3**.

10   pp 54–6 | §5

*A Law is the Deed of the whole Body Politick, whereof if ye judge your
selves to be any part, then is the Law even your Deed also.*

A fiction of Law, for the purpose of giving to that, which is
necessarily empirical, the form and consequence of a Science—to the
reality of which a Code of Laws can only approximate by compressing
all liberty and individuality into a Despotism—As Justinian to
Alfred, and ⟨the the Consuls, and Senate of⟩ Constantinople to the
Lord Mayor, Aldermen, and Common Council of En London; so
the Imperial Roman Code to the Common, Statute and Customary
Law of England.[1]—The Advocates of Discipline would, according
to our present notions of civil rights, have been justified in putting
Fact against Fiction; & ⟨might⟩ have challenged Hooker to shew,
first, that the Constitution of the Church in Christ was a congruous
subject of parliamentary Legislation; that the Legislators were bonâ
fide determined by spiritual views; and that the jealousy and arbitrary
Principles of the Queen, aided by motives of worldly state policy, ex.
gr. the desire to conciliate the Catholic Potentates by retaining all,
she could, of the exterior of the Romish Church, its hierarchy, its
Church Ornaments, and its Ceremonies, were not the Substitutes for
the Holy Spirit in influencing the majorities in the two Houses of
Parliament. It is my own belief, that the Puritans and the Prelatists
divided the Truth between them; and as half-truths are whole
Errors,[2] were both equally in the wrong—the Prelatists in contending
for a Church in Christ (i.e. the collective number τῶν
ἐκκεκλημένων, = ἐκκλησιᾳ)[3] which only belonged, but which right-
fully did belong, to a National Church, as a *component* Estate of the
Realm (sc. *En*clesia) the Puritans in requiring of the Enclesia what
was only requisite or possible for the Ecclesia.[4] Arch-bishop Grindal
is an illustrious exception.[5] He saw the *whole* truth; and saw, that

10[1] For C's praise of the wisdom of
British common law see e.g. *Friend (CC)*
I 246, and cf ENCYCLOPAEDIA LON-
DINENSIS 7.

10[2] Cf HOWIE 6 (from n 1 onward).
On "half-truths, the most dangerous of
errors" see HAYLEY 1 and n 8.

10[3] "Of those called out [of the
world], that is, the Church". See FIELD
6 and n 1 and cf n 4, below. C refers to
this annotation in N 36 f 33ᵛ (25 Dec
1827) (*CN* v). For HOOKER v §13 on the

origin of the word "Church" see *C&S*
(*CC*) 125 n 2. Cf *CL* v 455 (c 16 May
1825).

10[4] See HACKET *Scrinia* 33 and n 2.
See also 14 and 15, below.

10[5] Edmund Grindal (c 1519–83),
Abp of Canterbury ("the last of the Race
of Luther & Melancthon" in BLOMFIELD
6), whose *Life* by John Strype (1710) C
annotated. C seems to be thinking of the
letter of 20 Dec 1576 to Queen Elizabeth
in which Grindal defined the relations

the functions of the *Enc*lesiastic and those of the *Ecc*lesiastic were not the less distinct, because both were capable of being exercised by the same Person; & vice versâ, not the less compatible in the same subject because distinct in themselves. The Lord Chief Justice of the King's Bench is a Fellow of the Royal Society.[6]   S. T. C.

11   pp 56–7 | § 6

*] *God was not ignorant, that the Priests and Judges, whose sentence in Matters of Controversie he ordained should stand, both might and oftentimes would be deceived in their judgement. Howbeit, better it was in the eye of his understanding, that sometime an erroneous sentence Definitive should prevail, till the same authority perceiving such oversight, might afterwards correct or reverse it, than that strifes should have respite to grow, and not come speedily unto some end...*

* It is difficult to say, which most shines thro' this whole passage, the Spirit of Wisdom or the Spirit of Meekness![1] The fatal error of the Romish Church did not consists in the inappellability of the Councils, or that an acquiescence in their decisions and decree was a duty, binding on the Conscience of the Dissentients—not, I say, in contending for a practical infallibility of Council or Pope, but in laying claim to an actual and absolute immunity from error, and consequently for the unrepealability of their decisions by any ~~after~~ succeeding Council or Pope.[2] Hence even wise decisions—wise under the particular circumstances & times—degenerated into mischievous follies, by having the privilege of immortality without any exemption from the dotage of superannuation. Hence Errors became like Glaciers or Ice-bergs in the Frozen ⟨Ocean⟩ unthawed by Summer, and growing from the fresh deposits of each returning Winter.—

between the spiritual and temporal power when he declined to accept the Queen's order to suppress "prophesyings" (clerical meetings for the exposition and discussion of scripture). The Queen then ordered all the bishops to suppress prophesyings in their dioceses and suspended Grindal for six months from his jurisdictional, but not his spiritual, functions as Abp of Canterbury. See STRYPE *Grindal* App x. See also **36**, below.

10[6] It is not certain that C has a particular person in mind; at least no Lord Chief Justice of King's Bench who was also a Fellow of the Royal Society has been identified.

11[1] On 6 Sept 1826 C noted: "Reading Hooker's Preface. See p. 56. 57—The Spirit of Wisdom and of Meekness equally translucent.—" He continued with a "Mem.—" that "No sophistry more pitiful...than that of reasoning by possible...consequences...". *CN* IV 5437.

11[2] A key statement of C's on the error of the doctrine of the infallibility of the Roman Catholic Church. Cf CHILLINGWORTH COPY A **8**, COPY B **5**.

12 p 57

An Argument necessary and demonstrative is such, as being proposed
unto any man, and understood; the mind cannot chuse, but inwardly
assent. Any one such reason dischargeth, I grant, the Conscience, and
setteth it at full liberty.

I would not concede even so much as this. It may well chance, that
even an argument demonstrative if understood, may be adducible
against some one sentence of a whole Liturgy; and yet the means of
removing it without a palpable over-balance of evil, may not exist
for a time—& either there is no command against schism, or we are
bound in such small matters to offer the sacrifice of willing silence
to the public peace of the Church—This would not, however, prevent
a Minister from pointing out the defect, in his character as a *Doctor*
or learned Theologian, to the Learned.[1]

13 p 59 | § 8

For adventuring to erect the Discipline of Christ, without the leave of
the Christian Magistrate, haply ye may condemn us as fools, in that
we hazard thereby our estates and persons, further than you which are
that way more wise, think necessary: But of any offence or sin therein
committed against God, with what conscience can you accuse us, when
your own positions are, That the things we observe, should every of them
be dearer unto us, than ten thousand lives; that they are the peremptory
Commandments of God; that no mortall man can dispense with them;
and that the Magistrate grievously sinneth, in not constraining
thereunto?

~~This~~ Hoc argumentum ad invidiam, το συκους φαινειν, nimis
sycophanticum est, quam ut mihi placeat a tanto Viro![a] Besides, it
contradicts Hooker's own very judicious Rule—that to discuss and
represent is the office of the Learned, as Individuals—because the
Truth may be entire in any one Mind; but to *do* belongs to the

a At first sight ." But probably trouble with the pen

12[1] The minister would then be acting
not as a member of the Church of Christ,
the *ecclesia*, but speaking to his fellow
members of the *enclesia*, the clerisy, the
learned class in general. Cf **10**, above.

13[1] "This argument appealing to
hatred, informing against figs, is—from
so great a man—too sycophantic to
please me!" It was a commonplace that
in classical Greek the sycophant—from

συκους φαίνειν, "to show figs"—was
the vexatious informer on trivial matters,
one explanation being that he informed
about evasions of the laws relating to figs.
The modern meaning of "flatterer" or
"toady" would arise from the fact that
the informer curries favour with the
authorities. In *CN* IV 4970 C plays upon
both meanings. Cf also *BL* ch 10 (*CC*)
I 188–9.

Supreme Power as the Will of the whole Body Politic—and in effective Action Individuals are mere Fractions without any legitimate Referee to add them together.

14 pp 59[a]

Again, it may justly be feared, whether our English Nobility, when the Matter came in tryal, would contentedly suffer themselves to be always at the Call, and to stand to the sentence of a number of mean persons, assisted with the presence of their poor Teacher...From whom...no Appeal may be made unto any one of higher Power...

Hooker's Objection from the Nobility & Gentry of the Realm is unanswerable, and within half a century afterwards proved insurmountable.—

Imagine a Sun containing within its proper Atmosphere a multitude of ~~circling~~ transparent Satellites, lost in the Glory or all joining to form the visible Phasis or Disk. And then beyond the precincts of this Sun a number of opake Bodies at various distances, and having a common center of their own, around which they revolved, and yet more or less according to the lesser or greater distance partaking of the Light and natural Warmth of the Sun, which I have been supposing; but not sharing in ~~the~~ its *peculiar* influences, or in the Solar Life sustainable only by the vital air of the Solar Atmosphere.— The opake Bodies constitute the National Church, the Sun = the Church Spiritual.[1]

15 pp 60–1 | referring to **14**

—/The defect of the Simile overleaf, arising necessarily out of the incompossibility of spiritual prerogatives with material Bodies under the proprieties and necessities of Space, is—that it does not, as no Concrete or visual Image can, represent the possible duplicity of the Individuals, the aggregate of whom constitutes the National Church— so that any one Individual, or any number of such Individuals, may at the same time be by an act of their own Members of the Church Spiritual—and in every congregation may form an Ecclesia or Christian Community—and how to facilitate and favor this without any schism from the *En*clesia, and without any disturbance of the Body Politic, was the Problem which Grindal and the Bishops of the

---

[a] This note looks like a continuation of **13**, and is so printed in *LR*

14[1] C found this figure defective: see **15**, below.

first Generation of the Reformed Church sought to solve,[1] and it is the Problem which every earnest Christian endued with competent gifts, and who is at the same time a Patriot and a Philanthropist, ought to propose to himself, as the ingens Desiderium proborum![2]

S. T. Coleridge.—8 Sept[r] 1826.—

16 p 62

*] *Baptism of Infants, although confest by themselves, to have been continued even sithence the very Apostles own times, yet they altogether condemned, partly because sundry errors are of no less antiquity; and partly for that there is no commandment in the Gospel of Christ, which saith,* Baptize Infants; *but he contrariwise in saying,* Go Preach and Baptize....

* Q[y]—I cannot say what the Fanatic Anabaptists of whom Hooker is speaking may have admitted; but the more sober and learned Anti-pædobaptists, who differed in this point only from the Reformed Churches, have all, I believe, denied the practice of Infant Baptism during the first Century[1]

17 pp 70–3 | Bk I § 2

All things that are, have some operation not violent or casual: Neither doth any thing ever begin to exercise the same, without some fore-conceived end for which it worketh. And the end which it work-eth for, is not obtained, unless the Work be also fit to obtain it by; for unto every end, every operation will not serve. That which doth assign unto each thing the kind, that which doth moderate the force and power, that which doth appoint the form and measure of working, the same we term a *Law*.

See the Essay on Method, FRIEND, Vol. III.[1]—Hooker's words literally and grammatically interpreted seem to assert the Antecedence

15[1] See the last three sentences of **10**, above.

15[2] The "great desideratum of honest men".

16[1] For C's assertion "not that Infant Baptism was *not*; but—that there exist no sufficient proofs that it *was*, the practice of the Apostolic Age" see *AR* (1825) 361n. See also BAXTER *Reliquiae* COPY A **8**.

17[1] C quoted the last sentence of textus, ascribing it to "the judicious HOOKER" (for which see title-page, and cf **19** at n 2, below) in Sect II Essay IX on the principles of method, as parallel to Plato and Bacon on the nature of ideas and laws. *Friend (CC)* I 493. He also used a long quotation from HOOKER p 70 (not annotated) as epigraph to the essay "On the Grounds of Government...": in the 1809–10 *Friend (CC)* II 123 (cf II 81n) (I 186, cf I 114); repeated selectively in *BL* ch 4 (*CC*) I 88.

of *the Thing* to its *kind*, i.e. essential characters; $\langle \& \rangle$ to its force & ~~to~~ together with its *form* and *measure* of working, i.e. to its specific and distinctive Characters—in short, the words assert the pre-existence of the Thing to all its constituent powers, qualities and properties. Now this is either—I. equivalent to the assertion of a prima et nuda Materia,[2] so happily ridiculed by the Author of Hudibras,[3] and which under any scheme of Cosmogony is a mere phantom, having its whole and sole substance in an impotent effort of the Imagination or sensuous Fancy; but which is utterly precluded by the doctrine of Creation, which it in like manner negatives.—Or, II[ndly] the words assert a self-destroying Absurdity—viz. the antecedence of a thing to ~~the grounds~~ thing itself—as if having asserted that Water *consisted* of Hydrogen = 77 and Oxygen = 23,[4] I should talk of Water as existing before the creation of Hydrogen and Oxygen—All *Laws*[a] indeed are ~~not~~[b] constitutive;[5] and it would require a longer train of argument that[c] a note can contain, to shew what *a Thing* is; but this at least is quite certain that in the order of *thought* it must be posterior to the Law that constitutes it. But such in fact was Hooker's meaning, and the word, Thing, is used prolepticè, in favor of the imagination—as appears from the sentences that follow, in which the Creative Idea is ~~d~~ declared to be the Law of the things thereby created.[6] A productive Idea, manifesting itself and its reality in the Product, is a Law: and when the Product is phænomenal (i.e. an object of ~~the~~ outward Senses) a Law of Nature. The Law is Res *noumenon*; the Thing is *Res* ~~P~~ *phænomenon*.[7] A physical LAW, in the

<hr>

[a] Underlined in pencil
[b] Cancelled in pencil
[c] A slip for "than"

17[2] A "first and naked Matter".

17[3] Samuel Butler *Hudibras* I i 560–3. With the help of special drops in the eyes, Hudibras
    had *First Matter* seen undresst:
He took her naked all alone,
Before one Rag of *Form* was on.

17[4] The approximate proportion of hydrogen to oxygen in water, by weight, is 11 per cent and 89 per cent. For Beddoes's guess at 27 and 73 see *Logic* (*CC*) 192 and n 1.

17[5] Cf "...the Supreme Reason, whose knowledge is creative, and antecedent to the things known, is distinguished from the understanding or creaturely mind of the individual, the

acts of which are posterior to the things, it records and arranges". *SM* (*CC*) 18–19. Cf *Friend* (*CC*) I 515 n 2: "the Reason or Law of a thing constitutes its abstract Being, the ground of its Reality".

17[6] Pp 70–1, still in § 2, reads: "...only the Works and Operations of God, have him both for their Worker, and for the Law whereby they are wrought. The Being of God, is a kind of Law to his working, for that Perfection which God is, giveth Perfection to that he doth."

17[7] The Law is "a *noumenal* Thing"; the Thing is "a *phaenomenal Thing*".

right sense of the term, is the *sufficient* Cause of the Appearances/ causa *sub-faciens*—[8]

P.S.[a] What a deeply interesting Volume might be written on the symbolic import of the primary relations and dimensions of Space[9]— Long, broad, deep or depth; superficies; upper, under or above and below; right, left, horizontal, perpendicular, oblique. And then the order of Causation, or that which gives intelligibility, and the reverse of order of Effects or that which gives the conditions of actual *existence*. Without the higher the lower would want its intelligibility, without the lower the higher could not have *existed*. The Infant is a riddle of which the Man is the Solution; but the Man could not exist but with the Infant as its ante[ce]dent.[b]—

18   p 71

Our God is One, or rather very Oneness, and meer Unity, having nothing but it self in it self, and not consisting (as all things do beside God) of many things. In which Essential Unity of God, a Trinity Personal nevertheless subsisteth, after a manner far exceeding the possibility of mans conceit.

If "conceit" here means *Conception*, the remark is most true: for the Trinity is an Idea, and no Idea can be rendered by a conception. An Idea is essentially inconceivable.[1] But if it be meant, that the Trinity is otherwise inconceivable, than as the divine Eternity, & as *every* attribute of God is & must be—*then* ⟨neither⟩ the *commonness* of the Language here used, nor the high authority of the users, can deter me from denouncing it as untrue and dangerous. So far is it from being true, that the Trinity is the only Form, in which an Idea of God is possible—unless indeed it be a Spinozistic or World-God.[2]

19   p 75 | 1 § 4

But now that we may lift up our eyes (as it were) from the Foot-stool to the Throne of God, and leaving these Natural, consider a little

---

[a] This follows in the same line of ms but is written in a different hand and ink
[b] Letters supplied by the editor

17[8] "Sufficient (adequate)" is etymologically the same as *sub-faciens*— "making from underneath"; the sufficient cause is literally the basic cause.

17[9] On interior or psychic space see e.g. *CN* I 1771, 1823 and n, II 2402 ff 128v–9.

18[1] I.e. beyond the field of conception. See 3 and n 3, above, and **23**, below. Cf *C&S (CC)* 20.

18[2] Cf *AR* (1825) 169–70: "I am clearly convinced, that the scriptural and only true Idea of God will, in its developement, be found to involve the Idea of the Tri-unity."

the state of Heavenly and Divine Creatures: Touching Angels, which are Spirits Immaterial and Intellectual, the glorious Inhabitants of those Sacred Palaces, where...all joy, tranquillity, and peace, even for ever and ever doth dwell.

All this disquisition on the Angels confirms my remark, that our admirable Hooker was a Giant of the Race, Aristotle ⧸✳ Plato.[1]— Hooker was truly *judicious*—the consummate Synthesis of Understanding and Sense.[2] An ample and most ordonnant Conceptionist, to the tranquil Empyrean of *Ideas* he had not ascended. Of the passages cited from Scripture how few would bear a strict scrutiny— either namely 1. Divine Appearances/ Jehovah in human form/ or 2. the Imagery of Visions, and all Symbolic—or 3. Name of Honor given to Prophets, Apostles & Bishops: or lastly, mere ⟨accomodation to⟩ popular notions.[3]

20　p 75

The fall of Angels therefore, was Pride: Since their fall, their practices have been the clean contrary unto those before mentioned; for being dispersed, some in the Air, some on the Earth, some in the Water: some amongst the Minerals, Dens and Caves that are under the *]* Earth, they have, by all means, laboured to effect an Universal Rebellion against the Laws, and as far as in them lieth, utter destruction of the Works of God.

* Childish; but the childishness of the Age, without which neither Hooker nor Luther could have acted on their contemporaries with the intense and beneficent energy, which they (God be praised!) did act.[1]

21　p 76

Thus much therefore may suffice for Angels, the next unto whom in degree are Men.

19[1] See **22** (at n 4), below. For the contradistinction between Aristotle and Plato see **22** and n 2. In *CN* IV 5288 C refers to Aristotle as "that Goliath in Understanding".

19[2] Cf, however, "I must acknowledge, with some hesitation, that I think Hooker has been a little over-credited for his judgment." *TT* 29 Aug 1827.

19[3] For C on angels see also **20** and **21**, below, and HACKET *Century* **16** and nn.

For examples of the four types of scriptural passages on angels see (1) e.g. GREW **39** on Acts 6.30, 38; (2) e.g. Jacob's Ladder in FICHTE *Bestimmung* **11** and n 1, and cf *Friend (CC)* I 58–9; (3) e.g. HACKET *Century* **16** (at n 3) on 1 Cor 10.11; (4) e.g. GREW **25** n 3 on the messenger in Job; cf BIBLE COPY B **71** n 1. Cf BIBLE COPY B **139** on Eph 2.2—"mere fictions".

20[1] Cf HACKET *Scrinia* **15, 26**, and **29**.

St Augustin well remarks that only three distinct Genera of ⟨Living⟩ Beings are conceivable—1. The Infinite Rational: 2. The finite rational: 3. The finite irrational—i.e. God: Man: Animal. Ergo— Angels can only be Men with wings on their shoulders—Were our Bodies transparent to our Souls, we should be Angels.[1]

22   pp 86–7 | I § 10

*] It is no improbable opinion therefore which the Arch-Philosopher was of, That as the chiefest person in every houshold, was alwayes as it were a King, so when numbers of housholds joyned themselves in Civil Societies together, Kings were the first kind of Governours amongst them.

* There are and can be only two Schools of Philosophy/ differing in kind and in Source. Differences in degree and in accident may be many; but these constitute Schools kept by different Teachers ~~of~~ with different degrees of Genius, Talent &c—Auditories of Philosophizers, not different Philosophe~~ries~~.—Schools of Philopsophy (the love of empty noise) of Psilology, and Misosophy are ~~numer~~ out of the question.[1] Schools of Philosophy there are but two—best named by the Arch-philosopher of each—viz. Plato and Aristotle. Every man capable of philosophy at all (& there are not many such) is a *born* Platonist or a *born* Aristotelean.[2] Hooker, as might have been anticipated from the epithet of Arch-philosopher applied to the Stagyrite *sensu monarchico*,[3] was of the latter family—a comprehensive, rich, vigorous, ~~and~~ *discreet* ~~or~~ and discretive, Conceptualist—but not an *Ideist*.—[4]   S. T. C.—

21[1] For St Augustine on the "Genera of Living Beings" see *C&S* (*CC*) 169 n 4. In Jul–Sept 1809 C copied into a notebook a passage from Hooker p 80 (not marked in C's copy) together with a quotation from Theophrastus taken from a shoulder-note on the same page, and used the Hooker passage as an epigraph in *Friend* (*CC*) I 464. *CN* III 3574 and n. He also quoted the Theophrastus passage in *Logic* (*CC*) 204. This extract ends with a passage from I § 10 that C also quoted in Lect 8 of the 1811 series, combining it with a long quotation from I § 11. *C on Sh* 90–1 n 2. Also in *CN* IV 5443 (14 Sept 1826) C cites and quotes from Hooker pp 81 and 82; see also **23** n 5 and **26** n 4, below.

22[1] Philo-psophy—from ψόφος, noise mere sound, high-sounding words. Not in *OED* (through HNC's muddling his transcript the word does not appear in *LR* III 33). Psilology—"mere or empty talk": *OED*, citing the incorrect text of *LR*, attaches to this word the parenthesis that belongs to "Philopsophy". Misosophy—hatred of wisdom, the reverse of philosophy (love of wisdom): *OED* cites this instance from *LR*.

22[2] For other versions of this well-known statement see *P Lects* Lects 2, 5 (1949) 107, 186–7, and 403 n 44. See also *TT* 2 Jul 1830 and cf *CN* III 3756 (c Feb–Apr 1810) and Tennemann VIII i ⁻4–⁻2, referring to 130.

22[3] "*In the sense of monarchic*"—i.e. he is sole king of philosophers.

22[4] Cf **19** and n 1, above, and **42** n 3, below.

23 pp 88–9

*] Of this point therefore we are to note, that sith Men naturally have no full and perfect power to command whole Politick Multitudes of Men; therefore utterly without our consent, we could in such sort be at no Mans commandment living. And to be commanded, we do consent, when that Society whereof we are part hath at any time before consented, without revoking the same after by the like Universal Agreement. Wherefore, as any Mans Deed past is good as long as himself continueth; so the Act of a Publick Society of Men done Five hundred years sithence, standeth as theirs, who presently are of the same Societies, because Corporations are Immortal; we were then alive in our Predecessors, and they in their Successors do live still. Laws therefore Humane of what kind soever, are available by consent.

* No nobler or clearer example could be given of what an IDEA is, as contra-distinguished from a Conception of the Understanding,[1] correspondent to some Fact or Facts, quorum Notæ communes con-capiuntur[2]—the common characters of which are taken together under one distinct Exponent, hence named a Conception—and Conceptions are internal subjective Words. Reflect on an original Social Contract, as an *incident*, or historical *fact*: and its gross improbability, not to say impossibility, will stare you in the Face. But an ever originating Social Contract *is* an Idea, which exists and works continually and efficaciously in the Moral Being of every free Citizen, tho' in the greater number unconsciously or with a dim & confused Consciousness.[3] And what A POWER it is ![4]—As the vital power compared with the mechanic, as a Father compared with a Moulder in wax or clay, such is the Power of Ideas compared with the influence of Conceptions and Notions![5]—S. T. C.

23[1] See **17** and n 1 and cf **3** and n 3, above.

23[2] C translates as he goes on—"the common characters of which are taken together"—playing upon the Latin origin of the word "conception", *con-capio*, as he does in *C&S* (*CC*) 13, *Logic* (*CC*) 68n, and elsewhere.

23[3] For C on the social contract see esp *C&S* (*CC*) 14: "Now if this be taken as the assertion of an historical fact...I shall run little hazard at this time of day, in declaring the pretended fact a pure fiction...". Cf e.g. *Friend* (*CC*) I 174, 175.

23[4] For "Ideas" as "Truth-powers" see **28** (at n 2), below.

23[5] In an entry of 14 Sept 1826 C noted: "P. 89. Eccles. Pol.—An exquisite passage on the instinctive *Humanity* of Men. 'A manifest token that we wish after a sort of universal fellow-ship with all men appeareth in the wonderful delight, men have, some to visit foreign Countries, some to discover Nations not heard of in former Ages; we all (*all of us*)

24 pp 90–1

*] Be it for the ending of strifes, touching matters of Christian belief, wherein the one part may seem to have probable cause of dissenting from the other; or be it concerning matters of Polity, Order and Regiment in the Church; I nothing doubt but that Christian men should much better frame themselves to those Heavenly Precepts, which our Lord and Saviour, with so great instancy gave, as concerning Peace and Unity, if we did all concur in desire to have the use of Ancient Councils again renewed, rather than these proceedings continued, which either make all Contentions endless, or bring them to one only Determination, and that of all other the worst, which is by Sword.

* This is indeed a Subject that deserves a serious consideration: and it may be said in favor of Hooker's proposal (sc. that the use of anc. Councils be renewed) that a deep and universal Sense of the Abuse of Councils progressively from the the Nicene to that of Trent, and our knowlege of the Causes, Occasions, and Modes of such Abuse, are so far presumptive for its non-recurrence ~~that~~ ⟨it⟩ is as to render it less probable that honest Men will pervert them from ignorance, and ~~will be~~ more difficult for unprincipled Men to do so designedly. Something too must be allowed for an honourable ambition on the part of the Persons so assembled to *disappoint* the general expectation, and win ~~from~~ for themselves the unique title of The Honest Council.—But still comes the Argument, the Blow of which I might more easily blunt, than parry—that if Catholic and Protestant, or even Prot. Episcopalian and Prot. Presbyterian Divines were ⟨generally⟩ wise and charitable enough to form a *Christian* Gen. Council, there would be no need of one. S. T. C.

25 p 91 | referring to **24**

N.B. The reasoning in the Mss Note below,[a] as far as it is in discouragement of a recurrence to General Councils, does not, me saltem judice,[1] conclude against the Suffering our Convocation to

---

[a] I.e. **24**, this afterthought being written in the head-margin, and marked "2" for a copyist (see also **27** n *a*, below)

to know the Affairs and Dealings of other People, yea, to be in league of Amity with them....'" *CN* IV 5443, cited above. Again in Sept–Oct 1829 he noted from p 89: "the Well-spring of that Communion is a natural delight which Man hath to transfuse from himself into others and to receive from others into himself, especially those things wherein the excellency of his kind doth most consist." N 42 f 10ᵛ (*CN* v).

25[1] "In my opinion, at least".

meet. The virtual abrogation of this branch of our Constitution ~~to~~ I have long regarded as one of 3 or 4 Whig-patriotisms, that have succeeded in de-anglicizing the mind of England.[2]

26 pp 92–3 | I §11

With us... although the Beauties, Riches, Honours, Sciences, Vertues and Perfections of all Men living, were in the present possession of one; yet somewhat beyond and above all this, there would still be sought and earnestly thirsted for. So that Nature, even in this life, doth plainly claim and call for a more Divine Perfection, than either of these two that have been mentioned.

Whenever I meet with an ambiguous or multivocal Word, without shewing its meaning fixed, I stand on my guard against a Sophism.[1]—I dislike this term, NATURE, in this place. If it mean the Light that lighteth *every* man that cometh into the World,[2] tis an inapt term: for Reason is Supernatural.—Now that reason in man must have [been][a] first actuated by a direct Revelation from God, I have myself proved[3]—and do not therefore deny, that FAITH as the means of Salvation was first made known by Revelation; but that Reason is incapable of seeing into the fitness and superiority of this means, or that it is a Mystery in any other sense than as all spiritual Truths are Mysteries, I do deny—and deem it both a false and a dangerous doctrine.—[4]

s. t. c. 15 Sept[r] 1826.

a Word supplied by the editor

25[2] Cf BAXTER *Reliquiae* COPY B **115**. By ancient custom two assemblies of the Church of England were held (Convocations), one at Canterbury, the other at York, each by the fifteenth century sitting in an upper house (of bishops) and a lower house. The function of Convocations was to establish the church taxes and to pass canon laws. In pre-Reformation times the deliberations of Convocations were not subject to the civil power, but under Henry VIII (in 1534) they lost their independence. In the early eighteenth century the government secured a bench of bishops in the upper houses whose Whig sympathies ran counter to the generally High Church and Jacobite sentiments of most of the clergy. The resulting conflict was settled in 1717, when the Convocations were prorogued by royal writ and their meetings reduced to formality. Not until 1852 did the Canterbury Convocation return to discussion of substantive matters; York followed in 1861. See also *C&S (CC)* 84, 99, 124.

26[1] See also **41** (at n 1), below. The earliest use of "multivocal" noted in *OED* is quoted from the *LR* version of this annotation.

26[2] John 1.9 (var).

26[3] See e.g. *AR* (1825) 144: "the Image of God in us, which we call REASON".

26[4] In an entry of 14 Sept 1826 C refers to HOOKER "P. 92. All creatures below man seek that ~~reality~~ which is best for them; the perfections of Man alone consisteth in that which is simply best. Love supposes Likeness—in the very act of loving Men Dogs acquire a mysterious affinity to Man...." *CN* IV 5443.

27 p 94

Concerning that Faith, Hope and Charity, without which there can be no Salvation; was there ever any mention made saving only in that Law which God himself hath from Heaven revealed? There is *] not in the World a syllable muttered with certain truth concerning any of these three, more than hath been supernaturally received from the Mouth of the Eternal God.[1]

* [a]That Reason could have *discovered* these divine truths, is one thing; that when discovered by Revelation it is capable of apprehending the beauty and excellence of the things revealed, is another. I may believe the latter, while I utterly reject the former.

28 pp 94–5

Laws therefore concerning these things are Supernatural, both in respect of the manner of delivering them, which is Divine; and also in regard of the things delivered, which are such as have not in Nature any cause from which they flow, but were by the voluntary appointment of God ordained, besides the course of Nature, to rectifie Natures obliquity withal.

That all these Cognitions, together with ⟨the⟩ feälty or faithfulness in the Will whereby the mind of the flesh[1] is brought under captivity to the Mind of the Spirit (the Sensuous Understanding to the Reason), are super*natural*, I not only free[ly][b] grant but fervently contend. But why the very perfection of Reason, viz. those Ideas, or Truth-powers[2] in which both the ⟨spiritual⟩ Light and the spiritual Life of the Soul are co-inherent and *one*, should be called super*rational*, I do not see. For Reason is practical as well as theoretical.—Or even tho' I should exclude the practical Reason, and confine the term Reason to the highest *intellective* power—still I should think it more correct to describe the mysteries of Faith ⟨as⟩ plusquam-rationalia, than *super-rational*.[3] But the Assertions, that provoke this remark,

[a] Above **27** ms is marked "1" for a copyist, and above **28**—as for **25**—"2"
[b] Letters supplied by the editor

27[1] C included **27** textus, with the whole long prefatory section of the same sentence, in a literary lecture of 13 Mar 1818: *Misc C* 217.
28[1] φρόνημα σαρκός (of Rom 8.6–7), for which see Baxter *Reliquiae* copy B **115** n 10.

28[2] Cf **23** (at n 4), above. See also Donne *Sermons* copy B **60** and n 1 and **62** §2. See also *C&S* (*CC*) 17n and cf 58.
28[3] Apparently C's "*super-rational*" means "above reason, more than rational" and "plusquam–rationalia" means "rational more than other things, supremely rational".

arose for the greater part and still arise out of the confounding of the Reason with the Understanding.[4] In Hooker and the great Divines of his age it was merely an occasional carelessness in the use of the Terms, using Reason when they meant the Understanding, and when from other parts of their writings it is evidently[a] that they knew and asserted the distinction, nay the diversity, of the things themselves—to wit, that there was in Man another and higher Light, than that of "the faculty judging according to Sense", i.e. our Understandings.[5] But alas! since the Revolution it has ceased to be a mere error of language, and in too many amounts to a denial of Reason!—

29   p 111 | Bk II § 5

To urge any thing upon the Church, requiring thereunto that Religious Assent of Christian Belief, wherewith the words of the Holy *] Prophets are received; to urge any thing as part of that supernatural and celestially revealed Truth which God hath taught, and not to shew it in Scripture, this did the ancient Fathers evermore think unlawful, impious, execrable.

* Even this must be received cum grano salis.[1] To be sure, with the licences of interpretation which the Fathers of the 3 or 4 first centuries allowed themselves, and with the arcana of evolution by word, letter, allegory, yea, punning which they applied to detached sentences, or single phrases, of Holy Writ, it would not be easy to imagine a position which they could not "shew in Scripture."— Elucidated by the Texts even now cited by the Romish Priests for the truth of Purgatory, Indulgence, Image-worship, Invocation of dead men, and the like.—The assertion[b] therefore must be thus qualified—The ancient Farther anathematized any doctrine not consentaneous with scripture, and deducible either pari ratione[2] or by consequence—as when Scripture clearly commands *an end* but

---

[a] A slip for "evident"
[b] Here C, having used all the space in the foot-margin, has written "(turn to the top of this page)" and continued in the head-margin with "(*continued from the bottom of this page.*)"

28[4] See e.g. DONNE *Sermons* COPY B **29** and cf *AR* (1825) 245–6.

28[5] This definition, phrased with only small variations, C ascribed to Kant in *AR* (1825) 208, 224, in LACUNZA, and in LEIGHTON COPY C; for an earlier approximation see *Friend* (*CC*) I 177. The phrase is C's mnemonic for several pas-

sages in the *Critique of Pure Reason* rather than a direct quotation. Cf e.g. *Logic* (*CC*) 208, 224, 239, 255.

29[1] "With a grain of salt".

29[2] "By the same reasoning", or—as C in HUGHES 1 (at n 5), and others, translate it—"by parity of reason".

leaves the means to be determined according to the circumstances—
ex. gr. the frequent Assembly of Christians.—The appointment of
a Sunday or Lord's Day is evidently the fittest and most effectual
means to this end—but yet it was not practicable, i.e. the means did
not exist—till the Roman Government became Christian. But as soon
as this event took place, the duty of keeping the Sunday holy is truly
tho' *implicitly* contained in the Apostolic Text.—[3]

30 ̄ pp 115–16 | II § 6

Again, with a Negative Argument *David* is pressed concerning the
*] purpose he had to build a Temple unto the Lord: *Thus saith the
Lord, Thou shalt not build me an House to dwell in. Wheresoever I
have walked with all Israel, spake I one word to any of the Judges of
Israel, whom I commanded to feed my people, saying, Why have ye
not built me an house?*

* The wisdom of the divine Goodness both in the negative (the not
having authorized any of the preceding Judges from Moses downward
to build a Temple) and in the positive, the having commanded David
to prepare for it, and Solomon to build ᵴ it, I have not seen put in
the full light, as it so well deserves to be. The former or negative, or
the evils of a splendid Temple Worship and its effects on the character
of the Priesthood, ⟨(evils)⟩ when not changed to good by becoming
the antidote & preventive of far greater evils), would require much
thought both to set forth, and to comprehend. But to give any
reflecting reader a sense of the providential foresight evinced in the
latter, and thus a foresight beyond the reach of any but the
Omniscient—it will be only necessary to remind him of the Separation
of the 10 Tribes, and the Breaking up of the Realm into the two
Kingdoms of Judea and Israel, in the very next reign. Without the
continuity of succession provided for by this vast and splendid
Temple, built and arranged under the divine sanction attested by
Miracles, what criterion would there have existed for the purity of
this Law and Worship? What security for the preservation &
incorruption of the Inspired Writings?—&c &c &c.

31 p 118 | II § 7

*] That there is a City of *Rome*, that *Pius Quintus* and *Gregory* the
thirteenth, and others have been Popes of *Rome*, I suppose we are

29[3] 1 Cor 16.1–2. See *TT* 19 May 1834.

certainly enough perswaded. The ground of our perswasion, who never saw the place nor persons before named, can be nothing but mans testimony. Will any man here notwithstanding alledge those mentioned humane infirmities as Reasons, why these things should be mistrusted or doubted of? yea, that which is more, utterly to infringe the force and strength of mans testimony, were to shake the very Fortress of Gods truth.

* In a Mss Note on one of the Volumes of the Rev^d — Skelton's Works (belonging to my nephew, the Revd E. Coleridge)[1] I have detected the subtle sophism that lurks in this argument as applied by later Divines in vindication of proof by testimony, in relation to the Miracles of the O. & N. Testament. As thus applied, it is a μεταβασις εις αλλο γενος,[2] tho' so unobvious that th a very acute & candid Reason^a might use the argument without suspecting the paralogism. It is not testimony as testimony that necessitates us to conclude that there is such a City as Rome—but a Reasoning that forms a branch of Mathematical Science.

So far is our conviction from being grounded on our confidence in human testimony, that it proceeds on our knowlege of its fallible character, and therefore can find no sufficient reason for its coincidence on so vast a scale but in the real existence of the Object.[3] That a thousand lies told by as many several and unconnected Individuals should all be one and the same, is a possibbility expressible only by a fraction that is already to all intents and purposes $= 0$. The preceding Unit is diluted to evanescence in the long series of 0^s that follow it $\frac{1}{1000,000,000}$.[4]

32   p 131 | Bk III § 3

The mixture of those things by speech, which by Nature are divided, ∧ is the Mother of all Errour.

∧ with the division in thought of those things which in Nature are distinct yet one—i.e. distinguished without breach of unity, is the

^{a} A slip for "Reasoner"

31[1] The ms note is written on the text of *Deism Revealed* in Philip SKELTON (1707–87) *The Complete Works* (6 vols 1824) IV 29–35.

31[2] "A transition to another kind": see BAXTER *Reliquiae* COPY A **29** n 1.

31[3] See also **2**, above, and cf **41**, below.

31[4] On p 119 Hooker writes of truth as an "intuitive beholding", which may account for C's claim that Hooker's definition of intuition as "an immediate beholding" prefigures Kant and Fichte. See *Logic* (*CC*) I 151 and n 1. Cf also *BL* ch 10 (*CC*) I 172 and n 2 and *AR* (1825) 216.

C quoted from p 124 at the end of Bk II in a letter of 21 Sept 1826: *CL* VI 617.

Mother &c.—*So I should have framed the position.* Will, Reason, Life; Ideas in relation to the Mind, are instances—entia indivisè d̶i̶s̶t̶ interdistincta[1]—and the main arguments of the Atheist, Materialist, Deniers of our Lord's Divinity, all rest on the asserting of Division as a necessary consequence of Distinction/—

33   pp 208–9, pencil | Bk v § 19

Of both Translations, the better I willingly acknowledge that which cometh nearer to the very letter of the Original verity: yet so, that the other may likewise safely enough be read, without any peril at all of gain-saying, as much as the least jot or syllable of Gods most sacred and precious Truth.

Hooker had far better rested on the 1. impossibility, 2. the uselessness, of a faultless translation—and admitting certain Mistakes and over-sights recommended them for notice at the next revision—& then asked, what objection such harmless trifles can be to a Church that never pretended to infallibility?—But in fact, the Age was not ripe enough even for a Hooker to feel, much less with safety to expose, the protestant idol—i.e. their Bibliolatry.[1]

34   pp 218–19 | v § 22

Their only proper and direct proof of the thing in question had been to shew, in what sort, and how far mans Salvation doth necessarily depend upon the knowledge of the Word of God; what Conditions, *] Properties and Qualities there are, whereby Sermons are distinguished from other kinds of administring the Word unto that purpose; and what special Property or Quality that is, which being no where found but in Sermons, maketh them effectual to save Souls, and leaveth all other Doctrinal means besides destitute of vital efficacy.

Doubtless, Hooker was a theological Talus with a Club of Iron against opponents with paste-board Helmets and armed only with Crab-sticks![1] But I yet I too, too often find occasion to complain of him, as abusing his superior strength. For in a good man it is an

32[1] "Entities indivisibly interdistinct". On distinction and division see BAXTER *Reliquiae* COPY B 82 n 2.

33[1] On "Bibliolatry"—Bible-worship —see CHILLINGWORTH COPY B 2 n 1.

34[1] C has in mind Spenser's Talus, the iron man, "Who in his hand an yron flaile did hould, | With which he thresht out falshood, and did truth unfould". *Faerie Queene* v i 12. For the character of Talus as "the boldest effort of [Spenser's] powers" in "fancy under the condition of imagination" see a literary lecture of 3 Feb 1818: *Misc C* 38.

abuse of his intellectual superiority not to use a portion of it in stating his Christian Opponents' cause, his ~~Broethers'~~ren's (tho' dissentient & perhaps erring, yet still ~~Brothers~~ethren's) Side of the question, not as *they* had stated and argued it, but as he himself with his higher gifts of logic and foresight ~~wc~~ould have set ~~i~~ft forth.[2] But Hooker flies off to the *General*, in which he is unassailable; and does not, as in candour he should have done, enquire whether the question would not admit of nay ~~require~~ demand a different answer, when applied solely or principally to the ~~con~~circumstances, the condition and the needs of the English Parishes and the Population at large at the particular time, when the Puritan Divines wrote & he, (Hooker) replied to them.[3] Now the cause tried in *this* way, I should not be afraid to attempt the proof of the paramount efficacy of Preaching on the scheme & in the line of argument* layed down by himself—p. 218, 1. 28.[4] In short, H. too frequently finds it convenient to forget the homely proverb—the proof of the Pudding is in the eating. Whose parishes were the best disciplined, whose Flocks the best fed, the soberest Livers, and the most awakened and best-informed Protestant Christians, those of the zealous preaching Divines? or those of the prelatic Clergy with their *Readers*?[5] In whose Churches and Parishes were all the other pastoral duties, Catechizing, Visiting the Poor, &c &c, most strictly practiced?

35   p 219

The People which have no way to come to the knowledge of God, no prophesying, no teaching, Perish. But that they should of necessity perish, where any one way of knowledge lacketh, is more than the words of *Solomon* impart.

But what was the *fact*? *Were* those Congregations that had *those* Readers of wh~~at~~om the Puritans were speaking—*were* they, I say, equally well acquainted with and practically impressed by, the saving truths of the Gospel? Were they not rather perishing for lack of Knowlege?—To reply—it was their own fault! They ought to have been more regular in their attendence at Church, & more attentive,

---

[2] C's first principle in criticism and in the fair conduct of controversy, as characterised in his habits as a reader.

[3] One of C's main objections to theologians, as to *Naturphilosophen*, is their resort to generalities rather than to specific points in arguing a case.

[4] Marked in textus.

[5] "Readers"—in the Church of England, lay readers, who by ancient custom read lessons and conduct minor offices in the absence of the curate or incumbent. William Cowper for a time performed such duties at Olney.

when there, to what was there read—is too shocking, too un, nay, anti-christian! *S. T. C.*

36 p 220

Now all these things being well considered, it shall be no intricate matter for any man to judge with indifferency on which part the good of the Church is most conveniently sought; whether on ours, whose opinion is such as hath been shewed, or else on theirs, who leaving *] no ordinary way of Salvation for them unto whom the Word of God is but only read, do seldom name them but with great disdain and contempt who execute that Service in the Church of Christ.

* If so, they were much to be blamed. But surely this was not the case with the better and wiser part of those who clinging to the tenets and feelings of the first Reformers, & honoreding Bishop Grindal as much as they dreaded his Arminian Successors, were entitled Puritans![1] ⟨They⟩ limited their censure to *exclusive* Reading, to Reading as the Substitute ⟨for—⟩ and too often for the purpose of doing away with—Preaching.[2]

37 pp 298–9 | v § 65

Thus was the Memory of that Sign which they had in Baptism, a kind of bar or prevention to keep them even from apostasie, whereunto the frailty of Flesh and Blood, over-much fearing to endure shame, might peradventure the more easily otherwise have drawn them. We have not now... those extream conflicts which our Fathers had with blasphemous contumelies, every where offered to the Name of Christ, by such as professed themselves Infidels and Unbelievers. Howbeit, unless we be strangers to the age wherein we live... there is not the simplest of us, but knoweth with what disdain and scorn Christ is dishonoured far and wide.... When they that honour God, are despised... when they which pretend to honour him, and that with greatest sincerity, do with more than Heathenish petulancy trample under foot almost whatsoever, either we, or the whole Church of

36[1] For Edmund Grindal see **10** n 5, above. For the controversy between Arminians and Calvinists see BUNYAN COPY B **7** and n 3. Grindal's most formidable anti-Puritan successor was William Laud, Abp of Canterbury 1633, whose failure to recognise the legitimate power of the Puritans led eventually to his impeachment on charges (*inter alia*) of popery.

36[2] The Puritans, essentially Calvinists, placed strong emphasis on preaching, and objected to the use of lectors or lay readers who were not competent to preach.

God, by the space of so many ages, have been accustomed unto, for the comelier and better Exercise of our Religion...we cannot think, that the Sign which our new Baptized Fore-heads did there receive, is either unfit or unforcible...

I begin to fear that Hooker is not suited to *my* nature. I cannot bear round-abouts, for the purpose of evading the short cut straight before my eyes.[1] Exempli gratiâ. I find myself tempted in this place to *psha*! somewhat abruptly—and ask: How many in 20 millions of Christian Men and Women ever reverted to the make-believe impression of the Cross on their forehead in unconscious infancy by the wetted tip of the Parson's Finger, as a preservative against anger and resentment? "The whole Church of God"![2] Was it not the same Church, which neglecting and concealeding the Scriptures of God, introduced the adoration of the Cross, the worshipping of Relics, Holy Water, and all the other countless mummeries of Popery? Something *might* be pretended for the material Images of the Cross, worn at the bosom, or hung up in the Bed Chamber. These may and doubtless often do serve as silent monitors; but this eye-falsehood or pretence of making a mark that is not made, is a gratuitous Superstition, that cannot be practised without leading the Vulgar to regard it as a *Charm*. Hooker should have asked—*Has* it hitherto had this effect on the Christians generally? Is it likely to produce this effect, and this principally?—In common honesty he must have answered—No!—

Do I then blame the Church of England for retaining this ceremony? By no means. I justify it as a wise and pious condescension to the inveterate Habits of a People ⟨newly⟩ dragged rather than drawn out of Papistry; and as a pledge that the Founders & Fathers of the Reformation in England regarded innovation as per se an evil, and therefore requiring for its justification not only a cause, but a weighty cause. They did well and piously in deferring the removal of minor spots and stains to the time when the good effects of the more important Reforms had begun to shew themselves in the minds and hearts of the Laity—But *they* do not act either wisely or

37[1] Cf C as pointer rather than greyhound, and as a chamois-hunter, in BAXTER *Reliquiae* COPY B **82** n 3.

37[2] On p 298 Hooker writes: "But to prevent some inconveniencies which might ensue...we neither omit it [the crossing]...nor altogether make it so vulgar, as the Church heretofore hath been: Although to condemn the whole Church of God, when it most flourished in zeal and piety, to mark that age with the brand of Errour and Superstition, only because they had this Ceremony more in use, than we now think needful ...is...a censure of greater zeal than knowledge."

charitably who would eulogize these Maculæ[3] as Beauty-spots and vindicate as good what their Predecessors only tolerated as the lesser Evil.

S. T. Coleridge
12 Aug. 1826.

38 p 300

For in actions of this kind, we are more to respect, what the greatest part of men is commonly prone to conceive, than what some few mens wits may devise in construction of their own particular meanings. Plain it is, that a false Opinion of some personal Divine excellency to be in those things, which either Nature or Art hath framed, causeth always Religious Adoration.

How strongly might this most judicious Remark be turned against Hooker's own mode of vindicating this "ceremony"!

39 p 303 | v § 66

The Church had received from Christ a Promise, that such as believed in him, these signs and tokens should follow them, *To cast out Devils, to speak with Tongues, to drive away Serpents, to be free from the harm which any deadly Poyson could work, and to cure diseases by Imposition of hands.*

The Man who verily and sincerely believes the narration in St John's Gospel of the Feeding of three and again of four thousand persons with a few loaves & small fishes,[1] and of the raising of Lazarus,[2] in the plain and literal sense, cannot be reasonably suspected of rejecting or doubting any narrative concerning Christ & his Apostles, simply as miraculous. I trust therefore that no disbelief or prejudice against ~~the~~ miraculous events and powers will be attributed to me, as the ground or cause of my strong persuasion that the last Chapter of Mark's Gospel was an additament of a later Age, for which Luke's Acts of the Apostles ⟨misunderstood⟩ supplied the Hints./[3]

"SEVERAL OTHER TREATISES"

40 p 476 | [Miscellaneous Treatises.] "A Supplication Made to the Council by Master Walter Travers"

...to condemn all the Fathers, I said directly and plainly to all mens understanding, *That it was not indeed to be doubted, but many of the*

37[3] Spots or stains. For the same attitude, but not the word, see *C&S* (*CC*) 160 and n.

39[1] John 6.1–15.
39[2] John 11.1–44.
39[3] See BIBLE COPY B **101** and n 1.

Fathers were saved; but the means (said I) *was not their ignorance, which excuseth no man with God, but their Knowledge and Faith of the Truth, which it appeareth God vouchsafed them, by many notable Monuments and Records extant in all Ages.*

Not certainly, if the ignorance proceeded directly or indirectly from a defect or sinful propensity of the Will. But where no such cause is imaginable—in such cases this position of Master Travelrs is little less than blasphemous to the Divine Goodness, and in direct contradiction to an assertion of Sᵗ Pauls,[1] and to an evident Consequence from our Saviour's own words on the Polygamy of the Fathers.[2]

S. T. Coleridge
12 August 1826

41 p 484 | *Mr. Hooker's Answer to the Supplication That Mr. Travers Made to the Council* § 9

The next thing discovered, is an opinion about the assurance of mens perswasions in matters of Faith. I have taught, he saith, *That the assurance of things which we believe by the Word, is not so certain as of that we perceive by sense.*

A useful instance to illustrate the importance of distinct and the mischief of equivocal or multivocal terms.[1] Had Hooker said, that the fundamental Truths of Religion tho' perhaps even more *certain*, are less evident than the facts of Sense, there could have been no misunderstanding. Thus, the Demonstrations of Algebra possess equal *Certainty* with those of Geometry, but cannot lay claim to the same *evidence*. Certainty is positive, Evidence relative; the former *strictly taken* insusceptible of more or less, the latter capable of existing in many different degrees.[2]   *S. T. C.*

P.S. (a year or more after the preceding.) I am sorry to say, that Hooker's Reasoning on this is sophistical throughout. That a man must see what he sees, is no *persuasion* at all nor bears the remotest analogy to any judgement of the mind. The question, whether men have a clearer conception ⟨and a more stedfast conviction⟩ of the objective reality, to which the Image, Moon, in their eye appertains, than of the objective reality of the Things and States spiritually

40[1] Rom 2.12.
40[2] Matt 19.8. Cf HACKET *Scrinia* 24.
41[1] See **26**, above.
41[2] Cf **2** and **31**, above. For the difference between algebra and geometry see

e.g. *Friend (CC)* ɪ 440–1 n 2. On the alleged "apodictic force" of the truths disclosed by geometry see *SM (CC)* 98–9 and n 1 and cf *C&S (CC)* 19, 179. See also HARTLEY **6** (at n 2).

discovered by Faith?—And this Travers had a right to question, where ever a saving Faith existed. 12 Aug. 1826.

42 p 509 | *A Learned Discourse of Justification, Works, and How the Foundation of Faith Is Overthrown* § 31

But we say, our Salvation is by Christ alone; therefore howsoever, or whatsoever we add unto Christ in the matter of Salvation, we overthrow Christ. Our Case were very hard, if this Argument, so universally meant as it is supposed, were sound and good. We our selves do not teach Christ alone, excluding our own Faith, unto Justification; Christ alone, excluding our own Works, unto Sanctification; Christ alone, excluding the one or the other unnecessary unto Salvation.... By this speech we never meant to exclude either Hope or Charity from being always joyned as inseparable mates with Faith in the Man that is justified.... But to shew that Faith is the only hand which putteth on Christ unto Justification; and Christ the only Garment, which, being so put on, covereth the shame of our defiled natures, hideth the imperfection of our Works, preserveth us blameless in the sight of God, before whom otherwise, the weakness of our Faith were cause sufficient to make us culpable, yea, to shut us *] from the Kingdom of Heaven, where nothing that is not absolute can enter.... As we have received, so we teach, that besides the bare and naked work, wherein Christ without any other Associate finished all the parts of our Redemption, and purchased Salvation himself alone; for conveyance of this eminent blessing unto us, many things are of necessity required, as, to be known and chosen of God before the foundation of the World; in the World to be called, justified, sanctified; after we have left the World, to be received unto Glory; Christ in every of these hath somewhat which he worketh alone.

* No where, out of Holy Scripture, have I found the root and pith of Christian Faith so clearly & purely propounded. God, whose thoughts are eternal, beholdeth the END: and in the completed work seeth and accepteth every stage of the process.[1]

P.S. I dislike only the word "purchased"[2]—not that it is not scriptural, but because a metaphor well and wisely used in the enforcement & varied elucidation of a truth is not therefore properly employed in its exact enunciation. I will illustrate, amplify, and

42[1] For C on faith see DONNE *Sermons* COPY B **30** and n 2. See also "Essay on Faith" (nd) in *LR* IV 425–38.

42[2] See Acts 20.28, Eph 1.14.

"divide" the word with Paul; but I will propound it collectively with John.[3] If in this admirable passage aught else dare be wished otherwise, it is the division & yet confusion of Time and Eternity, by giving an *anteriority* to the latter.[4]   *S. T. C.*

I am persuaded, that the PRACTICE of the Romish Church *tendeth* to make vain the doctrine of Salvation by Faith in Christ alone; but judging by her most eminent Divines I can find nothing dissonant from the truth in her express decisions on this article. Perhaps, it would be safer to say. Christ alone saves us, working in us by the Faith which includes Hope and Love. See Ep. to the Gal. Ch. I. v. 20.[5]

43   p 512 | § 34

If it were not a long deluded Spirit which hath possession of their Hearts; were it possible but that they should see how plainly they do herein gainsay the very ground of Apostolick Faith?... By Grace, the Apostle saith, and by Grace in such sort as a Gift: a thing that cometh not of our selves, nor of our Works, lest any man should boast, and say, *I have wrought out my own Salvation....* The Apostle, as if he had foreseen how the Church of *Rome* would abuse the world in time by ambiguous terms, to declare in what sense the name of Grace must be taken, when we make it the cause of our Salvation, saith, *He saved us according to his mercy...*

In all Christian Communities there have been & ever will be, too many Christians in name only; too many in belief and notion only; but likewise, I trust, in every acknowleged Church, Eastern or Western, Greek, Roman, Protestant, many & those in *belief* more or less erroneous, who are Christians in *faith* & in Spirit. And I neither do nor can think, that any pious Catholic did ever in his heart attribute any Merit to any work as being *his* work. A grievous error and a mischievous error, there was *practically* in mooting the question at all of the condignity of Works & their Rewards!—In short, to attribute Merit to any *Agent* but God in Christ, our Faith

---

42[3] By "Paul" C means Eph 1.14 (cf 1.13); from John he would assemble examples of salvation by faith in Christ alone.

42[4] See ETERNAL PUNISHMENT 1 and n 6, **18.**

42[5] A slip for Gal 2.20: "I am crucified with Christ: nevertheless I live; yet not I, but Christ liveth in me: and the life which I now live in the flesh I live by the faith of the Son of God, who loved me, and gave himself for me."

say, This is true. If it were so in matters of Faith, then, as all men have equal certainty of this, so no Believer should be more scrupulous and doubtful than another. But we find the contrary. The Angels and Spirits of the Righteous in Heaven have certainty most evident of things spiritual: but this they have by the light of Glory. That which we see by the light of Grace, though it be indeed more certain: yet it is not to us so evidently certain, as that which Sense or the Light of Nature will not suffer a man to doubt of. Proofs are vain and frivolous, except they be more certain, than is the thing proved: and do we not see how the Spirit every where in the Scripture proving matters of Faith, laboureth to confirm us in the things which we believe by things whereof we have sensible knowledge? I conclude therefore that we have less *certainty* of *evidence* concerning things believed, than concerning sensible or naturally perceived. Of those who doth doubt at any time? Of them at sometime who doubteth not? I will not here alledge the sundry confessions of the perfectest that have lived upon Earth, concerning their great imperfections this way; which if I did, I should dwell too long upon a matter sufficiently known by every faithful man that doth know himself.

The other, which we call the *certainty* of *adherence*, is, when the heart doth cleave and stick unto that which it doth believe: This certainty is greater in us than the other. The reason is this, The Faith of a Christian doth apprehend the words of the Law, the promises of God, not only as true, but also as good; and therefore even then, when the evidence which he hath of the Truth is so small; that it grieveth him to feel his weakness in assenting thereto, yet is there in him such a sure adherence unto that which he doth but faintly and fearfully believe, that his Spirit having once truly tasted the heavenly sweetness thereof, all the world is not able to quite and clean remove him from it: but he striveth with himself to hope against all reason of believing, being setled with *Job* upon this immoveable resolution, *Though God kill me, I will not give over trusting in him.* For why? This Lesson remaineth for ever imprinted in him, *It is good for me to cleave unto God, Psal.* 37.

Now the minds of all men being so darkned as they are with the foggy damp of original corruption, it cannot be that any mans heart living should be either so enlightned in the knowledge, or so established in the love of that wherein his Salvation standeth, as to be perfect, neither doubting nor shrinking at all. If any such were, what doth lett why that man should not be justified by his own inherent righteousness? For Righteousness inherent, being perfect, will justifie. And perfect Faith is a part of perfect Righteousness inherent; yea, a principal part, the Root and the Mother of all the rest: so that if the fruit of every Tree be such as the Root is, Faith being perfect as it is, if it be not at all mingled with distrust and fear, what is there to exclude other Christian vertues from the like perfections? And then what need we the Righteousness of Christ? His Garment is superfluous: we may be honourably cloathed with our own Robes, if it be thus. But let them beware, who challenge to themselves strength which they have not, lest they lose the comfortable support of that weakness which indeed they have.

Some shew, although no soundness of ground, there is, which may be alledged for defence of this supposed perfection in certainty touching matters of our Faith; as first, that *Abraham* did believe, and doubted not: secondly, that the Spirit, which God hath given us to no other end, but only to assure us that we are the Sons of God; to embolden us to call upon him as our Father; to open our eyes, and to make the truth of things believed evident unto our minds; is much mightier in operation than the common light of Nature, whereby we discern sensible things: wherefore we must needs be more surer of that we believe, than of that we see; we must needs be more certain of the mercies of God in Christ Jesus, than we are of the light of the Sun when it shineth upon our Faces. To that of *Abraham, He did not doubt*; I answer, that this *negation* doth not exclude all fear, all doubting, but only that which cannot stand with true Faith. It freeth *Abraham* from doubting through Infidelity, not from doubting through Infirmity; from the doubting of Unbelievers, not of weak Believers; from such a doubting as that whereof the Prince of *Samaria* is attainted, who hearing the promise of sudden Plenty in the midst of Extreme Dearth, answered, *Though the Lord would make windows in Heaven, were it possible so to come to pass?* But that *Abraham* was not void of all doubtings, what need we any other proof, than the plain evidence of his own words? *Gen.* 17.17. The reason which is taken from the power of the Spirit were effectual, if God did work like a natural Agent, as the fire doth inflame, and the Sun enlighten, according to the uttermost ability which they have to bring forth their effects: But the incomprehensible wisdom of God doth limit the effects of his power to such a measure as it seemeth best to himself. Wherefore he worketh that certainty in all, which sufficeth abundantly to their Salvation in the life to come;

but

but in none so great as attaineth in this life unto perfection. Even so, O Lord, it hath pleased thee; even so it is best and fittest for us, that feeling still our own Infirmities, we may no longer breath than pray *Adjuva Domine, Help Lord our incredulity*. Of the third Question, this I hope will suffice, being added unto that which hath been thereof already spoken. The fourth Question resteth, and so an end of this Point.

That which cometh last of all in this first branch to be considered concerning the weakness of the Prophet's Faith is, *Whether he did by this very thought* [The Law doth fail] *quench the Spirit, fall from Faith, and shew himself an Unbeliever, or no?* The Question is of moment; the repose and tranquility of infinite Souls doth depend upon it. The Prophet's case is the case of many; which way soever we cast for him, the same way it passeth for all others. If in him this cogitation did extinguish Grace, why the like thoughts in us should not take the like effects, there is no cause. Forasmuch therefore as the matter is weighty, dear and precious, which we have in hand, it behoveth us with so much the greater chariness to wade through it, taking special heed both what we build, and whereon we build, that if our Building be Pearl, our Foundation be not Stubble; if the Doctrine we teach be full of Comfort and Consolation, the Ground whereupon we gather it be sure: otherwise we shall not save, but deceive both our selves and others. In this we know we are not deceived, neither can we deceive you, when we teach that the Faith whereby ye are sanctified cannot fail; it did not in the Prophet, it shall not in you. If it be so, let the difference be shewed between the condition of Unbelievers and his in this or in the like imbecility or weakness. There was in *Habakkuk* that which St. *John* doth call the *Seed of God*, meaning thereby the *first Grace* which God poureth into the hearts of them that are incorporated into Christ; which having received, if, because it is an adversary to Sin, we do therefore think we sin not both otherwise, and also by distrustful and doubtful apprehending of that which we ought stedfastly to believe, surely we do but deceive our selves. Yet they which are of God do not sin either in this, or in any thing, any such sin as doth quite extinguish Grace, clean cut them off from Christ Jesus: because the *seed of God abideth* in them, and doth shield them from receiving any irremediable wound. Their Faith, when it is at strongest, is but weak; yet even then, when it is at the weakest, so strong, that utterly it never faileth, it never perisheth altogether, no not in them who think it extinguished in themselves. There are, for whose sakes I dare not deal slightly in this Cause, sparing that labour which must be bestowed to make plain. Men in like Agonies unto this of the Prophet *Habakkuk*'s are through the extremity of Grief many times in judgment so confounded, that they find not themselves in themselves. For that which dwelleth in their hearts they seek, they make diligent search and inquiry. It abideth, it worketh in them, yet still they ask, where? Still they lament as for a thing which is past finding: they mourn as *Rachel*, and refuse to be comforted, as if that were not, which indeed is; and as if that, which is not, were; as if they did not believe when they do; and, as if they did despair when they do not. Which in some, I grant, is but a melancholy passion, proceeding only from that dejection of mind, the cause whereof is the Body, and by bodily means can be taken away. But where there is no such bodily cause, the mind is not lightly in this mood, but by some of these three occasions: One, that judging by comparison either with other men, or with themselves at some other time more strong, they think imperfection to be a plain deprivation, weakness to be utter want of Faith. Another cause is, they often mistake one thing for another. St. *Paul* wishing well to the Church of *Rome*, prayeth for them after this sort. *The God of hope fill you with all joy of Believing.* Hence an Error groweth, when men in heaviness of Spirit suppose they lack Faith, because they find not the sugred joy and delight which indeed doth accompany Faith, but so as a separable accident, as a thing that may be removed from it; yea, there is a cause why it should be removed. The light would never be so acceptable, were it not for that usual intercourse of darkness. Too much Honey doth turn to Gall, and too much joy, even spiritual, would make us Wantons. Happier a great deal is that mans case, whose soul by inward desolation is humbled, than he whose heart is through abundance of spiritual delight lifted up and exalted above measure. Better it is sometimes to go down into the pit with him, who beholding darkness, and bewailing the loss of inward joy and consolation, crieth from the bottom of the lowest Hell, *My God, my God, why hast thou forsaken me?* than continually to walk arm in arm with Angels, to sit as it were in *Abraham's* bosom, and to have no thought, no cogitation, but *I thank my God it is not with me as it is with other men*. No, God will have them that shall walk in light to feel now and then what it is to sit in the shadow of Death. A grieved Spirit therefore is no argument of a faithless mind. A third occasion of mens misjudging themselves, as if they were faithless when they are not, is, They fasten their Cogitations upon the distrustful suggestions of the flesh, whereof

D d d d 2

as Christians forbids us; and to dispute about the Merit of Works abstracted from the Agent Common Sense ought to forbid us.[1]

S. T. Coleridge—

44 p 522 | *A Remedy Against Sorrow and Fear, Delivered in a Funeral Sermon*

*] Desolate and comfortless I will not leave you; in Spirit I am with you to the Worlds end. Whether I be present or absent, nothing shall ever take you out of these hands.

* O how grateful should I be to be made intuitive of the truth intended in the words "*In Spirit* I am with you."[1]

45 p 525[a]

Touching the latter affection of Fear, which respecteth evil to come, as the other which we have spoken of doth present evils; first, in the *]nature thereof it is plain, that we are not of every future evil afraid. Perceive we not how they, whose tenderness shrinketh at the least rase of a Needles Point, do kiss the Sword that pierceth their Souls quite thorow?

* In this and in sundry similar passages of this venerable Writer there is, ὡς ἐμοίγε δοκεῖ,[1] a very plausible but even therefore the more dangerous, Sophism—but the due detection and exposure of which would exceed the scanty space of a marginal Comment.—Briefly— what does Hooker comprehend in the term, PAIN?—Whatsoever the Soul finds adverse to her well-being, or incompatible with her free action?—In this sense Hooker's position is a mere Truism,[2]—But if Pain ~~mean~~ be applied exclusively ⟨to⟩ the Soul *finding* itself as *Life*—then H. errs.

46 p 525

Fear then in it self being meer Nature, cannot in it self be sin, which sin is not Nature, but therefore an accessary deprivation.*

* I suspect a misprint, & that it should be "de*pra*vation—"—is not

---

a 45 was written after **46**, as shown by the small writing at the end to fit into the space left above **46**

43[1] In a letter of 19 Jan 1824 (*CL* v 324) C provided a quotation from Hooker's sermon "On the Nature of Pride" (p 521) for *AR* (1825) 188–9: "What is Virtue but a Medicine, and Vice but a Wound?..."

44[1] Cf the last words of Jesus in Matt

28.20: "...lo, I am with you alway, even unto the end of the world". For Hooker's additional phrase "in Spirit" there is no gospel authority.

45[1] "In my opinion, at least".

45[2] On the relation of pain to evil see DONNE *Sermons* COPY B **114** n 2.

nature; but if not nature, then it must [be]*ᵃ* a super-induced and incidental depravation of Nature. The Principal, viz. Fear, is Nature; but the sin, i.e. that it is a sinful Fear, is but an Accessary

47   p 527 | *A Learned and Comfortable Sermon of the Certainty and Perpetuity of Faith in the Elect...*

The following truly admirable Discourse is evidently the concluding Sermon of a Series, unhappily not preserved.[1]

48   p 528 (misprinted 328)

If it were so in matters of Faith, then, as all men have equal certainty of this, so no Believer should be more scrupulous and doubtful than another. But we find the contrary. The Angels and Spirits of the Righteous in Heaven have certainty most evident of things spiritual: but this they have by the light of Glory. That which we see by the light of Grace, though it be indeed more certain: yet it is not to us so evidently certain, as that which Sense or the Light of Nature will not suffer a man to doubt of.

Hooker's *Meaning* is right; but he falls into a sad confusion of words/—blending the *thing* and the relation of the *Mind* to the thing. The 4ᵗʰ Moon of Jupiter is *certain* in itself; but *evident* only to the telescopic Astronomer.[1] See M.S. Note—Life, p. 15—[2]

49   pp 528–9, marked with an ink line in the margin

The other, which we call the *certainty* of *adherence*, is, when the heart doth cleave and stick unto that which it doth believe: This certainty is greater in us than the other. The reason is this, The Faith of a Christian doth apprehend the words of the Law, the promises of God, not only as true, but also as good; and therefore even then, when the evidence which he hath of the Truth is so small; that it grieveth him to feel his weakness in assenting thereto, yet is there in him such

ᵃ Word supplied by the editor

47[1] In a letter of 31 Aug 1826 C told Tulk that he had "derived...much support" from "Hooker's Sermon on the perpetuity of Faith, appended to his Ecclesiastical Polity". *CL* VI 607. C refers to it in BIBLE COPY B **97** and again in BUNYAN COPY B **21** (c 1831).

48[1] On evidence and certainty cf **41**, above. Galileo discovered the first four moons of Jupiter (of twelve now known) by telescope in 1610, first I–III, then IV six days later. (These four are visible through good binoculars.) No V was not discovered until 1892, XII in 1951. A copy of Galileo's *Mathematical Collections and Translations* (perhaps 5 vols 1661–5) was in Wordsworth LC 469, twice marked as C's. Cf *CN* I 937D.

48[2] I.e. **2**, above.

a sure adherence unto that which he doth but faintly and fearfully believe, that his Spirit having once truly tasted the heavenly sweetness thereof, all the world is not able to quite and clean remove him from it...

Now the minds of all men being so darkned as they are with the foggy damp of original corruption, it cannot be that any mans heart living should be either so enlightned in the knowledge, or so established in the love of that wherein his Salvation standeth, as to be perfect, neither doubting nor shrinking at all. If any such were, what doth lett why that man should not be justified by his own inherent righteousness? For Righteousness inherent, being perfect, will justifie. And perfect Faith is a part of perfect Righteousness inherent...And then what need we the Righteousness of Christ? His Garment is superfluous: we may be honourably cloathed with our own Robes, if it be thus. But let them beware, who challenge to themselves strength which they have not, lest they lose the comfortable support of that weakness which indeed they have.

Some shew, although no soundness of ground, there is, which may be alledged for defence of this supposed perfection in certainty touching matters of our Faith; as first, that *Abraham* did believe, and doubted not: secondly, that the Spirit which God hath given us to no other end, but only to assure us that we are the Sons of God; to embolden us to call upon him as our Father; to open our eyes, and to make the truth of things believed evident unto our minds; is much mightier in operation than the common light of Nature, whereby we discern sensible things: wherefore we must needs be more surer of that we believe, than of that we see; we must needs be more certain of the mercies of God in Christ Jesus, than we are of the light of the Sun when it shineth upon our Faces. To that of *Abraham, He did not doubt*; I answer, that this *negation* doth not exclude all fear, all doubting, but only that which cannot stand with true Faith. It freeth *Abraham* from doubting through Infidelity, not from doubting through Infirmity; from the doubting of Unbelievers, not of weak Believers...But the incomprehensible wisdom of God doth limit the effects of his power to such a measure as it seemeth best to himself. Wherefore he worketh that certainty in all, which sufficeth abundantly to their Salvation in the life to come; but in none so great as attaineth in this life unto perfection....

Should be written in gold!—O may these precious words be written on my heart!/

1. That we all need to be redeemed: & that therefore we are all in Captivity to an Evil. 2. That there is a Redeemer. 3. That the Redemption relatively to each individual Captive is if not effected under certain conditions, yet manifestable as far as is fitting for the Soul, by certain signs and consequents. and 4. that these Signs are in in myself, that the conditions, under which the Redemption offered to all Men is promised to the Individual, are fulfilled in myself—these are the four great points of Faith, in which the humble Christian finds and feels a gradation from full assurance to trembling Hope./ Yet the *Will*, the *Act* of Trust, is the same in all. Might I not almost say, that it rather increases with the decrease of the consciously discerned evidence? To assert, that I have the *same* assurance of mind that I am saved as that I need a Saviour, would be a contradiction to my own feelings—and yet I may have an *equal*—i.e. an equivalent— assurance/. How is it possible that a Sick man should have the *same* certainty of his Convalescence as of his Sickness?—Yet he may be assured of it.—So again, my Faith in the Skill and Integrity of my Physician may be complete—but the application of it to my own case may be troubled by the sense of my own imperfect obedience to his prescriptions—[1]

The *sort* of our beliefs & assurances is necessarily modified by their different Subjects. It argues no want of saving Faith on the whole, that I can not have the same trust in myself as I have in my God! That Christ's Righteousness *can* save me—that Christ's Righteousness *alone* can save—these are simple positions, all the terms of which are steady and co-present to my mind. But that I *shall* be so saved—that of the Many Called I have been one of the chosen[2]—this is no mere conclusion of mind on known or assumed Premises.—

50   p ⁻2, referring to pp 528–9

If R. Hooker had written only the previous pages 328, 329[a]—I should hold myself bound to thank the Father of Lights and Giver of all good Gifts,[1] for his existence and the preservation of his Writings.

S. T. Coleridge.

[a] Actually pp 528–9, the folio of p 528 being misprinted "328". See the marked passage, **49** textus

49[1] Cf *AR* (1825) 311–16.
49[2] Cf Matt 20.16, 22.14, etc.
50[1] "Father of Lights"—James 1.17. The phrase "Giver of all good Gifts" is not biblical, but appears in BCP in the Form...of Making Deacons, or Ordering of Priests, and the Consecration of Bishops; it also appears in a prayer to be said on Ember Days "for those who are to be admitted to Holy Orders". Cf Matt 7.11, Luke 11.13.

51 p 530^{*a*}

I ~~can~~ remember no other discourse that sinks into, and draws up comfort from, the depths of our Being below our own *distinct* Consciousness, with the clearness and godly loving-kindness, of this truly evangelical, God-to-be-thanked-for Sermon—Yet how large, how important a part of our spiritual life goes on like the Circulation, Absorptions and Secretions of our bodily life, unrepresented by any specific Sensation, & yet the ground and condition of our total Sense of Existence! *S. T. C.*

52 p 530^{*b*}

While I feel, acknowlege and revere the almost measureless superiority of the Sermons of the Divines, who labored in the first and even the two first Centuries of the Reformation, from Luther to Leighton, over the prudential morals and *apologizing* theology that have characterized the unfanatical Clergy since the Revolution in 1668—I cannot but regret—especially while I am listening to a Hooker—that they withheld all light from the truths contained in the words, Satan, the Serpent, the evil Spirit, & this last used plurally.[1]

a Possibly a continuation of 49, being in the same hand and ink
b Possibly a continuation of 51, being in the same hand and ink

52[1] See e.g. BÖHME **84**, DONNE *Sermons* COPY B **115**, HILLHOUSE **1**, HOWIE **8** n 12. See also *AR* (1825) 297 and 302n.

EDWARD THOMAS STANLEY HORNBY

c 1782–1825

LOST BOOK

[Identity of author and title uncertain]
Childhood. London 1821. 12°.

Not located; no record of marginalia.

In a letter to C. A. Tulk dated "Sunday Night"—conjecturally dated 5 Oct 1823—C wrote: "I have perused Mr Hormby's Poem with great interest and have taken the liberty of adding some *Pencil* marks of several passages that I especially admired, and of a few easily removeable faults ὡς ἔμοιγε δοκεῖ. They all arise either from the dire necessity of rhyme compelling a change & choice of Metaphors which the Judgment and imagination would not have of themselves suggested or from inattention to the *quantity* of words which must be consulted no less than the *accent* in order to harmonious verse." *CL* v 303. Printing his text from a transcript, Griggs may have repeated an error of the transcriber. No other mention of the name has come to light in C's papers.

JOHN HOWIE

1735–1793

Biographia Scoticana; or, an historical account of the lives, characters, and memorable transactions, of the most eminent Scots worthies, &c. [Anonymous.] 2 pts in 1 vol. Leith 1816. 8°.

University of Indiana

Allan Cunningham's copy, with his autograph signature at the foot of the title-page. Bookplate of William Harris Arnold and Walter Chrysler.

When C was making final preparations to write his "Apology for the Life of Leighton" as preface to *AR*, he wrote to his publisher J. A. Hessey asking for certain books that he urgently needed to complete the work, among these the "*Bibliographia Scoticana*". Of these, he secured three from Sion College (BURNET *Memoires*, LAUD, and Kirkton), but there was no copy of Howie in Sion College or in Dr Williams's Library; perhaps the BM had it (the 1st ed was published in 1774), and he had asked Davy to recommend him "as a Reader there". *CL* V 300–1. Hessey seems to have inquired among the regular contributors to the *London Magazine* (which Taylor & Hessey had acquired in Apr 1821). A notebook entry of c 13 Oct 1823, in which C refers to an edition of Scottish mss needed for the Leighton life, records receipt of what was surely Cunningham's copy: "Am reading the Biographia Scoticana —published in 1816...attacking & deprecating religious Toleration...". *CN* IV 5015. *CN* IV 5021–5040 (13 Oct–Nov 1823) record several details of this reading (as noted below). See also LEIGHTON COPY C 1 n 3.

Allan Cunningham (1784–1842), Scottish autodidact and miscellaneous writer, first came to London in 1810, contributed stories to *Blackwood's* in 1819–21, then transferred to the *London Magazine* and so became an associate of Lamb's—one of "our old chums of the London"—rather than a close friend. See *LL* II 298, 324, III 158. C's deferential apology to Cunningham for "thus bescrawling a leaf of his Book" (4) suggests a formal rather than personal relationship. Whether or not Cunningham meant C to keep the book, C never returned it: it is item 6 in Green LC.

MS TRANSCRIPTS. (*a*) VCL LT 49a: transcript of **9–11** under EHC's title "Transcript of passage from Work on Scotch History by —— McClelland— together with transcript of Marginal Notes [on M'Clelland] by S T C." This also includes, without C's annotation, **7** textus (ii 126), the marked passage cited in **2** n 1 (i 385), and passages from ii 75 (on Andrew Melville) and ii 131 (on Viscount Kinmuir).

(*b*) Cornell (Wordsworth Collection) Healey 2248: a sheet with transcript of **9–11**, with textus, in an unidentified hand, inserted in a copy of Malcolm

Laing *The History of Scotland* III (of 4) (1804). Healey 2248 does not associate this paper with HOWIE.

DATE. From c Oct 1823 (*CN* IV 5015, cited above) to 1825.

1 i 14 | Preface

[Footnote:] This doctrine of original sin is plainly evinced from scripture, canonical and apocryphal...asserted in our church-
*] standards, illustrated and defended by many able divines, both ancient and modern, and by our British poets, excellently described: Thus,

> Adam now ope thine eyes, and first behold
> Th' effects which thy original crime hath wrought
> In some, to spring from thee, who never touch'd
> Th' excepted tree, nor with the snake conspir'd,
> Nor sinned thy sin; yet from that sin derive
> Corruption to bring forth more violent deeds.
>
> PARADISE LOST, Lib. ix.

> Conceived in sin (O wretched state!)
> before we draw our breath:
> The first young pulse begins to beat
> iniquity and death.
>
> Dr. WATTS.

* Capital! He ought to have meant Taliessin, Hoel &c[1]—But a your true Scot could ⟨not⟩ bring himself to say "Our English Poets"—even while he is imagining himself to be writing English.[2] And then the *Dual.* Milton and DOCTOR WATTS![3]

[1] Taliesin, sixth-century Welsh bard, claimed by mediaeval Welsh poets as their great exemplar, yet named by Nennius in *Historia Britonnum* as a British poet. By "Hoel" C presumably means Hywel Dda (Hywel the Good) (d 950), Welsh lawgiver. If, as seems likely, C's source was Thomas Warton *History of English Poetry* (e.g. 4 vols 1824) he would have found the two names, spelled "Taliessin" and "Hoel [Dha]", in two consecutive sentences on I 1.

[2] It was a commonplace of nineteenth-century writers to speak of Welsh as the "ancient British language"—as Sharon Turner does in *A Vindication of the Genuineness of Ancient British Poems* (1803) 12, citing Taliesin but not Hywel— and so to call the early Welsh bards the first British poets.

[3] Isaac Watts (1674–1748), dissenting pastor and writer of some 600 hymns, one of the most popular writers of his day, to whom Johnson accorded a *Life*, and whose *Horae Lyricae* (1706) were reprinted in both *B Poets* IX and Chalmers XIII. C was early aware of his poems in *B Poets*—see *CN* I 84, 161 [*a*] n; cf *Watchman* (*CC*) 69, 287, and nn—but never expressed special admiration for them.

C apparently summarises, or refers to, i 11–15 in *CN* IV 5023, 5035, and 5038.

2   i 23

Again, some sceptical nullifidian or other may be ready to object further, "That many things related in this collection smell too much of enthusiasm; and that several other things narrated therein, are beyond all credit."

Turn to p. 385 & 388!!¹

2A   i 28 | Introduction

King Cratilinth built a church for them, which was called the church σωτηρ] of our SAVIOUR, in the Greek αωσηρ...

3   ii 60–1 | Life of Mr David Black

The liberties of the Church, and discipline presently exercised, were confirmed by divers acts of parliament, approved of by the Confession of Faith, and the office-bearers of the church, were now in the peaceable possession thereof; that the question of his preaching

2¹ On i 385 C has marked with an enclosing ink line a paragraph in the "Life of Capt. John Paton" describing an incident in the Covenanter's resistance to Montrose in Jul 1645. The Covenanters under Lieutenant-General Baillie, in an action near Stirling, were driven "into a standing marsh or bog, where there was no probability either of fighting or escaping". The marked paragraph reads: "In this extremity, the Captain [John Paton], as soon as he could get free of the bog, with sword in hand made the best of his way through the enemy, till he had got safe to the two Colonels, Hacket and Strahan, who all three rode off together: but had not gone far till they were encountered by about fifteen of the enemy, all of whom they killed except two who escaped. When they had gone a little farther, they were again attacked by about thirteen more, and of these they killed ten, so that only three of them could make their escape. But, upon the approach of about eleven Highlanders more, one of the Colonels said, in a familiar dialect, Johnny, if thou dost not somewhat now, we are all dead men. To whom the Captain answered, Fear not; for we will do what we can before we

either yield or flee before them. They killed nine of them, and put the rest to flight."

Unmarked, i 388 continues the life of Paton. After the rout of the Scottish army in Sept 1651 in their assault on England, Paton returned home to his farm and worked peacefully there until in 1660 he joined a group of Covenanters determined to resist "some insolencies committed in the south and east by Sir James Turner". On 28 Nov 1660, at Rullion, Paton with a force of Covenanters under Captain Arnot was attacked by General Dalziel and the King's forces. After getting the worst of the action for most of the day, Dalziel forced Arnot's men to give ground. "Here Captain Paton...behaved with great courage and gallantry", first outfacing Dalziel himself in an encounter with pistols, then—surrounded and outnumbered—broke into the open with two other horsemen "when there was almost no other on the field of battle, having in this encounter, stood nearly an hour". The story continues to i 389, telling how Paton dealt with three mounted men sent by Dalziel to capture him, and so "got safe home at last".

*] ought first, according to the grounds and practice foresaid, to be judged by the ecclesiastical senate, as the competent judges thereof at the first instance.

[*] This and numerous similar attempts to form an absolute Theocracy in Scotland, are pregnant with instruction. It is observable, that all Theocracy commences with an assertion, express or implied, of *Infallibility* in one or more Individuals, without proof. *If* A. be an Ambassador from the King of Kings, *all* Kings must yield obedience to his words, and not pretend to be his Judges. But I = A am an Ambass. &c—: Ergo.—Negatur *Minor*:[1] till proved.—The Proof was not given: nor could be given but by some Exertion of miraculous Power that would have *made* A. a King & the King A's Subject; & thus superseded the necessity of a Proof. Facile *pre*scribit, qui *pro*scribere possit.[2]

4   p ⁻2, referring to ii 82 | Mr Patrick Simpson

On a Tuesday morning, about day break, he went into his garden as private as possible, and one Helen Gardiner, wife to one of the bailies of the town, a godly woman, who had sat up that night with Mrs Simpson, being concerned at the melancholy condition he was in, climbed over the garden-wall, to observe him in this retirement; but, coming near the place where he was, she was terrified with a noise which she heard, as of the rushing of multitudes of people together, with a most melodious sound intermixed; she fell on her knees, and prayed, that the Lord would pardon her rashness, which her regard for his servant had caused. Afterwards she went forward and found him lying on the ground; she entreated him to tell her what had happened unto him, and, after many promises of secrecy, and an obligation, that she should not reveal it in his lifetime, but, if she survived him, she should be at liberty, he then said, "O! what am I! being but dust, and ashes, that holy ministering spirits should be sent with a message to me!" And then told her, that he had had a vision of Angels, who gave him an audible answer from the Lord, respecting his wife's condition: and then returning to the house, he said to the people who attended his wife, "Be of good comfort, for

3[1] "The *Minor* [premiss] is denied".
3[2] "He will easily *pre*scribe (lay down the law), who may be able to *pro*scribe (lay your life on the line)." A variant of

a Latin epigram by Macrobius, for which see FLÖGEL **3** and n 3.
C made note of "P. 60, Bibliog. Scot., 157–60" in *CN* IV 5021. For pp 157–60 see **9–11**.

I am sure that ere ten hours of the day, that brand shall be plucked out of the fire."

P. 82. God keep me from uncharitable Thoughts—It may have been a Posthumous Fancy, or a Prose Epic, of Mrs Helen Gardiner, suggested perhaps by the wind in a Scotch Fir at the moment she was peeping at her pious Pastor on his knees in his Garden—But it does look horribly like a pia-fraudish confabrication.[1] If intended only for Mr Simpson's solace & as enabling him to predict with confidence, what need of the rushing of a Mob of Spirits or of the melodious Voice intermixed? And if intended for a bono publico[2] Miracle to the honor and glory of Misepiscopy (no worse word than Misanthropy),[3] whiley the injunction of Silence till after the Death of the only person who might have contradicted it & who alone could have confirmed it? At all events, this excuse for posthumous testimony (which is [of]^a frequent occurrence in Puritan Biography) is an injudicious, ⟨not to say, profane⟩ imitation of our Lord's Prohibition to his Disciples respecting his Messiahship, his Crucifixion, & Resurrection on the third day.[4] For here the Motive[s]^b for injoining Silence were evident & the suggestions of Mercy no less than of Wisdom—For to have proclaimed himself the Messiah i.e. King of the Jews, would have been High Treason to the Civil Government, i.e. the Roman Magistrates—& to have declared that the Messiah would be *hung* would have been justified his apprehension for Blasphemy by the Sanhedrim, in the exertion of the privileges accorded to them by the Roman Emperor & Senate./^{5}

S. T. Coleridge.^{c}

who intreats & trusts in, Allan Cunningham's pardon for thus bescrawling a leaf of his Book. A. C. may be assured that S. T. C.

---

^{a} Word supplied by the editor
^{c} Signature underlined twice in pencil

^{b} Letter supplied by the editor

4^1 Neither "pious-fraudish" nor "confabration" is in *OED*. The phrase "pious fraud", probably in its earliest use a play on *impia fraus* (a criminal or wicked fraud) from Cicero *De divinatione* 1.7, is cited by *OED* from Foxe's *Martyrs*, Cudworth, and Addison, and may have been given fresh currency from Burke's use of it in *Observations on a Late State of the Nation* (1769). For C's early use of the phrase see e.g. *EOT* (*CC*) I 149 (3 Feb 1800), *Friend* (*CC*) II 39 (10 Aug 1809) (= I 37–8).

4^2 For "the public good".
4^3 Hatred of episcopacy...Hatred of man. *OED* ascribes "misepiscopist" to Gauden (1659). Cf "misosophy" in HOOKER 22 and n 1.
4^4 See e.g. Matt 16.20–1, 17.9 and Mark 8.30.
4^5 See EICHHORN *Neue Testament* COPY B 9 and n 1. For Christ's denial that he was "King of the Jews" see John 18.33–9, 19.14–15 and parallels in other gospels.

is not so devoid either of genial Taste, or of gratitude for pleasures enjoyed, as to have treated a Book of A. Cunningham's own creation so irreverentially[6]

5 ii 90 | Mr John Scrimgeour

[Mr Scrimgeour, having witnessed the death of "several friends and children", found his only surviving daughter "seized by the king's evil". He went out in the fields and prayed:] "Thou, O lord, knowest that I have been serving thee in the uprightness of my heart, according to my power and measure; nor have I stood in awe to declare thy mind even unto the greatest in the time, and thou seest *] that I take pleasure in this child. O that I could obtain such a thing at thy hand, as to spare her!" [And she recovered.]

* a similar anecdote is related by Cotton Mather of a John Smith in New England.[1] Both were, I doubt not, true—i.e. as to the daring familiarity with God—& a score others. It was the fashion among the High-fliers[2] in Anthropomorphism.

6 p +1, concluded on p l,[a] referring to ii 118 | Mr Robert Bruce

He had a very notable faculty in searching the scriptures, and explaining the most obscure mysteries therein; and was a man who had much inward exercise of conscience anent his own personal case, and was oftentimes assaulted anent that grand fundamental truth,

[a] I.e. the last page (verso) of the appendix, facing p +1

4[6] In view of C's slight acquaintance with Allan Cunningham (see headnote), the length and fervour of **8** is remarkable, unless it may be supposed that the book was not to be returned to Cunningham.

5[1] Cotton MATHER *Magnalia Christi Americana* (1702) iii 47 (bk III pt i ch 3 §19), " The Life of Mr. John Wilson": "When one Mr. *Adams*...was followed with the News of his Daughter's being fallen suddenly and doubtfully sick, Mr. *Wilson* looking up to Heaven, began mightily to wrestle with God for the Life of the Young Woman: *Lord* (said he) *wilt thou now take away thy Servants Child, when thou seest he is attending on thy Poor unworthy Servant in most Christian Kindness; Oh! do it not!* And then turning himself about unto Mr. *Adams, Brother* (said he) *I trust your Daughter shall live, I believe in God she shall recover of this Sickness!* And so it marvellously came to pass, and she is now the fruitful *Mother* of several desireable Children." In the same §19 Mather gives two other examples of miraculous cure by prayer. His own son John fell from a loft four stories high; battered and bruised, he was taken as dead; "But Mr. *Wilson* had a wonderful Return of his *Prayers* in the Recovery of the Child, both unto *Life* and unto *Sense*...". Again, his last daughter "fell sick of a *Malignant Fever*, whereunto she was gone so far, that every one despaired of her Life", but prayers offered up by several ministers caused her to live.

5[2] I.e. Evangelicals. See *OED* 3b. C referred to ii 87–90 in *CN* IV 5024.

the being of a God; insomuch that it was almost customary to him to say, as when he first spoke in the pulpit, "I think it a great matter to believe there is a God;" and by this he was the more fitted to deal with others under the like temptations.

P. 118. l. 12.—Martin Luther was of the same mind: and I am persuaded, that the notion inculcated from childhood and the after confirmed habit of considering the existence and attributes of God as a sort of self-evident truth, so little beset with difficulties, that it is a doubt with them whether there ever was such a creature as an Atheist—I am persuaded, I say, that this prepossession among the Learned & those educated for the Ministry has been most injurious to the faith—and it is not the least among the causes of the prevailing indisposition to the mysteries of the Gospel—the Trinity, the personality of the WORD, and his incarnation in the Man Jesus, &c.—Every error has its opposite: and*a* The effects of the opposite error ⟨in this instance,⟩ viz. the too exclusive direction of the mind to the divine *personality*, the contemplation of ⟨the Filial⟩ God⟨head⟩ in the *Subjective* only without duly attending to that which he is *objectively*, as the WORD, the LIGHT that lighteth every man,[1] the energic Reason and Law of the World[2] present over all, are seen in the theology of the Scottish Confessors and Martyrs under the Stuarts, and at once constitute and explain its peculiar characters. Missing the Objective in the Highest they ~~sought for~~ clung to it ~~with~~ more eagerly & in the same ~~exclusiveness~~ spirit in the ⟨visible⟩ *Church*—& to the outward Kingdom & its forms they attached all the ~~momentous~~ and indispensability, all the ~~deeps~~ interests of faith and conscience, which ~~belonged~~ to the *Subjective* or Spiritual Church, to the Kingdom within! Hence their Judaizing sabbatarian principles, their predilection for the Old Testament, their equal readiness to suffer or to inflict ~~marytyrdom~~ for points of Church Government; hence lastly their indecent familiarities in prayer,[3] their anthropomorphic, yea, sarcomorphic[4] notions of the Supreme, and their anile Superstitions, and devil-combats. S. T. C.

a Here C has written " ∧ ∧ *turn to the leaf fronting this.*"—i.e. p l (last page of the appendix)—and has resumed the note with " ∧ ∧ "

6[1] John 1.9 (var).

6[2] For C's use of "energic" of his own reason see *Lines on a Friend Who Died of a Frenzy Fever* line 40: *PW* (EHC) i 77. See also: "My mind is always energic—I don't mean energetic: I require in everything what...I may call *propriety*,— that is, a reason, why the thing *is* at all, and why it is *there* or *then* rather than elsewhere or at another time." *TT* 1 Mar 1834.

6[3] See e.g. **5**, above.

6[4] "Attributing the form of flesh", on the analogy of *anthropomorphic*, "attributing the form of man". Not in *OED*.

7 ii 126, pencil, marked in the margin with a pencil line | John Gordon, Viscount Kenmuir

The minister finding him claiming kindness to Christ, and hearing him often cry, "O Son of God, where art thou, when wilt thou come to me; Oh! for a love-look" said, "Is it possible my Lord, that you can love and long for Christ, and he not love and long for you? Can love and kindness stand only on your side? Is your poor love more than infinite love, seeing he hath said, Isa. xlix. 15 *Can a woman forget*, &c?"

Visc. Kenmuir[1]

8 pp [+1]–[+3], referring to ii 142 | Mr James Mitchell

One time, in conference concerning the sin in the godly, his father said to him, "I am sure you are not now troubled with corruption, being so near death." He answered, "Ye are altogether deceived, for as long as my foot remaineth on this earth, though the other were translated above the clouds, my mind would not be free of sinful motions."

p. 142—

I have at sundry times been disturbed and assaulted by the question—If it pleased God to restore me to Health and Strength, have I any sufficient ground of confidence, that the sense of the sinfulness of Sin,[1] of the unworthiness and baseness of the sins, to which my constitutional softness, sensibility, and craving for sympathy, render me most prone, would either prevent or instantly suppress the workings of Sin on my members, or secure me against temptations, and opportunities of indulgence?—The inward Conviction of my weakness forces me to forego all hope of such a result from ~~any~~ the power or strength of any principle or habit of Will in myself—& to rest my only hope on the daily, hourly, nay, momently assistance of the free Grace of the Spirit of Christ.[2] And yet according to Bishop Jer. Taylor (Tract on Repentance) less than than such a Victory over Sin is delusion,[3] and even Archbp Leighton asserts the

7[1] C referred to ii 125, 131, in this "Life", in *CN* iv 5024.

8[1] See Rom 7.13.

8[2] The confessional intimacy of the beginning of this annotation is not unlike the tone of the marginalia in the earliest (1814) set of LEIGHTON (COPY A).

8[3] *Unum necessarium, or the Doctrine and Practice of Repentance*, in Jeremy TAYLOR *Polemicall Discourses* i 582–837. See n 5, below. At i 715 Taylor writes: "I deny not but all persons naturally are so that they cannot arrive at Heaven, but unless some other principle be put into them, or some great grace done for them, must for ever stand

necessity of the same Holiness, ~~as~~ which the Redeemed have in Heal~~th~~ven, as the indispensable condition of our ever getting thither.[4] Of Taylor's Book I have elsewhere avowed my opinion, that it partakes of the worst characters of ~~the~~ Romanism, and the Salvation by Works[5]—But Leighton was a Divine of a better School:[6] and ~~of~~ concerning his judgement I would remark—that if he means ~~the~~ by Holiness, the Righteousness of Christ, what disciple of John and Paul would hesitate to receive it? But if by Holiness while yet in the perishable Body he means such a strength already united with the "*I*", with the whole Man, as to exclude all danger, so that Temptations no longer act as Temptations—then he seems to me to make the ~~passio~~ Cross of Christ, his Blood shed for us, and the mediatorial ~~effe~~cticacy of his perfected Right̅ness[a] of no effect[7]—and the Redemption from the Body for which Paul prayed with such fervent groans and taught us to pray for,[8] no *deliverance* at all, or a deliverance only from a few incommodities which to a Soul fearing Sin &

> [a] Written "Right̅ness" for "Righteousness"

separate from seeing the face of God." In a long critical summary (pp +2-+3) C gives as an example of the way Taylor's works "contain dogmas subversive of true Christian Faith", especially "the Unum Necessarium, which reduces the cross of Christ to nothing".

8[4] Robert Leighton (1611–84), Abp of Glasgow, the annotation of three sets of whose *Works* brought C from a projected "Beauties of Leighton" to *Aids to Reflection* (1825); C had borrowed HOWIE to help him prepare a prefatory Life of Leighton. He may here refer to the passage on which he says he wrote "the first marginal Note I had pencilled on Leighton's Pages". *AR* (1825) 158. See LEIGHTON COPY C I 7 textus: "But this is the wisdom of a Christian, when he can solace himself against the meanness of his outward condition, and any kind of discomfort attending it, with the comfortable assurance of the love of God, that he hath called him to holiness, given him some measure of it, and an endeavour after more; and by this may he conclude, that he hath ordained him unto salvation." Cf e.g. *AR* (1825) 152–3.

8[5] See *AR* (1825) 251–75. C may also refer to his long note written on Jeremy TAYLOR *Polemicall Discourses* pp

+2-+3, in which he analyses "the Errors of this Great, & excellent Genius at their fountain-head, (the question of Original Sin)...". Cf "He [Taylor] was the Origen of our Church...but in his tremendous book on Repentance, he transcended not only all the Arminians of his own party, but even the most ascetic writers of the Romanists themselves. It is remarkable that it is the least eloquent of all his works, and the most prolix; without splendor, without unction...". "Thoughts on the Church", in *The Christian Observer* XLV (Jun 1845) 328–9, in *C 17th C* 266–7.

8[6] Cf LEIGHTON COPY A I 136–7: "Other divines [than Leighton], Donne & Jeremy Taylor for instance, have *converted* their worldly gifts, and applied them to holy ends: but here [in Leighton's *Commentary on 1 Peter*] the gifts themselves seem unearthly."

8[7] For more detailed discussion of this issue by C see *AR* (1825) 152–69.

8[8] Rom 7.24: "O wretched man that I am! who shall deliver me from the body of this death?"—which C in the later years often quoted in a personal sense (sometimes with the phrase "the/this body of death"), as he does at n 10, below. Cf. however, *CN* III 3078, 3189.

feeling the root of weakness in himself, must appear almost nothing. Therefore, tho' this be not the only instance in which the ascetic Spirit of Thomas a Kempis joined with a platonizing View of the Beauty of Virtue[9] has somewhat tinged and refracted the Rays of the Faith, as it shines thro' the ~~Pauline~~ Preaching of S[t] Paul—I am inclined to interpret this sentence of the Archbishop's ~~a~~ by its immediate purpose (the rousing of *loose*-living Believers from the lethargy of a false Conscience) rather than as a universal proposition, to be received without limit or qualification. And doubtless, there is a great need of guarding the Believer against turning the Grace of God into wantonness—or imagining that we can be saved without such a hatred of Sin as will make the Soul deliberately prefer any loss of temporal and bodily pleasure or advantage to a return under its tyranny. I trust that I sincerely & with my whole spirit pray to God thro' Christ, that he will preserve me in that state in which the temptations are not greater than my strength—the state, in which the portion of Grace, which he has bestowed, shall be sufficient for me—tho' it should be a continuance in weakness and languor of body and an incapacity of all the enjoyments of this world. Yet it would follow from Jer. Taylor's doctrine, that this very Prayer, supposing me to die immediately after, would be a presumption, that I had perished! But no! never never can I receive a doctrine which forbids me to believe, that there is any thing to be forgiven and supplied by and thro' Christ to my Soul, or that I shall leave behind in the deliverance from the *Body of Death* aught,[10] that I had not in fact & completion, and not only in firm principle & sincere desire, already been detached from! Extremes generate each other.[11] The truth lies between the Judaizing Pelagian and the presumptuous Antinomian[12]—hard to be

8[9] Thomas [Hemerken] à Kempis (c 1380–1471), German ascetic, traditionally the author of *The Imitation of Christ* (1418), which C regarded as a landmark in Christian history. In making to John Murray a proposal for "The Beauties of Leighton" in Jan 1822, C proposed "a sort of appendix, some short biographical and critical notice of that...class of Writers, before and immediately following Thomas à Kempis, whose works and labors were the...Pioneers of the Reformation". *CL* v 205. Thomas à Kempis was Leighton's favourite devotional writer.
8[10] See n 8, above.

8[11] An unusual, and illuminating, version of his favourite aphorism, "Extremes meet". See BLANCO WHITE *Practical Evidence* 9 n 2. In *CN* IV 4830 (c 1820–1) C had wondered whether his delight in "adages or aphorisms of universal or very extensive application" was "a peculiarity of my own mind", and continued: "I cannot describe how much pleasure I have derived from 'Extremes meet' for instance...".
8[12] Here the "Judaizing Pelagian" is Leighton, the "presumptuous Antinomian" Jeremy Taylor. The Pelagian holds that the first steps towards salvation are taken through a man's own initiative,

expressed in *words*, that may not be misunderstood, but easily found by a Soul that seeks a Saviour, in humility, and prays earnestly for the Spirit which is already given to whoever asks in faith by Christ.—

It seems to me as sufficient answer to the scheme of J. Taylor, that Christ has instructed us to pray—Lead us not into *Temptation*, but *deliver* us from the Evil one.—[13]

9   ii 157–9 | Mr John McClelland

[Letter of McClelland 20 Feb 1649:] "Englishmen shall be made spectacles to all nations for a broken covenant, when the living God swears, *As I live, even the covenant that he hath despised, and the oath that he hath broken, will I recompense upon his own head.*...His [i.e. the Lord's] assertion is a ground for faith, his oath a ground of full assurance of faith, if all England were as one man united in judgment and affection, and if it had a wall round about it reaching to the sun, and if it had as many armies as it has men, and every soldier had the strength of Goliah, and if their navies could cover the ocean, *]* and if there were none to peep out or move the tongue against them, yet I dare not doubt their destruction; when the Lord hath sworn by his life, that he will avenge the breach of covenant...."

* It is to be hoped that M^r M'Clellan did not mean the extirpation of the whole People & the Extinction of the very name of England. If not, this was a safe Prophecy, sure to be fulfilled, sometime, and somehow, if only a M'Clellan should be at hand as an Interpreter.— The great Fire, the great Plague &c[1]—Unless God expressly commanded the *covenant* itself in addition to the Contents or things covenanted, this is weak Reasoning. For God either did and does command the things covenanted, or he did & does not. If he did, the things are binding on the conscience without reference to the

---

not through the grace and assistance of God; the Antinomian holds that Christians, by grace, are released from observance of any moral law. Arminians held, against the determinism preached by Calvinists, that the sovereignty of God was compatible with the real exercise of free-will in man.

8[13] From the Lord's Prayer: see Matt 6.13, Luke 11.4 (AV in both "deliver us from evil"). The Greek phrase τοῦ πονηροῦ is ambiguous, meaning either

"evil" as an abstract noun or "the evil one". *NEB* reads: "and do not bring us to the test, but save us from the evil one". In *CN* IV 5078 C draws an opposition of τὸ πονηρόν (neuter), "evil principle", to ὁ πονηρός (masculine), "evil person".

9[1] The Great Fire of London burned from 2 to 8 Sept 1666 and destroyed most of the City, including St Paul's. The Great Plague of 1665 took c 75,000 lives in London.

Covenant. If he does not, then the Covenant is a presumptuous Will-work—the Imposers of which we humbly leave to the Mercy of Him who can alone know their motives. But how *their* act should be more obligatory on us, than the Covenant of another & far more numerous portion of our Ancestors/ viz. an Act of Parliament ~~to~~ in both Kingdoms ~~that~~ speaking the mind of not only all the constituent Parts of the State, Kings, Lords & Commons but beyond doubt of a vast majority of the People (in England at all events) ~~is perfectly~~ a covenant renouncing & forbidding the former Covenant, is perfectly incomprehensible.—

10 ii 158

A very little after he [John McClelland] wrote this letter, in one of his sermons he expressed himself much to the same purpose, Thus: "The judgments of England shall be so great, that a man shall ride fifty miles through the best plenished parts of England, before he hear a cock crow, a dog bark, or see a man's face." Also he farther asserted, "That if he had the best land of all England, he would make sale of it for two shillings the acre, and think he had come to a good market." And although this may not have had its full accomplishment as yet, yet there is ground to believe that it will be fulfilled, for the Lord will not alter the word that is gone out of his mouth.[a]

Mr M'Clelland continued near twelve years at Kirkcudbright. About the year 1650, he was called home to his Father's house to the full fruition of that which he had before seen in vision.

He was a man most strict and zealous in his life, and knew not what it was to be afraid of any man in the cause of God, being one who was most nearly acquainted with him, and knew much of his !!*] Master's will. Surely the Lord doth nothing but what he revealeth to his servants the prophets.

* If by the Prophets the writer means M'Clellan & other Heroes of this Biog. Scoticana, this is a most amusing!—the very *impudence* of Folly!

11 ii 158

A little before his death he made the following epitaph on himself.

> Come, stingless death, have o'er, lo! here's my pass,
> In blood character'd by his hand who was,
> And is, and shall be. Jordan, out thy stream,
> Make channels dry. I bear my Father's name,

[a] This paragraph and the whole of p 158 up to the opening of the new chapter are marked with pencil lines

Stampt on my brow. I am ravished with my crown,
I shine so bright, down with all glory, down,
That world can give. I see the peerless port,
The golden street, the blessed soul's resort,
The tree of life, floods gushing from the throne,
Call me to joys. Begone, short woes, begone,
I lived to die, but now I die to live,
I do enjoy more than I did believe.
The promise me unto possession sends,
Faith in fruition, hope in having, ends.

N.b. These are very fine Lines in their way. There is an intensity, a glow, a lyrical Burst and *Up-swing*,[1] that entitles them to preservation in some more accessible Museum.[2]

12 ii 472, pencil, marked with a pencil line in the margin | Mr Robert Fleming

... I bless God, (said he), that in fifteen years I have never given any man's credit a thrust behind his back; but when I had ground to speak well of any man, I did so with faithfulness, and when I wanted a subject that way, I kept silence.

worth transcribing.

11[1] Not in *OED*.
11[2] In *CN* iv 5039 C referred to ii 364–5 (on Robert Garnock) and to ii 408–9 (on

John Nisbit of Hardihill), and in *CN* iv 5040 to ii 423 (on John Blackadder).

HUGH OF SAINT VICTOR
1096–1141

Hugo de Sancto Victore De sacramentis. 2 pts in one vol. Strassburg 1485. Fᵒ.

Printed by Jordanus de Quedlinburg. Text in two columns.

Collection of N. F. D. Coleridge

Inscribed by C on p ⁻5: "This rare and intrinsically valuable Volume was presented to me, S. T. Coleridge, by my friend, the Revᵈ Edward Irving, 2 July, 1829—Grove, Highgate." On p ⁻3 some erasure of earlier writing in ink both above and below C's note. There are annotations in another hand.

This is the only incunable C is known to have owned. The initial letters are finely executed throughout in red and blue.

For C's relations with Edward Irving, whom he considered more Luther-like than any other contemporary, see IRVING headnote.

In Jan 1824 C recommended Hugh of St Victor to Tulk as "one of the incomparable Mystics before the Scholastic Æra". *CL* v 326. In *TT* 25 May 1832 C declared: "Hugo de Saint Victor, Luther's favourite divine, was a wonderful man, who, in the 12th century, the jubilant age of papal dominion, nursed the lamp of Platonic mysticism in the spirit of the most refined Christianity."

DATE. After 2 Jul 1829.

1 p ⁻3

[A note in pencil in an unidentified hand:] The 9 vital energies accordᵍ to Sir G. Blane

    Generative
    Conservative
    Temperative
    Assimilative
    Formative
    Restorative
    Sensitive
    Motive
    Sympathetic

"Medical Logic."[1]

May not Animal Life be defined The aggregate of these nine.

1[1] Sir Gilbert Blane (1749–1834) *Elements of Medical Logick*...(1819) 22–3.   The list represents the "properties peculiar to animated nature...the ulti-

Answer. The Catalogue is both defective and erreoneous. Names that ought to have h̶a̶d̶ a place in it, are missing: and two or three, that are mentioned, are mere modifications of other energies. But were the Catalogue as compleat as the Querist assumes it to be, still I should answer—No! It might be a *Description*; but not a Definition. Even in Euclid a description, or diagnostic attribute, is substituted for a definition: viz. in that of the Circle, which we may indeed distinguish from other figures by its being equi-radial; but which must be defined, "The Figure formed by the circumvolution of a strait line, having one end fixed."[2]

mate facts, or primary elements, which form the groundwork of physiological and pathological science....It is meant to comprehend all the properties in which the essence of life consists, and which characterize and distinguish it from inanimate matter on the one hand, and from moral and intellectual nature on the other." In the 2nd ed (1821) ten "*elementary principles* of life" were listed, adding "The Appetitive"; in the 3rd ed (1825) there were eleven "Elementary Attributes of Life"—"Sensitive" was removed, "Appetitive" was retained, and "Imitative" was added.

Blane had served at sea under Rodney with such distinction in the West Indies that he was appointed physician to the Fleet at the age of thirty; he returned to London in 1783, secured a position at St Thomas's Hospital and developed a large private practice, attracted a high reputation for his *Observations on the Diseases*

of Seamen (1785) and other medical books, and was elected FRS.

1[2] In an extended discussion of the difference between definition and description, in a letter of 24 Oct 1826 to James Gillman, Jr, C used this same illustration of a "*constitutive*" definition, "as all legitimate mathematical Definitions ought to be: and inasmuch as they supply the ground and condition of the reasoning...they are of necessity antecedent. Ex.—A Circle is the Figure formed by the circumvolution of a strait line fixed at one end.—Thus is a circle constituted." Of a "*diagnostic*" definition he gives the example: "A circle is a figure, having all the lines from the center to the circumference equal." But, he remarks, "This enables you to *distinguish* a circle from all other figures; but it is only *one* of the numberless properties of the Circle, and therefore, tho' adopted by Euclid, it is not a legitimate *geometrical* Definition." *CL* VI 635–6.

JOSEPH HUGHES
1769–1833

The Believer's Prospect and Preparation, described in a discourse delivered in Broadmead Meeting House, Bristol, on Sunday morning March 6, 1831, on occasion of the death of the Rev. Robert Hall...To which is annexed, the address delivered at the interment, on the previous Wednesday, by the Rev. T. S. Crisp. London 1831. 8°.

Bound as seventh in "PAMPHLETS—DIVINITY", a made-up volume of eight sermons and addresses 1824–33.

British Museum C 126 h 2 (7)

C first met Joseph Hughes at Cottle's house c 1795, when Hughes was assistant minister of the Baptist Church, Broadmead, Bristol. In 1796 Hughes moved to the Baptist Church in Battersea, which he served for the rest of his life, and became one of the first secretaries of the British and Foreign Bible Society (founded 1804). The surviving records of their relationship suggest that it was at best intermittent. C sent Hughes tickets for his 1812 lectures (*CN* III 4159). When they met in Nov 1819, C seems to have talked effusively out of pleasure at meeting somebody "at once competent and interested in religion *theologically*", for he sent Hughes an annotated and affectionately inscribed copy of *The Friend* (1818) with a letter, partly of apology and explanation, asking him to comment on any passages that he found "*objectionable*". *Friend* (*CC*) II 390, 503–4 (*CL* VI 1048–50). In 1823 and 1825 Hughes (to the knowledge of C's publisher) gave advice about *AR* (*CL* V 300, 455), and in May he encouraged C to sketch out (reluctantly) themes for three discourses in support of the proposed London University (which he did not deliver). *CL* V 447, VI 1053. See also *CL* IV 965, VI 1055.

DATE. After mid-Mar 1831.

1   pp 13–23

How different from those of a former period are the convictions, the confessions, the supplications, the propensities, the sources of comfort and hope, and the proofs of gratitude and obedience, when, being regenerated by the Holy Spirit, fallen creatures justly "reckon" themselves "to be dead indeed unto sin, but alive unto God through *] Jesus Christ our Lord;" "being born again, not of corruptible

1184

seed, but of incorruptible, by the word of God, which liveth and abideth for ever."

* Birth is the passage of *Being* to *Existence*. The *Potential* becomes ACTUAL.[1] The potentiative Cause, i.e. the actualizing Agent, of our Birth into our present state of Existence, is "the corruptible Seed".[2] Now a finite, conditional, and impermanent *Cause* must necessarily manifest itself in a finite, dependent, & transitory Effect or Product. And in this, if ever, we must find, I presume, the true ultimate ground and Rationale of the universality of *Death*/ and on the same principle it must remain uncertain whether Adam before the Fall was immortal/ for he was *created*, & not begotten—. But Cain, Seth, &c were begotten—and "of corruptible Seed"—and *therefore* quoad hoc[3] *mortal.*—But thro' Christ we are *born again*—begotten of an *incorruptible Seed*[4]—and by parity of reason "heirs of immortality".—The slight & irregular connection of Death with Disease, the frequent contrast between Health & Longevity—the very fact, of healthy Old Age—/ seem to confirm this view. The healthful instinct-obeying Stag or Elk dies in his 20th or 30th year—and many an intemperate & thro' intemperance sickly, Man retains his Life to the 90th.—But I confess, that I find nothing in Reason to authorize me, nothing in Scripture that requires me, to believe an actuality, or full *existency*, of the Soul separate from the Body[6]—even as I am utterly incapable of conceiving a *Body* without a Soul. A carcase *is* not a Body[7]—any more than a Dendrite is a Plant—tho' it bears the impression of a Plant, and proves the past existence of a Plant.—But *the Man* by necessity of his finite nature at once potential and Actual exists, as *Soul and Body*. The Man in a mere potential Being you may, if you please, *call* the Soul; but then recollect, that the moment this potential ~~Being~~ is *actualized*, the opposite ~~Being~~ Mode instantly takes place—and the

1[1] For this (originally Aristotelian) distinction between "*potential*" and "*actual Power*" see e.g. *C&S* (*CC*) 95–6 and especially the PS at the end of this annotation. See also n 11, below.
1[2] 1 Pet 1.23 (in textus).
1[3] "As far as this [applies]".
1[4] Still 1 Pet 1.23.
1[5] Not in NT; but cf 1 Cor 15.53–4, James 2.5.
1[6] Cf e.g. *AR* (1825) 302n, in which C rejects "the notion of a rational and self-conscious Soul, perishing utterly with the dissolution of the organized

Body", on the grounds that the soul would then be "a quality or Accident of the Body—a mere harmony resulting from Organization". See also HACKET *Century* 22 and n 2.
1[7] On the relation between soul and body see—in addition to HACKET *Century* 22—e.g. BÖHME 155 and n 2, DONNE *Sermons* COPY B 76 and 126, and *CN* III 3320. This recurrent issue assumed prominence in the marginalia on IRVING *Sermons*, LACUNZA tr Irving, and LEIGHTON COPY B and COPY C.

unit, Man, appears in the *Dyad*, or corresponding opposites, Soul and Body—/ not that Soul and Body *compose* the Man, as Carbon & Hydrogen compose Oil, or Hydrogen & Carbon compose Alcohol—/ But rather as the *Magnetic Power* realizes itself in the two Poles, Attraction & Repulsion. Hence, I hold that the Gospel *first* presented the true idea of Immortality[8]—layed the first *ground* of future *existence*—The *Stoics* substituted for this the delusive conception of *imperishable Being*[9]—which tho' true is futile—for it applies with equal ⟨truth,⟩ yea, with far greater evidence, to a Molecule of Sand, a Mote in a Sun-beam, as to a Man./ Whatever *is*, is necessarily: for it is, because God *is*—but it is not necessarily *actual. S. T. C.*[a] for this is the incommunicable Attribute of God, as the Absolute—that he is the Supreme, in whom the Real & the Actual are one & the same[10]—in whom the Actual comprizes all Reality—or in the language of the Schools, "*Actus purissimus sine ullâ potentialitate.*"[11] But in every Creature *the Real* is the *Prothesis*, of which the Actual and the Potential are the Thesis & Antithesis, or + and − Poles.[12] For *us* the Real exists only as the *Identity* of the Actual & Potential. My power of Walking & my power of Sitting are equally *real*; but at this moment the latter is actual, the former potential—So in all Being ~~in~~ there is the *Bothness*[13] of Finite & Infinite—~~but~~ & in all, but God, the Potential is infinite, the Actual finite. In every finite Actual there is a potential infinite—(presented theorematically in the infinite divisibility of Matter.)—But even this is only the first & simplest view—The Problem expands when we take in, as we must do, the equally necessary terms of Multëity and Unity, as the character of every *creature*.[14] For in God alone is true *Unity*. He alone is *the One*.[15] The highest of Creatures, the Angels even, are but *Numbers*[16]—i.e. Multëity brought under Unity. Now Man is a *Number*, and in his present state of a lower Order—And it is this which renders the problem of our Immortality so difficult for the *Reason*—and which

---

a C evidently ended the note, as at first conceived, with "not necessarily *actual.*", wrote his initials, and then—in the same line of ms—resumed the note in what seems to be the same hand and ink

[8] Sée e.g. *LS* (*CC*) 175 (at n 1).

[9] On the transitoriness of life, and the soul as "a rambling sort of a Thing"; see AURELIUS **27**, **28** n 3 (on suicide), **44**, **46**, and nn.

[10] See *C&S* (*CC*) 234 (of c 1830).

[11] "Absolutely pure actuality without any potentiality"—for which Scholastic phrase see BAXTER *Catholick Theologie* **1** n 2.

[12] See the diagram in *C&S* (*CC*) 234.

[13] Not in *OED*. Cf "the *Dyad*...Soul and Body", above.

[14] See e.g. ATHENAEUM **31** n 3. See also the last sentence of this note.

[15] See *AR* (1825) 161–2.

[16] For C's scepticism about angels see e.g. HOOKER **19** and n 3.

ought to make us so thankful for a *Revelation*. As natural men, we feel the underswell of our Multëity, of the complexity and dissonances of our Being, so manifoldly & intrusively as to perplex and *unsteady* our Sense of the *Unity*.[17]

2 p 19, continued on p [64]

Inquiry, pursued through the sacred volume, shall be met with the assurance that "there is forgiveness with God," his own Son* having "suffered, the Just for the unjust," that "by the sacrifice of Himself he might put away sin," and that "through Him we might have access, by one Spirit, to the Father."

* *This*, THIS, THIS, is what I complain of, in so many good & pious discourses—viz. the assignment of a *reason* for a position, left incomparably more difficult & strange than the position itself/[a]

That "there is forgiveness with God",[1] all within me renders me ready to believe; but that it is, because an innocent & most righteous Being has *suffered*[2]—that God gives Good to the Miserable only on account of the Misery of the Good—this startles the mind—& should not thus nakedly be presented to it. Yet I trust, I am as firm a believer in Redemption by Christ Jesus, and in the necessity of that Redemption, as even the excellent & by me most affectionately esteemed Author of this Discourse.

S. T. Coleridge.

[a] Here C has written "See last page, 64.—" and continued the note with "MS marginal Note from p. 19."

1[17] On the unique "*Contradiction* in the Human Being"—"the Riddle of Man"—see *AR* (1825) 343–4.

2[1] Quoted in textus, but not in NT. Cf however Ps 130.4, Dan 9.9, Acts 5.31, 26.18, Eph 1.7.

2[2] See 1 Pet 3.18, quoted in textus. For C's insistence that the "*Mystery*" of Redemption is to be understood—as St John understands it—"without any metaphor", identifying it "with a *fact*, not with a Consequence", see FIELD 12 and n 4 and cf HOOKER 42 and n 3. This is also a central point of attack in C's adverse analysis of Jeremy Taylor *Unum necessarium*: see HOWIE 8 n 3.

HYMAN HURWITZ

c 1775–1844

The Elements of the Hebrew Language. London 1829. 8°.

Victoria College Library (Coleridge Collection)

Inscribed on the title-page, probably not by Hurwitz: "To S. T. Coleridge Esqr with the Authors Comp^ts". Light pencil marks on pp 9 (Roman and Greek equivalents of Hebrew characters), 24, 25, 56, 57, 71.

C read the proofs of *The Elements of the Hebrew Language* in May 1829. *CL* VI 791. Although Hurwitz did not take into the final version the few revisions that C is known to have proposed, much of the Preface and "Introductory Observations" to the companion volumes, *The Etymology and Syntax...of the Hebrew Language*, which C was discussing with Hurwitz in detail a few months later, sound Coleridgian, and at least two paragraphs sent by C were included in the text. *CL* VI 816–18. Whether C made substantive contribution to either book has not been determined. The *Elements* (1829), published probably to mark Hurwitz's appointment in 1828 as first professor of Hebrew language and literature in University College, London, was a completely rewritten version of his *Elements of the Hebrew Language*...(1807) Pt i "Orthography"; Pt ii, announced in 1807 as "Etymology and Syntax", was not published until 1831.

When Hyman Hurwitz, with the rest of his family, followed his father to England from Posen in Poland in 1796 or 1797, he was already highly educated and quickly found an appointment as a schoolmaster. In c 1799, at the invitation of certain influential Jewish families, he set up in Highgate a seminary for Jewish boys. In 1804 he took a sixteen-years' tenancy of Church House, 10 South Grove, two houses away from Moreton House, where the Gillmans were living when C joined their household in Apr 1816. By that time the Academy had an enrolment of about a hundred boys, being the only considerable school of its kind in the country.

The circumstances of the early acquaintance between C and Hurwitz are not recorded. In c Nov 1807 C prepared a verse translation of Hurwitz's *A Hebrew Dirge...on the Day of the Funeral of Her Royal Highness the Princess Charlotte*, and in Mar 1820 *The Tears of a Grateful People...on the Day of the Funeral of King George III*: see *PW* (EHC) I 433–5, 436–8 (and *CL* V 40). The friendship, however, had a more learned and biblical basis than those verses might suggest: for C, who had been made a "tolerable Hebraist" at Christ's Hospital but had allowed his Hebrew to fall into disuse, found that Hurwitz could add an important dimension to his own biblical studies, not only in matters of Hebrew language, but also in interpreting the Jewish way of thought. See e.g. *CN* III 4418 f 11 (c Aug 1818), DAVISON **12** and **16**, N 36 ff 36–36^v (27 Dec 1827) (*CN* V). Two letters from C to Hurwitz

1188

in Jan and Mar 1820 provide a concentrated statement of C's view of the relation between Jew and Christian and between the OT and NT. *CL* v 1–9, 19–22. These letters were evidently responding to the ms or proofs of Hurwitz's *Vindiciae Hebraicae, Being a Defence of the Hebrew Scriptures as a Vehicle of Revealed Religion* (1820), in which Hurwitz paid C a compliment to which C drew attention when he sent a copy of the book to Blanco White in Dec 1825. *CL* v 522, 523n. C praised the book publicly in *AR* (1825) 205n, and in the same year described Hurwitz to John Taylor Coleridge as "the first Hebrew and Rabbinical Scholar in the kingdom". *CL* v 440; cf 443. But by then Hurwitz had left Highgate.

Much of what is now known about Hurwitz is recorded in a paper by Leonard Hyman—"Hyman Hurwitz: the First Anglo-Jewish Professor"– –delivered by his son Robin Hyman to the Jewish Historical Society of England on 13 May 1964, a month after Hyman's death, and published in the Society's *Transactions: Sessions 1962–7*. It is also known that Hurwitz was a Freemason and that he founded the liberal Western Synagogue.

Hurwitz renewed the lease on Church House in 1821 for seventeen years, but shortly afterwards decided to retire for reasons of health, transferred the direction of the school and the remainder of the lease to his assistant, Leopold Neumegen, and in 1821 or 1822 moved to Grenada Cottage, Old Kent Road. See *CL* v 441 and cf 135. Neumegen (d 1875) continued to be a friend of C and the Gillmans—see e.g. *CL* vi 709 (Nov 1827) and N. L. Broughton *Some Letters* 107 (11 Aug 1830)—and directed the school in Highgate until 1841.

A reference to EICHHORN *Allgemeine Bibliothek* in Jan 1820 (*CL* v 3) suggests that there was interchange of books between Hurwitz and C. Beginning with the *Vindiciae* in 1820, if not earlier, C evidently undertook to read Hurwitz's mss and to advise him in preparing his books. In 1825 C encouraged Hurwitz to prepare for Murray a collection of *Hebrew Tales*: these were published in 1826 with three of the "Specimens of Rabbinical Wisdom" that C had rendered from the German in 1809 (see BLANCO WHITE *Practical Evidence* 2 n 3). *The Elements of the Hebrew Language* and the *Etymology* followed, and probably other smaller pieces such as Hurwitz's *Introductory Lecture* as professor of Hebrew, which C had read before publication late in 1828. *CL* vi 775n. C's close editorial concern for Hurwitz's work, first as next-door neighbour, then at a distance with the fluency that came from some years of scholarly friendship and collaborative biblical study, may account for the absence of marginalia in the copies of the books Hurwitz presented to him: in addition to a copy of *Vindiciae Hebraicae* (1820), a second copy of the *Elements*, and a copy of the *Etymology* (1831), all in Green's library (but none of them acquired by the BM).

For C's letters recommending Hurwitz's appointment as professor of Hebrew see *CL* vi 668, 709–10. Hurwitz died at Artillery Place, City Road, on 18 Jul 1844; his library was advertised for sale at auction by Evans on 23 May 1846 but was not sold.

DATE. Shortly after 20 Nov 1829 (1).

1 p⁻1

I have had no Sleep, at least but an hour and a half, for two nights—thro' torture of symptomatic Rheumatism accompanied with oppression of Spirits worse than the pain, (tho' that is more than I have fortitude to bear). It seems to alternate with the Appearance of the Erysipelas on the right Leg—.[1] I am so weak, I really cannot write—which I will do when a little better. Lord Lyndhurst's letter was a kind one—I shall send him my Book on the Constitution with a letter[2]—Heartfelt Love to Mary & the dear Boy.[3] Shall I yet be permitted to kiss him?[4]

S. T. Coleridge—
20 onilthiy[a] Nov[r]
1829.

---

[a] The reading is uncertain. C probably intended "something"—and Griggs reads it so in *CL* vi 823

[1] Cf *CL* vi 823–4 (4 Dec 1829); the symptoms had begun to appear when C wrote to DC in Aug—see *CL* vi 814.

[2] C ordered the book from Hurst on 6 Dec 1829: *CL* vi 824. For the inscribed copy of *C&S* that C sent at this time to John Singleton Copley, Baron Lyndhurst (1772–1863)—now in HEHL—see *C&S* (*CC*) 237 and cf liv.

[3] DC married Mary Pridham on 6 Dec 1827. Derwent Moultrie—the "little Dervy" of *HCL* 105 (30 Aug 1830)—was born 17 Oct 1828. Cf *CL* vi 814–15.

[4] This annotation is also printed in *CL* vi 823 as a letter addressed to DC.

LUCY HUTCHINSON

1620–c 1676

Memoirs of the Life of Colonel [John] Hutchinson [1615–1664], Governor of Nottingham Castle and Town...with original anecdotes of many of the most distinguished of his contemporaries, and a summary review of public affairs: written by his widow Lucy, daughter of Sir Allen Apsley....Now first published from the original manuscript by the Rev. Julius Hutchinson, &c. &c. to which is prefixed the life of Mrs. Hutchinson, written by herself, a fragment. 2 pts in 1 vol. London 1806. 4°.

British Museum Ashley 4780

Inscribed on p ⁻3 in an unidentified fair hand: "Mʳˢ Gillman". At the head of i xiii, in pencil in C's hand, "Assembly"; at the foot of i 273 "prejudice"; at the head of ii 445, in ink "H A G" (Henry Gillman's initials). Pencil lines in the margin, possibly C's, on i vi, vii, viii, ix, x, xii, xiii, xiv, 1–2, 12–15, 16n, 17; ii 1–3, 6–7, 12–13, 15, 16, 17, 24, 34, 45 (**4** textus), 48n, 51, 69 (**6** textus), 189.

The enthusiastic response of the Wordsworths to this book when Lady Beaumont gave them a copy in Feb 1807, at Coleorton while C was still with them, and the fact that C referred to the book in HAYLEY 3, written in Nether Stowey in the summer of 1807, and again in BROWNE *Works* 4 (Jan–Jun 1808), suggest that C had probably read the book early in 1807. See *WL* (*M*2) i 133, 140. There is no evidence in the annotations themselves that they were written as early as 1807–8.

MS TRANSCRIPT. VCL LT 48: 2 notes (**5, 6**) in HNC's hand; and others (**7–19**) in two unidentified hands.

DATE. 1831 (dated in **1**) and perhaps earlier, c 1825. Two references in marginalia—BAXTER *Reliquiae* COPY B **88** and PEPYS II i 13 (**4**)—both of 1825, suggest that some of the annotations may have been written as early as that, for they do not all seem to have been written at one time. C refers to the *Memoirs* in c Sept 1821: *CL* v 170n.

1   i 3, pencil, overtraced | The Life of Mrs. Lucy Hutchinson, Written by Herself

The people, by the plenty of their country, not being forc'd to toyle for bread, have ever addicted themselves to more generous employments, and bene reckoned, allmost in all ages, as valliant warriours as any part of the world sent forth...

Alas! the change!—1831—*a*

Q*y*—Whether the Nation,—whose mechanic and manufacturing class is merely adequate to the supply of its Learned & Landed Gentry, and its Agriculturalists, is not a nobler & more prosperous, tho less powerful, than manufactories stimulated by a widely extended Commerce now presents?[1]

2   ii 9 | Mrs. Hutchinson to Her Children Concerning Their Father

*] In matters of faith his reason allwayes submitted to the word of God, and what he could not comprehend he would believe because 'twas written, but in all other things, the greatest names in the world could never lead him without reason...

* Well may I *believe* what I do not *comprehend*, when there are so many things which I *know* yet do not *comprehend*—my Life, for instance, my Will, my rationality, &c.—But let us be on our guard not to confound *com*prehending with *ap*prehending—I do not, even because I *can* not, believe what I do not *ap*prehend—i.e. I cannot assent to the Meaning of Words, to which I attach no meaning—tho' I may believe in the wisdom of the Utterer.[1] But this is to believe the veracity of the Doctor, not the truth of the Doctrine.[2] S. T. C.

3   ii 11

He was as faithfull and constant to his friends as mercifull to his *] enemies: nothing griev'd him more than to be oblieg'd, where he could not hope to returne itt.

a C has written this phrase in the outer margin beside the textus; the second paragraph is written in the spacious foot-margin

1[1] On the social effects of the growth of commerce and manufacture see *LS* (*CC*) 194–5 and cf 160–1, 169–70, 203–9, 213–25. See also *C&S* (*CC*) 50.

2[1] On comprehension see *CN* iii 3311, 3517. See also Böhme **56** n 2 and cf FIELDING *Tom Jones* **9** n 2, for Augustine's dictum "Unless ye believe, ye will not understand". The distinction between apprehension and comprehension corresponds to the difference between reason and understanding, understanding being—as C in his marginalia on Jeremy Taylor ascribes the meaning to Leighton and Kant—"the Faculty that judges according to Sense". In attacking

Taylor's treatment of original sin in *Unum necessarium* C says of "Luther, Calvin & their Compeers & Successors" that they made "an awful Fact of Human Nature...contradictory & absurd by a vain attempt at explication". "It was a *fundamental* fact, & of course, *could* not be comprehended: for to comprehend, & thence to explain, is the same as to perceive, & thence to point out, a something before the given fact, & standing to it in the relation of cause and effect." Jeremy TAYLOR *Polemicall Discourses* p +2.

2[2] On veracity and truth see e.g. BAXTER *Reliquiae* COPY B **46** n 1.

* The youthful Reader should be made see, that this was a defect, tho' a defect symptomatic of a noble nature. Besides, except to God, we cannot be obliged without the power of making the right return; for ⟨where no more is in our power,⟩ to feel, to acknowlege, and duly to appreciate an obligation, is to return it.—Nay, God himself accepts our thankfulness & obedience as a *return* for his free gifts & mercies.

4 ii 45, pencil, overtraced | The Life of John Hutchinson

The greatest excellencie she had was the power of apprehending and the virtue of loving his: soe as his shadow, she waited on him every where, till he was taken into that region of light, which admitts of ?] more, and then she vanisht into nothing.

none—i.e. of no shadow.

5 ii 47–8, pencil, overtraced

The gentleman that assisted him he converted to a right beliefe in that greate poynt of predestination, he having bene before of the Arminian iudgment, still upon the serious examination of both principles, and comparing them with the scriptures, Mr. Hutchinson *] convinc'd him of the truth, and grew so well instructed in this principle, that he was able to maintaine it against any man.

* A most instructive instance of the delusions, consequent on the logic of Dichotomy: or the antithesis of terms precluding each other or assumed so to do. Ex. gr. Necessity ⚹ Freedom, Real ⚹ Unreal, Spirit ⚹ Body, Cause ⚹ *a* Effect, &c*bl*—The doctrine of Predestination is built on the assumption that the distinction of the Terms implys a division of the Things[2]—ex. gr. the Divine Reason & the Divine Will. The ~~latter*c*~~ former is arbitrarily taken as the Antecedent & the *Cause*, the latter, as the *effect*, as a passive Clay, receiving the impression of the former—Deny this, or (as you safely may do) affirm the contrary, namely that the Will is the Antecedent and the Reason the form or Epiphany of the Will—and the whole Argument of the Predestinarian is quashed.[3]

a Incorrectly overtraced "χ"   *b* Not overtraced
c This word, cancelled by C, is not overtraced

5[1] On the virtue of trichotomy as against dichotomy see *Logic (CC)* 241–3. See also BAXTER *Reliquiae* COPY B **103** and nn.

5[2] On the error of mistaking a conceptual distinction for a real and exclusive division see e.g. HUGHES **1** and n 1.

5[3] See e.g. BUNYAN COPY B **21**.

6 ii 69

If any one obiect the fresh example of Queene Elizabeth, let them remember that the felicity of her reigne was the effect of her submission to her masculine and wise councellors; but wherever male princes are so effeminate as to suffer weomen of forreigne birth and different religions to entermeddle with the affairs of State, it is always found to produce sad desolations...

But what was the cause of that submission, to Men chosen? of that choice of Men, worthy to be submitted to?—This is an old but just Answer to an old Detraction from Elizabeth's personal Character.

7 ii 74, pencil, overtraced

The King's designe in going to Scotland...retarded all the affaires of the government of England...but yet the parliament shew'd such a wonderfull respect to the king, that they never mention'd him, as he was, the sole author of all those miscarriages, but imputed them to evill councellors, and gave him all the submissive language that could have bene us'd to a good prince, fixing all the guilt upon his evill councellors and ministers of state, which flattery I feare they have to answer for: I am sure they have thereby expos'd themselves to much scandall.

[Editor's footnote:] This is an oversight of Mrs. Hutchinson's, of which she is seldom guilty. Good policy required then, as it does now, that the king should be held incapable of wrong, and the criminality fixed on ministers, who are amenable to the law. If the patriots of that day were the inventors of this maxim, we are highly obliged to them.

I am yearly more and more inclined to question the expediency of falsehood of any kind[1] and therefore doubt the wisdom of M^{ra} J. Hutchinson's censure of his high-minded Ancestrèss.[2] Had the Parliament as soon as the King's own principles and passions were known to be prime movers of his Council, declared the same, it might

a "M^r" incorrectly overtraced as "M^{rs}"

7[1] Cf "What apology can be made for falsehood...". *EOT* (*CC*) ɪɪ 72; cf ɪɪɪ 59 (conjectural ascription to C). See also Essay vɪɪɪ "On the Communication of Truth" in *Friend* (*CC*) ɪ 58–66. For C on Charles ɪ as a liar see HACKET *Scrinia* **44** n 1.

7[2] Rev Julius Hutchinson (c 1751–1811), who edited Lucy Hutchinson's *Memoirs*, was a descendant of the colonel's half-brother Charles. See the Hutchinson family tree facing Preface.

have prevented the Civil War, at all events the apparent inconsistency of their own proceedings.

8 ii 115

There was one Mr. Widmerpoole, a man of good extraction, but reduc'd to a small fortune, had declin'd all the splendor of an old house, and sunke into the way of the middle men of the country; yet had a perfect honest heart to God, his country, and his friend...

The Ellipsis of the pronoun relative after the Conjunction is a frequent and, I think, a graceful idiom in our elder Authors—"But reduced" for "but who, reduced"—

9 ii 115

As a Port[r]ait-painter,[a] M[rs] H. unites the grace and finish of Vandyke with the life and sub[s]tantive[a] Reality of Rembrandt.[1] By the bye, among the numerous points, that make up that most notice-worthy Contrast of the old English Republican, and the modern mongrel-bred Jacobin,[2] one of the most striking is the

[a] Letter supplied by the editor

9[1] Sir Anthony van Dyck (1599–1641), painter to Charles I from 1632, whose portraits of Charles and his court are remarkable for fineness of execution and for their haunting penetration of character. Rembrandt Harmenszoon van Rijn (1606–69) was as much preoccupied, particularly in his early and later years, with portrait painting as with the exploration of the qualities of light; sixty-two self-portraits are recorded. The specificity of C's comment suggests that he had actual paintings in mind. He could have been familiar with the work of both painters, in some sense, from "reading" —with Lamb and Hazlitt—engravings of their work. C could have seen the Rembrandt *Portrait of a Jewish Merchant*, which Sir George Beaumont owned and later (1826) presented to the National Gallery. Farington *Diary* VII 118 (21 Oct 1812). Other Rembrandts and Van Dycks he could have seen in various exhibitions, especially those held at the British Institution, where Van Dyck's portrait of Cornelius van der

Geest was exhibited in 1815 (Farington *Diary* III 17n). From 1806 the British Institution, with the support of Sir George Beaumont and—among others— C's acquaintance Sir Thomas Bernard, held two exhibitions a year in Boydell's Shakespeare Gallery to show modern works and Old Masters, the Old Masters being lent by their owners. The Angerstein collection, which C visited with WW in 1808 (*WL—M* 2 I 208) and no doubt on other occasions, included Rembrandt's *Woman Taken in Adultery* and *The Birth of Christ* and Van Dyck's *Emperor Theodosius Refused Admittance to the Church of Milan by Archbishop Ambrose* and *Portrait of Rubens*.
9[2] For C's definition of a Jacobin see *EOT* (*CC*) I 369–70 (21 Oct 1802); this he considered "the first philosophical appropriation of a precise import to the word Jacobin, as distinct from Republican, Democrat, and Demagogue". *Friend* (*CC*) I 221n. See also BAXTER *Reliquiae* COPY B 16 n 1.

reverential value of ancient family,[3] entertained by the former, with comparative contempt of the court-derived Titles, which the latter hates ⟨both alike,⟩ because he envies both.

10　ii 196–7, pencil, overtraced

[Editor's footnote:]... the road still lay open to Lincoln, but probably Prince Rupert was too strong and too active to let the besiegers escape any way unless they had acted with better accord amongst each other.

There is something almost fantastic in the thought, that this Prince Rupert, whose character of Temerity, Brutality, Insolence, Impetuosity, & *Unreasonableness*, (ex̶ i.e. the abandonment of Bristol) is given almost in the same words by the Royalist and the Parliamentarian Historians,[1] should have been the Inventor of Mezzo-tinto Engraving[2]—The Superstition of Royal Blood in its most exclusive intensity, acted on Charles's mind in the instance of this his Nephew, most ruinously for his affairs. If Charles did not authorize, he

9[3] See *LS* (*CC*) 170 (as emended in annotated copies of *LS*): "...this reverence for *ancientry* in families acted as a counterpoise to the grosser superstition for wealth".

10[1] Prince Rupert (1619–82), Count Palatine of the Rhine and grandson of James I, afterwards Duke of Cumberland and Earl of Holderness. On his arrival in England in Jul 1642 at the outbreak of the Civil War, he was appointed by his uncle Charles as general of horse in an independent command. Through his almost Wellingtonian understanding of military tactics and equipment, his innovative flair, and the force of his presence he quickly instilled in Charles's soldiers a resolution and professional skill that they had hitherto lacked. After an uninterrupted series of successes he was defeated by Cromwell at Marston Moor (2 Jul 1644). Arrogant, overbearing, impatient of direction even from the King, many times neglecting to restrain his men from looting and killing in the towns he captured, he was nevertheless appointed commander-in-chief. Largely through disregard of the military advantage he held before the battle, he was decisively defeated again at Naseby (14 Jun 1645). In Sept 1645, he surren-

dered Bristol—which he had captured in 1643—to Fairfax. For this Charles considered him guilty of dereliction of duty, stripped him of his command, and ordered him to leave the country. This, however, was by no means the end of his career as commander in the field and at sea.

10[2] The art of mezzotint engraving was invented by Ludwig von Siegen (1609–c 1680), military officer and artist, who in 1654 showed his work to Prince Rupert, himself an amateur artist. Rupert brought the process to England at the beginning of the Restoration, and in Mar 1661 demonstrated the process to the virtuoso John Evelyn (1620–1706), who immediately publicised it in his *Sculptura; or the History and Art of Chalcography* ("to which is annexed a new manner of engraving, or mezzo tinto, communicated by his Highness Prince Rupert") (1662) with fulsome—and no doubt inadvertent—acknowledgment to Prince Rupert as inventor of the process. The ascription was plausible because of Rupert's restless and prolific ingenuity as an inventor, particularly of military devices and of ways of compounding and manipulating metals.

passively sanctioned, and perhaps inwardly approved of Rupert's *overly* treatment of the Duke of Newcastle and thus baffled & disgusted the chivalrous Loyalty and Devotion which nothing could alienate.[3] Prince Rupert was the Evil Genius of Charles's *Military Enterprizes*/

11   ii 197, pencil, overtraced

Indeed, such a blow was given to the parliament interest, in all these parts, that it might well discourage the ill-affected, when even the *] most zealous were cast downe and gave all for lost: but the governor, who in no occasion ever lett his courage fall, but, when things were at the lowest, recollected all his force, that his owne despondency might not contribute aniething to his mallicious fortune, at this time animated all the honest men, and expresst such vigor and cheerefullnesse, and such stedfast resolution, as disappoynted all the mallignants of their hopes.

* Beautiful! A Woman only, (tho' certainly a Woman κατ' εξοχην) could have so appreciated the true grandeur of Masculine Virtue.[1]

12   ii 198, pencil, overtraced

One great moral Benefit results from the study of History/ that it tends to free the mind from the uncharitable, the calumniating spirit, of party Zeal. Take the warmest Zealot of Charles, the Martyr's Cause, & let him only be an *honest* man and with the feelings of a Christian and the reflection—"*But yet* Col. Hutchinson was a Regicide"—could not but attemper his Heart, ⟨could not but⟩ Christianize his antipathies.[1]   *S. T. C.*

10[3] William Cavendish (1592–1676), Duke of Newcastle, was sent by Charles from York in the summer of 1642 to secure Newcastle and take command of the northern counties. After some success in the north, he should have advanced south to join the King, but neglected to do so perhaps under Prince Rupert's orders. Driven to retreat to York, he was surrounded by Fairfax's army; in the first day of the battle Rupert intervened but failed to save Newcastle from defeat next day in the battle of Marston Moor. Declining requests from both Charles and Rupert to remain in command, he left the country.

C's use of "*overly*" in this sense, in BAXTER *Reliquiae* COPY **102**, is cited in *OED*; cf *CN* IV 5097.

11[1] See also **18**, below. The Greek phrase means "in the highest degree/ *par excellence.*"

12[1] Hutchinson was reluctant to accept appointment as one of the commissioners of the King, yet "looking upon himselfe as call'd hereunto, durst not refuse it, as holding himselfe oblieg'd by the covenant of God and the publick trust of his country repos'd in him" (ii 301). Cf HAYLEY **3** and n 5. After the Restoration, because of his own submission of repentance and the influence of his

13 ii 199–200

[Editor's footnote:] ...it is proper here to state, that in the outset all those sects, which have since taken so many various names, joined their forces to repel the encroachments of the *Prelates*,—it would not be fair to say of the *Church of England*, whose characteristic is moderation itself,—but when they had almost crushed the Episcopalians, the Presbyterian ministers began to rise pre-eminent in power, and to shew that though they had changed the name, they by no means intended to diminish the dominion of the hierarchy.

It seems (and if it were so, it is much to be regretted) that the Editor had not read Baxter's own Life, published by Silvester.[1] The Revd Julius Hutchinson is an honor to the C. of E: O si sic omnes![2] His kindred Soul would have *felt* Baxter's veracity and integrity:[3] his freer Judgement would have discovered without difficulty the good old *Church*-presbyter's unconscious declinations from verity: & he would not here or elsewhere have used the term, Episcopalians, as synonimous with the Prelatists. Even the phrase, Presbyterian Ministers, and Presbyterian Party, Mr H. would have found reason to place among the vulgar errors of History. The fingers of one hand would suffice to number all the *proper* Presbyterians in the Parliament at this time, or among the London Ministers. A large number of those who were afterwards ejected on the twice-infamous St Bartholomew's Day[4] would have been content even to retain the Prelates under the name of Patriarchs (Cant. and York) and Arch-bishops: and as to

kinsmen, he was not punished as a regicide, but "he was not very well satisfied in himselfe for accepting the deliverance" (ii 377). Arrested in Oct 1663 on suspicion of complicity in the Yorkshire plot (the evidence was not conclusive), he was imprisoned and, finding himself at peace with his conscience, made no effort to extricate himself. Less than a year after his trial he died of fever contracted through the severity of his imprisonment.

13[1] BAXTER *Reliquiae Baxterianae* ed Matthew Sylvester (1696).

13[2] "O that all [spoke] like this!" Cf Juvenal 10.123–4. See also *EOT* (*CC*) III 244.

13[3] Cf BAXTER *Reliquiae* COPY B **88** n 3.

13[4] First infamous because at dawn on St Bartholomew's Day (24 Aug) 1572, at the instigation of Catherine de' Medici, a massacre began in Paris that brought nearly 10,000 Huguenots to their death. The second infamous association of the saint's day was the Act of Uniformity. Receiving royal assent on 19 May 1662, it required that all ministers of religion who had not been ordained by a bishop were to be deprived, and required all ministers publicly to declare by St Bartholomew's Day of that year that they accepted the authority of the Book of Common Prayer. About 2000 Presbyterian clergy, including Richard Baxter, refused to conform and were ejected from their livings. See also BAXTER *Reliquiae* COPY B **72** n 1 and **115** nn 5 and 7.

the main characteristic of the Genevan, or true Presbyterian, Discipline, the introduction of Laymen as Deacons & Ruling Elders, they were almost to a man against it. Let it not be forgotten too, that their very intolerancy, to which Mr H. does not attribute more than may be unanswerably laid to their charge, was the intolerancy of the established Church, inherited from the Re-founders of the Church under Elizabeth, & grounded on an interpretation of Schism common to them & the Prelatic and Anti-parliamentary Party of the *same* Church.[5] Remember, that the Reformers in the Church before the War approached far more nearly to a Majority, than the Protestants in the Western Church: & if the latter were not Schismatics, neither were the former.

14   ii 203

To rayse this siege, Prince Rupert came with a greate armie out of the south; the besiegers rise to fight with the prince, and Newcastle drew all his force out of Yorke to ioyne with him, when both armies, on a greate plaine call'd Marston Moor, had a bloody encounter, and the Scotts and my lord Fairfax were wholly routed...

This appears to have been forced on Newcastle by Prince Rupert.

15   ii 253, pencil, overtraced

[Editor's footnote on the publication of the King's letters:] The public is in possession of these, they having been printed by the parliament, which some thought a hardship, but surely without reason....

I altogether agree with the Editor and regard the outcry raised by late writers against the indelicacy of publishing the King's correspondence, as sickly sentimental Cant.[1]   *S. T. C.*

16   ii 270–1, pencil, overtraced

[Editor's footnote on the account of Col Hutchinson and his wife's doubts concerning infant baptism:] Surely this shews an unbecoming propensity to speculate in religion; the story is, however, told with candour.

Surely this is the strangest note that ever came from a man of the Editor's sense. Mrs H. has been speculating in Politics from the very

---

13[5] For C's view that the Church of England at this time "detested every form of Freedom" see HACKET *Scrinia*

49. See also BAXTER *Reliquiae* COPY B 115.
15[1] See H. COLERIDGE 23 and HACKET *Scrinia* 45 n 1.

commencement, and all to the Editor's approbation and admiration. She & Col. H. speculate on the most unbecomingly speculative part of Theology, God's absolute decrees, and the Editor finds no fault. Now as Parents about to exercise a duty to their own Child, they endeavour to square their conduct with the commands of their Redeemer—examine the sacred Scripture to learn what they are—find them in apparent contradiction to the common practice—[1]

17 ii 322–3

The collonell prosecuting the defence of truth and iustice, in these and many more things, and abhorring all councells of securing the young commonwealth, by cruelty and oppression of the vanquisht, who had not laid downe their hate, in delivering up their armes, and were therefore, by some cowards, iudg'd unworthy of the mercy extended them, the collonell, I say, disdaining such thoughts, displeas'd many of his owne party, who, in the maine, we hope, might have bene honest, although through divers temptations, guilty of horrible slips, which did more offend the collonell's pure zeale, who detested these sins more in brethren then in enemies.

These and of this sort were the too notorious Practices, the disappointment, disgust, and indignation at which misled Milton for a time into a Supporter and Apologist of Cromwell's violent ejection of the Parliament, and Assumption of the Dictatorship under the name of Protector.[1] Good men bore too little, and expected too much: and even wise men, comparatively wise, were eager to have an Oak, where they ought to have been content with planting an Acorn. O that Col. Hutchinson & his Co-patriots throughout England could at this period have brought themselves to a conviction of the Necessity of a King, under that or some other name—& have joined with Lord Brook & others in offering the Throne to Cromwell, under a solemn national Contract![2] So, and so only, might England

16[1] For C on infant baptism see e.g. FLEURY **51** and n 1 and HOOKER **16** and n 1.

17[1] C has in mind particularly Milton's panegyric on Cromwell in *Pro populo anglicano defensio secunda* (1654), in which he approves of Cromwell's forcible dissolution of the Rump and assumption of dictatorship, and his resumption of dictatorship after the failure of the Barebones Parliament.

Milton did not consider his position inconsistent with genuine republicanism. See HAYLEY **3** n 5.

17[2] "Lord Brook"—Robert Greville, 2nd Baron Brooke (1608–43), the parliamentary general whom Milton called "a right noble and pious lord" and whose *Nature of Episcopacy* (1641) Milton praised in *Areopagitica*—was the leading Puritan among the peers. He was killed in battle some years before Cromwell

have been a republican Kingdom—a glorious Commonwealth with a King as the Symbol of its Majesty, and Key-stone of its Unity!—[3]

S. T. C.

18   ii 344, pencil, overtraced

It is believ'd that Richard himselfe was compounded with, to have resign'd the place that was too greate for him; certeine it is that his poore spiritt was likely enough to doe any such thing. The army *] perceiving they had sett up a wretch who durst not reigne, that there was a convention mett, by their owne assent, who were ready, with a seeming face of authority of parliament, to restore the Stewarts, were greately distrest...

* There is something delightful to me in this the true *Woman* in all Woman-hood breaking forth—the high, accomplished, and Christian minded, the contra-distinctive[a] masculine intellect, ⟨of⟩ Mrs Hutchinson![1] But in a Woman's Soul, no virtues in a man can atone for Pusillanimity; for either bodily or mental *Cowardice*. Woman can not look *down* and love. Even her Children are *Angels* to her, and she clasps her Babe to her Bosom with a participation of the Feeling, with which the Catholics describe the Holy Mother to embrace her God-enshrining Child./   *S. T. C.*[b]

19   p +1, pencil, overtraced

As the only-begotten Word was incarnate in Christ Jesus, so is the Spirit that proceedeth from the divine Word incarnate, as it were, in the written inspired Word and by the Written Word with the Spirit, and by the Spirit in and thro' the written Word do the Father, the

---

a C first wrote "the contra-distinctive Woman-hood" and then marked the words for transposition. The overtracer missed this detail and left the complex, but clear, sentence in a muddle
b The initials may not be in C's hand

---

was first offered the title of King in 1653. Declining the crown, Cromwell was installed as Protector under an "instrument of government" on 16 Dec 1653, and after declining the crown for a second time was again made Protector with far more extensive powers on 26 Jun 1657.

17[3] For "the king, as the majesty, or symbolic unity of the whole nation" and "the one point in which ten million rays concentered" see *C&S* (*CC*) 41 and *Lects 1795* (*CC*) 295; cf *EOT* (*CC*) I 136, *C&S* (*CC*) 20. In *Friend* (*CC*) I 177n C remarked upon the "fashion in the profligate times of Charles the Second" of ignoring the difference between "the Person and the King" in order to "prepare the minds of the people for despotism". See also HACKET *Scrinia* 47 and n 3.

18[1] See **11**, above.

Son & the Spirit, manifest the holy[a] Will, Truth, and Wisdom ⟨of God⟩ to the Redeemed thro' and in the Church.

The Word

The Written Word　　　The Spirit　　　The Church

The Preacher

The Word is the Prothesis, the Written Word the Thesis, The Church the Antithesis, the Spirit in ~~or~~ and by the written Word and in and by the Church the Mesothesis, and the Preacher declar~~ed~~ing the w. word & representing the Church, the Synthesis.[1]　　　S. T. C.

---

[a] Word not overtraced; perhaps intended to be omitted

19[1] For a general explanation of "the great scheme or formula of all logical *Distribution* of our Conceptions...entitled the Logical Pentad", see *C&S* (*CC*) 233. The formula appears many times, especially in late notebooks, and promi- nently in Jeremy TAYLOR *Polemicall Discourses*; this particular pentad ap- pears also in DONNE *Sermons* COPY B **49**. See also H. COLERIDGE **2** and e.g. *CIS* p [xlvi] (facing fly-title "LETTERS ON THE INSPIRATION OF THE SCRIPTURES").

JAMES HUTTON

1726-1797

An Investigation of the Principles of Knowledge, and of the progress of reason, from sense to science and philosophy. In three parts. 3 vols. Edinburgh 1794. 4°.

British Museum C 126 k 2

Inscribed on II ⁻2 in pencil, in a large sprawling hand, presumably Josiah Wade's, and crossed out: "boᵗ of reading Society" (perhaps the Bristol Library Society), and, not crossed out, "Wade request the favor of Mʳ Coleridge to accept this Work—". "S. T. C." label on the title-page of each volume, and the initials "S. T. C." (not in C's hand) on the title-pages of Vols II and III. Inscribed by John Duke Coleridge in ink on I ⁻4: "C Coleridge Heath's Court 1892 This book belonged to S. T. C".

In 1890 EHC discovered, loosely inserted at II 270/1 (where the leaves are still unopened), a letter from WW to C dated 7 Nov 1806. For the letter and EHC's note see *WL* (*M* 2) I 90–1. In a blank space of this letter the name "William Hoffer" was written, around which C wrote: "Sara Sara Hutchinson my Beloved—Who is William Hoffer, Sara?"

C had acquired these volumes by 22 Jun 1796: see *CL* I 222. Some time thereabout he copied into the Gutch Notebook a passage from III 548, providing the reference. *CN* I 243; also quoted in a sermon of Jan 1796—see *Lects 1795* (*CC*) 353, cf 101–2 n 1.

MS TRANSCRIPT. Transcript of 1 by EHC tipped into Vol I, adding a reference to Hutton in "Scott's *Antiquary* cap. XIII. p. 148.".

DATE. After 1 May 1808, when Hazlitt married Sarah Stoddart (see 1), and before C left Allan Bank for London on 18 Oct 1810 (Wordsworth LC 431, twice marked as C's); perhaps also earlier—see *CN* II 2912 and n (c Oct–Nov 1806) and n.

---

1   I title-page, pencil

"I can not walk *with* them, because I could walk *in* them", said a Wag of a very much too large Pair of Shoes. Something of the sort might be applied to this Work. There is great metaphysical Talent displayed in it; and the Writer had made an important ~~advance~~ Step beyond Locke, Berkley & Hartley—and was clearly on the precincts of the Critical Philosophy—with which & the previous Treatises of

1203

Kant he appears to have had no acquaintance.[1] In short, there is Sense, and strong Sense: but it loses itself in its own enormous House, and is ~~benighted~~ in the Wilderness of the multitudinous Chambers & Passages.—As poor Sarah Stoddart, (afterwards, poor Lass! Mrs Hazlitt)[2] complained to me of her Brothers Lectures & Remonstrances—"He drives it *in*, ~~and~~ *in*, ~~and~~ *in*, (to my head) till he drives it out, out, out, again. I feel as if there was a Hole thro' my head and nothing remaining but a Buz."[3]

S. T. Coleridge

1[1] By the "Critical Philosophy" C means the *Critique of Pure Reason* and the two other *Critiques*; by the "previous Treatises" he would mean the Inaugural Lecture—*De mundi sensibilis atque intelligibilis forma et principiis* (1770)—and perhaps at least the *Theorie des Himmels* (1755) and *Principiorum primorum cognitionis metaphysicae nova dilucidatio* (1755), which are included with the other precritical writings in *Vermischte Schriften* (4 vols Halle 1799, Königsberg 1807).

1[2] Sarah Stoddart (d 1842 or 1843), sister of (later Sir) John Stoddart (1773–1856), married William Hazlitt 1 May 1808 after about two years' acquaintance. By Sept 1803, when she was about to leave for Malta with her brother, who was to be HM Advocate at the Admiralty Court in Malta 1803–7, Sarah was already a close friend of Mary Lamb. Mary's letters suggest that Sarah had probably met C before he went to Malta; they also show that Mary told Sarah about C's ill-health and asked her to be kind to him when he arrived—a request that she honoured (*CN* II 2099, 2310, *LL* I 399)—and that she was not only "unfit to flourish in a little, proud Garrison Town" but also uncomfortable and unhappy living with her cantankerous brother and an unsympathetic sister-in-law. See *LL* I 358–60, 366–8, 406–7. RS described the Hazlitts in 1816 as "a worthy couple—they quarrel, fight, make it up over the gin bottle, and get drunk together". *S Letters* (Curry) II 144–5. They separated in 1819 and in Apr 1822 secured in Edinburgh a divorce of questionable legality.

1[3] It was Stoddart who, in c Aug 1803, invited C to Malta: see *CL* I 977 and cf *CN* II 2099n. In Malta, however, C soon felt that he was not being treated hospitably by the "moody" Stoddart, and there was little warmth between them. When Sarah came home by herself in c Sept 1805 Mary Lamb asked her whether "your brother and Col argue[d] long arguments, till between the two great argue-ers there grew a little coolness, or perchance the mighty friendship between Coleridge & your Sovereign Governor Sir Alexander Ball might create a kind of jealousy". *LL*(M) II 175. For a glimpse of Stoddart's opinionated and importunate talk, and the trouble it could cause among friends, see *WL* (*M* 2) I 242–3 (May–Jun 1808). The relationship between C and Stoddart was never to be that of friends. In the spring of 1807 Stoddart brought back from Malta C's "Books & *MSS*" that Noble had "rescued from the French at Naples", but so neglected to send them to C that he suspected Stoddart of putting the mss to his own use in composing a book on Malta. *CL* III 20, 30, 42–3. In 1811 C's friends accused Walter Scott of plagiarising *Christabel*, and Stoddart was the one who had transmitted a ms of the poem to Scott in 1802 without permission. *CL* III 356 and n. In 1818 it was Stoddart who so "interpolated" C's "Essay on Method" for the *Encyclopaedia Metropolitana* that C said he would be "equally ashamed of it as a man of letters and as a man of common honesty". *CL* IV 817. For Stoddart's bull-headed critical "*integrity*" see *CL* IV 821.

2 III 50 | Pt III sect ii ch 4 "Of the Defect of the Physical Systems Already Received"
§ 4

It must be here observed, that the resorting to absolute hardness as only placed in the unperceived parts, is nothing but a feeble effort to stave off this question, how comes the figure of the perceived thing to be changed. For, if it be only those parts that are altogether imperceptible which are hard, and do not change their figure, this is to involve philosophy in an opposite difficulty, which it is impossible upon those principles to resolve, namely, how come perceptible bodies ever to be hard?

Surely the component particles of any body may be moved ~~into~~ from their place; drawn closer to, or removed farther from each other; without any necessity of denying their hardness or impenetrability?—

3 III 136 | III iv ch 1 "Of Efficient and Final Causes" §3

But, atheism, so far as this is an assertion, that there is no first cause, is an expression which has not properly a meaning. For, they who are to make this assertion, must either found the negative proposition upon some principle, or they only persuade themselves that they believe what they cannot comprehend. But, if atheism is to be founded upon some principle, I confess myself ignorant of what this principle may be.

An atheist regards cause & effect, as events no otherwise different from each ~~time~~ other than in *time*—as *conjunoined* by precedence & consequence; not ⟨as⟩ *connected*—the latter with the former—by a *creative power* in the former.—Of such events he believes an infinity *in time* as well as space—i.e. a co-existing infinity, and an infinite number of similar events pre-existing to ~~each one~~ every & each event in that co-existing infinity.[1] He charges *the Theist* with the Absurdity of believing an event without a cause.—

The first sentence of this Chapter is, I think, founded in error & absurdity;[2] but granting it, a species of atheism may be legitimately deduced—at least, as *a thing possible*/[3]   S. T. Coleridge

3[1] Cf HUGHES 2 n 2 and HUTCHINSON 2 n 1.

3[2] "Cause and effect are considered as events, things that have happened or come to pass; and this is the only light in which we can conceive them: For, although we may be convinced that there is a first cause, which has been always,

this is only because we cannot conceive an event to happen without a cause; and therefore, we suppose that the first cause is no event, but has been always, and will be without end."

3[3] As C himself recognised: see Allsop I 88–9, also quoted in *Lects 1795 (CC)* 249 n 1.

4 III 440, pencil | III vi ch 4 "The Theory of Virtue Illustrated..." pt 5 §5

But when, instead of offending the personal feelings of my neighbour, I shall endeavour to persuade him that he is wronged in the political constitution or administration of the state; when I thus incite him to desert his duty to the public, or not to comply with the orders of the magistrate; when I sow dissension in the state, by making the common people, or the lower ranks of society, discontented with their political lot, then I am not simply vicious, in seeking improperly that which naturally pleases, but I please myself with seeking evil; I am criminal, in doing evil to the state without the immediate solicitation of a natural indulgence; I am criminal, in forming a plot against the common interest of society, a conspiracy to which I am not naturally led in seeking my immediate personal satisfaction; I have then entered the dangerous carreer of political ambition; and, so far as I shall have transgressed the law of benevolence to that government to which I owe my protection, and every* social advantage, I have committed a crime for which, in the wisdom of political justice, I am punishable in my person.

* I owe every advantage to Society. Society is the Blessing, and Government demands my gratitude as being the means of preserving this blessing—~~But~~ Safety & Public Spirit are the advantages, for which my body & mind are indebted to Society.[1] Now if instead of promoting these Government by wars murders, or by corruptions makes selfish, it disorganizes Society & tends to reduce men to a savage state: and of course becomes the object of resistance & abhorrence, not obedience or love—even as if the Physician employed for the preservation of Health should be detected in administering Poisons.[2]

S. T. Coleridge

5 III 551, pencil | III vi ch 8 "Importance of Philosophy to the Art of Social Life..." §19

Despotism is the government of a monarch ruling by his will alone, without the restraint of any law or custom.

4[1] For the principle that man is "a creature of society" rather than "a creature of nature" see *Friend (CC)* II 200–2 (30 Nov 1809) (I 250–3). See also **5**, below.

4[2] C often used this image: see e.g. *LS (CC)* 149—"If then to promise medicine and to administer poison..."—and *EOT (CC)* I 78 (6 Jan 1800), II 141 (13 May 1811).

No such state exists—except perhaps among the savage Africans. Despotism is a government, in which the People neither by any Law or custom exercising ₽ any *power* have no *Security* against oppression: ᴡ the possession of which *Security* is the sole discriminating mark of political Liberty.[1]

S. T. Coleridge

5[1] On despotism see GODWIN **2**. See also *Friend* (*CC*) ɪ 71, 256; but cf 220.